THE GREAT
CONTEMPORARY
ISSUES

EDUCATION, U.S.A.

The New York Times

ARNO PRESS

NEW YORK/1973

JAMES CASS

Advisory Editor

Copyright © 1973 by The New York Times Company.
Library of Congress Cataloging in Publication Data
Main entry under title:
Black Africa.
  (The Great contemporary issues)
  Selections from The New York Times, 1870 to the
  present.
  "A Hudson group book."
  Bibliography: p.
  1. Africa, Sub-Saharan—History—Sources. I. Lynch,
Hollis Ralph, ed. II. New York Times. III. Series.
DT352.5.B55   916.7'03   73-8774
  ISBN 0-405-04165-9
Manufactured in the United States of America by Arno Press, Inc.

The editors express special thanks to The Associated Press, United Press
International, and Reuters for permission to include in this series of
books a number of dispatches originally distributed by those news services.

A HUDSON GROUP BOOK
Produced by Morningside Associates. Edited by Gene Brown.

Contents

Publisher's Note About the Series

It would take even an accomplished speed-reader, moving at full throttle, some three and a half solid hours a day to work his way through all the news THE NEW YORK TIMES prints. The sad irony, of course, is that even such indefatigable devotion to life's carnival would scarcely assure a decent understanding of what it was really all about. For even the most dutiful reader might easily overlook an occasional long-range trend of importance, or perhaps some of the fragile, elusive relationships between events that sometimes turn out to be more significant than the events themselves.

This is why "The Great Contemporary Issues" was created—to help make sense out of some of the major forces and counterforces at large in today's world. The philosophical conviction behind the series is a simple one: that the past not only can illuminate the present but must. ("Continuity with the past," declared Oliver Wendell Holmes, "is a necessity, not a duty.") Each book in the series, therefore, has as its subject some central issue of our time that needs to be viewed in the context of its antecedents if it is to be fully understood. By showing, through a substantial selection of contemporary accounts from THE NEW YORK TIMES, the evolution of a subject and its significance, each book in the series offers a perspective that is available in no other way. For while most books on contemporary affairs specialize, for excellent reasons, in predigested facts and neatly drawn conclusions, the books in this series allow the reader to draw his own conclusions on the basis of the facts as they appeared at virtually the moment of their occurrence. This is not to argue that there is no place for events recollected in tranquility; it is simply to say that when fresh, raw truths are allowed to speak for themselves, some quite distinct values often emerge.

For this reason, most of the articles in "The Great Contemporary Issues" are reprinted in their entirety, even in those cases where portions are not central to a given book's theme. Editing has been done only rarely, and in all such cases it is clearly indicated. (Such an excision occasionally occurs, for example, in the case of a Presidential State of the Union Message, where only brief portions are germane to a particular volume, and in the case of some names, where for legal reasons or reasons of taste it is preferable not to republish specific identifications.) Similarly, typographical errors, where they occur, have been allowed to stand as originally printed.

"The Great Contemporary Issues" inevitably encompasses a substantial amount of history. In order to explore their subjects fully, some of the books go back a century or more. Yet their fundamental theme is not the past but the present. In this series the past is of significance insofar as it suggests how we got where we are today. These books, therefore, do not always treat a subject in a purely chronological way. Rather, their material is arranged to point up trends and interrelationships that the editors believe are more illuminating than a chronological listing would be.

"The Great Contemporary Issues" series will ultimately constitute an encyclopedic library of today's major issues. Long before editorial work on the first volume had even begun,. some fifty specific titles had already been either scheduled for definite publication or listed as candidates. Since then, events have prompted the inclusion of a number of additional titles, and the editors are, moreover, alert not only for new issues as they emerge but also for issues whose development may call for the publication of sequel volumes. We will, of course, also welcome readers' suggestions for future topics.

Introduction

The nation's schools and colleges lie close to the heart of American life. Over the years they have been the object of perennial attention, concern, and, often enough, bitter controversy. On occasion they have enjoyed broad public understanding and support; more often, perhaps, they have been the battleground of special interests, or conflicting philosophies of education. But always, the passion inspired by issues affecting the schools has reflected the profound faith of the American people in the benefits that flow from education. The schools have always been democracy's instrument for achieving the bright dream of equality of opportunity for all men. Therefore, no issue was too insignificant to be ignored.

At the turn of the century a New England historian of the public schools in Massachusetts wrote: "Questions involving the fate of nations have been decided with less expenditure of time, less stirring of passions, less vociferation of declamation and denunciation, than the location of a fifteen-by-twenty district school house. I have known such a question to call for ten district meetings, scattered over two years, bringing down from mountain farms three miles away men who had no children to be schooled, and who had not taken the trouble to vote in a presidential election during the period."

Finding means for informing the public about their schools, then, has always been a crucial issue. The local newspaper, quite naturally, has provided the primary channel for information. All too often, however, school affairs were not considered news of sufficient interest to merit continuing coverage until controversy erupted. In the simpler days of the early Republic, when communities were closer to their schools, an informed public was not so difficult a goal. But as the educational establishment grew larger the problem of community grew more acute, management of the schools became progressively more remote from the people, teachers were increasingly professionalized, educational issues grew more complex, the costs of the enterprise rose alarmingly,

and the difficulties of insuring an informed public multiplied accordingly.

The current issues of size, complexity, and cost are not new—they go back many decades. But it was following World War II that the pace of growth, and its attendant problems, accelerated dramatically. Ex-G.I.s swarmed into the nation's post-secondary institutions, and soon their children swelled the ranks of elementary schools. Progressively during the decades of the 1950s and 60s the pressures for expansion moved from the elementary schools to the secondary schools to the institutions of higher learning. And during this period a variety of forces outside of education helped to focus public attention on the schools with new intensity.

The National Citizens Commission for the Public Schools, for instance, was formed in 1949 to mount a national campaign to stimulate broad public involvement in the solution of school problems. Local and state citizens' committees were formed throughout the country to study educational issues and to generate support. Through the example of the nationally known members of the Commission it became increasingly fashionable for young business and professional men and women to devote their time, energy, and intelligence to active involvement in school affairs.

By the end of the fifties, Sputnik was providing new impetus for school reform. Suddenly it seemed to the public (albeit inaccurately) that the nation's schools were failing to perform as well as they should, since the Soviet Union apparently had surpassed the United States in scientific achievement. But the public took a degree of comfort in James Bryant Conant's *The American High School Today,* because it seemed to provide an educational blueprint for schools in the space age. And the nation set about making sure that their classrooms reflected the academic rigor that Dr. Conant recommended.

During the decade of the 1960s the focus of public interest in the schools shifted significantly. The Civil Rights Movement, growing out of the Supreme Court's 1954 and 1955 decisions mandating desegregation of the schools "with all deliberate speed," turned national attention first toward the dual school systems of the South, and then, progressively, toward the inadequacies of the inner city schools of the North and the increasing *de facto* segregation taking place there.

By mid-decade the second major movement of the 1960s, the student rebellion, was focusing national attention on the colleges and universities. Starting with the Berkeley uprising in the fall of 1964, and fanning out across the country to disrupt campus after campus, the movement was primarily white, even when black militants were involved. Beginning with Columbia, in 1968, black activists progressively disassociated themselves from white tactics and goals. Although their objectives often coincided with those of white militants, black leaders had become convinced that their cause could be adequately served only when it established a separate identity. Otherwise, they felt, their goals too often would be sacrificed to the desires and the designs of the white majority. As a result, the following year at San Francisco State, Cornell, Swarthmore, Brandeis, City College of New York, and elsewhere the student challenge was primarily black. Only at Harvard, among the major eastern institutions, were the militant demonstrations predominantly white.

The tide of campus violence reached a watershed in the spring of 1970 at Kent State. The following fall the president of Yale could speak of the eerie quiet that pervaded the nation's campuses, and as we moved farther into the decade it seemed clear that the attitudes as well as the actions of a majority of students were changing. But the fruits of both the Civil Rights Movement and the student rebellion were still emerging. The growing interest in open classrooms, schools without walls, and other innovations that provided a more flexible and humane environment for students, remained strong. And the efforts to open up the educational process at the undergraduate level were even more dramatic as requirements for graduation were modified or eliminated, student designed programs of study became popular, credit by examination programs proliferated, and attempts to make the community into a classroom for some studies at a growing number of institutions gave added meaning and relevance to classroom work.

It is the reporting of the education scene by *The New York Times* during the tumultuous decades of the Fifties and Sixties that provides the major focus of this volume. As such it offers a fascinating study of both the strengths and the limitations of the daily paper as an instrument for informing the public about complex issues.

For many years the *Times* has been the nation's leader in offering its readers full, thorough, and sophisticated reporting of educational affairs. Long before other major metropolitan newspapers recognized the need for highly professional, specialized reporting in the area, the *Times* was employing a full-time education editor. During the late forties and early fifties the in-depth reporting of issues and events by Education Editor Benjamin Fine and his colleagues was rarely, if ever, equalled by other newspapers. During the sixties Fred Hechinger replaced Fine and, with the education staff, continued the *Times* tradition of extensive coverage and added thoughtful and sophisticated analyses both of local events and national issues.

It is clear from reading these pages that, day-by-day, in-depth reporting of current events in education, when done by skilled specialists, can play a major role in informing the public. It is not capable, however, of insuring understanding of issues and events. This is the role that Mr. Hechinger's interpretations and analyses played during the sixties. However, since he moved up to membership on the newspaper's editorial board in 1969, only rarely has he found time to perform this function.

The pages that follow clearly mirror the ebb and flow of events over the years, the vast changes that have taken place—and the many areas of education that seem to have changed so little. They provide not only an example of the role of a newspaper in reporting the education scene, but also useful perspectives to the student of contemporary events.

JAMES CASS

THE GREAT
CONTEMPORARY
ISSUES

EDUCATION, U.S.A.

hn Dewey.
e New York Times.

CHAPTER **1**

The Background

SUPT. MAXWELL DEFENDS FADS IN THE SCHOOLS

Offers Proof That 1905 Pupils Beat Those of Sixty Years Ago.

PEOPLE FAVOR NEW IDEAS

Annual Report Says Part-Time Classes Will Soon Be Ended—Wants Police Census of Pupils.

City. Supt. Maxwell submitted his annual report to the Board of Education yesterday. In it he recommends that a school house site be purchased for every square half mile of those portions of the city which are still "farm land"; that the Police Department be required by law to register every child in the city for the better enforcement of the compulsory education and child labor laws; that the Board of Education establish special schools for the deaf and dumb, the blind, and for crippled children; that the two evening trade schools be made more efficient and a complete system of trade "continuation" schools be established, and that self-government be introduced in the upper half of the elementary schools and in the high schools.

Aside from these specific recommendations, the most interesting features of the report are Supt. Maxwell's discussion of the part-time problem and his defense of the much-assailed so-called fads and frills system.

The pupils on part time, all schools, on June 30 in each year since 1902 are given as: 1902, 35,347; 1903, 56,071; 1904, 66,925; 1905, 55,292. Supt. Maxwell says if school building operations are continued at the present rate part-time classes will disappear in four years.

Of the so-called fads and frills the report says:

The past year has seen a most persistent attack on the teaching of special branches—singing, manual training, sewing, and cooking—by those in charge of the finance department of the city. That their attack on these subjects is not supported either by the people of this city or by the educators of the country is conclusively established by two things—the first, a popular vote of the people which showed them to be overwhelmingly in favor of such teaching; the second, the declaration of policy by the National Education Association.

The opponents of modern educational methods who would abandon the present rich courses of study and return to the barren instruction of sixty years ago, which was limited to the so-called "Three R's," have for a long time been deploring the alleged fact that children to-day do not spell and cipher as well as did pupils of half a century ago. To-day it is the singular good fortune of those who believe that education has become more valuable, to be able at last to offer facts which establish the truth that children in the eighth year of New York City's elementary schools are better in spelling and arithmetic than were much older pupils in the high schools of sixty years ago.

Dr. Thomas M. Balliet, while Superintendent of Schools in Springfield, Mass., discovered in the archives a volume of examination papers in spelling and arithmetic written by eighty-five pupils in the Springfield High School in 1846. With these papers were the original questions. Mr. Riley, the present Principal of Elm Street school, last March gave these questions to 245 pupils in the ninth year of the present elementary schools. The results of this test were as follows:

	1846.	1905.
Number of pupils, Springfield	85	245
Spelling, per cent. correct	40.6	51.2
Arithmetic, per cent. correct	29.4	65.5

The need of a plan for selecting school-house sites, which is the first recommendation, is occasioned by the necessity of getting rid of part-time classes and of limiting the classes to forty pupils. Supt. Maxwell's plan is outlined as follows:

In all farming neighborhoods within the city sites should be selected and purchased at once on some carefully prepared plan. Possibly these districts should be platted into sections half a mile square. A school site should then be secured at or near the centre of each plat. The proximity or advent of electric or steam railroads—population always follows rapid transit facilities—should then determine the order in which these sites should be built upon. Population would be attracted away from the congested sections, (population invariably clustering round a schoolhouse;) the taxable value of what is now rated as farm land would be vastly increased; provision would be made in advance of the settlement of population; no child would be required to walk more than half a mile to school, and all children would be accommodated.

The board received from the Finance Committee a proposal for reforming the board's present system of keeping its accounts. The plan was referred back to the Finance Committee for further consideration. The new plan is designed to meet the criticisms of the Association for the Improvement of the Condition of the Poor.

The Board adopted the amendment to the by-laws providing that a teacher who is absent for five days shall receive refunds according to a sliding scale, which, in all, amounts to two and a half days' pay for the five days' absence. For the fifth to the twentieth day full pay will be given. From the twentieth to the ninety-fifth, half pay will be given.

Chairman Harrison of the By-Laws Committee submitted a resolution providing that all the special committees appointed prior to Feb. 5 be discontinued, except the Committees on Educational, Museum, Examinations, and Central Supply and Depositary, each of which shall have five members. It was voted to retain the present personnel of the Museum and Examinations Committees.

March 1, 1906

Corporal Punishment in New York's Public Schools

WHEN the New York Board of Education forbade the practice of corporal punishment in the public schools it took a long stride toward a finer and a nobler pedagogy. It was indeed more than this, for no one who gives an observing attention to the work in the elementary schools will deny that the modern methods of discipline are superior in every way to the old, and certainly far more effective. The use of the rattan was always degrading and often brutal.

The new régime has brought about a co-operation between parents and Principals; a friendly, rational discussion of the pupil's faults, and the best remedies for them, has raised the standard of discipline, and induced an era of much better feeling between the master and his charges.

It is one of the elements which have made the wonderful New York schools a model for the world. In spite of the protests of associations of teachers and Principals in some of the boroughs, it has given birth to a finer spirit in school life.

This may be observed especially in the very large schools in Manhattan, some registering as many as 5,000 pupils, and more particularly on the lower east side, where the congestion is greatest, the success of the reform might have been regarded as most desperate.

※ ※ ※

Here parents are frequently called into consultation. a code of class honor has been established, whereby an offender suffers that most severe chastisement to the husky youth, the loss of prestige among his fellows, and the making of the school record in conduct and scholarship a factor in the choice of candidates to represent the school on the athletic field. The latter is an extremely powerful influence, for now in many of the schools an aspiring athlete must attain a certain standard of record if he wishes to enter the lists as a champion for the honor of his school.

In some instances this ruling has been very severe. In one of the biggest schools in Lower Manhattan, with a registration equal to the population of a New England factory village, the basketball team just lost the championship because the Principal insisted upon its application. His inflexibility showed no inconsiderable courage on his part. Since he has remained obdurate the boys in that school are observing a much greater care in their behavior.

The writer has visited several hundred of the schools of Greater New York, has talked with the Principals in every borough, and is convinced that the banishment of the "hickory rod" has improved school conditions wonderfully. No doubt there are often times when a flogging is a highly beneficent operation on a child. It will give birth to a more serious view of life, and arouse the sober-thinking faculties as nothing else can, unless something can be substituted that will cut deeper and induce a greater sacrifice of the pupil's privileges. This has been accomplished very cleverly in the best schools. When the pupil has been convinced that loss of caste and deprivation of certain advantages are the inevitable price of careless mischief, he is likely to think twice before he indulges in it.

☙ ☙ ☙

Dr. Maxwell has been and is now meeting with a constant and determined opposition to the rule forbidding corporal punishment. It is one of the greatest of his reforms, and experience has taught him that he should adhere to it. In talking with many teachers one finds that the majority of them are opposed to the doctrine. Frequently they confess to an eager itching to get hold of the young offender by the "scruff of the neck," and with a good, old-fashioned shaking to send him with beating heart and frightened mien to his seat. All sorts of associations—Principals, heads of departments, and teachers—have passed resolutions disapproving of the law; but the sober-minded minority supports Dr. Maxwell, and he has sufficient reason, in their saner opinion, to continue.

An interview with one of this minority who has been a teacher for a generation, and is now at the head of one of the larger schools, was extremely interesting. In his early days he had ruled by the rod, and had used it freely. It was the one panacea for bad lessons, bad conduct, truancy, and tardiness. But he had a habit of thinking over the condition of his school before he went to sleep, and became more and more satisfied that the practice was more of an abuse than a remedy. He practiced it less and less as the years passed, until he abandoned it altogether. He confesses now to the "itching" to get hold of the culprit, but on the whole he can govern much more effectively without it.

His strongest argument against a return to old methods was this: In the hands of many it would certainly be abused, and although there might be a few who would use it with wisdom and discretion, that fact had but small weight in his mind, when the greatest good was to be conserved.

☙ ☙ ☙

One very practical reason for the success of the regulation in the larger Manhattan schools in the crowded districts is the fact that the young folks are more keenly alive to their rights and privileges. Only a few weeks ago a subordinate teacher in one of these schools seized a young culprit quite violently. Not long after he was facing a Magistrate in a court, with the young victim and his father seeking the effective vengeance of the civil law for the infraction of the school law. The Principal of the school was also present to secure an amelioration of the judicial authority, and referred to the "eager itching" teachers often felt. But this did not seem to win a great deal of sympathy with the Magistrate, whose feelings were more disposed to favor the boy. He referred to the obvious fact that the teacher must have known his legal limitations and had scouted them. It must have been a very remarkable and comfortless scene to the offending pedagogue in the presence of pupil, father, and Principal.

But the ghost of the "hickory rod" still walks in certain spots. It is not a little amusing to listen to some of the expedients used by Principals to call it into service in the maintenance of discipline.

In an upper Manhattan school, where there is a higher percentage of "incorrigibility" than in most schools, the Principal told how he had visited the woody sections of New Jersey this Spring on a holiday ramble, and had returned with a stout hickory stick. It reposes now in a convenient corner of his big building. He has christened it "General Jackson." The Principal has never used it; but he has been clever enough to reap the advantages of its healing powers occasionally when the itching becomes quite unbearable. He summons a parent to his office, and can sometimes convince him of the need of a chastisement of the ancient vintage. The suggestion that "General Jackson" be called in to help is adopted and the "itching" vicariously satisfied. How humiliating it must be to a naughty Manhattan boy to have his father called over to the school to "warm his hide."

There was once a master in Brooklyn, who has, presumably, been called to a higher and more heavenly school, who adopted this same expedient; but in order that he might secure the advantage of the chastisement, opened the doors of all the surrounding classrooms that the music might be heard by all.

Along the outer fringe of Father Knickerbocker's school domain the rule against whipping is more frequently disregarded. One master smiled mysteriously and observed that he "guessed when he and a boy were up in an area on the top floor, if a question of veracity arose between himself and the boy, he would be the least likely to suffer." This was really quite shocking. It gave rise to educational requirements of even greater importance than corporal punishment.

☙ ☙ ☙

Elsewhere there were guarded admissions, sufficiently convincing, that the regulation, in that vicinity at least, was frequently honored in the breach. These youngsters are not so well advised on the matter of school law as they should be.

In Boston some months ago a Principal of gray hairs and of over forty years' experience was summoned before the "School Committee" to explain why he had administered nearly 600 whippings within the present school year. Three or four boys the past Winter had been "warmed" almost every school day.

It was a trying ordeal for the old, white-bearded man, since the order had been passed at an open public meeting, and all "Beantown" knew about it. The boys felt that the old man was going to "get it in the neck," and he had to run a gantlet of newspaper camera artists that must have been equal to all the punishment he had inflicted. But he explained that he had no better method of suppressing misdirected boyish energy.

If he had been stationed in New York, at least he would have had to employ his brain, as has been done here, to devise a better and more effective mode of punishment.

That has undoubtedly been the effect of Dr. Maxwell's sweeping regulation here. There can be no question that it has brought about a revolution in school government and given birth to improved modes of correction, more civilized, more benevolent, more intelligent, and more effective than have ever been known before.

INSTRUCTION IN WORK.

Discussing the need for a change in the kind of schooling given to the negroes in the public schools of the South, and the charge that negro labor is not now so valuable as it was, The Tradesman of Chattanooga remarks:

Who is there that can say the present complaint generally made against the efficiency of the negro in the field of labor is wholly to be placed on the black race? What steps were taken to increase his usefulness in that direction or even to maintain his former habits for industry? When history is correctly written of that transition period the negro will not stand so much in the darkness of censure as he does to-day, for he was the "ward of the Nation" and the special subject, whom the dominant race undertook to guard and guide in its future career. If we went astray or became weaker in any respect the fault was not his, but rather should belong to those who took such charge over him.

But having made mistakes in the past is no reason why they should be continued. A system of industrial education will do much for the negro now, and it will do more for the South. This is entirely without sentiment, without thought other than what will best serve to advance the South in its changed career from an agricultural to an industrial section.

That is a view that will command general approval among all the true friends of the South within or without her own borders. Much patient and intelligent effort has been made in this direction by private persons and in institutions maintained chiefly by subscription. But the underlying principle applies with full force to the public schools, which must always supply the great body of instruction for the children of any State. Sensible industrial education is entirely possible in such schools, and it is of incalculably more worth than any other kind beyond the essential elementary subjects.

CHILD LABOR LAW HAS AIDED SCHOOLS

Prof. John Dewey of Columbia Says Much More Should Be Done for Young Workers.

PLEA FOR DULL CHILDREN

They Most of All Need Vocational Training — Praise Henry Street Settlement.

That the new Child Labor law of the State of New York has increased the demand for schools and for courses of study better adapted to the needs of boys and girls about to enter industrial pursuits, is the assertion of Prof. John Dewey, of Columbia University, in an introduction to the Directory of the Trades and Occupations taught at the day and evening schools in Greater New York.

This directory is published by the Committee for Vocational Scholarships of the Henry Street Settlement at 265 Henry Street, and was compiled by Mrs. Mortimer J. Fox. Among those who are interested in the movement to enable boys and girls to secure employment for which they best are fitted are Mrs. Max Morgenthau, Jr., Miss Elsie Borg, Mrs. William Ehrlich, Miss Margaret Brown, Miss Harriet West Knight, Miss Alice Lewisohn, Miss Irene Lewisohn, Mrs. Wesley C. Mitchell and Miss Lillian D. Wald.

According to Dr. Dewey, the educational problem faced by the city of New York, as by every other great industrial centre, is whether the community shall care for the education of the children or whether the education of the largest number shall be left to the unregulated conditions of factory life.

"Child labor laws have, upon the whole, approached the question from the negative side," Dr. Dewey writes. "They have kept the children out of industrial pursuits until they have reached a certain age, and have presumably secured a certain amount of schooling. The problem will not be adequately dealt with on its positive and constructive side until the community furnishes to the large number of boys and girls, who are about to become wage-earners, educational facilities that equip them intellectually and morally for their callings in life; and until continuation schools, in some form or other, are provided for at least all children between fourteen and sixteen, who are engaged in factory work.

NOTES AND GLEANINGS.

In a comparison of white and colored children measured by the Binet scale of intelligence, Dr. Josiah Morse of the University of South Carolina finds that, in the same course of study and with equally good teachers, 29.4 per cent. of

"The new child labor law of the State of New York, while more stringent as a preventive measure than the older law (since it requires the boys and girls to have attained the Grade of 6B or the age of 16 years), actually increases the demand for more schools and courses of study better adapted to the needs of those going into industrial pursuits. Naturally, it is the duller children who, not reaching the 6B Grade, have to remain in school till they are 16 years old. To a large extent these children, backward in book studies, are just the ones to whom instructions that use the hands and the motor energies would appeal. Meantime, they are kept out of industry, and yet are not adequately prepared for any useful activity in life.

"The public is indebted to the Henry Street Settlement, which maintains a system of scholarships for the benefit of those boys and girls who might otherwise leave school and go to work at 14. The purpose of the scholarships is to give as many children as possible two years of further education and vocational training during that period which has been called the "two wasted years." The giving of scholarships to the comparatively few children fortunate enough to secure this protection and the supervision of their education keeps the committee in close touch with the educational agencies throughout the city.

"While we must rejoice that the showing is as good as it is, and that such excellent work is done by these schools, nevertheless we must confess that the showing is a meagre and inadequate one. When one considers the thousands and thousands of children destined to wage-earning pursuits, the obvious conclusion from the exhibit found in this directory is that neither by public activity nor by voluntary agencies has the City of New York as yet made more than a bare beginning. The directory should thus serve a double purpose, in that it gives information—otherwise very difficult to procure—regarding existing facilities, and in that it makes evident the immense work that remains to be done."

The Scholarship Committee of the Henry Street Settlement offers its second directory of the educational resources of the city to teachers and settlement workers, parents and children because it often becomes the duty of both teacher and settlement worker to advise boys and girls about to leave school as to their future occupation. The committee hopes that the directory may render the choice less difficult and insure a vocation more appropriate to the capacity of the various boys and girls who apply to it for aid.

Conferences on vocational guidance and training, held during the past two years in Boston and New York, demonstrate that interest in this problem is growing. Meanwhile, opportunities for vocational education have not increased proportionately either to this interest or to the school population. In 1909 there were 27,152 children graduated from the elementary schools, and in 1913 there were 41,151. To meet this increase of 50 per cent., three new public trade schools have been established, and eight schools conducted by private organizations, four of which are special schools for the blind and the crippled, the other four, electrical, corporation and Children's Aid Society schools. Since the first directory was published in 1909 two schools have been discontinued.

the colored children are more than one year "backward" to 10.2 per cent. of white children; that 69.8 per cent. colored are "satisfactory" to 84.4 per cent. white, and but 0.8 per cent. of colored children are more than one year "advanced" as compared with 5.3 per cent. of white children.

HIGH SCHOOL PUPILS GO OUT ON STRIKE

Boys and Girls of Long Island City Institution Make List of Their Grievances.

150 HAVE QUIT STUDIES

Principal Demarest Hints That Some Striking May Be Done by Irate Parents Before Long.

Of the 1,200 pupils in Bryant High School in Long Island City, 150 went on a strike yesterday morning. Calling attention to many grievances they sought for the support of all the pupils in the school. The strikers have taken as their slogan, " Objection to Tyrany Is Obedience to God." The ranks of the strikers remained firm throughout the day, and last evening the leaders said that they had obtained several recruits. The real test, they said, would come on Monday morning, when it would be found that nearly half of the pupils of the school would be out on strike, including many of the prettiest girls.

Several of the strike leaders in order to prevent thinning of their ranks by hunger at the noon hour took up a collection from sympathizers among the hundreds of trolley passengers who transfer at the Bridge Plaza Station, two blocks from the schoolhouse. With the proceeds of the collection they bought pie and doughnuts at a bakery and distributed them among the strikers.

Dr. Peter E. Demarest, Principal of the school, last evening refused to admit that there had been a strike, saying that twenty or twenty-five pupils had played truant, and they would have to answer for this infraction of the rules later. In the course of the day the Principal communicated with the parents of boys who were not in school, and he felt that parental influence would break the strike.

Harry Walker, 17 years old, a senior, living at 157 Pearsall Street, is the leader of the strike. He was busy last night detailing his followers to picket duty and directing them to visit pupils who had continued in school and get them to agree to remain away on Monday. He also was making arrangements for a meeting to be held at a hall in Astoria to which he asserted he intended to invite parents and pupils to discuss the situation.

The strikers, under Walker's leadership, drew up a list of grievances and had them printed on slips of paper, which they passed around in their efforts to make converts. Here are the demands of the strikers:

1. We demand a general school organization.
2. We demand more self-government and student representation on the Faculty Board.
3. Control by the students of the funds raised by entertainments for the support of the athletic clubs and other school organizations.
4. Opportunity for pupils to be heard in their own defense when accused of infraction of the rules.
5. That Miss Julia Garrity be either transferred from the school or be shorn of power.
6. That students be not expelled without apparent cause.
7. That students be not treated as guilty before both sides have been heard.
8. That unnecessary and disagreeable rules be abolished.
9. That rules for taking Regents' examinations be revised.

The strike was in a measure due to the dismissal of Walker from the school on last Friday by Principal Demarest. He had been popular among the pupils since the political campaign last Fall, when he held mass meetings and obtained the promise of candidates for local offices to urge the construction of an addition to the high school. According to Walker, on last Friday at the noon recess he was snowballing with other pupils and got his hair filled with snow. He then went to the study room, which was in charge of Harry K. Monroe, teacher of English. Walker says he began writing an essay on " Child Labor " and absentmindedly ran his hands through his hair, which is cut in the long style affected by students.

His hair, he said, became badly tousled, and as some merriment was aroused Mr. Monroe sent him to Principal Demarest's office for causing a disturbance in the study room. Principal Demarest censured him, and Walker says he told the Principal that he thought the class had a poor sense of humor. Thereupon, according to Walker, Mr. Demarest replied: " That is enough for you. You go home."

Walker was not reinstated in the school, and as a result the pupils got together on Thursday afternoon, formulated their grievances, and decided to strike.

One of the chief grievances is that Dr. Demarest will not permit the pupils to have a general school congress to discuss matters of school welfare. The strikers say that every high school in the city but Bryant has an organization of the kind.

The strikers also say that Miss Garrity, who was appointed a teacher in the Long Island City schools when Gleason was Mayor of Long Island City, has too much authority in the school.

Principal Demarest said yesterday: " There is no strike—merely truancy on the part of twenty or more pupils. The trouble has been started by Walker, whom I have not permitted to return to school, and he has persuaded these others to quit school, thinking I will let him return. I believe that the real striking will come when some of these pupils return to their homes to-night. I have been talking with some of the parents, and I expect some such result. " Miss Garrity is one of the best teachers we have in the school, and there is no complaint against her, at least from pupils who do their school work. The demonstration that we have had here to-day shows that these pupils ought not to have a general governing body of their own. They have more clubs and societies in connection with their athletics and studies than any other school in Queens."

March 14, 1914

ASSERTS IMMIGRANT IS SCHOOL PROBLEM

Research Director Lays Stress on Education's Part in Work of Assimilation.

CITES OLD PREJUDICES

Albert Shiels Says Critics of the Foreign-Born Are Apt to Generalize Too Much.

The school and the immigrant are the subjects of a report made to the New York Board of Education by Albert Shiels, Director of Reference and Research. Within the last thirty years, he says, there has been considerable uneasiness over the continuous flow of immigration, and the question has been raised as to the power of this country to continue successfully to assimilate so many variant types that might imperil American institutions, customs, traditions, and standards of living.

Whatever justification there may be for this feeling, says Mr. Shiels, its existence is a fact. It has been formulated in magazine articles, books, public discussions, and Governmental reports. It is interesting to note, however, that the present protests affect to be less against immigration, as such, than against the present character of the immigrant laborer, usually referred to in terms of his geographic origin. In the period from 1810 to 1883, 95 per cent. of the total immigration was from countries west of the Russian boundary and north of the Mediterranean and the Balkan Peninsula. From 1883 to 1907 81 per cent. of the immigration was from Italy, Austria-Hungary, the countries of the Balkan Peninsula, Spain, and Asiatic Turkey. Out of the total immigration for the year 1913 the latter type of immigration represents 74 per cent. of the total.

In a discussion of present-day immigration, he declares, we should be mindful that our judgment is always likely to be affected by possible illusions, and that impressions and prejudices may be confounded with fact. One frequent illusion is due to a prejudice derived from familiarity with the newly arrived immigrant, as we may meet him in person—his physical condition and his habits. We are likely here to confound the accidental and temporary with the fundamental and permanent. An immigrant may be unclean in person, repellent in his habits and apparently content to live under offensive conditions. Yet in such matters he may, in many cases, be but a creature of circumstances, perhaps their victim. The real question is whether he is inherently vicious, criminal or indolent, and, on the other hand, whether he may not under favorable conditions develop into a desirable citizen.

Critics Prone to Generalize.

A second illusion, Mr. Shiels finds, is the acceptance of generalizations, which are themselves based on very hasty and superficial inferences. One example is the tendency to repeat what appears on a printed page, without thoughtful reflection. Thus it is frequently stated that recent immigration implies a disproportionate increase in poverty, disease, and crime. Some of the opponents of the immigrant movement affirm this, others are very cautious. There do not seem to be many convincing statistics to prove the validity of all these assertions. Another charge is that immigration displaces native labor, reduces wages, and increases unemployment, or, at least, contributes to under-employment.

A third illusion, and a very real one, in Mr. Shiels's opinion, is a manifestation of what Lord Bacon called an idol of the tribe, meaning our own human tribe. It is the attitude which most persons have against any stranger. To the degree that he differs in nationality, or race, there is always apt to be a corresponding intensity of suspicion and dislike.

Our welcome to immigration, Mr. Shiels says, has been a splendid service to the world; it is necessary to remember, however, that our goodness has not been without reward. When we realize, for example, to what degree the development of mining industries depends upon foreign labor, or remember that three-quarters of all our laborers on railroad and construction work are foreign born, certainly we must hesitate to adopt policies of exclusion, even if we adopt methods so illogical as the imposition of a literary test.

The question, therefore, Mr. Shiels thinks, is not to be solved by personal prejudice, by unprofitable economic theories, nor altogether by the assumption of responsibility for the welfare of the unfortunate of other lands. What we need to know are the fundamental qualities of the immigrant as we are getting him, what promise he and his children hold for good citizenship, what influences, pro and con, he produces on wages, labor and opportunity, and—perhaps the most important question—what we are prepared to do to reap the richest advantage from his coming. What we are doing consciously and purposively is a question the answer to which would scarcely flatter our national pride. If we shall do no more than we have done, if we are content to depend upon the slow process of evolution that has worked fairly well under happier conditions, it is possible that, notwithstanding all the material contributions that the immigrant may make, immigration itself may be a bad thing.

Whatever may be done in the matter of future distribution, Mr. Shiels points out, the immediate problem for teachers is to consider the immigrant, not in the places where we might like to place him, but where he insists on going himself. It is true that many immigrants working in camps or as farmhands go to rural districts. Until State educational agencies evolve a more effective system, however, the main concern of public school teachers will be centred in the interests of immigrants in the cities.

Teachers Need Broad Culture.

It has been doubted, Mr. Shiels says, whether the regular public school teachers are best fitted for this special work. Whatever the merits of the contention for a special school system, the actual conditions are that for some time to come many day public school teachers will continue to do the work in evening classes. Many of them have already done it with conspicuous success. Whatever the system may be, every teacher should have an equipment greater than a mere command of special method, however necessary that is. He should have a real understanding of the questions other than curriculum and teaching technique. The broader understanding brings the deeper sympathy; the foreign pupil should not be a mere recipient for a certain mass of knowledge, or a lay subject for technical demonstration of teaching skill. The foreign pupil, appreciated in all his relations, becomes in the teacher's presence a man like himself, with hopes, aspirations, misadventures, misfortunes; a fellow-being to be aided and encouraged without contempt or patronage.

Our civilization, Mr. Shiels thinks, has indicated a somewhat naïve confidence in the public school teachers' abilities, which, though flattering, is embarrassing. The school is assumed to be the exclusive agency in education. Whatever faults the rising generation may have are calmly attributed to it. Such fundamental influences as the home, the street, the newspaper, the differences in individual instincts and experiences are all brushed aside, and the teacher is called upon to assume the rôle of mentor, parent, and inspired prophet. Omnipotence is the prerogative of divinity, and not even public sentiment can confer it on a corps of teachers. There is, however, one duty a teacher is required to perform and to perform well. That is the duty of effective instruction.

Now, in the case of the immigrant, Mr. Shiels says, the whole educational procedure is handicapped from the beginning. The evening school, in which the teaching of foreigners has so large a place, is, in the words of one teacher, the stepdaughter of the educational organization. When school funds must be reduced, it is the evening schools that bear the reduction. When other branches of instruction come to require more and more rigid conditions for the training of teachers, it is only among evening classes for foreigners, that in so many communities a place remains for almost any kind of teacher with any kind of license. When elaborate courses in special methods have been evolved in training schools, extension courses, and teachers' colleges, consideration of the critical problem of instructing our immigrants has alone been omitted.

July 11, 1915

HIGH SCHOOL PUPILS AIDED IN ENLISTING

Board of Education Will Give Diplomas to Volunteers on Entering Service.

ASKS TEACHERS TO PLEDGE

Loyalty Declaration Is Adopted and All Will Be Asked to Sign.

General George W. Wingate presented to the Board of Education yesterday, in behalf of Acting City Superintendent Straubenmuller, a resolution providing that all high school students who have expressed a desire to enlist in Government service be excused from further school attendance and given diplomas of graduation upon their entrance into the service, and that this fact be en-

tered upon their diplomas. The resolution was passed.

President Willcox referred again to the fine loyalty of the great majority of the teachers and to the few who "do not show themselves to be in a state of mind in regard to the country and flag that is desirable." He then offered a resolution, which was adopted, that all Principals and teachers be requested to join in signing the following declaration as a message to the city and to the nation from the teaching staff of the New York school system:

We, the undersigned, teachers in the public schools of the City of New York, declare our unqualified allegiance to the Government of the United States of America and pledge ourselves by word and example to teach and impress upon our pupils the duty of loyal obedience and patriotic service, as the highest ideal of American citizenship.

Mr. Willcox said it would be a good thing for the board to know the names of those who might refuse to sign this pledge. General George W. Wingate heartily approved the test of loyalty and spoke of reports he had received of the lack of devotion to the country on the part of some of the teachers.

President Willcox read a statement about Dr. Alexander G. Fichandler, whose transfer from Public School 165 to Public School 109 was disapproved by the board March 28 because his loy-

alty to the Government was not deemed strong enough. Dr. Fichandler, Mr. Willcox said, no matter what criticisms he might have made of war measures, was loyal to the Government, and taught his pupils to be loyal.

John Martin moved that the question of the rejection of Dr. Fichandler's name be referred to the Committee on Elementary Schools. Dr. Ira S. Wile, Chairman of that committee, said the board had not been fair to Dr. Fichandler. If he were not fit to be Principal of Public School 109, Dr. Wile said, neither could he be fit to be Principal of School 165, and charges ought to be preferred against him. John Greene said that no charges were made against Dr. Fichlander, but that the board had rightfully voted not to place him in charge of a larger school, where his influence would be felt by a great number of pupils. Mr. Martin's resolution was lost, and the case of Dr. Fichandler was dropped.

A communication was received from the District Superintendents' Association, pledging loyalty to the Government, expressing a wish to serve the country, and assuring the board that if any of the members should be called upon by the Government the remaining ones would cheerfully perform the duties of those in the service.

A resolution was offered that the Committee on the Care of Buildings be authorized to grant the use of school buildings for patriotic meetings by the National Security League and the Women's Security League, under the supervision of the Principals of the schools. The plan was referred to a committee.

April 12, 1917

Plays for a Boy.

To the Editor of The New York Times:

In the course of my day's work in an uptown branch of the New York Public Library yesterday I came across something I judged interesting enough to pass on to your paper. A lad of some 14 lean years, to judge from his appearance, came in with a list of dramas given him by his teacher of English in first-year high school. From the list he was to choose any one, read, and make a written report on it. I saw no reason to doubt that the teacher had given the list, just as the boy said, especially as he was most anxious to "get the shortest one, please." The list contained the following:

Ibsen's "Ghosts."
Tolstoy's "The Living Corpse."
Galsworthy's "The Fugitive."
Zangwill's "The War God."
Synge's "The Playboy of the Western World."
Maeterlinck's "The Bluebird."
Hauptmann's "The Weavers."
Shaw's "Man and Superman."

The librarian has it pretty well fixed as a conscientious aim to co-operate with the school. But could one connive at such a merciless disregard of psychology and the eternal fitness of things as this? Is this the sort of thing New York school authorities consider intellectually beneficial to the youth of the city? ELLEN BROWN.
New York, May 22, 1917.

May 24, 1917

EDUCATION GROWS DEAR.

It Costs the Country $4,752,197 a Day to Run the Schools.

It costs $4,752,197 a day to run the schools; in 1870 it cost only $479,551 a day. It now costs about ten times as much per day as it did half a century ago. The annual per capita expenditure for education for each person in the total population is $7.26; while in 1870 the corresponding cost was $1.64. The average annual amount for each person of school age is $23.28 for current expenses and $4.30 for new buildings and grounds, making a total of $27.58. In 1870 the corresponding total cost was $5.26.

The average annual cost for each child enrolled in the schools is $30.91 for current expenses and $5.71 for new buildings and grounds, or a total of $36.62. In 1870 the corresponding average was $9.23. The average annual cost for each pupil in average daily attendance is $41.45 for current expenses and $7.67 for capital outlays, or a total of $49.12. In 1870 the corresponding cost was $15.55.

October 10, 1920

INTELLIGENCE TEST FOR 40,000 PUPILS

Scheme to Group School Children According to Ability to Be Tried on Large Scale.

EXPERIMENTS SUCCESSFUL

Retardation of Students Eliminated at Public School 64, Says District Superintendent.

Intelligence tests as a means of grouping school children according to their ability are to be tried out on a large scale in this city next year for the first time. It is expected that 40,000 children will be tested.

The tests have been conducted experimentally for several years past at

Public School 64, on Ninth and Tenth Streets, east of Avenue B. District Superintendent William E. Grady said that the results of these tests have eliminated retardation of pupils at that school.

"The biggest element of waste in the public school system," he added, "is not in supplies, but in the crude way of handling children. The test is a real economy because it prevents the repeater in the grades."

A request has been made for $5,000 to supply the test blanks incidental to the work. The tests will be conducted by the Bureau of Reference and Research. Mr. Grady said that the value of the tests could not be measured in terms of dollars and cents. Director Nifenecker of the bureau said that as a result of the success of the tests given at Public School 64 his department had tested 6,000 children in the Spring, using unexpended balances to defray the cost.

The luncheon service will be introduced in ten additional schools next year. Six of these schools will be located in Manhattan and four in Brooklyn. The present organization has twenty-four of these schools in Manhattan and Brooklyn. Assistant Superintendent Gustave Straubenmuller says 800,000 hot lunches have been served to the pupils during the school year just ended.

July 24, 1921

COMPULSORY ATTENDANCE.

EVERY State now has a compulsory school attendance law, according to information recently furnished by the United States Department of Labor through the Children's Bureau. The bureau recently completed an analysis of education laws affecting child labor, the results of which are published in a chart entitled "State Compulsory School Standards Affecting the Employment of Minors."

In five States attendance is required until 18 years of age, in two of these in certain districts only; in three until 17, and in thirty-two until 16. One State requires attendance until 15, six others and the District of Columbia until 14, and one State requires attendance until the age of 12 years, but applies this to illiterates only.

Unfortunately, the exemptions in the majority of States are so numerous that they greatly limit the application of the law. The most common exemptions are for employment, or upon completion of a specified school grade. Four States specifically exempt for work in agricultural pursuits, three with no age provision. The laws of fourteen other States contain loosely worded provisions exempting a child at any age, which might be used to cover absence for farm work as well as for many other purposes. Several States exempt a child whose services are necessary for the support of himself or others, without any age or educational provision.

July 31, 1921

TESTS OF INTELLIGENCE.

Children of Higher Social Status Rank Best, Says Dr. Chassel.

A champion has appeared at last to deny the popularly acclaimed superiority in intelligence of the son of a grocer to the son of a professor, in the person of Dr. Clara Chassel, conductor of the recent intelligence tests at Horace Mann School. The growing conviction in the heart of the public that the road to intellect lay behind the grocery counter rather than behind the lecture platform, was vigorously attacked by Dr. Chassel, who says that we cannot generalize in the two cases, since environment and heredity would govern the result in either case.

"Intelligence tests which seem to show a superior intelligence on the part of the grocer's son as compared to the professor's son, show no such thing," she declared indignantly. "The higher intelligence is approximately five times as common among children of superior social status as among children of inferior social status."

In many schools the Stanford Revision of the Binet-Simon Measurement Intelligence Test is used as a basis for classification. Although this use is not universal, it is gaining more and more recognition. It aims to determine the child's status at the time the test is given, and usually the variance of this average as the child grows older is not marked.

About 60 per cent. of all school children test between 90 and 110 IQ. and 40 per cent. between 95 and 105 IQ. Edward Rochie Hardy, Columbia's much-discussed prodigy, has hit the bell here with a figure of 187. The children of the higher rank, composed largely from the professional classes or the fairly successful mercantile classes, approximate an intelligence quota of 110 to 120

Careful psychologists who have given special study to the subject are required to administer these tests, which include many branches of knowledge. A list of fifty words is offered, starting with such simple words as "gown," and gradually increasing to more difficult words on which an adult would fail. Fables are also sometimes read by the examiner, and the child is asked to give his interpretation of the lesson.

July 31, 1921

Wisconsin Restricts School Histories.

MADISON, Wis., April 6.—Governor Blaine signed today the bill prohibiting the use in Wisconsin schools of history textbooks which defame the nation's founders or contain propaganda favorable to any foreign Government. The act will take effect on publication within the next two days.

April 7, 1923

HIGH SCHOOL FAVORITES.

Boys Like Mathematics Best, and Girls Commercial Subjects.

The question, "What two subjects do you like best in high school?" was asked of students in various high schools throughout Massachusetts last year. In answer to this question 6,145 choices were made. The commercial subjects were most frequently named as favorite studies and were chosen by over a fourth of the seniors. Nearly a fifth selected English and literature. History and civics, modern language and mathematics were each selected by about one-tenth of the seniors. No one of the remaining high school subjects was selected by more than 5 per cent. of the seniors. Agriculture and gymnastics were each selected by less than 1 per cent. The three most popular studies among the boys are evidently (1) mathematics, (2) history and civics, and (3) English and literature, in the order named. Only one of these subjects appears among the favorite three chosen by the girls, which were (1) the commercial subjects, (2) English and literature, and (3) modern languages.

December 26, 1924

TEACHERS TO CONSIDER SCHOOLING FOR BABIES

Ask Themselves if State Should Take Charge—New York May Try Centres for Both Mother and Infant—What Is Done in Europe

By RITA BERMAN.

AT what age should public education begin? Does it lie within the province of the State to see that the elements of education are supplied at the proper age to each future citizen? Shall nursery education be supplied by the State if it is not available in the home? Of what does this education consist?

Next Friday evening, April 24, in the Teachers' Conference Room of the East Fifty-eighth Street Branch Library, representatives of educational and welfare bodies in New York City will come together for a round-table discussion on means of providing within the public education system of New York City for the training and education of the child of nursery age, the so-called pre-school child.

What researches and educational experiments justify this need? What legislative steps are necessary to provide for it? Under what departments of the Board of Education could a public experiment in the desired direction be undertaken? Shall the public kindergarten be the starting point, widening its scope to include the nursery school? Does this venture come more properly within the province of the home-making department of education which, it appears, is the course its development is taking in some places, as in Los Angeles, at Cornell University and the University of Minnesota? Or may not the mother and baby centres initiated by the Department of Extension Activities, under the supervision of Eugene C. Gibney, prove a logical channel for the development of experimental nursery schools and mother-training centres in this city?

These and other topics will be considered by citizen-parent-teacher representatives, and steps proposed to arouse a taxpayers' interest in the question.

Infant Schools Started in 1826.

A hundred and fifteen years ago, in December, 1809, De Witt Clinton, in an address before the Public School Society, referring to the large number of children between the ages of 5 and 15 who were "entirely destitute of means of instruction," called attention also to those children "of tenderer years who ought to be introduced into infant schools."

Such schools were established by Robert Owen in the year 1800 as a fundamental feature of his famous plan for the redemption of the human race, put into operation in the mill town of New Lanark, Scotland. This remarkable philanthropist came to America in 1824, and, purchasing the entire village of Harmony, Ind., he established there in 1826 the first nursery school on the continent. He saw in his mind's eye "a new moral world—an organization to rationally educate and employ all through a new organization of society which will give a new existence to men by surrounding him with superior circumstances only."

His infant school was the intended key to that consummation, and in it Owen aimed to gather together the young children of the community "to form their dispositions to mutual kindness." There were to be no punishments for these babies; their instruction was combined with singing and dancing and as much amusement as was found requisite for health and to render them "active, cheerful and happy. In fine weather they were much out of doors. * * * They were to be taught the uses and nature or qualities of common things around them."

"Pedestal to the Pyramid."

It is doubtful whether it was a real understanding of Owen's ideal, or simply a benevolent intention, that dominated the action of "a meeting of ladies" on May 23, 1827, in New York City, which resulted in the formation of the Infant School Society and the subsequent establishment of a number of classes in the basements of the common schools for "female scholars from 2 years of age and upward and male scholars from 2 to 6 years of age."

The first of these New York City Infant schools was opened in the basement story of the Canal Street Presbyterian Church and in a few months numbered 170 on its register, with an average attendance of from 60 to 100. Two teachers were employed, with an assistant, "who also attended to the fire, keeping the schoolroom in order and other general duties." Less than six months after its establishment, De Witt Clinton, then Governor of the State, made the following allusion to it in his message to the Legislature:

The institution of infant schools is the pedestal to the pyramid. It embraces those children who are generally too young for common schools; it relieves the parents from engrossed attention to their offspring, softens the brow of care and lightens the hand of labor. More efficacious in reaching the heart than the head, in improving the temper than the intellect, it has been eminently useful in laying the foundations of good feelings, good principles and good habits.

At the coming Friday evening conference of modern child welfare workers, educators' and psychiatrists' sympathy with Governor Clinton's enthusiasm for infant education is likely to be overshadowed with wonder at the temerity of those city fathers and city mothers who could attempt so difficult an enterprise with such scanty preparation, so limited a staff and so manifestly inadequate arrangement for the comfort and care of the children of nursery age who came in the early morning and remained till evening, even though, as the record states, they brought their dinners with them!

The "infant" of the year 1827 has become the pre-school child of this century; the "infant school," long since dropped from the New York public education system, is having its modern revival in the nursery school of today; and the educational concept which found "a basement story" adequate for the activities of a hundred toddlers and runabouts has given place to a different ideal.

Training Toddlers Under Four.

In such nursery schools as are to be found at the City and Country School on West Twelfth Street, the Manhattanville Nursery School on Old Broadway, the nursery school supervised by the kindergarten department at Teachers College, the one at Greenwich House on Barrow Street and a number of others carried on in connection with various day nurseries and health centres in New York City, modern equipment and educational skill combine to meet the needs of the young child in a scientific yet humanized way.

At the Manhattan Nursery School—which is the demonstration nursery school of the Institute of Child Welfare Research—one floor, containing two large sunlit rooms, is supplied with furnishings and equipment to receive the seventeen children, all under 4 years of age (the youngest 2), who are registered there. A trained directress, with two assistants, is in charge of the little group, and consultants are available and records kept to insure that each child is attaining satisfactory physical, mental and social-moral development. Here, as in the other nursery schools, domestic activities, creative activities and training in the formation of right health habits and social habits make up the child's day.

Such activities range from setting and waiting at table, hand and face washing and hair combing, to correct speech training, work and play with blocks, color and number, drawing, story-telling and musical rhythm; with many other activities indoors and on the roof, self-initiated or suggested by the informal environment.

On the roof playground of the Manhattanville Nursery School, which is provided with a large awning in Summer, but is open to the sun and snow of Winter, the children spend much time in "work" and play. There are a fascinating "jungle-gym," a "climbing-rack" (invented by Miss Marian Walker, the directress), a slide, a small rope-ladder, a see-saw, a rope-swing, a jumping-board, a sand-box, many paint-cans and brushes ("painting with water" is a favorite pastime), low work-benches, with hammer, nails and plenty of old boxes to play carpenter with, and a real dirt-pile.

Europe's Nursery Schools

Out here, where in the Summer there are vines trailing and plants growing, the doll-carriages, wagons, kiddy-cars, velocipedes and blocks are all put to hard usage by the babies. A large wooden chick and a larger wooden duck lend a rural touch to the scene, and a little dust-pan and brush set in a corner marks the presence of the ideal of domesticity always in the background.

The mothers who bring their toddlers here to this pleasant place, most of them, have all-day employment at machine, laundry, housework or in offices. One mother is a student, another sends her child here because she feels it needs contact with other children. All pay a small sum daily, twenty cents for one child, thirty-five for two. The directress is in touch with the mothers and visits their homes, and periodic mothers' meetings are held.

As an expedient to meet the needs of the working mother, the all-day nursery school has proved its value here as in England, where it influenced the Parliamentary enactment in 1819, whereby power is conferred upon local education authorities to supply nursery schools for children over two and under five years of age "whose attendance at such a school is necessary or desirable for their healthy physical and mental development."

Governmental recognition of the needs of the pre-school child has existed in other European countries for many years; in Belgium since 1880, where the State at the present time supplies funds for the greater part of the salaries of mistresses and superintendents of these écoles gardiennes and contributes fifty per cent. of the gross expenditures for buildings, furniture, &c., the remainder being a charge on municipal funds.

In France écoles maternelles for very young children have been an integral part of the national system since 1833, and there are at present 3,400 of such nursery schools, of which 2,622 are State-supported. In the United States, however, it is doubtful whether any legislation, mandatory if not permissive, has been passed by any State to cover this specific need.

That it is a need, and one with compelling points in the direction of establishing intelligent social control over the pre-school period of childhood, is indicated by the records available at child-welfare stations, research bureaus and laboratories and habit clinics. Workers in these fields are unanimous in concluding that the basis of physical defects and character defects is already fixed when the child first enters school and that standards and minimum requirements should be set up by the State to assure that every child is rightly environed, nourished mentally and morally, no less than physically, during the pre-school period.

State's Displacement of Home.

A child's earliest surroundings and associations are of basic importance, and it has become plain that the State cannot, as Arnold Gesell says, "entrust the welfare of even young children entirely to the dictates of the home." Just as minimum health standards have been established by Federal and State legislation, so legal cognizance must be taken of the right of the babe to be given full opportunity from the cradle to form right mental and moral habits.

Is the nursery school the social agency which can accomplish this? Can it serve the home in such a way that the responsibility of parenthood becomes keener, or does it hold within itself the grave danger of weakening the parent-child relation upon which the family, the foundational unit of the social structure, has rested? Doubt is expressed by many sober thinkers on this question, and emphasis is being placed rather on nursery centres which shall be mother-training stations or schools for mothers.

NEW WAYS OF TEACHING GAIN WIDE RECOGNITION

The Progressive School, With an Altered World in View, Overturns Some Old Classroom Traditions—The Teacher as Child's Consultant

MODERN leaders in education are seeking to fit the child to conditions of life in the new machine age. The following article gives an outline of the present modern movement in the elementary schools and the methods and experiments pursued in them.

By EUNICE FULLER BARNARD.

WHEN the historian of the future appraises our age, will he place our "educational revolution" alongside the radio and the automobile as precursors of social change? Certainly in the decade since the war men have been experimenting with education almost as avidly if not as spectacularly as with the airplane. In education they have come to see not only the instrument of literacy but the potential transformer of men's attitudes, habits, and emotions. Are we, also, experimenters are asking, soon educationally to cease trudging and to begin to fly?

Out in Missouri not long ago a class of country school children voted in lieu of regular lessons to spend a term in discovering and if possible removing the causes of recurrent typhoid fever on a neighboring farm. They were, in other words, to have no reading or writing or arithmetic or geography at all except as these formal subjects came incidentally into the course of the adventure.

So they set to work with their teacher to find out what the possible causes of typhoid are. They made a minute survey of the farm. They got the farmer to move a manure heap that was dangerously near the house. They bought fly traps and swatters and helped the farmer clean up the place generally.

Since then there has been no more typhoid on that farm. Oddly enough, too, the children who solved the problem learned more reading, writing and arithmetic than did other children of the same age, grade and mentality who had had routine lessons in two near-by rural schools. They graded higher on standard tests, and they had in addition admittedly gained a mature and inquiring viewpoint lacking in the other children. Moreover, in the opinion of several observers, they had energized the life of the whole countryside.

An Apprenticeship to Life.

The adventure in sanitation, reported by Carleton Washburne and Myron Stearns, was an experiment in education made under carefully observed conditions by a professor of the University of Oklahoma, acting on suggestions of Dr. W. H. Kilpatrick of Teachers College. But schooling in the manner of active apprenticeship to life is being tried the world around. It is education from a brand new viewpoint of its scope and purpose. And it opens a vista of speculation as to what the inert millions of children might, if given the chance, joyously and voluntarily contribute to community life.

In Russia school children are growing and testing out seeds for the farmers under different conditions of soil and cultivation. They are instructing illiterate adults in the workings of the local Soviets. They are taking younger children on excursions to model factories and farms. Here in New York, even, in dozens of progressive schoolrooms, children 8, 9 and 10 years old are running school banks and printing presses and stores for the sale of school supplies—running them on a business basis.

Ten years ago the progressive elementary school was just springing up, a fragile exotic growth largely in New York. Today it flourishes like a hardy vine, twining gradually around the world. From Hawaii to Russia, from tradition-haunted England to freest California, it blossoms with a new assurance. Indeed, in Russia, Austria and Germany, it has been adopted into the national system.

In our own country it still largely forces its way in fast multiplying private enterprises. The Progressive Education Association, formed by about thirty bold pioneers at the start of the present decade, drew to its convention in New York last year an attendance of 8,000 people. The Child Study Association with related aims now numbers 5,000 members and has branches in five foreign countries. Today to all the better established modern schools in this city—and there are now dozens of them—come observers from the four corners of the globe. One such school alone—the Lincoln School of Teachers College—last year had 2,500 visitors from forty-five countries, with notable numbers from Japan and Germany.

To Meet Modern Life.

The child and his school have suddenly become the centre of a world of investigators, innovators and inquiring parents. College professors, psychologists and doctors, all are combining to create the new school which shall fit the inner needs of the child on the one hand and the modern world blaring with motors, radios, airplanes and factories, on the other

Out of the chaos of small, unrelated experiments, three basic lines of inquiry emerge. At least, education as a science has found out what its problems are. Looking at the matter narrowly from the viewpoint of the little red schoolhouse, it recognizes that after all these centuries no one yet knows when or how the three R's may best be taught. To determine by tests as conclusive as those of chemistry just when the child is physiologically and psychologically ready for this kind of learning, and how the learning can be expedited, is thus the first field of modern endeavor. Already discoveries as to the workings of the eye muscles during reading have thrown light on right and wrong methods of teaching. Already practical tests have cast doubt on the time-honored system of class recitations.

In a second field, scientific education is trying to discover what other subjects beyond the three R's the child needs to study to meet the demands of modern life. Is it, for example, more important for him to master cube root than the workings of an automobile engine? Should he be taught to "bound" every country of the globe, or how to use the atlas, the encyclopedia and the public library? Will he be more successful for having learned the battles of the Civil War, or for having learned how to choose his meals with proper regard for vitamins and calories? What is the real basic curriculum as a preparation for present-day living?

Thirdly, scientific education recognizes that merely adapting the child to the modern world is not enough. If there is to be progress, school must also show him how to develop his own inherent talents. And this is perhaps the deepest difference between the old school and the new—that the new cherishes variation as well as uniformity. By giving each child freedom and time for experimentation as well as materials and technical help, it encourages the artist, engineer or poet to emerge.

Now, although experiments are being made with widely differing aims and in different places, they show a common laboratory approach to the problem. The little red schoolhouse, like its spiritual successors, looked at both the learner and the things to be learned as fixed and static. As a bridge between the two, it used literally or metaphorically the dunce cap and the switch. In practice it saw in the child little more than a certain mentality and will-power to be cajoled or coerced into the acquiring of annual quotas of the three R's.

The modern experimental school, on the other hand, looks at both the child and the curriculum as organisms, growing and imperfectly understood. It recognizes that ours is a changing world with rapidly changing demands. It therefore constantly questions the usefulness of the old curriculum and the advisability of the new. It sees in each child a complex and unique individual with individual interests, capacities and learning rate—a wild thing, to be encouraged, studied, fed and allowed freely to grow, till the laws of its being are better understood.

An Era of Experiment.

Indeed in respect to freedom, education stands today at about the same experimental stage that government stood a century and a half ago. Then the United States, and soon France was making the democratic experiment, with a passionate belief in men's individual rights to life, liberty and the pursuit of happiness. In certain progressive schools today there is the same conviction that the old class-room autocracy was wrong and that children as well as adults can reach their highest development only in an atmosphere of freedom.

But whether or not that freedom should be absolute and, if not absolute, how much it should be limited by the known demands of society, which the children have ultimately to face, are questions on which modern schools differ as fundamentally as do modern Russia and France on governmental forms. Each with some success is working out its own hypothesis, and there is as yet no comparative scientific standard of merit to judge them.

Take for instance those schools which are chiefly interested in the development of the child's individual talents. In some of the extreme left-wing schools compulsion is done away with altogether. Interest is the only motive of the child's work. Education, in this theory, is simply the free flowering out of the child's own nature when surrounded and stimulated by varied opportunities.

In such schools the compass, so to speak, has completely veered about. Where it used to point to a whole category of exact knowledge—tables, spelling lists and reading books which the child must be put through day by day and year by year—now it has swung around to the growing, inquiring child himself. This learning is secondary to his mental, physical and emotional development. In the most liberal schools it is introduced and taught only as the child himself feels the need.

Activities as a Stimulus.

Real activities, it is believed, bring their own desire for abstract knowledge, and the three R's become a by-product of such an education. The pupils would not, for instance, learn a list of the products of Holland. But they might go down to watch a Dutch liner unloaded. They do not learn about money by the ar'd route of decimals. They run a store, selling pencils and paper and paints to the other children, and make change themselves. Decimals of a sort are a natural record of the process. To be a responsible storekeeper trusted by the class one must know a few tables and be accurate in making change.

The teachers are the child's consultants. They do not set tasks for him. He appeals to them for help in carrying out his own ideas, whether in engineering, sculpture, cooking or arithmetic. One progressive school in New York has all sorts of special laboratories and shops at the children's disposal. With more freedom than many students have in college, children from 8 to 13 may choose. in a part of every afternoon, what they wish to do. A child may go to the "clay room" to model whatever he wishes, with a sculptor at hand to advise. He may go to the kitchen to cook, with the help of a domestic science expert. He may build an airplane in the laboratory or a ship in the woodworking shop. He may read or do reference work in the specially selected children's library, which he soon comes to use, as the adult does, to look up the things he wants to know.

On the right wing, at the opposite flank of the progressive movement, are those who "do not believe it is vicious to see to it that the child learns certain definite things." That is, they would keep the child more or less to the traditional objectives of schooling, but use the newer, freer methods to obtain them. The various activities, or projects, which in the left-wing school just decribed would be considered ends in themselves in the more conservative, progressive schools are used as devices to teach the facts of geography, history or the three R's.

Another Kind of School.

With a far richer curriculum than the traditional school, with a free classroom atmosphere and a beginning of arithmetic and reading far later in the life of the child, these schools, nevertheless, hold with the older theory that the core of education is exact knowledge.

"By the end of the fourth year," said the principal of the Horace Mann School, the demonstration school of Teachers College, "we believe that a child should have certain knowledge and certain skill, and we see to it that he has them, by sheer drill if necessary."

CHILD EDUCATION ALONG MODERN LINES

Interest, Rather Than Compulsion, Is the Motive Behind the Pupil's Work.

But where such compulsion comes in in this type of new school it is often compulsion of a new sort—compulsion on the school to assess a difficulty in learning. Many of these schools have psychologists and even psychiatrists on their staffs. If Johnny is not learning to read as fast as most of his classmates, often a little trained observation will establish the fact that there is nothing wrong with Johnny's mentality, but some emotional kink has turned him against reading. Such a kink, which in the old school might have marked Johnny as a lifetime dullard, in the new is patiently untwisted by counter-suggestion, without scolding or opprobrium.

Two other methods which have come into use in this type of school where academic accomplishment is adhered to as a primary aim are the famous Dalton plan and the Winnetka Individual Technique. Both of these abolish the old classroom recitation and lecture system. Each child advances at his own rate of speed, with the teacher as helper and adviser. Each reads or spells to the teacher by himself.

Under the Winnetka plan, which is particularly flexible, Johnny may take a year and a quarter to do the geography that most of the class can do in a year, but only three-quarters of a year to do the arithmetic. So he goes ahead exactly as fast as he is able and never, as in the traditional school, repeats a whole grade in every subject just because he is a little slower than the other children in one or two.

Staff Not Increased.

One of the unexpected discoveries of the experiment at Winnetka was the fact that it took no greater teaching staff than the old method, that the pupils advanced faster and had more time for other activities.

Between these two camps of modern schools—those centred wholly on the child's spontaneous development and those whose main aim is the swift and painless method of instilling the traditional types of knowledge—stands the third, already mentioned, which is trying to discover what new studies the pupil should have to fit him for the modern world.

While agreeing with the more radical group that children should learn what they like to learn, it does not believe that the matter may be left quite so freely to their unguided choice. Above all it desires "to cause them to wish to learn those things which life-needs show they ought to learn." Its aim, in the words of the Lincoln School of Teachers College, is to construct a fundamental curriculum which will represent the important activities, interests and possibilities of modern life.

Thus these schools take a completely realistic point of view. In this world of adding and computing machines, they would not put a child through the agony of intricate mathematical computations that he would never be called upon to make in real life. But they would, for instance, as a basic essential, teach him the principles of choosing a balanced diet.

It is not only new facts that these schools want to teach. It is new habits, new attitudes and new skills that are necessary to the dweller in the complex world of today and tomorrow. And all these things, if possible, must be woven into some one activity or unit of work into which children will throw themselves whole-heartedly.

This, in the opinion of John Dewey, as expressed in a recent address, is the most important next step for progressive education to take—to formulate and suggest to pupils lines of activity "which involve an orderly development and interconnection of subject-matter." Progressive teachers, he believes, should constantly be working out and presenting to other teachers for trial and criticism such projects with all their social, cultural and intellectual implications. Freedom the children must have to initiate and work out such projects for themselves, but it must be a more or less guided freedom, in which no educational implication must be passed by.

These, then, are the three forward thrusts which elementary education is making in our generation in its hope of becoming a science. It is trying to develop the natural aptitudes of the learner. It is trying by psychological and physiological studies to devise swifter and easier ways of teaching the traditional subjects. And it is searching for activities that will equip the child both in habits and knowledge more efficiently for modern life.

PROGRESSIVE SCHOOLS CUT 'THREE R' DRILLS

Era of Painless Education Is Hailed as New Devices for Catching the Interest of the Young Find a Widespread Acceptance

By EUNICE FULLER BARNARD.

Multiplication is vexation,
Division is as bad;
The rule of three doth bother me,
And fractions drive me mad.

To the youngster of tomorrow—if half the efforts now going on in his behalf succeed—that rhyme should be meaningless. Suddenly, as if in expiation of the millions of grimy, tear-stained arithmetic tests that have strewn the centuries, gray-bearded professors, earnest young Ph. D.'s and cooperating phalanxes of school teachers are devising experiments night and day to make the road to learning royal for him.

Some, spying from their statistical towers upon the arithmetic processes commonly used by business men, are proposing to rule out all others from the course of study. Others are charting the movements of the eye-muscles during reading with the scientific attention of a golf professional analyzing a drive. Still more assuaging spirits are setting up those Elysian schools where the three R's are relegated to an hour or two a day or almost lost sight of in some pleasant game of storekeeping or dramatization. Enter, the age of the painless learning.

No less an authority than Dr. Harold Rugg of Teachers College was recently reported to have said that the three R's could be taught as well as necessary in one-fifth of the present school day, thus releasing the remaining four-fifths for creative activities. And that was almost done in the experimental classes of Public School 61, New York City, from 1923 to 1928. Similar proportions of time are allotted in many of the private progressive schools. In the public schools of Winnetka, Ill., all the routine subjects are got throught with in half the school day.

In the two public schools here mentioned elaborate statistical studies have been made, showing that children taught in this way actually pass in a more satisfactory manner the standard tests in reading, writing and arithmetic and make better high school records than do the children who have given full elementary school time to those subjects. Colleges have also reported favorably on graduates of private progressive schools. According to Dr. John Dewey, the old question, once a bugaboo, as to what will happen when such pupils go to college or out into

life has in the last few years proved to be no longer an open one.

Doubts in Other Quarters.

Yet many a hard-headed parent has his doubts, and most boards of education would hesitate long before they would give up the good old-fashioned five-hours-a-day drill system. It does not seem rational to believe that in the long run the same results can be obtained in one hour or even two and a half hours as in five plus homework.

Take the matter first from the viewpoint of scientific management in a factory. The minimum aim of the school factory narrowly considered is to give its graduates enough of the three R's to enable them to get on successfully in life. One large group of academic experimenters today is working to find out whether there are any waste motions. Does all the memorizing of tables of square rods and of unknown spelling words, all the weary solving of complex fraction examples, stay by and function in adult life?

Two of the most vivid experiments performed to answer those questions have been made by Dr. Carleton Washburne, superintendent of the Winnetka schools. He took successful and intelligent business men and women in various Rotary and commercial clubs and parent-teacher associations in Northern Illinois and gave them the standard arithmetic tests required to be passed by the children. In plain addition and subtraction the adults far surpassed the children in quickness and accuracy Indeed, a prominent Chicago manufacturer, sitting beside a school principal, did two addition examples to the principal's one. But when it came to long division, the manufacturer trailed behind. And in fractions he got through but one example and his answer was wrong.

A Lesson In Fractions.

The successful adults on the whole could do fractions, according to Dr. Washburne, about as well as the fifth grade child who is just learning. A child in the upper grades could "work circles around them." In other words, he concludes that intricate fractions are so little used in life that it is a waste of time to teach more than the fundamentals. All the rest apparently is forgotten. But more time might profitably be spent on increasing the children's adding and subtracting speeds.

Similarly, he set his Winnetka

teachers to cutting out the names of persons and places found in some eighteen periodicals covering every month in the year for eighteen years back and comparing them with those emphasized in the textbooks. In all the periodicals they found that such names of textbook fame as Ponce de Leon, De Soto, Antietam, Bull Run and Shenandoah were not mentioned once. On the other hand, Plato, Homer, the Celts, Mecca and Bagdad were high on the periodical list but occurred in almost no textbooks.

Moreover, words like "meritorious" and "ascendancy," favorites of the school speller, were found not to be in the list of the 10,000 commonest words in the English language as drawn up by Dr. E. L. Thorndike of Columbia, while many of those in almost universal use the spelling books omitted.

But even more important than what should be added and what subtracted from the study of the three R's is the question of how they should be taught. We assume that we are a literate nation and that our elementary schools with their eight-year drill have made us so. Tests of drafted men during the war showed, however, according to researches of Dr. May Ayres Burgess, that there must have been a million of our soldiers and sailors who were not able to write a letter or read a newspaper with ease. Yet the overwhelming majority of them had been to school, attending the primary grades where reading is taught.

In the last twenty years, it is said, there have been more than 600 scientific investigations of the reading process. Yet it is doubtful whether any one yet knows when or how reading should be taught. Some progressive schools do not begin teaching it till children are 7 or 8. Others allow the children to begin at 5 or as late as 9 or 10, according to the children's own interest in the matter.

Yet all the experiments tend to confirm certain new trends. In progressive schools less time is being given to reading, yet the children grade higher on the standard reading tests. And that is because, it is believed, the shorter time is spent to greater advantage.

The two chief arts on which the new school relies to outdistance the old in reading, as in everything else, are those of interesting the child and of individual work. Books with no title or taint of the "reading book" about them, books with one story

running all through, instead of the old-fashioned miscellany, from primer grade up, are some of the offerings. Another is the fact that before any books are given to them the children are already used to reading signs and bulletins and rhymes and recipes which have come to them as a natural part of their other activities in schools. Reading is always first presented as the key to something they really want to know, rather than as a mechanical process full of hard letters and syllables.

New York Demonstration.

How this works out in actual academic success has been demonstrated by the six-year experiment, recently closed at Public School 61, New York City. In 1923 Miss Elizabeth Irwin started with a class of regular first-grade children. All through that year and half of the next she gave them no academic work of any kind. Instead they went on trips around the neighborhood and the city, talked about them and, in block-building or painting, reproduced the things they saw. Not until the latter half of the second grade did they begin any of the three R's. Then a total of an hour and a half a day was given to reading, writing and arithmetic, spelling and dictation. In the sixth grade this was increased to two hours a day.

At the end of the sixth year, when the children left Miss Irwin to go to junior high school, they were tested with an equal group in the same school who had had regular work in the three R's the greater part of the five-hour day for six years. In other words, Miss Irwin's experimental group was tested with a control group which had had more than three times as many hours of academic work, and had also, as it happened, a slightly higher average I. Q.

Nevertheless, two-thirds of the experimental group equaled or surpassed the control group in reading. In arithmetical reasoning the experimental group excelled the control in every case but one, where the score was equal, and in arithmetical computation it excelled or equaled in all but one instance. In only one subject, spelling, did the control group score higher. In this the test was given on spelling book words on which the control group had been drilled. Many of these the experimental group had not had, since they had learned to spell no words not familiar to them in use.

Experience in Winnetka.

More complex comparisons still have been made in Winnetka, where children of a whole suburban school system of four elementary schools and a junior high school gave but half their time for five years to the regular academic subjects. The other half of their school day, as in Public School 61, was given to dramatics, art, music, various crafts from printing to cooking, scientific experiment, sports, and projects such as publishing a school paper. In the three R's and other "common essentials" they had had only individual instruction.

To each child was given a set of "goals" in arithmetic, spelling, &c., and he worked toward them at his own rate, with as much of the teacher's help as was found to be necessary. Thus no child ever repeated a whole grade. He was allowed to take a year and a quarter if needed to do his year's arithmetic, and three-quarters of a year to do his spelling.

For one school year the Winnetka children, trained under the half-time plan, were tested in various ways by University of Chicago investigators, who compared them with those in another school system spending practically all their time on academic work by the class method. In reading, arithmetic and language the Winnetka children scored from 2 to 60 per cent above the average of the other schools studied. In spelling, exactly as in the New York experiment, they fell slightly below that average.

The significant features of the Winnetka experiment were that the children were in no sense precocious, and that the cost of teaching them individually was not excessive. On the contrary, it was suggested that Winnetka actually saved money by having no children repeating grades.

Experiments Far-Reaching.

Other experiments with the individual method in the three R's made in places as diverse as London, Detroit and San Francisco have resulted in similar findings. Most of the advocates of the method seem to feel that it has much the same advantages over the class method that a physician's method of diagnosis and treatment of the individual patient has over patent medicines and general health directions.

It should be noted, however, that in both the Winnetka and New York experiments described, a definite, if small, amount of time each day was set aside for drill in the three R's. And in Winnetka, at least, this was entirely distinct and aside from the time given to group and creative ac-

tivities. That is, in neither case was there the effort made in some progressive schools to teach the basic subjects more or less indirectly through projects.

If the Winnetka children ran a newspaper or a bank it was wholly for the social and semi-business experience involved, and not for the purpose of teaching languages, spelling or arithmetic. Admittedly, the children gained in this way new urges to conquer these subjects. But the two aims were not fused in the thought or practice of the school.

There is evidence, however, that in some private progressive schools where no regular drill hours are set aside, but where the children learn because they need to in order to run stores and postoffices, satisfactory results have also been obtained. No absolute statistical comparison has been made of any one group of such children with other groups more rigidly trained. But it is true that such children ultimately can and do pass the same standard achievement tests selected as criteria in Winnetka and New York. Moreover, they can

and do enter regular high schools and make excellent records.

No "goals," however, in the lower grades are set for them. The child's own interest and vision of the necessity of learning the tool subjects, in this philosophy, must precede his acquisition of them. These the teacher tries to stimulate, and in most cases the various activities that the group undertakes practically require the child to have some skill if he is to take his part. He cannot, for instance, be a trusted storekeeper if he cannot write out sales slips and make change.

Progress Not Uniform.

Under these conditions, it is apparently true that the children make a less uniform rate of progress. Some develop facility in the three R's much later than they would under another system, while others get on more rapidly, having a genuine social incentive.

At the ten-year level there is no essential difference in the abilities of the children, one school psychologist reports. "Above this age," she

says, "we find that the standard ability of groups is far above the average norm. The main results then at the end of the elementary school years show that all group averages are above the norm in the standard achievement tests. It is interesting to note that as a general fact the achievement in the understanding of sentences, in vocabulary and all factors in English pertaining to qualitative development are higher than what might be termed the mechanics in English, such as spelling," &c. Again the strength and weakness of this method seem to be similar to those of the public school case experiments.

In both cases—in the radical private school case directly, in the public school cases indirectly—the method depends for its success on the awakening both of the sense of responsibility and of active life interests in the children in the other and cultural side of their program. If the child has a hearty, satisfying life in school, with the chance to exercise all his latent talents, whether for sculpture or business; if the school opens his eyes to and makes him feel a part of the world today, then, in this partly proved theory, the three R's will be easily added unto him. "The academic becomes a by-product of a real education."

That such academic training stands by progressive school students up through college years has been variously attested. "In the four last years," says Dr. Helen E. Sandison of Vassar College, "at least fourteen of the newer schools have sent up to Vassar about one hundred applicants. Of these about 57 per cent have been accepted. Since not far from half (41 per cent) of the whole number were competing for a limited selective list, this is a reasonably high ratio of acceptance. In fact, it is exactly level with the acceptance ratio for all private schools in the last year or two, and slightly higher than that for all schools, public and private.

"It tallies with the opinion recently expressed by the director of admissions at one of the men's colleges, that the percentage of the boys entering from progressive schools is as high as that from any other type of school.

"At Vassar, as elsewhere, these students after admission prove themselves alert and vigorous. Withdrawals for poor work are apparently rare. Withdrawals for other reasons have been rare at Vassar. Of fifty-three entering in four years nearly one-third have maintained honor or honorable mention standing, and all but three have sustained work satisfactory at least for graduation."

May 26, 1929

Photograph Courtesy of the Lincoln School.

A LESSON IN BANKING

Children Learn How to Deposit and Withdraw Money.

Bible Reading in Schools.

Bible reading in public schools is now expressly required by statute in eleven States (and by order of the Board of Education in the District of Columbia); it is specifically permitted by law in five States; and is generally construed as lawful in twenty of the thirty-two remaining States whose constitutions and statutes do not expressly require, permit or forbid it, says the United States Office of Education. Bible reading in public schools is now held lawful by supreme court decisions of twelve States. Six of these decisions are found in States whose laws either require or specifically permit Bible reading, and six in States whose laws are silent on the subject.

October 5, 1930

SCHOOLS FIT PUPILS FOR A MACHINE AGE

Many Mechanical Devices Are Used in the Education of Modern Youngsters.

HOW WORK IS CARRIED ON

Moving-Picture News Reels Bring to the Child the Problems of an Ever-Changing World.

**By ROLLO G. REYNOLDS,
Principal, Horace Mann School.**

Dean William F. Russell in his last annual report to the trustees of Teachers College presents a striking picture of the difficulty which the American public school faces in adapting education to the rapidly changing world in which we live. He says: "Ingenious men make inventions. New processes are devised. A whole new life develops on the earth. Shall machines, shall inventions, shall industrial processes determine the life which we shall live?" There seems to be in the back of his mind, as he thinks of tomorrow's education in America, the picture of the machine and an industrialized age.

Professor George S. Counts of Teachers College, in the Inglis lecture delivered at Harvard University in 1929, suggests that our teachers are living in the days of Henry Ford and are preparing their pupils for the times of the village blacksmith.

Many of us, whose responsibility is the actual teaching of boys and girls, accept the challenge of a changing age and recognize the industrial, machine-served society in which our children are to live.

I cannot present a formula for successful living in a machine age; nor can I tell how schools should prepare children to live in it. There is evidence, however, that in many ways the school is adapting its curriculum, its methods and its equipment to this machine age; that it is using in the education of children some of the things belonging to the time of Henry Ford. I wish to present some of the ways in which the modern school is making the machine serve the child in a multitude of schools, public and private, throughout our land, and to picture these machines aiding in the education of children who will live in a machine age.

*Readin' and writin' and 'rithmetic,
Taught to the tune of a hick'ry stick.*

So went the old song. So was the school practice. A book, a child, a teacher, and a stick, if necessary. These were the materials by means of which the three R's were handed on. Those were the days of the quill pen, the country fiddler, the tally stick, and McGuffey's Reader. All good in their day but consigned to memory, that deposit vault of "The Good Old Days," by progress, change—call it what you will.

In Schoolrooms Today.

Let us step into a modern school and see what instruments are taking the place of the good old tools. I might take you into any one of a thousand public schools, but because I am more familiar with it let me take you into the Horace Mann School, the demonstration school of

FIRST STEPS IN MASTERING MACHINES.

Typewriters Are Regular Equipment at Horace Mann School.

Teachers College, visited last year by thousands of school teachers and administrators from every State in the Union and most of the countries of the world.

Here is a third grade having a lesson in music. Before the group stands the teacher, a violin tucked under his chin; on the table beside him, a cornet, a clarinet, a viola and other instruments, each of which in turn he plays to the children, bringing out the peculiar tone qualities and explaining the function of each instrument. And now comes the "machine." From the corner, for it is a regular part of the room's equipment, the teacher rolls out the latest in reproducing machines, and into the education of the children, to become a part of their experience, is woven the melody, the harmony, the rhythm of a great symphony played by a great orchestra and bringing to them in reality the tone qualities, the special functions of those instruments which the teacher has offered as his contribution of the day to their education. Here is no slavery to a machine but rather the beginning of a process by which this machine will serve them richly throughout their lives.

Science Made Vivid.

A crowd of fifth and sixth graders are filing into the science room. Here is a machine, a combination of microscope and lantern projector. The children gather around the teacher as he places a drop of ditch water on a glass slide. The lights go out, and there on the screen the "machine" throws before the wondering eyes of the children the teeming, moving, living life which occupies that drop of ditch water. The story of life in its simplest forms becomes a part of the children's possession. The teacher lifts out a lens for a split second thus applying heat to the drop of water and instantly

the busy life on the screen ceases—killed by the heat. The machine has brought into the child's educational experience the principle of sterilization.

On our way out we go by the clerical office. Here are a half dozen boys and girls intent on another machine and as we watch, out from under the round barrel of the school mimeograph come flowing the sheets of a class newspaper whose exaggerated counterpart, the metropolitan press, will be a part of the machine environment into which these children are going.

News Films for Schools.

With strains of a stirring march a young man at the piano is drawing the children, like the Pied Piper of old, into a vast cavern, the assembly hall. Again the lights go out and again a machine contributes to the day's educative experience. From the moving picture booth in the gallery down a shaft of light onto the screen comes the big world of which those children are a part. The weekly news reel. The great ones of the world repeat their last week's activities on the screen. Events momentous in their social and historical significance move past, events to be talked about and discussed when the children get back to their class rooms. It may be in employment; the President's Cabinet; the coronation of Ras Tafari; a disaster in France—the perfection of a new device full of possibilities, good or bad for the world and those who live in it.

Then follows a reel telling vividly the story of transportation, from the savage's floating log and the human burden carriers to the great Europa, the Graf Zeppelin and the 20th Century. The movie: a machine serving these boys and girls by bringing to them the great, complicated, ever-changing world whose problems are soon to be theirs.

The program has been accurately planned and just as transportation has been brought up to the minute and the lights flash on, from the huge loud speaker of the radio, specially built for and given to the school by a modern parent, comes the voice of our favorite announcer describing to us the scene and introducing to us President Hoover, whose words as he addresses a great conference on childhood become a part of our school day. Again a machine, an almost magic machine, serves us as we strive to learn how to live in a changing world. The school prepares each week in advance a radio bulletin, which gives to the teachers the results of a careful study of programs to be presented during the week so that these teachers may take advantage of them during school hours for the children or recommend "listening in" at home.

History by Way of Movies.

In the music room and in some of the class rooms are extensions with small speakers where more intimately the children may listen—this time to Dr. Damrosch and his orchestra. In the library we find small portable moving picture projectors, and a collection of 16 mm. films prepared by various large companies. With these in the class room the children can study the events of history, the story of coal, the achievement of science.

As we have gone throughout the school perhaps you have noticed a kind of machine, which has been present in every class room in considerable quantities—the portable typewriter. There are 180 of them in the school—a regular part of the equipment for every grade. How man has made his records, how he has expressed his ideas in writing, has throughout the history of education been one of the fundamental concerns of the school.

The chiseled hieroglyphics on blocks of stone, the wax tablet and the stylus, the hand-illumined parchments of the monks, the goose quill and its accompanying box of blotting sand, the steel pen, the slate pencil, the lead pencil, the fountain pen: these are the instruments by which man has made his records—each one a step in advance but all somewhat crude, inefficient and requiring much patient practice in their mastery.

These also are the instruments the mastery of which has not been an end in itself but rather a means to the end that by them man may express his thoughts and ideas and transmit them to others. The more perfect the machine for making records, the greater ease in recording ideas. Some years ago Dr. E. L. Thorndike, the psychologist, expressed his belief in the usefulness of the typewriter as an instrument of instruction in the elementary school. With the perfection of the portable typewriter this recording instrument, for a long time practically universal in the business world, became suited to the use of children.

For two years these machines have been a part of the equipment of the Horace Mann School. They are still in the experimental stage, but their usefulness and adaptability have been demonstrated to teachers and children. Their influence on the educational development of the child seems to be at least favorable.

In the third, fourth, fifth and sixth grades of the elementary school we find the typewriters used by the children for stories, poems, spelling words to be learned, arithmetic, history and geography. A machine not to take the place of handwriting but an adjunct to it.

Television's Promise.

As the machine age develops new machines, these will be turned to the education of children. Television, the scientists tell us, is just around the corner. If one allows one's imagination a bit of play it is possible to conceive, for example, the geography of the schools of tomorrow quite different from words in a book. Children may be able to sit in their class room seats and actually see the rushing Niagara and hear its roar.

There is nothing intrinsically evil in a machine. A machine age is not necessarily a retrogression. I believe that schools should utilize machines in so far as they can visualize and vitalize learning and aid the child to make his own the great store of human knowledge and experience, which is accumulating at a terrific rate.

A good school will hand on to its children control over machines in order that these soulless machines may free the human soul to build for itself a better world in which to live.

January 25, 1931

FEDERAL SCHOOL AID GIVES CITY $245,000

Vocational Training Subsidy Is Part of $63,500,000 Spent in Year on Education.

$15,000,000 TO HELP FARMS

$14,000,000 to Army and Navy and $16,000,000 for Interior Department Spent by Government.

Although public education in the United States is considered a function exclusively of the State and local governments, the Federal Government disbursed more than $63,500,000 for various educational projects throughout the country during the fiscal year ended last June.

In addition to its support of the army and navy schools and the public school system in the District of Columbia, the government gradually has become interested in several phases of education and in consequence provides subsidies to encourage them

One such field is vocational training. The appropriation for the Federal Board of Vocational Education totaled $9,400,400 in the year mentioned. This city alone will receive $245,000 from the Federal Government this year as "special moneys earned by reason of the maintenance of vocational activities," according to the Board of Education's budget estimate.

For educational work in the Department of Agriculture more than $15,000,000 was spent. Nearly $5,000,000 of this was for the maintenance of experiment stations and more than $10,000,000 went for the "extension service" connected with that activity.

The operation of the Office of Education in the Department of the Interior, the only specifically educational division of the Federal Government, called for an outlay of more than $1,250,000. Salaries and miscellaneous expenses accounted for $283,000, an investigation of secondary education for $100,000, an investigation of teacher training in the country for $50,000 and "education of natives of Alaska" for $823,000.

The total appropriation for educational work in the Department of Interior rose to nearly $16,000,000. Two and a half million was required for colleges of agriculture and mechanic arts and more than $10,000,000 for the support of Indian schools. In addition, there was an appropriation of $1,249,000 for Howard University in Washington, $125,000 for the Columbia Institution for the Deaf and $100,000 for "civilization of Sioux Indians."

Outlays for the educational activities of the Navy Department rose to nearly $4,000,000. Half of this was for the United States Naval Academy, $934,000 for the naval training stations, $732,000 for "recreation of enlisted men," $130,000 for the Naval Reserve Officers' Training Corps, $115,000 for the Naval War College and $75,000 for the State marine schools.

The largest single share of the $10,267,000 expenditure of the War Department was disbursed for citizens' military training, which cost $6,823,000. Nearly $2,500,000 was required for the United States Military Academy and the rest of the appropriation was distributed among the following departments: army war college, command and general staff school, engineer school, infantry school, cavalry school, field artillery school and instruction, coast artillery school and the National Board for Promotion of Rifle Practice. Thus army and navy activities account for more than $14,000,000 out of the total educational outlay of $63,626,000.

These figures were compiled by the research division of the National Education Association.

April 3, 1932

OUR SCHOOLS FACE A DAY OF RECKONING

Failure of Our Promise of Equal Educational Opportunity For All Children Impels a Move for a National Plan

By EUNICE FULLER BARNARD

ON hundreds of slowly greening hillsides in America today the little red schoolhouse, hopelessly locked for months, has opened its creaking doors. Carpenters, whistling over new-made jobs, reshingle its leaking roof, while over in the next township PWA workmen pour in the concrete foundations of a prouder scholastic structure suited to the modern age.

Thanks to the Federal Government, this is a better Spring than had been hoped for in American public schools. Yet in a way it is a false Spring. For without the government's hothouse forcing it would have been far from green in many educational purlieus. Ten times the 2,000 schools of last Winter would have been closed, it is estimated, and hordes of youngsters turned out to roam the streets. Even now, it is said, 3,000,000 adolescents are without jobs or schools and 200,000 certificated teachers are unemployed.

For the first time in the nation's history, to all intents and purposes thousands of schools are on a Federal dole. That dole will not last forever. Many of our children have been, and still may be, threatened with illiteracy, while others are assured as elaborate a public education as is offered anywhere in the world. Yet this is only an acute phase of a chronic condition. Educators admit that those free and equal educational opportunities, to which we have pointed as the charter of our democracy, are becoming only a scrap of paper.

* * *

A GREAT American tradition has been shaken. We have come to see that our school system, of which we have boasted as if it were as set and standardized as the flag itself, is in fact no system at all. Our claim that the sons of the farm hand and of the factory owner through our public schools have the same chance to make good fades daily further into the realm of theory. The inequalities, to be sure, are on geographic rather than strictly economic lines. But the fact remains that some of our children are paupers and some are millionaires in educational opportunity.

In present practice, even with Federal emergency aid, our schooling varies from California to Alabama almost as much as does education in London, let us say, from that in Labrador. An American public school at the moment may connote anything from an unheated, dilapidated one-room shack, closed until further notice, to a 200-room palace whose frescoed walls, swimming pool and air-conditioned interior a Roman emperor might envy.

The school teacher may be the "deserving" aunt of a school-board member, who has never finished high school, or she may be a vigorous, professional-minded Ph. D. Her annual salary may be $400, payable in scrip and owing for months, or it may run up to the $10,000 stipend of the New York high school principal, paid in good cash, with only a slight cut during the depression.

The school program ranges between similar antipodes. It may include the rudiments of almost every science and art, from Greek to aviation; or it may have little more than the reading and writing of pioneer days. Library, laboratories, studios, special teachers, sound-motion pictures, radio and gymnasium may lend their aid. There may be, as in New York now, school-room concerts by opera stars, and conducted trips to some of the finest art and natural-history collections in the world. There may be extraordinary opportunities, as in dozens of cities like Cleveland and Los Angeles, to learn in school choral singing and orchestra playing.

On the other hand, for millions of our children almost the only glimpse of art, literature, science and music must come through the pages of a few dog-eared books and the spare moments of a single teacher.

* * *

AMERICAN education is the apotheosis of localism and individualism. And individualism in practice has not been uniformly rugged. Around the fortu-

"Some of Our Children Are Assured as Elaborate a Public Education as Is Offered in the World," While—

nate in our public schools has been thrown every safeguard of medical and sanitary and psychiatric science. A white-capped nurse, sometimes also a doctor, a dentist and an oculist look after infections, malnutrition, eyes and ears and teeth. Learning and behavior difficulties have the expert diagnosis and help of psychologist, mental hygienist and visiting teacher.

Meanwhile other school children across the State or county line may be drinking from a common dipper: spreading measles about the classroom unobserved and unchecked, and reciting in a schoolroom whose mental atmosphere is that of the dunce-cap and birch-rod era.

As for the higher schooling, and lower too, for that matter, there is little of the vaunted equality as between Detroit, for instance, and a Kentucky mountain district. In Detroit a youngster may spend his whole life up to maturity or beyond, from the age of 4 perhaps to 24, ranging under public auspices through all realms of learning from kindergarten through college and even professional training. In many places in Kentucky he is lucky if he has access to a one-room elementary school.

Schooling, according to the political orator, is the birthright of every American child. But it is a birthright of very variable annual cash value, according to whether the youngster's home is in city or country, in New Jersey or South Carolina. And the parents who would give their children the most and best education would better choose with care the town and State in which to live. In actual dollars and cents an elementary ed-

ucation in these United States ranges all the way in value from about $12 a year in certain parts of Alabama to $103.75 in New York City. Before the depression it ran up to $192 in a few favored Eastern towns.

Moreover, the city child not only gets a princely education as against the five-and-ten variety offered in some rural districts; he gets more of it. In normal times, it is estimated, he has a five weeks' longer term than his country cousin, or a whole year more of schooling during the elementary course.

And the injustice of it all is that oftentimes father makes little saving in taxes by living in the district where the children have a short, cheap schooling. On the contrary he usually has to pay a higher tax rate in such a poor district than in a rich one which offers far better

schools. By and large it is true that the most inadequate schools are kept going by a killing local property tax on a few poor farmers. The best ones thrive by the aid of State taxes on income, inheritance, sales, corporations or chain stores in addition to local real estate levies.

* * *

AS Alice found in her adventures through the looking-glass in the checkerboard country,

Times Wide World.

—"Others Are Lucky If They Have Access to a One-Room Elementary School."

everything changes when you come to the next square. So it is here, educationally. And to make it the more confusing, there are an unbelievable number of squares of every size and shape. This country, theoretically, so far as school systems go, is a collection of States. But in practice, educationally speaking, it is some 127,000 well-nigh sovereign principalities, large and small, rich and poor. With more or less, usually less, State regulation, each levies its own school taxes, sets its own school term, hires its own teachers and picks out its own school sites.

You do not have to go from Arkansas to New York to get school contrast. Crossing from one rural district to another in the same State may provide almost as much. In one may be a tightly locked one-room school closed after its four-month term. In another, not twenty miles away, may be a big, prosperous "consolidated school," with plants in the windows, children swarming through its steam-heated corridors, and visiting special teachers for music, art and the gymnasium.

In other words, there are 127,000 varieties of schooling in these United States, ruled over by as many school boards with varying amounts of help or interference from the State. And there is absolutely no rule as to the size of a district or how many children it shall accommodate with school facilities.

Take the two adjoining States of Idaho and Utah, which have about the same number of teachers. In Idaho a school district averages less than sixty square miles. Across the border in Utah it measures something over 2,000. It takes thirty-five times as many school boards, programs and tax systems in Idaho as in Utah to do the same size educational job.

In the populous States of Illinois and New York, where motor service and highways abound, there is nevertheless a school district on the average of every five square miles. That means more than 12,000 boards managing school affairs in Illinois alone relics of the horse-and-buggy era when a school had to be a neighborhood matter.

One school board of seven members in New York City presides over the destinies of 1,000,000 pupils. One of like size in Cedar Hollow manages the affairs of Miss Sally Jones and her score of young charges. Almost four-fifths of the school boards of the country have their whole kingdom centring in a single common school.

Thus while businesses, railroads and banks merge, the school has "set itself against the major currents of American life," according to a recent pronouncement of the United States Office of Education.

EVEN with schools closing entirely, as they have in the past year in many of the poorer districts, the system still persists, largely, it is asserted, because of the inertia and the will-to-power of the school board members themselves. Service on the school committees is one of the popular and time-honored American amateur sports, enjoyed today by some 423,000 of our fellow citizens. Logically it should be listed in some of the new guides to leisure-time occupations. There is actually one school board member to every two teachers in the country. And in twelve States the board members outnumber the teachers, in some cases by several thousand.

Again and again, according to a former United States Commissioner of Education, it has proved impossible to unite two or more school districts for the benefit of the children involved, because the various board members wanted to keep their jobs.

Generally speaking, these persons who direct the educational policies of our youth are middle-aged business men little disposed toward change of any kind, if one may trust the various surveys that have been made of them. A recent study of a thousand of them in all parts of the country showed a majority apparently believing that all is well with our present social order and with the present citizenship training of the schools. More than half said they were opposed to free speech.

Moreover, when it comes to making up the course of study these legally empowered amateurs have plenty of volunteer help. Constantly at their elbows, prodding them to put in this or that subject, are dozens of special-interest groups ranging from the American Legion to the Women's Christian Temperance Union. Sometimes these "pressure" organizations start higher up, with the even more amenable State Legislatures. For though States have often been chary of financial aid to schools, they have always been free with advice. State laws throughout the country already list an average of twenty-seven subjects that must be taught in elementary schools.

In Pennsylvania, for instance, according to a recent report to the National Education Association, the law requires the teaching of English, including spelling, reading and writing; arithmetic, geography, the history of the United States and Pennsylvania; civics, including loyalty to the State and national government; regular instruction in the Constitution of the United States; safety education, the humane treatment of birds and animals, music, art; health, including physical training; physiology and hygiene with special reference to tuberculosis and its prevention, and to the effect of alcoholic drinks, stimulants and narcotics upon the human body; and regular and continuous study of the dangers of fire and the prevention of fire waste.

The teacher must also read ten verses of the Bible at the beginning of the school day; devote some time to the study of wild birds, including the value of the existence of such birds to the people; give instruction in the life and principles of Frances Willard on Sept. 28; commemorate the death of General Casimir Pulaski on Oct. 11, and the life of William Penn on Oct. 24. In addition she is requested to celebrate Education Week, Thrift Week, Safety Week, Good English Week, Music Week, Bird Day, Arbor Day, and so on.

This leaves the balance of the day free for character building, social studies and other subjects not prescribed by legislative action.

Other States have other programs, with many sorts of required studies, from cotton grading and forestry to oratory and manners. Seldom do the statutes lay out a course of study according to a professional modern plan. More often they are an accretion of a century of laymen's prejudices, wise or ignorant.

* * *

IN brief, then, our "system of education" throughout the United States has scarcely one standard unit. Not even in minimum requirements is there any answer to the questions: What is a teacher? What is a district? A school term? A school building? Or a course of study? Our twin philosophies of local initiative in school matters and equality of opportunity for all children have in practice proved compatible. Local initiative has run away with the game, to the immense benefit of some children and the equal disadvantage of others.

What the last few years have done is to sharpen the demands for national rules of fair play. Everywhere educators' associations are calling for a national plan for schools and for a voluntary agreement of the States upon standards. The American teacher, they are saying, should be as explicitly stabilized as the dollar. In the first place, a national survey should determine how many teachers are needed. Only that number should be admitted to the profession. And each of these should be a graduate of a training school of certified grade and length of course.

Likewise, the school district should be as clearly defined as the postage stamp in its size and powers, they hold. Already they are suggesting standards that would wipe out the little red schoolhouses in many a countryside. A district should be large enough, they say, to give sound schooling from kindergarten through high school under expert supervision, and to provide care of health and other special services.

They are asking, too, that teachers should work out nationally a new school course "appropriate to the demands of life in the middle of the twentieth century," to provide a "social intelligence superior to that required in the pioneer epoch just closed."

Finally, they would have us make good nationally on our traditional promise of a certain modicum of schooling to every child regardless of race, creed, color or sex. And this is possible, they believe, without killing local school pride and initiative.

"The time has come to proclaim the principles of a national minimum or foundation program of education for every child, whether he happens to be attending school in Maine, Florida, Arkansas or California," declared a commission of the National Education Association recently. "This national minimum educational opportunity should be financed jointly by the nation and the States according to their tax-paying ability."

To "those who would raise the bugaboo of Federal control," the commission replies that such control is avoidable if no clauses in the law directly or indirectly involve it, and if the government grants are made on an objective basis of so many dollars per child.

That would mean not an emergency relief fund for schools, but year in and year out a certain part of our tax dollar apportioned equally among the youngsters of these United States, so that the youthful Montanan may have basically the same schooling as the Manhattanite, and the pickaninnies the same as the Pinckneys.

TEACHER GOES MODERN

Traditional 'Schoolmarm' Type Gives Way To the Exponent of the New Freedom

The Spring term of the New York public schools, which opens tomorrow, finds 410 names added to the roster of teachers and members of the educational staff. Similar groups, infiltrating into the school system year after year, are responsible for the slow changing of the New York school teacher as a type. This article attempts to depict the personality and background of the average woman teacher of today.

By VICTOR H. BERNSTEIN.

THE school teacher, in her vulnerable position as guardian of the nation's youth, has always been a center of controversy. Once she was criticized as a "blue stocking," a paragon of forbiddingly angular rectitudes who carried her classroom didacticism too frequently into the parlor. Now she is often attacked as a radical, a mercenary trade unionist, who carries the modern woman's new freedom too frequently into the classroom.

What is she really like, this teacher of whom much of our knowledge comes second hand, relayed by not always unbiased youngsters?

The fact is that, in the larger cities at least, the teacher is evolving from a distinct type into middle-class anonymity. Meet her on the street, at a party, on a West Indies cruise, and she is difficult to distinguish from other women of her class. If the season calls for brown, she is wearing brown. She has poise, sophistication and independence, and in mixed company she avoids shop talk, horn-rimmed spectacles and bookishness.

She no longer has chosen teaching as a better-than-nothing substitute for marriage; nor need she, through idealism, renounce the second for the first. With increasing frequency she is managing to find a husband and keep her job too.

The "Average" Teacher.

It is significant, of course, that the contemporary teacher is almost invariably thought of as a "she." Of the more than 35,000 teachers in the New York City public schools, 27,500 are women. In the elementary schools, women outrank men nearly nineteen to one; in the high schools, the ratio is three to two. Throughout the public schools of the country the ratio is about five to one.

The average New York teacher, then, is a woman nearly 40 years old; there is nearly a fifty-fifty chance that she is married and about a 20 per cent chance that she is a mother. In the opinion of most educators, the fact that she is married does not at all detract

from her teaching ability; and if she has children her ability is likely to have been enhanced by an added sympathy. She has, to a large extent, escaped the cynicism of the post-war younger generation (she was already settled in her job when F. Scott Fitzgerald was depicting that generation in terms of bitter disillusionment).

The average teacher earns a little more than $3,000 a year in elementary schools and $4,000 in the high schools (less a 6 per cent reduction voted two years ago). It is an income which she can command for thirty more years, until her enforced retirement at the age of 70. The chances are, however, that she will retire shortly before she reaches 60 on about half-pay, which she has earned by putting an average of 5½ per cent of her earnings into the Teachers' Retirement Fund (to which the city contributes).

Her Security Assured.

This pleasing financial outlook gives the teacher a feeling—heightened during the depression—of security she had never known before. She comes from a home of but moderate comfort, and one of her primary objects in going into teaching was to help eke out the family income. More likely than not, her own schooling—for teaching in elementary grades she has had a two or three year training school course beyond high school—has been paid for by her father. Now, in an amazing number of instances, she is paying her debt by helping to support one or more of her relatives.

The teacher knows the intricate financial history of her profession. She recognizes that each increase has been won only through the hardest kind of propagandizing before the State Legislature. She will fight bitterly and unendingly against any attempt to lower her income. Her economic philosophy rarely goes further, however. The teacher's interest in the two union groups at her disposal here—the Teachers Union and the newer and more conservative Teachers Guild—remains sporadic and somewhat academic. The combined membership is under 3,000—fewer than 7.5 per cent of the city's teachers.

Politically, she is inclined to be an opportunist—which means, in this city, a registered Democrat. She finds that avowed fealty to that party is never a barrier to promotions and various administrative plums.

Cultural Levels.

A painstaking research worker recently made a survey of the cultural background of teachers' col-

Doris Day.

A Teacher Engages the Attention of Her Pupils.

lege students in a dozen representative communities, including New York. She found that the future teacher read two or three of the popular "smooth paper" magazines fairly regularly and digested a light novel about once a month. Her interest in authors reached its apex in Temple Bailey, Gene Stratton Porter, Dickens and Kathleen Norris; was moderate in John Galsworthy, Zane Grey, Warwick Deeping and Edna Ferber; began to peter out at Eugene O'Neill and Shakespeare, and was barely active in Sinclair Lewis and Upton Sinclair.

In music her taste ranged from the Irving Berlin genre of popular songs through sacred music, the "Old Kentucky Home" type of sentiment song, down through love songs, jazz, orchestra, bands and grand opera in the order named.

Opinion is divided as to how accurately this sketch reflects the background of the active New York teacher, who is nearly twenty years older than the student teacher, presumably more sophisticated and who certainly has more cultural opportunity.

Technical Ability High.

Little disagreement occurs among educators with respect to the average teacher's technical ability in her profession. The qualifying examinations for teachers have grown steadily more difficult. The teacher of today not only knows what is in her textbook, but knows how to maintain discipline and get her knowledge across to her pupils. She is conscientious about her job, but does not live, breathe and

eat it in the fashion of many teachers of an earlier day. She enjoys women's new freedom as much as the salesgirl or the stenographer, and has rather more money to pay for it. Her acquaintance with clothing and millinery shops is varied and enthusiastic; she sees the most popular Broadway shows, is fond of the movies and (so far as the younger group is concerned) has at least as many dates per week as the representative New York girl.

Because of her superior financial position she is the darling of mail advertising writers. She buys generously, most advertisers agree, and she has a characteristic womanly fondness for charge accounts.

Many Live With Relatives.

The unmarried teacher of the younger set, despite her independent means, rarely lives alone or even with a chum. Mostly she lives at home or with an aunt, a cousin or a sister. Naturally enough, the school personnel furnishes the majority of her friends. With them she talks "shop," discusses clothes, "dates," movies, drama and books in something of the order named. She does not read many of the technical educational journals, but she follows religiously the school pages of the daily paper.

The average 9-to-3 workday of the school teacher, coupled with the long vacations, brings her official working hours to something less than 1,000 a year. The factory or office worker puts in 1,000 hours at his job in six months or less.

17

In many instances, too, the ringing of the 3 o'clock bell does not mean release for her. Extra-curricular activities—clubs, meetings with parents, school conferences, sports, debating teams, school journals—take up an hour or two.

Inferiority Complex?

Dr. Olga Knopf, an acute commentator on women, believes that the unmarried teacher still retains an inferiority complex with respect to men—a heritage of the time when teaching was the only respectable method for an unmarried woman to make a living. If this is so, it is a rapidly decreasing phenomenon. The removal of the ban on marriages and provisions for a two-year maternity nave opened the profession to thousands of average girls who actively harbored every normal expectation of marriage.

There is now in process of evolution a new series of qualifications for the city's school teachers. The training schools, closed several years ago, are permanently to be replaced by a full four-year college course, in which general culture will share the curriculum with pedagogy. What effect this new plan will have on the personality of the average school teacher remains to be seen.

SCHOOLS DISCARD PUPIL DISCIPLINE

Negative Punishment Gives Way to New Psychology in the Classroom

CHILDREN ARE HAPPIER

Solemn Atmosphere Displaced by Friendly Spirit Between Teachers and Classes

By BENJAMIN FINE

With the long Summer vacation officially at an end, the 1,225,000 children who go back to school tomorrow morning will find that formal discipline—the kind that demands the child to sit up straight, march through the halls like a robot, stop fidgeting in his seat and never whisper or pass a note to his neighbor—is on its way out in the New York City school system.

Educational leaders disclosed yesterday that greater emphasis is to be placed on individualized instruction this year and that "negative" punishment will be discouraged. The teacher will be expected to gain the confidence of her class not by autocratic dictum, but through sympathetic cooperation with her charges. The new classroom psychology is expected to make school a happier place for both teachers and pupils.

Instead of treating the children as though they were hoodlums bent on mischief, the teachers have become imbued with the educational philosophy that considers them individuals with personalities, wants, desires and differences of their own. Natural conditions are found in the classroom, instead of the stiff, artificial situations that existed a generation ago. The solemn atmosphere has given way to the friendly, congenial spirit of children who go willingly to school. The day of the dunce-cap is over.

Discipline by Fear Is Over

A good teacher today, according to James Marshall, vice president of the Board of Education, thinks of discipline in terms of constructive accomplishments, rather than the iron rule and the rod. Good teachers have sufficient resources to cope with every classroom situation without resort to negative punishment in his opinion. Strict discipline through the use of fear is an admission of bankruptcy.

"The whole trend of modern education is an attempt to find some affirmative way of handling children who present disciplinary problems," he added. "We no longer accept formal negative discipline. If a childen does not listen to a teacher it is not assumed that the youngster is naughty.

"The teacher ascertains if the child is hard of hearing or suffering from some nervous disorder, and if so, prescribes medical attention. If a child falls asleep in class the teacher does not yank him out of his seat and make him stand in the corner as an object lesson to the rest of the class. Today the teacher tries to find out if he is undernourished or if the home conditions are such that the child gets no sleep."

Not long ago, Mr. Marshall said, the school exacted absolute obedience and subordination of self to the teacher. The classroom presented a picture of immobilized robots. Those who could not conform tended to become neurotic and often to enter criminal careers. Now, however, much greater freedom of movement and action are permitted. Good order is relative to the situation, he declared, and within the limits of decency and self-control, children obtain freedom as a necessary part of their development in learning to live with others.

Teachers Less Domineering

Dr. Benjamin Greenberg, Assistant Superintendent of Schools, in charge of several experimental projects where formal discipline has been completely abolished, said that a more natural "give and take" exists in the classroom today and the teacher is less domineering than she was in the past.

Whispering, moving about or getting out of the seat to confer with some one across the aisle is no longer considered a sign of disrespect or insubordination, he indicated. Accordingly, these acts are not considered a breach of discipline and punished. Through a "living and learning" process, behaviour patterns of a most wholesome kind are being developed in the classroom.

"Our new approach to the problem of discipline is a challenge to the teacher," he continued. "If the teacher can keep the child vitally concerned in his work no problem will arise. We are getting away from regimentation and formal discipline in the New York City schools in every progressive community in the country."

Children in sixty-seven schools of this city where the activity program is in process will find that discipline means self-control from within their own ranks, rather than obedience to a teacher. Under the direction of Dr. John J. Loftus, assistant superintendent of schools, this experiment, started a year ago, will continue, and the results will be evaluated.

Children Easier to Handle

Tentative conclusions show that the children are much happier and much easier to handle when the discipline is shifted to their own shoulders.

A teacher who takes the attitude that she is "boss" and must dominate the situation will fail, Morris E. Siegel, director of continuation and evening schools, said. A closer pupil-teacher relationship in which they discuss the problems of the classroom is in effect in many schools and has proved valuable.

The children's dicipline should be the result of genuine interest in their school work, Mrs. Johanna M. Lindlof, Queens representative on the Board of Education, declared. The old idea of sitting up straight with eyes forward, of marching into the assembly room and acting like robots is no longer tenable in the school system, she added. However, a "happy medium" is desirable, a point where freedom but not license is allowed the child.

"A certain amount of discipline is needed but it should be the sympathetic, understanding kind," she said.

CITY LIKELY TO DROP 8B GRADE SCHOOLS

Board of Education Committee Recommends That Junior Highs Replace Them

SWEEPING CHANGES ASKED

6-Year Elementary Training Would Cut Out Transition Period in High School

What may prove to be the death knell of the traditional eight-year elementary school in New York City was sounded yesterday when a committee of educators, appointed a year ago by the Board of Education, presented a sixty-page report strongly recommending that the junior high schools be made a permanent part of the city's public school system.

For the last decade the school system has been going in two directions simultaneously. On one hand the Board of Education has expanded the 6-3-3 plan (six years of elementary school, three years of junior high and three years of senior high), while on the other it has continued with the traditional 8-4 program (eight years of elementary school and four years of senior high school).

A year ago the Board of Education mapped out a six-year building program. At that time the educators decided that they would have to determine the future policy of the school system before it embarked on its projected construction plans. A committee headed by Henry C. Turner, chairman of the board's finance committee, was appointed by James Marshall, president of the board, and Dr. Harold G. Campbell, Superintendent of Schools, to study the question and recommend the policy to be followed.

All Phases Studied

Every phase of the problem was considered and analyzed by the committee. Various traditional elementary schools were compared with the newer junior high schools. According to the educators, the evidence indicates that the 6-3-3 plan is superior to the time-honored 8-4 type of educational program.

As a result, it is urged that the eight-year grade school, now in effect in 50 per cent of the system, be ended as soon as possible. The report suggests that all future schools, wherever feasible, be built along the newer lines of the junior high school plans.

If the Board of Education acts upon the report of its committee, it will mean basic changes in the set-up of the New York City school system. For one thing, the curriculum would have to be adjusted to meet the changes brought about by the new organization. All high schools would become three-year institutions, instead of four as at present.

Fundamental changes would also take place in the administration of the schools. There would be a transfer of elementary school teachers to the new junior high schools, and the approach to the teaching would differ drastically. As a relatively minor result, the traditional graduation exercises that now take place at the end of the eighth grade would disappear.

Better Articulation

What would happen, though, the educators point out, is that there would be a better articulation from kindergarten up through high school. The transition period that usually takes place between elementary and secondary school would disappear, as the student would continue through the grades and into high school without a break.

Recommendations for the improvement of the junior high schools, as they now exist, are made by the committee. It is proposed that girls receive shop training in electrical work and in woodworking and boy pupils "in cooking and some of the other household arts."

The committee found, in studying shop provisions for the junior high school student, that "general differentiation of shop activities into those for boys and those for girls has led to a narrowing of the industrial arts experiences of both sexes."

According to the committee, the "junior high school system is suffering from an enforced growth." This has resulted in including some of the schools in buildings not adapted to the needs of the junior high schools. It is suggested that each school be surveyed and improvements made where possible, and that if the school building or location is found inadequate, it should be discontinued.

Oppose Division in Groups

Opposition to the existing practice of dividing junior high school students into three groups—academic, commercial and industrial—was voiced by the educators. Children are too young to decide what future course to take while still in junior high school, they feel.

"Very little can be learned about these immature pupils in the seventh school year that can be a sound basis for an important educational decision," the committee reported. "Besides, what differentiation of courses at this age can be of much significance to most pupils in their later studies in the secondary schools?"

What these pupils actually need, it was suggested, is a sound general education, courses of study in basic subjects adapted to their abilities and interests, and rich experiences in the fields of appreciational, applied and industrial arts.

"Notwithstanding the desirability of completely reorganizing the school system into a 6-3-3 type of organization, it is plainly evident that many years will be required before this goal is reached," the committee declared.

In the meantime, 8B elementary schools will continue to operate. It is important, therefore, that whatever adaptations of the junior high school program can be made to advantage for the upper grade pupils of the 8B schools should be made."

MORE MEN ARE TEACHING

School Survey Shows Rise From 18 to 25 Per Cent Since 1920

WASHINGTON, July 19 (P).— Men, who made up 32 per cent of the country's school teachers in 1900 but only 18 per cent in 1920, gradually are returning to the school room.

Some 266,000 male teachers, composing one-fourth of the teaching total, were listed today in a government survey covering 1934-36 for the latest full report on education in the United States.

The survey showed that Latin, French and Spanish are losing popularity in public high schools. Where every other student took Latin in 1900, only four out of twenty-five were enrolled. The most popular subjects were English, mathematics, commercial studies, science and physical education.

More than 30,000,000 persons, about one-fourth the population, were enrolled in full-time day schools in 1935-36, with more than 2,000,000 in other type schools. Total expenditures for education, public and private, were listed as $2,650,000,000.

July 6, 1939

July 20, 1939

COLLEGE ENTRANCE BOARD

An Association for Examinations Organized at Columbia.

Middle States and Maryland Institutions Represented—President Low Chairman of the Organization.

The College Entrance Examination Board for the Middle States and Maryland met in the Trustees' Room, at Columbia University, yesterday. The meeting was for the purpose of perfecting a permanent organization.

The different colleges in the association were represented as follows: Barnard, Acting Dean Robinson; Br'n Mawr, President Thomas; Columbia, Prof. Nicholas Murray Butler; Cornell, Prof. H. S. White; New York University, Chancellor MacCracken; University of Pennsylvania, Prof. W. A. Lamberton; Rutgers, President Scott; Swarthmore, President Birdsall; Union, President Raymond; Vassar, President Taylor; Woman's College of Baltimore, Prof. Van Meter; Johns Hopkins University, Prof. Griffin.

The board organized by choosing President Seth Low as Chairman, President Thomas of Bryn Mawr as Vice Chairman, and Prof. Nicholas Murray Butler as Secretary. No Treasurer was elected. An Executive Committee was appointed as follows: President Taylor, Prof. W. A. Lamberton, and Dr. Julius Sachs of the Sachs School.

The plan of organization of the new association is as follows: A College Entrance Examination Board is established, to consist of the President, or an authorized representative of each college or university in the Middle States and Maryland, which has a freshman, or entering, class of not fewer than fifty students, (courses in arts and in sciences to be reckoned together for this purpose,) and of five representatives of secondary schools of the Middle States and Maryland, to be chosen annually by the Association of Colleges and Preparatory Schools.

This board has the power, from time to time, to adopt and publish a statement of the ground which should be covered and of the aims which should be sought by secondary school teaching in each of the following subjects, and a plan of examination suitable as a test for admission to college: Botany, chemistry, English, French, German, Greek, history, Latin, mathematics, physics, and zoölogy.

Not later than December of each academic year this board designates for each of these subjects a college teacher to act as chief examiner, and one additional college teacher and one secondary school teacher to act as associate examiners. It is the duty of the examiners so appointed to prepare examination questions in the several subjects, to be used at the annual examinations to be held under the direction of the College Entrance Examination Board. When the question papers have been agreed on by the respective groups of examiners, they are submitted for approval or revision to a committee to consist of the chief examiners and the five representatives of the secondary schools upon the College Entrance Examination Board.

These examiners will hold examinations on four days in the last week of June at two or three points in the Middle States and Maryland, and at other points in the West.

Such students as are successful in passing the examinations will receive a certificate, which will be accepted in lieu of further examination by all institutions represented on the board.

An examination fee of $5 will be charged, and it is expected that the expenses of the board will be met by these fees. It is believed that at least 1,000 students will take the examinations next June. Some of these, however, will be those who do not intend to enter college, but wish the certificate as a proof of completion of the college entrance course.

MORALS AND MANNERS OF COLLEGE STUDENTS

Topic Considered at the National Educational Association.

President Harris of Amherst Says Athletics Promotes Morals—Address by President Tucker of Dartmouth and Bishop Gailor.

BOSTON, July 8.—The Department of Higher Education connected with the National Educational Association considered to-day the question, "Shall the University Concern Itself More Directly with the Morals and Manners of the Students?"

Presidents George Harris of Amherst, William J. Tucker of Dartmouth, W. F. Slocum of Colorado College, and the Rev. Thomas F. Gailor, Bishop of Tennessee, were the speakers. President Harris, in the course of his address, said:

"The college should concern itself with the morals and manners of students, but not, I think, directly by specific methods and devices. The college must make requirements as to studies, and, for the most, must trust to influence. Work itself is the best moral power.

"Athletics promotes morals. Should football, baseball, and field athletics cease, the moral tone of the college would be lowered. Sports come more and more upon a moral basis.

"There is more genuine religion in the college to-day than in any period of our history. Cant and pretense are not tolerated. Irrational doctrine is discarded. But faith, hope, love, and character are exalted. The college should encourage sane, healthy, trustful, God-loving and man-serving religion."

President Tucker said in part: "The American college or university stands for social advancement as well as for intellectual discipline. The university is that gateway through which democracy passes to the refinement of its strength.

"Scholarship is not the first end of college or even of the university. The common product of each is not the scholar by distinction, but the man who is fitted for the largest uses of society and the State. In view of these considerations it becomes a matter of 'direct concern' for the college and university to take account of morals and manners.

"In carrying out this obligation constant stress must be laid upon the morality of work. We do not wish to produce any type of manhood in which honest work has no substantial place.

"I should urge with great emphasis the principle that nothing more can be expected from students either in morals or manners, but especially in manners, than is done for them or with them. If the college management is unbusinesslike, if the college buildings are without taste, if the whole social life is lacking in vigor or attractiveness, nothing more ought to be expected from students than careless and indifferent behavior."

Bishop Gailor said: "The universities of the country are the truest and surest nurseries of citizenship, and citizenship in its largest sense is rounded manhood.

"A university which does not concern itself directly and systematically with the morals and manners of its students fails to appreciate or discharge its duty to the country.

"When we come to consider more specifically what that moral development includes, I should say that the three virtues of honesty, purity, and reverence are the virtues that need most to be cultivated, because they are foundations of character and because they are not altogether encouraged by the conditions of modern life."

THE LATIN REQUIREMENT.

That the four-year Latin requirement for admission to Yale College "has now become almost unique"; that most of the high schools "except those within Yale's sphere of "influence" have either dropped or sidetracked this subject, and that Yale is therefore restricting admission from the high schools, and in consequence snobbishly encouraging admission from the special fitting schools, was the contention of the Chairman of the Committee on Entrance Examinations in the Sheffield Scientific School, printed in The Yale Alumni Weekly of March 27. Some one has gone after and searched these statements, and in the current issue of The Yale Alumni Weekly the facts are produced.

Examining the catalogues of twenty-one of the leading older endowed institutions with which Yale is classed, it is found that Dartmouth, Williams, Amherst, Boston, Brown, Columbia, Princeton, and Johns Hopkins have the four-year Latin entrance requirement; that five of the women's colleges, Wellesley, Mount Holyoke, Smith, Vassar, and Bryn Mawr, maintain it; and three years' preparation in Latin is required at Harvard, Bowdoin, and Trinity. Tufts requires two years. Only two universities, Cornell and Pennsylvania, confer the B. A. degree with Latin as an elective. At Bowdoin and Harvard, which require only three years' preparation, it is found that 60 per cent. of the candidates for the class of 1917 presented the full four years.

"Dead" Latin is not so moribund, it seems, as Greek. The high schools furnished students at the nine colleges entering with the four-year requirement in quotas ranging from 25 per cent. at Princeton to 60 per cent. at Columbia, 70 per cent. at Dartmouth, and 80 per cent. and more at Amherst. If these pupils come within "Yale's sphere of influence," certainly the five or six thousand students at the women's colleges, all of whom must have a four-year Latin course, are not within that influence. The girls come from all over the country. While 48 per cent. of the new students at Vassar during the last four years were from public high schools, only 41 per cent. were prepared at private schools, the remainder having had training at both. At Wellesley 64 per cent. of the two lower classes are high school pupils, 32 per cent. from the private schools; at Smith the proportions are 63 per cent. and 30 per cent. among sophomores, which is about the average for all the women's colleges. At Mount Holyoke 82 per cent. of the students come from the high schools.

As a component part of the English language Latin is very much alive—a fact which the schools and colleges seem to realize.

NEW WOMAN'S COLLEGE UNLIKE ALL OTHERS

Projected Institution at Bennington, Vt., Expects to Train Women for a Broader Life at Home—Has Approval of Leading Educators

COOLIDGE ASSAILS COLLEGE RADICALS

Sees Need for More Attention in Teaching Fundamentals to Students.

WOULD DEVELOP CHARACTER

More attention to teaching fundamentals to combat the influence of radical propagandists who are seeking to spread their doctrines among the students of American colleges, is suggested by Vice President Calvin Coolidge in an article in the August Delineator.

"As this is written," Mr. Coolidge said, "the attempt to open the colleges to undirected radical influences is going on. The press reports 250 students organizing such a movement at Harvard.

"There was a report in The New York Herald of April 26 of a serious difficulty at Valparaiso, Ind., which forced President Hodgdon to resign, and to say:

"'The University is a hotbed of Bolshevism, communism and other cults, and nothing we could do to thwart their propaganda has been of any avail because of sinister inside influences.'

"The same paper reports an article written for the Yale News by E. G. Buckland, Vice President and General Manager of the New York, New Haven and Hartford Railroad, in which he says:

"'Periodically, Yale is written to, visited and talked to by men who present ideas at variance with what have long been regarded as sound economics. This propaganda appeals to the sympathies and exploits the credulity of the younger part of their hearers and readers. It taxes the patience and offends the common sense of the older part.'

"'Again it must be said, 'Let the students hear all sides;' but undirected they do not hear all sides. Education is a leading out. What influence and who is to lead student thought?"

At a time when so many colleges are going to the public with pleas for funds to increase their endowments, Mr. Coolidge said that it was a pertinent question to ask what results they obtained from these funds.

"Are they missing the one true aim of all education, the development of character?" he asked. "In their scramble to teach commercialism have they forgotten that character does not come from economic development? Sound economic development comes from sound character and sound character alone."

Mr. Coolidge said that men in many countries had experimented many times with radical theories in great and small ways, and always with complete failure.

"Such theories are not new," he said. "They are old. Each failure has demonstrated anew that without effort there is no success.

"Of this the French Revolution is the classic example. As a rebellion against despotism it was to be commended. When it went beyond that and undertook to confiscate all Government and all religion, when there was no safety for property or life, it was foredoomed to failure. Rather than endure such a condition the people sought refuge in an orderly monarchy. They turned back.

"The same thing will take place—from all appearances it is taking place—in Russia. The theory of the revolution, which overthrew Government and religion alike for a form of communism, has broken down. The people are setting up authority. The rulers of Russia are beginning to recognize the right of life and property. They are doing this in order to save their country from complete devastation. They are turning back."

PLANS are being made to establish another woman's college in New England, different from all the others. The project is creating widespread interest in the field of education. Probably no question is more deeply discussed today than the failure of educational methods; and of all those who deplore the situation, educators and teachers are the quickest to speak their criticisms.

Within recent years there have been great improvements in the methods of teaching in kindergarten, primary and grade schools, changes accomplished because the teaching body was dissatisfied with the poor results hitherto obtained. Horace Mann School, connected with the Teachers College of Columbia University is a well-known example of such changes and improvements. But compared to the planning and efforts expended on secondary schools little has been done within the institutions of higher learning.

Now an opportunity has come to establish a college with the highest standards of scholarship, but different in many ways from the accepted characteristics of such an institution. Educators with vision and a clear sense of relative values are seizing upon the idea. The same amount of careful planning and testing will be used in the establishment of this college which has been used in latter years with schools for children. Unhampered by "traditions"—a word that has covered many coeducational sins—with a Faculty of men and women chosen not only for their scholastic achievements and teaching capabilities but because they have in their hearts the vision of effective education and the spirit of progress, the proposed new college has, in the opinion of competent observers, vast opportunities for effective work.

Supported by College Presidents.

It is significant that the presidents and deans of women's colleges of New England and near-by States are supporting the plan. Among them are the executives of Wellesley, Smith, Barnard, Mount Holyoke, Radcliffe, Teachers College, Bryn Mawr, and also of Cornell, Middlebury and the College of Physicians and Surgeons, as well as thirty-six other educators and leaders in the work of the nation. These people have found that there is an increasing demand for higher education among young women. Their own institutions are overcrowded. Girls now are registered for college when they are mere children because of the long waiting lists. Smith, for example, with its freshman class limited to 600, had 2,400 girls registered last October. It is felt that a new college, available for both New England and New York State, is a necessity.

How this new college will differ from its fellows is the natural question. It is planned to provide a curriculum expressly designed to meet the needs of the students as women. Girls go to college for various reasons. A few have

a definitely marked out plan to follow which will fit them for a chosen profession: a few have the type of mind which is happiest when deep in calculus or Greek prosody; but the majority are normal well-to-do active young women who are open to conviction on the matter of marriage and home and children. This new college will be especially built "to prepare for their high destiny the young women whose ambition it is to become mothers and the founders of beautiful, wholesome homes."

The curriculum will include modern languages, literature, past and contemporary; history, art, music and the social sciences, child psychology, biology, physiology, eugenics, sociology, economics, and chemistry and physics as applied to the needs of a home. These, one can judge easily, are all necessary to its purpose. The subjects which one misses are mathematics, Latin, Greek and pure science—those studies for which tradition demands a place in the orthodox college, and yet for which the average woman has little use. It is not that any one would lessen the value of these subjects or of their place in colleges, but rather that they be reserved, so to speak, for those who need and appreciate them.

For so many years it was believed that studying a difficult subject, which might be obviously of no value to the student, nevertheless strengthened the mind and prepared the student to grasp another subject more easily. That painful theory has apparently been exploded. Experiments and statistics have proved, according to educators, that there is no transfer of training, and that the agony spent in the mathematics class brings no immunity from further difficulties to the harassed student in the rhetoric course.

Another Disputed Theory.

Another theory which has been given a great deal of credit is that college is a preparation for life, not life itself. Several generations of young men and women graduated from college, and with the ink yet damp upon their cherished diplomas, set out to determine what they would do with life now they were all prepared for it, and found that it was often a series of cases of square pegs in round holes. Modern educators believe that the years at college are very much life itself, the time when foundations for the later years must be well and thoughtfully laid; years of habit formation and character building and of finding each his place in the scheme of things. "To see life clearly, and to see it whole" is the ideal of many teachers today. Wherefore the belief that a college for women according to the new plan will fill the space now left empty between the business or vocational school, designed primarily to fit women to earn their living, and the academic course as needed for the professions.

Statements from Dr. W. A. Neilson, President of Smith College, and from Miss Ada Comstock, President of Radcliffe, give viewpoints of two represen-

tative executives on the changes in curriculum which are in progress today, and of the need for a different type of woman's college.

"The curriculum in most women's colleges is pretty constantly undergoing modification," said Dr. Neilson. "In many cases attempts are being made to adapt it to different degrees of ability through grading the sections of large classes and providing special opportunities for the more able students. While most of the colleges are maintaining their general cultural character, consideration is being given more and more to what may be called pre-vocational studies, so that on graduation students may enter, for example, medical schools without loss of time. In certain cases, also, there is pressure to adapt a curriculum to the future careers of wives and mothers.

"In spite of all this and other possible modifications, the curriculum of the standard women's college is not fitted to students of many types who are still capable of higher education. The stress generally laid upon languages and mathematics excludes many able girls, and the need for a women's college of a new type seems to me to be due largely to the desirability of providing another sort of education for girls whose talents do not run along linguistic and mathematical lines."

Methods of Guiding the Student.

Miss Comstock said:

"In all the colleges, both for men and women, there seems to be a tendency to try to guide the student toward a more intelligent and fruitful concentration in the field of his greatest interest. At Harvard and Radcliffe the student is required to prepare himself for a general examination in the field on which he has concentrated his attention during his junior and senior years. In this preparation he must supplement by outside reading and study the work he has done, under supervision in the various courses he has elected. The process can hardly be called specialization for the field is often a broad one; but it does mean a more definite focusing of the student's attention upon a given subject than is probable if his work is carried on simply by means of courses.

"Through the honors system at Smith College such a focusing of attention on the part of the ablest students is also secured.

"At Vassar a new department—that of euthenics—is in process of organization, under the guidance of which, as I understand it, students must choose courses which have to do with the adaptation of the individual to environment and which will afford a foundation either for further training in the professional schools or for the general experience of the homemaker.

"It is an admitted fact, I think, that higher education is now being sought by a greater variety of types of student than ever before. All of these students wish higher education. Not all of them wish the type offered in the usual college course leading to the Bachelor of Arts degree. Nor are all of them suited to such a course. There is a fairly general agreement that we ought to have colleges of different types to meet these varied desires and capacities. A new college for women, founded in recognition of this need and adapted, with some ingenuity, to fulfilling it, would be an interesting and valuable addition in the field of education."

Dr. W. H. Kilpatrick, Professor of the Philosophy of Education at Teachers College, Columbia, is one of the moving spirits in the plan. He said they would have no difficulty in getting a Faculty to carry out the ideals of the new college.

"I know a number of teachers who would welcome the opportunity to teach in a college which would be established with the principles on which this one will be based. It will be a serious, thoughtful effort to improve methods and conditions in college work. Heretofore, we have had to confine our ideas and improvements to the lesser schools. Traditions and vested interests generally make it impossible to make changes in the colleges already established. But this will be a chance such as does not come in generations. I feel that it will be a matter of tremendous importance.

"We hope to gather together a Faculty which will not only represent the best of the new ideas today but will be open to conviction to other new theories as they present themselves. Of course, it is impossible to insure that such will be the case, but at any rate that will be our aim. There will probably be as many changes within the next three generations as there have been during the last. Girls nowadays have a much broader outlook than they have ever had before; economic problems are not by any means out of their realm, and they are aware of sociological conditions which our grandmothers never heard of.

"When women's colleges were first founded it was against very strong opposition. A hundred years ago when Mary Lyon, the founder of Mount Holyoke, and Emma Willard, founder of the Willard School in Troy, maintained that a means of higher education for women should be created, they had to work against the widely accepted theory that women's minds were incapable of mastering the subjects as taught in men's colleges. That notion has long since had to be discarded, perforce; but these women, in order to prove their contentions, had to lift the curriculum intact from the men's schools and show that their girls could handle them in exactly the same degree of difficulty. For that reason the old established colleges for women have stressed mathematics, the classics and pure science, much of which is unnecessary to the average young woman.

"We will have some adverse criticism, of course. That is to be expected. But we have the interested cooperation of many who can help us to overcome that difficulty."

Comparing the Old and New.

Dr Kilpatrick discussed the ideals of the new college as compared with those of the finishing schools of three generations ago.

"The finishing school of our grandmothers had for its purpose the teaching of social graces—how to enter a room gracefully, how to serve tea, how to make polite conversation and read a little French and play a bit on some musical instrument. There its scope ceased. The women of that generation learned what else they knew, which had chiefly to do with the management of a household, in their own homes from their mothers. With the broader outlook of the women of today and the decline of American home life as such, there is need for a college which can fit a young woman to fill the bigger place as well as to revive the art of making a wholesome and attractive home, in the old sense of the word. We hope to be able to point to great accomplishments within twenty-five years."

Old Bennington, Vermont, is the place where the new college will be built. A "Committee of Twenty-one" is in charge of the project, with Dr. Vincent Ravi-Booth as Chairman, an honor which is his by right, since the whole plan of the college originated with him. He told of its beginning:

"About five years ago I went to Old Bennington to live because my health was very poor and it was judged best that I should have a complete change of surroundings," he said. "The village is at the southern end of the valley made by the Green Mountains and the Taconic range, and there is no more beautiful spot to be found in the country. The mountains rise on each side in all their varied scenery, the air is crisp and invigorating, the water is pure and health-giving. Revolutionary history was made there and the neighborhood is rich with a background of historic deeds and the traditions of New England freedom and justice.

"From my study I could see three States, Vermont, Massachusetts and New York. One day it occurred to me that no better place could be found in all the east to build a college. Since Williams College is only fifteen miles away, there would be no point in making a rival men's institution, so we decided upon a woman's college. The rest of the plan has grown from these beginnings."

Bennington's place in Revolutionary history is best recalled by the exploits of Ethan Allen and the "Green Mountain Boys." General Burgoyne had to give up hope of gaining New England for the British after his defeat at the Battle of Bennington. Monuments marking places of interest are to be found in many spots in the neighborhood.

Those who have the planning of the new college in hand expect to see their dreams materializing within five years. As yet but few definite arrangements can be stated, but those few are: A small student body, limited to five hundred, a picked Faculty numbering perhaps fifty or sixty; a sum amounting to at least $3,000,000 as a basis of operations, and Colonial architecture, red brick with white pillars—simple, comparatively inexpensive, yet in keeping with the surroundings of the college in every way. The nucleus of the institution stands today in the building of the Second Meeting House, dedicated in 1806, a perfect example of Colonial church architecture. Around this chapel on the first slopes of Mount Anthony it is hoped that the campus and class life of the student body will move.

April 20, 1924

HITS COLLEGE 'PLUTOCRACY'

Dr. Lester Says Examiners Favor Private School Applicants.

PHILADELPHIA, Jan. 25 (P).—Accusations of "plutocracy" and "discrimination" were hurled today at certain of the better-known Eastern colleges by Dr. John Lester of Pottstown, speaking at a luncheon of Haverford alumni here.

Dr. Lester said that ordinary applicants for admission to such institutions as Haverford and Princton, with only public school educations and moderate means, are discriminated against by the college examining boards.

"Figures obtained from the college entrance board of Haverford show that 529 boys from private schools pass these examinations to 70 from high schools. Likewise the number of private applicants for these examinations has increased 23 per cent., while the number of high school applicants has decreased 20 per cent.

"A semi-moron can be trained to pass these examinations, but that training is not supplied in the public schools, and the public school boy loses out, regardless of ability."

January 26, 1926

IGNORES BAN ON NEGROES.

State Education Department Has No Complaint on N. Y. U. Rule.

Special to The New York Times.

ALBANY, N. Y., Dec. 31.—The barring of negroes from physical education and from the dormitories of New York University will be ignored by the State Department of Education unless a formal complaint is made. Charges by the National Association for the Advancement of the Colored People that negroes were so discriminated against at New York University have not thus far been filed with the department, Dr. Frank P. Graves, Commissioner of Education, said tonight.

"There is some question whether the department has any jurisdiction in the matter," Dr. Graves said. "No appeal has been made to the department. I do not care to discuss the matter or prejudge it."

January 1, 1928

COLLEGES DENY BIAS AGAINST ANY SECT

Columbia, Brown, Harvard and Dartmouth Say Jews Are Not Discriminated Against.

CURB ON QUOTA ALLEGED

Social Director at Columbia Says Number Is Kept Down by Psychological Test.

Columbia and Brown universities denied yesterday the charge made on Wednesday by Gustavus A. Rogers, Chairman of a committee seeking endowment for Yeshiva of America, the first Jewish college in this country, that Jews were the victims of discrimination in several Eastern universities, but Jacob Freedman, Social Director of Jewish Students' House at Columbia, endorsed last night Mr. Rogers's statement.

"No discrimination of any kind is practiced at Columbia University," said the statement from that institution. "There is no racial or religious test of any kind in connection with entrance requirements, either into Columbia or any of the professional schools connected with it."

"Jewish students in Columbia College are kept down to a quota of 20 per cent.," said Mr. Freedman, "regardless of whether they can meet the academic standards for admission. The basis of restriction here is not scholarship or social standards, but simply the fact that after a certain number of Jews have been admitted to college, no more are taken in."

Says Test Eliminates Some.

"The Thorndyke psychological test, which all applicants for admission to college are required to pass, is used as a mechanism of elimination of Jewish students after the quota is filled. In several discussions of the situation with university officers, I learned that the policy of the university was to enroll a cosmopolitan student body, and that racial restrictions were enforced for that reason."

Mr. Freedman asserted that the proportion of Catholics was about 22 per cent., Jewish about 19 per cent., and the remainder Protestants and students of miscellaneous faiths. Social solecisms in Christians were minimized and placed in the background by their fellow students, but the same faults in the Jews were emphasized and made the basis of argument against them, he declared.

Mr. Rogers's charge that the Eastern university did not want the "pious Jew" was disputed by Mr. Freedman, who said that Columbia authorities had more respect for the Jew who adhered to his religion than for the irreligious Jew. Herbert E. Hawkes, Dean of Columbia College, welcomed Jewish students at his house last year, Mr. Freedman said.

"There is no discrimination against the Jewish student after he enters the university," said Mr. Freedman, "except by men of other denominations in the student body. The Faculty and administrative officers show no partiality. The blame for the discrimination in admitting students rests on the Board of Trustees of the university."

April 30, 1926

COLLEGE CHAPEL BECOMES STORM CENTRE

Students on Many Campuses Object to Compulsory Attendance at Prayers

By W. W. SCOTT.

CONSIDER the college chapel, a venerable institution, voluntary in some colleges, compulsory in most, and now the focal point for rebellion. Yale, Williams, Amherst, University of Pennsylvania, Brown, Vassar and Oberlin are a few of the outstanding trouble centres.

At each amid sylvan scenes and ivy-covered halls, civil warfare rages with battles of words, editorials, referendums, petitions and more words. Year after year the talk continues. Student editors pass and others take their place to carry on the fight. At Dartmouth, College of the City of New York, and Dubuque University the persistent student agitation has actually succeeded, and compulsory chapel has been officially abolished by action of trustees, pestered beyond endurance by the torrents of petitions.

The war started it. Students matured by service returned to the colleges only to find what seemed to them mere kindergartens, Sunday schools. They were required to attend chapel, and it bored them. They protested, and though they were few and at first but faintly heard, they started something, and those who followed them took it up, until now in college after college the anti-chapel clamor rises even above the din of football victories.

Protest is not all. There is also a widely waged indirect guerrilla warfare of disrespect, the "chapel cough," whispering in chapel, newspaper reading and snoring sleep. In many of the colleges organized religion has fallen upon evil days.

Yet daily chapel of the collegiate brand is far from being an essentially devout affair. A hymn, a few Proverbs, a short prayer, an address by some semi-celebrity. * * * "It gives me great pleasure * * * bright young faces * * * the hope of the nation," * * * a few announcements and chapel is over until tomorrow. Religion as such is handed over to the minority groups of the Y. M. C. A. and the Y. W. C. A., and chapel remains, as one college paper has put it, an alarm clock, petty discipline, police regulation.

The campaign against chapel is not one of militant freethinkers forced to be present at church services. They are pious, more or less, these young rebels. Some of them even base their objections to chapel on the laws of true piety.

"Religious compulsion is a contradiction in terms," writes a student at Williams. "You can beat a man to his knees," he goes on, "but you can't make him pray. Every morning the college regulation beats 700 men to their knees, and then the college authorities and a few alumni wonder why these men don't pray, but read The Springfield Republican instead."

Why Chapel Is Unpopular.

In general, the resentment is not against chapel as religion but against chapel as a nuisance. The embattled students are not bitten by the microbe of atheism, nor do they roar with the rage of reformers. They have simply determined to be rid of the compulsion of going to chapel when the authorities think best, and they have set about it in the only way open to them, that of agitation and publicity.

Yale University, originally founded to "counteract the godless irreligion of Harvard," is the scene of the longest and most vigorous chapel fight. The Yale News, undergraduate paper, has for three years under three different editors carried in its platform a plank against compulsion. And the undergraduates, in their turn, have been noted for what might be termed passive resistance. Ask any chapel speaker. Says The News of this resistance, "We have a body of men who go to chapel under protest to sleep, read, or mainly sit while the choir sings and the leader reads and prays."

In November of the present college year the anti-chapel feeling at Yale took a more active turn when a referendum was held on the subject. Of the 2,300 undergraduates eligible nearly 2,000 voted, 1,681 for abolishing the compulsory feature of chapel to 241 for retaining it. So eager were they to vote that thirty-three men, The News reports, nullified their franchise by voting twice.

On the first day of circulation, a petition requesting the elimination of compulsory chapel gathered 1,312 names. It and the referendum results were presented to the trustees.

A few weeks later came the reply, "The special college chapel committee in reporting on the situation recommends that the rules remain unchanged, as graduate opinion and the Yale Corporation must be considered."

Harvard Incites Yale.

But The News through its editorials kept the issue alive, and the students through their disrespect keep the services dead, while throughout the whole college ran an undercurrent of grumbling and resentment. Christmas went by, and midyear exams, but chapel remained the same. Then late in February came unexpected aid. Harvard, the traditional enemy, godless and irreligious still, as old Eli Yale would have put it, having no compulsory chapel of her own, decided to strike a blow "for freedom of religion at New Haven."

An article by Lucius Morris Beebe, once a poet at Yale, now a joyous young pagan at Harvard, was featured in The Crimson. This article was caustic and vigorous. It mentioned names, spoke of hypocrisy and endowment drives. It was just the sort of thing, thought Harvard, for the Elis to read and meditate upon.

No sooner thought than accomplished. Automobiles were procured, and when The Crimson came from the press it was piled in by hundreds of copies, then away into the darkness sped the young editors to reach New Haven just as the sleepy-eyed Yale men left their morning worship. The article was read. For once Yale and Harvard were in accord.

Thus reopened the row, and this time the trustees yielded a point. Hereafter chapel at Yale is compulsory on week days only; attendance at the Sunday chapel is voluntary. The insurgents have, therefore, realized exactly one seventh of their demands. It is predicted that they will increase their gains before this time next year.

The referendum idea spread to Amherst, Brown, Vassar and Williams. In all the vote favored the abolition of the compulsory feature of chapel.

At Amherst there was action. Someone stole the records of chapel attendance. As but a single copy of the record had been kept, the theft was a serious affair. Who was to know how many cuts each student had to his credit? Who was to tell how many times each had been absent? The Faculty's answer to this problem was an announcement that no further chapel cuts would be allowed for the rest of the year. The innocent were to suffer with the guilty.

Indignant protests burst from the students. Mass meetings, parades were formed. A toy cannon was fired, the Dean's effigy was pushed beneath a street car, doorbells were rung, and, for some reason, "Onward, Christian Soldiers" was sung by the collegiate mob. The next day the ruling was changed. The students were put on their honor to remember how many cuts they had taken, and to take no more than the prescribed number. Compulsory chapel continues, and so does the campaign against it. All is normal again on the Amherst front.

Chapel for Freshmen.

The Student Council of the College of the City of New York recently laid itself open to a severe editorial drubbing by the student paper, The C. C. N. Y. Campus. Owing partly to a persistent campaign by The Campus, compulsory chapel at the College of the City of New York was quietly done away with last year, when the trustees failed to take their usual yearly vote for its continuance. There was then rejoicing among the students, and The Campus felt extremely pleased with itself. Imagine then its indignation when the Student Council, composed of undergraduates, presented to the trustees a plan of compulsory chapel for freshmen, "to foster college spirit in the entering class."

"Compulsory chapel must not return," cried The Campus in boldface type. "The principle of non-compulsion is far more important than any such petty thing as college spirit." And so the chapel issue under another guise was alive once more at the College of the City of New York.

Under one guise or another it is alive throughout the nation. There is hardly a non-denominational college in the country where compulsory chapel now exists unchallenged.

April 25, 1926

REMAKING THE AMERICAN COLLEGE

A Picture of the Situation Which Agitates Academic Circles and the Measures Proposed to Counteract the Evils Resulting From a Flood of Students and Extreme Specialization

By H. I. BROCK

THE American college is a key institution of the social system which has saved this country from excess of democracy. At the moment the higher educational pot is hissing and steaming at a great rate because the academic chief cooks —or some of them —think that the time has come to try to save the college itself from excess of democracy. The basic trouble may be roughly diagnosed as acute indigestion in the system due to extreme congestion.

In the first place, one out of every 150 in the population is trying to crowd through the campus gates where a short generation ago one in 1,000 was content to enter. In the second place, thousands of subjects, all tending to be specialties and most of them pretending to the privilege of a separate water-tight compartment, are contending for places in the educational scheme which the college or its synthetic successor, the university, is expected to administer. The college is swamped with undergraduate material, much of it of such low grade as to be unfit to take advantage of the opportunities which the college provides, at the moment when it is already submerged under the flood of specialization, which is the expression of diverse competitive university activity.

The many new experiments and reforms in the higher educational set-up are generally directed toward correcting or palliating evils resulting from one or the other of these two things or from a combination of both Some of the reforms seem to promise or to threaten radical changes in the system. Broadly they may be grouped, according to more immediate objective, as measures toward saving the college from the university or measures toward saving

the university from the specialists. Right understanding of the reformers' proposals, therefore, must be based on a clear idea of what the college originally was in this country and how the university arrived.

Both go back to European models, but neither is a slavish copy of any model. Both have become characteristically American institutions deep-rooted in our soil and protected by a lush growth of tradition produced by the hothouse conditions with which we surround all our cultural undertakings. The form of the college was brought from England and transplanted to New England and Virginia in the seventeenth century. Back of the first Colonial foundations and back of all later foundations for 200 years—State colleges and private colleges of the sort commonly tagged "freshwater"—was the idea that the prime purpose of the establishment was to train decent and able citizens to serve the Commonwealth.

Harvard came into being in 1636 to form stout fellows fit to carry on the torch of the Puritan civilization of Massachusetts Bay. William and Mary, more than half a century later (it had, like Harvard, an assignment of Indian missionary work), was devoted to training Virginians to carry on worthily. From Thomas Jefferson's time the "universities," so-called, hopefully set up by the several States of the Union as they emerged from the wilderness, were solemnly dedicated to that public service which consists in producing and conserving the best citizenship. This citizenship was conceived, of course, as the citizenship of a democracy. But the original democratic feature, common to all our older colleges, was chiefly this: The college by its comparative convenience of access to the region it aimed to serve, as well as by the modest cost of living and tuition which it afforded, created the door of opportunity which education opens to the poor but capable and energetic. This was democracy automatically rationed. Excess of democracy came later, roughly between the administration of Andrew Jackson and the Civil War.

Then began to sprout the rank crop of State-supported trade schools—first agricultural and mechanical colleges entitled to the benefit of Federal lands under the Morrill act of 1862, and then the so-called normal schools or teachers' training colleges. Clearly the springing up of these institutions was in response to the new needs of the community produced by changing conditions. The movement was destined to prodigious expansion under the economic pressure created by the industrial age which succeeded the Civil War and which has been accumulating mass,

speed and momentum ever since. Involved was a complete shift in the ideal of education. The old ideal of education for straight thinking, good living and good citizenship was replaced by the ideal of education for wage-earning, provided gratis by the State or heavily subsidized by private endowment.

Inevitably the new idea was exploited by politicians on the eternal panem et circenses principle. The game was to divert all State funds previously allocated to so-called higher education to institutions expressly devoted to training for specific money-making occupations. If the cherished State "universities," pride of an earlier generation, were starved to death, that did not matter. In his earlier populist days Ben Tillman literally applied this form of execution to the University of South Carolina. That was forty years ago. But within the last five years Thomas Jefferson's own University of Virginia itself seemed for a while in imminent danger of sharing the same fate in order that the trade and "normal" schools might benefit by a larger share of the tax money.

In the face of the drift, historically "liberal" institutions dependent on State aid were saved chiefly in two ways. Either they accepted degradation to the trade or "normal" school level—a thing which literally happened for a time to our second oldest college, William and Mary —or they survived under the weight of a mass of added schools and departments of all sorts, with just one thing in common among them.

Each frankly appealed as machinery to equip young people for wage earning, even though all that was practically done in some cases amounted to the issue of a certificate entitling the graduate to teach in the public schools—a certificate which came to be looked on by not a few as a meal ticket to the public crib.

So far, the college. It is at this point that we arrive at the university, which up to then had been merely a pretentious name assumed by certain colleges.

The idea of the university was imported from Germany after the trade school idea had seduced the public imagination to the "practical." The imported idea was accepted as a sort of container for the college and the accumulation of trade schools superimposed on the college. To the accumulation was added—Johns Hopkins having shown the way—the research laboratory or "original scholarship" feature which was the characteristic German contribution to the basic university idea.

The basic university idea, of course, was merely the collection, in a single quarter of a single town, of groups of curious and learned men experts in the arts of civilization upon which the world's progress in the long run depends. What made the university was the association, the discussions and the investigations of these men. What kept it alive and gave it name and fame was the fact that younger scholars flocked there to profit by the association and the discussion.

It is necessary to take this look backward from the modern American university and the modern German university in order to recover this basic idea, which later developments have almost totally obscured. For it is here that the train of thought begins which drives toward saving the university from its own pampered offspring, the specialist.

* * *

AT the same time that the imported idea of the German university was clapped like a cover on the clutter of trade school accumulations around the State colleges, that imported idea was grafted on the stem of the older and bigger endowed colleges, which had already got into the habit of calling themselves universities. This they did in right of possession or affiliation with a law school, a divinity school and perhaps a medical college. These older colleges had been handsomely adapted to the needs of our simple beginnings as a people. Though the idea of the founders, as we have seen, was always service public service, lay or religious the colleges they founded had regularly performed the function of providing initial equipment toward earning a living for a select class: for lawyers, parsons and teachers, and, to a certain extent, for doctors of medicine, in short, for the learned and quasi-learned professions of the day.

The rapid growth of the country and the progressive mechanization of life had, however, already at the third quarter post of the nineteenth

century left the old type of college far behind. What the country wanted and wanted badly at that stage was engineers, geologists, metallurgists, chemists, economists, trained specialists in medicine, the Arts and business. In order to prevent a rank growth of professional schools outside of the colleges, the colleges themselves had to undertake to provide such schools. Inevitably what happened was a competition among the leaders, striving each to furnish the most and the best such schools, and dragging along a comet's tail of fake professional schools based on the desire of the less fortunate colleges to keep in with the fashion and up with the procession.

It was at this point that the general lowering of standards in these less fortunate colleges came in, bringing the A. B. degree into disrepute and eventually resulting in the organization of the better colleges (backed by the Carnegie Foundation for the Advancement of Teaching) for a drastic reform. As a matter of fact, the reform was so drastic that it is one of the causes of the present trouble.

Standards of college entrance were jacked up on the theory (of which more hereafter) that the college was to be considered mainly as a prep school for Ph. D's. The entire system of higher education was regimented on this principle. So far had the university idea prevailed when the century index changed, so completely had the degree imported from Germany with the German university idea become the tag of professional competence and the sine qua non of advancement in the educational mill. The submergence of the college, considered as the agent of general education, became more and more complete as the teaching of undergraduates fell more and more into the hands of university professors primarily interested in serious professional students or in their laboratory work the academic pursuit called "research" which, valuable as the best of it is, sometimes covers acres of operations in intensive solemn piddling.

Naturally, the multiplication of scientific subjects, the opening up of vast fields of knowledge with a direct bearing on everyday life, had dislocated the value of the traditional curriculum of the American college, which itself was a remainder from the English college's heritage of basic learning sifted down through the Middle Ages and furbished up by the Renaissance return to classical sources. The fight to dislodge that curriculum from its vested right within academic halls to precedence of all other knowledge is history. It was a Homeric struggle. It was settled by the substitution for the older prescription, rigidly applied, of the free elective system of which President Charles W. Eliot of Harvard was the apostle and pioneer Something certainly had to be done.

But it is now the feeling, based on experience of the working of the elective system, that in passing the buck to the freshman—which in effect was what was done—the academic authorities simply avoided the real job which was theirs: the erection of a new set of requirements, more or less flexible in application, but backed, on the lowest estimate of its value, by a riper knowledge of the world than can possibly belong to the young man who finds himself projected into the midst of the thousand and one college courses, gets a fit of buck ague and shoots at random into the lot.

In fact, the mistake was so immediately recognized that Eliot's successor, President Lowell, promptly set about finding the antidote, if not the remedy, by the device of "fields of concentration." This device limited and incidentally directed the undergraduate's choice to some extent. It is prerequisite to a degree that one subject of some scope shall be broadly covered and adequately mastered—and this without the utter neglect of enough outside lines to give some balance to the general outlook.

Just as the Eliot plan knocked down the bars all over the country, so the Lowell plan has tended to put them back all over the country. The antidote to the free elective system was so badly needed that "the field of concentration" has become a sort of patent medicine label.

* * *

THIS brings us to the point where, the restoration of the colleges having got under way the rescue of the university from a state of growing up like Topsy began to seem desirable and even necessary. The state of growing up like Topsy consisted in sprouting specialties, ever more numerous, divergent, intensive, expansive and expensive. The university being the sort of organism it is, this meant the generation of forces mainly centrifugal in the amorphous and heterogeneous mass of instruction, instructors and instructed of which it had come to consist.

Some may object to the summing up of the educators' present problem as that of saving the college from the university and the university from its own pampered specialties. It may be urged that a grave and complex problem is translated into terms of melodrama. Yet it is a summing up which assists both the analysis and the synthesis of the remedies, applied or proposed, which are now distilling among hundreds of thousands of alumni pro and con so much acrimony.

What compels attention, even outside college and alumni circles, is the spectacle of our oldest institutions of learning vying with our newest in offering themselves to the knife for experimental major operations of vivisection and reconstruction. Before our eyes Harvard and

One Out of Every 150 in the Population Is Trying to Crowd Through the College Gates.

Etching of One of Harvard's Gates by Owen Selwyn.

Yale are competitively letting themselves be cut up into bits, called "houses" and "quads," for the avowed purpose of preventing the disintegration of the college ideal by the centrifugal forces of the university. This operation is submitted to after both of them, along with all the other bigger and better endowed institutions of so-called higher learning, have ruthlessly and by arbitrary rules limited, for the sake of the effectual working of the college as such, the number of those admitted to its privileges.

For obvious reasons the State universities may not resort to any such arbitrary limitation of a student body made up of the sons and daughters of the taxpayers upon whom they depend for support. Yet, as we shall see, they have had to invent means of sifting the collegiate material which are more effective than the coarse sieve of graduation from high school. Most of these institutions are considering more or less serious operations in reconstruction, and at the moment, one of the most outstanding of them, the University of Wisconsin, nursery of the Wisconsin idea and the eminent La Follette family of Washington and Madison, is actually on the table for vivisection. Official diagnosis of the trouble is urgent need of "greater integration of the curriculum, greater informalization of the teaching method, greater socialization of the student" which sounds formidable. However, it may be observed that these large words sum up very fairly the advantages expected to be gained by cutting up alive the big Eastern colleges. What these are doing is to substitute for a single amorphous mass groups of from 200 to 300 drawn from all three upper classes and housed together socially with their tutors in quarters furnished with a common dining room and lounging room.

* * *

REALLY Harvard and Yale between them are thus setting up more than a dozen experimental colleges. Wisconsin has one experimental college, so expressly labeled. It has been in operation for three years and is widely advertised because it is run by Alexander Meiklejohn, the same whose reforming spirit cost him the presidency of Amherst. Meiklejohn's college is admitted by Glenn Frank, president of the university, to be "an extreme application" of the principles which the other experimental colleges propose to apply in a less radical and a less missionary spirit. It represents the first stage of the operation on the university under the diagnosis quoted above.

Like the others, it assembles the students and teachers together "socially" with living and teaching quarters in the same building. Like them, it limits the number of students. Unlike them, it confines its attention to the freshman and sophomore classes — the so-called "junior college" field created by the diversion of the main energies of the college proper to service as a Ph. D. prep school. Unlike the others, it uses a special device for "integration of the curriculum." Study of the Greek civilization serves as a dragnet for the general consideration of the problems of civilization which must be faced in all ages and are vital in ours. This is a subject which calls for elucidation in a later article.

The essential fact here is that it is the preliminary stage of the major operation projected upon a university of 9,000 students with a faculty of 1,000. Its mere existence in the midst of such an institution registers an opinion in quarters of authority that, on the "cultural" side, college education has so far fallen down that something that is not a mere tinkering with "courses" needs to be done about it.

A less dislocating experiment toward injecting cultural values is that under way at St. John's College, Annapolis—an institution which has more than the color of a claim to rank ahead of Yale in the honorary seniority list of American colleges. The instrument of cultural injection in this case is the American cultural tradition itself, presented in the object lesson of a singularly well-preserved eighteenth century Colonial capital of real distinction. By this way the student's mind is opened to the excellence of good things.

These are samples or illustrations of the remedial measures designed to save the college and to restore to it its value as a place for young people to go to who do not intend to become Ph. D.s afterward, but who do aim at becoming men and women at ease at home in the United States of America and not quite lost in the great world which is the heir of so many ages and of which the United States of America is an integral part.

The program of reform for the world of the Ph. D.—the reorganization of the university in such a fashion as to correlate it more effectually with life and harness to practical problems the forces of its specialties which now tend to be dissipated centrifugally rather than applied cooperatively—is that which I have described as directed toward saving it from its own specialties and specialists. This situation is being faced in two large Middle Western universities as one of those major operations already referred to as so much in academic fashion. One of them—Wisconsin, itself, being a State university with two-thirds of its student membership undergraduate—is forced to include the saving of the college in the program of recasting the university. The other, the University of Chicago, may and does treat the college as so far secondary that the argument for bothering with it at all may be reduced to the convenience rather than the necessity of retaining it as a laboratory of observation (not one of experiment) for the Ph. D. candidates who intend to make teaching their business.

Allowing for this difference, the two programs are parallel. Each calls for a grouping into a few grand divisions or "institutes" of the entire subject matter of graduate work now split up into many divergent and centrifugal specialties. The physical sciences will be one group, the biological sciences will be another, the so-called social sciences will be another, with all humane letters making another. Educationally, it would be the grand division, with its greater perspective, which would control the students' "major" province of study, that selected with a view to his future occupation. Also, in the region of research, it would be the grand division which directed upon "projects" the converging expertise of the various intensive specialties composing the group and—where the project called for it—arranged for the cooperation of specialists from other groups toward getting at the whole truth.

Clearly this is a device for doing within the existent machinery of the university what is beginning to be done by those added agencies of specific private endowment which have already got tagged "institutes." The setting up of these "institutes" was an expression of the growing feeling that the inquiries of the specialists in the schools followed too narrow a line, of the conviction that getting at the truth of complex political and social situations required looking at the facts from a great many angles. It had become obvious, for example, that a mere "economist," operating as such, was incompetent to solve the simplest industrial problem. The establishment of the Institute of Law at Johns Hopkins, the Institute of Human Relations at Yale, the Institute for Research in Social Science at North Carolina, the Institute of Food Research at Leland Stanford, is a symptom of the realization that the system of specialization has reached the point where it needs to be reminded that its job is social synthesis as well as scientific analysis. Thus the saving of the university from the specialist began in several of them with the alarming phenomenon of the addition of another agency to the general clutter of agencies—to further duplication of machinery already too complex.

As it happened, Robert Maynard Hutchins, who has so recently achieved eminence at the age of 31 as the youngest university president, came to Chicago from a job which included a considerable part in the establishment of Yale's Institute of Human Relations. He promptly transferred the idea to Chicago, adopting the method of rearrangement rather than that of duplication of machinery. Whereas the problem selected for the converging points of view of the group of specialists at Yale was unemployment and bankruptcy, the obvious problem in Chicago was acute local crime conditions. Therefore, the new social science set-up, with medical assistance and possibly legal advice, is tackling that subject and has added to its faculty a police chief with years of practical experience in catching criminals.

Over at the other end of town Northwestern University is equally alive to the needs of the huge cosmopolitan community along Lake Michigan, which both are proud to serve and by which each is liberally supported. Northwestern's enterprise, however, is more like the other "institutes." It is an extra-faculty agency—a laboratory of crime detection. The purpose is to train experts—to standardize detective specialists—and to make this standard expertise available to the police and the State's attorneys.

Not quite incidentally, it is well known that a perpetual problem of every college or university is the getting of endowment to keep pace with its needs or its ambitions. It appears that the rich men who have the large sums of money which may be bestowed upon educational projects are at the moment captivated by the institute idea. They like the wide scope of the thing and the high visibility of the practical application to serious problems and flagrant evils. Perhaps that is one reason why the reform of the university is taking the line of the institute idea. However, the reform of the university, like the reform of the college, involves many elements upon which it has been impossible to touch in this introductory article. Each will have a separate article devoted to it in this series.

Cornell Offers Major Course in Fine Arts; Program Called an Innovation for America

Special to THE NEW YORK TIMES.

ITHACA, N. Y., April 28.—The study of the fine arts reached a new status at Cornell University with the announcement by Dean Robert Ogden yesterday that beginning this Autumn it will be a new major field.

The recent action of the faculty of the College of Arts and Sciences in offering an undergraduate course in which all the major arts have a place is regarded as an innovation in American universities. Hitherto graduate and undergraduate instruction has been given at Cornell in each of the fields of literary art, music and the visual arts. Students were also able to perform major work in esthetics under the direction of the Sage School of Philosophy. The new major includes related courses in all the arts.

The new program in fine arts emphasizes three points. The first is a requirement of introductory and advanced work in esthetics. The second is a distribution of required and elective courses in literary art, including dramatics, musical art and the arts of vision, such as drawing, painting, sculpture and architecture. The third requirement is a selection of advanced courses in the major divisions.

The student who follows this program will have opportunity to familiarize himself with the traditions and products of artistic endeavor. He will also be introduced to the principles of criticism and the recognized canons of good taste.

April 29, 1934

20,000 STUDENTS RALLY FOR PEACE

Meetings Here Orderly Except at City College, Where Dr. Robinson Is Booed.

HE BARS OXFORD PLEDGE

Faculty Participation in Move Against War Is Larger Than Ever Before.

About 20,000 college students in the city mobilized for peace yesterday. With classes suspended for an hour they gathered in auditoriums and on campus grounds to hear discussions of war. In contrast to similar demonstrations of previous years, in which the student attitude was rowdy and lighthearted, the meetings had an atmosphere of seriousness and order.

In only one instance did a meeting get out of control. That was at City College where a "breach of faith" by a student representative caused President Frederick B. Robinson to be booed and hissed by a number of students.

In general, the attitude of the students at the meetings was ascribed to participation by the faculty to a larger extent than ever before. At City College Dr. Robinson was chairman of the meeting. At Columbia, Dean Herbert E. Hawkes of Columbia College and Dean William F. Russell of Teachers College both spoke and at New York University Chancellor Harry Woodburn Chase had planned to speak but was prevented by laryngitis.

One Meeting Time Extended.

Dr. Robinson had originally intended that the City College meeting, attended by about 3,500 students and held in the Great Hall, would continue for an hour, between 11 o'clock and noon. However, the speakers, among whom were Charles H. Tuttle of the Board of Higher Education, and Dean Paul Klapper, had not finished and he extended the time.

The last speaker was Robert Brown, president of the Student Council. He presented four resolutions: to support genuine neutrality, for Ethiopian independence against Italy's campaign, to support legislation making the R. O. T. C. optional in colleges and remove it from City College and to further opportunities for relating education to such problems.

When he had finished, Dr. Robinson touched him on the arm and said, "Your time is up." The student representative ignored it and said there had been another resolution, but that "it was unfortunate that the administration and the Board of Higher Education did not permit us to introduce the Oxford pledge at this meeting."

"I am sure, however," Mr. Brown continued, "that were we allowed to vote on this resolution, City College would add its voice to those of hundreds of thousands of students throughout other nations who have adopted it." He then read the pledge: "We will refuse to support the Government of the United States in any war it may undertake."

Jeers Mingle With Cheers.

Dr. Robinson, who, as chairman, had put the other resolutions to a vote, declared that the Oxford pledge was "unconstitutional and illegal," and he was booed, there being, however, mingled sounds of cheering. The meeting had then gone half an hour past the scheduled time and he ended it. Later he declared that Mr. Brown's action had been "most discourteous and disrespectful," and said that the pledge had been ruled out at sessions at which arrangements for the meeting were made.

After the Great Hall meeting about 500 of the students gathered outdoors and took the pledge. About 200 of them marched to Columbia for a demonstration there, but they arrived too late.

The second meeting, held on South Field at Columbia, was attended by about 2,000 students. Dean Hawkes, who was introduced by Richard Stair, president of the Student Council, urged the assertion by each individual of social, personal or political influence which would "stem the tide toward war." Professor Harry J. Carman, head of the history department, suggested that lives be devoted to "spreading the anti-war gospel."

Dean Russell Speaks.

At the earlier meeting, in Horace Mann auditorium, Dean Russell declared, before about 700, he was glad to speak for peace. William Hinckley, president of the American Youth Congress, spoke at the same meeting.

Dr. Chase's speech was read to the downtown meeting of New York University students, held on the steps of Washington Square College by Harold O. Voorhis, university secretary. In it Dr. Chase declared that "peace is not effective when it attempts to bind youth not to support their country in war."

More than 4,200 students participated in meetings downtown and on University Heights. Other downtown speakers included Dean Martin E. Loomis of the Washington Square College and Dean John W. Withers of the School of Education. The faculty participants on the Heights were Professors Charles Gus and Harry Pratt Fairchild.

At Hunter College, President Edward A. Colligan opened a meeting attended by about 1,500 students by asking them to approach the promotion and maintenance of peace with tolerance and a determination to find the truth.

75 Take Pledge at Barnard.

Miss Elspeth Davies, president of the Student Council of Barnard College, explained to a group of about seventy-five students the Oxford pledge, after which they took it.

The peace demonstrations were planned by the Committee for Student Mobilization for Peace. A number of organizations cooperated, including the National Student Federation of America, the Y. M. C. A., Y. W. C. A., the Student League for Industrial Democracy, the National Students League, the American League Against War and Fascism, the American Youth Congress and the Intercollegiate Council.

A meeting also was held in Newark by the students of Dana College, and one was scheduled for Monday night at Rutgers University.

November 9, 1935

TELEVISION IS USED FOR N.Y.U. LECTURE

Questions of 200 Students Are Transmitted to Dr. C. C. Clark, as in Classroom

IMAGE IS CLEARLY SHOWN

Professor's Demonstrations Are Followed—First Use of New Medium for Teaching

For the first time in this country television was used yesterday as a medium of classroom instruction and at the end of a forty-minute demonstration the experiment was voted a "great success."

Two hundred New York University students gathered before television receivers on the sixty-second floor of the RCA Building, while on the third floor Dr. C. C. Clark, Associate Professor of General Science at N. Y. U. School of Commerce, delivered an illustrated lecture on the uses and principles of photo-electricity.

The students were in one of the studios before fifteen receivers. At 2:30 P. M. the room was darkened and on each of the fifteen screens flashed the image and voice of the instructor.

Professor Clark discussed the principles underlying television, demonstrating various steps. To most of the students this was the first experience with a television set.

Students Inspect Studio

At the close of the performance the students were taken through the studio where they were shown some of the latest designs in radio and television.

Before the demonstration, Dr. James Rowland Angell, N. B. C. educational counselor and former president of Yale University, who had arranged the experiment, told the audience that the possible uses of television in the classroom were virtually limitless. He said that he felt "enthusiastic" about the future developments in this field.

"This is the first attempt to use television as part of a classroom exercise," Dr. Angell continued. "What we are trying is purely an educational undertaking. We hope to learn from it some of the things we do not know."

After the broadcast, Dr. Angell declared that the experiment had been a "great success." "Five years from now," he predicted, "I expect to see television used very frequently in the classroom."

Questions Heard and Answered

At one point in his lecture Professor Clark asked casually, "Are there any questions?" He explained, "I can hear you if you are near the microphone."

It was revealed later by the N. B. C. officials, under whose auspices the experiment was conducted, that a special talk-back radio circuit had been installed to link the teacher with his students.

"I have a question to ask," a student volunteered, after a moment's pause. "Can you explain further the way the pictures go through the air? This is Lillian Chase speaking."

The teacher listened intently and then replied with a beckoning motion of his hand, "If you come here, Lillian, I will show you."

Five minutes later she joined Professor Clark. The other students applauded. She was visible on the screen, talking to their teacher, and although they were both sixty floors away every word and facial expression came to them distinctly.

"Am I being televised now?" Miss Chase asked.

Told that she was, she slumped into a chair, much to the merriment of the other students. Soon, however, she seemed to regain her composure and stood by while Professor Clark proceeded with his lecture.

With the aid of another student, Robert Harr, a senior at the Commerce School, the demonstration continued. Professor Clark illustrated the function of the photo-electric cell, demonstrated the production of sound by use of the device and discussed the fundamental principles underlying the RCA all-electronic system of television.

Professor Clark was interrupted several times when members of the student body asked questions. He explained that the program was being carried to N. B. C.'s Empire State tower transmitter by coaxial cable and there broadcast to the receiving room.

May 20, 1938

Higher Education for Women Stresses Role of Conserver

Dr. Havens Says Modern Liberal Curriculum Recognizes Natural Bent as Mediator

By Dr. PAUL SWAIN HAVENS,
President of Wilson College

The question of how the higher education of women should be planned has perplexed educators in this country ever since the colleges for women were established after the middle of the last century and women were admitted to colleges and universities originally designed for men. Today that question is less difficult to answer because educators have recognized that women are inevitably the conservers of life and of civilization. The modern liberal curriculum for women, therefore, attempts to prepare them for their particular responsibilities in the world at large and in the segments of life where their influence predominates.

But one basic assumption which has underlain the higher education of women from the beginning has not changed. It is the assumption that men and women have equal intellectual abilities. This is the starting point today of all discussion about women's education and gives added significance to the purpose of all college education, which is to train the mind and to stimulate it so that it will never slumber or sleep.

Women always have been, and always will be, conservers of life. Consequently, a curriculum for women should include sound work in biology, the life-science. They are mediators in the home, the school, the church and the community at large. This fact points toward the necessity of seeing to it that study is made available to them in the fields of history, psychology, sociology and political science, which help them to understand human relationships.

Health Education Expanded

We have come to think of athletics as a male prerogative, and so it is in its strenuous competitive features. But health based upon sound physical development is as necessary for women as for men. This fact has led to the establishment, in colleges and universities where women study, of carefully planned programs of physical recreation and sport, designed to strengthen the physique, teach a life-long habit of exercise, and, not least important, teach the intangible values of sportsmanship and fair play.

The women's colleges have felt the need also of a well integrated health program, not only to keep their students well, but also to show them, through their physical examinations, their work in hygiene and the college infirmary, what intelligent medical planning can mean to a community; for the bent of a life is often determined in college, and the college for women recognizes that its students, when they have learned how to keep themselves healthy and have observed the work done by a good infirmary or hospital, will better take the lead in securing similar benefits for the communities where they live.

With this thought in mind the institution where women study must make careful provision for the stimulation of interest of permanent rather than passing value. It must excite in young women an interest in books, so that their lives will be refreshed by good reading; it must encourage them to cultivate a hobby to which they can turn when perhaps their children are grown. It must also give them an intelligent appreciation of art and music, not as "female accomplishments" but as vigorous interests for a lifetime.

Extracurricular Work Added

Interests outside the curriculum also deserve attention. Whether rightly or wrongly, social work these days is largely woman's province. Extracurricular interests which excite an interest in social problems and give some experience in meeting them are essential. Again, if women are to meet the criticism that, having won the ballot they do not exercise it, they must learn in college the importance of the democratic process and through their own student government how that process works, what its pitfalls are and the measures necessary to perpetuate it.

Some colleges for women stop at this point. Others are wise enough to realize that the spiritual destinies of the future also lie with womankind, and so provide for the normal, well-rounded spiritual development of their students through an adequate provision for the study and practice of religion on the campus and by insisting upon the necessity in the busy college for a moment of leisure, when pressure relaxes and the mind and spirit orientate themselves anew.

December 17, 1939

Postwar Issues

WAR BABIES TO TAX SCHOOLS THIS FALL

First of Six 'Heavy' Years Will Increase First-Grade Rolls 9%, U. S. Reports

WASHINGTON, Aug. 2 (AP)—The first American babies born during the war will create a new school crisis this fall.

The United States Office of Education estimates that the upsurge in births following Pearl Harbor—babies born during 1941-42—will increase first-grade enrollments about 9 per cent in the next school year.

This, however, is only the first wave of war babies. The upswing in births has carried over into the postwar years. In 1946 the total reached 3,260,000, a record. Births this year are at a high rate.

This means the increased tide of pupils will last at least six years. Many educators predict facilities will have to be increased from one-fourth to one-third in elementary and high schools.

There were 17,047,539 babies born from 1941 through 1946. This is 3,631,358 more than were born from 1935 to 1940. The increase in 1946 over 1940 was about 50 per cent.

The school situation already is so acute that Chairman George D. Aiken of the Senate Committee on Labor and Public Welfare says:

"At least 2,000,000 children are suffering a major impairment in their schooling because of poorly prepared teachers.

"And according to United States Census estimates for the year 1945 more than 4,000,000 children between the ages of five and seventeen, inclusive, attended no school whatever."

The big problem is obtaining teachers. High salaries offered by other occupations enticed an estimated 350,000 qualified teachers from their profession during the war.

Dr. John W. Studebaker, United States Commissioner of Education, says:

"It is estimated we will need about 1,000,000 new teachers in the next ten years and about 350,000 new classrooms.

"On the basis of births during the last six years, the number of elementary school children will increase by about 6,000,000 in the next six years. This is a rise of about one-third.

"There will be about 1,000,000 more secondary (or high school) students and about 500,000 more people in colleges.

"That gives you a rough idea of the problem we face."

Dr. Studebaker suggests:

1. Give citizens more information concerning the educational problem.

2. Increase the number of schools.

3. Raise educational expenditures to provide first class buildings and equipment; put teachers' salaries on a professional level and give them acceptable working conditions.

August 3, 1947

Rearming Saps School Gains As Rolls and Costs Still Soar

By BENJAMIN FINE

Once again the nation's public schools are in serious plight. Eighteen months of defense mobilization have taken their toll. Danger signals are flying everywhere, but often are not heeded.

Many advances made in the first five years after World War II are being swept away.

The schools, like other aspects of civilian life, are beginning to feel the effects of the Korean conflict. As a result, they face a gloomy year. Many educators are worried lest the gloom continue for another decade.

Reports from state commissioners of education, correspondents of THE NEW YORK TIMES in each of the forty-eight states, and interviews with leading educators all point to a downward trend.

The schools are caught in a pincers. Four major factors are involved: Increased enrollments, inflationary costs, lack of building materials and an acute teacher shortage.

Educators Back Defense

Each is leaving its imprint on the schools, and on the children, too. It is not a question of tanks versus textbooks. Educators everywhere wholeheartedly support the Government's defense program. They applaud its efforts to make our democracy strong enough to withstand the challenge of Soviet Communism.

They say their problem is not one of more ABC's or more airplanes. They insist our economy is strong enough to provide both. Moreover, they insist that it is just as true today as it was a century ago, when first proclaimed by Horace Mann, that schoolhouses are the first line of our defense.

In the last year it appears schools have made few advances, and many backward steps. A number of communities report unexpected setbacks. Over the nation, 3,500,000 elementary and high school children—one out of eight pupils in the public schools—are suffering an impaired education because of inadequate facilities. A year ago a TIMES study showed 3,000,000 children were being deprived of an adequate education. Thus, there has been an increase of half a million in twelve months.

Incompetent teachers, poorly equipped classrooms, inadequate buildings and poor supervision combine to cheat these hundreds of thousands of young people. The number of pupils on double sessions is growing steadily. An estimated 400,000 boys and girls are not getting a full school day—some are attending school even on triple-session schedules. They go half a day, or a third of a day. What this does to the morale of the children, the parents, the teachers and the community is easy to imagine.

Educators emphasize that a child deprived of his schooling will be unable to regain the years lost—a child is 6 only once. One cannot postpone the growth of a pupil as one might postpone the building of a road or a garage.

This comment by Dr. Walter Maxwell, secretary of the Arizona Education Association, is typical: "At numerous schools I have seen children lined up in front of a schoolhouse door, marching in to take their places in the school as the first shift marched out—just like the changing of shifts in factories."

Costs Provide Headaches

Inflationary costs are a headache everywhere. School officials are haunted by rising prices. Everything they buy has gone up 50 or 100 or even 200 per cent. Teachers are insisting they get their share, too. Cost-of-living bonuses have been handed out, but not fast enough, the teachers complain, to keep pace with rising food prices. As a result, morale in many communities is poor. Last spring the 500 teachers of Pawtucket, R. I., went on strike for several months, closing all of the city's schools. They won part of the increase they sought—but at a serious cost to the schooling of their pupils.

In other communities the struggle for higher salary schedules goes on in the board rooms rather than on the picket line. The New York City teachers recently ended a-year-and-a-half "boycott" of extracurricular activities. Judging from the reaction of their spokesmen, they are far from happy at the compromise salary increases.

But the salary issue is only part of the educational picture. Competition has arisen from higher-paying Government jobs, war-related positions and the demand for skilled and semiskilled workers in various industries. More teachers are leaving the profession today than at any time since World War II, when 350,000 departed, never to return.

Frequently the community must employ substandard, unqualified teachers because trained personnel are lacking. Many school systems report they are "scraping the bottom of the barrel."

A smoldering discontent is detected. Never before have the schools been under such attacks. Frequently the controversy is artificially contrived, dishonestly designed to wreck the free public school. But there is enough discontent to make thoughtful educators and civic-minded citizens take stock.

The schools are in need of greater financial help—and they are unable to get it. Many communities already allocate a substantial part of their tax funds for the schools. Oftentimes real estate is taxed almost to the danger point. But education costs more today than ever before—and the money frequently is not there to spend.

Enrollment a Record

Enrollment is at its highest peak. THE TIMES survey indicates that the 1951-52 school enrollment is 26,525,115—representing a growth of 826,194 in a year. Most of this growth has occurred in the elementary grades, and more particularly the first grade. The private and parochial schools will add another 3,000,000 children or more, thus bringing the total elementary and secondary enrollment close to 30,000,000.

Moreover, the school rolls are going to increase for at least eight years, more likely ten.

Next year—1952-53—the schools will enroll 1,700,000 more children than were registered this year. This is a tremendous number to absorb, particularly since most of the classrooms already are overcrowded. The peak will not be reached before 1957-58, if by then, at which time it is estimated the enrollment in public elementary and secondary schools will exceed 32,000,000, an increase of 6,000,000 over that of today.

Educators are deeply disturbed by this condition. Typical is the view voiced by Dr. Earl J. McGrath, United States Commissioner of Education:

"The tidal wave of children bearing down on our schools bids fair to overwhelm us. We simply are not building enough new schoolhouses or training enough new teachers to meet the situation. We can't go on from year to year on the present makeshift basis without seriously undermining our whole public school system.

"Unless the American people are prepared to take positive action to remedy these deficiencies, millions of children will continue to get a makeshift education."

Today many thousands of children are attending classes in school basements, apartment-house basements, empty stores, garages, churches, inadequate private homes and even trailers. What is more, one out of five of the regular schools is either unsafe or obsolete.

Building Program Delayed

The defense program has played havoc with building plans. Even though the nation spent a record $1,200,000,000 for school construction in 1950-51, the communities were unable to keep pace with the number of children reaching school age. And in 1952, educators warn, steel and other critical materials will stymie the construction of many badly needed schoolhouses.

More than 1,000,000 school teachers are now employed, 46,000 more than last year. But with more than 1,000,000 children to be added each year for the next several years, the teaching rolls also will have to rise steadily. However, teacher-training institutions are not preparing enough men and women to do the job. All but four states report a teacher shortage even this year. They now could use 71,886 elementary and 15,121 high school teachers.

Despite the need for teachers, young people seem to shy at entering the profession. The teacher colleges report a decrease this year of 16 per cent in their entering classes. This means, in effect, that four years from now, when the school rolls will have increased by more than 5,000,000, there will be fewer trained teachers.

Although the number of teachers holding substandard or emergency certificates has decreased by 5,053, there are still 66,354 of them in the school system. For example, 8,500 of the 24,600 teachers in Missouri are on emergency certificates, and South Dakota reports 1,796 of its 7,159 teachers do not hold regular licenses.

But the "substandard certificates" tell only part of the story. The National Education Association estimates that of the 600,000 elementary teachers in the public schools 300,000 do not hold college degrees—the minimum standard. Of this number, the N. E. A. says, at least 100,000 are so inadequately prepared as to make their continued presence in the classroom dangerous to the mental and emotional growth of America's youth.

Slight Rise in Salaries

THE TIMES survey shows that teachers' salaries have risen slightly from an average of $3,097 to $3,290 annually. This $193 increase, or $3.71 a week, has been eaten up, the teachers declare, by increased living costs and higher taxes.

New York State, with an average annual teachers' salary of $4,500, leads the country, followed by the District of Columbia with a $4,300 average and California with $3,967. Mississippi again is at the bottom of the list, paying its teachers an average of $1,475 a year. Arkansas is next to Mississippi with $1,700, and South Carolina is third from the bottom with $2,130.

Six states pay some teachers less than $20 a week — Mississippi, South Carolina, Kentucky, Iowa, Georgia and Missouri. Ten others pay a minimum of $20 to $25 a week.

AS DANGER SIGNALS FLY IN NATIONAL EDUCATION FIELD

A crowded schoolroom presents a problem for the community

For the country as a whole, the public schools cost just a little more than five billion dollars, a slight increase over that in 1950-51. Two states—New York and California—spend more than $500,000,000 each. Because of spiraling costs, the funds needed to operate the public schools have risen higher than ever before. Educators complain, however, that the money they get cannot buy as much as their funds of as recently as two years ago.

Once more the effects of the Korean conflict can be seen in the classrooms of every community in the United States.

With Congress in session the N. E. A. and other school organizations again will seek Federal aid for the public schools. One member of Congress who has advocated a Federal aid bill — Senator Lister Hill of Alabama — asserted that the strength and security of the United States against aggression were bound inexorably to education. In a statement to THE TIMES he observed:

"Education has given us the widespread, high level of intelligence and general competency by which we have built history's most perfect example of democratic government and preserved it against the winds of alien ideologies. We face a long period of international tensions and big armaments that may last perhaps for five, ten or even twenty years. In terms of sheer numbers of people our potential enemies hold a heavy advantage and our intelligence sources tell us that Russia and her satellites are feverishly working to train large numbers of skilled workers, instructed by industrial experts taken out of East Germany since the last war.

"We must fix our educational sights accordingly and insure that every American boy and girl has the opportunity for maximum development of his or her capabilities. Only in this way can we meet the need for more scientists, more engineers, more chemists, more physicists, more technicians, more skilled workers of every kind, more nurses and doctors and leaders in other professions and business."

The status of public school education, in contrast to conditions a year ago, as shown by regions in THE TIMES survey, follows:

NEW YORK AND MIDDLE ATLANTIC

A heavy influx of young children has burdened schools in this region, and with no signs of relief in sight. Both New York and Pennsylvania report the largest enrollment increases. The registers of all the states and the District of Columbia have increased about 200,000. In face of the need for additional schools, all states report difficulty in obtaining building materials. Even so, most states are pushing school building programs. New York intends to spend $150,000,000 this year, compared with $100,000,000 last year.

Salaries in this area are among the best. No state except Delaware can get a sufficient number of elementary teachers. Pennsylvania cannot obtain enough qualified secondary, as well as elementary school teachers. The region employs more than 10,000 teachers who hold substandard certificates, an increase over last year.

NEW ENGLAND

New England offers a contrasting picture as regards teachers'

salaries. Three states—Massachusetts, Connecticut and Rhode Island—pay their teachers more than the national average, the other three do not. The salaries of Maine, New Hampshire and Vermont are not much better than those in some of the southern states.

Only Connecticut, Massachusetts and Vermont record large enrollment increases. Almost all the states report conditions are better than a year ago, and the number of teachers on substandard certificates has decreased. All but Rhode Island need additional teachers, largely in the elementary grades—Massachusetts and Connecticut need 500 elementary teachers each.

SOUTH

Conditions in the South, although steadily improving since World War II, are still poor. Enrollment has been increasing in some states but tapering off in others. The problem is largely one of improving school services and raising teacher standards. Absenteeism and school drop-outs also are serious issues.

Many southern teachers are on emergency licenses, although in some states the number has decreased in the last year.

However, a large number of Southern pupils receive an impaired education. In Arkansas, Alabama and Kentucky, 50 per cent of the pupils are affected by sub-standard teachers, inadequate buildings and double sessions. The lowest salaries in the country are paid in the South. Some teachers in Mississippi receive $500 a year, in South Carolina $600 and in Kentucky $640. All states in the region fall below the national teacher's salary average.

SOUTHWEST

Enrollment increased in all states, with Texas showing a gain of 29,000 in a year. All states report conditions are either "better" or "same as last year." Texas, however, has not increased its teaching staff despite its enrollment gain.

Salaries in New Mexico and Arizona are above the national average. Arizona, with $3,800, ranks fourth. Only Arizona reports it can obtain all the teachers, both elementary and secondary, it needs.

MIDWEST

School conditions are generally reported as improving in the twelve states in the region. Enrollment is on the upswing, due in large part to growth of defense industries, particularly in Michigan.

Some glaring contrasts are evident. Michigan pays its teachers an average annual salary of $3,700, seventh highest in the nation, and Illinois, with $3,600, is near the "top ten." But North Dakota with $2,162, South Dakota with $2,185 and Nebraska with $2,200 are forty-sixth, forty-fifth and forty-fourth, respectively, in the national standing. Although in many states the number of substandard teachers is negligible, approximately one-third of Missouri's, one-seventh of South Da-

kota's and one-eighth of Michigan's teachers hold substandard certificates. Large numbers of pupils are receiving second-rate or impaired schooling.

ROCKY MOUNTAIN

The post-war birth rate is evident in the Rocky Mountain public schools. Colorado reports an enrollment increase of 5,000, Utah 7,000, Wyoming 3,000 and Nevada 3,000. Considering the total number of pupils in each state, the gains are significant.

With the exception of Utah, where about one-tenth of the teachers hold emergency certificates, the problem of substandard teachers has been largely solved. Utah is making improvements. The average salaries range from $2,900 in Colorado to $3,316 in Nevada. All report they can obtain secondary, but none can get elementary teachers.

NORTHWEST

Montana and Idaho have approximately the same number of teachers—5,225 and 5,020, respectively—but Idaho has 16,000 more pupils. Idaho needs both elemen-

Dr. Earl J. McGrath, United States Commissioner of Education, who declares "we are not building enough schoolhouses or training enough new teachers to meet the situation."

tary and secondary teachers while Montana needs only elementary. Both have many emergency teachers. There is a big difference in teachers' salaries. Montana has an average of $3,415, Idaho $2,639.

FAR WEST

Teachers' salaries in the Far West are among the highest in the country. California, with a $3,967 average, is second nationally and Washington, with $3,690, is ninth, while Oregon, with $3,650, is tenth.

California now has 63,800, the second largest staff in the country. The number of teachers on emergency certificate increased 7,600. Oregon has 1,800 of its 12,350 teachers on substandard licenses. All need elementary, but Washington also needs secondary teachers.

THE TIMES study shows serious school problems in every section of the land. It also shows that not enough attention is paid to these roblems. Soaring enrollments, fewer buildings, a shortage of teachers and a lack of money to keep pace with school needs have combined to bring another educational crisis.

While this crisis is not yet in the acute stage, our system of free public education may be endangered unless the schools receive more financial support.

January 14, 1952

Another Record Enrollment Intensifies the Problems Faced by the Nation's Schools

By BENJAMIN FINE

As the 1954-55 academic year gets under way, the nation's public elementary and high schools have a record enrollment of 30,673,500 pupils. The increase over last year's record total amounts to 1,500,000.

In New York City 911,000 youngsters are scheduled to enter the public schools, and an additional 300,000 are enrolled in the parochial schools. Because of its size, the metropolitan school system has a set of problems all its own; but problems exist everywhere. Even the small town of Woodstock, Conn., with a school population of 400, is hard pressed to find space for the increased enrollment. It has had to take over a garage and to press into service an old one-room schoolhouse.

Educators and citizens generally are showing greater interest and taking a larger part in educational affairs than ever before in recent years. The newspapers, magazines, radio and television have in recent months highlighted the need for more public support of the schools. More persons are aware of the importance of education

and the need to maintain the public schools at the highest possible standard.

Outstanding Needs

As the schools reopen, various problems stand out sharply. There are too few teachers; the shortage is acute, and growing more so every day. The number of substandard teachers will be increased this fall. Classes are too crowded. Many schools are on double and even triple sessions; children are cheated of a first-class education. More buildings are needed to keep pace with the phenomenal growth in school attendance.

But for seventeen of the country's states, the "normal" problems will fade into the background as educators attempt to meet a new challenge: to change a dual system of education into a single system.

When the Supreme Court of the United States ruled last May 17 that segregation was unconstitutional, that issue became the number one problem for a large section of the country.

This fall many communities will face the problem realistically. It is no longer academic. But much litigation may be expected before a final solution is arrived at.

The seventeen states that, along with the District of Columbia, legally required segregation embrace 40 per cent of the nation's public school enrollment. Involved are 8,250,000 white children and 2,550,000 Negro in high school and elementary grades. Some 400,000 teachers are in this area. A total annual budget of $2 billion is spent in these Southern states for educational purposes.

Some of the states are adamant in their refusal to accept the Supreme Court decision. Georgia, Mississippi and South Carolina are prepared to give up their public schools if white and Negro children are required to attend classes together.

However, the reports reaching this department indicate that some states —Delaware, West Virginia, Missouri, and parts of Maryland—have already started the process of desegregation. The District of Columbia is taking the lead in setting up a "model" program that may well serve as a pattern for the rest of the country.

But as the new year gets under way the schools face problems beyond the issue of segregation, important as that is. In this city, for example, the question of providing sufficient school buildings and getting enough teachers is paramount. Under the direction of Charles J. Bensley, chairman of the Board of Education's building and sites committee, a tremendous construction program has been undertaken.

During the coming year the school board plans to build schools costing more than $75,000,000. Mr. Bensley appeared confident that within ten years, at the, present rate of construction, the city would be able to provide sufficient classroom space for the growing school population.

A survey of twenty-five school systems, representing every section of the country, made by this department indicates the gravity of the educational situation this year. Soaring enrollments will make a serious impact on urban school districts of over 100,000 population; overcrowding in elementary classes is worse than ever before.

Similar Conditions

Overcrowding, likewise, is the major problem in elementary grades in the smaller school systems. Thousands of children will be forced to attend classes of forty-five or more pupils each. (The recommended maximum is thirty-five.)

But it is not quantity that should be stressed this year—it is quality. America's most critical educational problem is the supply of competent, adequately trained teachers. Here the problem becomes complex—for not only is there a serious shortage of teachers, but there is a serious lack of competent students who desire to become teachers.

Warning that the situation has never been so serious, Dr. William G. Carr, executive secretary of the National Education Association, in an interview last week, pointed out that since 1950 the number of new teachers prepared annually for both elementary and secondary schools has declined from 115,000 to 91,000. This year there are 6.5 per cent fewer new teachers than last year; and the decrease will continue for at least another year.

What does this mean? This year all the teachers colleges graduated 35,000 elementary school teachers—scarcely enough to cover the new classrooms that were opened this fall. What about replacing the retired teachers? Or the 75,000 experienced teachers who left the classrooms last year for higher-paying jobs with greater opportunity for 'advancement?

The highest peak in public school enrollment is yet to come. By 1960, it is estimated, the schools will enroll 35,000,000 children. There simply are not enough teachers, buildings, classroom facilities or administrators to take care of this tremendous increase. Although the communities are building more schools than ever before, the rate of construction will have to be tripled if we are to keep pace with the number of children to be educated. And, even more important, the number of elementary teachers under training will have to be tripled. The country needs a minimum of 100,000 properly prepared teachers each year.

Probably the objectives for the coming year set forth by Superintendent Louis P. Hoyer of Philadelphia schools would be accepted by the majority of other schools reached in The Times survey. These goals are:

(1) To maintain an adequate teacher supply, particularly for special classes.

(2) To place salaries at a level in keeping with the rising cost of living.

(3) To extend the building program to meet needs of newly developed areas, older areas in which the population has become congested, and the increased enrollments due to the high birth rates of recent years.

(4) To expand special services such as counseling, psychological, psychiatric, recreational, school work programs for supplementary instructional purposes.

(5) To rehabilitate or replace equipment, and increase appropriations for books and supplies.

(6) To improve curricula and classroom techniques to secure maximum pupil achievement. Special emphasis will be placed on the three R's and all other fundamentals, one of the most important of which is character and citizenship training.

September 12, 1954

RISING ENROLLMENT TREND AS A NEW SCHOOL YEAR OPENS

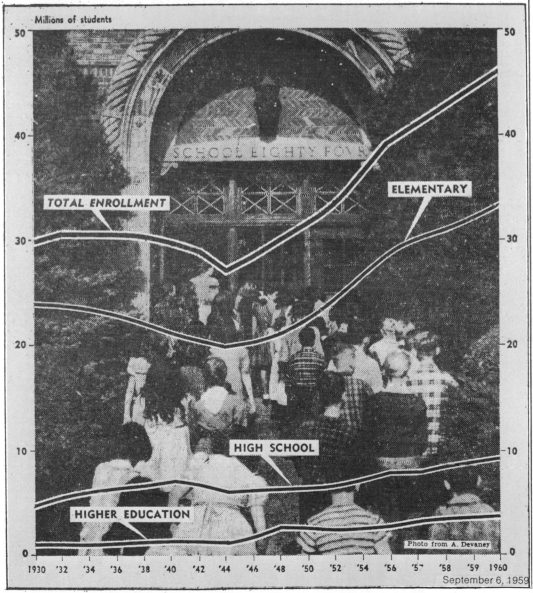

Millions of students

TOTAL ENROLLMENT

ELEMENTARY

HIGH SCHOOL

HIGHER EDUCATION

Photo from A. Devaney

1930 '32 '34 '36 '38 '40 '42 '44 '46 '48 '50 '52 '54 '56 '57 '58 '59 1960

September 6, 1959

20% Rise Is Reported In Half-Day Students

WASHINGTON, May 14 (AP)—The number of children attending half-day sessions in city grade schools has risen 20 per cent in two years and is still climbing, the National Education Association reported today.

And classes that continue full sessions are becoming more and more overcrowded, the association added.

The N. E. A., which has long advocated a Federal program of aid to school construction, cited figures from a new survey of city grade schools. The study covered 6,500,000 children—about 55 per cent of the total in school districts with populations of 2,500 or more.

There are now 300,000 such students on half-day schedules, the association said, compared with less than 250,000 in the school year of 1955-1956.

The association said more than half of all city grade school children were in classes of thirty pupils or more, compared with the N. E. A.'s ideal of twenty-five.

May 15, 1958

ILLITERACY IN U. S. DECLINES TO 2.2%

WASHINGTON, Feb. 4 (UPI) —The Census Bureau reported today that Americans—and especially Negroes—are continuing to improve their educational levels.

The bureau said a survey last March showed that the illiteracy rate had fallen to a low of 2.2 per cent and added:

"The ability to read and write is now shared by nearly all persons 14 years or older. The relatively small number of illiterates is concentrated mostly in the older age groups."

Most striking reductions in illiteracy and increases in general educational attainment have been posted by non-whites, the bureau said in a special report. It noted that in 1870 illiteracy among non-whites was 80 per cent. In 1959 it had dropped to 8 per cent.

The bureau also said "the persistent uptrend in the nation's educational attainment is being maintained." In 1959 half of all persons 25 years old and older had completed eleven years of schooling. This compared with 9.3 years in 1950 and 8.4 years in 1940.

The average for men was 10.7 years and for women 11.2 years, according to the 1959 survey.

The bureau said 20 per cent of all non-white adults had completed high school in 1959, compared with 8 per cent in 1940. It added that about 43 per cent of the nation's adult population had finished high school last year, about double the level in 1940.

February 5, 1960

U. S. Schools Enroll 46 Million; 52% Rise Cited Over 10 Years

Enrollment in United States schools and colleges last fall was 46,259,000, according to the Bureau of the Census.

The total ten years earlier was 30,276,000. The increase was 52.8 per cent. The Census Bureau, in announcing its survey, said the inclusion of Alaska and Hawaii in the 1960 statistics accounted for about 250,000 students and caused little distortion in the comparative statistics.

The figures showed that the greatest rate of increase was in kindergartens. In October, 1960, there were 2,092,000 in kindergartens compared with 902,000 in October, 1950. That is a ten-year increase of 131.9 per cent.

Elementary school enrollment rose in ten years to 30,349,000 from 20,504,000 for an increase of 48 per cent. High school enrollment rose to 10,249,000 from 6,656,000, an increase of 54 per cent. Students at colleges, universities and professional schools increased 61.2 per cent from 2,214,000 in 1950 to 3,570,000 in October, 1960.

Not only were striking increases recorded in numbers of persons attending schools, but also a significant increase was shown in the last five years in the proportion of the total population in classrooms.

In the whole age span from 5 to 34, persons attending school last October constituted 56.4 per cent of the total civilian non-institutional population in that age bracket. In October, 1955, the percentage was 50.8.

A breakdown by age groups showed that the highest proportion of school attendance was in the 7 to 13-year-old bracket with 99.5 per cent attending school last October compared with 99.2 per cent five years earlier. The enrollment totals were 25,621,000 last October against 21,028,000 in 1955.

The junior college age levels, 18 and 19 years, showed the greatest rise in percentage points. Attendance rose from 1,232,000 or 31.5 per cent of the population in that age bracket in 1955, to 1,817,000 or 38.4 per cent of those 18 and 19 in October, 1960.

The proportion of the increase in the last half decade was greatest at post-graduate age levels, reaching 50 per cent in the 30 to 34-year-old bracket. School attendance in this bracket rose from 192,000 or 1.6 per cent of the population in 1955 to 278,000 or 2.4 per cent of the population in 1960.

In the 25 to 29-year-old bracket nearly one person in twenty was in school last fall. The total last October in this bracket was 514,000 or 4.9 per cent of the population compared with 475,000 or 4.2 per cent in 1955.

January 18, 1961

FEWER SCHOOL DISTRICTS

While the enrollment in the nation's public schools has reached the highest number in education history, the total of school systems in which these students are being educated is smaller than ever. This news was reported last week by the United States Office of Education as a success story in the continuing battle for consolidation of small districts.

Preliminary figures of a survey undertaken for the office by the Census Bureau show that the number of public elementary and secondary school systems fell to 42,428 in the 1959-60 academic year. Of this number, another 7,029 are paper districts only and operate no schools. They usually pay tuition for students attending nearby districts.

The total represents almost a 40 per cent reduction since 1951 when there were 70,000 school systems. Indicating that consolidation is not nearly complete, the report cautions that there remain 14,862 systems with fewer than fifty pupils each.

September 11, 1960

44.6 Million Pupils in Schools
At Record $27.8-Billion Cost

WASHINGTON, Jan. 1 (AP) —The nation's public schools are educating a record number of students with the largest staff ever and at the greatest cost in history.

Enrollment in public elementary and secondary schools has reached 44.66 million, an increase of 2.3 per cent over the 1965-66 school year and 38 per cent greater than ten years ago, according to statistics released tonight by the National Education Association.

The million-member teacher organization reported that total expenditures for public schools this school year would be about $27.8-billion, 9.3 per cent greater than last year and a 131 per cent increase over the $12-billion spent only 10 years ago.

The current figure includes $22.4-billion for operating elementary and secondary schools, $3.6-billion for capital outlay, $913-million for interest on school debt and $862-million for other educational programs of local districts.

These other programs include adult education, community colleges, summer activities, community centers and recreational programs. This area is the fastest growing of all with a 23 per cent increase in expenditures over the 1965-66 school

year. The rise is partly a reflection of growing Federal involvement in these programs, the association said.

Preliminary estimates show that total Federal aid to elementary and secondary school systems will total $2.1-billion, up 12 per cent from last year. At the same time, states and local districts increased their school outlays by $1.8-billion, a rise of about 8 per cent.

Dr William G. Carr, N.E.A. executive secretary, said the increased local spending should help allay the fears of those who thought the states and communities might reduce their financial support of education in view of increasing Federal assistance.

State support for public schools is $10.7-billion, up 9.8 per cent, while local revenues account for $14-billion, an increase of 6.2 per cent. The figures include the 50 states and the District of Columbia.

$529 Per Pupil Cost

The average per pupil expenditure this year is $529, an increase of 7.5 per cent over last year and 68 per cent greater than the 1957-58 school year, the association said.

The number of classroom teachers is about 1.8 million with 996,000 in elementary schools and 763,000 in high schools. The figure is 3.7 per cent greater than last year as compared with the 2.3 per cent rise in total enrollment.

The trend toward a greater proportion of male teachers continued, the association said. The growth for men this year was 4.1 per cent compared to 3.5 per cent for women. Ten years ago 26 per cent of the teachers were men. The figure now is 32 per cent.

The association reported that children between the ages of 5 and 17 now make up more than one-fourth of the United States population, compared with one-fifth in 1950. About 28.2 million are enrolled in elementary schools and 16.4 million in secondary schools. There will be about 2.4 million high school graduates next spring.

The association reported that the average salary of elementary teachers was $6,609 and secondary teachers, $7,095. The average salary of the entire instructional staff — teachers, principals and other professionals — is $7,119 per year, 64 per cent greater than 10 years ago.

January 2, 1967

Elementary Schools Show Another Drop In Pupil Enrollment

WASHINGTON, Sept. 7 (AP) —The number of children in elementary school this fall will decline for the second consecutive year, in another note of bad news for aspiring teachers.

The Office of Education, in its annual back-to-school statistical roundup, said today that the sharp decline in births during the last decade would cut attendance from kindergarten through the eighth grade this year to 36.7 million, a decline from 37 million last fall.

The Government also projected 8,000 fewer jobs for elementary teachers—1,308,000, down from 1,316,000—and said the slump would last for at least another five years.

The Office of Education statistics followed a report from the Washington Center for Metropolitan Studies saying children under age 5 decreased from more than 20 million in 1960 to about 17 million in 1970.

Underlining the immensity of education as an American business, the education office said 63 million persons—30 per cent of the population—would be involved this year as students, teachers or administrators.

The cost of public and private education will increase by $9.7-billion to $85.1-billion.

The education office said the slump for elementary teachers would be offset by a 27,000 increase in secondary school teachers and a 30,000 increase in the number of college and university instructors.

In a related report released today, the National Academy of Sciences-National Research Council noted a marked worsening of job prospects for science Ph. D.'s who received their doctorates in 1970.

September 8, 1971

Report Points Up Magnitude of the Financial Problems Facing Nation's Public Schools

By BENJAMIN FINE

As a record number of children entered the nation's public and private schools last week, communities turned to the all-important question: How can the expanded school rolls be financed? They are facing a real problem—the "threatened" rise in enrollment has taken place, and with it the need to spend much more money on education than was considered necessary in past years.

Financing public school education has, in recent years, absorbed the attention of educators and laymen alike. With an estimated student body of 29,500,000 in elementary and high schools this fall, and with an expected increase of nearly 1,000,000 a year for the next seven or eight years, the nation must recognize that education will grow more costly for some time to come. More children in school will mean that more teachers will be employed, more textbooks bought and more buildings constructed.

It is appropriate to ask: Where will the money come from to support the public schools? Since the end of World War II the separate states have responded generously to the requests of the school systems for more money; yet costs have continued to rise at a steady pace, eating up the additional funds. At the close of the war the public elementary and high schools were spending slightly more than $3 billion a year for all educational purposes. Two years later this had jumped to $4 billion, and since then to $5 billion. While this $5 billion is a record sum, it is not enough, educators find, to maintain an adequate educational system. Increased requirements for school buildings, coupled with higher teacher salaries and the unprecedented enrollments, have more than absorbed the 60 per cent increase in school revenues.

Haphazard Financing

In an attempt to determine the financial needs and abilities of the states, experts in this field have just completed a comprehensive study. The 110-page survey, prepared by the United States Office of Education, the University of California School of Education and the Council of State Governments, presents an unhappy conclusion: That the states, by and large, are financing their schools on a haphazard basis, with the result that many communities are not offering satisfactory schooling to their children. Here are some of the more significant observations:

(1) There are many states and communities where sufficient funds have never been available to make possible an adequate school program.

(2) In states having small districts, the differences in ability to support the educational program from local sources are often as great as 10,000 to 1. In other words, one community may be 10,000 times better able than another town to carry a school program.

(3) As long as the funds available to support public schools in some communities—and even in some states—are inadequate, there is no real basis for expecting their educational opportunities to be satisfactory.

(4) The need for a thorough reappraisal of school support policies is extremely urgent in many states and local school systems. Making frequent adjustments in a program which is basically unsound may help to meet some of the immediate problems, but can never substitute for a careful systematic study which takes into consideration all pertinent factors and which is designed to meet all needs satisfactorily.

Variation in State Allotments

What is an adequate program for the financial support of education in the United States? The Office of Education report shows that there is great variation in the funds allotted for public schools in various parts of the country. Current expenditures among states range from an annual average of slightly less than $100 per pupil to more than $250.

States that are trying to run their schools on the basis of less than $100 per pupil are simply not doing an adequate job. Ten years ago it would have been difficult; today it is entirely impossible. The report suggests that a reasonably satisfactory program will cost a minimum of $200 a year per pupil. Unfortunately, many communities will be unable to reach this minimum without substantial help from other sources.

This brings up the question of Federal aid. Without some form of assistance from the Federal Government, many leading school authorities are convinced, equal educational opportunities will never be available for the poorer sections of the country. It is pointed out that the so-called poorer states now spend as great a proportion, if not more, of their income for schools than the more prosperous states, but that is not enough to provide adequate education for their children.

Citizen Support

Accompanying the issue of Federal aid is a basic question which must be answered by every state and community: How much should the citizens invest in the support of their public schools? Citizens of some states are now spending for public school support more than twice as great a percentage of their total income as are the people in some other states.

Here is a table that compares the states' "effort" to support their public schools. It shows the percentage of total annual personal income in each state that is spent for public schools:

	School year 1937-38		School year 1949-50	
	Per Cent	Rank	Per Cent	Rank
Alabama	2.71	39	2.77	16
Arizona	5.48	2	3.87	3
Arkansas	2.81	33	2.48	25
California	3.69	16	2.28	32
Colorado	3.76	12	2.74	18
Connecticut	2.24	47	1.79	48
Delaware	2.25	46	2.20	37
Florida	3.18	26	3.36	10
Georgia	2.71	38	2.41	26
Idaho	4.54	6	2.75	17
Illinois	3.47	18	2.04	44
Indiana	3.75	13	2.62	20
Iowa	4.25	8	2.58	23
Kansas	3.76	11	3.00	8
Kentucky	2.80	34	2.33	30
Louisiana	3.40	20	3.46	7
Maine	2.49	43	2.34	29
Maryland	2.33	44	2.14	38
Massachusetts	2.59	42	2.06	42
Michigan	3.32	22	2.61	21
Minnesota	3.54	17	2.60	22
Mississippi	2.74	37	2.24	33
Missouri	2.75	36	1.95	46
Montana	4.28	7	2.65	19
Nebraska	3.20	25	2.05	43
Nevada	2.59	41	2.37	27
New Hampshire	2.65	40	2.21	35
New Jersey	3.45	19	2.31	31
New Mexico	4.16	9	4.11	1
New York	3.22	24	1.95	45
North Carolina	3.71	14	3.50	5
North Dakota	5.27	3	2.80	15
Ohio	3.09	28	2.12	40
Oklahoma	5.03	4	3.04	11
Oregon	3.24	23	3.50	5
Pennsylvania	2.84	31	2.12	40
Rhode Island	2.19	48	1.80	47
South Carolina	3.10	27	2.90	13
South Dakota	5.99	1	2.21	36
Tennessee	2.82	32	2.57	24
Texas	3.70	15	3.50	5
Utah	4.87	5	3.98	2
Vermont	2.80	35	2.36	28
Virginia	2.32	45	2.24	34
Washington	3.05	29	2.85	14
West Virginia	3.38	21	2.90	12
Wisconsin	3.04	30	2.12	40
Wyoming	3.86	10	3.38	9
AVERAGES	3.24		2.39	

There are some other interesting statistics in the report. For example, New York State had in 1948 an income of $10,880 for each child of school age, whereas Mississippi had an income of only $2,745 per child. In this respect the differences between the wealthiest and poorest states have widened during the last ten years. In 1940 the eight wealthiest states had an average income of $4,205 for each child of school age; in the eight states with the least income the average was $1,049. In 1948 the average for the top eight states per child was $10,009, for those with the lowest income, $3,469.

Uneven Educational System

Because of the vast differences in financial abilities of the states, the nation's educational system is uneven; the type of education that many students now receive is largely a matter of geographic birth. Because the "poorer" states on the whole make a greater contribution, proportionate to their wealth, than the "richer" ones, the chances are that the disparity will continue in the future. This, of course, is one of the arguments used by the proponents of Federal aid.

An analysis of the Office of Education report shows that almost any conceivable type of school finance practice may be found. Nearly every state has some practices which may be seriously questioned.

American education during the coming year will play a vital role in helping to win the battle of ideologies. That the schools need adequate financial support can hardly be argued. The report, prepared by Prof. Edgar L. Morphet of the University of California and Erick L. Lindman of the Office of Education, can serve as a guide for better school support.

September 17, 1950

U.S. EDUCATION AID BACKED AT PARLEY

White House Conference and Folsom Support Plan

By BENJAMIN FINE
Special to The New York Times.

WASHINGTON, Dec. 1—Federal aid to education received strong support on two fronts today.

The White House Conference on Education, closing a four-day series of meetings, adopted a report calling for Federal funds for the nation's public schools. It opposed money for nonpublic schools.

And, at the final evening session, Marion B. Folsom, Secretary of Health, Education and Welfare, urged Federal aid without any strings attached to it.

He predicted that the Administration would present to Congress a bill to provide funds for school construction.

On Feb. 8 President Eisenhower asked Congress for a $7,000,000,000 building program. But most of this money was to go in the form of loans to the communities. The bill was attacked by school officials as unworkable and impractical. It never came out of Congressional committees.

The new Administration bill, suggested by Mr. Folsom, would be a "broadened and improved program of Federal assistance."

At the opening of the White House conference on Monday both President Eisenhower and Vice President Richard M. Nixon said that some form of limited Federal aid might be necessary. There were many "buts" and "ifs" attached, however.

Policy Is Reversed

Tonight the Administration through Mr. Folsom went further than it has done before on the controversial and politically dangerous question of Federal aid. It appeared to those who have followed this issue closely that President Eisenhower and his Administration are now ready to support the principle of Federal aid. This would be a dramatic reversal of Republican policies in this field.

What gave Mr. Folsom's talk added weight was his pointed statement that he had talked to the President before coming to the conference.

It was known that he had spent the morning in Gettysburg, and finished preparing his talk after returning to Washington. It was assumed, although Mr. Folsom did not say so, that the President knew what his Cabinet officer would say to the delegates.

"I talked with President Eisenhower this morning," said Mr. Folsom, "and he greatly appreciates the time and effort which all of you have put into this work."

Later in his talk he said "we shall study with great care the reports of this conference and the local and state conferences."

Since the Washington conference came out unreservedly for Federal aid, as did many of the local and state meetings, the delegates concluded that the President would accept their recommendations.

First Parley of Kind

About 2,000 delegates and observers, from every state in the union and many foreign lands, attended the conference. This is the first of its kind ever to be called in this country. President Eisenhower called it to advise him, he said, on questions dealing with the national school crisis.

Major issues confronting American education were discussed during the session. To the delegates they seemed to be a series of endless round-tables, meetings and panel groups, from 9 o'clock in the morning until nearly midnight daily.

Three reports were adopted at the closing session today. In addition to the controversial Federal aid document, the delegates adopted reports on "How Can We Get Enough Good Teachers—and Keep Them?" and "How Can We Obtain a Continuing Public Interest in Education?"

The teacher report attracted considerable attention. The report called for a salary schedule high enough to compete with other fields. It listed these characteristics of a good teacher: one who has an active interest in children, who is professionally competent, who has good physical and mental health, and who is proud of teaching as a profession.

Public Role Stressed

The report on how to continue interest in the nation's schools called for greater emphasis on the role that the public can plan in making the schools better. The delegates were told that this conference should be but the beginning of a renewed interest in American education by all segments of the population.

Long before the White House conference began the Federal aid issue dominated it. But it was not designed that way.

Conference officials had urged the delegates to study all issues, not to let Federal aid become the dominant one. But the delegates took the bit in their own teeth.

They heard from President Eisenhower that the question of finance was the heart of the nation's school problem. And they heard references, time and again, to the need for more money to develop a better school program.

The Federal aid report, adopted tonight, stirred a controversy. A number of delegates protested. They said that the two final chairmen who wrote the report were biased. They objected to techniques used at the conference.

The delegates met in 166 round-tables of ten to twelve members each. Reports of these panels went to sixteen tables of ten each; this was followed by two tables of eight each. Then by two final co-chairmen who prepared the last report.

This was a paradoxical twist. Before the conference opened, critics said it would be stacked with those who opposed Federal aid. Some charged that the Federal aid issue would not even be discussed at this conference. Today the charge was made that the Federal aid people had gained control.

Issue Thoroughly Studied

The White House report on Federal aid was prepared by Mrs. Pearl A. Wanamaker, State Superintendent of Public Instruction, Washington, and Dr. Edgar Fuller, executive secretary, Council of Chief State School Officers.

Before they met for the final statement, the delegates had threshed out the question of Federal support for many hours. The discussion began early yesterday afternoon and continued until 2:15 o'clock this morning. Then the two chairmen met at 8 A. M. and continued their deliberations until well in the afternoon. No other school issue had been so thoroughly considered. Or, for that matter, was met with so much praise on the one hand and so much criticism on the other.

Typical of the protest was this resolution adopted by Table 165.

"Regardless of our personal views and feelings, and leaving out all question of personalities, it is amazing to us, in view of the stated preliminary plans for the mechanics of this conference, that on the question of Federal aid to education, the final two chairmen should turn out to be persons of national prominence, who have publicly stated their stand on this subject."

The fifty delegates from Texas opposed the White House report on Federal aid in its entirety.

Plan Wins Wide Support

Despite the opposition and controversy aroused, both the White House report, and the Folsom statement, came out wholeheartedly for Federal aid.

The report said that the 1,800 delegates favored Government support by a 2-to-1 ratio. The overwhelming majority approved Federal funds for school building construction. On the issue of funds for the day-to-day operation of the schools, the delegates divided about equally.

A small majority said the report opposed Federal aid to education in any form.

The majority agreed that all states should be eligible for Federal funds. However, they said it should be granted only on the basis of actual needs.

There was almost unanimous agreement that Federal control should not be exerted in the use of the funds.

On the controversial issue of funds for private and parochial schools, the report said:

"While the participants recognize the right of parents to educate their children in nonpublic schools in accordance with American tradition, a large majority of the participants did not favor the use of tax funds for support of nonpublic educational institutions."

The report suggested that nonpublic schools should get increased support from private and corporate gifts, rather than from the tax rolls.

In his talk to the delegates, Mr. Folsom warned that the nation's schools face critical shortages in many areas. Despite much progress that has been made, the rate of classroom construction is seriously inadequate. He said we are moving too slowly in meeting the large backlog of classrooms that has accumulated.

If the greater number of children are to be educated, and the quality of education improved, the schools will need more support, he said.

Some communities do not have the necessary local resources, Mr. Folsom said. Unless the Federal Government provides help, they will not have good schools.

"If we are to meet our classroom needs soon enough, the Federal Government must help raise some of the funds for buildings," Mr. Folsom declared.

How much money should the Government provide? And how should the funds be allocated?

These questions, said Mr. Folsom, are now being studied by the Administration. The report of the White House conference will be analyzed with great care, he told the delegates.

Principles Outlined

Then Mr. Folsom outlined the following general principles for Federal aid to education:

¶Federal assistance in building schools should not reduce the incentive for state and local effort.

¶Federal assistance, while nationwide in scope, benefiting all states, should be distributed according to need.

¶The Federal Government should give assistance without in any way endangering the freedom of local school systems.

"This Administration," he said, "believes firmly, just as you do, in the American tradition of state and local control of schools. The danger is not that the freedom of local school systems will be lost by Federal aid for school buildings, but that it be gradually weakened through default.

"When you come right down to it, the freedom of local school systems will be preserved just as long as the American people insist upon it.

"The President told you in the opening hours of this conference that the lack of adequate school facilities can no longer be allowed. I am confident that in the weeks ahead this Administration will present to Congress a broadened and improved program of Federal assistance to help erase the classroom deficit and dispell this shadow over our children."

Campaign Issues

Both Candidates Favor School Aid, But Differ Widely on Size and Kind

By PETER BRAESTRUP
Special to The New York Times.

WASHINGTON, Oct. 28.—Senator John F. Kennedy and Vice President Nixon agree that a "challenge" in education exists, but they disagree on the response to the challenge.

Their disagreement covers both how much and what kind of Federal help should go to meet the shortage of classrooms and to raise teachers' salaries. Vice President Nixon and the Republican platform have stressed limited Federal aid for school construction only, primarily through paying the interest and principal on local school bonds in some areas. This method, according to Mr. Nixon, would free local funds that could be used to raise teachers' pay.

News Analysis

In his first television debate with Senator Kennedy on Sept. 26 Mr. Nixon said:

"I do not believe that the way to get more salaries for teachers is to have the Federal Government get in with a massive program. My objection here is the potential cost in control and eventual freedom for the American people by giving the Federal Government power over education."

President Shares Fears

President Eisenhower has voiced similar fears. Partly for budgetary reasons, he has repeatedly sought to curb or cut major outlays for school-aid programs urged by liberal Democrats in Congress.

The Eisenhower Administration has been backed in its antipathy to the liberals' programs by a bipartisan conservative coalition in Congress and by such anti-spending groups as the United States Chamber of Commerce and the National Association of Manufacturers.

On the other side, Senator Kennedy has stressed the pledge in the Democratic platform to supply "generous Federal financial support" to the states to "use as they see fit" for teachers' salaries and school construction, as well as for college classrooms and an expansion of current programs.

The Democrats have argued that limited local tax resources have proved insufficient in many areas to finance the education programs required. With Federal aid funneled through the states, they contend, local control would be fully protected.

They have criticized the Nixon-Eisenhower plan for financing school construction bonds as inadequate and unwieldy, contending that it would even force some states and localities to change their tax laws to participate.

Democratic proposals for omnibus aid have been supported by the National Education Association, many labor organizations and liberal groups such as Americans for Democratic Action.

Parochial Aid Mentioned

The candidates' differences over education, as the campaign has progressed, have also been touched by the "religious issue."

Senator Kennedy, a Roman Catholic, had repeatedly stated his opposition to "unconstitutional" aid for parochial schools.

Then on Oct. 10, Henry Cabot Lodge, the Republican Vice-Presidential aspirant, advocated Federal aid for both parochial and private schools. This suggestion was greeted without enthusiasm by Arthur S. Flemming, the Republican Secretary of Health, Education and Welfare, and by silence on the part of the Vice President. Mr. Lodge has not raised the issue again.

Federal aid to education is not a newly controversial topic. It has a history almost as old that of the nation.

As early as 1783, public lands were set aside by Congress for schools in the Northwest Territory. Similar policies were followed as new states came into the union. When public land became scarcer, money grants were made.

In passing the Morrill Act of 1862, Congress established a new policy of helping the states for only specific educational purposes. These included the land-grant colleges, vocational education and rehabilitation. Almost yearly thereafter, Congress passed costly but limited bills—free school lunches, the 1944 "G. I. Bill" to aid veterans, the 1958 National Defense Education Act.

Starting under the Hoover Administration in 1931, a succession of governmental advisory commissions urged that all future Federal grants to the states be made for general educational purposes — including school construction and teachers' salaries.

But comprehensive Federal school aid did not receive serious attention in Congress until 1948, when such a measure was introduced by Senator Robert A. Taft, Republican of Ohio.

In education, as in housing, the late Senator Taft was far less conservative than President Eisenhower and Mr. Nixon. He joined two other Republicans and four Democrats in sponsoring a $300,000,000 "educational finance" measure that passed the Senate and was favorably reported by a House subcommittee. It was widely predicted that the bill would go through Congress the following year.

The Taft bill was aimed at "equalization" of educational standards through the establishment of a minimum annual outlay of $50 a pupil in all states to subsidize "current expenses," including teachers' salaries. School construction was excluded. In segregated states, Federal funds were to be equitably apportioned between white and Negro schools. The question of aid to parochial schools was left to the states to decide.

The Taft bill passed the Senate again in 1949. But the measure died in committee in the House, stalled by bitter controversy over costs and the question of Federal aid to parochial schools.

Rider Attached in 1956

The segregation issue killed other education bills, notably in 1956, when an anti-segregation rider was attached to a Democratic measure providing $1,600,000,000 to the states on a matching basis for school construction. The "rider" was attached by Representative Adam Clayton Powell Jr., Democrat of Manhattan. A more limited $1,200,000,000 measure requested by President Eisenhower never got out of committee.

The fight over aid for education was resumed this year. The Senate passed a two-year measure carrying $1,800,000,000 for both construction and salaries. In May the House approved a $1,300,000,000 proposal to help construction only, with an anti-segregation rider attached. The bill died in the conservative-dominated House Rules Committee.

Meanwhile, the Eisenhower Administration has sought in vain to cut back aid to schools in "impacted areas"—communities affected by large influxes of Federal workers, military personnel and their dependents. This program, begun in 1950, has been popular with Congressional conservatives and liberals alike, even though it includes aid for teachers' salaries as well as for construction. It bars Federal control over curriculums and the hiring of teachers.

In answering Republican charges that their school proposals mean "Federal encroachment," liberal Democrats have pointed to the "impacted areas" program. This has earmarked or paid out almost $2,000,000,000 to 4,000 school districts without any apparent loss of local autonomy.

The Administration, Mr. Nixon and conservatives have shown no such enthusiasm.

Voting Records Differ

Even more than the respective party stands, the voting records of Senator Kennedy and Vice President Nixon reflect sharp differences.

Mr. Nixon, as a freshman Representative from California, did not vote in 1948 on an "impacted schools" bill. In the Senate, three years later, he favored an amendment reducing funds for school operating costs while voting to increase funds for surveys and construction.

As Vice President and presiding officer of the Senate, Mr. Nixon, by not voting to break a tie vote last February, killed a Democratic amendment to add $1,000,000,000 a year to provide both salaries and school aid. The same day, Feb. 3, he broke another tie vote and thus blocked reconsideration of the motion.

Senator Kennedy, on the other hand, has voted consistently with his party's liberals, with the exception of a House vote in 1950 opposing a five-year $163,000,000 program to promote library service in the states.

The same year Senator Kennedy voted to establish a National Science Foundation. In 1953 he supported a proposal to use revenue from Federal offshore property for educational purposes. Thereafter, he voted consistently with liberal Democrats for increased school aid.

Although the history of Federal aid to schools is long and tangled, the contrast between the Presidential candidates is clear. To the questions of how much and what kind of Federal aid to the states for education, Senator Kennedy's reply is essentially "much more on a broad front."

Vice President Nixon says essentially:

"More, but on a narrower front."

PRESIDENT SIGNS EDUCATION BILL AT HIS OLD SCHOOL

Hails $1.3 Billion Aid Plan —First Teacher Attends Ceremony in Texas

By CHARLES MOHR
Special to The New York Times

JOHNSON CITY, Tex., April 11—President Johnson signed today the $1.3 billion aid-to-education bill at the old country school where he had his first lessons.

"As President," said Mr. Johnson, "I believe deeply that no law I have signed or will ever sign means more to the future of our nation."

At Mr. Johnson's elbow during the ceremony was his first schoolteacher, Mrs. Kate Deadrich Loney, who is now 72 years old. The former Junction rural elementary school is a mile and a half east of the LBJ Ranch house. It has been converted into a farm home owned by Mr. and Mrs. Bert Alford of Oklahoma. It is not occupied.

Mr. Johnson sat at a rude wooden bench outside the building, which is covered in ancient galvanized metal siding meant to resemble cut stone. Flanking him were old wooden school desks and chairs, some of which had been in use when he attended the school.

The President, who has sometimes used more than 100 pens to sign a bill, used just one and handed it to Mrs. Loney. She seemed not to realize that it was meant as a souvenir for her and left it on the table as she walked away.

Students Are Guests

Mr. Johnson recalled that he first began to go to the school at the age of 4 when his mother would ask the teacher to mind him while she worked at housecleaning.

"They tell me, Miss Kate, that I recited my first lessons while sitting on your lap," he said. He attended the school for three years.

Mr. Johnson also recalled that he had been a teacher himself. He invited as guests to the ceremony some of the Mexican-

Associated Press Wirephoto

President Johnson gives the pen he used to sign the aid-to-education bill to Mrs. Kate Deadrich Loney, his first school teacher. The measure became a law yesterday.

American students he taught at Cotulla, Tex., in the late 1920's.

About seven of his former students visited him at his ranch house and came to the ceremony with him. Also on hand were several students he had taught at San Marcos State Teachers College in the 1920's. He shook their hands warmly, and smiled as one man shouted "speech class" at him as a reminder.

Also on hand were Senator Eugene J. McCarthy, Democrat of Minnesota, and the House majority leader, Carl Albert of Oklahoma, who were spending the night with Mr. Johnson.

The education bill passed the Senate Friday. It provides for $1.06 billion in aid to public schools under a formula designed to channel the aid to school districts serving needy children.

Under the formula the Federal Government will pay an annual grant equal to half the cost borne by the state in educating each child from a family with an income of $2,000 a year or less. There are about five million such children and almost every school district will receive some aid.

In addition the bill provides $100 million to purchase textbooks and library materials for both public and parochial school children and $100 million

for community education centers that will provide "shared-time" educational facilities for both public and private school students.

It is the first time Federal funds have been authorized to indirectly assist private, church schools. And it is the first major, general aid to elementary education to get through Congress, where there has been acrimonious disagreement on the church-state issue.

Mr. Johnson said he had chosen the time and place of the signing ceremony because "I do not wish to delay by a single day the program to strengthen this nation's elementary and secondary schools."

He said he "devoutly" wished his sense of urgency would be matched by those officials responsible for carrying out the aid program.

"Second," said Mr. Johnson, "I felt a strong desire to go back to the beginning of my own education—to be reminded and to remind others of that magic time when the world of learning was beginning to open before our eyes."

The President deplored the fact that the controversy over whether parochial schools should share in aid had blocked Federal aid to any schools.

"For too long children suffered," he said, "while jarring interests caused stalemate in efforts to improve our schools."

"I predict that all of those of both parties of Congress who supported the enactment of this legislation will be remembered in history as men and women who began a new day of greatness in American society," he said.

Mr. Johnson added that "by this act we bridge the gap between helplessness and hope for more than five million educationally deprived children."

He said he "devoutly" wished million new books into the hands of youth, "reduce the terrible time lag" in bringing newer teaching techniques to active classroom use and strengthen state and local education agencies.

This morning Mr. Johnson, Mrs. Johnson, Mrs. Loney and the President's sister, Mrs. Birge Alexander, attended Palm Sunday services at the First Methodist Church in Johnson City. Mrs. David Brinkley, wife of the National Broadcasting Company commentator, who flew to Texas as a guest of the Johnsons, was also in the party.

After church Mr. Johnson took the wheel of his white Lincoln sedan and led a motorcade of more than 40 vehicles on a tour of Johnson City and the surrounding countryside.

In Johnson City, the President and his party visited the home in which Mr. Johnson spent his boyhood.

A plume of dust hung in the sky as the President and the serpentine line of cars drove off a paved road and on a five-mile tour of dirt ranch roads.

Mr. Johnson will return to Washington tomorrow morning, arriving in time to throw out the first ball of the baseball season in the afternoon.

April 12, 1965

Federal Education Aid to Poor Is Found to Have Little Effect

By WILLIAM K. STEVENS

The nation's largest Federal aid-to-education program has improved the school performance of some poor children dramatically, but in most cases has produced minimal or uncertain results, according to interviews with school officials, teachers and parents in 15 states.

The aid program, Title I of the Elementary and Secondary Education Act of 1965, during the last four years has provided $4.3-billion to states and localities to improve the education of poverty-stricken children who are doing badly in school. About eight million pupils now are taking part in Title I projects.

Many localities in the survey pointed to at least one instance in which hard, objective test data indicated that Title I had improved significantly the reading ability of the poor. In such widely separated areas as rural West Virginia and Georgia, California, and the big-city ghettos of Chicago, Baltimore and New York, some pupils reportedly have reached national norms or made gains of from one to three grade levels in reading proficiency.

But these instances appear to be exceptions. Almost no school district could demonstrate, on the basis of objective tests, that a majority of children enrolled in Title I programs had been significantly affected.

In some places, tests showed no interruption at all of the typical pattern of failure in which poor children from the city slums, farms and mountains fall further and further behind national norms of achievement and ultimately drop out of school.

And in a majority of states and localities surveyed, officials said they simply did not have any conclusive test results by which to gauge the effect of most Title I programs.

In many areas there was evidence tending to justify recent critics of Title I. The critics have charged, among other things, that Title I funds have been used as general school aid, rather than for the particular needs of poor children, that the funds have in many instances been spread too thin to have much effect; and that representatives of the poor have not been included in the planning and execution of Title I projects. Dr. James E. Allen Jr., the United States Commissioner of Education, has named a special study group within his office to investigate the criticisms.

Red Tape and Resistance

The interviews also turned up evidence that in some large cities, the effective operation of Title I projects has been frustrated by red tape and bureaucratic conservatism and resistance.

Title I represented the first major breakthrough in Federal aid to education when it was passed in April, 1965. It provides money for a wide variety of school activities — for example, pre-school education, intensive reading instruction, free meals and free health examinations — on the theory that many benefits concentrated on one child will produce the best results.

This wide variety of Title I activities is being pursued in the 15 states surveyed, with a heavy emphasis on reading instruction and pre-school education.

The 15 states are California, Colorado, Georgia, Illinois, Kentucky, Maryland, Massachusetts Michigan, Mississippi, Missouri, New York, Pennsylvania, Tennessee, Virginia and West Virginia.

In virtually no instances were local school officials able to list all the services directed at a given child. Several officials said they were developing data systems that would make possible such accounting and thereby enable them to gauge the combined effect on individuals of Title I benefits.

'Intangible Things'

Regardless of the imprecision with which most school officials were able to assess the impact of Title I, almost all said they thought it was doing some good.

"So many of the results of Title I you can't put on a piece of paper," said James Screws, manager of Title I funds in Pierce County, south Georgia. "They're intangible things which we'll reap rewards from later on. When you help a child restore his teeth, and he holds up his head a little higher, and he's accepted, I don't know how you evaluate things like that.

Pierce County was one locality that reported some hard test results from Title I projects. For example, Mr. Screws said, fourth, fifth and sixth graders in four schools advanced in reading proficiency by one to three years in a single year. He and other educators in financially hard-pressed rural Georgia say Title I is "a godsend" for their poorer students.

'Nothing but Good'

"They [the children] get nothing but good from this," said Fred W. Gabbard, superintendent of Owsley County schools in eastern Kentucky. "If it were cut off we'd be lost. We've started all these programs [predominantly reading projects] and if we didn't get the Title I money I don't know what we'd do."

"For the hard-core deprived, it would appear that we haven't yet started to close the gap," said Leo D. Daugherty, chief of the New York State Department of Education's bureau of evaluation for urban schools.

The "gap" to which he referred was the one between the average academic attainment of poor children and that of the general school population. By "hard-core," he meant the most severely deprived children, estimated by Mr. Daugherty to constitute between 10 and 20 per cent of all those eligible for Title I aid.

"For all the rest of the Title I children," he went on, "my feeling is that we are slowly but surely closing the gap."

One of several examples he cited was a group of 5,000 New York City children enrolled in special reading classes during the first two years of Title I. They showed an average gain in reading ability of nine months after seven months' instruction.

Among other examples of demonstrable progress were two projects observed recently in McDowell County, W. Va., and Chicago. The West Virginia project, a remedial reading effort, produced substantial gains among students in all classes where it operated. The Chicago project, a group of child and parent centers where children received special instruction beginning at age 3, produced pupils who were reading at or above national norms at age 7.

Following are some other examples of what can apparently be accomplished with Title I funds, all of them appearing to be exceptions to the general pattern of performance.

¶In St. Louis, special reading classes in the elementary schools produced gains of 1.4

years in one year of instruction.

¶Memphis officials reported that remedial reading classes raised the reading level of some children by as much as a year in a year, indicating that normal gains were being made.

¶In Louisville, teachers indicated that children in some Title I classes were making "noticeable" progress. Teachers said they believed that tests would show the students to be reading at normal levels by the end of this year.

¶Baltimore school officials said tests showed that a group of 338 fifth graders in special classes last year made an average gain of one year in understanding paragraph meaning and eight months in word meaning, much larger gains than would ordinarily be expected from such a group.

A major exception to the general rule of spotty progress was in California, which reported to the Office of Education after a statewide sampling of school districts, that about 15 per cent of Title I participants were in classes where the average academic growth in a year was a year or more. About 10 per cent were reported to be in classes averaging a growth of a year and a half or more.

The most successful projects appear to embody one, or all, of the following features:

¶Clear, precise, realistic goals for pupil achievement, expressed in behavioral terms; for example, a goal that pupils be reading at national norms after three years. Mr. Daugherty of New York said he believed that more than half the projects in operation, both in his state and nationally, embodied vague objectives.

¶Reduction of class size to between 15 and 25 students, and provision of a full-time instructional aide to the teacher, so that more attention can be given to individual pupils.

¶Concentration of effort on children in the pre-school years and elementary grades.

¶Concentration of available money on a relatively few eligible children.

'Scattergun' Abandoned

Many school districts, in an attempt to concentrate the money more effectively, are beginning to reduce the number of children involved in Title I programs. An example is Baltimore, which, after taking a "scattergun approach" initially, has cut in half the number of children served.

The Office of Education requires that the per-pupil expenditure of Title I funds equal at least half the locality's per-pupil expenditure in state and local money. Most school systems appear to ignore this requirement.

Only California has adopted a statewide policy of concentration. It requires a minimum expenditure of $300 per Title I pupil, compared with a national 1968-69 Title I average of $141.53.

But in many districts, the money is still spread thin. A critic of Detroit's Title I program, for example, described it as being "a mile wide and one inch deep."

When a local school system concentrates Title I funds on children most in need, many deprived pupils must be left out. If they are to be included, many state and local officials say, Congress is going to have to provide more money.

Based on the number of poverty-stricken families in the nation, as shown by census data, Congress authorized the expenditure of $6.5-billion for the first four years of Title I. It has appropriated only $4.3-billion.

In many cases, Title I appears to have made little difference simply because regular classrooms remain overcrowded, thereby frustrating attempts to provide more individual attention to pupils. This is particularly true in the big-city ghettos, where school principals have sometimes used Title I funds for general purposes in order, as they say, merely to keep the school running.

Many school districts were criticized in the early years of Title I for spending inordinate amounts of money on equipment. There were two reasons for this spending. First, districts had to scramble to spend the money the first year so that they would not lose it, and it was easier to buy hardware than to plan academic programs. Second, equipment salesmen, who reportedly were more alert to Title I than some school officials were, made the most of the situation.

Indications are that indiscriminate buying of equipment has waned considerably in more recent years.

Dissent in Detroit

Resistence within the established bureaucracies of large-city school systems appears to have cut into the effectiveness of some Title I programs. An example is in Detroit, which seems to have had some success at improving the school performance of poor children by attacking their deficiencies in the pre-school years.

Dr. Louis Monacel, director of Title I operations in Detroit, has nevertheless been severely criticized by Negro leaders who want more control over the way money is spent and by other community groups who think

that some projects, such as jazz performances and poetry readings in the school are a waste of time and money.

Dr. Monacel, however, said these were not his greatest difficulties. "The biggest thorn in our side is our own organization," he said. "Change is coming very hard to Detroit public schools. Many teachers and administrators battle us daily."

Some of the most effective Title I programs have operated outside the conventional school organization. An example is Chicago's child and parent centers, which were created wholly out of Title I funds and operate with great autonomy and freedom from bureaucratic headaches.

Participation by Poor

Rarely in the interviews was there reported an instance of effective participation of community representatives and spokesmen for the poor in planning and executing Title I projects. In many instances the parents of pupils affected had never heard of Title I.

On the other hand, there are widespread indications that Title I has forced school officials to look more closely at the problems and needs of disadvantaged children.

"Through Title I, the disadvantaged child came into his own," said Louis Pasquini, acting coordinator of Title I programs for New York State. "We rediscovered poverty, and rediscovered that poor children were not doing well in school.

"Title I has been an eye-opener," said Miss Patricia Allen, director of curriculum innovation for the state of Massachusetts, who has generally been critical of the program's operations in her state. "It has brought the kinds with the problems to the surface."

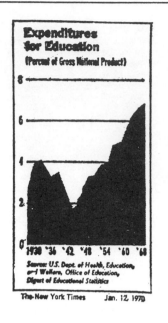

Expenditures for Education
(Percent of Gross National Product)

8
6
4
2
0

'1930 '36 '42 '48 '54 '60 '66

Source: U.S. Dept. of Health, Education, and Welfare, Office of Education, Digest of Educational Statistics

The New York Times   Jan. 12, 1970

Tax Revolt: 46,000 Shut Out of School

By WILLIAM K. STEVENS

A major revolt of taxpayers —believed to be the biggest and most serious of its kind to date —has shut 46,000 pupils out of classes in four suburban school districts north of St. Louis, and threatens to do the same for 35,000 students in two neighboring districts next month.

In all, more than a third of the pupils in St. Louis's 25 suburban school districts are affected by the rebellion, which has led to the consistent defeat of school tax levies—the three most recent last week— in the six predominantly white, middle-class districts that lie across the top of the city.

The revolt is a dramatic example of a financial crisis in public education across the country. The crisis appears to grow out of a tax structure that is widely criticized as placing too heavy a burden on localities. And it appears to be compounded of the twin pressures of inflation and recession; of sometimes heated clashes over education philosophy; of a deepening mistrust of educators by some of those who must pay the educational bill; and of a more skeptical attitude among voters that denies to education the no-questions-asked approval that many Americans have traditionally accorded it.

All of these elements have surfaced in the turmoil. "It is certainly the worst crisis we have had to face," said Dr. Robert D. Elsea, executive director of the cooperating school districts of the St. Louis area.

Thursday, voters in the 20,-000 - pupil Ferguson - Florissant district north and east of St. Louis municipal airport rejected for the fifth time a tax increase of 43 cents on each $100 of assessed valuation. Schools have not yet opened in the district, and its school board is scheduled to meet during the coming weekend to decide on a next step.

On Tuesday, voters in the 9,000-pupil St. Charles and the 10,000-pupil Riverview Gardens districts also rejected levies. Riverview Gardens plans to open its schools today, but will close them again Oct. 23

if the tax levy is not approved in a new vote Sept. 24.

St. Charles has set a new election for Sept. 26, and its board has deferred a decision on the opening of school until the State Attorney General rules on whether the board must pay a full year's salary to its teachers if classes do not run a full year.

The 25,000-pupil Hazelwood district, the area's largest, has opened its schools. But, like Riverview Gardens, it will close them Oct. 15 if a fourth levy election fails on Sept. 22.

Contingent on Levies

The remaining two districts involved—Ritenour, with 10,000 students, and Wentzville, with 7,000—had closed their schools pending new levy elections next Monday. If the levies pass, Ritenour will open its schools Tuesday and Wentzville Wednesday. In neither case has the school board decided what to do in the event of yet another failure.

Referendums on property tax increases to cover increased operating costs, as well as on bond issues for construction, have been defeated in record numbers across the country during the past two years. But in only a few instances have the defeats resulted in locked classrooms. That happened first in the winter of 1968-69, when Youngstown, Ohio, closed its 27,000-pupil school system for five weeks after rejection of an increased tax levy.

Since then, other Ohio cities have undergone similar experiences. Only last Tuesday, the 55,600-pupil Dayton system suffered its third levy defeat in the past 10 months. Its schools are open, but may have to close in November.

But so far, never has such an extreme situation involved so many pupils in a single locality as in the St. Louis area, according to officials of the National Education Association.

Two-Thirds Required

The situation is made more serious by the fact that Missouri's Constitution requires that levies must pass by at least a two-thirds vote. Of the six districts involved, levies have won a simple majority of the vote in five. Yesterday, for example, 53.6 of those voting in the Ferguson-Florissant district favored the levy.

School officials such as Dr. Warren M. Brown, Ferguson-

Florissant superintendent, believes the two-thirds requirement is highly unfair in that it gives "no" voters twice the electoral power of "yes" voters and thereby violates the Supreme Court's one-man-one-vote doctrine. About 15 states require more than a simple majority in school tax elections, and the Supreme Court is expected to take up the question next month.

The two-thirds rule notwithstanding, the pressures and issues here are perhaps representative of thos eat work in countless school districts across the country and Ferguson-Florissant is said to represent accurately the general situation in the six districts.

Fifteen years ago, Ferguson-Florissant had only a quarter as many students as it has today. In the intervening years it has become a residential community housing both blue-collar workers and some relatively affluent professionals and managers. The former have generally voted against the school levy, while the latter have generally supported it.

Homeowners Hit Hardest

The community is largely one of neat, modest brick and frame homes on wide tree-shaded streets. Its commercial and industrial contingent is relatively small, and as a result, its property-tax burden falls most heavily on homeowners.

The property tax continues to be the major source of revenue for schools. The Missouri Legislature last year tried to remedy this by passing "an excellent state support bill," in the words of Dr. R. L. Johns of the National Education Finance Project, a $1.6-million Federal study of public school financing. "But they didn't raise the money to support it," Dr. Johns said.

The reason the money was not raised is that the income tax that was to provide it failed in a state-wide referendum. Many suburban communities such as Ferguson-Florissant favored it, but outlying areas killed it.

Dr. Johns said that he believed the local school crises across the country are likely to continue unless the state and Federal governments pick up a larger share of the load. He predicts that by 1980, state and federal revenues will pay for 80 per cent of educational costs.

"If the state money had come through, the Ferguson-Florissant superintendent, Dr. Brown, said yesterday, "we wouldn't have had to ask for a local tax increase." Even so, he

January 12, 1970

said, certain economies would have been necessary. Already, the Ferguson-Florissant schools have stopped reducing their pupil-teacher ratio, which is now reported to be at about 28-to-1.

Inflation has had a double effect on the situation at Ferguson-Florissant. According to Dr. Brown, it is the major factor in driving up school costs, and also play a major part in the reluctance of taxpayers to part with their money—particularly when coupled with layoffs and lower raises in the depressed aerospace industry that provides many jobs for Ferguson-Florissant residents.

The tax increase hits retired persons on fixed incomes particularly hard. "Don't they stop to consider how hard it is on us retired folk when they raise taxes?" asked 73-year-old Leroy Kapller of the district's Cool Valley neighborhood. "Why, we just can't stand it."

There is also much evidence of mistrust on the part of Ferguson-Florissant voters. "What we'd like to know is what are they doing with all that money," said Mr. Kapller. "What I'd do is close down the school, send the kids out on the street to clean up the area and wait until the teachers feel the pinch in their bellies before offering another levy."

Ferguson-Florissant teachers last year earned an average salary of $8800, roughly equal to the national average. Most of the $700,000 tax increase this year would go for a 9 per cent salary increase, already incorporated in teachers' contracts.

Another form of disillusionment with school officials was expressed by B. T. Otto, a garage mechanic. "What I resent," he said, "was that the board said, 'You're either going to vote it in or we're going to close the schools.' That's strictly blackmail. If I had been for

the levy to start with, I would have voted it down, the way they put it."

To James Fox, who for five years was chairman of a suburban school board south of St. Louis, such views signal a shift in attitudes toward education. "There was a time when you felt that the schools, like flag and motherhood, were sacred," he said. "The fact of the matter is, the schools are doing a lousy job in many areas, and administrators have conned the public into believing that anyone who had the temerity to challenge the schools was a bad guy."

Superintendent Brown of Ferguson-Florissant concedes that there is some justification for this view. "We're perfectly well aware that our communication system needs to be overhauled," he said. "It is essential to get out into the blocks, face to face with the people."

In the view of Dr. Brown and others, a general disillusion-

ment with public officials, along with the general frustration over the nation's domestic problems, is focussed in the school issue because school referendums are the only occasions on which most citizens can directly vent their dissatisfactions.

Philosophical differences over education have also played their part in the controversy here. Mr. Buzzard and others favor an essentially conservative, back-to-basics approach and an end to "fancy programs" and "frills."

"My second-grade daughter just can't understand," said Mrs. Mary Beckemeier, who is adamantly in favor of the levy. "She says, 'I'm going to double up my fist and hit 'em.'"

Tense with anger and frustration, Mrs. Beckemeier noted that much hate had been sown in the community, and that it was now friend against friend and neighbor against neighbor.

September 14, 1970

SCHOOL TAX CRISIS FORCING CUTBACKS

Some Cities Planning Early Closings—Fund-Raising System Under Attack

By WILLAM K. STEVENS

The money crisis in the nation's public schools, compounded of sharply rising costs and shrinking local revenues, has entered a new, more acute and more threatening phase. At the same time, the perennial talk about reforming the school tax system is beginning to turn into action.

Some big cities for the first time are faced with the stark prospect of closing their schools for lack of funds. Last week, for instance, the Chicago Board of Education decided to end that city's school year 11 days

early next June unless other ways can be found to trim $22.8-million from a school budget that has already been drastically pared.

The cities are finding themselves in such straits largely because the local property tax, historically the main support of public education, has become inadequate to the job. That tax is under increasing attack in the state houses, in the courts, and in Washington, where efforts to replace it as education's chief support are gaining momentum.

"Reform is in the air," says Kenneth E. Buhrmaster, president of the National School Boards Association. "That wasn't true a year ago."

Some state governments for the first time are actively seeking to lift the major burden of school financing off the backs of the localities.

They have been spurred, in some instances, by lawsuits attacking the constitutionality of the local property tax. The latest such suit was filed in Boston on Dec. 2.

That same day, President Nixon committed his Adminis-

tration to "a complete overhaul" of the present system of financing education and said that "specific proposals" along those lines were being prepared.

Meanwhile, pressure for massive Federal aid to schools has become more intense than ever, and some observers believe the enactment of such aid to be inevitable. They see 1973, after the Presidential election, as the most likely time for action.

Those pressing for an increased Federal role, including most of the country's education lobbies, hope that Washington will assume at least a third of the cost of elementary and secondary education. Federal aid now amounts to less than 7 per cent of the total spent on schools.

"This thing has been smoldering a long time, and now it has burst into flame," Dr. Roe L. Johns, director of the National Education Finance Project at the University of Florida, said in describing the general situation.

One major reason why the situation has suddenly burst into flame is that the financial plight of the localities has both broadened and deepened. A year ago, the crisis was most visible in the taxpayers'

revolts that killed school bond issues and operating levies in community after community. Schools in some few localities, mostly suburbs and smaller towns, were forced to close for short periods because the voters would not provide enough operating money.

Problems Continuing

That pattern has continued. Independence, Mo., for example, closed its schools for two weeks this fall, and may close early next spring. Classes in Dayton, Ohio, were shut down for a week early in November, and Kalamazoo, Mich., plans to shorten its school year by 23 days.

But this fall, the school-closing syndrome has begun to invade metropolitan America as well.

Chicago's pupils originally were scheduled to get 12 extra days of Christmas vacation, beginning last week, so that $22.8-million might be saved. That city's Board of Education has put off the cut until the end of the year, in the hope that other economies might be made in the meantime.

Gary, Ind., with not enough money to meet its December

payroll, had planned to give its students an extra week of Christmas vacation. But the teachers voted by a 4-to-1 margin Friday to remain at work whether they got paid or not.

Gary will end the school year with a $20-million operating deficit and may not open its schools next September unless the Indiana Legislature increases the state share of operating funds, now one-third.

Portland, Ore., where two consecutive school levies have been defeated, will end the 1971-72 term 17 days early, or about the time that money is expected to run out.

Philadelphia, lacking $41-million of the $365-million it requires to operate at last year's levels, has made severe cutbacks in program and services, and has eliminated 800 teaching positions. It also plans to shorten its school year by five weeks.

In New York City, Isaiah E. Robinson, president of the Board of Education, has warned that the nation's biggest school system might be forced to shut down early, despite a state law prohibiting it, should the state government impose further budget cuts. The city this year has already cut out 5,000 teaching positions, reduced some services drastically, and cut back sharply on supplies.

Earlier this fall, 63 of the nation's largest school systems responded to a National Education Association survey on fiscal matters. On the basis of the survey, the N.E.A. concluded that at least 41 of the systems were operating under "crisis conditions."

A New York Times sampling of 27 states has revealed that only four of the states in the sample report no serious financial problems.

Both surveys found that teachers had been laid off by the thousands and that classes had consequently grown in size as the remaining teachers had to take extra students.

While class size has typically increased by only two or three students, this nonetheless represents the reversal of a years-long trend across the country toward smaller classes. Ironically, it has happened at a time when the rise in school population appears to be tapering off, and teachers are in more than adequate supply.

Further, the curriculum in school after school has been reduced to "basics." Often, this has meant that such subjects as art, music, physical education, driver education, dramatics, industrial arts, and such activities as band, athletics and debate have disappeared from school programs. (In Philadelphia, however, high school football was restored, with the help of private funds, after a public outcry.)

In addition, maintenance has been allowed to slide in many areas, leading to the deterioration of school plants; and supplies, textbooks and library stocks have suffered.

Underlying the fiscal problem of big-city education, according to most analysts, are two basic factors: Rising costs and a deteriorating property tax base.

Dollar for dollar, big cities get less education for their money than do other areas. To begin with, almost everything is more expensive in the city. Further, it costs more to educate the higher proportions of the poor and handicapped that are found in the cities. Land for school buildings costs more than elsewhere, and militant teacher unions have succeeded in forcing higher salaries. Add to this the pressure of inflation, and costs continue to rise even though enrollments may be stabilizing.

Since the 18th century, public education in the United States has relied, and still relies, on the local property tax for the bulk of its support. All across the country, overburdened taxpayers for the last two or three years have been rejecting property tax increases.

And in the cities, the problem is made more acute by the fact that affluence, both personal and corporate, is moving to the suburbs. The property tax base is therefore undercut.

Last Aug. 30, the California Supreme Court struck the match that, according to Dr. Johns and others, turned the smoldering school finance issue into a blaze. The court first found the local property tax for schools unconstitutional on grounds that it violated the 14th Amendment's equal protection clause by providing more school money from wealthy districts than from poor districts. Later it declared that its ruling had not been final. It said the tax system was still valid and it ordered further

ther consideraiton by a lower court.

Since then, as many as 30 similar suits have been or will be filed. State legislatures, taking notice, have begun or stepped up efforts to relieve localities of the burden of supporting their schools.

In Kansas, for example, the California decision has spurred legislators to explore a variety of alternatives to the local property tax for schools.

Minnesota has already increased the proportion of state support for schools from 50 to 65 per cent.

The present leadership of the Florida Legislature is committed to an increase in state support for schools. In that state, the proportion of the total school bill paid by the state has already risen from 41 to 54 per cent since 1965-66.

In Wisconsin, Gov. Patrick J. Lucey has announced that within 30 days he would name a special study group to "re-examine the whole base for financing elementary and secondary education."

In Ohio, Gov. John J. Gilligan's tax reform program, enacted last week by the Legislature, calls for a statewide income tax to supplant property and sales taxes for the support of schools.

Gov. William G. Milliken of Michigan is now leading a petition drive to put on the ballot a constitutional amendment that would allow a dramatic reduction in the use of the local property tax for schools, with the slack to be taken up by statewide revenues.

A STATISTICAL PRIMER ON PUBLIC ELEMENTARY AND SECONDARY EDUCATION IN THE UNITED STATES

State	Population (April 1, 1970)	Est. Birth Rate per Thousand (1969)	Pct. Population Urban (1960)	Enrollment (Fall 1970)	Enrollment as Pct. Total Pop.	No. of School Districts (1970-71)	Amt. Spent Per Pupil High	Amt. Spent Per Pupil Low	Est. No. of Teachers (1971)	No. Pupils Per Teacher (1970-71)	Est. Avg. Salary Per Teacher (1970-71)	Total Non-Instr. Staff (1969)	Total Personal Income (1969)	Pct. Residents Income Below $3K	Personal Income Per Capita (1968-69)	Pct. Per Capita Income	Pct. Per Capita Income Local	Educ. Exp. as Pct.	Est. Exp. for Public Schools (1971)	Local	State	Federal
Alabama	3,444,165	17.8	58.1	806,000	23.4	124	$581	$344	33,026	24.4	$7,376	13,006	$5,669	29.0	$2,365	14.4	4.2	40.2	$370	21.4	62.8	15.8
Alaska	302,173	24.2	35.8	80,000	26.4	28	$1,810	$480	3,821	20.9	$13,570	1,550	$950	17.6	$4,053	19.1	5.4	32.1	$106	12.8	69.7	17.5
Arizona	1,772,482	20.1	73.8	440,000	24.8	295	$2,223	$436	19,323	23.4	$9,285	9,343	$3,879	19.6	$3,026	14.7	5.3	49.6	$333	47.8	44.6	7.6
Arkansas	1,923,295	16.7	47.7	464,000	24.1	389	$664	$343	19,671	21.9	$6,668	8,178	$3,157	31.5	$2,315	13.1	4.0	35.5	$240	37.1	44.5	18.4
California	19,953,134	17.8	86.0	4,633,000	23.2	1,120	$2,414	$569	184,000	24.0	$11,022	98,332	$60,198	16.6	$4,010	15.9	4.5	35.5	$3,943	59.8	35.2	5.1
Colorado	2,207,259	18.0	75.1	550,000	24.9	181	$2,801	$444	23,402	22.3	$8,260	11,959	$5,233	17.6	$3,316	14.8	4.7	46.8	$399	62.4	30.3	7.3
Connecticut	3,032,217	16.4	76.2	662,000	21.8	169	$1,311	$499	31,442	21.1	$9,600	10,901	$9,626	9.6	$4,303	10.6	3.4	37.6	$600	71.6	26.3	2.1
Delaware	548,104	19.3	66.0	132,000	24.1	26	$1,081	$633	6,034	22.0	$9,780	2,510	$1,502	16.4	$3,842	12.8	3.8	42.1	$117	21.7	71.2	7.1
Florida	6,789,443	17.0	75.5	1,428,000	21.0	67	$1,036	$593	62,571	22.9	$8,805	34,509	$14,857	23.2	$3,192	12.0	4.3	44.3	$1,040	34.8	56.0	9.1
Georgia	4,589,575	19.6	55.5	1,099,000	23.9	190	$736	$365	47,419	25.0	$7,778	18,521	$9,425	22.5	$2,791	13.0	4.2	42.2	$656	31.8	57.7	10.6
Hawaii	769,913	19.8	78.0	180,000	23.4	1	$984	$984	7,654	22.6	$10,140	3,979	$2,135	11.7	$3,565	16.0	4.1	33.2	$167	2.9	89.4	7.7
Idaho	713,008	18.1	50.3	182,000	25.5	115	$1,763	$474	7,701	22.7	$7,059	3,045	$1,344	21.2	$2,600	14.4	4.3	39.3	$110	53.6	38.2	8.2
Illinois	11,113,976	17.4	81.6	2,357,000	21.2	1,174	$2,295	$391	107,785	21.1	$10,233	47,472	$33,992	14.1	$3,989	10.3	3.5	40.1	$1,968	56.4	38.2	5.4
Indiana	5,193,669	17.9	63.9	1,232,000	23.7	315	$965	$447	51,204	24.4	$9,272	23,375	$13,197	16.2	$3,415	10.8	4.1	51.0	$861	63.6	32.5	4.0
Iowa	2,825,041	15.4	55.6	661,000	23.4	454	$1,167	$592	31,843	20.2	$9,271	15,076	$6,889	19.9	$3,288	13.9	5.2	45.8	$590	67.7	29.2	3.1
Kansas	2,249,071	17.9	64.3	512,000	22.8	311	$1,831	$454	25,884	19.8	$8,034	10,876	$5,787	19.3	$3,283	12.2	4.3	45.7	$360	62.9	31.2	5.9
Kentucky	3,219,311	17.9	47.1	717,000	22.3	192	$885	$358	29,911	23.8	$7,190	14,245	$6,046	26.1	$2,630	13.2	4.0	40.1	$404	31.6	55.0	13.5
Louisiana	3,643,180	19.9	64.9	843,000	23.1	66	$892	$499	38,500	23.1	$8,340	21,721	$6,681	25.8	$2,644	15.6	4.6	37.5	$621	28.8	60.0	11.2
Maine	993,663	17.9	52.5	245,000	24.7	288	$1,555	$229	11,170	21.9	$8,127	4,372	$1,984	16.4	$2,830	13.7	5.0	39.7	$175	60.1	31.9	7.9
Maryland	3,922,399	16.1	71.5	916,000	23.4	24	$1,037	$635	40,811	22.5	$10,091	20,490	$10,784	12.5	$3,780	12.3	4.3	41.7	$808	58.9	35.3	5.8
Massachusetts	5,689,170	16.8	81.8	1,168,000	20.5	416	$1,281	$515	91,441	21.1	$9,613	21,805	$16,107	9.3	$3,888	13.8	3.3	29.8	$938	72.3	21.7	6.1
Michigan	8,875,083	18.2	73.1	2,181,000	24.6	630	$1,364	$491	93,287	23.4	$10,647	45,214	$24,258	13.2	$3,715	13.4	4.5	47.5	$1,879	50.9	45.5	3.7
Minnesota	3,805,069	18.7	64.9	921,000	24.2	500	$903	$370	44,940	21.0	$9,271	19,198	$9,271	17.4	$3,346	14.6	5.3	45.0	$896	51.9	43.4	4.6
Mississippi	2,216,912	17.8	41.6	535,000	24.1	150	$825	$283	22,533	23.7	$6,008	9,424	$3,048	34.5	$2,074	15.4	4.8	39.7	$463	25.2	52.4	22.4
Missouri	4,677,399	17.5	69.1	1,039,000	22.2	621	$1,699	$213	43,352	21.5	$8,373	22,702	$11,036	22.2	$3,264	11.7	4.0	42.7	$686	59.4	32.2	8.4
Montana	694,409	18.8	50.0	177,000	25.4	744	$1,716	$539	8,900	21.0	$8,173	2,696	$1,476	22.3	$2,906	14.5	5.0	40.9	$142	68.0	24.0	8.0
Nebraska	1,483,791	16.8	60.0	329,000	22.2	1,700	$1,175	$623	17,161	19.1	$8,120	7,679	$3,739	19.2	$3,200	13.1	4.5	45.9	$214	75.3	17.6	6.6
Nevada	488,738	18.8	74.9	127,000	26.0	17	$1,679	$746	5,086	25.7	$9,551	2,306	$1,434	16.7	$3,971	15.0	4.1	33.2	$95	56.3	36.8	6.9
New Hampshire	737,681	16.8	56.8	159,000	21.6	168	$1,191	$311	7,125	21.3	$10,050	1,713	$1,696	16.2	$3,272	13.8	3.2	41.4	$106	86.2	9.6	4.3
New Jersey	7,168,164	16.0	87.2	1,482,000	20.7	599	$1,485	$400	70,900	20.5	$8,214	27,839	$21,834	11.3	$3,963	10.4	3.8	40.0	$1,530	69.2	25.9	4.9
New Mexico	1,016,000	21.6	71.6	282,000	27.8	89	$1,183	$477	11,620	24.2	$9,298	5,081	$1,898	22.2	$2,666	18.4	4.6	48.5	$209	20.0	63.4	16.6
New York	18,190,740	17.1	83.6	3,477,000	19.1	760	$1,889	$669	178,135	19.6	$11,100	82,054	$58,080	14.2	$4,141	16.2	3.9	33.9	$4,336	47.7	47.9	4.3
North Carolina	5,082,059	18.1	41.6	1,192,000	23.5	152	$733	$467	49,565	24.1	$8,168	24,406	$9,924	22.5	$2,658	11.2	3.9	46.8	$713	18.8	66.2	15.0
North Dakota	617,761	18.4	40.8	147,000	23.8	411	$1,623	$686	7,005	19.2	$7,260	3,048	$1,260	20.6	$2,657	18.3	5.2	41.9	$98	66.2	25.8	8.0
Ohio	10,652,017	17.2	73.4	2,425,000	22.8	631	$1,685	$413	104,680	23.2	$8,798	48,943	$28,278	15.3	$3,480	10.5	3.8	42.2	$1,750	64.5	28.8	4.7
Oklahoma	2,559,253	16.2	66.1	627,000	24.5	665	$2,566	$342	28,184	22.2	$7,360	11,836	$5,280	26.5	$2,833	14.9	4.1	39.8	$385	46.7	43.5	9.8
Oregon	2,091,385	17.0	62.7	479,000	22.9	350	$1,439	$399	21,700	22.2	$9,298	11,385	$5,025	19.8	$3,325	15.3	5.3	47.1	$411	74.5	19.6	5.9
Pennsylvania	11,793,909	15.8	70.9	2,358,000	20.0	597	$1,401	$484	108,800	22.1	$9,300	52,522	$29,954	15.2	$3,394	11.2	4.0	41.6	$2,089	47.8	46.2	6.0
Rhode Island	949,723	17.4	84.0	188,000	19.8	40	$1,206	$531	8,988	20.9	$9,442	2,785	$2,409	15.3	$3,611	12.5	3.2	35.4	$164	57.8	36.5	5.7
South Carolina	2,590,516	18.7	42.4	638,000	24.6	93	$610	$397	28,000	22.3	$7,000	10,781	$4,370	25.8	$2,390	12.1	4.4	47.0	$392	25.4	61.7	13.0
South Dakota	666,257	17.3	43.4	166,000	24.9	286	$1,741	$350	8,853	19.1	$6,793	3,838	$1,387	23.0	$2,584	16.0	5.6	46.5	$113	73.9	15.1	10.9
Tennessee	3,924,164	18.5	53.6	900,000	22.9	147	$766	$315	35,450	25.4	$7,400	20,080	$7,196	26.1	$3,019	12.0	3.8	40.4	$510	40.3	47.0	12.6
Texas	11,196,730	19.6	78.5	2,840,000	25.4	1,187	$5,334	$264	121,900	21.9	$8,325	53,342	$24,513	22.0	$2,793	11.0	4.0	45.9	$1,578	40.7	49.3	10.0
Utah	1,059,273	23.6	76.9	304,000	28.7	40	$1,515	$533	11,250	26.8	$8,073	5,678	$2,093	15.9	$3,053	15.6	5.7	53.2	$185	39.8	54.2	6.0
Vermont	444,732	17.8	39.9	103,000	23.2	277	$1,517	$357	5,582	17.9	$8,420	1,416	$983	17.6	$3,074	15.0	3.9	39.4	$108	63.5	33.9	2.5
Virginia	4,648,494	18.3	58.3	1,078,000	23.2	134	$1,125	$441	50,300	22.5	$8,700	23,429	$10,374	19.8	$3,074	13.4	3.9	44.6	$810	54.2	35.2	10.6
Washington	3,409,169	16.7	68.5	818,000	24.0	321	$3,406	$434	33,380	24.5	$9,520	17,488	$9,137	17.3	$3,674	14.4	4.5	45.5	$665	37.7	56.6	6.7
West Virginia	1,744,237	16.2	40.5	399,000	22.9	55	$722	$502	16,625	24.1	$7,800	9,353	$2,961	26.7	$2,433	14.4	4.7	42.0	$238	39.0	48.8	12.3
Wisconsin	4,417,933	17.4	64.7	993,000	22.5	455	$1,432	$344	49,052	21.4	$9,640	17,341	$10,792	16.0	$3,374	15.1	4.4	44.7	$872	67.6	29.3	3.1
Wyoming	332,416	18.5	62.9	86,000	25.9	131	$14,554	$618	4,621	19.0	$8,687	1,961	$764	19.2	$3,100	19.1	6.1	35.4	$76	51.6	25.8	22.6
U.S.	202,428,262	17.7	70.9	45,904,000	22.7	17,895	—	—	2,039,091	—	$9,265	944,788	$514,043	17.9	$3,425	13.2	4.2	40.5	$44,424	52.0	44.1	6.9

Sources: Population (April 1, 1970) Source: Bureau of Census; Est. Birth Rate (Live Births per Thousand) (July 1, 1969) Source: H.E.W.; Pct. Population that is Urban (Dec. 1, 1969) Source: Sales Management; Enrollment (Fall) 1970 Source: Office of Education; Enrollment as Pct. Total Population Source: Office of Education, H.E.W.; Number of School Districts (1970-71) Source: N.E.A.; Amount School District Spends Per Pupil (1969-70) Source: N.E.A.; Number of School Districts (U.S. Office); Est. Number of Teachers (1971) Source: N.E.A.; Number of Pupils Per Teacher (1970-71) Source: Office of Education, N.E.A.; Est. Average Salary of Teachers (1970-71) Source: N.E.A.; Total Non-Instructional Staff (1969) Source: Bureau of Census; Total Personal Income (1969) Source: National Income Project; Pct. of Residents Income Blocks with $3 Thousand Source: Bureau Sales Management; Personal Income Per Capita (1968-69); Pct. of Per Capita Income (1968-69); Pct. of Pct. Income and Local Functions; Educational Expenditure as Pct. of Per Capita Income Spent on Local Schools (1968-69) Source: Bureau of Census; Est. Expenditures for Public Schools (1971) Source: Office of Education, H.E.W.; Pct. of Revenue received by Public Schools by Source (1970-71) Source: N.E.A. Source: President's Commission on School Finance.

COURT, 5-4, BACKS SCHOOLS IN TEXAS ON PROPERTY TAX

Holds State Laws Are Not Void Just Because Their Benefits 'Fall Unevenly'

MARSHALL IN A DISSENT

He Terms Ruling a Retreat From the Commitment to Equality of Opportunity

By WARREN WEAVER Jr.
Special to The New York Times

WASHINGTON, March 21—The Supreme Court held today that the states could finance their public school systems in part with property taxes that provided more money and better educational facilities for pupils who lived in wealthier districts.

The decision, by a 5-to-4 vote, upheld the constitutionality of the Texas school finance system, which effectively prevents districts with relatively low property values from spending as much money on education as do those with higher property values.

If a single Justice had shifted his vote, reversing the Court's ruling, the school system of every state except that of Hawaii would have been materially affected, with residents of richer districts paying more taxes to help support comparable standards in poorer districts.

'Burdens Fall Unevenly'

But a bare majority of the Court concluded that state laws for financing public services should not be declared unconstitutional "merely because the burdens or benefits thereof fall unevenly, depending upon the relative wealth of the political subdivisions in which citizens live."

All five Republicans, four of them appointees of President Nixon, voted to sustain the Texas school plan. Associate Justice Lewis F. Powell Jr. wrote the majority opinion in which Chief Justice Warren E. Burger and Associate Justices Potter Stewart, Harry A. Blackmun and William H. Rehnquist concurred.

The minority consisted of four Democrats, with Associate Justices Byron R. White and Thurgood Marshall writing minority opinions, joined by William O. Douglas and William J. Brennan Jr.

School Quality Varies

Justice Marshall called the decision "a retreat from our historic commitment to equality of educational opportunity and . . . unsupportable acquiescence in a system which deprives children in their earliest years of the chance to reach their full potential as citizens."

The majority, he said, decided "that a state may constitutionally vary the quality of education which it offers its children in accordance with the amount of taxable wealth located within the school districts within which they reside."

Challenging the constitutionality of the Texas law were 15 Mexican-American families living in the Edgewood district of San Antonio, where the total public school expenditure in 1967-68, from Federal, state and local sources, was $356 per pupil.

In San Antonio's most affluent district, Alamo Heights, the comparable figure was $594 per pupil. The difference was largely attributable to the amount that the wealthier district was able to raise by property taxes.

Justice Powell wrote in the majority opinion that the equal protection clause of the Constitution did not require "absolute equality or precisely equal advantages," and that the relative poverty of the Edgewood parents "has not occasioned an absolute deprivation of the desired [educational] benefit."

"The Justices of this Court lack both the expertise and the familiarity with local problems so necessary to the making of wise decisions with respect to the raising and disposition of public revenues," the majority continued.

When educational experts disagree on how and where to raise and spend money, Justice Powell wrote, "the judiciary is well advised to refrain from interposing on the states inflexible constitutional restraints that could circumscribe or handicap . . . continued research and experimentation."

Although the majority felt it necessary to declare that its action "is not to be viewed as placing its judicial imprimatur on the status quo" in educational finance, the same justices said that the recommendations in the dissent would have produced "an unprecedented upheaval in public education."

The court's decision was criticized by the acting executive secretary of the National Educational Association, Allan M. West, who said, "The yield of crops and the concentration of wealth in individual communities will continue to determine the kind of education each child receives."

He emphasized that the Court's ruling did not prevent individual states from adopting school financing plans designed to produce greater equality than property tax systems generally do.

In his dissent, Justice Marshall did not hold out much hope that parents—like the plaintiffs in this case — could persuade a legislature to rewrite the education spending formulas in their favor.

"I, for one, am unsatisfied,"

Associated Press
Demetrio P. Rodriguez of San Antonio, Tex., was plaintiff against Texas school financing system.

he wrote, "with the hope of an ultimate 'political' solution sometime in the indefinite future while, in the meantime, countless children unjustifiably receive inferior educations that 'may affect their hearts and minds in a way unlikely ever to be undone.' "

The last phrase was a quotation from the Supreme Court's landmark decision of 1954 prohibiting segregation in the public schools.

In deciding the case, the Court produced five separate opinions totaling 136 pages.

Plaintiff Is Bitter
Special to The New York Times

SAN ANTONIO, Tex., March 21—Demetrio P. Rodriguez, the original signer of the petition that lead to the Supreme Court's ruling, said today:

"I cannot avoid at this moment feeling deep and bitter resentment against the supreme jurists and the persons who nominated them to that high position. The poor people have lost again, not only in Texas but in the United States, because we definitely need changes in the educational system."

Another signer of the petition, Mrs. Jose Fermin Rodriguez, who is not related to Demetrio Rodriguez, said that the ruling "is not going to help our poor children."

New Educational Methods Queried

To the Editor of The New York Times:

Among recent New York guests of mine were a mother and her nearly 7-year-old son. He was a youngster of great energy and surpassing curiosity; every radio knob, light bulb, knot holding up awnings, shutters, curtains, typewriter attachment, formed a challenge, to be met on the spot, with results often surprising to him and to me. The possibilities of shears, knives, matches, were greater than I had imagined.

It surprised me that, though he was obviously a keen and observant boy, he neither could read nor did he show any ambition to learn. His mother explained that he had been attending a New York public school where the first year is devoted to the development of personality and character, and to accommodation to environment; reading is taken up in the last few weeks, and he had missed them.

Of course, this boy might emerge unscathed from any educational process. I once tutored a Yale Sheff Junior who admitted he had never read but one book beyond those required. To my query what that book was, he could not recall its name or author, but did remember that "it was a red book."

But as I think back to the 6 and 7 year old boys and girls with whom I toed the crack (no figure of speech!) in Massachusetts district school nearly seventy years ago, I know every one of us could read, spell and figure fairly well toward the end of the first year, or our teacher, with a ruler, would know the reason why. We developed personality, character and accommodation to environment as we went along doing tasks under discipline, without taking time off and taxpayers' money for special instruction in those arts. Or am I merely a laudator temporis acti? CHARLES UPSON CLARK.

North Hatley, Que., July 6, 1948.

July 15, 1948

Resignation of California Official Points Up The Issue of Progressivism vs. Orthodoxy

By BENJAMIN FINE

Dr. Willard E. Goslin, nationally known as one of the foremost educational administrators, recently resigned under pressure as Superintendent of Schools of Pasadena, Calif. The importance of the case is not limited to Pasadena or even California: Fundamentally it epitomizes on a nation-wide scale the continuing attack on progressive education, and it points up again the controversy over what should be and should not be taught in public schools.

The National Education Association and the American Association of School Administrators, which together represent more than 800,000 teachers and administrators, have appointed a joint committee to investigate the Pasadena dispute and the circumstances surrounding Dr. Goslin's resignation. The committee will go to California soon for an on-the-spot study.

The character of Pasadena as a community forms the backdrop for the Goslin case. Pasadena, with a population of 104,000, is predominantly residential; it is a handsome city of more than average prosperity. It lies amidst a well-endowed intellectual atmosphere, with the California Institute of Technology and a fine Community Playhouse near by. Many of its residents are former New Englanders—indeed, they tend toward a rather Bostonian outlook.

A Divided Community

For some years prior to 1948, when Dr. Goslin went to Pasadena, the city had been divided over its system of progressive education. Some parents complained that the schools went "too far" in the advanced philosophies of education. They asserted that the Pasadena set-up produced a generation of high school graduates who could scarcely read and write.

Some compromises were made, and the educational pendulum swung between progressivism and orthodoxy. Yet the progressive idea was never wholly submerged, partly because California is a center of progressive education, with the concepts of that field fostered and developed by the state university.

It was against this background, two years ago, that Dr. Goslin was invited to become Pasadena's Superintendent of Schools at a salary of $18,000. He came well recommended, although he had just resigned as superintendent in Minneapolis because he felt the Minneapolis public did not support his program adequately. At Minneapolis Dr. Goslin had emphasized the development of the "whole child" rather than the teaching of the three R's. He also believed in the broader aspects of education—the training of youth who could develop into well-adjusted citizens of their communities.

In Pasadena everything seemed right for a long, compatible relationship between the new superintendent and the community. Dr. Goslin tried to develop the educational philosophy that prevailed when he took over. Reading, writing and arithmetic continued to play an important role, but the curriculum went far beyond these fundamentals. As is true in many schools today, the "whole child" was the objective of Pasadena training. The

child's physical, mental and emotional adjustment became the concern of school officials. A sound guidance program was established.

Techniques Used Elsewhere

One innovation is an example of Dr. Goslin's approach. Last June he asked the Pasadena Board of Education for funds to establish school camps in the near-by Los Angeles National Forest. He felt that grade school children could not only study botany and other outdoor subjects at first hand, but that they could acquire an appreciation of broad concepts, such as soil conservation, that were considered important to the national welfare.

Many of Dr. Goslin's techniques are accepted, in greater or lesser degree, in numerous other parts of the country. His "satisfactory-unsatisfactory" grading system is used in New York City public schools and elsewhere, as is the custom of promotion en masse for the lower grades.

Many prominent citizens and organizations have backed Dr. Goslin in the controversy surrounding his work. The Rotary Club, for example, rallied to his support when he was asked by the Board of Education to resign. A citizens' group, led by a former president of the Chamber of Commerce, has diligently worked with and for him. Other groups supporting him are local chapters of the League of Women Voters, the San Gabriel Central Labor Council, the National Association of Colored People and the Independent Progressive party.

Opposition to Goslin

The main group opposed to Dr. Goslin has been the Pasadena School Development Council, with a claimed membership of 4,000, headed by a physician. The association went to work two years ago, when Superintendent Goslin was appointed, and it has suc-

ceeded in crystallizing the sentiment against progressive education. It brought pressure on the school board—consisting of a paint dealer, an undertaker, a retired teacher, a lawyer and a housewife—which culminated in the board's request for Dr. Goslin's resignation.

In spearheading the drive against the superintendent, the School Development Council argued that "modern and advanced" techniques should be used to implement rather than supplant training in the conventional subjects. It contended that sex education "usurps a family prerogative" and that if the subject is taught at all, it should be presented only by medical authorities and only to high school classes sexually segregated.

The School Development Council urged that American history and "heritages" be taught before those of foreign countries. It charged that Dr. Goslin's administration had not adequately examined textbooks and other teaching materials for matter that "might subvert the loyalties of students." The council also complained against the showing of "The Brotherhood of Man," a film on racial tolerance.

Dr. Goslin has angrily denied the assertion that his methods are "super-progressive." He has attributed his ouster to "professional opposition" backed by "certain community minorities" who, he says, are "self-appointed saviors of the American scene who are afraid of the social and political consequences of free education."

The investigation to be made by the National Education Association and the American Association of School Administrators may throw some more light on the complex issues and motives behind this unfortunate controversy, which has an important bearing on education throughout the country.

December 10, 1950

Pasadena Backs Education 'Frills' Over Plain 3R's, Survey Reveals

By GLADWIN HILL
Special to THE NEW YORK TIMES.

PASADENA, Calif., Aug. 17—Another milestone in the protracted and acrimonious controversy over public education in this otherwise sedate residential city was reached last week with the publication of the findings in an exhaustive eighteen-month study of its school system.

The inquiry, which cost around $50,000 and involved more than 1,000 of Pasadena's 105,000 citizens, was precipitated by the nationally discussed dismissal in November, 1950, of the city's superintendent of schools, Dr. Willard Goslin.

The dismissal became a cause célèbre because Dr. Goslin, while denounced in some local quarters as a radical, was widely regarded as typifying the moderately progressive school of educational thought. This school of thought has been under attack in a number of communities from coast to coast by advocates of "three R's" education as opposed to the "frills" of contemporary school curricula.

Actually, Dr. Goslin's departure was surrounded by many strictly local issues and grievances that combined to obscure any clear-cut showdown between the conflicting views on education.

The report returned last week—2,000 pages long—left some of the broad questions unresolved, while it illuminated many points of interest.

The minute investigation of the school system was designed not to produce an indictment or a vindication of any individuals or points of view, but to be a constructive survey and guide to policy. As such, it was concerned largely with details of school operation and administration.

However, by implication, in its very lack of recommendations for radical alterations, it constituted an essential vote of confidence in the school system and a contradiction of the contentions of the system's more vehement critics.

These critics have ranged from state legislative investigators who adjudged instructional programs "unfit," to local groups who have asserted that students were being inculcated with socialistic and communistic notions.

The study was made under the auspices of a Citizens Survey Committee headed by a lawyer, James B. Boyle, who typified the large number of middle-of-the-road citizens simply anxious for a dependable diagnosis of their school system.

Co-directors of the survey were Dr. Clyde M. Hill of the Yale University Graduate School of Education and Dr. Lloyd Morrisett, Professor of Education of the University of California at Los Angeles.

Participating citizens were organized into some 140 specialized investigatory committees. Public opinions on key questions were appraised by approved scientific polling methods.

The Pasadena school system involves 24,000 students, 2,000 staff members and an annual budget of around $10,000,000.

Satisfaction in general with the education the system is now providing was expressed by citizens in a ratio of two to one. There also was preponderant satisfaction with the "6-4-4" plan (six years of grammar school, four years of junior high and four years of combined high school and college-level training) in which Pasadena pioneered.

On the key question: "Do you think that the school now is spending enough time teaching the 'citizenship subjects' of civics, American history and American geography?" equal proportions of the citizenry expressed assent and dissent, with 26 per cent undecided.

On broad questions of curricula, in regard to the complaints of "frills" of contemporary education, the report summarized survey findings as follows:

"Citizens overwhelmingly believe that students at all levels should be taught to get information on all sides of a controversial question before forming their opinions. * * *

"Morals and manners, they are convinced, must be taught in the schools. * * *

"Four out of five citizens desire one-half to three-quarters of the time spent in school to be devoted to basic subjects, i.e., reading, spelling, arithmetic and civics. A still larger proportion wish the skills to be learned in practical activities. * * *

"All junior high school pupils must study about other governments and about world affairs, declare 90 per cent of the citizens. * * *

"Junior high school pupils should receive vocational guidance. * * *

"By almost a three to one ratio, citizens desire their children to be taught moral and spiritual values. By almost the same majority they prefer a planned program within the school rather than released time for outside instruction."

On the touchy matter of sex education—exhibition of the film "Human Growth" had been one of the issues of the Goslin regime—designation of the field as a school responsibility was endorsed by citizens by a ratio of more than four to one. People favoring sex education in junior high school outnumbered those favoring it at the elementary level by a ratio of only five to four.

August 18, 1952

Dr. John Dewey Dead at 92; Philosopher a Noted Liberal

The Father of Progressive Education Succumbs in Home to Pneumonia

Dr. John Dewey, the philosopher from whose teachings has grown the school of progressive education and "learning by doing," died of pneumonia in his home, 1158 Fifth Avenue, at 7 o'clock last night. He was 92 years old.

His wife, the former Mrs. Roberta Lowit Grant, who was with him when he died, said he had been ill for twenty-six hours. He had broken a hip last November, and had been confined to the apartment, except for occasional trips to the roof for sunning.

The widow said Dr. Dewey had been carrying on various projects at home to the last, and had outlined several works. She had no idea how near to possible publication any of them might be.

Surviving also are two adopted children, Adrienne, 12, and John, 9. Five other children of his first marriage also survive—Frederick A. Dewey of New York, Mrs. Evelyn Smith of Kansas City, Mo.; Mrs. Lucy A. Brandaur of Syracuse, N. Y.; Miss Jane U. Dewey of Baltimore and Sabino L. Dewey of Huntington, L. I., the last also having been adopted.

Mrs. Dewey said the funeral service would be held at the Community Church of New York, 40 East Thirty-fifth Street, on Wednesday at 1 P. M.

As a philosopher—and he was acknowledged by many as America's foremost philosopher of his time—Dr. Dewey was not content to bring forth theories; he came forward to emphasize his ideas of liberalism, and, with the courage of a crusader, was willing to lend his name and reputation to causes that were frowned upon by staid society.

He was too big a man to be sneered at as an "armchair Bolshevist." His convictions were those of an essentially honest man, and although he might well have sat back to criticize the general order of things, he took an active part in the attempt to create a third political party, to lend his voice and influence to help the down-trodden, to do away with oppression in this country and elsewhere, and to strive for a finer universal education.

In his quest for betterment he

Dr. John Dewey
(from a photograph made three weeks ago)

met—and was prepared to meet—not only opposition but defeat. Some of his plans were quixotic and much too good for this world, but never wavered in a cause that he considered just and he commanded the respect of all who opposed him.

As the champion of an ideal and l :ral democracy, Dr. Dewey saw the good as well as the bad in countries where the masses were groping for new social systems. He visited Russia, China and Turkey; saw for himself, and maintained his views in the face of public opinion in this country. He condemned hasty judgment of the affairs of other peoples and pointed to the flaws at home in no uncertain terms.

Dr. Dewey had become attached to liberalism in his student days at the University of Vermont and at Johns Hopkins, where he came under the influence of Coleridge, Emerson and T. H. Green, but what finally emancipate. him from the cumbersome and academic sys-

tems of transcendentalism was his discovery in 1891 of William James' "Psychology." In this work, according to Prof. Herbert W. Schneider of Columbia, he not only found the "instrumental theory of concepts" on which Dewey's logic was based, but also experienced that contagious mental "loosening up" with which James influenced his generation and which made him the father of American philosophy.

Dr. Dewey's principal achievement was perhaps his educational reform. He was the chief prophet of progressive education. After twenty years that movement—"learning by doing"—had become a major factor in American education in the late Thirties, and in 1941 the New York State Department of Education approved a six-year experiment in schools embodying the Dewey philosophy.

But progressive education was long the center of controversy among educators, and in the early

Forties criticism was becoming more outspoken. The revolt against Dewey and pragmatism in education was strongest in Chicago, the scene of his first and greatest triumphs. At the University of Chicago, where Dr. Dewey was head of the Department of Philosophy and for two years director of the School of Education, President Robert Hutchins has sponsored a system of "education for freedom" which seeks to separate the teaching of the "intellectual" from the "practical" arts. Both Dr. Hutchins and Dr. Nicholas Murray Butler, long president of Columbia University, sharply attacked progressive education in 1944.

In a birthday interview that year Dr. Dewey dismissed as "a childish point of view" the criticism by Dr. Butler, in an address at the opening of the university, that progressive education, "a most reactionary philosophy," has led to undisciplined youth.

And replying to Dr. Hutchins' attacks, he said:

"President Hutchins calls for liberal education for a small, elite group and vocational education for the masses. I cannot think of any idea more completely reactionary and more fatal to the whole democratic outlook."

While Professor of Philosophy at the University of Michigan in 1893 Dewey wrote:

"If I were asked to name the most needed of all reforms in the spirit of education I should say: 'Cease conceiving of education as mere preparation for later life, and make of it the full meaning of the present life.' And to add that only in this case does it become truly a preparation for later life is not the paradox it seems. An activity which does not have worth enough to be carried on for its own sake cannot be very effective as a preparation for something else * * * if the new spirit in education forms the habit of requiring that every act be an outlet of the whole self, and it provides the instruments of such complete functioning."

June 2, 1952

Influence of the 'Progressive' School Is Now Found Throughout the Country

By BENJAMIN FINE

The Walden School in New York City, celebrating its fortieth anniversary this week, has had considerable influence on the nation's educational philosophy. One of the early progressive schools, Walden took the lead in breaking away from the rigid book-centered pattern of the traditional school program.

Walden, which started with ten children, two teachers and one room, has seen many of its ideas and principles incorporated in the public schools of the country. Today it has a staff of thirty-five, 350 pupils from kindergarten through high school, and a national reputation.

The story of Walden and of progressive education generally is told in a report issued last week by the school's present director, Dr. Vinal H. Tibbetts.

The theories of John Dewey, William H. Kilpatrick, William James and Francis W. Parker were still untried when Walden opened in 1914.

Most of the schools in those days stressed conformity. For example, children had to reach a certain level of reading ability by the end of the first grade, or they were kept back. Today educators recognize that children vary in their rate of intellectual development. The child who is unable to read at age 6 may be a superior reader at age 9. Holding him back in school for one or two grades will hurt, rather than help, his adjustment.

When Walden opened, its founder, Margaret Naumburg, explained its main objective in these words:

"The purpose of this school is not merely the acquisition of knowledge by children. It is primarily the development of their capacities * * *. The ability to absorb knowledge and information develops naturally."

Children as Individuals

Walden found that when children were allowed to develop their own

interests, they produced amazing results both academically and socially. Unlike the other schools of the period, Walden did not regard the children as an Army squadron, nor the teacher as a drill sergeant. Walden treated children as individuals. The youngsters were not forced to sit up straight in their seats, hands clasped on desks, eyes front, at constant attention.

Here were the beginnings of the progressive program as we know it today. Classes were small. Children moved about the rooms freely. They talked to each other as they worked or played. They felt at home with their teachers. Critics were shocked to learn that the pupils called their teachers by their first name. (They still do.)

Progressive education does not seem like a radical idea today. But four decades ago it was a jolting concept. The innovations at Walden raised many eyebrows. Some referred to it in shocked tones as "that school where the teachers wear smocks." When a prominent educator heard that Walden wanted the services of a trained psychologist, he asked sarcastically, "Are you running a school or a clinic?"

But slowly the work done at Walden attracted respect and gained the attention of the community. Educators were surprised to find that after some years of this seemingly "easy" education, most of the children equalled or even surpassed those who had studied in the traditional schools. After graduation, they did well in college. Some colleges now accept Walden students on certificate, instead of examinations.

Influence on Schools

Forty years after its founding, Walden School is taking a broad look at the future. What has been its impact upon American education? The public schools of today are vastly different from their predecessors. In many ways, the "progressive" philosophy has entered the public and private school programs of large numbers of communities.

But not every one, in or out of the educational profession, is ready to accept the validity of the progressive system. There has been considerable criticism in recent years and particularly in the past few months. Some say that progressive education has gone too far.

Last week a member of the Los Angeles Board of Education charged that the California school system was too "progressive." The State Department of Education, in a brochure, "Framework for Public Education in California," had suggested a departure from the traditional marking system in favor of "evaluation" of individual progress. It called for the measurement of "social maturity" rather than the use of fixed scholastic yardsticks.

"Such educational policies," said the board member, Paul Burke, "are permeated with progressivism—the theory that boys and girls may progress through school and through life without achieving objective standards of performance."

Pro and Con

As the Los Angeles incident shows, the question of traditional versus progressive education has spilled over into the community itself. In some quarters progressive education is a dangerous term. It connotes radicalism.

Here are the major arguments used against progressive schools:

(1) The discipline of the child is neglected. Progressive schools turn out children who are rude and undisciplined, with little respect for authority.

(2) The fundamental skills—reading, writing and arithmetic—are slighted. Children in these schools are unable to read or write properly.

(3) The curriculum is vague, indefinite and flexible. Pupils don't get a course in history or geography, but something called "social studies."

Proponents of progressive education speak loudly in its praise. They say:

(1) Progressive education develops a richer curriculum than does the traditional school, and attracts a higher caliber of teacher.

(2) Progressive education graduates have a high record of successful entrance to college and successful work after they have entered.

(3) Progressive schools develop better relationships among the children, teachers and parents than do other schools.

How many progressive schools are there in this country? Dr. Tibbetts estimated that about 100 private schools exist whose major emphasis is upon the "progressive" formula. They enroll from 10,000 to 15,000 students. In New York City such schools as Ethical Culture, the New Lincoln, Dalton, the Little Red School House, City and Country School and the Downtown Community School might well be classified, with Walden, as the followers of the Dewey-Kilpatrick point of view.

Accepted Elements

But this does not begin to tell the story. There is hardly a public school in the land that does not, in one degree or another, practice methods that a generation ago would have been considered as progressive education. Movable furniture has become an accepted part of the new school building. Teachers' conferences have replaced the traditional report card in a growing number of school systems. The permissive method of classroom discipline is frequently found in public schools. Formal recitation has been modified. Class excursions are used to supplement textbook learning. Emphasis is placed on creative expression in the arts and crafts. Special attention is given to the needs of the individual child.

These procedures, says Dr. Tibbetts, have been taken lock, stock and barrel from the pioneering private schools. The substitution of social studies for the rigidly separated study of geography, history and civics, the more general evaluation of students rather than the precise report cards, the school psychologist and the concept of parent participation in the schools are direct outgrowths of the "startling" doctrines adopted by Walden forty years ago.

PROGRESSIVE UNIT IN TEACHING TO DIE

Group Founded in 1919 on John Dewey's Philosophy Will Disband Saturday

ONCE POWER IN SCHOOLS

In Last Years It Has Fallen Into Disrepute, but Friends See Its Mission Fulfilled

By BENJAMIN FINE

American education is about to lose one of its most controversial school groups.

The Progressive Education Association, long a powerful influence in shaping teaching methods, will die quietly on Saturday at a meeting of its board of directors.

Dr. H. Gordon Hullfish, Ohio State University professor and president of the association, said yesterday that he did not expect to see more than two or three of the twenty-odd board members at the final "death-dealing" meeting, to be held at the University of Illinois, Champaign.

Founded in 1919, the Progressive Education Association was a protest movement against traditional education. It was based in large part upon the philosophy of John Dewey, noted scholar who died three years ago. "Learning by doing" has been a fundamental concept in progressive education.

The association made little headway in its early years. But it hit its stride in the Nineteen Thirties.

With the coming of World War II, the association went into an academic eclipse. Somehow, it never managed to achieve a come-back.

Reasons for the Demise

Ironically, one reason for the Association's demise is that many of the practices it has advocated have been adopted by the nation's schools, according to Dr. Hullfish.

"I'm sorry that I have to preside at the dissolution of this school group," the veteran educator said "Yet I believe that it

passes on with its work done, its influence great.

"Its influence within American education and American life is considerable and permanent. Democracy is stronger because education is stronger. The Progressive Education Association had some part in enhancing this strength."

But there is a more cogent reason for the end of the Progressive Education Association. And that is the disrepute, even contempt, in which the term "progressive" has been held in recent years. In many school systems it has been the educational kiss of death to be labeled a disciple of Dewey or a member of the association.

Period of Greatest Activity

In its most active period in the Nineteen Thirties the association received grants from the Carnegie Foundation and General Education Board to make a series of important school studies.

In 1933 began the "Thirty Schools Experiment," also known as the "Eight-Year Study." At a cost of close to $1,000,000, the association provided an opportunity for thirty schools to experiment with their courses of study. More than 300 colleges cooperated with the commission set up by the Progressive Education Association.

Beginning with the class of 1936, the colleges admitted graduates of the thirty schools without regard to the usual subject and unit admission requirements. It thus freed the schools to experiment with curriculum reorganization.

The study concluded that the traditional college entrance courses could well be modified.

It is not easy to get educators to agree on just what progressive education is or what it stands for.

In general, however, it is conceded that these factors are present in a school system under the influence of progressive education:

¶There is a friendly, informal atmosphere in the classroom between teacher and pupils.

¶Emphasis is placed on self-discipline rather than imposed discipline.

¶More student activities take place, often originated by the students themselves.

¶The child is treated as an individual, with individual differences and learning abilities.

It is generally recognized that the leadership of Frederick L. Redefer, who was executive director of the Progressive Education Association from 1932 to 1945, kept the organization on a respected basis in the academic world.

June 21, 1955

Pupils Today Seem to Know the Three R's Better Than Pupils of Twenty Years Ago

By GENE CURRIVAN

Parents who have been wondering whether modern education has more entertainment than academic content may find some solace in the results of a study just completed at Evanston, Ill. It dealt with junior high school boys and girls in fifteen schools.

They were given the same achievement test that had been taken by pupils of their age and grade back in 1933, and they made a splendid showing. The fields covered were reading, spelling, vocabulary and arithmetic. With the exception of the arithmetic computation test, in which both groups earned the same score, the so-called modern class made a far better mark.

While the schools of Evanston are not typical of the nation as a whole, they are generally considered representative of residential suburbs of any metropolitan area. For years Evanston has been used as an edu-

cational testing ground with educators throughout the country paying close heed to the results.

This latest study was conducted last September and October under the direction of O. M. Chute, superintendent of Community Consolidated Schools, Evanston. It was in response to queries by parents and other interested persons as to whether the "fads and frills" in today's schools had caused lower achievement in the basic skills. The report on the experiment concluded:

"On the basis of the findings of this and other local 'then and now' studies completed at representative grade levels, it can be stated that children in Evanston, on the whole, are achieving as well as or better than Evanston children did a generation ago."

Questions Used

When plans were made to conduct the examination, it was re-

called that Grade 8-B pupils had been given the New Stanford Achievement Test twenty-one years before as part of a routine testing program. The test was in five parts. Here are some sample questions:

Reading: Paragraph Meaning — Pupils were asked to write in one word on each dotted line such as in the following example: "Gulliver could put five of the Lilliputians into his coat pocket, but the Brobdingnagians could pick him up between their thumbs and forefingers. The Lilliputians were .... than Gulliver and very much .... than the Brobdingnagians."

Reading: Word Meaning—Pupils were asked to draw a line under the word that makes the following sentence true—"Usury has to do with—chivalry, fiction, homage, loans, work."

Spelling: Sentences were dictated by the examiner and written by the pupil, to test spelling and punctuation.

Arithmetic Reasoning: "A recipe for jam calls for 3 lbs. of sugar to 4½ lbs. of fruit. If 6 lbs. of fruit are used how much sugar is needed?"

Arithmetic Computation: Such as "Write the following expression in the simplest form: —11b — (—2b)."

The same research staff that gave the original tests administered the repeat performance with conditions as nearly duplicated as possible. Scoring was the same with Dr. Edward L. Clark of Northwestern University acting as statistical consultant.

The test was taken by 158 boys and 143 girls. It was found that the girls in the modern group had a higher intelligence quotient and mental age than their sister pupils of 1933 and that the boys, while showing a higher I. Q. than those in the class of '33, had about the same mental age. The 1954 group was also younger in chronological age, probably because of changes in promoting practices since 1933.

Results of the Test

The final analysis of the combined test scores of the boys and girls showed:

"In the reading, vocabulary and arithmetic reasoning comparisons the 1954 group was five months (one-half school year) ahead of pupils in 1933. There was a three

53

months' difference favorable to the 1954 group in spelling. The same grade-equivalent score was earned by the 1933 and 1954 groups on the arithmetic computation test.

A breakdown of the boy and girl categories indicated that the boys' were a bit brighter but not too much.

Girls—The 1954 group were five months higher in reading comprehension, vocabulary and arithmetic reasoning than those of 1933. They also were three months ahead in spelling.

Boys—The 1954 group was six months higher in reading comprehension, five months higher in vocabulary, four months higher in spelling and three months higher in arithmetic reasoning. Both groups (1933-1954) had the same score for arithmetic computation.

The results show that the greatest strides forward were made in the reading area, which at the moment has attracted nation-wide attention. The question of whether Johnny can or cannot read has become a controversial topic wherever modern education is discussed. New fuel was thrown on the fire by Rudolf Flesch's best selling "Why Johnny Can't Read," which accused educators of failing to teach properly.

Mr. Flesch held that reading has become a problem because the phonic method has been discarded in favor of sight recognition. Phonics teaches reading letter by letter and syllable by syllable while sight recognition is concerned with the whole word.

In Evanston, a combination of phonics and sight recognition is used depending on the needs of the individual child. The teacher decides whether or not Johnny can read and if he can't she sets about seeing that he does. School authorities think the system has worked out satisfactorily.

Teachers Doing Home's Work?

While on vacation from their pupils, teachers this week spanked their other problem children: the parents. At a meeting of the executive council of the American Federation of Teachers in Chicago, one of the organization's vice presidents charged that "the teaching of initiative, responsibility and adaptability" had been shifted from the home, where it belongs, to the school, where it interferes with the serious business of education.

Miss Sophie Jaffe, a sixth grade teacher from New Britain, Conn., lodged the complaint. She said what teachers have been saying in private conversation for some time—that the schools, and especially elementary school teachers, have been forced "to take over the traditional functions of the home in order to create basic attitudes for learning."

'Mothers on the Go'

"The American mode of living in eight-cylinder cars and one-room apartments" and the lack of responsibility of "mothers on the go" have brought the problem to a head, she said. She made it plain that she considered "mothers on the go" the women who prefer to devote their time to matters other than their children. Working mothers who take seriously the responsibilities of the home, she added, not only are not to blame but actually often manage to do a better job of preparing their children for the business of learning.

The problem is real. But Miss Jaffe overlooked two important historical aspects of the cause:

First, it is not too long since many educational theorists created the impression that the schools could, and should, do many things that traditionally had been considered the job of the home. Miss Jaffe, for instance, singled out "character development," and there is little doubt that this ought to be a prime concern of every family. But too much of the educational literature of the Thirties talked about "character building" and about "citizenship training" and such things as "social attitudes" and "human relations" in a way that, at least by implication, encouraged parents to think that the school had found new secrets which might relieve the home of burdensome responsibilities.

Second, carried away by the promise of "permissively" raised children, parents found themselves encouraged to tolerate unruly youngsters at home and to send them untamed to school.

There is little gain in denying the mistakes of history—even of educational history. When educationists in the Twenties and Thirties wisely pointed to newly acquired knowledge about child psychology and the child's mind, overenthusiastic disciples permitted the now notorious misinterpretation of "teaching the whole child" to create the impression that the schools could, and would, do the whole job.

The child-centered home and school bred the self-centered child. By putting adolescence on a pedestal, school and home together ran the risk of making society permanently adolescent. By coincidence, at another meeting in Chicago on the same day, another educator looked back on the cause of present failures. Prof. Lawrence A. Cremin, of Teachers College, Columbia University, told the American Historical Association that "popular misconceptions" of the theories of John Dewey led to perversions of his real purpose. "Baby does not know best, Dewey insisted," Dr. Cremin said. The problem, he implied, was that the home and the school too often refused to admit that baby needed to be told.

Return Swing

These are the days of the return swing of the pendulum. Discipline is being taken out of the mothballs; strong guidance is considered more constructive than unchecked self-expression. Now, as the news from teachers' meetings underlines, the home is again stressed as crucial in a child's educational odyssey.

The time may have come to divide again more effectively the tasks of home and school. This cannot be done with an inflexible rule book. The school must tell "the mother on the go" that her children are her most pressing social obligation. But the child without a mother, or with parents incapable of doing their job, will continue to need the school for extra help.

The problem, as in most matters of education, is to avoid new extremes. Essentially, Miss Jaffe's plea confirms a sound trend: teachers want to get on with the job of teaching, and the home is asked to shoulder, within the limits of varying ability, its own important educational task. If more homes again tackle "life adjustment" and "social values" the schools may find it easier to concentrate on learning.   F. M. H.

MAKING CONVERTS—

A "middle of the road" reform program, announced last year as the new experimental curriculum of Amidon Elementary School in southwest Washington, D. C., is beginning to spread to other schools in the capital.

The "Amidon plan" seeks to combine the best features of traditional and progressive education. It calls for the allocation of "prime school time" to the basic subjects of reading, spelling, arithmetic, speech, science, geography and history, with great stress on written homework and textbooks. Most controversial is the school's return to the teaching of reading by way of letter-by-letter and sound-by-sound method, rather than word recognition. Extensive instruction in speech, composition and writing is supported by memorization and choral reading. Formal grammar begins in fourth grade.

Washington's superintendent Carl F. Hanson, widely considered the father of the program, reports that the Amidon plan is meeting with enthusiastic response from parents, teachers and pupils. Several other schools have announced that they intend to adopt the new pattern.

ROUT OR PROGRESS

The Rigorous New School Is Seen As More Than Counter-Revolt

By FRED M. HECHINGER

In almost every public appearance the new United States Commissioner of Education, Sterling M. McMurrin, calls for "more vigorous" education. Abraham A. Ribicoff, the Secretary of Health, Education and Welfare, in his current appeal to the nation asks that the schools "prune away the frills and insist on a high standard of quality." In Washington, D. C., School Superintendent Carl F. Hansen reports that the district's one-year-old Amidon Elementary School has demonstrated that children enjoy achieving "difficult goals by the sweat of their brows."

A natural reaction to all this tends to be puzzled questions: "Isn't this where we came in? Is not this new and rigorous school simply a reactionary return to the tough and regimented days before 'modern' or 'progressive' education?"

Some educators, committed to the more permissive and less demanding idea of education, try hard to create the impression that the current move is a primitive counter-revolution. Actually, a number of new developments must be understood, if the new trend is to be fairly interpreted. Granted that the aim is to cope with a more competitive world and greater stress on individual achievement, the new elementary school is as different from the old rote, rod and repetition as it is from the extremely "child-centered" school of the Thirties and Forties.

Some Key Differences

These are some of the key differences:

(1) *Child and teacher:* Not unlike the old schools, the post-progressives put firm priorities on such basic knowledge as expression through the written and spoken word and the mastery of numbers. They assume that without language and numbers, all progress is severely limited, if not impossible. But instead of arguing whether this fundamental curriculum is "child-centered" or "subject-centered," the new school insists that every known method and every human effort must be devoted to it.

In the process, the "rigorous" school is firmly committed to the lessons of child psychology. It neither reverts to the original, unbending view that every child must clear the same hurdles or fall by the wayside nor to the permissive idea that the school should let the child bypass the hurdles. "We try," said Dr. Hansen, "to make maximum use of our knowledge of children and to link it to a curriculum thought out by adults." The teacher returns to the front of the class, without apologies, "to teach what needs teaching."

The aim is not an authoritarian dictatorship, but a system of well-defined responsibilities leading to a feeling of security on the part of the youngsters.

(2) *The process of learning:* The curriculum is carefully mapped out but not "fixed" at the same level for all pupils. It is neither based on limited advances and dull repetition nor on the postponement of what is difficult or unpleasant. The new approach to learning is best defined by Jerome S. Bruner, the Harvard psychologist, in his book, "The Process of Education." He sees a curriculum which deals thoroughly with basic ideas and concepts and then "revisits" these repeatedly while continually building on them through so-called "spiral reinforcement."

Changing Concepts

The new school, less permissive in what it considers essential, is more permissive and less dogmatic about the timing of learning. It has been aided by Dr. Bruner as well as the experiments of sociologist Dr. Omar K. Moore of Yale, permitting 2- and 3-year-old children to "teach themselves" how to read and write. If the Amidon School, for instance, introduced concepts of geometry and formal reading into kindergarten, writing of compositions into first grade and formal grammar into fourth, it responds to the natural drive of youngsters—provided the school gets out of their way.

Pre-school children have always taught themselves to talk and form sentences. This is not considered drudgery. The "rig-orous" new school wants to encourage continuation of this drive. It takes issue with the progressive idea of sugar-coating learning with play or fun—not because learning should be unpleasant but because the child's mind should not be made to believe that play is fun and learning is not.

(3) *Substance and method:* The new school tries to unscramble the two. It is not subject-centered nor anti-method. But it insists that mastery of the subject and teaching effectiveness are two separate entities and should be approached separately.

(4) *Rejection of doctrine:* An ironic consequence of the progressive movement has been the unprogressive, rigid stance of its disciples. Reading is the prime example. The word-picture (or look-say) method, which eliminated phonics (the teaching of separate letters and syllables) entirely, replaced the original phonics-only method. Just as the old phonetic approach had become a sterile science, forgetful of the children, the word-picture method turned into a religion to be questioned at the risk of charges of heresy.

The open-mindedness of the new school is documented by the use of a reading method called "phonovisual" at Amidon. It is a non-doctrinaire exploitation of everything that is useful in old and new methods. It combines phonics, word and word-picture. Thus, the reading chart would show a cat's picture, together with the whole word "cat" and the letters c-a-t. It is neither all abstract nor all pictorial.

Previous Attempts

This might not be startling—except for the fact that the "inventors" of the phonovisual approach tried to introduce their heresy in the public schools of their district some ten years ago. They could not get a hearing. For years, they therefore operated, like rebels-in-exile, from a private school, the Primary Day School, in Bethesda, Md. Only recently have they been permitted to reestablish a beachhead in the public schools.

These are some of the facts which show the "rigorous" school to be far from a reactionary swing-back of the pendulum. Inevitably, this new school will appear tougher if only achievement is measured. But much of its success will be the result, not of harder push, but of greater release of energies, talents and enthusiasm.

October 15, 1961

SCHOOL POST GOES TO CONSERVATIVE

By BILL BECKER
Special to The New York Times

LOS ANGELES, Nov. 7—Dr. Max Rafferty, outspoken anti-progressive educator, was elected California State Superintendent of Public Instruction today over his liberal opponent, Dr. Ralph Richardson.

In a race even closer than the bitter battle for Governor, Dr. Rafferty pulled ahead as tabulations from conservative areas of Southern California mounted. At midday, Dr. Richardson conceded defeat.

With more than 80 per cent of the votes counted, Dr. Rafferty had 2,090,861 and Dr. Richardson 1,925,351. For months, the two educators debated face to face in a campaign that aroused parents throughout the state.

By a 165,000 margin, parents apparently favored the "back-to-fundamentals" approach of Dr. Rafferty. He is a forthright critic of John Dewey's progressive education theories.

Dr. Rafferty, former Superintendent of Schools in suburban La Canada, was endorsed by a committee of prominent conservative industrialists. He disclaimed any tie with the John Birch Society.

He is nationally known as the author of the book "Suffer Little Children" and other controversial writings about modern schooling.

Dr. Richardson, an associate professor of speech and English at the University of California at Los Angeles, has been on leave as president of the Los Angeles City Board of Education.

The $20,000-a-year position, nominally nonpartisan, for which they contested was open for the first time in seventeen years. Dr. Richardson had been endorsed by the retiring superintendent, Dr. Roy E. Simpson. The 44-year-old Democrat, formerly served on Gov. Edmund G. Brown's staff.

Dr. Rafferty, a 45-year-old Republican, contended that his opponent lacked administrative experience. Dr. Rafferty has served as superintendent of a number of smaller California school systems.

He pledged today that his first step in January would be to make a comprehensive survey of the State Education Department.

He says he does not advocate a return to "the three R's" but a revival of solid subject matter in the classical tradition.

November 8, 1962

The democratic heritage of academic freedom—This inscription appears on a gate leading into the Harvard Yard.

Should Communists Be Permitted to Teach?

No, says Professor Hook, who argues that party members are not free to search for the truth.

By SIDNEY HOOK

THE academic community throughout the United States is currently being disturbed by the perennial issue of the nature and limits of academic freedom. The specific event which has precipitated intense interest and discussion, not only in college classrooms but in all circles interested in education, is the expulsion of some professors from the University of Washington for being members of the Communist party. The arresting thing about this case is that for the first time in the history of education the grounds given for the expulsion of the professors is that *they* have been guilty of violating the principles of academic freedom, and therefore of "conduct unbecoming a teacher."

Here is certainly a startling reversal which reflects the emergence of new problems in culture and education not dreamed of when John Dewey and Arthur T. Lovejoy organized the American Association of University Professors to further the interests of their profession and defend academic freedom and tenure.

Because the decision may set an important precedent in higher education, it invites a reconsideration of first principles in the light of the facts.

If, as Cardinal Newman has observed, the function of a university is the discovery and publication of the truth in all branches of knowledge, then academic freedom is essential to its very life. For without the freedom to inquire, to challenge and to doubt, truth cannot be well-grounded or error refuted. Since not everything which has been accepted is true, nor everything which is newly proposed is false, the result of inquiry sometimes undermines the customary and supports the novel. When this takes place in non-controversial areas, it is recognized as the natural operation of the discipline of scientific inquiry; when it affects controversial issues, vested interests and emotions are often aroused and attempts are made to safeguard some special doctrine and conclusion from the consequences of critical scrutiny.

ANYTHING may be regarded as a controversial subject, from the heliocentric hypothesis and the theory of evolution to the causes of World War II and the wisdom of the Marshall Plan. That is why universities from the time of their origin have been compelled to fight the battle for academic freedom over and over again. Although in the West, in matters of pure science, there are no longer powerful special interests that can be outraged by the progress of inquiry, in the social studies, arts and philosophy, convictions are not so clearly a function of evidence. Conclusions in these fields touch on issues of contemporary political or social concern in relation to which almost everyone believes he is something of an authority. One man's truth is often another man's propaganda.

None the less no distinction in principle can be drawn between noncontroversial and controversial themes, especially if we recognize that all human judgments are fallible. The presumption is that university professors engaged in the search for truth are qualified by their professional competence. The judges of their competence can only be their intellectual peers or betters in their own fields. If this is denied, the university loses its *raison d'être* as an institution, not only for free research but critical teaching.

IN consequence, any doctrinal impositions, no matter what their source, which set up limits beyond which the professor cannot go, affect him both as a scholar and a teacher. As a scholar, he loses professional standing in the intellectual community if it is suspected that his findings must fit the predetermined conclusions and prejudices of those whose first loyalty is not to the objective methods of seeking the truth. As

a teacher, he cannot engage in the honest presentation and reasoned investigation of all relevant *alternatives* to the theories and policies he is considering. He runs the risk of forfeiting the respect of his students, who look to him for candid evaluation and intellectual stimulus, if they believe that he is time-serving or prudent beyond the call of scientific evidence.

IF in the honest exercise of his academic freedom an individual reaches views which bring down about his head charges of "Communist," "Fascist" or what not, the academic community is duty bound to protect him irrespective of the truth of the charges. And since these words are often epithets of disparagement rather than of precise description, there is all the more reason why the university must stand firm. It places its faith in the loyalty of its teachers to the ethics and logic of scientific inquiry. The heresies of yesterday are often the orthodoxies of today. In the interests of winning new truths, it is better to err on the side of toleration than of proscription.

This means that the professor occupies a position of trust not only in relation to the university and his student, but to the democratic community which places its faith and hope in the processes of education. ("If a nation expects to be ignorant and free, in a state of civilization," wrote Jefferson, "it expects what never was and what never will be.") Academic freedom therefore carries with it duties correlative with rights. No professor can violate them under the pretext that he is exercising his freedom. That is why the graduate faculty of the New School of Social Research explicitly declares that in the interests of academic freedom, "no member of the faculty can be a member of any political party or group which asserts the right to dictate in matters of science or scientific opinion."

SO far the analysis of principles can take us. There remains the important question of fact. Is a member of the Communist party, so long as he remains a member, free to exercise his rights and fulfill his duties as an objective scholar and teacher? To answer this question we must look at what the Communist party itself teaches, its conditions of membership, and what has come to light about the actual behavior of known

members of the Communist party. We are not dealing now with the right to hold Communist *beliefs* but with what is entailed by the *act* of membership in the Communist party as it affects educational practice.

First of all, it is important to recognize that there are no "sleepers" or passive members of the Communist party. The statutes of membership define a party member as one who not only "accepts the party program, attends the regular meetings of the membership branch of his place of work" but "who is *active* in party work." Inactivity as well as disagreement with the decisions of any party organization or committee are grounds for expulsion. The concluding sentence of the pledge which the member inducted into the Communist party takes since 1935 reads: "I pledge myself to remain at all times a vigilant and firm defender of the Leninist line of the party, the only line that insures the triumph of Soviet power in the United States." (Daily Worker, April 2, 1936.)

THE "place of work" of the Communist party teacher is the school or university. How is a Communist party member active in party work at the university? Here are some directives from the official organ of the Communist party (The Communist, May, 1937):

"Party and Y. C. L. fractions set up within classes and departments must supplement and combat by means of discussions, brochures, etc., bourgeois omissions and distortions in the regular curriculum. *Marxist-Leninist analysis must be injected into every class.*

"Communist teachers must take advantage of their positions, without exposing themselves, to give their students to the best of their ability working-class education.

"To enable the teachers in the party to do the latter, the party must take careful steps to see that all teacher comrades are given thorough education in the teaching of Marxism-Leninism. Only when teachers have really mastered Marxism-Leninism will they be able skillfully to inject it into their teaching at the least risk of exposure and at the same time conduct struggles around the schools in a truly Bolshevik manner."

TWO things are significant here. The first is the injunction to cooperate with Com-

munist party fractions among students in order—I am still quoting from official sources—"to *guide and direct that spirit of rebelliousness which already exists.*" The practice, many years ago, was to organize Communist students and teachers in the same cells, but since this led to exposure when students dropped out, teachers and students are now separately organized and meet only through carefully selected committees.

The second noteworthy thing is that the Communist party teachers are fearful of exposure and quite aware that their practices violate accepted notions of academic freedom and responsibility. That is why when literature appears under their imprint it is anonymous. Since no one takes personal responsibility, what is said about things and persons, including non-Communist colleagues, is not likely to be scrupulous or accurate. Sometimes it is downright scurrilous.

HOW is it possible for the Communist party to control the thinking of its members who teach in so many different fields? What have literature, philosophy, science and mathematics got to do with its political program? The answer is to be found in the fact that according to the Communist party itself politics is bound up, through the class struggle, with every field of knowledge. On the basis of its philosophy of dialectical materialism, a party line is laid down for every area of thought from art to zoology. No person who is known to hold a view incompatible with the party line is accepted as a member. For example, if he is a historian he cannot become a member if he teaches that the economic factor is not the most decisive factor in history or, if a political scientist, that the state is not the executive committee of the ruling class or that the Soviet Union is not a democracy. Individuals have been denied membership in the Communist party because they did not believe in "dialectics" in nature.

If a philosopher, to cite cases from my own field, accepts the theories of Mach or Carnap or Husserl or Alexander or Dewey or T. H. Green or G. E. Moore, upon joining the Communist party he will criticize the doctrines he had espoused previously. He cannot ever criticize dialectical materialism or the theories of Lenin and Stalin whom he now regards as great philosophers.

If a physicist or mathematician becomes a member of the Communist party he is required, wherever it is possible for him to do so, to relate his subject to the growth of technology, its impact upon social divisions, the class uses to which discovery is put, and the liberating role it can play in a Communist economy. The general theme is: science under capitalism makes for death and poverty; under communism, science makes for life and abundance.

THE party line, however, is not constant in all fields. It changes with political exigencies. The life of a Communist party teacher, therefore, is not a happy one, since he may have to prove the opposite of what he once so fervently taught. His difficulties are mitigated by the fact that in different terms he faces different students whose memories are apt to be short in any event. But English teachers who have been members of the Communist party during the last few years have had to reverse their judgments about the same novelists, and sometimes even about the same books, e.g. Malraux's "Man's Fate," Dos Passos' "U.S.A.," Wright's "Native Son," because of changes in the party line toward these authors.

In the social sciences, Communist party teachers taught in 1934 that Roosevelt was a Fascist; in 1936, during the Popular Front, a progressive; in 1940, during the Nazi-Stalin Pact, a warmonger and imperialist; in 1941, after Hitler invaded the Soviet Union, a leader of the oppressed peoples of the world.

Whether with respect to specific issues Communist teachers have been right or wrong in these kaleidoscopic changes is not the relevant question. What is elevant is that their conclusions are not reached by a free inquiry into the evidence. To stay in the Communist party, they must believe and teach what the party line decrees. If anyone doubts this we have the objective evidence provided by Granville Hicks in his public letter of resignation from the Communist party. Hicks resigned because he was refused even the right *to suspend judgment* on the Nazi-Stalin pact. "If the party," he writes, "had left any room for doubt, I could go along with it. * * * But they made it clear that if I eventually found it impos-

sible to defend the pact, and defend it in their terms, there was nothing for me to do but resign." (New Republic, Oct. 4, 1939.)

IT is argued by some civil libertarians, who are prepared to grant the foregoing, that this is still not sufficient evidence to impugn the integrity of teachers who are members of the Communist party. They must be judged by their individual actions in the classroom; they must, so to speak, be "caught in the act" of inculcating the party line in the minds of their students.

This has two fatal difficulties. It would require spying in every classroom to detect the party line, and disorganize or intimidate not only Communist party members but the entire faculty, since a member of the Communist party admits membership only when faced with a charge of perjury, and not always then. The academic community would wrathfully and rightfully repudiate any such practice.

Second, it would be very difficult to determine when a teacher was defending a conclusion because he honestly believed it followed from the evidence, and when he was carrying out his task as a good soldier in the party cause.

Those who contend that membership in the Communist party is *prima facie* evidence that a teacher does not believe in or practice academic freedom, insist that such membership is an *act*, not merely an expression of opinion. They deny that they are invoking the principle of guilt by association, for no one who joins and remains a member of the Communist party could be ignorant of what classroom practices are required of him. If he were ignorant, the Communist party itself would drop him for "inactivity."

IT is interesting to note that this position is independent of the questions whether a teacher has a right to be a member of a legal party or whether the Communist party is or should be a legal organization. Paraphrasing Justice Holmes' famous remark about the Boston policeman, a man may have a constitutional right to be a member of the Communist party but he has no constitutional right to be a college professor unless he is free to accept the duties as well as rights of academic freedom.

Anyone is free to join or leave the Communist party: but once he joins and remains a member, he is not a free mind.

Some administrative authorities have taken the position that they would not knowingly engage members of the Communist party, otherwise thought competent, but that they would not discharge them after they discovered the fact of their membership. This is obviously inconsistent. The reason which explains their reluctance to take on a member of the Communist party, if valid, still operates when he has already joined the faculty. If on educational grounds a Communist party member is objectionable *before* he has begun working for the party line, is he any less objectionable when he is actually in action? If anything, a person, known from the very outset as a member of the Communist party, may be assigned to a post where he can do far less damage than someone who has successfully concealed the fact of his membership.

THERE remains the question as to whether expulsion on grounds of membership in the Communist party does not set a dangerous precedent. Communists under fire in a sudden accession of concern for Catholics, express fear lest this threaten the tenure of teachers who are members of the Catholic Church.

As one who cannot be taxed with undue sympathy for Thomist doctrine, I should maintain there is no evidence whatsoever of the operation of Catholic cells in nonsectarian universities which impose a party line in all the arts and sciences that must be followed by all Catholic teachers on pain of excommunication. The comparison is a red herring. The danger to free inquiry in education from Catholic quarters comes not from teachers but from outside pressure groups.

If any other organization exists which operates like the Communist party, its members should be treated equitably with the members of the Communist party. Members of the Nazi party were under similar discipline. But in their case, before and after the Stalin-Hitler alliance, the Communists demanded their peremptory dismissal.

THE problem of the "fellow-traveler" is even a more dif-

ficult and involved question. But its solution, paradoxical as it may appear, is simple. It must be left entirely to the enlightened good sense of the academic community, which can apply various sanctions short of dismissal. The term "fellow-traveler" is hopelessly vague. "Fellow-travelers" come and go. They are of all varieties. No one is wise enough to pick out the dumb, innocent sheep from the cunning and dishonest goats. So long as they are not under the discipline of the Communist party, they may still be sensitive to the results of honest inquiry. Whatever harm they do is incomparably less than the harm that would result from any attempt to purge them. Without the steel core of the Communist party fraction on the campus to magnetize them, they will fly off in all the directions their scattered wits take them.

Although the exclusion of Communist party teachers from the academic community seems justified in *principle*, this by itself does not determine whether it is a wise or prudent action in *all* circumstances. Sometimes the consequences of removing an unmitigated evil may be such as to make its sufferance preferable. If removal of Communist party members were to be used by other reactionary elements as a pretext to hurl irresponsible charges against professors whose views they disapprove, a case might be made for suspending action. On the other hand, failure to act in a situation where the academic process has been flagrantly suborned may lead to public suspicion and reprisals that injure innocent and guilty alike.

HOW to protect the innocent, as well as those who have genuinely broken with the Communist party, from dangers attending a policy justified in principle is too large a theme to explore here. But I am confident that *if the execution of the policy were left to university faculties themselves*, and not to administrators and trustees who are harried by pressure groups, there would be little ground for complaint. In the last analysis there is no safer repository of the integrity of teaching and scholarship than the dedicated men and women who constitute the faculties of our colleges and universities.

Should Communists Be Allowed to Teach?

Yes, says Professor Meiklejohn, who argues that democracy will win in the competition of ideas.

By ALEXANDER MEIKLEJOHN

In a recent issue THE NEW YORK TIMES *Magazine published an article by Professor Sidney Hook of New York University in which he argued that known Communist party members should not be allowed to teach in American colleges because, as adherents to the party "line," they are not free to seek the truth. Herewith is an article challenging Professor Hook's views, written by Dr. Alexander Meiklejohn, former president of Amherst, teacher, philosopher and author of "Freedom and the College" and other works.*

BERKELEY, Calif.

THE president and regents of the University of Washington have dismissed three professors and have placed three others on probation. That statement fails to mention the most significant feature of what has been done. The entire faculty is now on probation. Every scholar, every teacher, is officially notified that if, in his search for the truth, he finds the policies of the American Communist party to be wise, and acts on that belief, he will be dismissed from the university.

In one of the dismissal cases, the evidence is not clear enough to enable an outsider to measure the validity of the decision. But the other five cases force an issue on which everyone who cares for the integrity and freedom of American scholarship and teaching must take his stand. Cool and careful consideration of that issue should be given by all of us, whether or not we agree with the teachers in question, but especially if we do not agree with them.

The general question in dispute is that of the meaning of academic freedom. But that question has three distinct phases. The first of these has to do with the organization of a university. It asks about the rights and duties of the faculty in relation to the rights and duties of the administration. And the principle at issue corresponds closely to that which, in the Government of the United States, is laid down by the First Amendment to the Constitution. Just as that Amendment declares that "Congress shall make no law abridging the freedom of speech," so, generally, our universities and colleges have adopted a principle which forbids the administration to abridge the intellectual freedom of scholars and teachers. And, at this point, the question is whether or not the president and regents at Washington have violated an agreement, made in good faith, and of vital importance to the work of the university.

The principle of academic freedom was clearly stated by Sidney Hook in THE NEW YORK TIMES Magazine of Feb. 27, 1949. After noting that "administrators and trustees" are "harried by pressure-groups," Mr. Hook concluded his argument by saying, "In the last analysis, there is no safer repository of the integrity of teaching and scholarship than the dedicated men and women who constitute the faculties of our colleges and universities." On the basis of that conviction, the Association of University Professors has advocated, and most of our universities, including Washington, have adopted, a "tenure system." That system recognizes that legal authority to appoint, promote, and dismiss teachers belongs to the president and regents. But so far as dismissals are concerned, the purpose of the tenure agreement is to set definite limits to the exercise of that authority.

THIS limitation of their power, governing boards throughout the nation have gladly recognized and accepted. To the Association of University Professors it has seemed so important that violations of it have been held to justify a "blacklisting" of a transgressor institution—a recommendation by the association that scholars and teachers refuse to serve in a university or college which has thus broken down the defenses of free inquiry and belief.

It is essential at this point to note the fact that the fear expressed by the tenure system is a fear of action by the president and regents. Since these officers control the status and the salaries of teachers, it is only through them or by them that effective external pressure can be used to limit faculty freedom. To say, then, as we must, that the explicit purpose of the tenure system is to protect freedom against the president and regents, is not to say that these officials are more evil than others. It says only that they are more powerful than others. Theirs is the power by which, unless it is checked by a tenure system, evil may be done.

UNDER the excellent code adopted at the University of Washington, it is agreed that, after a trial period in which the university makes sure that a teacher is competent and worthy of confidence, he is given "permanence" of tenure. This means that he is secure from dismissal unless one or more of five carefully specified charges are proved against him. And the crucial feature of this defense of freedom is that the holding of any set of opinions, however unpopular or unconventional, is scrupulously excluded from the list of proper grounds for dismissal. The teacher who has tenure may, therefore, go fearlessly wherever his search for the truth may lead him. And no officer of the university has authority, openly or by indirection, to abridge that freedom.

When, under the Washington code, charges are made against a teacher, it is provided that prosecution and defense shall be heard by a tenure committee of the faculty, which shall judge whether or not the accusations have been established. In the five cases here under discussion, the only charge made was that of present or past membership in the American Communist party. Specific evidence of acts revealing unfitness or misconduct in university or other activities was deliberately excluded from the prosecution case. And, further, since the alleged fact of party membership was frankly admitted by the defense, the only question at issue was the abstract inquiry whether or not such membership is forbidden under the five provisions of the tenure code.

UNDERLYING and surrounding the Washington controversy is the same controversy as it runs through our national life. The most tragic mistake of the contemporary American mind is its failure to recognize the inherent strength and stability of free institutions when they are true to themselves. Democracy is not a weak and unstable thing which forever needs propping up by the devices of dictatorship. It is the only form of social life and of government which today has assurance of maintaining itself.

As contrasted with it, all governments of suppression are temporary and insecure. The regimes of Hitler and Mussolini flared into strength, and quickly died away. The power of the Soviet Union cannot endure unless that nation can find its way into the practices of political freedom. And all the other dictatorships are falling, and will fall, day by day. Free self-government alone gives promise of permanence and peace. The only real danger which threatens our democracy is that lack of faith which leads us into the devices and follies of suppression.

UPON that issue, the faculty committee decided unanimously that, in the cases of the ex-members of the Communist party, there were, under the code, no grounds for dismissal. And, by a vote of eight to three, the same conclusion was reached concerning the two men who were still members of the party. In the discussions of the committee, the suggestion was made that the code should be so amended that party membership would give ground for dismissal. But that action was not recommended. In its capacity as the interpreter of the code which now protects academic freedom, the committee, in all five cases, declared the charges to be not supported by the evidence presented.

In response to this judgment upon teachers by their intellectual peers, the regents, on recommendation of the president, dismissed the two party members. And, second, going beyond the recommendation of the president, they placed the three ex-members "on probation" for two years. These actions are clearly a violation of the agreement under which faculty members have accepted or continued service in the university. They deserve the condemnation of everyone who respects the integrity of a covenant, of everyone who values faculty freedom and faculty responsibility for the maintaining of freedom.

THE second phase of the general question goes deeper than the forms of university organization. It challenges the wisdom of the tenure code as it now stands. It may be that, though the regents are wrong in procedure, they are right in principle. Here, then, we must ask whether President Allen is justified in saying that a teacher who is "sincere in his belief in communism" cannot "at the same time be a sincere seeker after truth which is the first obligation of the teacher." In a press interview, Mr. Allen is quoted as saying, "I insist that the Communist party exercises thought control over every one of its members. That's what I object to." Such teachers, he tells us, are, "incompetent, intellectually dishonest, and derelict in their duty to find and teach the truth." Can those assertions be verified? If so, then the tenure code should be

amended. If not, then the action of the university should be immediately and decisively reversed.

No one can deny that a member of the American Communist party accepts a "discipline." He follows a party "line." As the policies of the party shift, he shifts with them. That statement is in some measure true of all parties, whose members agree to work together by common tactics toward a common end. But the Communist discipline, it must be added, is unusually rigid and severe. Our question is, then, whether submission to that discipline unfits for university work men who, on grounds of scholarship and character, have been judged by their colleagues to be fitted for it.

FOR the judging of that issue we must examine the forces by means of which the discipline of the American Communist party is exercised. It is idle to speak of "thought control" except as we measure the compulsions by which that control is made effective. What, then, are the inducements, the dominations which, by their impact upon the minds of these university teachers, rob them of the scholar's proper objectivity?

So far as inducements are concerned, good measuring of them requires that we place side by side the advantages offered to a scholar by the Communist party and those offered by the president and regents of a university. On the one hand, as seen in the present case, the administration can break a man's career at one stroke. It has power over every external thing he cares for. It can destroy his means of livelihood, can thwart his deepest inclinations and intentions. For example, in very many of our universities it is today taken for granted that a young scholar who is known to be a Communist has not the slightest chance of a faculty appointment. He is barred from academic work. And, as against this, what has the American Communist party to offer? Its "inducements" are the torments of suspicion, disrepute, insecurity, personal and family disaster.

Why, then, do men and women of scholarly training and taste choose party membership? Undoubtedly, some of them are, hysterically, attracted by disrepute and disaster. But, in general, the only explanation which fits the facts is that these schol-

ars are moved by a passionate determination to follow the truth where it seems to lead, no matter what may be the cost to themselves and their families. If anyone wishes to unearth the "inducements" which threaten the integrity of American scholarship he can find far more fruitful lines of inquiry than that taken by the administration of the University of Washington.

BUT Communist controls, we are told, go far deeper than "inducements." The members of the party, it is said, "take orders from Moscow;" they are subject to "thought control by a foreign power." Now, here again, the fact of rigid party discipline makes these

Dr. Alexander Meiklejohn.

assertions, in some ambiguous sense, true. But, in the sense in which President Allen and his regents interpret them, they are radically false.

LET us assume as valid the statement that, in the American Communist party "orders" do come from Moscow. But by what power are those orders enforced in the United States? In the Soviet Union, Mr. Stalin and his colleagues can, and do, enforce orders by police and military might. In that nation their control is violent and dictatorial. But by what form of "might" do they control an American teacher in an American university? What can they do to him? At its extreme limit, their only enforcing action is that of dismissal from the party. They can say to him, "You cannot be a member of this party unless you believe our doctrines, unless you conform to our policies." But, under that form of control, a man's ac-

ceptance of doctrines and policies is not "required." It is voluntary.

To say that beliefs are required as "conditions of membership" in a party is not to say that the beliefs are required by force, unless it is shown that membership in the party is enforced. If membership is free, then the beliefs are free.

Misled by the hatreds and fears of the cold war, President Allen and his regents are unconsciously tricked by the ambiguities of the words, "control," and "require," and "free," and "objective." The scholars whom they condemn are, so far as the evidence shows, free American citizens. For purposes of social action, they have chosen party affiliation with other men, here and abroad, whose beliefs are akin to their own. In a word, they do not accept Communist beliefs because they are members of the party. They are members of the party because they accept Communist beliefs.

SPECIFIC evidence to support the assertion just made was staring President Allen and his regents in the face at the very time when they were abstractly denying that such evidence could exist. Three of the five men whom they condemned as enslaved by party orders had already, by their own free and independent thinking, resigned from the party. How could they have done that if, as charged, they were incapable of free and independent thinking? Slaves do not resign.

At the committee hearings, these men explained, simply and directly, that, under past conditions, they had found the party the most effective available weapon for attack upon evil social forces but that, with changing conditions, the use of that weapon seemed no longer advisable. Shall we say that the decision to be in the party gave evidence of a lack of objectivity while the decision to resign gave evidence of the possession of it? Such a statement would have no meaning except as indicating our own lack of objectivity.

In these three cases, as in the more famous case of Granville Hicks who, some years ago, resigned party membership with a brilliant account of his reasons for doing so, the charge made cannot be sustained. The accusation as it stands means nothing more than that the president and regents are advocating one set of ideas and are banning another. They are attributing to their victims their own intellectual sins. And the tragedy of their action is that it has immeasurably injured the cause which they seek to serve and, correspondingly, has advanced the cause which they are seeking to hold back.

THE third phase of our question has to do with the wisdom, the effectiveness, of the educational policy under which teachers have been dismissed or put on probation. And, on this issue, the evidence against the president and regents is clear and decisive. However good their intention, they have made a fatal blunder in teaching method.

As that statement is made, it is taken for granted that the primary task of education in our colleges and universities is the teaching of the theory and practice of intellectual freedom, as the first principle of the democratic way of life. Whatever else our students may do or fail to do, they must learn what freedom is. They must learn to believe in it, to love it, and most important of all, to trust it.

What, then, is this faith in freedom, so far as the conflict of opinions is concerned? With respect to the world-wide controversy now raging between the advocates of the freedom of belief and the advocates of suppression of belief, what is our American doctrine? Simply stated, that doctrine expresses our confidence that whenever, in the field of ideas, the advocates of freedom and the advocates of suppression meet in fair and unabridged discussion, freedom will win. If that were not true, if the intellectual program of democracy could not hold its own in fair debate, then that program itself would require of us its own abandonment. That chance we believers in self-government have determined to take. We have put our faith in democracy.

BUT the president and regents have, at this point, taken the opposite course. They have

gone over to the enemy. They are not willing to give a fair and equal hearing to those who disagree with us. They are convinced that suppression is more effective as an agency of freedom than is freedom itself.

But this procedure violates the one basic principle on which all teaching rests. It is impossible to teach what one does not believe. It is idle to preach what one does not practice. These men who advocate that we do to the Russians what the Russians, if they had the power, would do to us are declaring that the Russians are right and that we are wrong. They practice suppression because they have more faith in the methods of dictatorship than in those of a free self-governing society.

FOR many years the writer of these words has watched the disastrous educational effects upon student opinion and attitude when suppression has been used, openly or secretly, in our universities and colleges. The outcome is always the same. Dictatorship breeds rebellion and dissatisfaction. High-spirited youth will not stand the double-dealing which prates of academic freedom and muzzles its teachers by putting them "on probation."

If we suggest to these young people that they believe in democracy, then they will insist on knowing what can be said against it as well as what can be said for it. If we ask them to get ready to lay down their lives in conflict against an enemy, they want to know not only how strong or how weak are the military forces of that enemy, but also what he has to say for himself as against what we are saying for ourselves.

Many of the students in our colleges and universities are today driven into an irresponsible radicalism. But that drive does not come from the critics of our American political institutions. It comes chiefly from the irresponsible defenders of those institutions — the men who make a mockery of freedom by using in its service the forces of suppression.

March 27, 1949

RED TEACHER BAN URGED

Norman Thomas Says Party's Members Are in 'Conspiracy'

ROCHESTER, March 19 (P)—Norman Thomas, Socialist party leader, said today that Communist party members had no right to teach in public schools.

In a speech prepared for the Rochester City Club, Mr. Thomas called members of the Communist party members of "a conspiracy" and added:

EDUCATORS INSIST ON OUSTER OF REDS

Professors Would Drop Party Members, Saying Academic Freedom Has Limits

SEE NO CURB ON RIGHTS

They Are Concerned Only at the Threat in Dismissals for Political Activity

By BENJAMIN FINE

Many leading American educators are concerned at the threat to academic freedom caused by the dismissal of college teachers because of their political activities. However, they are virtually unanimous in upholding the ouster of Communist party members from their faculties.

Representative college and university presidents questioned in a survey believe that there are limits beyond which academic freedom should not extend. Any teaching of subversive doctrines, it is generally held, cannot be permitted to use the cloak of academic freedom. A man who belongs to the Communist party disqualifies himself from the teaching profession, many educators assert.

The dismissal of communist teachers will not impair our traditional principles of academic freedom, leading college and university heads maintain. The use of the protection of academic freedom by those who are opposed to the American form of government is dishonest and hypocritical, many contend.

"No member of a conspiracy has the right to teach in our public schools if we are to continue to believe in democracy."

Mr. Thomas said, however, he did not believe what he termed the excitement of a Communist hunt was justified by contemporary conditions.

"We must rethink the problem of separating church and state," he said. "We must rethink the problem rising with the increasing concentration of control by private owners, not by the Government, of our means of communication, press, radio and movies."

March 20, 1949

It is necessary, although it may be more difficult, to maintain the principles of academic freedom during the present "cold war," according to the educators. Unless the pattern of free inquiry and expression is continued the entire concept of democratic education in this country may collapse, they warn.

Inquiring Mind as Ideal

Typical of the comments is that made by Dr. Edmund E. Day, president of Cornell University. Although academic freedom has been under attack during recent months it has not been seriously impaired, Dr. Day said. The elimination of avowed members of the Communist party from our educational institutions is fully warranted and does not weaken academic freedom, he declared.

"The faculty of any college or university should be made up of free, honest, competent, inquiring minds, seeking to find and disseminate the truth," Dr. Day held. "The mind of a member of the Communist party is enslaved to the party line. It cannot possibly claim to be either free or honest. It is manifestly disqualified for membership in a faculty of higher learning in a free and freedom-loving society such as ours.

"But in undertaking to eliminate these traitors to the American academic tradition we must be careful not to sacrifice free and inquiring minds that are honestly engaged in the pursuit of truth, however disturbing this truth may appear to be. The untrammelled pursuit of truth, wherever it may take us, is an indispensable part of any long-range defense of freedom."

The Communist issue is receiving considerable attention because of the ouster of two avowed Communists from the University of Washington faculty. The dismissed professors have appealed to the American Association of University Professors, which is studying the case. A decision is expected by the end of the summer.

Many educators agree with Dr. Clarence R. Decker, president of the University of Kansas City, that the ouster of Communists will not impair academic freedom but "the ouster of left-wing or liberal teachers would." Similarly, Dr. Stewart H. Smith, president of Marshall College, Huntington, W. Va., said that his faculty showed little concern over the ouster of Communists, except that "there was some concern that a program of ouster tactics might make teachers timid in expressing their beliefs."

Hutchins Expresses View

Taking an opposite view, Chancellor Robert M. Hutchins of the University of Chicago declared that Communist or "left-wing" activities of teachers might or might not influence his qualifications as teachers. This is a matter for their fellow members of the faculty to determine, as a matter of their competence, Chancellor Hutchins said.

"Disqualification of teachers for their political beliefs alone, by boards of regents or trustees, is an attack on academic freedom," he stated.

Most of the educators reached in the study expressed opposition to loyalty oaths or to laws that require teachers to stay out of "subversive" groups. Chancellor Hutchins observed that the means by which most organizations are designated as "subversive groups" are generally not subject to legal safeguards or determinations. Since virtually any organization can be termed "subversive" by its opponents, he pointed out, teachers may be subjected to penalty without adequate safeguards or recourse.

Dr. Ludd M. Spivey, president of Florida Southern College, declared that laws requiring teachers to take loyalty oaths tended to endanger academic freedom. He added that "it would be difficult for a group of human beings to make a general and final statement as to what is subversive."

"I think that the passing of laws requiring teachers to take loyalty oaths and stay out of subversive groups is quite dangerous and unfair to the teaching profession," Chancellor J. D. Williams of the University of Mississippi declared. "In order to be fair it seems that all citizens should be included, not just teachers. Why not require lawyers, doctors, research workers, industrialists and all other groups to take loyalty oaths and to stay out of subversive groups?"

Dr. Theophilus S. Painter, president of the University of Texas, asserted that the state laws requiring faculty members to take loyalty oaths did not endanger academic freedom.

"The trouble with such legislation," he added, "is the difficulty of defining what groups are subversive and what are not, and this is likely to lead to witch-hunting which will impair academic freedom."

Says Loyal Fear No Oath

On the other hand, Dr. Smith of Marshall College declared that a loyal person had no objection to taking such an oath.

"I doubt if any of our faculty would object seriously to taking a loyalty oath," he commented.

However, he added, "I often wonder why teachers as a group should be singled out for such attention. Why not require a loyalty oath of all citizens?"

There are some areas in which academic freedom can or should be legitimately circumscribed, such as the teaching of the overthrow of established governments by force or violence, the educators held. Many of them agreed with this principle, outlined by Dr. Day:

"In America we are irrevocably committed to effecting social and political change by peaceful methods. We have established constitutional arrangements and procedures under which the will of the people can express itself without resort to violence. Any teaching that advocates overthrow of our Government by force and violence has no place within the concept of academic freedom for it abuses academic freedom and betrays the obligations it involves."

Other educators agreed that while academic freedom must be protected that freedom must not become a matter of license. As President Painter observed, "academic freedom does not authorize any faculty member to teach or to support the violent overthrow of legitimately established governments." Advocacy of such doctrine would be treason, and "academic freedom does not license treason."

Similarly, Dr. Decker asserted that academic freedom does not imply or include the freedom to destroy academic freedom. However, he held that there must be maximum opportunity for disagreement and for discussion about the workings of democracy. On the other hand, those who would use the privilege of academic freedom to promote a type of government that opposes academic freedom "may legitimately be circumscribed."

Smith College has always welcomed diversity of opinion and has never been frightened by independent thinking on the part of its faculty or students, President Herbert Davis declared. Neither scholarship nor research can flourish in an atmosphere of suspicion or under a threat of suppression, he warned.

"I do not fear the influence of any extreme opinions in the academic world as much as I fear the attempt to stifle them and limit freedom of debate," he said.

It is important to preserve academic freedom, the educators agreed, warning that otherwise a danger existed that the democratic way of life might be impaired.

"There can be no such thing as complete freedom of inquiry without academic freedom," Chancellor Williams maintained, "The teaching profession itself should pass on its own members who are unethical or who violate the trust and responsibility which must go hand in hand with academic freedom. There is always a real danger of the intrusion of authoritarian controls into the American educational system, but it is a danger that an enlightened people will resist. So long as we can keep our educational system highly decentralized, the danger of authoritarian control of any large segment of American education is greatly reduced."

Academic freedom can be retained in a time of world tensions and in the "cold war" of today, the college heads declared. Asserting that academic freedom must be maintained, Dr. Day conceded that in these times when the alien ideologies give rise to uncertainty, confusion and anxiety, the practice of open-minded thinking is not easily maintained.

Vigilance Price of Freedom

"All sorts of prejudices threaten it; all sorts of pressure groups undertake to throttle it," he said. "Unless we are to be misled by false reasoning, unless we are to be lured by doctrines that employ deceit, chicanery and treachery, we must be free to examine such doctrines and to know their errors. The price of freedom is vigilance."

Dr. James B. Conant, president of Harvard University, declared:

"Admittedly we are living in a world in which an ideological rivalry that goes as deep as the religious hatred of four centuries ago breeds similar poisonous incidents and inflames suspicions. But I am convinced that our American doctrines in which tolerance plays so large a role will prove to have unsuspected stamina and resilience. The disruptive forces, however, will be powerful at times, and near-panic may be threatened; strong points will be required by the friends of freedom. That is why our universities are of so great importance."

Similarly, Dr. Robert G. Sproul, president of the University of California, asserted that the protection of academic freedom was equivalent to the safeguarding of the ideal of the true university. If universities were to be denied such freedom, he said, then democracy as provided for by the constitution of the university would be lost.

"We would be well on our way to some form of totalitarianism whether we still called it democracy or not," he said. "I believe such academic freedom can be maintained even in a time of world tension."

May 30, 194?

Eisenhower and Conant in Group Barring Communists as Teachers

By BESS FURMAN
Special to THE NEW YORK TIMES.

WASHINGTON, June 8—Communists should be excluded from employment as teachers, a group of prominent education advisers declared today. The group, which included Gen. Dwight D. Eisenhower, president of Columbia University, spoke through a fifty-four-page handbook made public by the National Education Association.

General Eisenhower and fifteen associates drafted the book, "American Education and International Tensions," as members of the educational policies commission, set up under the auspices of the association. Dr. James B. Conant, president of Harvard University, also served on the commission. William G. Carr, an officer of the National Education Association, served the commission as secretary.

In urging the exclusion of Communist members from the teaching profession, the commission insisted that no abridgement of academic freedom was involved. Such a prohibition would serve a contrary purpose, it asserted.

"Such (Communist) membership involves adherence to doctrines and discipline completely inconsistent with the principles of freedom on which American education depends," the report said. "Such membership, and the accompanying surrender of intellectual integrity, render an individual unfit to discharge the duties of a teacher in this country."

The report declared that advocacy of communism should not be allowed in the schools. However, as a second principle, the report stressed that teachers should not be called Communists "carelessly and unjustly." Textbooks, which must give information on principles and practices of totalitarianism to safeguard the youth of America, must not be called "Red" when in fact they do not advocate communism, the report added.

The educators urged that much more be taught about recent United States foreign policy.

By coincidence, the House Un-American Activities Committee

disclosed today that it had sent letters to seventy-one state boards of education, colleges and high schools, for lists of textbooks used to find out if any were written from a Communistic slant.

Representative John S. Wood, Democrat of Georgia, chairman of the Un-American Activities Committee told reporters that the querying of schools on texts was "no investigation." The schools were chosen at random, he said, and assurances had been given to the National Education Association that no infringement whatever was being made on academic freedom.

The policies commission's handbook held that if schools failed to provide accurate, objective information on the practices of the Soviet Union and of the Communist party in the United States "the education of American youth will be incomplete to the point of national danger." Lacking "objective exposures of facts in the classroom," the report said, "youth are left a prey of propaganda through out-of-school channels—often possessing the enhanced appeal of forbidden fruit."

The handbook continued that "violent attacks by some sections of the public on the schools and the teaching staff" as "subversive" or "leftist," and, less often, as "reactionary" or "a tool of capitalism" were to be expected.

"Hazard" of Teaching

"Educators are accustomed to this attack from all sides and recognize that a certain amount of it is a necessary hazard of their occupation," the report said. "However, if such charges, with their usual accompaniment of 'investigations,' book-banning and efforts at intimidation, become too violent, frequent and widespread, they can seriously impair the efficiency of the school system. The educational profession will need to explain and defend the true role of education in American life.

"The whole spirit of free American education will be subverted unless teachers are free to think for themselves. It is because members of the Communist party are required to surrender this right, as a consequence of becoming part of a movement characterized by conspiracy and calculated deceit, that they should be excluded from employment as teachers."

The book discusses the fundamental cleavage between East and West; between communism and democracy. It discusses the new international position that aggressive warfare is a criminal act, and that it is the duty of all states to resist such acts, aid those attacked, and punish the criminals. The threat of such aggression, the report holds, is the reason for our part in the "cold war," which must depend for its strategy on day-to-day decisions.

"While there will be differences of opinion in marginal cases," the report said, "it is surely possible on the basis of careful study to set up a program of minimum factual essentials that every youth and adult in America needs to know about the major issues, facts and trends of international relations."

June 9, 1949

College Freedoms Being Stifled By Students' Fear of Red Label

By KALMAN SEIGEL

A subtle, creeping paralysis of freedom of thought and speech is attacking college campuses in many parts of the country, limiting both students and faculty in the area traditionally reserved for the free exploration of knowledge and truth.

These limitations on free inquiry take a variety of forms, but their net effect is a widening tendency toward passive acceptance of the status quo, conformity, and a narrowing of the area of tolerance in which students, faculty and administrators feel free to speak, act and think independently.

A study of seventy-two major colleges in the United States by THE NEW YORK TIMES showed that many members of the college community were wary and felt varying degrees of inhibition about speaking out on controversial issues, discussing unpopular concepts and participating in student political activity, because they were fearful of:

1. Social disapproval.
2. A "pink" or Communist label.
3. Criticism by regents, legislatures and friends.
4. Rejection for further study at graduate schools.
5. The spotlight of investigation by Government and private industry for post-graduate employment and service with the armed forces.

Such caution, in effect, has made many campuses barren of the free give-and-take of ideas, the study found. At the same time it has posed a seemingly insoluble problem for the campus liberal, depleted his ranks and brought to many college campuses an apathy about current problems that borders almost on their deliberate exclusion.

A number of the nation's leading educators held that such a developing unwillingness to pursue free inquiry, fostered by pressures that promote prejudice and fear, struck a body-blow at the American educational process, one of democracy's most potent weapons, and that it was a long step toward defeating one of the basic purposes of the university.

But at the same time it also gave new impetus to a small but growing resistance to conformity and stimulated a new appreciation of America's free heritage.

Convinced that adolescence was a normal period of rebellion and a time when the young student challenged accepted doctrines, the educators maintained that the student's continued exploration of new horizons was "a normal symp-

tom," a part of the process of growing up and of developing critical faculties and the ability to evaluate. The latter, in their option, was a virtual "must" in today's market of conflicting ideologies.

A little more than a fortnight ago, Earl J. McGrath, United States Commissioner of Education, told a group of educators in New York:

"Education for life in the world community of nations * * * begins in the school and on the campus in which democratic respect for personal and social differences is nourished."

The campus study revealed in the main a growing restrictive atmosphere, and that while there were few instances of reprisal or overt action against free expression, there was considerable evidence of self-censorship.

Controversies Skirted

Discussions with student leaders, teachers and administrators—in most instance names were withheld for fear of reprisal or criticism—disclosed that this censorship, wariness, caution and inhibition largely took these forms:

1. A reluctance to speak out on controversial issues in and out of class.
2. A reluctance to handle currently unpopular concepts even in classroom work where they may be part of the study program.
3. An unwillingness to join student political clubs.
4. Neglect of humanitarian causes because they may be suspect in the minds of politically unsophisticated officials.
5. An emphasis on lack of affiliations.
6. An unusual amount of serio-comic joking about this or that official investigating committee "getting you."
7. A shying away, both physically and intellectually from any association with the words, "liberal," "peace," "freedom," and from classmates of a liberal stripe.
8. A sharp turning inward to local college problems, to the exclusion of broader current questions.

Part of the wariness and apathy —the latter is a marked characteristic on many college campuses— is not solely a product of current "hysteria," or as a majority of students and faculty put it, "the pressures generated by Senator Joseph McCarthy of Wisconsin."

While this was an important contributing factor, they said, it stemmed also from the "times," the probable inevitability of the draft, the fear and uncertainty in national life and a fatalistic and frustrated conviction that little can be done in the college area to alter international developments.

Other Factors Noted

Other contributing factors toward decreased liberal activity

were a mature awareness of the true nature of communism, with the result that it has lost much of its former fascination, and the feeling that under present conditions a firm, unswerving allegiance to established concepts is in the national interest and should be accepted.

How much each contributed, however, was almost impossible to assess.

According to the study, municipal colleges and large state universities in large cities felt the impact of the pressures most, with lesser state universities, large private colleges, smaller private institutions and denominational colleges following.

The concern with the problem shown by educators is apparent in this comment from Dr. Alvin Eurich, president of the University of the State of New York:

"Freedom of inquiry, thought and speech are indivisible human rights in a democracy. In recent months justifiable fear of communism has set in motion unjustifiable behavior denying these very principles. Such extreme counter-actions are as dangerous as communism itself, because they seek to deny to our citizens the freedoms for which our nation was originally founded."

Stresses Importance of Inquiry

"We as educators are concerned daily with these attitudes creeping onto the college campus. There has been much discussion of loyalty and academic freedom for professors. An exact parallel to this issue is academic freedom for the student. Nowhere is it more important to cherish and protect freedom of inquiry, thought and speech than on college campuses— the training grounds for some 2,-500,000 future citizens who must understand the values and responsibilities of democracy."

Some random examples taken from the study turned up these indications of repressionism and inhibition on the college campuses:

At the City College of New York, a student leader said he was "extremely reluctant" to express any opinions that might be considered left-wing, even when asked to write a theme in class on a political issue.

A student editor held that his fellow-students were unwilling to speak out, particularly in engineering, where, he said, "the wrong word at the wrong time might jeopardize their futures." He said agents of the Federal Bureau of Investigation were constantly inquiring about students applying for Government jobs, and that some graduate schools, with Government-classified projects, were extremely reluctant to accept students who had committed themselves to an unpopular point of view.

"It Can Only Be Felt"

The current issue of one of the undergraduate papers at the college explored another phase of the problem in this way: "The willingness of instructors to express their own honest viewpoint has been slowly ebbing. Evidence in support of this statement cannot be given in black-and-white. It can only be felt in the classroom."

At Queens College, Dr. Harold Lenz, dean of students, declared that students were now more afraid of controversial issues and speakers than in previous years. A student editor declared that the students "were playing it safe."

Student leaders at Hunter College reported that students were fearful of signing petitions, because they were reluctant to get their names on "any list." Letters to the editor of the undergraduate paper, they said, in explaining the greater caution, now open with "It appears that," rather than with the "I think," and "I believe," of years ago.

A number of the teachers offer qualifying apologies during their lectures, particularly when they move from the black-and-white realm of the textbook, to analysis and interpretation, saying, "Don't get me wrong," and "Don't think I'm a Communist."

Dean Millicent C. McIntosh of Barnard told of a meeting with dormitory students recently. She said she summoned the girls because some had indicated that speakers at a political institute had skimmed over vital issues and made only "patriotic speeches."

"Obscurantism" Noted

The dean said she found some girls held that anything identified with peace, freedom of speech or negotiation to resolve differences was suspected of Communist influence.

"Girls are becoming afraid to advocate the humanitarian point of view," Dean McIntosh declared, "because it has been associated with communism. The most fearless will not be influenced, but the middle group is made to feel the confusion and fear involved in the 'obscurantism' that is, McCarthyism."

The president of the college's political association noted that she had found a definite emotional reaction to anything verbally tinged with ultra-radicalism. The president of the Liberal Action Club, which has no set platform or outside affiliation, reported that students were fearful of joining any political clubs on the campus, because they were afraid that such affiliations would hurt them in Government work.

In the college placement office, Miss Ruth Houghton, director, said the word "liberal" was "a poisonous word" to many would-be employers, who conceived of the "liberal girl" as an "obstructionist" and "organizer against employer interests."

At Columbia University, responsible student spokesmen said a generally good record on academic freedom for faculty and students was slowly being marred by the national "hysteria." Prof. Robert S. Lynd, sociologist, said students were "pretty apprehensive and cautious," but the precise difficulty and the reasons for the wary attitudes were difficult to identify.

Vassar Situation Similar

At Vassar, the evidence was repeated by the leaders of liberal clubs, who said fear of future reprisal was the motivating factor

that kept their club rolls small. They pointed to a recent anonymous letter to the editor of The Miscellany News, one of the two undergraduate papers on the campus, in which the writer noted that she did not now belong to, nor did she intend to join any political association on the campus. The decision, she said, involved careful thought on her and her parents' part.

"In today's world of 'witch hunting,' 'subversive actions' and 'pink tinges,' such factors as these must be taken into consideration by every student," the writer declared. "It is particularly important if the student might some day want a position with the Government."

At Rutgers, several student leaders told this story that pointed up the problem:

A number of students who were asked to sign the widely publicized, anti-Communist Crusade for Freedom Scroll refused, because they were suspicious of the words "crusade" and "freedom" and unsure of the sponsors. After the scroll was explained, a few came into the fold, but others remained adamant, maintaining that they didn't want their names on any suspicious lists.

At Yale University, as a result of a recent campus incident, The Daily News, student newspaper, explored the problem in a long editorial in which the editors declared:

"We cannot believe that the American people will indefinitely tolerate this control over youthful lives by looming up before them the spectre of the 'loyalty check.' We cannot believe that this virtual blockade of the marketplace of ideas to young men can go on for a lifetime.

"And yet, despite hope, we see the sky growing darker, the night of thought-conformity closing in. We see college men growing more and more docile, more and more accepting the status quo, paralyzed by the fear of their futures, radicalism snuffed out where it should flame the brightest."

Leaders See "Reticence"

At New York University, a group of student leaders reported "a reticence" on the part of their classmates to express liberal viewpoints for fear of reprisal in graduate school, thus failing to take advantage of a liberal policy on student and faculty freedom.

At the University of Michigan, Dean Erich A. Walter explained that students were quite obviously more careful in their affiliations, recognizing that Federal security officers were making careful checks of the memberships of liberal organizations.

Student leaders also reported a shrinking of the numbers and membership rolls of campus liberal organizations.

Students at the University of California were also pictured by their leaders and faculty as being increasingly more careful about choosing their associations and committing themselves to actions they might later regret.

Student leaders here and at many other colleges and universities also cited the social dis-

approval factor as an important inhibiting influence, indicating that in many respects the college community had ceased to be an arena for divergent views.

Several student leaders at the University of North Carolina asserted that students with radical views were not accepted socially as formerly. John Sanders, retiring student body president, explained:

"The liberal traditions of the university are still intact. I do not feel that there has been any particular increase in restriction of student expression over the past year by the university administration.

"We, however, are not by our academic status isolated from the prevailing climate of opinion. The growing fear of new ideas and of different ideas, largely a consequence of the McCarthy witch-hunts, has had its effect on students, as on citizens everywhere."

Henry Bowers, newly elected president of the student body, believes that students with radical opinions are discouraged "only through social action." He added that "the academic freedom of the administration has been limited by the inclusion of a non-Communist oath."

John R. Harris, assistant attorney general for the student body, said that while the student newspaper was free to say what it pleased, there was an atmosphere on the campus, "as in most of the country, which tends to equate criticism with disloyalty and liberalism with communism."

At the University of Wisconsin, John Searle, president of the student body, pointed to the rejection of Max Lerner, newspaper columnist, as a lecturer; the refusal to permit an instructor to take part in a debate with a Catholic professor on "Scholastic Sociology vs. Scientific Sociology," and to a general tagging of the student board as "subversive" because it had issued a statement opposing the views of Senator McCarthy.

George Rucker, president of Students for Democratic Action at the University of Oklahoma, said the lack of opposition to a recently enacted loyalty oath law in that state has been "nothing short of tragic in its evidence of the extent to which fear reigns in our nation." Student reaction, he added, has been on the whole "appallingly apathetic."

Mr. Rucker said that the faculty, which is "almost completely in intellectual opposition to the oath, has done nothing about it."

Article Is Withdrawn

At the University of Nebraska, a faculty member advised a student who had completed an article for publication critical of the McCarran (National Security) Act that such an article might damage his reputation. The article was withdrawn. Student spokesmen cited the case of a woman student who informed a faculty member that her name had been put on a Communist-front mailing list, and faculty members called in the F. B. I. to investigate.

They reported that a student who submitted an article comparing modern subversive investigations with witch trials was told

that it could not be printed because it was too controversial.

They also noted that the university organization to which all foreign students belonged halted programs on political and international issues when students from Asia and elsewhere were accused of being communistic.

At six Midwestern campuses—Iowa State, Indiana University, Purdue, Oberlin, Kenyon, Washington University—college and university authorities, deans and student leaders said they detected greater caution on the part of students. Students, it was reported, were aware of the increased activity of the F. B. I. and other investigative units. Political expression appeared to have faded on these campuses in the last year and a half.

Purdue students, according to Paul Schule, head of the Student Union Board, were more willing to express and explore liberal ideas when in intimate groups, or fraternity, sorority or small dormitory bull sessions.

"McCarthyism" Prevalent

"But in public and off campus," Mr. Schule continued, "McCarthyism, or call it what you will, is disgustingly prevalent. Students fear being tagged by others who might say of their views, 'This is the same as something (left-wing line) else.'"

Similar evidence was reported at Ohio State University, Bryn Mawr College, the University of Colorado, Haverford College, and to a lesser degree at Princeton, Stanford and perhaps twenty to thirty other colleges.

In New England's privately endowed colleges—Williams, Bowdoin, Amherst, Smith, Wellesley—left-wing liberalism has been ebbing for some time, even before Senator McCarthy began his drive to rid the State Department of what he termed Communist influence.

The reluctance to speak out on controversial issues for fear of reprisal has caused more of a ripple than a wave in this area, with the chief sufferers seniors who are thinking of Government jobs after graduation.

Harvard showed the greatest effects of the current pressures in the New England area, although these were compared to effects in colleges elsewhere. Student and faculty spokesmen here said that organizations still were willing to speak out in a nonconformist vein, but individuals tended to be more reticent.

The pattern at the bulk of other private New England schools, which reportedly have never seen much political activity, remained virtually unchanged.

Catholic Schools Different

At the country's leading Catholic colleges, deans and students explained that any pressures toward conformism were virtually nonexistent because student and faculty thinking and action were consistent with the Catholic point of view.

At Manhattanville and Fordham, students reported that the current pressures had resulted in a more militant Catholicism, and in a growing awareness of social and economic problems with which most of the colleges were now dealing. They said that rare expressions of extreme liberalism might bring social disapproval and "constructive criticism."

The sameness of background and belief almost erased the area of debate on most controversial issues of the day, but did not preclude discussion. Similar views were expressed at Georgetown University, Holy Cross College, Loyola University and Notre Dame University.

May 10, 1951

RED-TEACHER BAN IS UPHELD BY 6 TO 3 IN SUPREME COURT

FEINBERG ACT WINS

State Held to Have Right to Protect Immature Minds of Children

AID TO A 'SENSITIVE AREA'

Douglas Dissent Sees Threat to 'Cradle of Democracy'— Calls It Invasion of Rights

By LUTHER A. HUSTON
Special to THE NEW YORK TIMES.

WASHINGTON, March 3—The Supreme Court upheld in a 6-to-3 decision today the constitutionality of New York's Feinberg Law.

The statute prohibits employment in that state's public school system of any person who advocates overthrow of the Federal or State Government by force or violence or who is a member of any organization that preaches such doctrine. It makes membership in such an organization prima-facie grounds for dismissal.

Associate Justice Sherman Minton delivered the majority opinion in which Chief Justice Fred M. Vinson and Associate Justices Stanley F. Reed, Robert H. Jackson, Harold H. Burton and Tom C. Clark concurred. The dissenters were Associate Justices William O. Douglas, Hugo L. Black and Felix Frankfurter.

Differing Views Stressed

Divergent philosophies of the court's members were accentuated in the prevailing and dissenting opinions. The basic tenet of the majority decision was that the state had a constitutional right to protect the immature minds of children in its public schools from subversive propaganda, subtle or otherwise, disseminated by those "to whom they look for guidance, authority and leadership."

In the minds of the dissenting justices, especially Mr. Douglas, the Feinberg Law should have been struck down as an invasion of the civil rights of citizens that denies them freedom of thought and expression.

Condemning witch-hunting, Mr. Douglas said that "the law inevitably turns the school system into a spying project," then added:

"Regular loyalty reports on the teachers must be made out. The principals become detectives; the students, the parents, the community become informers. Ears are cocked for telltale signs of disloyalty. The prejudices of the community come into play in searching out the disloyal."

The case was brought by Irving Adler, George Friedlander, Mark Friedlander, Marta Spencer, Samuel Krieger, William Neuman, Dave Tiger and Edith Tiger. The first four named are teachers. The others brought suit as parents and taxpayers.

The Supreme Court's ruling sustained a decision of the New York Court of Appeals, the state's highest bench, which reversed a ruling by the New York Supreme Court that the Feinberg Law was unconstitutional.

Law Aimed at Reds

The law was enacted in 1949 chiefly to keep Communists and fellow-travelers out of the school system. Its proponents argued that despite other statutes designed to keep those held to be subversive from getting jobs in the public schools, subversive persons were infiltrating the school system and were using their positions to promulgate their doctrines.

Introduced by Benjamin J. Feinberg, Plattsburg Republican who was then the Majority Leader in the State Senate, the law also provided for the removal of superintendents, teachers and employes in the public schools who disseminate subversive propaganda. It directed the Board of Regents of the state's public school system to establish rules and regulations for its enforcement.

The attack on the law was on two grounds. The first was that it was an abridgment of the right to freedom of speech and assembly guaranteed by the First Amendment.

The second was that the rule making membership in an organization listed as subversive an automatic grounds for dismissal violated the Fifth Amendment, which prohibits the taking of life, liberty or property without the process of law.

Justice Minton held that there was "no constitutional infirmity" in the Feinberg Law on either of these grounds.

The schools, he said, were a "sensitive area" and the state has a vital concern to preserve their integrity. It cannot be doubted, he added, that the authorities have a right to screen the officials, teachers and employes as to their fitness to maintain the integrity of the schools.

In so doing, Justice Minton ruled, the authorities do not deprive the teachers and other employes of any right guaranteed them by the Constitution.

They may still "assemble, speak, think and believe as they will," he said, and only their freedom of choice between employment in the school system and membership in an organization held to be subversive is limited. The police power of the state may properly be exercised to impose such a limitation, he declared.

The contention that the provision providing for dismissal because of membership in a subversive organization denies due process also found no support with the court majority. The appellants' argument on this point was that the fact that an organization was found to be subversive was not reasonable ground for presuming that a member of that organization was disqualified for employment in the schools.

Due Process Held Satisfied

Justice Minton held that the law was full of such presumptions, and that in this case, the statute was a "legislative finding" that the member by reason of his membership supported what the organization stood for, and that "disqualification follows therefore as a reasonable presumption from such membership and support." The requirements of due process are satisfied, the justice held.

Justice Douglas dissented sharply from these conclusions of the majority. He asserted that the public school was the "cradle of our democracy," and none needed more than the teacher the protection of the Constitution against denial of freedom of thought and expression.

The law, he said, embraces the principle of "guilt by association" and this was "repugnant to our society."

"The very threat of such a procedure is certain to raise havoc with academic freedom," he asserted. Mistakes of the past, he added, become "the ghosts of a harrowing present."

A "party line" as dangerous as that of the Communists "lays hold," according to Justice Douglas, when a "problem cannot be pursued with impunity to its edges" because orthodox thinking must prevail. Then, he said, "fear stalks the classroom."

The First Amendment, the justice said, was designed to protect the pursuit of truth, and "we forget the teachings of the First Amendment when we sustain this law."

Issue Held Speculative

Justice Black agreed with Justice Douglas' opinion, but dissented from the implications he saw in the Feinberg Law that it was dangerous for school teachers "to think or say anything except what a transient majority happen to approve at the moment." The law, he said, was another of "those rapidly multiplying legislative enactments" that espouse this doctrine.

Justice Frankfurter's principal ground for dissenting was that the court's past course had been to avoid "constitutional adjudications on merely abstract or speculative issues" and base them on actual controversies.

This was not the case in the present appeal, he held, because the regulations involved were "formulated partly in statutes and partly in administrative regulations, but all of it is still an unfinished blueprint."

Therefore, he felt, the limits the court has put on its own jurisdiction should prevent it from sustaining the appeal in this case.

March 4, 1952

RED TEACHERS LOSE AID OF FEDERATION

A. F. L. Union Reverses Policy of 36 Years, but Demands Fair Play for Accused

By MURRAY ILLSON
Special to THE NEW YORK TIMES.

SYRACUSE, Aug. 21—For the first time in its thirty-six-year history the American Federation of Teachers, A. F. L., voted overwhelmingly here today not to defend any teacher proved to be a Communist party member.

The 500 delegates at the federation's thirty-fifth national convention cast a voice vote after more than two hours of heated debate. Only a few scattered "no's" were heard.

The federation thus reversed its stand at its 1949 convention in Milwaukee that, in effect, a person's membership in any legal political party should not of itself be a bar to a teaching job.

The new resolution, based on a majority resolution submitted by the convention's Committee on Civil and Professional Rights of Teachers, declared it the "duty" of any federation local "to see that a teacher accused of being a member of the Communist party or any other totalitarian organization has every opportunity to clear himself of the charge."

Cites Union's Constitution

Observing that the federation's own constitution barred from membership Communists, Fascists and others "submit to totalitarian control," the approved resolution declared that the A. F. T. "cannot logically insist that boards of education employ or retain such persons" as teachers in the public schools.

All locals of the American Federation of Teachers, the resolution declared, shall "further the use of the democratic principle which entitles every citizen to a fair trial through due process of law keeping in mind the tradition, long cherished in free countries, that the accused is assumed innocent until proven guilty."

The resolution, as approved by the convention, also called for instructing all locals to consult with area vice presidents and the national office of the federation "in respect to defending any teacher accused of being a member of the Communist party or other totalitarian organization."

Before adopting its new stand, the delegates defeated a minority motion, submitted by Herbert Hackett, an instructor of English at Michigan State College, seeking to have the federation reaffirm its 1949 position. In defending the motion, Mr. Hackett asserted that the

"American tradition of the free labor movement is built on the rights of the individual" and that "out of the rights of the individual grow the rights of the group."

He added that democracy was "a calculated risk, not a cowardly, not a fearful thing." One of the "risks of democracy," he said, is that some persons might "do some damage" through the use of democratic freedoms.

Seven delegates spoke for the 1949 stand, and seven opposed it. Speaking for reaffirmation, Robert Lowenstein of Newark, N. J., declared that if the federation reversed itself on the position that teaching competence should be the sole criterion for a teacher's fitness, the tenure rights of all teachers, Communist and non-Communist, would be endangered.

Advocating the new anti-Communist position, Meyer Halushka of Chicago observed that a stand satisfactory in 1949 might not be "fully adequate" in 1952. Warning against an "unwarranted risk," he pointed out that this country was "now fighting Communist aggression."

The resolution was approved by the convention with the strong backing of the New York Teachers Guild, Local 2.

August 22, 1952

Supreme Court Decision Renews Controversy Over Loyalty Oaths for Teachers

By BENJAMIN FINE

Educators generally are opposed to loyalty oaths for school or college teachers. They object to being singled out as a profession, holding that by being required to declare their loyalty to this country they are placed in an inferior position. At the same time, the educational leaders of the country are opposed to the employment of any teacher who is in any way subversive or is a member of the Communist party.

These views were made known to this department in a sampling of opinions of college presidents and school spokesmen, as the question of loyalty oaths was brought to the fore again last week by a decision of the United States Supreme Court. The court held unconstitutional an Oklahoma law requiring state employes to take a loyalty oath.

The case arose out of the refusal of seven teachers at the Oklahoma Agricultural and Mechanical College to sign the oath. They asserted that they were not Communists or members of any disloyal organization—they objected to the oath on principle. The oath required of the Oklahoma state employes read in part:

"* * * I am not affiliated directly or indirectly * * * with * * * [nor have I] within the five years immediately preceding the taking of this oath * * * been a member of * * * any agency, party, organization, association or group whatever which has been officially determined by the United States Attorney General or other authorized public agency of the United States to be a Communist front or subversive organization * * *."

Safeguards Lacking

In voiding the statute the Supreme Court held that it did not offer adequate safeguards to persons who may, out of innocent motives, have joined organizations that have since been listed as subversive.

As was pointed out by some educators in response to this department's inquiries, the Oklahoma case involved only the validity of a local law with certain unique provisions. The court's findings cannot easily be applied to loyalty requirements set up by laws of other states.

On the question of loyalty oaths in general, however, almost without exception the educators reached by this reporter objected to the oaths' purpose and intent.

They insisted that taking an oath would not make a teacher a better citizen; the mere signing of a paper, they said, would not change a person's viewpoint. And the educators also asserted that only a small fraction of the American teaching profession was of questionable loyalty—and that these teachers could be screened out of the classroom by other means more effective than loyalty oaths.

Dr. Ralph E. Himstead, secretary of the American Association of University Professors, said that the administration of loyalty oaths would tend to stifle the freedom of mind of many educators. Dr. Himstead declared:

"Test oaths for loyalty currently required of teachers are not loyalty oaths; they are non-disloyalty oaths. They are based on a presumption of guilt, which is contrary to our law and Constitution.

"The traditional American loyalty oath is an affirmative oath which pledges affirmative loyalty to the Government of the United States, and is based on the presumption of innocence. Non-disloyalty oaths are alien to America and contrary to American legal and constitutional principles. I oppose non-disloyalty oaths because they are as futile as they are un-American. Estimates provided by the Federal Bureau of Investigation indicate that the number of disloyal Americans is small. The number of disloyal teachers is infinitesimally small."

Discrimination Charged

Dr. Himstead said that he opposed the discriminatory application of "non-disloyalty" oaths to teachers as a class because it impairs their professional morale to the detriment of education and the general welfare. He continued:

"My opposition to non-disloyalty oaths is not based on rights of teachers; it is based on the fact that such oaths create an atmosphere inimical to the freedom of the mind, an atmosphere dominated by suspicion and fear which deters forthright expression of opinion on any subject which may be regarded controversial."

In the opinion of Dr. Katharine E. McBride, president of Bryn Mawr College, loyalty oaths are not an effective bar to the Communists. She felt that the use of these oaths might bring about the danger of limiting freedom of thought. Also, she added, the simple loyalty oath is likely to be complicated by additional provisions, such as the matter of membership in other associations, as in the Oklahoma oath. This raises the objections noted in the main opinion of the Supreme Court.

"Schools and colleges themselves are the best judges of the loyalty of their staffs," said Dr. McBride. "They should be given full responsibility and held to their responsibility for this function. Loyalty oaths are infringements of the essential rights of citizens, whether teachers or not, as well stated in the concurrences of Justices Black and Frankfurter."

Oaths Held Ineffectual

Dr. David D. Henry, executive vice chancellor of New York University, declared that since subversives are not likely to hesitate to tell an untruth, loyalty oaths, in general, are an ineffectual way of dealing with disloyalty. Their only possible value, he suggested, is to lay the groundwork for perjury as a cause for dismissal. This, at its best, is an indirect way of getting at the problem, Dr. Henry said, adding:

"Loyalty oaths do not harm, however, any more than do the oaths traditionally required of public officials and in many professions, if all people are treated alike. When teachers are singled out for special oaths, they should object, for such treatment is an unjustified suspicion of the profession as a whole. When teachers are treated as are all other citizens in similar employment, they should not seek to be exceptions."

According to Dr. Henry, the only effective method to maintain a teaching force of the highest standards is through employment screening, which permits the appointment only of those who meet the objectives of the profession. When employment errors are made, professional disapproval of those who do not comply can be brought into play.

Loyalty oaths are not necessary for the loyal teacher, and are ineffectual for those who are subversive, Dr. Buell G. Gallagher, president of City College, said. Dr. Gallagher declared:

"I am not in favor of compulsory loyalty oaths, particularly for one profession only. They do not accomplish their ostensible purpose of keeping Communists out of the school system. The dishonest and disloyal will always swear loyalty except under certainty of conviction for perjury while the honest and loyal need no oath either to discover or to protect them.

"Loyalty oaths required of the teaching profession only are an infringement of academic rights in that they place peculiar restrictions on the profession and assume that all teachers are suspect until proved loyal. This has the effect of inhibiting the teacher from speaking his mind or joining groups on the ground that at some later date these groups might be changed in character and be declared subversive."

Church View

Declaring that no loyalty oath is needed or desired at Marquette University, the Rev. M. G. Barnett, vice president of the institution, said that "just as it expects its members who are soldiers, the Catholic Church expects its teachers to be loyal fighters for America."

"To expect a teacher to be loyal to the country that protects him and enriches his life is elementary logic," Father Barnett declared, adding: "How could such an expectation have anything to do with academic freedom to teach the truth?"

According to Dr. Richard B. Kennan, executive secretary of the National Education Association's democracy commission, teachers do not oppose affirmative loyalty oaths. They have been administered for years without protest. Teachers oppose, however, oaths that go beyond the question of loyalty to require denials of associations of prior years or that differ from oaths administered to other public employes in positions of comparable responsibility.

Oaths have proved to be ineffective as a means of discovering subversives, said Dr. Kennan. He held that the best assurances of teacher loyalty are through the careful selection of faculty members and through the provision of adequate supervisory assistance.

Colleges Vote Freedom Code Banning Reds From Faculties

37 Universities in U. S. and Canada Demand Staff Members Be Loyal Citizens and Fearless in Ideas and Teaching

By RUSSELL PORTER

The Association of American Universities declared yesterday that full academic freedom must be guaranteed to professors and scholars, but it should not include the right to membership in the Communist party.

Dr. Harold W. Dodds, president of Princeton University, is head of the association, which speaks on matters of common policy for thirty-seven leading American and Canadian educational institutions.

In a report that took six months to prepare, the association explained that it shared the "profound concern" of the American and Canadian people over an international conspiracy that would destroy all free institutions, including the universities. But it also stressed its desire for the public to understand the nature and function of the university and why freedom of expression should be guaranteed to faculties in the public interest as well as their own.

On one hand, the association condemned Russian communism and its subversive activities, along with all other totalitarianism; on the other, in defining academic freedom, it asserted "free enterprise" was as essential to intellectual progress as it was to economic progress.

To protect its members and their faculties against Communist infiltration, the association laid down these principles for universities to follow:

¶Loyal citizenship, integrity and independence as well as professional competence should be required in appointing and retaining faculty members.

¶Loyalty, integrity and independence are incompatible with membership in the Communist party or adherence to the Soviet Union and its satellites.

¶Therefore present party membership "extinguishes the right to a university position."

¶Those who follow the party line and silence criticism of it in classrooms also have no right in American universities, and forfeit the protection of academic freedom.

¶Qualifications of professors who invoke the Fifth Amendment against self-incrimination in refusing to answer questions asked by competent authorities should be "re-examined," and the professors should bear a "heavy" burden of proof of their fitness to continue teaching.

¶Cooperation should be extended to legislative investigating commitees, and abuses should be met by appealing to public opinion rather than by non-cooperation or defiance.

¶Cooperation should also be given to law-enforcement agencies when faculty members are charged with violations of the law.

¶Professors owe to their universities and to the public "complete candor and perfect integrity, precluding any kind of clandestine or conspiratorial activity."

¶Academic freedom does not include freedom from criticism, and is not a "shield" to protect violation of the law.

¶Faculties should recognize their responsibility to maintain the highest standards of appointment and promotion.

¶Not only governing boards but also faculties have public obligations because of the public benefits they enjoy, including support of state universities by funds and aid to endowed universities by tax exemptions.

Academic Freedom Protection

On the protection of academic freedom against interference with free expression the association held:

¶Faculty members must continue to examine all ideas, even "unpopular, abhorrent and dangerous" ones, on the same theory that deadly diseases and enemy military potentials are studied to perfect defenses against them.

¶Even in the face of popular disapproval timidity should not lead a scholar or teacher to stand silent when he must speak in matters of truth and conscience, particularly in his own special field of study.

¶The spirit of the university requires "investigation, criticism and presentation of ideas in an atmosphere of freedom and mutual confidence," relying upon "open competition as the surest safeguard of truth."

¶Faculty members who meet the requirements of citizenship, competence and good taste are entitled to "all the protection the full resources of the university can provide."

¶Unless a faculty member violates a law his discipline or discharge is a university responsibility and should not be assumed by political authority.

¶Discipline on the basis of irresponsible accusations or suspicion can never be condoned.

¶Professors, while not entitled to special privileges in law, should not be subject to special discriminations, such as loyalty oaths that others are not required to take.

¶Academic freedom and freedom of expression are not merely faculty rights, but are vital to the American system and the general welfare.

¶Insistence on complete conformity would do "infinite" harm to American freedom.

Five Members Drafted Report

The report was drafted by a committee of five headed by Dr. A. Whitney Griswold, president of Yale University, as chairman. Other members were Dr. Arthur H. Compton, Chancellor of Washington University, St. Louis; Dr. Franklin D. Murphy, Chancellor of the University of Kansas; Dr. John E. W. Sterling, president of Stanford University, and Dr. Henry W. Wriston, president of Brown University.

In preparing the report the committee consulted with Dr. Dodds as association president, Dr. J. L. Morrill, president of the University of Minnesota and association vice president, and Dr. C. E. de Kiewiet, president of the University of Rochester and association secretary.

Other members of the association, all of whom have approved the report, are:

Lee A. DuBridge, president, California Institute of Technology;

The Rev. Patrick J. McCormick, rector, Catholic University of America;

Howard B. Jefferson, president, Clark University;

Grayson Kirk, president, Columbia University;

Deane W. Malott, president, Cornell University;

A. Hollis Edens, president, Duke University;

Paul H. Bush, chairman of the administrative committee, Harvard University;

Herman B. Wells, president, Indiana University;

D. W. Bronk, president, Johns Hopkins University;

F. Cyril James, principal, McGill University;

J. R. Killian Jr., president, Massachusetts Institute of Technology;

J. Roscoe Miller, president, Northwestern University;

Howard L. Bevis, president, Ohio State University;

Virgil M. Hancher, president, State University of Iowa;

Robert G. Sproul, president, University of California;

Lawrence A. Kimpton, chancellor, University of Chicago;

George D. Stoddard, president, University of Illinois;

Harlan H. Hatcher, president, University of Michigan;

F. A. Middlebush, president, University of Missouri;

R. G. Gustavson, chancellor, University of Nebraska;

Henry T. Heald, chancellor, New York University;

Gordon Gray, president, University of North Carolina;

William H. DuBarry, acting president, University of Pennsylvania;

James P. Hart, chancellor, University of Texas;

Sidney E. Smith, president, University of Toronto;

Bennett Harvie Branscomb, chancellor, Vanderbilt University;

Colgate W. Darden Jr., president, University of Virginia;

Edwin B. Fred, president, University of Wisconsin;

Henry S. Schmitz, president, University of Washington.

Broad Red Invasion of Education Reported by Senate Investigators

Group Says Inquiries Reveal a Dangerous Undercover Plot Guided by Hard-Core Communists—Urges Local Attacks

By C. P. TRUSSELL
Special to THE NEW YORK TIMES.

WASHINGTON, July 26 — The Senate Internal Security subcommittee declared that it had developed convincing evidence that the American school and college systems had been invaded to a dangerous degree by teachers bent on distorting education to Communist advantage.

Directing the work of this force of instructors, it asserted, was a group of hard-core Communists that had brought under its influence not only professors and others who willingly accepted Communist party orders and carried them out but also many dupes who had bitten at Red bait.

Reporting unanimously on investigations that started last year and recessed recently but did not adjourn finally, the subcommittee set forth conclusions based on testimony taken from more than 100 witnesses.

The hearings proceeded under widespread charges that the Senate group was intruding upon academic freedom. The subcommittee, headed by Senator William E. Jenner, Republican of Indiana, contended that, instead of stifling academic freedom, it was operating to preserve it.

Support of Views Cited

The report cited confirmation of the subcommittee view by educational organizations and individuals, including Dr. William Jansen, Superintendent of Schools for New York City; Joseph B. Cavallaro, chairman of the New York City Board of Higher Education, and Dr. Harry D. Gideonse, president of Brooklyn College.

The report emphasized that at no time had the subcommittee attempted to deal with the administration of educational institutions or with what they should teach; or had recommended what such institutions should do about faculty members, instructors or other employes after testimony was taken from them.

From the testimony, taken through months of public and closed hearings, the subcommittee, with most of its questioning being conducted by Robert Morris, chief counsel, reached these conclusions:

¶World Communist leaders had made schools and colleges of this country a target of infiltration and activity as a part of their program to destroy the United States.

¶A Communist educator, because of his submission to a totalitarian organization, could not maintain the standards of academic freedom and objective scholarship and be loyal to the regulations of local authorities.

¶Communist teachers used their positions in the classroom and in extra-curricular activities to subvert students and other teachers and the public to promote the objectives of communism.

¶Communist teachers exercised as part of an organized conspiracy an influence far more extensive than their numbers would indicate.

¶Communist penetration of the schools was becoming more covert, and Communist teachers were being organized into a secret underground more difficult to detect.

¶Teachers, students and educational authorities, public and private, did not have the means to identify—unassisted—secret members of the Communist party or to trace their conspiratorial activities.

¶Exposure of Communists by Congressional and state legislative committees has helped local authorities protect themselves against organized subversion and had given authorities the evidence by which some hidden Communists could be removed from teaching positions.

¶Since the great majority of present-day secret Communists could, with great difficulty, only be identified by evidence sufficient to justify legal action, it fell upon the educators themselves to devise criteria and methods to deal with teachers whose adherence to the Communist conspiracy, though not easily legally provable, made them morally unfit to teach as well as a threat to national security.

¶A teacher who invoked his constitutional privilege against incrimination rather than deny membership in the Communist organization before a duly constituted authority, violated his trust and forfeited his right to shape the character of American youth.

Recommendations Made by Group

On the premise of those conclusions, the subcommittee recommended as follows:

¶That the educational authorities give consideration to the establishment of criteria and the initiaton of procedures whereby schools, colleges and universities could eliminate teachers who had demonstrated their unsuitability to teach because of their collaboration with the Communist conspiracy.

¶That state governments and their educational institutions consider a program such as has been adopted in California, under which classroom and campus activities are watched by trained investigators and there is a free exchange of security reports between colleges and legislative committees.

¶That school authorities, colleges and local boards of education institute "positive" programs, under qualified experts in the field of combatting communism, to teach both teachers and pupils the nature of the Communist conspiracy.

¶That legislation already adopted by the Senate but not yet passed by the House of Representatives, designed to force witnesses to answer questions concerning Communist affiliation, receive the support to enact it into law.

If this legislation went onto the law books, the subcommittee said, it probably would recall many witnesses who have invoked constitutional protection to refuse to answer questions. This privilege, given by the Constitution's Fifth Amendment, it was conceded, had been a great frustration to the investigating group.

The report, which was interspersed freely with quotations from questions and answers set down officially as hearings were held, dealt largely with testimony taken in the New York area one of the four "sample" points—New York, Washington, Boston and Chicago—where the investigations were made.

The subcommittee held that much progress had been achieved in delving into Communist infiltration into the education system by the Rapp-Coudert investigation by the New York General Assembly in 1941. It added, however, that when this investigation ended apparently nothing else had been done about communism in education in New York until the Senate subcommittee picked up the inquiry last year.

The report declared also that it appeared that for at least twelve years many suspects who had denied to the New York legislative committee that they were Communists were permitted to continue in their posts, but invoked the Fifth Amendment when called by the Senate subcommittee to repeat their denials.

Charter Provision Noted

By the time the Senate subcommittee resumed the investigation, the report said, the New York City Charter included a provision that subjected any city employe, including teachers, to suspension or dismissal or both, if one refused to answer questions posed by an official inquiry.

Early witnesses, the report pointed out, were all officials of the Teachers Union of New York. Of the thirteen responding to subpoena, the subcommittee stated, ten refused to answer questions under protection of the Fifth Amendment. The three others testified that they were not Communists. Further check-ups, the report added, indicated that the three who openly denied Communist affiliations had testified truthfully, but the ten others were left in doubt but under suspicion.

The subcommittee appeared to be much pleased with New York's efforts to ferret out Communist infiltration in education, through its charter provision and additional measures taken by school officials themselves. Dr. Jansen reported that more than 100 teachers had been suspended or separated from service and that some 180 still were under investigation.

Signing the report, besides Mr. Jenner, were Senators Arthur V. Watkins of Utah, Robert C. Hendrickson of New Jersey, Herman Welker of Idaho and John Marshall Butler of Maryland, Republicans, and Senators Pat McCarran of Nevada (who was chairman when the investigation began last year), James O. Eastland of Mississippi and Olin D. Johnston of South Carolina, Democrats. The group constituted a subcommittee of the Senate Judiciary Committee.

Commenting upon the subcommittee's report Miss Selma Borchardt, vice president and Washington representative of the American Federation of Teachers, said there were "relatively few" places in this country in which there had been Communists in the school systems. Proof of the rarity of instances in which Communists have succeeded in infiltrating schools, she added, is the shocked outcry that arises when Communist intrusion has been established as a fact.

With reference to the subcommittee's recommendation favoring legislation designed to force witnesses who invoke the Fifth Amendment to testify, Miss Borchardt said that her organization was critical of such a proposal.

"We believe that the methods of American jurisprudence must be applied," Miss Borchardt added. "Judicial procedures set up by the Constitution must be respected. They should not be put aside just because they prove inconvenient."

2 Leaders Here Back Findings

Two spokesmen for teachers and administrators of the New York school system agreed yesterday with the Jenner subcommittee that local school administrations should cleanse their own systems.

Raymond F. Halloran, president of the High School Teachers Association, said the organization was in favor of local policing of the school system but did not believe that outside help was necessary. He held that the local educational boards had sufficient power to cope with the situation without calling on Congressional bodies to interfere. He pointed to the fact that none of the teachers who were suspended or dismissed by the Board of Education was a member of the association.

Mr. Cavallaro felt that the commitee's report on Communist infiltration into the school system was "very disquieting and alarming" and called for immediate action.

"I am in favor of the recommendation that local authorities must clear their own systems of infiltrators and obtain outside help if necessary," he said.

July 27, 1953

STUDY OF RUSSIAN FALLS OFF IN U. S.

Such Courses in 183 Colleges Draw Only 5,000 Students, Drop of 35% Since '50

By BENJAMIN FINE

Despite the growing demand for specialists in Russian and other Slavic languages, the number of students enrolled in such studies in American colleges and universities has dropped sharply since 1950.

At present 183 colleges in this country offer courses in Russian, with twenty-two others providing courses in Polish and eight in the Czechoslovak tongue. Five thousand students of the 2,500,000 attending American institutions of higher learning are enrolled this fall for Slavic languages.

This is a drop of 35 per cent from the high of 1950. Interest in Russian and related studies began in World War II and continued until the outbreak of the Korean conflict. Then interest fell rapidly. Several colleges dropped studies in Russian because of the lack of student enrollment.

At West Point, where Russian is one of five elective languages taught, one-fifth of the 475 members of the senior class are taking it. When they finish the 200-hour course they will be able to speak for five minutes without interruption and read well enough to understand its meaning.

College officials report that many students are afraid to take any subject connected with the Soviet Union or the satellite nations. The students are worried lest at some future time the fact that they had studied the Russian language in college might be considered "suspicious" by a super-sensitive investigator.

Moreover, the students have told their professors that they have experienced pressure from their parents to stay away from anything that might tie them in with "communism." In some instances students have dropped their Russian studies because of eyebrow raising from classmates or friends of their families.

Such Studies Valuable to U. S.

At the same time, a study made by The New York Times brings out, many college authorities agree that more students should know the Russian language, and

know more about the Soviet Union. They emphasize that a knowledge of Russian is of growing importance, particularly in the field of science. Many Russian scientists can read the American reports written in the English language; but few Americans are able to read the Russian studies in the original.

However, fear is not the only reason for the sharp decline in the number of students taking Russian. Many students feel the language is too difficult, and they would be required to work too hard to master it.

In other institutions the drawback is inability to get an adequate teaching staff. In some instances the college itself is not eager to expand its offerings in this area.

Dr. Fan Parker, Russian instructor at Brooklyn College and president of the American Association of Teachers of Slavic and East European Languages, said that the most important reason for the decline in Slavic studies was that of fear. Many students have told her, she said, that they do not want the word "Russian" to appear on their college record. They do not want to risk being questioned at some later date.

"What are we afraid of?" asked Dr. Parker. "For our own national security it is important that we know more about the Soviet Union, and certainly more about its language. This seems like a short-sighted attitude on our part."

Even at the large Russian study centers, found at Columbia, Harvard, Cornell, Michigan, Maryland and Stanford, the decrease is noticeable. Columbia had a high of 525 students taking Russian and other Slavic languages in 1950-51. It dropped to 364 last year, and this fall only 211 students enrolled.

Dr. Philip E. Mosely, director of Columbia's Russian Institute, said that this drop was attributable in part to the fear of some students that "an interest in the Russian language or in Russian studies would fall under the rubric of subversion." He added that the interests of national security would be strengthened if students brought to the service of our Government not only a knowledge of Russian but also a thorough training both in a major discipline and in the related disciplines of a given area, such as Russia, China or India.

At Cornell University, where enrollment in Russian has dropped steadily, the officials declared that "Government investigations have hurt enrollment." One student at Cornell "audited" the Russian languge course so it would not be listed on his transcript.

Typical of what is happening elsewhere is the drop in the Russian and other Slavic language enrollment at the University of Maryland. Dr. Wilson H. Elkins, the president, reports that 120 students were enrolled in 1950-51. This dropped to eighty-one last year, and this fall fifty-five students registered for courses in Russian.

"The Foreign Language Department definitely urges upon students the advantage of knowing Russian," said Dr. Elkins. "We point to the posts held now by former Russian majors."

Prof. William R. Parker of New York University, secretary of the Modern Language Association of America, said that the enrollments in Russian and other Slavic languages should be greatly increased. He said that the number of Russians studying English far exceeded the number of Americans studying Russian.

"There seems to be a general nervousness about American students taking a course in Russian," Dr. Parker observed. "Many students shy away from anything that deals with the Iron Curtain countries. It's not a rational fear, but it is an attitude that must be dispelled if we are to strengthen our own national security."

The enrolment in the Russian language dropped from 133 last year to 108 this fall at the University of Michigan. Associate Dean Burton D. Thuma noted that the suggestion that a student take Russian was sometimes met with amusement or incredulity. Those who do take it report that "my friends back home ask me why I'm taking Russian," or "my folks can't understand why I want to take Russian." This seems particularly true in the case of students from small towns.

"More students should be encouraged to take Slavic languages," said Dr. Thuma. "When representatives of C. I. A. [Central Intelligence Agency], N. S. A. [National Security Administration], State Department and other government agencies come to the campus they are keenly interested in students with a good knowledge of Russian."

At the University of Kansas City, where fewer than a dozen students are taking courses in Russian or other Slavic languages, Dr. Earl J. McGrath, president of the university, said that in the interest of national security more students should have a knowledge of the Russian language and the history and government of the Soviet Union.

"A knowledge of the Russian language," said Dr. McGrath,

former United States Commissioner of Education, "would enable the student to obtain firsthand knowledge of Communist writings and thus be able to evaluate their falsity."

At some institutions the enrollment in Russian has disappeared. At the University of Denver it dropped from forty-six students in 1950-51 to none this year, and at Tulane University it dropped from nineteen to none. At the University of Wisconsin the drop has been, since 1950, from 339 to 188 and at the University of Texas from 294 to 141.

Need for Students Emphasized

Typical of the comments of the educators, stressing the need for more students in the Russian field, is this from Dr. W. Boyd Alexander, vice president of Antioch College:

"From the point of view of national security more students should be encouraged to take courses in Russian or other Slavic studies or languages. For every American who has studied Russian there are 100 Russians who have studied English.

"We are handicapped in trying to understand what they are up to by this disproportion. In war, either hot or cold, this handicap is serious. But there is another side to the coin. If we hope to work out some sort of co-existence with the Russians we need to know much more about their language and their culture than we do now."

Similarly, Dr. Nathan M. Pusey, president of Harvard University, said that "the more Americans know about the Soviet Union and the Slavic countries, the better prepared we shall be as a nation to face the power situation in which we find ourselves today."

At Bowdoin College, where the enrollment dropped from twenty-two last year to thirteen this year, Dr. James S. Coles, the president, declared that "in the interests of the security of the United States, the security of our Western way of life and our basic freedoms, and in the interests of eventual world understanding and world peace, I believe it to be of utmost importance that many, many more students should be encouraged to study the Slavic languages and Slavic culture."

Dr. Coles said that there had been a deterioration with respect to the study of all foreign languages throughout the United States. With our increasing burden of world leadership, he warned, "this may prove disastrous not only to the United States, but also to many other peoples of the free world."

YALE, HARVARD SPURN U.S. LOANS

Drop Aid Plan for Students in Protest on Loyalty Oath

By The Associated Press.

NEW HAVEN, Nov. 17—Yale and Harvard Universities teamed tonight to withdraw from the Federal student loan program in protest over the loyalty affidavit that it requires.

The action by the two universities meant that they would relinquish almost $500,000 in funds available to them from the Federal Government as loans to needy students..

Dr. A. Whitney Griswold, president of Yale, said his university would make no further commitments for loans under the National Defense Act of 1958 as long as the "negative affidavit" was required in addition to the oath of support for the United States Constitution.

Dr. Nathan M. Pusey, Harvard's president, said the university was relinquishing $357,873 in Federal funds. He described the "affidavit of disbelief" as "misguided."

A spokesman for Yale said the university had been allocated $210,000 since the act went into effect, of which, all but about $50,000 had been received. The spokesman said most of the remaining $50,000 would go back to the Government.

Later, the spokesman said Dr. Griswold and Dr. Pusey discussed the matter as late as this morning in a telephone conversation.

The two presidents had been talking about the loan program and the affidavit since last winter, he said.

Yale's withdrawal was announced in a letter from Dr. Griswold to Arthur S. Flemming, Secretary of Health, Education and Welfare. The announcement by Dr. Pusey in Cambridge, Mass., was addressed to Dr. Lawrence G. Derthick, United States Commissioner of Education.

Dr. Griswold said the loyalty affidavit "is contrary to the classic principles of our colleges and universities."

The affidavit requires a student applying for a loan to swear that he does not believe in, belong to, or support "any organization that believes in or teaches the overthrow of the United States Government by force or violence or by any illegal or unconstitutional methods."

Dr. Griswold said the affidavit "partakes of the nature of the oppressive religious and political test oaths of history, which were used as a means of exercising control over the educational process by church and state."

"The universities of the free world, especially those of England and the United States, have taken the lead in resisting and doing away with such oaths," Dr. Griswold said.

Loyalty, he declared, "cannot be coerced or compelled, it has to be won. Loyalty oaths are inherently futile as no subversive or treasonous person hesitates to use them as a cloak for his intentions."

November 18, 1959

'Citizenship Education' Is Social Studies Again

Special to The New York Times.

ALBANY, Nov. 18 — The Board of Regents today went back to the term "social studies" to describe elementary and secondary school courses in geography, history, government and economics.

The Regents had dropped "social studies" in favor of "citizenship education" in 1950 because some members of the board at the time believed that the original phrase smacked of socialism.

In reversing themselves today, the Regents noted that "social studies" described the subject matter more accurately, that it had been in use for more than fifty years and that it was accepted by colleges and professional groups.

November 19, 1960

President Signs Repealer Of Student Non-Red Oath

By BEN A. FRANKLIN
Special to The New York Times

WASHINGTON, Oct. 17—President Kennedy has signed a bill repealing the controversial non-Communist disclaimer affidavit that had been required of college students and scientists seeking Federal loans and grants.

The President signed the measure last night, capping a three-year effort by liberals in Congress to abolish the affidavit requirement. As a Senator in 1959 and 1960, Mr. Kennedy led the opposition to the disclaimer provision.

In a statement issued at the White House today, he said he was "glad to approve" the legislation. He noted that the repealed provision had caused 32 colleges and universities to stay out of the student loan program because they believed the requirement "discriminated against college students and was offensive to them."

However, the new measure contained several provisions that seemed certain to stir new controversy.

Can Revoke Stipends

Among them was a stiff, new criminal penalty of $10,000 or a prison sentence of up to five years, or both. This would apply to persons who are members of "any Communist organization" that is required to register with the Subversive Activities Control Board and who apply for, use or attempt to use any Federal scholarship or fellowship funds.

Another provision gives the Office of Education and the National Science Foundation new authority to revoke, for reasons "in the best interest of the United States," any fellowship or stipend awarded to a graduate student or researcher.

Several groups have indicated that they are less than enthusiastic about these and other provisions that were inserted in the measure to obtain the necessary support in Congress for passage. The groups include the American Association of University Professors, the American Council on Education and the American Civil Liberties Union.

The bill the President signed yesterday was the result of a carefully executed compromise. In parliamentary maneuvering on it last month, organizations that had long favored repeal of the non-Communist affidavit maintained almost total silence as the measure advanced through committees and onto the Senate and House floors.

"We tried very hard not to rock the boat," a spokesman for one of these groups said. He noted that the repealer had been "slipped through quietly," without the necessity of a roll-call vote on either side of the Capitol. Passage was by voice vote or by unanimous consent.

Applies to Fellowships

The bill was said to be "something of a coup" on another count, as well. Its provision repealing the non-Communist affidavit requirement applied not only to loans and grants under the National Defense Education Act but also to graduate fellowships and research stipends administered by the National Science Foundation.

Since 1950, applicants for the latter have had to sign disclaimer affidavits. The National Defense Education Act was passed in 1958.

The repealed provision required the applicant to attest that he did not "believe in," was not a member of and did not support "any organization that believes in or teaches the overthrow of the United States Government by force or violence or by any illegal or unconstitutional methods."

Applicants for undergraduate loans are still required to take an affirmative oath of allegiance to the United States. In addition, applicants for graduate fellowships and research stipends will have to file statements of any convictions of serious crimes and of criminal charges pending against them.

All applicants, whether for loans or grants, will be subject to the new criminal penalties against members of proscribed organizations. For the moment, pending further action by the Subversive Activities Control Board, this appeared to apply only to members of the Communist Party.

The Office of Education and the National Science Foundation will also have authority to revoke any graduate-level grant summarily for any reason.

Applications Are Pending

Twenty-one of the 32 protesting colleges have pending applications for participation by their students, awaiting favorable action on the repeal. Several others, however, have indicated that they will continue to hold out for unqualified repeal of all student loyalty provisions.

The 32 institutions are Amherst College, Antioch College, Beloit College, Bennington College, Brandeis University, Bryn Mawr College, Colby Junior College, Goucher College, Grinnell College, Harvard University, Haverford College, the Illiff School of Theology, the International Theological Seminary, Mills College, Mount Holyoke College and Newton College of the Sacred Heart.

Also, Oberlin College, the New School for Social Research, Pacific Oaks College, Princeton University, Radcliffe College, Reed College, St. John's College (Maryland), Sarah Lawrence College, Smith College, Swarthmore College, the University of Chicago, Vassar College, Wellesley College, Wesleyan University, Wilmington College (Ohio) and Yale University.

October 18, 1962

HIGH COURT VOIDS LAWS ON LOYALTY IN STATE SCHOOLS

'Vague' Wording on Banned Activities and Threat to Academic Liberty Cited

JUSTICES SPLIT 5 TO 4

Dissent Says 'Blunderbuss' Decision Destroys 'Right of Self-Preservation'

By FRED P. GRAHAM
Special to The New York Times

WASHINGTON, Jan 23—The Supreme Court declared unconstitutional today New York State's laws designed to keep subversives off the faculties and staffs of public schools and state colleges.

In an opinion written by Justice William J. Brennan Jr., the Court swept away the state's "complicated and intricate scheme" of antisubversive laws and regulations, some of which dated to 1917.

Among the affected provisions were one requiring school and college teachers to sign a statement saying they were not Communists and another requiring that teachers be removed for "the utterance of any treasonable or seditious word."

Another result of the decision is that no state employees—including Civil Service personnel as well as teachers—can be dismissed solely for being members of the Communist party.

Emphasis on Education

The decision declared unconstitutional a provision that said public employment could be denied to Communist party members, on the ground that the law did not specify that such employes must agree with the party's illegal aim before they could be dismissed.

Officials of the state and city Civil Service agencies said yesterday that they had not seen the Supreme Court's decision. They said that a determination on whether the ruling extended to all Civil Service employes would have to await a careful study by the agencies' lawyers.

The decision found virtually all of the state's subversive legislation constitutionally defective, but noted that "there can be no doubt of the legitimacy of New York's interest in protecting its educational system from subversion" with properly drafted laws.

The vote was 5 to 4, with the Court dividing along liberal-conservative lines.

Chief Justice Earl Warren and Justices Hugo L. Black, William O. Douglas and Abe Fortas joined in the majority opinion. The dissenters were Justices Tom C. Clark, John M. Harlan, Potter Stewart and Byron R. White.

The decision followed the pattern of a series of recent cases, in which the Supreme Court majority indicated its hostility to loyalty-oath programs by striking them down on narrow grounds, while upholding in principle the right of states to bar subversives from their payrolls.

The decision found virtually all of the state's subversive legislation constitutionally defective, but noted that "there can be no doubt of the legitimacy of New York's interest in protecting its educational system from subversion" with properly drafted laws.

Three basic laws were involved in today's ruling.

The first, enacted in 1917, required the removal of public school personnel for treasonable or seditious words or acts.

The second, passed in 1939, denied public employment or school jobs to anyone who advocated the overthrow of the Government by force, published material advocating such overthrow or joined groups advocating overthrow of the Government.

The third was the so-called Feinberg Law of 1949, which directed the Board of Regents to adopt regulations to enforce the earlier laws, and to prepare a list of subversive organizations.

In 1953 employes of state colleges were brought under the Feinberg Law. Three years later the regents began requiring teachers in both colleges and the public schools, as a condition of employment, to sign "Feinberg certificates" stating that they were not members of the Communist party.

The present court challenge came when the University of Buffalo was merged into the State University system in 1962, and all staff members were required to sign "Feinberg certificates." Five refused to sign and asked a special three-judge Federal District Court to declare the laws unconstitutional.

On June 10, 1965, a week before the case was to be tried, the requirement that all employs sign the certificates was eliminated. The lower court subsequently upheld the Feinberg Law, relying on a 1952 Supreme Court decision that had declared the law constitutional.

Justice Brennan said the 1952 decision was no longer valid because it was based on the then-prevailing doctrine that public employes may be required to sacrifice certain rights enjoyed by the public at large.

Subsequent decisions have eroded that doctrine, Justice Brennan said.

A public employe cannot now be fired for membership in an allegedly subversive group without proof that he intended to advance the illegal aims of the organization. Since the Feinberg Law condemns mere membership in the Communist party, it is therefore void, he said.

He also declared that the New York laws had not been attacked in 1952 as unconstitutionally vague, as they were in today's appeal.

Examining the provisions one by one, he found that each contained vague terms that failed to inform the public what was being outlawed, and that this might intimidate teachers into steering away from controversial activities.

Among the vague terms was the prohibition of "treasonable or seditious words or acts," and the barrier to employment of persons who distributed written material "containing or advocating, advising or teaching" the doctrine of violent overthrow of the Government.

"Our nation is deeply committed to safeguarding academic freedom, which is of transcendent value to all of us and not merely the teachers concerned," Justice Brennan said. "That freedom is therefore a special concern of the First Amendment, which does not tolerate laws that cast a pall of orthodoxy over the classroom."

Justice Clark, in his dissent, charged that the court reached beyond the facts of today's case in "blunderbuss fashion." He noted that the Court struck down Section 105 (3) of the Civil Service Law, and Section 3021 of the Education Law, although neither applied to college personnel.

The two provisions, which contain similar wording regarding the discharge of employes who utter "treasonable or seditious words," apply to civil service personnel and public school teachers and staff.

He also disputed Justice Brennan's statement that public employes could not be discharged for mere Communist party membership, and concluded that "the majority has by its broadside swept away one of our most precious rights, namely, the right of self-preservation."

Although today's decision directly affects only the New York statutes, a number of states and cities have loyalty provisions that are drafted along the same lines and would be subject to the same objections.

Maryland's "Ober Law," which requires state employes to sign a loyalty oath, has been professor of English; Newton widely copied by other states and is also before the Supreme Court.

The five appellants from Buffalo University were Harry Keyishian, an English instructor; George Hochfield, an associate Garver, a lecturer in philosophy; Ralph N. Maud, an associate professor of English, and George E. Starbuck, a librarian.

Richard Lipsitz of Buffalo argued for the appellants. Ruth V. Iles, Assistant Attorney General of New York, and John C. Crary Jr. of Albany argued for the state.

January 24, 1967

Training School Children in the Event

of a 'Sneak' Air Attack on the City

Pupils at Public School 75 taking shelter under their desks

The children find shelter against the walls of a corridor

First 'No Signal' Atom Bomb Drills Are Staged in the City's Schools

Imaginary enemy planes slipped through New York City's radar defenses without detection yesterday and dropped equally imaginary atom bombs on the metropolitan area—but only the city's teachers were aware of it. In classrooms throughout the five boroughs the teachers put their pupils through the first of a series of "no signal" air raid drills, designed to acquaint the youngsters with what to do in event of a sneak attack.

At 10:45 A. M. Mrs. Bertha Smith, a sixth-grade teacher in Public School 75 at 735 West End Avenue, observed a hypothetical "sudden white flash" and gave the "take cover" signal to her class. Almost immediately the youngsters dropped to the floor, their backs to the windows, and covered the exposed parts of their bodies. It took only a fraction of a second.

When Mrs. Smith gave the "all clear" the youngsters came up beaming. A visitor to the class, impressed with the pupils' remarkable speed and lack of alarm, asked them whether they were playing a game.

"Oh, no," replied Jeanette Silverman, who is 11 years old. "We were taking cover in case of a sneak attack."

"Like Money in the Bank"

"We hope it won't ever be necessary," said Mrs. Martha R. Frey, the principal. "But it's good to know that we are ready for everything—it's like having money in the bank."

Although yesterday's drill was the first of the "no signal" type, the youngsters—like the rest of the city's school children—had previously been briefed on what to do, and had practiced "forewarned" drills.

In addition, all pupils had distributed to their parents in the last week an official message from the Board of Education explaining why the drills were being held and what they could do to protect themselves and their children. The parents are required to sign a receipt saying they have read the message and return the slip to their child's teacher.

Regard It as Fire Drill

In another part of the school building a first-grade class was going through the same routine. These pupils, who are 5 and 6, were not told the purpose of the drills, Mrs. Frey explained, to avoid any undue alarm. The children regard it as a fire drill and they enjoy it, she added.

"We have taken every precaution to see that no child is frightened or alarmed," the principal declared, "and we have met with our Parents' Association and assured them so. Our parents are giving excellent cooperation. They feel that even if their children were alarmed, which they are not, it is still more important to have them ready for any eventuality."

Later in the day, Dr. William Jansen, the Superintendent of Schools, reported that a sampling of the city's schools showed that the "no-signal" drills were "taken by the children in their stride."

"No single incident of panicky or uncooperative behavior was reported," Dr. Jansen declared. He added that "sneak attack" drills would be held next Wednesday and on the following Wednesday and that students would regularly practice "no-signal" and "shelter-area" drills until they develop "automatic reactions."

Instructions are continued in a corridor during the drill

February 8, 1951

RAID TESTS SHOW CHILD ANXIETIES

Increase in Nail Biting and Thumb Sucking Reported During School Drills

By DOROTHY BARCLAY

The statement that most children take "sneak attack" atom bomb drills in school "matter of facly or as welcome interruption of classroom routine," is not so in the opinion of Dr. Wilfred C. Hulse, psychiatrist at the Children's Center and Mt. Sinai Hospital.

Dr. Hulse said yesterday that close observation of youngsters during such a drill would show a marked increase in thumb sucking, nail biting or other repetitive compulsive movements that represent defenses against anxiety. He spoke at a meeting of the Conference Group on Child Care of the Welfare Council of New York at the Academy of Medicine, 2 East 103rd Street.

To lessen the tension during such drills, Dr. Hulse recommended, the prohibition against children's speaking should be removed. "Talking is one of the best means for relieving accumulated tension," he said. "It is nonsensical to increase the anxiety and pressure in the child by putting him under a restriction not to speak. The children should be encouraged to speak in a low voice during the drills. The supervising adults always find plenty to say!"

To increase the children's security further, he added, the teacher should "take cover" herself.

"No leader should ever segregate himself from his group," Dr. Hulse said. "If taking part in the practice drill makes observation difficult, two classes could be combined, one teacher taking part and one observing."

Discipline Is Scored

Instances of abuse of the drill idea for disciplinary purposes have come to his attention, he said. He told of one teacher who used the command "take cover" whenever her class became unruly. Such actions will confuse air-raid precautions with punishment in the children's minds.

"Freedom from fear does not depend on environmental circumstances, not on reality, but on a close relationship to a secure and protecting adult," Dr. Hulse asserted.

June 13, 1951

1,250,000 PUPILS ARE CALM IN DRILL

City's Schools Go Through Air Raid Routine Unexcited and With Precision

The city's 1,250,000 school-age youngsters took yesterday's air-raid drill in their stride. If they were excited or alarmed by the wail of the sirens and the signals of the school bell, they did not show it and no major incidents were reported to school civil defense officials.

After nearly a year of practice drills and classroom instruction, the youngsters—from the kindergartners to the senior high school students—reacted almost instinctively to the alarm. As the "red" or "take shelter" signal sounded—a three-tenths-of-a-second ring, followed by two-tenths-of-a-second of silence, repeated for three minutes—teachers and pupils in public, private and parochial schools throughout the five boroughs sprang into instant action.

Teachers and pupils put away their work and got their coats. As window shades were pulled down and curtains drawn—a protection against flying glass — youngsters in some instances had a fleeting glance of traffic being halted and pedestrians scurrying for cover. All lights were turned out in the rooms.

Then quietly and orderly, without needing to be told where to go or what to do, they filed from their classrooms and trooped to assigned shelter areas. They were at their stations in many schools before the initial three-minute signal was over.

No Sign of Excitement

In some schools the students sat huddled against the thick walls and covered their bodies with their coats. The younger children took the drill with extreme seriousness; the older ones often whispered bright remarks. But there was generally no sign of fear or excitement.

"They know what to do," a principal explained. "They know more than most adults. If it was the real McCoy they would still react the same way. There would be no panic."

For most pupils, the ten-minute drill passed quickly. Led by their teachers, some classes sang songs, like "Rudolph the Red-Nosed Reindeer," "Jingle Bells" and "Mocking Bird Hill." Teachers of young classes read stories. Pinnochio's fate inside the whale's stomach held more excitement for many children than the eerie echo of the sirens outside.

A 5-year-old sitting timidly in an East Bronx school was asked whether he knew why he was in the corridor and not in the classroom.

"Sure," he replied, "we're having an air raid."

"Oh no," cut in his teacher firmly, "we're having an air raid drill—this is just practice, like a fire drill."

The teacher's remarks seemed to

73

register and she was about to turn away, when the child asked:

"Say, what's an air raid anyway?"

Knew It Wasn't Real

In a mid-Manhattan school, a sandy-haired youngster exclaimed, "It's not a real raid. It it was, I would go into a refrigerator and eat up all the stuff."

But a first-grade pupil in the Bronx, said:

"The sirens sound frightening."

"That's not a word we teach in first grade," her teacher asserted. "She picked it up at home. Some parents seem more alarmed than their children and needlessly worry them."

The majority of the school children who were issued identification disks, wore their "dog tags" yesterday, teachers reported, but a goodly number did not for various reasons. Some were acting on the orders of the parents, who can decide whether their children should wear them or not. Others—as many as one-third in one class—forgot them. One little lady decided that the metal tag didn't go well with her pretty outfit.

One teacher reported that many children "swap" tags or play for them, as they do with picture cards and marbles. One youngster, she said, came to class wearing five different tags.

Most children, however, wear their tags and the majority of their parents have no objections, a school official pointed out. The tags had been criticized by some individuals and organizations on grounds that they tended to foster "war hysteria" and created the impression of immediate peril.

When the "white" or "all clear" signal sounded at 10:43 A. M., regular school activities were resumed almost as quickly as they ceased.

During the drill, Dr. William Jansen, Superintendent of Schools, and members of his staff, were in the emergency control room located in the sub-basement of the Board of Education building, 110 Livingston Street, Brooklyn.

SCHOOL CHILDREN GET IDENTIFICATION TAGS

William Jansen, right, Superintendent of Schools, starts distribution to selected students from different boroughs in move to provide identification for children in lower grades. With Dr. Jansen is James Marshall, chairman of the subcommittee on Identification Tags. The children are Michael Garey, Caroline White (partly hidden), Nicholas Petrides, Henry Tabon and Frances Altman.

The New York Times

Metal identification tags were distributed yesterday to 200,000 second and third grade pupils in the city's public, private and parochial schools. Designed as a civil defense measure in case of enemy attack, the disks are similar to the "dog tags" worn by members of the armed forces.

Students in other grades will receive tags as soon as they can be made and distributed, said John C. Cocks, administrator of the school civil defense program.

By the end of February it is expected that all pupils in the kindergarten through fourth grade will have their tags. The distribution procedure will continue grade by grade until all pupils are covered.

The tags, which must be worn at all times, give the child's name, address, date of birth, parents' name and school. The disks are attached to a beaded chain and can be worn around the neck or wrist.

The first tags were distributed by Dr. William Jansen, Superintendent of Schools, at a brief ceremony in his office at school headquarters, 110 Livingston Street, Brooklyn.

The officials decried the criticism of the identification program that has come from certain organizations that contend the distribution of tags is promoting "war hysteria" among school children. The officials held it is better to be safe than sorry.

October 19, 1951

Photo-Record Project to Begin

Special to THE NEW YORK TIMES.

LINDEN, N. J., Jan. 12—The photographing of public school children for a permanent identification card system for the public schools of the city will begin next week, Herman Mopsick, municipal safety supervisor, announced today. All children will be photographed, and prints will be attached to the identification cards. Two master files will be kept in connection with the public school civil defense program.

January 13, 1952

HIGH COURT BACKS STATE RIGHT TO RUN PAROCHIAL BUSES

Rules 5 tc 4 in New Jersey Case That School Funds Raised by Taxation May Be Used

HELD A PUBLIC BENEFIT

Black Writes Majority Opinion —Rutledge Dissents, Sees 'Public Aid for Religion'

By LEWIS WOOD
Special to The New York Times.

WASHINGTON, Feb. 10—In a decision of far-flung interest the Supreme Court by 5 to 4 ruled today that New Jersey public school funds raised by taxation can be used to pay for transportation of children to Catholic parochial schools.

The controversy which the tribunal settled by this narrow margin revolved around the interpretation of the first amendment to the Constitution which forbids Congress to pass a law "respecting an establishment of religion, or prohibiting the free exercise thereof."

For the majority, Justice Hugo L. Black held that a New Jersey law permitting the payments amounts to religious or public benefit legislation and that no person may be barred from these benefits because of his religion. Justice Black was joined by Chief Justice Fred M. Vinson and Justices Stanley F. Reed, William O. Douglas and Frank Murphy.

Every Form of Aid Opposed

The minority view expressed by Justice Wiley Rutledge, held that the First Amendment's purpose was to separate religious activity and civil authority by forbidding "every form" of public aid or support for religion. The dissent was shared by Justices Felix Frankfurter, Robert H. Jackson and Harold H. Burton.

In an independent objection, Justice Jackson, supported by Mr Frankfurter, charged the majority with "giving the clock's hands a backward turn," because the prohibition against establishment of religion cannot be circumvented by a "subsidy, bonus or reimbursement."

The case, which required three opinions totaling seventy-three pages to dispose of, arose through a protest by Arch R. Everson, a taxpayer of Ewing Township, near Trenton in Mercer County He contested the right of the township Board of Education to reimburse parents of Catholic children for transportation to the parochial schools on regular buses. A State court supported his protest, but was reversed by the New Jersey Court of Errors and Appeals, which was upheld by the Supreme Court today.

The Board of Education had authorized payment of $8,034 to be paid to parents of children for transportation to school, and of this $357.74 was reimbursed to the parents of the Catholic boys and girls.

Typical expressions from the three documents presented in the Supreme Court follow:

Majority, by Justice Black: "New Jersey cannot exclude Catholics, Lutherans, Mohammedans, Baptists, Jews, Methodists, non-believers, Presbyterians, or the members of any other faith, because of their faith or lack of it. We must be careful, in protecting the citizens of New Jersey against State-established churches, to be sure that we do not inadvertently prohibit New Jersey from extending its general State law benefits to all its citizens without regard to their religious belief.

"We cannot say that the First Amendment prohibits New Jersey from spending tax-raised funds to pay the bus fares of parochial schools as a part of a general program under which it pays the fares of pupils attending public and other schools. The First Amendment has erected a wall between church and State. That wall must be kept high and impregnable. We could not approve the slightest breach. New Jersey has not breached it here."

Burden of Taxes Cited

Minority, by Justice Rutledge: "No one conscious of religious values can be unsympathetic toward the burden which our constitutional separation puts on parents who desire religious instruction mixed with secular for their children. But if those feelings should prevail, there would be an end to our historic constitutional policy and command. No more unjust or discriminatory is it in fact to deny attendants at religious schools the cost of their transportation than it is to deny them tuitions, sustenance for their teachers, or any other educational expense which others receive at public cost.

"Two great drives are constantly in motion to abridge, in the name of education, the complete division of religion and civil authority which our forefathers made. One is to introduce religious education and observances into the public schools. The other, to obtain public funds for the aid and support of various private religious schools. In my opinion both avenues were closed by the Constitution. Neither should be opened by this court."

Independent dissent by Justice Jackson, with Justice Frankfurter: "Catholic education is the rock on which thee whole structure rests, and to render tax aid to its church school is indistinguishable to me from rendering the same aid to the church itself. The State cannot maintain a church and it can no more tax its citizens to furnish free carriage to those who attend a church. The prohibition against establishment of religion cannot be circumvented by a subsidy, bonus or reimbursement of expense to individuals for receiving religious instruction and indoctrination.

"It (the church) does not leave the individual to pick up religion by chance. It relies on early and indelible indoctrination in the faith and order of the church by the word and example of persons consecrated to the task. The effect of the religious freedom amendment to our Constitution was to take every form of propagation of religion out of the realm of things which could be directly or indirectly be made public business and thereby be supported in whole or in part at taxpayers' expense."

In deciding this case, Justice Black dealt with two main attacks against the New Jersey practice. These were: 1. That the State law and Board of Education resolution take by taxation the private property of some persons and bestow it upon others for private use, thus violating the due process clause of the Fourteenth Amendment. 2. That the law and resolution force persons to pay taxes to help support Catholic schools, thus violating the First Amendment.

Right Pass Beneficial Law

As to the first contention, the majority spokesman held that New Jersey must not be precluded from passing a law for the public benefit, and:

"The fact that a State law, passed to satisfy a public need, coincides with the personal desires of the individuals most directly affected is certainly an inadequate reason for us to say that a legislature has erroneously appraised the public need."

Justice Rutledge, in his forty-seven-page dissent, described in detail the fight by Madison to separate church and state. New Jersey's action, he said, "exactly fits the type of exaction and the kind of evil at which Madison and Jefferson struck." Under the test they framed, "it cannot be said that the cost of transportation is no part of the cost of education or the religious instruction given."

The dissenting justice said an appropriation from the public treasury to pay the cost of transportation to Sunday school, or weekday classes at the church or parish house or to meetings of young people's religious societies such as the Y. M. C. A., Y. W. C. A., Y. M. H. A. or Epworth League "could not withstand the constitutional attack" brought against the New Jersey bus payments.

In his lengthy objection, Justice Rutledge also stated:

"The realm of religious training and belief remains as the amendment made it, the kingdom of the individual man and his God."

Justice Jackson in his separate opinion said he originally wished to join the majority. He said he had a sympathy "though not ideological" with Catholics who had to pay taxes for public schools and also felt it necessary to support schools for their own children. But, saying he had been forced to change his mind, he criticized the majority ruling.

"The undertones (of the majority) opinion," he added, "advocating complete and uncompromising separation of church from state seem utterly discordant with its conclusion yielding support to their comingling in education matters."

The Ewing Township Board of Education resolution authorized transportation of pupils from Ewing to "the Trenton and Pennington high schools and Catholic schools by way of public carrier."

Stanza of 'America' Naming God Ordered Into Daily School Ritual

The Board of Education directed the public schools yesterday to begin each class day with the singing of the fourth stanza of the patriotic hymn, "America," as an act of reverence intended to help strengthen moral and spiritual values.

The board's unanimous action ended a long-simmering conflict that divided board members as well as school, community and religious leaders.

The board also directed Dr. William Jansen, Superintendent of Schools, to review the curriculum to insure that it includes "appropriate programs of instruction emphasizing the spiritual interest and patriotic motivations of our pioneering ancestors; the devotion and self-sacrifice of the Founding Fathers, and their abiding belief in the principles of democracy."

In authorizing the singing of the fourth stanza of "America," fol-

lowing the daily Pledge to the Flag, the board modified a plan proposed last October by Arthur Levitt, Brooklyn member, which suggested the singing of the first and fourth stanzas. The first stanza is patriotic in nature, and it was reported that the board's Committee on Instructional Affairs, which recommended the modification, felt that this theme was amply covered in the Pledge to the Flag.

Mr. Levitt's plan was offered as a substitute for the daily prayer urged in November, 1951, by the Board of Regents, a suggestion which touched off mixed reaction throughout the state. Only 300 of 3,000 school districts in the state have followed the Regents' proposal, as many educators expressed the fear that a formal prayer would open the door to religion in the schools.

Mark Price, public relations assistant to the school board, said that the schools would put the board's order on "America" into effect as soon as possible, probably when the new term begins next month.

"America" was written 120 years ago by Dr. Samuel Francis Smith while a student at Andover Theological Seminary. The fourth stanza reads:

Our fathers' God, to Thee,
Author of Liberty,
To Thee we Sing;
Long may our land be bright
With freedom's holy light;
Protect us by Thy might,
Great God, our King.

The tune of "America" is the same as that of the British anthem "God Save the King." Many other nations also have used the melody. According to some musical historians Dr. Smith copied the tune not from the British anthem but from the German version.

At yesterday's meeting, held at school headquarters, 110 Livingston Street, Brooklyn, Mr. Levitt said:

"It is difficult to comprehend how this patriotic hymn, whose hallowed lines have been sung by generations of Americans of every creed, could possibly offend any critic of formal prayer. In com-

bination with the Pledge of Allegiance to the Flag it will constitute a truly effective devotional exercise—devotional in the broadest and deepest sense—to the concept of freedom, to the nation and to the Supreme Ruler of the universe.

"I support the proposal in its present form since I find in it no substantial impairment of my original suggestion. I perceive no justification for the expressed fear that there is here involved a threat to the doctrine of separation of church and state."

Mr. Levitt said that "an intelligent and fervent loyalty to moral and spiritual values and to our tradition of devotion to the democratic ideal is essential to the survival of this nation." The resolution adopted by the board, he added, will serve as a mandate to the education staff to re-emphasize teaching the values that have made America great.

On recommendation of Dr. Jansen, the school board re-elected Dr. Frank J. O'Brien to his third six-year term as associate superintendent in charge of the division of child welfare. The position pays $16,250 a year. Dr. O'Brien, who is 62 years old, is a psychiatrist and holds doctorate degrees in philosophy and education.

January 16, 195

Jersey Supreme Court Bars King James Bible in Schools

Special to THE NEW YORK TIMES.

TRENTON, Dec. 7—The New Jersey Supreme Court today forbade the distribution of the King James version of the New Testament and two books of the Old Testament in the public schools of this state. In a unanimous decision the court ruled that the works in question were sectarian and that their dissemination in public schools would be a violation of both the United States and the New Jersey Constitutions.

The ruling was expected to have far-reaching effects, since the Gideons International, an Illinois corporation, has started similar programs in other states. The twenty-page opinion was written by Chief Justice Arthur T. Vanderbilt.

"To permit the distribution of the King James version of the Bible in the public schools of this state," it said, "would be to cast aside all of the progress made in the United States and throughout New Jersey in the field of religious toleration and freedom."

The case before the court was instituted in 1952. It followed the adoption by the Board of Education of the Borough of Rutherford of a resolution permitting the Gideons International to distribute in the schools volumes including the New Testament and the books of Psalms and Proverbs from the Old Testament.

The volumes were to be given only to children whose parents gave their consent. To test the constitutionality of the program, Bernard Tudor, a Jewish parent, and Ralph Lecoque, a Roman Catholic parent, obtained an injunction forbidding further distribution of the book. Mr. Lecoque later withdrew his child from a Rutherford public school and dropped out of the case. Mr. Tudor then received the backing of the American Jewish Congress.

Last March, Superior Court Judge J. Wallace Leyden handed up a decision in which he denied that the program was a violation of either the New Jersey or the Federal Constitution. At the same time he expressed the opinion that the action of the Rutherford Board of Education was "bad policy."

December 8, 195

SPELLMAN PUSHES EFFORT TO WIDEN SCHOOL MEASURE

Calls Kennedy's Bill Unfair —Cites Ways of Including Non-Public Institutions

Cardinal Spellman repeated yesterday his opposition to any program of Federal aid to education that excluded private and parochial schools on the elementary and secondary levels.

In a statement issued through the chancery office of the Roman Catholic Archdiocese of New York, the Cardinal praised President Kennedy's program of assistance to higher education as "fair and equitable to all students, all colleges and all universities."

But he declared:

"I am still opposed to any program of Federal aid that would penalize a multitude of America's children because their parents choose to exercise their constitutional right to educate them in accordance with their beliefs."

Three-Sided Program

The President's aid program has three facets: grants to states for public elementary and secondary education, loans to colleges for construction and grants for college scholarships. Mr. Kennedy has excluded private and parochial schools from the first category on constitutional grounds.

Cardinal Spellman called the Administration's proposal for elementary and secondary education "not fair and equitable."

"It would limit Federal aid to public schools and thereby withhold benefits from millions of children attending private and church-related schools," he said.

"It is not for me to say whether there should be any Federal aid to education. That is a political and economic matter to be decided by the Congress in compliance with the will of the American people.

Asks 'Equal Treatment'

"However, if the Congress decides there should be Federal aid, then certainly any legislation should conform to principles of social justice, equal treatment and non-discrimination."

An aid program providing equivalent benefits to children attending private and church-related schools without violating the Constitution would seem to be an "attainable objective," the Cardinal said.

If this is not feasible, he observed, Congress should weigh other means.

These might include, he said, long-term, low-interest loans, tax benefits to parents, tuition subsidies and "other forms of help" such as assistance for the non-religious aspects of church-related schools.

Last Jan. 17, the Cardinal assailed a Kennedy task force proposal that Congress enact a multi-billion-dollar program of Federal aid to public schools.

He said then it was "unthinkable that any American child be denied the Federal funds allotted to other children which are necessary for his mental development because his parents choose for him a God-centered education."

March 14, 1961

PAROCHIAL TEXTS CALLED BAR TO AID

Protestant Study Says Aim of Books Is Sectarian

By JOHN WICKLEIN

A report to the National Council of Churches has declared that parochial school courses in mathematics, science and foreign languages are permeated with religious indoctrination, and that therefore the schools should not get Federal assistance of any kind.

The 100-page report was based on a survey of Roman Catholic textbooks now in use. The conclusions were those of George R. La Noue, who made the study at the request of the Protestant council's Department of Religious Liberty.

A spokesman on national Catholic educational matters declined to comment on the report for the time being.

The report said that problems in many arithmetic texts were used to make students familiar with Catholic parish life, religious vocations, the saints and various other sectarian information.

In science, parochial schools were found to "inject a considerable amount of religious interpretation and even some sectarian doctrine" into subjects such as biology and psychology.

As for languages, the report said that at the elementary school level, religious themes were introduced in vocabulary drills, and that at higher levels reading lessons referred primarily to Catholic culture or interests.

Mr. La Noue challenged the constitutionality, on church-state grounds, of the National Defense Education Act, which provides loans for equipment to be used in the teaching of these "secular" subjects.

The legal rationale for these loans, Mr. La Noue said here yesterday, is that Federal funds can be used to promote the teaching of these subjects because they are without religious content and thus do not violate the separation of church and state.

"The purpose of this study," he said, "is to show that under the current practice of parochial schools the argument's major premise is empirically false."

A spokesman on national Catholic educational matters declined to comment on the report for now.

Mr. La Noue, a doctoral candidate at Yale, reported on his research last night in a lecture at the School of Education of Syracuse University. The data will be published later in full in a scholarly journal.

One of the questions most frequently asked by defenders of Government aid to parochial schools, Mr. La Noue said, is "How can there be any religious doctrine in an algebraic formula?"

"Religious doctrine can be taught in an algebraic formula," he replied, "or, at least, in an arithmetic book." To show one way, he quoted this problem from an arithmetic text:

"The book about St. Theresa costs $2.00. The book about St. Joseph costs $1.05. Find the difference in the prices of the two books."

Dean M. Kelley, director of the Department of Religious Liberty of the church council, said the study had been made to determine whether, as had been stated in hearings on the National Defense Education Act, no religion is taught in church-sponsored courses in mathematics, science and modern languages. Documentation from Catholic textbooks shows that it is, he said.

"This study," he commented, "does not criticize the objectives or methods of parochial education—quite the contrary. Christians must respect the dedication and zeal that have gone into the effort to integrate religion completely in the teaching of all 'secular' subjects.

"It is an admirable effort, but one which we insist must be financed on a strictly voluntary basis by the adherents of the religion taught.

"It would be a loss for all Christians if, in order to qualify for tax funds, the patrons of parochial schools were to recede from their high concept of integrating religion and general education. It would be an equally serious loss if taxes paid under coercion by citizens of all faiths were to be used to finance the teaching of religion. Somewhere between these two hazards, we are confident that a constructive solution can be found."

The National Council of Churches embraces thirty-four communions with 39,000,000 members, including the leading Protestant denominations and several branches of the Eastern Orthodoxy.

The council has gone on record in support of the right of any church group to maintain parochial schools. It has also held that Government aid to religious schools violates both constitutional principles and sound public policy.

It is likely that the report to the council will be used in future hearings on the Kennedy Administration's proposal for general Federal aid to public schools.

The National Catholic Welfare Conference, administrative organization of the Catholic Bishops of the United States, has been urging that the bill be extended to include aid to parochial schools. One of the arguments used has been that direct aid could legally be given to Catholic schools for the teaching of subjects that are non-religious in nature.

Catholic Policy Given

In his report, Mr. La Noue said the opponents of Federal aid to parochial schools thought the Catholic argument—that the "secular" and the "religious" parts of the parochial school curriculums could be separated—was "amazing." The argument, he said, contradicts the traditional educational phi-

losophy of the Roman Catholic Church.

Mr. La Noue said that the "secular subject" argument had apparently been accepted by the Department of Health, Education and Welfare. In its "Memorandum on the Impact of the First Amendment to the Constitution upon Federal Aid to Education," the department stated:

"At the present time, the National Defense Education Act permits the U. S. Commissioner of Education to make loans to private schools to acquire science, mathematics, or foreign language equipment. We believe such loans are constitutional because the connection between loans for such purposes and the religious functions of a sectarian schools seems to be nonexistent or minimal."

Examples Presented

Mr. La Noue said his survey of Catholic textbooks widely used in parochial schools showed that these books emphasized spe-

cifically Catholic aspects of the culture, and integrated Catholic doctrines with the subject matter wherever possible.

He cited these examples:

"Sister Mary Amanda Taylor et al., 'Science and Living in Today's World,' Doubleday, 1958, Book 8 — Unit 1 begins: 'The world is a huge book written by God. Its words are His works—the fishes of the sea, the birds of the air, the growing things in the earth.' In a chapter on the struggle against disease: 'The Church is opposed to mercy killing because mercy killing is contrary to Divine Law.'

"Sister M. Aquinas, 'Science 7 With Health and Safety,' Laidlaw Brothers, 1961: 'Vega, Deneb and Altair are visible soon after dark in summer, and the Northern Cross a little later (You can think of this constellation as symbolizing the victory through the Cross.)'

"William A. Brownell, Sister Mary Gerardus. 'Finding Truth in Arithmetic' (teachers' edi-

tion), Ginn & Co., 1959. Nature of book stated in preface: 'Therefore, a textbook on arithmetic written in the spirit of Christian philosophy should be a welcome contribution to Catholic education.'

"Most of the religious content comes into the course integrated with the problems to be solved, for example: P. 58 'It was Mother Mary's birthday. Ann brought 3 flowers and Jerome brought 2 flowers to put in front of Mother Mary's statue. How many flowers in all were put in front of the statue?'"

Such examples, and the study as a whole, Mr. La Noue contended, make it clear that Federal grants or loans to aid parochial schools in teaching these subjects violate the religious separation clause of the First Amendment to the Constitution.

The council's Department of Religious Liberty has offices at the council's headquarters, 475 Riverside Drive.

May 11, 1962

SUPREME COURT OUTLAWS OFFICIAL SCHOOL PRAYERS IN REGENTS CASE DECISION

RULING IS 6 TO 1

Suit Was Brought by 5 L. I. Parents Against Education Board

By ANTHONY LEWIS
Special to The New York Times.

WASHINGTON, June 25— The Supreme Court held today that the reading of an official prayer in New York public schools violated the Constitution.

The prayer was drafted by the New York Board of Regents and recommended in 1951 for recital aloud by teachers and

children in each classroom at the start of every school day. It is non-denominational and just twenty-two words long. It reads:

"Almighty God, we acknowledge our dependence upon Thee, and we beg Thy blessing upon us, our parents, our teachers and our country."

By a vote of 6 to 1 the court held that the reading of the prayer was "an establishment of religion" forbidden by the First Amendment to the Constitution.

Impact Far-Reaching

But the impact of the decision goes far beyond the New York prayer. The clear implication of the ruling was that any religious ceremony promoted by the state in public schools would be suspect. That would include, for example,

reading of verses from the Bible—a practice now under challenge in Pennsylvania.

Many of the public school systems in the United States have such religious ceremonies. The practice is most common in the South, where chapel exercises and Bible readings are commonly used.

Thus, today's decision would have a major and controversial impact on public school practices across the country. And beyond that, it might indicate a stricter attitude in the Supreme Court toward breaches of what it has called the "wall of separation" between church and state.

The prayer case was one of seventeen decided by the Supreme Court in a crowded final session today before it adjourned for the summer. In addition to those opinions the

court issued hundreds of brief orders to clean up the docket. It returns next Oct. 1.

In an unusual ceremony at the start of today's session, Justice Hugo L. Black was honored for serving through twenty-five terms of the court. The Solicitor General, Archibald Cox, and Chief Justice Earl Warren joined in a brief but dramatic tribute to the justice.

Justice Black wrote the opinion of the court in the prayer case. He was joined by the Chief Justice and Justice Tom C. Clark, John Marshall Harlan and William J. Brennan Jr. Justice William O. Douglas concurred in a separate opinion.

Justice Potter Stewart was the sole dissenter. Not participating were Justices Felix Frankfurter, who is in the hospital, and Byron R. White, who joined the court after the case was argued.

The case was brought by five parents of children in the public schools of New Hyde Park, L. I., N. Y. Two of the parents were Jewish, one a member of the Ethical Culture Society, one a Unitarian and one a non-believer. They said the form of the prayer conflicted with their religious beliefs.

The highest New York State court, the Court of Appeals, rejected their protest against the prayer by a vote of 5 to 2.

Established Clause Violated

The complaint of these families, as Justice Black phrased it today, was that the prayer violated the establishment clause of the First Amendment because it was "composed by governmental officials as a part of a governmental program to further religious beliefs."

"We agree with that contention," Justice Black said.

"In this country, it is no part of the business of government to compose official prayers for any group of the American people to recite.

School officials had argued that the prayer was inoffensive because parents who did not want their children to say it could get them excused. The children could then either leave the room or remain seated and silent while their classmates stood and prayed.

In New Hyde Park, only one child had sought to be excused since the prayer was adopted, in 1958.

Justice Black rejected this argument. He said, first, that placing "the power, prestige and financial support of government" behind a particular form of religious observance does tend to coerce religious minorities to conform.

Purpose of Ban

But the purposes of banning "an establishment of religion go much further," Justice Black said. He declared that the clause "does not depend upon any showing of direct governmental compulsion and is violated by the enactment of laws which establish an official religion whether those laws operate directly to coerce nonobserving individuals or not."

In stating the opinion from the bench today, Justice Black added these extemporaneous comments:

"The prayer of each man from his soul must be his and his alone. That is the genius of the First Amendment.

"If there is any one thing clear in the First Amendment, it is that the right of the people to pray in their own way is not to be controlled by the election returns."

Justice Stewart, in his dissent, criticized Justice Black's "uncritical invocation of metaphors like the 'wall of separation.'"

"I cannot see how an 'official religion' is established by letting those who want to say a prayer say it," Justice Stewart wrote.

"On the contrary, I think that to deny the wish of these school children to join in reciting this prayer is to deny them the opportunity of sharing in the spiritual heritage of our nation."

Reviews Government References

Justice Stewart reviewed historical examples of references to God in American governmental procedings. He noted that Congress begins its sessions with a prayer and that the crier of the Supreme Court itself says at every session: "God save the United States and this honorable court."

He said none of these amounted to establishing an "official religion," and neither did the New York prayer. All, he argued, simply recognized "the deeply entrenched and highly cherished spiritual traditions of our nation."

Justice Black, for his part, dismissed in a footnote the comparison of the New York prayer with references to God in such places as the Court and Congress. He said these were "patriotic or ceremonial occasions" bearing "no true resemblance to the unquestioned religious exercise" at issue today.

Justice Douglas, on the other hand, suggested in his concurring opinion that all these practices were unconstitutional. He said the audience for a prayer in a school, court or legislature was a "captive audience."

Some indication of the impact of the decision is given by the fact that twenty states came into the case as friends of the court to urge upholding of the prayer. The American Civil Liberties Union, which supported the case for the plaintiffs, and some Jewish and other groups were on the opposite side.

Comment By Southerner

Immediate reaction in Congress was dominated by unfavorable comment from Southern members. Representative George Andrews, Democrat of Alabama, said:

"They put the Negroes in the schools and now they've driven God out."

The Supreme Court had a chance ten years ago to rule on a similar case. But it dismissed the case on procedural grounds.

That case, from New Jersey, challenged the reading of verses from the Bible in public schools. But the children involved had all graduated by the time the case reached the Supreme Court, and the court held that the complaining parents lacked standing to sue simply as taxpayers.

The first important church-state decision from the modern court came in 1947. By a vote of 5 to 4, the court upheld the use of state funds to provide bus service for parochial school pupils.

Interestingly, Justice Douglas—who was one of the majority of five in the Buas case—said in his opinion today that it should be overruled. In retrospect, he said, it seems "out of line with the First Amendment."

In 1948 the court held 8 to 1 that the use of public school classrooms for religious instruction in a "release time" program was unconstitutional. But in 1952 it approved, by vote of 6 to 3, a New York program releasing children from public school classes for religious instruction elsewhere.

The prayer case was argued for the school district by Bertram B. Daiker of Port Washington for the school district by Bertram B. Daiker of Port Washington, L. I., and for a group of parents supporting the prayer by Porter R. Chandler of New York.

June 26, 1962

SUPREME COURT, 8 TO 1, PROHIBITS LORD'S PRAYER AND BIBLE READING AS PUBLIC SCHOOL REQUIREMENTS

2 CASES DECIDED

Government Must Be Neutral in Religion, Majority Asserts

By ANTHONY LEWIS
Special to The New York Times

WASHINGTON, June 17 — The Supreme Court decided today that no state or locality may require recitation of the Lord's Prayer or Bible verses in public schools.

An 8-to-1 majority wrote what appeared to be a final legal answer to one of the most divisive issues of church and state. The opinion of the Court was by Justice Tom C. Clark.

Even the sole dissenter, Justice Potter Stewart, said that religious ceremonies in public schools could violate the constitutional rights of dissenters. But he found the record in today's cases inadequate and would have sent them back for further hearings.

The prayer cases were among a dozen decided today in what turned out to be the final session of the present Supreme Court term. The Court recessed until October.

Insists on Neutral Stand

Justice Clark sounded the theme that government must be "neutral" in religious matters. His opinion ended with these philosophical phrases:

"The place of religion in our society is an exalted one, achieved through a long tradition of reliance on the home, the church and the inviolable citadel of the individual heart and mind.

"We have come to recognize through bitter experience that it is not within the power of government to invade that citadel,

whether its purpose or effect be to aid or oppose, to advance or retard.

"In the relationship between man and religion, the state is firmly committed to a position of neutrality."

Seek to Soften Criticism

Today's decision was a follow-up to last year's ruling against the recitation in New York public schools of a prayer composed by the State Board of Regents. The Justices were evidently concerned to prevent, as best they could, the bitter criticism that greeted the New York case.

In his opinion Justice Clark stressed the importance of religion in this country's tradition. He took care to say that the decision did not affect the right to use the Bible for teaching purposes or did not deal with such other matters as Army chaplains.

Justices William J. Brennan Jr. and Arthur J. Goldberg, in concurring opinions, also sought to disarm potential criticism. The Goldberg opinion was joined by Justice John Marshall Harlan.

Varied Voices Speak

It was particularly noted by courtroom observers that the voices of a Protestant, a Catholic and a Jew on the Court spoke up for the principle of church-state separation.

Justice Clark is a Presbyterian active in the affairs of his church here. Justice Brennan is the Court's only Roman Catholic and Justice Goldberg the only Jewish member.

The Court's decision dealt with two cases, from Maryland and Pennsylvania. Each involved both the reading of Bible verses to the students each morning, and the recitation of the Lord's Prayer by the classes in unison. The factual settings differed slightly.

In Pennsylvania a state statute requires the reading of "at least 10 verses from the Holy Bible, without comment, at the

opening of each public school on each school day."

The law was amended in 1959 to allow children to be excused at their parents' request.

A suit challenging the practice was filed by Edward Lewis Schempp, a Unitarian, his wife and two children, Roger and Donna. The children attend Abington Senior High School, near Philadelphia.

In that school the practice is for selected students to read verses from the Bible over the public address system each morning. Then the students in every classroom stand and repeat the Lord's Prayer in unison.

Find Conflict With Beliefs

The Schempps said these exercises conflicted with their religious beliefs. They did not seek to have Roger and Donna excused, feeling—Justice Clark said—that their "relationships with their teachers and classmates would be adversely affected."

The Maryland case involved a ruling of the Baltimore school board requiring the reading of a Bible chapter "and/or The Lord's Prayer" at daily opening exercises in schools.

The case was brought by Mrs. Madalyn Murray and her son, William J. Murray 3d, both professed atheists. They said that William had been subjected to taunts and physical assault in school because of his having objected to the morning exercises.

The lower courts came out opposite ways in the two cases.

A three-judge Federal District Court in Pennsylvania held the prayer and Bible-reading unconstitutional. Maryland's highest tribunal, the Court of Appeals, voted 4 to 3 to sustain the Baltimore practice.

The legal issue was the meaning of the First Amendment's religious provision — "Congress shall make no law respecting an establishment of religion or prohibiting the free exercise thereof."

'Decisively Settled'

First, Justice Clark said the Supreme Court had "decisively settled" that these two clauses -- on establishment and free exercise of religion — were made applicable to the states

by the 14th Amendment. He cited cases back to 1940.

Second, he said the Court had "rejected unequivocally the contention that the establishment clause forbids only governmental preference of one religion over another."

He noted that 16 years ago the Court said the clause also forbade laws aiding "one religion or all religions."

No party to the case had questioned these two "long-established" points, Justice Clark said. But he said others had, and so the Court was emphasizing that any doubts about them could only be "academic exercises."

The Regents prayer opinion last year, which was written by Justice Hugo L. Black, rested entirely on the establishment clause of the First Amendment. Justice Clark eventually did so, too, but he discussed the free exercise clause at length along the way.

Both clauses, Justice Clark said, enforce governmental neutrality on religion. If the purpose or effect of legislation is to inhibit or advance religion, he concluded, the Constitution is violated.

But in a free exercise case, the opinion continued, the citizen must show some coercive effect of government action on his religious practices. The establishment clause can be violated without coercing any individual.

Justice Clark said there was no question but that the required recitations in public schools, with children under compulsory school attendance laws, were an establishment. The logic of his opinion would doubtless apply to any teacher's undertaking a prayer exercise without official orders.

Argument Dismissed

The opinion dismissed the argument, made by both Baltimore and Pennsylvania authorities, that these were not religious exercises but were merely designed to promote "moral values."

Justice Clark said:

"Surely the place of the Bible as an instrument of religion cannot be gainsaid."

"It certainly may be said that the Bible is worthy of study for its literary and historic qualities," Justice Clark said.

Pointedly, he remarked that today's decision did not rule out any such study in public schools "when presented objectively as part of a secular program of education.

"But the exercises here do not fall into those categories," he continued. "They are religious exercises, required by the states in violation of the command of the First Amendment that the government maintain strict neutrality, neither aiding nor opposing religion."

Justice Stewart, in his dissent, conceded that the prayer and Bible-reading requirements would be "extremely doubtful" under the establishment clause of the First Amendment if they plainly insisted on a "a particular religious book and a denominational prayer."

But in fact, he said, the Maryland and Pennsylvania practice was to allow the use of varying versions of the Bible —Protestant, Catholic and Jewish. Thus he said the effect was to allow the majority of each community to exercise its religion freely in the public schools.

The real issue, Justice Stewart said, was whether in the course of such exercises minorities were being coerced in their beliefs — denied the free exercise of their religion.

"The dangers of coercion" are greater in a schoolroom than in adult situations, Justice Stewart noted.

He conceded that religious exercises with no provision for students to be excused or to give them some "equally desirable alternative" to occupy their time would be "unconstitutionally coercive."

Says Proof Is Required

But Justice Stewart said all these factors should not be assumed. There should be proof of coercion on any complaining child, he said, and there was none in these cases. Therefore he concluded that further evidence should be taken.

There were three concurring opinions, all expressly joining Justice Clark's views but going on to elaborate personal observations.

Justices Brennan and Goldberg each dismissed as without weight the contention that those cases were somehow different from the Regents prayer because they did not involve material composed by state officials. They called that constitutionally irrelevant.

Both opinions also went out of their way to say that other religious elements in public life would not be affected.

Justice Goldberg emphasized what he termed, here, "the pervasive religiosity and direct governmental involvement."

Some Activities Exempted

Justice Brennan listed a number of activities that he indicated would not be held constitutional violations — the provision of chaplains in prisons and military camps, the saying of prayers in legislatures, teaching about religion, uniform tax exemptions for religious institutions, public welfare benefits that incidentally aid individual worshipers.

The Brennan opinion, 77 printed pages long, canvassed the history of the church-state conflict to show long concern in this country about any breakdown of church-state separation. It concluded:

"The principles which we reaffirm and apply today can hardly be thought novel or radical. They are, in truth, as old as the republic itself."

The third concurring opinion was by Justice William O. Douglas. It briefly repeated a view he expressed in the New York case last year that any use of public funds for a church, however small, is unconstitutional.

Justice Douglas said, that the vice in any such aid is that "the state is lending its assistance to a church's efforts to gain and keep adherents."

The Baltimore case was argued for the Murrays by Leonard J. Kerpelman and for the city by City Solicitor Francis B. Burch; his deputy, George W. Baker Jr., and Attorney General Thomas B. Finan of Maryland.

Henry W. Sayer 3d of Philadelphia represented the Schempps. The state's case was argued by Philip H. Ward 3d of Philadelphia and John D. Killian 3d, Deputy Attorney General.

Mrs. Murray was in the courtroom today with a younger son, 8-year-old Garth. She said they had had stones thrown at their home because of the litigation and that despite today's victory, they were going to leave Baltimore.

United Press International Telephoto

OPPOSED PRAYER IN SCHOOL: Mrs. Madalyn E. Murray and son, Garth, on steps of U. S. Supreme Court yesterday. Mrs. Murray and another son, William, had brought the successful suit to bar prayer or Bible reading in Baltimore schools. William was said to have been taunted in school. At the rear is Mrs. Bonna Mays, Mrs. Murray's mother.

June 18, 1963

CHURCH COLLEGES LOSE AN AID TEST

High Court Leaves Standing Maryland Ban on Help for Nonreligious Purposes

Special to The New York Times

WASHINGTON, Nov. 14—The Supreme Court sidestepped a controversial church-state issue today by declining to review a decision in Maryland that declared unconstitutional public grants to church-affiliated colleges.

The action leaves in effect the ruling by the Court of Appeals of Maryland that colleges of sectarian repute cannot receive public grants, even when the funds were to have been spent for nonreligious purposes. According to the Maryland decision, such grants violate the prohibition contained in the First Amendment to the Federal Constitution, against an official establishment of religion.

Today's action does not indicate approval by the Supreme Court of that doctrine. State grants elsewhere and the Federal program of aid to education are certain to be subjected to new scrutiny now that the Maryland decision has been allowed to stand.

The Federal programs involved are the $1.6-billion program of aid to private colleges and the $1-billion plan for aid to elementary and secondary education.

Immediately after today's announcement, Democratic Senator Sam J. Ervin Jr., a stanch opponent of Federal aid to church schools, called for a law to allow court review of the increasing program of United States aid to private education.

Opponents of Federal grants to church colleges have been unable to obtain a court test because of the Supreme Court's rule, announced in 1923, in the case of Massachusetts vs. Mellon. This ruling held that Federal taxpayers lack standing to challenge in court expenditures of United States funds.

Senator Ervin, a North Carolinian, said that the constitutionality of Federal programs is in doubt and promised to press in the next Congress for a law authorizing taxpayers to challenge any Federal grant, despite the Mellon case.

In the Maryland courts, however, state taxpayers are allowed to contest state grants. The Horace Mann League filed suit in 1964 to invalidate state grants totaling $2.5-million to four colleges.

The league is an organization of several hundred, including some educators. It has been prominent in the fight against Federal aid to higher education.

The grants were earmarked to help construct dormitories, classrooms and science buildings at Notre Dame and St. Joseph Colleges, two Roman Catholic schools for girls; Western Maryland, a school with a Methodist background, and Hood College, which is affiliated with the United Church of Christ.

In a 5-to-4 decision handed down on June 2, 1966, the state's highest court analyzed in detail the religious aspects of each institution and concluded that the two Catholic colleges and the Methodist institution projected a religious "image." It voided the grants to them.

The court approved the grant to Hood College, which it found to be essentially secular in character. The Horace Mann League of the United States appealed this decision. Its appeal was also denied, a hearing today.

The Supreme Court has insisted in recent years on maintaining a wall between church and state, but it and the state courts have followed a varying course in applying the rule to specific situations.

In 1947, the Supreme Court struck down the use of state funds in New Jersey to transport children to parochial schools.

The following year it denied that the First Amendment prohibits the use of school facilities for religious classes. Then, in 1952, it held that the amendment does not prohibit the release of students from public schools for religious purposes.

On Aug. 18, 1966, Justice T. Paul Kane of the New York Supreme Court cited these decisions in declaring unconstitutional a new state law requiring public schools to lend textbooks to parochial school pupils.

The state has appealed the decision and is enforcing the law in the meantime.

Today, Justices Potter Stewart and John M. Harlan announced that they would have agreed to review both the Maryland appeals.

U.S. AIDE ASSESSES SCHOOL AID RULING

Says Maryland Case Won't Affect Federal Program

WASHINGTON, Nov. 15 (AP)—A legislative specialist in the Office of Education said today Federal aid programs under which grants are given to church-affiliated colleges would "continue as they have been."

August Steinhilber of the agency's Office of Legislation made the statement in response to questions as to what effect the Supreme Court's refusal yesterday to review a Maryland case involving state grants to such colleges would have on the Federal program.

In the Maryland case the State Court of Appeals ruled that grants to three church-affiliated colleges to help finance building construction violated the State Constitution. The Maryland court upheld a grant to a fourth, Hood College, because of the looseness of its ties with the United Church of Christ and the diversity of its staff and student body.

Grants to the College of Notre Dame in Baltimore and St. Joseph's College in Emmitsburg, both Roman Catholic schools, and Western Maryland College at Westminster, a Methodist institution, were held unconstitutional.

Certain Grants Authorized

Mr. Steinhilber pointed out that the Higher Education Facilities Act authorized Federal grants for construction of certain types of buildings at church-related colleges.

"The Court refused to hear the Maryland case, which involved only Maryland law," he said. "The Federal Government was not a party to the litigation in any way."

"Our programs will continue as they have been," he went on. "There will be no change in programs, policies and activities."

Existing Federal legislation does not authorize grants to private or parochial elementary or secondary schools.

No grants may be made to colleges for classrooms to be used for religious instruction or for chapels or for any facilities for schools of divinity or theology.

Grants may be made to private and church-related colleges to help finance institutes under the National Defense Education Act and to such schools under the developing college program.

Mr. Steinhilber said that under existing law and prior Supreme Court decisions there was no way that a taxpayer or an organization could seek a court ruling on constitutionality of the Federal programs.

Senator Sam J. Ervin Jr., Democrat of North Carolina, has unsuccessfully sought Congressional approval of legislation to open the way for such a test.

Pennsylvanians Lead School Prayer Revolt

Associated Photographers for The New York Times

Miss Donna Pomella reading a passage from the Bible to her pupils in the first grade at a school in Clairton, Pa.

By BEN A. FRANKLIN
Special to The New York Times

CLAIRTON, Pa. — At 9 o'clock each morning of the school week, Miss Donna Pomella reads a passage from the Bible to her first-grade class at the Fifth Street Elementary School here.

Then, after the children have bowed their heads, the pretty, dark-haired teacher leads the class in a recitation of the Lord's Prayer.

Thus is Scripture being bootlegged into the public schools of the Monongahela Valley—in direct defiance of the United States Supreme Court.

There is a special excitement to the revival of classroom devotion for the people of Clairton, for after six years of obedience they are knowingly performing an illegal if pious act. But the classroom scene here is being re-enacted inconspicuously in countless other communities where school boards have simply ignored the mandate that was handed down by the Court.

Although no precise current information is available, nearly 13 per cent of the nation's public schools—and nearly 50 per cent of the South's—were continuing devotional readings as late as 1966, according to figures compiled by Prof. Richard B. Dierenfield of Macalester College. And by all indications the practice has been spreading since then.

The Supreme Court ruled in 1963 that prescribed religious proceedings of any kind in public schools were unconstitutional because they tended to "coerce" students to take part and thus violated the First Amendment's prohibition against "an establishment of religion" by an agency of the government.

Like Prohibition, however, the prayer ban appears to have little popular acceptance. In Clairton, for example, many people feel that their youngsters "went to hell when God was put out of the classroom."

The combative mood here and in two other Pennsylvania communities that have decided by formal resolution to defy the prayer ban is only a more open form of the tacit defiance elsewhere in the country.

In Alabama, for example, no citizen has challenged the 1927 state law requiring public school teachers to make and report daily Bible readings in class on pain of losing a day's pay for each omission.

So the law there is still on the books and is still observed as if the Supreme Court had never spoken. Similar laws prevail across the Deep South, and there are repeated signs of pressures for a Bible-reading revival elsewhere.

In Maryland last week, the State House of Delegates voted, 87 to 34, in support of a measure that in theory would have restored worship to the classrooms. But then it reversed itself, 88 to 17, when Jewish legislators expressed their objections.

In much of the West and Midwest, according to various church spokesmen, Bible and prayer reading in school has never been a very widespread practice. Thus, outside the South, the Supreme Court's ban has had its main impact in the Northeast, and the new wave of open defiance appears to be centered here.

State Law Upset

In Clairton and in the rest of Pennsylvania, the Court's decision ended the observance of a 1913 state law requiring the daily reading of "at least 10 verses" of some holy writ—from the King James, Douay, or Revised Standard versions of the Bible or from the Jewish Holy Scripture.

One of the prayer cases included in the decision, Abington v. Schempp, bore directly on the Pennsylvania law and specifically overturned it.

In 1964, the Cornwall-Lebanon joint school district in central Pennsylvania was challenged by a local citizen in the United States District Court at Lewisburg for attempting to reinstate a prescribed morning devotional period. The school board lost in a test case that seemed at the time to have settled the issue. The Supreme Court was upheld.

The state government subsequently published a seven-point guideline suggesting constitutionally appropriate alternatives to prayer that were widely accepted.

The guideline, still in effect, suggests as permissible silent meditation in the classroom and "the objective study" of the Bible "for literary and historic qualities," among other projects.

But it plainly bars prayer and Scripture reading, even where teachers have the nominal option of noncompliance, if the worship period is initiated by school authorities.

The defiance in Clairton, in Fayette County to the south and also in the little community of Phillipsburg near Pennsylvania State University seems likely to spread.

A school board in McKeesport recently failed, by a tied 4-to-4 vote, to follow Clairton's example. Prayer resolutions are expected to come before other Pennsylvania school boards soon.

Widespread Anger Noted

According to school officials, clergymen and lawyers familiar with the phenomenon here, much of industrial and mining western Pennsylvania is angry over the youth rebellion, over crime and permissive courts, over Negroes, taxes and welfare.

The back-to-the-Bible movement, they say, is the visible symptom of a desire to stop talking and start acting in fundamentalist terms that seem tried and true to many Americans.

It is the theory of Carmine V. Molinaro, a Connellsville lawyer and attorney for the Albert Gallatin area school district in Fayette County, that "people are mad at the Government, and since they can't get at the Federal or state government, the only government they can tackle is local government. So they are doing it."

Under public pressure, the Gallatin district school board voted unanimously last week to join Clairton in restoring Bible reading and prayer in the schools.

Lawyer's Advice Unheeded

Mr. Molinaro said he had strongly counseled his board that what they were asked to do in citizen petitions and in personal confrontations at a

public meeting was unconstitutional and ill-advised.

But among the 300 angry citizens at the meeting who were pressing for Bible and prayer reading was William E. Duffield, an outspoken Uniontown lawyer who was a Presidential supporter of George C. Wallace and is president of the Fayette County Anti-Tax Protest Committee. And the school board was apparently in no

The New York Times   March 26, 1969

School prayers are read or urged in underlined cities.

mood to invite the wrath of that rapidly growing and militant group.

"What we have here is really a revolution in a mild sense of the word," Mr. Molinaro said. Agreeing, Mr. Duffield commented on the acknowledged unconstitutionality of the board's prayer decision by declaring: "The Boston Tea Party was illegal too."

Students in the Gallatin district have not begun morning prayers yet because the school administration, on Mr. Molinaro's advice, is moving cautiously in implementing the board's resolution, which calls for "Mass nondenominational prayer" in language that appears to brook no voluntary or conscientious student evasion.

Interpreted as Optional

In Clairton and in Phillipsburg, on the other hand, the school board action is being interpreted as optional for teachers but not for the pupils. Thus, if a teacher chooses to read the Bible and have prayers—

and most reportedly do under the current emotional circumstances—objecting students would appear to have no recourse.

In any event, according to the thinking of the Supreme Court, voluntarism adds no saving quality.

Few here object. One person who is "of two minds" about classroom prayer is Nick Soich, the rotund, overworked, 40-year-old acting principal of the Fifth Street Elementary School.

"I have qualms," Mr. Soich said. "If you are asking me about prayer, period, I am for prayer, period. But if you are asking about the democratic process in the classroom, I have reservations. This whole question should be resubmitted to the highest court and resolved again so people can understand it."

At the Clairton Junior-Senior High School, a recent Student Council survey among 201 seniors found 116 for prayer and Bible reading, 78 for silent meditation and 7 for no classroom religious observance at all.

The principal, Neil C. Brown, said: "Of course, I don't think there is a Jew in this school, so there is no objection from that quarter."

The citizens of Clairton, with a population of about 18,000, are chiefly of East European and Italian stock. About one-third are Negroes, most of whom are Protestants, and that makes the Roman Catholic and Protestant sectors of the population nearly equal.

Two months ago, against the professional advice of its newly hired school superintendent, Dr. Robert LaFrankie, and against the legal advice of its attorney, the Clairton school board voted 9 to 0, with almost no discussion, to accede to the High School Parent-Teachers Association's request for Bible and prayer reading.

Dr. LaFrankie, at 42 a rather dashing figure in the context of Clairton, is a vigorous, strong-willed, liberal Roman Catholic who has recently held public high school principalships at Engelwood, N. J., and Orangeburg, N. Y. He makes no secret of his personal disapproval of classroom prayer, but

his view of Clairton's parents is a sensitive and understanding one.

'An Attempt to Survive'

"In a time of turmoil in the country," he said in an interview, "our parents think the loss of Bible reading in school has contributed to the deterioration of the United States. This is not only an act of defiance, it is an attempt to survive."

In this gritty steel mill town, 14 miles south of Pittsburgh, the decision has almost been uniformly accepted.

The Pittsburgh Post-Gazette, in a critical editorial, has asked: "How can children be taught to respect the law when their school authorities are deliberately and boastfully defying it?"

But the Clairton decision has brought Dr. LaFrankie close to 1,000 letters "from around the world," he said, and all but 20 were strongly and often emotionally in support of school prayer and Bible reading. Many of the letters came from servicemen, he said.

The schools' act of defiance, in any case, is more a symbol of frustration than an act of constitutional nullification carrying with it a clear-cut risk.

"What the hell," one school official said. "It's illegal, but they can't put us in jail. All they can do is get an injunction."

The Clairton school board has already decided to pay the legal costs of the court fight, if it comes.

The Pittsburgh office of the American Civil Liberties Union, which would like to locate a local plaintiff to file what it regards as "an open-and-shut lawsuit" to end Clairton's defiance, has been unable to recruit a single litigant here.

The only known public dissent came in a recent sermon by the Rev. William Hess, a Methodist five years in his pulpit here.

But the sermon, in which he held that the Supreme Court was on sound theological as well as constitutional ground in its ruling, brought him "some heat," Mr. Hess said.

The minister has declined the A.C.L.U.'s suggestion that he sue the school board.

"I just don't want to put myself on the block," he said.

SUPPORT GROWING FOR PAROCHIAL AID

State Assistance Is Viewed as Cheaper Than Sending Pupils to Public School

By GENE CURRIVAN

A drive for legislation to provide state funds for parochial schools is gaining momentum throughout the nation.

The traditional argument that direct aid is prohibited by the constitutional provision for separation of church and state appears to be overshadowed increasingly by the economic argument that it may be cheaper to aid parochial school pupils now than take on the full cost burden if those schools are forced to close.

Connecticut and Rhode Island this year have agreed to provide direct aid to parochial schools, following the example set last year by Pennsylvania. Similar legislation failed this year in seven states, but proponents are still pushing the idea in at least 22 states.

The Pennsylvania law was challenged several days ago in a key test case in the United States District Court in Philadelphia by six major organizations. The American Jewish Congress, involved in the Pennsylvania case, also plans to bring suits in Rhode Island and Connecticut.

The mounting legislative campaign, bolstered by a recent Supreme Court decision permitting textbook loans to nonpublic schools, has been characterized as "unprecedented" by Joseph B. Robison, director of the Congress' Commission on Law and Social Action.

"The drive is unusual," he said "not only in the amount of pressure generated but also in the kinds of demands made.

"The stress is no longer on such fringe benefits as free buses and textbooks but on outright financing—the payment of tax-raised funds directly into the treasuries of the schools," Mr. Robison said.

"In most of the states in which the legislatures have completed their work, these proposals were defeated," he said. "Notable were Michigan, where a well-publicized, hotly debated drive for various forms of 'parochiaid' was defeated, and New York where the Legislature rejected a variety of proposals — passing only one, which was then vetoed by Governor Rockefeller."

At Grass Roots Level

But the mounting drive "is very hopeful for the future of our schools," according to the Rev. C. Albert Koob, head of the National Catholic Educational Association in Washington. "The interest is considerable and it is mostly at the grass roots level—and spreading fast."

Earlier this year, Msgr. James C. Donohue, a director of the United States Catholic Conference who speaks for the bishops, said that about two million Roman Catholic elementary school pupils would be dropped in the next six years unless there was a vast upsurge in public support. This would represent about half the current enrollment.

In New York state, where all bills failed, the state aid advocates saw future hope in Governor Rockefeller's support for a constitutional amendment that would permit aid to sectarian institutions of higher learning. The present Blaine Amendment precludes state aid to any type of religiously affiliated schools.

Pennsylvania set the pace last year with an appropriation of $4.6-million from the proceeds of harness racing for nonpublic schools and is now seeking $45-million that would dip into cigarette tax revenues. The state's House of Representatives passed the latest measure, but there was doubt about Senate passage even before the Federal Court suit was filed.

"I don't think you can get $45-million out of this Senate for a program that is under legal challenge," said State Senator Preston B. Davis, chairman of the Education Committee.

"The parochial school system is doomed because of spiraling costs. The question is can we help them out during this phasing-out period?"

State Representative Martin P. Mullen, chairman of the Appropriations Committee, who has threatened to block any new taxes required to balance the budget unless the bill is passed, argued that the taxpayers would save "tremendous sums of money" by keeping nonpublic schools open instead of forcing the pupils into the public school system.

Mr. Mullen said four Catholic schools closed last year for financial reasons, 10 more will close in September, and 35 to 45 are expected to close over the next three years unless substantial tax aid is given.

The bill provides for nonpublic educational services in four instructional subjects — modern languages, mathematics, physical education and physical science.

The Connecticut bill, which anticipated a constitutional challenge, will pay $6-million over two years, provides for payment of 20 per cent of salaries of teachers who teach nonreligious subjects

The state also will pay for textbooks on secular subjects in the amount of $10 for each pupil from Grades 1-8 and $15 for each pupil from Grades 9-12.

Furthermore, to induce nonpublic schools to take disadvantaged children, the state will pay 50 per cent of teacher costs in nonreligious subjects where classes have a one-third enrollments of disadvantaged children and 60 per cent of teachers in classes having a two-thirds enrollment of disadvantaged children.

During debate in the Connecticut House, Representative Thomas J. Donnelly, Republican, lamented "the unseemly spectacle of my church scrambling for public funds."

The Connecticut Civil Liberties Union has already announced plans for a suit.

The bill allows for a test of its constitutionality in that payments will not be made until the second year.

Rhode Island came up with $375,000 for part payment of teachers salaries in Grades 1-8. The bill provides for underwriting 15 per cent of salaries of those teaching secular subjects and who receive a minimum of $4,000 a year but not more than the maximum in the public schools.

Gov. Richard B. Ogilvie of Illinois asked unsuccessfully for state grants totaling $32-million for nonpublic schools. The bill was sponsored by Representative Edward J. Copeland, Republican of Chicago, who is of the Jewish faith. The measure asked for $60 for each elementary grade pupil and $90 for each high school student. It passed the House, but failed in the Senate, where there is considerable opposition to the Governor's revenue program.

In Michigan, a bill that would pay up to 75 per cent of salaries of teacher of secular subjects failed by a narrow margin. It would have provided $44-million for 1970-71.

The opposition was composed mostly of the 70,000-member Michigan Education Association, Protestant Church groups and the American Civil Liberties Union. The Catholic proponents were aided by Dutch Reform Church groups in western Michigan working through the Michigan Association of Non-Public Schools.

The Missouri legislature killed a series of bills that would have provided for textbooks, scholarships, busing, driver education and classes for the handicapped. The Catholic groups in Missouri are trying to get a foot in the door rather than go all out for broad-based aid.

State aid bills enacted this year, besides those in Connecticut and Rhode Island, were a text book rental measure in Indiana and a transportation bill in Minnesota. Bills for a wide variety of state aid were defeated in Illinois, Michigan, Montana, Missouri, New Mexico, New York and West Virginia.

June 16, 1969

HIGH COURT, 8 TO 1, FORBIDS STATES TO REIMBURSE PAROCHIAL SCHOOLS; BACKS COLLEGE-LEVEL HELP, 5 TO 4

U.S. PLAN UPHELD

Fund for Constructing Campus Buildings Wins Approval

By FRED P. GRAHAM
Special to The New York Times

WASHINGTON, June 28 — The Supreme Court declared unconstitutional today state programs that reimburse Roman Catholic and other church-related schools for instruction in nonreligious subjects.

With only one Justice — Byron R. White — dissenting, the Court's eight other Justices ruled that direct financial aid of this type involved "excessive entanglement between Government and religion."

However, at the same time the Court upheld by a 5-to-4 vote the Federal Higher Education Facilities Act of 1963, under which $240-million in Federal funds has been paid for the construction of academic buildings on the campuses of private colleges — including church-related colleges.

Provision Is Voided

The Court struck down only one minor feature of the United States law—a provision that after 20 years the colleges could use the buildings for any purposes, including religious ones.

If such buildings were to be converted into chapels or other religious structures, "the original Federal grant will in part have the effect of advancing religion," the Court held.

It therefore declared that feature of the law unconstitutional under the First Amendment's prohibition against any official "establishment of religion."

Chief Justice Warren E. Burger wrote the majority opinion in the state-aid case and the prevailing opinion in the Federal-aid decision.

Division in Voting

The latter opinion was joined by Justices John M. Harlan, Potter Stewart and Harry A. Blackmun, but Justice White, who provided the fifth vote in favor of the law, filed a separate concurring opinion. The dissenters in the United States case were Justices Hugo L. Black, William O. Douglas, William J. Brennan Jr. and Thurgood Marshall.

The decision on direct state aid to parochial schools, which invalidated state laws in Rhode Island and Pennsylvania, marked the first time that the Supreme Court had struck down a law on aid to church schools.

In a series of decisions that began in 1947, the Court upheld such indirect forms of aid as the use of Government-owned buses to transport students to parochial schools and the lending of state-purchased books to parochial students.

This encouraged 36 of the 50 states to enact aid programs that benefit parochial school students in various ways, ranging from busing and free lunches, books and counseling services to the direct salary supplements of parochial school teachers that were declared unconstitutional today.

Further litigation will be required to disclose how many of these programs will fall under the principles announced today.

However, the Americans United for Separation of Church and State—a group that has been active in court challenges against these programs —asserted in a statement that similar salary-supplement laws of Ohio, Connecticut, New Jersey and Illinois will be struck down as a result of today's decision.

Chief Justice Burger took great pains to point out why the "entanglement" between church and state in the state-aid program was enough to invalidate them, while the Federal program could stand.

A key point, he said, is that pre-college church schools are more involved in religious indoctrination than colleges are. Noting the "skepticism of the college student," he held that "there is substance to the conclusion that college students are less impressionable and less susceptible to religious indoctrination" than are elementary and high school students.

He also found fewer entanglements between church and state in the "one-time, single-purpose construction grant" than in continuing salary-supplement programs. Finally, he said, colleges normally do not draw major support from one area, so that bitter state political battles are not likely to erupt over aid to colleges.

A Shift in Emphasis

On the other hand, a major reason for the Court's ruling against the state laws was their "divisive political potential." Mr. Burger's opinion noted that political pressures for increased state aid to hard-pressed parochial schools could be expected to continue.

The opinion stated that political division along religious lines was an "evil" that the First Amendment was designed to avoid, and it left no doubt that the Supreme Curt hoped to put an end to the spreading tendency toward political battles in state legislatures over aid to parochial schools.

Both decisions today marked a shift in the high court's emphasis in cases on aid to church schools.

Previously, the Court had emphasized a "child benefit" theory, which held that aid programs might be constitutional if they benefited primarily the student in the parochial school and not the school. Since most aid programs basically assist the children, aid programs tended to proliferate.

In 1970, the Court hinted at a new approach, when it upheld the New York law that granted real estate tax exemptions to church property. The major rationale of the decision was that if church property were taxed, the church and state might become embroiled in battles over tax assessments, and that excessive "entanglements" were avoided by the tax-exemption system.

This test was used in both decisions today.

Justice White's View

Among the potential "entanglements" that Chief Justice Burger cited were the "comprehensive, discriminating and continuing state surveillance" of parochial schools that would be necessary to see that teachers receiving state funds were not teaching religion or that the money was not otherwise being used to propagate a faith.

Justice White, the swing man in upholding the Federal law and the lone dissenter to the state ruling, said that he would uphold them all on the theory that aid to a separable secular function of a church-related school was not unconstitutional. The fact that religious interests "may substantially benefit" from the aid does not matter, he said.

Although Justice White said that both the Rhode Island and the Pennsylvania laws were constitutional, he dissented only to the Rhode Island decision because of a quirk in the disposition of the appeal in the Pennsylvania case.

In it the Supreme Court reversed the Pennsylvania courts because they had thrown out the suit challenging the law without a trial.

Justice White disagreed with the Supreme Court's further finding that the Pennsylvania law was unconstitutional, but he did not dissent because he felt that there should be a trial to consider if the law operated in an unconstitutional way by allowing religious schools to use public funds for religious purposes.

Justice Brennan, the only Roman Catholic on the Court, stated that all three laws were unconstitutional. He deplored what he saw as the secularizing impact of public assistance on church schools.

By accepting Government funds, Justice Brennan said, Roman Catholic teachers "surrender their right to teach religious courses" and promise not to inject religion into their secular courses.

He insisted that church schools and colleges properly attempt to proselytize, and said that there was no way to separate out the religious and secular functions. Thus, if a school or college was found to be a "sectarian" institution, he would deny it any direct aid.

In a final dissent written by Justice Douglas and signed by Justices Black and Marshall, it was argued that the only difference between the state laws, which were struck down, and the Federal program, which was not, was the theory that "small violations of the First Amendment over a period of years are unconstitutional while a huge violation occurring only once is de minimus."

The Rhode Island law paid up to 15 per cent of the salary of teachers in private schools, provided the teacher taught only "secular subjects." About 250 teachers in nonpublic schools had applied for the grants. All of them were in Roman Catholic schools.

The Pennsylvania law granted $20-million a year from taxes on cigarettes and horse racing to pay for salaries of teachers, textbooks and instructional materials for courses in mathematics, modern foreign languages, physical sciences and physical education.

The challenge to the Federal law arose out of grants to four Connecticut colleges to build libraries and science, arts and language buildings. The colleges were Annhurst College in Woodstock, Fairfield University and Sacred Heart University in Fairfield and Albertus Magnus College in New Haven.

Edward Bennett Williams of Washington argued for the Connecticut colleges and for the Rhode Island plan. F. Michael Ahern, Assistant Attorney General of Connecticut, argued in behalf of the United States law. Charles F. Cottam of the Rhode Island Attorney General's office argued to uphold his state's law. Daniel M. Friedman of the Solicitor General's office also argued to uphold the United States law.

William B. Ball of Harrisburg argued in support of the Pennsylvania law. Henry W. Sawyer 3d of Philadelphia argued for the taxpayers who challenged it. Leo Pfeffer of New York, special counsel of the American Jewish Congress, argued for the taxpapers who challenged the Federal statute and the Rhode Island law.

Milton Stanzler of Providence also argued against the constitutionality of the Rhode Island law.

Ohio Catholics Drop 1st Grade, Cite Costs

Special to The New York Times

CINCINNATI, March 5— The first grade in all primary schools in the Catholic Archdiocese of Cincinnati will be abandoned next September.

This was announced today by the Most Rev. Karl J. Alter, Archbishop of the diocese.

He attributed the decision to what he called an educational crisis that had created problems "universal throughout the Roman Catholic school system of the United States."

At a news conference Archbishop Alter listed these problems facing the schools of the diocese:

Overcrowding, inadequate salaries for teachers, difficulty in obtaining qualified lay teachers at these salaries, and too frequent dropouts of teachers.

About 10,000 children will be affected by the abandonment of the first grade. Some 6,000 reside in Greater Cincinnati—3,000 of them in Cincinnati proper—1,500 in Dayton and 2,500 in Hamilton, Springfield, Sidney and other towns in the 19 southwestern counties that make up the archdiocese.

Wendell Pierce, superintendent of Cincinnati public schools, expressed confidence this afternoon that the city's public school system would be able to accommodate the affected Cincinnati pupils with the same "high level of education that we offer our children throughout our school system."

Annual tuition and fees for students attending the 27 diocesan high schools will be increased to $200 from $185.

The archdiocese released a brochure today entitled "Vital Changes in Archdiocesan Catholic Schools." It said that enrollment had increased more than 100 per cent between 1950 and 1963 — from 49,923 to 100,246.

This increase was greater than in the previous 125 years, the brochure said.

The annual cost of operating the diocesan schools, the brochure reported, has increased from $5 million to $13 million since 1950. The brochure went on:

"Of this total increase of $8 million, $3 million represents the increased cost of salaries for lay teachers alone. It would have been $5 million if these teachers had received the equivalent salaries of public school teachers.

"Because the salaries of lay teachers are so much less than the salaries of teachers in the public schools, it is difficult to recruit qualified teachers.

"The biggest single problem facing the pastors of these parishes with enlarged schools is that of finding competent lay teachers at the meager salaries available. The second biggest problem is to build the necessary physical facilities at constantly mounting costs."

Some 27,600 Catholic schoolchildren in the diocese are enrolled in public elementary and secondary schools here, the brochure said. It continued:

'The ideal of every Catholic child in a Catholic school simply does not exist now. Of the 254 parishes in the archdiocese, 100 parishes have no Catholic school and no prospect of starting one.

"It is estimated that 75 per cent of our Catholic children now attend kindergarten in the public school system; adding one more year to their presence in the public schools will not interfere too seriously with their religious training."

March 6, 196[]

Catholics Here Expanding And Modernizing Schools

By GENE CURRIVAN

The Roman Catholic Archdiocese of New York is modernizing and expanding its schools at a time when some Catholic school systems in other parts of the country have begun to cut back services in face of financial pressures and staff shortages.

Rather than curtail the parochial school effort here, as some Catholic quarters have proposed, the archdiocese reports that it is improving the curriculum, extending modern methods of teaching, providing new equipment and reducing the religious permeation of secular subjects.

A spokesman for the system —the church's third largest in the nation, behind Chicago and Philadelphia—notes that broader interpretation is now given to biblical teaching, with credit to the Jewish tradition.

The new look also includes a more critical self-evaluation —there is greater readiness to admit weaknesses, including a lack of equipment, inadequate science instruction, a shortage of qualified teachers and overcrowding.

The underlying motive for improving the system while others are cutting back was explained by Msgr. Raymond P. Rigney, associate superintendent of schools.

"Since we are in the business of education," Monsignor Rigney said, "we are convinced we have an obligation to make our program as strong as possible, and we will continue to make every effort to accomplish that end."

While some of the smaller Catholic schools here are still little islands of conservatism, the system as a whole has undergone radical changes—although gradual—in recent years. For one important example, it has moved toward closer rapport with the public and the public schools.

There is continuous interchange of views by teachers, administrators and parents. Conferences, parent organization meetings and discussion groups have brought the two systems closer together to discuss mutual problems.

Since many of the Catholic elementary school graduates go on to public high schools, when there is no room for them in the Catholic schools, it is considered important that they be prepared for the transition. This also applies to those who go to college.

A diocesan spokesman said that some parents believed that the youngsters were going into an entirely different world and needed reassurance. He said that while the basic preparation was the same in public and parochial schools, the Catholic student had to be prepared for classes that were marked by the absence of daily prayers and spiritual guidance.

In the past, Catholic schools were often accused of living in a small protective world of their own with little regard for outside realities.

In some cases, it has been charged, their graduates were dissuaded from attending non-Catholic colleges. An admissions officer at Amherst College said that up to 10 years ago it was difficult to get a prospective candidate's transcript or recommendation from some Catholic schools.

An attempt to correct this was made in November, 1961, when the archdiocese sent a directive to all high school principals.

Prompt Return Ordered

"Application blanks and recommendation forms for secular colleges are to be filled out and returned promptly to those colleges in addition to the student's transcripts," the directive said.

"This is to be done even when school officials consider that the student lacks a valid reason to attend a secular college. Where a specific question implying approval of a student's attendance at the college is asked, it may be left unanswered or it may be answered negatively with an explanation. This question may be answered affirmatively wherever there is a valid reason for attendance at secular colleges."

Valid reasons, a spokesman said, may include courses not available at Catholic institutions.

The archdiocese's determination to strengthen its system stands in contrast to reports from other parts of the country. For example, mounting costs and enrollments have led to the curtailment of all first grade classes in the Archdiocese of Cincinnati effective next September. This involves 133 schools and 10,000 children.

These children will be sent to the public schools, for which most of their parents are already paying taxes.

5,539,475 Pupils

Estimates compiled by the National Catholic Welfare Conference show that of 10,374,336 Catholic school children in the country between the ages of 5 and 17, only 5,539,475 are attending elementary or secondary Catholic schools. The others are presumably in public schools.

Canon law says that Catholic children should be educated in Catholic schools, but this has long since been found impracticable and cannot be enforced.

There are too many children and too few schools.

An uncompleted National Catholic Educational Association survey shows that entire grades were dropped in 161 schools throughout the country during the last five years. Although this is but a small percentage of the more than 10,000 schools canvassed, there is speculation in some Catholic quarters that a trend may be developing.

The highly controversial book "Are Parochial Schools the Answer?" by Mary Perkins Ryan has, in fact, caused widespread discussion with its recommendaion that the schools be abolished gradually.

Mrs. Ryan, whose book carried the imprimatur of the Most Rev. Ernest J. Primeau, Bishop of Manchester, N. H., contended that parochial schools were the least effective and most costly way to provide religious education.

A Window Opened

While the Bishop did not support Mrs. Ryan's arguments, he contended that they provided food for thought and "opened a window—and perhaps a door—on this crucial subject."

The open door is welcomed by Msgr. John Paul Haverty, superintendent of the New York Archdiocesan schools.

"Critics of Catholic education are now being heard in the land," he said recently. "This is causing surprise in some quarters and even generating apprehension in the minds of a few.

"Actually this criticism is a welcome phenomenon. It is an indication of our progress. It shows, too, that the public is interested in how well Catholic schools are preparing the millions of future Americans now enrolled in classrooms of Catholic schools across the land.

"The answer given to these critics by the administrators, supervisors and teachers in the 429 schools of the Archdiocese of New York is not one of angry rebuttal. Rather, it is an invitation to examine our broadfront efforts to improve our curriculum, to advance the competency of our staff and to provide additional classrooms within all reasonable means."

New Courses Cited

Monsignor Haverty called attention to new courses in geography, mathematics, religion, art, science and music introduced in the last three years. He cited experimental programs in English, social studies and foreign languages; the inservice courses and institutes to help teachers interpret the philosophy and aims of programs, and the continuing building program.

"This is our answer," he said, "to those who suggest 'phasing-out.' It is the answer our Catholics want. It is the answer we are happy to give."

The monsignor is the administrative head of a private school system that caters to the educational and spiritual needs of 222,232 pupils in 429 schools (330 elementary and 99 secondary). This far-flung complex covers 4,717 square miles from Staten Island to Sullivan County and includes Manhattan and the Bronx and Westchester, Putnam, Ulster, Rockland, Orange and Dutchess Counties.

The other two boroughs of the city—Brooklyn and Queens —make up the Diocese of Brooklyn and have 219,970 pupils in 238 Catholic schools (194 elementary and 44 secondary). The system is similar but completely detached.

This also applies to the Diocese of Rockville Centre, L. I. which has 103 schools (90 elementary and 13 secondary) and 81,413 pupils in Nassau and Suffolk Counties. Both dioceses are similarly undertaking improvement programs.

Control Is Limited

Unlike the New York City Board of Education, which has direct control, financial and otherwise, over its schools, the New York Archdiocesan Board of Education could be better compared with the State Board of Regents.

The archdiocesan board supervises, directs and establishes standards, but the final word is with the schools themselves. All comply with the minimum standards as required by the Board of Regents for all schools in the state, but whether they go beyond that point depends to a large extent on each school's ability to do so.

Some of the poorer schools that depend largely on the donations of their parishioners do not fare as well as the schools sponsored by religious communities, such as the Jesuits or the Dominicans, which receive their support from broad geographical areas. Nor do the parish schools do as well as the archdiocesan high schools, which receive direct help from the archdiocese.

The board, for example, may establish a schedule of salaries for lay teachers, as was done last month, but individual schools may or may not conform immediately, depending on their resources. However, they do conform in the long run—with assistance, if necessary, from headquarters.

$8,300 Maximum

The secondary school salary range, among the highest in the nation for Catholic schools, is from $4,600 to $7,900 a year, with a possible maximum of $8,300 for additional preparation. The public school range here is from $5,300 to $10,575.

The board is like a shepherd with a flock of independent sheep. Some try to be rugged individualists but all manage to remain within the fold.

The titular shepherd is Cardinal Spellman, but the direction of the schools is in the hands of the board, which is headed by Auxiliary Bishop John J. Maguire. His colleagues are Msgr. Terrence J. Cooke, chancellor; Msgr. Edward J. Waterson, pastor of the Church of the Incarnation, Washington Heights, and Msgr. Arthur Scanlon, pastor of St. Helena's Church, Parkchester. The board post of secretary to the Cardinal for education is vacant.

The administrative staff, which has direct control of the schools, is headed by Msgr. Haverty, with headquarters at 31 East 50th Street, just east of St. Patrick's Cathedral.

The entire staff for the administration of schools is composed of only 11 persons, plus a secretarial unit of 10 persons. The priests receive a salary of only $100 a month and the staff budget does not exceed $100,000 a year for the others.

The associate superintendents are Monsignor Rigney, for elementary schools, and Msgr. Edward M. Connors, for secondary schools. Assistant superintendents are Msgr. John T. Doherty, for religious education, and the Rev. Joseph T. Riordan, for the Staten Island schools.

Members of this staff, which is ordinarily occupied with routine matters, now serve as discussion leaders in a rapidly growing grass-roots movement that has taken hold throughout the archdiocese. As one Catholic parent puts it: "They used to discourage parents who tried to take part in school affairs; now they invite us to speak our piece."

The new involvement by parents and teachers in the problems that confront Catholic education, plus particularly a growing and outspoken criticism by Catholic parents concerning weaknesses in the parochial educational process, have brought about an increasing series of regional meetings with greater lay participation than ever before.

The New York Times (by Neal Boenzi)

PRAYER IN PAROCHIAL CLASSROOM: Sister Jeanne Regis leading first-grade pupils in a prayer at the St. Francis de Sales elementary school at 166 East 97th Street.

May 4, 1964

CATHOLICS URGING LAY SCHOOL VOICE

Education Panel Calls on All Diocesan Boards to Halt Control by the Clergy

By GENE CURRIVAN

Recommendations that would end the absolute control by the clergy of Roman Catholic elementary school boards have been made to superintendents throughout the country by a special committee of the National Catholic Educational Association.

Under the plan, the boards, which are mostly controlled by local pastors, would have predominantly lay membership with parents having a voice in policy making.

There are now 110 lay boards throughout the country, mostly in the western states, with only two in the Archdiocese of New York, but the movement is gaining momentum despite opposition by some pastors. Those in New York are at Corpus Christi School, 535 West 131st Street, and Immaculate Conception School at Irvington-on-Hudson, in Westchester County.

The plan was disclosed yesterday by Msgr. O'Neil C. D'Amour, superintendent of Catholic schools at Marquette, Mich., and chairman of the Superintendent's Ad Hoc Committee on School Boards.

"We have had a hopelessly anachronistic structure in the past," he said, "but it must now reflect the Catholic community as it is today and not what it was."

He predicted that within five years 90 per cent of the parish boards would have lay members.

Under the recommendations the lay members would be elected from names selected by a parish-appointed nominating committee. All members of the parish would vote in the election. Other voting members of the board would be the pastor and the school principal. It would be a seven-member board with the bishop and diocesan superintendent as ex-officio but non-voting members.

The board's duties would include responsibility for annual budget, salary scales, tuition rates, retirement policies, hiring and firing of lay personnel; implementation of policies by the diocesan board of education; coordination of parochial educational activities; liaison with state bodies; evaluation of the effectiveness of programs; direction for all policies under which administrative officers shall operate the educational program of the parish; determination of policies relating to planning, operating and maintenance of facilities and equipment, and serving on the planning and building committee.

Reaction to lay boards was heard yesterday at a post-convention meeting of lay and religious leaders at the Hilton Hotel under the sponsorship of the school superintendents department of the association. The association ended its four-day annual convention here on Thursday.

Clerical Teachers Criticized

A discordant note was heard from William Holub, general manager of America, the Catholic magazine. He contended that the laity which, he said, had been virtually ignored by the educational clergy over the years, was now being asked to "come to the defense of education".

He was critical of the "untrained, incompetent and uncommunicative" members of the clergy "who qualified for their positions only because they lived long enough to become pastors."

Mr. Holub deplored the low salaries that were paid and said "it was a dodge at best to expect these teachers to be apostolic or work for God".

"A poor teacher", he declared, "is a poor teacher whether in habit, robe or suit".

James J. Fadden, Acting City Commissioner of Labor, proposed a lay board with 100 per cent lay membership.

Msgr. James C. Donohue, superintendent of diocesan schools at Baltimore, which has an operating lay board, said it was formed "to speak for the community and not be a rubber stamp for the superintendent, the pastor or even the archbishop".

April 24, 1965

VATICAN COUNCIL STIRS REVOLUTION IN THE CLASSROOM

Decrees Will Deeply Affect Schools, but Full Impact Will Take Some Time

By JOHN COGLEY

The decrees of the Ecumenical Council Vatican II will deeply affect Roman Catholic education all down the line.

It will take time for the full impact of the council to reach the local parish or even to penetrate a few universities still bogged down in pre-council thinking. But with the speed of modern communications, the catching-up period will be much shorter than the 30 years it took for the results of the 16th-century Council of Trent to be implemented throughout the church.

Roman Catholicism, specifically the Catholic education endeavor, can never be the same again, for Vatican II was revolutionary in its scope. It was a revolution in the best sense, in that it changed attitudes and did not simply overturn an existing order.

A Social Movement

When the changed attitudes reach the local level with full force, the impact of the council may mark as sharp a turning point in the classroom approach as the pontificate of Pope John XXIII did in the thinking of his bishops.

As the Rev. Andrew M. Greeley, a priest-sociologist of the University of Chicago, wrote not long ago in America, the Jesuit review:

"From the social science point of view, I am compelled to say that social movements (and make no mistake about it, the aggiornamento is a real winging of a social movement) cannot be stopped once they have begun. They may be challenged, they may be directed, they may be guided, but attempts to slow them behind their natural pace are usually a sure - fire guarantee of trouble."

New Guiding Spirit

The Vatican Council dealt specifically with education in only one of its 16 decrees, and it was not one of its outstanding products — indeed, in the opinion of many theologians and educators at the council it left much to be desired.

However, the more basic council doctrines, like the masterly "De Ecclesia" ("On the Church"), the declaration on religious liberty and on non-Christians and the decree of ecumenism, will count for more in the long run than the statement on Catholic schools.

These decrees express the guiding spirit of the council and deal directly with the new Roman Catholic attitude toward the world outside the church. The mood of the council, which is certain to permeate all the institutions of Catholicism in time, is expressed in them. It is this mood, however elusive, more than directives, that will shake up the church schools.

The mood of the Council of Trent, the great Counter-Reformation synod, was set by the events of its time. Christendom was breaking up; doctrines deemed central to Roman Catholic Christianity were being widely denied; the predominate religious energy of Europe was being poured into an enthusiastic, untried Protestantism.

In response, the Roman Catholic Church adopted a defensive, highly disciplined, militant posture. Reforms were decreed and implemented through tight regulations. The doctrines of the faith were formulated with a new rigidity. The church assumed the mentality of an institution under siege. Tremendous emphasis was placed on the importance of obedience to ecclesiastical rules and order in the ranks. The church itself was looked upon in pyramidal terms, rather like an army ever ready for combat that might come from anywhere in a hostile, highly competitive world.

Obedience and Readiness

At the peak of the ecclesiastical pyramid was the Pope of Rome; below him the bishops and the ordinary clergy, and the base was made up of the faithful, who were expected to accept the tremendous challenges facing the church in a spirit of willing obedience and ever-alert readiness.

That spirit hung on in Catholicism for 400 years. It deeply affected the tone of Catholic education, from kindergarten to graduate school. The mood of stern Christian apologies and group defensiveness touched the learning process throughout the vast parochial school system in the United States.

This had its advantages as well as its obvious disadvantages. It meant, for example, that Catholic education frequently was slow to adopt ex-

ST. JOHN'S STUDENTS PROTEST ACADEMIC POLICY: At the university's Queens campus, students rallied to demand greater academic freedom. Issue reached its high point with dismissal of more than 25 members of faculty.

perimental techniques and clung to traditional methods in the classroom. As a result, the church's schools were spared many of the disillusionments that came from excessive devotion to the latest revelation in pedagogy and mindless enthusiasm for the most recent fad.

It also meant that some Catholic schools passed up the more worthwhile developments in educational theory and lagged behind others in adopting fresh techniques.

The defensive, excessively parochial, overwhelmingly apologetic mood of the church sometimes reached almost absurd limits in the schools.

For example, it affected the teaching of history, which was sometimes taught as a constant series of high - noon confrontations between Catholic heroes in white sombreros and their black - hatted opponents.

Spelling words and examples of abbreviations as often as not were chosen from an ecclesi-

astical vocabulary: spell Eucharist, confirmation, hyperdulia; abbreviate monsignor, Right Reverend, requiescat in pace.

In arithmetic, little Johnny was asked to figure out the sum of four guardian angels plus 12 guardian angels.

At the higher levels, philosophy courses in the lesser institutions were sometimes little more than guided tours through the metaphysical realms of Thomism, with scant justice done to other towering figures of religious thought and practically none to those beyond the Christian pale. The Reformation, seen through sectarian eyes, became the Protestant Revolt.

Derived From Pope John

The new spirit, the spirit of the Vatican Council, could hardly be more different. Above all, the mood of the recent council derived from the spirit of Pope John.

It represented the altogether unexpected triumph of the late

Pope's "open," ecumenical, affirmative attitude over the old clerical fears and hesitancies about the world beyond the church. Almost certainly, though it is not clear yet, it also represented the defeat of narrowly conceived sectarian claims and tribal exclusivism among the laity.

In short, Vatican II marked the formal end of the Roman Catholic "siege mentality." The rest may be only a matter of the people catching up with their leaders.

Under the new dispensation, observers of the Catholic school system can expect a more expansive notion of the church and its commitments to prevail in the classroom. The student of "De Ecclesia" can hardly cling to the old-style view of the Catholic as a man caught in his religious ghetto, self - banished from participation in the modern world, and living in a

constant state of military qui vive:

According to that council decree, the church's responsibility for the world and its welfare is grave. The proper attitude toward other faiths, secular humanism and even atheism is a desire for mutual understanding and thoughtful dialogue.

The central problem for the modern Catholic, according to the council, is not to damn and denounce modernity, even in its most reprehensible form (the Council avoided condemning communism itself) but to understand it, to take what is good in it, and freely, almost enthusiastically, to accept the difficulties involved in integrating new knowledge with an old faith.

With such an assignment, Catholic schools may be the home of the most exciting developments in education in the next few years. The winds of revolution — bracing, invigorating, productive — are already blowing through them.

Catholic Schools May Drop 2 Million Pupils

By GENE CURRIVAN

A spokesman for the nation's Roman Catholic bishops has warned that the church's elementary schools will close their doors to almost two million pupils—about half the enrollment—unless there is a vast upsurge in public support for Catholic education over the next six years.

This means that many of the 10,000 elementary schools in the nation may close despite aid expected from state governments. The message to the Catholic laity, in substance, is that it must pay more if it wants to maintain quality parochial education.

The warning came from Msgr. James C. Donoghue, director of the Division of Elementary and Secondary Education of the United States Catholic Conference in Washington, which represents the nation's Catholic bishops. He said the impact on the high schools would not be as great because they are largely self-supporting.

Monsignor Donoghue made the declaration in a recent interview while pondering a constant flow of reports from around the nation on school closings, decreasing enrollments, dwindling finances and a scarcity of teaching nuns.

These problems will receive close attention at a meeting of the Catholic Educational Association, which opens today in Detroit.

In 1968, 360 Catholic elementary schools and 125 high schools were closed, and reports indicate many more closings will follow. Enrollment in elementary and secondary schools has dropped to 4,982,927 in the current school year from 5,600,519 four years ago.

The decline of parochial education has implications for non-Catholics because a steady rise in the flow of students from church to public schools seems likely to jam some already overcrowded urban schools without any compensating rise in school revenues.

Although the church makes public no over-all figures on costs and revenue, officials say the financial crisis stems from steadily mounting operating

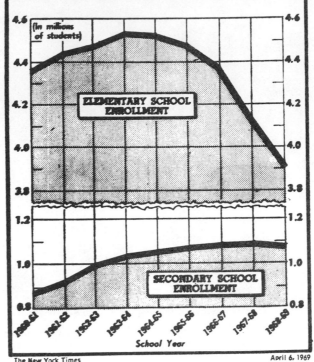

(In millions of students)

ELEMENTARY SCHOOL ENROLLMENT

SECONDARY SCHOOL ENROLLMENT

School Year

The New York Times   April 6, 1969

costs and decreasing revenues in the $1.7-billion-a-year operation.

They say Catholic parents, who already support public schools through taxes, are rebelling against increased tuitions, averaging $338 a year, and are sending their children to public schools.

While the preponderance of school closings so far has been in rural areas, the trend is showing signs of moving into the large cities as well.

The New York archdiocese has closed 17 schools since 1963, mostly in rural areas, but will close four this year in the inner city.

The Milwaukee archdiocese has announced that 18 elementary schools, mostly in rural areas, will close. Later, it said that three inner city schools originally scheduled for closing would continue as nondenominational schools under parental control.

In Boston, Richard Cardinal Cushing has made a direct public appeal for contributions.

He denied published reports that he would close down the high school system, but he told the parents of 9,100 pupils in 14 high schools that he was facing a debt of $10-million and that the operating deficit for 1969-70 was budgeted at $1.6-million, or $177.78 a student.

'Next 2 Years Critical'

In Buffalo, Msgr. Leo E. Hammerl said the operating loss this year would be $400,000, with a $1-million deficit in prospect next year. There have been no closings, but "the next two years will be critical," he said.

In Chicago, six high schools and one elementary school will close in June. Since June, 1967, 11 elementary schools and six high schools have been closed. Monsignor Donoghue said that while government aid would be helpful, the answer to the problem was more support from the Catholic lay public.

"There has to be a groundswell of public support," he said. "We have to know what the parents want. The bishops want to continue offering as much Catholic education as possible, but they can't maintain the present schools without help.

No System Closings Planned

"If the groundswell is great enough, the bishops will listen. I am sure that if the seriousness of the present predicament dawned on the people the situation could be reversed. If the

poor people of the country built the Catholic schools, why can't the more affluent support them?"

Many Catholic laymen have taken a different stand in their appearances before state legislators. Some of them have predicted the possible closing of entire diocesan systems if government aid is not forthcoming.

Monsignor Donoghue characterized this as "bordering on blackmail." He said he knew of no bishop who contemplated closing a school system.

"The total closing threat," he said, "is political and tactical. It may have some value in showing how parochial schools save money for public schools but I have my doubts about its use. However, it seems less fictional than ever before. I haven't met a bishop who has built a new elementary school in the past two years."

Seventeen state legislatures are weighing various measures to aid the parochial schools.

In New York, a bill sponsored by Senator John J. Marchi, Republican of Staten Island, would give each pupil from $50 to $250 a year depending on need.

Other proposals include busing and the loaning of textbooks in Missouri, tuition aid of $150 a pupil in Connecticut and payment of some teacher salaries in Michigan.

In Pennsylvania, where the Legislature earmarked $4.3-million for private education, the Philadelphia archdiocese is trying to raise more than $3-million from parishioners to guarantee continuance of the Catholic schools.

Msgr. Edward M. Connors, superintendent of the New York archdiocesan schools, said the closing of some schools was no longer a threat but "a general alarm."

"We have been trying for years to tell the Catholic laity that if they want Catholic schools they have to pay for them," he said. "Unfortunately the message doesn't seem to get across until we actually close a school. Threats impress no one. Just in the inner city schools alone we are helping with parish deficits to the amount of $2-million a year. We can't raise tuition much more, so the archdiocese has to pay the bill."

"There is little money in the ghetto areas" he continued, "although many mothers and fathers are holding extra jobs to keep children in school. If we had the finances, we could, for example, fill the Harlem schools three times over, but instead we must turn pupils away."

Tuition in the elementary schools runs from $3 to $10 a month with scaled-down rates for siblings. The average in the high schools is $30 a month.

Monsignor Connors said that the archdiocese would have to cut back about 50 per cent in enrollment at the elementary school level within 10 years unless there was massive public support.

In the diocese of Brooklyn, which includes Queens, Msgr. Eugene J. Molloy, secretary of education, and his superintendent, the Rev. Franklin E. Fitzpatrick, agreed that if there was not fuller public support by 1975 the system would be drastically cut.

There was no new building last year, and none is planned.

With class size reduced and more teachers needed, the Brooklyn diocese turned away 17,000 high school and elementary pupils this year.

Religious teachers receive about $1,600 a year in Brooklyn.

The diocese has just signed a new contract with its elementary school lay teachers for a minimum of $5,800 and a maximum of $8,800—an $800 increase. Public school salaries in New York City run from $6,750 to $13,750.

Bishops Nonplussed

Throughout the nation, bishops seem to be nonplussed with the situation. Many have ordered in-depth surveys, but in many cases the search for accurate statistics is unavailing because the schools are run under not one, but three systems—the dioceses, the parishes and the religious orders.

Coordination of facts, it has been found, is difficult because some of the orders jealously protect their virtual autonomy and computers are few and far between.

In Hartford, Conn., the archdiocese is holding the line pending the outcome of legislation to ease the financial strain. While no schools have been closed, a recent statement by Connecticut bishops said a "substantial" number of parochial schools will close within two years unless state aid is forthcoming. There are 94,000 pupils in the Catholic schools.

Rochester, N. Y., parents volunteered as janitors and secretaries to keep the Catholic schools open.

The Kansas City-St. Joseph diocese will close nine elementary schools this fall, and in Detroit, four elementary schools and five high schools are scheduled to close at the end of the year. A spokesman for the Detroit archdiocese said: "A good many more will have to close."

Viewing the national situation, Monsignor Donoghue said that even with massive government support, which he felt would not pay teachers' salaries or build schools, a cutback in Catholic education would still be necessary unless there was continuous public support.

However, he said, the cutback will not mean schools for the elite.

"The strength of the church is going to be in what will be done for the Negroes and Puerto Ricans," he said.

The nation's bishops, facing the necessity of denying a Catholic school education to half of the elementary school children who would ordinarily receive it, appear to be wondering how much faith they can put in the faithful, who, they feel, must ultimately pay the bill.

April 6, 1969

Catholic Schools:

Their Days May Be Numbered

A year ago, the former secretary of education for the Archdiocese of New York warned that the Catholic school system of the United States could be destroyed "from within" by the very persons who teach and administer in them. Msgr. George A. Kelly, a professor in contemporary Catholic problems at St. John's University, cited "some priests, some Brothers, and some Sisters" of Catholic teaching orders, who would pull their religious communities out of Catholic education, to meet new and different challenges.

Last Monday the Archdiocese of New York's school system — with 192,861 students spread over 10 counties, the fourth largest Catholic system in the country — was indeed threatened "from within," but from another source. The Federation of

Catholic Teachers, Local 2092, AFL-CIO, representing some 1,400 of the 2,800 lay teachers of the archdiocese, struck over wages and pay parity between elementary and high school teachers. The strike closed four schools in Manhattan and the Bronx—where the union's membership is heaviest — and disrupted 110 more of the diocese's 406 schools. F.C.T. is represented in 329 of the schools.

The Thanksgiving holiday blunted the initial impact of the strike, and today representatives of the union and of the Association of Catholic Schools, the administrative unit which is bargaining for the archdiocese, return to the negotiating table. Despite this move, the strike could still be lengthy particularly if F. C. T. president Barry F. Ryan stands firm on the issue of pay parity. He has maintained right along that it was "parity or bust."

The union's demands seemed hardly exorbitant. Its proposal of a 10-step, $8,500 to $15,400 salary scale would, if granted in full, still leave Catholic school teachers well behind their New York public school counterparts, who receive $9,400 to $16,950 in eight increments. Likewise, high school-grade school pay parity would give Catholic teachers a benefit which New York public school teachers have had since 1947.

The archdiocese, for its part, was not inclined to trumpet its offer of $200 more for elementary teachers, $400 for high school instructors, and $600 to those without degrees. "Every-

one is in favor of paying them as good a wage as public school teachers or better," said Msgr. Donald J. Pryor for the Association of Catholic Schools. "It means the caliber of our teachers would be better."

For the archdiocese, however, there is the problem that the money is not there to give. The Catholic school system operates on a deficit that could reach $31.4-million per year by 1972, according to one study. To meet the teachers' full demands would cost $10-million by one estimate, and swell the deficit to the point where, in Monsignor Pryor's words, "certainly one-third and perhaps as much as one-half" of the schools would be put out of business.

For the time being, however, the burden of a presumed settlement between the archdiocese and the lay teachers will fall on the parishes. Only about one-fourth of operating expenses come from tuitions, the remainder being made up primarily by parish subsidies. Some 60 to 70 percent of parish budgets are already going for support of the parish school, an imbalance at any time but never more so than in a period of tight money and declining church revenues. The net effect may be to make Catholic schools more and more a suburban institution, since only the more affluent suburban parishes will be able to afford them.

But even in the suburbs money is not the whole answer. In inner-city

93

and transition areas, seats are filled in Catholic schools, perhaps because the parochial school, with its discipline and tighter cultural knit, can be a seeming island of stability in an otherwise chaotic world. But in settled suburban areas, Catholic school officials are confronted with the phenomenon of open desks and empty seats, sometimes ranging as high as 30 percent.

Part of the explanation, of course, is the falling Catholic birth rate.

Part, also, is what a study conducted for the state's Fleischmann Commission terms "changing Catholic tastes." The study, done in conjunction with the commission's analysis of the "quality, cost and financing" of elementary and secondary education in the state, related the changing tastes to items such as better physical facilities and more convenient locations rather than to substantive qualitative differences between the public and the Catholic school systems. The academic quality of the two systems "compare favorably," the study stated.

Perhaps — but nowhere near all Catholic parents are so sanguine about the quality of Catholic schools. Larger class sizes, fewer top-qualified teachers, and an inability to match the enrichment programs of public schools in such fields as mathematics, music, science, languages and physical-education have prompted many Catholic parents to look elsewhere for a school for their children.

Another problem is the Catholic school system's retention of the old 8-4 grade sequence — eight grades of grammar school and four of high — years after the public school system has introduced the intermediate school and gone to a 6-3-3 grade sequence. This poses particular difficulty in areas where there is no parochial high school. To spare the child the adjustment troubles that come from moving from the eighth grade of Catholic school into the second

The New York Times/Neal Boenzi

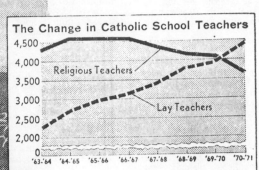

The Change in Catholic School Teachers

New York's Roman Catholic schools were disrupted last week by a strike of lay teachers, a growing percentage of the parochial schools' teacher body (see chart).

years of intermediate school, many parents prefer to transfer the child after the sixth grade into public school. This leaves the seventh and eighth grades of many suburban Catholic schools seriously depopulated.

The decline in religious vocations is another factor. Some parents conclude that if the drain-off of teaching religious means that their child is going to be taught by a lay person, then they might just as well send the child to public school. Among other considerations, the move saves tuition fees, an average of $150 for elementary school but which can be $900 for high schools.

Finally, there is a growing suspicion among increasing numbers of Catholics that the Catholic school may not be the place after all to prepare

a child for life in a pluralistic society. They worry that the low racial mix of the Catholic school and the absence of children of other faiths will give the child a distorted impression of the world in which he must one day function.

It is developments such as these which contribute to a feeling that the striking lay teachers and school officials of the archdiocese may actually be but bit players in a drama which is larger than both of them, and which will be settled by issues which are not even on the negotiating table.

—JOHN DEEDY

Mr. Deedy is managing editor of Commonweal magazine.

The Key Role of the Private School

Far from being superfluous, the 3,000 such schools that exist today face

new responsibility—not to replace the public schools,

but to help them gain strength and vigor.

By GRACE and FRED M. HECHINGER

ONE morning not long ago a distinguished professor at one of our large urban universities phoned for advice about a good private school for his teen-age daughter. He was apologetic about the inquiry because he had been known for his eloquent speeches on the importance of the public schools as the foundation of American democracy.

"It isn't that I don't believe in the public schools for my own family," he explained. "But the slums are moving in on our campus. I want to remain near the university. The public schools around our neighborhood are deteriorating, and even the way to and from school is getting to be a problem for our girl."

Unfortunately, the professor's case is not an isolated one. The recent curtailment of extracurricular activities in New York schools and the current threat of teachers' strikes dramatize the problem. True, the answer should be a renewed effort to improve the public schools; but for many parents the crisis is an immediate one, and often the alternatives are either to move to a better school district or to send their children to private schools. While, in the past, parents chose private schools mainly for reasons of exclusiveness, family tradition and even class consciousness, today the waiting lists are filled by those who simply want to permit their children to escape from the pressures and inadequacies of many urban public schools.

In addition, the prospect of overcrowded colleges and tightened admission policies hangs heavily over the scene. Many parents feel that acceptance by a good private school will pave the road toward higher education.

Nothing should obscure the fact that the public schools, with their enrollment of about 34,000,000 boys and girls, are the educational cornerstone of popular government and of an open society. No matter how good the private schools may be, the future of the country will depend on the over-all success of the public schools. And yet the present plight of public education, especially in the financially hard-pressed cities, has brought a new focus of attention on the private schools.

THE question is therefore valid: Is the private school merely a spare tire? If the public schools catch up with the demands of our time, will the private schools then be superfluous?

The answer is "No." If one vital aspect of freedom is based on the availability of tuition-free public education of high standards, freedom of choice is equally important. "It is sound American doctrine that a man is free to choose whatever school he pleases for his children and for whatever reason, regardless of whether his reason seems good or bad to anybody else," says Allan V. Heely, headmaster of The Lawrenceville School. "It is essential to our purposes as a nation to preserve that freedom."

Monopoly is rarely, if ever, good for democracy. It is in the best interest of the public schools themselves to prevent them from becoming a monopoly. This is assured by the existence, first, of the Catholic, Protestant and Jewish parochial schools (which enroll close to 5,000,000 students) and, second, of the roughly 3,000 independent schools which enroll only a little over 2 per cent of all elementary and high school pupils.

About the parochial schools there need be no further discussion. They guarantee the important right of parents to provide religiously oriented education for their children. But what about the independent schools? The amount of interest in them today shows that their importance is far greater than the size of their enrollment might indicate.

The real answer concerning the place of the private schools in the fabric of American education is not to be found in a debate as to which is better, private or public education. There are some shining, and some terrible, examples on either side of the fence. Besides, there are many kinds of private schools. Some are coeducational; others are "separate." Some are "progressive" and experimental; others adhere to the very essence of traditional education. Some are day schools; others are boarding schools; still others combine the two. Some specialize in problem children. Some are bastions of the intellect. The great majority have

as their special goal the preparation of students for higher education.

THE greatest value of the private schools, not only to their students but to the public schools as well, lies in the competition they have created in the nation-wide search for quality and high standards. Since the private schools are selective they can tailor their student bodies to the standards they believe essential. Thus their task is easier from the very start.

Yet by carrying out that task they continue to provide an invaluable yardstick for those public schools which also want to offer a demanding curriculum to their college-preparatory students. It is no coincidence that the study plan outlined by Dr. James B. Conant, former president of Harvard, as a minimum requirement for the top 15 to 20 per cent of the high school population comes pretty close to the traditional fare offered at the better private schools. If it is relatively easy for private schools to preserve such vanishing studies as Latin, ancient history and, occasionally, Greek, it is equally important that they are often free to try their hand at experimentation, without prior approval from school boards and representative town meetings. (The trustees of a good private school would hardly get involved in matters which they consider the headmaster and faculty competent to decide.) This is why some of the top private schools led the way in such experiments as the "early admission" to college. Having done this they cleared the path for forward-looking public schools to follow and, in turn, to lead the way for their more cautious contemporaries.

While some mediocre public schools, through envy, deny these private school advantages, the really good ones gladly acknowledge their debt. Some years ago, when the independent Park School in Baltimore celebrated an important anniversary, the city's public school leaders were among the most enthusiastic well-wishers.

In fact, public schools in the wealthy commuter suburbs have, by popular demand of their Ivy-League-oriented constituents, turned themselves into public college-preparatory schools cut to the private school pattern. While they cannot overlook the needs of a small, non-college-going minority (which in some Westchester, Fairfield County and Winnetka-type areas is less than 20 per cent), their curriculum is the mirror-image of the Andovers and Exeters. The town of Fairfield, Conn., has even organized its public high schools along a "house plan" which places small subdivisions of 400 students under separate house masters.

SOME less fortunate suburbs, of course, have not been able to keep pace with their own pressures. In his "Prep School Guide," Clarence E. Lovejoy writes: "Let us say that 10,000 new residents build homes and move into a suburban area. The hard core of old residents welcomes the new families but doesn't want to do enough for the children. * * * If more and better education means higher taxes, then they vote in the negative. No wonder newly removed families in some suburbs seek private prep schools!"

It is almost ironic that the two escape hatches from the hard-pressed city schools have been either the private schools or suburban public schools, created in the private school image.

Overcrowding is not the only public school problem which gives the private schools an advantage. It is never easy to make policy in a goldfish bowl. Yet, that is exactly what the public schools are often forced to do. At a recent meeting, when the public schools' tendency to add courses upon courses came under fire, an experienced high school principal spoke up. "Let me read you a list of organizations which, in our little community alone, demand to be heard," he said. The list included some thirty groups with a more or less legitimate reason for having a say about the curriculum. Then the school administrator added: "We need the support of many publics to get the funds we need. Many of these groups are truly helpful. But, of course, their ideas of what is good education are far from unanimous."

True, private school headmasters and trustees, too, must raise funds and appeal to their public. But their constituents' views on education tend to be fairly similar. Few of them, for example, are likely to pressure for the addition of a course in "citizenship." Nor are they apt to demand driver education, just because without it there will be a rise in automobile insurance rates. (Not long ago a State Superintendent of Public Instruction stated that it is no more important to learn to read than it is to drive a car.)

OF course, good public schools fight against such follies. But the struggle itself consumes valuable energy.

Nor is the private school as severely bound by the rules of teacher accreditation. When a visitor to an excellent Friends' school commented on the superior performance of a young English teacher, the headmaster said: "I must thank our state certification requirements for her presence. She had a brilliant college record, but lacks the teacher training requirements to teach in a public school."

Perhaps the very size of the public school system makes rigid ground rules inevitable. But the greater independence and reliance on personality judgment gives the private school an obvious advantage.

Since the private schools need not cope with unlimited numbers of students, they have been able to keep their teacher-pupil ratio at about 1 to 10, compared with the public schools' 1 to 28. In the case of the boarding school, this advantage is increased by the around-the-clock cohesion of campus life.

Sooner or later, the question is inevitable: What about the snobbery of the private schools? Do they consciously create a world of privilege, both in fact and in the minds of their students?

MUCH of this image is a hangover from the past. It is true that a few loyal "Grotties" still register their sons at Groton before they leave the maternity ward. But Sonny's acceptance is no longer assured, just because Dad went there. More important, most good private schools today admit a great many scholarship students. In the boarding schools, scholarship students average about 20 per cent. In some schools the figure runs to 50 per cent. Even in the day schools it is nearly 15 per cent.

The picture of the starched-collared and stuffed-shirted prep school boy, served by waiters and serviced by maids, is an anachronism. Today's boarding student is more likely to make his own bed, clean up his room and wait on table according to an alphabetical duty roster. How many of his suburban public high school contemporaries do as much? In fact, there are some wealthy public school districts where the snob dictate of living up to the Junior Joneses, in such matters as clothes and convertibles, is more compelling than in many private schools where the scholarship boy from Ohio looks and lives exactly like the alumnus' son from Tuxedo Park.

Those who worry about the stodginess of private education might be reassured by the story of Frank Boyden, the veteran headmaster of Deerfield Academy, returning disheveled and sweatshirted from football practice. Two sight-seeing matrons were admiring the lovely New England house which is the "head's" home and the frequent meeting place of faculty and students. Boyden asked if the ladies would like to tour the house. Delighted, they accepted the offer, and as they left slipped the amused headmaster a quarter tip.

Nothing should obscure the fact that a happy home, with a combination of parental love and supervision, plus a sensible schedule of study and play, is the best environment for any youngster. No boarding school can compete with that. But reality is often short of the ideal. For many boys and girls the "modern" home, frequently with both parents at work, does not provide either the care or the authority conducive to growing up, mentally and emotionally. The boarding school, under such circumstances, is a good alternative. Even the day school may at least prolong the hours of supervision and reduce the "door-key" children's dangerous vacuum, especially when the public schools are forced to operate on double (for which read half-time) sessions.

NONE of this would give aid and comfort to the fallacy that going to private school is an easy way to "beat the rush" into the "prestige colleges." Students don't get into college *because* they go to private schools. The fact is that good private schools select only those students who, if they had remained in public school (and had worked hard), would undoubtedly get into college on their own steam. On the contrary, since the colleges like a wide regional and social representation, the able student in the upper quarter of a public high school class may have a better chance for admission to one of the top colleges than the average student in prep school, where the queue forms hopefully along the Ivy League trail. And while college freshmen with prep school training generally do better for the first term or so, coasting on their superior study habits, public school graduates soon catch up and often overtake them.

A school is not good or bad because it is either public or private. There are inferior public schools as well as outstanding ones. And ever since Collegiate School in Manhattan was founded in 1638 as the first private school, there have been excellent private schools and shoddy ones, too. It would be folly to argue the case of American education as one of public versus private schools. It would be even worse if those who have turned to the private schools from personal choice—or from need, if the public schools seem substandard—used this as an excuse to withdraw their support from the public schools. The right to choose the private schools is a privilege to be paid for—over and above the support of public education, which is a national duty.

THERE is only one sensible way of looking at American education: it must be a cohesive fabric in which the public schools are the basic thread and the fundamental pattern. The "alternative" systems — whether denominational or independent, ranging from boarding academies to town or country day schools as well as military academies —are fibers which blend into the total cloth and add to its strength. If the public schools deteriorate, the entire fabric is weakened, and the country's educational health is in jeopardy. It is at such moments of crisis that the private schools must shoulder an additional burden, as they are called upon to do now, not to replace the public schools but to help them find their way back to strength and vitality.

Parents Face School Dilemma in City

*Benefits of Public vs.
Private Education
Are Weighed*

*Size of Classes Is One
Factor—Finances
Are Another*

By MARTIN TOLCHIN

"I COULDN'T stand going into my child's school," the mother said, "because I'd always hear teachers yelling. They seemed to spend more time on discipline than education. They didn't seem to enjoy teaching."

"My son was bored stiff," said another. "His grades were adequate and his knowledge small when he was graduated from junior high school. Had he been a good student, we would have left him in the public schools. But we felt that the public schools would have let him sit on his hands and just get by."

"Our neighbor's child had seven successive kindergarten teachers," said a third. "We heard about this and we were horrified. We couldn't face the prospect of sending our child into this kind of situation."

All these mothers were themselves educated in the public schools. They all believe in public education—but not for their own children. None feels that financially she can afford to send her children to private schools, or that educationally she can afford not to.

Fifty Private Schools

They are among a growing number of middle-income parents, motivated by neither family tradition nor religious ideals, who have enrolled their children in one of the city's more than fifty "independent, private non-public" schools. The schools range from the "conservative and haughty to the most progressive and radical," according to the Porter Sargent Handbook of Private Schools.

These private schools are now bulging with a student population in excess of 18,000. Virtually every one is filled to capacity, with applications exceeding openings by as much as five to one. Their tuitions range from $450 to $900 a year in the lower grades, and from $1,000 to $1,600 in the upper grades.

The inability of many city parents to pay these fees has been a major factor in the flight to the suburbs, in the opinion of Dr. Dan Dodson, director of the Center for Human Relations and Community Studies at New York University.

A first-rate, comprehensive high school on Manhattan's West Side would have stemmed the migration from that neighborhood, Dr. Dodson believes. Many of the middle-income families that left the neighborhood were unable to afford the private school tuitions and were attracted to the superior public schools available in the suburbs. They created a vacuum that was filled by the influx of Puerto Rican families, Dr. Dodson said.

Not First Rate

Most affected were parents of children who were not outstanding students and could not gain admission to the city's specialized high schools. Unlike the first-rate student who could more or less write his own ticket, the second-echelon youngster often got lost in the oversized classes and suffered from the lack of a more personal relationship with his teachers in the opinion of some parents and educators.

Small classes and a close relationship between pupils and teachers are one of the major attractions of the independent private schools. Contrasted to a maximum of thirty-nine pupils that is the aim of city schools, few private school classes exceed twenty-five pupils, and many have only fifteen or twenty.

The result is "a real interest in the child as a person, and more give and take between teacher and student," in the opinion of Mrs. Victoria Wagner, director of the private Ethical Culture Schools.

Another major attraction is the ability of the private schools to secure good college berths for their students. This is done through personal contacts, which are sometimes aggressively pursued, and because the private school graduate usually offers not only a higher degree of academic excellence than his public school counterpart, but also the likelihood that he will obtain a position of influence, and provide more funds as an alumnus.

Beginning at the first-grade level, the curriculum of a number of private schools is considered more challenging than the fare offered the public school child. For example, at the Trinity School, first graders study French, reading, writing and enough arithmetic to add and subtract three-digit numbers.

A more casual approach was cited by the mother of a city school child who complained to his teacher because he was a few grades behind on his reading.

"Don't worry," she was told, "there are other ways of acquiring information besides reading."

The junior high school years in the New York City school system are considered the most academically perilous by one observer of the education scene. These schools find it hard to attract good teachers. Subjects are taught by "retreaded elementary school teachers," he said. Between one-third and one-half of the teachers are substitutes. Confusion over curriculum aggravates the situation.

"I would have grave misgivings about sending a child to a public junior high school," he said.

Parents can judge the caliber of an elementary school, this specialist suggested, by how well the child learns the two essential subjects, reading and numbers. Another criterion, he said, is how excited a child becomes about wanting to learn.

Defenders of the public schools point out that its classes are smaller than classes in Roman Catholic parochial schools, a fact conceded by the Superintendent of Education of the Archdiocese of New York. Msgr. John Haverty said that classes in the city's Roman Catholic parochial schools averaged forty-five, with a strictly enforced maximum of fifty-five.

Those who point to the turnover of teachers in the public school system can point to an even greater turnover in the private schools. Half of the faculty of one local private school has been there less than five years. Four-fifths of the faculty of another have been there less than three years.

Dr. Thomas Nevins, an assistant to the city's Superintendent of Schools, believes that if the size of classes was reduced, the over-all city system would provide a better education than that at most private schools.

"Since the child will have to live in a world made up of all nations, creeds and nationalities," Dr. Nevins said, "he must learn early in life the contributions and peculiarities of all groups.

September 4, 1962

Military Schools Adjusting to New Irreverence

By ANDREW H. MALCOLM
Special to The New York Times

CULVER, Ind. — When the cadet lieutenant called the infantry battalion to attention at Culver Military Academy here the other evening, one student commander was full of proper military crispness.

"Sir, C Company all present or accounted for," he reported.

But the next company lined up on the prep school's windy Pershing Walk was strikingly informal.

"Yeah, we're all here," someone drawled and several dozen cadets burst into laughter.

Such irreverence—unheard of 10 years ago—is only one of the serious problems that confront the nation's more than 110 military colleges and prep schools these days.

Many of these schools have lived deep in traditions. Their ubiquitous campus cannons seemingly guard an educational system rooted in the late 1800's, when many of the schools were founded with a belief in the classical total education of a young man through strict mental and physical development.

But like practically all educational institutions today, military schools face vocal challenges by assertive youths who demand that a previously authoritarian form of education adapt to the times. "They'll have to cut a lot of the yessir, nosir bunk," said one cadet.

Another contemporary problem is the schools' military organization itself—a system that by its very nature arouses some opposition through association with the Vietnam war, which is particularly unpopular among draft-age men.

In addition, a Spartan military existence — complete with 6 A.M. reveille—appears less attractive than the generally affluent middle-class environment that has produced most of the students for military schools.

"Let's say we're worried but not panicked," said one admissions officer, "not yet anyway."

"Psychologically," says Gen. Hugh P. Harris, president of The Citadel, the state military college in Charleston, S.C., "there may be a little less enthusiasm for the military here

today. A permissive society eats on our youngsters and prohibits greater restrictions."

The problems have resulted in the following:

¶Enrollment has dropped. The National Association of Independent Schools reported in December that enrollment at 20 military prep schools was down 3.3 per cent this school year, to 6,720. Culver's enrollment, which was nearing 900 three years ago, is now 743. Enrollment at Pennsylvania Military College in Chester, Pa., dropped from 680 in 1964 to 380 today, prompting a study of abolishing the 150-year-old cadet corps.

Fewer students mean less income to cover rising costs. "If a decision was based solely on economics we'd drop the military tomorrow," said Dr. Clarence Moll, Pennsylvania Military's president. But elsewhere, such a financial pinch does not yet appear to be that serious.

¶Applications have declined. At The Citadel, applications fell almost 25 per cent in three years to under 1,300. At the nation's oldest military college, Norwich University in eastern Vermont, applications have dropped by one-sixth to 1,000, after 10 years of increases.

¶More aggressive recruiting campaigns, including films, frequent letters and colorful catalogues, have been adopted.

¶Regulations have been eased, such as shortening drill time and extending furloughs.

¶Consideration has been given—at Culver, at least— to the possibility of adding a girls school. And Penn Military's catalogue emphasizes that cadets attend classes and live on the same campus as students at its sister civilian — and coeducational — college, Penn Morton.

¶A greater voice has been given to cadets in policy formation. So far, this involvement is limited to such matters as entertainment, menus and regulations and has not extended to curriculum.

Some Congressmen have also reported increased difficulty in finding qualified high school seniors to send to West Point, Annapolis or the

Air Force Academy. But officials there said this was not true and that applications had actually increased. At Annapolis, for instance, applications so far this year total 6,883, or 1,000 more than last year at this time.

Officials at the military colleges and prep schools traced their immediate problems to an antimilitary feeling among youth and parents. They said that such cycles always follow wars. But, one added "This is the first time it's happened during a war."

Another problem for military schools, like that facing most private educational institutions, is that today's high costs are forcing parents of many potential cadets to look to public schools for their child's education, at least during high school.

The tuition and board at Culver, for instance, which is typical, totals $3,100 a year— almost as much as a year at Harvard or Princeton. Recent increases average $100 a year, also about the same as at private colleges.

School officials almost unanimously agreed that perhaps their most persistent obstacle was the image of military schools as rich boys' reform schools or training grounds for war-loving killers, an image they said was created by Hollywood or disgruntled former cadets.

"We're not running a prison here," General Harris of The Citadel said. "We assume each of our 2,000 cadets is here for an education within our system. If he isn't, we don't want him."

According to Bill Dryden, a 17-year-old junior here, the military system had little effect on his choice of Culver. "I think most kids came here because of the educational reputation," he said, "If I have to go through the military to get the education, fine."

Like many other cadets, Bill is against the Vietnam war and regularly hangs an antiwar poster in his room. Occasionally a member of the commandant's office rips it down.

But also like many other cadets here, Bill sees no hypocrisy in attending a military school while opposing a war. "I'm here to prepare

for college," he said, "not to learn how to kill."

Reserve Officer Training Corps classes are held only twice weekly, as are drill periods.

The schools enforce varying degrees of military strictness. But they believe generally that constant student exposure to a military system that stresses discipline, orderliness, teamwork and leadership pays personal dividends in self-discipline and motivation in life after graduation, regardless of vocation.

"It's more than just an education here," said one Citadel cadet, "it's a way of life."

Some alumni might have difficulty recognizing aspects of their alma maters that have undergone gradual changes in recent years.

Valley Forge's 1,000 cadets in spit-shined shoes and stiff, white collars still stand inspection daily at noon before marching in review to martial music and then to lunch.

But at Culver lunches have been made optional, instead of being required, and drill periods are less frequent.

At The Citadel plebes still run up stairs, turn square corners and walk in the gutter—never on the sidewalk— single file. But Norwich plans to eliminate such requirements, which one administrator called "the two-bit Mickey Mouse stuff."

Furloughs have been increased at many schools. At the military colleges, more students may drive cars, although marriage is still forbidden.

Much of the change is a result of more questioning and direct action by students, who, in fact, largely run the schools' day to day operations through their military chain of command.

"If there ever was a school where students have much to say about what goes on, it's here," said General Harris. He serves generally in an advisory capacity to the superintendent.

At Norwich, students elected by their peers meet frequently with the president to challenge and discuss policies. During last fall's Vietnam moratorium some schools

Steve Spahr of Sarasota, Fla., dons dress uniform at Culver Military Academy. The posters belong to his roommate.

mentioned cadet committees on food, entertainment and regulations.

A catalogue of the Virginia Military Institute, where officials declined to be interviewed, also speaks of involving students more in school committees.

Culver's cadets now share equal membership with the faculty on the Academy Senate, where one current topic is abolition of reveille a few days a week. The Senate was created last year and decisions are by majority vote. Although operational details have not been ironed out, it had pro and con student-run discussions on the war.

Every day brings new social changes, the V.M.I. catalogue asserts. "Although," it adds, "many of the developments may not meet with our approval, they nonetheless occur and take effect, and we must adapt."

March 25, 1970

Mr. Chips, abandoned by social evolution

By PETER SCHRAG

Twenty years ago it was easy to recognize them: Dirty white shoes, tweed sports coats, rep ties a little askew, coming down from Deerfield and Taft at Thanksgiving, or toting their bags and their prep-school paraphernalia into the freshman dorms of the Ivy League. For those of us who had attended urban public schools and met them for the first time in college, they were a strange breed who seemed to talk a special language, had actually been to deb parties and cotillions, and were—as we imagined them, often correctly—loaded with money. In the first year of college they performed well, seemed in fact, to possess some secret weapon of preparation; then they began to fade in the golden haze of booze, fraternities and weekend trips.

The preppies: They had their troubles even then. Pressed by the tough (and often nasty) competitors from the public schools, by new standards and by the gradual eclipse of their accustomed world, they became children of campus scorn and candidates for the contemptible occupations of the liberal world: advertising, banking, insurance. But neither they nor their parents nor the schools they attended could then imagine what would eventually hit them, could hardly suspect how thoroughly that world would be shattered.

If ever there had been a self-conscious élite in America—an élite, that is, which transcended mere power and privilege—then its bounds included not only the "good" clubs and colleges, was manifested not merely in particular styles and attitudes, but comprised just as surely the private schools and "academies" which reinforced or even formed them: Choate, Lawrenceville, Andover, Exeter, Milton, Groton, St. Mark's, St.

Mr. Schrag is an editor-at-large for Saturday Review and a freelance writer.

A World Of Our Own

Notes on Life and Learning In a Boys' Preparatory School.
By Peter S. Prescott.
400 pp. New York:
Coward-McCann. $7.95.

Paul's, Deerfield, Taft and perhaps a half dozen others. The schools are still there but they are being left high and dry by the receding certainties and declining values of the class they serve.

"A World of Our Own" is the world of Choate, which Peter S. Prescott calls "an excellent school," but it could be about almost any one: Five to six hundred "boys," 60 or 80 "masters," a headmaster named Seymour St. John, an ordained Episcopal minister (whose father was also headmaster of the school), and an 800 acre campus in Wallingford, Conn.

Although Prescott spent the better part of a year at Choate on his research, the book is, as the saying goes, "unauthorized," a fact which should become quickly apparent, despite the disclaimer about the school's excellence. Between Prescott's lines Choate comes out as a place whose vulgarity and repressiveness are matched only by its Waspy chauvinism, its pretentiousness and its unmitigated hypocrisy.

Its respect for intellectual distinction seems to be casual at best—"we try not to make them think," said a teacher, "because that's not taught here"—it honors expressions of individualism only in rhetoric and rarely in practice, and its understanding of the racial and social turmoil surrounding it appears, from Prescott's description, to be primitive. Although Prescott describes some highly attractive teachers and students (many of whom eventually depart for better climes) and although he portrays moments of courage and nobility in his account of a mild student

uprising two years ago, it is hard to imagine oneself comfortable in any of Choate's constituencies—teacher, administrator or student—let alone that of the exploited faculty wives who are expected to perform countless dirty jobs as unpaid accessories to their husbands' employment.

The prime objective of most prep schools, Choate included, is to keep people occupied, to have them running from compulsory class to compulsory athletics to compulsory chapel to compulsory meals to dormitories with little or no free time; to deny any person, teacher or student, the absolute privacy of his own residence; to encourage students to impose incessantly on teachers—something that many, at least, are gracious enough not to do; and to deluge all citizens of the community with endless sermons about values, leadership and responsibility. What those values are is never made explicit: vaguely Christian, vaguely "Western" but rarely distinct. They are obviously supposed to be in that Waspy woodwork, in the paneled walls, in the mud of the playing fields and in the unquestioned belief that if the school, its class and its system are not perfect, it would nonetheless be hard to imagine anything better.

Prescott's excellent descriptions of individual teachers and students—of students who decorate their rooms with posters and artifacts in an effort to hold out the world of Choate itself, who turn up their record players to drown out the surroundings, of masters so dependent on the structure and security of the school that they are lost during vacations—these descriptions make it clear that there are no identifiable tormentors, no real victims and that the destructive impositions come from the confining assumptions of a place which drives people at each other, which rarely lets them be. They also make it clear that without its covert rigidity the school could hardly function at all.

Choate, one finally has to conclude, is only as viable as

the system which created it, only as good as the class it was designed to serve. And both have plainly begun to go. All that talk about values, all that stoic discipline, justified themselves when their objects took for granted their positions of leadership and control. When these things can no longer be assumed, then all dependent practices begin to smell of the vulgar, the arbitrary and the repressive. We no longer have to discipline people, who, by virtue of birth, will become leaders, but to educate men for a world they have yet to understand. In their small rebellion against the strictures of the school, the students—hardly knowing what to ask or in which cause to protest—sensed the problem more acutely than the majority of their teachers or their headmaster who, in Prescott's account, never understood that communication meant the ability to listen.

Prescott's journalism is first-rate, although few people at Choate will appreciate what he has to say. At the same time, I kept wishing that he would provide a little more analysis, and more compassion for the plight of an élitist colony abandoned by the fall of its empire. Prescott himself once went to Choate and, I gather, liked it. Perhaps it was there that he acquired his restraint and his social *politesse*. Choate, from his description, is not an excellent school (or was he being ironic?); he should have said so, and then risked the dissection that the conclusion demanded. As it is, "A World of Our Own" is a superb social document. With less restraint, it might almost have served as a sympathetic epitaph to a class whose era has come to an end. ■

A Columbia Study Finds That the I. Q. of the Individual Varies With His Schooling

By BENJAMIN FINE

For many years educators and psychologists have insisted that the I. Q. remains constant. Allowance was made for slight variations, perhaps five to ten points, but this was termed the "margin of error." Basically, the belief existed that a person retained the amount of brains that nature endowed him with, and that very little could be done about it. Most textbooks on the subject upheld that belief.

Now this position is seriously questioned. A twenty-year study, conducted by Dr. Irving Lorge, head of the educational research institute at Teachers College, Columbia University, presents evidence that the intelligence quotient fluctuates with the amount of education an individual attains. A report of that study is published in the May issue of the Teachers College Record.

Dr. Lorge set out to discover whether a group of individuals tested twenty years ago had the same intelligence quotients today. In doing so he tested not only the individuals but also the theory that a boy, say, who had an I. Q. of 110 at the age of 14, would have the same I. Q., with slight variation, at the age of 34.

It did not turn out that way. Those who had additional years of schooling had raised their I. Q.'s by as much as fifteen or twenty points—with due allowance for the margin of error.

Method of Comparison

Here is the way Dr. Lorge came to his far-reaching conclusions: he compared sets of boys who, twenty years ago, were matched at the same intelligence score, let us say at 105. But one of the boys had continued his schooling and completed a four-year college course. The other boy had stopped at the end of elementary school. This boy retained his 105 I. Q.—he did not go backward. The student who had gone to college had raised his to 125. That was not according to the books.

Subsidized by the Carnegie Corporation, the study began in 1921, under the direction of Prof. Edward L. Thorndike, when a representative sampling of 863 boys in the eighth grade of New York City's public elementary schools received series of tests for abstract intelligence, mechanical adroitness and clerical ability.

In May, 1941, as the twentieth year of the experiment came to a close, Dr. Lorge, who by that time had succeeded Dr. Thorndike at Teachers College, invited the original group to come to the college for a retesting. In all, 131 responded, enough to provide a reliable cross-section of the original group, and thus of the larger student body.

In essence, the study showed that the men who had gone to college made higher ratings on their intelligence tests than those who had not. Strikingly enough, even as little as a year of schooling raised the I. Q. And the more education a person received, the higher his I. Q. became.

For example, a boy who at the age of 14 had an intelligence quotient of 100, raised that score to 115 or 120 by going to school. On the other hand, another boy who stopped going to school at the end of the eighth grade retained his 100 I. Q. While his intelligence score did not improve, neither did it go down.

Conclusions Reached

According to Dr. Lorge, the mental ages of the men who completed three years or more of college are two full years higher than those of the men who completed less than two years of high school. Men who had equal intelligence at the age of 14 revealed striking differences at age 34, depending upon the amount of education received in the meantime.

In other words, while the intellectual ability of a person is not lost as he grows older even though he does not go to school, his full abilities are not realized. It is not true that a boy who comes up the "hard way" has the same advantages as the person who receives formal schooling. However, even though education makes a profound difference, Dr. Lorge warns that "it would be overly optimistic to expect it to change the least able into the most able."

"An adult's measured mental ability is related to his intelligence as a boy and to the extent of his subsequent schooling," Dr. Lorge comments.

Because education can help develop a person's I. Q., it is essential that the opportunity for schooling be provided equally to all who can profit from it, Dr. Lorge suggests. Lacking opportunity, tens of thousands of men and women never reach their top capacities, he holds; and that, the Teachers College psychologist says, is a pity, since it means that society is losing "tremendous amounts of its fundamental human resources."

An intelligence test score of an adult, asserts Dr. Lorge, cannot be interpreted as direct evidence of the amount of brains he actually has. On the contrary, the only way you can be certain of the "inherent ability" of a person is to know how much education he has, and something about his background and environment. Too many men and women, it would seem, never reach the full height of their intellectual ability because they are denied an education.

That schooling makes a difference in a person's I. Q. is important not only to the individual but to society. It would follow from Dr. Lorge's provocative study that the community, to utilize its citizens to the fullest, should make it possible for all who can profit to continue their education. In the difficult post-war years ahead the world will need men and women who have developed their intellectual powers to the fullest.

The average American's instinctive belief in the value of an education now has received official scientific sanction.

A Child's Emotional State Can Affect an I. Q. Rating

FOR more years than educators care to count, the I. Q. (intelligence quotient) rating, now Exhibit A in a bitter custody fight in New Jersey courts, has been causing trouble for parents, educators . . . and children.

Many another battle has been touched off by a school's refusal to tell a parent his child's I. Q., by a parent's claim that his child has been incorrectly classified or by a difference between school and home over the type of instruction a "certified" little "genius" is being given.

The I. Q. rating, accurately determined and intelligently used, can help guide adults' decisions about the type of education and training most appropriate for a child.

How accurate is the I. Q. rating? There is evidence indicating that a child's score on an intelligence test is influenced not only by his intellectual ability, but by his emotional state at the time of testing. The child's motivation and morale play important roles in the final outcome.

I. Q. Can Change

Children from culturally impoverished homes, or those neglected or ignored by adults, consistently rate low on intelligence tests, research reports indicate.

But when such children have the benefit of pleasanter, more stimulating surroundings they may show a marked increase in I. Q. within a relatively short time.

Classifying children for educational purposes on the basis of I. Q. alone never has been approved by specialists, but it is increasingly relied on in overcrowded school systems, according to David Engler, author of "How to Raise Your Child's I. Q."

A New York City teacher, Mr. Engler points out that sometimes the differences of just a few points on an intelligence test can determine whether a child is selected for an "enrichment" class, or, at the other extreme, placed with "slow learners."

The effects of such placement are often accentuated with time, Mr. Engler said, because "it does not take a child long to sense I.Q.-based distinctions, and live up—or down—to them."

Can parents do anything to increase their child's I.Q.? How can they help the child with a good rating making the most of his potential?

The portrait of the child who can bring his full intellect to bear on intelligence tests reveals a youngster who is able to meet unusual conditions with youthful poise, a child who respects adults but does not fear them, and one willing and accustomed to follow directions accurately, according to Mr. Engler.

These are qualities developed from early childhood. They spring from the quality of the relationships the child has with his parents. They are nourished by discipline and guidance.

Going on family trips, being read to, talked with and listened to by adults and having opportunities to play freely with stimulating toys and equipment will prepare a child to tackle with confidence the kinds of questions and problems he will be asked to work out on intelligence tests.

March 10, 1960

PARENTS TO LEARN PUPILS' I.Q. RATING

City Schools Will Disclose Once-Secret Records to Meet State Ruling

By LEONARD BUDER

The city school system will soon lift the rule that has kept pupils' intelligence quotients and other school data from their parents.

Dr. C. Frederick Pertsch, Deputy Superintendent of Schools in charge of instructional affairs, said yesterday that the change would comply with a recent decision by the State Education Department directing public schools in the state to make such records available to parents.

The state decision, which went largely unnoticed in the city when it was made last month, said that parents and guardians, "as a matter of law," were entitled to see their child's progress reports, grades, I. Q. scores, achievement test results, medical, psychological and psychiatric reports and "evaluations by educators."

Disclose Interpretation

At present the city schools, as well as many others in the state, withhold I.Q. scores and psychological and psychiatric reports, as well as some other data, although they have generally passed on their interpretations of the findings.

The question of whether such information should be given to parents has been a matter of much controversy. Some educators have contended that parents should be told all that the school knows about their child—including test results.

Others have said that the specific information might be misunderstood, misinterpreted or wrongly used by parents. They have argued, for example, that parents might use I. Q. scores to make unfair and possibly harmful comparisons among children.

Another fear, expressed earlier this week at a meeting of the State School Boards Association in Syracuse, was that parents might sue school personnel for libel because of what might be written in the reports.

This was put to Dr. Charles A. Brind, the counsel for the State Education Department, who said at the meeting:

"If a school psychologist has any reservations about what he thinks, he should not put his thoughts on paper. But a genuine professional opinion as found by an examination would be, I think, a complete defense for libel."

Urges Caution

However, Dr. Brind cautioned that teachers should not make psychological judgments about pupils, let alone put them in writing.

In its ruling, the state department said the educational interests of the pupil could best be served by full cooperation between parents and the school, based on the complete understanding of the child.

But the department urged that when parents came to school for information, "appropriate personnel should be present to prevent any misinterpretation of the records."

The state delineated the new position in dismissing an appeal from a Levittown, L. I., school board member who objected to a new policy of the local board of making pupil records available.

Dr. Pertsch said that the matter of making confidential information available to parents would be discussed next month by the Board of Superintendents, which is composed of the heads of the major educational divisions in the city system.

At that time, he said, the superintendents will consider "methods of complying" with the state decision.

October 27, 1960

SCHOOLS WILL END GROUP I.Q. TESTING

Reading and Achievement Scoring to Replace Old Method Starting in Fall

BOARD PROPOSED SHIFT

Distortion and Unfairness to Minorities Had Been Laid to Mental Gauge

By LEONARD BUDER

New York City's schools will do away with group I.Q. tests starting next fall, the Board of Education announced yesterday.

The move is in line with a recommendation contained in the board's plan for integrating and improving the city system. Educators and psychologists have contended that the group I.Q. tests were aimed at middle-class white students and thus were unfair to minority group and underprivileged youngsters.

Many Negro and Puerto Rican parents have charged that misleading I.Q. scores have been used to keep their children out of special schools and educational programs. They have also asserted that teachers expect less and do not try as hard with pupils with low I.Q.'s.

Accuracy Questioned

Dr. Joseph O. Loretan, deputy superintendent for research and evaluation, told principals in a directive that the group I.Q. tests "can present a misleading picture of a student's abilities, resulting in an inappropriate instructional program."

He added that "the fact that a child obtains a low score on a group I.Q. test does not necessarily mean that he is incapable of learning, nor does a high score on a group I.Q. test necessarily mean that the child will not encounter difficulties in certain aspects of the curriculum."

To give teachers a more adequate measure of a pupil's strength and weaknesses for instructional purposes, Dr. Loretan said, achievement tests would be substituted for the group I.Q. tests.

He said the new tests would cover the study skills and major subjects—social studies, mathematics, science, English and reading. They will be given in grades 3, 6 and 9.

No such tests are now administered.

Reading Tests Planned

In addition, reading tests will be given to all pupils in grades 2 through 10. Up to now, reading tests have been given in grades 3, 5, 7, 8 and 9.

The board also announced the installation of a photoelectric scanning machine to speed the scoring of standardized tests. It said the machine could score tests and print the results at a rate of 1,750 sheets an hour.

The machine is already in use scoring a reading test given to sixth-grade pupils on Jan. 21. The board said the results of that test would be sent to schools on April 15.

It noted that scoring and tabulation of results of a test within three months of its administration would be unprecedented in the city school system.

The board added that with the new scoring machine and a computer it would be able to produce citywide summary statistics such as school, district and borough average scores and grade norms, which its Bureau of Educational Research could analyze.

March 3, 1964

Psychologist Arouses Storm by Linking I.Q. to Heredity

By ROBERT REINHOLD
Special to The New York Times

CAMBRIDGE, Mass., March 29—A storm is brewing over a suggestion by a leading educational psychologist that intelligence is determined largely by heredity and cannot be altered significantly by improving environment.

For this reason, argues the psychologist, Dr. Arthur R. Jensen of the University of California at Berkeley, compensatory education programs designed to raise the intelligence of disadvantaged children by enriching their cultural surroundings are misdirected.

Further, he theorizes, the measured mental differences between racial and ethnic groups are rooted in inborn genetic differences that are as much a part of group identity as skin color, hair texture and blood chemistry.

Such hereditary factors, he believes, may account for the fact that Negroes average 15 points below whites on I.Q. tests. Recent evidence, he adds, indicates that children from Negro and other disadvantaged groups do poorly in "cognitive" learning—the ability to reason abstractly—while they do well in "associative" learning, which involves rote learning and memory.

New Techniques Sought

If this theory can be substantiated, says Dr. Jensen, then "the next step will be to develop the techniques by which school learning can be most effectively achieved in accordance with different patterns of ability."

This is the chief conclusion of a controversial 123-page study by Dr. Jensen in the current issue of The Harvard Educational Review, a student-run publication of the Harvard Graduate School of Education.

Dr. Jensen's theories are not new, but the force with which he presents them has rekindled issues that have long divided geneticists, psychologists and educators. These include:

¶What are the relative roles of genetic endowment and cultural surroundings in determining mental ability?

¶To what extent can manipulation of the environment improve ability?

¶Do racial differences extend to mental attributes?

Such questions have defied close scientific scrutiny because humans cannot be bred and raised under controlled laboratory conditions like rats and because educators and psychologists have not settled on a strict definition of intelligence.

Predictably, the Jensen article has prompted heated reaction from those who say it lends support to racist claims that Negroes are inferior to whites intellectually.

"I believe Jensen is wrong and I hope he does not do too much damage," wrote William F. Brazziel, a Negro who is director of general education at the Norfolk Division of Virginia State College, in a letter to be published in the next issue of The Review.

Overinterpretation Feared

In addition, a number of geneticists and psychologists believe Dr. Jensen may have overinterpreted the limited scientific evidence available—particularly on the question of racial differences.

"From the standpoint of methodology, this is as difficult an issue as geneticists confront today," said a leading human geneticist. "It is conceivable there are significant mental differences between blacks and whites—but we simply do not have the information to reach a valid conclusion. Negroes have been subjected to so many subtle kinds of discrimination that we cannot compare the two groups."

However, Dr. Jensen says his study was intended as an objective scientific analysis of an area that he feels has long been taboo.

"As long as people assume there are no differences between races, then we are not going to understand them and give children the education they need," he said by telephone from California. "It's sort of like assuming everybody's digestive system is the same and will thrive on the same diet."

Dr. Jensen's conclusions, which deal only in small part with race, are based on a sophisticated statistical analysis of intelligence testing and heritability studies.

He set out on the premise that remedial education, such as the Federal Head Start program and the Higher Horizons program in New York, "has been tried and it apparently has failed."

To explain this failure, disputed by some experts, he mounts a strong attack on "environmentalists" who believe in the "almost infinite plasticity of intellect."

Compensatory education programs are based on the theory that scholastic performance of disadvantaged children can be raised by providing an enriched cultural environment that is lacking at home.

In his paper, which is based on evidence gathered by dozens of other experts in addition to himself, Dr. Jensen makes these points:

¶Intelligence tests are essentially measures of cognitive ability — the capacities for problem solving by means of classifying like and unlike. This is the key to higher mental functions.

¶Various studies, including those of identical twins reared apart, indicate that this kind of mental ability is largely fixed by inheritance.

¶The influence of environment seems to be limited by a "threshold" effect. That is, below a certain threshold of environmental adequacy, deprivation does have a marked depressing effect on I.Q.; but above that threshold, remedial action does little to raise intelligence.

¶Negroes tend to average 15 I.Q. points below whites on just about every intelligence test. Even so-called "culture-free" or "culture-fair" tests, designed to eliminate cultural biases in traditional I.Q. tests, give Negroes lower scores than whites on the average.

¶American Indians, generally considered to be more dis-advantaged than Negroes, consistently score higher than Negroes.

¶One study shows that the incidence of children with I.Q.'s below 75 (retarded) is 13 times as high among Negro families in upper social classes as among upper-class whites. This suggests environment is not an important factor.

¶Even I.Q. gains achieved by compensatory education have not proved to be lasting.

Urges Broad Inquiry

Such evidence has led Dr. Jensen to conclude that it is "not an unreasonable hypothesis that genetic factors are strongly implicated in the average Negro-white intelligence difference."

Therefore, he believes, attempts to increase cognitive learning ability are unlikely to succeed. "Educators would probably do better to concern themselves with teaching basic skills directly than with attempting to boost over-all cognitive development," he wrote.

"The techniques for raising intelligence per se, in the sense of general intelligence, probably lie more in the province of the biological sciences than in psychology and education."

Calling for a "no holds barred" scientific inquiry, he said:

"In other fields, when bridges do not stand, when aircraft do not fly, when machines do not work, when treatments do not cure, despite all conscientious efforts on the part of many persons to make them do so, one begins to question the basic assumptions, principles, theories and hypotheses that guide one's efforts. Is it time to follow suit in education?"

In an interview, Dr. Jensen indicated that he would not recommend widespread use of his ideas without further research. "I'm trying to stimulate more research," he said. "There should not be any fear in finding biological differences between groups."

Reaction to the article has been swift. At the Harvard School of Education, a special student group has formed to promote discussion of the question, and the editors of The Review have been criticized for not having any Negro psychologists review the article before publication.

Geneticists, while praising the scientific rigor of Dr. Jensen's presentation, said he may have gone too far.

"His interpretation may be a little overeager," said Prof. Steven G. Vandenberg, a leading behavioral geneticist from the University of Colorado. Professor Vandenberg added that he believed Dr. Jensen should have been more careful about the racial question, which was bound to raise emotions.

Like Shouting 'Fire'

"Quite apart from science, I think one should not shout 'fire' in a crowded theater without good evidence. He seems to go a little beyond what is known today."

Another leading geneticist, Prof. James F. Crow of the University of Wisconsin, said he agreed "for the most part" with Dr. Jensen's analysis of the high heritability of I.Q., but disagreed on the interpretation.

"No matter how high the heritability," Dr. Crow said, "there is no assurance that a sufficiently great environmental difference does not account for the differences in the two means [between Negro and white I.Q.'s], especially when one considers that the environmental factors may differ qualitatively in the two groups."

Reaction among educators and psychologists has been mixed.

"If you leave aside the discussion of race, it's probably the best thing that's been done on genetics and intelligence," said Christopher S. Jencks, a specialist in education of disadvantaged minorities at Harvard.

"You have to treat it as speculative argument, not as assertion that can be backed up by any appreciable body of evidence," he said. "His argument about the relative unimportance of environment is based on data on whites in England and the United States. But that does not say anything about what is possible in an environment you have not looked at."

In a reply to be printed in the next issue of The Review, Prof. J. McVicker Hunt, a psychologist at the University of Illinois, expressed unhappiness with the implications Dr. Jensen's piece held for public policy in education.

"As I read the evidence," he said, "the odds are strong that we can boost both I.Q. and scholastic achievement substantially, but we cannot know how much for at least two decades. However, we shall never find out if we destroy support for the investigation of how to foster early psychological development, for the development of educational technology, and for the deployment of that technology."

Another psychologist, Dr. Lee J. Cronbach, accused Dr. Jensen of girding himself for a "holy war against 'environmentalists'" that have led him to overstatement and misstatement.

"The genetic population we call races no doubt have different distributions of whatever genes influence psychological processes. We are in no position to guess, however, which pools are 'inferior.'"

I.Q. STUDY SCORED BY PSYCHOLOGISTS

They Challenge Link of Race Differences to Heredity

The policy-making body of a national organization of psychologists has unanimously challenged a recent contention published in The Harvard Educational Review that Negro-white differences in intelligence quotient scores are based largely on heredity.

The challenge was contained in a statement by the 18-member council of the Society for the Psychological Study of Social Issues. The statement was released by Dr. Martin Deutsch, society president.

Dr. Deutsch, director of the Institute for Developmental Studies and professor of early childhood education at New York University, described the challenge as a "position statement" and a "rebuttal." It was issued in opposition to the conclusions reached by Dr. Arthur R. Jensen, of the University of California at Berkeley, and published in the Harvard review.

Misinterpretation Feared

The rebuttal said in part:

"As behavioral scientists, we believe that statements specifying the hereditary components of intelligence are unwarranted by the present state of scientific knowledge. As members of the council of the Society for the Psychological Study of Social Issues, we believe that such statements may be seriously misinterpreted, particularly in their applications to the social policy."

The statement said that four decades of research had shown that "there are marked differences in intelligence test scores when one compares a random sample of whites and Negroes" but that "the evidence points overwhelmingly to the fact that when one compares Negroes and whites of comparable cultural and educational background, differences in intelligence test scores diminish markedly; the more comparable the background, the less the difference."

Dr. Jensen had said that various studies had shown that identical twins reared apart had shown evidence of mental ability fixed by inheritance, that Negroes tended to average 15 I.Q. points below whites; that American Indians, generally considered to be more disadvantaged than Negroes, consistently scored higher than Negroes, and that I.Q. gains achieved by compensatory education had not proved to be lasting.

Such evidence, Dr. Jensen said, led him to conclude that it is "not an unreasonable hypothesis that genetic factors are strongly implicated in the average Negro-white intelligence difference."

Inequalities Are Blamed

The council's rebuttal said that "social inequalities deprive large numbers of black people of social, economic, and educational advantages available to a great majority of the white population" and that "the existing social structures prevent black and white people even of the same social class from leading comparable lives."

"One of the most serious objections to Jensen's article is to his vigorous assertion that compensatory education has apparently failed," the statement said.

"It is obvious," the council added, "that no scientific discussion of racial differences can exclude an examination of political, historic, economic and psychological factors which are inextricably related to racial differences."

The statement was signed by Dr. Deutsch and the following:

George W. Albee, Case-Western Reserve University.
Kurt W. Back, Duke.
Launor F. Carter, Systems Development Corporation.
Robert Chin, Boston University.
Kenneth B. Clark, Metropolitan Applied Research Center.
William A. Gamson, Harvard.
Harold B. Gerard, University of California at Los Angeles.
Kenneth R. Hammond, University of Colorado.
Robert Hefner, University of Michigan.
Edwin P. Hollander, State University of New York at Buffalo.
Robert Kahn, University of Michigan.
Nathan Maccoby, Stanford.
Thomas F. Pettigrew, Harvard.
Harold Proshansky, City University of New York.
M. Brewster Smith, University of Chicago.
Ralph K. White, George Washington University.
Philip G. Zimbardo, Stanford.

May 11, 196

Boston Suit Charges Harm
From Faulty I.Q. Testing of Students

By WILLIAM K. STEVENS
Special to The New York Times

BOSTON, Sept. 14—A suit filed today in United States District Court here charges that the Boston school system, through a faulty method of testing and classification, has mistakenly shunted large numbers of poor but normally intelligent children into special classes for the mentally retarded.

The action contends that the school psychologists who test and classify such children are incompetent to do so. It seeks to place the testing and classification function under the supervision of a specially established, independednt commission until June 30, 1973.

Further, it asks that damages be paid to each of several children alleged to be "irreparably harmed" by the classification system.

The suit is believed to be the first to attack the process through which children in American schools are routinely and systematically sorted and grouped for instructional purposes. It is also one of the first to attack the way in which I.Q. tests are used. If t is successful, its backers believe, it will open the way for legal challenges by parents who believe their children are being mishandled by the schools in other ways.

The suit was filed on behalf of seven students and their parents and also as a class action in behalf of all children who might suffer from the alleged misclassification. It is being handled by staff attorneys of the Boston Legal Assistance Project and the Harvard Center for Law and Education. Both agencies are supported by Federal antipoverty funds. City and state school officials were named as defendants.

Among charges made in the suit are the following:

¶Children in the Boston schools are classified for instructional puroses solely on the basis of insensitive and narrowly based intelligence tests that cannot distinuish sufficiently between mental retardation, emotional disturbance, perceptual handicap, lack of facility in the English language and cultural differences. The tests used, the Stanford-Binet and Wechler intelligence tests for children, are commonly used by school districts throughout the nation.

¶Boston's school psychologists have been "minimally trained," are unqualified to interpret the intelligence tests used by the system and are not competent to administer more sensitive tests. Consequently, the psychologists' efforts result in an "incompetent, discriminatory and unprofessional classification."

¶Through faulty testing, many normally intelligent children have been placed in "special" classes for the retrrded where they are "irreparably harmed" because they do not get the education they need.

¶Such children were placed in "special" classes without sufficient notice to parents. In some cases, parents were not allowed to see the school system's information purporting to justify a child's placement in special classes.

A spokesman for the school district could not be reached for comment.

"We view this suit as a first step into examining the whole process of classifying children in the schools," Michael L. Altman of the Boston Legal Assistance Project, said today. "Misclassification causes harm, we're sure. On the question of what kind of harm, we'll have to get into the whole question of mal-education in this suit. And that takes us right into the heart of the educational process."

One of the more obvious kinds of harm, according to Dr. Milton Budoff, director of the Research Institute for Educational Problems in Cambridge and one of the suit's initiators, is that "when you tag a kid as a dummy, everyone understands he's a dummy, and he never again has a chance to show what he can do."

Mr. Altman and Dr. Budoff said the suit had been prepared at the urging of community groups including the Urban League, the Columbia Point Mental Health Center and the United South End Settlements.

The initial thrust was said to have been provided last year when 21 children who had been classified as retarded in Boston's predominantly black and Puerto Rican South End were retested. More than half were found to have been misclassified.

The suit asks that no child be placed in a "special" education class until a special "commission on individual educational needs" is appointed to oversee testing and classification. One commission member each would be named by the state commissioners of education, rehabilitation and mental health; the president of the Massachusetts Psychological Association; the Massachusetts Psychological Center; the Mayor of Boston, and the chairman of the Boston School Committee. Two members would be parents of children in the schools.

The commission's job would include assuring that all diagnostic tests were administered or supervised by a fully qualified psychologist; specifying adequate psychological tests; and assuring that students and parents were given full access to test results and a full hearing before placement in a special class.

The suit asks further that until the school system has sufficient professional staff to carry out the proposed remedies, it contract for such services from local psychologists and mental health agencies approved by the commission.

Changes

THE LONG HAUL

President Eisenhower seemed to be saying in his address to the nation last Thursday evening that we were doing all right in our short-term and long-term defense program but that from now on we must try to do better. It was for this purpose that he nominated James R. Killian Jr. to the newly created post of Special Assistant to the President for Science and Technology. If Mr. Eisenhower had been really satisfied with our progress in the field of defense technology, or if he had been certain that the public was also satisfied, Dr. Killian could have continued uninterruptedly with his useful work as president of the Massachusetts Institute of Technology.

The new emphasis on the underlying research that a modern defense establishment calls for is of course not merely a matter of spending money. We may need to invest quite a few billion additional dollars a year in this field, but not much will be accomplished if we tax ourselves merely to ease a sense of guilt. New weapons, new research agencies, increased numbers of fighting men in uniform signify nothing unless they are linked with a national policy and philosophy. It is the work done, not the means by which it is done, that counts.

What we are now running into is not so much the spending of vast additional quantities of money, but rather a diversion of our energies. We have failed, as the President said, "to give high priority enough to science education and to the place of science in our national life." One reason for this is that we can't compel persons to be interested in science. The recruitment of prospective scientists is a different problem from that of putting able-bodied young men in brown suits and teaching them close-order drill.

We have driven some men out of science by the absurd "security" regulations imposed by the Government. We have doubtless persuaded others to stay out of science because they do not choose to put up with this sort of nonsense. What we have to do now as a basic part of long-term defense is to make science study and scientific work attractive to original and independent persons. The choice must be free. We cannot draft unwilling young men to become creative workers in the sciences.

Doubtless the need will be met if the earth does not explode within the next few years. We will have our scientists, particularly the physicists, and we can count on them to make us so formidable that no one will dare to attack us. Out of their researches we will also derive what the Pentagon may consider by-products—new ways of preventing and healing diseases, new methods for feeding a growing population more abundantly, new tools for a more comfortable life. We are being forced by circumstances toward this development, just as conditions in our early history compelled peaceable young men to be good shots and capable woodsmen. But we must watch our step.

Perhaps it was the destiny of our civilization in any case to be increasingly creative in the scientific field to the possible detriment of some other fields of human creativeness. At any rate, this shift of emphasis is being forced upon us. But as we go into the long haul we must be careful not to change our civilization for the worse in our struggle to preserve it.

Valuing as we must that systematic approach to knowledge which is called science, we shall continue to need other means of self-expression. We shall continue to need a wholly disinterested inquiry into truth. We shall continue to need joy in life. Above all, we shall continue to need liberty: for if we do not have these things, what is there to defend? We may be more and more working with machines but we need not ourselves become machines.

Let us have more engineers but let us not discourage our poets, our musicians, our artists; for they, too, will help us win our battles for civilization.

3 SCIENTISTS GIVE PLAN TO IMPROVE U. S. HIGH SCHOOLS

Killian, Rickover and Tuve Suggest Harder Courses and Better Instruction

STRESS AID TO GIFTED

Assail Teacher Certification and the 'Mucker Pose' of Anti-Intellectualism

By JAMES RESTON
Special to The New York Times.

WASHINGTON, March 23—Three of the nation's leading scientists and educators outlined today a six-point program to improve high school education.

Dr. James R. Killian Jr., president of the Massachusetts Institute of Technology, who is now President Eisenhower's Special Assistant for Science and Technology; Rear Admiral Hyman G. Rickover, chief of the Atomic Energy Commission's Naval Reactors branch, and Dr. Merle Tuve, director of the Department of Terrestrial Magnetism at the Carnegie Institution of Washington, made these proposals:

1. Lift the standards that have to be met by all high school graduates.
2. Fight against what Dr. Killian called "the mucker pose that it's smart to be anti-intellectual."
3. Reward superior teachers with significantly larger salaries.
4. Give the high school teacher enough free time to become a scholar again.
5. Push the talented student ahead as fast as he can go, rather than holding him back with the dolts.
6. Bring into the high schools all the teaching talent possible, regardless of the "union card requirements" of educational "training and teaching techniques."

Teachers in Audience

These suggestions were made as a part of the fiftieth anniversary celebration of St. Alban's School for Boys at the Washington Protestant Episcopal Cathedral. The audience was composed of private and public high school principals and science and mathematics teachers in the capital.

The purpose of the meeting was to respond to President Eisenhower's challenge, made last November in Oklahoma City, that all school boards and parent-teacher's organizations scrutinize their curricula and standards to see whether they met the demands of the time.

Dr. Killian had some words of advice for parents. If we are to have better science education, he said, we must have better over-all education, and if we are to have better over-all education, we must have a shift in values so that intellectual interests are not minimized and ridiculed.

"There needs to be a greater interest in matters of the mind," he told a large and distinguished audience, "a weeding-out of the trivial, narrowly vocational subjects, and a more general acceptance by parents—particularly by parents—teachers, and students of the importance of intellectual qualities and high standards in all parts of the secondary school program."

All three agreed on the necessity to encourage a distaste for snap courses and anti-intellectual attitudes. Dr. Tuve and Admiral Rickover laid special emphasis on the need to get rid of state and local laws that forced teachers to meet "union card" requirements before getting a permanent job.

Dr. Tuve said that if responsible men and women really wanted to do something about improving secondary education in the United States, here was a good way to start:

"We can go after our local school boards and our own state

legislatures to change the laws which now restrict teacher certification to the products of the courses in education."

Admiral Rickover pointed out: "I hope this audience knows that neither Dr. Killian nor Dr. Tuve could qualify for a permanent teaching job in the high schools of this city."

Dr. Tuve had two other suggestions:

1. Build back the tradition of scholarship among high school teachers and insist that "the professional teacher be given some time to himself for his own scholarship."

2. Break the "equal pay" tradition so that the outstanding teachers receive significantly larger salaries.

Admiral Rickover said he would gladly see the defense budget cut, in the interests of national defense, to make adequate funds available to attract good teachers into the public schools.

Both Dr. Killian and Dr. Tuve appealed for a new and broader understanding of the nature of science and its relation to the humanities. Dr. Tuve expressed it this way:

"I believe that science must firmly be included among the liberalizing humanities in any honest assessment of modern thought and knowledge.

"The beauty and simplicity of the laws of nature which govern the world in which we find ourselves, the fantastic range today of man's ideas and studies and measurements, from the countless galaxies in the distant reaches of outer space far beyond the faintest stars of our own Milky Way, down to the structures inside the atomic nucleus, this is vision enough to humble the most arrogant.

"The poetically beautiful patterns of modern scientific knowledge bear fresh witness in a whole new range of thoughts and qualities and dimensions to the Psalmist's ancient cry:

"'The heavens declare the glory of God and the firmament showeth His handiwork.'"

"Lest anyone here has lost sight of it, let me tell you that this attitude, all too rarely spoken out in these days of secular support, is historically and still today the essential spirit of all scientific study and research. This spirit of wonder and exaltation is the ancient root and the modern strength of all our Western search for new knowledge.

"This is the spirit of science, and the content of science is knowledge. Science is not airplanes and missiles and radars and atomic power, nor is it Salk vaccine or cancer chemotherapy or anticoagulants for heart patients. These all are technological developments which have grown out of scientific studies. Science is knowledge of the natural world about us, it is the systematic ordering and interrelating of the huge body of information we already have acquired, it is the search for new knowledge about the marvelous world in which we find ourselves. Science is knowledge and the love of knowledge and teaching and research concerning nature."

Dr. Tuve and Admiral Rickover seemed to differ slightly, both on the need for more scientists and on the comparative quality of United States' education with Western Europe's.

Admiral Rickover said that the "chronic shortage of good scientists, and engineers," was due to "time wasted in public school." He gave the audience some figures to show that the school day in the Netherlands was 10 per cent longer than ours; the school week, 20 per cent longer; the school year 240 days or 33 per cent longer.

Dr. Tuve agreed that the standards were too low in this country, but he observed:

"I am not convinced that this is an educational problem. I think it is much more truthfully a problem in public administration. It is not obvious at all that we have a real shortage of technical men, but the distribution of these men has certainly been biased toward particular types of work for the Government.

"We would experience no great shortage if we could make really effective use of the technical men we already have without greatly increasing the output from our universities."

"Engineers and technologists, too often called scientists, are stacked three deep on most defense contracts. If these contracts were run more nearly on the old-fashioned American basis of competition and with rewards commensurate with the results obtained we would hear vastly less about any shortage of technical men."

CONANT ASSESSES U. S. SCHOOL NEEDS

Finds Only 8 High Schools of 55 He Visited Properly Fulfilling Objectives

OFFERS 21-POINT PLAN

Urges Challenges for Gifted and Harder Courses in His Report on 2-Year Study

The nation's public high schools have been found to be basically capable of meeting educational needs by Dr. James B. Conant, president emeritus of Harvard University.

Dr. Conant said that he believed that "no radical change in the basic pattern of American education is necessary in order to improve our public high schools."

After visiting fifty-five high schools in eighteen states in the last two years, Dr. Conant said he had one general criticism. Academically talented students, he said, are not being challenged sufficiently, do not work hard enough and do not follow study programs with a wide enough range.

His observations are to be published as a report entitled "The American High School Today" by the McGraw-Hill Book Company on Jan. 28, in paperback and hard-cover editions.

Dr. Conant's study was financed by a $350,000 grant from the Carnegie Corporation. It will continue for at least one more year and is being administered by the Educational Testing Service of Princeton, N. J.

Dr. Conant said that of the fifty-five schools that he had visited, only eight were in his judgment, satisfactorily fulfilling the three main objectives for a comprehensive high school.

Basic Objectives Noted

These objectives he set forth as a general education, good elective programs for those who wish to use their acquired vocational training immediately after graduation and satisfactory programs for those who will go to a college or university in achieving a vocation.

Dr. Conant made twenty-one specific recommendations for strengthening public high schools.

A point that he emphasized was that the number of small high schools must be drastically reduced by district reorganization. The cost of continuing the smaller schools, he said, was exorbitant.

Dr. Conant suggested that the number of high schools in the nation should be reduced from 21,000 at present to 9,000.

In urging greater challenges, more work and broader courses of study, Dr. Conant said:

"The able boys too often specialize in mathematics and science to the exclusion of foreign languages and to the neglect of English and social studies.

"The able girls, on the other hand, too often avoid mathematics and sciences as well as the foreign languages. A correction of this situation in many instances will depend upon an altered attitude of the community quite as much as upon action by a school board or the administrators."

Basic Program Listed

Dr. Conant listed a program of basic studies for every student in high school, regardless of academic ability.

The program would use about half of the classroom time of all students. It would include four years of English, three or four years of social studies—including two years of history and a senior course in American problems or American government—a year of mathematics in the ninth grade and a year of science.

The basic program would be supplemented by either vocational or academic elective courses with a vocational electives for students who do not intend to continue beyond high school.

For students who are academically talented, about 15 per cent of the national total, Dr. Conant urged stiffer programs. That would include four years of mathematics, four years of a foreign language and three years of science.

RICKOVER, IN BOOK, ATTACKS SCHOOLS

Vice Admiral Hyman G. Rickover, in a book published today, urges a more rigorous public school system. He also suggests changes in industry and government to give more freedom to the creative worker.

His book, "Education and Freedom," published by E. P. Dutton & Co., Inc., is written from speeches he has made in the last few years. It repeats his attacks on the public schools for not abolishing "frill" courses and for not adopting a European-style traditional curriculum. It also urges special schools for the talented on the ground that the comprehensive high school for all is undemocratic.

Education is the key to our survival, the admiral declares, and the nation cannot delay in building more schools, colleges and playgrounds, and paying higher taxes to provide "decent salaries" for a much larger and better-trained corps of teachers.

Admiral Rickover also says that this country will not make rapid technological progress unless it reorganizes its institutions to end their "exaggerated veneration for routine and protocol," and to make provision for creative workers and specialists to get things done without red tape.

The day of the organization man whose principal qualification is the ability to get along is nearing an end, he declares. "The man of the future is the technical expert," he says.

January 30, 1959

First Anniversary of Sputnik Sees More Awareness of Needs and Higher Goals

By LOREN B. POPE

Just a year ago the Russians put into orbit man's first earth satellite. This was a disaster, one educator observed, for which the nation immediately blamed the seventh grade.

Today Sputnik I is regarded by many in the educational world as one of the best friends the seventh grade has ever had, because it aroused much of the voting, taxpaying and parental public into informing itself about the seventh grade's needs.

The result was that a good many proposals for school improvement conceived before the sputnik orbited got a push. A Federal aid-to-education bill was enacted. More and more schools joined the lists of those requiring all students to take at least a basic academic program, and the abler ones to take more. Many schools added more language courses, including Russian, often in the elementary grades. Many schools lengthened the school day so as to provide more work. Summer school attendance in many areas became so great as to assume the proportions of an added term. After-hours and Saturday work projects for interested students were offered in a good many city and suburban high schools.

More Science Degrees

A United States Office of Education survey found that the nation's colleges in June will confer perhaps one-third more degrees in mathematics and science than they did last year.

Bond issues for school construction across the nation, the Investment Bankers Association reports, are ahead of last year's record high so far. Last year $2,361,000,000 worth of school bonds were floated, $1,627,000,000 in the first eight months. This year, in the eight-month period, the total was $1,647,-000,000.

This rate of construction is reducing the classroom shortage, but the states estimate it still may total 125,000 rooms. Last year the figure was put at 145,000.

Teachers' salaries were increased enough to ease markedly the teacher shortage in many states.

While progress is generally acknowledged, educators say there is still a long way to go. The National Education Association is still pressing for Federal aid for school construction and for higher teachers' salaries. And Dr. Lawrence G. Derthick, United States Commissioner of Education, said last week that there are three prerequisites to any thoroughgoing improvement of the public school system.

Three Imperatives

First is the job of reorganizing most of the approximately 53,000 school districts in the nation. This is one-half as many as in 1945. But in South Dakota, for example, Dr. Derthick said, there are 3,000 school districts, or one for every two teachers in the state. Of the state's 216 high schools, forty-three have only three teachers. Until such districts in all parts of the nation are consolidated in suitable reorganizations, it will be physically and economically impossible to offer the kind of comprehensive school programs needed.

Second, he said, is the need for everyone involved in education to find ways of stirring parental interest in school improvement.

Third is the need for research to discover basic information about the learning process, and to test existing practices.

Research men say that so little is known about how instruction changes the mind that education will be hobbled in designing a truly effective school until research on the scale of that in medicine is under way. At present the Office of Education has less than $3,000,-000 a year for basic research. The new Education Act will add $18,-000,000 in four years for research on television, films and other aids to teaching, but, by contrast, the United States Public Health Service has approximately $180,000,000 a year for medical and related research.

October 5, 1958

Poll Finds More Study Interest

A nation-wide poll of teen-agers indicating they have much more interest in their studies than they are given credit for is seconded by school administrators in this area.

The educators believe that student attitudes and their test results indicate a definite trend toward more interest in scholarship. They say the students are reflecting the temper of the times.

The opinion sampling of over 11,-000 students was planned by Dr. Harry Deane Wolfe, Professor of Marketing at the University of Wisconsin School of Commerce, and carried out for Scholastic Magazines. The survey was conducted in 284 junior and senior high schools of all sizes and kinds.

Nearly 95 per cent of those questioned thought good marks were important to their futures, and eight out of ten said the most important factors in success in life would be hard work, intelligence and personality, in that order. At the bottom of the list were money and influential friends or relatives.

Grades and Popularity

One-third of the students thought good marks were important for popularity. Nearly two-thirds thought marks made no difference and 2 per cent felt good marks were a liability when it came to popularity.

Nearly 60 per cent felt "fairly sure" they knew what their careers would be and another 13 per cent were "absolutely certain."

The most desirable courses, as rated by the boys, were mathematics, science and "occupational courses." With girls, secretarial courses led, with English second and science third.

Some indication that the survey answers were not merely teen-agers' gestures toward what they considered the "right" attitudes came from several local school administrators, who find their students more interested in studies than in past years.

Dr. Jordan L. Larson, superintendent at Mount Vernon, said results on quality tests indicate that pupils are achieving more than ever before.

In Farmingdale, Dr. Thomas Guilford, school superintendent, said that the consensus of a meeting of principals in his system Friday was that among their pupils there is a "general reawakening of the idea that scholarship is the thing to strive for." Dr. Guilford believes students are working harder because parents, as well as teachers, are now encouraging them more.

Flood of Paperbacks

In New York City, Assistant Superintendent of Schools Charles M. Shapp not only thinks teen-agers are working harder, but is apprehensive that good marks are being made too much of a fetish. He says schools and parents may be making children too fearful that their whole future is tied up in marks. Aside from marks, Dr. Shapp added, the fact that millions of 25-cent paperback books that were never sold before are now being sold through high school book clubs is evidence of new, serious interests.

Dr. Robert B. Foose, principal of the Westfield, N. J., high school, reported "a definite trend" toward serious student interests that "reflect the temper of the times." He anticipated it would be a topic of discussion at forthcoming high school principals' meetings in the state.

Dr. Philip B. Langworthy, school superintendent at Hastings-on-Hudson, said that there has been an increasing interest in academic work over the last few years.

October 5, 1958

112

PHYSICS REVISED FOR HIGH SCHOOL

Columbia Course Stresses Concept and Advanced Theory Over Fact

By ROBERT K. PLUMB

Columbia University Teachers College has developed a high school course in modern physics to be distributed to secondary school systems. It will also be given to teacher-training programs of colleges and universities associated with the Scientific Manpower Project.

Prof. Frederick L. Fitzpatrick, head of the Teachers College Department of Teaching of Science and director of the Science Manpower Project, said yesterday that a high school course in modern physics was needed.

Scope of Course

The recommended course is divided into units dealing with the foundations of mechanics, wave motion, the fluid state, heat-energy in motion, the nature and propagation of light, electricity and magnetism, alternating current phenomena, electronics, nuclear energy and relativity.

Classical concepts of time, space, force, matter and energy are extremely useful in understanding nuclear phenomena, Mr. Vitrogan said. They are retained to contribute to the student's grasp of the unifying principles of modern physics. Some other classical concepts are omitted from the recommended new course.

From an educational point of view, Mr. Vitrogan said, physics principles and concepts are more important than the facts they explain. Physics problems, and the methods of solving them, represent the heart of the "scientific method," he said. The reference books, he added, are the place for unrelated facts of little value.

Mr. Vitrogan said that some teachers might hesitate to use advanced material in high schools.

"But it is important to remember that a concept is not necessarily more difficult for the student because it may be unfamiliar to the teacher," he said. "Students are generally capable of learning far more than we have commonly thought. Where teaching basic concepts is concerned, no distinction should be made between elementary and advanced methods."

The new course has been distributed to several hundred school systems and to forty college and universities with teacher-training programs, Professor Fitzpatrick said.

A new course in modern chemistry and a course in biology and general science are being worked out, he added.

The Science Manpower Project was set up in 1956 at Teachers College to increase the number of qualified high school graduates entering science and engineering programs in college. Grants from leading industrial corporations and from foundations have supported the project.

"Most schools are teaching a type of physics that gives little recognition to the many recent advances in knowledge," Professor Fitzpatrick reported.

"The new course retains the key concepts of the older physics but reflects the tremendous growth of modern physical theory."

The course has suggestions for teaching electronics, nuclear energy and relativity. It emphasizes that students must know the fundamental theories, principles and laws of physics today.

An eighty-eight-page description of the recommended course of study has been written by David Vitrogan, a fellow of the Science Manpower Project and an Associate Professor of Electrical Engineering at Pratt Institute in Brooklyn. Mr. Vitrogan spent a year and a half studying the teaching of modern physics in high schools and discussed the subject with physicists, engineers, scientists and high school teachers.

March 15, 1959

The Teaching of Foreign Languages Is Undergoing a Revolution

By FRED M. HECHINGER

Except as a Broadway hit, the phrase "la plume de ma tante" may soon survive only as an epitaph to a dead language. The dead language is not just school-French but school-any-language. Dissatisfaction with conventional methods and purposes of language instruction has assumed the proportions of an educational revolution, and the fighting slogan of this new movement might well be: "It isn't a language unless you speak it!"

History and national circumstances have given aid and comfort to the revolutionary movement. There is shock value in the revelation by Theodore Anderson, director of the Foreign Language Program of the Modern Language Association of America, that 42.7 per cent of the United States' Foreign Service Corps lacks "adequate knowledge of any foreign language." A recent popular novel, "The Ugly American," drove home the point.

Last week's disclosure that the study of Russian everywhere in the country has skyrocketed, with more high school Russian courses offered in the New York and suburban area alone than were being given in the entire nation two years ago, is merely one symptom of the change.

Change in Purpose

The first change is one of purpose. Educators are beginning to discard the idea that language is merely another academic subject, useful either as a vocational tool (to a very small group) or as an exercise in training the mind. There is still much argument as to the percentage of students who should—and profitably could—study a foreign language. Only a minority of educators believe that all children can be made bi-lingual. One school superintendent in New York warns that this would simply make some children illiterate in two languages—their own and a foreign one.

But Abraham H. Lass, principal of Abraham Lincoln High School in Brooklyn, has no doubt that at least all those students with legitimate aspirations to go to college should speak a foreign language.

The major reason why languages are gaining favor among educators probably is not the popular one of more foreign travel in a smaller world. Nor is it only a question of great national need for expert linguists. Many educators list as a strong point in favor of foreign language study the fact that it

greatly increases mastery and understanding of *any* language—especially of English.

But if only the purposes and needs had changed, the American language revolution would be sure to fizzle. It must have new methods with which to arm the revolutionaries.

Years of Study

Basic to all new methods is the demand for a greater number of consecutive years of study of the same language. Dr. James B. Conant made this one of his priority calls for high school reform. He considers four years of one language an absolute minimum for useful achievement. Aimless flitting from one language to another is to be outlawed. Dr. Conant compares the study of a language for two years to drilling for oil and not waiting until you strike it.

Equally important is the new drive toward language instruction much earlier in a child's schooling. A poll showed that seven out of ten school administrators believe that language teaching (though not necessarily on a compulsory basis) should start in elementary school. This year, under a new program, about 20,000 junior high school students in New York City will study foreign languages. The Schenectady public schools introduced French for all children, from third through fifth grades, three years ago.

Laboratories Gain

Language laboratories, together with expert teachers, who themselves are fluent in the language, have made strong inroads on the public and private schools in the past two years, after they had already been adopted by many colleges. Several New York City high schools hope to have such laboratories available this fall.

The trend toward more and better language instruction is unmistakable. Recent reports that students are doing well even with such difficult languages as Russian are pulling the rug from under the legend that Americans "just aren't good" at languages—which is comparable to the "theory" that girls "don't do well" in science.

Some educators even feel that before long some students may be studying part of their science, history or literature in a foreign language, putting their ability to practical use. Even if this may be visionary for the majority of students, there may soon be fewer Americans who will feel as the late Heywood Broun did in France. "I've studied Beginners' French," he complained. "And when I got to Paris, I found that nobody there spoke Beginners' French."

Best Age

Mary P. Thompson, curriculum consultant in the public schools of Fairfield, Conn., says: "Children aged eight, nine and ten are in the stage of development when they can imitate sounds and patterns of expression with most facility. They are not selfconscious; they are eager and curious; and they are not bored by the kind and amount of repetition which is exactly what is most essential for making the foreign language patterns become unconscious habits." She suggests as a successful time sequence of language learning:

(1) A daily fifteen-minute period of foreign language instruction ir grades three to six.

(2) A forty-fifty-minute period, three times a week, in grades seven and eight for those who elect to continue and are advised to do so.

(3) A forty-five-minute period daily in grades nine and ten.

(4) A forty-five-minute period three times a week in grades eleven and twelve.

It is generally agreed that the specific methods of teaching languages should under any circumstances discard the old stress on writing, grammar, memorizing of vocabulary and translating. From the outset the instrument as well as the aim is to be speaking and hearing. Unfortunately educators, with their love for fun-killing terminology, have already invented the new definition of "the aural-oral approach" to make a simple matter sound less attractive.

A key to this new method is the language laboratory, with all it; electronic aids, tape recordings, op portunities for students to practice on their own and to compare their pronunciation with that of native voices. The result makes languages what is is: the spoken word and the communicated idea.

August 30, 195

CONANT ATTACKS STRESS ON FRILLS BY JUNIOR HIGHS

Urges Greater Emphasis on Academic Work in Second Major Education Study

By FRED M. HECHINGER

Dr. James Bryant Conant has outlined a junior high school program stressing academic preparation for high school. He warns against over-emphasis of athletics and pretentious graduation ceremonies in imitation of high schools.

His recommendations are contained in his second major study of American public education financed by the Carnegie Corporation, which was released yesterday by the Educational Testing Service.

He endorses some high school policies in junior high schools, such as departmentalization of classes. This, he says, can prepare the student for high school, if the teachers are specialists in their subjects.

Dr. Conant, former president of Harvard University, cautions against regarding junior high schools as training grounds for teachers who want to move on to senior high schools. The demanding nature of instruction in the seventh through ninth grade, he says, makes it imperative to train teachers who combine a sensitive understanding of early adolescence with expert knowledge of academic subject matter.

Ceremonies Assailed

Dr. Conant urges that the major portion of the junior

high school curriculum be devoted to "solid" academic subjects and the basic reading and mathematical skills.

The report, presented as "A Memorandum to School Boards," is gentle and conciliatory in much of its criticism, but hits hard at such things as elaborate graduation ceremonies as "without sound educational reason," finding that "too often they serve merely as public entertainment."

Dr. Conant's forty-six-page report is titled "Education in the Junior High School Years." It follows his earlier reform proposals for the senior high schools, "The American High School Today."

The new report contains fourteen specific recommendations based on observations in 237 schools in ninety school systems in twenty-three states during the last academic year. As for the debate over what grades junior high schools should encompass, Dr. Conant asserts that the physical arrangement is far less important than the academic content of those crucial years.

Charts Basic Course

Dr. Conant points out that the original junior high school called for algebra and foreign languages in grades seven and eight. He urges that henceforth all seventh and eighth-grade students study English, with stress on reading and composition; social studies, with stress on history and geography, and mathematics and general science. Biology or physics would be added in ninth grade.

In mathematics, most junior high school students would be required only to study arithmetic, but a small group (estimated at 3 to 5 per cent) of talented eighth graders would begin algebra, with an eye to completing freshman college mathematics in twelfth grade.

All pupils would be required to study art, music and physical education. In addition, boys

would get instruction in industrial arts, and all girls, home economics.

Dr. Conant urges that 60 to 70 per cent of classroom time be spent on the "solid" academic subjects—English, social studies, science and mathematics. A foreign language may be begun in the seventh grade by some students, Dr. Conant feels, but only if it can be continued for six years and if the community can assure the continuous staffing of junior and senior high schools with bilingual language instructors.

Reading Goal Set

The basic skills of reading and arithmetic, begun in elementary school, must be continued "as long as pupils can gain from the instruction," Dr. Conant warns.

By the end of the ninth grade, "even the poorest readers (except the mentally retarded) should read at least at the sixth-grade level," he says.

Dr. Conant sets as "a minimum goal" for future voters the ability, at the end of the ninth grade, to read "with comprehension the front page of a newspaper at a rate of about 200 words a minute."

"I have been in schools in which practically no one in the ninth grade was reading as low as grade six, and I have been in schools in which from 35 to 50 per cent of the ninth graders were reading at the sixth grade level or below," Dr. Conant reports.

Dr. Conant is severely critical of the frequent lack of coordination of subject matter between elementary, junior high and high schools, and even between different grades within a school. He urges that the teaching of all subjects be coordinated throughout a community's school system.

Dr. Conant confirms the belief that the junior high school years are among the hardest to teach and require more and better teachers than the senior high schools.

But he finds that, in fact, the junior high schools have fewer teachers. He calls for a minimum goal of fifty teachers for 1,000 pupils. A reasonable teaching load, he adds, would be five teaching periods with 125 to 150

pupils a day in grades seven to twelve. English teachers, because of the time needed for composition and reading, should not be required to teach more than 100 students in one term.

As for school boards "and other lay groups," Dr. Conant asks them to keep hands off the appointment of teachers, the judgment of the quality of teaching and the details of course content and the choice of textbooks.

At the same time, he adds, the superintendent should answer to the board for satisfactory operation of the schools and "should not have tenure."

Grade Size Suggested

Among his other recommendations are these:

¶A minimum of 125 pupils in each of grades seven and eight to assure economical operation. With smaller enrollment, these grades should be included in the senior high school, making up a total of six years. Otherwise, either a two or three-year junior high school is considered acceptable. Dr. Conant considers 750 pupils the optimum for a separate three-year junior high school.

¶The use of "block time," or the teaching of two subjects for two or more consecutive periods by the same teacher, at least in seventh grade, to enable at least one teacher to know his students well.

¶A sufficiently flexible schedule, best achieved through a seven-period day, or thirty-five-period week, to avoid the necessity for students "to make choices between, for example, science and foreign languages." Dr. Conant found "some school days are entirely too short."

¶A competent, full-time guidance specialist for every 250 to 300 pupils.

¶Homework from one hour a day in seventh grade to two hours by ninth grade for most pupils. But the report adds, "Drudgery, however, is not meaningful homework."

¶No automatic promotions if pupils fail to develop basic reading and mathematics skills, but they should not be held back for more than two years in the first eight grades.

¶A well-stocked library, a gymnasium, home economics and industrial arts rooms, an auditorium or assembly space for at least half the student body and cafeteria space for at least one-third. A professional librarian should not be responsible for more than 750 pupils.

¶An assistant principal for every 750 pupils; a clerk or secretary for every 250 pupils.

Copies of Dr. Conant's report are being sent to all school superintendents in the country for distribution to their school boards. A final report on the entire panorama of American public education will be added later, Dr. Conant said.

The new paperback volume will not be on sale in stores, but is obtainable for 50 cents a copy, or $1 for three copies, from the Educational Testing Service, Princeton, N. J.

October 9, 1960

TEACHING REFORM IN CLASSES SCORED

Self-Contained Classroom Is Upheld in Booklet That Criticizes Conant's Ideas

By FRED A. HECHINGER

Curriculum experts of the nation's largest public-education group opened a counter-attack yesterday against most school-reform proposals by rival experts.

Although the detailed brochure in defense of established practices, especially of the so-called self-contained classroom, mentions no names, it opposes some proposals made by Dr. James B. Conant in his recent report on the junior high schools.

Calling many present reformers "ignorant," the booklet opposes the teaching of special skills, such as reading, arithmetic or social studies, by specialists in departmentalized elementary and junior high schools.

Although it ascribes such reforms to "sincere, but often uninformed pressure groups," the statement makes no mention that the profession itself appears divided on these issues.

Among the kind of reforms the booklet denounces is the experiment, directed by Dr. George D. Stoddard, chancellor of New York University, that has introduced departmentalization in the Long Beach and Ossining, N. Y., elementary schools. These experiments are supported by the Ford Foundation's Fund for the Advancement of Education.

Other Proposals Cited

Many of the proposals for a less traditional school organization, including the use of teaching teams within one classroom, have actually been pioneered by another N. E. A. spokesman, J. Lloyd Trump, of the National Association of Secondary School Principals.

But Arthur W. Foshay, president of the curriculum unit, says in a foreword that many current reformers "have undertaken change in ignorance." He accuses "the innovators" of comparing "poor or average" existing schools with ideal dreams of future, non-existant schools. To underline the controversy, an accompanying news release calls the booklet an answer to "the recent hullabaloo over the need to raise educational standards."

Countering current demands for greater depth of learning through specialized instruction, the booklet urges retention of the traditional concept as the key to integration of knowledge.

Dewey Dispute Revived

The controversial booklet again conjures up the dispute between extreme followers of John Dewey who advocated a "child-centered" school and those who charge a deterioration of academic content, as a consequence.

The eighty-eight-page booklet, "The Self-Contained Classroom," was issued yesterday by the Association for Supervision and Curriculum Development, a department of the National Education Association.

It defines its ideal as "a type of curricular organization that allows one group of students and one teacher to be together for a major portion of the school day in the elementary school, and for a large block of time in the junior and senior high school."

Often, it adds, the elementary teacher might remain with one class for two or three years.

In addition to opposing departmentalized academic instruction, the booklet warns against rigid division of the school day into many periods of instruction. Dr. Conant asked for a seven-period junior high-school day.

Although the sharply worded booklet is likely to reopen the public controversy over what educators call the split between the "child-centered" and the "subject-centered" school, it also discloses a conflict within the N. E. A. itself.

October 26, 1960

BASIC REFORMS

Reading and Mathematics Changes Underline Grade School Trend

By FRED M. HECHINGER

At the beginning of the American school reform movement, which got under way about five years ago, it appeared as if the improvements might affect only the high schools. For one thing, the high school seemed to be the key to college admission. For another, the great catalyst of school improvement, Dr. James B. Conant, started out with that best-selling academic first-aid kit, "The American High School Today."

In recent years, however, it has become evident that if the school reform vaccine were to take, it would have to affect education all the way down the line. Last week's news left no doubt that elementary schools are part of the great change.

What are the major indications of change?

(1) *Reading.* The formation of the Leading Reform Foundation, with offices at Thirty-six West Forty-fourth Street in New York City, is merely a symptom—as was the immediate, widespread public interest in the group. Created with the admittedly controversial aim of advocating greater stress on phonetic or letter and syllable-conscious methods of teaching, the important aspect of the new group was that it had among its supporters prominent school principals and headmasters, as well as so influential a public school educator as the superintendent of schools of the District of Columbia. (It also has the support of some who in the past have been denounced as extremists in the battle against the present approach to reading and children's literature.)

What is important is not the question whether one extreme (the pure alphabet method) or the opposite extreme (the pure "whole-word" recognition method) will defeat the other. This is least likely to happen any way because few schools are any longer committed to any one method. The promise is that the roadblocks to research and comparison may be removed.

Improvement Expected

The current revolt promises that teaching materials—books, worksheets, slides, films and other aids—will improve. The most openly exposed targets of current criticism are the beginning primers and readers which, in spite of denials by some experts and publishers, are attuned to the limited vocabularies of extreme devotion to "whole-word" recognition. The "Go, Dick, go, go" type of children's literature is doomed, no matter what combinations of reading methods will emerge.

(2) *Mathematics.* By coincidence, the week also saw publication of the first part of a new approach to mathematics, from kindergarten through third grade, to be followed by similar materials through sixth grade by 1964. Although sponsored by the Educational Research Council of Greater Cleveland and to be published by Science Research Associates, educational publishers in Chicago, the new approach is the result of research and reform by more than a dozen scholarly groups, foundations and experts. It is already known that several other series of teaching materials will be offered by other groups, before the end of the year.

All have in common a new stress on fundamental concepts, permitting children to discover theories of mathematics before learning skills. Most of them appear to begin with geometric concepts rather than numbers—generally in kindergarten. In

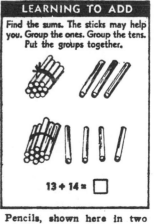

LEARNING TO ADD

Find the sums. The sticks may help you. Group the ones. Group the tens. Put the groups together.

13 + 14 = ☐

Pencils, shown here in two groups of ten and singly, illustrate the theory of how "sets" relate to numbers.

most of the new approaches, the idea of mathematics as "a language" rather than an exercise is basic. They seem to share the "set" theory rather than starting with numerals. Understanding of that theory on the children's level was recently illustrated when a five-year-old, asked to tell what was meant by a "set," replied: "A bunch of things."

Inadequate Preparation

(3) *Teacher training.* In the case of reading, there is agree-

LEARNING TO READ—TWO CONCEPTS EXAMINED

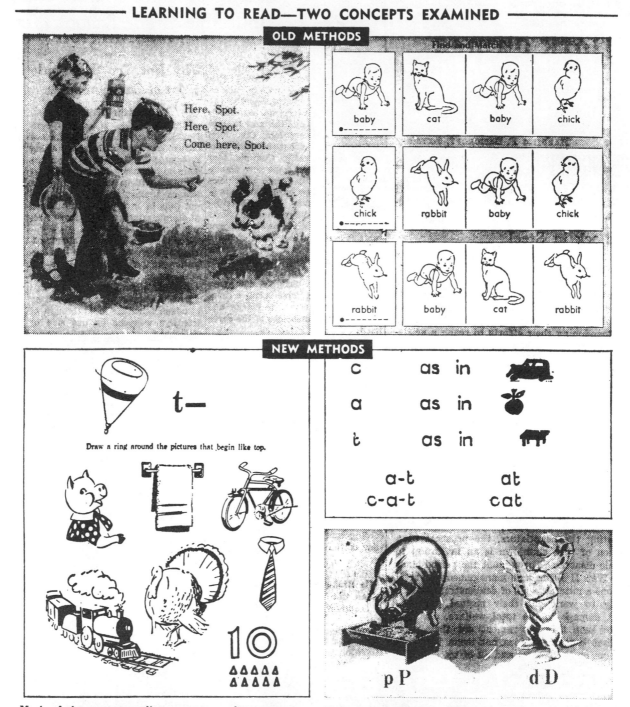

OLD METHODS

Here, Spot.
Here, Spot.
Come here, Spot.

Find and Match

baby	cat	baby	chick
chick	rabbit	baby	chick
rabbit	baby	cat	rabbit

NEW METHODS

t—

Draw a ring around the pictures that begin like top.

10

c   as in
a   as in
t   as in

a-t   at
c-a-t   cat

p P   d D

Much of the current reading controversy focuses on two theories, typified by these teaching materials. The page from "Sally Dick and Jane," (top left) one of the popular basic readers shows the stress on repetition of a few simple words which the child recognizes. The entire 48-page book uses only eighteen words. Typical for the process of getting children "ready" for this approach is the page (top right) from another basic reader series which associates "whole words" with pictures and asks the child to tell what the drawings represent, without reading letters or syllables.

The opponents of this approach stress early recognition of letters, as in the exercise (lower left) from the experimental "phonovisual" workbook or the newly designed beginning reader (top picture at lower right) of the Trent School in New York where single letters, first linked to familiar objects, are put to form new words. Another version of the phonetic approach is shown in the bottom pictures at lower right. This method introduces lower case and capital letters with pictures in Hay-Wingo method, named for authors Julie Hay and Charles E. Wingo. Thus, a controversy continues.

ment that, whatever the methods, present teacher preparation is inadequate. Recent studies at Harvard (described in "The Torch Lighters" by Mary C. Austin) showed that in the past practice teaching has been so ineffectively organized that few teacher-trainees ever got more than a fragmentary view of the problem and the task.

In mathematics, things are probably even worse. Most elementary school teachers have had little, if any, real mathematical training.

The reform movement has begun to re-train teachers, both in summer seminars and through television instruction after class. The new mathematics materials, published last week, will include films for teacher training. Even parents are, in complete reversal of the past "hands-off" theory, being taken into the confidence of the reforms, with special guides for parents who are interested.

(4) *Speed of Learning.* This remains the unanswered question and almost certainly the next general step in the reform. In the pre-reform school it was not at all unusual for the mother of a bright boy in kindergarten to be warned that he would have trouble in first grade "because he already knows so much that he will be bored." Second grade was often considered a holding operation, designed to give slower children a chance to catch up.

With greater stress on the natural momentum of children's curiosity and a more free-wheeling program, the rigid structure of grades is likely to give way increasingly to a more natural view of advancement. In some schools this has already led to the rediscovery of the "ungraded" elementary school idea of the early and truly progressive days.

This will lead some to say that the reform means simply a cruel speed-up, while others will charge that it is a return to the laissez-faire of progressive education.

Neither interpretation is correct. The new aim is to let children progress at "their own pace." Admittedly this was a progressive slogan. But the reform aims at not letting the pace be slowed down by low estimates of the power of young minds.

Two-Year-Olds Are Very Smart

Extremely young children can be taught almost any subject—if you know how to teach it.

By RONALD GROSS

"ANY subject can be taught effectively to any child at any age in some form that is honest and useful." This revolutionary hypothesis was put forward by Harvard psychologist Jerome Bruner, author of the provocative book, "The Process of Education," published in 1960. It has since become the creed of a growing number of American schoolmen and university scholars concerned with improving the public schools.

These pioneers are demonstrating that young children can grasp and apply difficult ideas if the curriculum is designed to engage their natural curiosity, intellectual initiative and level of interest—and if, too, the teachers know how to present it. In schools throughout the nation, experimental programs are demolishing many of the conventional assumptions about how children learn and what they can grasp. The results have implications not only for grade-schoolers but for children of all ages as well as all ranges and kinds of ability. The emerging conclusions could change the entire program of American education in coming decades.

A Rutgers psychologist, Omar Khayyam Moore, has shown conclusively that children from age 2 can be taught to read, not by being "pushed" but entirely through their own curiosity and drive to make sense of what Moore calls a "responsive environment" —in this case, a giant "teaching machine" consisting essentially of a computerized electric typewriter. The system is now being tried in Boston with underprivileged preschoolers, in a Freeport, L. I., kindergarten, and elsewhere.

In St. Louis, as well as in Scarsdale, N. Y., and Weston, Conn., mathematician Robert Davis guides elementary school children into "discovering" basic concepts of modern mathematics. At the University of Illinois, J. Richard Suchman leads youngsters into understanding the principles of original scientific investigations. In Elkhart, Ind., Purdue's Lawrence Senesh conveys the rudiments of college economics to second-graders.

Nor is this movement confined to scattered individual classrooms. Texas this year switched thousands of its elementary school pupils onto the "new math" which began, and still epitomizes, the movement. Meantime, "new

math" programs have reached three-fifths of all American high schools. And this fall some two-thirds of the nation's high-school physics students will be studying the "new physics," which uses diverse materials and more techniques to transform the standard, hopelessly outmoded high-school course.

In the words of Calvin Gross, Superintendent of Schools of New York City, "Everything has caught fire at once. These are very heady times in education."

* * *

ONLY by watching teachers in action is it possible to grasp the character and potency of the new programs. A good example is Prof. Robert Karplus, a bespectacled University of California physicist who is showing that second- and third-graders can engage in original inquiry concerning "physical systems, equilibrium, interaction and simple relativity." In San Francisco, under a National Science Foundation grant, Karplus trains regular public school teachers to start a typical lesson by showing the class two drawings. The first, labeled "Before," shows a beaker half-full of colorless fluid, with a small cube resting at the bottom. Bubbles are rising from the cube. The second picture, labeled "After," shows the beaker, still half-filled with fluid, but minus the cube and bubbles. Question: What has happened?

THE following responses were given by different children in one class:

Pupil: "It's sugar. It's a sugar cube. A sugar cube breaks up in water."

Pupil: "It's ice, and the ice melts in water."

Pupil: "No, if it was ice you'd have more water."

Pupil: "It's not ice. Ice would float at the top."

Pupil: "It looks like sugar. It's a sugar cube because it's square."

Teacher: "Could ice be square?"

Pupil: "Yes, but not all the time, so it's probably sugar."

Teacher: "Will sugar float at the top?"

The children say no, sugar will not float at the top, but they do not seem entirely ready to accept this idea.

Pupil: "It's a dice."

Pupil: "No, dice doesn't melt!"

Pupil: "Somebody might have taken it out of the water."

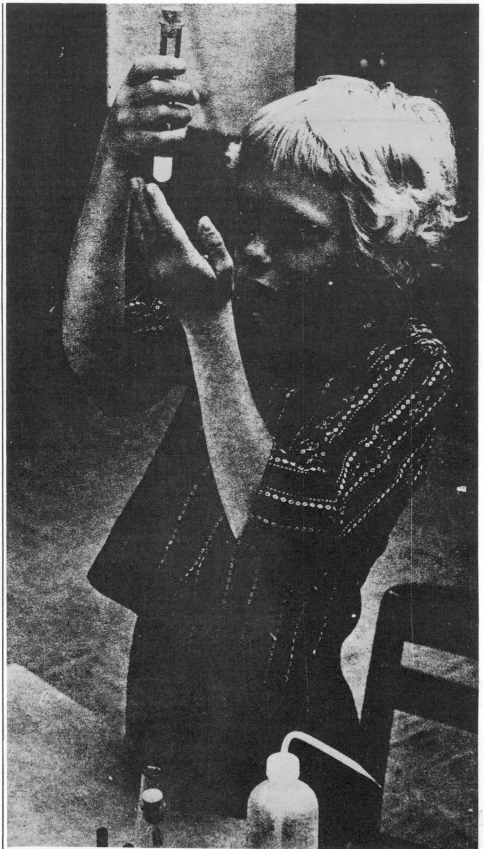

NEW PHYSICS—In a California second grade, children discover in an experiment the law of physics that matter is conserved even though its appearance may change dramatically. Unhampered by rigid curricula, they will venture into relativity physics in the third grade.

Pupil: "It's soap, because of the bubbles coming off."

Pupil: "It's not soap, soap takes too long a time to dissolve, and anyhow it forms lots of bubbles and lather."

Pupil: "I measured, the height of water in both is the same—about 16 inches."

The teacher writes down on the board all the things the class thought might be in the jar. The next day she places three jars of water before the children and has them try out each of the possibilities. One of the children who thought the object in the jar was ice obtains a piece from the school cafeteria for the experiment. Others bring a cube of sugar and a piece of soap. After observing and discussing the experiments, the class decides for sugar. Apparently the telling clue is the fact that the sugar cube in their own experiment gives off bubbles like those shown in the picture the day before.

The teacher could, of course, have given the children the relevant facts at the outset. Instead, 30 third-graders spent a considerable time observing, analyzing their observations and using them to defend or modify their conclusions. This type of lesson is sometimes called "How to Take Half an Hour to Teach What You Could Tell in One Minute."

"THE most difficult thing I had to do when I first began working in elementary classrooms," says Professor Karplus, "was to shut up and listen to the children's responses. Answers should be sought and found, as much as possible, not in the teacher or in a textbook, but in the behavior of the phenomenon observed by the student. That's why we publish no conventional textbooks, only student manuals which contain little scientific information. The only information to which the children have access is derived from the observations they make. The manuals suggest possible ways of interpreting the results or of getting more information."

Professor Karplus's Science Curriculum Improvement Study, like most of the curriculum revision programs, combines this kind of "learning by discovery" with conventional expository teaching. Basic scientific concepts are introduced by the teacher, but the children are then encouraged to discover interrelations and applications.

* * *

SO far, scientists and mathematicians have produced the most startling results with very young children, and they have new programs in the works, including a whole science curriculum for the elementary grades from kindergarten on up. But there are significant advances in the social sciences and humanities, too, including a nationwide "new economics" curricu-

NEW MATH—A 6-year-old builds, feels and sees numbers on a pattern board and thus begins to grasp their relatiohships.

lum recently announced by the Joint Council on Economic Education.

In Elkhart, Ind., for example, first-graders learn the basic concepts of economics—scarcity, division of labor, specialization, investment and unemployment—which build on the everyday life at home. "The program works by enabling children to analyze their own experiences and to discover the economic patterns and principles that underly them," says Lawrence Senesh, professor of economic education at Purdue University and designer of the project.

"The youngsters discover they can bring order into their own experiences—something they want desperately to do. There are just a few big ideas in economics, and our notion is to introduce and interrelate them all right at the start in

simple, concrete form, then come back to them term after term with richer, deeper study." Senesh thus defines the "spiral curriculum" that is at the heart of most of the new curricula.

First-grade pupils begin by analyzing the division of labor in their own families and the products and services they buy. But soon they generalize on these observations, helped by ingenious activities which bring alive the underlying concepts. In one class, two teams produce gingerbread men. Each child on Team A makes his own gingerbread man, starting from scratch — with visible waste of material, duplication of equipment, slowness of execution, and low production. On Team B, the youngsters form an assembly-line, with one child rolling dough, another cutting forms, a third pressing in the eyes, and the last child putting the cookies in the oven. The hypothesis that division of labor increases production is dramatically confirmed.

LATER in the term, Senesh's first-graders conduct surveys to find out how many of their neighbors are in production jobs, how many in service jobs, how many are unemployed and why. By the end of the year they can discern the relationships among such basic factors as consumer preferences, changes in the relative level of prices, and expansion or contraction of employment in different industries. It is not surprising by this time that one of the 6-year-olds, observing an increased demand for dresses in the first grade's mock economy, decides to expand his clothing business by borrowing from a bank run by a classmate.

Far from being vocationally oriented, like so many familiar efforts of the past, this program is keyed to basic economic ideas and the relations between them. In the second grade the program broadens out from the home to the neighborhood, and from neighborhood to city in the third grade. Economics is the core, but the children also delve into anthropology, sociology, history, political science and geography. Top university scholars in these fields have assisted Professor Senesh to make the course a general introduction to the social studies.

"We've shown that first-grade pupils are more curious

about their social environment than college freshmen," says Professor Senesh, who is extending his program through grade 12 and offering his materials to other schools. "They're ready to learn. The only question is — are the schools ready to teach them?"

* * *

DIVERSE as they are in form and origin, the radical innovations now challenging American education share certain common elements.

First, they have been initiated by distinguished university scholars rather than by professional educators. Evans Clinchy of Educational Services. Inc., a non-profit curriculum development organization, asserts: "This is perhaps the first time in history that so many richly endowed adults have lavished so much attention on what is or should be happening inside such small heads."

In the heyday of progressive education, it was the educators, especially the educational psychologists, who took charge. In the current reform movement, the academic scholars made the first move. It is significant, though, that in trying to plant their specialties in the *terra incognita* of the ordinary classroom, the scholars found they needed all the light that contemporary psychology and related disciplines could provide.

Second, the major reforms have been created outside the educational establishment of state departments of education, teacher-training institutions, professional curriculum committees, and commercial textbook publishers. The curriculum revisions are national in scope and support, if not in actual application. Most of the money has come from the Federal Government (National Science Foundation, U. S. Office of Education), the rest from private foundations such as Ford, Carnegie and Sloan.

Third, though the machinery of the educational establishment has been bypassed, the movement has won the support and enthusiasm of a great many practicing teachers and school administrators. Thus, the programs signal an unprecedented collaboration between academic scholars and schoolmen—the most hopeful outcome to date of the recent rapprochement of the two groups.

Fourth, the reformers have not merely issued dicta on what and how to teach.

The scholars have gone into the classrooms; they have brought real children and seasoned teachers into their laboratories; and, together, they have created, tested and revised materials and methods that will succeed in the schools.

Fifth, the most promising of the programs, whatever their particular form, draw from two broad streams of enlightenment: new understanding of the basic elements of each subject and new or freshly interpreted understanding of the capacity for learning inherent in youngsters. A pioneer in the field refers to this process as "the wedding of the key concepts of the disciplines with the mental-development of children."

One contributing influence is new insight into the teaching effectiveness of basing curriculum on the inner logic and relationships peculiar to each branch of learning. Here the scholars are discovering that improving education in the lower schools is no routine matter of updating and upgrading information: a complete analysis of the disciplines is prerequisite to making them understandable and useful to young children.

Another element is a new consensus on motivation. Cumulative evidence from many sources—animal experiments, studies of how children learn, everyday observations of the way they really behave—has shown up the inadequacies of old notions of motivation, based on reward and punishment, by demonstrating that human beings are born with the desire to know, the urge to explore and to master their environment, to achieve. Professor Robert White calls this basic human drive "competence motivation."

RELATED to these liberating ideas about human motivation are recent findings about human intelligence generally. No longer do scientists and educators concur, as they did for so long, in the stultifying concept of fixed intelligence and predetermined development. A sociologist, Robert E. L. Faris, puts it: "A half-century or so ago a miniature Dark Age descended over the field of human psychology and the doctrines of the mental testers convinced an impressed public with a secular variant of an infant damnation doctrine."

Now, however, an impressive array of findings is undermining this conception. Professor J. McV. Hunt of the University of Illinois has recently reviewed the evidence in his definitive book "Intelligence and Experience." After analyzing the relevant research, in fields ranging from the development of intelligence in children to the workings of electronic computers, Hunt concludes that "the counsel from experts on child-rearing during the third and much of the fourth decades of the 20th century to 'let children be' while they grow and to avoid excessive stimulation was highly unfortunate."

EVERYTHING points, says Hunt, to our ability "to discover ways to govern the encounters that children have with their environments, especially during the early years of their development, and to achieve a substantially faster rate of intellectual development and a substantially higher adult level of intellectual capacity. Moreover, inasmuch as the optimum rate of intellectual development would mean also self-directing interest and curiosity and genuine pleasure in intellectual activity, promoting intellectual development properly need imply nothing like the grim urgency which has been associated with 'pushing' children."

The reformers certainly want children left free to learn at their own best pace, but they know that each individual's rate of learning is largely dependent on the richness and complexity of his environment.

* * *

WHAT happens when children are provided with the most stimulating materials now available and then guided into "learning by discovery" in a wide range of subjects? Do the results force us to revise our notions about their learning capacity? What is the range of untapped intellectual resources in our youngsters? Why aren't students learning more than they are?

These questions are haunting American educators today.

What seems increasingly clear is this: Present limitations on learning are due not to children's incapacity or "unreadiness" to deal with complex ideas. These limits are due, rather, to adult incapacity to present ideas and facts in ways that will capture youngsters' imagination and interest. "I think that in many cases we have been boring children to death with the same information, the same materials," says Dr. Kenneth Wann, of Teachers College, Columbia.

In Melbourne, Fla., where high-school students are grouped by achievement and capacity in each subject, rather than by age or grade, they have shown astonishing progress following new curricula of all kinds, frequently on their own; even intelligence test scores have moved steadily upward for bright and average students alike.

THE only long-range solution, already being tested by some colleges and universities, is vastly to improve the preparation of prospective teachers, both in their knowledge of the disciplines and in their understanding of human capabilities.

When such teachers begin entering the schools in sufficient numbers, we can expect the new curricula to have a dramatic effect on the American school system. We will see children guided to intellectual discovery by teachers who know their subjects well enough to permit students to perceive facts and relationships themselves. Such an approach will run head-on into such current staples of our schools as the fixed curriculum to be "covered" in each grade, the whole concept of progression through the

"grades" for each student and the very notion of what a "teacher" is supposed to do in the classroom. In short, revolutionary changes are in the offing, because these experiments in stretching the limits of learning directly challenge education's "conventional wisdom."

Jerome Bruner, who formulated the hypothesis that underlies so much of the recent experimentation, has offered perhaps the most accurate and provocative comment on the future. "We are indeed on the edge of a great period of revolution," Bruner observes. "But it would be a great pity if our zeal were too easily assuaged by partial victories. We do well to recall that most revolutions have been lost precisely because they did not go far enough."

IN Brentwood, L. I., a modest New York suburb, the school system has developed a radically new curriculum which incorporates many of the new "national" revisions. Like Melbourne, Brentwood's reforms are keyed to each child's intellectual capacity and originality, and the school shows remarkable success in fostering intellectual initiative and self-respect among its students.

Melbourne and Brentwood are exceptional, of course. Not many schools have gone all out to validate the new assumptions about human learning. But from hundreds of classrooms, from experimental work in many subject areas, and from pilot projects like those described here, the evidence piles up.

Three-year-olds learn to read and write; first-graders grapple with the fundamentals of economics and algebraic reasoning; third-graders venture hypotheses in relativity physics; fifth-grade pupils "discover" set theory in mathematics: preadolescents deal with the principles of anthropology; and high-school students grasp aspects of physical theory usually taught in college How far, we may well begin to speculate, *can* we stretch the limits of learning in our schools?

The new teaching techniques have made it clear that we can teach such subjects as algebra and relativity physics, honestly and rigorously, to *some* elementary school pupils. And the implication is inescapable that we could, if we would, bring *all* children much further along in substantial learning than we have hitherto even hoped.

Even children at the low end of the ability scale benefit from instruction with the new techniques. In a conventional classroom the bright, verbal children often dominate completely. But when children are allowed to discover facts and relationships themselves, as with O. K. Moore's "talking typewriter" or in one of Professor Senesh's economics classes, the less bright youngsters often experience the exhilaration of intellectual success for the first time. Below-average students seem to thrive on increased independence in learning.

On a nationwide basis, the Biological Sciences Curriculum Study at the University of Colorado, leader in the reform of high-school biology, has developed a full-year course for "unsuccessful learners." The materials are designed for students with IQ's of 75-90, the lowest 20-25 per cent of high-school biology students — yet the course is built around the basic ideas of biology, not watered-down "hygiene." The course is being tested this year on 7,000 students throughout the country.

Professional mathematicians meeting in Cambridge (Mass.) last year, aware that their conclusions would be applied to other disciplines, boldly concluded that a mathematics program from kindergarten through high school "might be brought into being over the next few decades" which would be comprehensible to virtually all children and would lead to a level of competence "comparable to three years of top-level college training today."

Specialists in other fields are equally sanguine. But even the most enthusiastic reformers admit the enormous gap between what could *possibly* happen and what is likely to happen. In realistic terms, how will the instructional ferment affect the American school system in the years ahead? The answer depends primarily on the nation's schoolteachers.

It is one thing to retrain a few thousand high school physics teachers—as the National Science Foundation has done—but quite another to retrain close to a million elementary school teachers in the "new math" or the "new history." Current curriculum reforms have had to be designed within the limits of what present-day teachers with minimal retraining can handle. This has set a practical upper limit that is "uncomfortably close," says Francis Keppel, U.S. Commissioner of Education.

September 6, 1964

New Math Is Replacing Third 'R'

Some Experts Fear Haste in Change Is Hurting Teaching

School Pupils Learn Ideas Once Taught Chiefly in College

By HARRY SCHWARTZ

Warning to elementary and high school students, parents and teachers: Brace yourselves. The "new mathematics" of today may be followed by an even newer and stranger mathematics. You may look back on the present as "the good old days."

And yet, there are those who say the new mathematics already introduced has been thrown into the curriculum, in many cases, too hastily. They contend that the mathematics revolution has sometimes taken place so rapidly that teachers have not received adequate training to teach it.

The new mathematics is an attempt to introduce into elementary and high school teaching some of the ideas and points of view that have dominated mathematics research for more than a century. The aim is to help children to understand mathematics as well as to do it.

It is a good deal more advanced than the "old mathematics," which, say the proponents of the new, was little more than rote memorization.

One warning of possible things to come is contained in a published proposal that tomorrow's junior high school youngsters study derivatives, Diophantine equations and iterative procedures, and that high school students explore such other esoteric fields as the topology of the complex plane and the matrices of a transformation.

The proposal is in a report of the 1963 Cambridge Conference on School Mathematics, held at Cambridge, Mass.

New Reforms Urged

One influential elder statesman among American mathematicians thinks that even this proposal does not go far enough.

He recently submitted to the Carnegie Corporation a memorandum calling for even more radical revision of the curriculum below college level.

The reforms now being introduced, he said, are "timid and patently inadequate." The corporation asked that his name be withheld.

The United States Commissioner of Education, Francis Keppel, has declared that the schools must aim toward the more advanced curriculums that have been proposed. But he warned that not only would most teachers "be completely incapable of teaching much of the mathematics" set forth in the Cambridge proposal but also "most teachers would be hard put to comprehend it."

One of the voices raised against the speed of the mathematics teaching revolution in the elementary and high schools has been that of Dr. Max Beberman, the noted University of Illinois pioneer in the field.

Dr. Beberman, a stocky man, whose enthusiasm is infectious, told mathematics teachers in Montreal last month that "a major national scandal" may be in the making because of hasty introduction of the new mathematics in the elementary schools. He said this was harming the teaching of arithmetic to children who would need its skills for the tasks of adult life.

A survey by The New York Times of other leaders in mathematics education found this concern widely, though not unanimously, held.

Too Little Training

Prof. Howard Fehr of Columbia University's Teachers College said in an interview that there was ample ground for worry about the impact of the great changes in mathematics teaching. He believes that the new mathematics is being introduced more rapidly than teachers are being trained to give proper instruction in it.

Professor Fehr, a tall, gray-haired man who speaks precisely, said:

"About 75 per cent of all high school students are studying the new mathematics, but only 25 to 35 per cent of their teachers have been trained in the new subject matter. About

40 per cent of all elementary school students are studying the new mathematics, but at most only 5 per cent of elementary school teachers have been trained for the job."

Dr. Beberman has said that the proliferation of new-mathematics courses has resulted in "a large number of frightened teachers" terrified of a new subject matter they must teach although they understand it poorly or not at all.

If many teachers are frightened and baffled over the intricacies of the new math, millions more parents have scratched their heads over it in recent years.

The Idea of Sets

Many who can remember how they once were helped at home with their fifth-grade arithmetic homework have been shocked to discover they cannot do—or even understand sometimes — the homework problems of their own fifth-graders.

This is because the new subject matter goes into things Mommy and Daddy never learned in the fifth grade.

It introduces the idea of sets —any collection of well-defined objects, symbols or ideas—as basic to all mathematics. It seeks to put arithmetic and algebra on rigorously logical bases—complete with axioms, and theorems to be proved—on the style of Euclidean plane geometry. It goes into subject matter formerly rarely studied below the college level—for example, symbolic logic and probability theory.

Some mathematicians who would go further propose to put into the 12 years of elementary and high school mathematics study the essentials of the old curriculum plus most of the first three years of college mathematics, as far as advanced calculus and linear algebra.

It is the very speed with which the math teaching changes are being carried out that provides much of the explanation for the lagging development of teachers trained to do a good job.

Millions of Books

Dr. John M. Mays of the National Science Foundation illustrates the speed of the process by citing statistics on use of new-mathematics textbooks issued by the most influential single group seeking to develop materials in the field, Stanford University's School Mathematics Study Group.

In 1959-60, according to Dr. Mays, only 23,000 copies of experimental textbooks of the group were being used. Four years later, 1,300,000 copies were in use.

The field has now expanded to such an extent that commercial textbook publishers are busily issuing their own new or revised texts incorporating the new mathematics, in order to tap what promises to be a market for tens of millions of books.

Dr. Mays, as program director of the foundation's section on improvement of the content of mathematics and science courses, has played an important role in encouraging revision of curriculums.

What has led to the mathematics teaching upheaval?

It is the product of the great needs generated by two mathematics explosions of recent decades.

The first is the spectacular expansion of mathematical knowledge on the research level. Research findings are made in an intellectual stratosphere far above an adult who may have done well as an undergraduate mathematics major two decades ago.

New Uses for Mathematics

The second vast expansion has occurred in applied higher mathematics. Once necessary only for scientists, engineers and actuaries, it has now become indispensable in an array of fields.

In part because of the widespread availability of computers that have opened new possibilities in many areas, and in part because of advances in economics, business management, military strategy, biology, sociology and the like, higher mathematics is being used more widely than ever before.

For example, an advertising agency has $1 million to spend on advertising a new household cleanser. It wants to know how the funds should be spent among communications media—newspapers, radio, television, magazines, outdoor posters — to reach the largest number of interested housewives. A relatively new technique called linear programing can provide an approximate answer, since it embodies the mathematical tools required to take account both of the limited funds available and the relative number of housewives supposedly reached for each dollar in alternative media.

Economists for a large corporation are asked by the board of directors to forecast the state of the economy next year and the sales the corporation can make in such an economic climate. The economists may work with a model of the economy represented by an equation incorporating derivatives, logarithms and other mathematical relationships connecting such factors as consumer income, government spending and private investment.

Investigating a Drug

Another example of the use of applied mathematics is provided by a physician in a research laboratory who is asked to test a new drug. He finds that the medicine seems to help some patients and not to help others. But are these results pure chance, or is there a really significant effect produced by the drug? He turns to the theory of statistical inference and the mathematical techniques it provides for deciding whether observed results can or cannot reasonably be attributed to chance.

Assume that planners in the Pentagon are asked to study the economic implications of a future major war, on the assumption that no nuclear weapons are employed and it goes on a long time. The planners decide that such a war would require the United States to double its military budget.

Could this be done in a single year, and if it were done, what would its consequences be for the rest of the economy? The planners turn to the technique of input-output analysis, which provides a blueprint of the economy expressed in equations showing the detailed flow of goods and money through the entire economic system.

Such uses as these, the proponents of the new mathematics argue, must have their inception in grammar school.

They hold that tomorrow's scientists, engineers, businessmen and doctors will be gravely handicapped in learning the mathematics they must master in college and beyond unless the primary and secondary schools give them the basic ideas of the later subject matter.

The opponents of the new mathematics, many of whom feel they have been pushed aside in the wake of unjustified hysteria following the 1957 sputnik launching by the Soviet Union, are a varied group. Some say the new mathematics has introduced too little change. Most have other points of view.

It is held that the new mathematics is unrealistic in stressing abstract and theoretical aspects and ignoring the fact that for most people the concrete applications of ordinary arithmetic are most important.

'A Bill of Goods'

The reforms, it is charged, have confused many youngsters without producing compensating benefits. And the dissenters ask why so little attention has been paid to the needs of youngsters who will not go on to college.

A frequent view was stated by one this way:

"The mathematicians have sold the country a bill of phony goods, and we're going to pay a heavy price for it. The mathematicians don't care in the slightest for the needs of any kids but those who are going to become professional mathematicians, nuclear physicists or something of the sort. They couldn't be less interested in the problems of a youngster who will never need more mathematics than the arithmetic needed to fill out his income tax return."

But even among many mathematics educators who approve basically of the new mathematics, the Times survey found apprehension about the costs of introducing it.

Prof. Bruce Meserve of the University of Vermont, president of the National Council of Teachers of Mathematics, said many school administrators had hurried to introduce the new mathematics to get on a now fashionable bandwagon, but had neglected to make sure their teachers knew how to present the material.

Prof. Paul Rosenbloom of the Minnesota Mathematics and Science Teaching Project said: "I have seen some very shocking things taking place. Certain kinds of nonsense have been spreading very rapidly."

He assailed some commercial textbook publishers who, he said, have been hiring "hacks to do the same old rote job" on the new mathematics as was done in texts for the old mathematics.

Professor Rosenbloom was critical of teachers who emphasized new terminology at the expense of concepts.

Testing Project

The Minnesota mathematician has under way a major project to test the impact of the new teaching. He and his associates are studying 400 experimental classes in Minnesota, Wisconsin, Iowa, North Dakota and South Dakota to study the effectiveness of the various kinds of new courses.

The work is being financed by the National Science Foundation and the Minnesota Department of Education.

Other studies have been made of particular groups of pupils—by Professor Rosenbloom and others—that give ammunition to those who deny that the new mathematics threatens pupils' mastery of arithmetic and other fundamentals.

These studies, still few, suggest that children taught the new courses learn fundamentals as well as do youngsters studying conventional courses.

Supporters of the new mathematics also contend that the teaching innovations make even elementary arithmetic more exciting to youngsters.

Urges Re-education

Professor Rosenbloom said some of his recent studies indicated that a prime beneficiary of the new mathematics was the teacher. The second year a teacher uses the new methods, he said, the teacher does a better job on both the new and the old mathematics.

In Professor Rosenbloom's view, if the school systems of the nation want their mathematics teachers trained adequately for the new techniques they must finance the teachers' re-education.

Work on what would now be considered new-mathematics curriculums for the college level began at the University of Chicago in the early nineteen-forties. For the high school level it began at the University of Illinois in 1952.

In the mid-nineteen-fifties the College Entrance Examination Board—with financial aid from the Carnegie Corporation, which later aided the Illinois group and other pioneers—sponsored a report on curriculum reform.

Since 1957 the National Science Foundation has spent more than $8 million on projects to improve high school mathematics courses.

The largest single recipient of these funds has been the School Mathematics Study Group formed at Yale University by Prof. Edward Begle and subsequently transferred to Stanford.

It has published experimental texts for new courses from the fourth grade through the senior year of high school.

These have been, many observers believe, the most influential single factor in the mathematics teaching revolution.

The foundation also has helped support other projects at the University of Illinois, Syracuse University, Stanford, Wesleyan University and the University of Minnesota.

Independently, other groups have been working at Boston College, the University of Maryland, Ball State Teachers College, Southern Illinois University and other institutions.

Conference on the Future

The National Science Foundation also financed the 1963 Cambridge Conference on School Mathematics, which brought together mathematicians and scientists to consider a longer-range program of reform in mathematics teaching.

The recommendations for further changes cited at the beginning of this article come from one of the two curriculums published in the conference report, "Goals for School Mathematics."

The outlook is for continued ferment and experimentation. But there are signs that emphasis may turn toward teacher training.

The survey of mathematics educators found a widespread sense that the pendulum had swung too far and too fast toward introduction of the new mathematics without necessary preparatory work.

Education's New Guard

White House Talks Point Up Change; Leaders Are Now Ahead of the Troops

By FRED M. HECHINGER
Special to The New York Times

WASHINGTON, July 21—The most striking fact of the White House Conference on Education was the changing of the guard of educational leadership. The representatives of educational organizations who used to symbolize the Establishment seemed displaced by men and women who represent themselves and their own ideas.

News Analysis Symbolic of this new group is Francis Keppel, the United States Commissioner of Education, who not only came from the private preserves of Harvard and has never been part of the public education hierarchy but even lacks the trade union label of an advanced degree.

Moreover, the new men have, in the past, generally received more support from Washington and from the foundations than from the educational hierarchy.

Among the new group at the top are such "innovators"—the new badge of honor—as John Goodlad of the University of California, Los Angeles, the leading young fighter against the traditional arrangement of the school into a rigid succession of grades; James B. Conant, the former Harvard president who has tackled the reform of the public schools and of teacher training; Mary I. Bunting, the president of Radcliffe, who has shown impatience with conservatism in the education and employment of women.

Other Figure

Lest the list read like a conspiracy controlled by Harvard, it ought to include such people as Lawrence A. Cremin, the historian who a few years ago led the revolt of the young Turks against the Establishment at Teachers College, Columbia University; O. Meredith Wilson, the progressive president of the University of Minnesota, and Whitney M. Young Jr., the civil rights leader.

Perhaps typical of the new guard is Jerrold R. Zacharias, physicist at the Massachusetts Institute of Technology, who has become synonymous with the new breed of university scholars involved in the reform of the elementary and secondary school curriculum.

John W. Gardner, president of the Carnegie Corporation and chairman of the conference and his opposite numbers at other foundations have invested faith and funds in virtually all these new innovator-leaders. Mr. Gardner has probably been influential in raising many of them to their present positions.

'Courage and Flexibility'

Thus, when he said that the success of the conference depended on the educators' "courage and flexibility and imagination to innovate as the times require," he was not addressing the new guard of the leadership. He was speaking to the 700 delegates and to educators across the country.

Mr. Gardner told them that "giving up the old ways will be painful." He appeared to realize that many of the more tradition-bound educators, who are usually the leaders of such conferences, were still among the participants and would have to catch and carry the ball thrown by the new leadership.

This seems to have led to something of a reversal of roles. In most educational meetings, the leaders bring up the rear. The conference managers often try to prevent impetuous delegates from getting too far ahead. Occasionally, the management is pushed by the followers to move faster than it had intended.

This happened at the 1955 White House Conference when the delegates overwhelmingly voted for Federal aid to education, even though no such vote had been asked for or encouraged.

Different This Time

In 1965, the new leadership appears to have been ahead of the troops, a position that ought to be normal for leadership but is not often assumed.

The result, in some discussion sessions, seemed to be a reluctance to take up the challenge to "think boldly." The challenge is so rarely made at big conventions that some conferees may have been taken by surprise.

An example of the reluctance to respond to the leadership's challenge was the confused reaction to the meeting's most controversial proposal, the establishment of a measurement device to determine the success and accomplishments of American education in specific fields. Such an assessment might determine, for example, how well fourth-grade children read in Topeka, Kan., compared with fourth-graders in Palo Alto, Calif.

Greeted by Jargon

It was predictable in fact. Mr. Gardner predicted it—that there would be no immediate agreement. The real problem was that the response was not very sharp, either in support or opposition, and the revolutionary proposal was greeted with much old-fashioned jargon that had not grown more intelligible with age.

The real question, of course, is not what was said, or left unsaid, at the conference. Having moved out front, the new guard probably intended largely to wipe the old questions off the educational agenda and substitute a whole array of new ones. After all, the debate whether Federal aid is desirable, or even permissible, which preoccupied education meetings in the past, is over.

In some ways, as in the education provisions of the anti-poverty program, the political leadership had already outrun the educational leadership. It is therefore likely that Mr. Gardner and the new guard were more intent on updating the questions and the debate than in getting the answers, let alone instant consensus.

City to End Vocational Schools

DECISION SPARES ONLY FIVE IN CITY

Shopwork to Be Cut in Half At 24 Others—Critics Had Charged Misuse

By MARTIN TOLCHIN

A bizarre dispute over the purpose of vocational high schools has apparently ended with their scheduled demise in New York City.

Vocational educators and the Board of Education have long been at odds over a number of fundamental questions.

Were the vocational high schools intended to train non-academically oriented youths or those who had the potential to become skilled craftsmen? Why were superb shops wasted on retarded youths? Why were some students trained on obsolete machines and without regard to their eligibility to join trade unions? Why did only half the vocational students graduate?

Under plans formulated by School Superintendent Bernard E. Donovan, 24 vocational schools will become comprehensive high schools, and vocational subjects will be incorporated to some degree into the curriculums of the city's 60 academic high schools. Five remaining vocational high schools have been temporarily spared, but they are considered doomed.

Basic educational skills will be stressed in all the city's high schools. Vocational training at the present vocational high schools will be reduced by 50 per cent.

The Basic Issue

At issue, basically, was whether the problems were inherent in the system or injected by an unwritten policy of using the schools as a dumping ground for "difficult" students.

The critics charged that the schools failed woefully to fulfill their mission of providing training for students not academically inclined.

The vocational educators insisted that the schools were not designed for delinquents or retarded youths, but rather to provide training skills badly needed in a city where it is often easier to find a physician than a competent auto mechanic.

"Can a kid with no abstract intelligence, no visual ability and an I.Q. below 75 become a skilled electrician or a skilled machinist?" asked Charles A. Gilbert, principal of Alfred E. Smith Vocational High School.

"They send us kids who have no potential, and damn us when we don't succeed."

Particularly galling to vocational educators is the untapped reservoir of students in the academic high schools who receive general diplomas. Unprepared for college and untrained for a job, "they're all dressed up with no place to go," said Sidney Platt, the president of the Vocational High School Principals Association and founder-principal of Eli Whitney Vocational High School.

Paradoxically, civil rights leaders were in the forefront of the fight to close the vocational schools, although the Rev. Milton A. Galamison, the leader of two school boycotts, conceded that the schools had "a fair degree of racial balance."

Twenty-four per cent of the schools' 42,000 students are Puerto Rican, 28 per cent are Negro and 48 per cent are white and "other." Their education costs 75 per cent more than is spent on students in the 60 academic high schools.

Paradoxical, also, is the timing of Dr. Donovan's plan, which closes the schools at the very moment when vocational education is burgeoning across the country, thanks to the impetus of Federal funds made available by the Vocational Education Act of 1963.

Critics of the vocational high schools contend that the schools' inherent weakness stems from their misplaced emphasis on trade education rather than strong basic education. They also maintain that the schools require students to make a vocational choice before they are sufficiently mature.

'Adaptability' Called Key

"The best possible preparation for a job is a big, broad, basic education, emphasizing communication skills, social skills, basic math and science," said Frederick C. McLaughlin, director of the Public Education Association, in the forefront of the fight to close the vocational schools.

"What you have to prepare a student for is adaptability," he said.

Vocational educators scorn the concept that much of the training given by the schools could be given more efficiently by industry.

"A kid who walks in off the street you think they'll teach him how to work in a sheet metal shop?" asked one principal. "No, just how to use a pair of shears or a machine. These kids aren't rounded in terms of a total program."

Vocational educators cannot believe that students broadly trained as machinists or electricians will ever be unmarketable.

Moreover, the jobs exist. A follow-up study of 1963 vocational graduates showed that nearly 90 per cent found employment, with 90 per cent of that number holding jobs related to their high school training. By contrast, only 46 per cent of students holding general diplomas found jobs, with 36.2 per cent going on to more schooling and 4.5 per cent joining the armed forces.

Some Machinery Outdated

Obsolete machinery remains in use in some schools, largely because of the rapid rate of change and the indifference of some principals who do not fight for new equipment.

In the vast majority of schools, however, both the machinery and the techniques are current.

"Do you think industry would take our people if we weren't up to date?" asked Dr. Harry Lewis, the Board of Education's director of trade and technical education.

The principals believe that effective vocational training will end once the schools lose their individuality. They contend that the program will be torpedoed by academically oriented principals, teachers and parents associations.

Students at vocational high schools now are required to pass four years of English, three and a half years of social studies, two years of science, two years of mathematics and courses in art, health education and related technical subjects. A full half the school time is spent in shop.

The Public Education Association believes the new plan will expose a greater number of students to vocational training and, thus, enhance its status.

"All high schools should provide vocational exploratory programs, which, by surveying broad career areas, will help students make wiser and more realistic career choices," said the association's committee on education, guidance and work.

TRAINING FOR DROPOUTS: High school dropouts study engine in vocational course at Manhattan school.

January 12, 1966

CONANT REPORTS SCHOOL FINANCING IN 'CHAOTIC STATE'

New Study of High Schools Blames Shortage of Funds for Student Deprivation

URGES U.S. TAX REFUND

Finds Big Improvements in Curriculum in Decade but Inequities Still Remain

By FRED M. HECHINGER

Dr. James Bryant Conant, who triggered a nationwide high school reform movement 10 years ago, charged yesterday that the "chaotic state" of school financing continued to deprive many American youths of an opportunity for adequate education.

He called on Congress to return to the states a portion of Federal income tax receipts to be spent on public schools. He urged that fiscal responsibility for the schools be shifted from local communities to the states.

Dr. Conant reported that the high school curriculum in many schools had improved considerably since his original reform call, but he expressed serious concern over inequalities that remain.

Few Called Satisfactory

The 73-year-old president emeritus of Harvard University, who is widely considered the nation's most influential analyst of public education, offered his new appraisal in a report, "The Comprehensive High School: A Second Report to Interested Citizens," published yesterday by the McGraw-Hill Company and financed by the National Association of Secondary School Principals.

"If one accepts the criteria set forth in my first report, then one must conclude that only a few of the schools about which we obtained information can be regarded as highly satisfactory," Dr. Conant said. "On the other hand, the evidence indicates that the situation regarding academic studies in a great many schools is better than it was 10 years ago."

Only about 10 per cent of the schools, he added, measured up to all his original criteria.

The study begun at that time, under the auspices of the Carnegie Corporation, resulted in the 1959 report, "The American High School Today," which became a nationwide best-seller and a checklist for thousands of school boards that wanted to improve the curriculum.

Among his original recommendations was one that all academically oriented and college-preparatory high school students should be offered at least four years of English, mathematics and one foreign language and three years of science and social studies. He also asserted that any school with a graduating class of fewer than 100 students was too small to offer a full range of well staffed courses.

Quality Found Varied

In his reappraisal, based on questionnaires sent to principals of 2,000 high schools, Dr. Conant found significant improvements in the curriculum offered to students, but he also reported that the difference in the quality of educational content from state to state and from district to district was still far too great.

He aimed his fire primarily at what he considered insufficient financial support of public education.

"Inadequate finances spell an an unsatisfactory school," he said.

He added, "As one examines the returns from different schools and different states, it becomes apparent that the American ideal of equality of educational opportunity is far from being realized."

He concluded that "there is something wrong with the way we finance our public schools" and said that "a new look at an old problem is required by state legislatures and the Congress of the United States."

Big Variation in Share

In some states, he found, school districts received more than two-thirds of their funds from the state, while in others the figure might be as low as 6 per cent.

In addition, he wrote, the accidents of shifts in population and industries may dramatically change taxable resources, with the result that "what one board can afford is out of the question for its neighbor."

In his demand for "a radical overhaul of our thinking about financing public schools," he asked for a method of "apportioning to each of the separate states a share of the funds raised by the Federal income tax to be spent for education as each state sees fit."

In his reassessment of academic quality, Dr. Conant noted that the staffing of some fields, especially English, had improved. He called the situation in modern foreign languages, mathematics and the natural sciences "radically better."

He found, for example, that calculus was being offered in 816—or 40.3 per cent—of the 2,000 schools in the survey. The new physics program, developed as part of the recent nationwide school reform movement, was given in almost half of all the schools, and the new biology in 64.9 per cent of the schools. The survey also found that a four-year course in a foreign language was available in 1,290 of the schools, while his earlier study had reported that most high schools offered only two or three years of a language.

Among Dr. Conant's earlier criticisms was that the great majority of schools required English teachers to assume responsibility for far too large a number of pupils to permit proper instruction and critique. Although he originally called for a maximum of 100 pupils to each English instructor, he found that so few of the nation's schools were ready to satisfy this requirement that he reluctantly accepted the figure of 120 pupils as the norm. Even then he found that only one-fourth of the schools surveyed were able to report an English teaching load of 120 pupils or less.

In an interview, Dr. Conant conceded that even in the schools in which more of the basic and advanced academic subjects were being offered, there was still little assurance that all those students who were intellectually qualified actually enrolled in such work. But he warned that far more serious than the opportunity that is offered but not taken remains the damage done by schools that fail to offer these courses, thus depriving large numbers of students of the opportunity to develop their talents.

A Bar to Careers

Dr. Conant cites as an example the problem of the high school graduate who has had inadequate exposure to science and mathematics.

"Careers in engineering, science and mathematics become almost inaccessible when the decision has been made in high school to avoid mathematics and science as much as possible," he said.

He recommended that a comprehensive high school should as a minimum meet the following five criteria:

(1) Provide instruction in calculus.

(2) Provide instruction in a modern language for four years.

(3) Arrange the schedule so that a student may study in any one year English, mathematics, science, a foreign language, social studies, physical education, art or music.

(4) Provide one or more advanced placement courses (that is, courses of college-level content for able students).

(5) Afford a pupil load of fewer than 120 for each English teacher.

Lag in Technology

Dr. Conant reported that American educational leadership was highly conservative about the use of modern technology. Only 10.9 per cent of the principals who replied to his inquiry indicated that television was a major teaching device in one or more subjects in their schools. Only 16.2 per cent reported the use of teaching machines or programmed instruction—devices that permit students to tell instantly whether they have mastered the subject and answered the questions correctly.

Dr. Conant's survey limited itself to medium-sized comprehensive high schools -- schools that offer college preparatory, general and vocational education under the same roof. To assess average progress, he eliminated schools in slum areas and in prosperous suburban districts. Among the big cities, the survey included only one school in Chicago, two in St. Louis, one in Philadelphia, three in New York, four in Detroit, two in Los Angeles and one in San Francisco.

"I did not want to deal with the problems of New York City," he said. "I don't understand New York. It shouldn't really exist."

SCHOOLS CHANGE HISTORY TEACHING

Diaries and Treaty Texts Will Be Used in Effort to Enliven Courses

By GENE CURRIVAN

John Brown's diary and minutes from board meetings of companies in John D. Rockefeller Sr.'s oil empire will be used to bring alive the teaching of history and the social sciences in the city's public elementary and junior high schools this fall.

The program is designed to stimulate more emphasis on thought, discussion and individual research as opposed to the traditional system of memorizing dates and facts.

Instead of reading about treaties, the pupils will have true copies of them. Instead of taking for granted the written word of textbooks, they will be encouraged to do their own research and discuss the matters in class.

Where in the past there was classroom moralizing, for example, about the wrongs of slavery in the pre-Civil War years, specially trained teachers will now present documents from the period.

The documents will include newspaper clippings, letters from citizens and Brown's abolitionist writings.

There will be considerable stress on Negro and Puerto Rican history and culture, along with more readable and interesting texts on peoples in other parts of the world. Modern maps, tapes, film clips and other visual aids will help tell the story, which many educators feel has been buried in old textbooks and obsolete teaching methods.

The new approach was announced yesterday by the Board of Education, which also told of another program that will teach high school students the value of a dollar, good consumer spending and good shopping manners.

The social science curriculum will be taught in most schools in grades 1, 5, 6 and 9 but within two years will be taught from pre-kindergarten through high school, according to Dr. Leonard Ingraham, acting director of the school board's bureau of history and social science.

Sequential Teaching

"The program attempts to develop skills and research techniques sequentially," Dr. Ingraham said, "while providing students with the values, understandings and knowledge drawn from the disciplines of history and social sciences needed to cope with the pressing social problems of our age."

The work on the program to enliven the teaching began in 1964 and has since involved hundreds of teachers, supervisors, curriculum writers, textbook publishers and district representatives.

For the last year it has been under the supervision of Mrs. Helene M. Lloyd, acting deputy superintendent in charge of curriculum.

Mrs. Lloyd said the main purpose was to get the children thinking for themselves instead of memorizing something that had been said or written.

The new method will try to dramatize the roles of such figures from the past as Mr. Rockefeller by showing how he handled a board of directors meeting and presenting other material showing his weaknesses and strengths.

Mrs. Lloyd said: "We want the students to appreciate the impact of personalities on the business world. We not only tell them all that is generally known about Mr. Rockefeller, Andrew Carnegie of steel and James Fisk of the railroads, but we show how they operated in a competitive world that was not government-regulated."

Federal Funds Obtained

Research material used in the courses has been developed in many areas including the University of Chicago, Amherst College, Purdue University, Northwestern University, the New York State Department of Education and civil liberties organizations. More than $600,000 from the National Defense Education Act was used for textbooks, maps and treaty reproductions.

The other new program for about 10 high schools, although the exact number has not been determined, would teach the students how to get the most for their money in a supermarket or how to buy an automobile or a house.

It is assumed that much of this knowledge would be passed on by the youngsters to their parents. It includes budgeting, retail credit, insurance rates and the evaluation of advertisements and labels.

August 20, 1967

Study of Foreign Languages Declines

By ANDREW H. MALCOLM

The heavy emphasis placed on foreign language instruction in American schools and colleges for several years after the Russians launched their Sputnik in 1957 is under attack from some educators, students and parents.

At the same time, language teachers across the country are engaged in self-examination and serious debate over their goals and methods.

Faced with charges of irrelevance, declining student interest and stiff competition from such new subjects as minority studies, many foreign language instructors in colleges and universities have seen various entrance and graduation language requirements modified, reduced or eliminated in recent months.

Enrollment in some high school language courses, which generally have not been required but have been strongly recommended for college-bound students, has declined.

Language instruction in some elementary grades, once hailed as a sign of a truly progressive school system, has been cut back or is under scrutiny because of budgetary pressures and reassessments of academic priorities.

Emphasis on English

"We ought to make sure our kids can read and write English well before they start worrying about French or German," said one parent in Omaha. The remark was typical of those who see foreign languages as an academic "frill."

Such program cutbacks and eliminations are by no means universal. Some schools are satisfied with their language programs, although none could be found that were expanding greatly. And Americans, geographically isolated from exposure to many languages, have never exactly flocked to the tedious exercises believed necessary to learn another language.

But, in a series of interviews, several dozen experts said the current problems of foreign language instruction were representative of a general re-examination of academic curriculums and their relevancy to the needs and desires of today's students.

"Part of our problem," said C. Edward Scebold, executive secretary of the American Council on the Teaching of Foreign Languages, "is that we've gotten carried away with the way we have been teaching languages for the last 150 years."

"We have to step back and take a look at what we're doing and what the students want," he continued. "And I'm afraid that the foreign language experience these days has not been particularly useful to students."

The result has been enrollment drops. A few years ago, Denver's 96,000-student public school system had 15,000 studying various foreign languages (compared to 5,000 before Sputnik). Last year there were 10,-250 studying foreign languages. The system is experimenting now with combined classes from more than one school.

Faculty Reduced

Miami's Dade County school system has similar declines and the foreign language faculty is being reduced through attrition and transfer.

"I'm amazed that foreign language education has survived at all," said Mrs. Elizabeth Alonso, the only foreign language consultant left in the system, which has 250,000 students.

Spurred by the surge of interest and Federal money after the Soviet Union launched the first man-made earth satellite in 1957, the California Legislature required that foreign languages be taught in all public schools in that state.

But the economic realities of prohibitive costs have seen that provision watered down in elementary and junior high schools there in recent years.

Almost all those interviewed said the language hardest hit by enrollment declines is Latin, which is regarded by many students as a dead language.

French Still Popular

Generally, French still appeared to be the most popular, although some reported that Spanish was making a strong showing, sometimes exceeding French in enrollment.

On the college level, the academic controversy generally centers on whether a minimum

The New York Times

IT STARTED WITH SPUTNIK: An American student learns Russian. Launching of first orbital spacecraft by Soviet Union in 1957 spurred an interest in foreign languages.

number of college language credits should be required for graduation.

A growing number of colleges and universities, including Yale, Brown, Stanford, Trinity and Wesleyan, have abolished the undergraduate language requirement, often along with other required courses.

Duke, Haverford and the University of California at Los Angeles have reduced required language courses and similar action has been considered by many other schools. After much debate, Ohio State University abolished the foreign language requirement for its Ph.D candidates.

Changes Needed

"We face a clear-cut choice," Mr. Scebold said. "Either we start making some basic changes or we face a rather dismal future." Such changes, he said, should be away from the traditional orientation around foreign literature.

"Students are not just interested in reading 'Les Miserables,'" he said. "They want a speaking knowledge so they can talk about other countries' urban problems, family life and dating customs. Too often we haven't considered these other aspects."

Andre Paquette, the new director of the Middlebury Lan-

guage Schools at Middlebury College, said he feared the schools would not respond to student requests for relevant language instruction.

"Teachers of foreign language, as opposed to teachers of foreign literature, are rarely rewarded by schools for their efforts," he said.

"The result is that true professionals do not teach language," he added. "They leave that to the less-qualified graduate assistants and concentrate on such subjects as use of the past tense in 17th-century Burgundian dialects."

But he said he saw a "great opportunity" for true language teachers in the growing number of two-year colleges being established.

In addition, some high schools and colleges have begun to experiment with language instruction.

For instance, at Tufts University next month students will plunge into a total area of culture study, such as Germany or France, rather than begin with formal language instruction.

The foreign language department at California State College at Fullerton has founded a student consultation board, chosen by students, for their opinions on curriculum structure and teaching techniques.

Travel an Incentive

Some schools bring in outside lecturers or set aside certain dormitory wings for students of a particular language. Others include study and travel abroad as an incentive.

Next month, New York University will begin an accelerated program of longer and more frequent classes. Students will cover in one year what formerly took two years.

And many colleges and high schools across the country reported increased emphasis on teaching the more practical conversational uses of a language, rather than reading literature or writing essays. For this they rely heavily on up-to-date foreign periodicals.

But there was also much concern that the colleges' elimination or reduction of language requirements would undermine, in the high school student's eyes, the need for foreign language study, no matter how relevant.

August 23, 1970

The current cycle of change in reading instruction began in 1955 with the publication of Rudolf Flesch's book, "Why Johnny Can't Read." While the work was oversimplified and faulty in some respects, the main thesis was sound: that the whole-word approach to beginning reading instruction, advocated by most reading specialists and used almost everywhere in the country at that time, was wrong in theory and inferior in practice to a phonics approach.

The book set off a bitter argument between the reading experts and the public. The reading experts maintained that school reading attainments were satisfactory. When evidence mounted against that position, they shifted to saying that they had taught phonics all along.

Although the public and many school people believed that Mr. Flesch was right, there were no phonics-based reading materials to turn to, with a few minor exceptions. These obscure phonics programs were sought out and very slowly put into use here and there. It was not until 1963, however, that two publishers, not normally associated with large-scale textbook publishing, brought out complete series of reading textbooks on the phonics approach.

Imported From England

The next year, public attention was drawn to a new beginning reading approach that had been imported from England, the initial teaching alphabet, or I. T. A. This system, invented by Sir James Pitman, involved a set of 44 symbols that represented the 44 major sounds of English. The child was to use this special orthography to learn to read and to write and then, after one or several years, transfer to the standard letters. Bucking the entrenched position of all the major textbook publishers and the fraternity of reading experts, the two phonics series and I.T.A. made inroads slowly against the dominance of the whole-word materials. I.T.A. was admittedly still in an experimental phase. The controversy continued.

Then, in 1967, a book was published that put an end

Continuing Hassle Over How to Read

to the theoretical argument. "Learning to Read: The Great Debate" was written by Dr. Jeanne Chall, a professor at the Harvard Graduate School of Education, under the sponsorship of the Carnegie Corporation. Dr. Chall reviewed more than a half-century of research on beginning reading instruction. She found that most of the research was poor, but that the sound research pointed clearly to the conclusion that the whole-word or look-say approach (she called it the reading-for-meaning approach) was ineffective and should be scrapped in favor of the phonics approach (she called it the code-emphasis approach).

The enevitable howls were short-lived and came mostly from the old-line reading experts. The major textbooks publishers, seeing the handwriting on the wall, scrambled to begin overhauling their reading materials. The reading experts covered themselves as well as they could and resurrected everything they had ever said in favor of phonics.

No Instant Change

But something as fundamental as the approach to beginning reading instruction cannot be changed overnight. The teachers in the schools knew little or nothing about phonics because they had had no training in the subject in their colleges. Appropriate materials were not yet available from the major publishers, to which the schools look for most of their classroom materials. Teachers and other school people often had a natural resistance to changing what they had been doing for years. But change did take place slowly.

The pace of change was given an important boost in the fall of 1969, when the United States Commissioner of Education, the late James E. Allen Jr., started his right-to-read campaign. The signifi-

cance of the event was that, for the first time, a Commissioner of Education acknowledged serious deficiencies in reading attainments. Previously, the Office of Education had held that reading achievement was good and defended the old methods of instruction.

While sidestepping the question of method, Dr. Allen characterized the large number of reading failures as "a reproach to all of us" in education and called the situation in reading instruction "inexcusable" and "intolerable." Among the salient facts that he cited was that about half of the nation's unemployed young people between the ages of 16 to 21 were functionally illiterate.

A year later, in the fall of 1970, an event took place of considerable symbolic value. One of the major publishers of beginning reading textbooks, the one whose books made Dick and Jane and their dog Spot famous — and infamous — announced a new series of books that, at least in format, were radically different from the old ones that had been used in many schools for as long as a half-century. A company official told a reporter that "we prefer not to talk about the past."

The situation today seems to indicate that we are in the final stages of the change from the whole-word approach to the phonics approach.

There are five different kinds of programs being used in the classroom. The oldest and still the most popular consists of the whole-word books, perhaps updated somewhat, and usually accompanied by phonics materials supplied by the publisher or by a supplemental phonics program published by another company.

These programs still have

relatively limited vocabularies, chosen on the basis of frequency of occurrence in spoken language, and still utilize some of the old techniques of identifying new words. The other four types of programs are phonics-based in one way or another.

The first type—what might be called the pure phonics programs—introduces phonics early and explicitly and chooses words to illustrate the phonics principles.

The "linguistic" programs teach phonics principles by way of "word patterns." For example, instead of teaching the short "a" in isolation, they teach it in a man-Dan-fan pattern. Again, the words used are chosen on the basis of the phonics already taught.

The third type — phonics-based programed materials — generally uses the word patterns but arranges the content in a programed format so that each child can proceed at his own pace. One of the most popular programed series has been sometimes successful with the disadvantaged children for whom it was primarily designed, but it is paced too slowly for average and fast learners.

The last, and probably least-used category of programs, is the one using a special orthography, the initial teaching alphabet referred to above. Its special characteristics suggest that its use will continue to be limited.

The outlook is for a continued drift toward three of the categories of programs listed above: phonics, linguistic and programed. But in those cases where individual schools achieve a relatively high level of success with either a supplemented whole-word series or the initial teaching alphabet, they will be reluctant to abandon them.

Certainly, the schools are using a lot more phonics, in one way or another, than they did 17 years ago. Perhaps 10 years from now, most schools will be using phonics-based programs and the cycle of change will be complete.

GEORGE WEBER

The New Math Faces a Counter-Revolution

By HARRY SCHWARTZ

A decade ago the then "new math" was all the rage. Set theory was sweeping over all obstacles in the nation's elementary and high schools, while visionaries talked of teaching Diophantine equations to eighth graders and affine geometry to 16-year-olds.

The United States was in the grip of what now looks like the post-Sputnik panic. Moscow, the conventional wisdom of the early nineteen-sixties maintained, was going to conquer this country because Ivan and Svetlana learned more mathematics and science than Johnny and Dorothy. Suddenly every algebra classroom began to be looked on as a battlefield between freedom and slavery.

The panic is over now and the new math is faced by critical questioning in many areas. But in this reform's heyday, there were trusting souls who seemed to think they were going to save the republic by teaching youngsters Venn diagrams, Boolean algebra and the axioms of arithmetic rather than focusing on memorization of the multiplication table.

Parents No Help

At the height of the cultural revolution represented by the widespread introduction of the new math, parents all over the country were finding they couldn't help their fourth and fifth graders with their mathematics homework because the parents had never even heard of many of the concepts that their children rattled off so glibly. Publishers found it profitable to publish special new math textbooks for parents, with the result that some fathers and mothers had to seek help from their children.

Aside from the Sputnik-induced anxiety, the rationale for the new math movement was simple: Its proponents argued that traditional American arithmetic, algebra and geometry sequences were obsolete and included nothing that had been discovered by mathematicians during the last several centuries. Moreover, the proponents argued that American youngsters learned only the how of mathematical operations, not the why, and that they would be better in all phases of mathematics if they replaced memorization with understanding.

Adding weight to these arguments was the belief that the United States would need virtually limitless numbers of mathematicians and physical scientists to compete with the Soviet Union in the future. The new math was seen as the way to raise the most mathematically able generation in American history.

Set Theory Key

The key to the new math revolution was set theory, whose elements were sometimes even taught to kindergartners. A set is a collection of defined objects or entities, and set theory deals with the manipulation and interrelation of sets, actions often most easily demonstrated by geometric figures termed Venn diagrams.

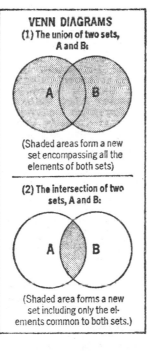

VENN DIAGRAMS
(1) The union of two sets, A and B:

(Shaded areas form a new set encompassing all the elements of both sets)

(2) The intersection of two sets, A and B:

(Shaded area forms a new set including only the elements common to both sets.)

A set is a collection of defined entities. Venn diagrams are used to teach relationships between sets shown above.

The New York Times/Jan. 8, 1973

Basic to the new math, also, was the idea of treating arithmetic axiomatically, i.e. building up a competence in addition and multiplication from basic definitions and premises in a manner akin to classical Euclidean geometry. In this treatment, one high point was the proof that a negative number multiplied by another negative number yields a product which is a positive number.

Many new math courses introduced children to the idea of number systems having bases other than the number 10, which is central to conventional numbers. Thus youngsters learned that in a basic six-number system, 532 was equal to five times 36 (i.e. six squared) plus three times six plus two times one or 200 in the usual number system based on 10.

Many Attitudes Cooler

Today the attitude toward the new math is much cooler in many quarters. The National Science Foundation, one of the chief backers of the innovations, expects to begin a new study of mathematics teaching that could be the beginning of a new policy. The most successful academic group sponsoring the new math, the School Mathematics Study Group at Stanford University, shut down last summer.

American astronauts having beaten Soviet cosmonauts to the moon, the old anxiety of Muscovite triumph in science is gone. With that bogey out of the way, the nation has suddenly found itself with a surplus of mathematicians, physicists and scientists, men and women whose unemployment has prompted questions about why so many were trained in the first place.

Simultaneously the focus of national attention has turned to the ghettos and the slums, and to the millions of disadvantaged youngsters who now go to high school and beyond but are still deficient in basic skills such as reading and computation.

Now there is the feeling voiced by George Grossman, head of mathematics teaching in New York City's schools: "The new math went too far toward abstraction and it was always primarily aimed at a small elite of top students, perhaps 5-10 per cent of the total. Our real problems now are with the great mass of ghetto students who do poorly in mathematics and for whom the new math is simply irrelevant."

Teaching the Disadvantaged

Much of the interest in innovation in mathematics teaching now lies in the search for better ways of motivating and instructing these disadvantaged youngsters. The difficulties are suggested by a recent article in the magazine, Mathematics Teacher, which asserts that when it comes to inner city children, "too many teachers tend to give up, to cop out. Many actually believe that teaching mathematics to black youngsters is an impossible task."

Now the interest is in individual instruction and the provision of mathematics laboratory facilities for these children, both needed for the technique of guided discovery that many educators see as the most effective means of helping the ghetto child learn mathematics, from essentials up.

Calculators Used

And with the rapid spread of computers and of powerful, small, transistor-equipped calculating machines, much mathematics teaching seeks to take advantage of these devices. In numerous high schools—over 50 in New York City alone—computer programming is now taught, while even slow learners are helped with the use of hand-operated calculating machines that easily demonstrate, for example, that multiplication is simply repeated addition.

The new math survives, and even its critics admit that it made a contribution by abolishing the old barriers between arithmetic, algebra and geometry. But with a surplus of theoretical mathematicians and the new emphasis on teaching ghetto youngsters to compute, the outlook seems bleak for Diophantine equations in eighth grade and affine geometry in the second year of high school.

January 8, 1973

Book Plan for Schools

A plan to provide literature for schools at low cost was announced yesterday by Bantam Books and Scholastic Magazines. The plan will offer books at 25 cents a copy to teachers and students.

October 16, 1947

Blackboards Turn Green

Special to THE NEW YORK TIMES.

ROSELLE, N. J., March 4—Blackboards in William L. McCord's mathematics classroom in Abraham Clark High School here are setting an early spring style note. As an experiment, the boards have been painted a special shade of green, supposed to be easy on the eyes. After initial trial, Mr. McCord said "green boards have great possibilities."

Pupils' Time Spent at TV Rivals Hours in Classes

By JACK GOULD
Special to THE NEW YORK TIMES.

STAMFORD. Conn., March 5—Children who have television sets at home are devoting almost as much time each week to viewing video shows as they are to attending classes in school, a survey conducted by the Burdick Junior High School of Stamford shows.

These boys and girls, ranging from 11 to 15 years old, are sitting in front of their television sets twenty-seven hours a week, or an average of 3.86 hours a day.

The schedule at Burdick calls for a pupil to be in school twenty-seven hours and fifty-five minutes each week.

Results of the survey, which became available here tonight, show that 79 per cent of the student body now looks at television on a regular basis.

Youngsters with sets in their own homes represented 50 per cent of the school.

Those who regularly see programs at the homes of friends or neighbors totaled 29 per cent. They spend eighteen hours a week, or an average of 2.64 hours a day, at television receivers, the survey found.

Those who do not see television programs regularly numbered 21 per cent of the total.

Other highlights of the survey, which for the most part dealt with children who had sets in their homes, included:

1. A majority of the pupils and their parents believe that television may interfere with the completion of homework.
2. A majority of children from time to time have their supper while watching a show.
3. An overwhelming majority of children believe that television has increased their interest in events outside the home and school.

In announcing the study of the social effects of television on the younger generation, Joseph J. Franchina, principal of Burdick, declared that "the figures have meaning for the educator, the parent and the broadcaster alike."

"Television presents new problems for all of us," he said, "but the first step toward their solution lies in a better national understanding of the sociological impact of this newest and most novel medium of communications and entertainment."

Will Compare Records

Mr. Franchina said that the Burdick school's next step would be to compare the individual scholastic records of students with the amount of time they spent looking at television.

The Burdick survey was made last Thursday as part of the regular classroom work. The final results were tabulated tonight. Questionnaires were distributed to every class under the supervision of the children's regular teachers. The children were told in advance that participation in the survey would have no bearing on their scholastic standing.

Children attending Burdick were believed by the school officials to represent a reasonably good economic cross-section of Stamford; they come from the Hycliff residential section and from lower-income homes near Pacific Street, in the business district.

Stanley C. Poltrack, vice principal of Burdick, who supervised the tabulation of the survey, emphasized that it made no attempt to measure mathematically the degree of change that television might have effected in such habits of the children as reading, movie-going and radio listening.

"The Burdick survey merely sought to give a general indication of the effects of television," he said. "The school is not undertaking any interpretation of the survey. As far as they go, the figures speak for themselves."

The detailed results of the survey follow:

SET OWNERSHIP

Of the 447 children who filled out the questionnaire, 223 said they had television sets at home and 130 looked at programs in the homes of neighbors. Ninety-four said that they did not view television shows regularly.

Of those having sets at home, ninety-four said they had had the sets "less than six months"; forty-nine, "more than six months," and eighty, "more than a year." Throughout the survey, however, there appeared no significant difference in the answers based on the length of time the set had been in the home.

HOURS OF VIEWING

Among the 223 whose homes had sets, the average hours a day of viewing were:

School days	3.7
Saturdays	4.2
Sundays	4.3
Daily Average	3.86

The breakdown of the hours that individual children look at video follows:

Hours a Day	Number of Children Mon.-Fri.	Sat.	Sun.
1	6	2	5
2	41	22	21
3	37	38	39
4	82	57	64
5	41	57	46
6	8	30	25
7	..	5	4
8	..	3	6
9	..	..	3
10	..	..	2

HOMEWORK

The questions asked on the subject of homework and the answers given by students having sets in their homes follow:

Has television made it more difficult for you to find time in which to do homework?

Yes	24
No	197

When do you do your homework?

After looking at television	6
Before looking	190
Between programs	27

Have your parents ever told you that they believe television interferes with doing your homework?

Regularly	16
Sometimes	110
Never	96

Do you think television interferes with completion of your homework?

Often	8
Once in a while	55
Seldom	60
Never	99

READING

Asked if television had affected the amount of time they devoted to reading, the students with home sets replied:

Devote more time	14
Devote less time	51
Devote same time	154

School officials believed this question might warrant further study, since the results did not appear too consistent with the time devoted to looking at television.

EATING SUPPER

To a question on whether they ate supper while looking at television, the children with sets at home replied:

Regularly	12
Occasionally	64
Infrequently	38
Never	106

PROGRAM PREFERENCES

Asked who selected the majority of the programs they see, the children with sets at home answered:

Select their own	74
Parents make the selection	89
Both child and parent choose	59

Asked to enumerate the types of programs they most enjoy, they gave preferences in this order:

1. Feature films.
2. Sports.
3. Vaudeville shows.
4. Musical programs.
5. Mystery shows.
6. Drama.
7. Quiz shows.
8. News programs.

March 5, 1950

Asked to name the program they most enjoyed, they listed preference in this order:
1. Milton Berle
2. Ed Sullivan's "Toast of the Town"
3. Six-Gun Playhouse
4. Wrestling
5. Captain Video
6. Arthur Godfrey and His Friends
   Roller Derby (tie)
7. Lights Out
   Paul Whiteman (tie)

The total number of shows mentioned was forty-seven. Of these, nine are designed primarily for a children's audience, thirty-eight for an adult audience.

Asked if some types of television programs had become "boring," the children replied:

Yes 184
No 37

Requested to list the types "most boring," they answered.
1. Discussion programs
2. Vaudeville shows
3. Musical programs
4. Wrestling
5. Quiz shows
   News programs (tie)
6. Boxing
7. Puppet shows
8. Western pictures
   Children's programs (tie)

It was believed that an influence on what was "most boring" might be the fact that parents of some children chose their programs.

OTHER ACTIVITIES

Asked if television "has increased your interest in events outside of school and home," the students with sets at home replied:

Yes 186
No 36

Asked how much they listened to radio programs after their families had obtained television receivers, the students replied:

More than before......... 4
About the same........... 47
Much less 94
Hardly ever 75

Asked how television might have affected their outside activities, the students with sets at home answered:

	More	Less	Same
Go to movies....	25	150	25
Outdoor exercise.	94	52	36
Attend sports events	86	46	39
Attend church...	100	10	50

While the answers on movie-going and sports were not inconsistent with surveys among adult television viewers, those on outdoor exercise and church attendance were regarded with reservation by school officials. It was believed that the parents might be better judges of whether the child was inside or outdoors more or less. The matter of church-going raised the question of whether parents might be requiring attendance as the price of their consent for the children to look at television.

TELEVISION IN EDUCATION

On the question of whether a program ever had been made part of a homework assignment, students with home sets replied:

Regularly 3
Sometimes 68
Never 150

A minority of students submitted suggestions as to specific programs that could supplement different courses, while a majority believed that several types of programs, such as vaudeville, amateur shows, comedy, drama and films, could be adapted to various uses in a school curriculum.

In commenting on the survey results, both Mr. Franchina and Mr. Poltrack expressed hope that other educational institutions would do similar research.

"Ours is only a small beginning," said Mr. Franchina.

March 6, 1950

HARVARD—Mechanical Aids

Use of mechanical and electrical devices to improve instruction in arithmetic, spelling and reading in the lower grades of elementary schools is under study in the Department of Psychology at Harvard University. These devices, according to Prof. B. F. Skinner, Professor of Psychology, would free the teacher for more important teaching where human guidance is crucial.

July 18, 1954

College Courses Given on Closed-Circuit Television Are a Promising Experiment

By BENJAMIN FINE

Closed-circuit television, which has been adapted to an increasing number of industrial uses, is appearing on the nation's college campuses as a partial solution to the growing shortage of personnel. Through the TV hook-up a professor can lecture to several classes at the same time.

In the closed-circuit method the program originates in one classroom, laboratory or studio, and is piped into other rooms with interconnected receivers. It does not go out to the general public.

Miami University in Oxford, Ohio, for example, has just received a substantial grant from the Fund for the Advancement of Education to experiment with television as a supplement to the instructors. Other colleges and universities now have experiments in the new medium under way.

Experiments in Progress

A report issued by the American Council on Education's committee on television last week shows that sixty closed-circuit television installations are now in use in colleges, universities and public school systems. Many schools are using television this semester for the first time.

This in-school television is one of two major forms of what is termed educational television. The other is regular telecasting of programs for the home audience. Such programs are now featured on eighteen noncommercial educational stations with a potential audience of 40,000,000, just about the same as the regularly enrolled school population of the United States.

Much has been written about the problems of these educational TV stations. But thus far little has been said about the closed-circuit operations which, in the long run, may make tremendous changes in the pattern of classroom instruction.

Many institutions of higher learning are teaching television techniques. In a few instances, as at Cornell University and the United States Naval Academy, the equipment is used primarily in the teaching of engineering courses; more commonly it is used to teach various aspects of production. There is a steadily increasing number of formal course offerings in this special phase of communications. Northwestern University has two separate closed-circuit training installations—one for use by Medill School of Journalism, the other for the department of speech.

Workshops for agricultural extension staff members, who often telecast their programs over commercial stations, are conducted by a number of institutions—among them Alabama Polytechnic Institute, the State College of Washington and the University of Missouri.

According to the American Council report, teachers' colleges are developing a two-fold interest in educational television. They are teaching its use as a medium of instruction. And they are finding that through closed-circuit television they enable students to observe teaching demonstrations at close range without actually being in the classroom. This permits discussion among observers without interruption of the class being taught. New Jersey State Teachers College at Montclair and Chicago Teachers College have made special studies with closed circuits.

Pioneers in TV

Notable among the closed-circuit television experiments this fall are the following:

Stephens College (Columbia, Mo.) One of the most comprehensive TV systems being used in regular teaching practice enables one instructor to lecture to fifty classrooms simultaneously at this women's college. These lectures provide the initial stimulus for independent discussion, which takes place in each classroom under the leadership of two faculty members. The ideas produced by television provide a common basis for the independent discussions developed by each class section.

The project is supported by grants from the Fund for the Advancement of Education and the Radio Corporation of America. An R. C. A. closed circuit links the college's TV studio with 21-inch home television receivers in several buildings around the campus. This semester a new orientation course is being televised twice a week to more than 800 freshmen in fifty classrooms.

New York University. Some 500 freshmen and sophomores are taking televised courses this semester in creative composition and in the literature of England. The students meet Mondays and Wednesdays in seven classrooms for closed-circuit sessions and Friday for discussion periods with special tutors. The lectures are conducted by senior faculty members and originate from the university's TV studios. The project is supported by a grant from the Fund for the Advancement of Education.

The experiment is directed toward determining whether tele-

131

vision can be useful to (1) extend the effectiveness of the individual teacher and improve the quality of instruction; (2) meet the teacher shortage, and (3) make it possible to raise faculty salaries by extending the individual teacher's effectiveness. Arrangements have been made for a special faculty viewing room so that interested staff members may have the opportunity of observing the course.

Pennsylvania State University. Teaching techniques in ten courses have been especially adapted for television. Among the courses taught are general psychology, chemistry and the psychology of marriage. This fall the university has broadened a research project, begun last year to compare the effectiveness of conventional instruction with the same instruction presented over closed-circuit television. Some 2,500 students are taking the TV courses.

At the end of the one-year trial run, the university reports that its experience indicates that closed-circuit television can channel excellent instruction from a single source to very large numbers of university students.

State University of Iowa. The emphasis here is on determining whether teaching by television can be used without sacrificing the values of classroom discussion. A two-way hook-up enables students in the viewing rooms and the lecturer in the broadcast room to communicate directly with one another.

High School Uses

Several high schools now have closed-circuit facilities. At South High School in Columbus, Ohio, a system was installed last spring. Vancouver (Wash.) High School has facilities for originating programs, picking up those of local stations and projecting films from a central source. Thirty-two classrooms are equipped with TV receivers.

After testing trainees in the Army Signal Corps at Camp Gordon, Ga., the Human Resources Research Office of George Washington University found that:

(1) Instruction time in one electronics course was cut in half when the course was presented on TV with cutaway models and other props.

(2) TV students remembered what they had learned as well as and often better than students taught by regular classroom instructors.

(3) TV training was particularly effective with low-I. Q. servicemen.

What of the future? Both educators and television experts are optimistic. Dr. Milton Eisenhower, president of Pennsylvania State University, believes that television may well be the greatest single aid to both resident instruction and adult education devised in this century. Brig. Gen. David Sarnoff, chairman of the board of the Radio Corporation of America, calls campus television "the modern counterpart of the blackboard and textbook."

N. Y. U. WILL TEACH LITERATURE ON TV

Will Offer Credit Course to Public Over WCBS for a Student Fee of $75

CLASS TO BE AT 6:30 A. M.

Enrolled Viewers of Program in Fall Will Have Use of Facilities on Campus

A college course carrying undergraduate credit will be offered over regular television by New York University beginning in September.

It will be the first commercially televised credit course to be given by a college or university in the metropolitan area. Such courses have been tried in other cities.

The course, Comparative Literature 10, will be presented Monday through Friday mornings at 6:30 to 7 o'clock over WCBS-TV, beginning Sept. 23 and ending Jan. 10. Viewers who wish to earn the three points of academic credit offered will have to meet admission requirements and enroll formally at the university.

Details of the course were announced by Carroll V. Newsom, president of New York University, and Sam Cook Digges, general manager of WCBS-TV, at a press luncheon yesterday in the Savoy-Plaza Hotel.

Dr. Newsom said that the undertaking was something of an experiment and that if it proved successful it could lead to other such courses in the future. For the last two years N. Y. U. has been experimenting with courses presented over closed-circuit television. Unlike the closed-circuit courses, which require a special receiver, the WCBS-TV programs can be seen by all.

Dr. Floyd Zulli Jr., assistant professor of Romance languages at N. Y. U.'s College of Arts and Science, will be the instructor for the course. It will comprise seventy-six half-hour sessions.

The course will deal with modern fiction from Stendhal's "The Red and the Black" to Ernest Hemingway's "The Sun Also Rises." Student viewers will be required to read prescribed major works by sixteen outstanding authors.

To receive the academic credit, which is applicable toward a bachelor's degree, students will have to take two home examinations and a final examination at the university, as well as submit a term paper. Special arrangements will be made for physically handicapped students. A total of 128 credits is required for an undergraduate degree.

Fee for Credit Is $75

The total fee for the course will be $75, which includes a $5 application fee. Because certain services, such as personal counseling, are more readily available to on-campus students, the total cost is less than the $90 that would be charged for a comparable nontelevised course.

Students enrolled in the television course, however, will be entitled to the same access to the university library and other campus facilities as regular students are.

N. Y. U. will provide the instructor and production personnel for the program and will administer the course. Warren A. Kraetzer, director of the university's office of radio-television, will produce the program. WCBS-TV will donate time and facilities and provide technical personnel.

Explaining the early hour for the course, Mr. Digges said that in planning the program it was decided that "the greatest potential in terms of interested audience was in people who are employed" during the regular business day.

This meant, he said, that the course would have to be presented either before these potential students went to work or after they returned home. However, the station's programming schedule ruled out the evening hours; so the morning time was decided upon.

November 13, 1955

June 18, 1957

The Three R's And Pushbuttons

Forward-lookers are experimenting with machines that teach, and traditionalists wonder if the schoolmarm is to be a mechanic

By DAVID BOROFF

THE Age of Technology has finally overtaken education, and the shape of the classroom of the future—assuming there will even be so retrograde an institution—is open to speculation. To the imposing array of television screens, films, tape recordings and language laboratories, there has now been added the teaching machine, the very name of which is either an affront or a sign that education has finally been inducted into the twentieth century.

The coming of age of the teaching machine was highlighted recently by the announcement of Encyclopaedia Britannica Films that it is adapting the entire high school mathematics curriculum, a large share of college mathematics, and eight years of foreign-language study for machine instruction. This climaxes more than thirty years of preliminary exploration of these devices. At present, courses in Russian, statistics, freshman English, music, genetics—even the Old Testament—are being prepared for teaching machines in a variety of institutions.

What are teaching machines? Can the classroom indeed be transformed into an aseptic assembly line of learning? Are schools going to be miniature Willow Runs replete with pushbutton instruction? Are teaching machines a pipe dream, Orwellian nightmare, or a soundly conceived breakthrough in educational method?

THE teaching machine, as developed by Prof. B. F. Skinner of Harvard University, is a simple mechanical device which presents information and questions to a student. The material is printed on a roll, which is fed to the student a little at a time. (It is called programed material; the term comes from the burgeoning field of computers.) The teaching machine itself is a small box about the size of a record player. Across the box are three rectangular windows or panels.

The programed material is presented in the left-hand panel. The student reads the information there, and in the second panel writes the answers to a question. He then turns a knob which reveals the correct answer in a third panel. If his answer is identical with that of the answer panel, he pulls a lever and goes on to the next item. If his response does not match that of the answer panel, he pulls another

lever so that when he has completed the lesson, the machine will return to the question incorrectly answered. The operation is as simple, according to one machine psychologist, as adjusting a television set—a statement hardly calculated to allay fears of this new wave of technology.

A few principles underlie teaching machines. One is that material has to be presented with absolute clarity and simplicity—information distilled to its essence. The second principle is that the machine offers what psychologists call "immediate reinforcement," or reward. In classroom terms, a reinforcement may be a good grade, a teacher's smile, or any of the numerous bribes by which children are motivated. With teaching machines, the reinforcement is the simple pleasure of being right—no small reward in our academically motivated culture.

ONE of the chief advances of the teaching machine over conventional methods of instruction is that reinforcement is immediate. The child absorbs information and applies it instantly in answering a question. In traditional arrangements, reinforcement—the satisfaction of being right—has to wait until homework is corrected in class or test papers returned a week or two after the material is initially taught. By that time, the reinforcement has lost a good deal of its potency.

Here is some material from a program in elementary physics. The machine presents one item at a time. The student completes the item, then uncovers the correct answer as shown at the right. Note how the information gradually grows in complexity, how it backtracks constantly to consolidate learning and how it uses techniques of hinting and prompting.

Sentence to be completed	Word to be supplied
1. The important parts of a flashlight are the battery and the bulb. When we "turn on" a flashlight, we close a switch which connects the battery with the _____.	bulb
2. When we turn on a flashlight, an electric current flows through the fine wire in the _____ and causes it to grow hot.	bulb
3. When the hot wire glows brightly, we say that it gives of or sends out heat and _____.	light
4. The fine wire in the bulb is called a filament. The bulb lights up when the filament is heated by the passage of a(n) _____ current.	electric
5. When a weak battery produces little current, the fine wire, or _____, does not get very hot.	filament
6. A filament which is less hot sends out or gives off _____ light.	less
7. "Emit" means "send out." The amount of light sent out, or "emitted" by a filament depends on how _____ the filament is.	hot
8. The higher the temperature of the filament, the _____ the light emitted by it.	brighter stronger
9. If a flashlight battery is weak, the _____ in the bulb may still glow, but with only a dull red color.	filament
10. The light from a very hot filament is colored yellow or white. The light from a filament which is not very hot is colored _____.	red

The following are questions from programed material in word study:

Sentence to be completed	Word or words to be supplied
1. An ache which "goes back" _____cedes; if it "comes again," it _____curs.	recedes recurs
2. The word real is a(n) _____. When you add -ity to it, you get _____, a(n) _____.	adjective reality noun
3. A sailor may be marooned or trapped on an island, but a maroon coat is not lost; it is a certain _____ of coat.	color
4. A stout stick is hard to break; stout is a synonym for s_____.	strong or sturdy
5. A person who believes in "looking before you leap" is cautious, wary, careful. Is calling a driver of a car "cautious" an insult?	No
6. The prefix re in "rebuild" and "refill" means _____.	again
7. The word length is a(n) _____. When you add -en to it you get _____. a(n) _____.	noun. lengthen verb
8. A group which has been split apart and then is "united again" is re_____.	reunited
9. Building a house is construction. Tearing it down ("unbuilding" it) is _____struction.	destruction
10. A flame emits or "sends _____" light. A person who has left his native country is an _____migrant.	out emigrant

It is apparent that through this process of breaking knowledge down into its simplest components, many subjects can be programed. Programing is particularly adaptable to skill and tool subjects—mathematics, spelling, punctuation, foreign languages. Even fact-crammed subjects like history can be programed by slicing away the fat and presenting the lean, hard facts which lie close to the bones of events. And, as indicated above, the pupil's assimilation of factual material is tested item by item as he goes along.

Proponents of teaching machines, a notably militant group, have a powerful arsenal of arguments. They assert that their machines lead not to the mechanization of learning but to the goal, so piously sought, of individualized instruction. Some call the machines "mechanical tutors" and argue that we now have within reach the optimal arrangement of one tutor and one pupil in each learning situation. (It was once said that the ideal college would be a log in the woods with educator Mark Hopkins at one end and a student at the other; now Hopkins has been implausibly transformed into a teaching box.)

MOREOVER, in the conventional classroom, the student has to wrestle with his own passivity and inertia. Using the machine, he is in constant interaction with programed material. Finally, if, as the psychologists insist, reinforcement is the key to learning, the machine can provide far more reinforcements than a teacher who has to distribute them among all her pupils.

"The simple truth," Professor Skinner has written, "is that as a mere reinforcing mechanism the teacher is out of date."

With teaching machines, students can move at their own rate of speed. Bright youngsters can romp through a program swiftly and move on to new ones. Dull students can take their time.

Another revolutionary feature of the teaching machine is that it is predicated on almost universal success. Instead of the current travesty of automatic promotion, a psychologist has argued, there will be automatic achievement. Everybody is expected to do well. The expertise of the programing will presumably enable even dull students—or those previously regarded as dull—to grasp the material presented.

In conventional classes, an examination in which everyone does well is immediately suspect. "I never regarded myself as sadistic," Skinner recently observed, "but when I started to program I realized that I was making things harder than I should. Teachers generally want students to be wrong. If everyone knows the answers to questions, teachers make them tougher. With teaching machines, you give the students every opportunity to be right."

A FINAL argument in their behalf is that teaching machines may provide a realistic solution for shortages of classrooms and teachers. Skinner envisions fifteen-minute machine sessions. This means a far shorter school day than at present. There is even the possibility of using the machines at home with only certain group activities taking place in what we now know as the school.

Nor are the claims of the machine psychologists mere rhetoric, for there are concrete results. At Harvard, Professor Skinner's students have been

ROBOT—Teaching machines vary in design according to their purpose. This one, "Tutor," is for industrial and military use.

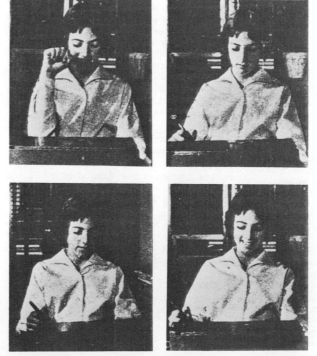

RIGHT ANSWER—A student ponders the question put by a teaching machine, writes her answer, checks it and discovers she's right. This prompt reaction, without a wait for test-paper grades, is claimed to be one of the machine's main advantages.

using machines in a psychology course and performing creditably.

Even more striking were the results last spring in Roanoke, Va., where a group of eighth-grade students in a junior high school studied algebra—a ninth-grade subject — *without teacher, textbook or homework*, using only machines and programed material. This experiment was under the direction of Dr. Allen Calvin of Hollins College. These children covered an entire year's work in one term—twice the normal quota. On national exams in algebra, their performance was impressive, despite the fact that they were competing with children a year older than they. The average score of the Roanoke test group fell in the lower end of the average category for ninth graders, but 41 per cent of the children surpassed the average score attained by ninth graders. Only one Roanoke child fell in the "very low" category.

THE consensus of other experimenters seems to be that, with teaching machines, students can learn at twice the speed of those being conventionally taught.

How did the Roanoke children react to the experience? Affirmatively, it would appear. At the conclusion of the experiment, only 16 per cent of the children preferred a return to regular instruction. More than half opted for a combination of teacher and machine.

Informal reactions ran a colorful gamut and demonstrated that, machines or no, children are stubbornly themselves. "I like not having to do homework," a boy said. A go-getting girl observed: "It challenges you to get ahead of someone else." Another youngster, sounding as if he had been well-reinforced by machines, stated magisterially: "In regular class you learn something and forget it and have to learn it again. Here you learn it the first time."

The principal of the junior high school manifested a wary enthusiasm: "I had a show-me attitude at first. You might say I'm from Missouri. But I'm real pleased now. I thought the novelty would wear off, that the youngsters would dawdle. But they didn't."

THE function of the teacher in this experiment was merely to straighten out mechanical breakdowns. She walked around, somewhat wanly, with a screwdriver instead of a rollbook. "I think education has not progressed as fast as other things," she said. "We're due for some changes. That's why I was glad to try this."

Despite the impressive results, the critics of teaching machines are vociferously unpersuaded. They range from a professor of history who said in accents of deep Spenglerian gloom, "It's the end of Western civilization," to uneasy collaborationists full of unresolved skepticism.

First, the very idea of mechanization in schools is repugnant to many people. "What will be the effect," a teacher asked anxiously, "of a generation of students who sit in front of a machine all day and go click-click?"

Objectors also point out the obvious limitations of teaching machines. At their present level, machines are admirably equipped to teach facts and skills, and, humbling as the thought may be, they seem to do so more efficiently than human beings.

But there is an immense area of education—perhaps the most crucial area—in which facts alone are useless. Values, feelings, convictions, the very things we live by—these cannot be precisely analyzed or programed. About the central questions of human existence there are no form answers—only other questions, partial answers, and infinitely complicated modulations of feelings and ideas. Here teaching machines are helpless.

MACHINE material is open to the same objections as all short-answer questions: there is only a right answer—and a wrong one. The modulated response, or what John Keats called "negative capability"—the capacity to sustain doubt —is unattainable with machines. There is danger of an intellectually efficient but robotized generation emerging from machine instruction.

Teaching machines, for example, can impart information about art, but they cannot teach us how to react to paintings—except in the most terrifyingly robotized fashion. Machines can provide facts about international politics and test students' absorption of them, but they cannot provide answers for international problems. Machines can show young people how to punctuate and how to negotiate the treacherous complexities of syntax, but they cannot teach them how to think through an idea or express themselves with grace and force.

IN that technological Arcadia of the future, the great decisions about life, for which education is designed to prepare us, will still be made in the lonely recesses of the human mind and heart. And they will issue from struggle and guesswork and passionate conviction, with the teacher fulfilling her traditional role as midwife in this agony of gestation and birth.

Comparing teaching machines to tutors is, in a real sense, disingenuous, for the essence of the tutorial process is free discussion, which may start with monetary theory and end with the values by which one orders one's life. No machine can do that.

The most strenuous objections, therefore, have to do with the role of the teacher. Everyone can remember a few magnificent teachers in his school career whose function far transcended merely imparting information. Through some special, indefinable gift, they were able to bring to life the high drama of ideas. It is through a kinetic encounter with a teacher of this kind that a student is recruited into the intellectual life. What will happen to teachers in an educational setting dominated by teaching machines? To bring up an everlasting question, who will inspire students? At best, teaching machines can merely motivate.

In a teaching-machine cul-ture, the best pedagogic talent will be drafted into the programing end of the profession. This has the obvious merit of providing excellent program material for all. (Just as we can remember the occasional giant among teachers, we also recall, with a shudder of distaste, the dreary procession of mediocrities.) But programing has the effect, too, of pulling good teachers out of the classroom and of reducing, or ending, the creative interaction among teachers, student and subject-matter.

CRITICS are keenly aware that teaching-machine spokesmen have been less than clear about the future role of the teacher. For the most part, they talk about interpersonal relations as the sphere of the newly liberated teacher—as if interpersonal relations can be practiced in any meaningful way independently of subject-matter. "The teacher will be a human being with some students, while others are on the machine," a psychologist said. There are those who invoke the talismanic word "enrichment."

In mathematics, it was suggested, the teacher, free of the bondage of algebra and geometry, would present the relationship of mathematics to the space age—an interesting subject but not mathematics.

Some of the moderate advocates of teaching machines see them merely as auxiliary instruments for rote instruction. The teacher, relieved of many mechanical chores, will continue to fulfill her time-honored functions of explaining, guiding and inspiring. But critics fear that hard-core machine proponents might be reluctant to let highly fallible teachers defile the work of the nearly perfect machines. They distrust the argument that a teacher, after all, merely deploys her own limited skills, while a machine program embodies the sophisticated efforts of a team of topnotch experimental psychologists (con-cerned with learning theory) and subject-matter specialists. They are not reassured by a psychologist's brusque assertion: "The teacher's function will be custodial—to keep children out of their mothers' hair."

One has to ask, also, what will happen to reading habits when students are conditioned to learn even complex material through a highly distilled, atomized presentation? The reading of discursive texts—a crude, nonreinforcing technique — might conceivably be a casualty.

Finally, those who have peered critically at the literature of the teaching-machine psychologists see in it a design for behavioral control. The strong emphasis on positive reinforcement seems somewhat Pavlovian. One psychologist, for example, sees education as "an integrated culture which [will undertake] the guidance of the individual's growth and development as a serious task of planned cultural conditioning." This kind of Faustian thinking worries some observers who point to the tragic miscarriage of Utopian ventures in the past.

ONLY the most defiantly old-fashioned would fail to agree that full exploration should be made of teaching machines. Incorporated within a context in which humane values are firmly anchored, machines may, indeed, bring about a new vitality and efficacy in our schools. The immediate task is to unite the machine more effectively with the classroom teacher, whose ministrations are even more vital in an increasingly machine-dominated world.

Educators, in making use of this revolutionary body of ideas, should avoid equally the delaying tactics of the inveterate enemies of change, and the headlong impetuosity of the new radicals, naively enchanted with their shiny technology.

MACHINE POWER—

As research increasingly becomes the province of the nation's colleges and universities, electronic computers become as necessary as blackboards and libraries. While the costs decline (the computer industry believes that even small liberal arts colleges can now afford the new low-cost computers), the search for qualified instructors and supervisors accelerates.

It is estimated that more than 100 colleges have active computational centers, with at least 100 more to be added in the coming year.

A program completed last week at Texas Agricultural and Mechanical College, one of seven supported by the National Science Foundation this summer, will enable thirty college teachers to man the computer centers that their institutions plan to install. In addition, during the last year, 250 students, including most engineering seniors at the college, received instruction in programing and use of the machines.

An article in the current issue of Chemical and Engineering News describes the training and enthusiastic response of A & M students. Students in any department, with training in calculus, learn the techniques of programing and get actual working experience on the simplest of the college's three computers. After completing the computer course, a student receives an "operator's license." This allows him to use the machine for his own problems during lunch hours, in the evening or on week-ends.

LIVE VS. TV—

An experiment to determine whether a teacher must be seen in person to be heard has found that a teacher of recognized ability can produce the same effect over television that he achieves in the college classroom. By means of kinescopes, the teachers were able to give identical lectures simultaneously by television and in person to different sections of a liberal arts course. The study also compared experienced and novice teachers, using the same techniques.

Dr. Lawrence Myers Jr., associate professor of radio-television at Syracuse University, who performed the study under a grant from the U. S. Office of Education, reported the following findings:

(1) Students will learn facts equally well from classroom or TV instruction.

(2) Both methods proved equally effective in teaching critical thinking, but the experienced teacher was generally more effective in getting students to apply principles, interpret data and integrate knowledge.

(3) Neither method proved an advantage in modifying student attitudes related to course content.

Dr. Myers suggested that educators might consider making better use of their teachers "by encouraging outstanding faculty members to use the television medium for lecturing to large classes, especially those introductory courses usually taught by graduate assistants."

Admission to High School Is Not Everywhere Easy

By DORIS DEAKIN

PAPERBACK books, in a switch on the usual experience of students these days, are having a tougher time getting "admitted" to high school than to college. Sales of paperbacks in college bookstores across the country have soared. University professors welcome paperbounds in their classes. Yet, although publishers began a strenuous effort in the mid-Fifties to interest secondary schools in paperbacks, comparatively few softcovers are going to high school.

The reasons most often cited:

(1) A lingering, if declining tendency to equate "paperback" with sex, sordidness and shooting.

(2) State rules on books used in public schools. Some serve as bars to paperbacks.

(3) The doubts of some school administrators about the durability of paperbounds.

(4) Uncertainty on the part of some publishers about who should be approached in the school system—the Board of Education, the superintendent, the principal or the teacher.

Less often mentioned is a factor that should perhaps head the list—the local distributor. Many—perhaps the majority—of the paperbacks that win acceptance on the college and university campus are titles in the higher-priced lines distributed through the normal hardcover trade book channels. However, virtually all the paperbacks now designed for the schools are the products of the so-called "mass-market" houses, which have to rely largely upon local magazine distributors. Publishers may push hard, but there is evidence that softcover classics reach high-school students most effectively in areas where the local distributor can discuss good books with school personnel and goes out of his way to sell them. This combination of qualities is rare and is particularly rare in New York City.

Frequently, paperback distributors are grizzled veterans of tough magazine circulation battles. They're accustomed to newsstand and drugstore sales and little inclined to serious reading. Distributor and high-school teacher tend to be strangers when they meet.

Striking examples of the key role local distributors with the correct approach can play in education are the Buffalo News Company of Buffalo, N. Y., and the District News Company of Washington, D. C. Because Washington is the larger city with perhaps more complicated problems, its story is particularly significant.

IN 1955, District News advanced the modest proposal that high-school administrators "give some thought" to the use of paperbacks as part of literature and other courses. The company noted that these books would "add a tremendous variety to the curriculum, enable you to make more copies available while staying within your budget."

One school administrator, expressing a nation-wide as well as a local attitude, replied "the [school] officers are unanimous in their feeling that paperbound books do not lend themselves to use in the public schools, where they must be passed from pupil to pupil [and] used over and over again."

But there has been a change. Today, Washington's Assistant Superintendent in charge of high schools, John D. Koontz, is an enthusiastic proponent of paperbacks. "In many areas," he says, "it's cheaper to buy these expendable books than to buy hardcovers."

Many school officials in the Washington area, while still weighing the question of the durability of paperbacks, are, as one administrator puts it, "surprised at the life of these things." Koontz notes that "in the [Army] cadet programs in the schools, they use all paperbacks. The paperbacks don't wear out appreciably faster

Mrs. Deakin is a freelance writer based in Washington.

han hard covers. Of course, in cadet programs, they don't carry the books home — and that's where books get beaten up." At least some other school officials are convinced that, even when paperbacks are carried home, their life expectancy is great enough to make them "worth considering."

What happened in six years? In a word—Hurowitz.

The District News Company hired Paul Hurowitz to head its paperback book department in 1956. Since then the company's paperback sales to high schools jumped from less than $10,000 in 1955 to more than $90,000 in 1961.

It takes more than one man to make a revolution, but Washington educators give Hurowitz much of the credit for the enthusiastic acceptance and extensive use of softcover books in the area's schools today. School boards in the metropolitan area—despite the handicaps sometimes posed by state regulations—have begun buying paperbacks for class libraries and supplementary reading. More than sixty high schools now have thriving paperback stores where students may buy approved books. Yorktown High School, just across the Potomac from the capital, boasts one of the largest high-school softcover stores in the nation, with a stock of 7,000 books and more than 2,400 titles. Paperback editions of Plato and the Greek tragedies are being assigned by teachers.

Hurowitz, a burly, 41-year-old, who likes good books and considers them good business as well, encountered an attitude at first every bit as bad as outright opposition - apathy. His approach was to go to the high-school teachers rather than the principals and administrators. Hurowitz knew he would have little chance of getting paperbacks into school libraries, so he aimed first at getting paperback bookstores set up in high schools. He talked to English teachers, Hurowitz explains, because "English students are automatic paperback supporters and they tend to work on the high-school quarterlies and newspapers. These groups are always in the red. What better way to put them in the black than to set up a project where they can sell books? Who's a more logical person to talk to

than the faculty adviser to these groups? And the adviser is usually an English teacher."

Hurowitz went into public, private and parochial schools. He explained the mechanics of setting up a bookstore and put the services of District News at the disposal of the teachers. The genial distributor's ambassador, equally effective in the separate worlds of truck driver and educator, regards his firm as a "utility" in the educational field, "basically a service operation for schools."

The meager initial results of visits to English teachers would have discouraged a salesman with less conviction. Hurowitz, however, remained convinced that paperback bookstores would prove profitable to students, schools and District News.

"Reading is habit forming," Hurowitz believes. "A student who won't pick up a textbook will read a paperback, especially if he feels a teacher didn't make him do it. If he reads a paperback, he may learn to like to read. And if he gets into the reading habit in high school he's a future customer for us."

A few parochial schools invited Hurowitz to set up bookstores for them. But the big break in the public schools

came in 1958 when a Fairfax County (Va.) English teacher, unsuccessful in her search for enough second-hand hardback copies of a classic for an entire class, happened into District News. "At first I thought I was in the wrong place," Mrs. Geraldine Lenvin recalls. "On one side of the room all the girls on the book covers seemed to be soaked in blood. But then I saw the *other* side. It was such a marvelous revelation. I found what I needed. Besides there were inexpensive Folger editions of Shakespeare, of Edith Hamilton's works and many others."

Mrs. Lenvin's enthusiasm led to the opening of a paperback bookstore in the Falls Church (Va.) High School. The store, set up in a supply room, consisted of one rack 8 feet tall and 110 titles. Within a month students had purchased more than 1,250 paperbacks.

Later, speaking before a group of Virginia high-school English teachers, Mrs. Lenvin described the store as well as the books and services available at District News. High-school officials in one Virginia county after another began asking Hurowitz to set up a bookstore. .

Secondary schools in Montgomery County, Washington's

next door Maryland neighbor, followed Virginia's lead. The District of Columbia school system continued to lag behind in paperback bookstores, but individual schools in the capital were installing them on their own. Hurowitz, traveling from school to school, helped teachers set up stores in closet-size spaces, in halls and, at least in one case, in a cafeteria.

The fear that sex will somehow slip into high schools between paper covers dies hard, even in upper-middle-class suburban areas. A high-school teacher in a Virginia area where paperbacks had generally been accepted wanted to use a softcover edition of Fielding's "Tom Jones." School officials reprimanded the teacher and banned the book. "It was probably the cover," Hurowitz says. "I believe one edition had a woman nude from the waist up on it."

"We screen books that go into schools," Hurowitz says. "We reserve the right to refuse to deliver books we do not deem acceptable." Freud is one of his pet peeves he refuses to supply the esteemed doctor to high schools. "The one great fear of a faculty," Hurowitz points out, "is that a paperback will get the school

Student-run paperback bookstore in Groveton, Va.

or faculty in trouble. This we intend to prevent."

In some schools, a faculty committee does the ...eening. In others, any judgment of Hurowitz' is good enough for the educators. The selection of titles to be displayed in a bookstore is frequently left to Hurowitz' discretion as well. Where school teachers, sometimes in conjunction with students, prefer to do their own choosing, order forms are delivered regularly.

District News has also furnished the racks of high-school paperback stores. It has specially designed financial arrangements for schools. No immediate payment for an initial order is asked. Schools, though regularly billed, can pay as the money comes in. Unsold books are returnable. "We have lost no money," Hurowitz says.

After the bookstores broke the ice, came school board orders for paperbacks. Although Hurowitz still encounters reluctance now and then, the vast majority of educators here have

reacted enthusiastically. School librarians, Hurowitz says, have given him the most trouble. "They don't feel a paperback is worth the trouble of cataloguing."

A high-school paperback store opened in a Washington slum area recently. It's one of the few that's not flourishing. Nevertheless, Superintendent Koontz says:

"I'm happy with it. Those students don't have much money. One little girl, who has to do her homework on the top of a washing machine because there's no other study area in the house, took home a paperback dictionary, probably the only book in the house. That bookstore is a little ray of light in a dark sky."

"We are a book centered school," says Dr. Harold M. Wilson, principal of Wakefield (Va.) High School, "as most American schools are. We should have available the materials the students need. The

paperback enables us to d[o] that."

Educators repeatedly mention these advantages of paperbacks

They enable teachers, once confined to survey textbooks to go into a subject in depth

Paperbacks provide up to-date information that standard textbooks don't.

Paperbacks enable, actually encourage, students to build their own home libraries.

Secondary school educator in the Washington area also have strong feelings about Pau Hurowitz. Says one teacher "He doesn't just do things t[o] make a fast buck. He's really excited."

Koontz summed up the opin ion educators have of Huro witz: "As the girls in ou schools would say—'he's a liv ing doll!'"

January 14, 196[2]

LANGUAGE TAPES FOUND MAJOR AID

School-System Study Backs Use of Laboratories by 10,000 Students Here

REPORT COVERS 3 YEARS

713 in Experimental Group Said to Exhibit Superior Standard of Fluency

A three-year study by the city school system has found that students who received instruction in language labora-tories did far better in some respects than those who were taught solely by conventional methods.

In a report prepared for the State Education Department and made public yesterday, the system declared that students in the experimental group had "superior achievement" in lang-uage fluency, intonation and lis-tening comprehension.

The study involved 713 stu-dents of French at Abraham Lincoln and Sheepshead Bay High Schools, both in Brooklyn. The students were divided into experimental and control groups to assess the quality of their instruction and their attitudes.

Supported by Grant

The project, designed to study the role of language laborator-ies, was supported by a state research grant.

More than 10,000 public school pupils here are receiving instruction in language labora-tories established at twenty-five senior and twelve junior high schools. Laboratories are also being installed this year in four elementary schools.

Part of the cost of installing and equipping the laboratories is provided under the National Defense Education Act.

The laboratories enable stu-dents to listen and respond to lessons sent by tape, phono-graph record, microphone or other devices and to hear their own responses.

The report noted that for those in the experimental group "sixty minutes a week were de-ducted from the regular class time for laboratory work while the control students were re-ceiving that much additional practice in traditional learn-ings."

Despite this, it said, on a standardized achievement test of vocabulary, grammar and reading comprehension, both groups performed equally well.

"This shows," the report as-serted, "that improvement in speech or in listening compre-hension was made without detri-ment to traditional skills.

"It is even possible that cer-tain traditional learnings may be reinforced through labora-tory activities. For example, lesson tapes that include struc-ture drills provide practice both in speaking and in acquiring control over patterns of lan-guage. Similarly, taped dicta-tion exercises provide listening practice as well as practice in the traditional skill of writing correctly."

The report also noted that al-though three years of language study were sufficient to meet college entrance requirements, 71 per cent of the students in the experimental group elected to continue French for a fourth year. This compares with 35 per cent of the non-laboratory stu-dents.

The study said this indicated that the language laboratory "stimulates a student's interest in French and his desire to con-tinue to study it."

The report was prepared by Mrs. Sarah W. Lorge, language consultant for the Board of Ed-ucation's Bureau of Audio-Vis-ual Instruction.

October 29, 196[ ]

New Teaching Methods Appraised In Language Laboratory Test

By FRED M. HECHINGER

A report on the effectiveness of language laboratories in high schools last week opened questions on the value of the new method of language instruction. Raymond F. Keating, research fellow in the Institute of Administrative Research at Teachers College, concluded from a preliminary study of 21 school districts near New York City that the laboratory as a "wonder drug" had been oversold to the public and to teachers. He added that, whereas he did not intend to say that the laboratories could not be used effectively, he found that many schools are doing as well—or even better—without them.

The final report, sponsored by the Metropolitan School Study Council, at 525 West 120 Street, New York 27, will be available in July.

Perhaps the most serious immediately visible limitation of the study was that all the school systems surveyed were far above average in wealth. Obviously, schools with superior teachers who have always been doing an above-average job are not a fair yardstick of what might be achieved in improving instruction elsewhere.

Although anti-laboratory educators will probably use the report to support their argument, the only undeniable points made in the Keating report are that the same errors are being committed in introducing language laboratories that have plagued film, television and teaching machines: in addition to over-selling by commercial interests, there has been a serious lag in the training of teachers on how to use the electronic aides, insufficient guidance in helping them select materials and, most important, too little concerted planning of how best to integrate the new approach into the total language curriculm.

Classroom Work

Ideally, much of the time spent in the laboratory should be in addition to the formal classroom instruction. But even when this is not possible, the laboratory's usefulness might still be considered like that of a good library, expertly and generously used.

If ability to speak a language is to be a first priority in foreign language study—and all but the most unreconstructed translation-minded educators today agree with this goal—then the usefulness of the language laboratory is self-evident. While laboratories vary in type, they typically provide students with microphones and earphones, with individual volume control. In addition, there is a control console for the teacher. The laboratory may be used under the teacher's direction or, like a library, for individual study and practice. Finally, laboratories have become an important part of intensive language instruction, of the crash program type, in the armed forces and elsewhere.

Expert language teachers in New York City who have been using language laboratories reacted to the research study with a vigorous defense of the new approach.

Perhaps the argument over the effectiveness of the laboratories is inseparable from the older argument about what should be studied. The old-school stress on language instruction used to be primarily on reading, with strong emphasis on grammar and translation. This led the late Heywood Broun to quip that he had studied Beginners' French, only to find on arrival in Paris that nobody there spoke Beginners' French. The "bookish" nature of such study often stifled student interest.

Subsequently, in the Thirties, a combination of post - World War I isolationism and the trend toward "life adjustment" education, which stressed the immediately "useful" skills in existing society, turned foreign language study into a "frill." Enrollment in languages declined from over 85 per cent of the high school enrollment in 1922 to less than 25 per cent in 1948. New stress on academic subjects, together with the excitement created by new methods of study, with early stress on the spoken word, have just begun to reverse that trend.

Some experts are worried—and this is reflected in the Keating report—that too much stress on speaking and listening may in the long run retard thorough knowledge of a language. They warn that, unless the speaking-listening (with the use of language laboratories) is quickly reinforced with grammar and reading, the result will be little more than tourist-guide conversational skills.

Finally, there is a minority of educators—probably the remnant of the life-adjustment group—who belittle the importance of language study as part of general education.

This view is opposed by educators who believe that language study is part of general education, helps in the comprehension of other cultures, strongly reinforces the understanding of language in general, including English, and easily transfers its benefits to later study of additional languages.

Buying Teachers

The most convincing warning on the role of the laboratory contained in the Keating report is that commercial and educational over-selling has induced schools to rush into the purchase of language laboratories—without preparation—because it was fashionable. It required no financial sacrifice since the equipment was offered free under the National Defense Education Act of 1958.

One argument sometimes used against the investment in laboratories is that an equal amount of money might buy teachers of such superior quality as to make the electronic device unnecessary. But since at present only two states require actual proof of a language teaching candidate's proficiency in the spoken language, the time is long distant when there will be an adequate supply of such teachers.

Even that, however, is a narrow view of the controversy. Whether or not the drill opportunities offered by the laboratory are essential, the potential use even for highly advanced work — including listening and response to foreign plays, discussions or readings seems almost unlimited, especially as the new devices which permit "dialing" continuously playing tape enter the field. The only important caveat highlighted by the Keating report, is to forstall hostility to the new process by putting a stop to extravagant claims of "French Without Tears." As with salesmen of television, teaching machines and, yes, books, the buyer must be sure he knows what he buys and how to use it.

May 19, 1963

VIDEO TAPE HELPS FUTURE TEACHERS

Coast System Lets Student See Himself in Action

Special to The New York Times

SAN FRANCISCO, Nov. 30—Student teachers scattered across the Bay area from the Stanford University School of Education can now see themselves in action and judge their teaching techniques.

These "teaching interns" in high schools are visited in class by two graduate students who form a television production crew.

The interns' classroom presentation is recorded on video tape by a portable recorder. It can be seen either immediately on a portable video monitor or later in the day back at Stanford. About 20 minutes of the presentation is recorded.

Prof. Robert N. Bush, who is the director of the secondary education project, supported by the Ford Foundation, said that the first nine months had proved the tapes very helpful to student teachers.

Keith Acheson and Alan Robertson, two former teachers who are working toward their doctorates in education, form the camera crew. They have two cartloads of equipment that they set up in the classroom between periods.

With this equipment, a teacher in a school many miles from the Palo Alto campus of Stanford can see himself in action immediately. Those who are doing practice teaching nearer to Stanford will go to the campus in the late afternoon or night to see their "screen tests."

The teacher watches his own performance, then asks help and comment from the faculty of the School of Education.

December 1, 1963

76,000 TV Receivers In Use in Classrooms

The television habit has tightened its grip on America's classrooms.

The Federal Communications Commission reports that 76,000 television receivers are being used in the public schools.

Twenty new educational TV stations are in the process of completion and about 20 others are expected to be under way in 1965.

Nine state educational TV networks are in operation and nine others are in the planning stage.

January 13, 1965

What the Talking Typewriter Says

By MAYA PINES

AN extraordinary learning device which children call a "talking typewriter" has been tried out, in the past few years, with almost every kind of learner—normal 3-year-olds, mentally retarded children, 17-year-old drop-outs, children with impaired sight or hearing—and to varying degrees all of them seem to have benefited from the experience.

Only a few weeks ago a "talking typewriter" was credited with spectacular improvement in the behavior of several children suffering from an extremely severe form of schizophrenia. One of these, a 6-year-old boy who spoke only in gibberish and was on his way to a state mental hospital has now begun to communicate with others and no longer needs institutional care.

In fact, so remarkable are some of the results achieved with this machine that the researchers working with the typewriter try to play down their enthusiasm. After all, the machine, called the Edison Responsive Environment — E.R.E. for short, is still a research instrument, not generally available in schools or hospitals; its cost is nearly prohibitive; and until recently, the few existing prototypes were still being debugged. Furthermore, in all the cases where it has proved effective so far, the device has formed only one part of a new approach to learning — a carefully worked-out system which provides the learner with a "responsive environment" in which he freely makes his own discoveries.

The fact that children like and benefit from the "responsive environment" method does not surprise its inventor, a quiet but intense man of 45 with graying hair and the unusual name of Omar Khayyam Moore. Born in Utah, brought up in Nebraska, Dr. Moore is now a professor of psychology at Rutgers University. He developed his system after years of research in human problem-solving, as a method of stimulating children to reason inductively. He believed that if children were allowed to teach themselves skills in their own way and at their own pace, without adult interference—as they could in a "responsive environment"—they would not only learn much more rapidly,

MAYA PINES is a writer (and mother of two) who is now working on a book discussing new educational techniques for pre-school children.

but also enjoy the process sufficiently to keep coming back for more.

The E.R.E. machine itself looks rather unexciting—it resembles a big steel cabinet with a typewriter attached. But it is a highly complex and subtle instrument that can talk, play games, read aloud, take dictation and show pictures. It consists of an electric typewriter with keys that cannot jam; a narrow window, called an exhibitor, on which letters, words or sentences may be shown; a slide projector; a microphone and a speaker—all connected to a small computer. The whole thing is about four feet high and weighs over 500 pounds. Only the keyboard is exposed to the child's fingers. To prevent its destruction by overeager explorers, the rest of the apparatus is enclosed behind gray steel or clear plastic. The long roll of paper on which the child types, the exhibitor and the slide projector remain visible, though out of reach. For the sake of privacy, as well as to encourage concentration, the E.R.E. and a chair facing it are usually placed in a small, soundproof booth.

When a child sits down alone in the booth before this "talking typewriter," he begins a process of free exploration. Whatever key he strikes, the machine responds by typing the corresponding symbol and naming it in the voice of the teacher who programed the instrument. No two children proceed in exactly the same way—some try each letter methodically, others play with the punctuation marks, others peck at keys apparently at random. The younger the child, the more fun this seems.

During a three-year demonstration project in a laboratory adjoining the Hamden Hall Country Day School in Hamden, Conn., Dr. Moore showed that children as young as 3 years of age could learn

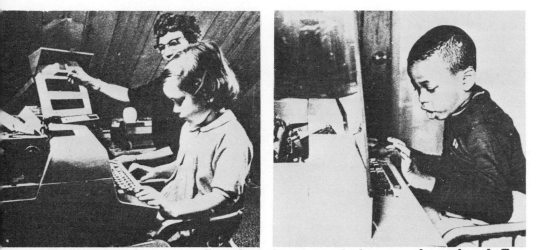

The talking typewriter says: An educational revolution may be at hand. For it has proved it really teaches—even disturbed children. Here, normal youngsters with the machine.

to read, write, take dictation and compose original stories by spending no more than half an hour a day in a "responsive environment." There they gradually made a series of interlocking discoveries about words and sentences, much the way that young children learn to talk.

Perhaps the most striking aspect of this "responsive environment" was its totally permissive atmosphere. The children came to the lab only if they wanted to; they were neither praised nor blamed; they could leave at any time.

ANOTHER remarkable feature was that the machine followed the interests of each child. The period of free exploration lasted only as long as the apparatus seemed to hold the child's attention. Outside the booth a trained monitor watched through a one-way mirror, and when she detected signs of flagging interest, she would adjust the machine so as to change the game to a puzzle.

Without warning, a letter would appear on the exhibitor facing the child, the machine would name the letter, and to the child's amazement all the keys would be blocked, except the one the machine had named. It was now up to the child to find the right letter. By trial and error, the child sooner or later hit the right key. Bingo! The key went down, the machine typed the letter, naming it again, and after a short interval a new letter appeared on the exhibitor.

Urged on by curiosity and a desire to hit the jackpot,

the children soon learned to find any letter that was named. At the same time, since their fingernails were painted to match colors dabbed on the typewriter keys, they learned to touch-type with correct fingering technique.

FROM then on, the "responsive environment" was tailored to each individual child. First one of the monitors would sit down with the child and talk with him for a while, recording the conversation on tape. Next this conversation would be broken down into its component words, sentences and paragraphs. This insured that the child was interested in these particular words, and also that he understood them. Instead of using an official word list, or a dull primer, the machine was then programed to use the child's own words in building puzzles that would help him bridge the gap from mere recognition of letters to reading.

Supposing the child had talked about playing in the park. During one of his sessions with the "talking typewriter," after a little free typing of letters and some letter-finding, he would suddenly see four letters on his exhibitor, instead of one, with a red arrow pointing to the first letter. The voice would say, "P-A-R-K, park." If the child tried to type "k" first, he would find the letter blocked. The keys responded only when he typed the letters in the right sequence, and then the machine again said, "P-A-R-K, park" before going on to another word.

At no time was the child actually "taught" anything. But after periods of varying lengths—weeks or, more frequently, months—the child would suddenly realize that the letters he knew actually made up words which had a meaning, and that he, himself, could now write such words. This discovery is so elating that when it happens, children have been known to jump up and down in excitement, or run out of the booth to talk about it.

In Dr. Moore's opinion, this is the way to introduce learning to children—to make it so exciting that they are "hooked" to it for life. "It's an affront to your intelligence to be always told, always presented with everything," he says.

The children who came to his lab during their nursery and kindergarten years learned to read and write so fluently that by the time they entered first grade they produced their own newspaper. They wrote and edited it by themselves, with the help of some kindergartners who dictated their stories into a tape recorder. Some of the children wrote poetry. Each one read books in fields that interested him particularly—from astronomy to the Boy Scout manual—as well as classics such as Aesop's Fables or "Alice in Wonderland."

Occasionally, for testing purposes, the children read standard film strips prepared by the Educational Development Lab of Huntington, L. I. This showed that the first graders read up to sixth-grade level, with the average about third-grade level, while the second graders who had

been in the program two years read up to ninth-grade level, with the average about sixth grade.

Originally, most of this was achieved without benefit of automation. When the demonstration program began at Hamden Hall in 1961, the only machines involved were electric typewriters (somewhat modified so the keys would not jam), exhibitors and tape recorders. Young women monitors named whatever key the child struck and pointed at letters on the exhibitor.

MEANWHILE, Dr. Moore and Richard Kobler, an engineer who is now manager of the Thomas A. Edison Laboratory of West Orange, N. J., a division of the McGraw-Hill Company, together devised the E.R.E. machine to coordinate all the equipment, increase its capabilities and also automate most of the monitors' functions. Components of this machine, in various stages of automation, became available at Hamden Hall, and finally in 1963, the last year of the demonstration project, one fully automated E.R.E. prototype was installed. There were then five booths for children enrolled in the program—one fully automated, three semi-automated and one nonautomated. The 65 children who participated that year were assigned to a different booth every day at random.

AT the small but splendidly equipped Mary Imogene Bassett Hospital in Cooperstown, N. Y., an article about Dr. Moore's work caught the eye of a pediatrician who was particularly interested in children with reading difficulties. For 10 consecutive summers, the hospital's pediatric department under Dr. T. Campbell Goodwin had sponsored a remedial-reading camp on a nearby estate. But both Dr. Goodwin and his wife Dr. Mary Goodwin, the energetic, white-haired director of the camp, had become so discouraged with available methods of helping such children that they were about to suspend the camp and concentrate on research. Then they read about the "responsive environment," and as soon as possible, Dr. Mary Goodwin went to Hamden Hall to see for herself.

"I was excited by what I saw there," she reports. Beside the reading activities, what impressed her most was

141

"the difference in the behavior of one blonde child when she was inside the booth and outside it. Inside the booth, she was a very relaxed, gay little girl; outside the booth, she seemed very withdrawn. I thought, here was surely something that ought to be tried with autistic children [those suffering from a severe form of schizophrenia], as well as with our retarded readers."

At the request of the pediatric department, the Cooperstown hospital then purchased one of the three existing prototypes of the E.R.E. Shortly before the machine was installed in February of last year, a 6-year-old boy with an unusually severe disturbance was brought to the hospital clinic. He had been excluded from his school because he was unmanageable. Completely withdrawn, Jackie spoke only in gibberish and often flew into tantrums, beating his head against the floor. Dr. Goodwin, a student of Dr. Leo Kanner of Johns Hopkins, characterized Jackie as "autistic"—a term first used by Dr. Kanner in the nineteen-forties, to describe certain schizophrenic children so withdrawn that they could not relate to people, only to things.

Three psychiatrists and two psychologists, Dr. Goodwin later learned, had already seen Jackie and diagnosed him as autistic. Since he clearly seemed to need institutional care, Dr. Goodwin helped his family make application at a nearby state hospital, but because of a shortage of beds there the boy could not be admitted immediately and had to remain at home. Meantime the E.R.E. arrived at Cooperstown, and Dr. Goodwin offered to let Jackie try out the machine. Without too many expectations, Jackie's mother agreed.

Dr. Goodwin recalls Jackie's first encounter with E.R.E.: "I led him up to the door of the booth. He touched a key, heard the voice and at once sat down. During the next half hour, without anybody in the booth with him, he typed off about 20 lines of apparently random letters, some of which made up recognizable words: Ivory liquid, clorox, arrid deodorint—that's the way he spelled it—Mr. Clean, and other brand names from television commercials. He was completely absorbed in what he was doing."

And so, for that matter, was Dr. Goodwin, who had been watching Jackie in amazement through a one-way mirror, together with some of her associates. "We really didn't know what we had there," she says, "except that it was very interesting." She asked Jackie's mother to bring him again.

ON the next occasion Jackie said, "Want to type"—his first words to the staff—and headed straight for the machine. He continued to come, two or three times a week, typing freely on the machine that could be trusted always to respond in exactly the same way (it was left in the free exploration phase for him). Once he played a lot with the carriage return, and then in the middle of the blank page he carefully centered the following three words:

BOXED

TAPED

WARPED

The staff still does not know what he meant—was he referring to some commercials, or to himself?

ONE of the hospital's three reading teachers always watched Jackie from outside the booth. After a few weeks the boy began asking this teacher to read back to him what he had just typed—thus turning the game into a sort of dialogue. Besides his half hour in the booth, Jackie spent an equal amount of time with another reading teacher in the library, playing with puppets, painting and having some juice and crackers.

Within two months of Jackie's first typing session his father reported that the boy had far fewer temper tantrums. Jackie was also beginning to show some interest in the child next door, whom he had always previously ignored. At the hospital he began to recognize some of the staff and call them by their names.

Today when he comes to the hospital Jackie goes up to one of the teachers, sits on her lap and plays with the typewriter. Then he presses a buzzer that connects with the booth room and announces over the intercom, "Jackie's here."

He has now paid nearly 70 visits to the laboratory. During this time he has changed from a noncommunicating, wild-looking, often violent child to one who for long periods seems perfectly normal. Although he is still far from well and his improvement may be only temporary, he is no longer a candidate for the

state hospital. The rapid change in his behavior is particularly striking since most of the other methods used to reach such autistic children have involved prolonged, round-the-clock relationships with therapists.

AT the Masters Children's Center, in New York City, psychiatrists have noted that very young autistic children can sometimes be reached through some inanimate object which they cherish to such an extent that it can be called a "psychotic fetish" — an extreme form of the attachment some normal children display toward a blanket. In the experience of Dr. Manuel Furer, medical director of the center, one autistic child of pre-school age used the piano as an intermediary between himself and people; another used a flag; a third an empty jar of baby food. Since older autistic children are particularly interested in machines, Dr. Furer speculates that they may come to use the E.R.E. machine in much the same way — partly for protection, since they are afraid of people; partly as a means of coming into contact with people.

DR. GOODWIN is well aware that case histories, unlike controlled experiments, do not prove much. She is also worried about stirring up false hopes among parents, particularly since E.R.E. facilities for treatment are so limited. But, she says, "something perfectly extraordinary has been going on in front of our eyes," and she has presented her clinical reports before two medical groups.

These reports include the stories of Jackie and of another 6-year-old, also diag-

nosed as autistic, who is now back in school, where he has no apparent difficulties. They tell of children sent over to Cooperstown from the state hospital. One boy of 14, a nearly mute schizophrenic who had failed to improve during 10 years of intensive psychiatric care, began to type, sing and talk when left alone with the E.R.E. He acted out an incident which, according to his records, happened to him when he was 2½. After 15 hours with the E.R.E. he had improved to the extent that he was able to reply, when asked where he was going, "To Cooperstown, to read a book."

Another group of children who have benefited from experience with the E.R.E. machine at Cooperstown are those with reading problems. According to Dr. Goodwin, children of all ages have used it, including a teen-ager who glowered at the machine when he first came but was all smiles as he left, declaring, "Gee, that's neat—you can't make a mistake!"

A 17-year-old boy who read at fifth-grade level was about to drop out of school before he started typing on the E.R.E. During each session he typed spontaneously a page of free association. He liked it so much that he still comes regularly, confides in the machine and has decided to stay in school.

"Older boys are so tired of having teachers tell them 'You can do it if you try'—they're bored stiff!" declares Dr. Goodwin. "But here's a fancy electronic gadget, and they find it extremely appealing."

The machine, of course, cannot play favorites, as ordinary teachers often do. It never tires of repeating things—in fact, its patience is such that

IA play with
I play with my teddy bear and his name is Fat Daddy. Sometimes I walk to the river near my house. It's fun to throw rocks in the water and watch them splash;

An example of work done on the "talking typewriter" by a normal 4-year-old. The child has recited a story, which is hand-printed by a teaching assistant.

aAt hpme I play with my friend
Coleen. I buy iee cream
at the store and go tothe
playground.

When I grow up I am going to
be a nurse so I can takd care
of sick people.

hen the child types the words, copying from the card; as each key is struck
nd the letter appears on the paper (above), a voice identifies and sounds it.

no mortal could match it. It never gets angry. It never compares the performances of students. In the privacy of the booth a retarded reader need not feel humiliated because he cannot keep up with his class. It is thus ideally suited to dealing with children with all kinds of problems.

A VERY different approach to the E.R.E. machine, totally at variance with the "responsive environment" system, is being tried out in Harlem in cooperation with the New York City Board of Education. There Dr. Lassar G. Gotkin, a senior research associate at the New York Medical College's Institute for Development Studies, hopes to develop a series of some 20 or 30 E.R.E. "lessons," lasting only 10 to 20 minutes each, for 5-year-old kindergarten children who have no knowledge of the alphabet.

At present the machine which Dr. Gotkin uses experimentally stands in a room reserved for research in a Harlem public school; eventually it would be placed in an ordinary classroom, thus eliminating the need for a booth. The lessons Dr. Gotkin is devising would be identical for all children, thus eliminating the task of obtaining individual material from each child. No semi-automated devices would be used, thus eliminating the need for a specially trained staff. No free exploration of the typewriter keyboard would be permitted — at first only six letters would be used, and at every stage of the game the child would be told what to do

I N a recent demonstration of the machine a little boy who had come for his fourth lesson sat down before the E.R.E. and, following instruc-

tions, typed the letters which appeared on the exhibitor.

"Very good," said the machine, "now type the next line." When the boy finished, a drawing of a cat flashed on the slide projector and the voice explained, "This is the picture of a cat. Now watch how we type cat.'"

The picture disappeared, a large C went on the slide projector and the voice continued, "First, type C." Then a large A appeared beside the C, while the voice said, "Then type A." Next, all three letters flashed on and the voice said, "Then type T. . . . Look, this is the word for 'cat.'"

The picture of the cat flashed on again and the voice said, "Type 'cat' again." repeating its instructions and showing the appropriate letters. After a while both the picture and the letters were removed, and the boy typed "cat" on the machine's oral instructions alone. The voice then said, "Very good, you've finished the lesson for today." By the end of the lesson the boy had typed "cat" 15 times.

In crowded city schools, Dr. Gotkin believes, one cannot afford the time it would take for hundreds of children to discover for themselves that a word is merely a sequence of letters — particularly in view of the machine's high cost. He does not envision a full use of the E.R.E. machine to produce maximum development of underprivileged children, but has, instead, aimed his program at economizing time, personnel and money and at preparation for the first grade.

A T Rutgers Dr. Moore is now busy devising ways to make the "talking typewriter" teach mathematics and languages. This is where the

E.R.E.'s flexibility will really come into its own: its audio components will be essential in teaching languages, its slide projector in teaching mathematics. For example, a student's voice can be recorded and played back automatically in such a way that he can compare his own speech with that of a pre-recorded model.

When fully programed, a single E.R.E. will be able to switch from English to any one of five other languages, as well as mathematics, at a flick of the wrist. Even adults who wish to learn a foreign language may then benefit from a "responsive environment."

Next year Dr. Moore will move to the University of Pittsburgh's growing Center for the Philosophy of Science, where he plans to build a laboratory for research on special aspects of the responsive-environment learning system. He will work with pre-school, mentally retarded and exceptionally gifted children, and even a few animals. Among other things, he hopes to determine the most satisfactory mixture of automated and nonautomated equipment. Also nobody knows whether children will continue to come to a fully automated E.R.E. day after day for a long period of time if they have no contact with the laboratory monitors.

R EGARDLESS of how much automation is desirable, Dr. Moore points out that a machine can never replace the classroom teacher, with whom the child in any E.R.E. program will still spend all but half an hour a day. Monitors will also be needed to watch the booths and to obtain individual programing material from the children.

An important feature of the E.R.E. machine in this respect is that it can be programed easily by people who have no special training in "computer languages." A teacher or monitor simply puts one of the blank program cards into the typewriter, sets a few dials and types out what he wishes —up to 120 words per card. These will then appear in any desired sequence on the exhibitor and also control the operation of the typewriter keys. The audio explanations are encoded simply by speaking into a microphone.

The real problem is to decide what to program. The buyer of an E.R.E. today buys, in a sense, a blank sheet of paper. What he does with it, Dr. Moore explains, is up to

him. He may decide to use the machine as the central tool of a "responsive environment" in which the child makes a series of linked disc veries through games in which the rules keep changing—as they do in our complex world — and at the same time learns many basic skills. Or the E.R.E. owner may look upon the instrument as merely another gadget with which to present traditional, formal instruction in a more efficient form. But given the promise of the "talking typewriter," Dr. Moore feels it would be a pity to settle for the latter.

A T any rate, the "talking typewriter" seems to be here to stay. Already the giants of the electronics industry are moving into the field, although none has yet developed an instrument to match the E.R.E. Westinghouse has announced a "talking typewriter" of its own, called SLATE ("Stimulated Learning by Automated Typewriter Environment"), which is still in the research stage.

At present the E.R.E. machine is so expensive—it costs $30,000 to buy, or about $1,000 a month to rent—that it is being used for research and demonstration purposes only. But, says Dr. Moore, who has no financial interest in the machine, "We already know how to drop costs, although it will take some time to do it. There will be low-cost instruments available for practical use with large numbers of children."

It should then become possible to hook many "talking typewriters" in different places to a single, general-purpose computer which could simultaneously monitor the activities of the children at al these typewriters and change each child's program individually, no matter how far away he might be. Such a system could serve thousands of children simultaneously. Although its initial cost would be very high, in the long run it might prove cheaper than the present system of education, with its many failures.

"For the first time in human history," Dr. Moore points out, "technology allows us to have an educational scheme truly tailored to the individual person—even if we are dealing with millions of people." He believes that, if properly used, this technology can bring about an educational revolution, and that it may result in "a truly humane treatment of humans."

May 9, 1965

Back-to-School Time Underlines Just How Big the Education Business Is

EDUCATION IN U.S. BIG AND GROWING

54 Million People Heading for Classes Mean Outlays Totaling $39 Million

FURTHER GAINS ASSURED

Government Aid a Factor— TV Plays a Key Role in New Methods of Teaching

By RICHARD RUTTER

Education is now big business and promises in the not-too-distant future to become the biggest of all.

This is back-to-school time and some 54 million children, teen-agers and young people are trekking to classrooms from the kindergarten to college graduate school level. It breaks down to about 48.5 million pupils enrolled in elementary and secondary schools and some 5.45 million students in colleges and universities. It also adds up to a massive outlay for education in all aspects of some $39 billion.

This sum is second in size only to the national defense budget and there are many who think in a few years it will surpass even that expenditure now running at about $49 billion.

One reason is the phenomenal growth of spending for education. Expenditures in 1950, for instance, were about $9.3 billion, or 3.5 per cent of the gross national product (the sum of all goods and services). Between 1954 and 1964, outlays rose 142 per cent to $33.7 billion, or 5.4 per cent of the gross national product. A rise to $50 billion or 6.1 per cent of the gross national product, has been projected by 1973.

Growth Is Assured

The population trend alone assures that the educational market will continue to grow. From 1955-64, school and college enrollment increased from 37.9 million to 52.6 million, or 39 per cent. Elementary school attendance rose from 27.7 million to 35.2 million; that in high schools, from 7.6 million to 12.6 million, and in colleges from 2.7 million to 4.8 million.

The Office of Education in the Department of Health, Education and Welfare foresees total enrollments of 62 million by 1973. The greatest increase is expected at the college level, already beginning to feel the impact of the post-World War II "baby boom."

Then there is the growing importance of Federal aid to education. It is now assuming gigantic proportions. Government outlays for education in the fiscal year ending June 30, 1966, are expected to be more than $2.7 billion.

The Elementary and Secondary Education Act of 1965 provides for outlays of $1.3 billion. It also authorizes up to $100 million for school libraries, textbooks and related materials. The Higher Education Act of 1965 authorizes about $250 million, with $65 million allocated to college libraries.

But that's not all by any means. Just last week the Senate Labor Committee unanimously approved a $4.7 billion higher education bill for funds to aid needy students and help colleges meet the enrollment flood now building up. Approval by the Senate is expected soon.

Construction Mounting

Where does business fit into all this?

Educational construction in 1964 alone amounted to more than $4 billion, may reach $4.25 billion this year and climb to $4.5 billion next year. Expenditures on all types of classroom equipment—teaching machines, audio-visual devices, television, textbooks, desks and so on—are running well above $1 billion a year and the curve is sharply upward.

The most striking recent development is in the audio-visual field. Television plays the key role here. At latest count, there were 102 educational television stations on the air in 36 states beaming lessons to more than 10 million students at all levels of education from kindergarten through college. The figures come from Educational Services of the Radio Corporation of America.

These programs go into homes in those cities where educational television stations are situated.

Then there is closed-circuit television, (CCTV), which has been used for educational purposes since at least 1946. There are an estimated 750 closed-circuit installations in schools and colleges today, at least half of which are at the higher educational level.

R. C. A. is a pioneer in a new instructional television fixed station service for the transmission of visual and aural instructional material to students. The company makes studio equipment of all types, transmitters and translators, antennas, converters, distribution systems and educational television receivers.

G. E. Gets Big Order

Puerto Rico recently placed an order with the General Electric Company for nearly 1,800 educational TV sets in a move that is expected to have far-reaching effects in the educational television field.

The $537,000, five-year contract was awarded to International General Electric, Puerto Rico, which will supply, install and service the sets designed specifically for school use. This is one of the largest educational television orders ever placed.

The order is considered especially significant in view of the heavy effort being made by Puerto Rico's Department of Education to improve the quality of education in the island commonwealth. Through expansion of the educational television program, it will be possible to offer a broader curriculum to the greatest number of students.

Eventually, with more sets in operation in a network, educational television will reach almost every school on the island. Large urban elementary and high school buildings as well as rural one-room school buildings will be included in the government - operated educational television network.

International General Electric, Puerto Rico, won the contract in international competition with 10 other television set manufacturers from the United States, England, Germany and the Netherlands.

The education field will receive a new system of learning Sept. 20 when "blackboard-by wire" is introduced at Texas A. & M. University.

The General Telephone & Electronics Corporation has announced that communications techniques will enable industrial personnel to "attend" advanced college courses that are being conducted on distant campuses.

Lecturer at Texas A. and M. draws diagrams on electronic writing unit as he talks to students 250 miles away. Diagrams are reproduced by General Telephone and Electronics system in the distant classroom.

The lectures in both courses will be transmitted complete with handwritten equations, formulas and diagrams.

A somewhat similar system has been developed by the International Telephone & Telegraph Corporation, which is now sending television pictures over ordinary telephone lines between the Los Angeles, and Berkeley campuses of the University of California. The pictures, sent 450 miles and accompanied by voice, are transmitted by means of the Videx system of the ITT Industrial Laboratories of Fort Wayne, Ind. The laboratories are a division of International Telephone.

The pictures are still pictures. By sending them over ordinary telephone lines, at phone-call cost, the use of expensive coaxial cables, was avoided.

Computer-assisted instruction is an aid developed by the International Business Machines Corporation. It examines the potential of the electronic computer to meet the individual learning needs of students — from kindergarten through graduate school.

A Computer Assist

Computer-assisted instruction is not intended as a substitute or a replacement for a human teacher. The educator, not the computer expert or the computer, must ultimately decide what value computer-assisted instruction holds for better education.

The instructional aid is based on the simultaneous use of many individual student "stations" linked to a central computer. Such a system maintains continuing control over a wide variety of learning materials, and it does this so that each individual student can progress at his own rate. At the same time, the system evaluates student responses and guides each one, individually, to the goal of mastery of the subject being presented.

So far, experiments are under way at several universities. These include Florida State, Penn State, the University of California and Stanford University. Thi is only a start, according to I.B.M.

The business of education, in classrooms inside and outside of schools as such, has increasingly attracted the atten-

Thousands of publications are held in vaults of University Microfilms, Inc., at Ann Arbor, Mich., subsidiary of Xerox Corporation.

Telephone Circuits Used

The Southwestern States Telephone Company, a subsidiary of General Telephone & Electronics, has installed a communications system at the university that transmits written data through conventional telephone circuits for visual display before an audience.

Termed "blackboard-by-wire," the system utilizes an electron-

ic writing unit. Handwriting produced on the master unit is transmitted over telephone circuits in the form of voice-frequency electrical tones to a receiving unit within the remote classroom, where it is projected on a display screen.

A one-and-a-half hour course on inorganic chemistry will be transmitted twice a week over telephone circuits to chemists 250 miles away at the Pittsburgh Plate Glass Company in Corpus Christi, Tex. A one-and-a-half-hour course in Physical chemistry also will be relayed twice a week to employes of the Dow Chemical Company in Freeport, Tex., which is 150 miles south of College Station, Tex., where the university is situated.

Using American Seating Company's experimental carrel, a student aims light seeker to select her audio material.

A Science/Math Discovery Work Center for elementary school level is introduced by E. H. Sheldon Equipment Company of Muskegon, Mich. Sheldon is a subsidiary of Raytheon.

tion, the funds and the managerial talents of some of the leading corporations in the United States.

Xerox is a representative case in point. It has moved into the educational field in earnest via the carefully selected acquisition route. Three years ago it made its first move with the purchase of University Microfilms, Inc., of Ann Arbor Mich. — a modest adjunct to Xerox's basic line.

Consolidating its position since then, Xerox has acquired Basic Systems, which prepares programed instruction materials for educational purposes in school classrooms and industry. It has also acquired American Education Publications from Wesleyan University Press, said to be the largest educational publishing enterprise anywhere. It publishes, among other things, a junior and senior high school sheet entitled Current Events.

The upshot is that Xerox is linked to the educational business in hardware (copying machines), storage and research (microfilm), texts and reading material (American Education Publications) and the still unrealized future of programed instruction and the so-called teacherless classrooms (via Basic Systems).

The Raytheon Company established its position in the growing educational electronics field earlier this year when it acquired the Dage-Bell Corporation. Dage-Bell is a leading manufacturer of closed-circuit and broadcast-television equipment for educational, broadcast, industrial and military markets, and is the nation's oldest and largest manufacturer of language laboratories and learning systems.

The Educational Electronics division of the recently acquired corporation has developed a new system known as Model 2000 Learning Center System. This system makes both audio and video taped programing available to educators in one package.

Student Pushes Buttons

To hear or view one of these programs, the student merely pushes two or three buttons on the control panel in front of him in his study alcove, according to his printed study schedule. The system provides for as many as 240 audio program sources and up to 26 video programs.

The instructor at his console or the attendant in the control room can shut off, listen, check the source program, take over, or talk to the student.

Students at Grand Valley State College, Allendale, Mich., are at work on experimental Astra-Carrels, made by the American Seating Company. The electronic equipment allows students to choose from a wide selection of audio material by aiming light seekers, mounted like small telescopes atop their alcoves, at one or another of the light sources on the classroom wall.

The light is then converted into sound by a system of battery-powered photoelectric cells and audio amplifiers built into the alcoves. Students may also watch study material offered on television monitors through transparent alcove fronts.

Grandmother, father and mother would not recognize the education scene as it is today.

A new Radio Corporation of America language teaching system will be used this fall at Shippensburg State College in Pennsylvania. Instructor at console can communicate with all or any of her students.

September 5, 196

A ROBOT TEACHER IS HIRED ON COAST

170 First Graders to Begin Daily Use of a Computer

By THOMAS O'TOOLE

Starting next fall, 170 first graders at the Brentwood School in East Palo Alto, Calif., will be introduced to the three R's by an infinitely patient, infinitely tactful teacher who knows all the answers: a computer.

Other students, from elementary school children to doctoral candidates, have received computerized instruction during experiments, but the Brentwood pupils will be the first in the nation for whom learning from a computer will be routine. Every day they and their regular teacher will work with the machine for at least an hour.

The developer of the Brentwood computer's curriculum, Dr. Patrick Suppes of Stanford University's Institute for Mathematical Studies, and other experts in the field view the program as a fascinating social experiment as well as an advance in technology.

Negroes May Be Helped

About 80 per cent of the Brentwood School's students are Negroes, most of whom were described by Dr. Suppes as "culturally underprivileged" with little incentive to learn. Perhaps a computer, which never expresses scorn or impatience, will help such youngsters develop a desire to learn, researchers feel.

The computerized teacher differs from other teaching machines in the flexibility, speed and variety of its response.

Plugged into the computer will be 16 teaching consoles at which children will sit.

Built into each console will be four different modes of teacher-student response — a television screen, a typewriter, a movielike screen and a headset, over which the child gets spoken commands, suggestions and encouragement.

The Computer Is First

"This capability of speaking to the child is too easy to underestimate," Dr. Suppes says. "It alone puts the computer ahead of all other teaching machines."

If the child told the machine that three plus three was seven, for instance, the computer would signal a soothing prerecorded voice to tell the child it had given the wrong answer. It might take one second to do this, most of it spent finding the correct vocal response out of thousands that are on the tape. The next second it would spend suggesting a new approach.

"All right," the same voice would say, "now let's go back and add up two and two." Dr. Suppes says that rapid response is almost as important as vocal response. "You don't get that kind of speed in a regular classroom."

The Brentwood computer will also tutor the child by flashing colored slides onto a screen and asking the child what they mean. Here, again, the computer's speed is its great advantage, since it can scan a cartridge of 1,000 slides at the rate of 40 a second to find the one it wants to show the child.

TV Screen to Be Used

A third means of communication will be a television screen onto which the computer can write questions with cathode ray signals.

A fourth will be a simple teletypewriter with a printout device facing the child.

How will the child answer the machine? In three ways—with a pen that casts a beam of light onto the cathode tube at the back of the television screen, over a microphone or by typing his replies onto the teletypewriter.

Typewritten response is unlikely in the Brentwood project because of the children's ages, but it would be a prime means of answering for older children.

The computerized teaching machine to be used at the Brentwood School is the first of about a dozen that are expected to be in American classrooms in the next two years.

The machine has been named the I.B.M. "1500" by the International Business Machines Corporation, which says it has spent eight years and "millions of dollars" developing the device.

Several universities have been conducting tests with bits and pieces of the I.B.M. "1500" for the last two years.

Although the machine costs $6,000 to $12,00 a month to rent and $450,000 to buy autright, most educators who have worked with it feel the machine has a big role to play because of its flexibility.

If the student decides to get smart - alecky, the computer could be programed to snap right back at him, even to refuse to go on with the lesson. Indeed, this is one thing about the machine that educators like best.

April 4, 1966

Teaching Machines: A Long Way to Go

By FRANCIS KEPPEL

In the middle of the 1960's it was freely predicted that technology would remake the schools and colleges in the following decade. Hardware and software (a rather unfortunate word to describe intellectual content) would combine either to replace the teacher or to make him more efficient, or both.

The Industrial Revolution, it was said, had passed education by, leaving it one of the few "labor intensive industries" in modern society. The revolution of the computer and the information sciences would bring about drastic change, for the first time making John Dewey's dream practical: individualized instruction for all, for each at his own pace.

It was not only educators in their ivory towers who saw these visions of the future. They were joined by many Wall Street investors.

Few observers would now make the same prediction for the next decade. Change there will be; educational technology will play more of a part—but at a much slower pace. Some harsh lessons have been learned by both education and industry. The message of the medium is that it has to earn its way.

Ranking in Influence

As one looks in more detail into the potential of scientific aids to learning, it seems likely that some kinds of technology will have more influence in the upcoming decade than others. If one arbitrarily divides the field into audiovisual technology, instructional television, teaching systems and computers in instruction, one can estimate that the United States today allocates to instructional technology roughly 1 per cent of its total expenditures for schools and colleges, and industrial and adult education. Clearly this suggests that educational technology is a long

Mr. Keppel, a former United States Commissioner of Education, is chairman of the board of the General Learning Corporation.

way from taking over the schools, even though the 1 per cent amounts to something like $650-million a year.

It is important to note that more than three-quarters of these expenditures—perhaps as much as 85 per cent—are in the audiovisual category alone. The other three groups have a tenuous foothold, with the computer barely visible on a financial chart which uses one million dollars as a unit of measure.

Even if one assumes a dramatic annual growth rate during the 1970's in any one of these categories—15 to 20 per cent a year—it seems clear that the field of educational technology as a whole will still play a small part of the nation's investment in education and training by 1980, though it is a big business in itself.

There are at least three factors that have to be considered in trying to peer into the coming decade. To begin with, there is the nature of our school and college system—or perhaps nonsystem would be more accurate.

Classroom Needs

Neither Washington nor any state capital can give orders to local schools or colleges and make them stick. Radical change will have to come from within, and those within are very human teachers and learners. They can easily restrain their enthusiasm for being treated as interchangeable parts of an industrial process.

Educational technology will have to be seen as something that helps the teacher to teach or the learner to learn, not as something to which they will have to adjust. It would seem that the audiovisual technology is slowly making its case, but obviously it has a long way to go. The technology of talking motion pictures, after all, has been available commercially for at least a third of a century. Why has it not made deeper inroads?

The answer leads us to a second factor. To be useful to teacher or learner, the technology has to be both flexible and nearly foolproof.

Television has had hard going in the schools because of the tyranny of time, and more teachers have given up using films because the projector won't work when they need it than they have because they dislike films.

Add to these troubles the problem of finding a film or television program that fits the need of that day. and hour and class, and it seems reasonable that the human voice, the book, and the blackboard seem both better and cheaper.

Justifying Costs

The third factor is cost. The educational world is not yet persuaded by studies and experiments that any one of the technologies can produce either more learning or faster learning than conventional methods.

To justify substantial capital expenditures for complex equipment, those who manage our schools have to have good reasons to think that the investment will pay off. So far the evidence is fragmentary and inconclusive.

It should be no surprise that a good many schools and colleges use "outside" money —from the Federal Government or from gifts—to purchase educational technology, reserving their own funds for traditional needs.

These are some of the lessons that have been learned the hard way. Add to them the increasing resistance by the public to the escalating costs of education, and the increased militancy of school and college faculty, and the result can only be a cautious prediction of expansion in the next 10 years.

The cliché of the nineteen-sixties said that the software was not up to the hardware, which was true enough but did not touch the real problem. The cliché of the next decade may be that the educators are not up to either— but I doubt it

There are signs that the naiveté is gone, that those involved now realize that progress will have to be made a step at a time, undramatically and carefully. By the end of the decade we should be able to report that some scientific aids to learning have been used effectively and economically to make individualized teaching and learning a reality. The nineteen-eighties may turn out to be the decade of John Dewey in practice.

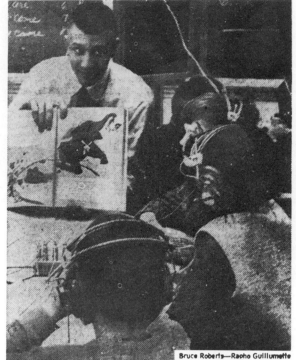

Bruce Roberts—Rapho Guillumette

SOUND—MEDIUM AND MESSAGE: Youngsters listen to recorded dramatization of a tale as the teacher displays illustrations. The simpler, cheaper techniques for teaching are used more widely than the sophisticated methods.

January 12, 1970

Cassettes:

A Machine At the Other End Of the Log

They're compact, cheap and even a child can operate them. All of which helps explain why cassette tape recorders are having a major impact on education.

● In a New Jersey kindergarten the children are using them in conjunction with visual aid cards to learn initial consonants.

● In Westchester County, re-tarded students are using them as adjuncts to film strips. Teachers say the cassettes bolster the students sense of responsibility and confidence.

● In high school civics classes, students are using them to hear the speeches of John F. Kennedy, Franklin Roosevelt and other major world leaders.

The tape revolution, sparked by the development of the cassette player, has come to the schools, and cassettes are making audio-visual education more practical, more widespread — and more controversial.

Some educators have hailed the introduction of cassettes—if used properly and not to excess — as a way of opening new horizons. They can relieve teachers of some classroom burdens, allowing students to follow lesson programs along with workbooks and other visual aids and permitting the teachers to spend more time on individualized instruction.

But other teachers are not so sure. "Used very cautiously, this can be helpful," says Ruth Grady, a veteran Long Island elementary and secondary teacher. "But," she adds, "too often such aids can lull students into passivity, when their learning experience should render them active. Too much electronic and mechanical teaching can take away the necessary personal equation in student-teacher relationships. I want a student to come out of school with what a teacher gave him, not just with what he got from a machine."

Despite such resistance, the use of the cassette and the expansion of its potential show no signs of a let-up. Sony/Superscope, Inc., for example, has developed a Superscope Library of the Spoken Word that is now being used in about 200 schools. In Nassau and Suffolk Counties, about a third of the school districts are now using cassette-cum-worksheet kits developed by 3-M Wollensack. A 3-M representative thinks, however, that some districts are buying only a single copy of the program and then copying it and sending it out for use in a number of different schools.

While the cassettes can be used alone to listen to lectures — or by students in place of the traditional paper and pencil for notes — most experts feel their real future, and their major impact, will be in conjunction with such auxiliary media as film strips, slides, worksheets and other text material. In this way, the students will be forced to use not just their ears in the learning process. What most agree upon, though — advocates and skeptics— is that the cassette is in the schools to stay, and that educators are going to have to learn how to deal with it as advantageously as possible.

—GEORGE DEVINE

Mr. Devine is chairman of the religious studies department at Seton Hall University.

July 23, 1972

Sunny, Colorful 'Dream Schools' Gaining Favor Throughout Nation

Special to THE NEW YORK TIMES.

NEW CANAAN, Conn., April 12—Something new is rising on suburban landscapes near New York. It is a variety of one-story "dream school" that combines the indoors with the outdoors to provide intimate, friendly, colorful classrooms bathed in natural light.

The schools, flat and sprawling, with tall chimneys, will differ sharply from "monumental" structures of the past. Architects report that those seeing the design for the first time "either hate it or love it." The bitterest critics say that externally the places resemble factories. Proponents contend that functionalism is more important than cornucopias.

Multi-million-dollar contracts being signed by boards of education indicate that schools of the new vogue will become legion in many areas. The South School of New Canaan, one of the first of its kind to be completed in the East, reports visits by educators and architects from twenty-six states and eleven foreign countries to plan similar buildings.

Stemming from influences of the Southwest, sixty schools of this type have been built in the Mid-west by the Chicago architectural concern of Perkins & Will. Entering the East recently, the company found interest in the design so high that it now has contracts, some in association with local architects, for schools that will exceed $20,000,000.

Architect Explains Ideas

Lawrence B. Perkins of the Chicago concern explained that influences from the Southwest call for unpretentious buildings to make the "outdoors and indoors all part of the same environment" and to keep facilities on one level for convenience.

"Our work," he said, "has been in the direction of taking these living values and finding ways to achieve them in form suitable for cold climates. Technical improvements in building have made this increasingly practical in recent years."

The school in New Canaan was designed by Sherwood, Mills & Smith of Stamford after study of contemporary design in the Middle and Far West and Europe. Its complete cost is $931,550; it accommodates 475 pupils and occupies a twelve-acre site. Sites up to thirty acres are being chosen elsewhere.

The design includes square classrooms with movable furniture, green chalkboards, low ceilings, sinks in every classroom, individual washrooms for all lower grades, built-in clothes closets and abundant storage space.

Fireplaces are in kindergartens and lounges. Every classroom has a door opening onto walks, gardens and playfields, and every door is painted a different vivid color to make identification easy.

Warm sunlight in every corner of every classroom distinguishes the schools from most in the East. The South School achieves it by using large windows on one side of a classroom and a bilateral lighting system to bring light into the customarily dark side of the room.

April 13, 1951

SCHOOL FURNITURE GETS MODERN LOOK

Curves for Comfort and Color for Eye-Appeal Are Evident in New Designs by Wright

By BETTY PEPIS

Russel Wright, the industrial designer, went back to elementary school to do research for his newest designs. The result of Mr. Wright's eighteen months of study in classrooms in many cities is a new collection of school room furniture. The group was scheduled to be shown to the press and dealers in Chicago yesterday.

These new desks, tables and chairs, while not revolutionary, present a marked advance in the field. Although many parents will remember the buff walls and brown furniture of their school days, few realize that public schools were standardized in color and equipment because they had been furnished according to practices recommended by the Bureau of Standards of the United States Department of Commerce.

A series of recommendations issued by the bureau in 1930 decreed that a brown-buff color scheme be considered standard,

NEW SCHOOL LOOK: Chair and desk designed by Russel Wright apply modern design principles to school furniture.

and it was even made possible for manufacturers to be supplied with "color blocks" (samples) that assured the consistent use of "school furniture brown."

Although the beige walls have given way in the past decade to a palette of pastels, and more recently, even to walls of glass, the large space of the room itself, Mr. Wright said in a recent interview, has remained "dirty, drab, dull, institutional and depressing."

Curves and colors are the two elements Mr. Wright has added to the furniture he designed for Schwayder Brothers. Bent, colored metal bases, shaped wooden seats, back rests of curved gray plastic, curvilinear metal desk drawer, round work tables in addition to square ones—these are all details meant to eliminate the formal regimented look of most school furniture.

Although his chairs, according to Mr. Wright, are strong enough to resist the onslaughts of the most restless adolescents, they should eliminate some squirming because of their new comfort features. Chairs have adjustable backs "because I can still remember how those stiff, unmovable backs felt on my scrawny anatomy," Mr. Wright continued, and the seats are rounded in front and at the corners as "a token to the memory of the discomfort to my protruding hipbones."

Nine sizes of chairs and ten of desks should assure correct scaling to youngsters in various stages of growth.

November 29, 1954

Flexible Arrangement of Teaching Areas Characterizes a School to Be

Built in Connecticut Town

TEACHING BY TEAM DUE IN GREENWICH

School Designed for New Concept Will Be Started

By LEONARD BUDER
Special to The New York Times.

GREENWICH, Conn., May 15 —A steam shovel will unceremoniously bite into a clump of earth in the Havermayer Park section of town this week to mark the start of construction of a new public school that will revolutionize the educational program here.

The school, the Dundee Elementary School, has been specifically designed for team-teaching. This approach does away with the traditional one-teacher-to-a-classroom concept, and, instead, employs teams of teachers to work with groups of pupils.

Because of this arrangement, the pupils can be organized into different-sized groups for different kinds of activities.

First of Kind in Area

While a large number of pupils may be listening to a lecture or watching an educational film, for example, smaller groups of children may be receiving advanced instruction or remedial work. The set-up gives the children the advantage of a wide range of teacher skills.

Although team-teaching has already been introduced in a few schools throughout the country, most such programs are handicapped by the fact that school buildings, with their standard-sized classrooms, are not suited to the new approach.

Dundee, which is expected to be completed by September, 1962, will be the first school in the New York suburban area planned for team-teaching. The architect is Perkins & Will of Chicago and White Plains. Initial research was made possible by a grant from the Educational Facilities Laboratories, which was established by the Ford Foundation.

Dundee will also break with the conventional grade grouping of pupils. Instead, there will be three major groupings of children — kindergarten through second grade, third and fourth grades, and the fifth and sixth grades.

Each group of pupils will have its own team of instruc-

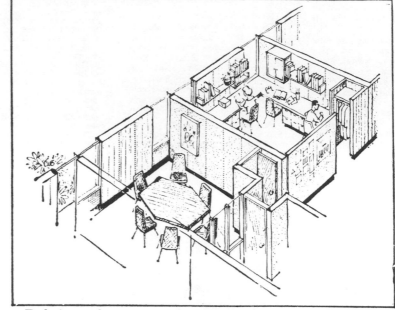

Each team of seven or eight persons will have an office, upper right. Other rooms are for instruction of small groups of pupils.

tors, Dr. John B. Smith, the Superintendent of Schools, noted. Each team will consist of a team leader, a senior teacher, four or five other teachers and a clerical assistant.

Dr. Smith, who came here in 1958 from Lexington, Mass., where he helped to pioneer the team-teaching concept, said the arrangement made it possible for the school to offer a flexible program geared to individual needs and abilities.

To provide the necessary physical flexibility for the team approach, Dundee will contain rooms of various sizes, many of which can be made smaller or larger by opening or closing movable walls. Unlike the make-

This is an architectural rendering of the Dundee Elementary School, designed by Perkins & Will for team teaching in Greenwich. Teams, rather than individual teachers, will give instruction.

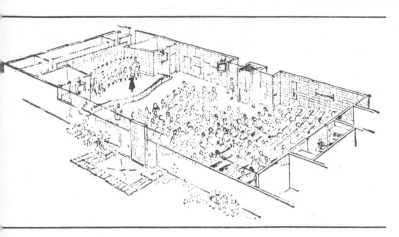

The Dundee school's pupils will be divided into groups—kindergarten through second grade, third and fourth grades, and fifth and sixth grades. Instead of classrooms, teaching areas will be used. This is the largest, open at left as auditorium, and divided by movable wall for two classes.

shift partitions often used in old school buildings. Dundee's "operable walls" will provide complete sound-proofing.

The main section of the building will be multilevel. Adjoining this is a gymnasium and cafeteria wing. The intermediate level of the main section will contain three large group spaces, which the architects describe as "the school's most radically flexible space."

One is a tiered area seating 00 pupils that was designed for lectures, demonstrations and films. Next to this will be a large hall, with a stage, which can be used for television teaching or special presentations. If the wall dividing these rooms is opened—it will take only thirty seconds to open or close the wall—the area will become a large auditorium that can accommodate 200 to 300 pupils.

The lower level will have the kindergarten and primary grade rooms, as well as some "medium group" rooms.

The upper level contains what Dr. Smith describes as the "heart of the team teaching operation." This is a complex of team offices and small group of seminar rooms. The seminar rooms can accommodate eight to fifteen pupils.

Dundee will be able to accommodate 550 pupils, including 100 kindergarten children. The total cost of the school, it is estimated, will be about $1,000,000.

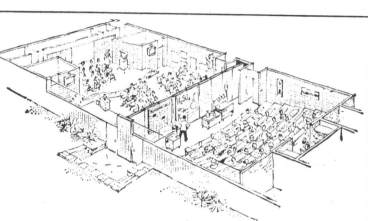

May 16, 1961

CAMPUS: NURSERY TO COLLEGE

This week near Fort Lauderdale, Fla., a school will open which, its sponsors believe, may be a prototype for education of the future. Nova High School, featuring the most advanced curriculum and plant facilities, is to be the first phase of the South Florida Education Center, which will eventually offer continuity of education from kindergarten through post-doctoral study, on one campus.

This educational complex is planned to include the Junior College of Broward County, which will move to its new buildings at the Center this Fall, and an Institute of Technology to be built in 1964.

The "Nova Plan" will follow an ungraded approach to learning. The student may progress as far as he can, at his own speed. New forms of testing will determine when he is ready to proceed to the next level of learning.

In the development of the plan, economies of dollars, space and time have been a welcome by-product. There will be no cafeteria; instead there will be lunches from home, snack bars and catered meals for the faculty. Lecture halls will be in constant use, doubling as classroom and auditorium. There will be no spectator gymnasium.

At Nova High School, time will be at a premium. The gifted student may work out an experiment in the laboratory until midnight, if he wishes. All elective subjects, as well as participation in sports, must take place before or after the regular school day. The school will be open longer each day and more days each year, thus providing 40 more of them in which to learn about today's complex world.

Growing out of an overcrowded area's need for additional schools, the South Florida Education Center master plan has received strong support in the local community.

OLIVE. EVANS.

Drawing of a new type of high school opening in Florida.

September 1, 1963

A Growing Number of Students Taught Behind Glassless Walls

Classroom instruction for elementary, junior high and high school students is going behind solid walls and even underground in increasing numbers of instances across the United States.

Windowless school buildings, an innovation started about six years ago, are now attended by more than 150,000 youngsters in 23 states from New York to California.

According to a recent nationwide study by Joseph Platzker, a New York building code consultant, a trend to windowless schools is expanding rapidly. He estimates that classroom space for one million students in such structures will be in use within 10 years.

The 96 windowless schools now in operation include 24 junior high schools, 36 high schools and 36 elementary schools. There are 11 under construction in eight states and four more in the planning stage in three states.

Mr. Platzker became interested in the new concept and decided to explore the trend fully while doing research for a speech to be delivered at San Francisco earlier this year before the National Association of Metal Manufacturers. He said he completed the research and prepared a 17-page report as a public service.

Many conflicting views on windowless schools were advanced in various parts of the country, but Mr. Platzker said his estimate of their growth was based on several factors listed by school and building officials. The sharp curtailment of vandalism and noise nuisance was a major factor; fear of nuclear bombing, and creation of atmosphere conducive to academic work without outside distractions were among others.

Mr. Platzker's information, most of it provided by officials of departments of education in all 50 states, shows that windowless school construction to date represents capital investment of almost $100-million.

The structures contain accommodations for from 300 to 3,000 students and range from those that are completely underground with landscaping over the tops to one-story and multistory buildings.

Many are air-conditioned, but some have only forced-air ventilation. They have been constructed in rural areas and in cities of various sizes.

The consultant found also that the subject is highly controversial. Some educators firmly declared that they would not have such schools in their jurisdiction. Most states simply have no mention of windowless schools in their building regulations, but some have codes that call for windows.

New York State's planning standards for school building, for example forbid construction of schools without windows. However, the cities of Albany,

Buffalo, New York, Rochester, Syracuse and Yonkers are exempt from state building regulations.

One who was strongly against the windowless school was Charles D. Gibson, chief of the school planning bureau of the California Board of Education. In a letter to Mr. Platzker, he said the bureau was officially opposed to the design and construction of such buildings.

Nevertheless, Mr. Platzker pointed out that California has more windowless schools in operation than any other state. Its 21st windowless school was dedicated last month in Los Banos; five more are under construction in the state and still another is in the planning stage.

New Mexico, with 16 windowless schools, was a pioneer in using the new concept. It is second to California in the number of such schools in operation and under construction.

Vernon R. Mills, now superintendent of the Clovis (N. M.) Municipal Schools, was a leader in planning and building the nation's first underground school. Called the Abo School, it was completed in April, 1962, at Artesia, N. M.

A joint study by the United States Department of Health, Education and Welfare and the New Mexico State Education Department showed no adverse effects on teacher-pupil relations, anxiety, attitudes or scholastic achievement in the 540-pupil building. Artesia's junior high school, also built underground, was completed two years ago.

According to Mr. Platzker, comparative construction costs show the underground, torna-

do-proof, bomb-shelter type of schools to be the most expensive. His estimates include $11.44 a square foot for schools with conventional windows; $12.56 for windowless aboveground structures, and $13.85 for underground building.

Mr. Mills said that the windowless classrooms have proved to be the best available for the Southwest, but that he would not give a blanket recommendation that the concept be adopted for every situation. He said it should be given consideration by communities faced with building programs.

Mr. Platzker cited the elimination of window breakage by vandals as a factor in favor of the windowless buildings. He quoted recent New York City Board of Education figures showing that vandalism in the schools was costing the city $5-million a year, including $934,-800 for replacing broken glass windows last year.

The four windowless schools in New York State include the 1,800 - student Intermediate School 201, which was recently completed at Park Avenue and 127th Street in Manhattan. It is mechanically ventilated, fully sprinklered and also air-conditioned.

The state's three other public schools in the windowless category are in Syracuse. They include two senior high schools and a junior high school, all air-conditioned structures.

Mr. Platzker says that copies of his 17-page survey report may be obtained by school officials at no cost by writing him at 45 John Street, New York, N. Y., 10038.

June 19, 196

Schools and Air Space

While urban universities are being urged to assume a new role of leadership, the problems of finding space for all educational institutions, from kindergarten through graduate school, in overcrowded cities becomes increasingly acute. The day when the elementary school could spread out on a large lot and rise only two or three stories may soon be past.

Last week the Ford Foundation's Educational Facilities Laboratories, an agency designed to help education solve its physical problems in unconventional ways, published a 46 - page pamphlet. "The Schoolhouse in the City," is

available without charge at the organization's headquarters, 477 Madison Avenue, New York 10022.

With too many city schools "aged, crumbling, ill - equipped," the booklet warns, the educational structure often is "a symbol of the decay surrounding it." Moreover, the demand for integration has resulted in new approaches to school planning. "The city school, wherever it is placed and whatever its size and facilities, is inextricably enmeshed in the sociology of the city," the report says.

The emerging patterns include "joint occupancy" plans which, in view of high real estate costs in the cities, place schools in high-rise private or public housing or

even commercial office buildings. Such plans are now under consideration in New York and Chicago. The New York City Education Construction Fund, recently created, hopes to lease the air rights above new schools for apartment and office space.

In Chicago, the 6-story classroom wing of the new Jones Commercial High School was designed to support the future construction of a 15-story commercial tower.

In another approach, the new campus of New York City's Bronx Community College is planned to straddle the tracks of a subway yard. Other New York school construction plans call for buildings over highways also and, in the case of the private United Nations School, on a renovated pier in the river.

Last week, to speed the process of adjusting the urban schoolhouse to the urban condition, the Educational Facilities Laboratories' board voted grants totaling over $300,000. It includes $140,000 to the Great Cities Program for School Improvement to intensify research on how best to remodel and modernize outmoded schools in 17 cities, New York among them.

Another grant will support the Friends' Select School in Philadelphia in its plan of a school as part of a $12-million, 20-story office building.

And Syracuse received $25,000 for plans of an "educational park system" which may eventually lead to the creation of four such school campuses to replace all of the city's 33 elementary schools.

December 11, 196

IMPROVEMENT SET IN KINDERGARTEN

Schools to Stress Approach to Reading and Add Hour

The Board of Education's efforts to improve the school program will reach down to the kindergarten level next fall.

Dr. John B. King, associate superintendent in charge of elementary schools, said yesterday that kindergarten programs would put greater emphasis on preparing youngsters for the formal learning that comes in the higher grades.

Increased emphasis will be placed on getting children ready for reading, he said, so that some children will be able to start reading instruction earlier in the first grade.

The system will also experiment with a longer afternoon session. At present, kindergarten children attend either morning or afternoon sessions. The morning sessions run three hours; the afternoon, two.

Under the experiment, the afternoon program in twenty-five selected classes will run three hours.

Kindergarten teachers now handle both morning and afternoon classes.

PRE-SCHOOL PLAN FOR SLUMS TRIED

Ford Foundation Sponsors Programs to Instill Good Learning Habits Early

By ROBERT H. TERTE

Inoculating slum children against the deficiencies that often lead to disaster in school may prove more effective and less costly than treating the deficiencies at an advanced stage, many educators now are convinced.

Since much of the damage is already done by the time the child reaches school age, the Ford Foundation is sponsoring a series of pre-school projects in New York, New Haven, Baltimore, Boston and Oakland, Calif., and in Pennsylvania to find an effective preventive.

The primary aim is to develop programs that will systematically introduce children from economically, physically and culturally restricted environments to the kinds of experiences and the ways of thinking that will enable them to do well in school.

The studies are also expected to provide a "better understanding of the nature of the child and of how he learns," Edward J. Meade Jr. pointed out. Mr. Meade, a program associate for the foundation, added that "this hopefully will provide a sounder basis on which to build a school program as a whole."

Worsens With Time

Studies of the culturally deprived child have shown that the longer he stays in school, the further behind he gets, Henry Saltzman, also of the foundation, said. This progressive retardation or cumulative deficit begins to appear at the third and fourth grade when the educational program shifts from emphasis on the tool skills of basic reading, writing and arithmetic to content areas, which build on concepts and language not specifically developed in the earlier grades.

The middle-class child makes the transition and continues to develop, but the child of the slums begins to stumble, Mr. Saltzman said. "He reflects intellectually the scars that are visible when you look at where and how he lives." He emphasized that the problem affected children of all races and national origins growing up in such circumstances.

Among the influences believed to affect the child's ability to learn in abstract situations are the quality and amount of speech between parent and child, the variety of experiences provided by trips and visits, the kind and quantity of books and toys available, the amount of reading to the child and similar experiences.

Parents a Factor

In addition to developing programs specifically for the children in the academic realm, the projects sponsored by the Ford Foundation seek to involve the parents to improve their influences on the educational development of their children. They are also seeking more effective relationships between health and service agencies and the schools to provide better assistance to children and parents in other areas—such as health and family stability—that influence the child's school performance.

Because special education is expensive compared with regular education, it is hoped to develop cost-sharing arrangements between the various agencies and different levels of government, from the local to the Federal, Mr. Saltzman said.

While remedial programs at higher levels will have to continue—including such efforts as Higher Horizons and projects to reclaim potential dropouts— "investments at earlier age levels begin to appear far more promising than at later ages," Mr. Saltzman observed.

Remedial work is costly not only in dollars but in the lost potential of students. And the chances of rapidly developing a large enough supply of expert teachers to meet the need for such programs are considered negligible. With these facts in mind the foundation is stressing the prevention of the development of learning deficiencies through its grants for the pre-school programs.

The New York project, in its second year, is under the direction of Dr. Martin Deutsch, director of the Institute for Developmental Studies in the department of psychiatry of New York Medical College.

One hundred and sixty pre-school and kindergarten children are taking part in the study in eight experimental schools in Harlem and on the Lower East Side. Because of lack of funds only about half of the group will continue in the project through the third grade.

Both the New York City Board of Education and the Department of Welfare are cooperating in the project. Dr. Deutsch hopes to develop a fairly detailed "therapeutic" curriculum with materials and

PRE-SCHOOL TRAINING: A child listens to recorded story and is encouraged to follow it with written text.

techniques for overcoming specific weaknesses in various intellectual areas where problems are found.

The Baltimore public school system has agreed that in the second year of its pre-school program next year it will lower the age for school enrollment of children who are considered culturally disadvantaged. This will in effect make the program part of the general educational services offered to them.

Funds have been provided within a larger project for the Oakland Board of Education to experiment with the assignment of language arts teachers to pre-school day care centers. And in New Haven, funds have been made available to the Board of Education for the organization of voluntary pre-school centers in slum areas.

Seven Projects Planned

The Pennsylvania program is under the state's Council on Human Services, which includes the Department of Public Instruction and the State Welfare and Health Departments. A full scale study has been inaugurated in one school district, with a revised curriculum for the primary grades to be developed and articulated with the pre-school and kindergarten classes. The five years from pre-school through third grade will be developed as a nongraded program.

Seven additional projects in Pennsylvania will provide summer programs for pre-school children, with follow-up programs when they enter school, and various smaller-scale projects. In conjunction with each of the state's programs there will be special programs of teacher training and coordinated community services.

January 16, 1964

Let the Child Teach Himself

By RONALD and BEATRICE GROSS

THE year was 1906. In the basement of a housing project in the slums of Rome a ragged, unruly gang of children filed into a sparsely furnished room that was their new nursery school. Suspiciously, they looked over the teacher.

She was Maria Montessori, the first woman to receive a medical degree from an Italian university and a person of great gusto, intelligence and determination. But in addition to having a remarkable character, she had devised a remarkable educational method. Within a few months Montessori's pupils were transformed into an attentive, friendly, neatly dressed class of model students. And they were learning—learning more quickly than the middle-class offspring of educated parents who attended conventional schools.

Today the educational theories Montessori used in her *Casa dei Bambini* are enjoying a phenomenal resurgence throughout the United States. Her books, long out of print, are being republished. Many educators are convinced that Montessori techniques and insights can correct some basic flaws in American primary schools. Parents in New York, Chicago, Washington, Los Angeles, Houston, St. Louis, Philadelphia and a score of other cities—eager for their preschool tots to learn reading, writing and arithmetic—have organized more than 100 Montessori schools in the past six years. Not since the nineteen-twenties, when private schools spearheaded progressive education, has a teaching method evoked such enthusiasm among the public.

The Montessori revival is part of a wave of reform sweeping American education, based partly on the fear that existing schools and teaching methods do not develop the full intellectual ability of pupils. Substantiating such doubts, recent demonstrations by educators and psychologists have shown that children of 3, 4 and 5 need and thrive on a solid academic diet. Then, too, Montessorians make persuasive claims to teach children more, and at younger ages, by converting the children's own intellectual steam into "real learning." Particularly relevant for American children is Montessori's success with the kind of child we call "culturally deprived"—the big-city slum youngster who is a major target of President Johnson's antipoverty program.

THE Montessori method is based on several distinctive concepts. Though in practice Montessori schools differ widely in applying the doctrine—a flexibility that sometimes pained the authoritarian *dottoressa* — all Montessorians share a common philosophy based on three primary principles. The theories concern early childhood, the learning environment and the role of the teacher.

Montessori believed that from birth to the age of 6 the child has an "absorbent mind" that endows him with a great capacity for disciplined work and a voracious appetite for learning. She held that the years from 3 to 6 are a particularly "sensitive" period, during which children can benefit enormously from serious knowledge.

"LA DOTTORESSA" — Maria Montessori, Italy's first woman physician and founder of the ground-breaking Casa dei Bambini, in Rome.

Montessori argued that if the school exploits these sensitive periods, the child's mind will develop from within. Quite naturally, the child provides his own stimulus to achievement. Adult pressure, or imitation of adult behavior, is frowned on; so are group activities. Instead, the child chooses his own tasks, works at his own pace, and progresses individually in ungraded classes that span a three-year range. The result, according to Montessori enthusiasts, is independent, self-reliant children who are eager to tackle work.

Related to this awesome view of child development is observance of Montessori's second canon—the "prepared environment." On the theory that "things are the best teachers," the Montessori teacher provides special teaching materials that subtly develop the child's ability to see, feel and discriminate between shapes, sounds, textures. Later, the child will use materials and perform exercises that prepare him for reading, writing and computation.

A youngster of 2½ or 3, for example, will execute "practical life" tasks, such as learning to tie his shoe laces, scrub a table and open the door for the teacher. He may sort buttons with his eyes blindfolded, or trace sandpaper letters with his fingers. Delighted with learning to do these jobs correctly, the child will practice them for hours. Thus does he learn to master simple requirements and follow directions—critically important abilities, as psychologists have discovered, to the growth of general intelligence.

The sandpaper letters, for example, help train the muscles of the hand for writing. He then learns the phonetic sounds of each letter, progresses to composing short words with a movable alphabet, and soon may make up whole sentences. From that point, it is a short step to the child's demand for story books that he can read to himself.

In the strictly utilitarian atmosphere of the Montessori classroom, there are none of the usual toy animals, dolls, trucks or dress-up costumes. Children in "pure" Montessori schools are virtually restricted to materials she devised, which are intended to suppress fantasy and imaginative play. Children should not make believe, Montessori proclaimed; to encourage them along such lines is to encourage defects of character.

With didactic materials carrying the burden of instruction, the Montessori teacher operates discreetly in the background, which constitutes the third basic aspect of the method.

The Montessori teacher's principal task is not "teaching" but diagnosing each child's interests, level of understanding and most fruitful line of development. Then she guides the child to those materials and experiences that will build on his interests and needs. Because the children work without constant supervision, Montessori classes may run to 40 or more, with several assistants to the teacher.

"A man is not what he is because of the teachers he has had, but because of what he has done," said Montessori. She insisted that at most the teacher should "artfully intervene" to insure that the child is successful and productive.

NO educational theory, of course, can guarantee that the intervention will be artful. That sensitive skill depends on the person, not the precepts. Yet when the Montessori teacher is both professionally well trained and personally sympathetic to children (a combination that is no more common among Montessorians than among conventional teachers), the results are impressive and exciting.

About one-fourth of the children in a typical Montessori class read before they are 6. Even more students can add and subtract large sets of numbers. Thomas Laughlin, a former screen actor who founded the Sophia School in Santa Monica, claims that his 5-year-olds are beginning to learn algebra. Before they enter first grade, he says, "they are parsing sentences, composing music and speaking French. By the time they're 12 they can have accomplished everything the 18-year-old accomplishes in a conventional American high school, and many will have completed the equivalent of two years of college."

❝The problems Maria Montessori faced in the slums of Rome are the problems that, on a vastly enlarged scale, face us today.❞

This is the dazzling—perhaps somewhat exaggerated—image of Montessori which has attracted so many middle-class and upper-class parents. But academic achievement by Montessori pupils is less uniform and automatic than Laughlin suggests, because most Montessorians are not that interested in "speeding up" the educational process. A visit to a Montessori classroom reveals what and how the children actually learn.

At St. Paul the Apostle's School on West 60th Street in Manhattan, 17 children ranging from 3 to 4½ years old are working on individual mats or at tables. The room is quiet and purposely spartan. Softly but firmly, the atmosphere says: Learn.

Robert, 4, is intently pushing long, brown blocks along the floor and clacking them together. The teacher, Miss Elizabeth Stock, lays the blocks carefully down in order of size, placing her hands on both sides of the formation to align the sides. Once the blocks are properly arranged, she takes the thinnest one and, sliding it carefully and quietly, "walks up the stairs." Then she takes the formation apart piece by piece and leaves the boy to do it himself. What is Robert learning? By discriminating size, weight and thickness, and doing things in a prescribed pattern, he is learning skills basic to arithmetic.

Betty, 3, goes through a repeating ritual. She places a pink towel near her small table, then neatly puts soap, a basin, a pitcher and a brush on the towel. Carefully, she pours from the pitcher into the bowl, soaps the brush, shakes it off, and with large, rounded movements scrubs the already clean table. When she has covered the table with soapy scrub marks, she dips the sponge, squeezes it dry, and methodically wipes the soap off, first vertically, then horizontally. Nearby a boy polishes his shoes, his work spread out on a piece of white paper so he can tell when he's getting the polish on the wrong target.

"The children are free to move about and choose what they'll work on," Miss Stock explains. "But they must adhere to certain rules. The children are expected to use each object as it was designed to be used; if they don't, I ask them to put it away. And they must finish a self-chosen task before setting themselves another." As she spoke, a girl who had been cutting paper was sweeping the scraps into a dustpan.

Walking around the room, we notice that some children have changed their materials. A child who was fingering a sandpaper letter is trying to solve a three-dimensional puzzle. The boy who was polishing his shoes is now matching up small color tablets.

Sometimes the teacher calls several children together for a demonstration of a new device, but the general emphasis is on individual learning rather than group activities. "After I demonstrate the proper use of each piece of apparatus," says Miss Stock, "the children can tell for themselves if they're doing it right. These objects make the child want to correct his mistakes. So you see, Montessori is not really a method of teaching, but a method of facilitating learning."

Each day the students silently practice sitting, getting up, moving chairs, closing the door. The room at the end of the day is as neat as when it began.

IN contrast to the rigorous climate of St. Paul's, the "prepared environment" of the Whitby School in Greenwich, Conn., is more relaxed. The classroom is bright and cheerfully decorated. Children sprawl on the floor, gather in groups at tables, or walk around the room at their pleasure.

This school is an Americanized version of the European doctrine. It stresses the *dottoressa's* techniques, but eclectically borrows from native experience. Thus, three young girls listen intently to a recording of Peter Rabbit, while at the other end of the room two boys meticulously count beads. They attach tabs after every ninth bead, soon mastering multiples of nine through 270.

Is all this Montessori? "No," replies the teacher, Miss Lesley Ann Bruce, "only the cumulative, independent work with the special materials constitutes 'the method.' But we believe that the other activities are consonant with Montessori's broad strategy—to engage the child early in his own learning."

In a Washington, D. C., Montessori class of 35 children and two teachers, a girl of 5½ dismantles a huge, wooden puzzle map of the eastern hemisphere. Accurately, she attaches tiny tabs to the separate countries and sounds out the names of each: "Ceylon, Syria . . ."

Next to her another girl, 4, lays out 10 words ending with "it" on her mat, using red and blue cardboard letters. A boy of 5 runs his finger over triangular insets, then fits them into their proper places on a wooden board as he softly murmurs "isosceles, equilateral . . ." On another mat, a 5-year-old boy serenely sorts out cylinders by holding each one next to his ear and discovering a subtly different sound.

"This is Montessori at its purest," the teacher, Sibyl Devereux, explains. "All over the world children in Montessori classrooms are doing pretty much what you see here. Our method is designed as an aid to life, and life and people are essentially the same all over the world."

Miss Devereux teaches at the D. C. Society for Crippled Children. Most of her pupils

Basic to Montessori theory is utilitarian ' play."

Each child has his own mat to work on.

Scrubbing a table is among prescribed "practical life" exercises.

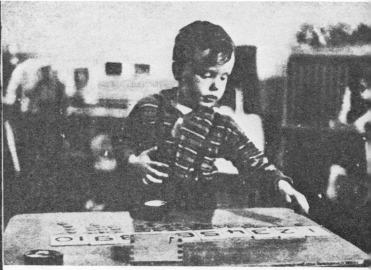

Identifying numbers by matching them to the same number of objects

"Things are the best teachers," said Italian educator Maria Montessori, whose aim
was to teach the child to teach himself and whose theories are having a
remarkable revival in the U.S. Above, preschool children deeply absorbed in teaching
themselves with a variety of "things," at St. Paul the Apostle's School, Manhattan.

New York Times photographs by SAM FALK

A frame with snap buttons develops dexterity and ease with fasteners on clothes.

years behind the times, Hunt argues that she may have been just about that far *ahead* of her time

According to Hunt, modern research corroborates the existence of Montessori's "sensitive periods" for certain kinds of learning; if development is not cultivated, children will have great difficulty later. Intelligence, as Montessori insisted, is not fixed, nor does it develop in a predetermined pattern. Early stimulation is all-important, and the senses play a more prominent part in intellectual growth than has been assumed.

EVIDENCE from many sources over the past decade—how children learn, careful observations of their everyday behavior—has revealed the inadequacies of old notions of motivation, based on reward and punishment. Recent findings demonstrate that human beings are born with the desire to know, the urge to explore and the need to master their environment. In short, to achieve.

Related to these specific liberating ideas about human motivation are discoveries about human intelligence generally. No longer do scientists and educators concur, as they did for so long, in the stultifying concept of fixed intelligence and predetermined development. On the contrary, says Hunt, creating an interesting, challenging environment for the child, especially during the early years, leads to a "substantially faster rate of intellectual development and a substantially higher adult level of intellectual capacity."

Moreover, adds Hunt, since the optimum rate of growth would mean "genuine pleasure in intellectual activity, promoting development properly need imply nothing like the grim urgency which has been associated with 'pushing' children." In other words, children should be free to learn at their own pace, but each individual's rate of learning is largely dependent on the richness and complexity of his environment.

A NUMBER of teaching innovations illustrate this approach: ungraded schools, programed learning and teaching machines, Cuisinaire Rods for teaching mathematics, and curricula based on the "discovery" method of learning. They are all strikingly similar to Montessori's basic strategy.

are mongoloid, brain-damaged or physically handicapped.

MARIA MONTESSORI died in 1952, having lived to see her theories take root and thrive in Western Europe (especially Holland), India and elsewhere. In the United States, where she lectured widely and drew capacity crowds, about 100 Montessori schools flourished by 1915. A few years later, however, the movement was dead.

The chief reason for the doctrine's demise was opposition by John Dewey's disciples, principally William Heard Kilpatrick of Columbia University's Teachers College. Kilpatrick, in print and in person, declared that whatever was good in Montessori theory was contained in Dewey's thought. What was original he criticized as excessively rigid and psychologically obsolete.

Similar controversy surrounds the current revival of Montessori methods, which has inspired among American educators the full range of reaction from enthusiasm to enmity.

One of the most enthusiastic is J. McV. Hunt, professor of psychology at the University of Illinois and one of the nation's leading experts on the development of intelligence and learning capacity. Pointing out that the progressive educators of 1915 condemned Montessori because her psychological theories seemed 50

However, most American educators and child phychologists argue that the best elements of Montessori have become standard practice in United States nursery schools. At the same time, they say, American educational theory has raced far ahead of the *dottoressa's* ideas in encouraging flexibility, freedom and individuality. In fact, the critics see much in Montessori methods that is potentially harmful to children.

Their major objection is Montessori's concentration on intellectual work in the classroom, to the virtual exclusion of the child's imagination. Children need dramatic make-believe play, the critics declare. It compels them to explain what they are pretending, to communicate their thoughts. As for the anger, jealousy and fear that a child may express in such play-acting, most teachers believe that such emotions should not be bottled up, but expressed in an understanding environment.

Rather than the impassive neutrality of Montessori teachers, American teachers are, of course, more actively didactic. They are also more openly sympathetic, creating a bond of intimacy that brightens the school environment.

Nor do the opponents of Montessori concede that American nursery schools neglect the student's intellectual development. A good nursery school is stocked with the materials that develop the sensory skills Montessori emphasized. It provides instruction in subjects that range from science and woodworking to counting and reading. A visit to a construction site or a garbage disposal plant is not a waste of time, American educators argue. Such field trips, they explain, deepen the child's understanding of his community and of himself.

AS with many other doctrines that take their inspira-

TEACHER—Elizabeth Stock with her Montessori class of pre-schoolers at St. Paul the Apostle's School in Manhattan.

tion from a single source, the Montessori movement has had its schisms. What may be called the "reform wing" in the United States is led by Nancy McCormick Rambusch, who founded the Whitby School in Connecticut in 1958 and the American Montessori Society. Occupying a middle-ground between all-out opponents of the Montessori method and its purist followers, Mrs. Rambusch advocates "an American approach to Montessori."

She admits that some current interpretations of the method are restrictive, out-of-date and unsuited to American children. She believes the special materials, used alone, are "anemic" by present-day standards and that American children are too permissively reared at home to adapt to the regimen of the orthodox Montessori classroom. Much has been learned in the past 50 years, she says, which must supplement Montessori methods.

"But the essential insights of Montessori are just as valid today in America as they were in Rome half a century ago," Mrs. Rambusch insists. "First and foremost, Montessori recognized that the early years, from 2 to 6, are critically important for the child's future education. Some psychologists maintain that half of all the growth in intelligence takes place before the age of 4—and the next 30 per cent between 4 and 8. Children need intellectual challenge in these years if they're to achieve their maximum development.

"Secondly," Mrs. Rambusch points out, "Montessori tells us that the only really important thing in education is to teach the student to want to learn and how to learn—and that the motivation for learning must come from within the child. Most American teachers still haven't learned that lesson, with the result that our schools still lean heavily on grades, tests, ex-

ternal pressures and rote-learning. Even in the early grades most teachers spend most of the time maintaining discipline and suppressing noise and movement.

"But Montessori demonstrated conclusively that the most efficient and effective education takes place when the teacher stops trying to make the children attend to her *teaching,* and devotes herself instead to helping them *learn,* by themselves, through artfully contrived experiences, exercises and materials. Our teaching machines, for example, are belated recognition of the importance of the *tools* of learning."

Even more belated, perhaps, is the growing awareness that the educational problems Maria Montessori faced in the slums of Rome are the problems that, on a vastly enlarged scale, confront us today in trying to teach disadvantaged children.

Nancy Rambusch has turned her energy to working with Negro and Puerto Rican children at the New York Foundling Hospital and to training other teachers to do the same kind of job in an integrated public-school program in Mount Vernon. Many other educators also believe that Montessori's system for building self-confidence and developing the senses by means of stimulating materials is the first step in educating youngsters from culturally barren backgrounds.

Indeed, the conviction that this task is possible, and worthy of the best efforts of our best teachers, may turn out to be Maria Montessori's greatest contribution to education. Her *Casa dei Bambini* in Rome was a social institution designed to redeem the lives of children who seemed doomed. That its mission succeeded remains Montessori's triumph—and our inspiration.

'HEAD START' PLAN FOR PUPILS BEGUN

Johnson Approves Preschool Centers to Aid Poor

By CHARLES MOHR
Special to The New York Times

WASHINGTON, May 18—President Johnson announced today approval of the first group of preschool summer guidance centers in Project Head Start. The program is aimed at giving culturally deprived and poverty-stricken children a better chance when they enter school next fall.

The President made public a list of 1,676 project grants that will result in the creation of 9,508 preschool centers to serve 375,862 children.

In about two weeks he is expected to announce a second and final list of projects for 1965 that will train 154,000 more children.

New York City will have the largest program in the nation, the White House announcement showed. In today's action Mr. Johnson approved the creation of 288 Head Start centers to train 25,689 New York City children this summer. The Federal Government will grant $4,668,-868 for these centers, and local financing will furnish $820,496.

A total of 301 preschool centers to train 6,749 children in New York State outside the city were announced today. These projects will receive $1,277,076 in Federal grants.

Mr. Johnson said in a speech in the White House Rose Garden that "5- and 6-year-old children are inheritors of poverty's curse and not its creators."

"Unless we act, these children will pass it on to the next generation, like a family birthmark," he said.

Mr. Johnson spoke before newsreel cameras and reporters in the presence of a group of officials and volunteers associated with the program, which is being run by the Office of Economic Opportunity as a part of the antipoverty program.

The Head Start projects will give many deprived children their first look into a story book, their first chance to play with alphabet blocks and their first glimpse into the middle-class environment around which educational systems and teaching aids are built.

The total Federal cost for this summer's pioneer effort will be $112 million. The cost of the first group of projects, announced today, is $65.7 million.

It is hoped to expand the program by next year to cover a half million more poverty-stricken children.

"These children," Mr. Johnson said, "will receive preschool training to prepare them for regular school in September. They will get medical and dental attention that they badly need, and parents will receive counseling on improving the home atmosphere."

A White House statement said that as many as 500,000 part-time volunteers, mostly mothers and housewives, would be needed to help 41,000 professional experts man the Head Start nursery school centers. In addition, more than 47,000 poor adults will be employed by the centers.

Four children who will attend Head Start centers this summer were present as Mr. Johnson spoke. They shyly shook hands with the tall President and Mrs. Johnson, who is honorary chairman of the Head Start program.

The children were Trait Burell of Gum Springs, Va., Harry Hill of Bethesda, Md., and Ronald Hennessey and Renee Davis of Washington. All are 5 years old.

May 19, 1965

HEAD START PLAN TO BE PERMANENT

President Cites Success of Preschool Training for Needy Youngsters

By JOHN W. FINNEY
Special to The New York Times

WASHINGTON, Aug. 31 — President Johnson announced today that the Head Start program to provide preschool training for poor children had been so successful that it would be made a permanent part of the American educational system.

Starting this fall, the program will be placed on a year-round basis, with both winter and summer programs for needy children.

Mr. Johnson announced the extension of the program in a speech before several hundred doctors, psychologists and educators who had gathered to assess the results of the program this summer.

Project Is Praised

Project Head Start, part of the Administration's antipoverty program, was begun as an experiment in helping needy children of preschool age. Nearly 560,000 attended 13,400 centers in 2,500 communities this summer. In addition to preschool training, the children were provided free lunches and medical checkups.

Mr. Johnson declared that the project, "which began as an experiment, has been battle-tested—and it has been proved worthy."

As a result of the program, he said, "hope entered the lives of more than a half-million youngsters who needed it most."

"Before this summer, they were on the road to despair—to that wasteland of ignorance in which the children of the poor grow up and become the parents of the poor," the President declared, continuing:

"But today, after the first trial of Project Head Start, these children are ready to take their places beside their more fortunate classmates in regular school."

As one example of the "many victories" made by the project, the President noted that in New York City, "where the Spanish-speaking population is hemmed in by the language barrier, 95 per cent of the Head Start children learned enough English to fit them for school."

The President also cited a New York case, declaring:

"In Staten Island, New York, a 16-year-old girl made a tiny Head Starter her special project. This little girl would not talk, would not eat, would not react.

"But through the care and patience of one volunteer, the child made such progress that now she is able to take her place in school. Without Head Start, that child might well have been classified as mentally defective—and condemned to life in a dark and narrow world."

Under the three-part extension of the project announced by the President, year-round centers will be established for children 3 years old and older. Mr. Johnson said that 350,000 needy children would be enrolled in the first sessions, "and many more within the next five years."

Summer programs, involving more than 500,000 children next year, will be continued for those not included in the year-round classes.

In addition, "follow-through" programs, such as special classes, home visits and field trips, will be established for children limited to summer sessions as a way of sustaining the progress made by the children.

Mr. Johnson said that with the success of the project "we have reached a landmark—not just in education, but in the maturity of our democracy."

September 1, 1965

HEAD START FOUND BADLY CRIPPLED

Protests Rise on Shortage of Funds and Red Tape

By JOSEPH A. LOFTUS
Special to The New York Times

WASHINGTON, Nov. 30 — Project Head Start, probably the most popular of all the anti-poverty programs last summer, was described by some of its best friends today as seriously crippled.

Stamped by President Johnson as "battle tested and proved worthy," the pre-school program for poor children is short of funds and trapped in a bureaucratic reorganization.

Even when the administrative snarl is untangled, the money now available will fall far short of the demand that Mr. Johnson helped to generate.

The President probably can use some Office of Education funds to enlarge the Head Start budget, but there is no way to put the money to work retroactively. The public relations, and perhaps political, damage has been done.

Letters and telegrams of dismay and protest are piling high at the White House and at the Office of Economic Opportunity. The Head Start staff is demoralized. Many members, not seeking a career in Government, joined the project for the pleasure of helping children.

For example, the director is Dr. Julius B. Richmond, dean of the medical center at Syracuse, N. Y., who is a distinguished pediatrician.

Dr. Richmond said in reply to questions that he thought the local disappointments derived chiefly from high expectations relative to low funds and the requirement to share with other local projects. He attached less **importance to the reorganization, although he said that the new regionalization was a problem.**

The project commanded such support in the field that Sargent Shriver, director of the antipoverty program, once said that the value of volunteer time exceeded the amount of Federal funds allotted to the project.

A spokesman for Mr. Shriver had this comment tonight:

"In Head Start, as in many other programs, we are paying the penalty for success. We realize and have realized that the demand by the end of the year is going to exceed our resources.

"We are not satisfied but we are pleased that so many young children are receiving assistance who just a year ago had nothing available."

He said that by Jan. 1 he expected 140,000 to be in Head Start classes and that the number would reach 300,000 by next summer.

Nyack, N. Y., is one community from which have come many protests to Mrs. Lyndon B. Johnson, members of Congress and Mr. Shriver's office.

One telegram from Nyack to Mrs. Johnson said:

"I serve as a volunteer in the Nyack Community Nursery School and we have been promised Head Start funds by the O. E. O. Our program has serviced about 125 families of the poverty segment of our population out of economic depression, atrocious housing, joblessness, **and despair. A glimmering of hope and trust are just beginning to emerge . . .**

"Suddenly we are told 'no funds are available.' This kind of irresponsibility is immoral and simply cannot be."

A letter to Mrs. Johnson from Mississippi said:

"I would like to know from President Johnson will the Head Start program begin again like I heard him say on television that the program did so good till he decided it would run year round. Many people are hurt terrible because now it is so hard to get any more money."

A Head Start worker in Austin, not far from the LBJ Ranch, commented:

"I have closets filled with applications and I haven't the **courage to open them, knowing how much time, effort, love and hope have gone into their making, and knowing I'm the S.O.B. who is going to have to write and say it is not going to be."**

In a Rose Garden statement on Aug. 31, President Johnson said the Head Start summer program had been so successful it would be extended year-round. Communities all over the country got busy with their applications, leased space and made commitments to teachers.

Within a month it became evident that the allotment of $150 million was far too little. The local Head Start programs were so notified and the protests began.

Even the $150 million is being put to work only in a few places.

For example, Mr. Shriver took away Head Start's independent status and made it a component of Community Action programs. Also, communities were advised that no more than a third of their Federal antipoverty funds could be devoted to Head Start.

Officials of the Community Action Programs here say that they can finance local Head Start projects separately, without waiting for a complete community action application. They cite several such separate findings to support their point. However, there are exceptions to general practice.

The communities themselves lose time figuring out how to allocate the money they might get from Washington. Thus, the Head Start application is delayed with everything else.

A form asking more than 70 questions has proved discouraging to many communities. Hundreds of applications that reached Washington were returned for processing through local community action agencies. They are delayed there, and then in regional offices, a relatively new level in the Office of Economic Opportunity structure.

Applications are estimated at $650 million. Head Start officials also pleaded with Mr. Shriver to administer the program as a separate unit, instead of as a unit of the Community Action Program as the Job Corps and Volunteers in Service to America are administered.

The House Appropriations Committee offered Mr. Shriver more than the $1.5 billion budget request, but Mr. Shriver was limited by the Administration fiscal policy and perforce said he could not effectively use more.

Head Start reached about a half-million children as a summer program in about 2,500 communities. Poor children received medical examinations and a general educational and social orientation to prepare them to deal with conventional schooling later.

December 1, 1965

Why Some 3-Year-Olds Get A's— And Some Get C's

By MAYA PINES

CAMBRIDGE, Mass.

THE all-American, exceptionally competent 3-year-old — the model for future generations, if a group of Harvard researchers has its way—is a frighteningly mature and verbal creature who scores high in 17 abilities which seem to hold the key to his success.

He can, for example, "dual focus." (While two children argued and one screamed, "I'll murder you!" Sally barely looked up from her block-building, muttered, "Not me, though!" and continued what she was doing.) He can sense dissonance or discrepancy. (When another boy held up a streaked drawing and an-nounced, "It's the moon," Jimmy replied at once, "A moon doesn't have hair!")

He can anticipate consequences. (Seeing his friend carelessly pick up a basket filled with toys, George shouted, "Carry it, carry it, use both hands!")

Relying on thousands of simple,

detailed observations like these, rather than on I.Q. tests, the Harvard School of Education's Pre-School Project believes it can now pick out the abilities which distinguish the most able 3-year-olds from the most inept. Nine of these abilities, including the three above, involve intellect (or "intellectual skills," if you like). The eight others involve social factors; for illustration, the Harvard researchers note that when something gets in the way of the inept child (they tag him "C"), he may be reduced to tears, or throw a tantrum, while the competent child ("A") will be quietly persistent (he might even "con" someone into giving him what he wants—in a socially acceptable way). Also the "C" child may be locked into either sheeplike docility or rebellion, while the "A" child knows both how to lead and how to follow. And as early as 2 years of age, the most competent group will be able to understand complex, unexpected instructions, such as, "Put the spoon under your foot," or the reverse, "Put your foot under the spoon," while the "C" group cannot.* (The average, or "B," child was not covered in the study.)†

The goal of the Harvard project is to find out how the two groups of children got that way—what it was in their earliest environment that produced the startling differences between them. But why concentrate on youngsters of age 3 and under especially? "There has been a striking shift of interest unprecedented in history, toward the first three years of life," declares Prof. Burton L. White, the Pre-School Project's director. A no-nonsense, pipe-smoking man whom everyone in

*Other intellectual abilities include: dealing with abstractions, making interesting associations, planning and carrying out a sequence of activities, making effective use of resources. Other social abilities: showing pride in accomplishment, making-believe being adult, expressing both affection and hostility to peers and adults.

†The researchers concentrate on the A and C children because they provide the greatest contrasts in abilities. These contrasts become focus points for the researchers, who otherwise would lose their way in the mass of material involved in so broad an undertaking as a study of over-all competence in children. The exclusion of B children—whose middle-level abilities do not provide such visible contrasts for investigation—cuts down the workload of researchers enormously. This does not mean, however, that B children are not studied at all. "Our errors allow us to study the B's," says one Harvard psychologist —that is, many children classified and studied as A's and C's are, upon later assessment, reclassified as B's.

his group calls "Bud," he notes that the original conception behind the Government's Project Head Start was that "something's wrong with these children at age 6. There was no appreciation of how early that something comes about."

"Head Start began," he says, "with a few weeks in the summer before the child entered kindergarten or first grade—the Head Start summer program. Then they decided to take the child for a whole year before he is 6. Next they decided to take him two years before he is 6. And now, at last, they've begun to run parent-and-child centers for children from birth on. It's always seemed clear to a number of us that the place to begin is with the first days of life."

Throughout the nation, large numbers of psychologists, computer experts, educators, sociologists, linguists and others are coming to the same conclusion. Working backward to a younger and younger age, they are creating a new field, encompassing what Harvard's Jerome Bruner has dubbed "the growth sciences." This new composite discipline concentrates on the period other researchers had chronically neglected because the child seemed so inaccessible— the time between his fifth day of life, when the newborn usually leaves the hospital, and his entry into nursery school at 3. Abandoning their rats, pigeons and other experimental subjects, including older children, hundreds of scientists are now focusing on the young child's mind—encouraged by the influx of Government funds for programs to stop the epidemic of school failure among the children of the poor, and by some new developments in psychology itself.

JUST five years ago Benjamin S. Bloom of the University of Chicago shook up his colleagues with "Stability and Change in Human Characteristics," a thin book filled with statistics based on a thousand different studies of growth. Each of these studies followed up certain children and measured them at various points in their development. Although made by different people over the last half-century, these studies showed such close

agreement that Bloom began to see specific laws of development emerging, rather than mere trends. For each human characteristic, Bloom found, there is a growth curve. Half of a child's future height, for instance, is reached by the age of 2½. By age of 4, his I.Q. becomes so stable that it is a fairly accurate indicator of his I.Q. at 17. To a large extent, therefore, the die may be cast before a child ever begins his formal education.

Bloom emphasized that the child's environment has a maximum impact on a developing characteristic — during that characteristic's period of most rapid growth. Thus, since human intelligence grows most rapidly before the age of 4, this is the time when the environment can influence it most easily. As time goes on, Bloom declared, more and more powerful forces are required to produce a given amount of change in a child's intelligence, if it can be produced at all—and the emotional cost of this change is increasingly severe.

Meanwhile, other researchers were focusing on the differences between the children of the poor and the affluent. By kindergarten age, these differences are painfully obvious, with poor children's I.Q.'s running 5 to 15 points below those of middle-class youngsters, and their verbal ability trailing ever further behind. The Head Start programs were showing it was not easy to bridge the gap at that stage. So, when President Nixon announced that "Head Start must begin earlier in life, and last longer, to achieve lasting benefits," people in the growth sciences took new hope — especially those increasingly vocal, who want to concentrate on reaching children even before the age of 3.

If their research confirms that the first three years of life largely determine a human being's future competence, these years can no longer be left to chance, they believe. Thus, armies of tutors could conceivably be sent into the homes of disadvantaged infants, and thousands of expectant parents enrolled in crash programs to teach them modern child-rearing. We may be witnessing the end of society's traditional laissez-faire about the earliest years of a human being's life.

Harvard has clearly taken the lead in the growth sciences at this point, with at least three nuclei of research on the child's early development. Each one, in its own way, has had to start practically from scratch, devising new tools to measure young children's progress and new techniques to rate their environment. "Assume that you are studying the great-chested Jabberwocky," Bruner advised his students.

The Pre-School Project, for one, had not originally intended to focus on children so young, but began by studying 6-year-olds. And, initially, it did not even try to measure competence, but looked for "educability" — how ready a child was for formal education by the age of 6. This turned out to be a knotty problem, however, all tied up with certain virtues which the school system rewards — passivity, obedience, being "a nice, organization child," as one of the researchers put it — but which the project did not much like. "Is the child who's geared up to the Boston educational system the kind of child we want to set as a model?" the Project's Dr. E. Robert LaCrosse recalls asking himself. And the answer was, "My God, NO!" Therefore, they decided to look for competence — all-around excellence in coping with problems in the yard as well as the schoolroom.

"What specifically is competence at 6?" Dr. White wanted to find out. "If you don't know the answer to that question, you can't have any idea of what you're trying to achieve." With disadvantaged children, at least you know clearly that you want to wipe out their deficits in language and whatever else goes into poor I.Q. development, he says, and there are programs for 4- and 5-year-olds that do this with some efficiency. "But

that's not the same as asking, how are you going to rear your child so he will be *optimally* developed? We're not just responding to an emergency; we're looking for answers that will help *all* children."

THREE years ago, then, White and a dozen other researchers armed with clipboards and tape recorders set out like naturalists to look for examples of excellent as well as poor development in children. In weekly visits to various local nursery schools, kindergartens and Head Start centers, they selected one group of outstanding 3-to-6-year-olds, their "A" group, and a parallel group of children who were not sick, but couldn't quite cope, their "C" group. They followed 440 "A" and "C" children closely for a year, noting the differences between them and checking their ratings of the children against the teachers' ratings of the children, and then they realized that they had come too late: "With our "A" kids, the 3-year-old children had basically the same cluster of abilities, in perhaps less polished form, as the 6-year-old children," says LaCrosse, "and, in fact, they were more advanced than the 6-year-old "C's" in terms of both social and non-social skills."

This came as a shock to the project. "We were surprised, really, and kind of excited," says LaCrosse, one of the strongly committed young psychologists who have been flocking to the growth sciences. "Big Daddy Freud had said everything was over at 5, with the resolution of the oedipal conflict, but we tended to disbelieve this. Then suddenly, we found that if you're talking about competence, the action comes before the age of 3."

As a result, the Pre-School Project did an about-face and began studying children between the ages of 1 and 3—in their natural habitat, of course. Off went LaCrosse and four associates into the homes of 30 toddlers to take regular running records of

what actually goes on in a small child's life. Their assignment was to construct a new maternal behavior scale, later to become "a *human* behavior scale, that we can plug any human being into," LaCrosse explained. They followed the mothers and children from kitchen to bedroom to bathroom, furiously recording in the manner of a sports announcer what happened to the child and what the mother was trying to do.

At first these intrusions into the privacy of the home seemed strange. "We had to fight the 'girdle-on' phenomenon," recalls LaCrosse. "You know—the first day we arrive, there's the mother with false eyelashes and hair freshly done, and the house perfect, at 9 o'clock in the morning! Then one day, perhaps three visits later, we'll arrive and find the mother in a housecoat and the kitchen in chaos, the beds unmade—at that point, the girdle is off and we have achieved a certain rapport." The families were all known to the project from its earlier work with older children, and they were paid $5 a half day for their services.

WHILE LaCrosse and his group concentrated on the mothers, other project teams visited 170 different homes to record how the children spent their time and to study the development of specific characteristics. It took a year and a half to boil down their material on child activities to 36 categories of things that these youngsters do. It is taking even longer to work out useful scales covering the development of the selected characteristics.

Now the information from all these probes is just beginning to produce promising patterns, as the children's activities are related to their development and to their mothers' behavior. "We think we have spotted five prototype mothers," says LaCrosse. "There is, first of all, the Super-Mother. She wants to provide educational opportunities for her child; she slips in

from time to time to teach the kid something, but she's not frantic about it. She enjoys the child as he is. She tends to do a great deal of labeling with him—'This is a ball'—and to elaborate on his sentences, adding new bits, such as 'This is a *red* ball,' or related ideas. There is a good balance between activities that she initiates and those initiated by the child.

"Then there is the Smothering Mother. All the kid does all day is respond to her commands. She seems discontented with where the child is right now. She's very busy preparing him for Harvard.

"The Almost Mother enjoys and accepts her child, but she is confused and frequently unable to meet his needs. She may lack a capacity for intellectual input — she usually waits for the child to initiate activities, then often can't understand what he wants. If she reads to her child, her spontaneous comments may be, 'See the ball!' or 'See the hill!' while the Super-Mother may ask, 'What's he going to meet at the bottom of that hill?'

"The Overwhelmed Mother finds just living from day to day so overwhelming that she has almost no time for her child. The children may be raised by older siblings, or by themselves, in a chaotic home. Usually the mother has eight kids and a $30-a-week food budget, but there are middle-class mothers of this type, too.

"Finally there is the Zoo-Keeper Mother, who tends to be middle- to upper-middle-class. She has a highly organized household routine, and the child will be materially well cared for, but will spend most of his time alone—perhaps in a crib filled with educational toys. She doesn't monitor her child's behavior, doesn't interact—in fact, there's a striking lack of contact between this mother and her child. This produces a child with highly repetitive, stereotyped behavior, despite the variety of toys."

These five mothers represent extreme types—since the mothers of "B" children were not included in this study. The Super-Mother naturally raises an all-around "A" child. The Smothering Mother's offspring rates "A" in cognitive* capacity, but not in emotional maturity—he tends to be shy or incredibly infantile. The Overwhelmed Mother produces a "C" child. The Almost Mother does a very good job until the child is 14 to 16 months old, when the mind-stretching aspects of care become more important, and then she fails. While the Super-Mother's child continues to grow rapidly, the child of the Almost Mother reaches a plateau which eventually turns him into a "B" child.

THESE differences cut across class lines. The project knows of at least one woman from a very poor neighborhood, a black activist, who is a Super-Mother, as well as numerous middle-class women who raise "C" children. However, the central tendency favors the middle-class child, both black and white, and one of the project's main contributions, so far, is that it documents for the first time just how the daily experiences of poor and middle-class children differ in the second and third year of life.

Take the matter of purposeless behavior — sitting and doing nothing, without looking at anything in particular, or else moving about in apparently aimless fashion. According to preliminary data, the child of an Overwhelmed Mother, who is usually very poor, spends 41 times as much of his waking hours in such vapid behavior as the child of a Super-Mother, who tends to be middle-class. Since the Overwhelmed Mother often attempts to cope with her children by giving them food or candy, he also spends much more of his time eating.

*The word **cognition** is used in psychology to mean the study of how knowledge is acquired, retained and used. The child rated "A" above has a good learning capacity.

The child of a Super-Mother, on the other hand, spends nearly one fifth of his day at an activity almost unknown to the offspring of an Overwhelmed Mother: make-believe, pretending to be someone or something else, a characteristic of children who are doing well around the age of 2. Throughout this study, middle-class youngsters were found role-playing five times more frequently than lower-class children of the same age.

Since poor children are often accused of lacking a drive for achievement in school, it is very revealing that the middle-class children in this study spent 50 per cent more of their time constructing things or practicing skills which give a sense of mastery. They also benefited from far more tutorial experiences. And they devoted more of their day to the one predominant occupation of nearly all children between the ages of 1 and 3: staring at a person or thing with intensity, as if to study its features.

The extraordinary amount of time spent staring in this way—an average of 22 per cent of the children's day—is "a revelation," says White. "It has authenticity and is not disputable." He warns that the relationship between the types of mothers and the children's activities remains to be verified, however.

These differences occur mostly after the baby is one year old, White believes, because until then most parents do things that are essentially the same. There are, of course, instances of extreme deprivation which can seriously retard or damage a child. But, in general, parents don't yet know how to enrich their babies' environment in a meaningful way, and even researchers such as White have only limited information on the subject. A few years ago, White showed that when infants in a bland hospital nursery were given a chance to look at and touch colorful stabiles, they learned to reach for objects above them — a landmark in development—in less than half the time it

took other infants in the same nursery. He has raised his own 3-year-old on the same principle, offering him plenty of interesting things to interact with at each stage in his development. Yet a lot more research needs to be done before parents can be given firm recommendations about the first year of life, he believes.

Meanwhile, White is convinced that the behavior of parents really begins to diverge during the child's second year, when the growing baby — now walking around and talking—forces himself on the attention of adults. The toddler's insatiable curiosity at that age, his zest for learning and his obvious grasp of language, all lead the effective mother to produce a rich flow of talk and try in various ways to satisfy his drives. To other types of mothers, however, this growth means only two things: danger to the child, and much more work for them. In an extremely poor family where the mother is barely able to get through the day and has many other children to take care of, "you can predict what that will mean," says White. "She'll concentrate on keeping him out of the way; she cannot nurture his curiosity, and she won't do much talking."

In a two-year follow-up of the original "A" and "C" children, now 5 to 8 years old, the project has found amazing continuity in their levels of ability. The "A" group is still doing extremely well in kindergarten through second grade and also testing high on the 17 critical abilities. The "C" group is still inept— some sad and teary, some just oblivious, some every bit as likable as the more competent children—a diverse group that has one thing in common: Whatever its members are given to do, they don't do it well, either through lack of persistence or through lack of skill.

As soon as White has collected enough solid information about what causes these early differences, he plans to start teaching the Almost Mothers and the average

mothers to use the best methods. Within 30 to 50 years, he predicts, the kind of child who is rated outstanding today will be considered merely normal, as a result of more skillful child-rearing.

THE Pre-School Project's offices in Cambridge are cluttered and busy. Across Harvard Square, on the 11th floor of the imposing concrete structure known as the William James Hall for the Behavioral Sciences, one encounters a more rarefied atmosphere. Here is the Center for Cognitive Studies, headed by psychologist Bruner, a man of electric energy who paces up and down his spacious study, speaking volubly, with gestures. Until recently he studied how children between the ages of 3 and 12 process information — how they acquire it, retain it, transform it and communicate it. But now, to find the *sources* of intelligent action, he concentrates on infancy. Under his guidance the entire center, with its staff of psychologists, linguists and researchers, has turned to an examination of the first two years of life—though no one here follows individual children, studies homes, or tries to intervene in the domestic situation in any way.

These researchers seem filled with a sense of wonder at how the human infant—so helpless and limited at birth —learns to control his environment and himself. At first, they find, the baby appears stupider than chimpanzees of the same age. But by the age of 2 or 3, the normal child has achieved one of the most difficult intellectual feats he may ever perform: he has reinvented the rules of grammar, all by himself, and he has learned to speak. He begins with what the linguists call holophrases—single words such as "Mummy" or "see," or very short phrases that are used as one word ("gimme"). Then, suddenly, around 18 months of age, he takes one holophrase and combines it with many other

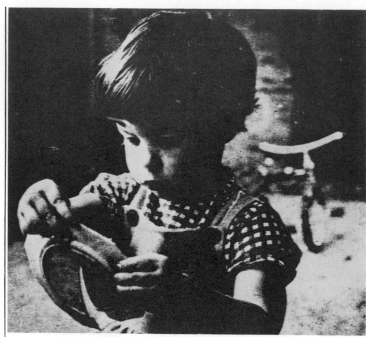

words ("see doggie," "see light.")

"At this particular point," notes Bruner, "as far as I am concerned, he enters the human race as a speaker, because I think you can find examples of holophrastic utterances in higher primates, but you will never find combinatorial grammar."

Besides learning language, the normal 2-year-old constructs a fairly complex mental model of the world. (This allows him to manipulate various aspects of the world in his thoughts and fantasies.) He has also learned to control his own behavior so accurately that he can mobilize various skill patterns whenever he needs them. This is a formidable set of achievements, and the Center for Cognitive Studies is only beginning to unravel how the baby attains them.

Behind a partly closed room at the center, overlooking all of Harvard, a mother nurses her 3-month-old infant. He has just been to a specially constructed baby "theater" where, reclining on a tiny chair resembling a car seat (safely strapped to it, in fact, by belly-and-breech cloth), he watched a swinging red ball, with exciting black and white bullseye stripes and a central row of shiny pearls, as it moved gently before his eyes.

It was an experiment in depth perception, to discover whether infants of that age have any idea of what is graspable: Would the baby move his arms more when the shiny ball was up close than when it was far away? Did he have any sort of mental map of where he was? Finding, on both questions: Yes. Three-month-old infants have much more depth perception than was thought possible only a few years ago, the center finds. On the day of their birth, it has been determined, infants can track a triangle with their eyes. By one month of age, they notice when objects have been changed. In fact, infants are in every way much more aware of their surroundings than scientists had surmised — which helps explain the speed with which they build their model of the world.

To trace the development of this world-model, Bruner and two associates recently put three groups of babies of different ages through an experiment in which a jingly toy was placed behind a small transparent screen, open on one end. The youngest babies, only 7 months old, simply reached for the toy with the nearest hand and bumped into the screen. After banging on and clawing at the screen for a while, they lost interest and

gave up. The next group, the 1-year-olds, began in the same fashion, but then let their hands follow the edge of the screen and reached behind it in a sort of backhand grasp until they got the toy. Only the 18-month-olds knew right away how to reach the toy efficiently, and did so. Over 16 trials each, none of the babies ever changed his initial strategy: this was the best he was capable of at that stage.

THE babies who take part in these experiments are usually the offspring of graduate students, brought there in response to ads in The Harvard Crimson. Asked how much time he actually spends with these babies, Bruner gestured helplessly. "Depends on what's going on in the Yard!" he exclaimed. "Which babies do you have in mind?" During the student strike, the faculty meetings took up most of his time. Now that the troubles seem to be over, he can go

back to his main interest— studying how babies discover how to use their hands intelligently.

In babies' hands, Bruner believes, lie clues to much of their later development, and he particularly wants to find out how babies learn the value of two-handedness. Nobody teaches infants this skill, just as nobody teaches them to talk. Yet around the age of 1, a baby will master the "two-handed obstacle box," a simple puzzle devised by the center to study this process. Seated on his mother's lap, he will suddenly use one hand to push and hold a transparent cover, while the other hand reaches inside the box for a toy.

To Bruner this is extraordinary, for it shows that the baby has learned to distinguish between two kinds of grip—the power or "holding" grip, which stabilizes an object, and the precision or "operating" grip, which does the work. Monkeys and apes have

developed a precision grip, Bruner says, but "it is not until one comes to man with his asymmetry that the power grip migrates to one hand (usually the left) and the precision to the other." From then on, he emphasizes, many routines can be devised for holding an object with one hand while working it with the other, leading to the distinctively human use of tools and tool-making.

The experiments at the center are essentially very simple, but their interpretations are not. Some of these interpretations parallel Noam Chomsky's "transformational" approach to linguistics, which reduces language to basic kernel sentences, each one made up of a noun phrase and a verb phrase. Early in childhood every human being learns the logical rules which allow him to transform these kernels into any possible sentence. Bruner speculates that when a baby learns to differentiate between the two kinds of manual grip, this foreshadows "the development of topic and comment in human language" — the basic sentence form of subject/predicate, which may be found in all languages, with no exception whatsoever, and which a baby expresses when he combines a holophrase with another word. Thus, man may be uniquely predisposed, at birth, to re-invent the rules of grammar, to process information, and to develop "clever hands." He is born with a highly complex programing system, the result

Learning a part

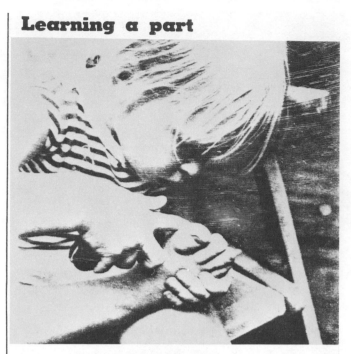

Here the child-watchers record Audrey Lyndon "easing discomfort" (that is, attending to a splinter in toe) . . .

. . . while her sister Laura, right, is playing adult-on-the-telephone. Frequent role-playing is a characteristic . . .

. . . of the competent, early-maturing child, which means life might be a piece of cake for play-baker Hilary Gresser, too.

of millions of years of evolution.

WHAT about disadvantaged children, then — why should they be different, if they are born with the same programing system? "Mind you, you can *ruin* a child's inheritance, too," warned Bruner, "with an environment where he acquires helplessness. You can also be trained to be stupid."

Before man's marvelous programing system can be activated for language, for instance, a baby must learn a series of primitive codes—and these require interaction with an adult. "What seems to get established very quickly between infant and parent is some sort of code of mutual expectancy," Bruner said, "when the adult responds to an initiative on the part of the child, thus converting some feature of the child's spontaneous behavior into a signal." Right from the start,

parent and infant are busy communicating through eye-to-eye contact, smiles and sounds. As early as at 4 months of age, an infant will smile more to a face that smiles back than to one that does not respond; and if the adult face then stops smiling back, the infant will look away. In some cases, he may even struggle bodily to look away. A child's other attempts at learning can similarly be brought to a halt when his expectancy is thwarted, and things stop making sense.

Much of the center's work is based on the findings of the famous Swiss psychologist, Jean Piaget, who first described the stages through which young children construct their mental model of the world. How well and rapidly this model is built depends largely on the children's environment: the more new things a child has seen and heard, Piaget noted, the more he wants to see and hear. The greater variety of

Two misses are hits . . .

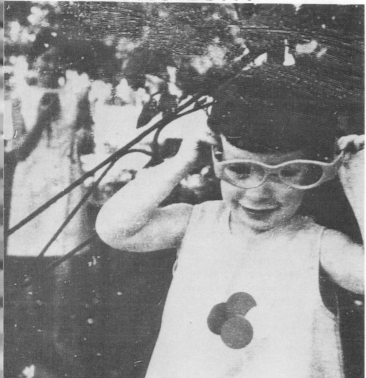

. . . with Harvard psychologist Burton L. White and his assistant, Itty Barnett, who are "covering" the activities of their 2-year-old subjects like radio reporters. Here they are seen tape-recording . . .

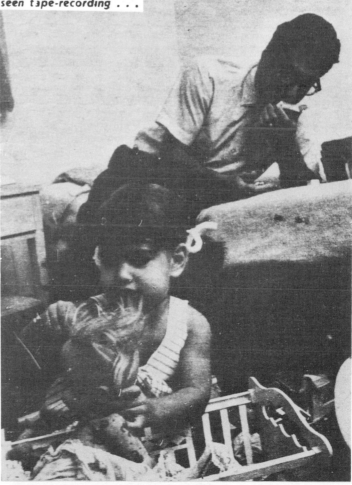

. . . descriptions of the play routines of Ellen Gallagher, with glasses and blocks at top, and Michelle Cukor, with doll and Lego (building-toy) set. White is director of Harvard's at-home child study.

things a child has coped with, the greater his capacity for coping, and the more new methods he is able to invent by combining or re-combining what he has learned before. Both Piaget and Bruner disclaim an interest in early childhood *education*, however. What they are studying is early childhood itself. The mind of the human infant is still so deep a mystery, said Bruner, that he himself intends to stay with it for the rest of his life—"or until we give up, in final despair."

WHILE Bruner concentrates on the process of learning, and White attempts to find the keys to individual children's competence, Prof. Jerome Kagan of Harvard's Department of Social Relations focuses on differences in the development of young children from different social classes. These are sometimes so acute, he has found, that poor homes can be considered actually crippling — at least for life in our society. This is not a racial matter: Kagan's study of 180 youngsters deals entirely with white families. For nearly three years he saw and tested these 180 children at regular intervals in his laboratory, beginning when they were 4 months old.

"Class differences emerge clearly by 12 months of age, and show up even earlier for girls—in some cases as early as at 8 months," Kagan declares. They appear in every one of the basic skills which the child learns during his first three years. Middle-class children are at an advantage, for instance, in learning specific "schema" for the events around them. By one year of age, they are way ahead of poorer children in discriminating between similar stimuli. As Kagan explains it, the reason for this superiority is the middle-class youngsters' greater experience with *distinctive* stimulation— slight transformations or discrepancies from what is ordinary.

"Middle-class mothers seem unconsciously to try to surprise their infants," he says,

"and that's very good! They play peek-a-boo, or make unexpected sounds. In slum areas the mothers don't do this—they don't think of it, or may have no time—yet it's important." Infants who live in crowded homes where they are surrounded by noise all the time, from television and from many voices, learn to "tune it out" right from the beginning. "You don't learn anything in a Tower of Babel," says Kagan. "The main question is, is the mother distinctive?"

Kagan was among the first to use electronic equipment to record babies' heartbeats during tests of attention. This is a useful way to determine whether an infant is actually looking at something, or just staring blankly: when a baby's heartbeats slow down, he is alerted and paying attention. With this equipment lightly and painlessly hooked up to the child's chest, Kagan could display various kinds of normal-looking or distorted masks and know exactly which ones surprised the infants. He learned that by the age of 1, middle-class children are more attentive to unusual events— they look longer at strange faces and forms. Kagan interprets this to mean that middle-class children have a bigger stock of schemata with which to try and explain unexpected things in their environment, which makes them less likely to turn away until they understand the event.

He also found that middle-class babies form closer attachments to their mothers, and therefore, he says, are more likely to accept the mother's values and goals. This closer attachment, which can be observed by the greater amount of crying among middle-class infants between the age of 6 and 10 months when their mother leaves the room, has nothing to do with the quality of the mother's love, he points out. "The fact is that the human caretaker is a target for the baby's clinging, scanning, vocalizing and smiling," explains Kagan. "The mother is a toy — just like the terry-cloth 'mothers' with which [psychologist Har-

ry] Harlow's monkeys were raised in an experiment, and which they preferred [for reasons still unknown] to the wire 'mothers,' even when the latter provided them with milk. The more you play with this object, the more you get attached to it." And, according to a recent study by one of Kagan's graduate students, middle-class mothers do indeed spend a lot more time entertaining their babies — talking, smiling, playing face-to-face — than do poorer women.

"We don't imply that the lower-class mother doesn't love her child," Kagan warns. "There is no difference in kissing, nor in the total amount of talking, as opposed to face-to-face talking. However, the

lower-class mother is more apt to talk from another room, or issue orders, and not take time for long periods of reciprocal play with her child."

This leads to obvious differences in the quality of language among the poor and the affluent. The poor child, then, is at a disadvantage in all these things — learning schemata, forming the kind of attachments which lead him to accept the mother's values, and speaking. He is also less persistent at difficult tasks, Kagan has noted; worse at nonverbal problems, such as perceptual puzzles; and, in addition, has learned a sort of impotence.

"When a mother tends to a child in distress as soon as he cries, this leads the child to believe there is something

LEARNING SITUATION—*Cambridge mothers who have brought their infants for testing chat with noted Harvard psychologist Jerome Bruner. "You can ruin a child's inheritance with an environment where he acquires helplessness," he says. "You can be trained to be stupid."*

he can do," says Kagan. "He learns he can have an effect upon the world—make things go, or stop. If he is not tended, he will learn helplessness." He describes a recent study with newborn dogs and cats which were placed in a situation where there was nothing they could do to ward off mild electric shocks. When these animals were later given the opportunity to act on their environment, they could not learn to do so.

Since all these differences occur so early, "we should think of changing the behavior of the mothers of poor children during the first two years of the child's life," Kagan suggests. He believes this will require a major national commitment.

EACH in its own way, then, the three Harvard groups conclude that some fundamental learning patterns are set very early in life—well before the age of 3 and that during this period the child is particularly open to environmental influences, for good or for bad.

Does this mean that, once past the age of 3, a child who has not learned the right patterns is doomed and cannot be changed? "No," replies Kagan. The child remains quite malleable during his first 7 years, but the longer you wait, the more radically you need to change his environment — and the *probability* of change becomes a little less with each successive year.

Is it true that "compensatory education . . . apparently has failed," as psychologist Arthur Jensen wrote in a recent issue of the Harvard Education Review? No, answer the growth scientists, compensatory education has not failed, because it has never really been tried — at least never properly, or on a large scale. They tend to dismiss the only massive effort, Head Start, as too little, too late, and too unfocused in its present form. "Just eight weeks [of training], a couple of hours a day? That's not very much!" says Kagan.

"That's not a radical change in a child's environment." The growth scientists also object that Head Start children are comparatively old (two-thirds of them are 5 or 6, and only 5 per cent of the total are under the age of 4.) More powerful programs, they believe, are needed for children between the ages of 3 and 6, lasting the full year, and focused so as to teach cognitive skills.

WHAT the people in the growth sciences really want, however, is not emergency treatment for disadvantaged children, but *prevention* of handicaps. And for this, they are convinced, you need to start before the age of 3. There are two possible strategies:

(1) Starting kibbutz-like day-care centers in which trained teachers would give children an excellent education from earliest infancy. In a reply to Jensen, Benjamin Bloom has just suggested that we learn from Israel's experience with the children of poor and mainly illiterate immigrants from North Africa and Yemen. These Oriental children have extremely low I.Q.'s when reared at home — an average of 85, compared with the 105 scored by Jewish children of European origin. When both kinds of children are raised in the same communal nurseries from birth on, however, both have an average I.Q of 115—a jump of 30 points for the Oriental children. Bloom points out that these children had spent 22 hours a day in the kibbutz nursery for at least four years.

(2) Producing major improvements in the way parents raise their children—the solution which Bloom, Kagan and many others in the growth sciences prefer, and for which White is actively preparing. This, too, is a form of prevention, apparently more palatable than widespread day-care centers, but not necessarily easier to carry out. After spending $2-million on projects in which social workers, clinical psychologists and psychiatrists tried to change the child-rearing practices of

lower-class parents by means of counseling, for instance, the National Institute of Mental Health's Committee on Social Problems learned from its chairman, J. McV. Hunt, that "nothing, absolutely nothing, so far as I can ascertain, has come of it." Hunt's book, "Intelligence and Experience" (1961), played a major role in sparking the current interest in the first three years of life. He now believes that when poor mothers are given something useful to do with their children they sometimes become just as effective as professional teachers.

The Growth Sciences

Just as medical research was organized around concepts of pathology, so today we would do well to organize our efforts anew around the concept of growth. Those sciences that can help us understand and nurture human growth — biological, behavioral, and social sciences alike—should find ways of joining forces as the growth sciences. Let them then make their knowledge relevant to those who are practitioners of the nurturing of growth: parents, teachers, counselors. It is bizarre that no such organization has yet emerged, though it is plainly on its way.—*Jerome Bruner.*

One "serendipitous finding," according to Hunt, was that infants in a Durban, N.C., ghetto actually benefited from a research program aimed only at studying their psychological development, not interfering in it. After two years of tests at a Duke University laboratory, once a month, these

toddlers scored close to 110 on the Binet I.Q. test, while other 2½-year-olds from their neighborhoods scored only 70 to 80. Hunt thinks that the babies' mothers — who were present throughout the tests—must have noticed which items they did well on and which they failed, and then given them practice where they needed it. "They appear to have been exceedingly effective as teachers," he says. "This suggests that poor children's decline can be prevented."

When Merle B. Karnes of the University of Illinois trained the mothers of 15 disadvantaged 3-year-olds to make inexpensive educational materials—sock puppets, lotto and matching games, etc—to use at home, she made a similar discovery. These mothers also served as assistants in Karnes' experimental nursery school, being paid $3 for each two-hour training session. Within less than three months after they began, their own children, who had stayed home, suddenly gained 7.5 points of I.Q. Later on these children did as well as those in Karnes' professionally run nursery school. Karnes concluded that teachers should take on a new role: Training parents, rather than just teaching children, and involving the entire family in the education of preschoolers.

The burden of the new research, then, is to put ever more burden on parents — which generally means mothers, since fathers have been strangely ignored by the growth sciences. Interestingly, when the mothers in Karnes' group realized how much time and effort are required to do a good job of raising preschool youngsters, they headed en masse for the local chapter of the Planned Parenthood Association — they felt they could never teach their children enough if they had babies every year, as before.

This does not solve the problem for the 1.5-million youngsters under the age of 3 whose mothers work away from home, however. Few of these women can either afford or find a first-rate nurse who is interested in stimulating their babies' intellectual and social growth. Even fewer have access to a day-care center with a strong educational component. The government has utterly failed to take their needs into account, but now private industry is beginning to enter this field and an upsurge in specialized day-care centers may be expected in the near future.

BOTH approaches—the educational day-care centers and the training of parents—have already come under attack. "What do you mean, have a white professor come here and tell us how to raise our kids?" sputtered a black militant when he heard about a new program for parents. Others object to the idea of "taking children away from their mothers and putting them in day-care centers from birth on—it's totalitarian!" Sociologists argue that one shouldn't impose middle-class values on the poor, who have their own culture. Community leaders declare that if any day-care centers are opened in their area *they*, not outsiders, should decide what will be taught.

The people in the growth sciences know it's going to be an uphill fight, but they are fascinated by the possibility of giving each child a chance to "realize his full potential." According to Hunt, "Most of the skills we are talking about — cognitive skills, language skills, pride in achievement, and so on—are not a matter that is black or white or green or yellow. In order to survive in a technological culture, one *must* have these skills." The best time to acquire them is in early childhood. He also points out that if one wishes to maximize a child's development, "you need to maximize it all along. Competence—like deprivation —is cumulative."

As these ideas spread, the nation's educational efforts are likely to include ever younger children, and soon the years from birth to 3 may become a target of first priority. ■

July 6, 196

Head Start Pupils Found No Better Off Than Others

By ROBERT B. SEMPLE Jr.
Special to The New York Times

WASHINGTON, April 13—The most comprehensive study ever made of the Government's widely admired Head Start programs asserts that poor children who participated in them were not appreciably better off than equally disadvantaged children who did not.

Accordingly, the authors of the study have told the Nixon Administration that the preschool program for disadvantaged children is not worth the cost in its present form and ought to be radically revised.

The study will be released to Congress tomorrow by the Office of Economic Opportunity after weeks of speculation about its content.

It has already made a great impact on Mr. Nixon's domestic policymakers at the White House—indeed, it directly influenced some of his recent recommendations on Head Start—and it may well have explosive ramifications among friends and foes of the program on Capitol Hill.

The study was carried out by the Westinghouse Learning Corporation and Ohio University between June, 1968, and March, 1969, under contract with the O.E.O., which administers Head Start and other antipoverty programs.

Under the terms of the contract, Westinghouse attempted to measure the extent to which children in the first, second and third grades who had attended Head Start preschool programs differed "in their intellectual and socio-personal development from comparable children who did not attend."

In all but one test, the differences were found to be statistically "insignificant."

Since it was beyond their contractual mandate to do so, the Westinghouse researchers did not attempt to explore in depth the reasons why Head Start children did not do better than other children in later grades. But they did not rule out two of the favorite hypotheses turned up by earlier, more limited studies.

The first is that Head Start does indeed make an impact, which is frittered away by poor teaching later on.

The second and more recent hypothesis—for which there is yet only limited statistical evidence — is that poor children have been so badly damaged in infancy by their lower-class environment that Head Start cannot make much difference.

In other words, even though the children who attend Head Start are only three or four years old, the program comes too late to do much good.

The White House, which has thoroughly reviewed the bulky, chart-filled document, regards its findings with mixed feelings.

Mr. Nixon endorsed Head Start during the campaign, and his aides firmly believe that the Government must support some kind of "early intervention" program to help poor children in their early years.

They are therefore fearful that the report's discouraging conclusions will be used by conservative Congressmen as a weapon against any kind of expenditure for disadvantaged children, especially Negroes.

At the same time, however, they regard the report's findings as bolstering Mr. Nixon's case for moving Head Start from the antipoverty agency to the Department of Health, Education and Welfare, where it would become part of a new office of Child Development.

They also believe that the findings support "deepening" of the program to make its benefits available to children at an earlier age and lengthening of the program to make certain that whatever benefits children receive from it are not lost as they proceed through later grades.

Mr. Nixon prosposed transferring Head Start to Health, Education and Welfare in a message to Congress Feb. 19. He said that such a move would surround the program with "supportive" services that only a large, well established agency could provide.

In a follow-up message last week, he and the H.E.W. Secretary Robert H. Finch, announced a limited expansion of the agency's Parent and Child

Center program for disavantaged children under the age of three.

They also announced a "substantial" expansion of the follow-through program — which seeks to carry the Head Start experience through later grades —by encouraging school boards to divert other program funds to the follow-through effort.

In addition, White House officials believe that the report provides strong statistical justification for Mr. Nixon's proposal to reduce drastically the number of summer Head Start programs but increase the number of year-round programs.

The report found that the year-round programs had at least a marginal impact on poor children but the summer programs were wholly "ineffective in improving cognitive and affective development."

Some of the President's recommendations have already caused consternation on Capitol Hill. Head Start is a popular program, and many Congressmen want to leave it alone.

The Democratic chairman of the House Education and Labor Committee, Representative Carl D. Perkins of Kentucky, has expressed fears that Head Start would lose its identity and momentum if allowed to be swallowed up in the huge welfare agency.

The White House hopes that the report will persuade allies of the program that Head Start needs substantial revision without, at the same time, providing ammunition for those who wish to do away with such programs altogether.

"One of the principal implications of this report is that we really do not know as much

as we thought we knew about improving the lives and the minds of poor children," one ranking White House aide declared last week.

"Thus the question is whether we proceed down the same old path, which might soothe our egos but will certainly damage the children, or whether we take a new look and surround this thing with some science."

The Westinghouse researchers studied 104 Head Start centers in all regions of the country. They subjected Head Start "graduates" in the first, second and third grades to a battery of tests, then compared the results with those obtained from similar tests administered to "control" groups of equally disadvantaged children who had not attended Head Start.

The principal findings were as follows:

¶On the Illinois test of psycholinguistic abilities, a measure of language development, Head Start children from both the summer and full-year programs "did not score significantly higher" than the control groups in any of the three grade levels.

¶On the Metropolitan Readiness Test, a measure of a child's readiness to begin first grade, the Head Start children who had attended full-year programs and who had just begun first grade "were superior to the controls by a small but statistically significant margin."

¶The Stanford Achievement Test, which contains subtests of a child's verbal and mathematical skills, was administered in grades two and three. "The Head Start children," the report said, "did not score significant-

ly higher at either of the two grade levels."

Similarly, the Westinghouse team found no "significant" differences on three tests designed to measure a child's self-esteem, his desire for achievement and his attitudes toward "school, home, peers and society."

These findings struck the Westinghouse researchers with particular force, since one of the major advertisements for Head Start was that it improved a child's sense of personal worth.

"The improvement of the child's emotional and social development is one of the major goals of Head Start. . . . However, the findings of this study show that affective development . . . has not been improved by either full-year or summer programs," the report said.

Marginal Superiority

Of the six tests, therefore, only one — the Metropolitan Readiness Test — suggested that Head Start children were superior to their non-Head Start peers. But even in this case such superiority was marginal and was limited to those who had participated in a year-round Head Start program.

The study also found that in some of the subtests administered as part of the survey that "control" groups that had not attended preschool Head Start sessions did better than their Head Start peers.

The study did not seek to measure Head Start's impact on the health and diet of the children, or its role in the family, the community and the schools.

It acknowledged that the program might well have a beneficial impact in all of these areas but refused to concede that large expenditures on Head Start could be justified on these grounds alone.

At the same time, however, the report said that despite Head Start's apparent failure the search for child-help programs should not be abandoned.

"We would like to urge in the strongest possible terms that these findings not be used as [a] basis for concluding that early childhood remediation programs for the disadvantaged are a waste of time and money," the authors declared.

"Our findings do not provide much evidence that the Head Start program as it is now operating appreciably improved the intellectual or social-personal development of disadvantaged children.

"But as we pointed out, our study did not examine other objectives in other areas of impact of the Head Start programs.

"Furthermore, we think it is of the utmost importance for policymakers to appreciate the fact that the remediation of disadvantaged children is an area where straightforward answers and clear techniques are yet to be produced.

"And because it is in the best interests of the country at large, we strongly recommend that large-scale efforts and substantial resources continue to be devoted to the search for finding more effective programs and techniques for remediating the effect of poverty on disadvantaged children."

April 14, 1969

Day Care Plans Stress Education Role

By JEROME KAGAN

The need for child care services outside the family, an obscure theme less than a decade ago, is in the forefront of the nation's consciousness today.

We used to ask whether preschool educational services were good or necessary; now we ask how these services should be implemented and who should pay for them.

The numbers explain the rapid change in attitude. In 1969 about 30.5 million working women had 11.6 million children under 16 years of age, a figure that is eight

times the comparable totals in 1940. Close to five million of these children were under six years of age.

Major Federal Issues

Since only 12 per cent of this group can be cared for in licensed day care centers, the vast majority of preschool children who do not have grandmothers, aunts, or older sisters to care for them while their mother is working, either had a "babysitter" come to the home or were taken to another woman's home for most of the day.

This service is viewed by

both the mother and the substitute caretaker as custodial, not as growth enhancing. Several bills have been introduced in the Congress that might authorize Federal funds for the construction and maintenance of preschool centers and the training of a large cadre of personnel.

There are several issues surrounding acceptance of Federal aid in this crisis: Who should get priority of enrollment in these preschool centers? Who should determine the content of the programs? What should the content of these programs be?

The general consensus is that priority should be given to low-income families. Since poverty is correlated with ethnicity in the United States the choice of values to be promoted by the preschool center becomes a more critical issue than in most European nations, which are less ethnically diverse.

Local Control Demanded

Some blacks, Puerto Ricans, Mexican - Americans, and American Indians are demanding local control of hiring and determination of program content so that the ethos of the subculture and the life style of the family can be celebrated, not suppressed.

America's permissive attitude toward the identity of its ethnic groups makes it important that preschool educational plans not invent structures that violate the validity of these needs. If this wish is to be honored, funds should be funneled to the local community rather than through a complex network of bureacratic agencies at the state and Federal level.

There is, finally, a belief that these preschool centers should have a strong educational program, preparing children for the first grade tasks of reading, writing, and arithmetic, as well as playing a socialization function for development of beliefs and values.

Although the requirements for healthy personality development cannot be stated in absolute terms since optimal development can never be divorced from the culture in which the child lives, we can make a guess about adaptive personality traits in our culture.

Society's Value System

Our technological society continues to value the traits of independence, autonomy, verbal facility and an almost super self-confidence that causes adults to wink at each other when they see an exaggerated display of self-assuredness in a five-year-old.

This quality of boldness, which is not encouraged in most societies, probably requires a special set of experiences during the first five years of life.

If we are to develop these personality traits, the interpersonal atmosphere of the preschool setting becomes more important than its architectural design or the number and quality of books, toys and games on the shelves.

Preschool centers must provide the five-year-old with an opportunity to gratify his natural tendency to attach himself to adult heroes or heroines whose actions and values he is tempted to adopt. This emotional relation with the teacher is most likely to occur if the child has an opportunity for frequent interaction with her or him. Hence the teacher's humanity and the adult-child ratio are critical determinants of the success of the center.

Since the five million children who will be in preschool will require over 300,-000 licensed teachers before this decade is over, it is clear that we cannot arrange the optimal ratio of adult to child unless the core personnel of the center includes parents, neighborhood adults and high school students interested in working with young children.

There are, of course, many different kinds of organizational arrangements that can satisfy the need for preschool care, and they have acquired different names.

Industrial day care places the center at the place of work; parent-child centers require the parent to be actively involved in the day-to-day running of the center. An increasingly popular solution is the comprehensive child development center where physical, medical and psychological needs are met in a coordinated unit that is viewed as a support to the entire family, not just the child.

Mistakes to Learn From

During the early part of the 19th century many American cities, especially those in the Northeast, established preschool centers for the children of European immigrants because citizens believed the centers would be better socialization agents than the homes.

Unfortunately, administrative efficiency rather than humanity became the catechism of these centers, and they did not perform the mission required of them. We must learn from history.

Many contemporary American families want help in the education, socialization, and care of their children. But we must not make the mistake of creating institutions that supplant the family.

Parents must not relegate the responsibility for the child's development to any agency or preschool center. Some countries that have done this have promoted an insidious erosion of the quality of parental involvement with the child.

The center should supplement the resources of the family, not replace it. It is admittedly difficult to knit a group of unrelated people into a coherent unit that feels a sense of responsibility toward children of families it may not know.

But given the current mood of our community and the acknowledgement that these new structures are necessary, perhaps we shall make this social movement work.

Dr. Kagan is a professor in the Department of Social Relations at Harvard University.

January 11, 197

NURSERY SCHOOLS GROWING RAPIDLY

Head Start Gets Credit for Much of the Increase

By JACK ROSENTHAL
Special to The New York Times

WASHINGTON, March 9 — The Census Bureau reported today an explosive growth between 1965 and 1970 in the number of children aged 3 and 4 enrolled in nursery schools and kindergartens.

According to a new current population survey, one of every five children of those ages was enrolled in some kind of formal preschool institution in 1970. In 1965, the figure was one in 10.

Much of the increase, according to Federal and private authorities, is explained — directly and indirectly — by Operation Head Start and other Federal child care programs for the poor, which have been started since 1965.

These programs account for about two-thirds of the increased enrollment. Beyond that, however, they are credited with stimulating nursery school demand among families that are not poor.

"Head Start awakened the lower middle and the middle middle to recognize the value of such programs," Sam J. Granato, of the Federal Office of Child Development, said.

Other authorities credit Head Start with changing "middle-class mothers' guilt feelings" about not staying with young children.

The census data were contained in a report on school enrollment, which also included the following findings:

¶Enrollment in all schools in October, 1970, totaled 60.4 million, a 56 per cent increase over the total in 1965. About 99 per cent of all children aged 7 to 13 were enrolled.

¶College enrollment, in the same period, increased 31 per cent, to 7.4 million. Black college enrollment jumped 91 per cent, to 522,000.

¶Sharp decreases were found in private school enrollment at all levels, reflecting declines in financially pressed Catholic parochial schools around the country.

Increase of 600,000

Authorities interviewed today found the preschool findings the most dramatic.

In 1965, out of 8.4 million children aged 3 and 4, 890,000 were enrolled in preschools, the census survey found. In 1970, the total number of children aged 3 and 4 had fallen to 7.1 million, but the number enrolled had jumped to 1.5 million.

In the five years, the total number of children enrolled thus increased by about 600,-000. Head Start, a comprehensive child care program for disadvantaged families, now accounts for fewer than 260,000. Other Federal day care programs for the disadvantaged cover 110,000 other children.

Authorities believe that the rest of the increase — about 230,000 — is accounted for by the rapid growth among private nursery schools.

"The times of growth have always coincided with efforts to help the poor—in the Depression, the war and now Head Start," in the view of Barbara Jeanne Seabury. She is director of the National Child Research Center, in Washington, one of the oldest nursery schools in the country.

Such efforts give the middle class an awareness of the advantages of such schools, she said, like "giving a child a chance to develop a sense of trust in other adults."

She cited an increasing desire by middle-class parents "who are willing to make the financial sacrifice" to send their children to such schools. But this desire, she said, is often accompanied by frustration when these parents discover that they are applying too late.

The costs of nursery schools and day-care centers range from less than $500 to more than $2,000.

Middle-class parents are increasingly willing to pay such costs for two reasons, said Mr. Granato of the Office of Child Development. One is the benefits for the child. The other is the convenience for the mother.

"The benefits of such programs are greater for poor children," he said, "but they are nonetheless real for middle-class children."

And, he said the existence of quality facilities make it possible for women who need or want to work to do so without feelings of guilt.

March 10, 1971

'Sesame Street' Getting High Marks

By ANDREW H. MALCOLM

Little Stevie Boyer knelt to say his prayers the other evening and began reciting the alphabet. His surprised father, Dr. Ernest L. Boyer, chancellor of the State University of New York, asked the 5-year-old boy where he had learned his letters.

"Oh, from Sesame Street,'" the youngster replied, "but my teacher thinks she's teaching me them."

The incident has since caused Dr. Boyer some serious concern. "I can't help wondering," he said, "what new things Stevie could have been learning."

Many parents, as well as a number of the nation's 1.3 million elementary-school teachers, are beginning to ask similar questions about the impact on the schools of the popular television program for 3 year-olds and 4-year-olds.

Brighter Each Year

A survey revealed many individual teachers who are adjusting their teaching styles and lesson plans as they encounter more demanding parents and, in the last two or three years, batches of kindergartners who seem to be brighter each year.

Prompted by the same phenomenon, a few school districts have ordered evaluations of existing teaching in primary-school subjects, although there has so far been little formal revision of curriculums. One teacher in Chevy Chase, Md., was ousted by 15 sets of parents who were convinced that, after 45 years of service, she was not prepared to handle "Sesame Street" graduates.

Such pressures on the traditional school systems are not likely to ease. Last week, as millions of "Sesame Street" "alumni" finished their first month in kindergarten, an expanded cast videotaped the first show of the program's third season, which begins Nov. 15.

About 300 public and private stations — more than broadcast any other program on American TV—will carry "Sesame Street." Each week, an estimated two-thirds of the nation's 12 million, 3 and 4-year-olds watch the antics of Bert, Ernie, the Cookie Monster and the rest of the fictitious population.

'The Electric Company'

On Oct. 25, the creators of the program, the Children's Television Workshop, will premiere "The Electric Company," a fast-paced television show for pupils with reading problems.

Added to this is a range of other children's television programs, more educational toys and the burgeoning enrollments in nursery schools and early childhood programs.

"We're getting a different kind of child now," said Pauline Mahon, San Francisco's elementary education supervisor. "Four years ago they came without any knowledge. Now they are singing the alphabet."

At the North School in Portland, Me., Mrs. Marilyn Todd said: "You can't help but notice a difference in children who have been exposed to ["Sesame Street"]. They come to kindergarten knowing numbers, the alphabet, colors and recognition of shapes."

More Electricity

Mrs. Todd uses "Sesame Street" materials in her class and notices "more electricity in the air" as a result.

"I'm absolutely amazed at what the kids know," said Mrs. Laura Avery, a kindergarten teacher at the Cabot School in Newton, Mass. "There's a much greater degree of cooperation. They're more ready for school and it means we can start at a much higher level. I can't find any other reason for the advancement. It may be that two years of 'Sesame Street' has made the difference."

Some principals in Chicago said they had to move up some portions of their kindergarten curriculums because the pupils were more advanced. In less structured schools, such adjustments were unnecessary since students already progress at their own speed and easily fit in at their own level.

Mrs. Marge McDow, a kindergarten teacher in Northbrook, Ill., asked her class for some words beginning with "V" the other day. "Venus, victory and vulture," the youngsters replied.

"I was so excited," Mrs. McDow said, "I rushed to the teachers' lunchroom to brag about them." She discovered that youngsters spouted the same examples in other classes. All three words are part of an animated "Sesame Street" sequence on the letter "V."

At Public School 144 in New York City's impoverished Ocean Hill-Brownsville area, youngsters regularly view the program and teachers urge them to watch at home. Teachers say the program helped a number begin to read. "'Sesame Street' is not the whole answer," said Harriet Brown, a library supervisor, "but it can be a vital spark, a common base."

At some schools, including La Salle Elementary School in Washington, "Sesame Street" draws more children than the playground during play periods.

Jerome Kagan, a child psychologist at Harvard University, said that "Sesame Street" had proven that children "can learn some cognitive skills through television."

More important, he said, the program "has changed a fundamental attitude."

"It is telling millions of people that learning itself is important" he said, "and maybe the youngsters will carry this attitude toward learning with them even when the TV set is off. That accomplishment has far greater potential significance than the specific letters and numbers it teaches."

Others had reservations.

Many said that "Sesame Street" was only one of many factors affecting preschool children.

Some say the program only widens the gaps between disadvantaged children—its prime target — and those from homes where learning is encouraged.

Program officials deny this. Dr. Edward L. Palmer, the Children's Television Workshop's vice president for research, said:

"The real question is how many are now crossing that literacy line that will enable them to function in society."

A number of educators interviewed said that the program taught specific facts well by rote but that it was weak in conveying relationships and concepts. For instance one principal said: "They can count rapidly to 20. But if you stop and ask what's on either side of 15, they can't tell you."

Staffers of "Sesame Street," which receives almost half of its $13.8-million budget from the Federal Government and most of the rest from foundations, concede that their program is only one way of teaching and that it has some flaws. But they say that they are constantly evaluating and changing the program to meet new needs and criticisms.

There will be, for example, more concentration on improving instruction of such things as social interaction and developing a child's sense of self-esteem, they said.

After all, said Dr. Palmer, teaching numbers and letters, "while perhaps more memorable than other aspects," only takes 20 per cent of the program's time.

He emphasized that, throughout its instruction, the program "never imposes a performance mandate on these youngsters."

"No kid ever flunks 'Sesame Street,'" he said. "He just soaks up his learning in a palatable form." Why, he asked, "shouldn't such learning be fun?"

October 17, 1971

SCHOOLS ADVANCE IN WEALTHY AREAS

Survey Finds Rich Suburbs Lead in New Methods

WASHINGTON, Aug. 25 (UPI)—The National Education Association said today that the nation's wealthier suburbs, "as might be expected," were leading the way in modernizing educational systems."

Experiments such as team teaching and ungraded classrooms have become almost conventional in many of these better-off communities, the N.E.A. said.

Team teaching involves two or more teachers instructing more than one class group, with each instructing the entire group in a subject in which he has special competence. It also involves small group discussions guided by the various teachers on the team.

It reported on a survey of new educational practices in suburban school districts with enrollment of more than 1,000 and with family incomes of more than $10,000.

Replies from seventy districts indicated a trend toward increased use of courses usually taught at the college level. Courses in world culture and the humanities were reported at Scarsdale, N. Y., Mount Lebanon, Pa., Beachwood, Ohio, Riverside, Ill., and University City, Mo. A course in logic was reported at Lake Forest, Ill.

But not even these wealthy communities were getting all they wanted in the way of financial help to develop new programs. Two — Highland Park, Ill., and Mountainside, N. J.—reported they were cutting back their programs because the taxpayers had denied necessary funds.

Two California districts said they were getting their students ready for the space age. Burlingame will introduce geometry in the second grade, and East Whittier will start astronomy in the fourth, fifth and sixth grades.

Other innovations reported in the survey included:

¶One of the first schools specifically designed for team teaching, at Greenwich, Conn. Teachers were trained in the method for three years.

¶"Custom tailoring" of education based not on age or grade standards but adapted to individual achievement, at Newton, Mass., on a Ford Foundation grant.

¶Using parents in a classroom at Bronxville, N. Y., for clerical chores and to assist children having special difficulties with reading, language or arithmetic.

¶A high school course in digital computers for advanced mathematics students, at Westbury, N. Y.

¶Two periods each week of typing for all students, at Glen Ridge, N. J., and additional work for those desiring proficiency for employment purposes.

¶Introduction of French and Spanish language classes this fall by the Maywood, N. J., junior high school.

¶Experiments with three approaches to the teaching of reading in kindergarten and first grade, at Ardmore, Pa.

¶Merit pay for exceptionally effective teachers, at Wayne, Pa., and creation of a file of citizens with special skills and interests available for classroom appearances.

¶A special program for slow learners, at Oakwood, Ohio, which sends 90 per cent of its graduates to college.

¶A Ford Foundation-financed "learning center" to stimulate independent study, at Shaker Heights, Ohio.

¶Team teaching for reading in grades 1 to 6, at Munster, Ind., which will be extended through junior high school later.

¶New curriculums, different instruction, different texts and higher standards for fast learners with an intelligence quotient of 130 or more, at Elmhurst, Ill. But foreign languages are being dropped from early elementary grades in favor of a more intensive program for grades 5 to 8.

¶A junior high school learning center to encourage self instruction and creative work beyond the classroom, at Winnetka, Ill.

¶Experiment in ability grouping in the first grade, at Skokie, Ill., testing results against a heterogeneous group at another school.

¶Classes in study skills for laggards, at Oak Park, Mich., with emphasis on how to study as well as on mastery of content.

Beverly Hills, Calif., is coordinating with high school courses a new program of foreign language for grades 1 to 8. The school this summer sent seventeen talented students to study in Spain and Austria.

NONGRADE SCHOOL BOTH OLD AND NEW

Plan Set for Ocean Hill Used by 16 Principals Here

By M. A. FARBER

The idea of the nongraded elementary school, which will be implemented as an experiment in the Ocean Hill-Brownsville Demonstration School District starting Monday, is as old as the one-room rural schoolhouse and as new as the latest innovations in city and suburbia.

But few of the nongraded schools today practice the same program. What they hold in common, for the most part, is a philosophy that children of varying abilities and readiness should be freed from the "lockstep" of education by removing specific grade levels.

"The curriculum," according to the city Board of Education, "should meet the child where he is and take him as far as he can go" — irrespective of traditional grade formalities.

Ideally, nongraded schools provide greater individualized education by allowing youngsters, under appropriate guidance, to work at their optimum pace and to gain self-confidence.

Many Needs Considered

"If we think of the many needs of children — academic, social, emotional, physical, creative — and the uneven patterns of child development, we can see how a nongraded primary is designed to meet all needs of the child," said Mrs. Reba Mayer, principal of Public School 219 in Flushing.

The city school system— with 650 elementary schools— has 16 that are fully or partly nongraded. It had none in 1963, when Mrs. Mayer started a nongraded effort at Public School 89 in Elmhurst, where she was then principal.

"I love it," Mrs. Mayer said yesterday of the nongrading idea. "Team teaching was the first major step out of the box and nongrading is the biggest step forward."

Mrs. Mayer said that parents at P.S. 89 and P.S. 219 had accepted nongrading "on faith" but were "a little apprehensive." The parents of older children, she explained, "worry some whether their children are going to lose out. But actually those kids gain from responsibility and leadership in groups of mixed ages," she said.

Choices to Be Broad

The scheduled experiment in nongrading at P.S. 144 in Ocean Hill-Brownsville appears to differ somewhat from current methods here in its heavy Goodland, dean of the School struction and in the latitude that is to be afforded students for choosing their own study programs.

In its wider opportunity for selection by students the experiment is suggestive of the long-controversial "progressive" education.

The National Educational Association, in a poll taken this year of 2,000 principals in school systems with more than 25,000 pupils, reported that approximately 11 per cent of first and second grades were introducing nongraded plans, as were 3 per cent of fifth and sixth grades.

August 26, 1962

November 21, 196

Students Flock to Philadelphia

'School Without Walls'

By WILLIAM K. STEVENS
Special to The New York Times

PHILADELPHIA, Jan. 21 — About a year ago, amid great fanfare, high hopes and some skepticism, the Philadelphia school system initiated one of the nation's boldest experiments in public education, the Parkway Program, in which high school students choose their own subjects of study and use the city's institutions and businesses as classrooms.

The program was designed as an alternative means of education for teen-agers who find conventional schools repressive and oppressive and conventional instruction dull and unrelated to their own concerns. It is directed toward students who want to attend college and those who do not.

Now, as the program's first anniversary approaches (the first 140 students were selected by lot from a group of volunteers last Jan. 31), many of its supporters — especially students and parents — feel that the high hopes are mostly being fulfilled.

"For the first time," said one parent, [my son] is actually being educated. He has learned more in his first session than in all his previous years of school. For the first time he likes school."

Final Judgment Deferred

But many of the approving parents have some reservations, often centering on whether the program deals adequately with basic skills like reading and writing and basic disciplines like history and science. Final judgment, in most quarters, is therefore being deferred.

So attractive has been the program's inherent freedom, however, that more than 10,-000 students applied for the 500 places open this year. Partly because of this response, other cities are considering the merits of the program. One, Chicago, will open its own "school without walls" on Feb. 2.

Essentially, the philosophy behind the Parkway Program is that people learn only what they want to learn, not what someone else imposes on them, and that they learn best by grappling directly with the rich material in the world around them.

"School is not a place but an activity, a process," says John Bremer, the 42-year-old, British-born director of the program. He further conceives of school as "a service organization" whose function is to help the student as he pursues his own self-initiated learning scheme.

The Parkway Program "is an attempt to break down the dichotomy between living and learning, and to that extent it's extremely significant," says Mario Fantini, who has been monitoring the project for the Ford Foundation. The foundation helped the program to get started with a $100,000 grant.

'Not a Total Solution'

"It's an important option for kids who aren't profiting from school," Mr. Fantini said, "but it's not a total solution. For some kids it may work, for others it may not."

The program is set up this way:

Students are organized into four "communities," each of which is governed informally through a "town meeting" held once a week. Teachers and students together decide what courses will be offered.

Credits in broad subject areas such as English and social studies are required so state demands may be met, but within each general area students decide what, specifically, they are to study.

"Alpha" community, the original group of Parkway students, now offers 95 separate courses—many of them conventional academic and vocational subjects, many of them unknown to the ordinary high school. Some examples of the latter are psychology of the adolescent, game theory, computer programing and a seminar on Vietnam.

There is also an encounter group, in which students attempt to strip away each other's psychological defenses and communicate more directly and openly. Many courses involve social service projects, for example —working with post-psychiatric patients or the aged.

"Classes" are held at various sites around the city — newspaper offices, hospitals, an art museum, university laboratories, corporate offices, print shops, garages, a drama institute, a music academy, to mention some — where workers, managers and professionals in the adult world become volunteer teachers.

More-or-less conventional classes are conducted by certified teachers in churches and lofts.

There are no grades, except for pass or fail. Teachers assess students' progress on a personal basis, and students evaluate teachers' performance. If a student does not like a class he can drop out and attend another one. Some do.

Equality between student and teacher is not only encouraged but is pursued almost fiercely. Sometimes it is difficult to distinguish long-haired, bearded teachers from teen-agers. Students call instructors by their first names and in general wear their newly found equality like a badge.

Help Is Available

In one class yesterday, a student challenged a teacher's statement with an expletive that would have got him thrown out of some schools. The teacher, obviously used to such things and not in the least disturbed, simply entered into what turned out to be a rational discussion with the student.

"If you need help, the teachers will help you," 15-year-old Janet Sloan said as she sat and talked in Alpha group's cluttered headquarters at 1801 Market Street yesterday. "There's no attitude like 'It's just another stupid 15-year-old, so what's the difference!'"

Some students complain that they detect such attitudes in ordinary classrooms.

Photographs by The New York Times by JACK MANNING

Students in a psychology class, given at the First Baptist Church in Philadelphia, in connection with the Parkway Program, begun nearly a year ago

Some parents worry that their children are not independent enough to handle the increased freedom and responsibility; that they flounder and need more direction. Students say some classes degenerate into bull sessions. In some instances, classes turn into a routine lecture, and students usually are quick to call the teacher to task for it.

There is no objective way so far to determine, in traditional terms, how much and how well the students are learning. The major indication along these lines is expected to come when students who have spent most of their high school careers in the Parkway Program take college entrance examinations. This is what leads many parents to suspend judgment.

Some Parents Concerned

Despite their children's liking for the program, some parents are concerned lest it fail to provide a solid subject-matter undergirding and philosophical framework for what the students learn from their encounters with the city's life.

"There is considerable value to learning by doing, by touching, feeling, making mistakes, etc.," one parent wrote in a generally favorable critique, "but often this has the limitation of provoking only a superficial or surface knowledge."

"On this," said Mr. Fantini of the Ford Foundation, "we'll just have to wait and see what happens. To just make the students happy and deny them the skills they need to survive in a technological society, well, that's not fair."

January 23, 1970

Parents With $300 and an Idea: Free School Is Born

By JOAN COOK

MOST families faced with the conditions that prevail in New York City schools have done one of three things: moved to the suburbs, turned to private or parochial resources or tried to cope as best they could with existing conditions.

Most families, but not all.

From a nucleus of six determined women and their families—all of whom had been active in their local public schools—has come yet another alternative to the status quo, an ungraded, racially balanced, free school called the Children's Community Workshop.

Taking the British Infant School as their model—with its emphasis on child-initiated activity and flexibility of movement between classes—the six women determined to start a school of their own, one that would bring together effectively the poverty of Harlem and the relative affluence of the Central Park West area.

Passed the Hat

The program started with the women passing the hat among themselves.

"One girl wrote a check for $25, another for $10, whatever anyone could scrape together, that's how we started. The determination was fantastic," Dorothy Arfer, one of the founders whose 8-year-old son, Joshua, attends the school, recalled over cake and coffee in the main building at 55 West 88th Street.

The group raised about $300 "and then," Mrs. Arfer said, "we went out and recruited pupils and space; we begged."

The group began with two store fronts, a basement and subsequently added a $1,000 grant from the Episcopal Church, Diocese of New York, Urban Crisis Fund, to help it on its way. That was in September, 1968.

Since then, it has grown to include 65 households, between 90 and 100 youngsters from kindergarten through the eighth grade. It has also received a charter from the state of New York.

"In the beginning we had to send to the corner candy store for pencils," Mrs. Anita Moses, the director, said. "Every time we wanted something Xeroxed, we'd have to send it to the Chrysler Building where Anita had a contact who would let us use the machine," Mrs. Ruth Messinger, the assistant director, remembered.

Presently, the school is housed on two floors of a five-story house that is scheduled for demolition by the city; some of the younger children are quartered in a spacious basement across the street.

"See our reading loft," Mrs. Messinger said, pointing to a narrow ladder leading up to a private perch for youngsters who want to do their reading away from the hurly-burly of the classroom. "One of our teachers designed it and the parents helped build it."

Parents are very much involved in the school's activities, according to Mrs. Moses. On a recent snowy night more than 40 mothers, fathers and teachers crowded into what had once been the paneled library of the house.

The subject (discussed both in Spanish and English) was funding the school, with all sources of public funding—city, state and Federal—to be explored.

In addition, a suit against the state of New York for per capita funds by next spring is anticipated as a test case. (The school's total expenses for the past year ran between $1,200 and $1,300 per child; the Board of Education budget for an elementary school child is $728, a figure that does not include pupil transportation, building construction and maintenance or debt services.)

The gist of a statement by the group's finance and publicity committees was that the current public school system is segregated and inadequate and does not respond effectively to parents and other members of the community who fight for change.

By establishing a free community school, the Children's Community Workshop says it has offered an educational alternative with open enrollment on a first come-first served basis. The balance between black, Spanish-speaking and white children is maintained despite a waiting list for white children and the availability of a few places for Spanish-speaking youngsters).

"We provide a model of what public education could and should be like," the statement said.

Obviously the school is fine for some children but not necessarily all. Mrs. Moses, who stresses that this is one alternative, but not necessarily the only one, to the public school system, estimated that about eight families have withdrawn their youngsters since the school's inception.

Missed Organization

"We loved the idea of the school and what it stands for but our daughter found the lack of structure too chaotic and wanted to go back to public school," Mrs. Susan Feingold said, "and my husband and I felt the decision was right for her."

Others found that while they objected strenuously to the existing public school system, this was not the answer either, and at least one family moved away.

The school's approach, as Mrs. Moses explained it, is based on a concept that goes back to Socrates.

"In other words, to take advantage of a child's potential when he is tuned-in, we must allow him to tune-out," Mrs. Moses, whose sons, Marc, 8, and Elan, 5, attend the school, said. "We believe that children learn not by being given ready-made answers but by becoming aware of questions."

Most of the parents would agree with Mrs. Michael Good whose 9-year-old son, Anton, attends the school. "We love it," Mrs. Good said. "You have to go there during the day and see the kids and how they function and how they feel. It's very organic. My son feels better and I feel better."

Children are permitted to move at their own pace, to leave or join study group at will. Teachers take interruptions to show off a pet in stride.

February 7, 1970

O.E.O. TO TEST PLAN TO AID EDUCATION

2-Part Experiment Intends to Provide Incentives

By JACK ROSENTHAL
Special to The New York Times

WASHINGTON, May 14 — The Office of Economic Opportunity disclosed plans today for a two-part experiment that, if successful, "could revolutionize education" for all, not just poor, chidren.

The more dramatic part of the experiment, styled "performance contracting," involves payment of incentives to students, teachers, and private educational contractors, depending on improvements in student performance. The incentives would take different forms, including cash, trading stamps and prizes.

The heart of the experiment lies in the second part—reliance on advanced programed instruction techniques. These ermit students to learn at their own speed from special materials, often with the help of teaching machines.

The one year experiement is to begin next fall in 24 school districts. It will include from 12,000 to 17,000 students and will cost between $3.5-million and $5.5-million. The selection of six private contractors and of the school districts will be made late next month.

Evaluation is Challenged

Donald Rumsfeld, director of the poverty agency, expressing the belief that the experiment could revolutionize primary and secondary education, challenge today present forms of evaluation of educational performance.

"Historically, we have measured our concern by asking how many millions we spend, how many textbooks we buy, how many schools we build. But those are all inputs. They don't tell us anything about the impact on human begins."

The new experiement will seek to confirm and enlarge early evidence that performance contracting dramatically improves educational achievement.

The experiment derives from a small privately operated program that is underway in Texarkana, Tex., under a grant from the Office of Education.

This 400-student program has had rather phenomenal results" even though not intended as a measurable experiment, in the opinion of John O. Wilson, planning director of the O.E.O.

Since last September, according to Mr. Wilson, students have shown a 2.4 grades improvement in reading and a 1.9 grade improvement in mathematics. This program involves an hour a day of intensive instruction, coupled with incentive payments.

Texarkana has also noted dramatic decreases in the dropout rate, vandalism and opposition to desegregation, Mr. Wilson said, possibly as a consequence of the performance contracting program.

The new experiment, aside from being far larger, will seek to pinpoint the important factors behind such gains. Different parts of the experiment will test the impact on poor inner-city and rural children of incentives alone, of new instructional methods alone, and of both together.

The results of tests taken during and after the experimental year will be compared with the performance of children in ordinary school situations. Evaluation will be done by a private contractor, Indewho will conduct the experipendent of any of the concerns ment.

"We're not starting this to make it work," Mr. Rumsfeld said today. "We want it to work, but the aim here is to find out if it does work."

In separate comments, Mr. Rumsfeld denied that any of the poverty agency's money would be diverted to help fulfill President Nixon's commitment to provide $500-million this year to assist schools involved in desegregation.

"To my knowledge, there no intent to divert any O.E.O. money" for that purpose, he said, "and I try to stay currently informed." He said that most of the total could be collected from, for example, funds for programs that Congress has been slow to authorize.

May 15, 197

The revolution that failed,

Turning on The System

War in the Philadelphia Public Schools. By Henry S. Resnik. 299 pp. New York: Pantheon Books. $6.95.

By RONALD GROSS

In the fall of 1967 Henry Resnik, a 27-year-old freelance journalist, went to Philadelphia to do a story on an experimental school for seventh and eighth graders. He found the whole city in a ferment of educational reform, and stayed to observe and participate in it (briefly as a teacher) for one and a half years. In that period he prowled the city covering as best he could the various manifestations of a reform school administration. This book is the result.

It had all started in December, 1965, when Philadelphians, sick of their moribund school system, elected a new Board of Education headed by Richardson Dilworth, the legendary ex-mayor who had reformed the city's political affairs. This Board, in turn, hired Mark Shedd, a young school superintendent from Englewood, N.J., and brought in a group of nonprofessional educators (the "Ivy Mafia") as new, central-office administrators; their average age was 36, and they were committed to "turning on the system."

Together, Shedd, the Board and this new team introduced to Phila-

Mr. Gross is vice president of the Academy for Educational Development and co-editor, with his wife Beatrice, of the recently published "Radical School Reform."

delphia an array of experimental programs unparalleled in American education since World War II. The Advancement School, for example, recruits bright kids who aren't making it in school, and tries to spark their learning with a program of unconventional studies including psychodrama, experimental arts and multi-media courses. At the same time, Terry Borton and his colleagues in curriculum development at the Board created a course of study focused on the cultivation of the emotions, rather than on mastery of conventional school subjects. In nine pilot schools the "integrated day" approach, which was revolutionizing British primary education, got a widespread tryout in the elementary grades. Among other experiments were the use of work-study students from Antioch College as change-agents in the schools, T-group retreats in which white and black teachers tried to work out their hostilities, a mini-school along the lines recommended by Paul Goodman, one of the largest computer-assisted instruction projects in the country and a "school without walls" — Parkway — which uses the city's cultural institutions and businesses as its classrooms.

Shedd's innovations fully justify Resnik's initial judgment that "Philadelphia was special because it seemed to be well on the way, more than any other American city, to coping successfully with the failures of urban education. The movement for educational reform held enormous promise. . . . Alienation and *anomie* would be supplanted by involvement and creativity. Everyone in the system, fulfilled by new roles and attitudes, would be 'turned on.' It was a magnificent dream. . . . not really a plan so much as a basic commitment to humanitarian values and the liberated, anti-establishment style of the turned-on youth movement."

In portraying all this, Resnik's book breaks new ground in educa-

tional reportage. His canvas is broad, encompassing the entire system from the political machinations between the Board of Education and the Mayor, right into the classrooms and the lives of individual teachers and kids.

Taped interview transcripts, diary entries, profiles of leading figures in the fray and children's writings make up Resnik's montage. The author himself is very much part of the story — a young journalist, honestly trying to learn but also on the make. He haggles for months with a militant black leader who wants a split of the royalties on his book, wins and loses the confidence of a bright drop-out, is attracted to and fears a gang of young toughs on a streetcar, falls under the spell of a brilliant (pseudonymous) poet - teacher and then sees how their relationship is based on mutual deception.

But the book is also somewhat formless and sloppy. Different chapters were obviously written at quite different times, with little effort to coordinate them or to keep them current. (The account of the Advancement School is particularly obsolete, even taking account of book production lag-time.) Annoying repetitions of background facts are frequent, and there are glaring errors such as a reference to the "U.S. Department [instead of Office] of Education."

The worst flaw is the absence of an in-depth portrait of Mark Shedd, the Superintendent of Schools at the center of this system during its period of reform and crisis. Shedd's chief lieutenants get the full-dress treatment, with Rick deLone, his administrative assistant, given an entire chapter. But while we read much about Shedd's actions, we never meet the man, hear his voice, get the opportunity to size up his stlye, see what makes him tick. This is a serious omission—particularly in a book so filled with interviews and profiles—since what happened in Philadelphia is unimaginable without Shedd. This is particularly critical because Resnik's final judgment is that Shedd's reform program came a cropper. As Resnik tells the story, the awesome forces of conflict and confusion in American cities today shattered the dream of educational renewal. Racial clashes shook Shedd's administration, budgetary squeezes slowed the flow of money for innovation, educators' notorious resistance to change prevented the new practices from spreading, a feud developed between the Mayor and the school board. Shedd himself (though still in command today) became aloof and unresponsive as his chief lieutenants, younger men with other fish to fry, drifted away out of frustration.

"After almost two years of Mark Shedd and a full three years of the new Board," Resnik concludes, "the Philadelphia public school system remained essentially the same institution that it had been before the battle began. . . . No sensible person could talk about revolution in the Philadelphia school system with a straight face, and 'turning on' had gone the way of all slogans. The great revolution had failed to deliver, had suffered

so many defeats that it seemed never to have been more than a wild, clever dream. Slow reform was all too often the best one could hope for."

This is, of course, Resnik's interpretation, and he admits that his book is neither comprehensive nor objective, but rather a highly personal account of "what I have learned." Often — as in the pervasive use of martial metaphors —the book tells us more about the author than about his subject.

Resnik admits that "During Shedd's first two years a tone had been set for the Philadelphia schools that would probably enable the system to survive most of the battles to come: the system had indeed opened up; barring some cataclysm that might wipe out the liberal regime at 21st Street, it would remain open. . . . The changes encouraged and brought about by the Shedd administration were, and probably continue to be, the kind that made the Philadelphia school system better."

This is no small achievement: one desperately wishes the same could be said for the New York City school system,

or that of Boston, Detroit, Los Angeles or virtually any other major city. But, to the degree that one must admit that school reform in Philadelphia has lost momentum and failed to transform the whole city school system, the question remains: If a powerful and progressive administrator, backed by a politically savvy board and armed with a cadre of creative teachers, and a bundle of outside money, cannot turn around an urban school system then what hope is there?

Radical school critics like John Holt, George Dennison, Herbert Kohl and Paul Goodman would put their money on independent, grass roots, "free schools," like Kohl's Other Ways in Berkeley or the ill-fated First Street School described by Dennison in "The Lives of Children." Others, no less dedicated to reform in education, insist that only by truly decentralizing the power which is now congealed within the central bureaucracies, can urban schooling be revitalized. The recent literature on school reform suggests, sadly, that both approaches may be needed, but that neither is adequate to the present crisis. ■

May 24, 1970

COMPANY TO TEACH GARY, IND., PUPILS

Private Group to Run Entire School for Four Years

By ANDREW H. MALCOLM

The Gary, Ind., public school system has contracted with a private company, Behavioral Research Laboratories, to run one of its elementary schools this fall. It is believed to be the first city in the nation to turn over the entire operation of a single school to such an experiment.

Under the four-year contract agreement, which was announced here this week, the

company will reorganize, and operate Gary's Banneker Elementary School, receiving $800 per student annually, the current cost to the city of educating each student.

The agreement provides that B.R.L. will bring the students achievement scores up to or above the national grade-level norms in all basic curriculum areas or refund to the city the fees paid for each child who does not reach those levels.

Evaluation will be undertaken after three years by an independent agency chosen by B.R.L. and the city. Afterward a second evaluation of the first will be made. Otherwise, the fourth year of the contract will provide a transition back to city control.

Other Contract Teaching

The Gary agreement on a single school is among a grow-

ing number of educational performance contract ventures in which private companies are paid in accordance with the academic progress of the students whom they instruct.

To date, however, the companies have been limited to teaching such subjects as reading or mathematics, rather than running an entire school. This, for example, is the case in Texarkana, Tex. and Texarkana, Ark., the most publicized of the performance contract efforts.

In Camden, N. J., the RCA Corporation has joined school officials and community leaders in a joint effort to reform the entire city school system and some of RCA's sub-contracting to other companies is expected to be on a performance basis.

The system to be used in Gary relies heavily on the use

of teaching techniques tailored to the individual pupil.

"We'll be handling everything at Banneker," said Donald Kendrick, a B.R.L. executive, "from the requisitioning of pencils to the texts, teacher hiring and the instruction." The company will also rent the school building from the city.

All-Negro Enrollment

Last year the school, a one-story brick structure built in 1957, had 744 students, all Negroes. An enrollment of 800 is expected this fall.

The school is situated in Gary's central Tolleston area, inhabited predominantly by steel workers and their families.

Gary officials said the school, where classes run from kindergarten through grade six, was chosen for the experiment because the neighborhood is a

179

relatively stable one and because students there have traditionally been under-achievers. The principal, Clarence Benford, said that in various subjects the students had been performing from two months to two years below grade level.

Mr. Benford said the community "was quite enthused, indeed thrilled over the project's possibilities."

"With the company's guarantee," he said," we feel we have everything to gain and nothing to lose."

Complete operational details will be worked out in a series of intensive staff meetings at the school next month. But some general organizational lines are already clear.

Reallocation of Resources

"The basic concept is to reallocate resources—the people, the money and the facilities— for maximum instructional efficiency," Mr. Kendrick said in an interview. "There is, for instance, no reason why six people, including instructional staff, should be involved in ordering new erasers."

The staff of about 30 instructors—plus 20 "paraprofessionals" or neighborhood people who will help teachers and provide contact with the community—will be hired by B.R.L.

All existing union contract provisions will be retained. The teachers' union is not expected to object to the reassignment of a number of its members, the company says, although a meeting to work out details has not yet been held.

The school will be run by a manager, with a learning director under him to serve in place of a principal.

Five curriculum managers, all of them teachers, will be chosen to specialize in the areas of reading and language arts, mathematics, social studies and foreign languages, science and enrichment (arts, music, drama and physical education).

The remaining teachers and paraprofessionals will be divided among those areas to develop their own expertise and pass it onto teachers in the other fields.

Upon registration a pupil will take a series of diagnostic tests to determine his competence in such fields as reading and mathematics.

Using special texts designed by the company and individual instruction, he will progress at his own rate according to a prescription designed to meet his own particular academic weaknesses and strengths.

July 26, 197

Report Hails Oregon High School's Experiment in Free Study

By WILLIAM K. STEVENS
Special to The New York Times

PORTLAND, Ore.—The clean-lined, futuristic colonnades, courtyards and skylights of Portland's John Adams High School symbolize a fresh view of how teen-agers should be educated.

Opened just over a year ago on a site south of the Columbia River, it houses what may well be the country's "most important experiment in secondary education," according to the recently published report of a three-and-a-half-year study of American schools commissioned by the Carnegie Corporation.

Adams High seeks to determine whether ordinary teen-agers are willing and able to accept day-to-day responsibility for their own education—planning their own studies, sometimes developing their own tailor-made courses and managing their own time.

Thus a black senior, Don Bilbrew, is free to embark on a two-year independent study of black history in Portland that requires him to make use of the disciplines of sociology and economics as well as history. At the same time he can, and does, study such subjects as Shakespeare, drama, biology and journalism.

And Diane Crane, a sophomore, can branch out from her state-required biology course and undertake an independent study of genetics.

Conceived at Harvard

The Adams experiment is attempting to eliminate what the Carnegie study found to be some of the most damaging features of the typical American high schools: Encouragament of docility and conformity; over-regulation of students' lives; and a pallid, uniform curriculum.

The experiment was conceived three years ago by seven young PhD. candidates at the Harvard University Graduate School of Education. One of them, Robert Schwartz, 32 years old, is now the principal of the school.

Similar ventures in "free" or "open" education for teen-agers are going on elsewhere, but in relatively small, especially constituted environments with selected or volunteer students. Adams, by contrast, is a regular district high school operating within political and economic realities. Its student body of 1,600 is drawn from all social strata, with a heavy contingent from white working class families. A quarter of the students are black.

"If the approach works here," says Mr. Schwartz, "it will work anywhere."

Rules Are Few

The Adams approach begins with the proposition that the overall climate of a school may have a stronger effect on student learning than the formal curriculum.

"If you require a kid to have a hall pass you're saying you don't trust him," Mr. Schwartz said. "You then undercut the value of any 40-minute lesson in self-direction."

Except for the fact that students must come to school and participate, and that they must obey civil laws, Adams has few rules and regulations.

Legitimate authority at Adams is held to be rooted in experience and knowledge. Since adults are by and large more experienced than children, it is reasoned, they have a kind of "natural" authority that makes itself felt when an adult deals with a youngster on an equal, respectful footing.

Teachers are viewed as helpmates and colleagues, not dictators. "We try not make decisions for kids," Mr. Schwartz said. "We press the student to confront himself and what he's going to do with his life, and to make responsible choices. We are not permissive."

For many students accustomed to being told what to do, the pressure to choose has been uncomfortable, even painful. Some students have simply refused to act for themselves or to go to class, but Mr. Schwartz said that a large majority adjusted to the new way of doing things.

Curriculum for Generalists

Students at Adams choose as electives many essentially traditional courses—for example, physics, chemistry, electronics and industrial arts. Often students work independently in such courses, checking with the teacher only when help is needed.

But the pride of Adams's effort at curriculum reform is an interdisciplinary "general education" course set up this way:

Students and faculty are divided into seven "teams," each of which designs its own learning program that will lead students to explore key concepts in the state-required subjects of English, social studies, mathematics and basic science. Typically, a team will do this by focusing on some real-life problem—race relations, for example—that can be attacked through the application of several disciplines.

Thus, a team headed by teacher David Mesirow has begun a unit called "the psychology of self," designed to enable students to become surer about their own identities and their relationship to the rest of the world. The team will focus in sequence on politics, students' rights and the process of change; values, advertising and the media; the experience of poverty; the black experience; alternative life styles; and the urban environment of Portland.

General education meets for half a day every day, but a student may skip the group sessions in favor of independent study if he wishes. Should general education spark several students' interest in some particular subject—say, general philosophy—a six-week "mini-course" is organized.

Each student has two free option periods a day, during which he can do anything he likes, or nothing. Some do nothing.

Students choose whether to be given letter grades or to receive a "credit-no credit" rating.

Parents' reaction to the experiment has been mixed.

A survey of students indicated that they considered Adams a "humanized" school. "At least you feel like a person here," said one student. But the same survey found that many students felt the intellectual content of the curriculum should be strengthened.

October 19, 1970

"IT is not possible to spend any prolonged period visiting public school classrooms without being appalled by the mutilation visible everywhere—mutilation of spontaneity, of joy in learning, of pleasure in creating, of sense of self."

This is but one of the melancholy findings of the now much-discussed report on American public education, "Crisis in the Classroom," commissioned by the prestigious Carnegie Foundation of New York and authored by Charles E. Silberman.

Most American public schools, the Carnegie report charges, are "grim," "intellectually sterile," "esthetically barren" places, governed by "oppressive" and "petty" rules. Teachers and principals are seen by the report largely as victims of an educational system divorced from the realities of child development. Specifically, the Carnegie report's indictment against the traditional American school cites the "preoccupation with order and control, the slavish adherence to the timetable and lesson plan, the obsession with routine qua routine, the absence of noise and movement, the joylessness and repression, the universality of the formal lecture or teacher-dominated 'discussion' in which the teacher instructs an entire class as a unit, the emphasis on the verbal and de-emphasis of the concrete, the inability of students to work on their own, the dichotomy between work and play."

Silberman and his staff, observing schools in every part of the United States, did discover what they regarded as oases of hope. These were schools or portions of schools where teachers had introduced the informal classroom methods adopted by a growing number (at least one-third) of the state primary schools in Great Britain. The approach is now stirring considerable interest, comment and excitement in American educational circles.

The underlying assumption of "informal" schools, both British and American, is that in an enriched and carefully planned environment that supports *the natural drive toward learning* children are able to learn mostly by themselves, from each other and from books. They learn in

WALTER and MIRIAM SCHNEIR, writers who frequently work as a team, co-authored "Invitation to an Inquest," a study of the Rosenberg-Sobell case. She is a former elementary school teacher.

The Joy of Learning —In the Open Corridor

By WALTER SCHNEIR and MIRIAM SCHNEIR

encounters with the things and people around them, and they do so at their own irregular and individual pace. They learn most intensely when they are interested and see the pertinence of what they are doing. The role of the teacher is important, but quite untraditional: there are few, if any, whole-class lessons, no standardized tests, no meticulously detailed and rigidly enforced curriculum.

Informal methods are being tried in New York City and in the Westchester communities of New Rochelle, Greenburgh and Irvington, and across the country in such cities as Washington, Detroit, New Haven, Newark and Berkeley, as well as such states as North Dakota, Vermont, Maine and Arizona.*

ONE of the most interesting experiments singled out for mention by the Carnegie report is taking place at P.S. 84, a school in a racially and economically varied neighborhood along Manhattan's Upper West Side. The school, with 900 children in pre-kindergarten through sixth grade, has an enrollment that is about one-third black, one-third white and one-third Spanish-American.

Today at P.S. 84, the visitor can see in operation the most dramatic physical innovation of the British primary schools: the use of hallways as extensions of the classroom. The British were forced to adopt this plan because of overcrowded schools. But necessity proved to be a virtue when classroom doors were thrown open and the children were allowed free access to the corridors. The arrangement made possible a sense of community among students and staff, a spirit of mutual help and learning. The educator who has promoted this

---

*But in the United States there is probably only one authentic informal school on the British model, and that is the all-girl primary school of the Convent of the Sacred Heart in Greenwich, Conn. Most of the pupils are daughters of affluent suburbanites, and the teaching staff is British.

particular approach in New York, Mrs. Lillian Weber, describes it as the "open-corridor" program.

The sight of a small boy sliding down a bannister greets the two visitors to P.S. 84, situated at 92d Street between Columbus Avenue and Central Park West. The sliding boy and a companion, who is taking the more conventional route down a short flight of stairs from a first floor landing, are conversing animatedly.

Walking up a half dozen steps, we come upon a first floor corridor that is the connecting passage between four primary classrooms that open off it. At 10 A.M. in the corridor, four kindergarten girls, seated cross-legged on some cushions with a pile of magazines, a paste pot and a very large sheet of brown paper, are cutting and pasting. Nearby, a third grader is reading a story to a younger child; both are giggling at the antics of "Curious George." Two girls sitting side by side on the corridor floor are each absorbed in a book, as is a boy leaning against the opposite wall. Several youngsters are writing in notebooks or on loose sheets of paper. A large, bright yellow wooden tub on wheels, with two children and an oversized stuffed dog crowded into it, is being pushed along the corridor by a highly energetic boy.

The children who are working do not look up as the cart rolls by. No adult is present in the corridor aside from the visitors. From time to time, a child gets up and goes into one of the classrooms to ask some available adult a question; occasionally, a child turns to us for help. One asks, "How do you spell Morison?," the name of the school's principal to whom she is writing a letter. Presently, a teacher comes out of a classroom and offers the four kindergarten girls a few more illustrated magazines. The girls speak English to their teacher, and converse quietly in Spanish together.

The institutional tile walls of the corridor are covered with a variety of art work and posters. Any child who wants to can tape up his work.

Open Corridors=Open Minds. *At Manhattan's P.S. 84, the kids can gambol in the corridors during classes under an experiment that is freeing both pupil and teacher from regimentation—and attracting interest across the country.*

It is not long past Halloween and a group of highly individualistic jack-o'-lanterns leer down. A poster, one of many, provides the following information: "We guessed how much our pumpkin would weigh. Risa thought it weighed 21 pounds. She weighed it and it weighed 20 pounds. After we took out the seeds and pulp, it weighed 16 pounds." In the corridor we are nearly surrounded by words, words of songs, poems, stories, announcements, news items —all placed at a convenient height for children to read.

A third-grade classroom opens off the corridor. At first our eyes are assailed by the apparent chaos of the scene—a profusion of movement, sounds, colors, shapes. Gradually, however, the organization of the class reveals itself. The room is perhaps a little smaller than is standard and has a class register of 30 children, a few of whom are in the corridor or visiting other classes. What is most striking is that there are no desks for pupils or teachers. Instead, the room is arranged as a workshop.

Carelessly draped over the seat, arm and back of a big old easy chair are three children, each reading to himself. Several other children nearby sprawl comfortably on a covered mattress on the floor, rehearsing a song they have written and copied neatly into a song folio.

One grouping of tables is a science area with equipment ranging from magnets, mirrors, a prism, magnifying glasses, a microscope, a kaleidoscope, batteries, wires, an electric bell, to various natural objects (shells, seeds, feathers, bones and a bird's nest). Also on nearby shelves are a cage with gerbils, a turtle tank and plants grown by the children. Several other tables placed together and surrounded by chairs hold a great variety of math materials such as shaped blocks known as "geo blocks," combination locks and Cuisenaire rods, rulers and graph paper. A separate balance table contains four scales.

THE teacher sits down at a small, round table for a few minutes with two boys, and they work together on vocabulary with word cards; her paraprofessional assistant is at the blackboard with several children who are writing. A student teacher (available in the mornings only) praises a

drawing a girl has brought over to show her; other children display their work to the visitors with obvious pride.

Children move in and out of the classroom constantly. The teacher seems alert to the nuances of all the activity. To a boy trying to explain to a classmate how to construct a rather complex paper fan, she suggests, "As a game, see if you can describe it to her with your hands behind your back." To a child who has produced a collection of ink-blot pictures, she casually introduces the idea of "symmetry." She keeps a record book handy in which she jots notations on each of the children. Seeing a child filling and emptying different sized plastic containers at the sink, she stops for a moment and talks about pints and quarts. Weighing, measuring and graph-making appear to be favorite activities.

In spite of all that is happening— the constant conversation, the singing—the noise level is quite subdued. The children look engaged, bright-eyed, happy. A little boy breaks into an impromptu rock 'n' roll dance;

Photographs by MICHAEL GOLD

Work+Play=Discovery. "Work and play are not opposite but complementary" in the program at P.S. 84, which is modeled after British informal education. Whether the activity is drawing, singing or just rolling a bicycle wheel, there is lots to learn. Moving between classroom and corridor, the teacher encourages each child to make his own discoveries and each can thus develop at his own rate. The approach might help in urban schools with pupils with different achievement levels. (The eye was drawn in a class of the "T.E.S.L." — i.e, "Teacher of English as a Second Language.")

nobody takes any particular notice. Apparently satisfied, he returns to the math area.

In the corridor on the second floor of P.S. 84, a tumbling mat is taken out for the first time this year. Children from classrooms off this hallway line up and take turns: handstands, cartwheels, but mostly somersaults. They are good. One boy does a headstand and holds the pose. After a few moments, the "corridor

66 'People had gotten adjusted to things and I wanted to unadjust them,' says Mrs. Weber, who sold the open-corridor approach. 'The big word in education was control.'99

teacher" begins to count and the children chime in. They get up to 47 before the child stands again and proudly struts to the end of the line.

In a first-grade classroom a prominent sign suggests: "Things to Do. Play at the math table. Paint a picture. Make a book. Play with sand. Use the typewriter. Use the chalk board. Play a reading game. Listen to a record. Read a book. Play checkers." Most of these activities are being sampled. The level of noise and movement, though noticeably higher than in the older third grade, is not overpowering. As in the other class visited, the teacher has a record book in which she makes notes about individual children, such as: "Speaks in monosyllables," "Counts to 15, recognizes number symbols to 8," "Built huge bridge out of blocks—I promised to bring book on bridges."

A box labeled "story starters" contains pictures that are employed to suggest narrative. On a wall is a collection of such stories dictated by the children and copied down by an adult. A Chagall print adorns one wall and beneath it is a story by a child named Rachel:

"This bird is playing in the water. The flying horse is watching it play. The bird is having fun playing in the water. Now the bird is chasing its tail while the flying horse is shaking the weeds. The flying horse is getting closer to the river while the bird is getting dizzier and dizzier. The flying horse is getting closer and closer to the bird near the river. Then the bird

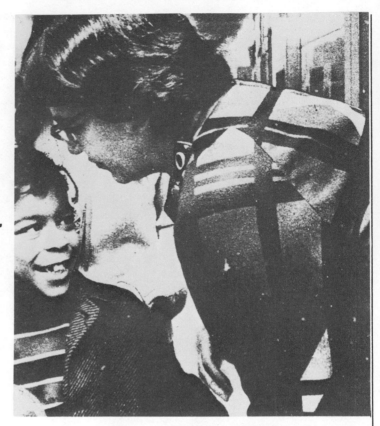

Woman + Mission = Change. *Mrs. Lillian Weber, professor of early childhood education at C.C.N.Y. Her zeal—and her conviction that change was possible—led to the open-corridor program in a number of New York schools.*

sees the flying horse and then the bird paddles away."

DESPITE superficial similarities, informal education is by no means a reincarnation of the progressive schools of 40 or 50 years ago. A major reason for the substantial difference between progressivism and informal education is that far more information is available now than in Dewey's day on the cognitive growth of the child.

The American progressive schools, as the Carnegie report notes, too often were characterized by "anti-intellectualism." Dewey himself attacked progressivism for "casual improvisation and living intellectually hand to mouth" and scored excesses such as "deplorable egotism, cockiness, impertinence and disregard for the rights of others." Whatever progressive education was meant to be, in practice it was frequently weakened by a sentimental view of the child and his mental growth. The bias of progressivism was too

strongly in the direction of the child's doing his own thing—on freedom without an understanding of how children develop and learn.

Informal education, aided by the insights of Jean Piaget and others, seems able in England to provide relative freedom and emotional warmth without sacrificing either a high intellectual level or constructive adult direction. "What chiefly distinguishes the contemporary English informal schools...from the American child-centered progressive schools of the nineteen-twenties and thirties, which they resemble in many ways," the Carnegie report states, is the "recognition of and indeed insistence on the teacher's central role."

As teachers in Britain frequently point out, lack of formality in their classrooms should not be confused with lack of structure, plan, organization and careful thought. They are firm in their assertion that the teacher's primary responsibility is to create an environment in the school that stimulates learning and to see to it that the environment is altered and expanded as the needs of each child change and his interests become more complex.

Traditional education with the teacher up-front lecturing and the pupils seated silently in neat rows, apparently conceives of the child's mind as little more than a tape recorder or camera that records what it hears and sees. If the child can deliver back on a test what he has read or been told, he is said to have "learned" the subject matter. But has he? Does he necessarily comprehend the material on a deeper level? Will he retain it for a month or year after the test? Those who believe in informal education answer with a resounding no.

The mind of the child, as described by Piaget, does not make a photographic copy of reality but, employing reason and experience, actively comes to grips with the raw data of the world outside himself and transforms it in the manner of an artist.

According to Piaget, each child— starting at the earliest age — constructs in his mind his own unique model of the world, in an attempt to gain understanding and mastery. This self-created conception is, of course, replete with errors and the child constantly revises it. He does so by testing reality through innumerable direct experiences with people and objects in the environment. Though memory plays a vital part in this process, learning which is based on memory alone is shallow. The child learns most meaningfully by means of his own self-motivated discoveries. In the words of a Chinese proverb quoted in the Carnegie report, "I hear, and I forget; I see, and I remember; I do, and I understand."

Intellectual growth, reports Piaget, proceeds in stages roughly related to age. Each child, painstakingly building his own model of reality, moves through these stages at his own individual pace. Thus, whole-class teaching of a uniform curriculum is at best inefficient, since some will be bored while others are confused.

HOW did so unorthodox a program take root in the arid soil of the New York City educational system?

The answer to that would seem to differ according to whom one talks with—parents, teachers or administrators. Like the proverbial blind men describing the elephant, each of these groups is most aware of those aspects of the process of change which they actively experienced and participated in.

Yet, inevitably, in any conversation with anyone who was involved in the arduous and, provisionally at least, successful process of change at P.S. 84, one name soon comes up. That is Lillian Weber's.

In the foreword to "Crisis in the Classroom," Silberman wrote: "This book, and I, owe much to Professor Lillian Weber of the City College of New York . . . she profoundly influenced the course of my own thinking and hence the shape of this book." Elsewhere in the Carnegie report, Mrs. Weber is referred to as "the most sensitive and best-informed American student of informal education."

A close colleague and admirer of Mrs. Weber describes her as "a little fierce." A district supervisor who has dealt with her calls her "a terror," and a teacher who is still awed after witnessing a confrontation between Mrs. Weber and a principal, says she is "a real tiger."

In her moments of repose Lillian Weber's face appears gentle, her features soft and relaxed. But these tranquil moments are rare, at least in public, for she is a woman engagée, an individual passionately possessed by an idea. It is an idea that sets her apart from many of the most scathing critics of American schools, with whose critiques of traditional education she generally agrees. For she believes fervently that it is possible to bring about substantial educational change within the confines of the public school system.

IN 1963, Mrs. Weber was among a group of British and American educators who met at Vassar College for a three-week summer conference of the British Nursery Association. The Americans who attended were largely educators associated with universities and respected private nursery schools such as Bank Street and the Vassar Demonstration School. The English representatives, headmistresses and teachers, showed an impressive film — about the state-run primary schools.

Such was the parochialism of the American educators in 1963 that they were totally unfamiliar with the fact that momentous changes had been taking place in the British schools.

At that time, Mrs. Weber recalls, American early childhood educators who were concerned with quality education felt that "basically, if you were terribly interested in children's growth and learning, you'd try to go to one of the well-known experimental places or perhaps get a job at an outstanding small and independent private school like Ethical Culture or Walden. But if you went into the system you had no choice or freedom of methodology within public education. You simply had to adjust."

"Now, here were the English and they were showing their film and everyone was nodding and saying, 'Isn't that nice, we're all the same.' Gradually, however, a striking discrepancy in this appraisal, apparently missed by other delegates, impressed itself on Mrs. Weber: if public education in England looked similar to the very best private nursery schools in America, then the English obviously were far ahead of the Americans.

"I said to myself, 'You have to go see.'"

THE British successes were even more impressive than Mrs. Weber had thought at first. For the informal methods depicted in the film were not being used with preschool children but with children in the first few grades of primary school. To an American educator, used to the jarring discontinuity in teaching styles between kindergarten and the first grade, this was a really mind-bending innovation.

In England, the primary grades consist of two divisions: the "infant school" for youngsters 5 to 7 or 8 years old, and the "junior school" for children up to about 12. (The infant schools typically are very small by American standards—200 to 300 pupils.) Traveling through England studying schools in 1965 and 1966, Mrs. Weber discovered that the British were relying on fewer whole-class lessons to teach the three R's than even those American private schools that were considered "progressive." Moreover, not only many infant schools but some junior schools were beginning to adopt the new method. The technique appeared applicable with much older children than Mrs. Weber had imagined — at least in Britain.

She correctly anticipated what has proven to be one of the more persistent American criticisms of informal education: that it cannot work in urban schools with large classes containing a high ratio of poor, intellectually "deprived" children. Her response to such criticism is that she frequently saw the system working in England under just such circumstances.

As a scholar attached to London University while pursuing independent research, Lillian Weber had entree to infant schools everywhere, including those situated in what Mrs. Weber calls "gin-soaked, depraved slums" of London and those with large immigrant populations. In her research, one account by a British educator written in the mid-thirties particularly fascinated her; it contained a description of the poor verbalization of lower class English children. "If you put your finger over the words 'East End of London,' " she says, "you would think it was written about Harlem."

At the time in America, it was widely asserted that the schools could do little for children who, during a brief so-called "critical period" in the preschool years, had not been exposed to intellectual conversation, books and other cultural experiences. Deprived of these in his early years, the argument went, the child was probably doomed to a cycle of disappointment and failure; the reasons for his inability to learn were to be found in the child, not in the school. In England, however, Mrs. Weber said she saw just such children being successfully educated in informal schools.

Classes in the infant schools are frequently as large as 40 children to a room and school buildings often somewhat deteriorated and designed for another type of education altogether. Yet within these classes Mrs. Weber saw British teachers dealing with children as individuals, carefully observing and maintaining records on each child. They were particularly adept at seizing every opportunity for teaching — without pushing the children—and also at using the same material with children in different stages of learning development. However, the British teachers made clear that no material they used was as crucial to their program as simple talk — spontaneous and companionable conversation, storytelling, playacting, communication with interested adults. From such experiences, both reading and writing skills grow

—an insight which clashes sharply with the traditional restrictions on talking in the classroom.

Mrs. Weber insists that the teachers she saw in England were by and large *not* geniuses. Though British classrooms were as distinct from one another as those in most American schools, the use of corridor space brought about "a unity of life" within the walls. "It was the mood of the school that transcended," she says. "I mean a particular teacher might not be so hot, a particular teacher might be inadequate, but if the headmistress was good then the school transcended that, and the life of the child transcended that."

In early 1967, a British parliamentary commission published a lengthy study entitled "Children and Their Primary Schools." This study, named the Plowden Report after the chairman, disclosed that British primary education was undergoing sweeping changes. These changes, which had developed slowly in the infant school over several generations, had accelerated greatly in recent years. The informal approach had been such a success the commission urged that it be extended to still more schools. In a chapter discussing the aims of education, the report described the philosophy of this type of school:

"The school sets out deliberately to devise the right environment for children, to allow them to be themselves and to develop in the way and at the pace appropriate to them. It tries to equalize opportunities and to compensate for handicaps. It lays special stress on individual discovery, on first-hand experience and on opportunities for creative work. It insists that knowledge does not fall into neatly separate compartments and that work and play are not opposite but complementary. A child brought up in such an atmosphere... has some hope of becoming a balanced and mature adult.... Not all primary schools correspond to this picture, but it does represent a general and quickening trend."

Answering critics of informal education, the report noted:

"Some people, while conceding that children are happier under the modern regime and perhaps more versatile, question whether they are being fitted to grapple with the world which they will enter when they leave school. This view... assumes, quite wrongly, that the older virtues,

as they are usually called, of neatness, accuracy, care and perseverance, and the sheer knowledge which is an essential of being educated, will decline.... Society is right to expect that importance will be attached to these virtues in all schools.... What we repudiate is the view that they were automatically fostered by the old kind of elementary education. Patently they were not, for enormous numbers of the products of that education do not possess them."

Professor Vincent Rogers, head of the department of elementary education at the University of Connecticut, told a recent seminar on British primary schools that when he arrived at one English infant school the teacher had announced: "Children, we have a visitor from America today. How much do you estimate he weighs?" Afterwards, Rogers watched the children counting the stones in an old church in an attempt to arrive at the weight of the building and, later, trying to decide how they might discover the number of daisies in a large field. Professor Rogers told the gathering with a wry smile: "You won't find the answers to those questions in the back of the book."

WHEN Mrs. Weber returned to City College in late 1966, she was a woman with a mission: to tell Americans what was being done in England and to "test the possibility" of adapting the British model of informal education to American inner city schools. To help her begin the proselytizing, she had made a film of one informal curriculum in action at a "rather ordinary" infant school in a racially heterogeneous London neighborhood.

She was hardly naïve about the rigidity of the New York City educational establishment, nor unaware that an educational system grows out of cultural and historical factors unique to each nation. "When I say that I came back determined to test the possibility, it was not with ignorance of all the difficulty. It's that I decided that you have to *defy* all the difficulties and that then maybe you'd break through."

Colleagues who saw the film Mrs. Weber was showing wherever and whenever she could warned her that the informal approach would be impossible in New York.

"It was the old story, that you needed gifted teachers, you needed

186

special children, and so on. I thought, 'Is it conceivable that if we can figure out a way to cut down the size of a school and get the teachers to begin to work together that they can begin to function in a somewhat different manner?' Not of course with the fluidity and serenity that you see in England, because you can't do that overnight. I thought, 'Is there a piece of a school I can slice off?'"

Her duties as professor of early childhood education at C.C.N.Y. included supervision of student teachers in nine Manhattan elementary schools. Thus, her job coincided with the personal task she had set for herself. "I wanted to be in a lot of schools, because I was casing the joint to see what the architectural possibilities were," looking for a "little configuration" of classrooms and corridor which might work together as a sub-school of sorts.

At the same time, her contact with the schools as they existed made her more and more impatient. She began to "state the obvious," as she expresses it now, "because people had gotten adjusted to things and I wanted to unadjust them. The whole underground legend was that no matter how you trained teachers, six months out of college and the student adjusts to the system. In the lunchroom, you hear the older teacher telling the beginner: 'Oh, forget what you learned at school. This is reality. This is it.' The big word in education was control.

"My students came to me and said, 'The teacher hit a kid today.' You know, there is rampant hitting in the schools. I guess everyone knows that big kids hit teachers, but do you know that little kids are hit by teachers? Well, one of my students came to me and mentioned casually that she had hit a child." Mrs. Weber, who is never casual, exploded: "I practically split. I said, 'Listen, dear heart, it's not just illegal but you know what? You're going to flunk, because the fact is that I'm going to support the law on this whether the school does or not.'"

AFTER a great deal of talk aimed at "unadjusting" everyone she could buttonhole, Mrs. Weber convinced her colleagues at City College that "we couldn't place even one student in a class where it was possible to see children learn or the teacher relate to an individual child. Everything was a whole-class lesson in

1967. So they said I could try this other [open corridor] thing. And I said, 'It will be a model for the student teachers.'"

As the site for her first limited experiment, Mrs. Weber chose a corridor in Harlem's P.S. 123 — a school affiliated with the college's teacher-training program. With the support of her faculty heads and the district office, she obtained permission from the school's principal to try out her ideas.

In the spring of 1968, after months of preparation, Mrs. Weber and some of her students invited the teachers to send children into the corridor. It was stocked with materials such as a water table, clay, musical instruments and a math table. In addition, a small grant made possible the purchase of special materials selected by the teachers: a workbench, animals, a phonograph for dancing, and an oven. During "corridor time" (one hour, three days a week), groups of children were released from class to visit the hallways or adjacent rooms. By the end of the term, the participating classroom teachers, as well as the student teachers, all agreed that the children had enjoyed and profited from the experience. Moreover, the dire predictions of some that the children would run wild, hurt each other or destroy equipment had never proved accurate.

BUT the learning that took place during the corridor period at 123 (for example, from measuring for shop projects, reading recipes for baking and counting with Cuisenaire rods) was almost incidental; the teachers still relied on their whole-class lessons for instruction in the three R's. What Mrs. Weber needed was a place to try out the open-corridor principle as the sole instructional methods for children in a number of classes. P.S. 84 in Manhattan provided the setting for this experiment.

Currently within the Community School District, P.S. 84 was previously part of one of the city's decentralized demonstration districts. In the first half of 1968, preparations were under way for the election of a governing board. During this seemingly inopportune period of political ferment, Lillian Weber's film came to the attention of a group of parents and teachers at the school.

They heard Mrs. Weber speak. They circulated among themselves an influential series of articles on informal education by Joseph Featherstone in The New Republic. Some of them visited the corridor at P.S. 123 and came away impressed. But whenever anyone tried to talk education, recalls one parent, Hannah Hess, "the community control people would say, 'First you have to get the control. Then you can talk about education.'"

At that time, Jack Isaacs, an assistant superintendent in the district, was director of a state-funded "balanced-classes" project, which was designed to counteract the de facto racial segregation of classes by grouping the children in ways that would reflect the racial balance of the community without respect to academic performance. Some of these untracked classes were in P.S. 84, and Isaacs had come to the conclusion the children could be taught successfully only by means of some individualized technique. Thus, he became a powerful ally of those who were working for innovation in P.S. 84.

A few teachers in the school had already begun on their own to rearrange their classrooms and to teach more informally. Under parental pressure, the principal of the school agreed—reluctantly—to permit a trial of the new approach.

That summer, Isaacs asked Lillian Weber to serve as a consultant at P.S. 84, assuring her that she would be working with "balanced" classes. (She was resolutely opposed to testing the program on any group not representative of an inner-city population.) Four classrooms, two kindergartens and two first grades, were set up along one corridor in the school. The teachers were all volunteers and the children, too, were volunteered for the program by their parents. Some state funds were budgeted for equipment through Isaacs, who became director of the program.

Then in the fall of 1968, came the teachers' strike.

JACK ISAACS, a big, affable man with the rapid-fire delivery of a Borscht-Belt comedian, still groans when he recalls the period. "All the difficulties you read about today in public education applied to that school at the time. The staff was torn apart. The parent group was torn apart. And the principal wasn't much help."

That description would be regarded as kindly understatement by those parents and teachers who favored the open-corridor program and were critical of the principal's handling of it. Isaacs, though, can sympathize to a degree with principals who are faced with a new program that they cannot understand or control.

"The principal would come into the class and she'd say to the teacher that she wants to see a reading lesson. Now, there are four kids sitting on the floor in a corner reading by themselves. The teacher says, 'That's your reading lesson.'

"Or, the principal asks for lesson plans. Weber announces: 'We don't do lesson plans.' Weber intimidated everyone. She's not in the system at all and her ideas are clearly laid out in her own head. She says to the principal, 'This is it. You don't want it?' She'll tell them to forget it, start walking out. The parents who do want the program are then screaming and the principal says, 'Wait. Come back.' So there is this threat to the principal that she is no longer in control of her school." Isaacs is quick to add that P.S. 84 teachers do submit their weekly goals, rather than any tight scheme for the week's activities.

While the strike was in progress, many parents and teachers worked together closely to keep P.S. 84 open, and this joint struggle created a mutual commitment to improving the quality of education at the school. Afterwards, those parents who had long been dissatisfied with the principal escalated their campaign for her removal and in January, 1969, she was transferred to the district office. The woman who was president of Parent-Teacher Association through most of this fight, Jane Mills, summed up the change-over this way: "I think it all came about as a result of cooperation between parents who are interested in education and a group of teachers within the school who are similarly interested, coming at a time when parents and teachers were being listened to more."

THE fledgling open-corridor program survived its first year despite the turmoil of the strike. After an unsuccessful interlude with a second principal, a third was appointed, Sidney H. Morison, a former district math coordinator. Morison, a tall, youthful-looking, modishly attired man with long sideburns and mustache, is hardly the stereotype of the old-fashioned principal.

"I've been to many schools and the atmosphere in most places is dead," he says, "Teachers often don't realize that they have been as oppressed in this educational system as the kids. . . . Their own creativity has been stifled in many different ways. . . . There's a certain feeling of life here at 84 that I didn't find any place else. Along with that there goes a lot of other things; we've had a lot of problems, lot of conflict, lot of turmoil. I'd rather live with that than be in a place where nothing is happening."

In the spring of 1970, three second-grade classes of open-corridor children at P.S. 84 took the Metropolitan Achievement test, which measures vocabulary and reading comprehension. The three classes surpassed the national norm of 2.7, averaging 3.35. Their individual range of reading varied widely from 1.1 to 6.0. But of the 73 children tested, 47 were reading on or above grade level — 24 of these, a year or more above.

Broken down ethnically, the scores show that of 38 black or bilingual (largely Spanish-speaking) children, 17 tested on or above level—six of these, a year or more above. By comparison, of 33 black and bilingual second-graders in classes not in the program, only four were reading on grade.

These initial scores suggest that children in the open corridor will do *at least* as well on reading tests as children in traditional classrooms, if not better. But many of those associated with the open-corridor classes feel strongly that no tests — certainly none presently available—can properly evaluate the gains to the children under the program. Principal Morison notes:

"Children have improved not only in skills but in attitude toward learning, in attitudes toward one another, in development of self-reliance, in many ways. But," he emphasizes, "we are *absolutely* not saying that we're trying to develop a certain social milieu, without the skills. The program is content-oriented as well as child-oriented."

Jacqueline Sanders, a young, black kindergarten teacher in the program, told us that last year 14 of the 25 pupils in her class had learned to read. This year, she is reacting more quickly to the children's interest in reading, and she expects that most of them will be reading to some extent by the end of kindergarten. Each child is able to move ahead with reading and other learning experiences as quickly as he wishes; since these children will all be staying in the program, Miss Sanders is not concerned that knowing how to read will make life in first grade boring.

Parental acceptance of the new program at P.S. 84 appears to be generally good. A number of doubts are voiced persistently and, in an effort to answer them, Hannah Hess, now president of the P.T.A., has prepared a booklet in English and Spanish. A few of the complaints dealt with are: "But Do Children Really Learn if They Don't Sit Down and the Teacher Doesn't Teach?" "But All That Playing—That May Be All Right in Kindergarten, But My Children Can Play at Home. I Send Them to School to Learn," and "What About Discipline?"

The responses to these thorny questions presented by Mrs. Hess, who has two daughters in the program, are clear and direct. She explains that formerly half the children of P.S. 84 left the sixth grade several years behind in reading and math; the open classroom was started to try to "change this high rate of failure." She points out that learning is something a child must do for himself, the teacher "can't *learn* for the child." What looks like or is described as "play" really involves a lot of intellectual activity and learning.

As for discipline, Mrs. Hess points out that the traditional classroom, by setting up standards of silence and immobility that are unnatural for children, actually "creates discipline problems." Under a program that supports children's natural drives, there are "*fewer* discipline problems, and they're less serious." There are rules, "but they're real rules . . . and they create real discipline—self-discipline." For the nervous parent, the *pièce de résistance* of the booklet is the information that: "Last year, 99 per cent of the children who were in an open-corridor class were reading by the time they left the first grade. That *never* has happened before in this school."

PRESENTLY, in New York City, notably in the East Bronx and Brooklyn, many teachers are changing their classroooms on their own to permit an informal approach.

Today more than half of P.S. 84's classroom teachers are officially part of the open-corridor program. Many other teachers at the school, through the sixth grade, are working informally on their own. Eight other schools in District 3 now have open corridors, with a total of 65 teachers officially working under the guidance of Lillian Weber. For some time now, she has been prepared to state flatly that the period of testing is over and has proved that the British model can be adapted for use with American urban children. "There isn't any doubt in my mind," she says. "That doesn't mean there aren't a million obstacles."

Not the least of these obstacles is the lack of preparation of American teachers for an informal setting. Although pleased at the rapid expansion of the program within District 3, Mrs. Weber is concerned that teachers with too thin an understanding of what informal education is all about may feel pressured to join. Initially, any teacher who expressed an interest in the program was accepted; now, Mrs. Weber feels that no teacher should begin to change her classroom until she has had a course on informal methods and has read a good deal about it. (She herself has written a book scheduled for publication soon, "The English Infant School: The Model for Informal Education.")

What one sees at P.S. 84 is both typical and unique compared with other District 3 schools in the program. One of the most important points that can be made about informal education is that just as each teacher and therefore classroom is different, so each corridor is different and each school is different.

P.S. 144, an all-black school in south central Harlem is now in its second year in the program. Mrs. Weber believes that 144 is "far, far ahead" of where 84 was at the same

stage of development. She is particularly impressed by the strong sense of community that has been achieved among the teachers.

At P.S. 75, on the other hand—perhaps because of the newness of the program—we encountered great unevenness in the quality of the teaching. For instance, at P.S. 75, a booklet prepared by the pupils about their visit to the Hall of Science in Flushing Meadow Park contained forms with multiple-choice questions, such as: "We went through the —— Bridge to get there. (George Washington, Triboro, Queensboro.)" Clearly, this heavy-handed attempt to have each child learn from a class trip certain information the teacher wants him to learn is antithetical to the goals of informal education. In one classroom, a half-dozen second-graders attired in costumes and directed by an adult put on a skit with memorized lines. The audience of kindergarteners was enjoined to be "polite," which evidently meant no talking or moving about. One felt the imposition of adult standards of neatness and order. Yet at this same school one saw marvelous life-sized cutouts that children had drawn of themselves. And at least one class in this school was as rich educationally as any classroom we visited.

Mrs. Weber says:

"I recognize that at this point teachers come from a different base of training: they've been grade-oriented, homogeneous-group-oriented, lesson-oriented. . . . By changing the classroom, we create a new situation where the teacher can at least begin to see children. And actually I would say that all of last year this is all we did and with any new teacher this is all we're doing. In addition, most teachers have previously functioned in empty classrooms. They are not oriented to materials. So, in addition to giving them an opportunity to get to know children, we also have to help them to know the world — to see the possibilities in materials."

As for the principals, Mrs. Weber declares that they must somehow get out from under their paperwork, have more contact with children, and do more supervising of teachers beyond checking whether their plan books, desks and bulletin boards are

in good order. "Believe it or not, these principals have had a lot of years of teaching and study and then they're stuck in the schools—patrolling halls, making up schedules and yelling in the lunchroom. They ought to be insulted. Some way or other, one must bring this to their notice, so they get a sense of shock and revolt."

LIKE Lillian Weber, Morison regards the informal method as an educational alternative that can co-exist with traditional teaching. "I would like to support all teachers who are doing a good job. Informal does not automatically mean that it's going to be a good class, and the other way around. We have formal teachers who do good jobs."

A similar view has been expressed by other partisans of informal education, including Silberman, who has observed that "a good formal teacher is to be preferred to a poor informal one. Some children, moreover . . . may require more structure, more teacher-direction, and more specificity of goals than the typical informal classroom provides." Albert Shanker, head of the United Federation of Teachers, has said: "Instead of mandating the open classroom as a replacement for the traditional one, we should provide a choice of classroom styles for both teachers and parents."

Yet Shanker has spoken enthusiastically about the open-corridor program, as have Dr. Ewald Nyquist, New York State Commissioner of Education, and Dr. Harvey B. Scribner, Chancellor of the New York City Schools. The willingness of the educational hierarchy to thus endorse an attempt at profound change is just one sign of the predicament of American education.

"The fundamental trouble today," says Dr. Scribner, "is that for large numbers of students the schools do not appear to work. . . . For every youngster who gains intellectually and psychologically as he passes through our schools, there is another who is pushed out, turned off or scarred as a result of his school experience." ■

April 4, 1971

Education Voucher Plan Is Making Slow Progress

By WILLIAM K. STEVENS

The Federal Government's plan to experiment with "education voucher" systems in a few willing communities — almost given up for dead a few months ago—is now making slow headway in a handful of localities on both sides of the continent.

Under the highly controversial scheme, all parents of elementary school pupils in a given locality would receive public funds with which to "buy" whatever kind and style of education they wanted for their children — at either a public, private or, pending future legal tests, at a parochial school.

The parent would receive the full cost of a year's education in the form of a voucher, to be presented to the school he chooses. The school would then get its operating funds by presenting vouchers to a special educational agency set up at the local level to set standards, and generally administer and regulate the program.

The stated objectives of such a plan are to stimulate the growth of tuition-free "alternative" schools; to provide relief for parents and students who are dissatisfied with their neighborhood public schools but cannot afford any other kind of schooling, and to create a wider range of educational choices for students and parents.

On June 24, the voucher cause hurdled a major obstacle when the California Assembly passed a bill, 47 to 23, authorizing voucher experiments of from five to seven years' duration in no more than four school districts, starting in 1972. Such enabling legislation is required in virtually all states.

Gov. Ronald Reagan supports the California bill, and its chances of passage in the state Senate are considered good.

Feasibility Studies Set

Two of six school districts that have undertaken or plan to undertake feasibility studies of the voucher system, financed by the Federal Office of Economic Opportunity, are situated in California. They are Alum Rock Unified District, which includes territory in both the city of San Jose and surrounding Santa Clara County, and San Francisco.

Alum Rock has, in the words of an O.E.O. official, "tested the water and found it neither too hot nor too cold."

Preliminary surveys there have indicated that a number of "alternative" schools would be established, some of them by teachers now in the public schools, if a voucher system were established.

Further, an opinion survey showed that although many organized interest groups opposed the idea, favorable opinion generally outweighed unfavorable. The survey showed also that many citizens were reserving judgment until they knew more details about precisely how their children would be affected.

Alum Rock is now biding its time, pending passage of the enabling legislation, before drawing up a more detailed "model" of the voucher system and submitting it to more extensive public discussion.

San Francisco's school board voted on June 17 to accept a $53,000 grant from O.E.O. for a preliminary feasibility study. On the other side of the continent, Rockland, Me., has been awaiting such a grant and New Rochelle, N.Y., is expected to receive one about Aug. 1.

2 More Studies Completed

Besides Alum Rock, two other communities have completed preliminary feasibility studies: Gary, Ind., and Seattle.

Interviews with school officials in Seattle indicate the school board, already mired in controversy over its recent decision to begin mandatory busing to achieve school integration this September, is having second and third thoughts about becoming embroiled in arguments over the voucher system as well.

Nonetheless, public hearings on the voucher plan may begin next month. After that, the board is expected to decide whether to continue.

Gary and Seattle, unlike Alum Rock, decided to drop the voucher project upon completion of the initial feasibility study, not so much because of opposition to the plan itself, apparently, but more because of Gary's preoccupation with other problems.

"There wasn't a great deal of sentiment one way or the other on the subject," said Dr. Gordon McAndrew, president of the Gary school board. "O.E.O. wanted us to go ahead with a second phase development of a detailed voucher 'model,' but I had kind of a gut feeling we should call it at this point. I was convinced it was feasible, but in the present context of Gary it wouldn't go over."

Interviews in most of the communities where feasibility studies have been undertaken, or will be, indicate that none are about to plunge headlong into a voucher experiment. For the most part, they are simply keeping open minds for now.

Major political battles almost surely lie ahead in any community that decides to proceed. Beyond that, O.E.O. officials foresee a strong possibility that any voucher system would be attacked in the courts on constitutional grounds, because it would provide aid to students attending parochial schools.

The Supreme Court declared on Monday that direct aid to parochial schools was unconstitutional. But backers of the voucher plan have contended from the beginning that "indirect" aid, such a sthe "scholarships" provided under a voucher system, is constitutional.

More threatening for the voucher scheme, its proponents believe, is the Court's prohibition this week against "excessive entanglement between government and religion." They point out that under the voucher plan, a local educational voucher agency, would be able to prohibit the use of voucher funds for religious instruction.

"One would guess that this is still an issue the courts are going to have to decide," Dr. Thomas K. Glennan, the O.E.O.

research director, said yesterday.

Whatever the outcome of the parochial aid issue, many other types of schools apparently would be legally eligible to receive voucher money. And Dr. Glennan says he is "optimistic that within the next two or three years, a voucher system will be tried."

Opposition Developed

Originally, O.E.O. had hoped to have at least one experimental voucher system in operation by this September. But immediately after the agency announced in June, 1970, that it planned to try such an experiment, vigorous opposition developed.

Opponents of the plan charged, among other things, that it would damage the public schools; promote "educational hucksterism," and violate the principle of church-state separation.

So intense was the opposition, particularly from teachers' groups, that the project was said to be on the verge of extinction last fall. One national news magazine reported that it had been scuttled.

But as the opposition's first thrusts died, O.E.O. decided to stick by its original commitment, and the first feasibility study grants were awarded to Alum Rock and Gary last January.

Government Would Pay

Under the O.E.O. plan, the Federal Government would pay for the cost of vouchers tendered to private or parochial schools. The state treasury would reimburse vouchers presented to state-owned schools.

The plan would require that no vouchers be used to maintain racial segregation; that private schools participating in the scheme could not charge tuition above the value of the voucher (which likely would match the local per-pupil expenditure for public schools); and that no voucher funds could be used for religious instruction.

Further, the plan would require that all schools provide, well in advance of registration, full, complete and verified information as to their programs and operations, so that parents could make informed choices.

July 2, 197

190

Learning-Plan Test Is Called a Failure

By JACK ROSENTHAL
Special to The New York Times

WASHINGTON, Jan. 31 — The Office of Economic Opportunity pronounced a reluctant but blunt judgment of failure today on performance contracting—the use in public schools of private concerns, teaching machines and incentive payments in an effort to conquer slow learning by poor children.

The verdict derived from a massive, year-long test of variations of the widely heralded contracting approach at 18 sites, including the Bronx.

Performance contracting held out such promise that last year it was tried by 54 school districts in 24 states. The experiment was designed and financed by the O.E.O., the Federal antipoverty agency, as a comprehensive guide to the nation's schools.

The O.E.O.'s conclusions are thus likely to have wide impact and to strike a possibly fatal blow to enthusiasm for the contracting approach.

Fearing such a result, several of the private contractors in the experiment challenged the O.E.O. findings today as too hasty or incomplete.

O.E.O. officials expressed disappointment today, even sadness, at their findings. "We wanted it to work as much as any one, knowing that we will have no solutions to teaching poor kids better," Thomas K. Glennan Jr., O.E.O.'s research director, said.

"But there is a great value also in learning which basket we should not be putting our eggs in," he continued. "Better to stop now, rather than wait until hopes—and spending—have become enormously inflated."

There have been earlier, more tentative indications that contracting did not accelerate achievement among the disadvantaged. But because of the extremely detailed and varied nature of its experiment, O.E.O.'s assessment is regarded as decisive.

As expressed today in a written report and a press briefing, that assessment was blunt. Is performance contracting more effective than traditional classroom methods?

"The answer," the O.E.O. report said, "is No."

Private concerns can provide needed educational services, the O.E.O. report said. They should continue to play an important part in developing and marketing educational materials.

But, the report concluded: "There is no evidence to support a massive move to utilize performance contracting for remedial education in the nation's schools. School districts should be skeptical of extravagant claims for the concept."

Six Companies Involved

The experiment was conducted during the 1970-71 school year. It involved six private concerns working at three sites each. They contracted to bring about larger gains than the half-a-grade annual advance common among disadvantaged children.

About 13,000 children in Grades 1 to 3 and 7 to 9 were involved directly. They received about two hours a day in special reading and mathematics instruction. Another 10,000 children outside the experiment were used for comparison.

The O.E.O. found that overall, there was essentially no difference between the two groups of children.

In reading, for example, experimental children did slightly better in some grades. In other grades, they did slightly worse.

While some contractors had hoped for gains exceeding a full grade per year, the largest difference shown was one-tenth of a grade over the comparison group.

Another measure showed that of 212 classes in the experiment, slightly better achievement than in the comparison group occurred in 31, slightly worse in 54 and identical achievement occurred in 127.

Conclusion Is 'No Gain'

Seeking some measure of success, the O.E.O. analyzed the results in a variety of ways. But it found the general conclusion of "No gain" applicable regardless of the particular form of contracting and regardless of whether the children were better or worse pupils.

Children in smaller school districts and children in the South did slightly better than the others. But this difference, Mr. Glennan said today, is barely significant statistically, let alone educationally.

Thus the results in large Northern sites such as the Bronx, Philadelphia and Seattle were at the bottom, but none of the results were very far ahead.

The O.E.O. conclusions will affect the private contractors financially. Applying the incentive philosophy to their own efforts, they had agreed to payment according to performance —the greater student achievement, the greater their payment.

Now, the O.E.O. is embroiled in negotiations over the amounts of final payments. Some contractors are insisting that allowances be made for class interruptions such as fire drills and assemblies and for class periods shorter than an hour.

Only one of the six contractors has settled so far, for 78 per cent of the possible maximum payment. If the O.E.O. were to pay maximums to all, the total cost of the experiment would reach $7.2-million.

One contractor, Alpha Learning Systems, Albuquerque, N. M. said today that it feared the O.E.O. results were inaccurate and complained that it had not yet been given the O.E.O. data. In addition, a spokesman said, the O.E.O. failed to consider such beneficial side effects as increased attendance and decreased vandalism.

Behavioral Research Laboratories of New York City said that it still was certain that "a performance contract properly done can be a great asset to American education."

February 1, 1972

Gary, Ind., Ends Pact With Concern Running School

GARY, Ind., Dec. 14 (AP)—An experimental program in which a Palo Alto, Calif., company operated a Gary elementary school has been discontinued because it was not working, school officials said.

Behavioral Research Laboratories had a three-year contract through next June to operate Banneker Elementary School in Gary's inner city. A fourth year was included in the contract for a study of the program.

The Gary School board voted 4 to 0 Tuesday night to terminate the agreement effective Dec. 31.

Frederick C. Ford, a board member, said the experiment was "to see if the incentive of business would improve education and if you do a good job you get a raise and if you don't you get canned."

"Well," he added, "they're getting canned."

Dr. Allen Calvin, chairman of the board of Behavioral Research Laboratories, said he knew of no criticism that the program was not working.

"We anticipated in the contract turning the program back over to the school system, and we're just doing it a few months early," he said. "We see this as a natural evolution of what was planned from the beginning; and, from our point of view, we're very satisfied."

When the $630,000 yearly contract was awarded, it was reported to be the first in the nation where operation of a public school was turned over completely to a private company.

School officials said they would continue to use the lessons learned, including continuation of individualized instruction and ungraded classes, use of aides and use of the research laboratory's materials.

The first-year tests, after the program started in 1970, were encouraging, the Gary school superintendent, Dr. Gordon L. McAndrew, said. During the second year, tests were delayed and inconclusive, he said.

The school administration later conducted tests in connection with other schools in the city and found Banneker lowest of about 33 elementary schools in the system, the same as two years ago.

December 15, 1972

5 Oyster Bay Boys Pledge to Stick It Out All Term

Long-Haired Students Isolated

By RONALD MAIORANA
Special to The New York Times

OYSTER BAY, L. I., Sept. 9 —Five high school boys here who have been described by their principal as "apparitions" have been barred from regular classes because of their long hair.

The students ended their first week of school today assigned to a previously unoccupied floor of the four-story, red brick high school building.

During school hours they have been kept out of sight of and out of communication with the student body of about 1,200, one of them said. Since the start of school Wednesday, they have studied assignments given to them by their regular teachers under the surveillance of a specially assigned teacher.

Three of the five youths agreed today that they were prepared to spend the entire term away from the student body "to defend the principle that we are individuals and entitled to our rights."

"This is a rash injustice." George Scott, 16 years old, said. "The only way we can get out of what the other students are calling the 'zoo' is to get our hair cut. We are being persecuted because our hair is long."

An Educational Matter

Young Scott was one of 12 youths assigned to the special class on Wednesday by the principal, Richard E. Nodell.

Mr. Nodell said today that the youths had been told that they could return to their regular classes if they cut their hair. Seven of the 12 did so.

"It's a little educational matter," the principal explained. "We don't forbid long hair unless it is excessive and poor in appearance.

"They are in violation of a student code, majority rule, that deals with appearance. These kids aren't rebels. They have minds of their own. But they can't be different to the point where they disrupt the education of other children in the school."

Mr. Nodell said that letters explaining the school's position had been sent to parents of the youngsters involved.

"Your son is one of a very few students who have chosen to ignore a personal appearance code . . ." the letter started out.

The letter listed three findings by educators in Oyster Bay that were said to warrant barring offenders from class: first, that the wearing of long hair is "upsetting the morale" of other students; second, it is "distracting" other students;

The New York Times

From the left: Todd Nardin, 13 years old, George Scott, 16, and Edward Yberg, also 16

and, last, that teachers "feel their teaching is adversely affected in the presence of these apparitions."

Young Scott, who has long brown hair, parted on one side, and blue eyes, was interviewed a short distance from the school, which is situated in a residential section of one-family homes.

"Look at this," he declared, dropping his school books to a cement stoop. He held aloft a plastic water container that was empty.

"They won't even give us water," he said. "They keep us up there all day long, away from everybody and everything, and let us out just once, to go to the lavatory. I was thinking of becoming a teacher before this, but that is out now."

Two of his classmates in what Mr. Nodell described as a "special study situation"

came by also carrying water canteens.

Edward Yberg, 16, with blond hair in long bangs and a gold earring in his pierced right ear, said: "We are ready to pay the price for the way we look. This is a matter of principle."

Todd Nardin, 13, with longest hair of the three, said that "it is unfair to deprive us of an education because of our hair."

All asserted that their parents agreed with them and had told them to decide for themselves the wisest course of action.

The mother of a fourth youth in the special class, Mrs. Morton Sugarman, said that her son, Robert, "has every right as an individual to wear his hair as he sees fit."

"I think that what they are doing to him and the other youngsters is absolutely dis-

graceful," she said. "He is in a penal institution rather than a place of learning."

Support from the Ranks

The fifth student was identified by his classmates as Gary Fitzgerald.

None of the parents planned to bring legal action against the school districts, according to Mrs. Sugarman and the other youngsters.

The students in the high school circulated a petition today calling on the principal to permit the boys to keep their long hair and be returned to regular classes.

John Hawley, a 17-year-old senior, summed up the position of the students this way:

"We figure it's up to them," he said. "If they want to wear their hair long, that's their business. Personally I don't like it."

September 10, 1966

192

High Court Upholds A Student Protest

By FRED P. GRAHAM
Special to The New York Times

WASHINGTON, Feb. 24—The Supreme Court ruled today that public school officials may not interfere with students' rights to express political opinions in a nondisruptive way during school hours.

In a 7-to-2 decision, the Court held that school officials in Des Moines, Iowa, had violated the First Amendment rights of three children, 13 to 16 years of age, when they suspended them for wearing black armbands to protest the Vietnam war.

The ruling provoked a heated dissent from Justice Hugo L. Black, who insisted that it would encourage students to demonstrate and would embroil the Supreme Court in public school affairs.

Justice Abe Fortas emphasized in the Court's opinion that school children's free speech rights are limited to conduct that does not disrupt discipline or interfere with the rights of others.

He also said that their rights included only political expression, and that the Federal courts would not become involved in disputes over the permissible length of students' hair or skirts.

But he noted that some students in Des Moines had been permitted to wear political campaign buttons, and some had worn the Iron Cross. The school principals ruled out only the armbands protesting the Vietnam war. Justice Fortas saw this as an attempt to suppress expressions of opposition to the war.

"In our system, students may not be regarded as closed-circuit recipients of only that which the state chooses to communicate," he said. "In the absence of specific showing of constitutionally valid reasons to regulate their speech, students are entitled to freedom of expression of their views."

The Supreme Court declared as early as 1943 that schoolchildren have First Amendment rights, when it struck down a West Virginia law that required students to salute the flag, even if they had religious scruples against it. Lower Federal courts have extended this to safeguard the rights of students to wear political or civil rights insignia.

However, today's ruling marked the Supreme Court's first ruling on the question of free speech rights, and Justice Fortas emphasized that the decision related only to "symbolic speech" or speech itself, and not to protest demonstrations.

He said that the courts should consider if curbs school officials imposed on students' political expression were reasonable in the light of the probability of disruption, and

should enjoin unreasonable restrictions.

Despite efforts by Justice Fortas to confine the ruling to narrow limits, it may make it more difficult for public schools to censor student publications or to purge school libraries or curriculums of "objectionable" material. Principals and deans may also encounter legal difficulty when they attempt to discipline student protesters.

Justice Black insisted that after today's ruling many students "will be ready, able, and willing to defy their teachers on practically all orders."

"This is the more unfortunate for the schools," he said. "since groups of students all over the land are already running loose, conducting break-ins, sit-ins, lie-ins and smash-ins."

He objected that young persons are currently too prone to try to teach their elders rather than to learn from them, and that today's ruling would make the situation worse. Moreover, he said, the Court's "reasonableness" standard would put the Federal judiciary in the position of second-guessing actions of school officials without clear standards to guide either.

Justice John M. Harlan also dissented in a short opinion.

Justice Black, whose dissents have tended to become longer and more acid in recent years, spoke extemporaneously for about 20 minutes this morning.

At one point he used mocking tones to quote from an old opinion with which he dis-

agreed, and he finished by stating that "I want it thoroughly known that I disclaim any sentence, any word, any part of what the Court does today."

Justice Black will observe his 83d birthday next Thursday.

The events leading to today's decision go back to December, 1965, when antiwar groups in Des Moines began to plan the armband protest. The Board of Education voted to prohibit the wearing of armbands.

Seven children defied the rule and wore armbands. Those who refused to remove them were suspended and were permitted to return later without the armbands.

The suit, sponsored by the American Civil Liberties Union, was brought in the names of three of the suspended students: John F. Tinker, then 15; his sister Mary Beth, then 13, and Christopher Eckhardt, 16.

The father of the Tinker children is a Methodist minister employed by the American Friends Service Committee. Young Eckhardt's mother is an officer in the Women's International League for Peace and Freedom.

The United States District Court in Des Moines refused to enjoin the school officials from forbidding the armband protests, and the United States Court of Appeals for the Eighth Circuit affirmed.

Dan Johnsston of Des Moines argued for the children. Allan A. Herrick, also of Des Moines, argued for the school board.

February 25, 1969

High School Unrest Rises, Alarming U.S. Educators

By JOHN HERBERS
Special to The New York Times

WASHINGTON, May 8—Government officials and educators have become deeply concerned about the sharp increases this year in student protests and disruptions in high schools and junior high schools. The unrest has emerged in every region of the country, disrupting schools in suburbs and rural areas as well as in cities.

And officials and professional education groups are expecting, with growing anxiety, an even greater wave of protests in the future.

The extent of the unrest below the college level was disclosed in recent national studies by private and Government sources, in a New York Times check and in interviews with educators and officials.

"Three out of five principals report some form of active protest in their schools," according to a survey conducted this

spring by the National Association of Secondary School Principals. "Many who note no protest as yet add that they expect it in the near future.

"One of the surprises of the survey was the fact that protest is almost as likely to occur in junior high schools as in senior high schools. Among junior high schools, 56 per cent report protest activities."

Robert H. Finch, Secretary of Health, Education and Welfare told a Chamber of Commerce audience here last month that "we must be prepared for much greater disorders in the secondary field" than have been seen in the colleges.

"The high school principal," said an official of the National Education Association, "is replacing the college president as the most embattled American."

Newspapers Studied

Alan F. Westin, director of the Center for Research and Education in American Liberties at Columbia University, has been monitoring 1,800 daily newspapers to determine the extent of disruptions. Dr. Westin is working under contract with the United States Office of Education.

In a four-month period, November through February, he counted 239 "serious episodes" of disorder—strikes, sit-ins, demonstrations, riots or other violence—in high schools. During the same period, 348 high schools in 38 states underwent some form of disruption that was reported in the newspapers studied.

Dr. Westin said in a telephone interview that the disruptions increased threefold from November through February. No detailed count has been made since then, he said, but the disorders have continued to increase. A conservative estimate, he said, is that 2,000 high schools have undergone disruptions from November through today.

A check by correspondents of The New York Times in 15 major cities across the country showed that the majority of high schools in some cities—San Francisco and Chicago, for example—experienced disruptions during the current school year. There has been a high incidence of violence, and police patrols at urban schools have become common.

Racial Conflict

In the large cities, racial conflict and protests are reported to have been the major cause of disruptions and of violence. Englewood High School on the South Side of Chicago, which is predominantly Negro, provides a current example.

Two weeks ago, the white principal, Norman E. Silber, notified a Negro teacher, George Spencer, that he would be dismissed for unsatisfactory performance. This sparked a campaign among blacks to have Mr. Silber dismissed.

On Monday, there was an outbreak of window-breaking and false fire alarms. A group of militants forced their way into Mr. Silber's office, and the police were called. The school was closed.

When Mr. Spencer refused Mr. Silber's order to report to the central personnel office for the public schools, he was arrested and charged with resisting arrest and criminal trespass.

The school was reopened yesterday under police guard, but about 500 students walked out in protest. Mr. Silber was removed by his superiors, and an assistant principal, a Negro, was named to replace him.

Freedom Central Issue

However, most protests outside the major cities, both disruptive and peaceful, appear to have been nonracial. The central issue is the growing effort toward more student freedom and involvement in school policy, according to the surveys.

Dr. Westin classified 361 disruptive cases as follows:

Type of Protest	Number of Incidents	States Involved
Racial	132	27
Political (including Vietnam)	81	21
Against dress regulations	71	25
Against discipline	60	28
For Educational reforms	17	14

The Secondary School Principals survey, compiled by J. Lloyd Trump and Jane Hunt, included all forms of protests and concluded:

"While dress and hair account for more protests than any other single topic, the principals enumerate many other regulations which students oppose. In fact, 82 per cent of the schools have protests against school regulations."

In suburban schools across the country, students have organized protests against everything from the food in the cafeterias to lack of toilet paper in the rest rooms.

A favorite target is the student councils, which in the nineteen-twenties were considered a daring innovation, but are now labeled by the students as meaningless or instruments of the administrators.

Underground newspapers, which have spread from the colleges to the high schools and junior high schools, are considered an important part of the protest movement. Three months ago, Government officials estimated there were 500 such papers being published in the secondary schools.

Underground Newspapers

Douglas W. Hunt, director of administrative services for the National Association of Secondary School Principals, said the number was now "probably closer to 1,000."

B. Frank Brown, director of informational services for I/D/E/A, an educational research organization affiliated with the Charles F. Kettering Foundation, said in a speech to the Education Writers Association last February:

"The current wave of organized high school revolt has its origin in a position paper prepared by a Los Angeles high school student for the Students for a Democratic Society in 1965. This paper, entitled 'High School Reform,' was circulated in mimeographed form for a couple of years and published for wider distribution by the S.D.S. in 1967."

"The purpose of the position paper was to inform high school students on the best techniques for taking over a high school," he said. Part of the strategy was the establishment of an underground paper.

"If the underground paper is indeed a prelude to more militant activity as inferred by the S.D.S. pamphlet," Mr. Brown said, "then the high schools of our country had best prepare for an excruciating era."

Most educators, however, attribute the protests mostly to changes in the society and the fact that teen-agers no longer automatically respect conventional values.

"In my view," said Dr. Westin, "it is a more decentralized and localized kind of thing. I haven't found any indication of a conspiracy, no blueprint. There is a common pattern, but this is more a cultural phenomenon."

School disruptions have occurred in such unlikely places as Edcouch, Tex., population 2,800, and Billings, Mont., 55,000, according to Dr. Westin's findings. Part of the trouble, he said, is that the public school system has been one of the last basic institutions to adapt to changes in the society.

Efforts to prepare school administrators for continued protests are encountering some difficulty. The National Association of Secondary School Principals prepared a 22-minute filmstrip on the subject for showing to parents and administrators.

It showed, among other things, teen-agers explaining the protest point of view, and it carried the voice of Thomas E. Hayden, the S.D.S. leader, presenting the view "of an increasing number of students."

The filmstrip was shown at a recent convention of the association. Principals from the large cities, a spokesman said, found it to be rather mild, but it created a furor among some of the principals from suburban and rural areas.

One reason for Mr. Finch's concern about the high school disorders is a belief among Federal officials that there is little the Government can do about the situation or even to collect meaningful intelligence about the scope of the trouble. There are 20,000 public school districts in the nation with 45 million students enrolled.

The Times check showed that much of the racial trouble in the city schools was occurring in those that had been fully integrated—a reflection of the increased tension between black and white adults.

In Pittsburgh, a spokesman for the Board of Education said the most difficulty had been in the schools with "the kind of racial balance we are striving for throughout the city."

"Appalling racial tensions have set black students against whites and whites against blacks," said Bernard McCormick, the Pittsburgh school superintendent. "I blame racial tensions that exist in our neighborhoods and are poisoning our city. Students bring into schools attitudes and hostilities that are bred in their homes and neighborhoods."

City Issues Behavior Code For High School Students

By LEONARD BUDER

A new policy statement that details the rights and responsibilities of the city's 275,000 high school students and declares that "no student has the right to interfere with the education of his fellow students" has been approved by the Board of Education.

The new policy, intended to "establish a new trust" among students "based on self-respect and respect for others," will take effect in September when the city's 91 academic and vocational high schools reopen.

The statement defines the personal and political freedoms of students in senior high schools and acknowledges their right of peaceful dissent and a voice in school matters that concern them.

It provides for the establishment in each school of a "representative student government" by balloting in which every student would be eligible to vote and the formation of a parent-student-faculty consultative council to work closely with the principal.

Dress and 'Badges'

It also recognizes that students have, within certain limits, the right to determine their own dress, to wear buttons, armbands and "other badges of symbolic expression" and to distribute leaflets and other literature on school property at specified times and locations.

In the past there has been no comprehensive citywide policy on students' rights, and principals have had the primary authority in such matters

Board officials expressed hope that the new policy would "de-fuse" the student unrest and dissatisfaction that have been growing in recent years and would redirect student action into constructive channels.

A directive detailing the new policy will be issued within the next few days by Irving Anker, the Acting Superintendent of Schools. Copies of the circular will be sent to each high-school principal at his summer address and at his school.

Mr. Anker said yesterday that it was "rather unusual" to send circulars to principals during their summer vacation, but said he did not want to make them wait two months for the information.

The statement was a revision of one informally approved last fall by the Board of Education but never implemented. The original version provoked considerable controversy.

Some students an organizations had charged that the earlier statement did not go far enough, but principals asserted it went too far and would undermine school authority and discipline.

Two public hearings held by the board were disrupted and cut short by outbursts from militant students.

The chief author of both versions was Dr. Seymour P. Lachman, the Brooklyn member of the board who is on leave as a dean of Kingsborough Community College in Brooklyn.

Dr. Lachman said yesterday that the revised statement was more explicit and, in some instances, went beyond the previous version in detailing the rights of students. But the new document also placed greater emphasis on the responsibilities of students, he said.

Literature Rights

The new policy declares that students should be allowed to distribute political leaflets, newspapers and other literature "on school property at specified locations and times designated." The earlier version had required students to obtain "prior authorization" before they could distribute such materials.

However, the board said that the principal and the student government should establish guidelines "governing the time and place of distribution" and providing "sanctions against those who do not adhere to prescribed procedures."

The present statement contains a new section that begins, "Rights also entail responsibilities," and an appended explanation that says the new policy does not "diminish the legal authority of the school officials and of the Board of Education to deal with disruptive students."

Dr. Lachman said that in formulating the new policy the board considered a wide range of views, including those of principals and students, during the last year.

Ordinarily, board policy resolutions must be officially acted upon at a public meeting. But some members were of the opinion that a public meeting might be used, in this instance, as another occasion for disruptive.

Administrative Act

With the concurrence of Mr. Anker, who worked closely with the board in drawing up the document, the decision was made to implement the new policy by means of an administrative circular, which the Superintendent has the authority to issue. This, in effect, makes the new policy an administrative act of the Superintendent, rather than a ruling of the board.

High schools have long had student governments or G.O. (General Organization) Councils, but these have come under mounting criticism by students as being meaningless and often unrepresentative bodies. In some schools students must pay G.O. dues to be eligible to vote in student government elections.

July 8, 1970

Road to 1984?

COMPULSORY MIS-EDUCATION. By Paul Goodman. 189 pp. New York: Horizon Press. $3.95.

By JOHN KEATS

"WE already have too much formal schooling," Paul Goodman writes, "and under present conditions, the more we get the less education we get." From this different point of view, he goes on to say that "there is no right education except growing up into a worthwhile world. Indeed, our excessive concern with the problems of education at present simply means that the grownups do not have such a world. A decent education aims at, prepares for, a more worthwhile future, with a different community spirit, different occupations, and more real utility, than attaining status and salary."

Instead of serving such ends, he says that our vast public educational systems, from primary grades through graduate schools, principally produce manipulated little conformists; that they are maintained at public expense primarily for the exclusive private benefit of faceless corporations. His thesis is that we do not have better schools that help to produce better communities, but that ours is a sick society full of spurious values that has produced sick schools that compound the social ills by catering to false values.

He sees the academic Establishment as having a vested interest in its own aggrandizement, run by "administrators, professors, academic sociologists and licensees with diplomas" who "have proliferated into an invested intellectual class worse than anything since the time of Henry the Eighth."

IN his passionate new book, "Compulsory Mis-Education," Mr. Goodman says it is wrong to say our schools are geared to middle-class values: "Some of the most important strengths that have historically belonged to the middle class are flouted by the schools: independence, initiative, scrupulous honesty, earnestness, utility, respect for thorough scholarship. Rather than *bourgeois*, our schools have become *petit bourgeois*, bureaucratic, time-serving, grade-grind-practical, timid, and *nouveau riche* climbing. In the upper grades and colleges, they often exude a cynicism that belongs to rotten aristocrats."

In such a case, he argues, "long schooling is not only inept, it is psychologically, politically and professionally damaging," and he can hardly blame students for dropping out of it. Indeed, he doubts whether, under present circumstances, "going to school is the best use for the time of life of the majority of youth," and in any event he believes "very many of the youth, both poor and middle-class, might be better off if the system did not exist, even if they then had no formal schooling at all."

Such thoughts lead the author to offer startling suggestions. One, that makes more sense in context than it might seem to make here, is to give school funds directly to high-school students for "purposeful travel" instead of handing it to educators who fail to teach much worth learning. "We should be experimenting with different kinds of schools, no school at all, the real city as school, farm schools, practical apprenticeships, guided travel, work camps, little theaters and local newspapers, community service," he says.

Schools

FACING a confusing future of automated technology, excessive urbanization, and entirely new patterns of work and leisure, the best educational brains ought to be devoting themselves to devising *various* means of educating * * *. We should be experimenting with different kinds of school, no school at all, the real city as school, farm schools, practical apprenticeships, guided travel, work camps, little theaters and local newspapers, community service. Probably more than anything, we need a community, and community spirit, in which many adults who know something, and not only professional teachers, will pay attention to the young.—"*Compulsory Mis-Education.*"

Mr. Goodman suffers no delusions that his suggestions will be immediately embraced. "My purpose," he says, "is to get people at least to begin to think in another direction, to look for an organization of education less wasteful of human resources and social wealth than what we have. . . . I do not think we will change along these lines. Who is for it? The suburbs must think I am joking, I understand so little of status and salary. Negroes will say I am down-grading them. The big corporations like the system as it is, only more so. The labor unions don't want kids doing jobs. And the new major class of school monks has entirely different ideas of social engineering. Nevertheless, in my opinion, the present system . . . is leading straight to 1984."

Mr. Goodman is a lonely humanist, crying in a Philistine market place, where the largest single share of public wealth is devoted to the strategies of overkill, and where another enormous amount is dedicated to putting blinders on the probable victims. He has written an eloquent book that could be read with profit by any parent who actually has his child's welfare at heart—to say nothing of his own.

Mr. Keats has looked at American culture and its products in "The Crack in the Picture Window" and "Insolent Chariots."

September 27, 1964

Scared-Eyed in the Classroom

By ELIOT FREMONT-SMITH

HOW CHILDREN FAIL. By John Holt. 181 pages. Pitman. $4.50.

CERTAIN books, fiction and nonfiction, are acts of recognition. They are also a means for new discoveries about ourselves, what we are, what we really feel and think and do. They force us into profound, if momentary, focus. The experience involves some pain; discovery or insight (a part of learning) is our surmounting of that pain in shock, surprise and awe: we see. This perhaps is what is meant when we say a book is moving: it moves us, almost literally, through pain to recognition. Such books are not all works of art — though the authors manner has everything to do with our willingness to become involved. Nor are they as rare as we suppose. They come in many guises; their subject matter can seem limited or special, even esoteric; the author's tone is often modest. Yet intensity, the excitement of discovery, vibrates off their pages; we are made to see what we think we could have always seen.

"How Children Fail" is such a book. Written from a three-year journal John Holt kept while teaching and observing children in fifth-grade classrooms, it is an eloquent and anguished record of his discovery of what anyone who deals with children has in his heart always known. Mr. Holt's great achievement was to become consciously aware of how children fail in school and how we unknowingly fail our children—of how, specifically, "they fail to develop more than a tiny part of the tremendous capacity for learning, understanding and creating with which they were born and of which they made full use during the first two or three years of their lives."

"Most children in school fail," he writes in his introduction. "For a great many, this failure is avowed and absolute. Close to 40 per cent of those who begin high school drop out before they finish. For college, the figure is one in three.

"Many others fail, in fact, if not in name. They complete their schooling only because we have agreed to push them up through the grades and out of the schools, whether they know anything or not." It is all the more remarkable, then, that the children Mr. Holt observes—and what a leap that apparently is, to perceive children as they actually are, as they really behave—are not "typical" children in public schools, but supposedly bright and privileged children in two of the country's best, most enlightened private schools.

"What really goes on in the classroom?" he asks. "What are these children who fail doing? What goes on in their heads? Why don't they make use of more of their capacity?"

Mr. Holt calls his book "the rough and partial record of a search for answers to these questions." It is much more, for it deals with the most basic elements of learning and the stifling of learning—from the way a baby armed with curiosity and undaunted by repeated mistakes, explores and tries to make sense of the world around him, to the way this curiosity and persistence is subverted in school by fear, boredom and taught confusion, and by an emphasis not on problems and understanding but on producing right answers.

All of this Mr. Holt documents with examples that are so routine and obvious, so much a part of everyday schoolroom life, that one is shocked (as he was) to discover what they mean. He talks about 10-year-olds whose primary response is, "I don't get it" or who use the "mumble strategy," about daydreamers and the scared-eyed children who *must* be right, the "answer-grabbers" and "teacher-pleasers," about the countless unconscious devices children employ, not to learn, but to avoid being wrong and being thought stupid, and to get through somehow an experience that is for most children most of the time unpleasant, threatening and meaningless.

Mr. Holt offers few specific remedies, and on the surface his book is a despairing one. Yet the book itself exemplifies the first and most important, and most difficult, step that must be taken—which is to see and understand what children really do in school, what they really think and feel. This requires considerable courage, for if Mr. Holt is right—and his book has the stirring knell of truth—most of our assumptions about what school is like for children are wrong, dishonest and destructive to intelligence.

"How Children Fail" is a short book. It is full of anger and despair, but it also carries in it the exhilaration of discovery. It is possibly the most penetrating, and probably the most eloquent, book on education to be published in recent years. To anyone who deals with children and cares about children, it cannot be too highly recommended.

July 26, 1965

That They May Become All That They Can Be

COMING OF AGE IN AMERICA. Growth and Acquiescence. By Edgar Z. Friedenberg. 300 pp. New York: Random House. $5.95.

By ROBERT COLES

WE Americans do not simply give birth to children and send them to school for the proper length of time. Many of us ponder almost feverishly the rearing of children and are anything but indifferent to how and what they are taught in school.

In this strong-minded and often brilliant book, Edgar Friedenberg warns that, for all our concern, the hypocrisy and callousness of the market place or the political arena have saturated the schools. It is not easy to read Mr. Friedenberg; he has an unsettling willingness to speak sharply about what he sees, even when to do so is to raise doubts about the cherished values of the American middle-class and the purposes of our system of compulsory public education.

Put briefly, it is his conviction that in large measure the schools of this nation encourage, and if necessary demand, a kind of obedience and compliance from children that may well prepare them for their various "places" in American life—but at the relentlessly exacted price of whatever independence of mind and spirit they may somehow have acquired, or be capable of acquiring. That is, children do not simply learn their letters and numbers at school: they learn to think, feel and act in the manner our society expects; they slowly relinquish their powers of critical observation, their integrity, their inclination to form from what they

Dr. Coles is a psychiatrist who works chiefly with children and young people. He is on the staff of the Harvard University Health Services.

learn their own vision of the world.

To document so broad an indictment the author, professor of sociology at the University of California at Davis, has devised an interesting and sensible experiment. He describes how he constructed a series of incidents that take place in an imaginary high school. For each incident or "problem" he drew up a number of alternative solutions, then presented them to high school students all over the country. For example, the students are asked to choose among profiles of several "candidates" to greet a foreign king visiting their school, having in mind that their choice should reflect the king's expressed desire to meet "spirited" youths, and the school's desire to show the best of its students. Friedenberg offered his subjects a wide range of candidates, from scrubbed, automatically smiling boys and girls, who seem destined for billboard advertisements, to rather moody, sensitive youths extraordinarily intent on heeding the stirrings of their own minds. Again and again the "well-adjusted," genial types were selected over what David Riesman would call the "inner-directed" ones.

For Mr. Friedenberg the moral is clear: a ready grin and an eagerness to fall in with the crowd go a long way in our society, and they start doing so in the schools, where children too often develop fears about their own ideas. Eventually they submit to rote learning and an uncritical acceptance of every regulation, regardless of its good sense or justness.

Not that the book rests simply on an imaginative research design (no small achievement in itself, considering the tired uselessness of so much social science research at present). The author has supplemented his tests' results with long hours of interviews. His shrewd, ironical mind has missed little of the moods in school life: the hard-pressed bitterness of some teachers, often enough envious or resentful of their pupils; the dreary, stultifying atmosphere in so many of our schools (as though it were built into the shape of their bricks); the quality of their nearby surroundings; the character of their institutional life; and finally the means by which not simply good behavior but a kind of narrow-minded conformity are obtained, through rules, through punishment meted out, some of it devious, some of it even devilish.

Several times Mr. Friedenberg shows how "guidance" programs and "counseling" or "treatment" of one sort or another can be used to wring consent and allegiance from children whose "problem" may be a stubborn refusal to stop questioning the conventions of the willful (and perhaps thoughtless) majority. No honest teacher, or for that matter psychiatrist, can ignore this practice. When children are indiscriminately called "sick" or "troubled" instead of accepted as the dissenters they have the right to be, a new refinement in tyranny has been accomplished.

What is to be done, if we intend somehow to preserve our most independent, unorthodox youth, many of them unlikely to be successful in business or the professions, but likely to contribute a good deal to our intellectual and cultural life? In his last chapter the author suggests doing away outright with *compulsory* public education. He recognizes the general value of the public schools in binding together a large and exceedingly diverse population. He would not at all wish to impair what strengths or virtues they possess. On the contrary, he recommends a thorough reform of the teaching profession, so that overworked schoolmasters will be less burdened with insulting, exhausting, enraging bureaucratic details, or less often forced to give police work priority over instructional responsibility. To be blunt as Mr. Friedenberg is: we have tended to look down upon teachers (as against lawyers, doctors and bankers say) and the result is not only a relatively underpaid and demoralized profession but one with perhaps more than its fair share of incompetents or worse.

More controversial is the author's final advice that a new "Federal Education Authority" be established to provide boarding schools for those of the poor who are commonly least able to make a go of it in public schools. Specially planned and staffed, such institutions would compete with our regular schools. In addition, the author recommends "direct payment of fees to private schools," which he envisions attracting students who are "too energetic, creative and original to flourish in the public school and too poor or disadvantaged to attend these [private] schools without subsidy."

THIS book is another in a recent run of books that examine critically the values of our essentially middle-class society and relate them—always despairingly—to the way our children are educated. Paul Goodman's "Compulsory Mis-Education" worked on the same theme, and in a different way so does John Holt's recent "How Children Fail." For that matter even the less radical commentary on education today shares the essentially sociological (and thus potentially optimistic) viewpoint these books take: children—at least a good lot of them—are pictured as coming to the school rather hopeful, imaginative and lively; slowly they become fearful, constricted with anxiety, their eventual "success" measured by adjustment to the school's authority.

The implication in all this—a reasonable one, I think—is that various changes in the schools (and other institutions) would make for more authentic, more spontaneous and generous youth.

There is, however, more that affects human growth and development than the influence of the social order. True

enough, for a number of years we heard so much about the mind in its depths that one might have thought we all grew up in a vacuum, or in a social environment never explored, never seen in its pervasive ability to affect not only our daydreams but our nightmares. Yet one excessive concern does not justify another; and I think Mr. Friedenberg's book weakest in this respect, in its almost unqualified emphasis on the school's power to compel acquiescence. The author largely ignores the complicated interplay of individual psychological growth and its needs for social organization

Though Mr. Friedenberg acknowledges his admiration for Erik Erikson, he might well have drawn more heavily on his extraordinary work, and for that matter, the excellent psychoanalytic literature on youth and adolescence—the writings of August Aichorn ("Wayward Youth"), Peter Blos ("On Adolescence") and Anna Freud (in a number of books and periodicals that deal with child development in the family). There are, after all, thousands of American youth whose lives, past and present, put into question some of Mr. Friedenberg's fears, or those of Paul Goodman.

In the Peace Corps, in the civil-rights movement, in the Appalachian volunteers, in the social service organizations that have proliferated on American campuses, thousands of students are showing a remarkable degree of dedication and idealism. I have been working with many of them for years now, and the fact is that these youths have come overwhelmingly from our middle class, and have attended our public schools. In instance after instance they have described their schools as very much like those described in this book. Beyond that, they have described their own past boredom, insensibility, eagerness to go along with this or that crowd. Some of them might well have answered Mr. Friedenberg's questions in ways hardly pleasing to him or me—once.

Seized by a historical moment, moved by the appearance of concrete possibilities for action, these young men and women

have done us all proud, regardless of what their teachers or parents—and for that matter, they themselves, upon occasion in the past—did or did not do. Life in this nation is simply not as grim and empty as some critics insist. And human beings are very complicated and very unpredictable. The schools are but one part of life. Any critic of the schools must somehow account for the large number of young people who do conform to admittedly shameful trends in our classrooms and go on to live genuinely kind, useful and thoroughly imaginative lives.

As Erikson and others have shown so clearly, growing children go through developmental stages of acquiescence, times of fierce orthodoxy and of desperate, apparently senseless disobedience or moody rebelliousness—and all this quite possibly in the face of the most solicitous, compassionate and sensitive parents and teachers. No society can be fairly judged by turning every riot of its youth, every scrap of silliness on its campuses, every evidence of conformity in its children into an apocalyptic vision of its decay. Put differently, the character of our institutions simply does not explain or account for all of the possibilities in our people, or for their deeds either.

Precisely what in life makes for excellence and compassion in people? The lives of our heroes, of great philosophers, writers or artists—or the lives of "ordinary" men of virtue and kindness—filled as they often are with hurt, confusion and tension, trailing histories of "bad" parents, or "poor" teachers, or even no teachers, offer us only the awesome truth of the paradoxes they exemplify.

Edgar Friedenberg is also concerned that we see the fatal consequences to our children of our various public sins. At times he has strained too hard; nevertheless, his intention is that the hearts of more youths be sustained. One can only hope that such a spirited voice—in many ways so very angrily, fervently, and morally American—will be heard over the land.

Freedom to Grow

SUMMERHILL: A Radical Approach to Child Rearing. By A. S. Neill. With a Foreword by Erich Fromm. 392 pp. New York: Hart Publishing Company. Paper, $1.95.

By GEORGE DENNISON

IN "Summerhill" A. S. Neill describes the theory and practice of the school called Summerhill, which he founded 45 years ago in Leiston, England, and which is still under his guidance. The book was first printed in the United States in 1960. In England, where it appeared two years later, there was no subsequent paperback edition. But in the United States the paperback, printed in April, 1964, is among the best-selling books in a great many stores. American interest is further reflected in the fact that a number of schools have been founded here modeled to a greater or lesser extent on Summerhill. There are at least six in New York State alone.

Neill is not an educational theorist. His primary concern is with communal relations, and his observations in "Summerhill" are the fruits of a personally conducted experiment, or "demonstration," as he prefers to call it. In his rural school, about 100 miles from London, classes are held and subjects are taught, but formalized learning comprises only one part of the children's experience—and, like other parts, is subject to their own wishes. They are the free citizens of the community.

Self-regulation is the key principle that underlies all activity at Summerhill. The young are not compelled. The bearing of this practice on problems of learning can be seen in these words of Neill's: "When we consider a child's natural interest in things, we begin to realize the dangers of both rewards and punishment. Rewards and punishment tend to pressure a child into interest. But true interest is the life force of the whole personality . . . Though one can compel attention, one cannot compel interest."

Indeed, "the life force of the whole personality" is the chief concern of the school communi-

MR. DENNISON is a playwright and poet who has taught in an experimental school.

ty. Neill gives many examples of the dazzling speed with which children learn when they are free to cultivate this force and are permitted to bring it to bear, at their own discretion, upon books, maps, equations, and so forth.

But as the book's subtitle suggests, the author is ultimately concerned with the impact of education on society as a whole. There would be little point to his faith in the innate joyousness and goodness of humankind if he did not believe that the application of that faith was universal. At the same time, Neill admits that Summerhill is like an island, and that he himself can improve the lives only of a relative handful of children. The distinction he makes here is something more than merely modest.

There is a terrible temptation in an experiment of this kind to treat the subjects (in this case the children) as if they were the exemplars of a new world, thus exposing them, perhaps unwittingly, to a subtle and damaging exploitation. Disciples of Neill have been guilty of this practice. It is an inevitable phase in the dissemination of a powerful idea. Neill himself, however, is as much a pragmatist as an idealist and has the kind of rugged worldliness that prevents this short-circuiting of experience. When he speaks of the children of Summerhill, there is no doubt that he has known them as persons. They may prove the value of freedom, but they remain persons, not exemplars.

Neill's message is basically a simple one. Rather, it is simple because it is basic. The premise on which he operates is that coercion breeds fear and fear breeds hate and destruction. The human organism is so constructed as to seek its own good. The two important things adults can give children are freedom and care.

But what is freedom? How do we define this elusive good? It varies from moment to moment; and, since no one possesses it, it is no one's privilege to give. The manner in which this books attempts to define "freedom" is what makes it unique and valuable. First, Neill gives us hundreds of examples drawn from life; and, second, he writes with unflag-

ging personal presence. We hear the voice of the man; we judge his character, and our sense of his character helps us understand abstract concepts that by themselves are impossibly vague.

Neill comes through to us in his writing as a man of great integrity and rectitude, with a passion for justice and an aversion to punishment and violence, with a remarkable sense both of communal pleasures and communal duties. Though he seems a little cantankerous, a little hardheaded, he is gentle in action and absolutely reliable. To these qualities one must add courage, patience and

Copyright © 1964 by Herb Snitzer.
A Summerhill student.

devotion. When such a man speaks to us of the place of sexuality in our daily lives, and of the effects of freedom and self-regulation, he conveys a concrete and trustworthy sense of these things.

This presence of the man in his thought is surely one of the reasons Americans are reading "Summerhill." As a nation we are at present hag-ridden by Experts, and since we are suffering severe crises in communal life, family life and school life, we have been deluged by Expert Opinion on communications, marriage, and education.

The trouble with Experts is not that we cannot figure out what they are saying—we can almost always accomplish that task — but that we can never quite figure out whom they are talking to. (They are notorious for respecting the wishes of their employers.) They are, in fact, inadequate to a crisis, for

in a crisis we desire action above all things. It may very well be that Neill's voice is falling like rain on parched ground.

Although the crises in American life have been a long time growing, there is a strong American tradition and many contemporary voices that have spoken directly to these issues. Our receptivity to A. S. Neill represents the welcoming of a comrade as much as it does attendance upon a leader.

THE movement toward freedom in education passes through Dewey and Whitehead, and that toward self-regulation through Wilhelm Reich and the Gestalt therapists.

Both tendencies have been powerfully synthesized by Paul Goodman in such books as "Growing Up Absurd," "Compulsory Mis-Education," "The Community of Scholars," "People or Personnel." John Holt's recent book, "How Children Fail," has called attention to the damaging conventions of the ordinary classroom. And while American compulsory education has been verging on collapse ever more spectacularly, scientific experimentation (as at Harvard's Center for Cognitive Studies) has quietly —all too quietly—confirmed many of Neill's principles. In several of the public schools of New York grading will be abandoned experimentally in some classes and subjects, and there is currently a movement afoot to introduce solid literature instead of pap into the early grades—as Whitehead recommended many years ago.

Neill's book has appeared, then, under the following circumstances: our public-school system has failed; our most eloquent voices have been urging freedom and true communal values; our cognitive researches have indicated that compulsion, grading, testing, and regimentation are harmful; our parents are desperate and our children bewildered. Obviously a man will be listened to who under these circumstances says, "Start new kinds of schools. Don't coerce the children. Don't test them and grade them. Don't pretend that they are all alike. Have patience, and have faith in the innate powers of life. I have done it myself, and here's how."

October 16, 1966

School was a friendly place

The Lives of Children

*The Story of the First Street School.
By George Dennison.
320 pp. New York:
Random House. $6.95.*

By HERBERT KOHL

"The Lives of Children," to be published next month, is a moving account of a school that worked yet failed to survive, an important contribution to the philosophy of education and a practical handbook on the creation of small neighborhood schools. George Dennison's ideas are not new — he constantly refers to their sources in Wewey, Tolstoy and A. S. Neill. But there is no book I know of that shows so well what a free and humane education can be like, nor is there a more eloquent description of its philosophy.

Dennison manages to achieve these different ends by alternating selections from the diary he kept during the year he taught at the First Street School with discussions of such diverse subjects as freedom, learning theory, the sociology of being an expert, technology and education, and educational research. He ends with a concise handbook on the specifics of creating and financing a small school. For all its apparent complexity the book is not disconnected; the philosophy is constantly illuminated by descriptions of the lives of children and adults (the author included) who are trying to live it.

The First Street School was a small private school on the Lower East Side. It had four teachers (Dennison, his wife Mabel Crystle, Susan Goodman and Gloria Aranoff), 23 students, and no principal or administrators. The school functioned on about $850 per pupil per year, the same as the New York City Board of Education. The extremely low ratio of students to teachers (6-1) could be afforded because there was no expensive and unwieldy bureaucracy eating up more than half the money available.

Staff as well as students lived in the neighborhood of the school, which rented space from a local Y. The kids, black, Puerto Rican, Oriental and white, knew their teachers on the

Mr. Kohl is the author of "36 Children," an account of his experiences in teaching in a public school in Harlem.

streets and in their apartments as well as in school. They all participated in a community which included parents and friends.

The kids in the First Street School were mostly "problem" students. They had what educational experts call "learning" and "behavior" disorders. Translated into ordinary language this means they were suffering from brutal schools and indifferent teachers. Many had been kicked out of the public schools; some were hostile and defiant, others had given up even attempting to read or write. They were demoralized and cynical about adults, especially those in positions of authority.

Dennison describes the visit of some local school bureaucrats, who saw the familiar faces of students who had given them trouble for years and smiled incredulously at the sight of these hopeless kids actually having fun and learning. The officials gave the school no trouble, for as Dennison says, "In their eyes we were one of the Safety Valves of the [school] district, and they didn't want to clog us in any way."

If for school officials the First Street School was a way of taking care of problems they had created and couldn't handle, for the kids involved it was a new way of life, based on respect for them as autonomous individuals. The first and most apparent difference from their life in public school was that the students were not compelled to show up every day. No matter how much freedom exists within a public school, the teacher still must play the role of enforcer of the compulsory attendance laws. Students who don't show up are chased like criminals by truant officers and when they are caught can be sent to prison. There is no way for pupil or teacher to feel free under this pressure. Many of my own problems as a public school teacher developed from the fact that students had to be hounded to attend school for their own safety.

Lack of compulsion is really the essence of free education. Freedom is not a positive attribute that can be isolated from the way people exercise control over their own lives and the lives of others. Rather, as Dennison says, "There is no such thing as 'freedom,' but only the relations between people." He adds: "The idea of freedom to be intelligible must be stated in terms of actions and individuals."

Some people presume to control the lives of others and make decisions for them. This is easier with children than with other adults, and public school in our society is predicated upon compulsion. Students must attend, they must study certain things in a predetermined order, they must

take tests, they must spend their time with the teacher they are assigned to, they must arrange their time as the school insists, they must even accommodate their toilet habits to the convenience and often the whims of their teachers. I have often wondered whether the demands upon schoolchildren are not violations of the Bill of Rights, assuming of course that children are people and have rights.

Not only were the students in the First Street School not compelled to attend, they were not forced to sit through lessons or relate to adults they didn't like. They were free to talk and move about and explore. This doesn't mean they were entirely free to do as they pleased. As Dennison puts it, "freedom is not movement in a vacuum, but motion in a continuum . . . Our concern for freedom is our concern for fulfillment of activities we deem important and of persons we know are unique. To give freedom means to stand out of the way of the formative powers possessed by others."

The staff tried to create an environment that would encourage the students to explore the world and each other. Dennison calls it a "healing environment," where some of the damage done to young children in authoritarian schools can be undone. He believes in children's innate desire to know as much as possible about the world and in the joy they naturally take in learning. Throughout the book, he uses words that hardly ever occur in books about schools, children or educational philosophy — care, concern, justice, patience, forgiveness, acceptance — the components of healthy love.

It is not inconsistent with this love to be demanding, to want students to read and write and listen to you. Under the rhetoric of freedom one often finds adults who don't care, who let children do whatever they want to do no matter whom it damages. The staff of the First Street School brought things they cared about to class and attempted to teach as much as they could. They tried to enrich the environment by bringing in books, tape recorders, records, junk — things to play with and touch and learn from. Yet they didn't force the kids to learn what they wanted them to learn or punish them for saying no to adult demands. The teachers were as natural and open as they hoped their students would become.

At one point Dennison talks about being so frustrated with one of the boys that he grabbed him and spanked the hell out of him. This was not the institutionalized corporal punishment that Jonathan Kozol describes in "Death at an Early Age." It was a personal response to specific actions of an individual child. As Dennison says, "Spanking Stanley made me realize that I couldn't handle him. Not that the spanking was wrong. It was exactly right (and could not be repeated). He is terribly alienated from the

child in himself and is consequently driven by the child's fears. I treated him as a child by spanking him. I had set up relations with the part of him he had rejected."

Many of the students made phenomenal academic gains. Others just began to feel free to learn for themselves rather than for the teacher. The school made sense to all of them. It was familiar, comfortable and welcoming. It's really that simple. School can be a place where it's fun to learn or play or relax or meet people.

Most schools are not comfortable or welcoming They are forbidding and hostile. These public schools survive unchanged while the pressures of

raising money and continually struggling to do one's work take a heavy toll on those like the First Street School, which survived only a year and a half.

"The Lives of Children" is the story of a success and of a failure. Most of the students returned to the public schools or the streets; some retained what they learned. A year or two of humane education is not enough. Though Dennison quit the First Street School after a year, he experienced what is possible in a small authentic situation and proposes that there be many First Street Schools. He knows that "running a primary school — *provided it be small* — is an extremely simple thing. It goes without saying that the

teachers must be competent (which does not necessarily mean passing courses in a teacher's college). Given this *sine qua non*, there is nothing mysterious. The present quagmire of public education is entirely the result of unworkable centralization and the lust for control that permeates every bureaucratic institution.

"In saying this, I do not mean that the work in a free school is easy. On the contrary, teachers find it taxing. But they find it rewarding, too — quite unlike the endless round of frustrations experienced by those at work in the present system."

There is nothing mysterious. All that is left is for us to act. ■

September 14, 1969

Study Calls Public Schools 'Oppressive' and 'Joyless'

Report, Commissioned by the Carnegie Corporation, Finds That Children Receive Inadequate Education

By WILLIAM K. STEVENS

In an unusually outspoken indictment of the nation's public schools, a three-and-a-half-year study commissioned by the Carnegie Corporation has found that most schools not only fail to educate children adequately but also are "oppressive," "grim" and "joyless."

The study report, written by Charles E. Silberman, an editor, author and former college teacher, is the first of its magnitude and prestige to agree with the severest critics of present-day American education. Some educators who have read the report expect that it will have major impact on educational debate in the United States.

The report recommends a radical reordering of the classroom along more informal lines, so that a student would be free to use his own interests as a starting point for education and would no longer be dominated by the teacher.

It contends, among other things, that most schools are

preoccupied with order, control and routine for the sake of routine; that students essentially are subjugated by the schools; that by practicing systematic repression, the schools create many of their own discipline problems; and that they promote docility, passivity and conformity in their students.

Further, the report charges that students in most classes are taught in a uniform manner, without regard to the individual child's understanding of or interest in a subject; and that despite attempts at reform during the late nineteen-fifties and early nineteen-sixties, the curriculum in use is often characterized by "banality" and "triviality."

One result of all this, says the report, "is to destroy students' curiosity along with their ability — more serious, their desire—to think and act for themselves." Thereby, it is charged, the schools deny students sufficient ability to understand modern complexity

and to translate that understanding into action.

"When we began, I thought the severest critics of the schools were overstating things," Mr. Silberman, director of the study, said in an interview. "But now I think they were understating them."

The gloomy picture is relieved, he writes in the Carnegie report, by examples of successful reform scattered across the country. The schools involved are said to encourage the freedom, informality and individuality associated with the "child-centered" progressive schools of the Nineteen Twenties and Nineteen Thirties. But they reportedly avoid the lack of concern with subject matter and intellectual discipline that many believe sent the progressive movement into disrepute.

Hope at 'Informal Schools'

Such "informal" schools, the $300,000 Carnegie study concluded, provide models of what education should be, and at the moment offer the main hope for improvement.

The report asserts that reform within the system is possible, in that most teachers and principals would be receptive to the informal approach if they were given the encouragement and support necessary to master it.

Mr. Silberman is a onetime Columbia University teacher, a senior editor of Fortune magazine, and the author of "Crisis in Black and White," a much-praised 1964 study of race relations, and a later book, "The Myths of Automation."

He also directed a year-long

private study of education for Time Inc.

He was chosen to direct the Carnegie study largely because the Carnegie Corporation "wanted to reach outside the professions of education themselves and because they wanted someone who was already familiar with many of the problems," says Prof. Lawrence Cremin of Columbia University Teachers College, chairman of a 12-man commission of educators and scholars that frequently advised Mr. Silberman. Dr. Cremin advised the Carnegie Corporation on the selection.

The Carnegie study, Mr. Silberman said, was based on a review of existing literature on the subject; extensive interviews and correspondence with contemporary educators and critics; and first-hand investigations in more than 100 schools, by himself and in about 150 more schools by his three-member staff.

Publication Date

Random House will publish the report as a book by Mr. Silberman, entitled "Crisis in the Classroom," on Oct. 12. Advance copies of the 553-page book are now circulating in education circles.

"It is clearly one of the best studies on education that has appeared in the last 20 years," said Dr. John Fischer, president of Columbia Teachers College. The study's findings rest on "quite responsible investigation," Dr. Fischer said.

"I think [Mr. Silberman's] findings are quite accurate," said Dr. John I. Goodlad, dean of the Graduate School of Education at the University of California, Los Angeles, one of the country's leading authorities on such issues. "The study gives a clear, comprehensive, sober picture of reality without being a polemic."

In "Crisis in the Classroom," Mr. Silberman contends that in some respects the schools are better than they ever were before, noting for example, that more people are learning to read. But, in most respects, he charges, the schools are "intolerable."

This is so, he argues, not because teachers are incompetent, indifferent or cruel. Most teachers are characterized by Mr. Silberman as "decent, honest, well-intentioned people" who are victimized by the current system as much as students are.

Teachers Held Victims

The teachers are said to be treated as subservient employes whose job is to take orders and punch the time clock every day, and whose competence is judged not by what and how their students learn, but by how well they control their classes.

The central cause of the difficulty, Mr. Silberman writes, is that schools and teacher training institutions are afflicted by "mindlessness."

By this, he means that educators fail to think seriously about the purposes and consequences of what they do — about the relationship of educational means to ends—and that they seldom question established practice. Lacking any considered philosophy of education, he writes, teachers tend to do what teachers before them have done.

In assailing both the quality of education and the quality of life in the classroom, Mr. Silberman asserts that schools "operate on the assumption of distrust." Teachers assume that pupils cannot be trusted to act in their own best interests, he contends, and principals make similar assumptions about teachers.

This lack of trust produces a kind of school in which virtually every aspect of behavior is governed by minute and petty rules, he argues.

"The most important characteristic the schools share in common is a preoccupation with order and control," the report says. Teachers become primarily disciplinarians, and discipline is defined as "the absence of noise and movement."

Through "the unnatural insistence that children sit silently and motionless," and through "the unreasonable expectation that they will all be interested in the same thing at the same moment and for the same

Charles E. Silberman, author of the study on public schools

length of time," the report says, the formal classroom seems to produce its own discipline problems—in the form of restlessness, misbehavior, and baiting the teacher.

"It is not the children who are disruptive," says the report, "it is the formal classroom that is disruptive—of childhood itself."

Some of this might be tolerated as the price for a "good" academic education, Mr. Silberman writes, except that most students are not getting that, either.

He contends that the high school curriculum reform movement that swept the country around the time of Sputnik 1 in 1957 "has been blunted on the classroom door" — largely because the reformers, mostly university professors, concentrated on subject matter and paid little attention to how children learn.

In the elementary schools, much of what is taught "is not worth knowing as a child, let alone as an adult, and little will be remembered," Mr. Silberman continues. "The banality and triviality of the curriculum in most schools has to be experienced to be believed."

Furthermore, the report says, schools "discourage students from developing the capacity to learn by and for themselves," because the schools are "structured in such a way as to make students totally dependent upon the teachers." The result is said to be an authoritarian system that "educates for docility."

In examining the schools, Mr. Silberman leaned substantially on the thought of Jean Piaget, the Swiss psychologist who demonstrated, in the words of the Carnegie report, "that the child is the principal agent in his own education and mental development;" and that each child's path to understanding is unlike any other child's.

In view of this, Mr. Silberman questions many common assumptions about schooling, including the assumption that "teaching" means teaching a group of students at once from a uniform lesson plan, or any lesson plan at all; and the assumption that all children in a group should be studying the same subject at the same time, even when each child is allowed to go at his own pace in what is often described as "individualized instruction."

'Tyranny of Lesson Plan'

The Carnegie study contends that under the "tyranny of the lesson plan," and of the rigid time schedule it usually requires, lessons often start before children become interested —if, indeed they get interested at all—and end before interest is exhausted or understanding achieved.

In one of more than 200 "items," or concrete examples of school practice that stud the report, Mr. Silberman describes

a cluster of children who are "examining a turtle with enormous fascination and intensity." The teacher tells the children to put the turtle away because "we're going to have our science lesson."

In an "informal" or "open" classroom of the kind Mr. Silberman favors as an alternative, the children's natural fascination with the turtle would be used as a springboard into science. But the subject would be pursued only as long as the children were interested. Then each child's ensuing interest would be pursued in a similar manner.

Such schools — operated by ordinary teachers — are said by the Carnegie report to be widely established in England, and to be operating successfully in every section of the United States, although so far they constitute a very small minority in this country.

In such a school, the teacher's job is said to be to apprehend each child's interests and to provide an environment — filled with an abundance of concrete materials and books— to stimulate those interests.

Informal Atmosphere

There is no "up front" in such a classroom, and a teacher seldom teaches a group of children as a whole. There are no rows of desks, and few tables and chairs. The main burden of activity shifts from the teacher to the children, who actively pursue their own interests. With the burden thus shifted, the teacher finds herself free to work with individual children.

Although such a classroom is child-centered and offers considerable freedom and informality, Mr. Silberman reports, it is not and should not be completely given over to "doing your own thing," as some reformers would favor.

Adults have a responsibility to guide children toward an understanding of the best man has done and thought, the Carnegie report argues. In Mr. Silberman's words, "some things are more important than others and adults have to make conscious choices about which is which" and guide children in the most important directions.

When working with adolescents, who for the first time in their lives are thinking consistently in the abstract, the informal approach might well involve more book work and more conventional research, Mr. Silberman says.

In the high school years, he adds, the teacher has a further responsibility to see that the student acquires the intellectual tools and disciplines that add rigor and validity to inquiry that is fired by natural curiosity.

Mr. Silberman reports that disciplinary and motivational problems largely disappear in informal classrooms; that there is "great joy and spontaneity and activity" coupled with "great self-control and order."

"One simply does not see bored or restless or unhappy youngsters, or youngsters with the glazed look so common in American schools," he writes.

But is informality and joyousness purchased at the price of learning the three R's in the early grades and solid subject-matter in the later years?

Generally, Mr. Silberman reports, "the answer would appear to be no" in the English schools, where the approach has been in effect longest.

Mr. Silberman writes that such schools demontrate what the American reformer John Dewey argued but many of his disciples ignored—"that a deep and genuine concern for individual growth and fulfillment not only is compatible with but indeed demands an equally genuine concern for cognitive growth and intellectual discipline, for transmitting the cultural heritage of the society."

September 20, 1970

From 'Crisis in the Classroom'

The result of a three-year study commissioned by the Carnegie Corporation, Mr. Silberman's report combines his reactions to the schools he observed with a survey of the literature on the subject and his own philosophy of education, which, he says, he acquired in the course of making the study. Following are excerpts from his report:

It is not possible to spend any prolonged period visiting public school classrooms without being appalled by the mutilation visible everywhere—mutilation of spontaneity, of joy in learning, of pleasure in creating, of sense of self. The public schools—those "killers of the dream," to appropriate a phrase of Lillian Smith's—are the kind of institutions one cannot really dislike until one gets to know them well. Because adults take the schools so much for granted, they fail to appreciate what grim, joyless places most American schools are, how oppressive and petty are the rules by which they are governed, how intellectually sterile and esthetically barren the atmosphere, what an appalling lack of civility obtains on the part of teachers and principals, what contempt they unconsciously display for children as children.

Schools can be humane and still educate well. They can be genuinely concerned with gaiety and joy and individual growth and fulfillment without sacrificing concern for intellectual discipline and development. They can be simultaneously child-centered and subject- or knowledge-centered. They can stress esthetic and moral education without weakening the three R's. They can do all these things if—but only if — their structure, content, and objectives are transformed.

Education should prepare people not just to earn a living but to live a life—a creative, humane, and sensitive life. This means that the schools must provide a liberal, humanizing education. And the purpose of liberal education must be, and indeed always has been, to educate educators—to turn out men and women who are capable of educating their families, their friends, their communities, and most importantly, themselves.

Our preoccupation with the urban crisis must not be permitted to blind us to the important, if less urgent, defects of public schools everywhere. In good measure, the defects and failures of the slum schools are but an exaggerated version of what's wrong with all schools. To be sure, the schools in middle-class neighborhoods seem to do a better job of teaching the basic skills of literacy and computation, hence their students are better equipped to earn a living. But this "success" is due far less to the schools themselves than to what has been called "the hidden curriculum of the middle-class home."

After 12 years of dull, repressive, formal public schooling and three and a half years of uninspired formal college teaching, six months of practice teaching in the same kind of classroom is almost bound to convince the student teacher that that is the way teaching is—worse, that that is the way teaching has to be. Almost inevitably, therefore, that is the way he tends to teach when he finishes his training and takes over his own classroom.

If our concern is with education, we cannot restrict our attention to the schools and colleges, for education is not synonymous with schooling. Children and adults learn outside as well as—perhaps more than—in schools. To say this is not to denigrate the public schools: as the one publicly controlled educating institution with which virtually every child comes into close and prolonged contact, they occupy a strategic, perhaps critical, position in American society. Nor is it to denigrate the colleges and universities, which for different reasons occupy a position of great and growing importance. It is simply to give proper weight to all the other educating institutions in American society: television, films, and the mass media; churches and synagogues; the law, medicine, and social work; museums and libraries; the armed forces, corporate training programs, boy scout troops.

The tragedy is that the great majority of students do not rebel; they accept the stultifying rules, the lack of privacy, the authoritarianism, the abuse of power—indeed, virtually every aspect of school life—as The Way Things Are.

While the inadequacies of teacher education are more serious for teachers going into urban slum schools, I have yet to meet a teacher in the middle-class suburban school who considered his preparation even remotely adequate. On the contrary, the great majority agree with the judgment of Seymour Sarason of Yale, that "the contents and procedures of teacher education frequently have no demonstrable relevance to the actual teaching task."

Students need to learn far more than the basic skills. For children who may still be in the labor force in the year 2030, nothing could be more wildly impractical than an education designed to prepare them for specific vocations or profesions or to facilitate their adjustment to the world as it is. To be "practical," in education should prepare them for work that does not yet exist and whose nature cannot even be imagined. This can only be done by teaching them how to learn, by giving them the kind of intellectual discipline that will enable them to apply man's accumulated wisdom to new problems as they arise — the kind of wisdom that will enable them to recognize new problems as they arise.

© 1970, Charles E. Silberman

September 20, 1970

Abolishing Schools: I

By IVAN ILLICH

CUERNAVACA, Mexico—The entrenchment of institutionalized schooling in the U.S. social structure was recently checked by the Supreme Court in *Griggs et al. v. Duke Power Company.*

Chief Justice Warren Burger, speaking for a unanimous Court, held that the requirements—as a condition of employment—of either a high-school diploma or of success in a standardized general education test are prohibited under certain conditions by the Civil Rights Act of 1964.

This case may set us on the road to the legal recognition that schooling requirements, in and of themselves, constitute a discrimination which hampers social advancement and thus violates public policy.

Tests relevant to job competency are not prohibited by the act, but the employer has to prove that any given standard is necessary for his business. The Court extends the application of the concept of "job relevance" which appears in the legislative history of the 1964 Civil Rights Act to the requirement of a high-school diploma as well. The Court rules that any tests used "must measure the person for the job, not the person in the abstract."

This decision encourages those of us who refuse to believe in the benefits of schooling. It sustains our argument that an individual's economic or social advancement should not be made to depend on his ability or willingness to attend age-specific small-group meetings, under the authority of a teacher, for 500 to 1,000 hours every year. This constitutes the hidden curriculum of schooling which seems irrelevant both to the goals of a liberal educator and to preparation for any specific job.

The Court In *Griggs* tells us that "diplomas and tests are useful servants, but Congress has mandated the common-sense proposition that they are not to become masters of reality." This mandate has now received a big assist from the Court itself. It was gravely needed. The proponents of compulsory schooling have taught us that diplomas and, more recently, general tests are indeed the masters of reality. Americans take this mastery for granted.

I rejoice in *Griggs* because the present Court headed by and spoken for by so American a Chief Justice as Burger has seen fit to demolish this myth. But I rejoice even more, because I see in this decision and in the reasoning on which it is based, implications far wider than the Court had any occasion, in this context, to consider. The decision represents an exemplary breakthrough in the present, worldwide crisis of schools. It is the first juristic step towards the disestablishment of the school—a move as necessary today as the separation of church and state was in 1789.

Employers will find it difficult to show that schooling is a necessary prerequisite for any job requirement. It is easy to show that it is necessarily antidemocratic because it inevitably discriminates.

I believe it can be shown that al-most the entire American structure of schooling is irrelevant for gaining competence in the vast majority of American jobs. I also believe it can be shown that our open-minded structure of schooling is inherently discriminatory. It is evidently so for those who are denied a fair part in the school budget because of their color. It is equally discriminatory for anyone who does participate in it without climbing the very last rung.

Michael Crichton worked for his doctorate at the Harvard Medical School with the rather specialized purpose of qualifying to write about the medical profession. He claims that being trained as a medical scientist, as all medical schools train their pupils, has little relevance to medical practice.

Everybody knows that some of the most successful practitioners of the law, present as well as past, have achieved their success without the benefit of any legal schooling whatever. It is even more significant that the legal schooling of some of the greatest jurists of our time (Hugo Black, the late Robert Jackson) was negligible. Justice Story, the father of American legal schooling, had none at all. We also know of cases—Caryl Chessman is just one example—where the confinement, discipline and leisure provided inmates of penitentiaries with unusual opportunity to become competent lawyers. Schooling may perhaps be a useful servant, but not when, as today, we have let it become the master of reality and of ourselves.

Ivan Illich, author of "De-Schooling Society," is director of Centro Intercultural de Documentasion in Cuernavaca. This is the first of two articles.

May 3, 197

Abolishing Schools: II

By IVAN ILLICH

CUERNAVACA, Mexico—The hidden curriculum of compulsory schooling discriminates by its very nature. It serves as a means to apportion scarce resources and jobs to the person who qualifies for them through the largest consumption of public funds. It makes out of the loser a failure. Compulsory schooling establishes the presumption that the person who has consumed more professional treatment under the supervision of certified teachers is therefore socially more useful—and unquestionably entitled to the choice privileges society has to offer.

The social structure as a whole has organized itself into operating departments, fitting various levels of drop-outs. Persons who have failed, for whatever reason, to accumulate a certain number of packaged units of schooling are automatically excluded from positions whose level within the structure provides money, power, and social prestige in an ascending order. This happens, no matter how irrelevant the prescribed schooling may be to the jobs in question.

One of the diabolic features of this system is that it teaches the individual who is caught up in it to discriminate against himself. He is taught to disqualify himself as incompetent, uneducable or unworthy of a job for which he has no formal credentials. The hidden curriculum of schooling trains him to know his place. The discriminatory nature of certified schooling as the puberty rite of a technological tribe can be neatly illustrated by the organization of school itself. No one may teach in a public grade school or high school, no matter how great his abilities as a teacher, or what his mastery of his subject, unless he has been certified as schooled in the theory of teaching and the bureaucracy of schools.

If this structure is not in fact designed to assign privilege, disqualify the self-learner, and train clients for an economy based on increasing dependence on futile service but instead meant to serve the communication of skills and the awakening of political discernment and critical judgment, then it has ceased to be a useful servant. It has become the master of reality.

In yesterday's article I expressed optimism as to the impact of the Supreme Court's decision in the Griggs case. This optimism might seem extreme to some people, even to people favorably inclined to my over-all view of the need to de-school society. They may question the foundation of my hope that Griggs set us on our way to the legal recognition of the inherently discriminatory nature of schooling or of tests which are calibrated by it.

True, Griggs is limited to the problem of discrimination against certain clearly definable classes. True, it is limited to the application of a particular statute. But an earlier Court, in Brown v. Board of Education, managed to prohibit a clearly undesirable discrimination without the aid of a statute, on the basis of constitutional guarantees of due process, and due process is guaranteed to all citizens, not just to those who belong to particularly vulnerable classes. May we not hope that a Court as daring as the Burger Court may extend its present ruling further to diminish the discrimination inherent in our system of publicly established and compulsory schooling? May we not hope Congress together may eventually abolish the mastery over contemporary reality of an overgrown institution of past centuries?

If I were of a less sunny disposition, I should worry more about social scientists who will be employed in the meantime to "prove" the relevance of schooling requirements that employers may see fit to impose on prospective employes.

May 4, 1971

Who Pushed Humpty Dumpty?

*Dilemmas in American Education Today.
By Donald Barr.
341 pp. New York: Atheneum. $10.*

By JOSEPH FEATHERSTONE

In education, maybe even more than in other realms of our cultural life, the old controversies keep recurring, the combatants frozen into ritual postures like mastodons embalmed in icebergs. Recently the stage has been held by progressives and radicals. Now, on cue, comes Donald Barr, a self-proclaimed reactionary who occupies an interesting pulpit, the headmastership of Dalton, a New York City private school once noted for its progressivism. Barr rules in the great tradition of undemocratic, imperious headmasters, and you may be sure that he has occasioned gnashing of teeth and rending of garments among the progressive faithful. Others like his espousal of intellect and discipline, and some may feel uplifted by the spectacle of a man willing to take on the poisonous and deformed mushroom philosophies that are springing up everywhere to challenge old certitudes.

Barr has an elegant, witty pen, and a cultivated mind. This collection of essays spans 10 years and covers a host of subjects from campus unrest and sex education to curriculum reform. Barr provides a running commentary, explaining what he was doing when he wrote a particular piece and what he now thinks about the matter, and the reader is often treated to brief autobiographical snippets, such as a reminiscence of Joyce Cary. The effect is personal and charming, although Barr's determination to have the last word on every subject can be a bore.

The less bitterly polemical pieces in "Who Pushed Humpty Dumpty?" are full of sharp observations and sensible points about schools, public and private. Barr has, for instance, long argued that all tests ought to be for the benefit of the students who take them, and should therefore be returned with grades and comments; he is particularly devastating on multiple choice and college board exams. He expresses eloquent dismay over the reluctance of schools—even the poshest—to link the teaching of reading to the cultivation of children's powers of written expression. He has many wise things to say about science teaching, in which he takes a knowledgeable interest.

When he wants to be, this reactionary can be the soul of reason: thus he argues that there is and ought to be a recurring dialectic in education between developmental views—stressing the needs of the child—and scholastic views—stressing the demands of the world: "We need new ways of letting each child progress at its tempo, without losing the social character of knowledge."

This last point—the fundamentally dialectical nature of all sound thinking on education, and the craziness of pushing matters to a logical conclusion—will be especially useful to keep in mind during the inevitable silly seasons of the new progressive counter-counterattack that is upon us, in the shape of the fad for open, informal classrooms.

So much for Barr the man of reasoned judgments. There is another, far less interesting Barr in chapters of "Who Pushed Humpty Dumpty?" This Barr has forsaken the conservative's prime task, the promulgation of sound values, and has instead succumbed to a particular hazard of the conservative enterprise. The scholastics used to say that all beings, including angels, risk characteristic forms of corruption. Radicals can be corroded by their hatreds and (as Barr notes) by the distinctions they too readily draw between micro and macro moralities, the universal causes they serve and the web of human relations they actually inhabit. One occupational disease of conservatives and reactionaries is the recurring temptation to appeal to two enduringly conservative traits in any audience, the sense of complacency and the sense of fear.

There are some remarkable complacencies in these essays. When Barr says that the culture has rendered youth nearly superfluous—an increasingly prolonged and pointless way of life spent in poor schools preparing for exams—this is plainly a tactical concession, for he is not mounting a reactionary counterattack on the relevant institutional arrangements. His agenda is much more simple, as a proposal from a different context shows: "On the day that parents stop paying tuition for non-

Joseph Featherstone, author of "Schools Where Children Learn," is on leave from the New Republic to write a book on John Dewey.

education; on the day they stop handing out allowances for strike funds and narcotics and reeking apartments, the student revolutions—impatient with reason, violent against restraint, a holiday from self-control — will wither away . . ." Parents might have forestalled all this trouble years ago, by taking to heart a smug little catechism: "Q. 'What are we to do?' A. 'Help your child develop a Superego.' Q. 'What did we do wrong?' A. 'You failed to help your child develop a Superego. You were permissive.' "

When it comes to fear, Barr paints a scary picture: "Students are discovering that violence is psychedelic. Girl graduate students patronize paroled rapists. Freshmen carry around the works of the Marquis de Sade." Barr is against all this, the strange implication being that everybody else supports it.

Almost everybody is against hard drugs and violence in schools, both of which are ominous realities. The question is whether anything is helped by lashing out at students in general or some vague bogey man called the New Left. Barr is less than precise in his indictments, choosing to sneer rather than argue: "Raskolnikov, the murderous antihero of Dostoevski's 'Crime and Punishment,' would feel at home at Harvard." Is this really what the Dalton alumni at Harvard report back to Barr? Has he then stopped sending students to Harvard? (In any case, it seems to me that a better comparison for Cambridge would be the world of "The Idiot" with its mixed lunacy, pathos and possibility.)

All this diminishes confidence in Barr's basic seriousness, particularly when he suddenly snaps off a discussion and asks the reader for a quick vote of confidence in author-

In the great tradition of imperious headmasters

ity, responsibility and leadership. These are necessary qualities in any institution, but they are subject to abuse in schools, as in politics, and an abstract appeal to them should not be allowed to do service for either a philosophy of education or a political program. Barr emphasizes the importance of the principal as a symbol of adult authority in a time when all adult authority is shaky, and that is good, as far as it goes. I suspect that part of the subtle appeal to youth of A. S. Neill's libertarian idyll, "Summerhill," is that Neill, for all his dated Victorian rebelliousness, is a genuine adult authority: a benevolent Scottish patriarch presiding over a children's commune (not a school), throwing people out if they smoke.

But Barr tells us little about the nature of legitimate authority in a school. How important would he think it for teachers, and students too, to be models for each other of straightforward conduct, decency and open reasonableness? How can a teacher set an example of responsible adult freedom in a school where the headmaster says he is free to dictate the curriculum? You can't tell from "Who Pushed Humpty Dumpty?" because Barr defines his position on important points solely by angry negations.

The intelligent, tart pieces on specific educational matters in the later portions of the book demonstrate that Barr is capable of surmounting these gloomy simplicities. Plainly it needs saying that the counterculture in education, as in politics, all too faithfully mirrors the inane sloganeering, shoddiness, greed, twisted values, absence of workmanship and discipline, susceptibility to mass commercial exploitation and hunger for violence of the social order from which it springs. But to criticize one without touching the other, or to imply that deranged students and irresponsible critics are the main educational problems today, is to engage in that sour-bellied demagoguery we have all heard too much of. Among its several defects, this sort of performance increases the odds that our educational practice will continue to follow the arc of a tedious pendulum — misguided and half-baked reforms alternating with peevish reaction. ■

Education as Tragicomedy

By ANATOLE BROYARD

WHO PUSHED HUMPTY DUMPTY? Dilemmas in American Education Today. By Donald Barr. 341 pages. Atheneum. $10.

When a liberal educator behaves in a dogmatic manner, his action is ascribed to a "passionate concern." It is not that he is forcing his personality or his convictions on someone else: Rather, he has taken "a selfless position" in the best interests of the community. But should a conservative insist on *his* principles, he is immediately anathemized as "coercive," "autocratic" or "imperious." His sincerity and his seriousness are questioned by committees.

This is what has happened to Donald Barr, headmaster of the Dalton School and author of "Who Pushed Humpty Dumpty?" Mr. Barr has complicated the picture by being witty, even ironical. Is irony appropriate to headmasters? Would you want your child to go to an ironical school? In this book, Mr. Barr has laid his cards on the table, presented his collected writings for the outraged parents' inspection. He has confessed his guilt: He *is* witty; he *is* ironical. At a time when most educational theorists are tragedians, he has dared to write a tragicomedy.

In reading a book for review, I generally jot down particularly quotable lines or points: In this case, I soon had to abandon this practice. I was writing down almost as much as I was reading. Mr. Barr's aphorisms and insights came at me so thick and fast—his texture is so rich—that I often had to put the book down after a few pages to give my intellectual appetite a chance to burp.

Insights Thick and Fast

But lest I be suspected of hyperbole, let me give you a few samples: "To the modern liberal mind, the word discipline has an almost pornographic sound." "Though discipline and freedom seem antithetical, each without the other destroys itself." For the alienated young, "The meaning of every experience leaks away even at the instant of occurrence, so that life is like sitting and endlessly eating a sort of dry existential bran." "A few years ago, adolescence was a phrase; then it became a profession; now it is a new nationality." "Parents who would never give their children an unbalanced physical diet proudly give them an unbalanced psychological diet." "We think unthinkingly (so to speak) that 'yes' is a loving word and 'no' is a hostile word." "It is by waiting (for the gratification of their desires) that children learn what time is."

Of the "sexual revolution," Mr. Barr says: "An adolescent in his joyless round of promiscuity is no more a revolutionary than a pickpocket is a socialist." "They go through the motions of emotion . . . like robots in heat." What is needed, he urges, is not education in sex, but in sexuality—and especially in passion, because passion is the most difficult thing adolescents must learn to cope with.

On the use of drugs as a means of extending awareness or intensifying perception, he writes: "There is no point in asking 'Perception of what? Awareness of what?' These perceptions need no object. It is masturbatory awareness. The children 'turned on' by marijuana, cocaine (now common), LSD, or methedrine are like radios tuned to nothing, they play the noise of their own tubes."

"When a bright child begins to do badly in his studies, the question to ask him (but not in so many words) is: 'Whom are you punishing?' " "The permissive fallacy is that children learn good things from bad experiences." "The trouble with many children is that their fathers are mothers and their mothers are sisters." "When should a parent turn over authority to a child? When the child stops reaching for authority and reaches for responsibility."

Of Student Revolts

Speaking of student revolts, Mr. Barr says: "The more arbitrary their demands the more 'idealistic' it will seem to the sociology department and to the radicals' parents." Many of the disaffected young, the author feels, are suffering from "the enormous fatigue of trying to live without religion." About the feeling of superfluousness so many young people have, the sense that the world doesn't need them, he writes: "Many men begin to die when they retire from their jobs, and something like this is going on at the other end of life as well."

The college student, the author points out, has become the new proletariat for the revolutionary. The old proletariat is too prosperous to be proselytized, while the student is ideal material, because he sees himself as a serf at school. While student radicals are fond of espousing large causes —what Mr. Barr calls "macro-morality"— they are often indifferent to the personal or "micro-morality" of cheating on tests, stealing, being cruel to their parents, lying and destruction of property. In fact, he says there may be a negative connection between these two moralities. "Consistency is only a kind of chastity of the head; the times do not regard it much," and finally we must learn not to think always of the child as the victim: Often it is the parent.

If I seem to have given over most of this review to quoting Mr. Barr rather than criticizing him—as a critic is supposed to do—it is because I found very little to criticize. And what little there might have been for me to say seemed so much less important—and less interesting—than the author's ideas that my sense of proportion left me no choice. In self-defense—if I need any—I will say that it was no easy job to decide which of Mr. Barr's lines would have to be sacrificed to the exigencies of space.

September 30, 1971

The Great Myth

By COLIN GREER

It is fashionable these days to point to the decline of the public school, as if there were a time in some golden past when the schools really made equal opportunity available to children of every economic and social class. The truth is that our public schools have always failed the lower classes—both white and black. Current educational problems stem not from the fact that the schools have changed, but from the fact that they continue to do precisely the job they have always done.

Public schools have, in fact, only been public in the sense that what happens inside them is typical of what happens outside. For at least the last eighty years socioeconomic class, as signified by employment rates and levels, has determined scholastic achievement as measured by dropout and failure ratio. Our public schools have done no more than carry out the program written for them by society. They have not tried to change that society in the slightest. Outsiders were kept out; insiders prospered.

Yet the claims of the schoolmen and the authority of the major educational historians, who swallowed whole the schools' rhetoric without checking the facts, has created a powerful legend whose influence, it seems, we still cannot shake off. This Great School Legend asserts that credit for building American democracy should be given to the American public school system. The public schools, so the story goes, took the backward poor, the ragged, ill-prepared immigrants who crowded into the cities, educated and Americanized them, and molded them into the homogeneous productive middle class that is America's strength and pride.

It is a lovely legend. Would it were true. If it were, perhaps today the urban public schools could work for the black urban poor instead of merely insulting them with the invidious and erroneous comparison to the alleged success of the immigrant poor who, as the legend claims, made such good use of the public schools fifty years ago.

But the actual performance of the public schools fifty years ago offers little support for the great school legend. In virtually every school effectiveness study since the one made in Chicago in 1898, more children have failed in urban public schools than

Jan Faust

have succeeded, both in absolute and in relative numbers. Among the school systems which had large numbers of immigrant and poor pupils, in Boston, Chicago, Detroit, Philadelphia, Pittsburgh, New York and Minneapolis, failure rates were so high that in no one of these systems did the so-called "normal" group exceed 60 per cent, while in several instances it fell even lower—to 49 per cent in Pittsburgh, and to 35 per cent in Minneapolis.

The truth is that the upward mobility of white lower classes was never as rapid nor as sure as it has become traditional to think. The 1920 census, for example, showed that even the favored English and Welsh migrants found half their number tied to the terrifying vulnerability of unskilled labor occupations. And school dropout rates for all groups, including blacks, were in direct proportion to rates of adult employment. Compulsory attendance at higher levels only pushed

failure rates into the upper grades throughout the nineteen-twenties and nineteen-thirties in such cities as Chicago, Boston, New York, Philadelphia, Detroit and Washington, D. C. And this trend continues today, though now failure is postponed to the community college.

Historically, academic effort has never been relevant to the place of the American poor, and the urban poor in particular; the public schools did as they are doing for the black poor today. Yet the legend that our schools have been effective agents of social change persists and supports the illusion that they can now, in like manner, address the problems we so fervently wish would go away. The truth is, the public schools have never done what they are now expected to do.

Colin Greer is executive editor of Social Policy magazine and author of "The Great School Legend."

Denny Hermanson

Do Better Schools Make a Difference?

If poor children are provided better schooling, will they get better jobs when they grow up? Most education reformers have said yes in pushing such efforts as racial desegregation in schools, compensatory education, preschool programs and increased school spending.

But last week a Harvard University study, which seems certain to provoke much controversy, said no—better education does not necessarily open the door to economic opportunity. Schools not only do not affect inequalities in "cognitive skills"—the ability to manipulate words and numbers, assimilate information, make logical inferences and the like—but even if they did, this would have little impact on how good a living children would make as adults, the report concluded.

The conclusions were based on a three-year study by an eight-man research team directed by Christopher Jencks. The team made an extensive, computerized analysis of much of the data about family, schooling, jobs and income gathered over the last decade.

Brushing aside desegregation and unequal distribution of money among schools as insignificant factors in determining the effects of schooling on cognitive skills, the report argued that the primary factor is the characteristics of the children entering school. "Everything else—the school budget, its policies, the characteristics of the teacher—is either secondary or completely irrelevant," it added.

As for economic success, the report estimates that only a quarter of the variation in incomes is explained by differences in schools, cognitive skills, genes, home background and I.Q. For the most part, earning power depends on personality ("the ability to persuade a customer") and luck ("chance acquaintances who steer you to one line of work rather than another"), Mr. Jencks theorizes.

September 10, 1972

CHAPTER **4**
The Minorities

*hody McCoy at his Brownsville office during the New York City teacher's
rike of 1968.*
he New York Times.

Southern Educators Study the Implications of Supreme Court Rulings on Segregation

By BENJAMIN FINE

The Supreme Court decisions last week on segregation and racial discrimination reopened an old educational controversy in the South. Educators generally were unwilling to admit that the traditional policy of the dual educational system in the seventeen Southern states was on the way out. Their immediate reaction was: "Nothing can change that policy." However, they were plainly worried.

In directing the Universities of Texas and Oklahoma to admit Negroes to their graduate schools, the high court did not break down all existing barriers, but it did chip away at the South's doctrine of separation of white and Negro students.

The Court told Texas that Heman Marion Sweatt must be admitted to the all-white University of Texas Law School, and that G. W. McLaurin must be permitted to sit and eat with the other students at the University of Oklahoma. The doctrine of "separate but equal" facilities was not considered specifically by the Supreme Court, but the implications of its rulings were serious enough to cause a shudder among Southerners.

One aspect of the Court decisions, as expressed by Chief Justice Fred M. Vinson, received wide attention in education circles. He noted that the University of Texas Law School "possesses to a far greater degree (than the Negro school) those qualities which are incapable of objective measurement but which make for greatness in a law school." The Negro school, he said, excludes 85 per cent of the population of Texas and most of the lawyers, witnesses, jurors, judges and others with whom Mr. Sweatt would deal when he became a member of the Texas bar.

Not Substantially Equal

Then came this significant statement by Chief Justice Vinson:

"With such a substantial and significan segment of society excluded, we cannot conclude that the education offered (Mr. Sweatt) is substantially equal to that which he would receive if admitted to the University of Texas Law School."

This statement was immediately seized upon by those who are opposed to the segregation policy. They saw in it an opening wedge that might lead to the final and complete overthrow of all educational segregation in the South. For, they argued, under this interpretation, it would be utterly impossible for any Negro college or university, no matter how adequately equipped or financed, to provide "equal" opportunities to the Negro student.

If a student is required to go to a separate state university, one for Negroes only, he is bound to be cut off from a "substantial and significant segment of society." And whether he is studying to be a lawyer, doctor, accountant or teacher, under the Vinson ruling he can show that he is being handicapped by exclusion from the white universities.

Walter White, executive secretary of the National Association for the Advancement of Colored People, said the Supreme Court decisions "struck a blow against discrimination and segregation in higher education." And he served notice that Negro students intended to press for the abolition of segregation in all academic circles. It is impossible, he said, to achieve equality in higher education within the framework of segregation.

Suits Are Pending

Several lawsuits have already been started challenging the "separate but equal" principle. The expectation is that a number of others will follow as a result of the Court's action.

In North Carolina, four suits involving segregation in education are pending. One affects the University of North Carolina and three the public schools. Four suits are awaiting disposition in Louisiana, where Negroes are demanding equal education in public schools. In Florida, six suits are pending in which Negro students seek admission to various professional and graduate schools in the University of Florida. Two suits demanding equality in public schools are before the Georgia courts.

Southern educators, in some cases, have admitted Negroes to higher education institutions, particularly on the graduate levels. The University of Arkansas enrolls Negroes in its graduate schools of law and medicine. In Kentucky, a state law which becomes effective next week permits boards of trustees to vote to let Negroes take courses not provided by the Negro state college. West Virginia University admits Negroes to its graduate school.

But the question of admitting Negroes to white public elementary and secondary schools is another matter. A survey of the State Education Commissions of the South, conducted by this department, shows a unanimous "no" to the question: "Will you admit Negroes to your white public schools?"

A. R. Meadows, Superintendent of Education in Alabama, commented: "I do not think that Negro parents and pupils want that to happen."

Warnings from the South

Several educators warned that even if the South agreed to take Negro children in the white schools, individual communities would not permit it. They held that any such attempt at ending segregation would lead to a dangerous situation. Several warned that the parents would oppose this step, and that the pupils themselves would not sit beside the Negroes.

"You can't legislate social mores," is the way one of the educators put it. "We've solved the problem of the two races in our own way, and it would be dangerous for anyone from the outside to come in and upset the applecart."

But that view was challenged by those who believe that the segregation controversy is "synthetic."

Dr. White said:

"The N. A. A. C. P. is prepared to challenge whatever obstacles Southern reactionaries may seek to interpose. Negro young men and women of the South are entitled to equality of educational opportunity. A Jim Crow system cannot offer such equality. Southern Negroes are insisting upon an end to segregation."

It would appear that the question of "separate but equal" educational facilities is rapidly heading for a showdown.

Southern educators generally admit that Negro schools are not equal to those provided for white children. However, they are quick to point to the tremendous progress that has been made in recent years. Many millions of dollars have been spent by the South, they say, to bring the Negro schools within striking distance of the white schools. However, even the most sanguine will admit that the two systems are far from equal at this moment.

COLLEGES IN SOUTH EASE COLOR CURBS

Survey Reveals Enrollment of Negro Students in White Institutions Exceeds 2,000

By BENJAMIN FINE

The color line is slowly giving way in many Southern colleges and universities.

More than 2,000 Negro students —most of them on the professional or graduate levels—are attending white institutions of higher learning at present in the seventeen Southern states and in the Districtm of Columbia where educational segregation is mandatory. The number of Negroes in the colleges ranges from one at William and Mary in Virginia to 275 at the University of Louisville in Kentucky.

The growth of Negro enrollment in what were until recent years all-white colleges has taken place without any disorder or major disturbances of any kind. The Negro students eat in the same cafeterias with white students, go to athletic contests, and to a lesser extent to social activities.

These conclusions are based on a survey of representative colleges and universities in the South. The study shows that once the color line is broken, Negro students are absorbed into the life of the college or university without disturbance.

Court Rulings a Factor

The enrollment of Negro students has taken place, the survey indicates, as a direct result of the recent United States Supreme Court decisions that directed states to provide equal educational facilities for Negro and white students. These facilities are lacking, in most Southern states, on the graduate or professional levels. For that reason, the bulk of the Negro registration is found today in the graduate schools. However, in some colleges the Negroes also are entering the undergraduate classes.

Five cases are now pending before the Supreme Court involving the right of Negroes to attend white public schools. The previous decisions had been taken on the higher educational level only. The cases before the highest tribunal go beyond the "equal but separate" doctrine. The entire question of segregation itself is involved. A decision is expected soon.

Segregation laws are found in the District of Columbia and in these states: Alabama, Arkansas, Delaware, Florida, Georgia, Kentucky, Louisiana, Maryland, Mississippi, Missouri, North Carolina, Oklahoma, South Carolina, Tennessee, Texas, Virginia and West Virginia. In addition, local option regarding segregation is found in Arizona, Kansas, Wyoming and New Mexico.

Despite the Supreme Court rulings, four states—Mississippi, South Carolina, Alabama and Georgia—have not admitted any Negroes to their colleges.

Actually, the Supreme Court rulings are applicable to the publicly supported institutions of higher education only. Few private colleges or universities have admitted any Negroes. But, the study shows, a growing number of private institutions is beginning to accept Negroes, even though not required to do so by law.

Reaction to Change Varies

For the most part, it was found, the students and faculty have accepted the presence of Negro students without opposition. They just seem to take them for granted, after the novelty has worn off. But here and there, reports indicate, parents, college trustees and community residents raise more than eyebrows. In some instances they have raised a row over this breaking down of a tradition that long has been taken for granted.

Among the pertinent conclusions reached in the survey are these:

¶Between 2,000 and 3,000 Negro students are attending white colleges and universities in the Southern states.

¶In general, the student body and the faculty accept the Negroes on terms of academic equality.

¶The admittance of Negro students has not left any scar or brought any new tensions to the classroom or campus.

¶Negro students, when admitted to white colleges, are eligible for scholarships, fellowships and other grants on the same basis at white students.

¶The number of Negro students in the white colleges has shown a steady annual increase since 1950, when the Supreme Court ordered equal educational opportunities on the higher level.

¶Few Negro students are found on the undergraduate level or in private colleges and universities.

Educators Voice Optimism

Of course, in terms of numbers, the 2,000 or so Negro students in Southern white colleges is only a minute percentage of the total.

There are more than 100,000 Negro youths in colleges, most of them in the 105 Negro colleges and universities in the South. These institutions have not slackened their work in any way. Realistically, they recognize that for some time to come the Negro colleges will be needed to train and educate the Negro students.

But the educators reached in this study are hopeful that a gradual change will take place in the general attitude of the community itself. The Southern college presidents and school leaders urge a "hands off" policy from outside sources. The position taken is something like this: Let us alone, and let us solve this problem in our own quiet way. We will find the answers if we are not pushed too hard.

Comments from leading college educators indicate that the presence of Negroes on formerly all-white campuses has been taken in good stride. At the University of Kentucky, for example, ninety-three graduate students and one law school student were admitted. According to Dr. H. L. Donovan, university president, the attitude of the student body toward Negro students on the campus is "excellent." He asserted:

"From the very beginning our students have treated the Negroes with the utmost politeness. Not a single embarrassing incident has happened since the Negroes were first admitted in 1948."

The faculty, too, has accepted the Negro student at the university, the president added. The Negro student eats in the cafeteria, and sits wherever he desires in the classroom. A minority of the local citizens was critical when the Negroes first entered the university. However, Dr. Donovan said, there appears to be less criticism each year.

'Solved Delicate Problem'

"It is my opinion that so far as Kentucky is concerned, we have met and solved the problem of the admission of Negroes to the university," he continued. "We realized that it was a delicate problem when the Federal court directed us to admit Negroes.

"The greatest care was exercised in orienting both the white students and the Negroes, as well as the faculty, to the new situation. The Negroes who applied for admission to the university were advised of the delicacy of the problem and they themselves recognized that it was essential that good judgment be used in meeting every situation that might lead to an embarrassment. We could not have had finer co-operation from the Negroes than we secured.

"As a result of an understand-ing of the problem and the general cooperation of both the white and Negro students, no embarrassing incident occurred. Now the presence of Negroes at the university is taken for granted, and it is no longer a problem."

The University of Kansas City reported that fifty Negro students were enrolled in the undergraduate Liberal Arts College, or from 5 to 7 per cent of the total undergraduate enrollment.

First admitted in the fall of 1949, the Negro students have been generally accepted by the rest of the student body and by the faculty, Dr. Wheadon Bloch, Dean of Students, said. The Negro and white students mix in the classrooms and the cafeteria. Negro students participate on both the intramural and intercollegiate athletic teams. They attend the athletic contest, the plays and musicals, convocations and dances.

Private Institutions Report

Kansas City is essentially a segregated community. The public school system and the motion picture houses are segregated.

"In the light of this," Dr. Bloch said, "it would appear that there has been an unusual acceptance of non-segregation in this private institution. The segregation in the community does make it difficult for mixed student groups to find suitable places off-campus to hold social affairs."

St. Louis University, a private institution, reported 276 Negro students, 191 of whom are undergraduates. Both the Dean of Men and the Dean of Women reported "complete acceptance" by the student body of the Negroes on the campus. Negroes are handled in exactly the same manner as other students, and are taken for granted in the classroom. All university-owned cafeterias are open to Negro students.

At the University of Tulsa (Okla.), the Negro students have been accepted by white students and the faculty "without any apparent struggle or awareness that they should be treated in any way other than as fellow-students," the president, Dr. C. I. Pontius, reported.

Commenting on the admission of Negroes to the Southern colleges, Lester B. Granger, executive director of the National Urban League, asserted that the rapid absorption of these students into Southern colleges was both significant and inspiring.

"This process has moved so smoothly that there is no reported case of any unpleasantness between white and Negro students," Mr. Granger added. "This is a most dramatic example of what can be done in community situations once the errant demagogue is removed from the picture."

March 15, 1954

HIGH COURT BANS SCHOOL SEGREGATION; 9-TO-0 DECISION GRANTS TIME TO COMPLY

1896 RULING UPSET

'Separate but Equal' Doctrine Held Out of Place in Education

By LUTHER A. HUSTON

Special to The New York Times.

WASHINGTON, May 17—The Supreme Court unanimously outlawed today racial segregation in public schools.

Chief Justice Earl Warren read two opinions that put the stamp of unconstitutionality on school systems in twenty-one states and the District of Columbia where segregation is permissive or mandatory.

The court, taking cognizance of the problems involved in the integration of the school systems concerned, put over until the next term, beginning in October, the formulation of decrees to effectuate its 9-to-0 decision.

The opinions set aside the "separate but equal" doctrine laid down by the Supreme Court in 1896.

"In the field of public education," Chief Justice Warren said, "the doctrine of 'separate but equal' has no place. Separate educational facilities are inherently unequal."

He stated the question and supplied the answer as follows:

"We come then to the question presented: Does segregation of children in public schools solely on the basis of race, even though physical facilities and other 'tangible' factors may be equal, deprive the children of the minority group of equal educational opportunities? We believe that it does."

States Stressed Rights

The court's opinion does not apply to private schools. It is directed entirely at public schools. It does not affect the "separate but equal doctrine" as applied on railroads and other public carriers entirely within states that have such restrictions.

The principal ruling of the court was in four cases involving state laws. The states' right to operate separated schools had been argued before the court on two occasions by representatives of South Carolina, Virginia, Kansas and Delaware.

In these cases, consolidated in one opinion, the high court held that school segregation deprived Negroes of "the equal protection of the laws guaranteed by the Fourteenth Amendment."

The other opinion involved the District of Columbia. Here schools have been segregated since Civil War days under laws passed by Congress.

"In view of our decision that the Constitution prohibits the states from maintaining racially segregated public schools," the Chief Justice said, "it would be unthinkable that the same Constitution would impose a lesser duty on the Federal Government.

"We hold that racial segregation in the public schools of the District of Columbia is a denial of the due process of law guaranteed by the Fifth Amendment to the Constitution."

The Fourteenth Amendment provides that no state shall "deny to any person within its jurisdiction the equal protection of the laws." The Fifth Amendment says that no person shall be "deprived of life, liberty or property without due process of law."

The seventeen states having mandatory segregation are Alabama, Arkansas, Delaware, Florida, Mississippi, Missouri, North Carolina, Oklahoma, Georgia, Kentucky, Louisiana, Maryland, South Carolina, Tennessee, Texas, Virginia and West Virginia.

Kansas, New Mexico, Arizona and Wyoming have permissive statutes, although Wyoming never has exercised it.

South Carolina and Georgia have announced plans to abolish public schools if segregation were banned.

Although the decision with regard to the constitutionality of school segregation was unequivocal, the court set the cases down for reargument in the fall on questions that previously were argued last December. These deal with the power of the court to permit an effective gradual readjustment to school systems not based on color distinctions.

Other questions include whether the court itself should formulate detailed decrees and what issues should be dealt with. Also, whether the cases should be remanded to the lower courts to frame decrees, and what general directions the Supreme Court should give the lesser tribunals if this were done.

Cases Argued Twice

The cases first came to the high court in 1952 on appeal from rulings of lower Federal courts, handed down in 1951 and 1952. Arguments were heard on Dec. 9-10, 1952.

Unable to reach a decision, the Supreme Court ordered rearguments in the present term and heard the cases for the second time on Dec. 7-8 last year.

Since then, each decision day has seen the courtroom packed with spectators awaiting the ruling. That was true today, though none except the justices themselves knew it was coming down. Reporters were told before the court convened that it "looked like a quiet day."

Three minor opinions had been announced, and those in the press room had begun to believe the prophesy when Banning E. Whittington, the court's press information officer, started putting on his coat.

"Reading of the segregation decisions is about to begin in the court room," he said. "You will get the opinions up there."

The courtroom is one floor up, reached by a long flight of marble steps. Mr. Whittington led a fast moving exodus. In the courtroom, Chief Justice Warren had just begun reading.

Each of the Associate Justices listened intently. They obviously were aware that no court since the Dred Scott decision of March 6, 1857, had ruled on so vital an issue in the field of racial relations.

Dred Scott was a slave who sued for his freedom on the ground that he had lived in a territory where slavery was forbidden. The territory was the northern part of the Louisiana Purchase, from which slavery was excluded under the terms of the Missouri Compromise.

The Supreme Court ruled that Dred Scott was not a citizen who had a right to sue in the Federal courts, and that Congress had no constitutional power to pass the Missouri Compromise.

Thurgood Marshall, the lawyer who led the fight for racial equality in the public schools, predicted that there would be no disorder and no organized resistance to the Supreme Court's dictum.

He said that the people of the South, the region most heavily affected, were law-abiding and would not "resist the Supreme Court."

Association Calls Meetings

Mr. Marshall said that the state presidents of the National Association for the Advancement of the Colored People would meet next week-end in Atlanta to discuss further procedures.

The Supreme Court adopted two of the major premises advanced by the Negroes in briefs and arguments presented in support of their cases.

Their main thesis was that segregation, of itself, was unconstitutional. The Fourteenth Amendment, which was adopted July 28, 1868, was intended to wipe out the last vestige of inequality between the races, the Negro side argued.

Against this, lawyers representing the states argued that

214

since there was no specific constitutional prohibition against segregation in the schools, it was a matter for the states, under their police powers, to decide.

The Supreme Court rejected the "states rights" doctrine, however, and found all laws ordering or permitting segregation in the schools to be in conflict with the Federal Constitution.

The Negroes also asserted that segregation had a psychological effect on pupils of the Negro race and was detrimental to the educational system as a whole. The court agreed.

"Today, education is perhaps the most important function of state and local governments," Chief Justice Warren wrote. "Compulsory school attendance laws and the great expenditures for education both demonstrate our recognition of the importance of education in our democratic society. It is the very foundation of good citizenship.

"In these days it is doubtful that any child may reasonably be expected to succeed in life if he is denied the opportunity of an education. Such an opportunity, where the state has undertaken to provide it, must be made available to all on equal terms."

As to the psychological factor,

the high court adopted the language of a Kansas court in which the lower bench held:

"Segregation with the sanction of the law, therefore, has a tendency to retard the educational and mental development of Negro children and to deprive them of some of the benefits they would receive in a racially integrated school system."

1896 Doctrine Demolished

The "separate but equal" doctrine, demolished by the Supreme Court today, involved transportation, not education. It was the case of Plessy vs. Ferguson, decided in 1896. The court then held that segregation was not unconstitutional if equal facilities were provided for each race.

Since that ruling six cases have been before the Supreme Court, applying the doctrine to public education. In several cases, the court has ordered the admission to colleges and universities of Negro students on the ground that equal facilities were not available in segregated institutions.

Today, however, the court held the doctrine inapplicable under any circumstances to public education.

This means that the court may extend its ruling from primary and secondary schools to include state-supported colleges and universities. Two cases involving Negroes who wish to enter white colleges in Texas and Florida are pending before the court.

The question of "due process," also a clause in the Fourteenth Amendment, had been raised in connection with the state cases as well as the District of Columbia.

The High Court held, however, that since it had ruled in the state cases that segregation was unconstitutional under the "equal protection" clause, it was unnecessary to discuss "whether such segregation also violates the due process clause of the Fourteenth Amendment."

However, the "due process" clause of the Fifth Amendment was the core of the ruling in the District of Columbia case. "Equal protection" and "due process," the court noted, were not always interchangeable phrases.

Liberty Held Deprived

"Liberty under law extends to the full range of conduct which an individual is free to pursue,

and it cannot be restricted except for a proper governmental objective," Chief Justice Warren asserted.

"Segregation in public education is not reasonably related to any proper governmental objective, and thus it imposes on Negro children of the District of Columbia a burden that constitutes an arbitrary deprivation of their liberty in violation of the due process clause."

Two principal surprises attended the announcement of the decision. One was its unanimity. There had been reports that the court was sharply divided and might not be able to get an agreement this term. Very few major rulings of the court have been unanimous.

The second was the appearance with his colleagues of Justice Robert H. Jackson. He suffered a mild heart attack on March 30. He left the hospital last week-end and had not been expected to return to the bench this term, which will end on June 7.

Perhaps to emphasize the unanimity of the court, perhaps from a desire to be present when the history-making verdict was announced, Justice Jackson was in his accustomed seat when the court convened.

A Sociological Decision

Court Founded Its Segregation Ruling On Hearts and Minds Rather Than Laws

By JAMES RESTON
Special to The New York Times.

WASHINGTON, May 17—The Supreme Court not only upheld Justice John M. Harlan's famous dictum that "the Constitution is colorblind" today but also based its decision on the primacy of the general welfare.

At a time when the Executive and Legislative Branches of the Government were involved in a major conflict over their respective powers, the principal court of the land managed to agree unanimously on what heretofore had been one of the most controversial questions of the century.

In ruling out racial segregation in the nation's public schools, it rejected history, philosophy and custom as the major basis for its decision and accepted instead Justice Benjamin N. Cardoza's test of contemporary social justice.

Relying more on the social scientists than on legal precedents—a procedure often in controversy in the past—the court insisted on equality of the mind

and heart rather than on equal school facilities:

"To separate them [Negro children] from others of similar age and qualifications solely because of their race," Chief Justice Earl Warren said for the court, "generates a feeling of inferiority as to their status in the community that may affect their hearts and minds in a way unlikely ever to be undone."

The court's opinion read more like an expert paper on sociology than a Supreme Court opinion. It sustained the argument of experts in education, sociology, psychology, psychiatry and anthropology in the Gebhart case, namely, that even with equal school buildings, segregated Negro children received a substantially inferior education.

Two arguments seemed to impress the court: the testimony in the South Carolina, Kansas and Delaware cases on the effects of segregation on the Negro students in those states; and the testimony of social scientists on the effects of discrimination on personality development.

In the South Carolina case, witnesses testified that compulsory racial segregation in the public schools of that state injured Negro students by:

¶Impairing their ability to learn.

¶Deterring the development of their personalities.

¶Depriving them of equal status in the school community.

¶Destroying their self-respect.

¶Denying them full opportunity for democratic social development.

¶Subjecting them to the prejudices of others.

¶Stamping them with a badge of inferiority.

The South Carolina Argument

The argument in the South Carolina case, which the court sustained, was this:

In a democracy, citizens from every group, no matter what their social or economic status or their religious or ethnic origins, are expected to participate widely in the making of important public decisions.

The public school, even more than the family, the church, business institutions, political and social groups and other institutions, has become an effective agency for giving to all people that broad background of attitudes and skills required to function effectively as participants in a democracy.

Thus, this argument continues. "education" comprehends the entire process of developing and training the mental, physical and

moral powers and capacities of human beings, and these capacities cannot be developed properly, even in the finest of school buildings, if the students are segregated from the majority by law.

The appellants in the case presented to the court a brief by what they described as a "consensus of social scientists with respect to the issue * * *." This "Brandeis-type" brief seems to contain the major arguments on this key question of the detrimental effects of segregation in the schools.

The report argued that segregation damaged not only the minority Negro students in the segregated schools but the majority group students as well. It made these points about the effects on Negro children:

¶Negro children, observing that they are kept apart from the white children who are better treated, "often react with feelings of inferiority and a sense of personal humiliation."

¶Some Negro children—usually of the lower socio-economic classes—"may react by overt aggressions and hostility directed toward their own group or members of the dominant group."

¶Middle-class and upper-class minority group children are "likely to react to their racial frustrations and conflicts by withdrawal and submissive behavior."

Defeatist Attitude Seen

"Minority group children of all social and economic classes," the

215

report said, "often react with a generally defeatist attitude and a lowering of personal ambitions.

"This, for example, is reflected in a lowering of pupil morale and a depression of the educational aspiration level among minority group children in segregated schools.

"In producing such effects, segregated schools impair the ability of the child to profit from the educational opportunities provided him."

The report to the court also noted that white children, under these circumstances, were hurt because they were encouraged to think of whole groups of people as inferior. This, it was contended, set up conflicts in the white child's mind because he was taught principles of equality that were not applied to the Negro children.

The report also made these points:

¶The child who is compelled to attend a segregated school may be able to cope with ordinary expressions of prejudice by regarding the prejudiced person as evil or misguided; but he cannot readily cope with symbols of authority, the full force of the authority of the state—the school or the school board, in this instance—in the same manner.

¶Segregation leads to a blockage in the communications and interaction between the two groups. Such blockages tend to increase mutual suspicion, distrust and hostility.

¶Segregation not only perpetuates rigid stereotypes and reinforces negative attitudes toward members of the other group, but also leads to the development of a social climate within which violent breaks of racial tensions are likely to occur.

Thus the court today added one more illustration to Justice Cardoza's power of prophecy:

"When the social needs demand one settlement rather than another," he said, "there are times when we must bend symmetry, ignore history and sacrifice custom in the pursuit of other and larger ends.

"From history and philosophy and custom, we pass, therefore, to the force which in our day and generation is becoming the greatest of them all, the power of social justice which finds its outlet and expression in the method of sociology * * *.

"The final cause of law is the welfare of society * * *."

May 18, 1954

YEAR'S GAIN NOTED IN DESEGREGATION

But Anniversary of Court's Ruling Barring School Bias Finds Picture Indecisive

By RUSSELL BAKER
Special to The New York Times.

WASHINGTON, May 16—Tomorrow is the first anniversary of the Supreme Court decision against school segregation, but the day still has not earned its red letters on the calendar.

In the year elapsed since the court spoke, the South has witnessed considerable confusion, much indecision, more uneasiness and a few bold experiments.

The biggest and the boldest experiments look like successes. But it is too early to give them the unqualified accolade.

A few of the smaller ones failed.

The Deep South, which announced at the beginning that it would not desegregate, has not. Political leaders in Georgia, Mississippi and South Carolina have been actively planning ways to evade the spirit of the court's ruling.

In Georgia the man who ran for Governor declaring, "Come hell or high water, races will not be mixed in Georgia schools," was elected.

In the absence of a court decree to give the decision effect, however, areas planning resistance have been working in a vacuum. Not knowing what the law will demand, they have had nothing but a statement of principle to plan against.

While the Deep South awaits the decree, many communities in the border states have moved toward compliance without it. In the most daring tests—notably in Baltimore and Washington, where complete desegregation was ordered, and in St. Louis, where the high schools were desegregated—the big problems that will characterize desegregation's aftermath are beginning to emerge.

Two long-range problems, one for the Negro and one for the educators, have already come into focus.

To the Negro it has become apparent that physical desegregation of school buildings is not the end-all and be-all of his striving for equality. A large degree of segregation is being maintained in the schools by segregated housing patterns in the border cities.

Children normally go to the school in their community. When the community is all white or all Negro, the color of the school reflects the segregated character of the community.

In Baltimore and Washington, Negro leaders agree that there will be a great deal of school segregation without fiat until housing patterns crumble. Thus, the first experiments have indicated the goal for the Negro's next major battle—to break out of the housing strait-jacket.

For the educators, the problem is finally to face squarely the question that has always plagued Southern education. That is how to give adequate education to a high proportion of students with low socio-economic backgrounds.

Baltimore and Washington school people agree with the accepted anthropological view that there is no correlation between race and intellectual ability. Yet social and economic environment, they agree, is reflected in a child's scholastic performance.

The Negro, who has generally had the worst of socio-economic life in the South, swells the proportion of slow learners, the maladjusted and the backward student in the all-white schools.

This, the administrators believe, will intensify an old problem, not create a new one.

While the Negro students were segregated, educators had the problem on a smaller scale in the white schools, among the lower proportion of white students with poor socio-economic backgrounds.

The problem was there, too, in the Negro schools, and on a large scale. But while segregation lasted, some administrators will privately admit, there was no strong compulsion to solve it in the Negro schools.

Admitted to white schools, the Negroes have brought the fruit of second-class education with them and dropped it with dramatic impact before white eyes.

The result in Washington, for example, has been a sudden increase in demand for remedial reading classes. One Negro teacher in a formerly white high school reports that of twenty Negro students in her class, twelve are five to six years below the grade level in reading ability.

The history of desegregation for the year was written largely in the border states. St. Louis, having integrated its high schools without incident, is ready to lower the color bar in its elementary schools this fall.

Wilmington, Del., culturally closer to Philadelphia than to Richmond, has desegregated smoothly. At Milford, in southern Delaware, however, the school board attempted it in the fall and promptly revoked the order in response to public demonstrations.

White Sulphur Springs in Greenbrier County, W. Va., had a similar experience. Yet in the deeper South, the small towns of Charleston and Fayetteville, Ark., desegregated without disturbance.

It is argued that, since the number of Negroes involved in the Arkansas cases was small, the cases were not typical and had little significance.

With equal force, it is contended that the Milford test failed because local authorities wavered instead of standing firm in the face of disturbances inflamed by a professional agitator.

Balanced against West Virginia's one setback is the fact that integration has been completely effected in twelve of the state's fifty-five counties and partly in eleven others.

The test areas are still too few and specialized and their results too diffuse and complex to form any pattern indicating what might happen with desegregation in other Southern communities.

Interviews with school administrators, principals, teachers, students and Negro leaders in Washington and Baltimore, however, produced some interesting points.

¶After a few tense days at the beginning of the school term, when students at a few scattered schools "struck," there has been nothing approaching violence in either city.

Dr. John H. Fischer, superintendent of Baltimore schools, believes this was because his city was moving gradually since the beginning of World War II toward desegregation.

The color bars had gone down in the city's legitimate theatres, in the Police and Fire Departments, and against employment by the cab companies and the public transit system.

Furman L. Templeton, executive director of the Baltimore Urban League, noted a complete absence of vocal or organized resistance to integration since its beginning.

"It seems that it's become almost unfashionable, or bad taste here for white people to get up on a soapbox and preach prejudice," he commented.

Community Trend Favorable

Dr. Fischer believes desegregation worked because it was consistent with a "community trend." He is reluctant, though, to advise other communities contemplating the move.

"You just can't be confident that what works in one community will necessarily work in another," he said. "The public school system of any community is and must be internally related to the community.

"I just don't believe any school superintendent can make a sharp break with the traditional patterns of the community unless the substantial elements of the community are willing to support it."

¶There is no desegregation after school hours. With rare exceptions, the educators agree, white and Negro children go their separate ways back to their segregated communities when the school days ends.

¶Even in the classroom, the cafeteria and on the playing field, Negro and white students

216

tend to bunch separately and avoid mingling. At a typical lunch-hour at McKinley High, Washington's most completely integrated high school, Negro and white children form separate islands in the cafeteria, each group automatically segregating itself from the other.

¶McKinley has five Negro teachers in charge of integrated classes. Dr. Charles E. Bish, the principal, reports that "not a single white parent has complained about the grades they've given or the activities of these teachers."

Mrs. Elizabeth W. Smith, one of the five, said she has had "no reason to feel that any pupils in the building have resented me."

She, too, noted the tendency of her students to form classroom cliques along color lines.

"But everybody knows you can't force friendships on people," she said. "I think this kind of separation is an inevitable result of the way they've grown up."

¶Desegregation has worked easiest in sports. The boy who performs well on the athletic field is accepted on his merits.

A Negro boy is one of the stars of the Baltimore Polytechnic swimming team. McKinley had several on its football team even before the school term began.

Integration?" said the Negro boy who quarterbacks the McKinley football squad. "I don't even think about it any more unless somebody says something to me about being at an integrated school."

There are sore spots, however, in the athletic story. A Baltimore junior high school bowling team organized on a segregated basis because the private alleys that it used refused to drop the color bar.

The Carver Negro high school in Baltimore had its application for membership in the Maryland Scholastic Association rejected this spring.

The association, which arranges athletic schedules for both public and private schools in Maryland, explained that it wanted to experiment for two years with "nonbody contact" sports before it accepted new applicants who would take part in interracial contests.

¶Desegregation has been most difficult in school social activities, particularly dances. McKinley High, where integration is complete enough to create a social problem, has held no dances this year.

This is a source of complaint among white students. The school is planning to go ahead with its commencement prom

next month, however, on a desegregated basis. Dr. Bish, after conferences with his students, has a prior stipulation that there will be no mixed couples on the dance floor.

Getting hotel ballrooms for such dances poses an additional problem, particularly in Baltimore's color-conscious hotels.

There, despite the local joy about the city's recent acquisition of a major league baseball team, hotel keepers have not been sufficiently infected to admit Negro ballplayers with visiting teams.

¶Student reaction to integration has been mixed. The comment most frequently heard is that integration "had to come eventually" and that the students must learn to live with it. But the general picture is a crazy quilt of prejudice and liberalism.

"They're just as good as we are," comments a Baltimore high school girl, "and I think it's terrible the way some kids act toward them."

'Like Everybody Else'

"You know," a McKinley High school girl tells you, "you'd always thought of them before as being jazzy — you know, hep cats, slangy. You'd never thought of them before as being like everybody else." The same girl accepts integration as inevitable and hopes it will work. But not so completely, she added, that "one day one of my children might marry one of them."

"The mere fact of a change of policy," Dr. Fischer commented, "doesn't mean that automatically everybody loves everybody else. But we have demonstrated that you can desegregate schools and they will keep on operating."

¶The built-in housing check against desegregation shows itself clearly in Washington's fall enrollment figures. Four high schools in predominantly white communities had a total Negro enrollment of fifty-eight. Their white enrollment was 4,071.

Of some 130 elementary schools, twenty-eight had no integration. Forty-nine had been "integrated" with ten or fewer students of the opposite race.

Thirty-two grade schools, less than one-fourth of the total, were integrated by a ratio of 10 to 1 or less. The ratio of Negroes to white students in the total public school population is about 60 to 40.

This statistical picture is modified somewhat by the fact that some Negro children, given the option of moving into white schools or staying in their old ones, elected not to transfer.

But the effectiveness of housing segregation as a social force against school integration is recognized by Negro and white leaders alike.

"How do you get fully integrated schools in segregated communities?" asked Dr. Fischer. "It is just as wrong to manipulate children to create integregation as it is to create segregation."

"We're going to have largely colored and largely white schools in Baltimore for a long time, and it won't be because of prejudice," conceded Mr. Templeton.

¶Gradualism in desegregation is indicated, too, in the reluctance of Negro students in higher grades to uproot from their old schools to move into formerly white ones.

Baltimore offered every student the school of his choice. Yet transfers from Negro to white high schools were few. Southern High, which had the largest number of Negro admissions, has only sixty in a total enrollment of about 1,800.

Many Refuse to Shift

In Washington, Negroes who could have transferred to a formerly all-white high school from the city's highly-respected Dunbar High "elected to stay where they were by the hundreds," one school official reported.

He ascribed this to reluctance of older, well-adjusted students to break from a comfortable educational and social environment on a doubtful chance for self-improvement.

Integration of white students into former Negro schools has been virtually nil. In Washington, only one white student was enrolled in the city's four big Negro high schools with a total population of 5,412.

¶Though statistics are lacking, the gravity of the purely educational problem in Washington has apparently been heightened by the reluctance of well-adjusted Negro students to leave their old schools.

School officials cannot say with certainty, but they believe that the Negro students who made the transfer last fall represented a poor cross-section of the Negro community.

Mrs. Margaret J. Butcher, Negro member of the Washington school board, has charged that the poorest Negro students were "dumped" indiscriminately into the white schools.

"It's reasonable," another school administrator said privately, "that the successful and happy student would prefer to stay where he is. I suspect this has been a strong factor in

fostering the movement of the below average Negro children into the old white schools. There are no figures to prove it, but I'm convinced the old white schools didn't get a fair shake."

Whatever the reason, the Negro transfers have aroused the school board to the existence of an urgent need for new remedial reading and social adjustment classes.

A white junior high principal announced recently that 135 of 300 students admitted to his former white school had I.Q.'s below 75; i.e., that they were mentally retarded.

In the three lowest ranking of ten seventh-grade classes, he said, all the students were Negroes. "All these children should have been in special classes during earlier years," he added.

This school drew Negroes from the city's lowest socioeconomic level.

Some in Transfer Excel

The consensus of informed opinion is that the white schools are finally reaping the bitter fruits of the old "separate but equal" doctrine.

A Washington school officer who refused to be quoted stated that the need for special instruction in the Negro schools had never received compelling attention when the city operated "separate but equal schools."

Not all the Negro students have done badly. One white principal reported that of six in her school with 818 white students, two were above average, one was a slow learner and the others were average.

Dr. Bish reported that the best French student at his school was a Negro transfer. So was the captain of the school's best cadet company, he added.

In Baltimore, Negro students are graduating this year from the Baltimore Polytechnic Institute's special "A" course in engineering, one of the hardest courses of its kind in the country. Completion of the course entitles the graduate to admission as a second-year student at many of the country's best engineering schools.

The explanation of the high proportion of backward Negro students is not racial, Dr. Fischer believes, but purely social and economic.

"What we face is nothing new because the schools have been integrated," he said. "We've had this problem always. What is happening now is not essentially different from what happened here about forty years ago in the high schools when we began taking in all white students, whereas previously we had taken in only the gifted."

May 17, 1955

217

HIGH COURT TELLS STATES TO END PUPIL SEGREGATION WITHIN 'REASONABLE' TIME

NO DEADLINE SET

Federal District Courts Get Job of Checking on Compliance

By LUTHER A. HUSTON

Special to The New York Times.

WASHINGTON, May 31—The Supreme Court directed the states today to end racial segregation in the public schools within a "reasonable" time.

Regional Federal courts were entrusted with the responsibility for determining whether local authorities made a prompt start, whether their plans were effective, and whether they were submitted and carried out in good faith.

No deadlines were fixed in the unanimous opinion written by Chief Justice Earl Warren. The court devised a flexible formula to effectuate the court's ruling of May 17 last year that separation of school pupils because of color was unconstitutional.

Full consideration was accorded the "complexities" involved and the wide variety of local conditions that must be dealt with by the authorities.

The court's opinion, however, plainly warned those who disagreed with the ruling not to attempt to frustrate today's judgment by unreasonable or unnecessary delays. The jurisdiction of the Federal courts to act against those who "drag their feet" was retained.

Prompt Compliance Ordered

Compliance with the ruling, the court said, must begin promptly. It must be carried out in a "systematic and effective" manner and in good faith.

Officials of the Eisenhower Administration generally were gratified by the court's ruling. President Eisenhower said last November that he understood

the high court did not intend to be arbitrary in establishing procedures.

The Department of Justice, in briefs and arguments submitted to the court, advocated a "middle-of-the-road" approach to the problem. Officials of the department noted with satisfaction that today's ruling included most of the basic proposals they had put forward

Congressional reaction, for the most part, indicated relief that the court had not ordered a summary end to segregation under a rigid mandate. By permitting a gradual transition from segregated to integrated school systems, many felt, serious repercussions probably had been avoided.

Most Senators and Representatives from southern states appeared to believe, however, that complete integration of their public schools was many years away.

Negro lawyers had asked the high court to order segregation ended not later than September, 1956. No great disappointment was expressed, however, that the court had adopted the more gradual approach.

The Chief Justice delivered the opinion in the same manner that the constitutional ruling was announced a little more than a year ago. That, too, was a unanimous decision.

No announcement is ever made of opinions that are to be handed down. Persons in the courtroom get their first inkling of what is coming when a member of the court begins reading.

Today, as last year, the unusual procedure was adopted of withholding release of the opinion until the Chief Justice had finished reading. Customarily the decisions are given out in the press room, one floor below, as soon as the reading begins.

An amplifying system installed a few months ago carried the Chief Justice's words more clearly than last year to all parts of the courtroom. The chamber was filled with the usual throng of lawyers, reporters, sight-seeing groups and individual spectators. A few

notables, including Mrs. Warren, were in the section reserved for guests of the court.

The scene did not differ, however, from any normal day when the black-robed justices, from their bench in the high-ceilinged, sedately decorated courtroom, hand down their judgments.

At the outset, the Chief Justice made it clear that any Federal, state or local law that permitted racial discrimination in public education was invalid. This was a position urged by the Government.

Solicitor General Simon E. Sobeloff had argued that such a declaration was necessary so that there could be no misunderstanding that the prior judgment applied to all racial discrimination in all public schools.

In the opinion of lawyers, this broadened the decision beyond the five cases that were before the court and made it apply to areas not involved in the litigation under review.

The five cases came from Kansas, South Carolina, Virginia, Delaware and the District of Columbia. The high court reversed the decisions of lower courts in each of these cases except Delaware. In South Carolina, Virginia, Kansas and the District, lower courts had upheld the constitutionality of segregation laws.

Delaware Ruling Reversed

In Delaware, however, the State Supreme Court had ordered the immediate admission of Negro pupils to white schools, on the grounds that equal separate facilities for the colored students were not available. The state appealed from this ruling, as contrary to its Constitution, as well as the Federal Constitution. The United States Supreme Court upheld the Delaware court's decision.

Except in Delaware, the cases had been heard by what is known as a "constitutional court." This consists of three judges, one from the Federal Court of Appeals and two from the Federal district courts.

The United States Code requires that a three-judge court must rule in cases where the constitutionality of a state statute is challenged.

The Supreme Court remanded the segregation cases to the three-judge courts in all but Delaware. Lawyers said that this meant that the "constitutional courts" would be the bodies that would pass upon enforcement procedures.

If a case of noncompliance arose in Virginia, for example, a judge of the Fourth Circuit Court of Appeals would be a member of the judicial body that would pass upon it. This would also apply it was stated, in states that were not parties to the current suits.

An effect would be, in the opinion of some lawyers, to prevent a Federal district judge who might, because of his origins and background be sympathetic toward community attitudes, from tolerating dilatory tactics or plans not submitted in good faith.

State Plans Invited

The Government had suggested that each community be required to submit within ninety days a plan of integration for the approval of the lower court. The high court imposed no such requirement but it invited the submission of such plans.

"They [the lower courts] will also consider the adequacy of any plans the defendants may propose to meet these problems and to effectuate a transition to a racial nondiscriminatory school system," the court said.

The primary responsibility for the solution of the complex problems involved, the opinion stated, rests upon the school authorities. The cases were remanded to the lower courts because, Justice Warren said, these courts were familiar with local conditions and best qualified to appraise the merits or demerits of suggested procedures.

Courts would be guided by equitable principles, the Chief Justice said.

"Traditionally, equity had been characterized by a practical flexibility in shaping its remedies and by a faculty for adjusting and reconciling public and private needs," he said.

Once a start has been made, the opinion stated, the courts may determine how much time is required to bring about elimination of segregation in their areas. But the "burden rests on the defendants," the court asserted, to establish how much time is necessary in the public interest and "consistent with good-faith compliance."

Case Began in 1952

As far as the Supreme Court is concerned, today's judgment disposed of an issue that has been before it since 1952. Arguments were first heard in the 1952 term. Unable to reach a decision, the court ordered rearguments in the following term, which began in October, 1953.

A decision on the constitutional issue was reached during that term but the question of the decrees the court should issue to effectuate it was put over to the session that began last October. Originally set for argument on Dec. 6, the cases were postponed because of the death of Justice Robert H. Jackson and Senate delay in confirming Justice John M. Harlan as his successor.

Seven members of the present court, Justices Hugo L. Black,

Stanley F. Reed, Felix Frankfurter, William O. Douglas, Harold H. Burton, Sherman Minton and Tom. C. Clark, have heard arguments all three times. Chief Justice Warren participated in the constitutional hearings as well as those involving the nature of the decrees. Justice Harlan took part only in the decision announced today.

Seventeen states and the District of Columbia have mandatory segregation laws. The states are Alabama, Arkansas, Delaware, Florida, Mississippi, Missouri, North Carolina, Oklahoma, Georgia, Kentucky, Louisiana, Maryland, South Carolina, Tennessee, Texas, Virginia and West Virginia.

Kansas, New Mexico, Arizona and Wyoming have permissive statutes, although segregation has not been practiced in Wyoming.

June 1, 1955

'With Deliberate Speed' Is the Coming Phrase

WASHINGTON, May 31 (AP) —The Supreme Court in its opinion today said school segregation must be ended "with all deliberate speed"—a phrase likely to keep lawyers arguing for a long, long time.

Under one dictionary definition of "deliberate" the phrase is self-contradictory. This definition is: "slow in action; unhurried."

It seems likely, however, that the high tribunal did not have this definition in mind. Others include:

Arrived at, or determined upon, as a result of careful thought and weighing of considerations.

Carried on coolly and steadily.

Careful in considering the consequences of a step.

Characterized by reflection; dispassionate; not rash.

In the coming legal struggles in district courts, opponents of school integration are likely to put a lot of emphasis on the "deliberate" part of the Supreme Court's language; foes of segregation are expected to lay more stress on the word "speed."

June 1, 1955

4 Southern Governors Join To Fight Pupil Integration

Heads of Mississippi, South Carolina, Virginia and Georgia Meet to Map Opposition to High Court Ruling

By CLARENCE DEAN
Special to The New York Times.

RICHMOND, Va., Jan. 24— The Governors of four Southern states agreed here today to stand together in challenging the United States Supreme Court's ruling outlawing public school segregation.

The united front, as announced in a statement after a six-hour meeting, contemplates three measures: a resolution of interposition in each of the four state Legislatures, a request for Congressional action and the use of "legal measures" within the states to prevent school integration.

This program was accepted by Govs. Thomas B. Stanley of Virginia, Marvin Griffin of Georgia, J. P. Coleman of Mississippi and George Bell Timmerman Jr. of South Carolina. The Legislatures in these states are now in session.

Gov. Luther Hodges of North Carolina, the Legislature of which is not in session, also attended the meeting. While he did not join in the plan of action, he said that he had found the discussion of "substantial benefit and encouraging to us."

The program of the other states, he added, will "be given serious consideration by the advisory commission on education and myself for possible submission to the General Assembly at its next meeting."

An atmosphere of tension hung over the capitol, where the meeting was held. Mr. Timmerman read the statement after the meeting in the presence of the other Governors. No questions were permitted.

The statement follows:

"This conference composed of the Governors of the four Southern states whose Legislatures are in regular session does declare:

"That the states have not delegated to the Federal Government or any agency thereof the power to prohibit the segregation of the races in the public schools and we, therefore, shall recommend to the Legislatures of our respective states that the following action be taken:

"1—That there be adopted a resolution of interposition or protest in appropriate language against the encroachment of the Central Government upon the sovereignty of the several states and their people.

"2—That a call be made upon the Congress of the United States to take such action within the limits of its constitutional authority as to protect the states and their people against present and future encroachment by the Central Government.

"3—That each state exercise its right to enact and utilize such other appropriate legal measures as it may deem advisable to protect its sovereignty and the rights of its people."

The significance of the program, or exactly how it would be carried out, was not made clear.

Interposition Plans Offered

Resolutions of interposition, in varying strength of language, have been proposed in several Southern Legislatures. One of the milder versions was introduced in Virginia last week and referred to a Senate committee.

Essentially the resolutions would "interpose" the sovereignty of the state between the Federal Government and the people in an endeavor to obstruct Federal action that the state holds to be in violation of the Federal Constitution.

The call on Congress to take action "within the limits of its constitutional authority" was interpreted to mean Congressional action leading to a constitutional amendment declaring segregation in schools unconstitutional. Since three-quarters of the states would have to approve such an amendment, the South believes it would be defeated.

However, before such an amendment could be submitted to the states, a two-third vote of each chamber of Congress would be needed. Supporters of the interposition idea concede that they are not sure the two-third votes could be obtained.

States' Rights Stressed

One effect of the plan, however, might be to delay any immediate action toward integration. State Senator Harry F. Byrd Jr. of Winchester, son of the United States Senator, said today he believed that during such a move "no drastic action" would be ordered.

Mr. Byrd declared he wished to make clear that his position, and that of many other Virginians was not so much concerned with the school integration issue as the question of "Federal encroachment upon states rights."

The third point in the Governor's program, "appropriate legal measures" within the states, apparently would apply to such actions as the Virginia proposal to make state tuition funds available to private schools. A constitutional convention to implement this will be held March 5.

January 25, 1956

Segregation Ban Extended To Colleges by High Court

By LUTHER A. HUSTON
Special to The New York Times.

WASHINGTON, March 5—The Supreme Court affirmed today a lower-court ban on racial segregation in tax-supported colleges and universities. The effect was to extend specifically to higher institutions of learning the decision of May 17, 1954, in which the high court outlawed segregation in the public schools. That opinion dealt only with cases involving elementary and high school pupils.

A three-judge Federal court, sitting at Greensboro, N. C., agreed last Sept. 10 that the decision of 1954 had been limited to the facts before it. However, it added, "the reasoning on which the decision was based is as applicable to schools for higher education as to schools on the lower level."

The high court unanimously affirmed that interpretation of its earlier decision.

Today's action was on an appeal from the lower court's order directing the University of North Carolina to admit three Negro students. That order decreed that applications of the Negroes "and other Negroes similarly situated" must be processed on their qualifications regardless of race or color.[1]

The students were LeRoy Benjamin Frasier Jr., Ralph Kennedy Frasier and John Lewis Brandon. The university admitted them, pending the outcome of the appeal to the Supreme Court, and they now are attending classes at Chapel Hill.

Each of the Negroes is a graduate of a Durham, N. C., high school. They applied for admission to the university in April, 1955. When their applications were rejected, they sued to compel the university to admit them.

Their contention was that the refusal to admit them had violated their constitutional rights and privileges.

The university based its rejection on the ground that equal educational facilities were available for Negroes in institutions maintained by the state at great expense. North Carolina University averred the wisdom of the "separate but equal" policy and contended that Negroes got better educations in their own schools than if they attended integrated schools.

Judges Morris A. Soper and Armistead M. Dobie of the Fifth Circuit Court of Appeals and Federal District Judge Johnson J. Hayes heard the case.

Judge Soper wrote the unanimous opinion of the court. He rejected as "without merit" the contention of Attorney General William B. Rodman Jr., of North Carolina, and other attorneys for the university, that the Supreme Court ruling of 1954 did not apply to higher institutions.

Warren's Opinion Cited

Chief Justice Earl Warren, speaking for a unanimous court in that earlier ruling, held that segregation deprived Negroes of equal protection of the laws and that "in the field of public education the doctrine of separate but equal has no place." This was the "reasoning" Judge Soper said applied to colleges and universities as well as to lower schools.

North Carolina, in appealing Judge Soper's ruling, contended that the earlier judgment of the high court had been erroneous and asked that it be overruled. Congress, in submitting the Fourteenth Amendment, and the states, in ratifying it, "did not contemplate and did not understand that it would abolish segregation in the public schools," the state's brief asserted.

Furthermore, North Carolina asserted, the decision of 1954 should be set aside because "it is not within the power or authority of the [Supreme] Court to amend the Constitution."

No constitutional language, the state contended, forbade racial segregation in the public schools.

In any case, it was asserted, the lower court's decision should not apply to Negroes seeking admission hereafter. That would confer rights on persons not parties to the suit before the court, lawyers for the state declared.

Negroes' Lawyers File

On this point Judge Soper ruled that the right of the university's board of trustes to pass on the qualifications of applicants was not restricted.

"We decide only that the Negroes as a class may not be excluded because of their race or color," he said.

Lawyers representing the Negro students filed a motion to affirm the judgment of the the Supreme Court's 1954 ruling had "announced a constitutional doctrine which was to guide American courts in decisions concerning the Fourteenth Amendment with regard to questions of racial discrimination and segregation in general."

The Fourteenth Amendment provides that no state shall deny any person the equal protection of the laws. This was the basis on which the Supreme Court held school segregation to be unconstitutional.

The Supreme Court disposed of North Carolina's appeal in a per curiam opinion, meaning that the full court was speaking for itself rather than a single justice writing an opinion for the court. The opinion said:

"The motion to affirm is granted and the judgment is affirmed."

Tax-supported schools are those that receive their support from public funds raised by taxation. This usually means state schools, colleges and universities.

Whether the term would apply to institutions that accept tax exemptions, land grant colleges and so forth, probably could be decided only by further litigation.

Lawyers who represented the Negroes were Conrad O. Pearson, Floyd B. McKessick, John H. Wheeler, Thurgood Marshall and Robert L. Carter.

March 6, 195

---

96 in Congress Open Drive To Upset Integration Ruling

Declaration of Constitutional Principles by Southerners Vows 'Lawful' Fight to Maintain School Segregation

By ALVIN SHUSTER
Special to The New York Times.

WASHINGTON, March 11 — Ninety-six members of Congress pledged today to use "all lawful means" to reverse the Supreme Court decision of 1954 against racial segregation in the public schools.

They called the decision an abuse of judicial power that ran contrary to established law and the Constitution and encroached upon the rights constitutionally reserved to the states.

The result, they declared, has been to destroy "amicable relations" bewteen the white and Negro races and to replace friendship and understanding with "hatred and suspicion."

Nineteen Senators and seventy-seven members of the House, representing eleven Southern States, joined in the statement they called a Declaration of Constitutional Principles.

It will be read in both houses tomorrow, but it asks no action by them.

Although one of the sharpest criticisms of a Supreme Court decision by a group of lawmakers in years, the statement was milder in its wording than original drafts some Southerners had refused to sign.

The preliminary versions had called the court ruling "illegal and unconstitutional," but this phrasing was dropped. Moreover, the earlier draft had supported resolutions of "interposition" adopted by some states seeking to "interpose" their sovereignty to prevent implementation of the court's decision. This, too, was omitted.

As finally shaped, after three weeks of consultation, the manifesto reviewed the arguments against integration ruling, commended the states for plans to resist "forced integration by lawful means," and decried "outsiders" for meddling in the affairs of the South.

Throughout, the Southerners stressed "lawful means" and urged their constituents not to be provoked to disorder and lawless acts by "agitators and troublemakers invading our states."

There were words of caution for citizens outside the South. The statement said they should study the constitutional principles involved lest they also become "victims of judicial encroachment."

The signers—all Democrats but two—included both Senators from Alabama, Arkansas, Florida, Georgia, Louisiana; Mississippi, North Carolina, South Carolina and Virginia.

Senator Lyndon B. Johnson of Texas, the Senate majority leader, did not sign the document. His colleague, Senator Price Daniel, did. Mr. Johnson said he had not been shown the document because the majority of the group did not want to appear to be trying to "formulate Democratic or Senate policy."

Another Senator said it had not been submitted to the Democratic leader because it was realized "he had to work with all sides" on the Senate floor.

Senator Johnson did not comment directly on the document, but said he did not believe the solution could be found on the Federal level. He expressed hope that "wise leaders on the local level wil work to resolve differences."

Estes Kefauver and Albert Gore, Tennessee's Senators, did not sign. Mr. Kefauver, an aspirant for his party's Presidential nomination, said "I just don't agree with it." He added he had not taken part in any of the meetings of the Southern group. These were usually held in the office of Senator Walter F. George, Democrat of Georgia.

The Supreme Court's decision is now the law of the land and must be followed, Mr. Kefauver said.

Senator Gore declined comment.

Means Not Specified

The manifesto did not specify what "lawful means" its signers had in mind. A check of a few of them turned up a variety of interpretations on what was meant.

One Senator, for example, said "lawful means" might be the establishment of private school systems. But the statement itself cautioned against destruction of the system of public education.

Other signers said such efforts could include proposals for constitutional amendments, a boycott of candidates favorable to the court's ruling, or resolutions such as that sponsored by Senator Willis A. Robertson, Democrat of Virginia.

The Robertson bill, now before the Senate Judiciary Committee, would put Congress on record as declaring that a state could meet the requirements of the Constitution either by desegregating public schools or by providing separate but equal school facilities for white and Negro students.

It was the long-standing "separate but equal" doctrine that the high court struck down in its ruling in 1954.

In the declaration, the Southerners denounced the court for overturning the doctrine that "became a part of the life of the people of many of the states and confirmed their habits, customs, traditions and way of life."

By this action, they added, the Supreme Court Justices undertook to substitute their "personal political and social ideas" for established law.

"We pledge ourselves to use all lawful means to bring about a reversal of this decision which is contrary to the Constitution and to prevent the use of force in its implementation," they added.

The declaration originally was drawn up by Democratic Senators Richard B. Russell of Georgia, John Stennis of Mississippi and Sam J. Ervin Jr. of North Carolina. Other Senators proposed changes.

The two Republican signers were Representatives Joel T. Broyhill and Richard H. Poff, both of Virginia.

March 12, 1956

PRESIDENT SENDS TROOPS TO LITTLE ROCK, FEDERALIZES ARKANSAS NATIONAL GUARD

EISENHOWER ON AIR

Says School Defiance Has Gravely Harmed Prestige of U. S.

By ANTHONY LEWIS
Special to The New York Times.

WASHINGTON, Sept. 24—President Eisenhower sent Federal troops to Little Rock, Ark., today to open the way for the admission of nine Negro pupils to Central High School.

Earlier, the President federalized the Arkansas National Guard and authorized calling the Guard and regular Federal forces to remove obstructions to justice in Little Rock school integration.

His history-making action was based on a formal finding that his "cease and desist" proclamation, issued last night, had not been obeyed. Mobs of pro-segregationists still gathered in the vicinity of Central High School this morning.

Tonight, from the White House, President Eisenhower told the nation in a speech for radio and television that he had acted to prevent "mob rule" and "anarchy."

Historic Decision

The President's decision to send troops to Little Rock was reached at his vacation headquarters in Newport, R. I. It was one of historic importance politically, socially, constitutionally. For the first time since the Reconstruction days that followed the Civil War, the Federal Government was using its ultimate power to compel equal treatment of the Negro in the South.

He said violent defiance of Federal Court orders in Little Rock had done grave harm to "the prestige and influence, and indeed to the safety, of our nation and the world." He called on the people of Arkansas and the South to "preserve and respect the law even when they disagree with it."

Guardsmen Withdrawn

Action quickly followed the President's orders. During the day and night 1,000 members of the 101st Airborne Division were flown to Little Rock. Charles E. Wilson, Secretary of the Defense, ordered into Federal service all 10,000 members of the Arkansas National Guard.

Today's events were the climax of three weeks of skirmishing between the Federal Government and Gov. Orval E. Faubus of Arkansas. It was three weeks ago this morning that the Governor first ordered National Guard troops to Central High School to preserve order. The nine Negro students

221

were prevented from entering the school.

The Guardsmen were gone yesterday, withdrawn by Governor Faubus as the result of a Federal Court order. But a shrieking mob compelled the nine children to withdraw from the school.

President Eisenhower yesterday cleared the way for full use of his powers with a proclamation commanding the mob in Little Rock to "disperse."

At 12:22 P. M. today in Newport the President signed a second proclamation. It said first that yesterday's command had "not been obeyed and willful obstruction of said court orders exists and threatens to continue."

The proclamation then directed Charles E. Wilson, Secretary of Defense, to take all necessary steps to enforce the court orders for admission of the Negro children, including the call of any or all Arkansas Guardsmen under Federal command and the use of the armed forces of the United States.

Later in the afternoon the President flew from Newport to Washington, arriving at the National Airport at 4:50 o'clock.

He began his broadcast speech with this explanation of the flight:

"I could have spoken from Rhode Island, but I felt that, in speaking from the house of Lincoln, of Jackson and of Wilson, my words would more clearly convey both the sadness I feel in the action I was compelled to take and the firmness with which I intend to pursue this course. * * *"

It was a firm address, with some language unusually strong for President Eisenhower.

President Traces Dispute

"Under the leadership of demagogic extremists," the President said, "disorderly mobs have deliberately prevented the carrying out of proper orders from a Federal court. Local authorities have not eliminated that violent opposition."

The President traced the course of the integration dispute in Little Rock. He noted especially that the Federal Court there had rejected what he called an "abrupt change" in segregated schooling and had adopted a "gradual" plan.

"Proper and sensible observance of the law," the President said, "then demanded the respectful obedience which the nation has a right to expect from all the people. This, unfortunately, has not been the case at Little Rock.

"Certain misguided persons, many of them imported into Little Rock by agitators, have insisted upon defying the law and have sought to bring it into disrepute. The orders of the court have thus been frustrated."

The reference to "imported" members of the mob was seen as a sign that the Federal Bureau of Investigation had information, obtained through agents in Little Rock, on the organization of yesterday's violence.

The President tried to make it plain that he had not sought the use of Federal power in Little Rock, nor welcomed it. Rather he suggested that as Chief Executive he had no choice.

"The President's responsibility is inescapable," he said at one point. At another he said that when the decrees of a Federal court were obstructed, "the law and the national interest demanded that the President take action."

"The very basis of our individual rights and freedoms," he said, "is the certainty that the President and the Executive Branch of Government will support and insure the carrying out of the decisions of the Federal Courts, even, when necessary with all the means at the President's command.

"Unless the President did so, anarchy would result.

"There would be no security for any except that which each one of us could provide for himself.

"The interest of the nation in the proper fulfillment of the law's requirements cannot yield to opposition and demonstrations by some few persons.

"Mob rule cannot be allowed to override the decisions of the courts."

The President appeared fit and vigorous when he stepped into his White House office tonight to face a battery of news and television cameras.

His face showed the ruddiness of the outdoors exercise he has been enjoying on the golf links.

The President, who wore a gray single-breasted suit with blue shirt and tie, spoke calmly and his voice, after setting a steady deliberate pace, rose only occasionally as he sought emphasis for certain words and phrases.

It rose on the word "firmness" when he spoke of his course in this grave situation, and "mob" when he referred to the perpetrators of the Little Rock violence, and "agitators" he said were brought in from the outside.

At either side on the wall on either side of him as he spoke hung portraits of the four leaders whom the President has stated he regards as the greatest American heroes—Benjamin Franklin, George Washington, Abraham Lincoln and Robert E. Lee.

But in his thirteen-minute address tonight, General Eisenhower mentioned only Lincoln.

September 25, 195

U. S. TROOPS ENFORCE PEACE IN LITTLE ROCK AS NINE NEGROES RETURN TO CLASSES

SCHOOL IS RINGED

Mob Taunts Soldiers —Man Is Clubbed With Rifle Butt

By HOMER BIGART
Special to The New York Times.

LITTLE ROCK, Ark., Sept. 25—An impressive show of Federal force cowed racist agitators at Central High School this morning, permitting the integration of nine Negro students without serious disorder.

Soldiers of the 327th Airborne Battle Group of the 101st Airborne Division set up a cordon around the school. With bayonets fixed on their M-1 rifles, troops in battle dress broke up small, sullen knots of civilians as soon as they formed.

At least seven persons were seized by the troops and turned over to the local police. One man, accidentally pricked by a bayonet, tried to wrest a rifle from a sergeant. The sergeant struck him on the head with the rifle butt, inflicting a minor scalp wound. Another man whose right arm was jabbed slightly by a leveled bayonet was subsequently arrested when he returned to the scene muttering threats.

1,500 in School Area

These were the only "casualties" of the military operation.

In a city of 117,000 (20,000 of them Negroes) agitators could draw not more than 1,500 whites to the school area. The vast majority of Little Rock citizens went about their normal business. Downtown was quiet.

Integration at bayonet point was effected at 9:25 A. M., forty minutes after the opening bell. An army station wagon, sandwiched between two jeeps filled with troops, drew up at the main entrance and unloaded the Negro students.

Students Escorted In

Amidst a phalanx of thirty soldiers, six girls and three youths marched up the wide steps and disappeared within.

Tonight federalized troops of the Arkansas National Guard

222

relieved paratroopers from guard duty at Central High. The paratroopers remained in bivouac at the stadium directly behind the school, and officers said there was no immediate plan for moving them out.

They said paratroopers probably would be back manning the cordons at dawn tomorrow.

The relieving units are troops of the 153d Infantry, and come from towns in southwest Arkansas. They were not among the National Guardsmen employed by Governor Faubus to keep Negroes out of Central High.

The 153d, commanded by Col. John Beakley, began assembling at Camp Robinson in North Little Rock early today.

Decision to employ Arkansas troops at Central High was based on a desire to have National Guardsmen "phased in" on this operation as soon as possible.

General Walker said earlier today that he hoped that the 327th Airborne Battle Group would be able to return to Fort Campbell, Ky., as soon as possible but that the timing would depend on restoration of tranquility in Little Rock.

Gov. Orval E. Faubus was not visible today. His aides said he intended to remain inside the Governor's mansion all day. They said he would see no reporters.

Tonight Governor Faubus said he had "no comment on the naked force being employed by the Federal Government against the people of my state." He said he would make a radio-televisoin address to the state tomorrow night.

Meanwhile, about 1,250 white students, assembled in the Central High auditorium, had received a lecture on civics by Maj. Gen. Edwin A. Walker, commander of Federal forces in Arkansas.

General Walker, a tall, lean Texan who had been a Commando officer at Anzio beachhead in World War II, told the students that the United States was a nation governed by law and not by mobs.

Some Leave Classes

He assured the students they had nothing to fear from the troops. But in solemn voice

and with steely deliberation he warned that any students who interfered with the integration plans would be removed by officers and handed over to the local police. Most of the students applauded.

But as soon as the Negroes took their classroom seats, a slow trickle of students began moving out. There were not more than thirty. But an estimated total of 750 failed to show up at all.

General Walker, in his first press conference since taking over responsibility for area security, admitted that some minor brushes had occurred between troops and civilians outside the school. He said "there will be none when I get through."

There are Negroes among the troops of the 327th Airborne Battle Group, but none were seen among the 350 paratroopers guarding the school today. The Negro soldiers were kept out of sight within the Little Rock University Armory.

The white paratroopers were subjected to taunts and insults by groups of segregationists.

Shortly after 10 A. M., Little Rock police received a telephone call from a youth who warned that a bomb had been planted in the school. It sounded phony. All last night the school building had been tightly guarded by paratroopers.

But when, after an hour, the same youth phoned a second warning, the police notified the school superintendent, Virgil T. Blossom. Although the police still regarded the warnings as the work of an agitator trying to keep the school in turmoil, Mr. Blossom held emergency consultations with General Walker and with Col. William A. Kuhn, commander of the battle group.

It was decided to evacuate the building while a search was made. Alarm bells were rung. Students, told it was a routine fire drill, emerged in orderly fashion, remained in the schoolyard about thirty minutes, then went quietly back to their classes.

Soldiers Posted in School

Long before school opened, Colonel Kuhn had his troops disposed around Central High to deal with the mobs. Twenty-four soldiers with rifles were posted strategically inside the building. They were to remain in corridors and were instruct-

ed not to enter classrooms unless a teacher called for help.

No trouble developed within the school. But for the more than 300 soldiers on cordon duty outside it was a day of incipient violence and bitter abuse.

The taunting started early. A bus driver heading downtown threw open his door to shout "all you need now is a Russian flag."

A woman driver lowered her window to cry "Heil Hitler."

She could hardly have known that the last action of the 101st Airborne in World War II was the capture of Hitler's aerie at Berchtesgaden.

Occasionally the troops encountered passive resistance as they tried to disperse groups. Lawns and porches of houses near the school were favored sanctuaries for hecklers. They sensed that without a declaration of martial law, troops could not invade private property.

General Walker had, in fact, instructed the troops to keep off private property.

So front lawns in the area were pre-empted at intervals by groups of twenty to thirty persons who stared morosely across Park Avenue to the single line of troops guarding the school yard.

At first these groups regarded the soldiers in sullen silence. The soldiers, unsmiling, returned the stares. Told to betray no softness, the paratroopers seemed alien and unapproachable.

Later when squads of paratroopers came dog-trotting down the street to push groups back from the curbs and sidewalks tempers worsened.

"You call yourselves élite troops but boy you look like bums to me," cried a scrawny, red-necked man from behind a wire-fenced lawn.

Loiterers Dispersed

Troops made their first move against crowds after Maj. James Myers of San Antonio ordered a squad to disperse a dozen men and boys loitering in front of a service station across the street.

"Move on out," Major Myers told the group. "Move on out."

"Can't I finish my coke?" one man protested.

"Nope," said a soldier leveling his M-1.

The man threw down his soft drink bottle and stalked away.

A block east of the school a larger crowd gathered at the

intersection. Major Myers picked up a mobile speaker.

"You are again instructed to return to your homes peacefully," he said. "Disperse and return to your homes."

The crowd refused to budge. Major Myers called for troops. Confronted by bayonets, the crowd pushed back on the lawn. C. E. Blake, 46 years old, an employe of the Missouri Pacific Railroad, was brushed by a bayonet. He thrust it aside and, according to a sergeant holding the weapon, made a grab for the rifle.

The sergeant struck him on the head with the rifle butt. Mr. Blake started bleeding from a scalp wound. Mrs. Blake screamed. Another woman fell over a hedge and screamed.

Mr. Blake was treated at a hospital. He was not among those who were arrested. But another man, also pricked by a bayonet when he refused to move, was spotted and seized by paratroopers when he returned some minutes later.

He was identified as Paul Downs, 38, an unemployed salesman from out of town.

Apart from the nine Negro students, few others of the race ventured into the school area. At mid-morning two Negro youths, one of them wearing a jacket stamped "Rochester, N. Y.," were turned away by paratroopers as they neared the school. As they walked down a sidestreet, a crowd of white youths started chasing them. The Negroes ran for several blocks until they were rescued by a jeep-load of paratroopers.

Later a Negro delivery boy was forced to take refuge in a house when threatened by a crowd. The crowd smashed his bicycle. Soon paratroopers arrived in a jeep and took him and his broken bicycle out of the area.

General Walker had called a press conference for 11 A. M. in a downtown hotel. But the bomb scare at Central High delayed his appearance for an hour.

The general dodged questions on the use of Negro paratroopers and on employment of the Arkansas National Guard.

Asked whether Negro troops would be deployed at Central High, the general said: "They will be used in accordance with my instructions."

September 26, 1957

SUPREME COURT FORBIDS EVASION OR FORCE TO BALK INTEGRATION

9 WRITE OPINION

It Goes Far Beyond Little Rock Case— Officials Warned

By ANTHONY LEWIS

Special to The New York Times.

WASHINGTON, Sept. 29— The Supreme Court said today that neither direct opposition nor "evasive schemes" could nullify its ruling that racial segregation in the public schools was unconstitutional.

In an opinion written by all nine justices, the court gave its reasons for rejecting any delay of integration in Little Rock, Ark. The court, which had met in special term, had announced its decision against delay on Sept. 12.

But today's opinion went far beyond the issue in the Little Rock case—whether violent local opposition could justify postponement of a plan to admit Negro children to white schools.

The court spelled out in strong language—stronger than the original school decisions—the duty of state and local officials to end school segregation as promptly as possible.

State Plans Rejected

It warned that its 1954 decision against school segregation applied not only to regular public schools but also to any school "where there is state participation through any arrangement, management, funds or property." This was an evident allusion to plans for setting up "private" school systems in Little Rock and elsewhere.

Finally, the opinion discussed in historical terms the power of the Federal courts to interpret the Constitution and the obligation of state officials to follow those interpretations.

"Every state legislator and executive and judicial officer," the court said, "is solemnly committed by oath" to support the Federal Constitution. It went on:

"No state legislator or executive or judicial officer can war against the Constitution without violating his undertaking to support it."

Quiet Drama in Court

The courtroom scene today was one of quiet drama. Suppressed excitement could be sensed among the spectators as it became apparent, at the start of the reading by Chief Justice Earl Warren, that this was more than an ordinary opinion.

The Chief Justice began by saying that all nine members of the court had been joint authors of the opinion.

He looked at each of the justices in turn as he read their names. All were in court except William O. Douglas, who is traveling in the West.

Plainly, this device of joint authorship was intended to emphasize the high court's continuing unanimity on the school issue. Followers of the court's work could remember no previous occasion on which all its members had been named as authors of an opinion.

Chief Justice Warren read the printed opinion without change except to omit legal citations. The other justices followed him from their copies of the text.

The reading took forty-five minutes. At the end the Chief Justice said, "The special term is now adjourned."

The opinion summarized what the court said in 1955, when it spelled out how its 1954 decision invalidating segregation should be implemented. The 1955 decree said integration should proceed with "all deliberate speed."

Some of the same phrases that were used in 1955 were used again today. But the emphasis was different. The effect was a considerably firmer injunction to end segregation soon.

In many locations, the court said, obedience to the duty of desegregation would require the immediate general admission of Negro children.

Following the logic of 1955, it went on to say that lower Federal courts "might conclude" in some areas "that justification existed for not requiring the present nonsegregated admission of all qualified Negro children." This passage specifically ruled out as a factor to be considered "hostility to racial desegregation."

The opinion said that lower courts "should scrutinize the program of the school authorities to make sure they had developed arrangements pointed toward the earliest practicable completion of desegregation, and had taken appropriate steps to put their program into effective operation."

Delays Denounced

"It was made plain," the court said of its 1955 opinion, "that delay in any guise in order to deny the Constitutional rights of Negro children could not be countenanced, and that only a prompt start, diligently and earnestly pursued, to eliminate racial segregation from the public schools could constitute good faith compliance."

"State authorities were thus duty bound to devote every effort toward initiating desegregation and bringing about the elimination of racial discrimination in the public school system."

Legal observers saw the effect of that language as greatly stiffening the attitude of Federal courts toward dilatory tactics on the part of state and local officials. To this extent it is a clarification of "deliberate speed."

But the language still allows time for those areas that do make a start.

One point noted especially by observers was a critical reference in the opinion to a "pupil assignment law," one of several moves by Arkansas that the court said were designed to "perpetuate racial segregation." The Supreme Court itself has not yet passed on the constitutionality of any pupil assignment plan in the South.

Three times in the opinion the court made the point that any state action in connection with a school would subject it to the rule of non-discrimination. It cited two Court of Appeals cases upsetting efforts to lease a courthouse cafeteria in Texas and a state park in Virginia in attempts to continue segregation.

Cannot Be Nullified

"In short," the court said. "the Constitutional rights of children not to be discriminated against in school admission on grounds of race or color can neither be nullified openly and directly by state legislators or state executive or judicial officers, nor nullified indirectly by them through evasive schemes for segregation whether attempted "ingeniously or ingenuously."

At the end the court again emphasized its unanimity.

Since its 1954 decision, the opinion said, "three new justices have come to the court."

"They are at one with the justices still on the court who participated in that basic decision as to its correctness, and that decision is now unanimously reaffirmed.

"The principles announced in that decision and the obedience of the states to them, according to the command of the Constitution, are indispensable for the protection of the freedoms guaranteed by our fundamental charter for all of us."

The three justices since the 1954 decision are John Marshall Harlan, William J. Brennan Jr. and Charles Evans Whittaker.

State Bench Upsets Basis of 'Massive Resistance' to Racial Integration

By HOMER BIGART
Special to The New York Times

RICHMOND, Va., Jan. 19—Virginia's "massive resistance" laws against racial integration in the public schools were struck down today by the state's own highest tribunal.

The Virginia Supreme Court of Appeals ruled, 5 to 2, that the package of laws supporting the state's posture of total segregation violated the state Constitution. The decision cannot be appealed.

The ruling overshadowed a Federal court decision in Norfolk a few hours later invalidating a Virginia law for the automatic closing of any integrated school. Gov. J. Lindsay Almond Jr. has used the law to lock out since early September 13,000 white children from nine schools of Norfolk, Charlottesville and Front Royal. These nine schools were under order by Federal courts to enroll a few Negroes. The Virginia court not only struck down the school closing law but also ruled against related laws by which the Almond Administration had hoped to avoid even token integration. These laws included:

¶A provision for cutting off state school funds from any community operating an integrated public school.

¶A statute providing for tuition grants for the private education of pupils assigned to integrated public schools.

¶The so-called "Little Rock laws," under which the Governor could shut down permanently schools policed by Federal authority or disturbed by such policing in a near-by school.

The Governor's Powers

On the Little Rock law, the Virginia court held that while schools policed by Federal troops could be closed temporarily under the Governor's inherent powers, their control could not be taken permanently away from local school authorities.

The majority ruling said that the other statutes violated a constitutional provision requiring Virginia to "maintain an efficient system of public free schools throughout the state."

The Almond Administration had argued that this requirement was wiped out when the United States Supreme Court invalidated the segregation section of the state Constitution.

Pleased by the ruling, moderates hoped that the Almond Administration would fall back from "massive" to a more flexible form of resistance. They favored this avenue of retreat: Return the schools to local control and possible token integration, but provide tuition grants for the private schooling of children whose parents were unshakeably opposed to integration.

Agitation for Repeal

Diehard segregationists were expected to demand the repeal of the constitutional provision requiring a state public school system.

Governor Almond declined comment. He said he would carry out his previously announced plan of appointing a legislative study commission to devise new laws for consideration by a special session of the General Assembly.

He said he intended to study the decision carefully. Then, perhaps tomorrow night, he will make a televised broadcast that will include some advice to the three communities where schools are closed, he said.

Today's ruling was made on a friendly test brought last September by the Almond Administration. Governor Almond told newsmen that he had "implicit faith in and high respect for the capacity and integrity of each and every member of the court."

The majority opinion was written by Chief Justice John W. Eggleston of Norfolk, with Justices C. Vernon Spratley of Hampton, A. C. Buchanan of Taxewell, Kennon C. Whittle of Martinsville and Lawrence W. I. Anson of Portsmouth, concurring. Dissenting were Justice Willis D. Miller and Harold F. Snead, both of Richmond.

Justice Miller contended that Section 129 of the Constitution, obliging the state to maintain a system of "efficient free public schools," had been made inoperative by the United States Supreme Court desegregation decree invalidating Section 140, which provided that "white and colored children shall not be taught in the same schools."

The prevailing opinion forbade the Legislature to take the state out of the field of public education and said the state would have to support even those schools where "pupils of both races are compelled to be enrolled and brought together, however unfortunate that situation may be."

January 20, 1959

U.S. JUDGE WEIGHS GEORGIA U. ACTION

300 of Faculty Deplore Riot, Ask Return of 2 Negroes

By CLAUDE SITTON
Special to The New York Times.

ATHENS, Ga., Jan. 12—Lawyers met with a Federal District Judge today in an attempt to return two Negro students to the University of Georgia. Pending a further conference, no action was taken.

The students were suspended early today by university officials after one of the most serious riots in the South in opposition to desegregation.

A mob, made up of students and a handful of Ku Klux Klansmen and other outsiders, last night stormed the dormitory in which one of the students had been housed.

United Press International Telephoto

RIOT IN GEORGIA: The scene Wednesday evening as students demonstrated outside the dormitory where Charlayne Alberta Hunter lived at University of Georgia in Athens.

About 300 of the university's 600 faculty members met tonight and adopted a resolution condemning the riot and calling for the return of the two Negroes. The resolution said in part:

"We deplore and condemn the incidents and regret that officials of the State of Georgia were unable or unwilling to protect the rights and property of the university and its students.

"We also deplore and condemn the behavior of certain outside elements and those university students who regrettably joined in lawless demonstrations.

"Let the Governor of this state, its law-enforcement officials and the people know that we, members of the faculty of this great institution, will not retreat from the responsibility of standing steadfastly by the rules of law and morality."

"Believing this, we insist that the two suspended students be returned to their classes and that all measures necessary to the protection of students and faculty and to the preservation of orderly education be taken by appropriate state authorities."

During the day, lawyers for the Negroes prepared a motion asking Federal District Judge William A. Bootle to revoke the students' suspension, but did not file it. After a closed meeting in the judge's chambers at Macon, they said another conference would be held tomorrow.

Judge Bootle, meanwhile, issued a permanent injunction against Gov. S. Ernest Vandiver and other state officials. It forbids the implementation of a segregation clause in an appropriations act that would cut off funds to the university. The judge described the clause as "patently unconstitutional."

He handed down the initial desegregation order against the university last Friday. The two students started classes yesterday.

It was expected that the Negroes, Charlayne Alberta Hunter, 18 years old, and Hamilton E. Holmes, 19, would be readmitted shortly. Deputy Federal marshals in several southeastern states have been alerted for possible duty here to protect them.

Miss Hunter, sobbing and holding a religious symbol, was removed from her dormitory shortly after midnight. She and Mr. Holmes, who was living off the campus, were driven to their Atlanta homes by the State Highway Patrol. They were accompanied by William Tate, Dean of Men, and Edith Stallings, Dean of Women.

Joseph A. Williams, Dean of Students, ordered their suspension "in the interest of their personal safety and for the safety and welfare of more than 7,000 other students.

"They are withdrawn until such time as members of my staff and I determine that it is safe and practical for them to return," he said.

Militant segregationists hailed the suspension as a victory over the Federal courts. Peter Zach Geer, Governor Vandiver's executive secretary, commented that "the students at the university have demonstrated that Georgia youth are possessed with the character of and courage not to submit to dictatorship and tyranny."

Many faculty members, students and the state's moderate leadership were shocked and outraged. They felt that the state had failed after making a peaceful start toward reluctant acceptance of the first desegregation in its public education system.

Governor Vandiver issued a statement calling for an end to violence. He denied that he had hesitated in dispatching state troopers to the aid of the forty-man Athens police force.

Tear gas and firemen's hoses finally dispersed the rioters after they had raged uncontrolled in the area for more than an hour.

January 13, 1961

3,000 TROOPS PUT DOWN MISSISSIPPI RIOTING AND SEIZE 200 AS NEGRO ATTENDS CLASSES

SHOTS QUELL MOB

Enrolling of Meredith Ends Segregation in State Schools

By CLAUDE SITTON
Special to The New York Times

OXFORD, Miss., Oct. 1—James H. Meredith, a Negro, enrolled in the University of Mississippi today and began classes as Federal troops and federalized units of the Mississippi National Guard quelled a 15-hour riot.

A force of more than 3,000 soldiers and guardsmen and 400 deputy United States marshals fired rifles and hurled tear-gas grenades to stop the violent demonstrations.

Throughout the day more troops streamed into Oxford. Tonight a force approaching 5,000 soldiers and guardsmen, along with the Federal marshals, maintained an uneasy peace in this town of 6,500 in the northern Mississippi hills.

[There were two flareups tonight in which tear gas had to be used, United Press International reported. A small crowd of students began throwing bottles at marshals outside Baxter Hall where Mr. Meredith was housed.

They were quickly dispersed by tear gas. Soldiers also broke up a minor demonstration at a downtown intersection.]

200 Are Seized

The troops seized approximately 200 persons.

They were seized in the mobs of students and adults that besieged the university administration building last night and attacked troops on the town square this morning.

Among those arrested was former Maj. Gen. Edwin A. Walker, who resigned his commission after having been reprimanded for his ultra-right-wing political activity. He was charged with insurrection.

The university's acceptance of Mr. Meredith, a 29-year-old Air Force veteran, followed Gov. Ross R. Barnett's retreat from his defiance of Federal court orders that the Negro be enrolled.

The 64-year-old official, a member of the militantly segregationist Citizens Councils, had vowed he would go to jail if necessary to prevent university desegregation.

Mr. Meredith's admission marked the first desegregation of a public educational institution in Mississippi. It reduced the Deep South bloc of massive-resistance states to two — Alabama and South Carolina.

Although the step brought an apparent end to the most serious Federal-state conflict since the Civil War, its cost in human lives and bitterness was the greatest in any dispute over desegregation directives of the Federal courts.

Two men were killed in the rioting, which broke out about 8 o'clock last night after Mr. Meredith had been escorted onto the campus by the marshals.

The victims were Paul Guihard, 30 years old, a correspondent for Agence France Presse, and Ray Gunter, 23, a jukebox repairman from nearby Abbeville, Miss.

The number of injured could not be determined definitely. But Mr. Guthman told newsmen 25 marshals had required medical treatment. One of them, shot through the neck, was reported in critical condition.

A military spokesman said 20 soldiers and guardsmen had been injured, none of them seriously.

Dr. Vernon B. Harrison, director of the Student Health Service, said between 60 and 70 persons, including some marshals, had been treated at the university infirmary.

Others who were wounded or were burned by exploding teargas grenades obtained aid from local physicians or from Army doctors who moved into the infirmary last night.

Corps Chief in Command

Lieut. Gen. Hamilton Howze, commander of the 18th Airborne Corps, arrived here from Fort Bragg, in North Carolina, to take over the field command. The corps includes the 82d and the 101st Airborne Divisions.

Lieut. Col. Gordon Hill, Army public information officer here, said General Howze was accompanied by his corps command. There were reports that other units of the two famed airborne divisions were moving into the area.

The general's presence indicated that a major build-up of Army troops was under way here, in Columbus, Miss., and at Memphis.

General Howze took over command from Brig. Gen. Charles Billingslea, assistant commander of the Second Infantry Division, Fort Benning, Ga.

Mr. Gutnman said Federal forces were prepared to remain as long as necessary.

"Our mission is to see that the orders of the courts are enforced," he said.

Asked if the mission included the preservation of order in the town, he replied:

"I think we have a duty to maintain law and order."

The toll of property damaged included five automobiles and a mobile television unit that were burned.

Garden Ripped Up

Bricks, lumber and other building materials were stolen from a construction site and used as missiles or roadblocks.

United Press International Telephoto

WALKER IS STOPPED BY TROOPS: Former Maj. Gen. Edwin A. Walker is detained by soldiers near the courthouse in Oxford. He was turned over to U.S. marshals and is being held in $100,000 bail on charges stemming from his role in Sunday's campus riots.

The rioters ripped up the garden of a home in their search for brickbats and commandeered a fire engine and a bulldozer.

A hard core of 70 to 100 youths, most of whom appeared to be Ole Miss students, touched off the riot. They were soon joined by students from other universities and colleges in this area.

Youths and men from Lafayette County, of which Oxford is the seat, and from surrounding counties joined the fray.

Some members of the mob wore jackets from Mississippi State University, at Starkeville, and Memphis State College, in Memphis.

Members of the Ku Klux Klan and similar racist groups in Alabama and northern Louisiana reportedly had threatened to join the opposition against Mr. Meredith's enrollment.

State Charge Denied

In briefing newsmen, Mr. Guthman flatly denied assertions by state officials that Chief United States Marshal James J. P. McShane had precipitated the riot by ordering use of tear gas prematurely.

The Justice Department spokesman said tear gas had been used only after the students had showered the marshals with rocks and one deputy had been struck with an iron pipe, which left a deep dent in his helmet.

A force of 200 state troopers, used by Governor Barnett to block one of Mr. Meredith's three previous attempts to register, stood by on and around the campus last night. The troopers made no effort to break up the mob at the administration building, called the Lyceum. Some made it plain they sided with the students.

The troopers pulled back from the riot scene shortly after 9 o'clock, leaving the marshals to defend themselves.

The action was authorized by State Senator George Yarborough of Red Banks, the President pro tem of the Senate and Governor Barnett's official representative on the campus.

"We had been assured by the Governor that the state police would assist us in maintaining law and order," Mr. Guthman said.

The besieged marshals, commanded by Chief Marshal McShane and Nicholas deB. Katzenbach, Deputy United States Attorney General, held their redoubt at the Lyceum until shortly after midnight.

They got reinforcement then from Troop E, Second Reconnaissance Squadron, 108th Armored Cavalry, of the Mississippi National Guard.

The first unit of combat military policemen called up by the President did not arrive until 4:30 this morning. This was Company A of the 503d Military Police Battalion, from Fort Bragg, N. C.

Other troops poured into Oxford by truck and by plane. They included the 716th Military Police Battalion, which came overland from Fort Dix, N. J.; the 720th Military Police Battalion from Fort Hood, Tex.; the Second Battle Group, Second Infantry Division, from Fort Benning, Ga., and the 31st Helicopter Company from Jacksonville, N. C.

The Mississippi National Guard units sent here included the 108th Armored Cavalry Regiment from Tupelo and the Second Battle Group, 155th Infantry, from Amory.

A detachment of the 70th Engineering Battalion from Fort Campbell, Kentucky, operated a "tent city" for the marshals 15 miles north of here, in the Holly Springs National Forest.

The unit included medical and communications specialists from the 101st Airborne Division.

The 101st had been ordered to Little Rock, Ark., in September of 1957 by President Eisenhower to put down rioting and to enforce Federal court desegregation orders directing the admission of nine Negroes to Central High School.

The first military policemen to arrive helped the marshals and National Guardsmen repel a final assault on the Lyceum at 5 A. M. Barrage after barrage of tear gas and smoke grenades drove back the howling mob, whose strength had dwindled from a peak of 2,500 to 100.

It was difficult to estimate the number of persons who actually took part in the riot. Acrid clouds of smoke and tear gas billowed across the front of a campus area called the Grove, a tree-shaded oval in front of the Lyceum.

Virtually all the street lights were shot out or broken by rocks early in the evening. Observers edging as close to the action as the tear gas and prudence would permit got a view of shadowy forms racing back and forth behind Confederate battle flags.

The rioters cranked up the bulldozer twice and sent it crashing driverless toward the marshals. Both times it hit trees and other obstructions that stopped it before it reached their ranks.

Shouting members of the mob raced the fire engine back and forth through the trees and strewed links of hose across the Grove. At one point the engine careened down the asphalt drive only a few feet from the marshals, who peppered it with blasts from their tear-gas guns.

Several persons were burned as canisters of tear gas struck them or exploded near them.

Snipers Fire in Darkness

Snipers operated under the cover of darkness, aiming blasts of birdshot and pistol and rifle fire at the marshals and others.

Mr. Guihard received a bullet wound in the back. Mr. Gunter was shot in the forehead.

A sniper fired three quick shots at Karl Fleming, a reporter in the Atlanta bureau of Newsweek magazine, but the bullet struck the doorway of the Lyceum.

Other newsmen were attacked and beaten. Gordon Yoder, a Telenews cameraman from Dallas, and Mrs. Yoder were set upon by the mob. State troopers rescued them.

A group of teen-agers and a few men massed on the town square before the three-story Lafayette County Courthouse about 9:30 A. M. today. Many of them wore gray caps bearing Confederate battle flags.

They took up positions on the southeast corner of the square, facing two platoons of military policemen on the southwest corner. About a third of the M.P.'s were Negroes.

The youths began hurling bottles at the soldiers, drawing lusty cheers from adult bystanders when they scored a hit. The soldiers remained in ranks.

The platoons fixed bayonets, formed two wedges and scattered the assailants. But the mob returned and began tossing bottles and rocks at the soldiers again.

The M.P.'s donned their gas masks, formed in a line and moved across the square, throwing tear-gas grenades. The youths retreated.

The mob returned again, and squads of eight to ten soldiers chased them back along the streets, firing rifles over their heads. This broke up the mob.

Business establishments that had opened this morning closed their doors hurriedly. Except for the troops, the square was deserted at noon.

October 2, 1962

ALABAMA ADMITS NEGRO STUDENTS; WALLACE BOWS TO FEDERAL FORCE; KENNEDY SEES 'MORAL CRISIS' IN U.S.

GOVERNOR LEAVES

But Fulfills Promises to Stand in Door and to Avoid Violence

By CLAUDE SITTON
Special to The New York Times

TUSCALOOSA, Ala., June 11 — Gov. George C. Wallace stepped aside today when confronted by federalized National Guard troops and permitted two Negroes to enroll in the University of Alabama. There was no violence.

The Governor, flanked by state troopers, had staged a carefully planned show of defying a Federal Court desegregation order.

Mr. Wallace refused four requests this morning from a Justice Department official that he allow Miss Vivian Malone and James A. Hood, both 20 years old, to enter Foster Auditorium and register.

This was in keeping with a campaign pledge that he would "stand in the schoolhouse door" to prevent a resumption of de-

segregation in Alabama's educational system.

Students Go to Dormitories

The official, Nicholas deB. Katzenbach, Deputy Attorney General, did not press the issue by bringing the students from a waiting car to face the Governor. Instead, they were taken to their dormitories.

However, the outcome was foreshadowed even then. Mr. Katzenbach told Mr. Wallace during their confrontation:

"From the outset, Governor, all of us have known that the final chapter of this history will be the admission of these students."

Units of the 31st (Dixie) Division, federalized on orders from President Kennedy, arrived on the campus four and a half hours later under the command of Brig. Gen. Henry V. Graham.

A Birmingham real estate executive in civilian life, General Graham is the former State Adjutant General who enforced modified martial law in Montgomery, the state capital, following the Freedom Rider riots in 1961.

'Sad Duty' Emphasized

In a voice that was scarcely audible, General Graham said that it was his "sad duty" to order the Governor to step aside.

Mr. Wallace then read the second of two statements challenging the constitutionality of court-ordered desegregation and left the auditorium with his aides for Montgomery.

This sequence of events, which took place in a circus atmosphere, appeared to have given the Governor the face-saving exit he apparently wanted.

Whether the courts find that he actually defied the order issued last Wednesday by District Judge Seybourn H. Lynne in Birmingham remained to be seen. Significantly, Edwin O. Guthman, special assistant for information to Attorney General Robert F. Kennedy, noted that the students had not presented themselves for admission until Mr. Wallace had left the campus.

It thus appeared that the Kennedy Administration had saved itself the political embarrassment of bringing a contempt-of-court action against a second Southern Governor.

Gov. Ross R. Barnett of Mississippi now faces a trial for contempt as a result of his repeated defiance of orders directing the admission of James H. Meredith, a Negro, to the University of Mississippi last fall.

Tonight Mr. Guthman, in a news conference, said that it would be up to the courts to determine if Mr. Wallace should be prosecuted. He declined repeatedly to say whether the Jus-

tice Department would bring charges.

Governor Wallace gave no indication whether he still planned a show of defence Thursday, when another Negro is scheduled to register at the university's Huntsville branch.

He is Dave M. McGlathery, 27, a mathematician for the National Aeronautics and Space Administration at the George C. Marshall Space Flight Center in that northern Alabama city.

However, there was speculation among Wallace aides that the Governor would not seek to interfere with Mr. McGlathery's registration.

Mr. Guthman told newsmen that Federal officials did not now plan to send troops to Huntsville. "The situation will be handled by state and university officials," he said.

There were indications that the 500 to 600 Guardsmen dispatched to Tuscaloosa might not be needed for a lengthy period.

Stems From '55 Injunction

Judge Lynne's preliminary injunction against Governor Wallace followed a finding by District Judge H. H. Grooms that the university must admit the three students under a permanent injunction issued by Judge Grooms in 1955.

That order brought the registration of Miss Autherine Lucy, the first Negro to attend a formerly white public education institution in this state.

Miss Lucy, now Mrs. H. L. Foster, went to classes for three days in 1956. She withdrew and was later expelled after her lawyers had accused university officials of conspiring with the rioters who opposed her presence.

The injunction against Governor Wallace prohibited him from taking any of the following steps:

¶Preventing, blocking or interfering with — by physically interposing his person or that of any other person — the Negroes' admission.

¶Preventing or seeking to prevent by any means the enrollment or attendance at the university of any person entitled to enroll under the Lucy injunction.

The long-awaited confrontation between Governor Wallace and the Federal officials came shortly after 11 o'clock [1 P.M., New York time] on the sunbaked north steps of Foster Auditorium, a three-story building of red brick with six limestone columns.

Approximately 150 of the 825 state troopers, game wardens and revenue agents under the command of Col. Albert J. Lingo, State Director of Public Safety, lined the concrete walkways at the auditorium.

Others in this group, brought here to prevent any outbreak of violence, stood guard at entrances to the campus and patrolled the treeshaded stretch, which reaches westward to the banks of the Black Warrior River.

Shortly after 9:30 A.M., the Governor's aides and legal advisers arrived at the auditorium accompanied by two of his brothers, Circuit Judge Jack Wallace of Barbour County, and Gerald Wallace, a Montgomery lawyer.

General In Mufti

Maj. Gen. Albert N. Harrison, State Adjutant General, walked hurriedly in and out of the auditorium, conferring with the Governor's assistants and Colonel Lingo. He was dressed in civilian clothes, apparently realizing that he would not be asked to command the troops that might be used.

Governor Wallace and Seymore Trammell, State Finance Director, an ardent segregationist who is a top political adviser, rode up behind a highway patrol motorcycle escort shortly before 10 o'clock.

Mr. Wallace was dressed neatly in a light gray suit, a blue shirt, a blue and brown tie with a gold tie clip and black shoes. He joked with the some 150 newsmen waiting in the broiling sun that sent the temperatures near 100 degrees. Then he went inside to an air-conditioned office to await the arrival of the Negro students.

Four Federal officials entered the auditorium a few minutes later. However, the scheduled arrival time of 10:30 A. M. passed with no sign of the students.

Associated Press Wirephoto

CONFRONTATION: Gov. George C. Wallace, left, of Alabama blocks the entrance to Foster Auditorium at University of Alabama as Nicholas deB. Katzenbach, Deputy Attorney General, attempts to get two Negroes enrolled.

At 10:48 A.M., a white sedan followed by two brown sedans pulled up before the auditorium. Mr. Katzenbach emerged and walked to the entrance accompanied by Macon L. Weaver, United States Attorney for the Northern District of Alabama, and Peyton Norville Jr., the Federal marshal for this area.

Governor Wallace stood waiting behind a lectern placed in the doorway by a state trooper. He wore a microphone around his neck that was connected to a public address system.

Mr. Katzenbach said he had a proclamation from President Kennedy directing Governor Wallace to give way, but Mr. Wallace interrupted him and began reading a lengthy statement.

"The unwelcomed, unwanted, unwarranted and force-induced intrusion upon the campus of the University of Alabama today of the might of the Central Government offers a frightful example of the oppression of the rights, privileges and sovereignty of this state by officers of the Federal Government," he asserted.

Mr. Wallace cited the provision of the 10th Amendment that provides that powers not delegated to the Federal Government are retained by the states.

"I stand here today, as Governor of this sovereign state, and refuse to willingly submit to illegal usurpation of power by the Central Government," he said.

The Governor implied that there might have been violence were it not for his presence when he said:

"I stand before you today in place of thousands of other Alabamians whose presence would have confronted you had I been derelict and neglected to fulfill the responsibilities of my office."

He concluded by asserting that he did "denounce and forbid this illegal and unwaranted action by the Central Government."

"I take it from that statement that you are going to stand in the door and that you are not going to carry out the orders of the court," said Mr. Katzenbach, "and that you are going to resist us from doing so. Is that correct?"

"I stand according to my statement," replied Mr. Wallace.

"Governor, I am not inter-

ested in a show," Mr. Katzenbach went on. "I don't know what the purpose of this show is. I am interested in the orders of these courts being enforced."

The Federal official then told the Governor that the latter had no choice but to comply.

"I would ask you once again to responsibly step aside," said Mr. Katzenbach. "If you do not, I'm going to assure you that the orders of these courts will be enforced."

The Deputy Attorney General then asserted:

"Those students will remain on this campus. They will register today. They will go to school tomorrow."

Lips Are Sealed

After several pleas in a similar vein, including the one in which he forecast the students' admission, Mr. Katzenbach waited for the Governor to reply. Mr. Wallace stood defiantly in the door, his head thrown back, his lips compressed tightly.

The Federal officials returned to the car in which Miss Malone and Mr. Hood had been waiting. Mr. Katzenbach and Miss Malone then walked unmolested to nearby Mary Burke Hall, the dormitory in which she will live.

John Doar, first assistant in the Justice Department's Civil Rights Division, drove with Mr. Hood to Palmer Hall. Several student council members shook hands with Mr. Hood.

Both students ate lunch later in university cafeterias without incident.

Word of General Graham's arrival at 1:50 P.M. by military plane from Birmingham brought another series of consultations and preparations inside and outside the building. Troopers dispersed several hundred students who had filtered into the area.

At 3:16 P.M., three National Guard troop carriers escorted by Tuscaloosa motorcycle patrolmen and followed by a jeep roared up to Mary Burke Hall. Infantrymen, dressed in green fatigues and armed with M-1 rifles, jumped down and formed beside the auditorium.

Another convoy arrived on a street northwest of the auditorium. General Graham pulled up beside it in a green, unmarked command car.

The troops took up positions in the vicinity of the auditorium. Colonel Lingo walked over and saluted the general, who then returned the salute. They then shook hands.

Mr. Katzenbach and other officials conferred briefly with General Graham. A short time later, the officer strode purposely toward the entrance, followed by four unarmed special forces soldiers, all sergeants.

As the military party approached, Mr. Trammell turned toward the entrance and clapped on his straw hat. At this signal, Mr. Wallace walked out the door after an aide had straightened his tie.

General Graham walked to

within four feet of the Governor. Standing at attention and leaning forward, he began to speak in a grim voice.

"It is my sad duty——" and his voice sank so low that bystanders could barely hear it.

Governor Wallace pulled a crumpled piece of paper from his pocket and read a brief statement. He said that had the Guardsmen not been federalized, "I would at this point be your commander. I know that this [duty] is a bitter pill for you to swallow."

He then reiterated earlier requests that white Alabamians refrain from violence.

The Governor denounced what he termed a trend toward "military dictatorship" in the nation. "We shall now return to Montgomery to continue this constitutional fight," he said.

General Graham saluted the Governor smartly. After returning the salute, Mr. Wallace and his aides walked swiftly to waiting cars and were driven away, to the cheers of students.

Three minutes after their departure, Mr. Hood walked into the auditorium with Federal officials to register. Miss Malone followed a minute later.

WALLACE ENDS RESISTANCE AS GUARD IS FEDERALIZED

20 NEGROES ENTER

12 Whites Arrested in Birmingham—Other Cities Are Peaceful

By CLAUDE SITTON
Special to The New York Times

BIRMINGHAM, Ala., Sept. 10 — Twenty Negroes attended previously white schools in three Alabama cities today after President Kennedy's federalization of the state's National Guardsmen ended the defiance of Gov. George C. Wallace.

The police here arrested 12 whites in a rowdy, two-hour demonstration over the admission of two Negro girls to West End High School under a Federal court order. This, coupled with already existing racial tension, raised a threat of further disorder.

No major incidents marred the desegregation of two other schools here, four in Huntsville — where classes began yesterday—and one each in Tuskegee and Mobile. The 425 Guardsmen ordered to active duty by Federal officials remained in their armories.

Combined school attendance here at West End and Graymont elementary school, where two Negroes enrolled, dropped by almost 90 per cent. But Ramsay High School, which accepted one Negro, showed a slight increase.

Wallace Concedes Defeat

Only some 165 of an expected total of 550 students appeared for classes at the Tuskegee public school, which 13 Negroes are attending. Attendance figures at four Huntsville schools that have one Negro pupil each and at Murphy High School in Mobile, which has two, were near normal.

Governor Wallace conceded at a news conference in the state Capitol in Montgomery that for the second time in three months

he had been forced to retreat from a posture of massive resistance to desegregation in education. "I can't fight bayonets with my bare hands," he said.

A legal battle directed by Mrs. Constance Baker Motley of New York, associate counsel of the N.A.A.C.P. Legal Defense and Educational Fund, was largely responsible for the Governor's predicament. To preserve the right of admission this effort had won for the 20 students, Justice Department attorneys obtained a sweeping court order against Mr. Wallace last night.

The temporary restraining order, signed by all five of Alabama's Federal District judges, prohibited him and state troopers from any further interference with desegregation.

The Governor then ordered the troopers withdrawn from the schools in Birmingham, Tuskegee and Mobile, where they had denied entry to the Negroes yesterday. He followed this up by ordering National Guardsmen to replace the troopers.

But President Kennedy signed a cease-and-desist order against Mr. Wallace early today, federalized the Alabama National Guard and directed Defense Department officials to take all necessary steps to carry out the court order.

These actions, the Governor asserted in a formal statement, brought "the most potent instrument of force in the world, directed by the ruthless hand of the Attorney General, against the people of Alabama."

Wallace Arrest Avoided

The Kennedy Administration had given every indication that it would avoid, if possible, any confrontation with the Governor that might result in his arrest. This was the policy in the dispute over desegregation at the University of Alabama last June. Mr. Wallace staged a show of defiance there by blocking two Negro students, but he retreated in the face of National Guardsmen called out by the President.

Further, a Justice Department spokesman here emphasized that the 300 guardsmen being held in readiness at Birmingham, the 75 at Mobile and the 50 at Tuskegee would be

used only if needed by local officials to maintain order.

"No request has been made for them and none is anticipated," said Edwin O. Guthman, special assistant to Attorney General Robert F. Kennedy. Mr. Guthman, Nicholas deB. Katzenbach, Deputy Attorney General, and eight other Justice Department officials were sent here by the Attorney General to assist in carrying out the court orders.

The effect of the Administration's actions in Alabama was to clear the way for local officials in the four cities to implement plans for compliance, however reluctant, with the desegregation directives.

All these officials had demonstrated their willingness to do so last week after the scheduled beginning of classes. But through a combination of force and persuasion, Governor Wallace prevented this action on the ground that desegregation would bring violence.

The only serious threat of disorder began to develop at West End High School here shortly after two Negro girls arrived by automobile at 7:45 A.M. (9:45, New York time).

Few students saw them enter. But a blond girl standing nearby turned to a boy and began sobbing on his shoulder. Another girl sniffled.

"I hope my momma heard, so she'll come get me," said one girl among the group that began streaming out of the two-story, red brick building as the news of the Negroes' arrival became known.

'Go Home!'

Some 75 youths gathered across the driveway in front of the school, near the car that had brought the students.

"Keep the niggers out!" they shouted. "Go home!"

Other students soon swelled their ranks to more than 300 and they began chanting, "Two, four, six, eight, we don't want to integrate."

Some teachers smiled from the windows and students yelled encouragement to those who remained inside to leave the school, calling them "nigger lovers."

Led by a crew-cut youth in a yellow shirt and gray slacks, some 150 boys fell into a loose column. With the girls joining in, they marched around the driveway and lawn between the school and the street. Some waved Confederate battle flags and a student played "Dixie" on a trumpet.

with refusal to obey police commands.

Only 500 students registered for classes at West End, which has a normal enrollment of 1,400. And only 100 of these remained in school after the demonstrations began.

After the demonstrators were finally dispersed shortly before 10 A.M., the students wandered through the neighborhood or raced up and down the streets in cars, waving Confederate flags and segregationist placards.

Only a few spectators remained in the area into the afternoon. The policemen, who had little to do, played a spirited game of touch football on the lawn.

Associated Press

DEMONSTRATOR ARRESTED: Policemen subdue man protesting admission of Negroes to West End High School, Birmingham. Twelve white demonstrators were arrested there.

September 11, 1963

Some 50 parents, mostly mothers, gathered under a huge oak at the north end of the campus. They shouted at students in the windows to leave and cheered the demonstrators.

About 150 policemen in the area at the time kept the sidewalks and street clear in front of the school. But whites clustered at the two ends of the grounds. Negroes, many of whom live in houses directly south and west of the school, watched from a distance.

"We hate Kennedy!" chanted the students. "We hate niggers! We want Wallace!"

Police Capt. Glenn Evans, using an electric bullhorn, told the crowd:

"We're going to ask you to either go to your classes or leave the school ground."

The students shouted "No!" But they moved away.

Policemen on the south side of the grounds drove back a crowd of 100 students and adults after Captain Evans had called out:

'All right. Let's move 'em. Let's wedge 'em out. Let me see those nightsticks."

A scuffle broke out among the milling students and adults on the north end of the campus as the police seized David Stanley, a youthful Canadian who is a member of the National States Rights party. This anti-Semitic and anti-Negro group, whose membership is believed to number fewer than 100 persons, passed out Confederate flags and segregationist placards to the students.

Stanley fought back, but one policeman held his neck in a half-nelson, another twisted his arm behind his back and two others assisted them in handcuffing him and dragging him away. He was charged with inciting to riot.

A girl, knocked down accidentally in the skirmishing, fainted.

The police riot squad, armed with shotguns and carbines, arrived at the scene. And some Jefferson County sheriff's deputies pulled up at the school in squad cars.

The police began driving the crowd up both sides of the street to the north of the school. A man who sought to break through their lines was seized and began struggling. He was clubbed into submission with night sticks. A second white man who attempted to interfere was hurried away to a patrol wagon.

These two and nine other whites arrested were charged

Extent of Desegregation

The following table shows the extent of desegregation in the public schools of the Southern and Border states:

	Enrollment		Number of Negroes in Desegregated Schools	Percentage of Negroes in Desegregated Schools
	White	Negro		
SOUTH				
Alabama	*539,996	*287,414	21	.007
Arkansas	**328,023	**112,012	366	.327
Florida	*964,241	*237,871	3,650	1.53
Georgia	689,323	337,534	177	.052
Louisiana	**460,589	**301,433	1,814	.602
Mississippi	304,226	291,971	0	0
North Carolina	820,900	*347,065	1,865	.537
South Carolina	*368,496	*258,955	10	.004
Tennessee	*687,902	ᵛ184,940	4,486	2.72
Texas	2,045,499	*326,409	*18,000	5.52
Virginia	710,176	228,961	3,721	1.63
Total	7,919,371	2,894,563	34,110	1.18
BORDER				
Delaware	78,730	18,000	10,209	56.5
Dist. of Columbia	19,803	117,915	98,813	83.8
Kentucky	*611,126	*54,874	29,855	54.4
Maryland	540,667	160,946	76,906	47.8
Missouri	*793,000	*95,000	40,000	42.1
Oklahoma	*541,125	*43,875	12,289	28.0
West Virginia	*417,595	*23,449	*13,659	58.2
Total	3,002,046	514,125	281,731	54.8
Region Total	10,921,417	3,408,688	315,841	9.3

*Estimated total.
**1962-63.

May 18, 1964

HIGH COURT BIDS VIRGINIA COUNTY REOPEN SCHOOLS

SPEED DEMANDED

Closing of Classes in Prince Edward Is Upset, 9 to 0

By ANTHONY LEWIS

Special to The New York Times

WASHINGTON, May 25—The Supreme Court said today that Prince Edward County, Va., must reopen its public schools, closed since 1959 to avoid desegregation.

The Justices held unanimously that the Constitution does not permit the abolition of public schools in one county of a state while they remain open in other counties. The opinion was by Justice Hugo L. Black.

Today was 10 years and 8 days after the epochal decision of May 17, 1954, that held public-school segregation unconstitutional. And the Court was in effect answering one of the great challenges to that decision.

Whites Still Resisting

The white people of Prince Edward County, in rural Southside Virginia, were and are determined not to send their children to school with Negroes. Their lengthy and so far successful resistance to the decision of 1954 has been watched from elsewhere in the Deep South.

Justice Black's opinion had implications beyond the immediate question of school-closing. He hinted that the pace of desegregation generally must pick up, that the Court would now insist on more than the "deliberate speed" it called for in 1955.

"The time for mere 'deliberate speed' has run out," Justice Black said, "and that phrase can no longer justify denying these Prince Edward County schoolchildren their constitu-

tional rights to an education equal to that afforded by the public schools in the other parts of Virginia.

"There has been entirely too much deliberation and not enough speed in enforcing the constitutional rights which we held [in 1954] had been denied Prince Edward County Negro children."

The same hint was dropped in another school case decided today, this one from Atlanta. The issue there was whether desegregation at the rate of a grade a year, from the 12th grade down, was fast enough.

The Court, in a brief unsigned opinion, sent the case back for further hearings on recent actions by the Atlanta School Board. But it called attention to its warning a year ago, in another case, that the lapse of time since the decision of 1954 has changed the legal context and now requires swifter action.

The Prince Edward case was sent back to the District Court with orders to provide "quick and effective" relief, presumably designed to reopen the schools by next fall. These steps were outlined:

First, officials should be forbidden to give any financial aid to pupils in "private" schools so long as the public schools are closed. The county's white children have been attending a system of segregated "private" schools.

Second, if necessary, the District Court should directly require the county supervisors to levy taxes and "raise funds adequate to reopen and maintain without racial discrimination a public school system in Prince Edward County like that operated in other counties in Virginia."

Two Justices Demur

This aspect of the decision drew two dissents, from Justices Tom C. Clark and John Marshall Harlan. They said in a brief comment that they did not think Federal courts had the power "to order the reopening of the public schools," but they agreed with the rest of Justice Black's opinion.

Third, the Court indicated that as an ultimate step the District Court could prohibit state officials from helping to maintain public schools elsewhere so long as they do not exist in Prince Edward.

The purpose of such an order would be to force action by the state Government to maintain public schools in Prince Edward County. The state has consistently argued that schools are a local, not a state, responsibility in Virginia.

Justice Black ended by directing the District Court to enter a decree "which will guarantee that these petitioners get the kind of education that is given in the state's public schools."

He added the significant could bring in additional defendants if necessary. These might include, for example, the Governor and Attorney General, so that pressure would be directed at the highest state thought that the District Court level.

The Prince Edward case was one of the original group of cases decided by the Supreme Court in 1954. Since then it has dragged through the lower Federal courts, subject to what Justice Black today called "inordinate delays."

In 1959 the Court of Appeals for the Fourth Circuit ordered the county to begin admitting Negro children to white schools. Rather than do so, the county supervisors voted to cease taxing and spending for public schools. The schools closed.

Since then the county's white children have been attending a system of schools set up by a private foundation. Most of their costs were covered at first by state and county tuition grants. In addition, the county remitted 25 per cent of local taxes for contributions to these schools.

Negro children had no schools until last fall. A free school association, inspired by Attorney General Robert F. Kennedy and privately financed, is now running schools on an emergency basis for this school year only.

In 1961, when Negro families challenged the closing of schools, Federal District Judge Oren R. Lewis forbade the payment of tuition grants and giving of tax credits so long as the public schools were closed. He said they were part of a discriminatory system.

Tax Credits Stopped

That prohibition has continued to the present and will go on, under today's decision, at least until the public schools reopen. The county has repealed the tax-credit ordinance.

In 1962 Judge Lewis held that Prince Edward schools could not be closed to avoid integration so long as other Virginia schools were operating.

That decision was set aside in 1963 by the Appeals Court for the Fourth Circuit, which said the Federal courts should abstain from deciding that question until the Virginia courts had done so. Judge Lewis's ruling was reinstated by the Supreme Court today.

Justice Black first disposed of the Fourth Circuit's theory that

the Federal courts should have awaited state judicial action. The issues, he said, "imperatively call for decision now" by the Federal courts.

"The case has been delayed since 1951," he said, when the suit was originally filed, "by resistance at the state and county level, by legislation and by lawsuits."

Next, Justice Black noted that the all-white schools operated in Prince Edward since 1954, "although designated as private, are beneficiaries of county and state support."

He said the whole program had been undertaken "for one reason, and one reason only: to ensure that white and colored children in Prince Edward County could not, under any circumstances, go to the same school."

The opinion discussed a similar Louisiana plan, never put into operation but held unconstitutional in 1962, and said it and the Prince Edward actions had the same end:

"The perpetuation of racial segregation by closing public schools and operating only segregated schools supported directly or indirectly by state or county funds."

Justice Black then concluded that the Prince Edward system, viewed in this light, denied to the Negro children the equal protection of the laws guaranteed by the 14th Amendment.

Question Unanswered

The Court did not answer one question in which officials of Prince Edward County and others elsewhere in Virginia are deeply interested: Will payment of tuition grants be permissible if the Prince Edward public schools reopen?

Virginia wants to have tuition grants so that white families who deeply oppose integration can send their children to private schools instead of desegregated public schools. The state calls this a "freedom of choice" approach.

The possibility that tuition grants might again be available if public schools are provided could encourage Prince Edward officials to comply with today's decision.

The Supreme Court did not indicate any views on a state's constitutional power to close all its public schools rather than desegregate. That does not seem a possibility now in any state but Mississippi, which may face court orders to begin desegregation next fall.

Today's decision bore out a prediction by Chief Justice John W. Eggleston of the Virginia Supreme Court of Appeals. Last December, dissenting from his court's refusal to require public education in Prince Edward, he wrote:

"The refusal of the highest court of this state to recognize here the rights of the citizens of Prince Edward County, guaranteed to them under the Constitution of the United States, is a clear invitation to the Federal courts to step in and enforce such rights. I am sure that that invitation will be promptly accepted. We shall see!"

The Prince Edward case was argued by J. Segar Gravatt of Blackstone, Va., for the county officials, and by Assistant Attorney General R. D. McIlwaine 3d of Virginia for the state.

Robert L. Carter of the National Association for the Advancement of Colored People represented the complaining Negro families. Solicitor General Archibald Cox appeared as a friend of the court, decrying the school-closing as "an experiment in ignorance."

Mrs. Constance Baker Motley of the N.A.A.C.P. Legal Defense and Educational Fund, Inc. argued the Atlanta case. Burke Marshall, the Justice Department's civil rights chief, argued on her side as a friend of the court, and A. C. Latimer of Atlanta represented the school board.

Mrs. Motley and Mr. Marshall objected to the fact that Negro and white children still started out in separate schoool systems and could transfer only when the 12-year plan reached their grade level. But at the argument Mr. Latimer indicated that Atlanta was now changing the plan, and the Justices decided that the District Court should have another look at it.

May 26, 1964

RIGHTS ACT FORCES SCHOOL EQUALITY

Many Districts in the South Comply to Get U.S. Aid

By ROY REED
Special to The New York Times

ATLANTA, June 27 — John Baucum, the young superintendent of Richland County School District No. 5 a few miles south of Columbia, S. C., sat in his office one night recently, chuckling wryly over an incident that occurred last winter.

He had called together his school principals, Negro and white, for a routine meeting. He had to leave as it began and on his return learned that someone in the group had served refreshments.

Later, a parent approached him and said accusingly, "You had a mixed social here in the office."

"What do you mean?" Mr. Baucum replied. "We had an in-service training program."

"Oh, but you served cupcakes and Cokes," the parent said indignantly.

The incident does not exaggerate the general attitude toward racial integration among the white people of Richland School District No. 5, which has 4,100 Negro students and 2,375 white students. It is one of hundreds of districts in the South that will desegregate this fall to comply with the Civil Rights Act of 1964.

Negro Teachers Affected

The Civil Rights Act has pushed nearer the surface a couple of problems that have lurked since the Supreme Court school desegregation decision in 1954.

One that is beginning to crop up for the first time this year is the displacement of Negro teachers. Already, a handful of Negro teachers have lost their jobs because Negro students have been transferred to white schools and Negro teachers have not been.

Southern school superintendents agree with civil rights organizations that teacher displacement could become a major problem in the future. However, the superintendents oppose the "overnight" faculty desegregation advocated by civil rights groups.

S. P. Portis, superintendent of schools at Hamburg in southern Arkansas, said what others across the South have said: Negro teachers are not as competent as whites. The Negro teachers come from culturally deprived homes, inferior public schools and second-rate teachers colleges, he declared.

Mr. Portis suggested that a whole new generation of Negro teachers might have to be trained through desegregated public schools and colleges before they would be ready in appreciable numbers to enter the previously all-white schools

None of the districts contemplates faculty desegregation this year beyond integrated faculty meetings.

Mr. Campbell said the Greenville board had decided that it should start replacing incompetent Negro teachers with competent Negroes. However, he said the board did not want to clean house overnight and risk being unfair in weeding out "incompetents."

At the time of the Supreme Court decision, and even before, school districts across the Deep South had begun to spend millions of dollars building new Negro schools. The building boom was a frank admission that Negro schools were separate but not equal. Physical plants have been equalized but there is a possibility that large numbers of the new schools may be abandoned as Negro students integrate the white schools.

Up to now, however, even with the surge in desegregation this year, Negroes have not left all-Negro schools in large numbers, and the abolition of the dual school system has not arrived. Southern school officials believe it will survive a long time.

Negro Attitude Noted

One reason, according to Mr. Portis, Mr. Morris and Mr. Baucum, is that most Negroes still give every indication of preferring to stay in the Negro schools. Only a few have applied for transfers in the districts that have opened the doors of the white schools through "freedom-of-choice" plans.

Another reason cited is that whites are reluctant to send their children to predominantly Negro schools, which even the most liberal white Southerners believe to be inferior.

The Department of Health, Education and Welfare has been pressing for zoned attendance areas instead of freedom of choice. If it has its way, white children living nearer a Negro school will be assigned to that school. There is little prospect of zoned areas being imposed this year, but they may be next year.

Several Southern states have repealed their compulsory school attendance laws. Mr. Campbell said he feared that whites simply would withdraw from the public schools in Mississippi before they would attend "Negro" schools.

604 Desegregated in '64

As of last December, only 604 Southern districts had been desegregated. The region has

2,220 districts with both Negroes and whites.

Leslie W. Dunbar, executive director of the Southern Regional Council, has called the act "the most powerful coercive weapon the Government has had" in the fight against racial discrimination. It not only is bringing desegregation for the first time to rural districts, but also is speeding the process in urban districts.

Southern school administrators are no longer very fearful of violent white reaction to desegregation, but the potential remains in one otherwise obscure area, school bus desegregation. Buses travel thousands of miles a day carrying rural children to consolidated central schools.

Samuel F. Morris, superintendent of the Meriwether County, Ga., school district, notes that children restrained during the day by teachers come under the supervision of an untrained bus driver, who perhaps is an older student when they board the bus for home.

He is so fearful of the possibilities of violence against Negro children on the buses, he said, that he intends to advise all Negro applicants for previously all-white schools not to ride the white buses this year.

Policy Role Cited

Another problem that can be tied directly to enforcement of the Civil Rights Act is the effect of the Federal Office of Education's involvement in local school district policy-making.

Robert S. Davis, who has served 16 years on the Columbia school board, said the Department of Health, Education and Welfare had left so little leeway for decision by the local board in desegregation policy that he and his fellow board members believed that their responsibilities had been diluted.

Roy Campbell, a lawyer who heads the Greenville, Miss., school board, said board members had agreed that they would resign if the Federal Government should assume such a large role that the board was left with no substantial powers of policy.

Mr. Campbell is not a racist, and his city is by all odds the most enlightened in Mississippi. He views school desegregation not as an isolated problem but as a necessary part of the Negro's involvement in "the total fabric of American life." However, he also argues eloquently for caution on the part of the Federal Government.

"I think that the more we can govern ourselves at the local level—and do a decent job of it—the better nation we will have," he said.

233

No Letup of Pressure

The Federal department, which is administering the Civil Rights Act, has given little slack so far. The pressure has had some predictable consequences.

Former Gov. Marvin Griffin told the Georgia Legislature last winter, "I would sit here until hell freezes over before I would comply." He counseled raising local taxes and telling the Federal Government, "We'll educate our own, keep your Federal funds."

At least two Georgia districts and a relative handful in other Southern states are doing just that in face of Title VI of the Civil Rights Act, which bars Federal funds from being used to perpetuate discrimination.

However, even in Alabama, virtually all the local school people have disregarded the advice of Gov. George C. Wallace and submitted plans of compliance to the Office of Education.

Most local school administrators and trustees in the holdout areas seem resigned to desegregation but determined to inaugurate it as slowly as possible.

Columbia, however, desegregated its schools voluntarily

Justices Tell South To Spur Integration Of All Its Schools

Special to The New York Times

WASHINGTON, May 27—The Supreme Court ruled unanimously today that "freedom of choice" desegregation plans are inadequate if they do not undo Southern school segregation as rapidly as other available methods would.

In its first detailed review of the adequacy of the means being used to implement the landmark school desegregation decision of 1954, the Court declared that "delays are no longer tolerable." It stopped short, however, of granting the full relief that civil rights lawyers had requested.

The Court did not declare freedom of choice plans inherently unconstitutional. This would have required many Southern communities to begin taking affirmative steps to mix more Negroes with whites in the schools. About 9 out of 10 Southern communities now employ the freedom of choice plan, which permits children of all races to pick their own schools.

The Court also restricted its opinion to apply only to those Southern and border states that had legally sanctioned dual school systems when segregation in public schools was declared unconstitutional by the Supreme Court in 1954.

As a result, the strong condemnation of identifiable Negro schools in today's opinion will not require desegregation moves in the North, where de facto segregation often results from housing patterns.

Justice William J. Brennan Jr. wrote the opinions in the three cases decided today. They were appeals brought by Negro parents in New Kent County, Va., Gould, Ark., and Jackson, Tenn.

Upheld in Lower Courts

In each case a United States Courts of Appeals had held the school desegregation plan adequate on the ground that the Constitution forbids segregation of the races by law but does not require public officials to take affirmative action to reduce racial imbalance when it results from private choice.

The N.A.A.C.P. Legal Defense and Educational Fund, Inc., which represented the plaintiffs, contended that the freedom of choice system placed the burden on the Negro child to request a transfer to an integrated school. As a result, the fund said, few did, and many all-Negro school remained.

Lawyers from the fund pointed out that the United States Court of Appeals for the Fifth Circuit in New Orleans, which has jurisdiction over most of the Deep South states, has held that freedom of choice plans are not adequate unless they break down the dual school system that existed by law before 1954.

By agreeing, the Supreme Court required the United States Courts of Appeal for the Fourth, iSxth and Eighth circuits—sitting respectively, in Richmond, Va., Cincinnati and St. Louis—to apply the same standard and require school officials to take affirmative action to dismantle "the state-imposed dual system" and to create "a unitary, nonracial school system."

Maryland, Virginia, West Virginia, North Carolina, South Carolina, Kentucky, Tennessee and Arkansas are the states in the three Federal Court circuits that will be affected by today's ruling because these states had racially separate school systems in 1954.

"The burden on a school board today is to come forward with a plan that promises realistically to work, and promises realistically to work now," Justice Brennan said.

"We do not hold that 'freedom of choice' can have no place in such a plan," he said. "Rather, all we decide today is that in desegregating a dual system a plan utilizing 'freedom of choice' is not an end in itself.'

The opinion was vague as to what this might involve.

In the case of New Kent County, a rural community with 736 Negro and 519 white students, the Court noted that 115 of the Negro children had elected to go to the integrated school but no whites had chosen to go to the other school, which remained all-Negro.

It suggested a zoning system, which apparently would place all of the county's white children in predominantly-Negro schools. The court also suggested zoning for the Gould community, a farming area with a racial makeup similar to that of New Kent County.

In Jackson, the neighborhoods are divided into districts, which the lower court had said were not gerrymandered to foster segregation. But a "free transfer" variant of the freedom of choice plan permitted students to transfer. All white students transferred out of several of the schools, leaving them all-Negro.

The Supreme Court said that these students should not have been permitted to transfer, but otherwise it left it to the lower court to say what must be done.

Jack Greenberg, director council of the N.A.A.C.P. fund, who had argued the case for the Gould Negroes, announced in New York today that the fund would immediately reopen many of the 200 desegregation cases that it has brought in the South

Samuel Tucker of Richmond, Va., argued for the New Kent County appellees. Frederick T. Gray of Richmond argued for the county. James M. Nabrit 3d of New York argued for the plaintiffs from Jackson. Russell Rice, city attorney of Jackson, argued for the city.

SCHOOL INTEGRATION 'AT ONCE' IS ORDERED BY SUPREME COURT; NIXON BID FOR DELAY REJECTED

By WARREN WEAVER Jr.
Special to The New York Times

WASHINGTON, Oct. 29—The Supreme Court ruled unanimously today that school districts must end segregation "at once" and operate integrated systems "now and hereafter."

The decision will unquestionably apply to Southern states where dual educational systems exist. The initial reaction of most legal authorities in the civil rights area was that it would not affect de facto segregation in Northern cities.

The Court replaced its 14-year-old decision that school desegregation should proceed with "all deliberate speed" with a new and much more rigorous standard: immediate compliance.

The effect of today's decision is to write a legal end to the period during which courts have entertained various excuses for failure to integrate Southern schools. Its basic message was integrate now, litigate later.

The decision was a stinging setback for the Nixon Administration. The Justice Department had argued less than a week ago that delays were permissible in requiring integration in some districts and that providing a continuing education should take precedence over enforcing social justice.

View Rejected

The Court rejected this view unanimously in a two-page unsigned opinion.

The Court, which had heard the case on an expedited basis, released its decree in printed form as soon as it could be prepared rather than wait until Monday, its customary decision day.

It was the first major decision handed down by the Court with Warren E. Burger sitting as Chief Justice. He is President Nixon's first appointee to the Court, a man chosen to help restore a measure of conservative balance to the tribunal.

The ruling specifically affected 33 school districts in Mississippi, but its broad language will be a precedent for all pending Court cases involving school segregation and in all future suits that may be filed.

In the Mississippi cases, the Supreme Court held, all requests for additional time to present desegregation plans should have been denied "because continued operation of segregated schools under a standard of allowing 'all deliberate speed' for desegregation is no longer constitutionally permissible."

"Under explicit holdings of this Court," the opinion continued, "the obligation of every school district is to terminate dual school systems at once and to operate now and hereafter only unitary schools."

The Court specified directly that any exceptions to an integration plan sought by local school officials would be considered only after the plan had been put into effect, while it was operating.

When the disputed Mississippi school districts are operating on an integrated basis under an order that the United States Court of Appeals must now issue, the opinion said, a Federal District Court "may hear and consider objections thereto, provided, however, that the Court of Appeals' order shall be complied with in all respects while the District Court considers such objections or amendments."

The Supreme Court ordered an end to school segregation in 1954 in Brown v. Board, a case involving challenges in several states. Its establishment of the "all deliberate speed" standard came in an implementing decision a year later.

At the Justice Department, a spokesman said that the Supreme Court's action "now places the cases before the United States Court of Appeals for the Fifth Circuit, and the Department of Justice will await the Fifth Circuit determination."

In fact, the Fifth Circuit has no legal choice but to follow the Supreme Court order. The statement was apparently intended to give Attorney General John N. Mitchell time to draft some responsive comment.

The decision was applauded by the organization that had brought the Mississippi suits in behalf of 14 Negro children, the N.A.A.C.P. Legal Defense and Educational Fund, Inc.

"Now that the Court has accepted the principle which we urged of no further delays and that integration should exist during litigation, we are going to press for such relief in all pending school cases," Jack Greenberg, director of the fund, said.

The decision for immediate school integration appeared to place all eight Justices of the Supreme Court within President Nixon's definition of an "extreme group."

At his last general news conference on Sept. 26 the President replied to a question about delaying school segregation with this statement:

"It seems to me that there are two extreme groups. There are those who want instant integration and those who want segregation forever. I believe that we need to have a middle course between these two extremes. That is the course on which we are embarked. I think it is correct."

Political Strategy Seen

The Nixon Administration's decision to permit the Mississippi school districts to delay filing their integration plans had been regarded by critics of the President as further evidence that he had adopted a political strategy of favoring the South, to encourage Republican gains there in the elections of 1970 and 1972.

Such charges have emphasized that Attorney General Mitchell, who favored permitting delays in school integration, was Mr. Nixon's campaign manager in 1968 and has continued as one of his closest political advisers.

Today's decision raised officially the question of how integration plans could be enforced, one that Nixon Administration spokesmen had raised speculatively over a month ago.

At the Morristown, N. J., airport, where President Nixon was making a campaign speech, for Representative William T. Cahill, who is seeking the governorship of New Jersey, Ronald L. Ziegler, the White House press secretary, was asked about the ruling. "We may have a comment on it tomorrow," he replied, "but we haven't seen the decision or had the time to study it. So there will be no comment tonight."

Assistant Attorney General Jerris Leonard, head of the Justice Department's Civil Rights Division, had said that "there are just not enough bodies and people" in the division to enforce a decision for immediate integration.

"If the Court were to order instant integration," he said on Sept. 29, "nothing would change. Somebody would have to enforce that order."

Under today's decision, these steps were required by the Court for the Mississippi cases:

¶The Court of Appeals for the Fifth Circuit, which had authorized delay last August, must now issue an order that all the 33 school districts "may no longer operate a dual school system based on race or color and directing that they began immediately to operate as unitary school systems within which no person is to be effectively excluded from any school because of race or color."

¶The Court of Appeals may order the schools to accept all or part of integration plans prepared by the Department of Health, Education and Welfare. The Court may modify the plan, as long as the result is "a totally unitary school system for all eligible pupils without regard to race or color."

¶The Court of Appeals should take these steps "without further arguments or submissions."

¶While the schools are being operated on an integrated basis, requests for changes may be submitted to a Federal district court and cannot go into effect without approval by the Court of Appeals as well.

The Supreme Court also ordered that the Court of Appeals remain responsible for "prompt and faithful compliance with its order," which it may change as "necessary or desirable for the operation of a unitary school system."

October 30, 1969

Nixon Plans $1.5-Billion to Improve Segregated Schools

A 2-YEAR PROGRAM

President Vows to End de Jure Systems but Not de Facto

By ROBERT B. SEMPLE Jr.
Special to The New York Times

WASHINGTON, March 24—President Nixon committed himself today to elimination of officially imposed segregation in Southern public schools. But he said that until the courts provided further guidance he could not require elimination of de facto segregation, North and South, resulting from residential patterns.

At the same time, the President announced plans to allocate $1.5-billion over the next two years to help local school districts, North and South, to mitigate the effects of racial isolation stemming from de facto segregation.

These were the central themes of what Administration officials said was the most comprehensive statement by any President on the problems of elementary and secondary school desegregation. The 8,000-word document, judged to be too long for a television address, was handed to newsmen at the White House this morning.

Two Types of Segregation

A number of civil rights leaders reacted bitterly, saying that the President was honoring the concept of integration while signaling retention of segregation.

In an effort to resolve increasing national confusion resulting from conflicting court decisions and statements issued by his own Administration, Mr. Nixon drew a sharp distinction between the two generally recognized forms of segregation.

These are de jure segregation, which is largely a Southern phenomenon that results from the conscious discriminatory acts of public officials, and de facto segregation, which stems from segregated housing patterns in the larger cities, North and South.

The courts, the President said, have spoken fully on de jure segregation—most notably in Brown v. Board of Education, the historic Supreme Court school desegregation decision of 1954.

Mr. Nixon pledged to carry out the mandate of the courts—relying on court orders and the "good faith" efforts of local Southern officials to comply with those orders, while de-emphasizing the stern enforcement procedures that marked the Johnson Administration's approach to the same problem.

Mr. Nixon said that the courts had not spoken clearly on what, if anything, should be done to overcome de facto segregation. While such segregation is undesirable in practice, he said, it remains fully constitutional in theory. He therefore offered a set of suggestions on what might be done administratively.

Two Positions Repeated

Essentially, this prescription repeated both Mr. Nixon's oft-stated opposition to the busing of pupils to achieve integrated schools and his now-familiar endorsement of the neighborhood school concept. Some civil rights advocates have said that the surest ways to overcome racial isolation would be to promote busing and to lower the prestige of the neighborhood school concept.

The President, however, opted for a different and essentially middle course, relying heavily on innovation and experimentation. His main proposal was to offer funds for technical assistance to public school districts, North and South, that wish to eliminate de facto segregation on their own initiative or to soften the effects of segregation by providing compensatory educational help to minority group children in racially isolated classrooms.

The amount of money offered was unusually large—$500-million for the 1971 fiscal year, beginning July 1, and $1-billion in new money for 1972. The 1971 money would be shifted from other programs.

Speculation on Effects

The practical impact of the Nixon statement will not easily be measured for some time. But several results seemed probable, according to experienced civil rights observers within and outside the Administration.

First, the elimination of dual school systems—one white and one black, will probably proceed without serious interruption in rural Southern school districts, where desegregation requires few dislocations and little busing. Most rural school systems have eliminated, or are in the process of dissolving, the dual systems.

"Deliberate racial segregation of pupils by official action is unlawful wherever it exists," Mr. Nixon said. "In the words of the Supreme Court, it must be eliminated 'root and branch' —and it must be eliminated at once."

The statement set no deadlines for action and did not explain how the Government would enforce its desegregation policy. Last summer, however, in the first of a series of statements, the Administration forecast a gradual shift in enforcement responsibilities from the Department of Health, Education and Welfare and the Justice Department and the courts. H.E.W. had been cutting off funds to school districts that were found to be in noncompliance of the law.

Nixon Administration officials suggested today that even greater emphasis would henceforth be placed on the courts.

The second probable result of the statement is that desegregation in Southern cities, as opposed to rural areas, will probably move more slowly than it might have under the procedures in force until last year. Southerners close to the Administration have privately been forecasting this result all year.

Until last year, all Southern school segregation was assumed to be de jure, and Southern cities were exposed to the same strict enforcement procedures as Southern rural districts.

But in some Southern cities there is nearly as much de facto segregation, arising from racially "impacted" neighborhood patterns, as there is in Northern cities.

Southerners were quick to recognize and applaud this element of the President's statement.

"The mere existence of primarily white and black schools in an area is not conclusive evidence of true de jure segregation," declared Senator John G. Tower, Republican of Texas.

The third result, most observers agreed, was that the pace of overcoming either variety of segregation would depend heavily on the Administration's own day-to-day operational policies.

Mr. Nixon expressed a very strong preference for allowing local districts to devise their own solutions without heavy pressure either from Federal enforcement officers or over-zealous courts.

Court Cases Reviewed

Mr. Nixon's associates insisted privately, and repeatedly, that the funds would not be used to indemnify recalcitrant districts. Instead, they said, the funds would be used to replace the "punitive" aspects of the old enforcement procedures with new incentives to proceed with desegregation in good faith.

Mr. Nixon's statement was divided into four interrelated parts.

First came a lengthy summary of court decisions bearing on desegregation. The President endorsed the Brown v. Board of Education ruling and the decisions dealing with de jure segregation that have ensued since 1954, including those that call for the assignment of teachers on a nonracial basis. He noted that Chief Justice Warren E. Burger has said that the court had left unresolved a number of crucial questions dealing with how desegregation was to be carried out and whether a mathematical balance was required to satisfy its original mandate.

Mr. Nixon found greater confusion in the lower courts, especially those decisions that have attempted to come to grips with problems arising from de facto segregation. On balance, he concluded, the clear guidance of rulings on the Court of Appeals is that de facto segregation does not violate the Constitution.

A second section discussed the status of desegregation today. Mr. Nixon cited examples of progress but dwelt at length on the complexities. These included the process of "resegregation" caused when whites flee to escape desegregation; the existence of "deeply rooted racial attitudes"; the inability of the schools and the children to carry alone the burden of achieving "the kind of multiracial society which the adult community has failed to achieve for itself"; and the practical obstacles to desegregating a big-city school system already largely black.

In addition, he said, the impact of integration on raising the achievement levels of Negro pupils had yet to be clearly established. Also to be determined, he said, are the precise ratios at which blacks and whites function well together and the impact of factors such as social background and home environment on achievement.

A third section dealt with the principles of enforcement that Mr. Nixon offered for the guidance of his Cabinet officials.

He also called for efforts to equalize the "quality of education" in all schools, white and black; urged his associates to respect the judgment of local school boards "provided they act in good faith and within

constitutional limits"; reiterated his opposition to busing and his endorsement of neighborhood schools; and said that if a school system included both de jure and de facto segregation, the Federal Government could move against the former but not the latter.

A fourth section dealt with Mr. Nixon's proposal to spend money to mitigate the effects of de facto segregation, either by improving the quality of racially isolated schools or by financing local experiments in desegregation.

Mr. Nixon's proposals drew heavily on views expressed by Dr. James S. Coleman, a Johns Hopkins sociologist who recently conferred with the Presi-

dent. Mr. Nixon suggested a variety of unusual avenues to "interracial experiences" short of total integration, including integrated part-time, supplementary schooling outside a child's neighborhood school.

"This sort of innovation demonstrates that the alternatives are not limited to perpetuating racial isolation on the one hand, and massively disrupting existing school patterns on the other." Mr. Nixon said.

Officials said privately that the bulk of the money would not be channeled to upgrading slum schools. It would go, they said, to promote forms of desegregation short of the massive busing that Mr. Nixon continues to oppose.

March 25, 1970

SUPREME COURT, 9-0, BACKS BUSING TO COMBAT SOUTH'S DUAL SCHOOLS, REJECTING ADMINISTRATION STAND

OPINION BY BURGER

Segregation in North Based on Housing Is Not Affected

By FRED P. GRAHAM
Special to The New York Times

WASHINGTON, April 20 — The Supreme Court unanimously upheld today the constitutionality of busing as a means to "dismantle the dual school systems" of the South.

But the Court made it clear that today's decision did not apply to Northern-style segregation, based on neighborhood patterns.

In a series of decisions written by Chief Justice Warren

E. Burger and supported by the eight other Justices, the Court overrode the arguments of the Nixon Administration and the Justice Department, which had intervened on the side of Southern school systems in the four cases decided today.

Dismay Over U.S. View

To the dismay of civil rights organizations and the delight of many white Southerners, the Justice Department lawyers had argued that Southern school systems should be allowed to assign students to schools in their own neighborhoods even if this resulted in slowing the pace of desegregation in the South.

Southern lawyers had contended that the Northern areas were permitted to have neighborhood schools and that it would be discriminatory if the South were not allowed the same "privilege."

"Desegregation plans cannot be limited to the walk-in

school," the Court declared. It held that busing was proper unless "the time or distance is so great as to risk either the health of the children or significantly impinge on the educational process." Young children may be improper subjects for busing when the distances are long, the Court concluded.

Limits on Decision

The Court stopped short of ordering the elimination of all-black schools or of requiring racial balance in the schools. But it said that the existence of all-black schools created a presumption of discrimination and held that Federal district judges may use racial quotas as a guide in fashioning desegregation decrees.

This is expected to touch off a new wave of desegregation orders this summer in the cities of the South, where school segregation has persisted despite the 1954 Supreme Court decision that declared legally

required segregation to be unconstitutional.

Chief Justice Burger excluded "de facto" segregation of the North from today's ruling by declaring, "We do not reach in this case the question whether a showing that school segregation is a consequence of other types of state action, without any discriminatory action by the school authorities, is a constitutional violation requiring remedial action by a school desegregation decree."

The major portion of what Mr. Burger described as "guidelines, however imperfect, for the assistance of school authorities and courts" came in a 28-page opinion upholding a busing decree governing the joint school system in Charlotte-Mecklenburg County, N. C.

The court upheld the judgment of Federal District Judge James B. McMillan, who required massive crosstown busing of children in an effort to approximate in each elementary school the ratio of 71 per cent whites and 29 per cent blacks that exists in the entire school system.

Judge McMillan's ruling was overturned by the United States Court of Appeals for the Fourth Circuit on the grounds that it was unreasonable and burdensome. In upholding Judge McMillan, the Supreme Court stressed that the school board had failed to propose an acceptable plan and that this had forced him to produce his own plan.

In such cases a district court has "broad powers to fashion a remedy," the Supreme Court said. It said that Judge McMillan's solution was acceptable under those particular circumstances, although it did not mean that other judges were required to order similar measures.

The Court's guidelines contained the following points:

¶Desegregation does not require that every school in every community must always reflect the racial composition of the school system as a whole. However, if a judge wishes to use mathematical ratios, as Judge McMillan did, as "a starting point in the process of shaping a remedy," this may be within his equitable discretion.

¶The existence of "some small numbers" of schools of one race, or virtually one race, is not alone proof of racial discrimination. "But in a system with a history of segregation" the courts may indulge in "a presumption against schools that are substantially disproportionate in their racial composition." If such school districts have any all-black schools, the burden will be on them "to satisfy the court that their racial composition is not the result of present or past discriminatory action on their part."

¶It is not enough for school officials to draw school attendance lines that appear to be racially neutral. Officials must foster integration by such af-

The New York Times/George Tames

Chief Justice Warren E. Burger wrote Court's opinions

firmative measures as gerrymandering school boundaries to include both races, pairing "white" and "Negro" schools, and drawing school zones that combine noncontiguous areas in racially diverse neighborhoods.

¶The authority of Federal courts to require the assignment of students on the basis of race to achieve integration is not affected by antibusing language in the Civil Rights Act of 1964. The courts' obligation is to enforce the 14th Amendment's declaration that no state shall "deny any person within its jurisdiction the equal protection of the laws." Congress declared in the Civil Rights Act that it did not intend to enlarge the remedies of courts in enforcing the equal protection guarantee but that

it also did not purport to diminish these remedies.

A companion case today concerned a ruling by the Supreme Court of Georgia, which upheld the contention by white parents in Athens, Ga., that school officials had violated the 14th Amendment by making racial assignments to achieve desegregation.

Chief Justice Burger said that, on the contrary, racial assignments were necessary to enforce the 14th Amendment rights by upsetting the segregated status quo.

Using similar reasoning in a third case, the Court declared unconstitutional an antibusing statute enacted by the North Carolina Legislature. A similar law passed by the New York

Legislature has been declared unconstitutional by a three-judge Federal District Court and is pending before the Supreme Court.

In the fourth case the Court overturned the desegregation plan of Mobile, Ala., and ordered further desegregation. Mobile officials had avoided busing by adopting a neighborhood approach that left many Negroes in the eastern section of the city in predominantly black schools. The Court found this inadequate.

While the ruling today is its most sweeping school desegregation action since the 1954 case, it leaves some unanswered questions that may confound Federal District judges in the coming months.

The ruling said that "at some point" Southern school districts should have satisfied the 1954 ruling and become "unitary." However, it did not say how Southern communities would know when they had reached that point. Once there, the Court said the communities would not be "required to make year-by-year adjustments of the racial composition of student bodies."

The Court also did not say if comunities can close their inner city schools and bus Negroes out, or, if they must bus children of both races equally.

But the most vexing aspect of the ruling is likely to be the broad discretion given to Federal District judges. Having been told that they must do more to break down racial imbalance, but that they are not required to eliminate all "black" schools or achieve racial balance, any ruling is likely to be attacked as either too strong or too weak.

Jack Greenberg and James M. Nabrit 3d of the N.A.A.C.P. Legal Defense and Educational Fund, Inc., in New York, made the major arguments for more desegregation. Solicitor General Erwin N. Griswold presented the Government's argument.

NIXON DISAVOWS H.E.W. PROPOSAL ON SCHOOL BUSING

Bids 2 Members of Cabinet Work With Local Districts to Minimize Pupil Travel

OPPOSITION IS RESTATED

Steps Mark Major Change From Previous Position on High Court Ruling

By JAMES M. NAUGHTON

Special to The New York Times

WASHINGTON, Aug. 3 — President Nixon disavowed today his Administration's plan for extensive crosstown busing to desegregate the public school system in Austin, Tex., and reasserted his strong opposition to busing as a means of achieving racial balance.

The President directed Attorney General John N. Mitchell and the Secretary of Health, Education and Welfare, Elliot L. Richardson, to "work with individual school districts to hold busing to the minimum re-

quired by law" as school systems in the South seek to adjust to a Supreme Court ruling upholding the use of busing to desegregate schools.

Mr. Nixon instructed Mr. Richardson to submit to Congress an amendment to the proposed Emergency School Assistance Act "that will expressly prohibit" using any of the act's $1.5-billion to acquire buses. The bill is intended to help schools that are desegregating.

A Major Change

The actions signaled a major change by the White House from its earlier interpretation of the Supreme Court's April 20 ruling on busing.

The Court declared, over the opposition of the Justice Department, that busing was proper unless "the time or distance is so great as to risk either the health of the children or significantly impinge on the educational process."

In its first school desegregation proposal after the Supreme Court ruling, the Department of Health, Education and Welfare recommended on May 14 that a Federal District Court in Austin approve "extensive" busing to achieve a city-wide mixture of the Negro and Mexican-American minorities with the white Anglo majority.

At that time, J. Stanley Pottinger, director of the Office of Civil Rights, said that the plan was clearly "the first indication" of the Government's interpretation of the Supreme Court ruling.

Federal District Judge Jack Roberts rejected the Government plan on July 19 in favor of the Austin school board's proposal to create centers for fine arts, social sciences, avocations and science and to bus elementary school pupils to them for periodic "cultural" experiences.

In a statement issued late today by the White House, the President said that the Justice Department would appeal Judge Roberts's ruling "on limited constitutional grounds."

Mr. Nixon said the Attorney General had advised him that he "must appeal" the Austin school board's plan for periodic interracial experiences "because that decision is inconsistent" with the Supreme Court ruling.

In essence, the Government will contend that part-time desegregation does not meet the test of the Supreme Court mandate to put an end to the dual school system.

But the President's statement added:

"The Justice Department is not appealing to impose the H.E.W. plan. In the process of the appeal, the Justice Department will disavow that plan on behalf of the Government."

Gerald L. Warren, deputy White House press secretary, said he was sure that Mr. Richardson concurred in the disavowal.

Mr. Richardson was not available for comment. He left on a month-long vacation this afternoon.

Opposition Is Voiced

Mr. Nixon, who pledged in his 1968 campaign for the

Presidency to do all he could to prevent the forced busing of pupils, said that he "would also like to restate my position as it relates to busing." He declared:

"I am against busing as that term is commonly used in school desegregation cases. I have consistently opposed the busing of our nation's schoolchildren to achieve a racial balance, and I am opposed to the busing of children simply for the sake of busing.

"Further, while the executive branch will continue to enforce the orders of the Court, including court-ordered busing, I have instructed the Attorney General and the Secretary of Health, Education and Welfare that they are to work with individual school districts to hold busing to the minimum required by law."

The President's statement appeared to be a reply, in part, to a resolution adopted yesterday, 351 to 36, in the House of Representatives. It directed Mr. Richardson to furnish Congress with information on the extent of busing supported by his department.

Mr. Richardson sent a letter this afternoon to Speaker Carl Albert, saying that the vote yesterday "may reflect a fundamental misunderstanding" of his department's programs. He said that there was "no program administered by this department either designed or used to support, promote or require the busing of schoolchildren to achieve racial balance."

The Secretary recalled in the letter a statement of opposition to busing by Mr. Nixon on March 24, before the Supreme Court ruling.

When the Underprivileged and the Overprivileged Go to School

SLUMS AND SUBURBS: A Commentary on Schools in Metropolitan Areas. By James Bryant Conant. 147 pp. New York: McGraw-Hill Book Company. Cloth, $3.95. Paper, $1.95.

By FRED M. HECHINGER

IT may well be that "Slums and Suburbs" will turn out, in the perspective of history, to be James B. Conant's most important book. In his earlier studies, which offered valuable mind-lifting prescriptions for "typical" American schools, he overlooked the more controversial schools in the large cities and their suburbs. Now he has caught up with these schools, which enroll a crucial minority of the nation's children—the underprivileged and overprivileged. The result is a difference in tone: the difference between a management survey and a gale warning.

This time, the former Harvard president and Ambassador to Germany has rejected the language of educator or diplomat. He is writing with the controlled anger of a New Englander as he turns to the first of the two opposite extremes: the Negro slums. He fully expects to be attacked by squeamish liberals, white and Negro, for using this term. Yet it will be hard to challenge his belief, unpopular as it may be, that the crisis cannot be met "if we are deprived by terminology from knowing what the situation really is."

That situation is the Negro slum—not because of any racial inferiority but because "this republic was born with a congenital defect" — Negro slavery — which still condemns the Negro slum-dweller to a socio-economic confinement with few escape hatches. Discrimination in employment makes drifters of many of the slum men, while the women find employment more readily outside the ghetto. In contrast to the white immigrants in the slums of earlier periods, Negro youth in the slums faces practical and psychological "No-Exit" signs.

Mr. Conant is angry with those who want to apply routine, average-American school reforms, including his own earlier proposals, to these slums—where high-school girls' most serious problem is getting home unmolested; where between half and two-thirds of the boys between 16 and 21 are out of school and out of work; where children fall asleep in class be-

At Harlem's dilapidated P. S. 119, many classrooms and hallways are closed to pupils while needed repairs are made.

cause they have no place to sleep at home; where "home" is so transient that a teacher, absent for two weeks, may find few familiar faces in his class when he returns.

Controversy will rage over Mr. Conant's categorical rejection of forced integration of Negro slum schools by transporting children out of their neighborhoods. He would rather be called reactionary than be party to what he considers a popular delusion. While he is as adamant in his condemnation of *de jure* segregation and of gerrymandering to segregate children "solely" on the basis of race, he is convinced that the real problem is socio-economic, not racial. He challenges schools, labor unions and employers to prepare these children for jobs and place them effectively.

Even the social reformers' stress on housing seems to Mr. Conant a cart-before-the-horse fallacy: employment comes first. He considers the fight against drop-outs from school a mockery as long as Negro high-school graduates have little hope for employment after graduation. In his estimate, 300,000 jobs are needed at once for Negro slum boys, and he insists that they

---

Lesson

ONE lesson to be drawn from visiting and contrasting a well-to-do suburb and a slum is all important for understanding American public education. The lesson is that to a considerable degree what a school should do and can do is determined by the status and ambitions of the families being served.— *"Slums and Suburbs."*

---

be provided, if necessary through public works.

PERHAPS least satisfactory is Mr. Conant's approach to the kind of vocational training to be given to these youngsters, especially since jobs for them are scarce. But there can be no argument with his diagnosis that the slum schools are "social dynamite." The issue, he insists, is the improvement of the Negro slum schools in the Northern cities through more money and high-caliber, fully integrated staffs rather than through "token integration."

As Mr. Conant turns to the second half of the book—the wealthy suburbs—the first impulse is to ask: is this an attempt to equate cancer with the common cold, just because each is considered a disease? If it were not so clearly evident that sarcasm is foreign to Mr. Conant, his reference to the Great

Necks, Evanstons and Newtons as "lighthouse schools" might sound ironic, considering that their beacons offer so little light to slum schools, only a commuter ticket distant.

In the case of the slum schools, society does not care enough; in the wealthy suburban schools, society cares too much—for the wrong reasons. The slum schools lack relevancy if they fail to offer a transition into nondiscriminatory employment; the wealthy suburban schools feel they must send almost everybody to college, and thus ignore the relevancy of the student's limitations.

Mr. Conant is as impatient with hoarded suburban teaching talent, while the slum schools are starved, as he is with those who criticize American high schools for not offering a sufficiently demanding college-preparatory curriculum. Let the graduate schools and their product—the lawyers, doctors, professors and scientists—make graduate university degrees dependent on a truly demanding examination (in the European tradition), and the quality colleges may eliminate the educational status-seekers. This is a sound, if tough, prescription. It is the only one thus far offered that could free the suburban schools from the insane pressure by over-ambitious parents who want their children to be kindergarten-prepared for Harvard because "the right people" go there.

A brief excursion, toward the end of the book, into the progressive education debate seems an irrelevant aside. A terse, urgent summary, however, recaptures the theme and spirit of Mr. Conant's most powerful book. To make sure that nobody will mistake the first half of the report as mere educational slumming on the way to the suburbs, the conclusions reverse the order and leave the reader with an appeal for action "before it is too late." This is no checklist for eager P.T.A. chairmen; it is a grim warning to all Americans.

New Rochelle Plea On Schools Denied By Supreme Court

Special to The New York Times.

WASHINGTON, Dec. 11—A lower court decision that New Rochelle, N. Y., has segregated Negro pupils in the public schools and must now correct the situation was left standing today by the Supreme Court.

The original decision had been made by Judge Irving R. Kaufman in Federal District Court and affirmed by a 2-to-1 vote in the United States Court of Appeals for the Second Circuit.

As usual, the Supreme Court gave no reasons for denying a review today. It did so in a brief order that had the effect of making the lower court decision final without approving its reasoning.

The denial was not altogether a surprise. Since its original school segregation decisions in 1954 and 1955, the Supreme Court has agreed to hear argument in only one school case—the Little Rock case in 1958.

The decisions of Judge Kaufmann and the Second Circuit Appeals Court are of potentially great significance for both the North and the South. This is because the facts in New Rochelle demonstrated only partial, not total, segregatioin.

The complaint of Negro groups, including the National Association for the Advancement of Colored People, was not that Negro children were excluded from schools near their homes. This is the usual basis of segregation suits in the South.

Instead it was argued that school districts had been created and maintained so as to place most Negroes in one school. This was the Lincoln School, which last year had 94 per cent Negro pupils.

The New Rochelle Board of Education bitterly denied the charge that it had segregated anyone. It said its school districts were compact and reasonably drawn, not gerrymandered. The reason for the Negro predominance at Lincoln, the board said, was simply that most Negroes lived in its vicinity.

In a suit brought by parents of eleven children at Lincoln, Judge Kaufman found otherwise. He said "segregation at the Lincoln School was not a fortuity; it was deliberately created and maintained by [the School Board's] conduct."

The facts found by Judge Kaufman were that during the years before 1949 the New Rochelle board had several times juggled the boundaries of the Lincoln School District to put white children in other schools. Then, in 1949, the board adopted a policy of refusing any transfers from Lincoln.

The Court of Appeals opinion —written by Judge Charles E. Clark and joined by Judge J. Joseph Smith—emphasized these "crucial" findings.

After deciding that there was segregation, Judge Kaufman held further hearings on what relief to grant. He asked for and received suggestions from the Justice Department. Then he ordered the New Rochelle board to let children of either race transfer from Lincoln to other schools.

At the beginning of the present term, in compliance with this order, the board transferred 267 children out of Lincoln, leaving only 187 in the school. The Negro percentage there dropped from 94 to 90.

CIVIL RIGHTS SUIT OVER IMBALANCE IN SCHOOLS FAILS

Supreme Court Bars Review of Ruling Against Forcing Local Boards to Act

BUS-PLAN FOES BUOYED

No Legal Basis Is Found for Halting Inequity Due Only to Pattern in Housing

By ANTHONY LEWIS
Special to The New York Times

WASHINGTON, May 4—The Supreme Court left standing today a decision that school boards have no constitutional duty to end racial imbalance resulting from housing patterns.

The action was a major setback for civil rights forces attacking what they call de facto segregation in Northern cities. This is the situation in which neighborhood public schools are all, or predominantly, Negro or white.

The Supreme Court did not itself pass on the merits of the problem today. It simply declined, in a brief and unexplained order, to review the lower court ruling.

Nevertheless, those who oppose moving pupils by bus to end racial imbalance will doubtless take comfort from the Supreme Court's refusal to consider the contention that such action is constitutionally required.

School Board Absolved

The case came from Gary, Ind. According to the Negro plaintiffs, 97 per cent of that city's Negro public-school pupils are in predominantly Negro schools.

The Court of Appeals for the Seventh Circuit, in deciding the case last October, found that the school imbalance did not result from any official policy. The court said that school districts had been drawn originally on non-racial lines and that their racial characteristics had changed with population shifts.

In taking the case to the Supreme Court, the complainants did not challenge these findings. They did not argue that the Gary school board had deliberately caused the racial division of its schools.

The argument was, rather, that it is unconstitutional for a school board to "acquiesce" in such de facto segregation. The petition to the Supreme Court suggested that the Constitution's bar against racial discrimination required the school board to take affirmative action.

Such affirmative action could presumably be a redrawing of school zones to improve racial imbalance. It could be forced busing of pupils to distant schools. It could be pairing of schools, the so-called Princeton plan.

Nothing in the case ended today puts any legal roadblock in the way of such moves by local school boards. They may act to diminish racial imbalance. But the Constitution does not require them to, according to the decision of the Appeals Court.

Thus the way remains open for civil rights groups to press through political means and protests for better racial balance in northern schools. It also remains open for opposition by groups that have arisen to defend "neighborhood schools."

The National Association for the Advancement of Colored People supported the Gary case. The denial of its petition is certainly a blow to hopes for relief of de facto segregation through legal channels.

Significantly, the case did not have the support of the N.A.A.C.P. Legal Defense and Educational Fund, a separate organization that apparently did not think it was a well-advised lawsuit.

The N.A.A.C.P. petition to the Supreme Court said that the question was "whether the Constitution tolerates a school board's acquiesence in the operation of a school system which is segregated in fact, merely because it did not intentionally or overtly create it."

An Obligation Seen

The petition took the view that it was "incumbent upon a school board to mitigate segregation in education where possible."

The decisive legal difference between segregation brought about by school authorities and that created by other factors was nicely illustrated by an-

December 12, 1961

241

other case on which the Supreme Court acted today.

This case came from Jacksonville, Fla., whose schools were until recently wholly segregated by deliberate offical action. Now token integration has begun.

Last January the Court of Appeals for the Fifth Circuit held that the Jacksonville authorities must cease assigning teachers and administrators—as well as pupils—on the basis of race. It also prohibited discrimination in the budgeting of school funds.

The Supreme Court declined today to review that decision. The county school board had challenged the ban on racial assignments of teachers.

Again the court gave no reasons for letting the decision of the Appeals Court stand. But the decision was consistent with the view that a state may not act for reasons of racial discrimination.

The refusal to review leaves the Supreme Court free to consider either of today's question in future cases. Doubtless the de facto school issue will be pressed again.

Court's Action Hailed

Commenting on the Supreme Court's actions in the suit against racial imbalance in schools, Mrs. Rosemary Gunning of Ridgewood, Queens, executive secretary of the city-wide Parents and Taxpayers Coordinating Council, said yesterday:

"The Supreme Court action complete'y vindicates the position taken by P.A.T. This conclusively destroys the argument that the Supreme Court has mandated the assignment of children to achieve racial balance.

"This additional legal backing of the moral and practical grounds for the neighborhood school concept should put an end, once and for all, to the plans of the radicals to use our children as political pawns."

Robert L. Carter, general counsel of the National Association for the Advancement of Colored People, issued the following comment last night:

"We are greatly disappointed that the Supreme Court of the United States has denied certiorari in the Gary, Ind., case. However, it should be pointed out that the Court has made clear time and time again what its denial of certiorari means.

"This does not mean that the Court has validated de facto segregation or has held that such segregation is consistent with the United States Constitution or affirmed the judgment of the Court of Appeals.

"What the denial of the writ means is that 'the Court did not feel that the time was ripe, for whatever reason, for it to hear and review the issue at this time.

"Under these circumstances, it is our intention to continue to press this issue in the courts and, where appropriate, to apply for review by the Supreme Court in the hope that in some future time the court may decide that the cause is ripe for adjudication.

"In our judgment this is a crucial and critical issue affecting the whole course of the Negro struggle for equality. At some point a determination as to the constitutional validity of de facto school segregation must be made by the Supreme Court of the United States."

May 5, 1964

RACIAL FERMENT EMBROILS NORTH

Drives Gaining Momentum Against Housing Patterns

By FOSTER HAILEY

The 1954 school desegregation ruling by the Supreme Court started a revolution of thought and of conscience in the North as well as in the South.

It is a revolution that is gaining momentum. More demonstrations were staged and more desegregation battles won in the North during the last two years than in the previous eight.

Since 1962, the National Association for the Advancement of Colored People has extended integration campaigns to 86 school systems in 19 Northern states. In 26 of these systems, at least partial victory has been achieved.

The campaign has not been against segregation by law as in the South, but against de facto segregation brought about by housing patterns.

No Northern state had statutory segregation in 1954. But in four states — Arizona, Kansas, New Mexico and Wyoming —and in the District of Columbia there was permissive segregation.

Century-Old Battle

Further, virtually all had de facto segregation. This was especially true in the states with industrial cities to which Southern Negroes had been drawn in two world wars.

The struggle for school equality in the North did not begin in 1954, however. Familiar methods, including boycotts and demonstrations, had been used for more than a century. But it was not until the end of World War II, when the Negro had become a strong political force in many cities, that the struggle gathered momentum.

The 1954 decision gave it impetus. But the shock waves from the bombings in Birmingham, Ala., last year rattled the windowpanes of school boards from Malverne, L.I., to Tacoma, Wash.

And they continue to reverberate.

Well-manicured suburbs such as New Rochelle, N. Y.; Englewood, N. J.; Stamford, Conn.; Ardmore, Pa., and Pasadena, Calif., have heard the tread of marching demonstrators.

Consequently, either by voluntary action, or state or court order, they abandoned old segregated school patterns and distributed their colored youngsters among what were all-white or nearly all-white schools.

In many ways the drive for integration in the North has been more complicated than in the South. The argument for the neighborhood school — to have younger children within walking distance of home — is compelling for many Negro, as well as white, parents.

Some proposals, such as the pairing of schools or the busing of white children to schools in Negro neighborhoods, have aroused resentment among white parents who otherwise have been sympathetic to Negro demands for equality.

Integration Is Fought

In New York and some of its suburbs, parents have banded to oppose such methods of desegregation. Some 100 groups, loosely organized in a Parents and Taxpayers Association, have brought 32 court actions, at last count, to prevent integration in their neighborhoods. And they marshaled 15,000 persons for a protest march around City Hall in March.

Despite these and other setbacks, there is no indication that civil rights groups are abandoning the fight.

June Shagaloff, national special assistant for education of the N.A.A.C.P., gives this minimum aim:

"The N.A.A.C.P. is not proposing that children be distributed throughout a school system, from one end of a city to another, on the basis of race or color to achieve a proportional representation or fixed percentage of white and Negro children in every school.

"But we are insisting that school officials adopt comprehensive, city-wide plans to achieve maximum desegregation or to eliminate existing racial concentrations to the fullest extent possible."

School equality, the most emotional civil rights issue, has attracted the widest support and the most attention. But two other issues are no less vital — housing and jobs.

Housing patterns, Negroes say, have forced them into black ghettos and their children into neighborhood schools of inferior facilities. Inferior education and early school dropouts then restrict the jobs for which the Negro is qualified.

Whether the white man likes it or not, the Negro says, he intends to escape this circle of deprivation.

And he is escaping, says Harry Fleischman, Race Relations Coordinator of the American Jewish Committee, who has been watching and recording the civil rights struggle for many years.

Since the end of World War II he notes, the armed forces have been integrated, the median earnings of Negro workers have risen to 60 per cent of their white colleagues,' against only 30 per cent in 1939; Federal and local governments have sought to bar discrimination in employment; the color ban has been eliminated from the constitutions of all major labor unions; 30 states have forbidden discrimination in public accommodations, and 11 have forbidden discrimination in private, as well as public, housing.

May 18, 1964

SUBURBAN PUPILS CALLED DEPRIVED

Educator Says They Often Lose Touch With Others

By GENE CURRIVAN

A new type of deprived children — those who have moved to the fashionable suburbs and are isolated from the lower classes — is being developed in this country, according to a leading educator.

This observation was made yesterday by Dr. Harold Taylor, former president of Sarah Lawrence College, at a meeting of the Public Education Association School Volunteers at the New York Academy of Medicine, 2 East 103d Street.

The formula is simple, according to Dr. Taylor.

"People without money go without education, and where local and state taxes do not provide enough funds for good schools, the schools are not good and the children remain untaught," he said.

"On the other hand, people with money move to communities in the suburbs where they form communities of people with money, and build what amount to private schools, paying in taxes what otherwise would be called tuition.

"They are thus formed into closed communities of a separate class of citizens whose children learn to distinguish between their own class and other classes, who learn to believe that this is the natural condition of man, and too often go through life with a class attitude engrained in their minds as a by-product of their education. They are the new culturally deprived."

"What's so great about the white middle-class?" he asked. He told the volunteers, who work as teacher's aides with the underprivileged here, that Negroes, Puerto Ricans, Spanish-Americans and Indians have their own cultures and "have more to offer us than the white homogenized middle-class."

September 23, 1964

MEXICANS' PLIGHT IN U.S. SCHOOLS HIT

High Dropout Rate Linked to Use of English in Class

By M. A. FARBER

The "most acute educational problem" in the Southwest is the inadequate schooling for 1.75 million Mexican-American children, according to a 40-page report issued last week by the National Education Association.

The report, prepared after a year's study of the Spanish-speaking children in Arizona, California, Colorado, New Mexico and Texas, discloses a grim prevalence of low grades, high dropout rates and difficulties stemming from schools' insistence on the use of English as the classroom language.

As an example of the "limited" academic success of the Mexican-Americans, the report cites a California survey in 1960 showing that more than half of the Spanish-speaking males, and nearly half of the females, over 14 years of age, had not gone beyond the eighth grade.

Only 8.8 per cent of the males, and 6.2 per cent of the females, had completed one or more years of college.

Comparable figures for the total population in California disclose that 27.9 per cent of the males, and 25 per cent of the females, over 14, had quit school by the eighth grade, the report noted. Also it was noted that 23.4 per cent of all males and 19.4 per cent of all females in the state had finished at lease the freshman year of college.

In a profile detailing in-school experience, the report mentions the results of the California Achievement Tests administered to children in Lindsay, Calif., an agricultural community with a high percentage of Mexican-Americans.

In reading scores, it notes, 63.9 per cent of the Mexican-American children and 27.3 per cent of the "Anglo-Americans" were below grade level. Similar percentages in arithmetic were

38.7 and 20.8 and, in language, 55.5 and 30.6.

Quoting from an analysis of the Lindsay results, the N.E.A. report says that Mexican-American children "start school with a decided handicap, fall behind their classmates in the first grade, and each passing year finds them farther behind."

"They are conditioned to failure in the early years of their schooling," it goes on, "and each additional year only serves to reinforce their feelings of failure and frustration."

The "decided handicap" at the start of the Mexican-American's education is his almost exclusive use of Spanish.

"He knows some English but has used it infrequently," the report observes. "The language of his home, his childhood, his first years, is Spanish. His environment, his experiences, his very personality have been shaped by it."

But the student with this background often discovers that English is the only language acceptable in school, the report notes.

Spanish Forbidden

"In some schools the speaking of Spanish is forbidden both in the classrooms and on the playground" and "not infrequently students have been punished for lapsing into Spanish. This has even extended to corporal punishment," the report asserts.

In addition to the language barrier, the education association goes on, the Mexican-American student in the beginning "encounters a strange and different set of culture patterns, an accelerated tempo of living and, more often than not, teachers who, though sympathetic and sincere, have little understanding of the Spanish-speaking people, their customs, beliefs and sensitivities."

The association recommends the following remedies for the problem in the Southwest:

¶Bilingual instruction in preschool programs and early grades.

¶The teaching of English as a second language.

¶Emphasis on the reading, writing and speaking of good Spanish, since Mexican-American children are so often illiterate in it.

August 22, 1966

'TRACK' EDUCATION ENDS IN CAPITAL

But Dispute Over Divisions by Aptitude Continues

Special to The New York Times

WASHINGTON, March 18 — The "track" system of grouping public school students by ability, long the subject of bitter civil rights controversy in this most heavily populated Negro area among large American cities, appears to have finally ended.

The banishment of the system nearly cost its author his job and has been followed by an educational dispute with implications for other urban school systems.

Dr. Carl F. Hansen, who is the author of the 12-year-old track method of separating slow learners from more able students, came within one vote this week of not being reappointed to his fourth three-year term as the District of Columbia's Superintendent of Education.

He had been appointed without difficulty before, but this year his retention became an emotional civil rights issue.

Changes Demanded

Even school board members who provided the narrow majority for his retention demanded changes in the track system. But there was no agreement on what steps to take to replace it and critics of Dr. Hansen's continued advocacy of "basic" educational ideas predicted that his retention would lead to further turmoil in the city's schools.

One Negro leader has called for a school boycott on May 1, when the Superintendent's new contract becomes effective. Negroes make up nearly 65 per cent of the District's population, and support for the boycott proposal is reported to be strong in many predominantly Negro areas of the city.

The 61-year-old Nebraska-born educator is regarded by all but his most militant critics as a man of unquestioned goodwill on racial issues, and he appeared to have been deeply shaken by the 5-to-4 contract renewal vote of the school board.

"I think self-assessment and self-analysis at this point in my career are highly important," he told the board after the vote. "I need to know what it was which has caused a lack of confidence."

What it was, mainly the track system, has provided ammunition for Dr. Hansen's critics here and among professional educators for years. He has been accused of holding stubbornly to old-fashioned ideas about race and education in a ghetto school system.

The Superintendent, however, is noted for an outspoken low opinion of outside and lay innovators and reformers. He has called them dilettantes, and in the past the nine-member school board, appointed in this nonselfgoverning city by the judges of the United States District Court here, have tended to follow his lead.

Dr. Hansen has repeatedly made strong public commitments to "biracial education" as good for both white and Negro students. But he has also said repeatedly, usually with the preamble of "let's face it," that white parents and students tend to flee to the suburbs when the proportion of Negro pupils in a city school reaches 40 or 50 per cent.

According to Dr. Hansen's periodic explanations of the track system — and he has always defended the tracking of students as best for all — the method was initiated in part as a palliative to the dwindling white and middle class Negro public school minority here.

The idea was to mitigate the educational impact of integration on them in the hope of retaining middle class students and thus preserving meaningful integration.

At the same time, the plan was to offer vocational and basic academic education to students unable to absorb more, thus reducing the number of dropouts.

The Superintendent's four-track system, with honors, regular, general and basic segregation of students by classes, was begun in 1955 to cope with the admittedly large problems of race, poverty and previous educational deprivation in the Washington school system. The schools here have a Negro enrollment of about 93 per cent.

Dr. Hansen has often seemed to critics to be more concerned about retaining the remaining white and Negro middle class students in the school system than about "supervising the reality of the poorly prepared student majority," as one of his critics put it.

A study in 1965 by his staff of complaints about the track system showed that of 1,273 "basic track" students surveyed, 441 merited such low placement on academic standards. The study showed that many students had been assigned without testing, on orders of principals and counsellors.

Nine of the basic students were found to be severely retarded or emotionally disturbed, which heightened the charges that school officials were consigning difficult children to the lowest track as a matter of classroom convenience.

Study Indicates Pupils Do Well When Teacher Is Told They Will

By JOHN LEO

Four years ago Robert Rosenthal, now a 34-year-old professor of social psychology at Harvard, reported after tests that rats performed far better when the experimenters were told, falsely, that the rats had been specially bred for intelligence.

The same kind of rats consistently turned in poor performances when the experimenters had been told the animals were dull, he said.

Professor Rosenthal then began similar tests on schoolchildren, with what he termed similar results. A random sample of first and second grade children at a South San Francisco elementary school, who it was predicted would make dramatic gains in schoolwork, actually made those gains, while the rest of the student body did not. Only the teachers and not the pupils or parents had been told of the predictions.

Although, for ethical reasons, it was not predicted that any child would turn out dull, Professor Rosenthal believes that his tests provide important evidence supporting the common thesis that many children, particularly minority-group children, turn out dull because their teachers expect them to be dull.

"Pygmalion in the Classroom," his book on the experiment in South San Francisco and other school districts around the country, will be published in the spring by Holt Rinehart & Winston.

Dr. Lenore Jacobson, principal of South San Francisco's Spruce School — "Oak School" in the book—is the co-author.

Professor Rosenthal said in an interview yesterday:

"Kenneth Clark [professor of psychology at City College] and others have been saying for a long time that some children are victims of educational self-fulfilling prophecies, but they just haven't been able to come up with data to prove it. We think we have."

Three-Track System

About one-sixth of the 650 students at Spruce School are of Mexican descent, the only minority group enrolled. Mexican pupils in the "slow" track of the school's three-track system far outnumber the Mexican children in the "fast" track.

In the spring of 1964, with Dr. Jacobson's permission, Professor Rosenthal gave an I.Q. test to all pupils in the kindergarten and the first five grades.

Teachers were falsely told that the test would show which pupils were due to "spurt ahead" academically. The teachers were given the names

of 20 per cent of the student body, randomly selected from all grades and all three tracks, and were told that every pupil so listed would improve dramatically within a year.

A year later, when all the children still in school were retested, the "spurters" showed an average I.Q. gain of 12.22 points, compared with 8.42 for a control group representing the rest of the student body.

But the dramatic gains came only in grades one and two—increases of 27.4 in the first grade and 16.5 in the second grade for the "spurters." The control group rose only 12 points in the first grade and 7 in the second.

Seventy-nine per cent of the "spurters" and 49 per cent of the control group showed absolute gains of 10 I.Q. points or more in the first two grades.

Appearance an Element

The pupils of Mexican descent were found to be more advantaged by favorable expectations than were the other children, though the differences were not statistically significant.

Among the "spurters," Mexican boys—but not girls—whose faces looked somewhat Anglo-Saxon showed higher I.Q. gains than those with more identifiably Mexican faces.

"There is no clear explanation for this finding," said Professor Rosenthal, "but we can speculate that the teachers' pre-experimental expectancies of the more Mexican-looking boys' intellectual performances were probably lowest of all."

Contrary to Professor Rosenthal's expectation Spruce School did not car

Do They Know What They Do?

DEATH AT AN EARLY AGE. The Destruction of the Hearts and Minds of Negro Children in the Boston Public Schools. By Jonathan Kozol. 240 pp. Boston: Houghton Mifflin Company. $4.95.

By ROBERT COLES

I HOPE some of those Congressmen who are now looking into the causes of riots will find time to read this honest and terrifying book by Jonathan Kozol, a young teacher fired from his job by the Boston school system for using a poem by Langston Hughes that was not on the prescribed list of "reading materials." Mr. Kozol may even be called to Washington, and asked to tell our Congressmen what he experienced in an awful, hellish struggle, waged—of all places—in a city that fancies itself "the cradle of liberty," and dotes on its illustrious past. If he testified, perhaps the gentle, earnest, thoughtful quality of his mind, so apparent in this book, might be caught by the same television cameras that usually bring us our daily quota of evasive, pointless rhetoric from "important" people.

"Death at an Early Age" is not a long book. Its content can be easily summarized, but the heartbreaking story that it tells has to be read, and cannot be distilled into a review. Mr. Kozol entered the Boston schools as a substitute teacher in 1964, and the next spring he was summarily dismissed. Very simply, his book tells what happened in between, to him as a teacher and to the children, mostly Negro, he tried so hard to help and befriend. What emerges is an unsparing picture of American education as it exists today in the ghettos of our major Northern cities. Perhaps the United States Informa-

tion Agency will not want to use the book abroad.

Right off, Mr. Kozol found himself torn, confused and appalled. His "classroom" was the corner of an auditorium in which other classes were also held. In that same building children sat in a "dank and dirty urine-smelling cellar." One day a large window fell in as Mr. Kozol tried to teach his class. Not only was the school a disgraceful hovel—overcrowded, understaffed, something out of a Dickens novel—but the city did not provide police for the children who had to cross dangerous streets to reach the building, though once inside the teachers made sure no boy or girl felt at loose ends or unwatched.

In point of fact, the children were relentlessly and at times brutally tyrannized, and the major portion of this book documents exactly how. The rattan is used. The author describes the welts he saw, and even the serious injury one child sustained. All day long the children learn rules and regulations—to the point that whatever is original in them, whatever is *theirs* by virtue of experience or fantasy, becomes steadily discouraged and denied. What is even more awful to contemplate, boys and girls are taught by men and women who refer to Negroes as "black stuff" and worse.

The reader will find out about the cynicism, condescension, outright racism, and severely anti-intellectual attitudes that Mr. Kozol quite easily and openly encountered as a teacher among teachers. The city of Boston may someday (when is anyone's guess) tear down its already crumbling school buildings and provide its poor children with the best imagi-

nable "facilities" and "materials." But it is quite another question whether any American city is ready to look into its own soul, and admit to the subtleties of hate and terror that persist in the disguise of "education" or "law-enforcement."

The finest moments in this book are those in which the author quite openly examines his own, ordinary ("normal," if you will) willingness to go along with the rest, to submit to the very mean and stupid practices he so clearly recognized. Teachers in Boston and elsewhere may find him harsh on the "profession," but he does not spare himself, either.

Like the rest of us, he can excuse and condone—or simply ignore—events that threaten his "standing," his job, his yearly income, his day-to-day relationship with his peers. Like us he is capable of justifying the unjustifiable, or at least denying his own obligation to oppose what can easily be considered an impossible situation. There are moments in this life when to do the practical or wise thing is, in fact, to take the most corrupt and hurtful course possible. Mr. Kozol lets us see how those moments fall upon all of us—the would-be friends and supporters of what is "good" and "right," and of course "professional."

Eventually—inevitably we only now know—Jonathan Kozol slipped and brought down upon himself the self-righteous wrath of what emerges in his book as a hopelessly insensitive bureaucracy. The charges leveled against him were absurd: he taught Langston Hughes and Robert Frost to Negro children; he showed them pictures by Paul Klee, and read to them from Yeats—with surprising responses from his "disadvantaged" class.

Like so many of us, he can move on, obtain another job—and write this book. What of the children he describes, and their cousins and parents and neighbors? At the end of this book we are taken to a meeting of the Boston School Committee, to meet up with the vulgar, tricky and abusive comments of those "leaders" who control and direct the education of thousands of American children.

In the strongly worded title he has given his book, Mr. Kozol charges the Boston School Committee and the system they run with spiritual and psychological murder. Nothing in what they say, some of it supplied word for word in the book's notes, makes the accusation seem excessive.

October 1, 1967

Jonathan Kozol and his pupils, June, 1965.

WATERBURY, Conn. Sept. 27 (AP) — About 1,000 students from Waterbury's three high schools refused to attend class today in a dispute over the teaching of Negro history. They staged a protest rally in a park.

Two girls were said to have suffered cuts and bruises in incidents — one inside a school and the other outside. Brief skirmishes were reported at times between the angry students.

The demonstrators were in two opposing camps. One, made up of white youths, wants less Negro history taught. The other, made of Negroes, wants more Negro history given.

About 150 whites walked out of Crosby High yesterday to protest use of a textbook on Negro history in a course on American history. Some of the whites also said black students went unpunished for misbehavior.

Tuesday about 40 Negroes walked out of Crosby High when school officials refused to meet with them during class-time hours over the teaching of Negro history.

School Superintendent Michael F. Wallace went to the demonstration in Library Park today and urged the students to go back to classes until the problems — also involving the schools' dress code — could be solved.

But the youths refused, many of them saying they would stay away until an agreement was worked out.

Foundations Creating Climate for Change

By M.A. FARBER

Last July, school authorities in Philadelphia received $100,000 from the Rockefeller Foundation, mainly for establishing two experimental "mini-schools"—with 75 pupils each—in the city's predominantly Negro Mantua-Powelton section.

A major aim was to involve the community in educational affairs and provide "an environment for change." Local residents participated in all stages of planning from building and classroom design to the preparing of teaching materials. During that time, one resident remarked: "We're in at the take-off— not the crash-landing."

In both its hopefulness and its oversimplification, in what it noted and what it ignored, the remark told as much about the Rockefeller and

Rockefeller fund's design

other foundations that have turned their attention to the urban school crisis as about the situation in Mantua-Powelton.

Today the foundations are "in at the take-off" of the move to reform the schools in the cities, particularly in the slums. And it is a dramatic departure for many of them. But the foundations have had no corner on luck, wisdom or foresight about interwoven municipal ills; the very existence of a critical need for urban school reform is evidence of many previous "crash-landings."

In the decade before the nineteen-sixties, the foundations concerned with elementary and secondary school education were instrumental in advancing a variety of innovations, including team-teaching, the use of programed materials, educational television, independent study by pupils, the use of paraprofessional teachers' aides and an overhaul of curriculums in mathematics and science.

The problems peculiar to the cities and the slums or most exacerbated there — poverty and cultural disadvantage and race—did not top the agenda of the foundations, just as they were not paramount in the programs of the Government, the universities or civic organizations.

Warning of 'Dynamite'

In 1961, the Carnegie Corporation of New York sponsored a book by Dr. James B. Conant in which the former Harvard University president warned that out-of-school, out-of-work youth in the slums constituted "social dynamite." But it was not until the urban riots became an annual summer event several years later that the message of Dr. Conant's volume, "Slums and Suburbs," was really heeded.

Now the foundations, like other institutions, are paying significantly increased attention to the kind of advice Carnegie paid for. And a considerable part of philanthropy's new effort is being directed toward a "reconnection" of poor, often Negro, Puerto Rican and Mexican-American, communities with their schools and toward finding ways to overcome gross and widespread deficiencies in academic achievement.

The Ford Foundation has been a key, and continuing, financial supporter of the deeply controversial school decentralization concept in New York City, with its fundamental realignment of responsibility and power in the educational system. Decentralization, still under review, was a basic issue in the three

Ford Foundation's logo

teachers' strikes here last fall.

Ford also backed the planning for a privately operated, state-financed experimental school system in the Boston area last year. The racially integrated, urban-oriented project is expected to become the first nonsectarian, private system in Massachusetts— and perhaps the nation—to qualify for public financing where public schooling is available.

Rockefeller, in addition to its grant in Philadelphia, assisted slum schools in Los Angeles, Cleveland and Minneapolis to demonstrate that such schools "can have a vital role in all-around community development."

'Relevance for All'

"This has relevance for all of urban America today," declared J. George Harrar, the foundation's president.

A $200,000 Rockefeller grant went for a youth program in cooperation with four Harlem high schools here where disorders occurred last spring. Six-man teams of "streetworkers" were assigned to the schools to help youths "who are on the edge of dropping out of school and out of society."

This approach is an essential part of the growing, if still small, private educational network in Harlem that has been aided by foundations—including a $300,000 grant last year from Carnegie. On the lowest rung are 16 storefront "street academies" for dropouts; on the middle, two "academies of transition" that prepare youths for the third rung, a private preparatory school sending its graduates to college.

Carnegie last year assisted a private academy for dropouts in Chicago run by the Christian Action Ministry, an alliance of eight Protestant and Catholic churches. The high school dropout rate in the West Garfield Park area surrounding the academy is estimated at 50 to 65 per cent, which is suggestive of a major problem confronting all urban school systems.

Both the Chicago academy and the Harlem Preparatory School, sponsored by the New York Urban League, stress pride in the black race as well as scholastic accomplishment.

The support they give is indicative of the foundations' readiness to work outside the established school systems in the hope of finding new methods of motivating and teaching minority group youths. The backing is also clearly in line with the foundation's recent interest in the running of schools by the people who most closely represent the local community, black or white.

This interest has led the Ford Foundation into one of

Carnegie Corporation seal

the most bitter, emotionally charged conflicts in an American city today—the controversy over decentralization. The conflict, which at this point may only have begun, has resulted in more than strikes that have paralyzed the city schools; it has created or brought to the surface racial and political divisions

that under the best of circumstances would take long to mend.

But the dispute holds important lessons for foundations as they become more and more involved in sensi-

Danforth fund's symbol

tive public issues affecting millions of people.

It shows that if philanthropy is to encourage a reordering of entrenched and perhaps outmoded institutions —such as a vast centralized school system—it must be aware that the old definitions of what is "political" and what is not are probably inadequate guidelines.

Harsh Criticism Possible

Foundations that would be venturesome in the turbulent public arena will have to expect harsher criticism than has come their way in the past. And if the trusts themselves do not take a closer look at what is legitimate for tax-free organizations to be doing in this area, they must anticipate the likelihood of having Congress undertake the task.

Philanthropy, by its nature and according to its most highly regarded spokesman, has an obligation to be bold, to perform a job for the welfare of society that other, more constrained institutions might avoid or neglect. But if it must clash with powerful forces in the entangled urban situation—as Ford has done with the teachers' union here—it must be certain of its privileges as well as its goals.

School Segregation
—Northern Style

By ROY REED
Special to The New York Times

WASHINGTON, Feb. 22— The head of the Office for Civil Rights in the Department of Health, Education and Welfare believes that the South has perhaps pulled even with the North in desegregating its schools.

The North has slipped backward while the South has groped reluctantly forward, and now the gap has probably disappeared, according to Mrs. Ruby Martin. She is leaving the Civil Rights Office to enter private law practice later this month.

Mrs. Martin's observation during a recent interview probably would not be surprising if the lag in Northern school integration could be laid solely to hardening urban residential patterns and de facto segregation.

But there is a growing awareness in the Government, particularly in Mrs. Martin's office and in its counterpart in the Justice Department, that a great deal of the segregation in Northern schools is the accumulated result of outright discrimination—of official decisions calculated to separate Negro students from white.

Investigators are finding planned school segregation from New Jersey to California.

The roots go back two and three generations in some cases, and tracing them is requiring detective work never needed in the South.

Although President Nixon got much of the white backlash vote in last year's election, the Republicans are talking gamely about taking on the newly acknowledged problem of Yankee Jim Crowism.

Robert H. Finch, Secretary of Health, Education and Welfare, declared last week that the Republicans were ready to "go after" Northern school segregation.

The size of the job is not known. The Government does not know how many children are in segregated schools in the North.

Mrs. Martin's estimate that the South may have caught up with the North is based on contacts and long experience, not statistics. The first official figures on the number of Northern Negroes in integrated schools are only now being compiled. They will be available in a few weeks.

The Government has kept such figures on the South for several years, dating to the time when Jim Crow was considered a Southern offense. The latest figures from Mrs. Martin's office show that 20.3 per cent of the Negro students of the South attend integrated schools, up from 13.9 per cent last year.

News of this relative progress comes at a time when many Negroes and liberal whites, North and South, are losing interest in integration.

Increasing numbers of young Negroes are tiring of the steady abuse that comes with integrating white schools. Many are said to believe that integration has been too nearly a one-way street, with Negroes always leaving their schools to go to white schools, and that this somehow helps to place the stamp of inferiority on Negroes.

Negro separatists are openly denigrating the ideal of integration. Roy Innis, head of the Congress of Racial Equality, said here last Sunday on a television program, "The Evans-Novak Report":

"It seems to me we should stop kidding ourselves about this so-called—this mythical, illusionary thing called integration and talk about a serious way to organize black and white in a heterogeneous culture."

In spite of obstacles, the Government's attempt to extend school desegregation enforcement beyond the South has gained some momentum— more than an uninformed observer might gather from the tone of Mr. Finch's pledge to "go after" the Northern problem.

247

Mrs. Martin's office has more enforcement employes working on Northern school desegregation than on Southern. There are 52 in the North and 51 in the South.

Enforcement officials recognize that they rarely have enough people to make a dent in the Northern problem, considering the much larger number of school districts.

One of the last acts of the Johnson Administration was to deny a budget request that would have doubled the size of the staff of the Office for Civil Rights, raising it from 300 to 600.

Whatever measure of success thus far achieved in integrating Northern schools can be credited partly to Senator Richard B. Russell, a segregationist.

The Georgia Democrat attached a rider to the department's appropriation bill last fall requiring the department to begin giving as much attention to civil rights enforcement in the North as in the South.

A Possible Backfire

Some suspected that he wanted to squeeze the Federal enforcement officers out of the South. If so, the plan backfired. The department was able to put together a Northern team without unduly crippling its Southern effort.

Federal investigators have inspected 40 Northern school districts since last April, when the North program was started.

Six districts have been notified that they are running discriminatory systems and must produce acceptable desegregation plans or lose their Federal funds. They are Kansas City, Mo.; Union Township, N. J.; Penn Hills, Pa.; Ferndale, Mich.; Middletown, Ohio, and Wichita, Kan.

Union Township has produced a plan that the department is studying.

Two other districts — Pasadena, Calif., and Waterbury, Conn.—have been referred to the Justice Department for possible legal action. A citizens' lawsuit, in which the Justice Department has intervened, is pending against Pasadena.

The 32 other districts are still in various stages of investigation. The department has indications that several of them will be cited for discrimination.

Northern segregationists have been more resourceful than those in the South. The late Earl Long, three-time Governor of Louisiana, used to say, "There are more ways to kill a cat than stuffing him full of butter," and white Northerners have proved the truth of that.

Most of the Northern devices have been built around boundaries and school construction decisions.

A Negro community moves gradually westward; the school board moves the boundary of the Negro school westward with it.

Just Large Enough

A Negro area has 300 school-age children; the school board builds a school just large enough to accommodate 300 and places it in the middle of the Negro community, knowingly turning down a 500-pupil school that would draw some Negroes and some whites.

Gerrymandering has been imaginative. In Union Township in 1946, the school board drew a boundary down the backyards of the houses on Burnett Avenue to make certain that Negroes would continue to attend Jefferson, the Negro school, and whites Hamilton, the white school.

Is a school overcrowded? If it is "white" shift the boundaries or build a new building. If it is Negro, freeze the boundary and install portable classrooms.

Feeder systems can be manipulated. An all-white elementary school and an all-Negro elementary school feed pupils into the same junior high school. Because of shifting population, the Negroes gain in numbers more rapidly than the whites. The school board builds a new junior high, feeds all the whites there and lets the old school become all-Negro.

The Federal investigators sometimes have to dig into old records and interview elderly residents to establish a pattern of discrimination.

In Ferndale, Mich., they traced the beginning of the pattern to a school board decision in 1926. The board built a new school in the middle of what was then a pocket of Negroes, with the express purpose, the investigators assert, of serving only Negroes. The pocket has since become a small slum, and the school still serves only Negroes.

Echo of the Familiar

The investigators have had trouble persuading some school officials that they are presiding over discriminatory systems. Department officials say that most finally agree, however, after they are shown the evidence.

Once persuaded, a surprising number of Northern school officials have responded with an echo of the familiar, wounded cry heard so frequently from Southern school men: "We need

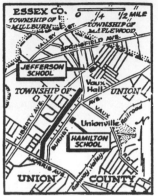

The New York Times   Feb. 23, 1969

A SCHOOL BOUNDARY: Heavy line, drawn through backyards, separates white school district (Hamilton) from Negro one (Jefferson) in Union Township, N. J.

a little time to work this thing out."

Negotiation seems to work a little better with Northern districts than with Southern. Officials say the Northerners seem more inclined to ask for technical assistance from the Federal agency and then are more inclined to accept the agency's recommendations.

In addition, 14 state governments have offices established to encourage school integration. Robert Stout and Gerald Stroufe, in an article in "The Center Forum," a publication of the Center for Urban Education, report that that is an increase of 13 since 1964, when only New York had such an office.

The Department of Health, Education and Welfare, which can only move administratively against recalcitrant districts, has yet to cut off Federal funds to any Northern district, as it has to 189 Southern districts.

But enforcement officials say the department is prepared to do so if necessary.

Glimmer of Hope

The department has not tried to cut off a Northern district's funds since it tried unsuccessfully to cut off Chicago's in 1965. Mayor Richard J. Daley interceded so imposingly with the White House that the attempt was dropped.

None of the nation's largest cities are involved in the latest moves. Department officials say the problems of de facto segregation in those cities are so complex that "we can't touch them."

They see a glimmer of hope, however, in a recent decision by Judge Richard B. Austin of Chicago in Federal District Court. He found the Chicago Housing Authority guilty of racial discrimination in the way it selected building sites and assigned tenants in public housing.

Judge Austin wrote:

"Existing patterns of racial separation must be reversed if there is to be a chance of averting the desperately intensifying division of whites and Negroes in Chicago."

Some department officials believe that breaking up the large concentrations of Negroes in the public housing of the slums would be a good start toward abolishing school segregation.

The judicial system is being used increasingly against Northern school segregation, as it has been in the South.

Justice Department lawyers filed their first lawsuits against Northern districts last year. They have five cases in various stages.

Stephen J. Pollak, head of the Justice Department's Civil Rights Division until he was replaced by the Nixon Administration, gave the department's philosophy Jan. 5 in a speech at Mobile, Ala., just two weeks before leaving office.

"The Supreme Court has held that segregated education is inherently inferior," he said. "It follows that if we are to achieve our national goal of high-quality education for everyone, we must attack segregation in the public schools wherever it appears and however caused, whether in Birmingham, Chicago or Pasadena."

Schools Hire Own Guards As Violence Rises Sharply

By WAYNE KING

Crime and violence appear to have increased sharply in public schools in urban areas.

This trend is documented in interviews with school officials in 20 major cities and in the preliminary results of a Senate subcommittee study to be released later this year.

The school officials also reported that some school systems were moving to meet the growing problem, in part, by bringing private guards and other nonteaching personnel into the schools to maintain order.

The Senate subcommittee study links what it calls a dramatic rise in school violence over the last few years with adverse socio-economic conditions, particularly in the inner cities. The study also says that the most dramatic rise in violence involves nonstudents who congregate in and around the schools. Examples of school violence abound:

¶In Washington last week, policemen were stationed at each of the city's 46 junior and senior high schools following several incidents on Jan. 5. On that day, a 15-year-old student was shot to death by a classmate; another, 14, was wounded in the leg when a derringer brought to school by a friend accidentally fired; a third was arrested for carrying a pistol, and a fourth reported being shot at on a school playground. The incidents occurred at four different junior high schools.

¶In Nashville, two students involved last year in a dispute with the band director at East Nashville High attacked him with their fists, knocking out several teeth and breaking his nose.

¶In Detroit, a 25-year-old substitute science teacher suffered a punctured lung last year when he was stabbed by a gang of youths who burst into his classroom during one of a series of disruptions at an East Side high school. Later in the year, a 26-year-old elementary school teacher was wounded when a youth, not a

student, asked for a match outside the school, then pulled a pistol and shot her when she said that she had none.

In the face of such incidents, coupled with student disruptions and evidence of racial polarization in some schools, a number of large urban school systems are relying on private guards, hall monitors and other nonteaching personnel to maintain order.

While the problem of violence in urban schools has been cited for several years by teachers' unions and others, no reliable system of reporting incidents on a nationwide basis has been developed.

However, the Senate Subcommittee to Investigate Juvenile Delinquency, headed by Senator Thomas J. Dodd, Democrat of Connecticut, is now compiling data from questionnaires sent to 153 school systems in all parts of the country.

The Dodd report, while it stresses that its figures do not reflect a definitive picture, concludes that "it is possible to say that homicide, forcible rape, robbery and other crimes on which statistics were developed have dramatically risen."

Statistics compiled so far, contained in a draft of a statement Senator Dodd plans to make in opening hearings on school violence in the early spring, show sharp increases in specific categories of crime and violence.

The statistics, based on responses from the 110 districts that replied to the questionnaire, showed that between 1964 and 1968 the number of homicides in the schools responding rose from 15 to 26, forcible rape from 51 to 81 and robbery from 396 to 1,508.

In other categories, the reports show that the number of aggravated assaults in the 110 districts increased from 475 to 680; burglary and larceny from 7,604 to 14,102; instances of vandalism from 186,184 to 250,544; weapons offenses from 419 to 1,089; narcotics violations from 73 to 854; drunkenness from 370 to 1,035; assaults on teachers by students from 1,601 to 4,267; other offenses from 4,796 to 8,824, and expulsions for incorrigibility from 4,884 to 8,190.

In another category, the report cited what it called "perhaps the most dramatic increase," a rise in crime by nonstudents from 142 in-

stances in 1964 to 3,894 in 1968.

The report continues: "There is every indication that despite his triumphant bravado, the dropout is deeply affected by his failure in school. In almost every case of vandalism, destruction of school property and attacks on students, former students who were dropouts are involved."

Cost of Vandalism

The report also notes that the nation's 36 largest cities reported that school vandalism, including arson, caused damage totaling more than $6.5-million in 1968.

The report tentatively suggests that the causes of school violence are the same as those listed as causes of general violence by the National Commission on the Causes and Prevention of Violence. These are:

Low income, physical deterioration of housing and surroundings; dependency; racial and ethnic concentration; broken homes; working mothers; low levels of education and vocational skills; high unemployment; high proportion of single males; overcrowded and substandard housing; low rates of home ownership or single-family dwellings; mixed land use and high population density.

The report said that these conditions were particularly prevalent in the inner city.

At the same time the statement suggests that laxity on the part of school officials may be a cause:

"It is in the interest of the school system that whatever untoward violence occurs be hushed up," the report said. "It reflects on the school system itself. . . . The fact that these events are treated so gingerly is not lost on the student body, which feels considerable encouragement from this failure to report violent incidents."

While teachers in some cities reported a reluctance to discipline unruly youngsters, sometimes out of fear of making a bad situation worse, there were also indications that more schools were turning to nonteaching personnel for discipline.

After the incidents in Washington last week, for example, school officials held an emergency meeting and authorized the hiring of 80 "community aides," mostly young men for duty in the schools. Uniformed city policemen, meanwhile, have been assigned to schools on a temporary basis, a step school officials had been trying to avoid as possibly inflammatory.

In New York, a $500,000 pilot program that puts 170 unarmed security guards in 29

high schools and 19 junior highs has been in operation less than a year. The Board of Education is requesting $2,656,901 to "provide additional security for pupils and teachers" and to make it unnecessary to call the city police to schools "except in rare instances."

Program Called Successful

Irving Anchor, assistant superintendent of schools, said that the guard program had been generally successful, although "some of the militants feel that these are pigs in the schools." About 60 per cent of the guards are Negro, 20 per cent Puerto Rican.

In Chicago, the public schools have recently increased the number of part-time security guards in the schools from 390 to 420. The guard program cost $912,000 last year and Edward D. Brady, director of security, said that he hoped for more money in the new budget.

As part of security arrangements, he has a direct-dial police phone on his desk that enables him to reach all police district stations and major police officials quickly. Other schools reported similar direct ties to police precincts.

With the increase in school security personnel, Mr. Brady reported that he was handling organization of a new school security directors association to be formed in Fort Lauderdale, Fla., in April.

In Philadelphia, the school system spends about $3-million a year to employ 532 nonteaching assistants, 48 fulltime security guards and varying numbers of "per diem security officers" hired as needed and numbering up to 170 at any one time.

The nonteaching assistants are not hired specifically to control violence, "but they come in pretty damn handy for unruliness," a school board spokesman said.

Public school officials in the last two years have also had to cope with student demonstrations and disruptions. Although disruptions in secondary schools have received far less public attention than incidents like those at Berkeley, San Francisco State and Columbia, the nation's public schools have been far from immune.

In a recent study titled "High School Student Unrest," published by the National School Public Relations Association, it was reported that 59 per cent of the high schools and 56 per cent of the junior highs had experienced some form of protest by January of last year. By May 25, according to Alan F. Westin, director of the Center of Research and Education in American Liberties at Columbia University, the number of protests had reached about 2,000.

January 12, 1970

Racial Strife Undermines Schools in City and Nation

National Trends Found

By WAYNE KING

Racial polarization, disruptions and growing racial tensions that sometimes explode into violence are plaguing school administrators in virtually every part of the country where schools have substantial Negro enrollments.

The degree of racial unrest was detailed in reports from a number of cities and in studies conducted by Government and private sources. They pointed to the following trends:

¶While there are indications that the dramatic increase in "issue-oriented" disruptions in the major urban areas last year may have leveled off, primarily as a result of some apparent accommodation by school officials, racial tensions continue at a high level and appear to be increasing.

¶The same kinds of disruptions and clashes that have occurred in major cities, particularly in the North, are cropping up increasingly in medium-size cities.

¶The pattern of school-oriented racial protest and tension is becoming more apparent in the border states and the South as schools there become more integrated.

¶Racial tensions seem to be moving downward in grade levels, with problems becoming more apparent at lower secondary levels and below.

¶Many of those studying or involved directly in school racial problems are outspoken in the attitude that an even-handed, "color-blind" approach will not work. Instead, administrators are increasingly being urged to become "color-conscious" and to meet problems head on.

No section of the country appears to be free of serious racial problems in schools.

39 Racial Incidents

In a study of "confrontation and racial violence," the Urban Research Corporation in Chicago collected newspaper accounts of racial incidents that occurred at schools in 39 cities, towns or counties, from the beginning of the school year, last September into January. The private research corporation monitors national trends and prepares reports for various subscriber groups and organizations, including governments.

The incidents occurred in the following places:

Phoenix, Ariz.; Little Rock, Ark.; Los Angeles, Oakland, Riverside, San Bernardino and San Francisco, Calif.

Also, Chicago, Blue Island and Harvey, Ill.; Muncie, Ind.; Kansas City, Kan.; New Iberia, La.; Springfield, Mass.; Pomfret and Prince Georges County, Md.

Also, Detroit and Pontiac, Mich.; St. Paul, Minn.; St. Louis, Mo.; Las Vegas, Nev.; Ashville, Chapel Hill, Lexington and Sanford, N. C.

Also, Atlantic City and New Brunswick, N.J.; Albany, Belport and Middle Island, N.Y.; Cleveland, Ohio; Portland, Ore.

Also, Philadelphia and Pittsburgh, Pa.; Greenville and Ridgeville, S.C.; Crystal City, Tex.; Arlington, Va.. and Charleston, W. Va.

John Naisbitt, president of the research corporation, noted that the study included only those incidents reported by the press and that some communities had had a series of incidents. Eleven reports, for instance, were gathered in Chicago alone.

'A Universal Tool'

Many of the incidents, Mr. Naisbitt continued, involved boycotts or closings of the schools. In Portland, Ore., for example, students at Roosevelt High School reportedly walked out over grievances, gained adult support and turned the protest into a citywide issue. "The school boycott," Mr. Naisbitt said, "is almost a universal tool."

He also noted rising black-white tensions. "In some cities like Chicago," he said, "bigotry is gaining respectability in the face of increased black awareness and black pride."

"These two social forces are on a collision course," Mr. Naisbitt added, "and one of the places it's finding its focus is in our integrated schools."

But the prevailing opinion of human relations directors and others involved with school racial problems was that polarization was traceable more to the quest for "black identity" and unity, and the reaction to it, rather than to racial animosities.

Rapid Integration

In some cases the two seem to overlap as blacks and whites come under the stresses of rapid integration.

In Detroit's Cooley High School, where fist fights between blacks and whites broke out last fall, black and white students tend to sit on opposite sides of the school cafeteria.

Other Detroit schools have had relative peace, however, and the difficulties at Cooley may be explained with some statistics. In 1964, more than 90 per cent of the students at Cooley were white. Today, more than 50 per cent are black.

White resistance to school integration has also generated some problems.

Gage High School in southwestern Chicago, for example, was integrated in 1965 and now has 400 Negroes in its enrollment of 2,600. The school has had a number of racial disorders.

About 120 arrests were reported in and near the school last fall, including 92 during the week of Oct. 28.

Explaining the clashes, a 16-year-old white student, Terry Conwell, said: "Only a few cause the trouble. Most of the whites [living in this area] want to keep this community white and resent integration of our school. But most of the kids have sense enough to know the fighting isn't worth it."

In Philadelphia, a spokesman for the school system's Office of Inter-group Education observed that "social separation [between races] has been total and complete."

The office operates in part on a principle it calls "conflict utilization." Once a conflict occurs, the office attempts to capitalize on the focus it creates to investigate and dramatize the underlying causes — community attitudes, conscious and unconscious discrimination, teacher attitudes, etc.—that often have little to

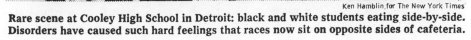

Ken Hamblin for The New York Times

Rare scene at Cooley High School in Detroit: black and white students eating side-by-side. Disorders have caused such hard feelings that races now sit on opposite sides of cafeteria.

do with the immediate cause of the incident.

'Fantastic' Gap

"The understanding gap," the Philadelphia spokesman said, "is fantastic."

A similar view was expressed by Dr. Alan F. Westin, a political science professor and director of the Center for Research and Education in American Liberties at Columbia University.

Dr. Westin, who was co-chairman of a panel that investigated the causes of the Columbia disruptions in 1968, has been monitoring 1,800 daily newspapers to gather data on student disruptions in secondary schools across the country.

"The color-blind approach, although it works in some areas such as treating everyone alike in restaurants and in public transportations, won't work in education," he said. "If there is a sudden influx of blacks into a school and school authorities take the attitude that they're color-blind, it's guaranteed to create disruption because of the special needs of blacks."

Dr. Westin found that, of 675 secondary school protests reported in the newspapers he monitored last year, 46 per cent were caused by racial problems. The study included only demonstrations, sit-ins, fighting or other disruptions And nearly one out of every five incidents—18.5 per cent—involved fighting between whites and blacks.

Although a detailed analysis of the protests in the current school year has not been complted, Dr. Westin said there were preliminary indications that the 'big city problems" of protest were occurring more frequently in medium-size cities.

"There is also a distinct pattern of protest developing in the border states and the South," Dr. Westin said, with Negro student demands centering on the hiring of more black school personnel, the revamping of school curriculums, and similar issues.

He also said there were indications that, in many big cities, the number of serious disruptions growing out of black demands for change had declined.

At the same time, Dr. Westin continued, there is no evidence that racial tensions have diminished. He noted, for instance, "a steady drumfire of fights in cafeterias and out of school, between blacks and whites."

Dr. Westin agreed with authorities who maintained that racial conflicts reflected the black students' striving for identity.

For example, he noted that a major issue last year was the lack of black cheerleaders. Other demands included the serving of "soul food" in school cafeterias and the placing of portraits of black heroes, such as Malcolm X, in school buildings.

Such demands were "symbolic of a need to imprint a sense of blackness on the schools," he said. "The black kids wanted to feel their heritage was as valid as the whites.'"

While school officials in many cities have tried to meet such demands, Dr. Westin believes that the current lull in racial protests is temporary.

"The changes have been very small and nowhere near meeting the problem," he said. "I think when the committees and studies fail to provide the things the black students want, they won't accept those answers next time."

February 9, 1970

National Push for School Integration Losing Momentum

By JOHN HERBERS
Special to The New York Times

WASHINGTON, March 21 — The national movement in support of public school integration, which five years ago was widely believed to be strong and viable, is now greatly diminished, divided and on the defensive.

In the mid-1950's, many political leaders, intellectuals and civil rights activists across the nation were committed to school integration, North and South, as a major means of healing racial divisions and extending equal opportunities to blacks.

During the last five years, there has been a gradual erosion of that commitment. In the last few months, the defections have been stepped up so that today Southern whites are for the first time since 1954 achieving an effective alliance with some Northern liberals and blacks in behalf of maintaining segregation.

"We now face the task of rearguing issues we thought were settled," Senator Walter F. Mondale, Democrat of Minnesota, said in summing up results of the last few weeks of controversy for liberals who still supported the desegregation cause.

Indicators

Elected officials, educators, scholars and civil rights leaders interviewed on the subject cited the following as indicators of the diminished national drive for integration:

¶When several Southern amendments designed to weaken enforcement of desegregation under the 1964 Civil Rights Act came before Congress in recent weeks, most Northern liberals found little public sentiment for opposing the move. Reaction of their constituents ranged from indifference to a "backlash" against rigid school integration plans.

¶A considerable segment of the liberal and Negro press, including several national columnists, has adopted the view that forced integration is either disruptive or accomplishes little and that more is to be gained by channeling energies into a drive to improve the quality of schools, whatever their racial composition.

¶Many educators, North and South, are skeptical about the benefits of integration and are inclined to look with disfavor on plans that require extensive reshuffing of students.

¶Groups that support school integration, including the N.A.A.C.P. Legal Defense and Educational Fund, Inc., which represents Negro plaintiffs in court cases across the country, have been having trouble raising the needed funds. "The liberal community is split wide open on this," said a foundation executive who had worked in the civil rights area for a number of years.

Disagreement Over Extent

There is disagreement, however, over how extensive the erosion of the integration movement has been.

"I think the failure has been overexaggerated," said Harold C. Flemming, director of the Potomac Institute, a nonprofit organization working for the elimination of racial discrimination.

Those who support this view point out that despite the move to separatism by militant black leaders, the polls continue to show: that the great majority of Negro citizens favor integration; that the finding of James S. Coleman of John Hopkins University — that integration is the most consistent mechanism for improving the quality of education for the disadvantaged—has been widely accepted by social scientists; and that integration has worked successfully for whites and blacks in a number of communities of various sizes across the country.

According to this view, the current crisis is due more to a failure of leadership than to a substantive change in the attitudes of the public.

"It is now painful for people to even think about it," said Thomas F. Pettigrew, a leading social psychologist at Harvard University. "If President Nixon had had a social psychologist advising him on the best way to generate resentments, he couldn't have done better."

251

"Sooner or later we'll muddle back to integration," Dr. Pettigrew predicted.

The support for integrated schools has been declining outside the South for several years as white liberals have joined urban black leaders in giving up the cause. W. H. Ferry, former member of the Center for the Study of Democratic Institutions, expressed this view in 1968.

"Racial integration in the United States is impossible," he wrote. "Like tens of thousands of other Americans I have supported, organized, and taken part in reformist projects, with integration always beckoning at the end of weary labors. Now such activities must be seen as nothing more than acts of good will, rather like Peace Corps expeditions into an undeveloped country that look toward the welfare and material progress of the natives but not

to their integration with the homeland."

"Unrealistic and Unwise"

Ben Holman, director of the Community Relations Service, the Federal agency established under the 1964 Civil Rights Act to assist in orderly establishment of racial justice, reflects the opinion of many Northern black leaders.

Mr. Holman has been saying that the integration drive was "unrealistic and unwise" because the majority of whites do not want integration. Mr. Holman, who is black, is promoting instead what he calls "Vietnamization of highly depressed areas of our inner cities," granting them self-determination, financial aid and technical assistance.

Members of Congress attributed the most recent deterioration of the integration drive partly to widespread disorders

that occurred in junior and senior high schools across the country, many of them integrated ones in Northern cities.

John Naisbitt, president of the Urban Research Corporation, which monitors trends in education and urban problems, said, however, that there was a tendency to make the causes more complicated than they were.

"Many whites have never favored integration in the first place," he said. "White liberals have always taken their cue from black people. Now they are all too ready to take the word of a few black leaders, which is in itself a form of racism.

"There also has been a shift in priorities from civil rights to civil liberties. Editorials in the black press are talking more and more of genocide. They are concerned with survival."

Black leaders such as Charles V. Hamilton, professor of political science at Columbia University, have been expressing concern about placing Negro children in "educationally racist" white classrooms, an apprehension expressed by W. E. B. Du Bois in the 1930's.

An idea that seems to be widely accepted by whites outside the South is that integration is not so important as it was thought to be five years ago. For example, The Lakeville (Conn.) Journal, said in an editorial the other day that although black children had been "shortchanged" in both Northern and Southern schools, "integration is only one part of our backward school system, and not really the most important."

"Education is most important," the editorial said. "Integrating schools, by forced busing, rezoning, or any other artificial means, does not upgrade the system."

March 22, 197

Use of Black English to Help Children Fit In at School Is Debated Here

By C. GERALD FRASER

Linguistics experts, teachers and college students yesterday discussed the issues surrounding the use of black English, and they agreed they don't be solvin' the problem.

Dr. Joey Dillard of Yeshiva University said experts agreed that there is such a thing as black English. The question now, he told a newsman, is whether to use it in the education of black children.

Another expert, Dr. William Labov of the University of Pennsylvania, said he saw advantages in using black English to teach black children "to break down the difference between the school and the child."

'Myth or Reality?'

The controversy was discussed at a conference on current issues in psycholinguistics and sociolinguistics, sponsored by the language and behavior program of the New York Language Center, of 80 Fifth Avenue.

More than 250 people, most of them white, attended yester-

The New York Times
Dr. William Labov, a linguistics expert from the Pennsylvania University.

day morning's conference session in the ballroom of the Retail, Wholesale and Department Store Union, at 13 Astor Place.

The session was titled "Black English: Myth or Reality?"

Experts now say that black English has an identity independent of white dialects of English. They also say that through developing descriptions of the many structures, they can conclude that black English has a linguistic integrity.

Black English is not so much black slang as it is variations in pronunciation and grammar. A favorite example linguists cite is the use of the verb "to be":

"Where Claude?"

"He be workin'."

By using the word be, the respondent indicated that Claude was doing something he usually does. Had the respondent said, "He workin'," he would have indicated that Claude was doing something he did not usually do in the given situation.

Also, in the question, "is" is unnecessary.

In the current issue of The Crisis, the magazine of the National Association for the Advancement of Colored People,

an editorial condemned academic and foundation recognition of black English as "black nonsense" and a cruel hoax.

Teach black children the language that "will best enable them to comprehend modern science and technology" and to communicate intelligently with other English-speaking peoples, the editorial said.

Educators had long held that there was a correlation between verbalization patterns and intelligence. Educators believed, the linguists say, that children who used black English had a low potential for high academic achievement.

Thus stigmatized, the experts say, black children, especially those in the early school years, were on the first step of a self-fulfilling prophecy that doomed them to educational failure.

Dr. Labov said there "may be a good case for teaching with vernacular primers." But he held that beyond the second grade dialects should be abolished.

May 16, 197

JUSTICES REBUFF PONTIAC ON BUSING

Supreme Court Declines to Review Lower Tribunal's Order for Desegregation

By FRED P. GRAHAM
Special to The New York Times

WASHINGTON, Oct. 25—The Supreme Court declined today to review a Federal court order for school busing that has touched off violence and boycotts in Pontiac, Mich.

By letting the lower court's decision stand, it avoided ruling on the volatile issue of busing to achieve racial balance in Northern schools.

At issue was whether a community is guilty of discrimination, and therefore must undertake busing aimed to eliminate all predominantly black schools, when school officials fail to adjust school district lines and when they build schools in all-black neighborhoods, knowing that the schools will be largely segregated.

Courts Free to Act

The Supreme Court has never considered if such "sins of omission" justify court-ordered integration plans. Its action today does not amount to a ruling that busing is required in these situations, but it does leave lower court judges free to order busing in other cases springing up in the North.

Without giving reasons, the Court denied a hearing to the Pontiac school board, which asserted that school segregation in that automobile manufacturing city was a result of neighborhood patterns and not of discriminatory actions by school officials.

The action today leaves in force one of the first busing orders to be issued by a Federal court in the North, an order that quickly released the intense emotions inherent in the busing issue.

Shortly after the order went into effect last August, 10 of Pontiac's school buses were dynamited. Five men, including a former Grand Dragon of the Michigan Ku Klux Klan, have been indicted in the bombing.

This week a boycott began after antibusing leaders charged that the busing had led to an upsurge of racial incidents in the Pontiac schools. School officials said that attendance fell by an average of 21 per cent yesterday.

These incidents came in reaction to a ruling by Federal District Judge Damon J. Keith, who ordered that about 10,000 of Pontiac's 24,000 public school students be bused. The object was to spread the city's Negro students, who make up about 32 per cent of the school population, throughout the city so that no school would be more than 40 per cent black.

Orders Rare in North

Under past Supreme Court rulings, Federal judges may order integration only if they find segregation is a result of discrimination by a government that denied Negroes the equal protection of the laws guaranteed by the Fourteenth Amendment.

Widespread busing has been ordered throughout the South to dismantle the segregation left over from the old school segregation laws, but busing orders have been rare in the North because school segregation appeared to be the result of neighborhood housing patterns and not discrimination by government officials.

Judge Keith held, however, that when the Pontiac school board built new neighborhood schools in areas that were all-black or all-white and continued to use school zones that had become segregated, it was guilty of intentional discrimination that violated the Fourteenth Amendment. "Sins of omission can be as serious as sins of commission," he said.

School officials protested that they had tried to counteract neighborhood segregation but that when they located schools conveniently for the students some of the schools were invariably segregated.

The United States Court of Appeals for the ixth Circuit, in Cincinnati, affirmed Judge Keith's decision, finding "a quantum of official discrimination" in the school board's actions.

Pressure Increases

The school board's appeal was the first Northern case to reach the Supreme Court since it upheld widespread busing in three Southern cases last April.

The Supreme Court has not heard an appeal from the North since it declared school segregation unconstitutional in 1954, and pressure for such a ruling appears to be growing in the form of a proposed constitutional amendment that would forbid school assignments on the basis of race. Senator Robert P. Griffin, Rpublican of Michigan, the Senate minority whip, became an outspoken advocate of such an amendment after busing was begun in Pontiac and Detroit was threatened with a similar order by a Federal judge

The Supreme Court also denied a hearing today to the school board of Winston-Salem and Forsyth County, N. C., where extensive busing has been ordered.

When the board asked for an emergency stay shortly before classes began, Chief Justice Warren E. Burger issued an unusual 10-page opinion declaring that some Southern judges appeared to have misinterpreted the Supreme Court's recent busing decisions by erroneously concluding that racial balance was required.

But he did not grant the stay because he said the entire Court should consider the question. He did not dissent today when the Court denied the school board a hearing on its appeal, leaving the desegregation order in effect.

The Supreme Court agreed today to decide if drive-in movie theaters violate obscenity laws when they show spicy films that can be seen by passing motorists or neighborhood children.

The appeal involves the conviction of William Rabe, proprietor of a drive-in in Richland, Ore., that showed the film "Carmen Baby." Courts in Rhode Island and New Jersey have found the film not obscene but the Oregon Supreme Court upheld a $600 fine against Mr. Rabe on the ground that the "context of its exhibition" made it obscene.

There was evidence that motorists and children outside the fence could see the film, and the Oregon court found that it violated the privacy of residents of nearby homes. In asking the Supreme Court to let the conviction stand, the state asserted that, even if a film was not so lewd that it could be banned from closed theaters, it should be a crime for a drive-in to show a film that "illuminates the nighttime sky of a residential area with a vivid portrayal of erotic sexual scenes."

Malverne's Bitter Legacy

By DAVID C. BERLINER

MALVERNE, L. I. — The busing issue may be boiling over in the nation's courts, in Congress, and along the Presidential campaign trail, but to the residents of this area, the controversy is nothing new.

Ten rancor-filled years ago, the patchwork Union Free School District 12, which takes in 6,000 families' portions of Malverne, Lynbrook and Lakeview, was divided on the broader issue: racial balance in the school system.

The district was the first in the state to be ordered to achieve balance. Busing was a natural offshoot.

Today, much of what took place in the years that followed seems remote, even insignificant, to many of those who were principals in the drama. Some, such as then-State Commissioner of Education James Allen, have died. Others have moved away. And still others discuss the past grateful for the benefit of hindsight.

In many cases, friendships between whites and blacks have faded away, amplifying between the races a gap that seemed too wide at the controversy's height. What re-examination that is present seems to be minimal and most often is described as strained.

Of the three lower-middle-class to upper-middle-class communities that make up the district, Lynbrook and Malverne are virtually all white, Lakeview all black.

●

In the early 1960's, the three elementary schools reflected the racial composition of the sections in which they were situated, particularly the crowded Woodfield Road School in Lakeview whose enrollment bordered on 90 per cent black.

This year, as it has been since 1968, the Woodfield Road building is not being used for classes. All black youngsters now attend the two elementary schools in the white neighborhoods and there is a technical and legal balance within the system.

There remains pervasive, however, the realization that the bitterness of the last 10 years may have been unnecessary and misdirected.

"We tried to relieve the overcrowding by requesting, unsuccessfully, that some of the black kids be sent to the other elementary schools," Burbank Mitchell, a postal employe who lives with his wife in an attractive two-story home at the end of a quiet dead-end street in Lakeview, recalled the other day. "The whole thing mushroomed into a case of trying to desegregate."

As the protest gained momentum, the National Association for the Advancement of Colored People filed a suit in September, 1962, in the name of Mr. Mitchell's 10-year-old daughter, Patricia Ann, charging that there was racial imbalance.

In June of the following year, Commissioner Allen ordered balancing, an order that was aimed at the district but swept across the state.

●

A special commission created by Dr. Allen to study the problem reported that there was no evidence of deliberate segregation in the district, but that de facto distribution had the effect of continuing a "ghetto-type situation." The community polarized. The suit and countersuits rose through the courts until October, 1965, when the United States Supreme Court refused to consider a petition to reverse Dr. Allen's order.

Makeshift schools were organized by residents; parents kept their children from attending classes; sit-downs, sit-ins and arrests occurred. The Princeton Plan, by which classes were reorganized by grades, ran into serious difficulties, not the least of which was the withdrawal from the system of white pupils by the parents when the time came for them to attend classes at Woodfield Road School.

Not until five years after Dr. Allen's order did the protesters and district officials settle on a compromise arrangement centered on a 4-4-4 grade division. As Mr. Mitchell maintains:

"As I look back, I see that we bought a bill of goods. The arrangement was explained that Woodfield Road School would be closed and the black students transferred to the other two schools with some portable classrooms brought over to take care of any students who could not be accommodated. The thing that was offered to us for acceptance of the closing of the school —and we had reservations— was a commitment by the state to pay the transportation costs for a (three-year) period. This appeared to be a solution with which we could live."

Instead of the community learning to accept the entire plan, as Mr. Mitchell says the black faction had hoped, it steadfastly resisted a key element after the state ended its financing last year. All three referendums proposing allocation of district funds have been soundly defeated and black youngsters, some of whom must travel almost two miles to class each day, are taken in car pools or pay for public transportation.

Where the population in the district had broken down two-thirds white and one-third black, today, according to the local Superintendent of Schools, 34 per cent of the pupils—virtually all of them white — attend non-public schools and the racial proportion within the system hovers at the 50-50 mark.

And Mr. Mitchell himself withdrew his daughter from the system in 1964 because "then the issue was not only race, but the quality of education."

"There generally are two purposes ascribed to these [balancing] plans," said Representative Norman F. Lent, an outspoken critic of the program as State Senator from the district from 1962 until his election to Congress in the fall of 1970. "One is achieving integration and the other is improving the education of the youngsters.

"I don't think either of these goals was achieved. Actually, it reversed the balance, if anything."

Sponsors Amendment

Representative Lent, who prodded the State Legislature into passing a bill prohibiting busing on the basis of race to correct imbalance (it was ruled unconstitutional last May), is currently proposing a controversial constitutional amendment that, he says, is similar and "seems to be the only recourse the people have" to fight forced busing.

"The Malverne ruling," he concluded, "rather than being as far-reaching as it seemed at the time, has almost been dwarfed into insignificance by the Richmond, Va., decision earlier this year which consolidated three counties—like taking Brooklyn, Queens and Nassau — and erased all school district lines in ordering school authorities to achieve a racial balance throughout the system."

Lincoln Lynch, at the time of the state order the chairman of the Long Island Chapter of the Congress of Racial Equality, has changed his views too from those he held when, he said, he "participated in every demonstration."

"Looking back on the issue," said Mr. lynch who currently is a member of the board of directors of the Urban Coalition, "the matter never was resolved. I think now that we made a very great mistake in forcing the closure of the Woodfield Road School. We should have worked to get the type of curriculum that would have made the black children not feel that in order to get a good education, they have to be sitting next to a white student in a white school."

Another key figure in the controversy, Dr. Bayard J. DeNoie, was elected president of the Malverne Board of Education only weeks after the Allen edict and served until 1965 when he returned to private life and his dental practice.

"One of the things that was lost over the years," he recalled last week, "was the fact that while the Malverne case was lost re: busing, it actually was not properly engaged. The wrong issue went to the courts.

"The issue that really was taken to the Supreme Court involved whether the Commissioner had the power to do what he did here. It never fully debated whether there was a good thing involved in integrating the schools along the Princeton Plan as Allen ordered.

"I felt, and I still feel, that this was the wrong approach. You might now call me one of the first black power advocates, although I wouldn't have accepted it at the time. What is interesting to me now is that in contrast to my period, when we had to deal with the violence generated by the parents, we have subsequently had to contend with the violence of the students."

Arrests of demonstrators in 1962 and 1963 drew national attention because prior protest activities in the district and elsewhere had rarely resulted in such drastic official action.

In the last several years, racial incidents have erupted among the 1,000 students at Malverne High School, the only high school in the district. At one point, Nassau County detectives were stationed in the building and last March, school was closed after fights between blacks and whites broke out.

To Dr. James Carnrite, Superintendent of Schools since 1967, the racial conflicts of the last three years not only have had nothing to do with the earlier controversy, but are "very normal and typical of a school system where you have black youngsters and white youngsters."

"It is very distressing and disturbing, and people cer-

tainly despair over the fact," he said, "but there again you return to the central question: How can we improve the instructional program so these things will not take place? The balancing, that is the opening and the closing of the schools, were mechanical things."

According to Dr. Carnrite, the system is continually improving both its teaching methods and its staff. Yet, while reading scores have improved substantially since the district instituted a new program two years ago, math scores have dropped.

The Superintendent says the decrease only "reflects the situation over all as far as the State of New York is concernd." Others cited the increase in the ratio of black to white students.

To one member of the school board, Ewell Finley, a black, busing never was the

issue at all, nor is it the issue today in the district or elsewhere in the country. No pupils here are required to commute farther than the legal limit allowable by law, he stressed.

He added, "The fact of the matter is that no matter what is said about the events in the district, each child now has an equal opportunity at a good education. That's what really counts, not whether black kids have to go a distance into white neighborhoods."

Just why district residents have three times turned down proposals for financing busing and upkeep of portable classrooms would seem to be easily answerable, if one were to believe that only white taxpayers voted against the plans.

But Charles W. Reardon, who now is vice president of the Board of Education

Charles W. Reardon, vice president of the Board of Education in Malverne.

and served as head of the Taxpayers and Parents Association formed to head off the eventual balancing edict, said he believed some black residents had helped vote the referendums down as well.

"Look at it this way," he said. "Transportation costs money and each and every homeowner would feel the burden of paying it, regardless if they had children in the system or not. I think black families without children in our system probably voted against it."

Was the entire effort to seek balancing worthwhile in the first place? Burbank Mitchell, whose daughter's name headed the original complaint, now is convinced it was a "learning experience at best."

"I wouldn't do it again, not at all in the way we did it," he said.

"We lost. We won the battle but lost the war. If we had spent the effort in upgrading the education in the black school instead of pressing for integration, then integration would have come as a natural course of events. But it's impossible to integrate before you achieve equality. And that means true equality, and in the minds of the people you're dealing with."

Photographs for The New York Times by ROBERT M. KLEIN
Mr. and Mrs. Burbank Mitchell in front of the closed Woodfield Road school.

March 12, 1972

Pupil Segregation Up in Chicago
While Faculty Integration Gains

By SETH S. KING
Special to The New York Times

CHICAGO, Dec. 16—Chicago's public schools were more tightly segregated this year, as white enrollment continued to drop and more neighborhoods "tilted" from white to black.

But integration of Chicago faculties continued to gain, with those in 56 more of the city's 624 schools now having no more than 75 per cent of their teachers of one race.

These findings are based on the Board of Education's annual racial census, taken last September and newly released.

The 1972 census confirmed the concern of school officials that the racial make-ups of elementary and high schools in "changing" neighborhoods (the euphemism for racially mixed districts) are not stabilizing.

Instead, schools that were once predominantly white are now more integrated, those that were integrated are becoming predominantly black, and those already largely black are remaining that way.

Southward Movement

The census illustrated the continuing shift in the city's racial patterns as black families kept pushing farther into southwest Chicago for their two large groupings on the South and West Sides.

There was also a spreading of black families into the previously all-white Northwest Side. And there was a sharp increase in Latin-American families, evidenced by an increase in Spanish speaking pupils from 9.7 per cent to 11.1 per cent of the school population.

The actual percentage of black students in schools having more than 90 per cent black enrollment increased only slightly. But among the 551 elementary schools, 142 are now all-black, while last year there were 124. There are now 267 other elementary schools that are 95 per cent, or more, black. The city has nine all-white elementary schools and 75 that are 85 per cent or more white.

There are no all-white schools among the 73 high schools. But 12 are all-black and 26 are 95 per cent or more black.

The number of white pupils in the total school population of 558,800 continued to decline. White enrollment dropped by 15,169 this year, declining from 34.6 per cent of all pupils two years ago to 31 per cent now. The number of black pupils declined by 2,822.

School officials said the drop also indicated a decline in the city's birth rate, as well as the exodus to the suburbs.

The Chicago Board of Education increased its efforts to integrate faculties three years ago after the Justice Department threatened to start court action.

New Teachers Assigned

The Justice Department's demand for more integration met with resistance from the board, as well as from the Chicago Teachers Union, many of whose black members insisted that they did not want to be transferred from all-black schools to make way for white teachers. Nor did white teachers want to be moved into ghetto neighborhoods from all-white areas, where they had been teaching for many years.

With the concurrence of the union, the board has been assigning new teachers in a pattern to achieve a level of integration in which no more than 75 per cent of each faculty is either white or black.

This year about 56 per cent of Chicago's schools meet this standard, compared with about 47.5 per cent last year. The number of schools with all-black faculties decreased from six to four and the number with all-white faculties declined from 32 to 22.

But the Chicago standards remain below Federal guidelines on faculty integration, which would limit the city's schools to no more than 70.1 per cent white teachers nor more than 47.1 per cent black teachers.

Board of Education Statement on Integration

Following is the text of a statement, in question - and - answer form, prepared by Dr. William Jansen, Superintendent of Schools, and Charles H. Silver, president of the Board of Education, on the board's position on integration in the city's public schools:

There has been some misunderstanding of several aspects of the integration program in New York City. Some anxiety has been generated among parents, teachers and other interested people because of these misapprehensions. To clear up certain areas of confusion, the [Board's] Integration Commission provides this simple question-answer review of the most widely discussed recommendations in the subcommissions' reports.

Q.—Why the concern about integration? Does New York City have segregation in its schools?

A.—There is no official segregation in New York City; it is outlawed by statute. However, there is a concentration of certain ethnic groups in some schools in New York City resulting from the residential patterns.

Q.—What has the Integration Commission done thus far?

A.—There are six subcommissions, five of which have already released reports. Three of these have been approved by the Board of Education. The first report calls for providing facilities to raise the level of achievement in schools in culturally deprived areas so that all children may receive the best possible education. The second report calls for increased guidance in these schools and greater stimulation of gifted students. The third report calls for improvement of school buildings in underprivileged areas. It also recommends the location of new buildings in fringe areas so that they will serve a mixed population. All three reports met with almost universal approval.

Q.—What has been the cause then of the recent criticism by some people?

A.—The reports of the subcommissions concerning zoning and teacher placement [which will be acted upon by the Board of Education on Feb. 28] have been the ones misunderstood. Let us now look at some of the provisions of these reports which have been most often misunderstood.

Rezoning to Spur Integration

Q.—What does rezoning of school districts mean?

A.—Zoning lines are constantly being redrawn as new housing and population changes occur. The rezoning now envisioned simply means that, wherever possible, zoning lines will be drawn in such a way as to encourage integrated instead of segregated schools. This would apply particularly to so-called "fringe" areas—neighborhoods made up of several racial groups. The subcommission noted that such procedures have been used in the past. It is democratic in an American community to have children of different racial background who live near each other attend integrated schools.

Q.—Does this do away with the principle of neighborhood school?

A.—Certainly not.

Q.—What of the "bussing" of children?

A.—Most "bussing" in New York City occurs because children live at a distance from the nearest school. "Bussing" of elementary school children occurs also when there is an overcrowded school not too far from an under-utilized one. It is now suggested by the Commission that integration be considered along with school utilization.

Q.—Does the zoning report require that children be bussed from one borough to another?

A.—Certainly not. As indicated in the answer directly above the "bussing" is the same type that is now being practiced for school children throughout the city.

Q. — What is "permissive zoning?"

A.—This would enable a child attending a non-integrated school in his neighborhood to transfer to an integrated school elsewhere if his parent so requests and school conditions permit.

Housing Pattern a Factor

Q.—Will all schools in New York City become integrated?

A.—Though this would be desirable, our segregated housing patterns make this impossible. Most elementary schools in racially homogeneous areas would probably have to remain virtually unchanged for the time being. The Commission on Integration has stated that only limited success is possible until the discriminatory residential patterns now in existence come to an end.

Q.—What about "rotation?"

A.—This is a word which has been bandied about very loosely. This report refers to an equitable staffing of all schools and the suggested methods to accomplish this. What is intended is that all schools will have the same ratio of experienced teachers to substitutes. In fact, this principle was approved by the Board of Education last June and some effort has been made to increase the number of licensed teachers in subject schools.

Q.—Some teacher groups have asserted that the subject schools should be staffed by volunteers. Why isn't the problem handled that way in order to avoid "drafting" teachers?

A.—This is precisely what is intended. It is only if there are not enough volunteers for the so-called subject schools, that some changes in teacher placement are intended.

Q.—It has also been asserted that if conditions in the subject schools are improved there would be no problem in staffing them. Has the subcommission on teachers assignments given thought to that suggestion?

A.—Of course it has. The subcommission's first recommendations were for reduction in class size, improvement in physical plant, more remedial teachers, increased supervisory help and more free time for the teachers in such schools.

Q.—Some teacher groups have recommended a salary differential for teachers in subject schools, similar to that now earned by teachers in "600" schools. Has the subcommission on teachers assignment given thought to that proposal?

A.—It has and it has peremptorily rejected that proposal. A subject school is not a school for delinquents. It is a school in an underprivileged and culturally deprived area. The additional funds required would be better spent in improving teaching conditions in these schools.

Teacher Transfers Possible

Q.—How is it intended to equalize the ratio of experienced teachers to substitutes in all the schools?

A.—If there are not enough volunteers, it may be necessary for teachers in some schools to be declared in excess and transferred to so-called subject schools, giving every possible consideration to distance from home. It is recommended, also, that a formula be established to regulate transfers.

Q.—Won't this be inconvenient for some of the teachers thus transferred?

A.—In some cases, yes. But the needs of the children are primary. It is likely that most teachers agree with that principle. Moreover, as conditions in the subject schools improve—more experienced teachers, smaller classes, better physical plant—the teaching conditions in the subject schools will be improved. The Board of Education in its budget request for the coming fiscal year indicated its wish to implement these recommendations. The subcommission believed it unfair to require the children to wait for all these improvements.

Q.—Since many more teachers than at present will serve in subject schools, won't this new policy have an adverse effect on teacher recruitment?

A.—On the contrary, it is believed that it will help, providing that new teachers enter the city school system with the assurance that they will begin work in relatively less complex teaching situations.

Q.—Isn't it a little harsh to uproot teachers who have been in the same school for many years?

A.—Admittedly, and under the recommendation, the Personnel Division of the Board of Education would not reassign teachers of twenty years service or more and would certainly consider individual cases of hardship when it makes assignments. However, it is not desirable to perpetuate the present conditions in which subject schools are staffed to such an extent by substitutes and inexperienced regular teachers.

Q.—If there is additional mixing of children from deprived areas with those from more favored areas, will the result be a lowering of standards in the fringe-area school?

A.—If anything, it should provide an additional educational stimulus. With the improvement of teaching conditions and the general quickening of the educational pulse, envisioned by the subcommission reports, the level of achievement should be raised in all schools.

Q.—Why then has there been some resistance to the subcommission reports on zoning and teachers assignments?

A.—A great deal of resistance is due to misunderstanding, which it is hoped this review will clear up. There is always resistance to change, especially change that means certain inconveniences. The Commission on Integration, however, is confident that the people of New York City will recognize their moral and democratic responsibilities.

We are not unmindful of the problems that the Superintendent will have in carrying out the recommendations in all of these reports, and it is understood that in the implementation of the recommendations, administrative discretion must be exercised by the Superintendent of Schools and his associates.

February 26, 1957

Wide Aid to Puerto Ricans Asked in City School Study

By LEONARD BUDER

A concerted attack on the problems of Puerto Rican school children here was recommended yesterday in a report made public by the Board of Education. The report, based on a four-year study that cost $1,000,000, called for a vast strengthening and expansion of efforts to speed the adjustment and education of Puerto Rican youngsters.

The study said that about half of the Puerto Rican children in city schools needed special help to overcome language difficulties, and that 17 per cent could not speak English.

The latest enrollment figures, for last October, showed that there were 137,000 Puerto Rican children in the system. This is 15 per cent of the total enrollment.

The 265-page report, "The Puerto Rican Study," dealt with the period from 1953 to 1957. The project was backed by a $500,000 grant from the Fund for the Advancement of Education of the Ford Foundation. An equal amount was spent by the school board.

The director of the study and author of the report was Dr. J. Cayce Morrison, former Assistant Education Commissioner of the state and a specialist in educational research.

The report was made public yesterday morning in the hall of the Board of Education, 110 Livingston Street, Brooklyn.

Dr. John J. Theobald, the Superintendent of Schools, said that a "substantial number" of recommendations and findings in the study had already been implemented. Teaching materials, courses of study and guides developed by the project, he said, are now being used. He said there were now 2,255 special classes for Puerto Rican children in the elementary and 346 such classes in the secondary schools.

Among those who took part in yesterday's presentation of the report were:

Dr. William Jansen, who retired last year as city school superintendent; Dr. Alvin C. Eurich, vice president of the Fund for the Advancement of Education; Dr. Joseph Monserrat, director of the Department of Labor of Puerto Rico; Miss Ethel F. Huggard, associate city superintendent of schools; and Dr. William H. Bristow, director of the Bureau of Curriculum Research.

The study found that although the heaviest concentration of Puerto Rican pupils was in the Manhattan public schools—where these pupils made up 28 per cent of the total register in 1956—the problem of meeting the special needs of Puerto Rican children was "rapidly" become city-wide.

"The area of rapid increase of Puerto Rican school enroll-ment," the report said, "is shifting from Manhattan to the Bronx and Brooklyn, and there is some indication that the tide is beginning to flow toward certain areas in Queens and Richmond."

The report said that, judging from the experience of other immigrant groups, the Puerto Ricans here could be expected to become reasonably well assimilated by the third generation. But the report said that neither the city nor the Puerto Ricans could "afford to wait" until then.

Misconception Cited

The report indicated that it was a misconception to lump Puerto Rican children together. Some youngsters, it said, are "island-born, island-schooled," while some are "island-born, mainland-schooled" and still others are "mainland-born pupils of Puerto Rican parentage." These groups, it said, often have different needs.

The report also deplored any idea that Puerto Rican youngsters had high truancy rates and posed more disciplinary problems than other children. A survey made in two Manhattan school districts, the report said, found that "the attendance record of Puerto Rican children as a whole appears to be quite as good as that of other children." But it said that Puerto Rican youngsters who become truants often were greater problems than other truants.

On court referrals in the two districts, the survey found that Puerto Rican children were offenders at the rate of 12 in each 1,000, while non-Puerto Rican children had a rate of 14 in each 1,000.

One of the major contributions of the study, Dr. Theobald said, was the development of a procedure to classify children by their knowledge of English.

Among the major recommendations contained in the report were these:

¶A uniform policy must be formulated for the reception, screening, placement and periodic assessment of non-English-speaking pupils.

¶In teaching English, the vocabulary, structure and quality of speech should be interrelated.

¶An auxiliary teacher should be assigned for each group of 100 non-English-speaking pupils in an elementary school and for each seventy-five in a junior high school.

¶Efforts should be made to bring Puerto Rican parents into a closer relationship with the schools.

¶Present teacher-training work on the needs of Puerto Rican youngsters should be expanded.

State Aid Formula

The report also recommended changes in the formula for awarding state aid to classes for non-English-speaking pupils. At present, it was said, small classes in which half the pupils cannot speak English qualify for special funds.

This, Dr. Theobald said, has prompted school officials to distribute non-English-speaking pupils in as many classes as possible while meeting the 50 per cent requirement.

But the study found that when this happened, the education of the entire class often suffered. The best concentration, the report said, was 30 to 35 per cent non-English-speaking pupils. It recommended that these classes be given state aid.

Dr. Theobald said that the schools would give up the practice of evenly mixed classes, even if it cost the system some state aid.

NONWHITE PUPILS INCREASE IN CITY

Population Change Found to Complicate Official Integration Work

RATIO NOW ONE TO TWO

One-Fifth of Schools Here Consist of 85% Negroes and Puerto Ricans

By LEONARD BUDER

A steady increase in the number of Negro and Puerto Rican pupils is making school integration here difficult, the Board of Education indicated yesterday.

Despite rezoning and out-of-zone enrollments, the number of predominantly Negro and Puerto Rican schools here rose in the last two years.

A board report showed that in 117 elementary schools and twenty-two junior high schools —about a fifth of the total— the enrollments last October were 85 per cent or more Negro and Puerto Rican. In 1958 the comparable figures were eighty-eight elementary and thirteen junior high schools.

Four schools were composed entirely of Negro and Puerto Rican children last October.

Dr. Herbert A. Landry, director of educational program research and statistics, who prepared the report, said: "If it weren't for the integration efforts, the situation would be far worse."

30,000 Others Lost

Since September, 1957, he noted, the city schools have gained 25,000 Puerto Ricans and 39,000 Negroes, but have lost 30,000 other pupils.

Elementary and junior high schools are largely neighborhood schools. Their enrollments thus generally reflect the populations of their districts.

The report, which dealt with a special school census made Oct. 31, showed that Puerto Rican and Negro children made up more than a third of the city's public school population of 986,679. The system had 153,697 Puerto Rican and 212,006 Negro pupils, 37.1 per cent of the total enrollment.

Negro and Puerto Rican children made up three-fourths of the elementary school enrollment in Manhattan, nearly half of the elementary enrollment in the Bronx. In Brooklyn, the figure was 41.7 per cent; in Queens, 19.1 per cent, and in Richmond, 10.2 per cent.

The percentage in the junior high schools was slightly lower. Here they made up 38.9 per cent of the total registration, compared with 43 per cent on the elementary level.

Negroes and Puerto Ricans made up 15.9 per cent of the academic high school students; 43.5 per cent of the vocational high school students.

48% Largely White

On the other side of the integration problem, there were 277 elementary schools, or 48 per cent of the total, that had 85 per cent or more white enrollments. Fifty-three junior high schools, or 44 per cent, were in this category.

Twenty-four elementary schools did not have one Negro or Puerto Rican child.

At 193 other elementary schools and twenty-eight other junior high schools, Negroes and Puerto Ricans accounted for 5 per cent or less of the total enrollment.

A school spokesman noted that the board's open enrollment program, which started on a limited basis in September, had had only slight impact on the distribution of pupils by the time the census was taken. The program, which has since been expanded, enables pupils attending schools that are predominantly Negro and Puerto Rican to transfer to other schools if there are vacancies.

The census, the fifth since 1957, furnishes data for many school operations, including open enrollment, assignment of additional teachers and applications for special state aid for classes for non-English-speaking pupils.

In enumerating Puerto Rican pupils, the report included all children born in Puerto Rico or the mainland when one or both parents is Puerto Rican.

TEACHERS ADVISED ON RACIAL TERMS

Pamphlet Tells Them Not to Talk of 'Your Kind' or 'You People' to Parents

'SLUM' ALSO RULED OUT

It Should Be Called 'Older, More Overcrowded Area,' School Report Says

By FRED M. HECHINGER

The school system asked the city's teachers yesterday to remember to speak positively in talking with parents. In a "compilation of observations of speech patterns that lead to difficulty in meeting with parents," it urged teachers to avoid words and phrases that "inadvertently suggest prejudice" of all kinds.

Among the phrases the pamphlet lists are references to minority groups like "you people" or "your kind."

The pseudo-complimentary terms it asks teachers to avoid are "Negroes naturally have rhythm," "thrifty as a Scotsman" or "smart as a Jew." It cites as offensive stereotypes such "symbols" as "watermelon for Negroes; pushcarts for Jews; laundries for Chinese; rice and beans for Puerto Ricans; spaghetti and meatballs for Italians."

Basis for Discussion

The report is suggested "as a basis for stimulating discussion by school staffs at conferences and as material for inservice courses in human relations for teachers, supervisors and other school employes."

It was prepared by a committee under the chairmanship of Dr. Frederick H. Williams, director of the school system's human relations unit.

It warns against the use of terms that remind anyone "of his group membership and of the status of his group in our social structure."

From a warning against camouflages for prejudice—"some of my best friends * * *," etc.—the report branches out into a discussion of what it considers misuse of professional terms.

It urges teachers to avoid or use "with extreme caution" such labels as "underprivileged children, culturally deprived, slum areas, low socio-economic," as well as "fear of walking in neighborhood" or "complete apathy of parents." Somewhat mysteriously, the same list includes the term "dedicated teacher."

Parents' Faith Cited

Negative words, the report says, "emphasize disadvantages" and destroy the parents' faith in "the upward mobility of their children."

In its glossary of positive words, the report suggests that "deprived, depressed or disadvantaged" children be described as "having a likelihood for good intellectual development, or children with untapped potential, or children with latent ability."

In a more elaborate list of substitutions, "low-income or underprivileged children" become "children unable to secure much beyond the necessities of today's world because of the modest finances of the family."

"Culturally deprived children," a term originally introduced by educators as a substitute for "poor," becomes, in the new glossary, the term "children whose experiences, generally speaking, have been limited to their immediate environment."

CITY WILL PERMIT PUPIL TRANSFERS FOR INTEGRATION

Negroes and Puerto Ricans to Be Granted Choice on a First-Come Basis

BUSES WILL BE PROVIDED

Gross, in Reporting to State, Calls Plan the Nation's 'Most Comprehensive'

The Board of Education reported yesterday that it planned to waive the neighborhood school policy for large numbers of Negro and Puerto Rican children to allow them to attend schools outside their districts.

The plan was disclosed in a report to the State Education Commissioner on the board's immediate and long-range program to achieve better integration. The program, which will cost $10,000,000 in the coming school year, includes both desegregation and improvement in the quality of instruction.

Schools that receive pupils transferring from areas where de facto segregation exists in housing will be given additional teachers. Educational opportunities will be increased through a wide range of activities including after-school tutoring and improved guidance in gaining admission to college and in getting jobs.

The report was submitted to comply with an order issued to all school districts on June 14 by the State Education Commissioner, Dr. James E. Allen Jr.

Plan Is Hailed

Dr. Calvin E. Gross, the city's Superintendent of Schools, called the plan "the most comprehensive effort to achieve maximum integration, both on the basis of past performance and future commitment, of any city school system in the country."

He said it would permit the city schools to "move toward complete ethnic integration to the limit permitted by feasibility and sound educational practice."

The plan represents "all possible steps we have been able to devise, short of the compulsory interchange of Negro and white students between distant communities," he said.

The board insists it will not yield to integrationist pressures to transport white children involuntarily to schools that, because of de facto housing segregation, are predominantly Negro or Puerto Rican.

Last week's meetings between Dr. Gross and integration spokesmen foundered on that point. It therefore is unlikely that these groups, which have threatened school boycotts in September, will consider this plan satisfactory.

The plan divides the areas in need of action into the "moral, desegregation, instructional and job" fronts. It proposes to convert the existing open-enrollment policy, under which about 14,500 Negro and Puerto Rican youngsters will attend predominantly white schools outside their neighborhoods this year, into a "free-choice transfer policy" by February, 1964.

Under the free-choice policy, any child in a school with a high Negro and Puerto Rican enrollment may transfer, at his parents' request, to any other school in the city where there is space available. Open enrollment affected only a limited number of "sending-receiving" schools.

The plan will apply to all levels of education. The transfers, to be offered on a first-come-first-served basis, will include free transportation.

As an immediate step, about 2,000 junior high school students who were declared ineligible for transfers at the opening of school next month will be recanvassed for immediate placement in predominantly white schools.

Immediate Changes Listed

Other immediate changes will include:

¶Approximately 100 zoning changes specifically to promote integration. A board spokesman said zoning changes were made regularly each year as neighborhoods changed and new schools were built. He added, however, that instead of merely considering numbers of children, all changes would now be made with integration as the first priority.

¶Monthly meetings by the Superintendent with civil rights and human relations groups to explore further integration measures.

¶Intensified recruiting of Negro and Puerto Rican teachers.

Immediate efforts to improve education in areas with large Negro or Puerto Rican concentrations will include:

¶Remedial instruction, giving special help after school hours and on Saturday mornings to pupils in need of tutoring or of a place to do homework.

¶Additional teaching staffs and materials for schools participating in the open-enrollment or free-transfer plan.

¶Improved instruction about the contributions by minority groups to American history and culture.

¶A full complement of teachers at the beginning of the new school year, with 10 to 25 supernumeraries assigned to each field superintendent as a pool to fill positions of teachers who do not report for work.

¶More than half of all first-grade pupils—about 46,000—will be put on a full five-hour day, instead of the prevailing four-hour day.

Conferences to Be Held

Other efforts will include conferences with the Board of Higher Education to explore ways of getting more students in minority groups into college, improved placement services for graduates seeking jobs, and improving vocational training and guidance.

The board also pledges to take "all reasonable steps to bar contracts for construction, building repairs and maintenance, or purchase of textbooks, school supplies and equipment from concerns and unions that practice discrimination in employment."

By the fall of 1964, the board hopes to be ready to experiment with the so-called Princeton Plan "in critical fringe areas." Under this plan, two or more schools close together are organized so each building is used only for certain grades for all pupils of a much larger area than is normally served by one school.

Other proposals, without a time schedule, include general reduction in class size. Although "reverse open enrollment"—the shipment of white children into de facto segregated areas—is listed among proposals for further study, sources close to the Superintendent disclosed that no such action was contemplated.

25 ARRESTED HERE IN SCHOOL PROTEST

3 Clergymen Among Those Prevented From Staging Racial Sit-In at Board

By THEODORE JONES

Twenty-five persons, including three ministers, were arrested yesterday for attempting a sit-in at the headquarters of the Board of Education in Brooklyn.

The demonstrators were protesting what they called "the complete failure" of the Board of Education to present a meaningful plan for the elimination of racial imbalance in the city schools.

The arrests were made as more than 100 Negro and white pickets marched, chanted and sang in front of the building, at 110 Livingston Street.

Among those arrested for attempting to sit in at the offices of Dr. Calvin E. Gross, the Superintendent of Schools, were the Rev. Robert Sherard of the Corona Congregational Church in Queens, and the Rev. Milton A. Galamison of the Siloam Presbyterian Church and the Rev. Martin Duffy of the Green Avenue Methodist Church, both in Brooklyn.

March Into Office

The picketing, which was staged by the Citywide Committee for Integrated Schools, began shortly before 9 A.M. and by 10 the building resembled an armed camp, with more than 50 patrolmen posted outside and on most of the 13 floors.

The first of a series of arrests came minutes after 14 persons, including the three ministers, had marched silently into Dr. Gross's office on the 10th floor and taken seats around a conference table.

August 26, 1963

Dr. Gross quickly held a conference with his aides and then, accompanied by Assistant Chief Inspector Patrick Whalen, entered his office.

"I don't want to duck the personal responsibility of asking you to leave," the Superintendent said, "I have a busy schedule today, but I would like to arrange for you to come back and talk."

None of the demonstrators spoke. However, a few, on hearing Dr. Gross's comments, stood up and began putting on their overcoats in anticipation of what was to follow.

When the demonstrators failed to leave the office, Dr. Thomas F. Nevins, an assistant superintendent, then asked Inspector Whalen "to arrest these people."

No Other Choice

When asked why he was in Dr. Gross's office, Mr. Galamison replied: "We are here, sir, because we have no other choice. If it means we have to be arrested, then so be it."

The demonstrators submitted to arrest without protest. All were charged with disorderly conduct and later released.

However, the arrests of 11 other demonstrators were more difficult. The police carried five persons—four men and a woman—from the 11th floor offices of James B. Donovan, the newly elected board president.

Six others—four men and two women—were carried from offices on the 10th floor. All 11 were charged with disorderly conduct and resisting arrest.

One demonstrator, Arnold Goldwag, a member of the Brooklyn Chapter of the Congress of Racial Equality, was also charged with malicious mischief. He was accused of breaking a glass panel in the door leading to the office of Dr. Joseph O. Loretan, Deputy Superintendent of Curriculum. Mr. Goldwag denied the charge.

Dr. Gross, apparently irritated by the demonstration, said later that the committee was making demands of the extremest kind. They want "instant racial balances" in the schools, he said.

Pairing of Schools Studied

"The things they apparently want," Dr. Gross added, "can only be achieved by the involuntary bussing of children over a long distance. I don't think any parent, Negro or white, would stand for this. It would lead to chaos."

Dr. Gross said that Mr. Galamison, who heads the committee, had told him that the demonstration had been called to express the committee's annoyance with his interim report on the progress of school integration.

The report, released last week, listed the system's efforts to improve education and promote integration. It also disclosed that studies on pairing some white and Negro schools in Manhattan to achieve better racial balances were under way.

Earlier, Mr. Galamison charged that Dr. Gross had failed to fulfill a commitment to the committee that "a plan and timetable for citywide desegregation of schools would be provided by Dec. 1."

Busing Held One Way

This plan, according to the Brooklyn minister, was also to have provided for substantial integration in all school districts by the first of the year.

Mr. Galamison said that involuntary busing was just one way of achieving integration. But he quickly added that "anyone who talks about integration and is against busing is not serious about the matter."

The minister described yesterday's demonstration as a "one-shot event." He said there would be more demonstrations and the committee would call for a boycott of the city schools in February if "some meaningful steps were not taken."

Twenty-two of those arrested yesterday were released after a hearing in Brooklyn Criminal Court. Their trial was set for Jan. 5.

Three others, arrested in the afternoon and charged with disorderly conduct and resisting arrest, were held for Manhattan Night Court.

The citywide committee is made up of the local branches of the National Association for the Advancement of Colored People and CORE; the Harlem Parents Committee, and the Parents Workshop for Equality in New York City Schools.

Negro and Puerto Rican Schools Have Doubled in City in 6 Years

By LEONARD BUDER

The number of predominantly Negro and Puerto Rican elementary and junior high schools in the city has more than doubled in the last six years, the Board of Education reported yesterday.

Despite this, the board said, there has been "an improved ethnic distribution" of pupils in the school system. It credited the school system's integration efforts with reducing the number of predominantly white schools and with increasing the number of schools with better ethnic balances.

The increase in the number of predominantly Negro and Puerto Rican schools was attributed to the growth of the city's Negro and Puerto Rican populations and their concentration in certain areas.

In a report on its ethnic census made last October, the board said there had been a sharp increase since 1957-58 in the number of Negro and Puerto Rican pupils and a decline in the number of other children attending the city schools.

The study, made by the Central Zoning Unit of the board, noted that the largest ratio of Negro and Puerto Rican pupils, about 52 per cent, was in the first grade of elementary school. This indicates, the board said, "that in the near future—estimated by 1966-67 or earlier—Negro and Puerto Rican pupils in the entire city will outnumber 'other' pupils in these schools."

The term "others" is used by the school system to refer to non-Negroes and non-Puerto Ricans. According to the United States Census Bureau, 96 per cent of the Puerto Ricans in the city consider themselves to be white. They refer to other whites here as "mainland whites."

Detailing the enrollment trend, the report observed:

There are now 264,616 Negro pupils in the system, an increase of 91,659, or 53 per cent, over the 1957-58 total of 172,957.

There are now 177,544 Puerto Rican children in the system, an increase of 48,564, or 37.6 per cent.

There are now 596,356 "others" in the system, a decrease of 54,324, or 8.3 per cent.

The board used 1957-58 as the base for comparison purposes because in that period the school system began to maintain ethnic distribution data. The census is based on the observation of teachers in the classrooms.

Despite the increase in Negro and Puerto Rican enrollments and the decrease in the number of other pupils, the board's announcement asserted, "an improvement in the ethnic distribution of pupils nevertheless is indicated in the Central Zoning Unit's report."

In 1957-58, the report said, 290 of the city's elementary schools had 10 per cent or fewer Negroes or Puerto Ricans. This year there are 186 such schools in a total of 581 elementary schools — "a decrease," the board explained, "indicating improved distribution."

Six years ago, 52 of the 123 junior high schools had 15 per cent or less Negroes or Puerto Ricans. At present there are 39 such schools in a total of 136 in the city, "also a favorable decrease," it was said.

At the other extreme in ethnic distribution were those elementary schools with 90 per cent or more Negro or Puerto Rican enrollments and junior high schools where the proportion of these pupils was 85 per cent.

The number of such elementary schools increased from 64 in 1957-58 to 134 this year and the number of such junior high schools rose during this period from 13 to 31.

This trend was cited in a recent report of the Urban League of Greater New York to show that, despite the board's integration efforts, the number of segregated schools in the city had increased in recent years. Board officials, however, have contended that without the system's efforts the increase would have been greater.

Between the extremes, the report noted, are the "mid-range" schools, "which are considered better integrated." In 1957-58, a total of 211 elementary schools were in this category compared with 261 at present. There are also 11 more "mid-range" junior high schools now —66, compared with 55 six years ago.

The report's admission that the increase in the number of predominantly Negro and Puerto Rican schools reflected neighborhood housing patterns is expected to reinforce the demands of civil rights groups here that the board do more than it has done to offset this factor.

BOYCOTT CRIPPLES CITY SCHOOLS; ABSENCES 360,000 ABOVE NORMAL; NEGROES AND PUERTO RICANS UNITE

PICKETS PEACEFUL

Integration Protest Is Hailed as Success by Its Leaders

By LEONARD BUDER

A peaceful one-day boycott emptied hundreds of classrooms in Negro and Puerto Rican sections of the city yesterday and kept many pupils at home elsewhere in the city.

School authorities said that 464,361 pupils, or 44.8 per cent of the total enrollment of 1,037,-757, had not attended classes.

Since the normal absentee rate is 10 per cent—a little more than 100,000 pupils—this means that the absences yesterday totaled about 360,000 more than the daily average.

The protest against racial imbalance started in the gloom of an icy morning, with pickets marching at 300 of the city's 860 public schools. It culminated with a cheerful, orderly march by 3,500 demonstrators, mostly children, on Board of Education headquarters in Brooklyn.

The police were everywhere, but there was little for them to do. The pickets—2,600 of them —braving the blustery winds of a 20-degree morning, made no effort to interfere with pupils or teachers who entered the schools.

Friction at a Minimum

With few exceptions, pickets were courteous and disciplined. The police were equally polite, and there was a minimum of friction between the two groups.

However, some parents said at the day's end that they had kept their children out of school because of the fear of violence.

As the pickets marched they chanted "Jim Crow must go," sang "We Shall Overcome" and handed out leaflets.

Teachers also joined the demonstration. Of the total of 43,865 in the system, 3,537 were absent yesterday. The absentee rate was 8.03 per cent, compared with 3 per cent on normal days.

Rustin Hails 'Success'

Bayard Rustin, who directed the boycott, called the demonstration "a tremendous success." He said it was the largest civil rights protest in the nation's history.

Mr. Rustin directed last summer's civil rights March on Washington, in which more than 200,000 demonstrators took part.

More significant than the statistics of yesterday's protest, Mr. Rustin said, was the fact that the Negro and Puerto Rican communities had joined together to work for common objectives.

Mrs. Thelma Johnson, Manhattan coordinator for the protest, described the boycott as a "whoopee success."

Her view was not shared by James B. Donovan, the president of the Board of Education, who called the boycott a "fizzle."

"All these people proved," Mr. Donovan said, "is how easy it is to get children to take a holiday instead of going to school. They also showed that parents could be frightened into keeping their children at home by a campaign of intimidation and threats of possible violence."

He referred to a statement made over the weekend by the Rev. Milton A. Galamison, chairman of the Citywide Committee for Integrated Schools, that "sociopaths" might take advantage of the boycott to cause trouble.

James Farmer, national director of the Congress of Racial Equality, later replied to Mr. Donovan's evaluation of the boycott.

"If this is a fizzle, we want more fizzles like this," Mr. Farmer said.

4 Initial Sponsors

CORE was one of the four initial sponsors of the boycott. The others were the National Association for the Advancement of Colored People, the Parents Workshop for Equality and the Harlem Parents Committee. Other groups taking part in the protest included the Urban League of Greater New York and the National Association for Puerto Rican Civil Rights.

The boycott leaders, Mr. Rustin and Mr. Galamison, appeared on television last night with Gilberto Gerena-Valentin of the National Association for Puerto Rican Civil Rights, Frederick C. McLaughlin, director of the Public Education Association, and Stanley H. Lowell, chairman of the City Commission on Human Rights.

In a special program on WABC-TV they analyzed the boycott.

Mr. Rustin called for the dismissal of Mr. Donovan, saying that his comments about the strike made it evident he did not have the "insight for the job" of president of the Board of Education.

During the day, some children attended improvised classrooms, known as Freedom Schools, that had been set up in churches and other community centers.

The Citywide Committee for Integrated Schools, which coordinated the boycott, also had set up emergency classrooms. Officials of the committee said that 90,000 to 100,000 students were in these classrooms yesterday.

But a spot check showed that many of these classes were not well attended. Boycotting students apparently preferred to take the day off or to participate in the demonstrations.

In the public schools, those with predominantly Negro or Puerto Rican student-bodies were the ones most affected. Some schools in white sections suffered only slight dips in attendance. Mr. Rustin estimated that a fifth of the demonstrators were whites.

100 Out of 1,350

At Junior High School 139 in Harlem, only 100 of 1,350 pupils attended. At Benjamin Franklin High School in East Harlem, only 350 students of 2,300 were present.

Schools in the neighborhoods bordering on predominantly Negro or Puerto Rican sections of the city had higher attendance figures, but even in these fringe areas many classrooms had only a sprinkling of pupils.

Opinions on yesterday's boycott were freely expressed by many people.

"I think it is one of the essential things in a democracy to learn that we have democracy by pressure," said Donald Morey, a white teacher of geography at Seward Park High School. "It's all pressure. You lean on the door and it opens. That's why I'm picketing."

"I can't understand what these people want", Mrs. Julia Stitch of 351 West 24th Street said as she passed by a picket line. "They have more freedom in our city than anywhere else. When I went to school they didn't allow such nonsense."

Gudrun Stiskovsky, 17 years old, a white senior at Seward Park High School, said: "I believe in integration. And I believe in being active—not passive. I don't think it's right to believe in these things and then sit home and let other people do the job."

Parents Accompany Children

Throughout the city parents in many cases accompanied their children to school because of a fear of what might happen.

Shortly after 9 A.M., two white mothers approached a police sergeant at the main gate of Andrew Jackson High School, Cambria Heights, Queens. Forty per cent of the school's enrollment is Negro.

"We're worried," one of the mothers said. "We're afraid that if our daughters go into the school, there will be trouble later."

The sergeant, also white, reassured them:

"There's not a thing to worry about, ladies," he said. "The pickets have been well-behaved. There hasn't been a word exchanged between them and the kids who have gone through the line this morning."

The mothers appeared relieved. They said good-by to their daughters, and the children entered the school without incident.

"It's a holiday," said a Negro teen-age picket in Harlem. "Why should we go to school?"

But a white student at the Bronx High School of Science stopped chanting "Jim Crow must go" long enough to explain that she felt that the integration problem was the most important one facing the nation.

"It's up to the young people to show the adults how we feel," she said.

The official view of the boycott was contained in a joint statement issued by Mr. Dono-

OUTSIDE FRANKLIN HIGH SCHOOL: Integrationist pickets marching yesterday

The New York Times

INSIDE FRANKLIN HIGH: Bernard Levine, history teacher, had about a third the usual number of students in this class. School is at East 116th St. and Pleasant Ave.

van and Dr. Calvin E. Gross, the Superintendent of Schools. They deplored the fact that so many pupils missed school and called upon all members of the community to help the system achieve its integration aims.

Dr. Gross, who resumed active duties yesterday after being away from his office for four weeks because of illness, sent his two school-age children to school. They walked past 20 pickets outside the virtually all-white Public School 81 at Riverdale Avenue and West 256th Street in the Bronx.

Mr. Galamison, as he had said he would, kept his 14-year-old son, Milton, Jr., home from the integrated private school he normally attends. The youngster helped out at boycott headquarters in his father's church,

the Siloam Presbyterian Church, 260 Jefferson Avenue, Brooklyn.

The number of pupils absent from public school yesterday exceeded all but the most optimistic predictions of civil rights spokesmen.

They had called the demonstration to register their dissatisfaction with the school system's integration plan, which was announced last week, and to press their demand for racial integration of all schools in the city.

'Ghetto' Schools First

The board's plan provided for the desegregation of about 30 of the city's "ghetto" schools —those whose enrollment is

more than 90 per cent Negro or Puerto Rican.

Civil rights leaders emphasized last night that they would call additional one-day demonstrations and perhaps a protracted boycott if school officials did not come up with an integration plan acceptable to them. However, Mr. Donovan reiterated that he would not be swayed by pressure tactics.

A Board of Education report showed that the pupil absentee rate for the city school districts ranged from 11.2 per cent for Districts 53 and 54 in Staten Island, which have no predominantly Negro schools, to 92 per cent for Districts 10 and 11 in Central Harlem.

In schools in the south Bronx, which are heavily Negro, the

absentee rate was 82 per cent; in the districts from central Harlem to Washington Heights, the rate was 73.5 per cent. Attendance was better in the predominantly white sections in the northwest part of Manhattan.

In the largely Negro Bedford-Stuyvesant area of Brooklyn and its racially mixed fringe areas, about three-fourths of the children were absent.

Heavy absences were also reported by schools on the Lower East Side, the West Side of Manhattan and East Harlem as well as various sections of Brooklyn, where there are large concentrations of Puerto Rican pupils. In Queens, schools in the southeast, which are heavily Negro, were most seriously affected.

The boycott hit schools on all levels—high schools, elementary schools and junior high schools. Nearly 61,000 of 204,000 pupils were absent in the academic high schools, and 15,604 of 38,459 students were out in the vocational high schools.

Negro and Puerto Rican pupils comprise 40.5 per cent of the city's public school enrollment.

Yesterday, designated as Freedom Day, pickets turned out before dawn at many schools, hours before the scheduled start of classes at 8:45. The early demonstrators said they wanted to take part before going to work. As some of the men left, women — including housewives with baby carriages—and students took up the picket signs. At one Bronx school, a student picket captain directed teachers in the line.

At George Washington High School in upper Manhattan, the principal, Henry T. Hillson, ordered coffee sent to the pickets. He said the demonstrators were "terribly misguided." But he added: We're not going to let them freeze to death."

While 50 students and teachers marched the picket line, a few boys gathered on a corner and shouted: 'Two-four-six-eight — we don't want to integrate." The police shooed the boys away. They also dispersed 100 students who were outside the building, telling them to "go to school or go home, but don't stay here."

In the Morrisania section of the Bronx, Puerto Rican pickets carried signs in Spanish. One read "Integración es una gran educación."

Miss Dorothy Bonawit, principal of Andrew Jackson High School in Queens, where about 60 per cent of the 4,600 pupils were absent, said that the demonstrators displayed "earnest conviction."

"I think the cold weather kept the lunatic fringe away," she added.

'One Way to Improve'

At De Witt Clinton High School in the Bronx, a teacher,

her teeth chattering from the cold, explained why she had not gone to work.

"I used to teach in Harlem," she said. "I know the conditions there—the water flowing from the toilets into the halls the doors hanging by one hinge, the children crowded in classrooms. I feel that the only way to improve things there—and everywhere in the system—is to integrate and improve all schools."

Kenneth Hines, a 13-year-old student at Junior High School 139 in Harmel, went to class because, he said, it was "more important to get an education than to demonstrate." He said that there were rats in the cafeteria, but "things aren't too bad at this school."

The turnout of 2,600 pickets was below the prediction of the boycott leaders, who had said they expected 8,000 to join the lines. This gave rise to early optimism at Board of Education headquarters that the boycott was not effective.

Because of the cold, some picket captains cut short the demonstrations before 11:45 A.M., the scheduled time to halt the picketing. The Bronx demonstrators then went to Governor Rockefeller's New York office at 20 West 55th Street; the Manhattan pickets went first to City Hall and then to School headquarters in Brooklyn, where they joined protesters from that borough and from Queens.

Dick Gregory, the Negro comedian, was a teacher at a Freedom School at boycott headquarters for 39 Negro pupils and one white child. He told the children that they would have to be "little soldiers" in the battle for Negro freedom.

Neighborhood movie houses in some sections reported that business was better than usual. The RKO Regent in Harlem, which had a double bill of "The Haunted Palace" and "Cry of Battle," said children lined up at noon but were not admitted until 3 o'clock.

At the Golden Gloves Billiard Parlor, 221 West 116th Street, Frank Chappell, manager, said "business was very good for a weekday morning." At one table, a junior from Benjamin Franklin High School was more concerned about his game than about the boycott.

More Than 10,000 March in Protest On School Pairing

By FRED POWLEDGE

Thousands of demonstrators, many of them homeowners from Brooklyn, the Bronx and Queens, marched on the Board of Education and City Hall yesterday, shouting that they wanted to preserve the tradition of neighborhood schools.

An unofficial police estimate put the size of the crowd at 15,000. Reporters estimated it at 10,000 to 15,000. An official of Parents and Taxpayers, the largest sponsoring agency for the march, said 20,000 persons took part.

More than 70 per cent of the demonstrators were women. Although the sponsoring organizations have said that they welcome Negroes, virtually no Negroes took part.

The organizers of the march contended that it was an unqualified success in alerting the city to the threat to the neighborhood school presented by school pairing.

The Board of Education is scheduled to announce on March 25 the names of 40 elementary schools and 20 junior high schools that will be matched in an effort to achieve better racial balance in the school system.

Each pair of schools will consist of one that has been predominantly white and one that has been predominantly Negro or Puerto Rican. Children from both neighborhoods would attend one of the schools in their first years, and the other in their later years.

The pairing will involve some bus transportation of students, and that is what the Parents and Taxpayers organizations and the Brooklyn Joint Council for Better Education were protesting about yesterday.

Their signs bore such slogans as "Can a bus bring a sick child home?" "Have child— Won't travel" and "Princeton Plan in the garbage can." The school-pairing system was first tried in Princeton, N. J.

Most of the demonstrators were taking their case into the streets for the first time. They marched jubilantly by the Board of Education offices at 110 Livingston Street, Brooklyn, in wet snow and 34-degree temperature. Then they walked across the Brooklyn Bridge to Manhattan, where the final demonstration was mounted around City Hall.

"This is the greatest day of my life," said one woman. "I'm going to remember this when I'm old and gray."

Leaders of the demonstration met briefly with Dr. Calvin E. Gross, Superintendent of Schools, and James B. Donovan, president of the Board of Education. The leaders said they were "courteously received."

Dr. Gross said the group had asked for a referendum on school transportation. "I doubt that the board would want a public referendum when every pressing decision comes about," he commented later at a press conference.

Mr. Donovan said he did not anticipate any major policy changes because of the demonstration.

After the demonstration at the Board of Education, the marchers trooped through downtown Brooklyn to the Brooklyn Bridge, with the Parents and Taxpayers of Canarsie group in the lead.

File Across Bridge

One of the two Negroes seen in the march was a young man who appeared on the fringe of the Canarsie group as the demonstrators filed across the bridge. He identified himself as Walker Williams and said he was from Manhattan and was not a parent.

Mr. Williams was spotted by Jerry Arkow, one of the leaders of the group.

"Put him in the middle, put him in the middle!" Mr. Arkow called through a red megaphone.

A poster was thrust into Mr. Williams's hand as he was led into the front row of marchers. He walked in the center of the front row, flanked by two banners proclaiming "PAT of Canarsie." After a few minutes, he disappeared.

The march continued into Manhattan through the snow.

The women wore everything from slacks and boots to tailored dresses and spike heels. There were imitation leopard coats and raincoats. Many women wore crocheted hats with metal or plastic spangles.

'Zoning, Zoning, Zoning'

The marchers were in high spirits despite the miserable weather. Some sang the following words to the tune of "Music, Music, Music":

"We've got troubles of our own,
"So why not keep us close to home?
"Please, oh, please, leave us alone,
"Stop zoning, zoning, zoning."

When a television camera or photographer appeared, the marchers slowed down and smiled. Some waved at the cameras.

"I can't wait until I get home tonight to see myself," said one man, who had sought out the cameraman for his favorite television station.

When the demonstrators from Brooklyn joined their fellow marchers at City Hall, the organizers were exultant over the size of the turnout. A solid band of demonstrators, four and six abreast, wound around City Hall Park for more than an hour.

"Even if you take the lowest estimate for the number of people," said one official of Parents and Taxpayers, "this is the biggest demonstration that's ever been held at City Hall."

Eleven of the leaders went inside City Hall in an effort to talk to Paul R. Screvane, City Council President. They were referred to Deputy Mayor Edward F. Cavanagh Jr., who frequently hears complaints from citizens who want to get the car of Mayor Wagner.

The leaders reported that their brief meeting with Mr. Cavanagh was unproductive.

White Parents Lose Case Against School Rezoning

By FRED M. HECHINGER

The Court of Appeals ruled yesterday that the Board of Education had the right to consider better racial integration as a factor in selecting school sites. The state's highest court thus upheld, in a 6-to-1 decision, a ruling by the Appellate Division in Brooklyn that school authorities could rezone a district, provided all pupils were still permitted to attend the school nearest their homes.

Chief Judge Charles S. Desmond, in the majority opinion, said that the question whether there was an "affirmative constitutional obligation to take action to reduce de facto segregation is simply not in this case."

The ruling on behalf of the board's action therefore was based solely on the fact that "it excludes no one from any school and has no tendency to foster or produce racial segregation."

Racial Issue Stressed

Associate Judge John Van Voorhis, in a dissenting opinion, said that race was the "dominant factor and controlling consideration" in the rezoning of the schools. He called that "the reverse of anti-discrimination" and thus a violation of the principle that "each person shall be treated without regard to race, religion or national origin." He declared that "if a person can be legally admitted to a school for racial or religious reasons, he can be excluded for the same reasons."

The suit was brought by a group of white parents in East Flatbush, Brooklyn, who contended that their children were being ordered out of their neighborhood and forced to attend a school elsewhere to bring about racial integration.

The court, however, held that the board's zoning had not been "arbitrary, capricious or unreasonable." It pointed out that none of the children, who had not attended junior high school before, were actually being transferred from a school in which they had been enrolled.

The decision constituted the second defeat for the white parents who charged that their children were being assigned against their will to a school outside their neighborhood. However, the ruling represented a more limited victory for the proponents of integration than they had won from the Appellate Division's.

While the Appellate Division said that a school board, under decisions of the Supreme Court of the United States was responsible for the zoning of new schools to "prevent the creation of a segregated public school," yesterday's ruling limited its concern to the question: "May (not must) the schools correct racial imbalance?"

The court held that the board had this right, provided that no child would have to travel further to the new school than to get to his "neighborhood" school. It found that in the Brooklyn case the children's rights were fully protected.

A spokesman for the Brooklyn parents expressed disappointment over the decision. He said the case would be taken to the Supreme Court.

The parents contended that their children were being assigned to Junior High School 275 in Brownsville solely on the basis of race to achieve better integration among the pupils. Brownsville is largely Negro and Puerto Rican. The school to which they ordinarily would have been assigned, Junior High 285, is in East Flatbush.

Quota System Charged

The parents had charged that by assigning their children to a school outside the East Flatbush neighborhood to bring about an enrollment of equal numbers of Negro, Puerto Rican and white students violated their rights and established a racial quota system.

The white parents won the first round when Supreme Court Justice Edward G. Baker ruled last September that the proposed rezoning was illegal. He cited Section 3201 of the State Education Law that holds that "no person shall be refused admission into or be excluded from any public school in the State of New York on account of race, creed, color or national origin."

In the second round, however, the Appellate Division said that section of the law had been introduced specifically to do away with actual segregation. It held that, if the law were now to be used as an instrument of segregation it would be unconstitutional under the 1954 Supreme Court ruling.

While upholding the neighborhood school as the nearest school to a child's home, the Appeals Court ruled that such terms as East Flatbush or Brownville were "purely artificial" and did not constitute a neighborhood in terms of school zoning.

Both the Appellate Division and the Court of Appeals made special efforts, however, to limit the impact of their rulings and to state specifically that their decisions did not imply that the board was required to bring about racial balance through rezoning in all schools. Yesterday's decision made it explicit that it was concerned only with "newly instituted" schools.

While the ruling thus may bring about integration in a specific school, it could serve as a precedent to prevent integration in any case that required pupils to go to a rezoned school further from their home.

Nevertheless, James Farmer, national director of the Congress of Racial Equality, said: "New York State's highest court has issued a very significant ruling. At long last, New York State has judicial clearance on reassigning pupils to break up racial imbalance."

Isidore Balaban of Brooklyn one of the parents who brought the suit, on the other hand, said: "We feel that the Court of Appeals based the decision on geography rather than racial quotas, which was what the original suit was based on." He declared that "the final say" would be up to the Supreme Court.

Judge Van Voorhis, in a long dissent, said that "it would be hopeless for any school board or other governing body to try to assemble an ideal amalgam by admitting the right quotas." He also referred to the refusal of the Supreme Court last Monday to review the Gary, Ind., case in which Negro groups charged that school zones had been drawn so as to maintain segregation.

May 8, 1964

Rights Groups, in Switch, Back Schools' Racial Plan

7 Organizations Drop Opposition After Gross Changes Setup on Transfers— Taxpayer Group Continues Fight

By LEONARD BUDER

Representatives of seven civil rights and community organizations switched their positions yesterday and said they would urge their members to support the Board of Education's integration plan.

The representatives acted after Dr. Calvin E. Gross, the Superintendent of Schools, agreed, as they put it, to eliminate "a number of objectionable features" in the plan, which is scheduled to go into effect in September. Dr. Gross described the changes as "refinements."

A key change will allow Negro children who were scheduled to attend sixth-grade classes in specified junior high schools next fall to transfer to specified integrated or white elementary schools. The groups had previously charged that the Negro pupils were merely being transferred from segregated elementary schools to segregated junior high schools.

Yesterday's development, which came as a surprise, ended for the time being the long controversy between civil rights groups and the school system.

All of the groups had previously denounced the board's integration plan because, they said, it did not substantially correct racial imbalance in the schools. Several had indicated that they might sponsor new demonstrations in the fall, including possibly a prolonged boycott by Negro pupils.

The organizations that announced they would support the school integration plan were the New York Urban League, the National Association for the Advancement of Colored People, the Congress of Racial Equality, the Harlem Parents Committee, the Citywide Committee for Integrated Schools, EQUAL, a group formed by white parents who support integration, and the Conference for Integrated Quality Education, an organization of labor, religious and civic groups.

Split Developed

The organizations announced their new stand after a meeting yesterday with school officials —the fifth since June 4. The joint statement represented the first time that such civil rights groups as the N.A.A.C.P. and the Citywide Committee for Integrated Schools had subscribed to the same announcement since last February. A split developed at that time within the rights movement over the conduct of the campaign for school integration.

The joint announcement came shortly after Dr. Gross disclosed that an agreement had been reached "within a framework that assures continuing discussion" between the school system and the organizations. "Cooperative planning for future [integration] steps will be resumed promptly," he said.

Although school officials achieved an unexpected gain in their negotiations with the civil rights groups, they suffered an expected setback in their efforts to gain support from officials of the Parents and Taxpayers organization.

The organization, which consists of autonomous local groups and a citywide coordinating council, is opposed to the provisions of the plan that will send some white pupils to schools outside their neighborhoods.

After an hour-and-a-half meeting with Dr. Gross, held at the Superintendent's invitation, officials of the Parents and Taxpayers said they were still "unalterably opposed to forced transfers of pupils." They added, however, that they would support the part of the plan that provides for the improvement of education in underprivileged areas.

In his announcement about the meetings with the civil rights representatives, Dr. Gross said he had pointed out that the steps slated for next fall were "in the directions indicated" in the recent report of an advisory committee appointed by Dr. James E. Allen Jr., the State Education Commissioner.

The state report, which called for a systemwide reorganization to reduce racial imbalance and improve education, had been generally approved by the civil rights groups.

The board's plan calls for the transfer of 4,500 ninth-grade pupils, who would normally attend primarily Negro junior high schools, to 36 designated integrated high schools. This will make it possible for these junior high schools to accommodate 5,800 sixth-graders, who would traditionally attend 44 elementary schools.

This in turn, will enable the elementary schools, which are largely Negro and Puerto Rican, to reduce class size, alleviate overcrowding, expand kindergarten programs and establish prekindergartens.

The civil rights groups, however, contended that the transfer of the sixth-grade pupils to junior high school would not improve integration, a point school officials conceded.

Dr. Gross said yesterday that parents of the sixth-graders affected would now be given an option. They can either have their children attend the 10 junior high schools or travel to certain integrated elementary schools.

Extends Programs

The new alternative will, in effect, extend the board's programs of "open enrollment" and "free choice" transfers. In the past some right groups have not been enthusiastic about these programs because they place the integration burden on Negro pupils, who must do the traveling.

Dr. Gross also announced that additional "educational complexes" — groupings of schools as recommended in the state report — would be established in September, 1965. These would include four-year primary schools and four-year middle schools, which were also proposed by the state. The plan for next fall provides for five such groupings.

The Institute of Urban Affairs of Teachers College, Columbia University, he added, will serve as a consultant in the development of the complexes. Dr. Robert Dentler, executive officer of the institute, was a consultant to the state committee.

Other groups attending yesterday's sessions between school officials and civil rights organization were representatives of the Migration Division of the Commonwealth of Puerto Rico and the City Commission on Human Rights.

June 16, 196

CITY TO ABOLISH ITS JUNIOR HIGHS, SHIFT TEACHERS

TARGET DATE '73

Union Issues Warning on Forced Transfers of Instructors

By LEONARD BUDER

The Board of Education said yesterday that it would abolish its 138 junior high schools by 1973 and take other steps to provide "excellence of education" for the city's one million public school pupils.

To replace the junior high schools, a new type of "intermediate" school will be established to achieve racial and economic integration. The new schools will start with the fifth or sixth grade and run through the eighth, in contrast to the junior high schools, which cover the seventh, eighth and ninth grades.

The creation of the intermediate schools will be part of a total reorganization of the school system that will dramatically alter the present pattern of education here. The elementary schools will lose some grades to the intermediate schools and the high schools will take over the ninth grade from the present junior high schools.

The changes thus will ultimately affect every child who attends public school.

To Start in 1966

Although the board specified a target date for completion of the changes, no details were given as to how these would be carried out during the intervening years. However, the board said that the changeover to the intermediate school should start in September, 1966.

The board also said it would seek to assure the "equitable distribution" of experienced and competent teachers throughout the system. This would involve the involuntary assignment of some experienced teachers — perhaps "a few thousand," one official said—to schools in underprivileged areas that are now staffed largely by new and inexperienced teachers.

This pronouncement by the board brought an immediate warning from the United Federation of Teachers, which represents the city's 46,000 teachers.

"Under no conditions will the U.F.T. allow the teachers to be forcibly transferred or rotated," Albert Shanker, president of the union, declared. "If necessary the schools will be closed."

But James B. Donovan, the president of the board, said that the system would not be deterred by opposition from the union.

"This is a matter of policy ant there can be no negotiation on this," he said. "The manner of accomplishing this objective, however, might be negotiable."

Significance Noted

The board's broad plans for the future were contained in a six-page statement of policy, titled "Excellence for The Schools of New York City." Specific measures will be adopted by the board next Wednesday.

Speaking at a news conference in the hall of the board's headquarters in Brokklyn, Mr. Donovan declared that the statement was the "most significant" document issued during his three-and-a-half years on the board.

The policy statement, he said in his opening remarks, "is a declaration by the board that both quality instruction and integration are essential components of excellence in education."

"It is possible to conceive of quality instruction without integration or integration without quality instruction," he continued, "but not of excellence of education without both in this multiracial city at this time."

Mr. Donovan said that the board's policies would "provide for excellence in education and rapid, consistent progress toward school integration."

To carry out these policies, Mr. Donovan said, "massive financial aid from all levels of government" would be required.

A total of $337 million. the board official continued, would be needed to build enough intermediate and high schools to accommodate all pupils on single session. In addition, he said, "there will have to be sizable increases in the operating budget."

The policy statement, which was adopted unanimously by the nine-member board, would move the school system in the direction suggested by a special advisory committee appointed by Dr. James E. Allen Jr., the State Education Commissioner.

4-4-4 Proposed

The state body urged that the system adopt a 4-4-4 pattern of education—four years of elementary or primary school, four years of middle school and four years of high school. The system now has six years of elementary school, three of junior high school and three of senior high school.

The board's new policies would give the city a 4-4-4 or a 5-3-4 setup, and possibly a flexible arrangement that would provide for both patterns. Civil rights groups and others have been in favor of such changes.

The new approach to education will place heavy emphasis on pre-kindergarten programs to enable children to overcome environmental handicaps that work against later success in school.

"From this pre-primary experience will emerge an elementary school concerned with using at least the next four years of schooling to teach the basic skills as the foundation of all further education," the statement said.

"The elementary program will emphasize those techniques and nongraded experiences"—programs that cut across formal grade lines — "in which small numbers of children are grouped and regrouped as their abilities indicate. The pivotal factor is the individual pupil and the teacher's ability to relate to him."

The intermediate school will represent the most drastic break from tradition. And it will undoubtedly provoke new protests from the junior high school principals, who have opposed previous proposals to abolish their schools. Some 212,-000 pupils now attend the junior high schools.

"The exact grades of this new program are not as important as are its nature and content," the board said in its statement. "this period of education must take the child from his elementary concentration on basic skills to the use of those skills in the acquisition of knowledge and the development of human and social relationships.

"One of the most important phases of his education in this period will be his introduction to other children who are different from those with whom he associated in his elementary school. It is obvious that many elementary schools in this city are going to be ethnically imbalanced by their location in the areas they serve.

"For the very early years of basic education, this disadvantage seems to be outweighed by the benefits of a quality educational program geared to basic skills training, parential involvement and community concern. But at or about the fifth grade there must be added to this program an extra ingredient of excellence — the sharing of learning experiences and life values with other children of different races, nationalities and economic status."

Mr. Donovan pointed out that the abolition of the junior high schools would not affect the status of the 1,250 teachers, principals and others who serve there. They will be assigned to other schools.

The educational experiences of the city's children, the statement noted, will culminate in the new four-year comprehensive high schools, which will offer both college preparatory and vocational programs.

HIGH COURT BACKS PAIRING IN QUEENS

Parents Lose Bid to Reverse Board of Education

By FRED P. GRAHAM
Special to The New York Times

WASHINGTON, Nov. 8—A challenge by a group of white parents in Supreme Court failed today to overturn the New York City Board of Education's efforts to reduce racial imbalance in two elementary schools in Queens.

The Court declined to review the board's action in merging school attendance districts. The move, made last year, put the predominantly white Public School 149 in Jackson Heights into the same district as the predominantly Negro P. S. 92 in Corona.

The brief order left standing state court decisions affirming the board's action.

Mrs. Remo J. Addabbo, president of the Parents and Taxpayers of Jackson Heights and 10 other parents contended that the school pairing denied their children the right to attend their neighborhood school because they are white.

They said the reorganization violated the Supreme Court's desegregation decision of 1954 inasmuch as their children were required for racial reasons to travel beyond the school they previously attended to study at a more distant school.

"The petitioners' children have not been made the objects of racial discrimination," the Board of Education told the Supreme Court in its brief, "for the simple reason that admission to both schools depends solely on the grade the child had attained and without regard to his race, color or creed."

It said that none of the children would have to travel more than six blocks farther than formerly and that some would travel less. In addition, the board said, the merger reduced overcrowding and a higher ratio of pupils to teachers at P.S. 92.

Today's case marked the first time a desegregation plan involving busing of students had reached the Supreme Court.

Twenty-nine white children are bused to P.S. 92, but the issue was not raised in the appeal because none of the plaintiff's children required busing.

Under the plan all children in the first and second grades go to P.S. 92 and those in grades three through six go to P.S. 149.

The pairing changed the racial composition of P.S. 92 from 99 per cent Negro to 46 per cent Negro. P.S. 149 changed from 88 per cent white to 75 per cent white.

Previous Pairings Upheld

Although the Supreme Court had previously upheld similar school pairings in Brooklyn and Malverne, L. I., interest in the Jackson Heights case was high because it had become a symbol of white opposition to desegregation efforts that eliminate neighborhood schools.

Bitter demonstrations flared at the Jackson Heights school last October and the police arrested 65 white parents who tried by force to put their children back into their former school. Some parents kept their children out of school and others sent theirs to two special private schools established by the parents and taxpayers.

By refusing a hearing to the Jackson Heights parents the Supreme Court underlined the "hands off" policy toward school racial imbalance that the Federal courts have evolved in recent years.

On the one hand the high court has refused to consider appeals by white parents challenging local officials' efforts to reduce racial imbalance. On the other it has left standing lower court decisions that school authorities are not required by the Constitution to make such efforts.

SEGREGATION UP IN SCHOOLS HERE

Board Finds 5-Year Rise— Gains in Integration Are Also Listed in Report

By LEONARD BUDER

The number of "de facto Negro and Puerto Rican segregated schools" has risen sharply in recent years, a Board of Education report said yesterday.

At the same time, the board noted, the number of "predominantly white" schools decreased substantially, and the system's "mid-range" schools—those with "better integration" — showed a marked increase.

The report attributed the growth of Negro and Puerto Rican schools largely to "the development of housing projects in ghetto areas with large numbers of families" and other factors beyond the board's control.

And it credited to its own integration efforts the improvement in ethnic balance in other schools.

Can Be Read Two Ways

A board spokesman observed that the report could be interpreted in contrasting ways.

"You could look at one set of figures and say we're making headway in school integration," he said. "Or, you could take another set of figures and say we're losing ground. We think we're making progress."

The report, based on an ethnic census conducted in the city system last fall, is certain to give new ammunition to civil rights groups and others who have repeatedly contended that the board has not been doing enough to combat racial imbalance in the schools.

Dr. Bernard E. Donovan, Superintendent of Schools, said yesterday he was "pleased that

the number of better integrated schools is increasing, and that many more of our white pupils are having the opportunity for an integrated education." But, he said, the increase in the number of de facto Negro and Puerto Rican segregated schools is "a serious concern."

"We are very much troubled by the situation," he added.

A board report made public last week, which was also based on the ethnic census, disclosed that there has been a steady influx of Negro and Puerto Rican pupils into the system in recent years. There has been a growing exodus of other children from the city schools, the report said.

The 1965 census showed that the system then had 19.8 per cent Puerto Rican pupils, 28.4 per cent Negroes and 51.8 per cent "others."

"In the face of the changing population of the city," the Superintendent said yesterday, "it is extremely difficult to implement the Board of Education's goal of quality integrated education—but it's not impossible. With the aid of all the other governmental agencies in the city and state, and the help of all citizens, it can be done."

Gain in Ratio

The new report, covering a five-year period, showed that last fall 201 of the system's 829 elementary, junior high and senior high schools were predominantly Negro and Puerto Rican. In 1964, 187 of 811 schools were in this category and in 1960, 118 schools of 782.

According to the board's definition, elementary schools are listed as "de facto Negro and Puerto Rican segregated" if 90 per cent or more of their pupils are Negro or Puerto Rican. In the junior and senior high schools, a ratio of 85 per cent or more is used.

Last fall there were 210 "predominantly white segregated schools," according to similar guidelines. In 1964, there were 268 such schools and in 1960 there were 327.

Many formerly "predominantly white" schools have become "mid-range" schools, the report said.

Much of this change, it went on, has been due to board policies that have enabled more Negro and Puerto Rican pupils to attend schools outside their ghetto neighborhoods.

November 9, 1965

June 16, 1966

Curtain for Higher Horizons

By FRED M. HECHINGER

Without fanfare—without even a press release—the New York City school system last week admitted that the Higher Horizon program is being closed down. Begun in 1959 with much publicity and subsequently hailed and imitated across the country, the plan was intended to raise the educational, vocational and cultural aspirations of elementary and junior high school students born and brought up in the slums, especially in the Negro ghettos.

At its inception, as a pilot project, its promise—and even its initial results—seemed limitless. It provided more of everything to the children who needed it most—more teachers, guidance counselors, psychologists, social workers and teacher aides. In addition to intensified instruction, it offered a host of extracurricular experiences. Children who had never left the confines of their shabby neighborhoods were taken to concerts, plays, operas and ball games.

College deans talked to them about higher education and invited them to spend weekends on Ivy-covered campuses to open their eyes to a world that would otherwise have remained out of view and out of reach. As their sights were raised, these children found new and concrete reasons to regard school as a road with a purpose.

Yet, for several years now, some observers have suspected that the early excitement and initial success were fading. A 298-page report ordered two years ago by the school system itself and only reluctantly made public in 1965, disclosed that Higher Horizons, which a United States Commissioner of Education not long ago hailed at a national meeting of educators, had had "virtually no measurable effect" in terms of educational achievement."

Official Post Mortems

Last week nothing was left but the official post mortems.

Why? The clue was in another admission of the 1965 report which said that Higher Horizons had "never achieved the saturation of additional services" envisioned by its founders.

This politely pedagogical critique contained the story of the failure of dozens of educational pilot projects across the country—imposing blueprints, without the expensive, time and manpower-consuming follow-through. This is the inherent danger, for instance, which experts also warn about when they urge that Head Start, the highly publicized pre-school project, must guard against turning into a false start.

The very success of such programs and the publicity-value of their labels and slogans invite the mistaken belief that, with a corner cut here and a little stretching of resources there, the same benefits can be offered to increasingly greater numbers, at bargain prices. The Higher Horizon story is a textbook case in point. Within a few years of its initial triumphs, it was expanded to include over 100,000 pupils in 52 elementary and 13 junior high schools. But at the original extra cost per child of $250, this would have required an additional annual budget of over $250,000,000, and an army of highly qualified teachers and specialists.

In fact, once a pilot project is translated into large-scale, routine operation, the number of staff needed to retain the momentum gets even larger. The founding cadre almost inevitably consists of enthusiastic, single-minded and devoted experimenters, ready to work overtime to prove their point. As the personal, emotional involvement is replaced by routine professional action, the extraordinary, self-propelling impact declines.

Other Flaws

There were other flaws in Higher Horizons. It was the outing to the ballet or the mock trial staged downtown in a real court or the visit to the United Nations that naturally caught public attention. The image was dramatic, full of human interest and so obviously photogenic that it was singled out and over-advertised.

Important as these extras are to stimulate minds and awaken aspirations, they are only the frosting. The essential nourishment of the cake is the everyday educational effort, with constant reinforcement by good teachers, in small classes or even in individual instruction.

It would be wrong to imply that nothing was gained before Higher Horizons was phased out. The lesson of what can—or might—be achieved was driven home. Some of the gains and experiences seeped into other programs—the new "More Effective Schools," with their extra staff, the Upward Bound projects elsewhere, even the intensive combination of educational-psychological-physical attention given to youngsters in Head Start and other pre-school programs.

Some of the special benefits provided under Higher Horizons furthermore were subsequently made standard operating procedure in all schools. For example, the provision of libraries for elementary schools was seen to be so crucial that the system is now providing them for all schools, or at least plans to do so.

Moreover, individual students expanded their personal horizons. Princeton University picked two or three students for scholarships. Mount Holyoke College took a busload of Higher Horizon girls and let them explore the mysteries of life in an exclusive women's college, not as a spree of reverse slumming but as a come-on to prepare for actual admission to such a college. For a segment of the group the well-intentioned theory did turn into concrete opportunities. The visibility of the group, through the project, helped to remind others that opportunities needed to be opened up to these youngsters.

But this, at best, remains the triumph of a lucky few, while the original goal was to find a way of blazing a trail for the many deprived.

To achieve its mass goal, New York's Superintendent of Schools Bernard E. Donovan admitted last week, the benefits of the program were "distributed so thinly, it did not really accomplish its purpose."

Like so many experiments in the education of the deprived, Higher Horizon proved what really needs no proof—that a heavy investment of money and talent in superior instruction leads to a high rate of educational success. But once, for reasons of economy, the contents are drained away, the attractive label cannot change the fact that the can is empty.

July 10, 1966

East Harlem's 'Model School' Is Still Turbulent

I.S. 201, Open 4 Months, Was Planned as 'Showcase'

By M. A. FARBER

Intermediate School 201 in East Harlem, the controversial school the Board of Education said would be "one of the best in the nation," is today gravely troubled.

Four months after its turbulent opening amid bitter disputes over integration, quality of instruction and community control of policy, the "showcase" school at Madison Avenue and 127th Street has a wary principal facing a still hostile community.

Many of its teachers feel encircled by tension and without support and its pupils are often defiant and undisciplined.

Near-bedlam prevails in a few classes, with the 10 to 13-year-old pupils, who attend fifth through eighth grades, darting about the rooms at will, punching one another in horseplay, tapping disconcertedly on chalkboard rims, and ignoring the teachers' occasional pleas for order, if not attention.

While unruliness is a common problem at many schools, it is so persistent in this "model" school that in some classes the chatter of even two or three students has sent teachers into rages.

"You know what I'm going to do to you?" shouted a mathematics teacher the other day, as she rushed to a cluster of students and shook her arms in fury.

At that moment, the principal, Stanley R. Lisser, happened to be at the door, and he hurried in to calm the distraught woman. Only a minute before, in the previous room, Mr. Lisser had seen another teacher screaming at a talkative girl.

Staff Is Experienced

I. S. 201, a red-brick, windowless building set on 14-foot concrete pillars, is air-conditioned and has many features designed to bring superior education to the youngsters, about 85 per cent of whom are Negro, 15 per cent Puerto Rican.

It has an experienced and evenly integrated staff of 56 teachers hand-picked by Mr. Lisser, a maximum class size of 24 pupils—six pupils fewer than in the average class in junior high schools—twice the usual help of school aides and a full-time "community relations specialist" to promote "closer parent and citizen involvement in the school program."

It has language laboratories, a social studies curriculum that does not neglect Negro and Puerto Rican history and culture, musical instruments and typing classes and an extensive after-school enrichment and tutorial program.

But the school has had to start a detention room for youngsters who will not go from class to class and who wander under fluorescent lights through long, blue-tiled corridors, often running from officials who try to corral them.

So frequently have pupils in the hallways reached into classes and turned out the lights —leaving the rooms dark—that switches operated by keys are scheduled to be installed next week.

Display Boards Bare

So often have pupils ripped down or defaced hallway display boards that today most are bare or scrawled upon and many teachers are discouraged from putting much effort into the next exhibit.

So at odds are parents and the school administration that a parents' group has not yet been formed and a leader of the organizing committee, Mrs. Helen Testamark, has complained about conditions in the school to District Superintendent Murray Hart. She has also requested a meeting with Superintendent of Schools Bernard E. Donovan.

Mrs. Testamark, a large, caustic woman who was in the forefront of the original opposition to I.S. 201 being opened, said last week that "there is no real administration going on" and that "morale is practically nonexistent."

"And if you can find any discipline," she added, "let me know."

Her comments were substantially the same as those of three professional educators, including an official of the school system, who have observed the operation of I.S. 201 independently of one another. The educators, who are especially concerned with ghetto schools, asked not to be identified.

Disenchantment with I.S. 201, and fear that it will become "just another slum school," is not new to Harlem residents.

Wanted Community Control

Their public demonstrations and boycott at the school four months ago received national attention and helped make the school a symbol of the problems of education in urban ghettos.

The residents first wanted the school to be integrated.

When the school system could not induce white parents to send their children to the school but promised that the school would have "unsurpassed instructional features," the community asked for a Negro principal and decisive control over the curriculum and the hiring and dismissal of staff members.

It has not been given any control by the board, which calls such a move a violation of its legal responsibility. The board has instead proposed the appointment of a city-wide task force to chart a course of improvement for slum schools, including I.S. 201.

But Harlem leaders have refused to serve on the task force, contending that it would just produce more recommendations that would not be implemented by the system.

"The board has acted in bad faith so many times," said Mrs. E. Babette Edwards, one of the protesters, who has rejected an invitation to serve on the panel.

The school system's hierarchy has also been criticized by the teachers at I.S. 201. They almost picketed the school in December over a dispute involving payment for after-hours work in an enrichment program for youngsters. Several teachers said they would not speak candidly for publication unless their identities were withheld.

A science teacher, when talking about the school, waves a 26-page list of supplies he has been trying to get for months. "The parents were right," he said. "As soon as you open the school, the system forgets about you."

An English teacher tells about a new curriculum that has never been used and says that "the same old thing is being taught in class to chil-

Stanley R. Lisser, principal of the troubled school.

dren who are used to seeing the unusual."

Several of the teachers are planning to leave in February.

Some of the teachers, who threatened to quit in September if Mr. Lisser was ousted as a concession to the dissident community, have retained their enthusiasm about the school. Yet even many of them now either say that "we need a principal who will stand up there and the kids will shake" or "we need a black principal."

Pupils Using the Feud

One English teacher, tidying up her well-decorated room after a class, said she did not have any disruptions. "I have a wonderful time and the kids are warm—same as other kids —and are just flipping, just dying to learn," she said.

"But these kids have had it with the system," she went on. "They have a sense of what's happening in the community and they use the feud to their advantage. When my mother didn't like someone, I got the feeling too."

Some of the trouble at I.S. 201 appears superficially to be confined to the school. But it is inextricable from the argument between the ghetto residents who want a larger role in the schools and the Board of Education, which is charged with operating the schools.

And this, Mr. Lisser said last week, is his dilemma. The 40-year-old, angular-faced principal, who has been a supervisor in Harlem schools for 10 years, said that "the basic problem"— the "extent and kind of involvement" of the community in the school—could only be resolved by the policy-setting Board of Education.

He said he had offered to meet anywhere with community leaders. But "we have not met," he noted, adding that it is hard "to build a discipline tone" in the school when the "status" people in the area and school officials cannot join hands.

Mr. Lisser described the disruptions at the school as "not excessive."

"Discipline," he remarked, "varies from day to day. That's the fragile nature of the school."

Commenting on his teachers, the principal said that "they have come out well, by and large, though difficulties here have tried some people." He would not comment on teachers' views that a change in principals would help the school.

Superintendent Donovan said last week that he had visited the school in late October and received reports on it regularly.

"Instruction of the children is going on satisfactorily," he said. "I haven't heard that the school doesn't have good sound leadership, but there have been some disciplinary problems and some tensions by teachers, largely growing out of community pressures. Remember that the school is being run in a goldfish bowl."

Dr. Donovan said that no bimonthly reports on "developments and accomplishments at P.S. 201" had been sent to Mayor Lindsay, as the Mayor had requested at the end of September. However, the Superintendent said that, as a substitute for the reports, "we're in constant touch" with the city Human Resources Administration, which is trying to create a broad community coalition in Harlem to better the schools.

Since the Mayor's request, the shouting demonstrators, the gray and orange barricades and the scores of policemen have disappeared from the front of P.S. 201.

The trouble has moved inside.

School Report Cards In Spanish Arranged

The Board of Education will issue report cards in Spanish to Spanish-speaking parents of pupils next fall.

The United Federation of Teachers announced yesterday that it had negotiated the change with the board and that the new cards would be distributed to more than 70,000 youngsters beginning with the September term.

Abe Levine, vice president of the federation, which is the collective bargaining agent for the 55,000 teachers, said the action was taken primarily for the benefit of parents as a means of helping them upgrade their children in areas where help was needed.

A spokesman for the board said school principals would be asked to determine the extent to which the Spanish-speaking parents prefer the report card in English or Spanish. Report cards have never before been issued in any language except English.

January 28, 1967

Negro and Puerto Rican Pupils In Majority Here for First Time

By FRED M. HECHINGER

For the first time in the city's history, Negro and Puerto Rican pupils now constitute the majority of New York's public school enrollment, the Board of Education reported yesterday.

In the last 10 years, the proportion of those two groups has risen from 31.7 per cent to 50.2 per cent of the city-wide enrollment. The remaining 49.8 per cent, designated officially as "others," include—in addition to white pupils—Asians, American Indians and other ethnic groups.

The city's total enrollment stands at 1,084,818. Of these, as of last October, 317,613, or 29.3 per cent, were Negroes and 226,614, or 20.9 per cent, were Puerto Ricans. There were 540,591 others.

In the 10-year period the total white enrollment, excluding Puerto Ricans, dropped by 17 per cent while the Negro and Puerto Rican enrollment rose by more than 80 per cent.

Dr. Nathan Brown, executive deputy superintendent of schools, said the statistics came "as no surprise."

"The Board of Education," he said, "has attempted through a number of procedures to promote ethnic balance in the schools." But the "continuing increase" in the number of Negro and Puerto Rican pupils, he declared, "makes it more difficult for us to provide the kind of integrated education that we would like to provide for every section in the city."

Dr. Brown added that "while the schools have the responsibility to develop programs which meet the needs of every child, they cannot alone provide the physical integration which we believe is desirable for the educational growth of all children in the city."

This, he warned, "can be provided only with the help of other city agencies." He meant housing and labor agencies.

Dr. Brown asserted, however, that New York had maintained a better record of integration than other major cities. He said that only 20.7 per cent of all Negro children here attended schools that were 90 to 100 per cent Negro, compared with 72 per cent in Detroit and Philadelphia and 89.2 per cent in Chicago.

Only slightly more than half of New York's Negro pupils, he said, attend schools in which Negroes constitute the majority, compared with over 90 per cent in the three other cities cited.

Contrast in High Schools

The ethnic census was prepared by the Board of Education's bureau of educational program research and statistics. It indicates that the change in the school population is the result both of a continuing absolute increase in the Negro and Puerto Rican population here and of the steady decrease in the white enrollment.

For example, in all types of schools the 10-year span showed an increase in Puerto Rican enrollment from 128,980 to 226,614 and of the Negro enrollment from 172,957 to 317,613. In the same period the enrollment of "others" declined from 650,680 to 540,591.

On a citywide basis, only the academic high schools still show a majority of white pupils—65.6 per cent of their total enrollment of 224,039. The vocational high schools on the other hand have the largest percentage of Negro and Puerto Rican students—58.6 per cent of a total enrollment of 41,463.

In the city's elementary schools now, 55.1 per cent of the total register of 599,528 are Negroes and Puerto Ricans.

Only in the academic high schools last year was there a slight numerical increase of the total white enrollment—about 3,800 students—over the year before. In the elementary schools, in the same period, they declined by 10,000.

The ethnic composition varies greatly in the different boroughs.

Variations Listed

In Manhattan 76.1 per cent of the elementary-school, 74.1 per cent of the junior-high and 60.1 per cent of the high-school enrollment are Negroes and Puerto Ricans.

"Others" still constitute close to 90 per cent of all the schools in Richmond and more than 70 per cent in Queens. But in the Bronx and Brooklyn the white enrollment represents the minority, except in the academic high schools. In the latter the Negro and Puerto Rican enrollment in the Bronx stands at 45.6 per cent and in Brooklyn at 31.4 per cent.

In compiling the figures, on the basis of the enrollment on Oct. 31, 1966, the schools were directed to obtain the count by "observation" only, without questioning the children as to their racial background.

In enumerating the Puerto Rican children, the schools were told to count all the children whether born on the United States mainland or in Puerto Rico, if one or both parents were Puerto Rican.

March 15, 1967

SCHOOLS CURTAIL OPEN ENROLLMENT

Overcrowding Prompts City High Schools to Suspend Policy, Starting in Fall

By PETER KIHSS

The open-enrollment program set up by the city school system to promote integration and more efficient use of buildings is being suspended in all city high schools this fall and will be limited in other Manhattan and Bronx schools.

The temporary halt was ascribed to overcrowding.

The move became known yesterday as the United Federation of Teachers said that "the failure of the schools" in ghetto areas was not the fault of teachers and threatened "temporary shutdown" of any school where teachers were targets of threatened violence. The union also warned against "racist" influence in teacher assignments.

About 25,000 children in elementary schools and junior and senior high schools are currently taking advantage of the program that lets them voluntarily go to schools out of their own neighborhoods, according to the Office of Education Information Services and Public Relations of the school system.

Now called the "free choice" system, the program started in the 1959-60 school year to give Negro pupils an opportunity to choose their own elementary schools. It gradually expanded to all levels and to white pupils as well.

But now the high schools in particular have become overloaded. In part, this has been caused by a policy of adding a ninth grade to high school, itself aimed at helping better racial balance. One result is that 224,039 pupils are attending the 61 academic high schools, whose capacity is rated at 180,633 this year, causing a 24 per cent overload.

With Negro and Puerto Rican pupils now a majority—50.2 per cent—of pupils in the city, the information bureau said better integration was being sought by a variety of measures. These include rezoning and a move to a system of four-year elemen-

271

tary, four-year intermediate and four-year high schools.

Under an April 7 directive following a central zoning unit survey, the Board of Education has notified superintendents and principals that high school crowding is "presently at a critical point." Accordingly, it said, "the high school open-admission program is to be suspended for the coming school year," except that "where a few seats are available, variances to improve integration have been arranged."

Present Students Unaffected

Students already in high schools are to continue where they are if they wish. In Grover Cleveland High School in Ridgewood, Queens, 160 Brooklyn residents will be allowed to shift to five Brooklyn schools; in East Harlem, 25 Benjamin Franklin High School students will be permitted to transfer to two other schools in Manhattan or one in the Bronx.

In junior high schools, the free-choice program is being suspended for the coming school year in Manhattan and the Bronx because of lack of space in receiving schools. However, brothers or sisters may join older kin, and sixth-graders may choose an elementary school instead of transferring to a junior high.

In elementary schools in Manhattan and the Bronx, the free-choice program for the coming year will be limited to students seeking relief from "short-time instruction" in overcrowded schools. An exception will be offered to brothers or sisters of older pupils.

In a news conference at 300 Park Avenue South, Albert Shanker, president of the United Federation of Teachers, said in a statement that "the failure of the schools is not the fault of teachers, who, for the most part, are attempting to do a job in conditions of scarcity

and neglect and who are often victims of the system along with parents and children."

But he followed up views expressed Sunday by Dr. Bernard E. Donovan, Superintendent of Schools, and Alfred A. Giardino, president of the Board of Education, asserting:

"We would be taking a giant step backward if we allowed unsubstantiated charges, sometimes taking racist forms — antiwhite or anti-Negro—made by a certain small segment of the community, to influence the judgment of professional performance or the hiring and firing of professionals."

To Ask Police Protection

Where teachers are threatened with violence, Mr. Shanker declared the union would ask police protection both within schools and "also to and from public transportation."

"Since education cannot take place in such an atmosphere," his statement went on, "should there be continued incidents at a school, U.F.T. will sponsor a temporary shutdown until such time as it is again possible to continue an educational program in a proper atmosphere."

However, Mr. Shanker said the union was promoting a positive program setting up "teacher - parent - community councils" in particular schools to seek open exchanges of views and "united-action programs for school improvements."

Mr. Shanker also made public responses by the Congress of Racial Equality to a union protest against "anti-Semitic remarks" ascribed to CORE representatives at an April 27 conference in a Brooklyn district superintendent's office.

In one, Oliver Leeds, the chairman of Brooklyn CORE, wrote that his organization was "completely opposed" to anti-Semitism and "steps have been taken to prevent a repetition of such incidents." But he added that teachers who can't lift "black kids" up to grade level" should go elsewhere — "this to us will be the best proof against anti-Semitism."

LOCALITIES TO RUN NEW SCHOOL UNITS

Parents and Teachers Will Gain Voice on Policy in 3 Experimental Districts

By LEONARD BUDER

The Board of Education has approved the creation of three experimental school districts in which parents and teachers would exercise city school powers never before granted to local groups.

The new districts, or units as they are officially called, will be run by elected boards consisting of parents, other community residents and members of the local school staffs.

The authority of these boards will include the selection of administrators to head the units, participation in setting educational policy for the areas and control of funds allotted by the citywide school board. In at least one unit, the new governing board will have the power to recruit and select teachers and supervisors, but within the framework of established standards.

I. S. 201 to Be Included

The three units will involve schools in East Harlem, including the controversial Intermediate School 201, the Ocean Hill-Brownsville section of Brooklyn, and the Two Bridges area on Manhattan's Lower East Side.

A fourth experiment, involving a single school in the Bedford-Stuyvesant section of Brooklyn, will also be undertaken.

Plans for the projects are being developed by parents, community representatives and members of the United Federation of Teachers. City school officials are working with the groups and the Ford Founda-

tion, it was learned, has promised to provide planning grants.

Although the city school board and Dr. Bernard E. Donovan, the Superintendent of Schools, have approved the "concepts" of the projects, the actual details will be given official review when they are worked out.

Part of Decentralization

Sources in the school system and the communities involved said that some of the experimental projects might be in operation within the year.

Alfred A. Giardino, the president of the school board, said yesterday that the new demonstration projects were in line with the system's announced intentions to experiment with various forms of decentralization to bring about greater community involvement in local school affairs.

He noted that a number of other projects were also being worked on and added: "The board hopes that from these decentralization experiences lessons will be learned that can have general application elsewhere."

Dr. Nathan Brown, who is Acting Superintendent while Dr. Donovan is on vacation this month, said that the Superintendent had approved in principle "the outlines, areas and objectives" for the projects.

In effect, the three demonstration units will be detached from their regular local school districts. Presumably, their governing boards will report directly to the central Board of Education, rather than to superintendents of the districts in which they are geographically located.

The city system is now divided into 30 local districts, each headed by an assistant superintendent and each with its own local school board. These boards have traditionally been advisory bodies, but under the central board's plans for administrative decentralization of the system additional powers are being shifted to the local school boards and the district superintendents.

May 23, 1967

The East Harlem unit will consist of I. S. 201 and the four primary schools — Public Schools 24, 39, 68 and 133 — from which it draws its students.

The opening of the windowless, air-conditioned "showcase" intermedial school was delayed for a week last fall because of a boycott. The controversy arose over the demands of some Negro and Puerto Rican parents and community representatives for "control" of the school's operation.

David Spencer, the president of the Parents Organization of I. S. 201, said that the new project will give parents a chance "to take a hand in their children's education so that we can see better results."

The unit will be governed by a board of 10 parents, 5 community leaders, 5 teachers and a school administrator. According to the proposal for the project, the board would recruit and select the staff of the five schools, with the exception of teachers and supervisors who are now there and want to remain.

The proposal also said that special programs would be introduced to overcome reading retardation and to meet other special needs of the pupils.

Drawn by Committee

The "Two Bridges" unit — so-called because the area is on the Manhattan side of the Manhattan and Brooklyn Bridges — will take in Junior High School 65 and Public Schools 1, 2, 42 and 126.

The Ocean-Hill-Brownsville experiment will involve J.H.S. 271 and its feeder schools, P.S. 73, 155, 87 and 137, and I.S. 55 and its feeder schools, P.S. 144 and 178.

The plans call for a governing body of eight parents, five community representatives, eight teachers and two supervisors. Features of the plan include the preparation of community-school workers and the in-service training of inexperienced or new teachers and members of the student governments at the schools.

The single school experiment involves P.S. 129 in Bedford-Stuyvesant. The school would be "overseen" by a committee of educators and community residents, but still would be under the local school board.

July 6, 1967

TEACHERS TIE UP CITY'S SCHOOLS; 400,000 PUPILS MISS OPENING DAY

SCHOOLS PICKETED

Volunteers Help Man Classrooms – Legal Test Due Today

By PETER KIHSS

The city's school system was disrupted yesterday as nearly 46,000 of the city's 58,000 teachers stayed away from the opening classes of the fall term. So did nearly 400,000 of their one million pupils.

Indications were that the disruption over a contract dispute would go on today, despite a temporary restraining order against the teachers' mass resignation tactic. The order is to be argued in Supreme Court at 2 P.M. today.

Both sides had met with Mayor Lindsay at Gracie Mansion for six and a half hours until 4:30 A.M. yesterday seeking to stave off the third teacher stoppage here in seven years.

Board of Education leaders asserted later they had come "close to agreement on the educational issues" but held the union was still seeking "substantial moneys" above a pending pay offer; the union insisted "no progress" had been made.

Volunteers in Classes

Inside many schools, parents and other community volunteers joined supervisors and still-working teachers to conduct some kind of program. "I love my children, I wanted to help them," Mrs. Carmen Ramos of 90 Avenue D, said in explaining why she helped out in second and third grade classes at Public School 64, Ninth Street and Avenue A.

Teachers marched on picket lines outside 740 of the city's 900 schools, according to the police. In front of Jamaica High School teachers carried signs saying, "We risk our job for a voice in schools" and, "Reduce class size now."

"The parents are better than teachers 'cause teachers scream too much," Josh Marlis, 10 years old, said in Public School 87, 160 West 78th Street. By the tens of thousands, pupils were dismissed early yesterday; they seemed unusually well-behaved, and Dr. Bernard E. Donovan, Superintendent of Schools, quoted the Transit Authority police as reporting that "the children went home like lambs."

11,662 Teachers Work

The Board of Education reported that 11,662 of 57,644 assigned teachers showed up yesterday morning for classes. Of the 1,030,967 enrolled pupils, 597,519 showed up.

About 50,000 other pupils were scheduled to start school in the afternoon. No attendance figures were available for the afternoon session.

The staffs in the schools were augmented by 8,577 volunteers, according to the board count. Alfred A. Giardino, president of the board, said 1,500 licensed staff members had been redeployed into the schools from usual nonteaching assignments in district and headquarters offices.

The board's figures indicated the highest proportion of teachers reporting was in the special schools, involving pupils with health or other problems — 341 of 520 teachers, or 66 per cent, reporting for work. The other turnouts varied from 10 to 37 per cent, the poorest tending to be in poorer areas and the next highest in Bay Ridge, Brooklyn.

The average teacher earns about $8,800, according to the board, and would lose $30.50 on such a salary for each day of an unexcused absence; this would indicate a teacher wage loss yesterday approximating $1.4-million.

The United Federation of Teachers, sponsoring the stoppage, estimated that 90 per cent of teachers were off the job citywide. This was based on reports from its area coordinators, Vito De Leonardis, staff director, said.

Dr. Donovan, in a broadcast over the school system's television and radio station, WNYE, said, "I wish to thank the staff, the children and the volunteers for an excellent job today — and a better day tomorrow."

In heavily Negro and Puerto Rican areas where pupil absenteeism and population mobility are frequently greater than elsewhere, yesterday's student turnout appeared generally close to — although slightly below — the city average of 58 per cent showing up.

Board figures indicated pupil attendance of 56 per cent in the Lower East Side school district; East and central Harlem, 51; North Harlem, 52; Stuyvesant, 53; Greenpoint-Williamsburg, 49; Crown Heights-Brownsville, 48. The lowest percentage was East New York's 37, but the St. Albans-South Jamaica area was as high as 69.

Donovan Thanks Aides

Dr. Donovan declared the schools would open again today, school buses would run as usual and lunches would be served. "If there has to be any dismissal for the safety of the school," he added, "handicapped and bused children should be given high priority."

The Superintendent asserted he was "confident thousands of other teachers will be back in school" today, and "there will be more volunteers so the instructional program can proceed."

But he also authorized principals to hire on a daily basis teachers and supervisors who have retired, except those with disability or against whom disciplinary charges had been pending; and others who had been on sabbatical leaves or unpaid leaves of absence. School officials later said that

273

pay for per diem teachers depended on experience but averaged $32.50 daily.

Supervisors Urge Discretion

On the other hand, the Council of Supervisory Associations, which had opposed efforts to keep the schools going during a teacher stoppage, telegraphed Dr. Donovan last night urging authority to each principal "to dismiss school when in his judgment conditions dangerous to the safety of pupils and remaining staff warrant it."

"Attempts to pretend that normal educational processes are going on and emphasis on keeping school buildings open regardless of result cannot continue," Joseph L. Brennan, council president, added in the telegram.

The Association of Assistant Principals called for closing the schools until teachers return. Mrs. Betty Ostroff, president, charged the Board of Education sought "to mask the fact that little or no instruction" could be given in most schools and asserted "we performed a holding operation today." She said "the breakdown of orderly procedures" had set an unfortunate example for children.

Support for keeping the schools open had come from the United Parents Associations; the City Teachers Association, which is a rival of the U.F.T.; the African-American Teachers Association, whose Negro members had sponsored workshops for parents, and the city-sponsored Puerto Rican community conference, among others.

Galamison Scores Both Sides

But the teachers union stoppage drew picketing support from two nationally known Negro civil rights leaders, A. Philip Randolph, president of the Brotherhood of Sleeping Car Porters, and Bayard Rustin, who led the 1963 March on Washington. Both picketed with Albert Shanker, the union president, outside Washington Irving High School yesterday afternoon.

Mr. Rustin joined Mr. Shanker in addressing 8,000 members of the union on Murray Street between Broadway and Church Street, after they

The New York Times (by Neal Boenzi)

ON A PICKET LINE: Teachers outside George Westinghouse Vocational and Technical High School at Bridge and Johnson Street, Brooklyn, in the union dispute with the city.

had staged an hour's march around City Hall.

"Most Negro teachers and parents are behind you in your fight to reduce class sizes and to set up more effective schools," the gray-haired Negro leader declared.

But another Negro leader, the Rev. Milton A. Galamison, who led the one-day boycott in February, 1964, that saw 464,362 children, or 44 per cent, stay out of classes in demands for better racial integration, criticized both the union and the Board of Education yesterday.

Mr. Galamison contended the union was interested only in "greater salaries," and its efforts to give teachers power to remove "disruptive" pupils indicated lack of understanding of ghetto needs.

The school system, he asserted, had been "consistently mulish" about ghetto problems and interested mainly "in pacifying the pathological forces in the white community."

Gilberto Gerena-Valentin, executive secretary of the Puerto Rican community conference, another leader of the 1964 boycott, had urged that schools be kept open. Mr. Gerena-Valentin said the Puerto Rican leaders were pro-labor and favored teacher wage increases but were "defending the community" by seeking to keep schools going.

Despite the intensity of feeling on all sides, yesterday's stoppage went off peacefully with only vocal clashes. At Intermediate School 201, 2005 Madison Avenue, at 127th Street, where an experimental school had been boycotted last fall in community demands for

a greater voice in policy, there were only six pickets at school opening.

John Marsh, union chapel chairman, explained, "most teachers did not wish it to appear that they were against the community by picketing here, so they have decided to picket somewhere else."

But Negro neighbors heckled the pickets, who included two Negro teachers, and Mrs. Alice Kornegay, president of the East Harlem Triangle Association, shouted at policemen that the teacher pickets should be made to walk "in the gutter" as she said the boycotters had been required to walk last year.

Shortly after 9 A.M., the teacher pickets went away, Mr. Marsh saying, "we don't want to antagonize the community." School cards indicated 54 of 72 scheduled teachers reported for work; volunteer aides included

The New York Times (by Don Charles)

IN A CLASSROOM: Ed Rosario, one of the teachers who worked, at I.S. 201, Harlem

not only parents but nuns from the All Saints Roman Catholic Church, 47 East 129th Street.

Mrs. Beryl Banfield, the acting principal, who is a Negro, said she was "overwhelmed at the quality of community support." She said parents had told her, "If no other school works, 201 is going to work—we're going to make it work."

A different experience was reported at nearby P. S. 175, 175 West 134th Street, where Harvey F. Nagler, the principal, said only 16 of 48 teachers showed up. About 25 other teachers—both white and Negro—went to two "freedom schools" opened by the union chapter in a joint effort with the school's parents' association.

Two such schools were operating at Bethel African Methodist Episcopal Church, 132d Street between Fifth and Lenox Avenues, and Metropolitan

A. M. E. Church, 135th Street between Fifth and Lenox Avenues. About 163 children attended the public school; the interim schools reported a lesser number, not given out.

46 Picket Bronx School

In the East Bronx, Junior High School 98, 1619 Boston Road, at 173d Street, scene of a three-day resignation by teachers last year in a protest over assaults by pupils, 46 pickets were on hand at school opening at 8:40 A.M.

But 30 counter-pickets, accompanied by two dozen children, showed up under leadership of Mrs. Evelyna Antonetty, president of the United Bronx Parents, to protest the teacher stoppage. "We're here to learn," the children's signs declared.

The teacher pickets left about 10 A.M., when the seventh and ninth grades were dismissed;

the school's eighth grade was dismissed at 11:40 A.M. About 1,000 pupils had attended, out of 2,100 enrolled; only 15 of 112 assigned teachers had reported.

In the Ocean Hill-Brownsville demonstration school district in Brooklyn, Rhody McCoy, unit administrator, reported that five of the seven schools "operated with great success." He said these were the ones "where the supervisory administration of the school accepted and cooperated with the desire of the community" to keep schools open.

His report said P. S. 87, P. S. 155 and J. H. S. 178, where community choices have been assigned as principals, had 85 parents at work although only 22 teachers showed up, while 40 parents aided four teachers at P. S. 137. At J. H. S. 271, Mr. McCoy said, 40 teachers ap-

peared, "almost all of Afro-American background." But at P. S. 73 and P. S. 144, he said, teachers failed to show up and he charged a lack of administration cooperation.

Herman B. Ferguson, who is fighting suspension as an assistant principal while resisting a murder conspiracy indictment, said yesterday he had joined the project as an after-hours consultant to Mr. McCoy to coordinate parent volunteers.

New School Opens

In South Jamaica, Junior High School 72, 133-28 New York Boulevard, opened for the first time. Only three teachers, all Negroes, reported for work out of a faculty of 72. Of the 1,338 pupils, 65 per cent Negro, 944 attended, according to Stanley Bloch, the principal.

Mr. Bloch kept 350 pupils in school, as the number he said he could handle on the basis of "safety and instructional aspects" in classes of 35 apiece supervised by teachers, volunteers and school aides. "I'm not assessing any blame in this, but it is sad," Mr. Bloch declared.

In a news conference at the Board of Education, Mr. Giardino, board president, said he was "happy to say that the new school year has begun." He said he expected more regular teachers to appear today— "after their initial duty to the union is fulfilled, they will then respond to their obligation to the pupils," Mr. Giardino declared.

Superintendent Donovan also told newsmen he expected teachers to return because of what he said was "a very fair settlement" and "the fact there are children in the city to teach."

"I am so concerned wit critical needs of this c' I cannot see stopping the four highest in for state aid; S' late-starting not norr'

Mr.
dent
at
2?
c

SCHOOL CONFEREES AGREE; UNION TO VOTE TOMORROW; CLASSES LIKELY THIS WEEK

The New York Times (by Neal Boenzi)

AGREEMENT: Mayor Lindsay, center, with Albert Shanker, left, teachers' union president, and Dr. Bernard E. Donovan, Superintendent of Schools, at City Hall following settlement.

TERMS IN WRITING

Shanker Calls Them 'Fantastically Good' —Board Acts Today

By LEONARD BUDER

A new agreement to end the two-and-a-half-week teachers' walkout, this time backed by a signed "memorandum of understanding," was announced yesterday by Mayor Lindsay.

The agreement must be ratified by the general membership of the United Federation of Teachers and be formally approved by the nine members of the Board of Education before the walkout is officially ended.

Mr. Lindsay expressed the hope that this would be done quickly "so that teachers can return to the schools as early as possible on Thursday."

The earliest teachers could return to work would be tomorrow afternoon. But there is a possibility the teachers might not be able to return before Friday morning if there is a delay in counting votes from the ratification election.

Albert Shanker, the president of the union, said: "I think it's an excellent agreement. It's fantastically good."

Union Meetings Today

Three of the 11 members of the union's negotiating committee, however, voted against going along with the agreement.

The 39-year-old union president conceded that there might be some opposition from the membership but he predicted that the new school contract would be approved.

The union's executive board will meet this morning and the local's delegate assembly will convene this evening to act on the proposed settlement. A general membership meeting is being arranged for tomorrow morning.

Superintendent of Schools Bernard E. Donovan also appeared happy at the agreement. He said that the school board would formally approve the contract at a meeting scheduled to start at 5:30 P.M. today.

The agreement, worked out earlier yesterday at a meeting at City Hall, cleared up the dispute that arose after last Wednesday's announcement by the Mayor that an oral understanding had been reached to end the crippling work stoppage.

The board and the union had accused each other of reneging and efforts to translate the oral agreement into contract language bogged down in a bitter exchange of charges and countercharges.

No details of the settlement were made public. But it was learned that the pact provided that at least half of a $10-million fund that will be set up next year for experimental school improvement programs would be used, as the union had insisted, for "intensive" projects.

No funds, however, are committed specifically for the expansion of the controversial More Effective Schools program for disadvantaged pupils. This originally had been a "top priority" union demand.

The dispute did not affect the over-all 26-month $135.4-million package of salary increases and other benefits that had been agreed to last week. Before the walkout, the teachers rejected a 24-month $125-million contract offer.

Part of the extra $10.4-million will be used to give all teachers $150 more a year than the previous two-year offer provided. This across-the-board increase, as well as an additional $150 that will be given to teachers with 30 credit hours of graduate study before...

Thus, the city systems salary scale on March 1, 1969, will range from a basic minimum of $6,720 annually for starting teachers to a top of $13,900 for those with more than 13 years of service and maximum qualifications.

The range under the contract that expired last June 30 was $5,400 to $11,900. Effective last Sept. 1, the range will be $6,200 to $12,600. Next Sept. 1, the range will go to $6,600 to $13,600. These increases had

276

been agreed upon before the walkout began.

The new agreement was announced by Mayor Lindsay at 3:35 P.M.

He stood at the speaker's lectern in the ornate chamber of the Board of Estimate on the second-floor at City Hall, flanked by Mr. Shanker and Dr. Donovan. The three men smiled broadly and looked relieved and relaxed.

"The City of New York has been through a great deal but I'm pleased to be able to state that within a very short time I expect that our schools will be open," the Mayor said.

Memorandum on Terms

He then read aloud the Memorandum of Understanding that had been signed —in signatures that were virtually the same size —by Mr. Shanker and Dr. Donovan. This said:

"It is hereby stipulated and agreed by and between the Board of Education and United Federation of Teachers, A.F.L.-C.I.O., that all of the terms and conditions of the collective bargaining agreement for the period commencing with July 1, 1967, through Sept. 7, 1969, have been agreed upon. There are no outstanding items which require further negotiation, discussion or clarification.

"The negotiating committee of the United Federation of Teachers agrees to immediately convene the necessary meetings in order to ratify this agreement."

The memorandum was also signed by a witness, Vincent D. McDonnell, chairman of the State Mediation Board. Mr. McDonnell and Harold G. Israelson, a labor lawyer, assisted in the recent conciliation efforts.

The two mediators had helped bring about last week's oral agreement and were called back by the Mayor when the new dispute developed last Friday.

After he made the announcement, the Mayor and the two chief adversaries in the school dispute clasped hands for the benefit of photographers.

Last Wednesday, when the first tentative agreement was announced at Gracie Mansion, the Mayor's home, the mood had been solemn. There were no smiles, no handshakes.

Leaving City Hall yesterday, Mr. Shanker and Dr. Donovan walked — separately — the two and a half blocks to the State Supreme Court building at Foley Square.

Defiance of Law Charged

There the trial of Mr. Shanker and two other union officers, which had been frequently delayed because of the contract negotiations, was already under way.

Mr. Shanker and George Altomare, union vice president, and David Wittes, treasurer, have been accused of criminal contempt by the board for disobeying a court order banning the teachers' walkout. The order had been granted under a state law, known as the Taylor Law, which prohibits strikes by public employes.

The trial ended at 6:15 P.M., after eight days of argument and the testimony of more than a dozen witnesses. Justice Emilio Nunez reserved decision.

If found guilty, the three officers can be sentenced to 30 days in jail and be fined up to $250. The Union, which is also a defendant, could be fined up to $150,000 for each day of the contempt.

While the three union officers were in court, Jules Kolodny, who is Mr. Shanker's assistant, and other teacher representatives went to Board of Education headquarters in downtown Brooklyn to put the written contract in final form to be printed. They met with school officials in the office of Miss Ida Klaus, the board's director of staff relations.

Under the union's policy, the printed version must be given to local's 50,000 members at least 24 hours before a vote can be taken.

Law Journal Prints Text

Jerry Finkelstein, publisher of The New York Law Journal, offered yesterday to print, as a public service and without charge, the complete text of the agreement between the board and the union. Mr. Finkelstein said he would print 60,000 copies, enough to supply each teacher in the system, and to have them ready for distribution this morning.

The union accepted the offer with thanks.

The last contract proposal, which was turned down by the teachers the day before the walkout began on Sept. 11, was printed at the school board's expense. This cost $37,525.

McNally Bros., Inc., the Brooklyn trucking concern that transported Michelangelo's priceless sculpture "Pieta," when it came here for the New York World's Fair in 1964-65, arranged to pick up the copies from the printers and rush

them this morning to various distribution points.

Teachers can pick up copies today at Central Commercial High School in Manhattan, Theodore Roosevelt H. S. in the Bronx, Brooklyn Technical H. S., John Bowne H. S. in Queens and Curtis H. S. on Staten Island and at the office of The Law Journal, 258 Broadway.

The dispute over the $10-million experimental fund and the More Effective Schools is resolved in the contract's preamble, it was learned. This section says in part:

"In addition to continuing present intensive experimental programs for educational excellence such as the More Effective Schools, the All-Day Neighborhood Schools, the five new primary schools and the newly strengthened program in the kindergarten through second grade in special service schools, the Board of Education agrees to set aside a fund of $10-million for the 1968-69 school year for the purpose of making progress in the development of new programs for the elementary schools.

"A work group will be established to make appropriate studies and to submit recommendations to the Board of Education for the utilization of the special fund. Recommendations of the work group will be subject to the final approval of the Superintendent of Schools and the Board of Education.

"Not less than $5-million of this fund shall be used by the board for intensive programs for the reorganization and improvement of additional schools.

"The work group will consist of two representatives of the union, two board representatives of parent or community groups chosen by agreement of the board and the union. It will be chaired by an eminent elementary school educator selected from outside the school system by the Superintendent of Schools."

The new agreement also provides for relief of junior and senior high school teachers from some administrative and clerical duties—a second major issue in dispute.

It specifies, for example, that "during the 1968-69 school year, no more than 35 per cent of home room teachers in high schools shall be given administrative assignments."

On Monday the board had offered to exempt only 50 per cent of the home-room teachers

from administrative assignments.

The contract contains new procedures for coping with problems posed by disruptive pupils. The agreement also provides that union representatives would be consulted on matters of educational policy and that a joint board-union committee would be established for "discipline planning and curriculum."

The matter of new procedures for handling pupil behavior problems had been one of the most bitter issues during the contract negotiations that preceded the work stoppage. The union, however, later dropped its original demand that teachers be given a contractual right to "permanently remove" pupils they considered to be disruptive from their classrooms.

The good feeling evident when the accord was announced yesterday contrasted with the acrimony that marked the discusions leading up to the new agreement.

On Monday night, with the negotiations still bogged down and no signs of a settlement in sight, Mayor Lindsay left City Hall and went to a midtown television studio. He taped a statement to be broadcast at 11 P. M.

But minutes before air-time, he ordered "Kill it," explaining he had just been informed that progress was being made in the talks.

In his prepared broadcast, never officially released, the Mayor urged that some issues be submitted to binding arbitration.

Mr. Lindsay, in the canceled broadcast, also criticized the Board of Education and the teachers' union.

"It has become apparent," he said, "that the children have been forgotten by the union leadership and the board amid all the hostility and mistrust between them."

It was learned yesterday that shortly before the broadcast was canceled, a high Board of Education official had telephoned Deputy Mayor Robert W. Sweet. Mr. Sweet was informed that the board was prepared to issue a statement of its own in the event that Mr. Lindsay made a public announcement that the board's opinion did not adequately reflect the situation.

The board official said that the Mayor and the mediators should publicly insist that the union honor the agreement reached last week.

400 Teachers Vote to Return to Slum Schools Despite Fears

By PETER KIHSS

Albert Shanker, president of he United Federation of Teachers, told teachers yesterday that it "will take personal heroism" for them to go back in some cases to their schools in slum areas because of community hostility, but he urged them to return.

Mr. Shanker, who led the teacher stoppage for 14 school days, addressed a meeting of 400 such teachers in Harlem and Brooklyn schools. The group met for several hours at the Americana hotel, and finally voted, with eight unexplained nays, to return.

"We must emulate the kids in Little Rock, who kept going to school despite harassment," Mr. Shanker said, recalling the 957 case when nine Negro children integrated a white school with aid of Federal troops. If teachers let themselves be driven away, he said, they would be "hastening the end of our school system."

Meanwhile, the planning board for the Intermediate School 201 School Complex in Harlem announced it would summon all teachers from that school and its four feeder elementary schools who took part in the stoppage to appear before a board committee as they show up this morning.

Screening Planned

The group said they would be asked to discuss why they stayed away, and would be screened "to determine their attitudes and motivation for returning to the schools in the I.S. 201 complex." David Spencer, executive secretary of the board, said the board "will decide who will work here," and Mrs. Babette Edwards, a member, said any teacher refusing to be screened "won't teach."

In Brooklyn, Rhody A. McCoy, unit administrator of the Ocean Hill-Brownsville school district, said he had seen a letter in which all 17 assistant principals in the seven schools in his area were said to be seeking transfers.

Mr. McCoy, whose appointment was confirmed by the Board of Education in a turbulent meeting Wednesday night, said he had met with the assistant principals last week after this letter. He said he had urged, "let's do a professional job," and believed some wanted to stay, but he was waiting for word from the Superintendent of Schools' office on what would happen.

Both the I.S. 201 and Ocean Hill-Brownsville areas are districts selected by the Board of Education for demonstration projects to promote community participation and to bring about more decentralization in school affairs.

The Harlem area is overwhelmingly Negro in population, and the Ocean Hill-Brownsville section has a high proportion of Negroes. Mr. Spencer, Mrs. Edwards and Mr. McCoy are Negroes.

The I.S. 201 planning board has set itself up with 35 members—four parents and two teachers from each of its five schools and five other community residents. It is operating with a Ford Foundation grant in a project in which it is to help organize elections for a governing board, which would nominate a unit administrator with whom it would work on curriculum, personnel and other problems, subject to Board of Education approval.

Mr. Shanker had been prevented from stating his union's objection to appointment of Mr. McCoy and three principals in the Ocean Hill-Brownsville area by a disorderly Negro audience shouting denunciations at the Board of Education session.

Yesterday morning, at Madison Square Garden, he told union teachers voting approval of a new contract that the board meeting had been "absolute chaos." He said more than 1,000 teachers faced "tremendous bitterness and hostility" in the ghetto areas.

"Now I know I express the view of all of you when I say we're not going to let those teachers down," Mr. Shanker said, and long applause followed. Later he told newsmen he didn't think the problem was racial — "some black teachers are being pushed out," he observed.

Fears Are Expressed

From there he went to the Americana hotel where teachers from the affected areas poured forth their concern. One woman told him.

"I don't want to be a dead hero. I'm afraid to return to school tomorrow. We have a National Guard—let's use it!"

One teacher said a "purge list" had been circulating in the I.S. 201 area with names of "the strong white male teachers" who had taken part in the work stoppage. A man who said he was from Public School 144 in Brooklyn told of finishing picketing one day and then driving away, only to be cut off by a car with four men who told him he ought to go into the school to teach.

Others said teachers had been kicked and slapped on picket lines in Harlem and that some individuals had told children the teachers were striking because they "hate the children." Others said they ought to seek mass transfers from the demonstration areas.

One complained of the activities of self-appointed goons." Another declared, "it's the same group of militants that go everywhere." A man from Junior High School 271 in Brooklyn said that "if the militants take over, the children will have an education of hate."

About a dozen Negro teachers were at the meeting. One was Mrs. Marguerita Fletcher, of Public School 178 in Brooklyn, who said she had stayed out during the stoppage, while her husband, Theodore, had kept teaching at the same school.

Mrs. Fletcher said "a black revolution is going on all over the country," and contended the militants "are actually expressing the feelings of the ghetto." She said teachers used to accuse parents of apathy; now that the parents had become active, teachers didn't like what was going on, but she said it was all a step in development.

Another Negro, Sidney Harris, the union's assistant secretary, insisted community participation must be given a chance to work.

The I. S. 201 planning board held a news conference in the library of the school, in part to answer statements made Wednesday by John Marsh, the union's chapter chairman. Mr. Marsh had declared that "at least two-thirds" of the 82 teachers at I.S. 201, wanted to be transferred, and said that "hate whitey" programs had been held at the school during the stoppage.

Paul Meyers, a white teacher who had kept teaching in the school during the stoppage, read a statement he said represented view of 27 of 35 teachers who had stayed at work.

The statement said they had seen "no traces of either teacher intimidation in this school or the use of the school to propagate racial hatred," and that they were "enthusiastic about the future possibilities" of partnership with the community.

Mr. Spencer, the planning board's bearded executive secretary, said the board was "fully integrated," and "the hysterical tone of Mr. Marsh's remarks underlines the urgency for parents, community and teachers to screen the attitudes and abilities of all staff desiring to be employed in the complex."

At the conference was Herman B. Ferguson, who has been suspended as an assistant principal after his indictment in an alleged Revolutionary Action Movement murder conspiracy. Mr. Ferguson, who denies the charges against him, said he had been hired by the planning board this week as assistant to Berlin Kelly, its chief consultant.

Mr. Ferguson said, "I was willing to be screened by the community." He added the planning board wants to screen teachers who "flouted the law" by failing to return to work after a State Supreme Court order against a work stoppage.

At the storefront headquarters of the Ocean Hill-Brownsville district at 1959 Fulton Avenue, near Saratoga Avenue, Brooklyn, Mr. McCoy said he did not personally know of any threats or violence directed by community representatives at any teacher in one of his seven schools.

The school system's Council of Supervisory Associations, through Max H. Frankle as counsel, sued this week in Supreme Court to block appointment of Mr. McCoy and demonstration principals as alleged violations of the State Constitution and civil service procedures. Supreme Court Justice Murray Feiden yesterday set a hearing for next Wednesday.

September 29, 1967

BOARD SEES CHAOS IF SCHOOLS ADOPT BUNDY PROPOSALS

It Says Decentralization Plan Could Increase Political and Racial Pressures

By LEONARD BUDER

The Board of Education charged yesterday that giving community school boards the power to hire teachers and supervisors would open the door to "personal and politically motivated appointment on a large scale."

Reacting to recent proposals for school reform made by a special panel appointed by the Mayor, the nine-member board declared that "the elimination of the present school system and the substitution of many full-blown new school systems" would hurt, not help, efforts to bring about needed school improvements.

The Mayor's panel, headed by McGeorge Bundy, president of the Ford Foundation, proposed earlier this week that a federation of 30 to 60 largely autonomous, locally governed school districts be established here. The plan would include parent-dominated community school boards with the authority to hire school personnel, determine educational policy and allocate funds from the city.

Assailed by Shanker

"Hiring by 30 to 60 different school districts of teachers and others could increase political, racial and religious interference in the selection process," the board said in its statement.

Albert Shanker, the president of the United Federation of

Teachers, also voiced strong criticism yesterday of some of the proposals. He said at a news conference that the panel's report, if enacted intact, would promote "years of chaos and eventual destruction of the city's school system."

He asserted that the panel's proposals on personnel appointment represented the "greatest piece of political patronage ever perpetuated."

However, Mario D. Fantini, the panel's executive secretary, said that the proposals would open the door to needed new leadership in school affairs, particularly on the local level.

Mr. Fantini, who is a program officer at the Ford Foundation, told a meeting of the Women's City Club of New York that the plan was not intended as a panacea but as an alternative to be considered.

"We are on a collision course unless something is done," he said.

At present, he said, there is too much "disconnection" and lack of communication at many levels of the city system, "even to the point that some teachers are not talking to one another."

He charged that the system did not have the "capability" to bring about necessary improvements and that a major reorganization was imperative.

Under the panel's proposals, the present nonsalaried Board of Education would be replaced by a three-man paid commission. Or it would be reconstituted, with the present members serving out their terms of office.

Under either setup, the board would cease to be the educational policy-making body for the city and would become a service and coordinating agency. It would operate only the vocational and specialized high schools and special schools for handicapped and emotionally disturbed pupils.

Alfred A. Giardino, president of the board, served on the Mayor's six-member panel. But he did not sign the report, which contained his dissent on behalf of the entire board. The

board's statement yesterday elaborated upon this dissent.

The board also commented on its objections at a news conference held yesterday morning at school headquarters, 110 Livingston Street, Brooklyn.

Called a 'Public Service'

Mr. Giardino, a lawyer, spoke to reporters from behind a long table in a wood paneled library on the second floor. He was flanked by Mrs. Rose Shapiro, the vice president Dr. Bernard E. Donovan, the Superintendent of Schools and two board members—Dr. Aaron Brown, and Thomas C. Burke.

"A great public service has been done by the report," Mr. Giardino said. "There are many excellent things in it. Unfortunately, the board does not share all of the recommendations and sees a number of dangers in them."

"The report seeks to achieve goals that we here at the board have long espoused," he added.

He explained that the board had been seeking greater involvement by parents and the community in the operation of the schools and had delegated increased authority to the system's 30 local boards and the district superintendents.

He said that state law now required these local boards to be largely advisory, and prevented the central board from delegating more of its authority to those on the local level.

New legislation is needed, he added, to enable the city board to delegate greater responsibility to the community boards, including the authority to hire the community or district superintendent on a contract basis. The community superintendents, he continued, should also have the right to hire teachers for the district, but with safeguards for the teachers.

The board asserted that under the panel's proposals, "all existing district superintendents and principals could be unseated at one strike" and that local teacher recruitment and selection would become "chaotic and divisive."

'Could Hurt Ghettos'

The board also pointed to various "practical operating difficulties." For example, it noted some teachers—those of

handicapped pupils, for instance—would be employed by the central board while others of regular classes in the same school would be employed by the community board.

The statement said that there would be curriculum problems for pupils who move from one district to another. It also said there was a need for a "common basic preparation" for high school students who will cross district lines.

Dr. Donovan said that the proposals for a "fragmented" network of local systems could hurt the very children—those living in the ghettos—who need help the most.

He said that the community school districts covering these areas might be the ones that would experience the most difficulty obtaining qualified personnel if teachers and supervisors were completely free to "shop around" for employment.

Mr. Shanker, at his press conference held in union headquarters, 300 Park Avenue South, said that the teachers' union had not taken a position on decentralization but that he wanted to discuss some "good points and bad points" of the panel's plan.

He said that among the good features were those proposals that "would help alleviate the bureaucratic setup that now exists in the present Board of Education."

Mr. Shanker also voiced concern that improper influences, political and otherwise, might figure in the appointment of teachers by the community boards.

He expressed fear that "Negro teachers would be hired in Negro areas and white teachers in white areas."

Mr. Shanker also asserted that reliable leadership would be lacking in many school districts because "extremists would have veto power."

Mr. Lindsay appointed the panel after the State Legislature directed him last spring to submit a school decentralization plan to qualify the city for additional state aid. The panel's recommendations are not binding on the Mayor, who must submit his plan by Dec. 1.

November 10, 1967

Negro School Panel Ousts 19, Defies City

By HOMER BIGART

The predominantly Negro governing board of a Brooklyn demonstration school district reached a major confrontation with the Board of Education yesterday over the power to hire and dismiss teachers.

The governing board sent registered letters to 13 teachers and six administrators terminating their employment in six schools of the Ocean Hill-Brownsville Demonstration School District.

But the Board of Education sent telegrams to the 19 directing them to ignore the dismissal notices and to return to their posts today. And the board warned the district administrator, Rhody A. McCoy, a Negro, that he was responsible for the safety of the teachers.

The United Federation of Teachers joined the Board of Education in denouncing the dismissals as illegal.

Albert Shanker, president of the teacher's union, said he would ask Mayor Lindsay to escort the teachers to their classrooms if they were threatened.

He said the teachers were victims of a "kind of vigilante activity." They were discharged "without due process," he said, holding that no charges had been specified against them.

Last night, about 400 of the 600 teachers in the school district voted overwhelmingly to ignore the dismissal notices and to appear for work today. The meeting at Ditmas Junior High School at 700 Cortelyou Road, Brooklyn, was called by the United Federation of Teachers.

Mr. McCoy said last night that the 19 were ousted because "the community lost confidence in them" and because they were suspected of trying to sabotage the demonstration project. It is one of three such districts set up by the Board of Education under a Ford Foundation grant to promote community participation and to bring about more decentralization in school affairs.

He said he had been told by the Superintendent of Schools, Dr. Bernard E. Donovan, that the dismissals were illegal, but he defended the action as the only recourse left to the community.

The letters of dismissal were curt, giving no reasons but suggesting that persons involved might attend a meeting of the governing board at 6 P.M. today in Intermediate School 55, at 2021 Bergen Street, Brooklyn, if they wanted to "question this action."

The letters said:

'The Governing Board of the Ocean Hill-Brownsville Demonstration School District has voted to end your employment in the schools of this district. This action was taken on the recommendation of the Personnel Committee. This termination of employment is to take effect immediately.

"In the event you wish to question this action, the Governing Board will receive you on Friday, May 10, 1968 at 6 P.M. at Intermediate School 55, 2021 Bergen Street, Brooklyn, New York.

"You will report Friday morning to Personnel, 110 Livingston Street, Brooklyn [headquarters of the Board of Education], for reassignment."

According to Mr. McCoy, the action was voted by a majority of the 19-member governing board Tuesday night. The meeting lasted four hours, he said, and some alternative courses of action were discussed. Some members wanted to wait until the end of the semester, he said, and some felt that the teachers ought to be granted a hearing.

Only one of the 19 dismissed persons is a Negro, Mr. McCoy said, and another is a Puerto Rican. He refused to identify them. The Board of Education also refused to give out the names of any of the 19.

However, a report to the governing board by Mrs. Clara Marshall, chairman of the personnel committee, had recommended the "removal" of the following:

Principal—Isidore Gordon, of Public School 137

Assistant Principals — Lawrence Greenberg of I.S. 55; Sylvia Shaefer of P.S. 178; Josephine Bernieri of P.S. 155; Joseph Lightcap Jr. of P.S. 144, and Paul Hirschfield of P.S. 137

Teachers—Theresa Galano, Richard Douglas, Daniel Goldberg, Barry Goodman, Frederick Naumann, Cliff Rosenthal and Mr. Steinberg (no first name given), of J.H.S. 271; Abraham Olener of I.S. 55; Steven Steinfeld of P.S. 155; Burt Landsman and Paul Satlow of P.S. 137 and Deborah Gelb and Mr. Bergen of P.S. 144.

In her report, Mrs. Marshall said that the governing board, in its struggle for control over school personnel, was frequently told by the Board of Education that its demands were contrary to state law.

"But we found," she said, "that the people in the street considered these laws written to protect the monied white power structure of this city."

She said that many teachers, white and black, had cooperated in the experimental program, but there existed "a small, militant group of teachers who continue to oppose this project."

May 10, 196

Frustration Is the Word For Ocean Hill

By MARTIN MAYER

THE Ocean Hill-Brownsville "demonstration unit" is a group of eight New York City public schools—two on the intermediate level and six on the elementary level—which since September has been more or less independently managed by a "unit administrator" chosen by a 19-member locally elected "governing board." Both the administrator, Rhody McCoy, and a solid majority of the board are Negro, as are about two-thirds of the pupils in the eight schools. (Most of the other pupils are Puerto Rican; about a sixth of the teachers are Negro or Puerto Rican.) To help him administer, McCoy has a standard district superintendent's staff of his own choice, plus the usual complement of principals inside the schools. The extraordinary attrition of school personnel in a neighborhood as rattled as Ocean Hill has enabled McCoy and his board to fill seven of these principalships (at least temporarily) with their own nominees—only three of whom, incidentally, are Negro.

Whatever else the Ocean Hill governing board has accomplished in seven months, it has held the loyalty of the neighborhood. On Manhattan's lower East Side, the board of a similar project has been publicly repudiated by the parent associations, which have requested the Board of Education to resume complete control over the neighborhood's schools. But the parents of Ocean Hill staged an effective boycott the two days before Easter vacation to demand that the Board of Education turn over to their governing board complete authority over the eight schools. And in seeking to dismiss from the unit the sole surviving regularly appointed principal, plus five assistant principals and 13 teachers — as they did on the day this article went to press — the governing board spoke the hearts, if perhaps not the minds, of the Ocean Hill community. The attempted dismissals have created an angry confrontation on the previously rather abstract issue of decentralization of the school system, and the outcome is still uncertain.

McCoy has his offices in a pair of apartments on the first floor of a new middle-income high-rise development still in process of construction on Atlantic Avenue. Unusual things are supposed to happen here, and sometimes they do. The other day, in the dining ell of the living room that serves the project as general office and reception area, about 15 ladies sat around an old conference table and listened while a consultant and saleslady for a publisher told them how to use, and why to buy, a set of new remedial reading texts.

All the Negro ladies were clustered around the far end of the table, and all the white ladies were at the near end of the table. At 11:30, the ladies at the front, who were teachers, left to go back to their schools; but the seven Negro ladies at the rear remained. They were "paraprofessional" aides, housewives who live in the neighborhood and have children in the schools, and this session was part of the training program which puts them in classrooms for half a week and in instructional sessions for the other half, preparing them for permanent appointments as teacher assistants. Their schedule called for them to remain at the office until noon.

McCOY, a short, squared-off man with a light tan complexion and a sandy mustache, who speaks softly around a thick-stemmed pipe that is a virtually permanent part of his physiognomy, emerged from his private office—the tiny middle-income-apartment bedroom—to talk things over with his neighborhood ladies. They had various concerns, some very practical and immediate, like the fact that after five weeks of

working as trainees they had not yet received their first pay checks.

Mostly, however, they were troubled by questions about their function and the function of their training, which to date had been almost entirely inspirational rather than practical. The practical work was to be done in Manhattan, at P.S. 148 in the middle West Side, a "600 school" for children with severe behavior problems, where McCoy, a product of Howard University in Washington, with a graduate degree from New York University, was acting principal before he received the call to Ocean Hill. McCoy explained that the P.S. 148 staff was already working with 10 parents from the demonstration unit and could not handle more than 10 at a time, and he was not going to bring them back to Brooklyn until the P.S. 148 people certified that they were ready to come.

"We want to be reasonably sure," McCoy said, "that when we turn this group into the classroom it will be effective —we want you parents to have the skills you need to work with children. We're working on the teachers, too —they worry about parents coming in with skills they don't have."

One of the mothers volunteered that she felt she was useful in the classroom right now: "We do pretty well without special skills," she said, "having went to New York schools ourselves."

Another of the paraprofessionals was puzzled: "She's the *teacher*. What do you mean she doesn't have the skills?"

McCoy nodded. "Well, an academic teacher may not be a reading specialist," he said. "You *will* have skills they don't have. And a teacher has a youngster who says 'street' without the final 't.' Well, the teacher just thinks, 'That's the way they talk in this culture.' You'll know he has a problem with final sounds, and when the teacher sends the kid to you, you'll work on final sounds. . . ."

FUTURE historians will have no difficulty dating precisely the moment of decision that

the New York schools could not be significantly integrated. It happened on the Sunday after Labor Day in 1966, when the president of the Board of Education, at the insistence of Mayor Lindsay and without consulting his board, announced that the new Intermediate School 201, on 125th Street, would not open that Monday with the rest of the city's schools, for fear of violent demonstrations by black militants.

This traumatic episode climaxed a year of mounting conflict between the school system and a fraction of the Harlem community, which resented the construction of this windowless fortress of a school on a site more than a mile from any significant English-speaking white community, guaranteeing a pupil population virtually 100 per cent Negro and Puerto Rican. Conscious of support from a quiet but large (probably majority) fraction of Harlem, which wanted new schools near home more than it wanted school integration, the board had brushed off the protestors with soothing words—including what looked like a pledge to bring white students to the school from other parts of the city. When this pledge was dishonored, as it had to be, the militants exploded.

IN what seemed to be a spasm reaction, the protestors announced that if this was to be a Negro school, they wanted a Negro principal, and they wanted a say in what the school would teach. This was a demand which parents who disliked busing their children could support; and after the board refused it, Mayor Lindsay's people in Harlem told him there would be trouble when the school opened. It turned out, however, that the militants' support in the community was far less than the Mayor's spies had claimed—the school opened a week late, and half the parents sent their children through a threatening CORE picket line marching to enforce a boycott. But something had to be done to get everybody (including the

Mayor) out of the situation—and from the groves of academe a call arose for "community control" of the ghetto schools.

For some months the Mayor, the board and assorted professors struggled to give meaning to this phrase, to define the functions of the "community council" proposed to supervise the work of I.S. 201 and the elementary schools which feed into it. Leading Harlem political figures, after investigating the situation, refused to touch the question; McGeorge Bundy, recently arrived in town as president of the Ford Foundation and eager for involvement in racial questions, considered undertaking the conciliation of the battling groups, then yielded to better advice and backed away.

But the I.S. 201 crisis had triggered a widespread, if previously latent, sense of the need for the "decentralization" of what Superintendent Bernard Donovan recently described as the city's "monstrous and overbearing" school system.

New York City has roughly 1,100,000 children in its public schools, almost 900 schools and about 60,000 teachers and other instructional personnel to man them. Such a system is obviously too large to run from a single center, and indeed the Board of Education is divided administratively into 30 districts, each headed by an "assistant field superintendent." But virtually all moneys are allocated directly from the central office; all personnel are assigned to specific jobs from the central office and their working conditions are held uniform under terms of a citywide union contract; all attendance zones are drawn centrally, and a single curriculum is mandated on all schools, regardless of whether it seems to be producing results. Parents and teachers perceive this monolith as the property of neither the public nor the profession, but of "the system" itself; and everybody who wants to get anything done treks down to 110 Livingston Street in Brooklyn, where the system has its lair.

Decentralization of the de-cision-making processes in the city's schools, to bring education within the range of possible influence by the people who send their children and the teachers who work in the buildings, became in 1966-67 a slogan of great political appeal. Among those adopting it was a group of black militants and white radicals who appointed themselves a "People's Board of Education" and advertised their existence by sitting in the big swivel chairs of the members of the board for an uproarious 24 hours before the police cleared the room. This People's Board encouraged the formation of little people's boards to compete with the powerless but official local advisory boards in each of the system's 30 districts.

Formation of a people's board for Ocean Hill-Brownsville was part of this movement, but it was more soundly based, and its administrative grievance was more uncomfortable for the Board of Education. Although this depressed area made up about one-third of District 17, there was in the fall of 1966 nobody from Ocean Hill-Brownsville on the existing local advisory board for the district. While officially denying that anything of the sort was in the works, the Board of Education began negotiating with the leaders of the unofficial People's Board with the idea of giving them a district of their own and some unspecified functions in its management. Meanwhile, the Board of Education was also negotiating with the chairmen of its local advisory boards to increase their influence by increasing the authority of the system's district superintendents—on terms that would require the superintendents to consult with the local boards before exercising authority.

A NEW element was introduced into this confused situation when the Lindsay administration proposed to the State Legislature a new gimmick to gain additional financial aid for the city's schools. This aid is calculated on the assessed valuation of the real estate within the school district. When New York City is taken as a whole, the value of its real estate makes it eligible for only the state's minimum per-pupil grant. But if the five counties are considered separately, the low values of real estate in the dormitory counties of Queens, Richmond and the Bronx produce extra state aid of more than $100-million a year.

The Legislature did not react kindly to the idea of appropriating additional state aid for New York City alone, and at one point threatened to insist that the city's school system be broken into five borough systems if state aid was to be given on that basis. Dissuaded from this course, the Legislature made new aid contingent on some alternative plan to decentralize the city's schools, to be submitted in time for the current session —and by the Mayor, not the Board of Education. The Mayor appointed a distinguished committee to produce such a plan, and McGeorge Bundy consented to chair it. The result was the Bundy Report, published last November, proposing the fragmentation of the school system into 30 to 60 almost autonomous districts, each to be run by a board of 11 local residents, six of whom would be elected (through an indirect process) by the parents of the district's school children.

Bundy's staff at the Ford Foundation, having kept in touch with the I.S. 201 situation, had come up with some ideas for "community control" which the foundation was prepared to finance. When the Board of Education reached agreement with its local advisory boards on a minimum (but not trivial) decentralization plan, which was adopted last May, a loophole was left for alternative experiments along the lines Ford was developing. In June, as the Bundy committee got to work on the over-all decentralization question, Ford announced that "demonstration units" of decentralized school administration, dominated by the local community, would be established in four small areas of the city with the help of $163,000 from the foundation.

One of the four units was to command I.S. 201 and its feeder schools; one was in the Two Bridges area on the lower East Side, where a Yeshiva University school project and Mobilization for Youth had presumably prepared the community (this is the unit where the parents' associations have repudiated their board); one was around Joan of Arc Junior High School in the marginally integrated middle West Side, and one was Ocean Hill-Brownsville. The ground work already done by the people's board there made it possible to organize quickly in Ocean Hill-Brownsville (the Joan of Arc unit has not been organized yet and the I.S. 201 unit was unable to agree on an administrator until late March). When the term began last September, the schools in Ocean Hill-Brownsville were under orders to report not to their district superintendent but to Rhody McCoy as unit administrator.

JURIDICALLY, the Ocean Hill-Brownsville unit is in an odd limbo. Except for $250 recently allocated by the Board of Education (with a stern and detailed prescription of how to account for its expenditure), the unit has no funds of its own. Anything it wishes to purchase must be funneled through the board's normal processes — which means, for example, that McCoy had to wait several months before he got authorization to have a telephone installed in his office, and that the Lord alone knows when some 10,000 new library books will actually be delivered.

The tables of organization for the unit's schools are set at Board of Education headquarters and may not be changed — though the new scheme of two teachers for each first-grade classroom is not working any better in Brownsville than it is elsewhere in the city ("It's like two women in a kitchen," a teacher said disgustedly the other day). McCoy cannot

HOUSEWIFE HELP—Master teacher Eva McEachern, left in striped blouse, briefs a group of teacher assistants selected to work in Ocean Hill-Brownsville classrooms.

shift any of these underemployed and unhappy teachers to other duty. The citywide union contract controls all assignment of instructional personnel in the unit and severely limits the possibilities for in-service training of teachers. Mary Alice Riddle, an alert young (white) former first-grade teacher whom McCoy chose as his co-ordinator of Early Childhood Education, has so far managed to set up a single half-day "workshop" for each of the 175 teachers in the unit's primary grades —"though our No. 1 need," she says, "is brainwashing sessions, to give our teachers the belief that these children are worth teaching and can learn."

One substantial special power granted to McCoy is the right to recommend for the principals' jobs men who have not achieved the normally required standing on the competitive examination for such positions mandated by state law. Superintendent Donovan and the Board of Education must approve and actually appoint the new principals, but they have in fact done so for all but one of the recommendations.

This new power, however, may turn out to be illusory: in response to a suit brought by the association of the school system's supervisors, a trial court has declared the special appointments illegal (and most lawyers who have looked at the case find it hard

to see how any court could rule otherwise, though the case is now on appeal and you never can tell). Moreover, the Board of Education has told the new Ocean Hill-Brownsville governing board that, even if the case is won, it intends to give the new principals tests similar to those it now administers, and to confirm only those who pass the tests.

THE problems McCoy and his board and his principals must meet with their limited authority are a summation of the condition of the urban poor. Though there are decent blocks of single-family housing in the area, most of it is a collection of tenements once described by Alfred Kazin, who was born in Brownsville, as "New York's rawest, remotest, cheapest ghetto." Most of the housing is more than 60 years old, put up during the unbelievable five years 1899-1904, when, according to Moses Rischin in his book "The Promised City," the population of Brownsville rose from 10,000 to 60,000, and 1,000 immigrants a month came off the boat to work in its sweatshops. Most of the school buildings date back to those days, too, and to say that they have not been well-maintained would be an understatement.

Nor have the schools changed much, as schools, from Kazin's time. "It was never learning I associated

with [my] school," he wrote in "A Walker in the City" in 1951; "only the necessity to succeed, to get ahead of the others in the daily struggle, to 'make a good impression' on our teachers, who grimly, wearily, and often with ill-concealed distaste watched against our relapsing into the natural savagery they expected of Brownsville boys. . . . My belief in teachers' unlimited wisdom and power rested not so much on what I saw in them—how impatient most of them looked, how wary—but on our abysmal humility. . . . You made the 'good impression' by sitting firmly at your wooden desk, hands clasped; by silence for the greatest part of the livelong day; by standing up obsequiously when it was so expected of you; by sitting down noiselessly when you had answered a question; by 'speaking nicely,' which meant reproducing their painfully exact enunciation; by 'showing manners,' or an ecstatic submissiveness in all things."

THE atmosphere has loosened just a little in 40-odd years; there are in most buildings tables and chairs instead of desks; more work is needed to maintain order; and the

teachers' enunciation is no longer exact—any speech is now acceptable except the slurred sounds of the black South or the singsong of a Spanish accent. Otherwise, Kazin's description is still serviceable for the Brownsville elementary schools.

These schools are a failure by any known measurement. Well over four-fifths of the children in McCoy's unit read below grade level, most of them well below; and something like a quarter of the junior-high population is essentially illiterate. Both teachers and children are unhappily bewildered, then stoical, about the inability of the usual teaching process to show results. It is hard to get teachers to work in Ocean Hill-Brownsville at all—about half the staff are substitutes; half the regularly licensed teachers have less than two years' experience; there are several vacant positions in each school, and the daily absentee rate among teachers is about 10 per cent.

Efforts to remedy the failures of the schools are further crippled by the almost unbelievable transiency of the students. Lou Fuentes, the new principal of P.S. 155 and

CONFERENCE—Administrator Rhody McCoy, left, talks with governing board members Agnes Hanson and Hattie Bishop and community liaison director Walter Lynch. Few give him more than an outside chance of success in helping "the 9,000 unlucky children in his area."

the city's only Puerto Rican to hold such a position, came to the unit from Farmingdale, L.I., where he had been a reading consultant (his background, incidentally, includes a term as principal of a white school in Georgia, where he was easily accepted, despite his tan skin, as some kind of foreigner). In Farmingdale, Fuentes had become a convert to the Initial Teaching Alphabet system of teaching reading to beginners, but he feels he can't introduce it in P.S. 155 because the children move in and out too fast—of the 1,100 in the school in September, fewer than 500 will still be there in June. New arrivals will have taken the place of the other 600.

What, after all, can a local governing board and a unit administrator and a handful of specially chosen principals do to cure pathologies like these? "Go see for yourself," said Rhody McCoy.

I.S. 55 is the showplace school, a brand-new building which opened Feb. 5 with 1,450 students and a staff of 103. "The eyes of New York and the entire nation are on *this* school and *this* community," said a Special Notice mimeographed and broadcast through the community on the occasion of the opening. ". . . Let it be known that we will raise our children to cherish I.S. 55 and make it grow as a symbol of what people can do when given a chance . . . THIS SCHOOL AND ITS COMMUNITY IS NOW A PART OF HISTORY. THE RECORDS MUST SHOW IT AS A POSITIVE CONTRIBUTION."

Designed long before anybody was talking of community involvement, I.S. 55 is a square, brown, brick fortress with crenelated walls. It has no obvious main entrance—its dark-brown steel doors blend into the walls—and its windows are hidden in the recesses of the crenelation, behind dark-brown metal grids. It seems admirably designed for defense: one feels looking at it that a handful of teachers armed only with a few pots of boiling oil could hold off the neighborhood indefinitely.

THE atmosphere inside matches the architectural impression, for this is a building where everybody — administration, teachers, children—is terrified of disorder. Seven to nine staff members are on hall patrol duty during every class period. Even when the halls are relatively empty, children are expected to stay on the right side of the permanent line down the middle, and to turn square corners. As anything left in a locker is stolen almost immediately, the children keep their coats and books with them at all times; but anyone who actually *wears* a coat in the halls is sent to a guidance counselor, possibly home for the day. Further problems are created by faulty acoustical planning which gave the classrooms hard-surfaced, ridged ceilings. The resulting extraordinary resonance blurs even precise speech and amplifies that screaming of teachers and children which gives junior high schools their characteristic zoo-like roar.

The school conducts grades 5 through 8 under the system's new 4-4-4 plan. Such organization supposedly permits individualization of instruction by mixing classes differently for English and math, creating small groups and forming teams of teachers. Every class has a daily period of Basic Skills — "to make sure they get spelling and writing," says principal Percy Jenkins, "and don't just read stories all day." The top groups in English achievement study French their last two years; most of the pupils in the school have classes in Spanish. There are 24 classes a week in "Afro-American and Puerto-Rican history and culture" to supplement the standard social-studies program. Next year Jenkins hopes to separate out "a real talent group," which will receive intensive instruction in music or art.

WITHIN the classrooms, however, it is hard to find any signs of originality. For reasons professors of education doubtless think they can explain, each lesson is to be directed toward a single pur-

pose, which the teachers dutifully write on the board. Thus, in a seventh-grade basic-skills class: "Aim: to gain an understanding of what America was like in 1492"—and underneath it four words, "unknown, nomads, united, primitive," each to be used in a sentence and defined. ("The tomb of the unknown soldier is in Washington.")

A teacher in a science class is performing for the students the classic experiment about saliva and starch, adding to the test tube without explanation "a substance we call Benedict solution, and when we add heat, if there's a little sugar, that solution is gonna turn green . . ." On the board the children can read "Aim: What happens to food in the mouth?" In the African-culture class the teacher is playing a Miriam Makeba record with a pure 19th-century European instrumental background, and has dutifully written on the board, "Aim: to improve our understanding of African music." In an eighth-grade English class the visitor is greeted with the announcement: "Are you the gentleman from The Times? This is a very bad class . . ." The teacher says to the class, "Everybody copy," and writes on the board, "Aim: we will talk about foods and dishes typical of different nationalities." Then she explains to the class, "Typical means certain people eat foods typical of what they eat in different countries . . ." The resonant room hums with conversations. "I can't believe," the teacher says sharply, "that some people can find so much to talk about when there's nothing to talk about."

On other days, the visitor goes on to some of the elementary schools. In one he finds a sixth-grade class working in third-grade readers of the green-grass-grows-in-my-yard variety. "At first," says their businesslike Negro teacher, "they objected, and said they'd already had this material. I told them they needed something in which they could make progress. But, of course, their attention span is so limited . . ."

In another school, by con-

trast, second-graders were getting reading instruction from pamphlet materials difficult enough to challenge third-graders. The visitor, pleased and impressed, sat down with one child and asked her to read from her book; and neither she nor any of the other children who clustered around could come anywhere near reading it. The school's principal was distressed; the teacher, who was not responsible for this material (it had been introduced by another teacher who had taken over the class during the regular teacher's daily "planning period"), paid no attention except to ask whether the visitor was being disturbed by the children who were crowding around.

When the visitor returned to McCoy's office a few days later, he said he thought things looked pretty bad.

McCoy said, "You mean the buildings . . ."

"No."

McCoy took his pipe out of his mouth and dropped his hands to the mass of papers on his desk. "Truthfully," he said, "I feel I can make changes. I'm a damned good educator and administrator. But everywhere I've ever been before, after a few months I've been able to show a success model. Here I can't show a success model yet. I know it. And it's killing me."

ACCORDING to observers at Harlem's I.S. 201 (among them several Negro teachers who left that unit in February to come to Ocean Hill-Brownsville), the antics of a publicity-hungry governing board without professional guidance have in fact made some bad schools even worse. At Ocean Hill-Brownsville, 70 or 80 teachers have quit, as have the 18 assistant principals in the schools for which McCoy imported new principals. (The Board of Education replaced the assistant principals from existing lists without consulting McCoy or his governing board, and they are now trying to fire three of the new men.) Yet it seems unlikely that McCoy has lost many people he really wanted to keep. What is wrong with the Ocean Hill-Brownsville unit

today is not, as has been charged, that black power fanatics have run down eight nice schools of the Board of Education, but that McCoy and his governing board have been unable to make significant changes in the way the schools work. They are no worse than they were; but, except perhaps in surface discipline, they are no better, either.

IT is not for lack of effort. McCoy, who lives in Roosevelt, L. I., arrives at his office every morning at 7:30; until recently all the principals met with him there at that hour every day. (Now there are only two preschool meetings a week, on the grounds that even a dedicated man does best if he isn't groggy from fatigue.) Most nights of the week McCoy has meetings of some sort—with his governing board, with parent associations in the unit, with city-wide civic groups concerned about decentralization or poverty, with black education groups or with "one of the kangaroo courts that's already trying to evaluate us." Consultants of all kinds come from universities, from publishing companies, from Government agencies, from Ford. McCoy meets with them, involves his principals and to the greatest possible degree involves his teachers — he desperately wants the teachers to choose for themselves the materials they will use and the programs they will teach. But very little happens.

"I have a few things going," McCoy said the other day. "There are the paraprofessionals. At I. S. 55 I have two college kids, one of them from Pratt, one with three years at Middlebury; both have backgrounds like these kids, and they're trying to teach them self-discipline—if kids take a teacher's room apart, I'll never be able to find out whether the teacher's any good or not.

"I have to do three things. I have to create an atmosphere where a teacher can work. I have to select those teachers who need exceptional help, and select the master teachers to help them. (We're going to tape outstanding

lessons by outstanding teachers, and make them available to other teachers.) Then I have to get rid of those teachers who don't work out. If I create an atmosphere of professionalism, and I give the teachers freedom, I can expect performance."

EVENTUALLY, McCoy envisages a system of teaching teams, with master teachers, licensed teachers and paraprofessionals working together. Some master teachers would have primary responsibility for subject matter, some would have primary responsibility for the over-all adjustment and performance of a group of children. McCoy is eager to introduce new programs (several phonics programs are already in use in classrooms where teachers volunteered to try them; Robert Davis's imaginative Madison Project mathematics is being taught to paraprofessionals in the hope that they will then carry it into classrooms, and Lou Fuentes has been encouraged to set up classes in first and second grade which will teach children to read Spanish before they even begin to study English).

But the heart of the future McCoy projects for his schools is the restructuring of the teaching job. The notion of specially recognized (and rewarded) master teachers has been anathema to the profession for years; presumably the United Federation of Teachers would have to approve.

McCoy grunted. "We meet with the U.F.T.," he said coldly, "once a month."

Of the many tragedies in Ocean Hill-Brownsville, none is so grim as the mutual antagonism of the teachers' union and the demonstration unit. Its roots, of course, are deep in the failure of the children, for which the teachers wish to blame the community and the community wishes to blame the teachers. (These attitudes, incidentally, are entirely independent of the skin color of the teacher.) In theory, decentralization offered a chance to shift attention from who's-at-fault to what-can-we-do-together. In-

stead, tensions in the unit have heightened the teachers' hostility to the children and their parents, and the community leaders' feeling that the teachers are racists.

The U.F.T. helped to draw up the original proposal for the unit and demanded and received a representation of eight teachers and one union delegate on the governing board. But when the time came to elect permanent teacher representatives, the union refused to participate; the best that could be done was the calling of a rump meeting of a handful of teachers supporting the unit, at which four "provisional members" of the board were chosen.

BY the first law of practical politics—that the weaker party is always at fault when something goes wrong — responsibility for the collapse of what once seemed a promising relationship must be placed upon the governing board and McCoy.

The first serious error was the board's nomination of Herman Ferguson to be principal of the new I.S. 55. This created considerable adverse comment in the press, because Ferguson was one of a group of black militants indicted on a charge of conspiracy to kill Roy Wilkins and Whitney Young. To the union, however, Ferguson was even worse than a suspect in a murder plot—he was a known saboteur of the union's cherished More Effective Schools program. As assistant principal of P.S. 40 in Queens, which according to the statistics was the most successful of the union-sponsored M. E. S. schools, he had denounced its principal, Harold Baron, for "practicing genocide on black children" and had stimulated a noisy CORE protest at the school. Because the children were in fact doing well, the all-Negro parent community was horrified by the protest and the N.A.A.C.P. promptly organized a much larger counterprotest. Ferguson's name was therefore mud with many people, especially with the union, and his nomination by the govern-

ing board was deliberate and senseless provocation.

The labor dispute that marked the beginning of the school year provided an opportunity to mend fences. The union leadership was uncertain how successful the strike would be in the face of the effort to break it by the Board of Education and the Mayor, and over the weekend before it began, U.F.T. officials offered the Ocean Hill-Brownsville governing board the union's support — at school headquarters, in the Central Trades and Labor Council and in Albany—in return for a gesture of support for the strike.

It was asking more sophistication than the governing board could supply. As the Rev. C. Herbert Oliver, chairman of the board, said the other day. "We felt we could not bargain with our children." This governing board denounced the strike and—from the union's point of view —sought to keep the schools open with scabs.

Whatever the political realities, however, anyone who actually visits the classrooms must sympathize first with the parents, who feel that too many teachers are just not teaching their children. The attitudes of many teachers, white and Negro, are contemptuous and punitive.

An unusually public and unforgivable example of some teachers' hard-heartedness came the last week in March, when a fire at 2:30 in the afternoon emptied I.S. 55 (and revealed something of the deficiencies of its ventilating system, as smoke from the one room actually blazing belched from the ducts into all the corridors). At 3 o'clock, out on the street, a few teachers simply turned over the keys to their rooms to their children, went over to their cars and drove away. Others dumped children's possessions in piles in the auditorium. In the bedlam which followed the reopening of the building, fights broke out among students, and a number of coats were stolen.

Principal Jenkins says that 80 per cent of his staff behaved "magnificently," but the other 20 per cent are still there. It was in response to this situation that the parents' associations of I.S. 55 and J.S. 271 staged their boycott on April 10, to demand full power—meaning the power to fire teachers — for the governing board.

MUCH as he sympathizes with the feelings of the community, McCoy is committed to the proposition that when the new leadership takes hold, the teachers' performance will improve. "My principals have to *solidify* the staff," he says, "so we won't have a mass turnover in September and have to start all over again." Yet, lacking a success model, there may be limits to how long McCoy can hold the unit on a constructive course.

One faction of the board, led by Father John Powis, a young Catholic priest who feels that "the oppression has got even worse this year," already wants to close down the governing board and turn the schools back to the district superintendent. When the time comes for this proposition to be discussed seriously, the governing board will probably find its hands tied by its human commitments to the unit staff and principals who gave up secure positions elsewhere to come to Ocean Hill-Brownsville. But McCoy, who has dominated the unit as a good administrator always dominates a school system, may find his leadership potential severely restricted by the politics of the neighborhood.

IN that event, McCoy's troubles are likely to be compounded by his feeling that because he is black and because he cares, he expresses in his person the will of the community. "I listen to the community," he says, "and I translate its wishes into programs. And it's part of my top-drawer operation here that I always have an alternative program to offer the board. I came here with years of experience in my hands, with 16 or 18 programs to try. The board understands that."

Mr. Oliver is not quite so sure. "Some members," he said cautiously the other day, "feel that they ought to know more about what's going to be brought to the board. All the principals so far have been McCoy's recommendations. There's a growing concern on the board — people want more consultation before candidates are brought to the board officially. He's often said, 'I don't know how to work with this board.' We're both learning."

On the subject of authority over the budget, the board and McCoy have worked out a charming contingency plan: "If the board gets the money," Mr. Oliver explains, "McCoy can't spend it; and if he gets the money, the board can't interfere. Of course, we haven't received anything yet."

The governing board feels itself abandoned by the Ford Foundation (which had once unwisely spoken of a possible $300,000 for paraprofessional training), rejected by the U.F.T. and despised by the Board of Education. ("If the board doesn't recognize us," says Mr. Oliver, "why should the teachers pay attention?") Nonetheless, the project enjoys considerable goodwill in all these institutions, and in the press: incidents which would be treated as sin if they occurred at I.S. 201 are dealt with as aberrations or ignored in Ocean Hill - Brownsville. And Ford will soon give McCoy another $275,000, through the Institute of Community Studies, to work on instructional programs.

KNOWING all his people's troubles with the unit, U.F.T. president Albert Shanker said recently, with some courage, "I think it's just possible that McCoy may make it." Superintendent Bernard Donovan says, "I'd like to see McCoy succeed. I've bent over backwards to assist him—but I can't go as far as I'd like because of the law." (The members of the Board of Education may be less sympathetic than Dr. Donovan, who recognizes McCoy's professionalism.) McCoy's powers, as the equivalent of a district superintendent's, are indeed considerable — but because they do not include the right to allocate budget or assign personnel, they are insufficient. They should be increased; and if the law forbids it, the law should be changed.

Giving McCoy and his board their heads will not guarantee moderation and tranquility in the unit. Behind the impassive professionalism McCoy is deeply hostile to much of American society. His administrative assistant Eduardo Braithwaite could serve as Mr. Arbuthnot in a Frank Sullivan piece entitled "The Cliché Expert Testifies on Black Power" ("Africa, man, that's the center of *everything*"). Fuentes is a Puerto-Rican separatist, who regards mastery of English as far less important to his students than mastery of Spanish — wandering around his school with him is a true venture through the looking glass, to a world where a New York principal gets annoyed with a child who answers in English when addressed in Spanish. But the important question now is not what these children think as the result of the instruction they receive, but their ability to think at all.

THERE must, of course, be grave doubts whether McCoy can make a significant difference in education in Brownsville.

The resources required to make a dent in the troubles of Ocean Hill-Brownsville are wildly beyond the capacity of the community to provide, and McCoy knows it: "They ask this community which they have degraded for X years to come up now with all the answers to urban education. Well, we can't; and don't expect it. But as long as I am here, things will be done. We won't create miracles, but things will happen, and this project will not die."

All things considered, it is an impressive and credible pledge. The debate on the decentralization of the schools this year has been discouraging in its intellectual level and obviously unproductive of political action. Emphasis has been placed consistently on those issues which most frighten the professional staff, rather than on the new opportunities for more responsible and responsive professional work.

But whatever else the Legislature may do in this session, it should give McCoy a chance to make good on his personal promise, by authorizing the Mayor or the Commissioner of Education to suspend whatever sections of the education law may need suspending to give a functioning community school board the power to carry through its administrator's ideas. No experienced observer could give McCoy and his people more than an outside chance at rescuing from ignorance and futility any substantial proportion of the 9,000 unlucky children in his area—but nobody really believes that the Board of Education as currently owned and operated can offer any chance whatever. ∎

May 19, 1968

GALAMISON NAMED WITH FOUR OTHERS TO SCHOOL BOARD

Lindsay Also Appoints First Puerto Rican Member and Negro Letter Carrier

LOCAL CONTROL IS GOAL

Enlarged Body of 13 Set Up to Give City Permanent Decentralization Plan

By M. A. FARBER

Mayor Lindsay added five members to the Board of Education yesterday, including the board's first Puerto Rican; a Negro letter carrier who is vice president of the United Parents Associations, and the Rev. Milton A. Galamison, who has led two massive school boycotts.

The board's enlargement to 13 members, mandated by the Legislature in May, moved the city school system a step closer to some form of permanent decentralization and local control by communities.

All of the new appointees are expected to share the Mayor's enthusiasm for faster, more thorough school reorganization than has been favored by the present board. Their views will be reflected in the permanent decentralization plan that the board must submit for state approval next year.

Terms to Be Staggered

Besides Mr. Galamison, a Negro who has previously urged removal of the board, Mr. Lindsay chose the following for staggered terms:

Hector Vazquez, executive director of the Puerto Rican Forum, a nonprofit organization that promotes educational and job opportunities.

William F. Haddad, a former official of the Peace Corps and the Federal Government's antipoverty program who is now chairman of the U. S. Research and Development Corporation, a management concern.

Salim L. Lewis, a philanthropist who is senior partner in Bear, Stearns & Co., investment bankers.

Ernest R. Minott, a letter carrier in the Post Office's Times Square station and former president of the Parents Association at Public School 11 at 1257 Ogden Avenue in the Bronx.

The selection of Mr. Galamison and Mr. Minott marks the first time that the board will have more than one Negro member. The only Negro on the board now is Dr. Aaron Brown, its vice president.

Mrs. Rose Shapiro, president of the nonsalaried board, said yesterday that she hoped there would be "no division and certainly no polarization on the board" as it devised a decentralization plan for consideration by the State Board of Regents and the Legislature.

"We should work together as a team to achieve the best possible educational system for all the city's children," she said.

Decentralization of the city's schools was one of the most controversial issues before the 1968 Legislature, and the bill that was finally passed was a compromise that put off final action for at least a year.

The Mayor, the Regents and Dr. James E. Allen Jr., State Commissioner of Education, supported strong reorganization bills that would have segmented the city at an early date into virtually autonomous local districts.

However, the city board and the United Federation of Teachers, while claiming devotion to decentralization, argued against those bills as being too radical.

Plan to Be Drawn

The outcome was a bill ordering the city board to prepare a detailed, permanent decentralization plan and expanding the board so that Mr. Lindsay could name advocates of speedy, broad reorganization.

The bill also authorized the city board to temporarily delegate many of its powers to the 30 existing local school boards, which now are mainly advisory. It also was understood that greater independence would be accorded the city's three school demonstration districts in East Harlem, Lower Manhattan and the Ocean Hill — Brownsville section of Brooklyn.

Mrs. Shapiro said that the board has started studying the transferral of a "substantial" portion of its authority to local boards for the coming year but

that decisions would not be reached before the new board members could vote.

A spokesman for the Mayor said that the new members would be sworn in "in the very near future." He did not know whether the oaths would be taken before the board's next public meeting on Wednesday.

The first action of the enlarged board will be the election of a president and vice president for terms ending next May. When Mrs. Shapiro and Dr. Brown were elected to these posts nearly two months ago—in a vote that Mr. Lindsay sought to delay — they promised to resign before the first public meeting of the expanded body. The next such session after Wednesday is Aug. 21.

Named to Fill Vacancy

Four of the Mayor's five appointments yesterday resulted from legislative decree this year. The fifth, Mr. Vazquez, was named to fill a vacancy created in May by the retirement of Alfred A. Giardino, who was both a member and president of the board. Mr. Vazquez will serve until 1975.

Mr. Galamison, the 45-year-old pastor of Siloam Presbyterian Church in the Bedford-Stuyvesant area of Brooklyn, led two one-day school boycotts in 1964 and a limited one last May. The two widespread boycotts in 1964 were to protest lack of school integration; the one this year was to dramatize demands for community control of schools.

In December, 1966, Mr. Galamison was among 12 persons arrested at the Board of Education headquarters, 110 Livingston Street in Brooklyn, after a three-day "occupation" of board members' meeting hall chairs. He called afterward for the board's ouster.

The minister, who said yesterday that he had been arrested nine times since 1963 in connection with school demonstrations, explained that he was joining the board because of the "opportunity for progress" in decentralization. He said he would resign if the board "does not move off dead center." His term ends June 30, 1971.

In early June Mr. Galamison signed a petition urging the Governor to veto the Legislature's decentralization bill because, the signers held, it was too weak.

Mr. Galamison asserted that the school system's basic problem was that it was "hopelessly bogged down in red tape, rigidity and bureaucracy." "Parents," he declared, "are not able to participate on a dignified level. When this is corrected a miracle will have taken place."

The minister said he did not now intend to give up directorship of the School and Community Organized for Partnership in Education, a group known as SCOPE that recently received $160,000 from the Ford Foundation "to enhance communications and cooperation among teachers, parents and other community residents and organizations." SCOPE, with offices in Mr. Galamison's church, at 260 Jefferson Avenue, has a paid staff of seven and five VISTA volunteers.

Mr. Galamison said he would "play it by ear" with regard to remaining as director but he said he did not see a conflict of interest between his keeping that position and being a board member. McGeorge Bundy, president of the Ford Foundation, was chairman last year of the Mayor's task force that recommended decentralization and the foundation financed the planning stages of the three demonstration districts that were designed to test community control.

Mr. Vazquez, who is 40 years old, was a dropout from Haaren High School who went on to graduate from the University of Miami and then earn a master's degree in economics and transportation from American University.

Directed Research

From 1957 to 1966 he was employed in the Puerto Rican Economic Development Administration office here, most recently as director of research. He assumed his current post a year ago after serving as assistant executive director of a manpower training program operated by the Puerto Rican Forum, the Urban League and Cornell University.

Mr. Haddad, 39, was graduated from Columbia University and was a reporter for The New York Post and The New York Herald Tribune before becoming associate director of the Peace Corps when it was formed in 1961. From 1964 to 1966 he was assistant director of the Government's Office of Economic Opportunity.

Last year Mr. Haddad was co-chairman with Percy E. Sutton, Borough President of Manhattan, of a group that fought removal of the State Constitution's ban on aid to church-related schols. The group was known as the Committee for Public Education and Liberty. In June, Mr. Haddad announced plans to start a weekly Manhattan newspaper with Roy Innis, associate director of the Congress of Racial Equality. His term expires in 1970.

Mr. Lewis, 59, will serve until June 30, 1972. He was formerly president of the Federation of Jewish Philanthropies, and of the Associated Young Men's and Young Women's Hebrew Associations of Greater New York. The Boston University graduate, who has been a trustee of Montefiore Hospital and the hospital for joint Diseases, has also served on the board of the Greater New York Fund.

Mr. Minott, 49, graduated from Haaren High School in 1938 and has worked for the Post Office for 20 years. He is chairman of the United Parents Associations executive committee and has served on the steering committee of the Board of Education's Bureau of Community Education, which oversees after-school and vacation programs. His term runs until next June 30.

Two of Mr. Minott's children graduated from William Howard Taft High School and a third will enter junior high school in the Bronx in September. Mr. Galamison's only child, Milton Jr., attended private school here before his present matriculation at Wesleyan University in Middletown, Conn.

Mr. Haddad has two preschool age daughters and a 6-year-old daughter who attends the Bank Street College of Education laboratory school in Manhattan. Mr. Vazquez has a 2-year-old daughter. Mr. Lewis's three sons and a daughter attended private schools, although the daughter went to public school here for a brief period.

Mr. Lindsay chose the new board members from a list developed by an official screening panel of university presidents and civic and public education leaders. Before the panel acted, Mr. Lindsay added three persons, including the body's first Negro and first Puerto Rican, to it.

Current members of the Board of Education are:

Mrs. Shapiro, a former president of the United Parents Associations.
Dr. Brown, professor of education at Long Island University's Brooklyn Center.
Joseph G. Barkan, vice president of the Prudential Steamship Lines.
Thomas C. Burke, a lawyer.
Lloyd K. Garrison, a lawyer.
Morris Iushewitz, secretary of the Central Labor Council.
John H. Lotz, vice president of Group Health Insurance.
Clarence Senior, professor of sociology at Brooklyn College.

July 15, 1968

BOARD APPROVES PLAN FOR SCHOOLS AS STRIKE LOOMS

33 Community Units to Get Authority Over Operation of Their Districts

SHANKER FOR WALKOUT

McCoy Hires 350 to Insure Opening of Classes in His Ocean Hill Section

By LEONARD BUDER

The Board of Education adopted a citywide school decentralization plan last night that would transfer substantial operating powers from central headquarters to the 30 regular and three experimental local school boards.

The board's action came at an uproarious four-minute public meeting a few hours after Albert Shanker, president of the United Federation of Teachers, said that he would recommend a strike by city teachers when the new school year begins next Monday.

Mr. Shanker said he would propose the walkout—which would violate the state law prohibiting strikes by public employes—because of the refusal of the local governing board of the Ocean Hill-Brownsville demonstration district in Brooklyn to reinstate 10 teachers "ousted" last spring. The district is one of the three created last year as experiments in community control.

2 Disputes Involved

With the start of the new school term fast approaching, the city board has been trying to resolve two bitter and partly related controversies — the clash in Ocean Hill-Brownsville and the broader dispute over the systemwide decentralization plan.

The Board of Education's decentralization plan, a modification of tentative proposals announced two weeks ago, would take effect as soon as it is approved by the State Board of Regents. The plan is intended as a short-range measure pending adoption of a more thorough reorganization later in the year. In an effort to mollify some critics of the tentative proposals, the board added a provision requiring local boards to carry out their new powers with advance consultation with parents and parent groups, members of the teaching and supervisory staffs and their organizations, and other community groups.

Local school boards would also be given authority to recommend the creation of new types of school licenses and positions to give them greater flexibility in staffing schools. Another new provision would allow two districts, by agreement, to transfer teachers between them without getting central approval.

The plan also specified that the local boards must give teachers charged in disciplinary proceedings the same rights they now have under the law, including the right of appeal to the central board.

Major features retained from the tentative proposals would give local boards the power to do the following:

¶Replace their present district superintendents.
¶Recruit and hire teachers who pass a required examination.
¶Discipline and dismiss teachers according to law.
¶Modify and add to the curriculum.
¶Select textbooks and prepare budget requests.
¶Manage school expenditures.

At a stormy 12-hour meeting last Wednesday, which ended in an uproar, the tentative proposals were generally denounced by those who charged that it either went too far or did not go far enough.

About 300 people showed up for last night's special meeting of the board. Most of them were advocates of total community control of local schools, and they made obvious their displeasure with the decentralization plan.

The meeting started shortly after 8 o'clock. Harold Siegel, the board secretary, read off the numerical designations of the four items on the calendar. Then Mrs. Rose Shapiro, the board president, asked, "All in favor? Any opposed?"

The actual vote—seven in favor of the plan, one opposed and one abstention — was drowned out by the din of the audience. Mrs. Shapiro then adjourned the meeting and the members quickly left through a side door as the spectators shouted: "This is illegal."

"What the hell's going on?" "Disgrace!" "Shame!"

Many were unaware that the meeting had been held and ended. "There's been no public meeting today," a man shouted.

During the uproar, a man called to spectators, "What right have you got to run the schools?"

Galamison Votes No

The lone negative vote was cast by the Rev. Milton A. Galamison, an advocate of total community control. He later told newsmen that he voted against the plan because "powers should not be delegated to local boards unless they are elected by the people" and the city board "did not give all that it could have given under the law."

At present only the boards of the three demonstration districts have been elected. The others were appointed by the central board. However, the city board has said that its future comprehensive plan would provide for the election of all boards.

William F. Haddad, another strong proponent of community control, said he had voted for the plan as "a first step." Others who voted in favor were Joseph G. Barkan, Dr. Aaron Brown, John H. Litz, Ernest R. Minott, Hector I. Vazquez, and Mrs. Shapiro. Morris Iushewitz abstained and two members, Lloyd K. Garrison, and Salim L. Lewis, were absent.

Mrs. Shapiro told newsmen that no public discussion had been permitted at the meeting because the board had already held a public hearing on the plan.

"We cannot hold meetings and do business when there are constant interruptions," she added.

One person was taken out of the meeting hall by police on the complaint of a woman spectator and given a summons for harassment. He was identified as John Duda, a 52-year-old custodian at P. S. 146 in Brooklyn. The woman who filed the complaint was Mrs. Cleotha Silvers of 764 Trinity Ave., Bronx.

3 Hear Complaints

After the brief meeting, most of the spectators, still angry, remained in the meeting hall. Three members — Mr. Galamison, Mr. Haddad and Mr. Vazquez—returned and listened to their complaints. After an hour the audience dispersed quietly.

Earlier in the day, Mr. Shanker told a boisterous meeting of union chapter chairmen: "It's a hell of a lot better to start fighting for things you believe in than start crawling."

"Rhody McCoy is striking against the community," he said, referring to the administrator of the Brooklyn demonstration district. "He has ruined a school system."

The chapter chairmen cheered his word.

The recommendation to strike

289

will be submitted — unless the situation changes dramatically — to a special meeting tomorrow of the union's delegate assembly and to a mass meeting of teachers Sunday.

Board of Education officials, however, were still hopeful that the controversy would be resolved in time to head off what could be a crippling disruption of the school system of a million pupils and 60,000 teachers.

A teachers' walkout last fall, called to press demands for higher salaries and other contract improvements, virtually shut the system for the first three weeks of the 1967-68 school year.

Shortly before Mr. Shanker convened the meeting of chapter chairman, Mr. McCoy announced through a spokesman:

"As o fthis afternoon, I have hired more than 350 new teachers to replace those who might strike. Applicants are still coming in.

"The schools of Ocean Hill-Brownsville will open Monday, strike or no strike, with a full staff and every classroom covered."

On Tuesday Mr. McCoy had asked the central Board of Education to approve the transfer out of the district of about 200 teachers who had taken part in a walkout last spring to protest the local governing board's refusal to reinstate the 10 ousted teachers, who were all used of being incompetent or trying to sabotage the demonstration project.

A total of 350 union teachers, most of them white, had taken part in that walkout, which crippled the demonstration district's eight schools for the last six weeks of the spring term. Since then 120 teachers have been transferred to other district at their request. The remaining 30 teachers have been told by governing board that they can return to their school posts.

The spokesman for Mr. McCoy said that the district actually had more new teachers than it needed. He said that the applicants were coming in "from all over the city."

During the day, members of the Board of Education worked on two fronts to try to ease the latest crisis to confront the school system.

While some members devoted themselves to work on the citywide decentralization plan, others tried to resolve the Ocean Hill-Brownsville controversy.

The board had expected to have the decentralization plan ready by midday but ran into snags. The actual document was not released until shortly before the board's scheduled night meeting.

Some members of the board also had hoped the dispute involving the Brooklyn demonstration district could be resolved before the meeting of chapter chairmen.

At one point, the hopes for a settlement rested on a compromise proposed by the city board to guarantee "union security" to teachers in the district, but to require the 10 teachers to accept transfers to other districts. But this was apparently unacceptable to the union.

Mr. Shanker emerged from a round of conferences at central board headquarters about 4 o'clock. The 39year-old former mathematics teacher looked grim.

"I have no other choice but to recommend a complete shutdown unles there is compliance," he told newsmen, referring to a recommendation from Judge Francis E. Rivers that the 10 teachers be allowed to return to their posts in the demonstration district.

Mr. Rivers, a Negro, served as trial examiner for the 10 teachers and cleared them of charges against them by the governing board and Mr. McCoy.

Mr. Shanker arrived at the meeting of about 700 chapter chairmen at 4:37 P.M. The session, which had been called for 4 P.M., was held at the Marc Ballroom, 27 Union Square. The chairmen gave him a rousing reception but a few boos were heard.

Dan Sanders, a spokesman for the union, said that the chairmen had no power to decide on a strike. Such a decision can only be made at a general meeting. The union's officers and executive board voted to recommend a strike at their meetings last Friday.

The union's delegate assembly will meet at 4 P.M. tomorrow at the Statler Hilton Hotel. The membership vote on a strike will be held Sunday at the National Maritime Union Hall, Seventh Avenue and 13th Street, at a time be announced.

Last May the Ocean Hill-Brownsville governing board originally attempted to transfer out 13 teachers and six supervisors without bringing formal charges against them. The local board later decided to let one teacher remain.

Dr. Donovan called the local board's action illegal and ordered the teachers reinstated. The local board refused. Hundreds of parents, children and their supporters blockaded one of the schools in support of the governing board. When the blockade was ended by police action, the parents boycotted the schools for several weeks.

The 350 teachers, meanwhile, stayed away in support of their ousted colleagues.

The governing board later brought charges against 10 teachers. These cases were heard by the trial examiner. Of the other eight educators involved in the original transfer, five have since asked for new assignments. The status of the other three educators is unclear.

September 5, 196

MOST CITY SCHOOLS SHUT; SHANKER, DEFYING A WRIT, REFUSES TO END WALKOUT

BOARD HAS OFFER

Plan for Job Security Will Be Submitted to Union Today

By LEONARD BUDER

A crippling teachers' strike forced the closing of most city schools yesterday, causing more than a million pupils to miss classes.

Last night the City Corporation Counsel, acting as attorney for the Board of Education, obtained a court order restraining the teachers' union from continuing the strike pending a court hearing tomorrow.

Albert Shanker, the president of the union, said later that the strike would continue despite the order.

"I did not enjoy the 15 days I spent in jail for last year's strike and I'm sure I won't enjoy it next time, but we have a union policy, of 'no contract, no work' and we feel that our contract has been broken," he said.

Gets News at Dinner

The 39-year-old former teacher was having dinner—a bowl of chicken soup and a glass of beer—at Connolly's Restaurant at 110 East 23d Street, near union headquarters, when a newsman told him of the order.

"I can't say I'm surprised," he said. "We've been expecting it for days. But it will not make any difference. The injunction won't put any children in the classrooms."

The court papers were served on Mr. Shanker at 8:40 P.M. while he was still in the restaurant.

The show-cause order was signed at 7 P.M. by Supreme Court Justice Harry B. Frank at his home at 300 East 74th Street. It is returnable at 9:30 A.M. tomorrow before Justice Jacob Markowitz.

The court order was obtained by Assistant Corporation Counsel John J. Loflin under the provisions of the state's Taylor Law, which bars strikes by public employes.

To Make Offer Today

At 9 o'clock last night, Superintendent of Schools Bernard E. Donovan announced that the

Board of Education had worked up "a firm offer of agreement" on a number of issues dealing with job security for teachers and supervisors.

"We are concerned now with the immediate resumption of instruction in the city," he said, "but we find ourselves unable to complete the agreement because of the unavailability of the union representatives. We have therefore, reluctantly agreed to delay the discussions until 9 A.M. tomorrow [Tuesday]."

He added that schools would be open today and expressed the hope that the teachers would return. He added that district superintendents "will continue to have the right to close such schools as may be considered necessary for the health and welfare of the children concerned." Many superintendents are supporting the teachers strike.

Mr. Shanker said he was "glad the Board of Education has reached a 'firm offer of agreement.'"

However, he added: "They have not shown it to us and there is still no agreement. It takes two sides to make an agreement."

The only thing definite, he said, is that "we will meet with the Board of Education in the morning."

The developments came after a day during which Mayor Lindsay and some members of the Board of Education had said that a settlement had been reached or was near.

Union Stresses Rights

A spokesman for the United Federation of Teachers said that the issues that led to the walkout on the opening day of the new school year could be settled in "five minutes or five months."

The union has maintained that it called the strike to protect teacher job rights and "union security."

The strike was the union's second in two years and fourth in the last eight years. It was also the most effective.

The Board of Education said that 810 of the 900 public schools did not open as 53,000 of the 57,000 teachers failed to report to work. Only about 50,-000 of the 1,129,000 pupils went to school.

Most principals did not even open their schools yesterday. Those buildings that did open were generally in Negro and Puerto Rican areas where community opposition to the strike had been strongest.

In the Ocean Hill-Browns-

ville demonstration district in Brooklyn, which has become a symbol of the current school crisis, all eight schools were open and operating under a staff augmented by newly hired teachers.

An aide to Rhody A. McCoy, the district administrator, said that the situation there was "beautiful."

Supervisors Back Strike

Meanwhile the Council of Supervisory Associations, which represents most of the principals, chairmen and district superintendents in the city, urged its members not to return to work until the teachers did.

The organization had earlier told principals not to open their school buildings in event of a strike as a safety precaution for pupils and to show support for the teachers' fight for "due process." During the 1967 strike, the supervisors remained on the job.

The court order obtained last night also enjoins the supervisors' council from participating in or assisting the strike.

At one point during the day, shortly after the school board announced the virtual shutdown of the city system, Mayor Lindsay told newsmen: "There is no strike."

But an aide later explained that what Mr. Lindsay had "obviously meant" was that "there was no reason for the illegal strike called by the union."

The Mayor said yesterday, as he had on Sunday, that the main issue that led to the union's original threat to strike had been settled.

He said that the agreement by the governing board of the Ocean Hill-Brownsville district not to "resist" the return of 10 teachers that the board had ousted last May had resolved the principal issue in the crisis.

But Mr. Shanker denied that a settlement had been reached.

He said that the Mayor, who had tried to mediate the school controversy on Sunday, was acting "completely irresponsible," was "not informed of the situation" and was "making a clown of himself."

Mrs. Rose Shapiro, president of the city school board, said that the Mayor had informed her that there had been a resolution of the Ocean Hill-Brownsville issue and "that is good enough for me." She added that there were apparently other issues standing in the way of a total settlement.

Major Remaining Issue

Sources at City Hall and the Board of Education that have been close to the negotiations said that the major

unresolved issue now was the union's demand that it be granted "agency shop" status.

This would enable the union to collect what amounts to a service fee from nonunion teachers. As the designated bargaining agent for the staff, the union negotiates in behalf of all teachers. Its membership has been placed at over 50,000.

One Board of Education member said that Mr. Shanker was trying to becloud the situation because he could not hope to get public support and perhaps not teacher support for a strike over the agency shop issue.

The member added that if the union wanted to make that demand it should do so when the present two-year contract expired next September.

Mr. Shanker, however, insisted that the agency shop issue was only one of many issues that had to be resolved before the teachers would call off the strike.

The union leader asserted that at one stage of the negotiations the Board of Education had offered to give the union an agency shop "if we would sacrifice the 10 teachers, which we refused to do." He said that obtaining an agency shop would be "a major breakthrough."

"As yet the Mayor and the board have not been able to put together a package satisfactory to us," he added.

Refused to Take Back 10

Until Sunday the Ocean Hill-Brownsville governing board had refused to take back the 10 teachers and some 200 others who had stayed out of the district's schools to protest the local board's action. It had insisted that the teachers be transferred to other districts.

Some of the 10 teachers had been accused of unsatisfactory performance. Others had been charged with "sabotaging" or criticizing the district, which was set up last year as one of three experiments in community control of neighborhood.

Superintendent Donovan ordered the 10 teachers reinstated after a trial examiner had cleared them of the charges.

Mr. Shanker and others have charged that the Ocean Hill-Brownsville governing board's "illegal" action was a forerunner of what could happen elsewhere if suitable protection of the rights of teachers and the union was not written into the Board of Education's newly adopted plan to decentralize the system and transfer greater power to local school boards.

Despite the Mayor's assurance that all teachers would be

allowed to return to the embattled experimental district, the union proceeded with its strike as had been planned.

Mr. Shanker said yesterday that the "vague and indefinite wording" of statements made about the 10 teachers did not "guarantee their status." He added that all he wanted was a "very simple assurance" that the teachers would be allowed to resume the same classroom duties they performed before their ouster.

The impact of the strike was tremendous.

Many parents did not bother to send their children to school. "What's the point in seding them?" a Flatbush mother of two school-age children asked, "They didn't do anything the last time there was a strike."

Lloyd S. Mapp, education coordinator for the East New York Community Corporation, an antipoverty organization, said that parents appeared to be divided along racial lines in their reaction to the strike.

He said that in the Canarsie-East New York section of Brooklyn, where there are about 30 schools, "the white community is supporting the strike and the black community is not."

Those youngsters who did go to school often found the school doors locked.

At Central Commercial High School, 214 East 42d Street, there were no pickets — only a picket sign hanging on a gate, reading: "Contracts must be honored."

At Public School 11, 320 West 21st Street, Murray Goldberg, the principal, allowed six teachers and a secretary who were opposed to the strike to enter the building but closed the school to pupils.

A group of teachers opposed to the strike succeeded in getting the custodian to let them into Thomas Jefferson High School, Pennsylvania and Dumont Avenues in Brooklyn. Then they obtained permission from the district office to open the doors to about 100 students who had waited patiently outside for an hour.

At Brandeis High School, 145 West 84th Street, a Negro boy came up to a white teacher, Willard Smith, who is also the union chapter chairman, and said, "I hope I'm in your class again."

For defying the court restraining order during last year's strike, Mr. Shanker later served 15 days in jail and his union was fined $150,000—the equivalent of about $3 for each member. The union also lost its dues checkoff privileges for a year—a penalty imposed under the Taylor Law.

September 10, 1968

SCHOOL STRIKE IS SETTLED; SHANKER CLAIMS VICTORY; CLASSES TO START TODAY

The New York Times (by Neal Boenzi)

ANNOUNCES SETTLEMENT: Mrs. Rose Shapiro, president of Board of Education, with Dr. Bernard E. Donovan, left, Superintendent of Schools, and Albert Shanker, union president. Levity is reaction to Mrs. Shapiro's standing on chair at request of photographers.

UNIONIST IS ELATED

Says 'We Have Won' on Basic Issue of Teacher Ousters

By LEONARD BUDER

A settlement of the two-day teachers' strike here was reached yesterday, and the school system was expected to return to normal this morning.

The settlement was ratified by a heavy majority of the United Federation of Teachers early this morning, after the union's delegate assembly voted overwhelmingly to accept it at a hastily arranged meeting last evening.

The vote of the union membership was 5,515 to 218 in favor of the agreement. The voting was held from 7:30 P.M. to 1 A.M. and the results were announced at 1:02 A.M. by George J. Abrams, a supervisor for the Honest Ballot Association.

Mrs. Rose Shapiro, the president of the Board of Education, jubilantly predicted that the "educational program will go into full swing" today.

Albert Shanker, the union president, received a standing ovation when he arrived for the 6 P.M. delegates' meeting in the auditorium of Washington Irving High School, 17th Street and Irving Place.

53,000 in Walkout

"We have won on every basic issue and shown that we are the strongest organization in this fight," he told the 600 cheering delegates.

The walkout by 53,000 of the city's 57,000 teachers had paralyzed the school system on the first two days of the fall term, preventing more than a million children from attending classes.

The school crisis had been triggered by the refusal of the Ocean Hill-Brownsville governing board to reinstate 10 teachers it had ordered "transferred" last May. The Board of Education had branded the transfers as illegal.

But the controversy soon took on larger aspects with the union insisting that teachers throughout the city must receive suitable guarantees of job security, due process and other protection when the new systemwide decentralization plan goes into effect short-

ly. It also asked for guarantees of "union security."

The settlement provided for the return of the 10 teachers if they want to go back to their former schools in Ocean Hill-Brownsville. It also contained the following provisions:

¶Full salary payments to some 300 teachers who stayed out of Ocean Hill-Brownsville's eight schools for more than a month at the end of last term to protest the governing board's ouster of the 10 teachers.

¶Those of the 350 teachers Brooklyn demonstration district can do so. Those who do not want to go back will be reassigned to other districts.

¶All present agreements between the union and the Board of Education will be binding on local school boards when the new decentralization plan goes into effect.

¶Any school employe who is dismissed or disciplined by a local board can appeal to a three-member arbitration panel.

¶No transfers of teachers who are union chapter chairmen, district chairmen or executive board members will be made by local superintendents or administrators "without the prior approval of the Superintendent of Schools."

The terms specify that these provisions would take effect even if they should be deleted from the decentralization plan by the State Board of Regents. The state board must approve the plan before it can be enacted and has the power to modify the school proposals.

A delegate asked Mr. Shanker whether the union had won its demand for an agency shop, under which it could collect a service fee from non-union teachers.

The union president said it did not. He asserted that the union had been offered a "deal" where it could have an agency shop if it did not press for the return of the 10 teachers.

He added: "We turned it down." The audience cheered.

The Board of Education, in releasing the terms of the settlement, declared:

"The Board of Education believes that the Ocean Hill-Brownsville governing board will act in good faith and that their public assurance to the Mayor on Sunday will be honored.

"To the Board of Education this means that each teacher who wishes to return to his former school and to his professional assignment will not be prevented from doing so and that these actions will be carried out in good faith and without reprisal."

Mayor Is Critical

Mayor Lindsay said in a statement from City Hall: "I am

delighted that the children of New York City can now return to school."

He said that the central issue in "this unnecessary and illegal strike" had been resolved at a City Hall meeting he called on Sunday at which the governing board reluctantly agreed to permit the 10 teachers to return.

The Mayor said that it was "inexcusable" for the teachers union to have called the strike after the governing board made its concession.

After the Sunday meeting, Mr. Lindsay announced that the controversy had been settled and that the schools would be open on Monday. But Mr. Shanker and union officials insisted that no settlement had been reached and that, moreover, the other issues involving decentralization remained unresolved.

The Mayor and Mr. Shanker were frequently critical of each other. One Board of Education member, who was recently appointed by Mr. Lindsay and asked that he not be identified, said that the acrimony between the two men had helped "prolong" the strike.

Announcement of the tentative settlement yesterday came after seven hours of sometimes stormy negotiations between officials of the school system, the teachers' union and the supervisory council.

No representatives of the Ocean Hill-Brownsville governing board took part. One of the Board of Education negotiators said that the Mayor had not personally been involved in the discussions since Sunday evening.

Newsmen standing outside the meeting room on the eighth floor of the Gramercy Park Hotel, at 21st Street and Lexington Avenue, could often hear angry exchanges. But throughout the day there were persistent reports that an agreement was near.

Then at 4 P.M., Mrs. Shapiro stood on a chair so she could be seen above the crowd of newsmen and said:

"The Board of Education is pleased to announce an agreement has been reached with the United Federation of Teachers and the Council of Supervisory Associations."

The council, which represents most of the system's 4,000 principals, chairman, district superintendents and other supervisors, had supported the teachers' strike. In three previous teacher strikes, the supervisors had remained on the job.

Walter J. Degnan, president of the council, said that the supervisors had joined in the fight because of their concern

for "law and order as opposed to anarchy."

Mrs. Shapiro expressed her thanks to Mayor Lindsay for bringing the disputants in the school controversy together last Sunday.

Mr. Shanker, who has sharply criticized Mr. Lindsay's role in the dispute, grinned broadly but said nothing.

Later Mr. Shanker said, "We will collaborate with the governing board [of Ocean Hill-Brownsville] and work on practical improvements to overcome the hostilities and bitterness that have become part of this conflict."

150 Were Reassigned

Of the 350 teachers who stayed off their jobs in Ocean Hill-Brownsville last spring in support of the 10 transferred teachers, some 150 have since been reassigned to schools in other districts at their request.

Referring to the 10 teachers and the remaining 200 who supported them, Rhody McCoy, the administrator of the Ocean Hill-Brownsville district, said last night: "As far as the governing board is concerned, they're able to come back."

But he added, "The city is going to have to pay for a double staff if they want them." He noted that the governing board had already hired 200 teachers to replace those who had stayed out last spring.

Both Mr. McCoy and the Rev. C. Herbert Oliver, chairman of the governing board, disavowed any knowledge of the agreement reached between the city school board and the teachers union.

"We have not had the privilege of seeing it," Mr. Oliver said. "We had nothing to do with it and have not been asked to be a part of it."

The official figures on the impact of the strike that were released yesterday by the Board of Education did not include the eight schools that are part of the Ocean Hill-Brownsville demonstration district or the five that belong to the Intermediate School 201 complex in Harlem.

The board reported that 228 of the 854 schools outside these two districts were open yesterday—128 more than on Monday—and that 4,301 teachers and 41,539 pupils came to classes. On Monday, the board said that 4,000 teachers and 50,000 pupils had shown up.

For the most part the situation was quiet, but minor incidents occurred at two schools.

Outside Public School 63 on the Lower East Side, police arrested Ralph Poynter, a 34-year-old dismissed teacher, on charges of felonious assault on

a policeman and inciting to riot.

The police said that Mr. Poynter, an outspoken advocate of community control of schools, had told a crowd of parents: "Let's charge the school." Several persons were knocked down in the melee that followed.

Mr. Poynter, wearing a motorcycle crash helmet and goggles, was a familiar figure during last spring's demonstrations outside Junior High School 271 in Ocean Hill-Brownsville. He was dismissed in June from his job at P.S. 175 in Harlem for "excessive absences."

Mr. Poynter was later arraigned before Criminal Court Judge Thomas G. Weaver. He was paroled until Oct. 10 when the charges will be heard.

In the Red Hook section of Brooklyn, a group of parents, nonstriking teachers and children forced school officials to open P. S. 27.

In the morning, the group tried to enter the building but were pushed back by the police. Some of the demonstrators called the policemen "pigs" and "racist cops," but the tense situation was averted by the decision to open the building.

Parents and teachers then conducted improvised classes for about 50 pupils.

One of the schools that was open and attempting to operate yesterday was Brandeis High School, which has its main building at 145 West 84th Street and an annex at 55 West 65th Street.

Fifty-seven of 213 teachers showed up as did 826 of 5,150 students. A policeman stood outside the main building, but there were no pickets.

Murray A. Cohn, the principal, would not discuss why he —unlike most of the city's other principals — kept his school open.

"Nothing I can say would shed any light on the situation," he remarked. "It's very complex and it may leave a great deal of unpleasantness."

Thirty-five of the nonstriking teachers said in a statement:

"We do not view this strike as a simple demand for union rights, but as a calculated effort on the part of the union leadership to destroy the concept of community control. We do not endorse the actions of Rhody McCoy or the governing board of the Ocean Hill-Brownsville district. We accept the thesis that they have acted improperly and have not accorded meaningful due process to the 10 teachers in dispute...

"This is a strike against the basic right of an educational community—parents, teachers and students — to determine educational policies. This is a

strike designed to perpetuate the essential failures of the educational system and to maintain the positions and privileges of those who control it — the supervisors, union leaders, and education bureaucrats.

The general membership vote took place in a large hiring hall in the National Maritime Union building at Seventh Avenue and 12th Street.

Mr. Shanker arrived at 8:55 P.M. and cast a "yes" ballot. Because he did not have his union card with him, he had to use a special blue-colored ballot. Members with union cards were given white ballots.

The 39-year-old union leader was surrounded by enthusiastic teachers.

"Thank you for protecting our rights," said Chet Gusick, a health education teacher at Forest Hills High School.

A group of about 50 persons representing the City-wide Coalition for Control of Community Schools, held a press conference in a reception room of the Board of Education during the afternoon and demanded that people of the communities be involved in any negotiations concerning their schools.

David Spencer, chairman of the governing board of the Intermediate School 201 complex, said that Mr. Shanker was against black and Puerto Rican control of schools and "could antagonize the communities to the point of violence."

In voting to approve the contract, the teachers authorized the union's executive board "to close the schools on 48 hours' notice" if the agreements concerning Ocean Hill-Brownsville should be broken.

Mr. Shanker told delegates at the 6 P.M. meeting that the Board of Education would not invoke "reprisals" against the union or school personnel because of this strike, "except for any sanctions that may be imposed under the Taylor Law."

This drew laughter from many in the audience. "See you in jail, Al," some delegates shouted.

The Taylor Law prohibits strikes by public employees. It took effect shortly before the start of last September's 14-day teacher strike.

For leading that strike in contempt of a court injunction, Mr. Shanker served 15 days in jail last December and the union was fined $150,000—the equivalent of $3 for each of its 50,000 members. The union also lost its dues-checkoff privileges for 18 months, under a provision of the Taylor Law.

Last Monday night, the Corporation Counsel's office obtained a temporary order against the union and the supervisors' group restraining them from continuing the strike. Officials of both groups must still appear this morning before State Supreme Court Justice Jacob Markewich in the case.

The Confederation of Local School Boards, which represents 27 of the 29 regular local school boards in the city, charged last night that the agreement between the central board and the union was "a complete sellout of decentralization."

Timothy Taylor, president of the confederation, said that the local boards "fere left with a shell of decentralization and yet we're required to be responsible to the community under a fake plan which really gives no powers at all" to them.

He added that the local members were wondering "when Al Shanker was going to be made Superintendent of Schools."

September 11, 1968

NEW TEACHERS' STRIKE IS CALLED FOR TOMORROW AS UNION CHARGES OCEAN HILL VIOLATED AGREEMENT

MELEE AT SCHOOL

Donovan Calls on All to Attend Their Classes Today

By LEONARD BUDER

The executive board of the United Federation of Teachers last night called a new city-wide teachers' strike for tomorrow morning. A vote by the union membership is not necessary.

The union board charged that the local governing board of the Ocean Hill-Brownsville demonstration district in Brooklyn had failed to honor the agreement settling the strike that crippled the city school system on Monday and Tuesday.

Superintendent of Schools Bernard E. Donovan said last night that the threat of a new strike should not stop pupils, teachers and supervisors from coming to school today as usual. He expressed hopes that the situation could be resolved in time to head off tomorrow's scheduled walkout.

Shanker Cites Violation

Albert Shanker, the president of the union, said that not a single one of the teachers involved in the dispute with the district had been allowed to resume teaching duties yesterday, in violation of the agreement that ended the two-day strike.

Earlier in the day, policemen battled through a crowd of jeering and cursing demonstrators outside Junior High School 271 to enable a group of teachers to enter the building.

The junior high is one of eight schools in the predominantly Negro and Puerto Rican Ocean Hill-Brownsville district and has been the center of much of the troubles there.

Three persons were arrested during the melee outside the school's front doors.

"You're dead!" a demonstrator shouted at the teachers. "We know your faces. We'll get you, your families, your children. We'll be where you live."

Once inside, the teachers were sent by school officials to a medical room where they remained until classes were dismissed.

The Rev. C. Herbert Oliver, chairman of the local governing board, told newsmen later that his board could not "control" the community's opposition to the teachers.

He was asked whether the community people would again try to block the entry of the teachers this morning.

"I think so—I hope so," he said.

Mayor Lindsay said last night that he deeply regretted and deplored "the scattered incidents that disrupted the first day in several schools." But he declared that it "would be even more deplorable" if the situation were to "escalate into a citywide strike."

Because of the school situation, the Mayor canceled his trip tomorrow to Washington and Baltimore. He was to have addressed the Federal Bar Association Convention in Washington and to have campaigned in Baltimore for Representative Charles M. Mathias, Republican Senate candidate.

Mr. Lindsay said that six of Ocean Hill-Brownsville's eight schools "were open and operating today with all teachers free to enter and to carry out their professional duties."

"In the two of the eight schools where assigned teachers were not allowed to enter today, they must be allowed to enter tomorrow," the Mayor went on. He urged that there be no interference with the teachers and, at the same time, he called on the union "not to penalize all the school-children in the city because of the unfortunate actions of a few persons in a few schools."

Mr. Shanker said later that "the Mayor just doesn't seem to understand the seriousness of the situation in Ocean Hill-Brownsville."

Other Incidents

Schools in two other districts as the city system resumed operations following the two-day strike, which kept 53,000 teachers and more than a million pupils out of classes:

¶About a dozen members of the Brownsville Education Committee entered Junior High School 275 in Brooklyn early in the morning and then locked the doors to prevent teachers and supervisors from entering.

The group said that "those teachers and supervisors who took part in an illegal strike cannot return without being screened" by the community.

The demonstrators dispersed at about 9 o'clock after being warned they would be arrested if they did not leave the building.

¶Militant parents in the Red Hook section of Brooklyn vowed not to allow the principal of Public School 27 to return to her post because she had "locked out" pupils during the strike. The principal did not go to her school yesterday, but said firmly, 'I'll be back.'

For most of the city's 57,000 teachers and more than 1.2-million pupils, however, the day was uneventful.

"Like any other other school-opening," a Bronx principal said, but then he added "—almost."

Pros and Cons Argued

For many of the staff and pupils the main topic of conversation in class and out was the pros and cons of the strike. Later in the day word began to spread among teachers of the new troubles in Ocean Hill-Brownsville.

A Queens first-grade teacher said that a youngster asked her at the end of the school day, "Will I see you again tomorrow?" "I didn't know what to say to her," the teacher said sadly.

The school crisis that led to the two-day strike, and has now raised the specter of a new strike tomorrow, was triggered by the refusal of the Ocean Hill-Brownsville governing board to reinstate 10 teachers it had ordered "transferred" last May.

A trial examiner cleared the teachers of charges brought against them—that they had either failed to maintain classroom order or had spoken critically of the demonstration district. The Board of Education branded the ousters as "illegal."

But the controversy took on larger aspects with the union insisting that not only should the 10 be reinstated but that all teachers throughout the city must receive suitable guarantees of job security, due process and other protection.

The union has voiced fears that without these guarantees similar abuses of teachers' rights may occur when the new systemwide decentralization plan takes effect shortly. Under the plan, considerable power to discipline and dismiss teachers would be shifted from the central Board of Education to all local school boards.

The controversy appeared to be resolved Tuesday when the Board of Education and the teachers' union reached agreement on new guarantees of teacher rights.

A key feature of the settlement was the provision—negotiated personally by Mayor Lindsay last Sunday—that the 10 teachers would be allowed to return to Ocean-Hill-Brownsville.

Mr. Lindsay said that the local governing board had reluctantly agreed to this, but had promised not to "resist" the teachers' return. He added later that the teachers would be allowed to resume "normal" duties.

In overwhelmingly approving the settlement terms, the union membership gave their executive board the power to call a strike on 48 hours' notice if there should be any violation of the agreement. Mr. Shanker said last night that the violation occurred at 9 A.M. yesterday.

Besides the original 10—the

Photographs for The New York Times by PATRICK A. BURNS

CLASH: A demonstrator struggles with patrolman as Chief Sealy, left, directs action

number actually was reduced to nine yesterday when one teacher put in for a voluntary transfer—the return of about 200 other teachers is at issue.

They, together with 150 others who have since been transferred, walked off their jobs last May to support the reinstatement of their ousted colleagues. The union has charged that when they later tried to return to work they were "locked out" by the governing board.

Only 100 of 200 teachers actually showed up for work yesterday. There was no explanation of what happened to the others, but a union spokesman said he assumed that they were applying for transfers.

Junior High School 271, at Herkimer and Saratoga Avenues, was the center of last spring's unrest. It continued yesterday to reflect the district's troubled state.

When teachers involved in the dispute arrived yesterday at the modern, sprawling red-and-turquoise brick building, the early morning rain had just stopped and the sun was beginning to break through.

Negroes Gather in Doorway

About a dozen Negroes, including Robert (Sonny) Carson, the bearded chairman of the Independent Brooklyn CORE, had gathered in the doorway.

Fred Nauman, a leader of the transferred teachers who was

union chapter chairman at J.H.S. 271, arrived at 8:05.

"We're here to teach," the stocky 38-year-old instructor told newsmen before mounting the five steps leading up to the door.

As Mr. Nauman and several other teachers reached the top step, a Negro man who refused to identify himself remained in the doorway and said: "We don't want you here."

At that moment, the door opened from the inside and Lloyd Sealy, assistant chief inspector of police, emerged with three Negro policemen and William Harris, the school's principal.

Chief Sealy, a Negro, asked Mr. Harris whether Mr. Naumann and his colleagues should be admitted to the school and the Negro principal said they should. There appeared to be no resistance, and the teachers went into the building.

At 8:40, hundreds of pupils who had been waiting outside the school were admitted. Half an hour later Mr. Nauman and other instructors came out of the school. All carried mimeographed notes asking them to report to the office of the district's administrator, Rhody McCoy, "prior to resuming your assignments."

An Explanation

Mr. Nauman, who explained that the meeting with Mr. McCoy had been changed to Intermediate School 55 in the district, said that the teachers had not found time cards to punch when they reported.

As he walked the four blocks to I.S. 55, Mr. Nauman said that once in J.H.S. 271, the teachers had been called "pigs

CONFRONTATION: Chief Inspector Lloyd G. Sealy asks parents to stop blocking doorway

and faggots" by Mr. Carson and others.

But, he added: "I don't think we should get out because of the words of a few people. I think what we have here is a game of intimidation."

Mr. Nauman and about 100 disputed teachers from the district's various schools went into the auditorium of I.S. 55 and occupied front seats in the large middle section. At the same time about 40 parents took seats on the right side, along with Mr. Carson and others. A few of the men carried crash helmets. Newsmen were barred from the session.

Mr. McCoy arrived for the meeting at 10:45 and told newsmen some parents were going to block the doorways of district schools in what he called "community action." Asked whether any of the controversial instructors would be allowed to teach, the pipe-smoking administrator said, "We'll see."

Mr. McCoy said that he could not guarantee the safety of the teachers under the circumstances. "I have enough trouble with my own," he remarked.

At 11:20 the teachers came out of the building, charging that the session with Mr. McCoy had been totally disrupted by screaming parents and community representatives.

Bitter Exchanges

As the teachers left the meeting at I.S. 55, there were bitter exchanges on the street between some of them and some local residents. Union officials said that a number of the teachers had been struck lightly by objects as they passed from the auditorium to the street.

Mr. Oliver, who had been in the auditorium, said on the street that the governing board had never agreed with the Mayor to let the disputed teachers return to actual classroom duties.

After the session at I.S. 55, the teachers went to lunch. They said they had been told by Mr. McCoy to report to their schools following the meal.

While the instructors ate in a nearby restaurant, Chief Sealy attempted to avert a confrontation between the returning teachers and the 30 to 40 men and women who were assembling on the steps of J.H.S. 271.

At 1:20, 15 teachers, including Mr. Nauman, arrived back at the school and faced the crowd on the steps. The police tried to clear a path up the steps for the teachers, but met resistance from several persons.

An order was given immediately to clear the steps and the police grabbed and shoved persons who would not move. Several were moved away with enough force that they either fell or were pushed down steps and to the cement.

Within 15 minutes the police, bolstered by reinforcements, had set up barricades separating the shouting crowd from the school. Teachers and pupils inside the building yelled from open windows: "Racist cops!"

Chief Sealy, perspiration pouring down his face, barked, "This isn't our fault, this is what we tried to talk you out of."

"You nigger," a man in the crowd called back. "You're next."

Mr. Nauman and the other contested teachers were ushered into the building, where they spent the closing hour of a shortened school day in the medical room.

"We didn't see any children and we didn't teach," Mr. Nauman said as he left the school at 2:40 under police guard.

After the teachers left, Mr. Oliver spoke to newsmen in front of the school.

"To bring them back in here," he said, referring to the returning teachers, "is to destroy decentralization in this district."

Mr. Oliver was asked whether the local board could control the community to keep residents from blocking school doors.

He responded harshly: "We are not in control of the people in this community. The Board of Education and the union have totally disregarded the community. We have not prevented the return of the teachers, but we cannot say that we'll prevent the community from not letting them in. The community is here. Look around. They're here."

He said, in reply to another question, that he had warned Mayor Lindsay on Sunday that this situation would develop.

What role will the teachers have in the schools, he was asked.

"What role?" Mr. Oliver replied. "Their role is to get out of the community."

The three persons arrested were accused of obstructing government administration and resisting arrest. One refused to give his name to police. The others were identified as Yashua Ben Levi, 25 years old, of 29 Dewey Place, Brooklyn, and Mrs. Leona King, a 17-year-old white housewife who lives at 1099 Gates Avenue, Broklyn.

One of the demonstrators, Ronald Simmons, who is employed as a school aide in the district, said that the fracas broke out because the police had pushed women down the steps.

"We didn't fight them," he said of the police.

About 75 school-age youngsters, led by a man and woman with Afro hair styles, gathered outside the East New York Avenue police station to protest the arrests.

Board Approves Pact

Even as the tenuous school strike pact was on the verge of coming apart, the Board of Education at a special 2 P.M. meeting formally approved Tuesday's agreement with the United Federation of Teachers.

The vote was 7 in favor and 2 against. The negative votes were cast by the Rev. Milton A. Galamison and Hector Vasquez. Two members—William Haddad and Ernest Minott—who voted in favor said they did so unhappily.

About a dozen speakers, many of them Negroes, spoke against approval of the agreement. They accused the city board of "irresponsibility" and of "selling out" community rights.

The union's executive board was called into emergency session on an hour's notice by Mr. Shanker. The members met at the Gramercy Park Hotel, Lexington Avenue and 21st Street, at 6 P.M. and quickly voted for the strike.

Mr. Shanker said that the teachers involved would not go back to Ocean Hill-Brownsville today because of what he said was the existent danger.

The union head also announced that he was calling a meeting for 9:30 A.M. today of the union's 900 chapter chairmen—all of whom will have to take time off from school duties to attend. The meeting will be in the Marc Ballroom, 27 Union Square.

In connection with the attempts of some Negro parents to keep out the principal of P. S. 27 in Red Hook, Dr. Anthony J. Ferrerio, the acting superintendent of district 15, said he was "investigating" the situation.

But the angry parents, led by Mrs. Gloria Oliver, said they would never let the principal, Miss Margaret M. Cooney, to return. Miss Cooney is white but the parents said that race was not an issue.

"She violated the law," Mrs. Oliver said of the principal.

Reached at home by telephone Miss Cooney, who has been principal of P.S. 27 for the past five years, said the school was closed during the strike "because I was acting for the safety of the children."

State Supreme Court Justice Jacob Markowitz yesterday morning adjourned for a week a hearing into an antistrike injunction against the teachers' union and the Council of Supervisory Associations, which supported the walkout. But he kept in effect the temporary restraining order that was issued against the strike Monday.

REQUESTS FLOOD PRIVATE SCHOOLS

Distress at Strike Expressed by Middle-Class Parents

Thousands of white, middle-class parents have been trying to get their children into private and religious schools since the public school strike began, and hundreds of others have been talking about moving to the suburbs.

"As soon as we can find a house in one of the suburbs where the schools are good, we're moving," said Mrs. Edward Shapiro, who have two children in the public schools. "We've already looked at a few places."

Mrs. Shapiro, who lives at 420 East 79th Street, said: "I moved here from Westchester two and a half years ago. I didn't realize then how terrible the school situation was here. I think New York will lose its middle-class because of this."

For many parents such as Mrs. Shapiro, whose well-dressed children live in comfortable apartments lined with books and records, long-time commitments to public education has been shattered by the current teachers' strike.

Transfers Daughter

A woman who asked to remain anonymous said:

"I'm being forced to change schools. I don't like it."

She has just transferred her 10-year-old daughter from a public school on the East Side to a private school on the West Side. "I prefer public education," she said. "The youngster rubs elbows with new people from different backgrounds. It's good for her, and she learns from the experience."

Mrs. Marion White, assistant director of the United Parents Associations of New York, which represents more than 400,000 parents affiliated with local associations, said: "We've had hundreds, thousands of calls from disgusted parents."

"They're exceedingly distressed that their children are losing all this valuable time, and they don't appreciate two teachers' strikes in two years.

"A great many parents have told us they're sending their children to private schools as soon as they get accepted, and even plan to move to the country."

The United Parents Associations has asked the State Board of Regents to postpone its statewide scholarship test scheduled to be given in early October because, Mrs. White said, "city children won't have any time to prepare—they'll be at a disadvantage."

The Trinity School, at 139 West 91st Street, is one of the many private schools flooded with calls from anxious parents. "About 60 families have tried to get their boys in here in the last week," said Richard M. Garten, headmaster of the school, where tuition ranges from $995 for younger pupils to $1,000 for the older ones.

"We're in the same situation as many of the other private schools," he said. "We haven't a square inch of space to take in new students. Our admissions have been closed since last March."

Switchboard Clogged

The chances of a child's being accepted to a private school at this time of the year are minimal. Most admissions quotas are filled during the spring.

"This teachers' strike has certainly filled whatever few places were left unfilled," said Paul H. Hornbeck, director of the School and College Advisory Center, 551 Fifth Avenue, a placement service for about 500 private schools.

"Our switchboard has been clogged since the strike began, and we have been quite successful in locating some openings in day schools here and boarding schools outside the city. Everybody I talked to was fed up with the situation here."

Mrs. Bernard Robbins of 4 East 89th Street is among the many parents who have tried unsuccessfully to place children in private schools this fall.

"I don't even remember how many schools I've called," she said yesterday. "Everybody I know wants to take their children out of public school. It seems to be impossible this year, but I'm preparing for next fall now."

Her 6-year-old daughter attends a parochial school, and her son is in the fifth grade at P.S. 6, at Madison Avenue and 81st Street.

"I just feel so terrible," she said. "My boy's not getting any education at all now. The public school system seems to be falling apart."

Mrs. Harold Brenner of 315 East 86th Street, whose four children have attended public school, explained why she was considering transferring her two small daughters from P.S. 190 at 311 East 82d Street to private school next fall.

"I'm afraid they'll be involved in violence," she said. "I know confusion goes along with change and I know there has to be change and I want the change, but I'm very concerned because this may seriously affect the quality of their education."

Mrs. Brenner, like many other parents, has been active in arranging temporary classes for her children.

In Brooklyn and Queens alone 4,000 students are expected to attend such special classes in 50 parochial school starting tomorrow, according to the Rev. Vincent Breen, assistant superintendent of schools for the Brooklyn Roman Catholic Diocese.

"The implications of this exodus from the public schools are very distressing," said Mrs. Eric Pleskow of 150 East 77th Street, who is president of the Parents Association at P.S. 190. "It means the system is losing many of its best parents. I know two other [Parents Association] presidents and five families who intend to move to the country because of the school situation.

"These are people who have worked like maniacs to improve the schools, but they feel their children are pawns in a big power game. Now they feel they have no choice but to leave."

SCHOOLS REOPENING TODAY; UNION AND CITY SIGN PACT; OCEAN HILL GETS OBSERVERS

5,825 FAVOR PLAN

Six Class Days Added to Schedule to Make Up for Lost Time

By LEONARD BUDER

The city's teachers voted last night to end their strike, permitting a reopening of school this morning.

The vote was 5,825 in favor of calling off the walkout and 592 against.

Earlier in the day, Mayor Lindsay announced that negotiators for the Board of Education and the teachers' union had resolved the differences that threatened to send the strike into its fourth week.

The agreement, worked out during a 16-hour negotiating session at Gracie Mansion, will send 110 teachers opposed by the Ocean Hill-Brownsville governing board back into the troubled Brooklyn district and return 52,000 striking teachers and more than a million pupils to their classrooms throughout the city.

Police to Be on Hand

Large numbers of policemen are expected to be on duty outside the eight schools in the predominantly Negro and Puerto Rican Ocean Hill-Brownsville district to make sure that the returning teachers are not prevented from entering. Teams of observers—including representatives appointed by the teachers' union—will be stationed inside the schools.

Albert Shanker, president of the United Federation of Teachers, told 1,000 members of the union's delegate assembly last evening:

"This is not a victory. When you deal with a messy problem, you get messy solutions."

McCoy Dissatisfied

Asked by delegates if he knew whether the Ocean Hill-Brownsville governing board would go along with the settlement, Mr. Shanker said:

"We don't know. We'd be a bunch of liars if we said we did. All we can do is try, and if it doesn't work, we've got to have the strength and the guts and the solidarity to win again."

Newsmen finally reached Rhody McCoy, the Ocean Hill-Brownsville district administrator, at 12:45 this morning. He expressed unqualified dissatisfaction with the agreement.

For most of the city's pupils, the strike settlement will not only mean a return today to normal classes, three weeks after the scheduled start of the fall term, but also a revised school schedule that will give them six days of "make-up" time.

To make up partly for the 11 school days lost during the strike, three normal school holidays—Election Day, Lincoln's Birthday and the day following Thanksgiving Day—will become instructional days and the spring vacation period was shifted and abbreviated.

Instead of being closed on Good Friday (April 4) and the week following Easter Sunday (April 6), city schools will conduct classes from April 7 through 11. Schools, however, will be closed on the two days before Good Friday.

Teachers will get extra pay for these additional schools days, which, in effect, will enable them to make up most of pay they lost during the strike. Because the teachers will be paid for the extra six days at a time-and-a-half rate, they will make up nine days' pay.

Big Question Remains

But the big question is what will happen when the disputed teachers go back to Ocean Hill-Brownsville in the face of expressed opposition from some elements in the community.

Once before, after two days of strike, it appeared that the dispute had been resolved on terms allloowing the disputed teachers to return to Ocean Hill-Brownsville. But when the teachers returned to work throughout the city on Sept. 11, some of the disputed Ocean Hill-Brownsville teachers were met outside one school by cursing, jeering demonstrators.

The police finally escorted the teachers inside, but, according to the union, school officials refused to allow them to take up teaching duties. This precipitated a new citywide walkout.

The dispute started last May when the Ocean Hill-Brownsville governing board ordered 10 teachers transferred. The teachers later were cleared by a trial examiner of charges that they had tried to sabotage community school control or done unsatisfactory work. The governing board opposed taking back the 10 teachers and 100 others who had stayed out of school last spring to support the original 10.

The militant local forces have viewed the strike as an attempt by a largely white teachers' union and, by extension, the white school Establishment, to crush their fight to exercise total community control over their schools. The teachers' union, backed by supervisory groups, saw the strike as a fight to protect the legal rights of the school personnel.

Local Board Informed

There was no immediate reaction to the Mayor's announcement from the Rev. C. Herbert Oliver, the chairman of the governing board of the Ocean Hill-Brownsville district. A spokesman for the Mayor said that the local board had been kept informed of the negotiations.

When Mr. McCoy was asked if he would allow the observers into the district's schools, he said:

"How would I stop them?"

Then he said, "We don't want them. We don't need them."

Asked about his plans in regard to the new developments affecting the district, Mr. McCoy said, "I don't have any idea at the moment."

Last week the city board, as part of a series of moves to try to end the school dispute, notified the local district that it could retain the teachers it had hired over the summer to "replace" those instructors the governing board opposed. These new teachers enabled the district to operate its schools throughout the strike.

There is also uncertainty about what might happen this morning at other schools outside the embattled district, particularly those in largely Negro and Puerto Rican areas where there was strong community opposition to the strike. Some local groups have warned that they would oppose the return of principals who shut down their schools in sympathy for the strike.

The break in the impasse that had stymied a strike settlement occurred after the teachers' union modified its demand, in the early hours of yesterday morning, that the observers sent into the Ocean Hill-Brownsville schools be given power to shut down schools if there is violence or threats of violence.

But the union won its demand to be represented on the team of observers. Previously, the Board of Education had said that the observers would consist only of members of the staff of the Superintendent of Schools.

The agreement signed yesterday provides that the observation teams will consist of members of the Superintendent's staff, which "will be augmented in each school by two observers selected by the United Federation of Teachers and one impartial observer selected by the Mayor."

The observers will report directly to a special committee of the city Board of Education that had been set up two weeks ago to first resolve the strike issues and then implement the settlement. This committee will have power to undertake whatever action it considers necessary, including the closing of the schools as a last resort if there is serious trouble.

During the night-long negotiation session, some of the negotiators tried to catch snatches of sleep during occasional lulls.

Toward morning, Mr. Shanker, unable to curl his 6-foot-3-inch frame into a comfortable napping position on a straight-back chair, stretched out on the floor and slept for 20 minutes.

An aide said later that this was the only sleep the union leader had had in 36 hours.

Despite considerable discussion, the deadlock over Mr. Shanker's demand for a voice in the appointment of the school observers and his insistence that the observers have the power to close schools continued as dawn broke.

Finally, according to one of the participants, "Al dropped the demand that the observers have the power to shut down the schools. That broke the jam."

After further talks led to an agreement on the composition of the observation teams, but then the negotiators for the city board and the union clashed over whether, as Mr. Shanker asked, the teams should make reports and recommendations. The city board objected to recommendations, and eventually that point was dropped by the union.

Mayor Announces Accord

Mayor Lindsay came out of Gracie Mansion at 2:20 P.M. yesterday to announce the agreement. He stood on the steps of the mansion, flanked on the left by Superintendent of Schools Bernard E. Donovan, and, on the right, by Mr. Shanker and Walter J. Degnan, the head of the Council of Supervisory Associations.

All four looked unshaven and weary after the marathon negotiating session. Mr. Lindsay, who had not had any sleep all night, read the following statement:

"After more than 16 hours of all-night discussions, the Board of Education and the United Federation of Teachers have signed a written agreement to reopen tomorrow. Mr. Shanker and Mr. Degnan have both agreed to recommend to their respective memberships that they return to school on Monday.

"This has been a difficult three weeks for our city—most especially for the more than 1 million school children and their parents. We are all thankful that the schools can now reopen.

"It is important now that we all return to the business of

education in accordance with law. The board and the city have provided appropriate safeguards for teacher rights and teacher safety. The board plan will also allow the important experiment in education reform in the Brownsville-Ocean Hill district to proceed.

"This agreement and the board's plan provide a framework for the proper operation of our schools.

"It is vital that the parties respect each other's rights and responsibilities. We can only move forward if all parties recognize that our school system like every other institution of government can only function under the rule of law. I am hopeful that out of this settlement a new relationship can emerge between teachers and parents, throughout our city, to work jointly for their common goal of improved education for all New York's school children."

Mayor Lindsay added to the prepared statement an expression of thanks to Vincent D. McDonnell, the chairman of the State Mediation Board, and Harold I. Israelson, a labor lawyer, for helping to bring about the agreement.

The written agreement was signed by Mr. Shanker, Mr. Degnan, Dr. Donovan, and Walter Straley, a member of the Board of Education's special committee. John Doar, the committee chairman, had left the mansion an hour before.

Mrs. Rose Shapiro, president of the Board of Education, said later she was "greatly relieved by the possibility that all children will go back to school tomorrow."

She praised Mayor Lindsay for his "strong leadership" and "persistency and determination in behalf of our city's children."

Mrs. Shapiro also lauded the "superhuman work" performed by Dr. Donovan and Mr. Doar as chairman of the special committee.

Court Order Issued

In another development yesterday, a Bronx Supreme Court justice signed an order directing State Education Commissioner James E. Allen Jr. to show cause why he had not removed the Ocean Hill-Brownsville governing board and cut off the district's state funds

for alleged refusal to obey the central board's directive to rehire the 10 ousted teachers.

The order is returnable Thursday in Bronx Supreme Court. It was signed at 4 P.M. by Justice Joseph A. Brust and was instituted by a former state senator whose two children attend a Bronx public school.

The order was obtained by Assemblymen Anthony J. Mercorella, Democrat-Liberal of the Bronx, and Burton G. Hecht, Democrat of the Bronx, acting as lawyers for Archie Gorfinkel, the former State Senator.

The Assemblymen said they would drop their action if the Ocean Hill-Brownsville board peacefully accepted the new settlement. If there is trouble in the schools today, they said they would press the court action.

From Gracie Mansion, Mr. Shanker went to union headquarters at 260 Park Avenue South, where he presided over a meeting of his 50-member executive board. The board voted unanimously to recommend acceptance of the agreement by the delegate assembly and general membership.

Then Mr. Shanker—looking relaxed and suddenly refreshed —went to a hastily called 5:30 P.M. meeting of the delegate assembly, held in the auditorium of Washington Irving High School, 16th Street and Irving Place. He received a standing ovation from the delegates.

"This is the greatest crisis that has ever faced us as teachers, a union, or a school system," the 40-year-old former mathematics teacher said.

Mr. Shanker said that the teachers had struck not for additional benefits, as in the past, but to hold on to the rights that they had.

He emphasized that under the settlement terms there would be "adequate police protection inside the schools and out." He went on, "We've had many a conflict with our Mayor..."

At this point, his remarks were interrupted by loud booing and hissing from the delegates.

Mr. Shanker quieted the audience and said:

"He didn't act in May or June, but he has acted now. He helped us get practically everything that was in our program. I am saying this as a

person who has no love or hate for the Mayor. He did a good job in the last few days."

"This union," he added, "should extend a hand of friendship to Rhody McCoy and to try to make that the best district in the city."

The rank-and-file vote, conducted by the Honest Ballot Association, got under way a little while later. The total of 6,422 votes cast, which included five blank ballots, represented a small fraction of the union's total membership of more than 50,000.

The membership vote took place at the National Maritime Union hall at 13th Street and Seventh Avenue. The teachers cast ballots marked either "yes" or "no".

At 7 P.M., when the polls opened, the hall was jammed by teachers, many of whom flashed V-for-Victory signs with their fingers.

Some Teachers Grumble

There were also some grumbling from teachers who charged that the settlement was "a sellout" by the union. The polls closed at 11 P.M. and the tally was announced soon afterward.

Mr. Lindsay was informed that the teachers had voted to end the strike after he completed his weekly television broadcast at the WNEW-TV studios. He said he was "very gratified."

Then, with his arm around his wife, Mary, he left the studio shortly after 11 P.M. for Gracie Mansion and, an aide said, "some much needed sleep."

Despite the end of the strike, Mr. Shanker and other leaders of the union and the supervisors' council still face prosecution for violating a court order obtained by the city under the state's Taylor Law. The statute prohibits strikes by public employes.

Last week State Supreme Court Justice Francis J. Bloustein, who is presiding over the proceedings, held that the teachers' walkout was an illegal strike under the provisions of the law.

A maximum sentence of 30 days in jail and a $250 fine can be imposed for criminal contempt. Last December, Mr. Shanker spent 15 days in jail for leading a 14-day teachers' strike in September, 1967.

STRIKE CRIPPLES SCHOOLS, NO SETTLEMENT IN SIGHT; POLICE REJECT CONTRACT

LINDSAY IS BITTER

Proposal by Donovan to Close J.H.S. 271 Rejected by Board

By LEONARD BUDER

A new strike by teachers, the third in less than six weeks, crippled the city school system yesterday and kept more than a million pupils out of classes.

There was no sign of a break in the walkout by some 48,000 teachers, which was sparked by union objections to the Board of Education's reopening of Junior High School 271 and other developments in the Ocean Hill-Brownsville decentralized district in Brooklyn.

The Board of Education last night rejected a recommendation from Superintendent of Schools Bernard E. Donovan that J.H.S. 271 "should be closed as a junior high school, its entire staff transferred out of the district and the school reopened as a high school," according to sources close to the board.

Explanation by Donovan

Dr. Donovan told the board in a confidential report that he was making the recommendation because "the atmosphere for school 271 is so hostile and inimical to effective instruction." The central board's rejection came at a closed meeting.

No meetings were held yesterday between the union and the city board and, as of last night, none was scheduled for today.

Albert Shanker, the president of the United Federation of Teachers, said that the strike could last "a month or longer."

He said that the city board should either close the junior high school or "get the gangsters out of the school so that teachers can teach."

Union Charges Harassment

The union has contended that its members at the school have been harassed and threatened with harm by other teachers and outsiders who object to their presence.

Mr. Shanker also charged that Dr. Donovan was suppressing a report from aides detailing "acts of terrorism," including death threats, at the junior high school. A copy of this report was obtained last night by The New York Times.

Dr. Donovan, in declining to make public the report, said that he would call to his office a number of teachers to question them about "alleged misconduct." He said he had already transferred two union teachers—not from J.H.S. 271 —because they were "in conflict with the administration of the school."

Last Friday, it was learned, Dr. Donovan told the city board that he wanted to transfer out about six teachers, including two Negro teachers at J.H.S. 271 who were allegedly leading the opposition to the returning union teachers.

However, strong objections to the removal of these two teachers were raised by a board member. He conceded that they were "troublemakers," but said that they could also help restore peace to the school if they wanted to.

Rhody A. McCoy, the administrator of the predominantly Negro and Puerto Rican district, which has been the focal point of the three strikes, said yesterday that he was exploring the possibility of running the district as a "private school district, financed by company funds and open to the public."

Improvement Seen

He added that with the union teachers absent because of the strike, the district's eight schools were running smoothly again and "everything is going beautifully."

Other developments in the tangled school controversy included the following:

¶The Council of Supervisory Associations, which represents most of the system's principals and other supervisors, voted to support the new strike, as it had the two previous walkouts. After taking the vote, 500 supervisors went to Board of Education headquarters demanding action to "get the militants out of Ocean Hill" and to declare the district-wide experiment in limited community control a failure.

¶Mrs. Blanche Lewis, president of the 400,000-member United Parents Associations, declared that the new strike was "not justified and must be vigorously condemned by all parents." She called on parents to demand the reopening of their schools and make it clear that they would "no longer tolerate the closing of the schools as the answer to every disagreement."

¶Mayor Lindsay again bitterly criticized the union for calling the strike without giving the Board of Education the one additional day—yesterday —it had requested "to test its conviction that the [Ocean Hill-Brownsville] community was willing to recognize the rights and protect the safety of the teachers—one day to try and ease a potentially explosive situation."

¶Acting on a request from the city, Justice Francis Bloustein moved up by a day — to today — contempt proceedings brought against Mr. Shanker and Walter J. Degnan, head of the supervisors' council, for calling the earlier strikes. The state's Taylor Law prohibits strikes by public employes.

More Teachers Show Up

The series of strikes has kept most of the city's pupils out of school on 12 of the first 23 days of the fall term.

The Board of Education reported that more teachers showed up for work yesterday than during last month's walkouts but that the number was still not sufficient to maintain any semblance of normal instruction except in a few instances.

These exceptions were mainly in Ocean Hill-Brownsville and in sections of Harlem, Bedford-Stuyvesant and other predominantly Negro and Puerto Rican areas, where community opposition to the largely white union is strongest. Negro teacher and supervisory groups are opposed to the strike.

The city board said that an incomplete tally showed that 352 schools were open and 510 were closed.

The board's figures showed that 85,190 of the system's 1,129,000 pupils attended school, along with 8,660 of the 57,000 teachers.

The tally did not include elementary schools in six of the city's 33 local districts and junior high schools in 33 districts.

During the earlier strikes, some 4,000 to 5,000 teachers came to work in all districts, and pupil attendance generally ranged from 28,000 to 50,000.

School Was Closed

The Ocean Hill-Brownsville controversy has centered on the locally elected governing board's refusal to reinstate a group of union members who it said were a detriment to the experimental district.

The return of these teachers —who now number 83—was a union condition for calling off the earlier strikes.

When local officials made a new move recently to remove the "unwanted" teachers from their classrooms, the Board of Education temporarily suspended the governing board and temporarily relieved Mr. McCoy, the district administrator, of his post.

Last Wednesday Superintendent Donovan relieved the district's principals after they had said they were still obeying the orders of Mr. McCoy and the governing board. He also said he closed J.H.S. 271 on Thursday and Friday to ease the tensions there.

Dr. Donovan's subsequent decision to reopen J.H.S. 271 and reinstate the principals, effective yesterday, led to the new strike. Mr. Shanker said that this action gave a "green light" for the removal of the 83 union teachers.

Dr. Donovan denied this. The Superintendent said that the situation had stabilized at the other seven schools in the district, where 67 of the disputed teachers are working, and he was hopeful that the conditions would be better at J.H.S. 271.

He said that if matters were not better, he would shut the

The New York Times (by Jack Manning)

McCOY SPEAKS AT RALLY: Rhody A. McCoy, left foreground, administrator of the Ocean Hill-Brownsville school district, addressing demonstrators at Murray Street, near City Hall. At his call, the group marched to Brooklyn.

school permanently, if necessary.

Mr. Shanker had warned that if the union went on strike, the city's teachers would not go back to work until the Board of Education dissolved the Ocean Hill-Brownsville district.

In a television interview last night on the Channel 13 program, "Newsfront," Mr. Shanker conceded that the new strike had cost the union some support from the public and from teachers.

He charged that Mr. Lindsay, who "knows what he's doing," had gone back on promises made when the teachers ended last month's walkout, because he knew public sentiment would be against a third strike.

"The public was with us the first time around, they were with us the second time around, but now the people are getting disgusted — and I'm one of them," Mr. Shanker added.

Mr. McCoy, at a news conference at district headquarters, before leaving for a City Hall rally called by supporters of the governing board, said he did not think that the union

would be able to prolong the strike.

"I don't think Mr. Shanker will be able to hold out this time," he said.

The administrator also noted that the district yesterday had no problem over the "unwanted teachers.

"Shanker has done a nice job by removing them," he said.

At a later rally, in J.H.S. 271, the more than 500 persons there gave Mr. McCoy a standing ovation as he rose to speak. He was applauded every few words.

"I met with the principals from a quarter of seven this morning, he said. "We heard rumors of an invasion of union teachers—all kinds of rumors —but they said, 'Don't worry, we're black, too,' and they went back into the schools, and from all reports, the schools are beautiful, too.

"We have something out here worth fighting for, and we're going to fight."

The city's pupils and their teachers went to sleep Sunday night uncertain whether they

would be in class the next morning.

The first word that the strike would definitely take place came at 7:15 A.M. yesterday from Dan Sanders, a spokesman for the union. "The strike is on in accordance with the vote of the membership," he announced.

Many teachers went to their schools as usual, some to picket, some to work and others to see what their colleagues were doing.

Some parents sent their children to school in the hope— often unfulfilled — that the schools would be open. Others did not even bother.

"I assumed it would be pointless," one father said dejectedly.

The first indication of the strike's impact came from District 20, which covers a largely middle-class section of Brooklyn, including Bay Ridge, Bensonhurst, Borough Park and part of Flatbush.

Twenty-seven of the 31 schools there were shut down by the strike, a Board of Edu-

cation spokesman reported. The four open schools had a total of 167 pupils. The district has an enrollment of 20,370 pupils.

District 1, which runs from the Lower East Side to 23d Street, was all but shut down by the strike. By mid-afternoon, only five of the 24 schools were open — Public Schools 4, 20, 22, 71 and 188. Pupil and teacher attendance at these schools was far below normal.

The district, which has been the scene of community unrest in recent weeks, was relatively quiet. But anger was expressed by some parents and teachers over school closings. Most principals did not attempt to open their buildings, saying they had either no teachers or an insufficient number to take proper care of the children.

At P.S. 40, a group of parents unsuccessfully attempted to have the building opened.

Seward Park High School, which had operated during the previous strike, was closed. The principal, Sidney Nanes, did not show up.

Anthony Amorosa, a teacher at P.S. 22, said:

"There were 23 teachers that showed up at the school at 8:30, out of a total teaching staff of 125. The police would not let us in. They said we had to see the acting superintendent. We met with [Jack] Landman, and he named Arthur Kaufman acting principal to open the school. We opened the school during the last strike with 14 teachers—this time we've got 23 the first day."

Public School 20 was opened with seven teachers when Mrs. Wilbert Mann, a teacher reported to Mr. Landman that a busload of retarded children had arrived to attend classes. She was named acting principal with authority to oversee the school. Policemen were stationed at the door, and everyone who entered had to be identified.

Teachers Try to Enter

Nonstriking teachers at one school in District 1 contended that they were "locked out" by their principal. They said the principal was standing with picketing teachers and when they asked him to open the school, he replied, speaking of himself in the third person: "He is not here this morning."

Groups of nonstriking teachers went to Mr. Landman's office during the morning to ask him to open their schools. He appeared at the door at 11:45 A.M.—amid jeers and boos—and announced he could not see any more teachers because he had to attend a meeting.

"You can't leave," shouted an irate teacher. "We've got to open the schools."

"I've got problems, too," Mr. Landman replied, "I've been here since 8:30."

"That's where you're supposed to be," came the retort. "Your first priority is to the students of the district—not to some meeting."

"I've run out of time," Mr.

Landman said as he disappeared inside the building.

Modesto Santiago, a member of the local board for District 1, said later: "Donovan left it up to the individual principal whether or not to open the schools. If you leave a loophole like that, how can you get the schools open. If a principal can just call up and say, 'I can't open the schools,' how can we get them open?

"I'm not in favor of breaking the strike or anything, but the teachers who want to teach ought to be able to teach."

In District 3, on the West Side, a group of parents and volunteer teachers from P.S. 41 in Greenwich Village operated emergency classes for 480 pupils in rooms provided by Greenwich House, the children's Aid Society, the New School for Social Research and two neighborhood churches. Thirteen striking teachers took part in the project.

At Joan of Arc Junior High School, 154 West 93d Street, 74 of the 96 teachers showed up for work. But only 500 of the 1,240 students came to classes.

A few pickets marched outside the school. John Traube, the union chapter chairman at the school, said that some youngsters had thrown blackboard erasers at the striking teachers.

A handful of students were also outside the building. They said that they had left their classrooms because their teachers were not present and they were not permitted to go to other rooms. The principal denied this.

A seventh-grade girl told newsmen, "Everything was chaos in my home-room class. Kids were throwing coats and everything. I went into another room, and the teacher said, 'We're too full, we don't want you.'"

Mrs. Lula B. Bramwell, the principal, said that the youngsters who left school were "just plain truants."

Racist and Anti-Semite Charges Strain Old Negro-Jewish Ties

By BILL KOVACH

Charges and countercharges of anti-Semitism and white racism have begun to intensify in the city as a result of the decentralization controversy that has paralyzed the school system.

Crystallizing around the Ocean Hill-Brownsville conflict — but fed by earlier troubles over New York University's appointment of John T. Hatchett, the author of an alleged anti-Semitic article, and the anti-Israeli position of some black militants — these charges have triggered ugly taunts dissemination of hate literature, and much anger and sorrow.

Although Jewish and Negro leaders are denouncing these expressions of prejudice (and some maintain the feelings are not widespread in the city), the fact is no one knows for sure how deeply these feelings run.

And many Negro and white leaders say Negroes are not basically anti-Semitic so much as they are antiwhite — that is, against whites whether Jewish or not.

Leaders of both the Negro and Jewish communities have been spurred into action in an attempt to develop a forum for Negroes and Jews to meet and discuss common problems — to open new lines of communications.

Last night a meeting between Jewish leaders and leaders of the black community continued a dialogue that has been established between the two groups in the past weeks. Rabbi Marc Tanenbaum, director of Interracial Affairs for the American Jewish Committee, said the meetings came because of the realization of the "urgent need for direct communications."

"We have been meeting," said the rabbi, "and will continue to meet to face up to the present very bad situation to begin to establish a dialogue."

Included in the meetings have been such community leaders as the Rev. C. Herbert Oliver, chairman of the Ocean Hill - Brownsville school district's governing board, and Dr. M. L. Wilson, president of the National Conference of Negro Clergy.

At the same time Senator Jacob K. Javits met with 45 rabbinical and lay leaders of the Jewish community to dis-

cuss black anti-Semitism and Jewish racism. It was reported that the strongest point of unanimity to come from the meeting, held at the Harmonie Club, 4 East 60th Street, was a feeling that none of these problems could be brought to meaningful solution until the schools reopened.

Many of these leaders are aware that in the history civil-rights movement, which originally tied Negroes and Jews colsely together, there were such signs that suggested future conflict as the following:

¶The move by black militants to control the direction of their own movement excluded whites — including many liberal Jews — from further participation in the civil-rights movement.

¶This influx of more and more Negroes in neighborhoods in the city where Negroes and Jews now compete for dominance, an influx that has increased fear and tension.

¶Increasing reports of crimes against property in slums that developed differing views of the law-and-order issue between Negro residents and Jewish shopowners.

¶The move by Negroes into such fields as teaching and social work, which had previously attracted a large number of Jews, a move that has contributed to economic and professional conflict.

Present jobholders are fiercely protective of the merit system that allowed them into the professions despite prejudices. They see a threat to that system from the practice of compensatory hiring to benefit Negroes.

¶The movement of black militants to the Muslim faith—carrying with it the traditional antagonism between Arab and Jew—was made even more ominous to some Jews when these militants supported the Arabs in their war with Israel.

The School Crisis

Many Negroes and Jews were aware of these historical developments when the city's school controversy began in the Ocean Hill-Brownsville district. In that situation, the United Federation of Teachers—largely white and about two-thirds Jewish—came into conflict with a predominantly black district when the local school board tried to summarily transfer 10 white teachers, nine of them Jewish.

The Ocean Hill-Brownsville governing board denies it is

anti-Semitic, citing the fact that 40 per cent of the teachers it hired for Junior High School 271 are Jewish.

The situation had been exacerbated to the point Monday that Vice President Humphrey took note. Speaking to a largely Jewish audience, he said he was "deeply troubled by the anti-Semitic remarks being made by some extremists" in the school dispute.

Interestingly, a leader of the Jewish community and a leader of the black community were discussing the problem the same day on a television program and agreed anti-Semitism was an artificial issue. They pointed out that the issue was being used by forces seeking to gain support either from the black or Jewish communities.

Other discussions have occurred in private meetings between Mayor Lindsay and leaders of Jewish organizations. A series of meetings was held in September to give the Jewish community an opportunity to express its concern about what they saw as growing anti-Semitism. At the meeting, the Jewish leaders urged firm reaction on the part of public officials to any anti-Semitism.

Resignation an Issue

Among those represented at some of the meetings were the New York Board of Rabbis, the American Jewish Committee, the American Jewish Congress and the Anti-Defamation League.

A specific complaint at the meetings was against the city's Human Rights Commission, from which a Jewish member had resigned in February, 1967, complaining that charges of anti-Semitism were ignored while the commission concentrated on Negro complaints.

Jewish leaders who attended the meetings further reported that complaints were aired against the city's hiring practices that tended to ignore experience and other qualifications. They urged the Mayor to speak out forcefully against anti-Semitism.

A report published last Thursday in The Long Island Press and other newspapers said that Mayor Lindsay had reacted bitterly to Jewish demands and accused Jewish leaders of complicating his problems. These reports were denied firmly by the Mayor's office. They were also denied by Jewish leaders who attended the meeting.

Nevertheless the reports were anonymously circulated as handbills and served to worsen an already touchy situation.

Mayor Shouted Down

This was shown in a way that shocked many New York-ers on Oct. 15. The bitterness confronted Mayor Lindsay like a wall when he stood before a crowd inside the East Midwood Jewish Center in Brooklyn that night. When the Mayor was shouted down in his attempt to discuss the school strike, Rabbi Harry Halpern admonished the crowd: "Is this the exemplification of the Jewish faith?"

To his surprise, the answer was shouted back: "Yes! Yes!"

The bitterness swept over Senator Jacob K. Javits campaigning the next day in Brooklyn. An observer described the mood of the predominantly Jewish crowds as "frightening" when the crowds heckled Mr. Javits as he tried to defend the Mayor.

"It is unacceptable," Senator Javits told his fellow Jews, "this Jewish backlash. There is a real Negro anti-Semitism, but physically, congenitally, ideologically, psychologically, it is impossible that this [backlash] should exist when there is such an identity of interests of the minorities."

It has been said the Jewish people are a people with a memory. That memory has been sparked anew by the ugliness released in the black-and-white lines forming around the decentralization controversy. There are visions of bigotry that have hounded them down the years being turned loose again here, in this city at this time.

Hate Literature

Those visions are stirred by the statements of some black militants and by the virulent anti-Semitic literature circulated among teachers and parents in the Ocean Hill-Brownsville district.

"It is impossible," says one anonymous tract distributed last week, "for the Middle East murderers of colored people to possibly task the insight, the concern, the exposing of the truth that is a must if the years of brainwashing and self hatred that has been taught to our black children by those bloodsucking exploiters and murderers is to be overcome."

The fear generated was more explicitly called forth by another anonymous handbill: "Get off our backs, or your relatives in the Middle East will find themselves giving benefits to raise money to help you out from under the terrible weight of an enraged black community."

Angry shouts from members of the community of "Jew pig," "You will go out in a pine box," have rained down on Jewish teachers.

Negro teachers have been subjected to similar anonymous threats. "Nigger lover" and "Communist traitor" epithets abound in unsigned letters received by Negro teachers, many of whom crossed picket lines to continue teaching.

Jewish Reaction

Antagonism is exhibited by some Jewish teachers. Walking the picket line earlier during the strike, one Jewish teacher argued:

"We don't deny their equality, but they shouldn't get it by pulling down others who have just come up. It's wrong and reactionary for them to pit their strength against a group that struggled for years to make teaching a profession."

A careful study of the hate literature being circulated in the community has been made by the Anti-Defamation League of B'nai B'rith. The league has found no evidence of an organized effort behind the material. Instead, the material shows no pattern and is sporadic both in issuance and content, according to a league spokesman.

That an antagonism should develop between two minority groups with similar histories of persecution would have been almost incomprehensible a few years ago. The Jewish community has been for a half century at the forefront of programs to eliminate prejudice—whatever its target. They have fought in behalf of Negroes for better housing, schooling and merit employment.

Martyrs for Cause

The rivers of racial hatred that swept through the country following the Supreme Court's school desegregation decision of 1954 were tinged with the blood not only of Negroes, but also of liberal white Jewish civil rights martyrs.

Observers of the civil rights movements in the South frequently noted the large number of Jewish whites who furnished manpower and money to keep the struggles alive. Many Southern Jews increased their personal jeopardy by adding to existing anti-Semitic feeling against them by courageously articulating their support of the Negro's struggle for equal rights.

Through the intensively active decade of the civil-rights struggle from 1955 to 1965, the Negro and the Jew were often singled out as a clear-cut example of how white and black could work together opposing the common enemy of prejudice and bigotry.

But, by the middle nineteen-sixties, the common purpose began to be marred by more overt resentment than in the past.

By 1966 and 1967 both Jewish and Negro leaders had become concerned by increasing attacks by Negro militants against Jews as a separate group in a developing "hate whitey" campaign.

Reference to Hitler

A Congress of Racial Equality member at a meeting in Mount Vernon in February, 1966, for example, suggested that Hitler had not done his work well enough, leading to protests from both Jewish and Negro leaders. The speaker was discharged the next day by CORE.

The Student Nonviolent Coordinating Committee issued a newsletter in the summer of 1967 carrying an attack on Jews as a result of the Arab-Israeli war. Articles began to appear in the Negro press discussing the basis for anti-Semitism among Negroes in the slums.

Negroes, on the other hand, began to see what they considered an anti-Negro backlash developing within the Jewish community. In 1966 many traditionally liberal Jewish voters, along with many other whites in middle-income areas, reacted negatively to the referendum to establish a civilian review board for complaints against the police. The proposal, which was strongly supported by the Negroes, was defeated.

Deeply troubled by the break in the traditional liberal voting pattern of the Jew, some Negro and Jewish leaders began to examine this new problem. They found a reaction among all whites, in general, to the increased militancy of the civil rights movement that coincided with the exclusion of whites from the radical civil rights organizations.

Historical Factors

According to a representative of the American Jewish Committee, there then began a public discussion of a whole series of historical factors involved in the split. The representative, who declined to identify himself, said:

"When the Negro moved into the large city he moved into those areas most recently occupied by the Jews and many of the Jews still had vestiges of their holds there—as landlords and shopkeepers.

"In this conflict situation the symbol of white 'oppression,' the slumlords, the overcharging of shopkeepers, was the Jew. Because, historically, Jews had been more helpful in early stages of the conflict between Negroes and whites, they expected more from Jews and resented the fact that they sometimes acted like other white men."

Each action produced a reaction among the other group. To keep this developing antagonism from growing into open, bitter conflict, a number of moves were begun to "set the record straight."

To the Negro argument that Jews dominate the slum and are the logical symbol for the Negro's antiwhite feeling, research done for the American Jewish Congress disclosed the following:

¶Sixty per cent of all stores in a 20-block area in the heart of Harlem are owned not by Jews, but by Negroes.

¶Black ownership of area stores is increasing.

Another study, done for the American Jewish Committee in late 1967 in New York's slums, confirmed national statistics indicating the Negro population was less anti-Semitic than the rest of the population.

Negro leaders, including Whitney M. Young Jr. of the Urban League, James Baldwin, the author, and Bayard Rustin of the A. Philip Randolph Institute, agree.

Where there is anti-Semitism, they say, it is merely the spin-off of a general antiwhite sentiment.

During all this debate, the Negro's struggle for equal rights had shifted from its rural-Southern orientation to the urban-Northern scene.

Recently, young Negroes have moved more into professional occupations, putting them more and more into conflict on a man-to-man basis for jobs.

Coupled with this is the question of merit versus compensatory preference—that is, to overcome years of neglect should the Negro move farther faster in his job.

Mort Yarmon, of the American Jewish Committee, suggested in an interview how the stage had been set for the current conflict.

"For various historical reasons—among them the Civil Service and merit hiring that opened professions to Jews when others were closed to them—the Jewish people have moved heavily into the social services and teaching fields, especially here in New York City."

These are exactly the two "pressure points" at which the Negro now makes his demand that "we be allowed to care for our own, to teach our own."

School decentralization, community power, community control, are all seen by some Jews as threats to these systems in which the Jewish professional has found his place.

"It is," said one Jewish leader simply, "a head-to-head conflict for the first time."

Warning flags had been flying for some time when the John T. Hatchett affair touched off a public outcry. Mr. Hatchett published an article in the November-December 1967 issue of The African-American Teachers Forum, in which he openly attacked Jewish teachers.

"We are witnessing today in New York City a phenomenon that spells death for the minds and souls of our Black children," Mr. Hatchett wrote. "It is the systematic coming of age of the Jews who dominate and control the educational bureaucracy of the New York Public School system and their power-starved imitators, the Black Anglo-Saxons."

A storm of protest broke. Jewish organizations across the country condemned what they considered was the anti-Semitic tone of the article. The protests were repeated when Mr. Hatchett was hired by New York University as director of the Dr. Martin Luther King Afro-American Student Center and were reiterated this month when he was dismissed.

"I am not an anti-Semite," Mr. Hatchett retorted. "The thrust of the article was not aimed at Jews just because they were Jews. The tone of the article was anti-Establishment—that is, it was against those in a position to change the system."

Some supporters of Mr. Hatchett see him now as a victim of racism and question whether the fear of losing contributions by wealthy Jews was behind N.Y.U.'s action in dismissing him.

Now, facing one another across picket lines at schools around the city, Negroes and whites—many of them Jewish—have begun mutual recriminations, threats and counter-threats.

Above it all hangs the fear that the masses in neither camp listen to the leadership.

If anything, however, as agitators and militants seek to develop the antagonism, the leadership of both are fighting desperately against time to find again that community of interest that has bound the two groups together over the years.

As one Negro observer put it: "The hope is always there as long as we are dealing with the Jews. With them we could always communicate. Were it some other group, we might think it hopeless, but not with the Jews."

Similarly, the United Synagogue of America, representing 825 Conservative synagogues in the United States and Canada, has announced its opposition to the developing mood.

The Jewish people, it said, should not confuse the mouthings of extremists with the entire Negro community. It urged continued support of the Negro's goals for achieving equal opportunity in housing, education and employment.

October 23, 1968

Study Finds Pathological Bureaucracy in Schools

Charges Insiders in System 'Sabotaged' Desegregation Plans in Early Sixties

By JOHN LEO

A four year study by a New York University sociologist finds that the New York City school system is "a pathological bureaucracy" that cannot fulfill its function without massive outside intervention.

The study charges that insiders in the system deliberately sabotaged desegregation plans in the early sixties, and that the Board of Examiners maintained testing standards that have kept most Negro and Puerto Rican applicants out of posts as teachers and principals.

The study, titled "110 Livingston Street," which is the Board of Education headquarters in Brooklyn, is by Dr. David Rogers. It will be published Nov. 8 by Random House.

Dr. Rogers is associate professor of sociology and management in the graduate school of business administration at N.Y.U.

Working on a grant from the United States Office of Education, Dr. Rogers completed a study of New York school desegregation last year, while he was senior research sociologist at the Center for Urban Education, a research and development laboratory chartered by the New York State Board of Regents. The book, an outgrowth of that report, makes these points:

¶Since the nineteen-fifties, the school system has been largely a Jewish system, and Jews are trying to protect themselves from Negroes and Puerto Ricans as Catholics once tried to protect themselves from Jews a generation ago when the system was largely Catholic.

¶Whether planned or unplanned, the system's use of hearings, studies, commissions and limited experiments serves to deflate pressure groups and maintain the status quo.

¶The system has developed a style of "crisis management" that involves enough delay and lack of leadership to polarize the community on each major issue.

Dr. Rogers writes of "extensive" evidence of sabotage from 1960 to 1964 during the city's Open Enrollment program—a voluntary pupil transfer plan for desegregation.

He said that in the receiving schools, principals and teachers "had many techniques to discourage transfer," reporting that "incoming pupils would often be placed in slow and/or segregated classes; more disciplinary measures would be used; they sent in false data to headquarters."

In the sending schools, he said, the transfer proposal was often announced too late for parents to act; parents who did apply were told that their applications were too late, and many principals talked against the program and withheld relevant information.

"It is clear," he said, "that the board put a tremendous burden on Negro and Puerto Rican parents to find out about the transfer option themselves," with the result that only 3 per cent of eligible pupils were actually transferred.

The Board of Examiners, which administers tests for teaching, supervisory and administrative appointments, also works to prevent integration, he said.

"They exclude blacks and Puerto Ricans by perpetuating standards that are irrelevant to what goes on in the ghetto," the study found. "The tests are geared to those who go through the city college system, and field personnel give coaching courses for colleagues. But blacks have been turned down for 'Southernisms' in their speech patterns."

'Irish Power' Recalled

Dr. Rogers said the examination system had always favored the ethnic group in power and was likely to keep doing so. "Irish power up to the nineteen-thirties was gradually replaced by Jewish power through the late nineteen-sixties, and it will soon be replaced by black and Puerto Rican power," he said.

He argued that civil service appointees, deeply entrenched in the system, viewed virtually every reform as an attack on the merit system, if not as a threat to their own careers.

The system, he wrote, "has an almost unlimited capacity for absorbing protest and externalizing blame, for confusing and dividing the opposition, 'seeming' to appear responsive to legitimate protest by issuing sophisticated and progressive policy statements that are poorly implemented, if at all."

"The system is like a punching bag," he said. "Protest groups can hit in one place, and it simply returns to its old equilibrium."

Dr. Rogers contended that the school system was both overcentralized and undercentralized.

"It has the worst kind of centralization," he said. "The most trivial routine requests — for maintenance and supplies — are passed on to general headquarters, but the key policy decisions made at headquarters are often subverted or redefined in the field."

Lindsay Urged to Act

The book, completed last February, calls on Mayor Lindsay to confront the system and decentralize it "with a massive show of political power."

In an interview, Dr. Rogers conceded that the recent decentralization controversy in Ocean Hill-Brownsville had dissipated much of the Mayor's potential political support.

"I think the Mayor can still do it by going out to the community and clearly labeling the system as sick," he said. "He has to build a coalition out of all the institutions that have sat on the sidelines up till now — the universities, corporations, banks, insurance companies and Port Authority — all the consumers of the school produc."

One of the costs of the current Ocean Hill-Brownsville turmoil, he said, is that the teachers are now on the side of the professional bureaucracy.

"The teachers might have been a force for reform," he commented. "It's a tragedy that they're now aligned with the bureaucracy."

October 24, 1968

TEACHERS ACCEPT AGREEMENT, 6-1, AND SCHOOLS WILL REOPEN TODAY; OCEAN HILL UNDER STATE TRUSTEE

M'COY MAKES PLEA

District's Principals Delay on Promise of Cooperation

By LEONARD BUDER

The city's 1.1 million public school pupils were scheduled to return to classes this morning after members of the United Federation of Teachers voted by a 6-to-1 margin yesterday to call off their citywide strike.

As soon as the strike settlement terms were ratified by the union, a state trustee officially took over operation of the controversial Ocean Hill-Brownsville district in Brooklyn.

The predominantly Negro and Puerto Rican district was the focal point of bitter conflict between community demands for full control over local schools and the union's concern for the job rights of teachers. The dispute raised racial tensions and broad questions on the future of plans to decontrolize the city school system.

The trustee, Dr. Herbert F. Johnson, Associate State Education Commissioner, announced that he had put off until tomorrow morning the return to the district of a group of union teachers whose reinstatement had been opposed by officials of the decentralized school district. He said that the extra day was needed to work out class assignments for the teachers.

Everyone Pleased

The end of the five-week teachers' strike, the third this fall, gratified city, school and teacher officials. Parents sighed

with relief, and even pupils appeared happy.

The three strikes kept 50,000 teachers and a million pupils out of classes for 36 of the first 48 school days of the fall term.

Some striking teachers and pupils went to school after the last teachers' vote was announced but most decided to wait until this morning.

A teacher returning to a Greenwich Village elementary school was greeted with a hug and kiss by a 9-year-old boy.

Community Gloomy

But a sense of gloom prevailed in Ocean Hills-Brownsville and early this morning there were signs of possible new difficulties involving the troubled district.

A meeting between State Education Commissioner Dr. James E. Allen Jr., and six of the district's principals that ended shortly before 2 A.M. today failed to result in any immediate promise from the local school officials that they would accept orders from the state trustee.

They said they would give their answer later today.

However, Louis Fuentes, one of the three principals who was reassigned as part of the settlement terms, said it would take "five or six of New York's Finest" to get him out of his office.

The strike settlement, worked out at Gracie Mansion during a 27-hour negotiating session that ended Sunday afternoon, was ratified by the teachers' union membership by a vote of 17,658 for, 2,738 against.

On Sunday night there had been signs of opposition to the pact, apparently from teachers seeking to punish the Ocean Hill-Brownsville board for pushing for strong community control and jeopardizing teachers' job rights.

A stormy meeting of the union's delegate assembly was hastily adjourned by Albert Shanker, president of the union, because, he said later, he thought the assembly might recommend that the terms be rejected.

The general sense of relief brought by the end of the strike, which had aroused racial tensions between white and Negro groups, was tinged in some parts of the city with uncertainty and new concerns.

Some teachers and school supervisors who had been on strike were apprehensive about the reception they would receive when they returned to their posts in predominantly Negro and Puerto Rican neighborhoods. Community opposition to the strike had been greatest in these areas.

The strike settlement only provided for the appointment of the state trustee to oversee the district and also involved the removal from their posts, for at least the present, of three community-selected principals and four popular Negro teachers.

The teachers were accused of harassing union teachers and the appointment of the principals has been declared illegal by a court because they were named in violation of Civil Service procedures. An appeal is expected to be made in the court case.

McCoy Urges Caution

Rhody A. McCoy, the district administrator, yesterday cautioned teachers who have sided with the local governing board in the dispute with the union not to create trouble when the union teachers return to the schools.

The local governing board had tried to transfer some of the union teachers summarily on the ground that they had harmed the experiment in community control; the other teachers were opposed because they supported their colleagues.

Addressing a districtwide staff meeting at Junior High School 271, Mr. McCoy said that the governing board had neither accepted nor rejected the agreement reached between

305

the union, the Board of Education and Dr. Allen.

"We are studying it," he said.

There were calls for protest actions from some of the teachers, most of whom are white, but Mr. McCoy urged them not to do anything on their own.

After settlement of the two previous strikes this term, union teachers walked off the job, charging that teachers in Ocean Hill-Brownsville had been harassed.

The big question throughout the city yesterday morning was whether the rank-and-file of the teachers would accept the pact and end the strike that had split the city into opposing factions.

The vote on the tentative agreement originally was scheduled to have been completed Sunday night.

But after opposition developed at the Delegate Assembly meeting, Mr. Shanker extended the voting until yesterday morning to make it possible for more teachers to participate.

More Votes Sought

This was a move to bring out those teachers who would not have bothered to vote in the expectation that the agreement was certain to be ratified.

About 9,000 teachers voted Sunday night at the National Maritime Union Hall in Greenwich Village. Another 11,000 came out, despite the poor weather, to vote yesterday at the 69th Regiment Armory at Lexington Avenue and 26th Street.

As it turned out later, the Sunday night vote would have easily ratified the agreement.

At noon yesterday, George Abrams of the Honest Ballot Association, who supervised the voting, announced that the polls were closed.

The ballots were dumped onto tables in the middle of the huge armory floor and 30 workers began sorting them into rubber-band-bound stacks of "yes" and "no" votes.

Fifteen minutes later Mr. Abrams was called to a side door where six women teachers stood in the rain and demanded to be allowed to vote.

"Girls, girls, let me tell you this," he said. "The vote is overwhelming. You are going back to work tomorrow." The teachers left happy.

At 12:35, Mr. Abrams announced the official tally.

"It's the largest turnout for the teachers for a vote of this kind," he told newsmen.

He said he had talked to hundreds of teachers who had told him that they had come because they were afraid that the agreement might be rejected otherwise.

At 12:50, Vito De Leonardis, the union's director of staff, said: "We urge all of the teachers to report as soon as possible to school."

The longest teachers' strike in the city's history was over.

Mr. Shanker, the union president, said in a statement that he hoped that the troubles of the city's teachers, pupils and parents were over. The union head was reported to be ill and his statement was issued through an aide.

The statement noted that under the settlement the State Commissioner had appointed a trustee for Ocean Hill-Brownsville and had established a three-man panel to make sure that all teachers and supervisors in the city system would be protected from local acts of harassment and intimidation.

Precedent Feared

In calling the recent series of strikes, the union had voiced fears that under the system's citywide decentralization plan, other local school districts might follow the example of Ocean Hill-Brownsville and try to remove school personnel from their posts without regard for their legal and contractual rights.

"The panel established under this agreement," Mr. Shanker said, "represents a strong hope that the schools and their teachers will be safe from harassment and intimidation.

"The city, its parents, teachers and children have paid a high price to achieve these important objectives," he continued. "The U.F.T. will now turn its efforts to work with parents and community groups."

Mayor Lindsay, taking note of the strike's end, said:

"Clearly no one is fully satisfied. But I think everyone in this city realizes that a settlement of the strike and a return to orderly education is essential for all involved.

"I hope we can begin now to heal the divisions this strike has opened and to turn our attention to the real possibilities for educational greatness this city can achieve."

Superintendent of Schools Bernard E. Donovan said that he expected the strike settlement to "work," although there might be some difficulties.

"When and if trouble develops," he told a news conference yesterday, "it will be dealt with at that time."

Governor Rockefeller said yesterday he was "deeply gratified" by the strike's end. The Governor, reading a prepared statement in the press room of his Manhattan office, 22 West 55th Street, said also that "we must take steps now" to avert future school shutdowns.

Mr. Rockefeller made his statement after he had met for about 45 minutes with 13 women who were involved last Thursday in demonstrations outside his office by several thousand parents urging him to convene the Legislature to act on the school strike. He described the meeting yesterday as "interesting and informative."

As news of the union's ratification spread, some teachers headed for their schools at mid-afternoon. Others came in before the vote was officially announced.

The Board of Education reported that 19,795 teachers—about 10,500 more than on Friday—showed up yesterday.

At Public School 40, 320 East 20th Street, a woman was overheard telling a returning teacher to take off the union button he wore on his coat.

Then, perhaps to show her impartiality, the woman remarked that she had told some pupils to remove their "Flunk Shanker" buttons.

Four striking teachers returned to P. S. 41, at 116 West 11th Street, where they were received warmly by a group of nonstriking colleagues.

No friction was evident but Irving Kreitzberg, the principal, told teachers at an impromptu staff conference to expect some problems requiring a readjustment of relationships.

However, he expressed confidence that both teachers and pupils could quickly recapture the "mystique" of the school.

Dr. Johnson, the state trustee for Ocean Hill-Brownsville, established his office at Intermediate School 55, not far from the district headquarters of Mr. McCoy and the governing board.

In the morning Dr. Johnson,

a former Superintendent of Schools in Rockville Centre, L. I., met with Mr. McCoy and his staff.

The official said that he had received Mr. McCoy's "assurance that it is his desire to work with the state trustee."

In appointing Dr. Johnson to oversee the district, Commissioner Allen had specified that Mr. McCoy could remain as administrator if he agreed to follow the directives of the trustee.

A spokesman for the State Education Department later was asked if this meant that Mr. McCoy had been restored to his position.

Last month Superintendent Donovan relieved Mr. McCoy of his duties after Mr. McCoy said he would take his orders from the local governing board. This came a few days after the local board had been suspended by the Board of Education.

The spokesman said that he was unaware that Mr. McCoy had not previously been officially reinstated. He added that Mr. McCoy was now the district administrator and would be as long as he cooperated with the trustee.

Dr. Johnson said that the three principals—William H. Harris, Ralph Rogers and Louis Fuentes—were being assigned to the district office.

The three and three others principals, Percy Jenkins, David Lee and Ralph Grandanetti, attended last night's meeting with Dr. Allen. Dr. Johnson and Mr. McCoy also were present.

When the session ended early this morning, Mr. McCoy told newsmen that while he had given assurances that he would cooperate on administrative matters, he was unhappy over the "vague" and unfair way the settlement terms treated the three principals and four teachers.

About 50 Puerto Rican supporters of Mr. Fuentes showed up outside 261 Madison Avenue, where the department has its offices, and demonstrated in the rain for 35 minutes.

They chanted "Fuentes si, Shanker no" and "Puerto Rican power." The demonstrators had earlier attended a rally that had been addressed by Mr. Fuentes.

Despite the settlement of the strike, the city's Law Department made it clear yesterday that it would press legal action against the teachers' union and its leaders for allegedly defying two court orders to end the walkout.

Highlights of School Bill

Special to The New York Times

ALBANY, April 30—Following is a summary of the major provisions of the compromise New York City school decentralization bill hammered out by the leaders of the Republican-controlled Legislature.

Interim Board—There would be appointed within 20 days after the bill is signed a five-member interim board with one member appointed by each of the city's borough presidents. This board would hire a Chancellor (whose functions would closely parallel those of the Superintednent of Schools)`and, after public hearings, divide the city into between 30 and 33 local community school districts.

The language is such that the present experimental school districts could be expanded (to meet the requirement that each district have a minimum of 20,000 students) and retained.

In addition, the interim board would provide for the election of community school boards (to consist of from 7 to 15 members each) to be elected by proportional representation Jan. 6, 1970. These board members would take office on Feb. 16, 1970.

Permanent City Board—Five members, one from each borough, would be elected on May 5, 1970, to succeed the interim board on July 1, 1970. In addition, By July 1, 1970, the Mayor would appoint two additional members to make a seven-member city Board of Education.

The central board would be the central hiring, assigning and negotiating agency on matters of personnel. It would also exercise veto powers over their Chancellor's decisions on courses, curriculums, estimated budgets and site selection.

The board would also sit as an appeals board to enforce or rescind orders of the Chancellor or hear appeals from community boards. The board could also, after a hearing, once each odd year, alter community district lines.

The board would have the additional power to supersede, suspend or remove a local district board or any of its members.

Community School Boards—Members would serve two-year terms with no salary. They would be elected the first Tuesday in May of each odd year by voters and parents (who have been residents of New York 90 days, are citizens and 21 years of age) who have children in the district's schools. The board would hire and fix the salary of a District Superintendent who would be the administrator of all schools through the junior high schools in the district.

The local board could select textbooks from lists approved by the Chancellor; contract for repair and maintenance up to $250,000 a year; recommend school sites and be involved in consultation on all construction in their respective districts.

The local boards would have limited power over personnel transfer and assignment, subject to city board authority and negotiated contracts.

Personnel—The rights of teachers and other professional personnel are to be closely guarded through complex appeal procedures and protection of tenure. The Board of Examiners, with the Chancellor as a member, would be retained to qualify teachers on open and competitive examinations. Teachers would be listed by the board on competitive eligibility lists. Supervisory personnel would be qualified by the board on the basis of qualifying examinations only.

A special provision has been inserted that would require that all persons on the existing list for elementary school principals be assigned by April 1, 1970, after which an entirely new list, based only on qualifying examinations, would be drawn up. The Chancellor would appoint and assign all teaching personnel to all schools under the jurisdiction of the city board.

Budgets—Local community boards would annually submit budget requests to the Chancellor, who would have the power to increase, decrease or modify requests in preparing a line item budget estimate for the entire system that he would submit to the Mayor and the Board of Estimate.

The Board of Estimate and the city board could increase or decrease the total amount of line items, subject to the Mayor's veto. The city board would retain full control of the capital budget.

Special Hiring Provision—Every year the city board would be required—during April and May—to give reading examinations to all elementary school students. Before Oct. 1 each year, the students would be ranked by scores on these tests, and all those schools that fall below the 45 per cent score (40 per cent the first year only) would be declared "eligible" schools. These schools would be allowed to appoint teachers who are not on any list, provided those appointed can pass the test or have passed the National Teachers Examination.

Special Provisions—The present community boards would remain in force until Feb. 16, 1970, when the new board members are to be elected. The city board is empowered to enter into contracts with the City University of New York for the administration of not more than five city high schools that exhibit the greatest degree of disadvantage.

Truancy Overwhelms the Truant Officers Here

The New York Times (by Edward Hausner)

Marguerite Johnson, an attendance teacher at Franklin K. Lane High School, counseling a truant in an office of the Bureau of Attendance in Queens. Thomas P. McNearney, a supervisor from the Bureau, is standing in the background.

By MICHAEL STERN

For tens of thousands of the city's teen-agers, going to school has become a some-time thing.

Some are so poor they have no time for anything but the struggle to stay alive; some are frustrated by their inability to do high school work; some are rebelling against parental and teacher authority; some are sapped of energy by asthma and other chronic ailments; some are living the half lives of drug addicts; some are turned off by studies in which they see no sense.

And there are some who stay home to avoid the gantlet of muggers, rapists and drug-starved predators they must pass on the way to school; some have been truants so long they think they cannot return; some play hooky simply because they know they will not be caught.

Taken as a group, these sometime students have dropped attendance rates for the 275,024 youths enrolled in the city high schools to the lowest levels since 1900 and have so overwhelmed the Board of Education's 522-man Attendance Bureau that it can no longer enforce the state's compulsory education law here.

"It's easy to stay out of school; no one bothers you," said Allen Harrell, president of the Student Council at Boys High School. "I know because I was one of the main hooky players here. But after a while I realized there was nothing for me on the streets and I came back."

Allen, who has raised his grades from failing to a 77 per cent average and hopes to go to college next fall, said: "I've made it, or at least I think I have, but how many other kids are out there on the streets still looking for **something they're never going** to find? Who cares? Who helps them?"

According to Bureau of Attendance figures, as many as 65,000 high school pupils are absent on an average day. Last November, at Eastern District High School, 44 per cent of the students enrolled were out each day; at DeWitt Clinton, an average of 33 per cent were out; at Julia Richman, 39 per cent.

At Boys High (46 per cent out), teachers report that hundreds of students are now on a self-declared Tuesday-to-Thursday school week, taking regular Friday-to-Monday weekend holidays.

'Phantom Classes' Cited

At Thomas Jefferson (40 per cent absent), teachers talk about "phantom classes," citing as an extreme example one official class of 50 habitual truants to which only two pupils reported during a 30-day period this term, one for one day and the other for two.

At Morris High School (35 per cent absent), irregular attenders fall so far behind in their work that in their senior year they must be coached up to eighth-grade reading level so they may qualify for high school diplomas.

At Benjamin Franklin (45 per cent out), more than 400 of the students sent to the school by the junior highs each year never show up. These "no shows" just disappear, some to other schools and neighborhoods, others to the streets of Harlem and the South Bronx where veteran attendance teachers are afraid to follow, even in pairs, and where school mail seems never to reach its destination.

School districts upstate report year after year to the State Education Department that 90 to 95 per cent of their high school students go to school each day. In the city, where records are available back to 1900, the average daily attendance had been running in the high 80's, but has been falling steadily for seven years..

Rolls in City Decline

It has dropped from 87.1 per cent for the 1962-63 school year—a high point for the past two decades—to 75.1 per cent for 1967-68, to an even lower percentage (not yet fully tabulated by the board's computer) for 1968-69, and with no indications of a significant turn-around this year.

Attendance also has been falling—but not so far—in the 27 vocational high schools and in the elementary and junior high schools.

The growth of absenteeism is causing frustration and demoralization among teachers who find their courses and lesson plans disrupted; deep disappointment among parents who hope the schools will lead their children out of poverty, and cynicism among students who see others breaking the law with impunity and are tempted to do the same.

It is adding millions of dollars to the cost of running the schools and, at the same time, making it harder for the city to bear the burden by reducing the amount of state aid to education, which is doled out according to the attendance figures.

It also is causing widespread fear that yet another lost generation of youths with no education, no work or study habits and no prospects is passing through the high schools on the way to an empty, unfulfilled adulthood.

"Our boys need education more than they need anything else," said Noel A. Louis, the black assistant principal of Boys High School. "But if they don't come to school, how can we teach them?"

A school-by-school study by the Bureau of Attendance of the average number of absences per pupils during the last five school years shows that almost every high school in the city has been affected by the growth of absenteeism. While the problem is most acute in schools drawing students from the poorest neighborhoods, it also is affecting schools with predominantly middle-class enrollments and even the elite high schools.

Among the slum-area schools, for example, the average number of absences has risen from 33 a year to 59 a year at Thomas Jefferson; among the middle class schools, from 25 to 36 a year at Lincoln; among the elite schools, from 12 to 23 a year at Stuyvesant.

Wide Variety of Causes

These figures record only the number of students who do not answer to their names when attendance is taken in official class periods. They do not record the large number of other students who report to official classes so that absence notices will not be sent to their homes, but who cut other classes.

According to Martin Miller, attendance coordinator at Morris, it is not uncommon for such students to come to school for their free lunch and to see their friends, but to skip all subject classes.

Parents, teachers, principals, pupils, guidance counselors and attendance officers interviewed offered a wide variety of explanations for the rise in absenteeism. Among the reasons they gave were these:

¶The frustration felt by thousands of pupils who come out of the junior high schools reading at third-, fourth- and fifth-grade levels and who find it impossible to keep up with high school work.

¶Skip zoning, an attempt by the board to establish better racial balance in the schools, which forces some students to travel up to an hour and a half to get to their out-of-neighborhood schools.

¶Overcrowding, which in some schools forces pupils to attend classes in auditoriums, cafeterias, gyms and other makeshift rooms; to wait as long as 45 minutes on lunch lines; to rise before dawn to attend a morning session or stay in school beyond dusk to complete an afternoon session.

¶Attacks on the relevance of the traditional curriculum of reading, writing, mathematics, science and history, which has lessened the value of these studies in the eyes of some students.

¶A decline in adult authority, which signalled itself to one attendance teacher by the defiance she meets now compared with the nervousness she used to find in truants she chased.

¶Drug addiction, which most teachers and students think is a growing and menacing problem.

¶The cumulative effects of five years of school boycotts, teacher strikes, welfare protests, peace moratoriums and other demonstrations, all of which has shown some students that it is acceptable—and even proper — to put others causes and interests ahead of a day in school.

¶The failure of many parents to recognize the importance of regular attendance at school, even though they may urgently want education for their children and may make enormous sacrifices for it.

¶The feeling among many poor blacks and Puerto Ricans that no amount of schooling is going to improve their chances in life.

¶The fear of parents in slum neighborhoods that their children are not safe on the streets alone, even in broad daylight.

Almost all those interviewed agreed that migration from the South and from Puerto Rico has brought to the city a large body of poor children, perhaps a larger body of the poor than the city's schools ever were asked to educate before.

There are no figures on income levels for previous generations of public school pupils, but one indication of the size of today's enrollment of the poor comes from the Department of Social Services, which administers the welfare program.

Its records show that last year some 600,000 children up to the age of 18 were being given support in the Aid to Families with Dependent Children category. Of these, about 450,000 were of school age, a group equal to 40 per cent of the 1,123,165 children enrolled in the city's schools.

While the schools always have had large numbers of impoverished children, the children in this welfare category have the additional problem of coming from broken, chaotic and unstable homes.

Most live without fathers, with mothers overwhelmed by the struggle to keep food on the table, or with aunts, grandmothers or other relatives, often in three or four different homes in a single school year.

"Most of our absentees aren't living in what you and I would call a normal home," said Gerald Barron, attendance coordinator at Benjamin Franklin High. "When I look at a referral card and see one name for the student and another name for the guardian, and I also see no telephone number, those are pretty good signs we're not going to be able to find that kid."

Children Defended

"Some of the homes these nonattenders come from are unbelievable," Arthur Clinton, director of the Attendance Bureau, said. "For such a child, just getting to school in a white shirt is something of a miracle."

And an attendance teacher in the South Bronx who never enters one of the neighborhood's festering slums without checking under the stairs for a lurking mugger agreed. "If I'm afraid to go into some of these buildings, think what it must be like for the kids who have to live here," he said.

In all schools with predominantly poor enrollments, teachers report large numbers of children suffering from asthma, emphysema, epilepsy, almost chronic colds and other ills. When these children need treatment, they cannot call a doctor to make an appointment the way a middle-class child can, but must skip school to go to a clinic and wait their turn.

Often, the high-school-age child is the eldest in the family and must stay home to take care of an ailing parent or a sibling when illness strikes.

Guidance counselors at several schools say that among the pupils they advise are some who live absolutely alone by scrounging what they can from friends and relatives and by doing odd jobs in their neighborhoods. Arnold Marcus, a counselor at Boys High, said after discussing one such boy:

"No real change is going to take place in the schools until there are fundamental changes in the society outside the schools. Adding new programs each year will not help. The situation will continue as long as the underlying social conditions remain the same."

Some of the high schools have tried to meet the special needs of their pupils with special programs. At Morris High School, for example, there are 18 different classes in remedial English for poor readers and a "core" program featuring a double period in speech and English for children of Spanish background.

At Benjamin Franklin, a "cluster" program was organized three years ago for ninth graders to see if a joint teaching effort and intensive counseling could start these pupils off on successful high school work. Groups of 120 children were assigned five teachers and a guidance counselor and, in addition, a psychologist was asked to help children with acute problems.

Neither program has had a significant effect on attendance rates, although both have provided other benefits for some pupils.

Often, the argument centers

Arthur Clinton, director of the Attendance Bureau.

on the chicken-and-egg question of whether children fail because they are truants or are truants because they are failing.

Morton Selub, principal of Franklin K. Lane High School, taking note of the failure of many remedial efforts, said that perhaps an entirely new kind of education was needed for the nonattenders.

"Some of these kids may need a social worker or a street worker more than they need a teacher," he said. "Perhaps street academies may be the answer for some, or smaller schools where everyone a pupil meets says, 'How are you, Charlie, how are you getting along? and means it."

Guidance Plan Backed

Herbert Von King, a black building contractor and president of the Parent-Teacher Association at Boys High, believes this kind of intensive interest and guidance can be provided by alumni volunteers.

"Seventy-five per cent of our students have no fathers at home," Mr. Von King said. "These boys get no supervision because most mothers can't cope with a teen-age boy."

To answer this need, Mr. Von King is organizing a "man behind the boy" program with the goal of providing an alumni counselor for every fatherless student who wants one.

At Benjamin Franklin, Leonard F. Littwin, the principal, also is skeptical of the efficacy of remedial programs.

"The core of the problem is what a kid sees school for," he said. "When a boy has college as his goal, he has no problem here. But how do you motivate the couple of hundred pupils we get each year who read at third-grade level and have never had any success in school?"

The answer being planned at Franklin is a new kind of program that would combine part-time work and full-time study leading directly to a career in health or electronics or some other field with wide-open opportunities. The children would be paid from the moment they started work in the ninth year, with regular raises as they acquired proficiency.

The program is being planned

The New York Times
Morton H. Selub, principal of Franklin K. Lane High.

by the school's Improvement Committee, a parent-community-teacher group, with the help of a grant from the Urban Coalition. It is roughly similar to the STEP and CO-OP Work programs already in operation in many schools for pupils 16 years old and older, but would be more comprehensive and would take in younger children.

For Mr. Littwin, the importance of a recognizable goal for a student is proved by the excellent attendance record achieved by students in the school's College Bound program. While the attendance rate for the school as a whole was only 55 per cent in November, it was 90 per cent for the College Bound classes.

Traditionally in the city, it was considered normal and tolerable for one of 10 pupils to be absent on an average day. Most of those absences were caused by illness, severe weather or unusual home problems. This left the attendance bureau with a managable work load of delinquents, truants and disturbed children.

Now, however, with an absence ratio higher than one in four in the high schools, and with as many as 65,000 high school students absent each day, plus thousands more in the elementary and junior high divisions, the bureau's 522 officers are swamped and cannot meet their responsibility of enforcing the compulsory school law, according to Mr. Clinton, the director.

Adding to the bureau's problems, and swelling the absentee rate, are many youths who are registered in school for non-educational reasons. Some keep themselves on the registers to avoid the draft. Some stay on to maintain their welfare grants, which continue through the 18th year if a child is going to school.

Some Move Into Jobs

Still others move away without telling their school or take jobs without formally resigning from school. The law requires children to attend school until their 17th birthday, unless they resign with parental consent to take a job after their 16th birthday.

Tracking down such children takes a large part of the working day of the attendance teachers and prevents them from doing the intimate counseling they are trained for.

Until such children can be found, or until an attendance teacher can conscientiously say they cannot be found after extensive efforts, they must remain on the school registers and must be programmed for and assigned teachers, classrooms and advisers.

Restoring the schools to normal compliance with the education law will require, as a first step, almost a doubling of the attendance staff, Mr. Clinton said. He has proposed adding 116 new attendance teachers plus 346 community liaison aides.

"Quite frankly, we have a mess on our hands," Mr. Clinton said. "For the past 10 years the size of our staff has remained constant, despite our annual pleas for increases. Now, the superintendent has put our request into the budget, and if we get the people we need, it will be a magnificent step forward."

The Board of Education, underlining the seriousness of the problem, has requested $10.4-million for a program to reverse the rising rate of dropouts and lower the rate of truancy.

Task Force Is Helping

Mr. Clinton and other members of the bureau have been encouraged by the work of an experimental task force led by Thomas P. McNearney, a veteran supervisor. With four attendance teachers and 12 community aides, Mr. McNearney's task force last year sought out in their homes 526 chronically absent 16- and 17-year-olds at John Adams High School.

Ninety-three of them could not be found or failed to come to conferences. Ninety-eight were discharged because they were over age, because they preferred to work or because they had medical disabilities. The others were given counseling and put under close supervision.

For the 325 youths in the last group, attendance rates improved, for a two-month period, from 59.1 to 73.9 per cent, and 30 per cent of them kept up their good attendance habits without any further counseling this year.

It is Mr. Clinton's hope that similar work will bring thousands of other pupils back into the schools.

Racial Strife Undermines Schools in City and Nation

City High Schools Affected

By JOSEPH LELYVELD

Racial fears and resentment are steadily eroding relations between white teachers and administrators and black students in many, possibly most, high schools here.

In a few schools, this erosion has gone so far as to create conditions of paralyzing anarchy in which large police detachments have been deemed necessary to keep classrooms functioning and put down sporadic outbursts of violence by rebellious students.

More generally, the widening gulf between white adults and black youths in the schools convinces increasing numbers of blacks and whites that the fading promise of school integration can never be more than a hollow piety.

A two-month survey by The New York Times of a cross-section of the city's 62 academic high schools—some predominantly black, others mostly white, some troubled and others ostensibly calm—indicated that racial misunderstanding appears in some schools not just as a fever that flares now and then but as a malignant growth.

In such schools adults and youths seize on narrow one-dimensional views of each other.

In the eyes of many teachers, students who express feelings of racial pride by donning the African shirts called dashikis and wearing talismans, or by sewing the emblems of various black power movements to Army combat jackets, surrender the status of children for that of "hard-core militants."

"We are faced with a very, very specific political movement," charged James Baumann, a co-chairman of the United Federation of Teachers chapter at Franklin K. Lane High School, a necolonial-style fortress on the Brooklyn-Queens border where a force of 100 policemen was stationed last October after an outbreak of racial violence. "A small, dedicated group of militants is trying to polarize the student body and establish a totally black school."

A respected Brooklyn principal, who didn't want to be quoted by name, talked not of small minorities but uncontrollable masses. "What can you do," he asked, "when you have 1,000 blacks in your school, all programed for special behavior and violence?"

In the eyes of many black students, teachers given to such interpretations lose their identity and vocation and merge into that monolith of rigid, hostile authority known collectively as "the Man."

'A Fallen House'

"As soon as they get the cops behind them, they show how racist they are," said a Lane student regarded by teachers as a "militant" leader. "We're trying to get ourselves together but they don't like that. They want to get us out. That's boss [great]! Black people shouldn't go to that school."

A black senior at George W. Wingate High School put his disaffection more broadly: "The school system? Like man, it's a fallen house."

Often under pressure the two sides conform precisely to each other's expectations with results that are mutually disastrous. Then teachers are openly taunted and abused, firebombs and Chemical Mace are discovered in stairwells, and racial clashes erupt between black and white youths who normally keep a safe, formal distance between them.

In 1969 incidents of this type were reported in more than 20 high schools here.

"The youngsters are militant—everyone's militant," said Murray Bromberg, principal of Andrew Jackson High School in Queens.

Much of the anger of teachers and students can be traced to the frustrations both suffer in classrooms.

'We Aim Higher'

In the furor over whether it is the schools that are failing to teach blacks and other nonwhites or the students themselves who are failing to learn there is one undisputed fact—that the results are catastrophic.

The level of educational achievement accepted as a norm in many schools was indicated last month by a letter sent to the parents of all students at Lane. "We are not satisfied just to bring every senior up to the eighth-grade level of reading," it said. "We aim higher."

Many black students are registered in watered-down "modified" courses that lead nowhere. Even in schools that boast of being integrated, these classes are often all-black.

But the small minority of students labeled "militants" are almost never drawn from the mass of undisciplined students, semiliterate dropouts, truants or drug users. Frequently they are among the most aware and ambitious black students in the school—the very students, teachers commonly say, who should concentrate on their studies and "make something of themselves."

Ironic Situation

Some observers regard it as ironic, even tragic, that these students and their capacity for commitment should be seen as a threat. "The fact is that they are an articulate and committed group of youngsters looking for change and reform," said Murray Polner, assistant to Dr. Seymour P. Lachman of the Board of Education.

But that has been distinctly the minority view, especially since the three teacher strikes over the community control issue in Ocean Hill-Brownsville late in 1968.

"That was the precipice," said Paul Becker, a Wingate teacher who broke with the union after the second strike and now is active in the Teachers Action Committee, which favors community control. "After that it was downhill all the way. It was 'us' against 'them.'"

Many black students are still outraged by the memory of epithets and abuse from U.F.T. picket lines. "There were teachers shouting, 'Nigger!'" recalled Billy Pointer, a Wingate senior, in the course of a recent group discussion on human relations.

"No, Billy, that's not right," said Martin Goldberg, a social studies teacher. "I have to admit that some teachers used unprofessional language but I'm almost sure that none of them used the word 'nigger.' That must have been parents."

Later, the teacher commented: "I hate it when people who aren't racists say 'nigger.'"

That the clash of values has not been exclusively racial was demonstrated at Jackson where black students last year agitated successfully for the appointment of a black assistant principal.

This fall the new man, Robert Couche, was stunned to find himself denounced as a "house nigger" after having been regarded himself, he says, as an "extremist" at his previous school.

More recently, these same black students threatened demonstrations to block the transfer of young white teachers whom they considered sympathetic.

Negro school administrators like Mr. Couche find themselves in a lonely, uncomfortable position where their motives are often over-interpreted or misinterpreted by both their white colleagues and black students. Nevertheless there are many who believe that the advancement of more blacks to positions of real authority in the system offers one of the few possibilities of blunting the racial confrontation.

At present few high schools have faculties that are less than 90 per cent white; only three have Negro principals. White teachers often complain that Negroes are being favored for promotion, while many blacks say that the system advances only the "safest" Negroes.

"Now if you don't bite your tongue, you're a 'militant,'" said Charles Scott, a former head of the U.F.T. chapter at Jackson who is a leader of a faculty Black Caucus there that sees itself as a counterpoise to the union.

Student 'Willing to Die'

Many white teachers are convinced that there is a carefully plotted conspiracy for a black 'takeover' of the high schools—those of North Brooklyn and South Queens, in particular—by the same forces that were active in Ocean Hill-Brownsville. The evidence they most often cite is the words and rhetoric of black student activists and adults who influence them.

A newsletter of the African-American Teachers Association calls for support of black students who "seek 'through any means necessary' to make these educational institutions relevant to their needs."

At Lane, a student sent tremors through the faculty by proclaiming his willingness "to die for the cause."

What do such declarations mean? John Marson, the self-possessed chairman of the African-American Students Association, replied that violence was the only power students had to "back up what they say," comparing it to the power of the U.F.T. to strike.

But he scoffed at the ideas many teachers hold about a conspiracy. No one can tell the students in the various schools what to do, he said.

That wasn't the way it seemed last semester to Max Bromer, the beleaguered Wingate principal. "It's all planned, it's all planned," he insisted when he was visited one day in his office, which looked like a stationhouse annex with four or five police officers lounging at a conference table and a police radio crackling in the background.

Pressure was building up in the school, he said, and he had reliable intelligence warning him of a likely cafeteria riot in the sixth period.

A white teacher came into the office and reported that the cafeteria was quieter than it had been in weeks "They're massing," the principal surmised.

When the sixth period passed without incident, his anxiety shifted to the eighth. Finally the school emptied. Was it all a false alarm? "No," he said, "it was psychological warfare."

Mr. Bromer's responses can't simply be written off as jitters, for he had seen his school brought to the edge of a breakdown by racial hysteria and violence, despite what he thought had been a successful effort the previous semester to negotiate an "understanding" with the "militants."

As regularly happens, he has also seen many of his most experienced white teachers flee the school as the proportion of nonwhite students shot past the 50 per cent mark.

Wingate's troubles last term boiled out of a controversy over where to draw the line on expression by black students —the starting point of most racial explosions in the high schools. That line had been clearly transgressed, most teachers felt, in an assembly program staged by the school's Afro-American club.

Two passages were seen as particularly offensive—a recitation of an old Calypso ballad popular among Black Muslims ("A White Man's Heaven is a Black Man's Hell") and a line from a skit ("Brothers and sisters, we can't live if we continue to support the pigs by buying their dope and kissing their —— and letting them label us.")

Blacks Aroused

White students weren't shocked by these lines but by the angry pitch to which black students in the audience seemed to have been aroused. "I was actually embarrassed to be white," one girl said, "because I thought they hated me for something I didn't do."

Teachers saw the program as a deliberate provocation. "The nerve! The nerve! The nerve!" one fumed.

A week later racial clashes broke out in which many more white students than blacks were injured. In fact, many teachers had assumed that a racial confrontation had been in progress ever since the assembly. Black students identified as "militants" complained that they immediately became objects of suspicion.

Many Wingate teachers as-

sumed the students were being manipulated by "outside influences." They singled out Leslie Campbell and Sonny Carson, two fiery figures in the Ocean Hill-Brownsville dispute.

'I Was Whitelisted'

Mr. Campbell, a 29-year-old Lane alumnus who is soft-spoken in conversation and anything but that in confrontation, lost his teaching post in the demonstration project last fall—"I was whitelisted," he says—and has just started a "liberated" nigh school, in Brooklyn for black students with the backing of the African-American Students Association.

Called the Uhuru Sasa (Freedom Now) School, its curriculum will include courses in martial arts, Swahili and astrology.

Asked to describe his relation to the students, Mr. Campbell didactically sketched a diagram on a pad before him.

"This is the soil," he said, pointing with a pencil. "The minds of these kids is fertile soil but it just lays there in the schools. We supply the seed —an understanding of black nationalism and the political situation."

Mr. Campbell said he was out of "the demonstrations bag." Mr. Carson, a onetime leader of Brooklyn CORE, is still in it. He likes working with students, he said, because they haven't been compromised by "the system."

"These kids are already liberated," he exulted. "They're beautiful."

Black students here reflect a mood of self-awareness that can be found at almost any high school or college in the country with a significant black enrollment. Some are imbued with sloganistic fervor. Some want an outlet for anger. Others are tentatively working out a life style. Many are just happy to "belong."

A few imagine romantic futures for themselves as black revolutionaries. But most think in conventional terms of gaining skills that will make them useful to their people.

Most of them seem more indifferent than hostile to whites. "I can only care about the people I relate to and the people I relate to are all black," said a youth in Panther garb at Jackson.

Linda Jacobs, a black senior at Thomas Jefferson High School in Brooklyn, was similarly casual when asked about her reaction to the flight of whites from her school, which has gone from 80 per cent white to 80 per cent nonwhite in only five years. "It doesn't bother me, not one bit," she said.

Fake Addresses Used

Many whites from the Jefferson district have used fake addresses to send their children across the racial boundary formed by Linden Boulevard to Canarsie High School, which is about 75 per cent white—"a nice, solid ethnic balance," according to its principal, Isadore S. Rosenman.

But Canarsie has had its troubles. After rioting last year it found it expedient to eliminate the lunch period, as a way of preventing racial clashes in the lunch room.

Canarsie has also tried positive measures to overcome the disinclination of black students to become involved in the school's extracurricular life. For instance, it is now routine to have two hands at all dances, one black, the other white.

Teachers use words like "magnificent" and "beautiful" to describe relations at Canarsie. But most black students appeared to agree with Vernon Lewis, a senior, who said, "Here you always have the feeling there is someone behind you, looking at you."

A Sharp Contrast

They contended that they would have more freedom of expression at a predominantly black school like Jefferson. The contrast between the bulletin boards of the Afro-American clubs at the two schools indicated the range. The Canarsie board told of scholarships available to blacks; the one at Jefferson carried the Black Panther newspaper.

Despite the publication of a code of students' rights by the Board of Education last October, there remain extraordinary variations in the degree of expression on controversial issues—racial issues, especially —permitted to students.

At Brooklyn Tech — a "special" school for bright students that is more than 80 per cent white—a dean last year ordered the removal of a picture of Eldridge Cleaver from the cafeteria on the ground that the author and Black Panther spokesman was a "fugitive from justice."

This year the principal, Isador Auerbach, summoned a police escort to remove a black "liberation flag" on the ground that state law forbade any banner but the American flag in the schools.

Ira Glasser, associate director of the New York Civil Liberties Union, termed this a typical case of "the lawlessness of principals." There is no such provision, he said.

Another View

By contrast, Bernard Weiss, principal of Evander Childs

High School in the Bronx, saw no need to react to the posting of a picture of Huey Newton, the Black Panther Minister of Defense, on a bulletin board in his school.

"We want kids to read, we want kids to discuss," he explained. "We don't teach revolution. But if that's what they want to discuss, at least we can make sure they hear both sides."

Evander is about 50 per cent white, and most of its white students are from predominantly Italian, deeply conservative neighborhoods of the Upper Bronx—the perfect ethnic mix, it is sometimes said, for an explosion. But though the school has had some close calls and thorny issues, it has had no major eruptions of racial violence.

The school that has come closest to a breakdown—and has thereby raised the specter of ultimate disaster for the whole system—is Franklin K. Lane, which is set next to the mausoleums of the Cyprus Hills Cemetery.

On one recent afternoon, Chemical Mace was released on a staircase, a fire was started in a refuse can in the lunchroom, and a tearful white girl, reporting that a gang of blacks was waiting to ambush her, demanded a police escort to her bus stop.

"Just a normal afternoon," said Benjamin Rosenwald, a dean.

Normality at Lane also included an ominous stand-off in the cafeteria between white policemen with little metal American flags stuck in their caps and black students standing guard beside a "liberation flag." Routinely, the students taunted "the pigs." The officers masked their reactions behind stiff smiles, but not one of them had his nightstick pocketed.

Many white students are afraid even to set foot in the cafeteria, known to them as "the pit." A handful have been kept out of school altogether by their parents for the last three months.

There are those who find a simple explanation for Lane's woes — the racial incongruity between the school and its locale.

Lane is about 70 per cent black and Puerto Rican but stands in a neighborhood that is entirely white and aroused on racial issues. Mainly Italian and German by ethnic background, the district sends Vito P. Batista, the Conservative, to Albany as its Assemblyman.

But, in fact, the residents were not the first group to become militant over the racial situation at Lane. Neither were the black students. Militancy began with the local chapter of the United Federation of Teachers, whose leaders complained five years ago that Lane was becoming "a dumping ground."

The U.F.T. Position

The U.F.T. demanded that the Board of Education hold the blacks to under 50 per cent and, when that point was passed, they demanded that a racial balance be restored.

The teachers insist that their only interest has been "quality integrated education." But the U.F.T. has never proposed that black students cut from Lane's register be sent to schools now predominantly white.

George Altomare, a union vice president and a social studies teacher at Lane, was asked recently if he thought a black-white balance would also be a good idea for a predominately white school like Canarsie. "Ideally yes," he replied slowly, adding the proviso that more high schools would first have to be built to relieve overcrowding.

But Mr. Altomare believes there must be no delay in implementing a union proposal to make Lane a "prototype" of effective integrated education—to be accomplished by cutting its register by one-third and introducing special training in job skills for students not continuing to college.

It is only on paper that Lane is now overcrowded, for its average daily attendance is under 60 per cent.

Black students find a simple explanation for the faculty's insistence on reducing the student body. "Lane doesn't like us and we don't like Lane," one declared.

Since the strikes in 1968, Lane has gone from crisis to crisis. Last year a shop teacher, identified in the minds of some students as a supporter of George C. Wallace, was assaulted by young blacks who squirted his coat with lighter fluid and set it on fire.

Action Overruled

The assault, which was followed by the threat of a teacher walkout, led to the placing of a strong police detachment in the school and the dropping of 678 students — mostly blacks—from its register, an action later declared illegal by a Federal judge.

Even before the assault, the union chapter had placed a special assessment on its members for "a public relations and publicity campaign" aimed at winning the support of "business, civic, political and parent groups" for its position.

This effort helped arouse the surrounding white community, which formed an organization called the Cypress Hills-Woodhaven Improvement Association specifically to protest disorders at Lane.

Michael Long, chairman of the group, said the union had hoped to use it as a "battering ram," then disowned it when it demonstrated for the removal of the school's principal, Morton Selub.

Now Mr. Long worries that he may not be able to control vigilante sentiment in the community if there are further disorders at Lane.

A Familiar Dispute

The breakdown at Lane last October had a familiar genesis —a dispute over whether black students had the right to fly the "liberation flag" in place of the American flag in a classroom where they studied African culture.

After the flag had been removed from the room two days running, the students staged a sit-in to protect it, setting off the cycle of confrontation, suspensions and riots.

Black student activists at Lane don't deny that they have resorted to violence to press their demands, or "raise tensions to help a brother," or to "keep things out in the open."

They also acknowledge that they have not tried to discourage assaults on whites by younger black students outside their own group who want, as one activist put it, "to express their anger and let the white students know how it feels."

What they do deny is that their insistence on the "liberation flag" was an attempt to do anything but stake out a single classroom where they would be able to express themselves freely.

"Students want to relate to what's happening in their school," said Eugene Youell who prefers the adopted name of Malik Mbulu to his "slave name" and now has enrolled in Leslie Campbell's new school.

Some schools see a point in struggling to prove to themselves and their most aroused black students that there is a place for them in the schools and an incentive to study.

At Jackson, a school that appears to be on its way to becoming all-black, the principal has become the focus of a wide range of pressures—from white teachers, black teachers, middle-class Negro parents who want their sons and daughters protected from radical influences, and some black students who believe they have the right to conduct public readings of the thoughts of Mao Tse-tung or anyone else.

Recently the principal, Murray Bromberg, went before a history class devoted to "the evolution of today's African-American experience" and boasted, "This is the school of the future."

He said it was time for white school administrators and teachers to revise their assumption that standards must inevitably be lower in an all-black school.

His audience seemed to be itching to provide the principal with a list of assumptions about black youths that white adults could revise. But if they were "militants," they were also very obviously teen-agers who found no incongruity in wearing a big "I Support Jackson Basketball" pin next to a "Free Huey" button.

In fact, the African-American Club at Jackson has discovered it cannot hold meetings on the same day as a basketball game. Too many of its members are boosters.

February 9, 1970

Schools

By NEIL POSTMAN

This is the story of the maiming of a school. A very good school. And a very good maiming. I should say almost the perfect crime, since all the suspects not only have a proper alibi but have behaved in such a manner as to make it appear that they are not suspects at all. And they are probably not. Which makes the mystery of the school even more intriguing.

The school is P.S. 146, located in East Harlem. An elementary school, it was one of twenty-seven schools funded by the Federal Government, advocated by the teachers' union, and nurtured by some dedicated teachers and administrators. For the record, 50 per cent of its students are Puerto Rican, and 45 per cent black, which when properly translated is supposed to mean: forget it. Except that for the past three or four years, P.S. 146 has been one of the finest schools in New York, perhaps in the entire country.

In "Crisis in the Classroom," Charles Silberman called it a place where "ordinary teachers perform in an extraordinary way." And Arlene Silberman, in a letter to Principal Matthew Schwartz, wrote that "a visitor can roam the length and breadth of your school without encountering a single instance of harsh treatment of a child, of adult authoritarianism, or of what I would consider poor teaching."

Under the leadership of Principal Schwartz and, this past year, of Acting Principal Seymour Fliegel, the teachers at P.S. 146 have proven that quality education in inner city schools is entirely feasible if commitment and a sound philosophy are backed up with enough money.

This term, much of what was happening at 146 will more or less stop.

In July, Community School Board No. 4, under whose jurisdiction P.S. 146 falls, adopted a resolution "that the program known as More Effective Schools is not to be funded out of District 4 Title I money. . . ." This decision has the effect of cutting approximately 43 people from the staff, just about half of last year's total.

The decision will pretty much undo P.S. 146. Cold-blooded deed? Hardly. The local school board feels that the Central Board should fund such schools, and that, in the absence of such funding, it would be unfair to deprive other schools in the District of sorely needed staff. The local board concedes that 146 is outstanding but has 22 schools to care for, and limited funds.

What about the Central Board? Under the decentralization plan, the Board feels it may not have the power to compel local boards to use Title I funds; in fact, it feels it may have no authority to administer these funds at all. Chancellor Harvey Scribner agrees. Moreover, he is committed to local control and no doubt believes that if an authentic decentralization is to be achieved, the Central Board must stop interfering with local people.

That leaves the United Federation of Teachers. The union included in the preamble of its last contract an in-sistence on the continuation of these programs. However, there is presently some doubt about whether the pre-amble of a contract is binding. The city's Corporation Counsel says no. The union has asked for arbitration, but it is not likely to press the matter too hard.

So there is it. All motives are good, and all consciences are clear. But the children at P.S. 146 are undeniably being harmed. But by whom? No one knows, and Acting Principal Fliegel, who fought desperately in the last few months to save the school, lost in the end because there was no one to engage — save the force of circum-stance, or progress, or some other abstraction.

———

Neil Postman is professor of educa-tion at New York University.

September 18, 197

Teachers' Union Planning Puerto Rican Culture Guide

Albert Shanker, president of the United Federation of Teachers, announced yesterday that his union would publish this fall the first teachers' guide on Puerto Rican history and culture.

The guide will contain lesson plans mainly for grades 7 through 12 on such topics as Puerto Rican identity, mi-gration to the United States, life in New York and the de-velopment of Puerto Rican cul-ture.

Mario Lemagne, chairman of the union's bilingual chapter, said that teachers believed it was important that students knew their ethnic heritage and that the guide met a major ed-ucational and intercultural need in this city.

School Board Will Create Office of Safety Director

By IVER PETERSON

The Board of Education will create a new position of safety director for the city's public schools and appoint Eldridge Waith, a former commander of patrolmen in Harlem, to fill it.

The move, which was con-firmed last night by board offi-cials, is apparently designed to counter the school system's growing problems with vio-lence, as well as to offset the United Federation of Teachers' contract demands for tougher policies on school crime.

The creation of the new post and Mr. Waith's appointment will be officially announced to-morrow. Mr. Waith broke the news yesterday in Charlotte Amalie, on St. Thomas, where he has served for the past 18 months as Commissioner of Public Safety for the United States Virgin Islands.

Dr. Harvey B. Scribner, Chancellor of the school sys-tem, would not comment pub-licly on the report.

Mr. Waith said he would leave his Virgin Islands job on Aug. 28. In New York, he will have under his command about 200 school guards who have been trained by the Police De-partment. This number is scheduled to be increased, a spokesman for the Board of Education said last night.

Mr. Waith's appointment comes at a time when the cen-tral board and the teachers union are sharply divided over the problem of handling crime in the schools, such as the sale of drugs, assaults on teachers, vandalism and shakedowns of students for pocket money.

The board has maintained that the teachers themselves are best suited to maintain con-trol over the students, a view that Albert Shanker, the union president, has sharply criti-cized. Mr. Shanker has also charged the board has under-rated the extent of violence in and around the city's schools.

The union has called in its current contract demands for the hiring of more than 6,000 trained security guards—one for every 175 students—in addi-tion to a mobile security patrol for each borough.

Some board members have called this demand an invitation for "an army of outsiders" to interfere with proper student-teacher relations.

One official of the central board characterized Mr. Waith's forthcoming appointment as a well-timed response to the un-ion's call for more guards.

"Shanker is making a big is-sue out of it," the official said, "so I guess they [the board] are retaliating."

Mr. Waith, a 29-year veteran of the city police force, had at-tained the rank of assistant chief inspector before he took a leave of absence to work in the Virgin Islands.

His last assignment in the city was as commander of Pa-trol Borough Manhattan North, which includes Harlem. He earned a reputation as an ag-gressive and tough-minded leader in that assignment.

The New York Times
Eldridge Waith

Teaching Juan His Name Is John

When Juan Ortiz began bringing his homework back from the second grade in Brooklyn, his mother noticed that he had changed the spelling of his first name on his papers.

"Well," the nine-year-old explained, "my teacher tells me my name isn't Juan. It's John."

The little episode, as insignificant as it may seem, touches on several elements at the heart of a growing concern among city educators—and growing militancy in the Puerto Rican community—over the quality of educational opportunity in New York's English-only schools for the children of the city's latest wave of immigrants.

Joseph Monserrat, president of the City's Board of Education and prominent champion of Puerto Rican causes, argues that the language barrier most Puerto Rican students face is not just an impediment to following what the teacher says, but—as with Juan Ortiz—it makes it hard to know who you are.

"The kid grows up in a Spanish-speaking house," he said recently. "He eats rice and beans, he has a language, and a certain way of being. This kid walks into a classroom when he's six and what the school proceeds to do then is knock his language out of him, in effect telling him that his whole world up till then is wrong. From an educational point of view, in terms of receptivity to learning and of self respect, the effect is negative to say the least."

How negative the experience has been for the city's Spanish-speaking students was illustrated in the figures of a Board of Education report issued last spring:

Of the 250,000 Spanish-speaking students, more than 100,000 speak little or no English; some 86 per cent are below normal in reading levels for their grade and age; more than 57 per cent drop out of school and do not finish, as compared to a 36 per cent drop-out rate of blacks and 29 per cent for white students.

These figures add up to disaster for a generation of first and second generation immigrants who are struggling for a toe-hold on the bottom rung of America's social and economic ladder. Senator Jacob Javits has for some time been charging that the record indicates a flagrant violation" of the 1964 Civil Rights Act by denying the Spanish-speaking students equal educational opportunity.

Ten days ago, Senator Javits announced a full-scale investigation of his charges of bias in the city school system by the Department of Health Education and Welfare. Ironically if the investigation confirms the charges, the city could lose more than $150-million a year in Federal subsidies—most of which is earmarked for remedial programs for unsuccessful students, such as the Puerto Ricans.

The city, meanwhile, has begun to take steps to help ease the way for Spanish-speaking students. The principal method is the bilingual education program, where students can study regular academic subjects in Spanish or English or both. But so far, only 800 of the city's 57,000 teachers are bilingual, and their efforts reach only 4,200 of the 100,000 or more Puerto Rican students who need them most.

Meanwhile, frustration over the plight of Spanish-speaking students has coalesced into firm action in some city school districts. The Community School Board for District One, which covers Manhattan's Lower East Side, stirred up a small storm of controversy last weekend when it appointed Luis Fuentes, a militant spokesman for Puerto Rican power in the schools, as District Superintendent in the overwhelmingly Puerto Rican community.

Mr. Fuentes, who has been accused of anti-Semitism and of various other instances of unethical personal conduct, gained an early following as a school principal in Brooklyn for his aggressive expansion of bilingual programs at his school. He has promised to do the same for the Lower East Side's 12,400 Spanish-speaking elementary and junior high students.

Nationally, education officials are beginning to discuss more widespread programs to help Spanish-speaking students across the country, especially in the Southwest and on the West Coast, where Mexican-American children face much the same problems as Puerto Rican pupils do in New York. Mr. Monserrat, for example, is working with officials from H.E.W. and others to devise a bilingual educational television show that will originate in Oakland, Calif.

But bilingual classes don't provide the whole answer. Like generations of immigrants before them who also spoke foreign languages—the Italians, Greeks, Poles, and Jews—today's Puerto Rican children have to deal with the indifference of many school officials who simply don't expect them to survive in school. They must also deal with some who believe that other immigrant groups managed to learn English and get an education without special programs and so Puerto Ricans should too.

A number of social historians have argued, however, that the public schools have historically failed the first generation of foreign-speaking immigrants, and, with a median age of 19, today's Puerto Ricans are the first to tackle the schools. In earlier migrations, studies have shown, the schools were not mastered by the various groups until the second and third generations, and neither the Board of Edu-

The New York Times/Patrick Burns

The Spanish-speaking child faces a major problem in New York City's schools. "Only 800 of 57,000 teachers are bilingual, and their efforts reach only 4,200 of the 100,000 students who need them most." Above, one of the city's bilingual classes.

cation nor the Spanish-speaking community want to wait that long.

Their problem is further removed from the experiences of earlier immigrants by the "education explosion" that has followed World War II. With a college degree as essential as a high school diploma was before the war, the Spanish-speaking leaders argue that just standing still today is the same as falling behind.

Mr. Monserrat sees little chance of progress until more basic problems of the city are solved along with changes in curriculum and teaching language.

"Historically, newcomers are the victims of the problems of the city, but are usually seen as the cause, so what happens is that we never solve the basic problems," he said. "Other groups have moved up and away, but look at the Lower East Side. Jacob Riis and Lincoln Steffens were writing about it at the turn of the century, but those houses are still there, the problems of education and recreation are still there. And now the Puerto Ricans are there." —IVER PETERSON

July 30, 197

How a School Tips From White to Black

By WILLIAM K. STEVENS

There is an almost classic quality to the ethnic switch that has taken place during the last decade at Brooklyn's Winthrop Junior High School 232 and in the East Flatbush neighborhood that surrounds the school.

Before 1962, more than 99 per cent of Winthrop's students were white. So were nearly all the people who lived in the red-brick homes on the leafy streets nearby. That year, 50 black students from Bedford-Stuyvesant, allowed under New York City's policy of open enrollment to seek a "better" school, entered Winthrop.

In 1967 the racial balance "tipped." Blacks then outnumbered whites in the school by 58 to 42 per cent. Two years after that the racial balance in the neighborhood "tipped," too.

The red-brick homes are still well kept and the streets are still leafy, but today Winthrop is again a segregated school. More than 99 per cent of its students are black or Hispanic, as are an estimated 80 per cent of the families living within half a mile of the school.

"We did a complete flipflop," said Mrs. Lillian Howitt, Winthrop's principal, who lives in East Flatbush and was at Winthrop both at the beginning and the end of the switch.

Fear of this urban dynamic, which has been repeated over and over in United States cities during the last quarter century, is said to be at the center of the last three weeks' school controversy in Canarsie, East Flatbush's neighbor in School District 18. White parents, afraid that their schools and neighborhood would "tip," have been resisting through demonstrations and a boycott the assignment of 32 black and Puerto Rican students from Brownville to Junior High School 211 in Canarsie, where blacks make up 30 per cent of the school's enrollment.

What is the nature of the "tipping" phenomenon? Why does tipping happen? Is it inevitable, once the process of school and neighborhood integration begins? Is there a precise, predictable tipping point?

Does tipping in a school spur tipping in a neighborhood, or vice versa? Is tipping detrimental to the quality of education in a school?

Some answers to these questions may be suggested by the case of Winthrop Junior High School, reconstructed through interviews with school officials and past and present neighborhood residents. The case displays many of the interacting factors—some of them tangible and real, some of them psychological—that are believed by social scientists to be involved in the matter.

The exact details, timing, precise interplay and relative weight of the factors is said to vary from case to case, but the essential process is thought to be the same.

In the not-so-distant past of the nineteen-thirties, East Flatbush was a young, spacious suburb where truck gardens still flourished. In those years Jewish shopkeepers, tradesmen and white-collar workers— eager to escape from the crowded decay of the Lower East Side, Brownsville and Williamsburgh—flocked to buy the bright new row houses that were going up just south of Eastern Parkway and just west of Rockaway Parkway.

For the next 30 years the neighborhood flourished as an enclave of lower-class and middle-middle class stability, and Winthrop Junior High developed one of the better reputations in the city. Its students had generally high I. Q. and reading levels, they won many academic prizes, and many of them went on to the city's specialized academic high schools. It was, in short, viewed as a "good school."

But the neighborhood aged, and so did its people. At the start of the nineteen-sixties, the original settlers of East Flatbush began moving out, a few at a time. The children, grown now, headed for outlying suburbs. The parents, old now, would move to Florida or move into smaller apartments elsewhere.

Blacks From Brownsville

Some, who did not like to walk stairs in their old age, moved off the top floors of the few four-story walkups near Winthrop. About 1960 lower-income blacks from neighboring Brownsville started moving into these rental apartments.

And as the sixties wore on, middle-income blacks from Bedford-Stuyvesant, by way of Crown Heights, followed. Seeking better surroundings and a better future for their children, they bought homes and began putting their children into Winthrop.

It is a classic pattern, according to Dr. Norman M. Bradburn of the University of Chicago, a social psychologist who has studied the phenomenon. "The major influence in changing a neighborhood," Dr. Bradburn said, "is black housing demand relative to white housing demand. People move the minimum distance necessary to find good housing."

As the younger white families gradually moved away, taking their children, the number of white students at Winthrop began to shrink. A nearby yeshiva drew away still more students. Yet, Winthrop in 1962 was still a predominantly white school.

Then came open enrollment. Under this new "freedom of choice" policy, designed to promote school integration, 50 blacks from other neighborhoods entered Winthrop in 1962.

In 1963, 250 of the school's 2,100 students were black. In 1964 blacks made up 32 per cent of the student body. In 1965 blacks comprised 44 per cent of the students and in 1966, 49 per cent.

Most of the increase, said Mrs. Howitt, could be attributed to open enrollment, inasmuch as the neighborhood was still overwhelmingly Jewish.

All during the middle of the nineteen-sixties—according to a former resident of the neighborhood who watched it all happen—white residents got edgier and edgier. For example, the black students from "outside" were welcomed at first

316

by some neighborhood store-keepers who wanted the students' lunchtime business. But these storekeepers, alleging pilferage by some of the students, closed their doors and eventually moved out.

In regard to the school itself, Mrs. Howitt said that whites in the neighborhood became increasingly concerned about the quality of education in the school. They feared that academically talented white students would be neglected in the rush to help the poorer, less well prepared blacks overcome their academic handicaps.

Despite a shortage of proper materials and resources, Mrs. Howitt attempted to individualize instruction, to serve all students' varying needs effectively and to convince parents that no one's child need suffer academically.

Tip Came in 1967

But in 1967, Winthrop "tipped" anyway. Blacks outnumbered whites by 58 to 42 per cent. A year later, the balance was 62-38. And with that, the neighborhood itself tipped. Exodus fever "spread like wildfire," in the words of a Winthrop teacher who still resides in the area. And by 1970 the neighborhood had switched from predominantly white to predominantly black.

Is there a fixed, predictable tipping point for a school or a neighborhood? Many believe that once a school in a white neighborhood goes above about one third black, tipping has already taken place. Others use higher figures.

School Quality a Factor

Deputy School Chancellor Irving Anker said that he believed that the quality of the school had much to do with it. "A well-run school with a 40 per cent minority may be more stable than one that is not so well-run," he said. Beyond that, he points out, neighborhood attitudes affect the tipping point, too.

Other educators agree. The degree of racial fear in a community, the degree to which residents feel boxed-in, the stance of the most vocal neighborhood leaders, and other psychological factors can raise or lower the tipping point, they say.

"Tipping points are in people's heads," said Dr. Thomas Pettigrew of Harvard University, one of the country's foremost authorities on matters of integration. "One community's tipping point may be another community's stability, depending on the circumstances.

"It's the sudden change in proportions that seems to upset people as much as the proportions themselves, that, and the fact that they're uncertain about what is coming."

Does tipping hurt the quality of education in a school? On this, opinions vary.

Mrs. Howitt and other educators believe quality need not suffer if proper steps are taken. These include genuine individualization of instruction and provision of the extra personnel and materials needed to deal with the special requirements of ghetto youths. Some predominantly black schools across the city and elsewhere are in-

deed attempting to do just that, and Mrs. Howitt believes that Winthrop has made some progress along these lines.

But other educators, as well as some black parents, believe that once a school tips, it inherits the considerable difficulties associated with any school serving lower-class black children. As explained by Dr. Kenneth B. Clark, a black who is a member of the New York State Board of Regents, black children are seen by many white teachers as being "uneducable."

"And being seen that way," Dr. Clark went on, "they are treated that way. They then tend to become that way. It is a self-fulfilling prophecy." Add to this a racial bias exhibited by some teachers, Dr. Clark said, and the result is a drop in the quality of education, even in terms of poor children's particular needs.

"I've been looking all across the country for predominantly black schools with high educational standards," Dr. Clark said, "and there are some, but few. The fact that there are a few means it [low quality] is not inevitable."

Teachers Said to Flee

Black parents also have complained that when a school tips, experienced white teachers tend to transfer to another school. Deputy Chancellor Anker said this has been true, but that the Board of Education's policies now attempt to discourage the practice.

Does tipping in a school spur tipping in a neighborhood, or vice versa?

The two are often inseparable, according to Dr. Bradburn, Mrs. Howitt and others. In the case of Winthrop, it is widely believed that official action by the city—namely, institution of the open-enrollment policy—contributed directly to the tipping of the school, and thereby to the tipping of the neighborhood.

Even so, Mrs. Howitt believes that white parents' fears could have been allayed had the school been provided with the resources it needed to deal with the first influx of black children, and had there been a more intensive effort to prepare the community for the children's arrival.

"This [tipping] might not happen if the whole situation were better understood by the community, if there were better preparation," she said. "You have to teach the teachers how to handle a kid from the ghetto, and teach the neighborhood how to be patient."

Still, many, including Dr. Bradburn, believe that given certain conditions in a white neighborhood—aging dwellings, an outward movement of older people for reason unrelated to schools, proximity to a lower-class black area — tipping is inevitable and conditions in the schools only hasten or delay it.

The conditions described by Dr. Bradburn applied to East Flatbush in the nineteen-sixties. Mrs. Howitt pointed out that they do not apply today to Canarsie, where both the houses and people are younger.

"When we started to integrate the school," she said, "this was already an old neighborhood. Canarsie has really just started building up."

November 6, 1972

CHAPTER **5**

The Teachers

GROUP UNITY URGED TO AID TEACHER PAY

NEA Calls 'Professional' Action Essential — Reaffirms Its Opposition to Strikes

By BESS FURMAN
Special to THE NEW YORK TIMES.

WASHINGTON, Jan. 1—The National Education Association today urged professional group action in obtaining pay rises for teachers while reaffirming its ethical code against teachers' strikes in a statement which one official called "among the most important in our ninety-year history."

"Group action is essential today," this statement said. "The former practice where teachers individually bargained with the superintendent of schools or the board of education for their salaries is largely past."

Under the plan presented, a "salary committee" would be "chosen by the entire group" and would be given "full authority to represent and act for the local education association."

Professional Methods Urged

The N. E. A. stated that such action should be taken "through professional organizations and by professional methods" as against trade union organizations. The N.E.A., in its State and local branches, would thus become the agency to talk salaries for teachers.

Willard E. Givens, executive secretary of N. E. A., in a news conference held to explain the statement, objected to the term "collective bargaining" being applied to this process. He said it might better be defined as "democratic persuasion."

He cited the State of California, where a constitutional amendment fixing a minimum of $2,400 for teachers was passed by a 3-to-1 vote on Nov. 5, as the most effective example so far of salary advances having been won by the democratic process.

Mr. Givens also said that the N. E. A. was aiming against trade unionism among teachers. A paragraph of the statement said:

"We believe that those who seek to place classroom teachers and school administrators in opposing camps do a disservice to the cause of education and to the teaching profession."

"We want no 'labor vs. boss' relationships," Mr. Givens said.

On teachers' strikes, the N. E. A.'s comment was:

"When teachers break contracts and strike, they deprive the children of the community of the educational opportunity which they agreed to provide. Such teachers set an example of breaking faith which the teaching profession cannot afford to justify."

Mr. Givens contended, however, that the action of the Norwalk, Conn., teachers came within N. E. A. code of ethics, since "they had not signed their contracts when they refrained from teaching until the city gave them $65,000 of the $93,000 in raises that they had been promised."

"That's not much different from John L. Lewis' system, is it?" a reporter asked.

Mr. Givens admitted that the two methods were not altogether dissimilar.

The NEA declared for a "minimum annual salary of $2,400 for a qualified beginning teacher who is a college graduate," with increments beginning with the second year and "leading to a professional salary level for experienced teachers ranging from $4,000 to $6,000 a year."

Such a scale is well within the resources of this country, the NEA held, since "the national income increased 400 per cent from 1932 to 1944, while school expenditures increased only 12 per cent."

"Teachers have not only the right but the duty to insist upon contracts or agreements calling for salaries in keeping with their preparation and responsibility," the statement said.

Stress Justification for Rises

"It is professional for teachers to seek adjustments in salaries during current contracts if conditions justify increases.

"As teachers fulfill the terms of current contracts or agreements, they should insist upon new contracts calling for salaries and working conditions which are acceptable."

The NEA promised "a resolute and unremitting campaign in behalf of the welfare of the American public school system and the teachers who make that system function." The organization called on the American people for backing, and demanded local, State and Federal action to increase school funds.

Mr. Givens pointed out that forty-four of the forty-eight States would be holding legislative sessions this year. The NEA statement urged "agressive" action for "adequate State minimum salary standards" and for "the development of State finance programs needed to support education."

Declaring that the Federal Government is "siphoning off tremendous amounts of tax money from the States and local communities and that 'more of these funds must go back to the States,'" the NEA pronounced it "imperative" that "additional Federal aid for public education be provided by the Eightieth Congress."

Mr. Givens said that the Hill-Thomas-Taft bill which would give to the thirty-five States least able to afford education the $40 per child minimum already enjoyed by the other States, would be reintroduced, but that this "$40 platform" would have to be raised to get teachers the $2,400 minimum for which NEA has declared.

January 2, 19[?]

TEACHERS COLLEGES NO LONGER ATTRACT

While Other Schools Show 50% Rise Over Peacetime Rolls, Education Study Lags

STUDENTS PLAN TO LEAVE

Many Will Shift to Liberal Arts Course—Profession Also Losing Appeal

By BENJAMIN FINE

Although the colleges and universities of this country are crowded far beyond capacity, averaging a 50 per cent increase over their peacetime records, the teachers colleges have not made any similar comeback.

During the war the schools of education and teachers colleges felt a drop of 50 to 75 per cent in their enrollment.

Today they have returned to their normal registration. However, they are being entered as a place of last resort by many students who cannot enroll anywhere else. The teachers colleges report that they could accommodate many more students, but the students are staying away.

Teaching has lost its appeal to the high school boy and girl. Boys, in particular, are keeping away from training schools. They are entering other professions.

While medical schools, engineering schools, business schools, law schools and dental schools are flooded with applicants, the teachers colleges are shunned.

Students Plan Shifts

The 189 teachers colleges of the country have an enrollment of 150,000, compared with 143,000 in 1940. However, this registration is misleading. A majority of the students do not intend to go into teaching. They have no other place to enter—and so they are going to a teachers college with the intention of shifting to a liberal arts college as soon as space becomes available.

For example, Pennsylvania State College found itself swamped with freshmen. Two thousand new students were farmed out to twenty-one other schools in the State, mainly State teachers colleges. The enrollment in the teachers colleges had slumped.

Similarly, 2,500 students at the University of Minnesota have been placed in the university's school of education, where they will get their first year or two of college work. After that, they will continue in the liberal arts division.

A million veterans have entered colleges and universities. Another 2,000,000 have been certified as being eligible, and will enter during the next several years. The veterans do not want the teachers colleges, however. To date about 20,000 veterans, or not more than 1 per cent, have enrolled in teachers colleges.

Both the hundred or so schools of education and the 189 teachers colleges report that they could accommodate many more students. The schools of education could accept an average of 300 more each, while each teachers college has room for an average of 200 more.

This condition is more disturbing when contrasted with the liberal arts colleges. The normal 1,500,-000 enrollment has gone beyond 2,000,000, with an estimated quarter of a million qualified students turned away.

Reports from the teachers colleges and the schools of education give this information as to average enrollment:

	1940-41		1946-47	
	Teachers Colleges	Schools of Education	Teachers Colleges	Schools of Education
Men	365	130	568	174
Women	480	257	370	237
Total	784	360	862	384

In both types of institutions for the training of teachers, the number of women has decreased. In the case of teachers colleges, it has decreased from an average of 48[?] women students for each college in 1940-46 to 370 today. The schools of education have dropped from 257 to 237. At the same time, the total gain for all teacher institutions is slight.

That the drop in women's enrollment is significant is conceded by informed educators. The increase in the number of men, as has been explained, is mainly brought about by the use of these institutions as over-flow places for the regular students of the colleges or universities. Women are beginning to scorn the teachers colleges and the teaching profession.

During the war the enrollment of women in teachers colleges dropped by 40 per cent. It is still 20 per cent less than it was in 1940.

Educators are alarmed at the decline in the power of teachers colleges to draw students. There has been a steady decline in the relative number of students who are entering the teaching profession.

A recent study covering twenty States, made by the North Central Association of Colleges and Secondary Schools, shows that the teachers colleges are becoming increasingly barren of students. Here are the comparisons:

In 1941, 10,182 students were completing their teaching preparation; by 1946 this number had dropped to 3,757. On the high school level, 9,327 were preparing to teach in 1941, and 4,954 in 1946.

The officials conclude that the available supply of elementary teachers will be less for the 1946-1947 school year than at any time during the war. The number of teachers preparing to enter the profession decreased by 55 per cent during the last five years.

Even after they enter the teachers colleges the percentage of those expecting to teach is much lower than it was before the war. Both the teachers colleges and the schools of education indicated that the students were not interested in teaching. This table is revealing:

Percentage of total enrollment expecting to teach:

	1940-41.	1946-47.
Men	74%	46%
Women	85	70
Both	81	60

Less than half the men in teachers colleges expect to teach today, compared with three-quarters of the total in 1940. Even the women show a 15 per cent decrease, while for both groups there is a 21 per cent loss in six years. Teachers colleges in every part of the country experience this loss.

Moreover, the best high school graduates do not go into teaching. Scores of college deans, presidents, professors of education and prominent educators told this correspondent that the brightest students entered other professions. Twenty-one per cent of the teachers college presidents said that the general ability of students entering teaching today was of poorer quality than it was in 1940.

Students Queried on Teaching

Last November Professor Raleigh Shorling of the University of Michigan, in charge of student guidance, queried the 1,288 seniors in the liberal arts college who were specializing in general science, physics, chemistry, biology and mathematics. Of the total only thirteen said they planned to go into teaching. One senior was preparing to teach physics.

"Last June I worked with sixty-five seniors in the School of Education," Professor Shorling remarks. "I said to them, 'if you could get a job in some other profession, would you go into teaching?' Three of the sixty-five said they would; eight said they might. The rest said they would not. It's a shocking situation."

"There is less desire to go into teaching today than at any time in recent years," President Alexander G. Ruthven of the University of Michigan observes.

"We can't get veterans to go into teaching," Chancellor Caleb F. Gates of the University of Denver reports. "They say they don't want any messy interference with their lives. They don't want every parent to be top sergeant and kick them around."

"We have not made the teaching profession valuable enough to students to get them to enter," President Franklyn Bliss Snyder of Northwestern University declares. "Topnotch students do not go into teaching . . . the upper 10 per cent of students will never even think of this field."

Why Teaching Is Avoided

Why don't the able students go into teaching?

Various answers are given by the top educators of the country as to ways of attracting better students into teaching. Beyond the question of salaries, which is mentioned by 90 per cent of all educators, the administrators call for better guidance and a more constructive philosophy.

"Too many of the best students are told that they are too good to go to a teachers college," President Martin F. O'Connor of Massachusetts State Teachers College observes.

Better students can be attracted by increasing the public regard for education and especially for the teaching profession, President Forrest A. Irwin of the New Jersey State Teachers College comments. Furthermore, he says:

"Develop in the public mind a conviction that the teaching profession is worthy of best equipped young people. Advance salaries to support this conviction as compared with other professions."

Dean William S. Taylor of the University of Kentucky College of education offers these suggestions to attract better sudents: Pay better salaries; provide better conditions for teaching; make teachers feel that their work is appreciated.

From Dean N. E. Fitzgerald of the University of Tennessee College of Education comes this advice to improve the profession: "Double the salaries; make teaching a real profession by providing and demanding good and continuous training for cultural educational leadership."

THE TIMES survey indicates that potential teachers are scared away from the profession because of the community attitude as well as the attitude of the school administrators. Many have heard about the meddlesome way in which their lives are circumscribed, and will have none of it.

Rightly or wrongly, these accusations influence and affect the careers that students follow. Men are refusing to enter it because they say teaching has become a woman's profession. Women are dropping out because they say that they are "fed up" with the public scorn and ridicule that frequently is heaped upon them.

Teacher Shortage, Growing Worse, Threatens Serious Damage to Nation's School System

By BENJAMIN FINE

The United States still faces a critical shortage of teachers. A rising enrollment, coupled with growing demands on the nation's manpower, will make it more difficult than ever to get an adequate supply of competent teachers. The pinch is already being felt on the elementary-school level and in many rural areas.

A survey conducted by this department indicates that the situation is worse this year than it was in 1941, when the U. S. entered World War II. Although most communities will be able to get instructors for their classrooms this fall, the teachers in many instances will not be professionally prepared for their jobs. And it is universally acknowledged that the real danger point will arise within the next two or three years. Educators everywhere warn that without enough teachers the nation's schools will deteriorate. They urge school administrators and responsible laymen to tackle the problem before it gets out of hand and causes serious damage to the nation's youth.

The teaching profession suffered severe losses during the war years—it is estimated that 300,000 teachers left the classroom between 1940 and 1945. Of this number, 85,000 went into the armed forces and the others entered business or war-related work. Most of these teachers did not return to their profession.

At the same time, as Dr. W. Earl Armstrong of the United States Office of Education points out, only a trickle of teachers was graduated from the nation's colleges and universities the first year after World War II. For the next few years the supply was below normal. Not until a year ago did the teacher-training institutions turn out more graduates than they did in 1941.

Competition for Personnel

Now the situation has once again become serious. The partial mobilization required by the Korean war, and the realization that the struggle against world communism is a long-range one, have combined to impose a large defense budget on the nation. As more billions of dollars are spent for military defense, comparatively less money will go for such civilian agencies as schools.

Moreover, there is even greater competition between the teaching profession and the other occupations than there was during the war. In earlier years the profession offered a sure, steady income, even though salaries were not high. Before the war a greater percentage of the total college enrollment prepared for teaching than is the case today. The slight shift toward teaching that became evident last year is all too likely to be wiped away during the current national-security crisis. If the emergency continues for any length of time, the schools will find themselves competing for the sorely needed personnel with the military services and with the war-related industries.

"The problem is not recruiting but the holding of good teachers," says Dr. Ralph McDonald of the National Education Association. "Our school systems cannot expect to keep their teachers if they maintain unbelievably low ceilings. Failure to provide adequate salaries for experienced teachers will prove disastrous for the country's school systems."

Estimates of Needs

Obviously, the increased birth rate has created a demand for new teachers, a demand that will grow as the school enrollment advances. By 1957 the public and private elementary schools will reach a peak enrollment of 29,500,000, as compared with 20,300,000 in 1947. Public and private high schools will enroll 7,300,000 by 1957, as compared with 6,500,000 in 1947.

Thus in a ten-year period the schools will have gained ten million students. Indeed, the gains will continue at least until 1960; this will mean that educators must prepare for a decade of almost continuous school growth. It will mean, particularly, that an army of teachers will be needed to accommodate the additional children.

February 16, 1947

October 1, 1950

RISE IN STANDARDS FOR TEACHING GAINS

Four Years of College Needed in 17 States for Position in Elementary Schools

STATES PUSH RECIPROCITY

Federal Office of Education Issues First Report Since '41 on National Trends

Special to THE NEW YORK TIMES.

WASHINGTON, Aug. 7—The first nationwide report in ten years on the upgrading of teachers' certificates through increased educational requirements was issued jointly today by the Federal Office of Education and the National Education Association.

The 182-page document — "A Manual on Certification Requirements for School Personnel in the United States" also listed, for the first time, the colleges and universities authorized by the States to train teachers, and the courses offered by each.

All States and Territories cooperated in furnishing information for the report, which is expected to provide useful comparisons for school systems seeking to improve their standards. The survey also provides facts for teachers about current requirements on certification in each state, and on the chances of moving from state to state under reciprocity agreements.

Some High Standards Noted

The study revealed that four states, New York among them, require five years of study beyond high school to qualify as a high-school teacher, and thirty-six other states call for completion of a four-year college course in order to so qualify. The others issue some high-school teaching certificates on less than a college degree.

Seventeen states require completion of a four-year college course for teachers in the elementary schools. Seven other states have set deadlines ranging from 1951 to 1960 for this minimum to become operative. The rest of the states range on down to two that currently are certifying elementary teachers on less than one year of college preparation.

The report commanded a noticeable trend "toward establishing the same quantitative requirements for elementary as for secondary teachers, thus ending an unjustifiable difference which has been quite general in the past."

Systems Are Being Simplified

A tendency toward simplification of the certification system also was commended.

New regulations in Mississippi, Virginia and Washington have set up only two types of certificates—a short-term certificate based on the four-year preparation level, and a long-term certificate issued on completion of five years of preparation. This would be in contrast to the situation in 1949 when a special survey showed about 1,000 separate name certificates—one state alone issuing sixty-three special subject certificates.

"The issuance of certificates by examination, once the universal practice and prevalent until recent years, is now practically extinct," the report said. The general rule now is for certification authority to be centralized in one state agency, usually the state's department of education.

Increasing reciprocity among the states in teacher certification was reported—at least thirty-nine states now having such agreements.

Reciprocity compact plans of wide scope include the completed thirteen-state Southern Association Compact on high-school teachers; the broader eight-state compact that will include the New England States, New Jersey and New York, and the six-state compact now being negotiated by California, Colorado, Nevada, New Mexico, Utah and Arizona.

Comment on "Conversion" Plans

An analysis of the "conversion" programs in sixteen states under which the oversupply of teachers trained for high-school instruction can qualify for work in the grades where there is a critical under-supply prompted this comment:

"Clearly the differences in these conversion programs are greater than the differences in conditions would justify."

The "conversion" requirements ranged from four hours of college work in one state to thirty hours in another.

"It is encouraging to see the trend toward establishment of higher teacher education requirements by many states during the last ten years," said Earl J. McGrath, United States Commissioner of Education, in commenting on the report as a whole.

"However, we must face the fact that there still is a wide variation from state to state in teachers' certification standards.

"Furthermore, the continuing use of emergency certificates shows that the requirements are not being maintained."

August 8, 1951

STUDY OF SCHOOLS STRESSES LOW PAY

Comparison With 1904 Notes Discouraging Prospect for Qualified Educators

By LEONARD BUDER

The inadequate salaries paid to many persons in the teaching profession, especially to those in executive positions, are discouraging qualified young persons from entering the field.

This was brought out in a report made public yesterday by the Fund for the Advancement of Education, which was established four years ago by the Ford Foundation. The report presents a fifty-year comparison of school and college salaries with those in other occupations.

The study was made by Beardsley Ruml and Sidney G. Tickton. In addition to supervising the undertaking, Mr. Ruml also wrote a section on "Inferences and Impressions" based on the findings. In it, he declared:

"The ablest young men and women eligible for graduate and professional training are not turning to education as they once did and as the nation's needs require. The graduate schools do not have students in the numbers and the quality that are desirable; and in the academic subjects, scholarships and fellowships are required to lure them in. No such subsidy is required to fill professional schools of medicine and law, and in these schools there is the necessity of selective admission so that the quality of the professions is likely to be maintained."

50-Year Period Covered

The study, which dealt with the period from 1904 through 1953, found that, taking the teaching profession as a whole, there had been little or no "absolute deterioration" in salaries except at the top. In fact, it said, all public school teachers, other than those in big city high schools, have gained.

This conclusion was arrived at after considering 1953 salaries in the light of 1904 purchasing power. For example, the average big city elementary school teacher earned $873 in 1904 and $4,817 in 1953. When the latter figure is "deflated" to 1904 purchasing power, it amounts to $1,394. Other comparisons, which are less exceptional, are:

¶Big city high school teacher: 1904 salary, $1,597; 1953 salary, $5,526, and "deflated" salary, $1,577.

¶Big city high school principal: 1904 salary, $3,552; 1953 salary, $9,156, and "deflated" salary, $2,497.

¶University professor: 1904 salary, $2,000; 1953 salary, $7,000, and "deflated" salary, $1,956.

¶University president: 1904 salary, $4,300; 1953 salary, $16,500, and "deflated salary, $4,196.

The most serious losses have occurred in the compensation of educational executives. The report observed that the Superintendent of Schools of New York City would have had to receive $50,400, as against the $32,500 he earned, to restore his economic status to the 1908 level, when the position paid $10,000.

However, it is in the matter of "relative deterioration"—that is, how the group has fared in relation to other occupational groups—that many educators have suffered the most. Teachers in big city high schools would require an additional $9,400 to give them economic status comparable with 1904. Similarly, big city high school principals would require an additional $14,644; professors in large universities an additional $5,070, and the presidents of those universities an additional $14,000.

But there are some exceptions. Elementary school teachers in big cities have gained 60 per cent in purchasing power in fifty years, and university instructors, 38 per cent.

Cost Held 'Not Unmanageable'

The study did not estimate the amount of money needed to rectify the salary situation of those on the top rungs of the academic ladder, but it expressed the opinion that the sum "is not unmanageable." It added that the correction "should be made over a period of time and on a merit basis."

What all this means, Mr. Ruml said in his analysis, is that "the American society is deteriorating in the sector most critical for future progress and well-being."

The economic situation, Mr. Ruml asserted, has also created "disaffection" at the "most sensitive point in our society."

"Pervading pessimism, extending in extreme cases to subversion, fellow-traveling, and other educational sabotage, springs basically from a sense of unfair treatment by a non-conscious social drift, not from a blazing passion to reform," he said. "The pessimism and disaffection expresses itself in lecture, classroom, and community activity. And the teacher, being literate and articulate, attracts both the other disaffected and the uninformed who earnestly wish for a better world.

"Adequate compensation is not a bribe nor is it a cure; it is simply an assurance that intellectual leadership maintains a balanced economic status with its contemporaries. On that foundation we can still expect deviation and criticism, but it can be sincere and rational, not poisoned by the facts of injustice, neglect and humiliation."

October 25, 19

Teachers' Pay—'04 to '55

The 1904, 1953 and 1955 salaries of some city schools and college employes follow. The data showing 1953 salaries in terms of 1904 purchasing power were taken from the report of the Fund for the Advancement of Education or were based upon the formula used in the report.

New York City Schools

Position.	1904 Salary.	1953 Salary.	1953 income required to provide same purchasing power as 1904.	1955 Salary.
Elementary school teacher				
To start	$ 600 (women)	*$3,000	$1,893	†$3,750
Maximum	1,240 (women)	*6,100	4,203	†7,050
To start	900 (men)	*3,000	2,885	†3,750
Maximum	2,160 (men)	*6,100	7,810	†7,050
High school teacher				
To start	1,100 (women)	3,200	3,675	4,050
Maximum	1,900 (women)	6,300	6,780	7,350
To start	1,300 (men)	3,200	4,450	4,050
Maximum	2,400 (men)	6,300	8,770	7,350
High school principal				
To start	5,000	11,050	20,345	11,900
Maximum	5,000	13,000	20,345	13,850

City College

Position.	1904 Salary.	1953 Salary.	1953 income required to provide same purchasing power as 1904.	1955 Salary.
Instructor	‡	5,350	......	5,853
Assistant professor	3,250	6,365	12,284	6,994
Associate professor	§	7,898	......	8,406
Full professor	4,750	9,472	19,110	10,193
President of college	8,250	20,000	39,858	25,000

*Teachers who hold master's degree or equivalent received $200 extra.

†Teachers who hold master's degree or equivalent receive $300 extra.

‡Salary figures not available.

§No such category in 1904.

NOTE: College salaries shown are averages.

October 25, 1955

TV ROLE

The High School Teachers Association of New York City issued a protest yesterday against television and radio programs that present, in its opinion, a "degrading and unwarranted stereotype of a teacher." It charged that "demeaning characterizations" had occurred on "Mr. Peepers," which is no longer on the air, "Our Miss Brooks" and a recent television play titled "Snow Job." The latter was featured on the "Playwrights 56" series.

The association's resolution, which was sent to networks and sponsors, read in part:

"Some of the qualities ascribed to teachers in these portrayals include timidity, lack of balance, lack of polish, inefficiency, unfairness and sheer ignorance. If these represent true teacher traits, then our American school system is indeed in dire straits."

December 1, 1955

SURVEY STRESSES TEACHERS' PLIGHT

73% of Men Forced to Take Outside Jobs—Extra Duty In School Also a Strain

PICTURE IS 'DISTRESSING'

In Spite of Drawbacks, N.E.A. Finds, Teachers Like Their Work and Stay at It

By BESS FURMAN
Special to The New York Times.

WASHINGTON, April 2—A comprehensive survey of the professional, economic and social life of teachers was released today. It showed that 73 per cent of men teachers and 17 per cent of women had to take outside jobs to meet their needs.

In addition, the survey found, teachers spend ten extra hours a week in nonteaching school tasks, such as planning and charity drives.

"It is a distressing picture of people who would like to give their time to teaching having to give it to something else," Dr. Hazel Davis declared. She headed the National Education Association's research staff that made the survey.

Questionnaires were sent out a year ago to a sampling of public school teachers regarded as typical of the total of 1,100,000. Usable replies numbered 5,602. The survey cost about $20,000.

'Crisis' in Summer

At a news conference, Dr. Davis read the plaint of a married man who taught English in a city high school:

"Every summer is a major crisis for my household," the teacher wrote. "In the past few summers, I have been dishwasher, ditchdigger, truck driver, gardener, screendoor salesman and tutor."

Dr. Davis said men teachers averaged ten years younger than women because the men usually moved to other professions as they added family responsibilities.

On duties other than teaching, the replies of both men and women told of hall-monitoring, club supervision, collecting money for milk, bank day, bonds, festivals, plays and the like.

"Don't ask the schools and teachers to assume responsibilities for the things that belong to the home and outside agencies," pleaded a teacher in a small-city school with forty-five years' experience.

The survey resulted in a picture of teachers that differed from long-believed stereotypes. For instance, most were married, lived in their own homes and had dependents.

Many Myths Exploded

Many myths about the habits of teachers were exploded. For instance, Dr. Davis said, teaching has been thought of as a pin-money, stop-gap job, not a lifetime profession. But the survey showed the median experience was thirteen years, half in the same system.

A theme that ran most strongly through the replies was that teachers, in spite of the drawbacks, loved their jobs.

To the surprise of the researchers, Dr. Davis said, it was found that 86 per cent of teachers voted in the last election. They had been typed as apathetic in politics and not rooted in communities.

"We were almost terrified at the extent to which they are joiners," Dr. Davis went on. "Only 7 per cent belonged to no community organizations, but 30 per cent belonged to four or more types of civic groups."

Although the classroom shortage was no object of the survey, it showed up in the replies as many complained of the heavy pupil load.

A small-city teacher with twenty years' experience, who handles two shifts of sixth graders, said:

"In the present age, the biggest barrier to best teaching is classes are too large for the best teaching. Our schools really are too well populated."

A woman high school English teacher in a big city commented:

"If the ends of education for democracy are to be achieved, teacher and student must know one another. Classes must be reduced to a size which makes possible each child's opportunity to be heard each day at least once in a thoughtful contribution."

Dr. William G. Carr, executive secretary of the N. E. A., said the statistical tables used in the sixty-three-page study would be distributed throughout the country in campaigns to recruit teachers.

He said the only other study along the same line dated to 1911. It was a doctorate dissertation by the late Dr. Lotus Delta Coffman.

April 3, 1957

TEACHERS PRESS RIGHT TO STRIKE

Federation Votes National Drive to Repeal Ban and Gain Bargaining Rights

By GENE CURRIVAN
Special to The New York Times.

MILWAUKEE, Aug. 29—A nation-wide effort to repeal no-strike laws for public servants was voted today as the American Federation of Teachers ended its week-long convention.

The inability to strike, the teachers said, has deprived them of a potent weapon in the battle to improve their status.

Realizing that this would be a long uphill fight, the federation took steps to make another approach in the same direction. It plans to sponsor legislation in every state for a collective-bargaining bill that would act as a guide for state and local units.

This would lay the ground-work for bargaining agreements between teachers and school boards. At present there are seven such agreements among federation locals, but they are weakened by the inability of teachers to back their demands by the threat of a strike.

Collective bargaining was a major issue at the convention. Despite the federation's affiliation with the A. F. L.-C. I. O., many critics contended that attempts at unionizing teachers and establishing contracts with school boards were inadequate.

In the face of this opposition, Carl J. Megel of Chicago won a close contest for re-election as president, defeating William P. Swan, a Negro, of Gary, Ind. Resolutions introduced on the last day reflected the feeling of the delegates, who represent 50,000 teachers, that increased efforts to unionize must take top priority.

Vote to Explore Plan

Another resolution urged federation members to "strive to introduce into the curriculum of their schools and districts the study of the true goals, values, history and methods of American unionism."

The New York Teachers Guild local, under Charles Cogen, recommended that every state establish a field service for union organizing, with the federation paying half the cost. However, the delegates voted only to explore the idea, since it appeared costly.

The federation went to the aid of its Evergreen Park local in Chicago. The local is 100 per cent organized but is losing tenure benefits for teachers because of alleged "union-breaking tactics of the school administration." The federation urged the State of Illinois to investigate conditions in the district.

A New York resolution was adopted for establishing of special pilot schools or classes for troublesome high school students. New York has such schools at the elementary level.

The federation, which now concentrates on elementary and secondary teachers, decided to start a campaign to bring in college teachers who lacked union protection.

SURVEY PICTURES SCHOOL PRINCIPAL

Study by N. E. A. Finds Men Outnumber Women in Job at Elementary Level

By BESS FURMAN
Special to The New York Times.

WASHINGTON, Oct. 25—The first comprehensive study of the elementary school principal in ten years, issued today by the National Education Association, shows more men than women on this job.

The survey showed that 59 per cent of the principals were men.

The N. E. A. gave this picture of the average man in charge of grade school children and their teachers:

"He's just passed his forty-third birthday and has had about eight years experience as a principal. About 5.8 years have been with the same school system. Most likely, he's had past experience as a classroom teacher. He now holds a master's degree. He's likely to have two or more full dependents and a small yearly income from outside earnings."

In the metropolitan areas, however, the study says, the grade school principal is more likely to be a woman. The average woman principal is 52, with about nine years experience as a principal and seventeen-and-a half years experience as a teacher. She, too, holds a master's degree. She has no outside income, no full dependents. Because she works for a big school system, her average salary is slightly higher than that of the man.

Pay Rises Found to Trail

The study stated that salary increases in the last two decades for elementary school principals had been proportionately less than the rises for classroom teachers.

The median salary of the principals reported on in the survey was $6,237.

"Salaries such as those paid to elementary school principals are too low to command the high level of professional leadership demanded of the principalship," the report said. "That a high quality of service is given by principals at present low salaries is a testimony to the devotion of the principals concerned."

It was recommended that the basis for salary schedule for principals be in a percentage relationship to that of classroom teachers so that the two would move upward in proportion.

However, it was stated that the grade school principalship is increasingly regarded as a career post, partially because "the amount of research and stress upon child growth and development has tended to make the elementary school principal a specialist in elementary education."

The study stated that the chief obstacle to the elementary school principal assuming effective leadership in his school and community was lack of clerical help. One principal was decribed as answering his thirty-fourth phone call for the day at 3 P. M.

Clerical Lag Reported

"When over 25 per cent of all principals reporting in this study agree that lack of clerical help is the main impediment to greater direct service to the classroom. the profession should take heed," the report said.

Survey Shows Teaching Loses Best Student Prospects

BARELY PASSING—

Teaching is described as a "profession in which a premium is placed upon mediocrity" in a report completed recently by the New York State Department of Education. It contains a statistical analysis of students who enrolled in 1949-50 as prospective secondary school teachers in sixteen upstate New York colleges and universities.

Of the 1,251 students originally enrolled, only 531, or 40 per cent, had become teachers by September, 1954. There were 310 who dropped out before graduation and 410 who completed their teacher education but did not enter the profession.

Students who did become teachers were found to be only one cut above those who dropped out because of academic failure. Candidates who dropped out for other reasons or changed to another curriculum tended to be two to three years younger and superior in the academic subjects; they had the other personal characteristics associated with effectiveness in teaching to a greater degree than did the group which actually became teachers.

The study was coincident with the Korean War and the draft, which may in part account for the high attrition rate, especially among the younger men. The group which dropped out during college to enter military service, or who did so following graduation, contained the highest proportion of men students who could be called the "cream of the crop."

Among the women, the high proportion of superior candidates changed to a curriculum other than teaching, married, or took a non-teaching position after graduation.

January 3, 1960

STATUS—

The preponderance of women in the teaching profession is one of the reasons that the teacher has low status in American society, according to Dr. Albert Reiss, a sociologist at the University of Wisconsin. "This is not because women are less capable," he explained, "but because of the status of women in our society in general."

American society tends to emphasize the woman's role as homemaker over her professional activity as a teacher, Dr. Reiss told a recent seminar of school administrators at the State University of Iowa. "Salaries paid to married teachers are usually supplemental," he said, "and the husband is thought of as the breadwinner."

July 24, 1960

Teacher Training Revised By States to Fit Space Age

By FRED M. HECHINGER

Nation-wide demands for school reform have led to rapid and far-reaching changes in teacher training standards since the launching of the first Soviet sputnik in 1957.

During the last two years, most of the fifty states have increased the requirements for the study of academic subjects by prospective teachers. Many of the remaining states are planning similar steps within the next twelve months.

At the same time, reform measures are made difficult by chaotically unequal standards that have resulted from lack of academic concern in the past. But even the most backward states now seem aware, for the first time, that a national pattern of standards is emerging.

Following revisions of requirements in New York State last fall, the forty-nine other states were canvassed as to whether similar steps had been taken during the last two years to improve teacher training. Replies were received from all but three states.

Flurry of Revisions

The replies leave no doubt that popular pressure after sputnik has led to nation-wide re-thinking of the minimum teacher preparation required, if the American schools are to be improved. A flurry of revisions, in 1959 and 1960, documents these major trends:

¶Stress on teacher preparation in the solid academic subjects, led by science, mathematics and foreign languages, but followed closely by English and the social studies, is reducing the time available for "professional" studies, often called "methods courses."

¶Although a small minority of states continue to leave changes to " local option," the trend is clearly toward a tightening of standards by state-wide mandate, reflecting national trends.

¶Along with the demand for better educated teachers, several states are beginning to yield to widespread calls to permit expert but uncertified persons to teach.

¶Some minimum specialized subject knowledge, especially in mathematics and science, is required increasingly of elementary school teachers.

Along with impressive moves toward improving teacher training, the inquiry revealed a chaos of different standards of quality that still prevents effective creation of corresponding minimum standards on a national scale. In some states the past levels were shown to have been so low that the present reform movement finds them in a position of laying firmer foundations and administering first aid.

This leads to a national picture in which some states struggle with the rock-bottom need to provide teachers with a complete undergraduate college education, while other states are moving into sophisticated graduate training of teachers.

It must also be remembered that even where standard requirements in different states look similar on paper, the quality of education depends both on the quality of the colleges and universities that prepare teachers and on the manner in which paper requirements are translated into practice.

Requirements Doubled

The New York State revisions, on which the inquiries were based, doubled the beginning or provisional, certification requirements for high-school teachers of foreign languages, mathematics and science and substantially increased the requirements for teachers of English and social studies. Specifically, the new requirements are thirty-six semester hours for English; twenty-four for foreign languages; eighteen for mathematics; forty-two for science, and thirty-six for social studies. An average one-semester college course constitutes three semester hours.

In a move typical of the attempt to start putting a floor under the lowest level of requirements, Georgia in 1960 stopped issuing certificates to beginning teachers with fewer than four years of college. At present, about 5,000 of the state's 31,200 teachers have less than that minimum.

Kentucky raised the minimum requirements for provisional elementary certifications to the four-year college level in 1959. Two years ago, only 67.1 per cent of the state's 24,106 elementary and high-school teachers were college graduates. This year, 74 per cent of the state's 25,000 teachers are college graduates.

A special cooperative program with the state's colleges and universities, the Kentucky Department of Education reports, has resulted in "greater depth in subject areas" and "some decrease in professional education."

3-Year Minimum in Maine

The State of Maine decreed in June, 1959, that "in order to raise the floor under teacher qualifications," no new teacher after 1960, could be granted any credential with less than three years of college education. An advisory committee has proposed that the requirement be raised to four years.

In Vermont, effective July 1961, a minimum of "two years of study beyond the high school" will be required for a provisional teaching certificate.

North Dakota reports that, beginning in 1960, teachers in one room rural schools must have completed at least two years of college. The next step toward a four-year requirement is hoped for in the near future.

The new State of Alaska is proposing a bill this year that would make two years of college preparation the minimum for anyone who wants to teach.

Arkansas, Montana, Illinois, Missouri and South Dakota have mandated within the last two years that the bachelor's degree be made the minimum requirements for elementary-school teachers. In South Dakota, where some rural districts up to last year required only one year of college for certification, the new standards will not be fully in effect until 1968.

Battle on Two Levels

For some states, the problem is not only long-range; it is also in the nature of a two-front battle, fought separately on the elementary and high-school level. Nebraska, for instance, has been able to increase only its lowest regular elementary teaching requirements, in the last two years. These it raised from twelve semester-hours (barely one semester's work) of college credit to forty semester hours for a certificate (valid only in its rural schools.) At the same time, however, the state's preparation in subject matter areas for high-school teachers has been increased from fifteen semester hours to twenty-four hours for fully accredited schools. Subject matter preparation required for teaching such courses as physics, chemistry, biology and history have been increased from eight semester hours in the subject to be taught by the teacher to fifteen semester hours.

On the other side of the educational spectrum, the Commonwealth of Pennsylvania acted several years ahead of New York—in 1957—to upgrade its subject teachers. From an original base of eighteen semester hours, for the provisional certificate, it raised to twenty-four the requirements

325

for physics, mathematics and foreign languages, and to thirty, thirty-six and forty for English, social studies and general science, respectively.

In addition, Pennsylvania's State Council of Education requires that foreign-language teachers pass a test in speaking ability as well as in knowledge of the culture and recent history of the language to be taught. It also recommends three to six months residence for native Americans in the country whose language is to be taught, prior to permanent certification.

Connecticut Changed Earlier

Connecticut reports that "the kind of s eps taken in New York recently were initiated in Connecticut back in 1955."

Specifically, science requirements were increased from fifteen to twenty-one semester hours; mathematics from nine to eighteen; English from twenty-four to thirty; social studies from fifteen to thirty. While foreign languages still remain at eighteen hours, a recommendation to increase the requirement to twenty-four "may be adopted soon."

In contrast to the other New England States—Maine and Vermont—cited above, Connecticut reports that the four-year bachelor's degree has been required since 1941 and that a fifth year of study was recently added "as a requirement for all standard permanent certificates." Not more than half of the fifth year may consist of "professional courses."

Texas also was ahead of the tide. Its new certification law, which became effective in September, 1955, puts much of the burden on reform on the colleges and universities. To be approved for the training of teachers, these institutions are required to offer "a well-balanced program of teacher preparation with approximately 40 per cent of the program devoted to basic education (arts and sciences), 40 per cent to the subject taught, and 20 per cent to professional preparation (teacher education)."

According to reports from superintendents, who in 1959-60 employed the first graduates under the strengthened programs of teacher education, these teachers are superior to the beginning teachers of former years.

New Laws in California

In sheer weight of massive legislative actions, California may be in the lead. In 1959, the Legislature passed "more than 400 bills aimed at improving and broadening education." Last year's session added thirty-four more.

Among the changes in California, was the requirement for college preparation in academic subject-matter, both major and minor, plus one year of graduate work.

"The greatest impact of this change is on the elementary teacher," the report says.

In addition, California attempted to cope with one major bone of contention by requiring that teachers be assigned "within their fields of preparation." A report to the State Board of Education is required where this rule is violated. For the time being, the letter admits, this ruling is not practically enforceable in elementary schools.

A strong hint that the raising of routine certification requirements alone is not enough comes from a new California move to permit outstanding experts in various fields to teach in the public schools. Under the new provisions, the State Board of Education may approve renewable, single-year credentials "to allow persons eminent in their fields to teach those subjects in public schools without meeting all formal credential requirements."

Among other states that have taken important action to upgrade teacher-training requirements in the last two years are Ohio, Wisconsin, Washington, Virginia, New Mexico, Mississippi and Florida.

Ohio Standards Raised

In Ohio, all high school teachers must now complete a minimum of thirty semester hours (about one college year) in general education courses. Such courses include language and literature, social studies, science and/or mathematics, fine and/or applied arts and religion or philosophy.

Subject-matter requirements have been increased from forty to forty-five semester hours in science, for science teachers; from fifteen to eighteen hours in mathematics; from fifteen to twenty-four in English; from fifteen to twenty in modern languages and from forty to forty-five in social studies.

The State of Washington stresses close cooperation between university faculties and elementary and secondary-school teachers rather than specific credit requirements.

The statement of revised standards recommends that approximately 35 per cent of the four years of undergraduate study of all future teachers be devoted "to broad education in the liberal arts and sciences" and that another 35 per cent be spent on "some field or area of learning," whether the candidate is preparing for elementary or high-school teaching.

Like California, the state is moving toward the greater use of available community experts who are not interested in regular teaching careers.

In Virginia, persons preparing for elementary-school teaching must, under the new standards, study mathematics and science in college. High-school teachers of the basic subjects are faced with substantially increased semester-hour requirements.

Minimum requirements in general education have been increased from thirty-six to fifty-nine semester hours for elementary-school teachers and from thirty-six to forty-eight for high-school teachers.

New Mexico Reports Gain

New Mexico reports that while almost half of its teachers had less than four years' college education in 1940, this year all high school teachers and 97 per cent of the elementary school teachers have a minimum of the bachelor's degree. The number of teachers with master's degrees has risen from 10.3 per cent in 1940 to 40 per cent this year.

Science teaching is being upgraded rapidly, with a requirement of thirty-six semester hours' preparation by 1963. This will include eight hours each in physics, chemistry and biology, with the remainder to be taken in those fields or in geology, astronomy and mathematics.

Mississippi, which has drastically increased all subject-matter requirements, now demands that high-school science teachers complete a minimum of forty-eight semester hours in science. The training of high-school mathematics teachers must include at least six semester hours in calculus.

Effective in 1962, teachers taking their master's degree must take at least half of their work in their special subject but may, if they wish, devote their entire master's study to that subject.

In Florida, certification requirements for foreign languages have been increased from eighteen to twenty-four semester hours and in mathematics from fifteen to twenty-one. Biology, chemistry and physics have been raised from fifteen to twenty semester hours each.

Nine other states are now shaping proposals for the improvement of teacher education. Generally, there are indications that the new trend calls for stronger enforcement of minimum standards at the state level. This indicates a move away from the extreme laissez-faire attitude, generally referred to as "local option."

The trend, however, is not yet nation-wide. Joe Morgan, Tennessee Commissioner of Education, for instance, wrote:

"Tennesseans, as a rule, function best in a volunteer capacity. The state, therefore, has a minimum amount of mandatory requirements and a wealth of means by which the 153 superintendents, boards of education, school personnel in the system anl laymen can exercise initiative to improve their schools."

But on a broad, national front, the years since Sputnik I have seen determined state action to improve education through higher standards of teacher certification.

February 26, 1961

TEACHERS' IMAGE
Strike Threat Highlights Issue Of Professions and Unions

By FRED M. HECHINGER

The news of collective bargaining, strike threats and mass rallies by New York City's United Federation of Teachers has implications far beyond the local scene. It involves key points about the professional status of organized teachers. In this light, the actions of New York's teachers —and their success or failure in achieving their goals—will be watched by their colleagues, by school boards, by parents and by teacher organizations across the nation.

Condensed to the bare essentials, this is the background of the dispute in New York: On Nov. 7, 1960, the United Federation of Teachers, a local of the American Federation of Teachers, A. F. L.-C. I. O. went out on strike. It lasted only for one day. Frantic behind-the-scenes efforts by municipal authorities and labor leaders led to an agreement which included a promise of no reprisals and speedier moves toward collective bargaining.

A referendum, a little over a year later, gave the U. F. T. a smashing vote of confidence as the bargaining agent for the city's 40,000 teachers.

First Round

Last week, the first experience with actual collective bargaining found the union's demands—$53 million for salary increases alone—far from the tentative offer by the Board— $27 million for salaries, in addition to about $45 million for improvements in educational facilities and better working conditions for teachers. A strike was threatened.

So much for the sketch of the local picture. What are the more fundamental implications?

Every teacher, whether independent, a member of a labor-affiliated group or of a professional organization, wants professional status. The question inevitably arises whether the labor and the professional images can be merged.

A serious conflict and one that will be of increasing national concern, is that between

The New York Times

School teachers in New York picketing outside City Hall.

the National Education Association, as the group which stresses the professional image, and the American Federation of Teachers, which follows the labor pattern.

The N. E. A. has over 780,000 members and wants one million by 1964. It has the equivalent of independent locals in the form of state and over 7,500 local education associations.

Its conventions attract vast crowds, relays of speakers and huge commercial exhibits of school equipment, comparable to industrial meetings or conventions of the American Medical Association. It publishes a mass of books, pamphlets and studies on educational issues.

Although at times accused of educational stodginess and conservatism, the N. E. A. has also been responsible for some of the more "far-out" studies. Even its detractors generally agree that its statistical research is the best available on American public education.

Against this colossus, the A. F. T., with fewer than 80,000 members, looks like an upstart. But it has, as the New York experience shows, made impressive gains on limited local fronts, particularly in areas of low teacher morale.

A. F. T. Eyes

In A. F. T. eyes, the N. E. A. is a "company union." Operating along employer-employee lines, the A. F. T. ridicules the large competitor which has thirty-three departments that include everybody from classroom teachers to school superintendents. The A. F. T. warns that professional status is an empty phrase unless salaries and working conditions make teachers economic equals among professionals.

Last week, in the backwash of the New York battle, the

leader of the Bridgeport (Conn.) Education Association underlined the conflict when he challenged the local school board to "take immediate steps to remove those conditions which attract these non-professional organizations (the A. F. T.) to take advantage of present teacher unrest."

In practice, on the local level, the difference between "professional negotiations" under the auspices of N. E. A.-affiliates and collective bargaining, as introduced in New York, may seem largely a matter of nomenclature to school boards or boards of estimate. But there is a tangible difference in this official N. E. A. policy statement: "The seeking of consensus and mutual agreement on a professional basis should preclude the arbitrary exercise of unilateral authority by boards of education and the use of the strike by teachers."

Board of Review

"Extreme differences," the statement says, should be resolved by a board of review consisting of members of professional and lay groups, in other words, a form of arbitration. But N. E. A.-affiliates have been known to urge members to refuse to sign contracts, a near equivalent of a strike.

Ultimately, whether trade unionism and professional status of teachers can be compatible will depend on the answers to these questions:

(1) Can teachers' unions consider conditions which improve their personal economic lot while considering the total effort to improve education? And can they consider the over-all effort without being made to subsidize, through personal sacrifice, the education of other people's children?

(2) Can they evolve a special relationship, different from that between industrial management and workers, in their dealings with the school board as the public representative of the children's and parents' interests?

(3) Can they achieve representation without widening the already serious breach between administrators and teachers which is damaging to education itself?

(4) Can they evolve bargaining procedures which eliminate the strike as a routine weapon, thus lessening the danger of an irreconcilable hostility between themselves and the school board, the administrators and the community?

The New York story will be watched for answers to these questions.

April 1, 1962

UNION BIDS TEACHERS HALT STRIKE; COMPLIES WITH INJUNCTION ORDER AFTER WALKOUT CRIPPLES SCHOOLS

25 BUILDINGS SHUT

City Hints It Will Not Penalize Any Who Go Back Today

By LEONARD BUDER

Leaders of the United Federation of Teachers called on its members early today to return to work and end the walkout that had disrupted classes yesterday for most of the city's 1,000,000 public school pupils.

At 3:30 A. M. Charles Cogen, president of the union, said the teachers would "comply with the slave labor injunction." He referred to a court order obtained by the Board of Education yesterday that prohibited further strike action.

The decision to return to work was made at a meeting of the union's executive board. The session began at 8 o'clock last night.

The injunction restrains the union from "causing, instigating, prompting, encouraging, sanctioning, authorizing, carrying on, continuing or lending support or assistance of any nature to any strike or work stoppage" against the Board of Education.

Cites Severe Penalties

Mr. Cogen said:

"We are complying with the injunction because its violation would have entailed penalties such as jail sentences and severe fines visited on rank-and file teachers."

"The United Federation of Teachers," Mr. Cogen said, "expects that all teachers who supported the strike will be restored to duty without reprisals or penalties of any kind, direct or indirect."

Mr. Cogen said he expected all teachers to return to their posts today.

"The U. F. T. as collective bargaining agent," Mr. Cogen went on, "further expects that negotiations will take place to complete a satisfactory contract which will reflect realistically the educational needs of our city's public schools. There can be no peace in our system until this is done."

Mr. Cogen said that Mayor Wagner, "by his intolerable fiscal policies with regard to education," bears a great responsibility for yesterday's "display of indignation by the city's teachers."

He called on the Mayor to remedy "this tragic situation" and said Mr. Wagner still had available funds for education and for bettering teachers' salaries and working conditions.

The strike, which began yesterday morning, forced the shutdown of at least twenty-five schools and disrupted classes for most of the system's 1,000,000 pupils.

Twenty thousand of the city's 40,000 teachers failed to report for work.

Max J. Rubin, president of the Board of Education, announced that the striking teachers had lost their jobs under the state's Condon-Wadlin Act, which prohibits strikes by public employes under penalty of instant dismissal.

However, early this morning, the board indicated that teachers who returned to work today would not be considered as having violated the law. A spokesman said the board had been advised that "we need not apply the full penalties of the law to those" who return.

In a statement, the board said that teachers who offered a "satisfactory explanation for their absence" would be presumed to have acted in good faith.

"All teachers," the statement said, "are urged to return to work for the sake of their professional futures and for the sake of the children."

A spokesman for the board said that "any teacher who does not return today would have a heavy burden in persuading the board that his explanation was satisfactory."

Last night a spokesman for the United Federation of Teachers, which called the strike, said its executive board was discussing an offer by the board not to penalize the teachers if they returned to work today. However, the Board of Education spokesman said no such offer had been made to the union.

Under the Condon-Wadlin Act, public employes who strike automatically vacate their jobs. They can be rehired, but would forfeit raises for three years and would be on probation for five years.

Yesterday the Board of Education obtained a court order restraining the federation from any further action that would interfere with school operations, including picketing. Although the board had said that in getting the injunction it wanted primarily to force the union to stop picketing and to stop encouraging other teachers to strike, the language of the court order was broadly interpreted in some quarters as an injunction against the strike itself.

Charles Cogen, president of the federation, and other union officials were served with the injunction when they arrived for last night's executive board meeting.

In invoking the Condon-Wadlin Act, Mr. Rubin had said the teachers "themselves terminated their employment."

The New York Times (by Arthur Brower)

STRIKING TEACHERS PICKETING yesterday at Junior High School 17, 327 West Forty-seventh Street, as pupils crowded the courtyard waiting to be admitted to school.

Last evening, however, Mr. Rubin and Mayor Wagner said that the Board of Education and the city's Corporation Counsel, Leo A. Larkin, were trying to work out procedures under which the striking teachers could return to their jobs.

Referring to the efforts of the board and Mr. Larkin, the Mayor said in a television broadcast that he hoped a way could be found to allow the teachers "to return with dignity to our schools."

There was no way of determining immediately how many teachers were actually on strike and how many were staying out of school because they did not want to cross picket lines set up by the federation.

Dr. John J. Theobald, the Superintendent of Schools, announced that all schools would be open today at the usual time and that "children and teachers are required to report as usual."

All activities and instructional programs, he said, will be conducted "to the extent practicable." He explained that it might be necessary to dismiss some pupils early, as was the case yesterday.

April 12, 1962

REGENTS INCREASE TEACHER TRAINING

5th Year Added to Standard for Elementary Grades— Specialization Stressed

By FRED M. HECHINGER

A substantial tightening of teacher-training standards for New York State's elementary schools was announced by the Board of Regents yesterday.

The new regulations significantly increase the general education required of teachers. They also call for a five-year program of college education for a permanent certificate, compared with the present requirement of a four-year bachelor's degree.

At the same time, colleges and universities were warned that they must improve their teacher-training courses and the quality of their faculties.

The new regulations call for greater breadth of study in the liberal arts and for concentration in at least one selected academic subject. The reform is in line with a nation-wide trend toward greater specialization in elementary schools and toward a declining stress on courses in educational methods apart from practice teaching.

The move, made public by Dr. James E. Allen Jr., State Education Commissioner, follows the raising of academic requirements for high school teachers in September, 1960.

The ruling for elementary school teachers will become effective for those seeking certification after Sept. 1, 1966. However, candidates preparing for elementary-school teaching will still be permitted to begin classroom teaching with a provisional certificate after four years of undergraduate study. They will be given five years in which to complete their additional work for the permanent certificate.

Under the new requirements, teachers applying for the provisional certificate will have to complete seventy-five semester hours of study in the liberal arts, instead of sixty semester hours demanded at present. A semester hour is defined as one fifty-minute classroom period a week for one semester of not less than fifteen weeks, or the equivalent in honors work.

Specialization Required

In addition, a concentration of at least twenty-four semester hours in a specific academic discipline will be required. This means that all future elementary-school teachers will have some specialist training in such fields as mathematics, English, foreign language, science, art or music.

The number of hours of supervised student teaching and

observation is simultaneously being increased from 240 to 300.

During the four years of undergraduate preparation, the semester-hour requirements for study in professional education, excluding practice teaching, will remain at the present twenty-four hours. This means that the proportion of "how-to-teach" courses to that of subject-matter courses and practical classroom internship is being decreased considerably.

The fifth year for the permanent certificate will call for a planned program of study, divided roughly between advanced work in the behavioral and social sciences related to teaching and advanced work in other fields of the liberal arts.

Allen Explains Need

In commenting on the new standards, Dr. Allen said:

"The schools of today and tomorrow must have a well-educated teacher in the classroom. The academic demands made on today's elementary schools require that the liberal education of the teachers in these schools be no less than that of their colleagues in the secondary schools."

The commissioner warned, however, that a change in certification rules would not automatically promise better teaching. He said the most important factor was "the selection and education of those persons who wish to teach." The responsibility for that, he said, rests squarely with the colleges and universities.

He called on those institutions to "strengthen their faculties and courses for the preparation of teachers."

Dr. Allen said the new requirements aimed at giving the teacher "a more realistic understanding of the nature of the intellectual pursuit in which students are to be guided." They also hope to give the teachers themselves a foundation for intellectual growth, it was said.

Dr. Harry B. Gilbert, chairman of the Board of Examiners in New York City, said the new provisions appeared to confirm the trend toward greater specialization in elementary schools. He called it "a wholesome step in the right direction."

At present, the New York City schools require only four years of college preparation for elementary-school teachers. Practice teaching here now calls for 240 hours.

The new standards were recommended after a two-year study made by an advisory committee, appointed by Dr. Allen, together with the Teacher Education Council, a permanent advisory group to the department.

It is known that the adoption of the revised rules has been delayed for almost six months as a result of controversy within the department and the Regents over the requirement of the fifth year.

In the preparations for the new standards, five regional conferences have been held. About 5,000 copies of the proposed requirements were distributed as a first draft to individuals and organizations. They were also presented to the presidents of the colleges and universities with teacher-training programs.

The State Education Department says that all those persons and groups agreed that the ruling was "a significant step forward in the development of quality programs for the preparation of elementary teachers for New York State."

End of Tradition Seen

The move throws new weight on the side of those education theorists who have complained that the conventional elementary school teacher, who was expected to teach all subjects to all children, had been rendered obsolete by new educational pressures and ideas.

An increasing number of schools have, in the last five years, been introducing specialized instruction in science, mathematics and foreign languages in the elementary grades.

June 1, 1962

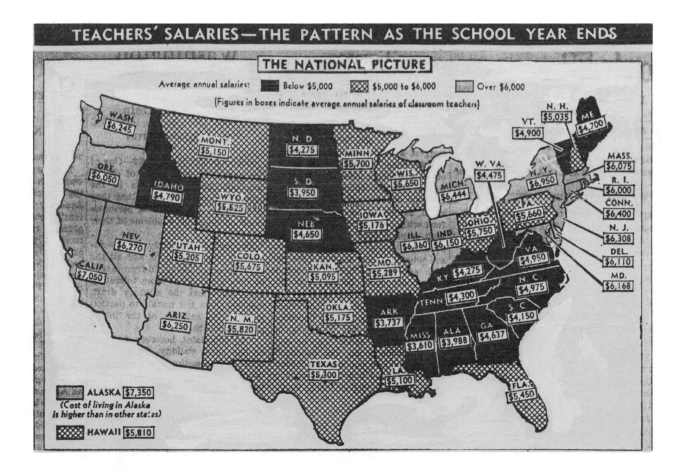

TEACHERS' SALARIES—THE PATTERN AS THE SCHOOL YEAR ENDS

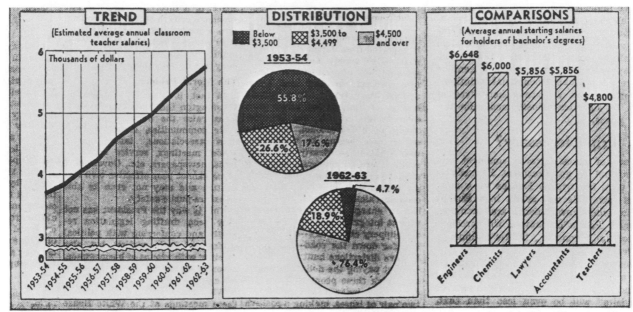

TREND	DISTRIBUTION	COMPARISONS

TREND
(Estimated average annual classroom teacher salaries)

Thousands of dollars

6
5
4
3
0

1953-54 1954-55 1955-56 1956-57 1957-58 1958-59 1959-60 1960-61 1961-62 1962-63

DISTRIBUTION

■ Below $3,500 ▨ $3,500 to $4,499 ▧ $4,500 and over

1953-54
55.8%
26.6% 17.6%

1962-63
4.7%
18.9%
76.4%

COMPARISONS
(Average annual starting salaries for holders of bachelor's degrees)

$6,648 Engineers
$6,000 Chemists
$5,856 Lawyers
$5,856 Accountants
$4,800 Teachers

Strike threats in New York City and salary negotiations for new contracts in many communities across the country have put the spotlight on teachers' pay. The map highlights the regional differences which recently were used by President Kennedy as a strong argument for the need to provide equalization through Federal aid. Charts at left and center indicate progress has been made. Problem (chart at right) remains to make teaching competitive with other fields.

June 23, 196[...]

TEACHER TRAINING SCORED BY CONANT AS U.S. 'SCANDAL'

He Says the Basic Criterion for Licensing Should Be Classroom Performance

---

ON-JOB TRAINING ASKED

New Book Calls for 4-Year Probationary Period and Broad Laymen's Role

By FRED M. HECHINGER

Dr. James Bryant Conant, in a sweeping critique of teacher training in America, has called for the abolition of the existing teacher certification system.

He has proposed measures that would make performance in the classroom the basic criterion for licensing the nation's public school teachers, And he has called for informed laymen to play a greater role in determining standards.

At the heart of Dr. Conant's proposals is the demand that, for certification purposes, the state should require only a bachelor's degree from a "legitimate college or university," evidence of successful and properly supervised student teaching, and the endorsement by a college or university vouching for the candidate's teacher preparation in "a designated field and grade level."

The proposals were contained in a 275-page book, "The Education of American Teachers," published yesterday.

Probation Time Urged

Teachers would gain certification with tenure after a four-year probationary period consisting of on-the-job training directed by specially selected "cooperating teachers."

Anyone thus certified in one state would be considered qualified to teach anywhere in the United States.

Although these proposals were believed certain to arouse violent controversy, it was learned yesterday that, even before publication of the book, New York State's Commissioner of Education had begun to move in the direction of some, but not all, of the Conant recommendations.

Immediate reaction to the report was varied.

Unqualified enthusiasm was voiced by Dr. Sterling M. McMurrin, a former United States Commissioner of Education, who has long criticized existing teaching standards. A guarded warning came from W. Earl Armstrong, director of the National Council for the Accreditation of Teacher Education, that the proposals might lead to low-quality academic programs.

Apparently anticipating the debate, Dr. Conant plans to make his personal services and efforts available to state education authorities interested in implementing his proposals, it was learned.

He will take the controversy to large professional audiences next February and hopes to meet with state education officials across the country in the fall of 1964.

Aid to States Offered

Dr. Conant is known to have expressed his willingness to guide and advise state education departments in preparing legislation that would make possible the implementation of his report.

A number of his recommendations would require legislative action either by state legislatures or by local school boards. Others would have to be dealt with by trustees and administrations of colleges and universities and by state education commissioners.

The 70-year-old scientist, educator and diplomat, who was president of Harvard University for 20 years, covered 77 colleges and universities in 22 states in his two-year study. He worked with education officials in the capitals of the 16 most populous states, in which two-thirds of all teachers in the nation are educated. The study was financed by the Carnegie Corporation.

The report called present state certification procedures "bankrupt." It described as "frightening" the rigidity of many branches of the teacher training and licensing "establishment."

Sees 'National Scandal'

It labeled as "a national scandal" the prevailing practice in most states, including New York, of permitting teachers certified in one subject field to teach practically anything else.

It "contemplates with horror" the fact that, as a result, 34 per cent of all seventh and eighth grade mathematics classes in the country are taught by teachers who have had less than two college courses in the subject.

Dr. Conant also called the majority of local school boards "scandalously remiss" in not providing new teachers with the proper help and opportunities to become expert practitioners.

In sharp contrast to his earlier efforts to reform the high schools without upsetting the existing school pattern, Dr. Conant appeared to be so alarmed by the deficiencies of the teacher training scene that he offered as the basis for improvement the "radical suggestion" of a break with the status quo. In addition, he demanded that teacher training candidates be selected among the top third of high school graduation classes.

Allen Hails Proposals

Dr. James E. Allen, New York State Education Commissioner, who had discussed the study with Dr. Conant before publication, said yesterday. "Once again Mr. Conant has designed a constructive program for the improvement of American education."

He added that he liked many of the recommendations. He considered plans to shift to the colleges responsibility for certification "in general, sound," provided these institutions "are ready to accept the wholehearted commitment" outlined in the Conant plan.

He warned, however, that in his opinion many colleges are not yet "ready or willing" to do this.

Dr. Allen urged colleges and universities to make proposals for carrying out the Conant plan.

Adding full endorsement to the need to improve practice teaching, he said that the state's 1964-65 budget includes a request for funds to assist local school systems to establish an effective partnership with teacher training institutions, as proposed by Dr. Conant.

Will Discuss Implications

Earlier this month, Dr. Conant said, he invited the heads of a number of colleges and universities in New York to confer with him during the remainder of the year to consider ways of improving the teacher training and certification picture. "In these conferences we shall discuss the implications of Mr. Conant's recommendations," he said.

Edgar Fuller, executive secretary of the Council of Chief State School Officers, who had only read the single recommendation concerning certification requirements, said the proposals might work fairly well for teachers who get all their training in one university but warned that it might be difficult to assure competence for those who have moved from state to state in their schooling.

He expressed serious concern over the idea of reciprocal recognition of certificates between states, considering the extent of the qualitative discrepancies between states and regions.

Until those discrepancies are eliminated, he warned, the proposals would result in "lower requirements" and would "put teaching on a lower level as a profession than it should be."

Dr. McMurrin, who has returned to the teaching of philosophy at the University of Utah, said, on the other hand, that "to adopt Mr. Conant's general principles would be a great step forward." He especially welcomed the idea of getting away from detailed specific requirements."

Dr. Armstrong, who had not yet read the full report, believed that leaving the responsibility to the colleges and universities might encourage them to be too loose and easy-going in granting statements of certification.

'Meaningless' Specifications

Dr. Conant argued that the present system under which state education departments list a certain number of courses in specific fields as certification requirements amounted to meaningless paper specifications.

He urged the substitution instead of pinpointed responsibility—by the college for the quality of the academic preparation, by the state education authorities for the quality of practice teaching, and by local school boards both for the selection of teachers and their continuing on-the-job training.

The book was sharply critical of courses in educational history, philosophy and psychology unless they are taught by persons who have completed basic academic work in history, philosophy and psychology.

Instead of leaving the teaching of education "methods courses"—often the center of controversy—to professors who have had little, if any, public school teaching experience, Dr. Conant urged the creation of the post of clinical professor of education.

These experts would be outstanding classroom teachers, who would supervise student teaching, preside over "methods" instruction and, in addition, continue their own teaching. They would, however, receive the full standing and pay of professors and would be employed jointly by the cooperating college or university and the public schools.

New Teacher Plan

Another new category of "cooperating teachers," also selected for outstanding performance in local schools, would train all newly licensed teachers on the job in regular public schools, during a four-year probation period.

The newly appointed "junior teachers," according to the Conant plan, would work in teams. At the end of the probation period, they would be carefully appraised, with a conscientious weeding out of those unsuited for the career. At the point of full certification of "career teachers," with tenure, salary scales would jump steeply.

The creation of the new teacher categories, based largely on the pattern of medical education, would significantly change the teacher salary structure. A considerable number of teachers, without giving up the classroom for administration offices, could command salaries equivalent to those at universities.

At the same time, Dr. Conant called for a wiping out of all future salary increment benefits based on what he calls "odd lot" courses, taken in university extension courses in the afternoon and on Saturdays.

Referring to many of these offerings as "Mickey Mouse" courses, he compared teachers enrolled in them to "opium smokers who were praising the habit of which they had long since become the victims."

Salary step-ups, he said, should be earned only through full-time study, financed in part by the local schools, or through summer courses, leading to master's and doctor's degrees designed specifically to improve the teachers' classroom effectiveness.

He admitted that, since universities have been doing "a landoffice business" in such courses, his recommendations would be violently opposed. But he insisted that teacher training should not have the responsibility of keeping academic institutions operating in the black.

Dr. Conant's earlier reports, especially his book on "The American High School Today," published in 1959, have been given credit for significant improvements in the quality of American public education.

Much of this success has been attributed to his missionary zeal and his readiness to take his message to school systems across the country, to confer with professional and lay people and to answer questions arising from local problems.

Although he is now in West Berlin as an adviser to the Ford Foundation, he will deliver two major addresses next February in Chicago, to take his proposals personally to the American Association of Colleges for Teacher Education and to the National Association of Secondary School Principals.

5,000 Copies Mailed

About 5,000 specially printed paperbound copies of the book were mailed to leading educators all over the country last week, but a paperback edition for general distribution will not be printed until next year. By now all college presidents, deans of schools of education and 131 cities as well as important state school superintendents in major education officials have received their free copy in envelopes labeled "Conant Report."

The six years of Dr. Conant's appraisals of American education have been underwritten by the Carnegie Corporation of New York, at a cost of about $950,000.

TEACHERS' UNION HITS ROADBLOCKS

Attempts to Organize Public School Groups Opposed

By GENE CURRIVAN

The nationwide movement to unionize public school teachers went into high gear last year but ran into a number of roadblocks set up by the National Education Association.

The association, whose 943,-581 members make it the largest teacher's organization in the country, believes that professionalism and unionism are incompatible.

Its principal rival, the aggressive 115,000-member American Federation of Teachers, is affiliated with the American Federation of Labor and Congress of Industrial Organizations.

Strikes or Sanctions

The federation, however, considers itself just as professional as the N.E.A. and scornfully refers to the larger organization as a "company union" because of the high proportion of members who are school superintendents and other administrators.

Although the federation gets stronger every year—it picked up 15,000 more members last year—the N.E.A. still considers it an upstart.

"The drive by the A.F.L.-Z.I.O. to organize the teachers of America is losing steam," according to Dr. William G. Carr, executive secretary of the N.E.A. "The union may achieve some additional local victories, but its effectiveness has been pretty well blunted."

The rival organizations have different approaches to major problems. When pressure is required "as a last resort," the federation generally resorts to strikes or strike threats. The association favors sanctions when all else fails.

When sanctions are applied against school systems, teachers throughout the country are advised to shun the schools and the general public is notified through widespread publicity of the conditions that brought the sanctions — low salaries, poor curriculums or generally inadequate conditions.

2 Strikes in Pawtucket

Oklahoma was under sanctions for four months until the Legislature came up with $28.7-million for the state's schools. Utah was under a ban for 300 days until its lawmakers produced an education budget of $26.4-million.

The federation showed its muscle in Pawtucket, R. I., where two strikes — one of a week and another of 10 days—produced salary increases. Perth Amboy, N. J., schools were struck for two weeks to get the right to a collective bargaining election. In Newark, there was a two-day strike to win the right of an election but the federation lost by a narrow margin.

There were also threats of strikes in New York, Chicago and Philadelphia.

The events that have contributed to the federation's alleged loss of steam have been defeats in direct contests between it and the association. There were, according to Dr. Carr, 39 such confrontations in which each sought to represent teachers in negotiations with the school boards.

The N.E.A. won 27 of these, including the hotly contested battle in Newark, where the final vote was 1466 to 1446.

The total number of elections won by the N.E.A. from December, 1964, to December, 1965, was 95. Included were elections in which the federation either withdrew or made no attempt to get on the ballot.

"The fact that the union is not on the ballot is indicative of its weakness in these areas," according to Dr. Carr.

A union spokesman disagreed, insisting that the N.E.A. victories in most cases were minor. "We go after the big fish," he said.

He cited the victory in Boston, where the N.E.A. did not enter the contest, and the largest one of the year—in Philadelphia—in which the N.E.A. lost to the A.F.T. by 5,403 votes to 4,671.

"Now that many of our locals have won the right to bona fide collective bargaining, we expect more and more outstanding teacher contracts such as the one in New York City," said Charles Cogen, the new president of the federation.

Mr. Cogen was president of the federation's New York City chapter in 1961 at the time the first contract with the city, covering almost 44,000 teachers,

was signed. When the third two-year contract was signed last year, Albert Shanker, the new chapter president, called it "the best teacher agreement ever negotiated in the United States."

But "the little ones" are still getting away from the union. An N.E.A. spokesman noted that while the federation won Hartford with a narrow margin of 29 votes out of more than 1,000 cast, the N.E.A. affiliate won 19 of 20 elections in Connecticut.

A major issue the two organizations have agreed on is the plight of displaced teachers, especially those who lost their jobs through school desegregation, in the South.

The N.E.A. is raising a $1-million fund to give them legal assistance and provide grants to tide them over while attempting to relocate them. The union is working along similar lines and also is continuing to establish and staff summer freedom schools in 11 states for 4,000 Negro pupils who have been receiving a minimum of education.

The New York Times

TEACHERS RALLY AT RANDALLS ISLAND: Thousands of the city's teachers met last summer to approve settlement of contract by the United Federation of Teachers.

January 12, 1966

Teaching License Is Hard to Get

Red Tape and White Paper Enmesh City Job Applicants

By MAX H. SEIGEL

New York City, like almost every other major metropolitan center in the country, is steering a careful course between the Scylla of slow growth in its teaching force and the Charybdis of a burgeoning school population.

And since no community can, or wants to, deny its children an opportunity to attend school, the emphasis everywhere is on recruiting enough teachers to maintain a proper classroom ratio.

The rivalry in recruitment has gone beyond competitive salary bidding. It has taken the form of an active search using various advertising media and special lures, such as private parking lots, housing aid, non-stop examination schedules and, in the case of many communities, no examinations at all.

If there is anything standing in the way of teaching as a career here in New York, it is not the pay (which is pretty good), or the hours (which are not too long) or the preparation (which is not too difficult). It may well be the red tape and white paper.

An applicant for a job is enmeshed in both almost as soon as he enters the threshold of 110 Livingston Street, Brooklyn, the staid gray-brick headquarters of the New York City Board of Education.

Last October, one applicant, armed with a Bachelor of Arts degree, a Master of Science in Education degree and a dozen or so additional credits in postgraduate work, turned up seeking a substitute's license. He wanted to qualify to teach English and French in the junior and senior day high schools.

Please Sign Here

The applicant was directed to the applications bureau. When he asked about qualifications, he was directed to the board of examiners. He then went to the office dealing with teachers of English.

Not Einstein, Either

The French office was 10 feet away, separated only by the common waiting room. But the applicant was not allowed to just cross over. Again there was a visitor's book to sign and, again, a white card to fill out.

As the applicant started to ask a question, a secretary halted him. He was told that he must first sign a visitor's book and then fill out a little white card. Both required that he list his name, address and the date. After a short wait, he was ushered in to meet an assistant examiner.

She was a kindly woman who tried to be helpful. She scrutinized the applicant's record painstakingly and then announced that he was not qualified to teach English because he had not taken enough English courses while at college.

The applicant protested: "I've been a visiting lecturer in English and journalism at the Baruch School of the City University for some 17 years. Surely, if I'm qualified to teach on the university level, I ought to be qualified to teach in a junior or senior high school."

"We're not allowed to give any credit for college-level teaching," was the reply. "Now, if you had taught anywhere on the elementary or high school level ... the state just doesn't accept college-level teaching as a substitute."

She paused.

"But the state does offer an equivalency examination that might produce some added credits."

The examiner did not know when, where or how often the equivalency tests were given.

"Why don't you try to get a license in French," she added, "you might do better there."

The second assistant examiner was another kindly woman who carried out another swift study of the college records.

"You seem to have enough credits in French," she mused, "but haven't you taught French in any of your courses?" The applicant could not remember, and the woman began to have doubts.

"You know, our rules are very strict, but don't feel this is any reflection on you. Do you realize that if Prof. Albert Einstein were alive today, he would not be qualified to teach in any of our schools?"

"Really?"

"Well, we had an actual case of an assistant to the late Mr. Toscanini who wanted to teach music. He couldn't qualify because he hadn't taken the courses in college. I'm sure he knew music. But the point is he had not taken the courses we require."

The applicant and the examiner decided then that perhaps he ought to take a chance and file for the examination. Further study of his records might qualify him, after all.

"What French should I study?" he asked.

"No French at all. The written test is just an English composition. The oral requires some French, but nothing you can study."

The candidate applied, paying $3 each for the applications to take examinations as a substitute teacher of French in the junior and senior day high schools. (He learned later that the senior high school examination would have been enough to qualify him for both, but no one had volunteered the information.)

The examinations, themselves, were assaults on the candidates' dignity and on human relations. Both the written and physical tests left the candidates smothered in white and yellow forms, sagging from waiting in line and bristling over the instructions for answering questions. Only the oral examinations came through as tests conducted in a suitable manner and on a proper level.

The written examination—an English composition of 450 words—was reduced in the instructions to an exercise in grammatical writing. The assault on the dignity of the candidates came in one sentence of the instructions, which asked pointedly that the applicants please use a few sentences containing more than one clause because the English language contained such sentences.

This coup de grace was delivered after the candidates had spent a half hour filling out forms and putting code numbers on all the papers handed them. One noted ironically that it had taken him only 20 minutes to complete the examination.

And Dress Neatly

The flood of forms was resumed when the candidates were called for physical examinations—so was the assault on the dignity of the applicants. Each was asked pointedly to come dressed neatly.

At the examination itself, there was a line for preliminary fingerprinting and a set of forms, then a line for registering—on another floor—then a line for height and weight and more fingerprinting. Next, a very short line for urine analysis—done, incidentally, in a room without a washbasin.

Finally, there was a seated line waiting for a call from a physician—almost like playing musical chairs, with the applicants shifting from seat to seat as their turn approached. Earlier, there had been two other fingerprinting sessions—one for a chest X-Ray examination and one for the written examination. All, obviously, were intended to prevent substitutes from taking the examinations.

The applicant, who had started in October, finally learned in December that he had been approved.

"I guess, if you love to teach, as I do, it's worth it," he said, and smiled.

CRITICAL SCARCITY OF TEACHERS HITS NATION'S SCHOOLS

Worst Shortage in Decade Follows Recent Gains— Officials Are Surprised

DRAFT CITED AS A CAUSE

Competition From Industry, Federally Aided Programs and Pay Also Blamed

By FRED M. HECHINGER

The most critical teacher shortage in a decade confronts the nation's classrooms at the start of the new school year.

The scarcity, which is reported from Maine to California, has taken local school systems and state education authorities by surprise. It comes after several years of steady improvement in the supply of teachers.

In contrast with indications in recent years that teacher shortages were a thing of the past, a check by The New York Times found public schools desperately trying to staff their classrooms.

Many states are resorting to the use of greater numbers of teachers without full professional credentials. Emergency calls are also being made to enlist college-educated housewives and to bring teachers out of retirement.

12,000 Needed in State

"It's the most serious shortage we have had since the nineteen forties," said Dr. Harry M. Sparks, superintendent of public instruction in Kentucky.

Dr. Vincent Gazetta, chief of the Bureau of In-Service Education in the New York State Education Department, said the situation had become serious. The state is short 12,000 fully certified teachers, about 8 per cent of the total.

"Areas that we thought were well covered in terms of people available—male physical education teachers, elementary school teachers and industrial arts instructors—are short," Dr. Gazetta added.

Despite the generally gloomy outlook, New York City, which employs 50,000 of the state's 150,000 teachers, is "cautiously optimistic" and hopes to have the schools fully staffed on Sept. 12, the opening day.

Draft Hurts in 2 Ways

Anticipating staffing problems, the city's school authorities signed up 2,000 prospective teachers for a special summer training program; hired 5,000 others through a stepped-up recruiting program that included trips to the South as well as newspaper, radio and television advertising campaigns, and hired 50 Negro teachers who were displaced by desegregation of Southern schools.

Nobody appears to have clear-cut answers as to why the national situation has changed so suddenly. Among the most frequently cited reasons are the competition for trained personnel by federally supported education programs, competition by industry and the inroads made by the draft.

The effects of the draft are felt not only by the induction of potential teachers into military service but also by the attempts of many to avoid the draft by attending graduate school.

Also, the mushroom growth of the two-year community colleges, which frequently recruit instructors from the high school level, has added to the shortage.

A spokesman for the United States Office of Education denied that there was a shortage of qualified teachers. The only shortage he insisted, is one of persons willing to go into classrooms at the going rate of pay.

"If the salaries were raised, there would be plenty of teachers," he said.

He estimated that about one million trained teachers were not in the schools and were not seeking employment there because they could find better-paying jobs.

Public school officials admit that Federal funds have helped to improve education by paying for greater numbers of teachers, especially for disadvantaged students, and for more specialists in such fields as remedial reading, guidance, science and other fields. Paradoxically, however, the officials blame the availability of Federal funds for much of the teacher shortage by paying for the greater numbers of teaching positions without supplying the teachers.

Shortages From Progress

In addition, there are new educational programs outside the schools that compete for teachers, such as the Job Corps, the various antipoverty projects and even the Peace Corps.

The total professional staff in the nation's schools and colleges of every description is estimated at 2,850,000 by the National Education Association. About 1.9-million are in the public elementary and secondary schools, employed at an average salary of $6,011 for the 10-month school year.

Progress made in the drive for greater educational quality brings with it the prospect of teacher shortages. For example, over the last 10 years, the ratio of elementary school pupils per teacher has decreased from 30.7 to 27.6.

While the number of pupils per classroom has been steadily reduced, the total enrollment in the nation's schools has established new records in each of the last 22 years. In the last five years, the number of children 5 to 17 years old has risen by 5 million to just below 50 million.

In addition, again with the aid of Federal funds, preschool education for children below the age of 5, such as Project Head Start, has become a popular addition to schooling. This, too, competes for manpower out of the total teacher reservoir.

This can be particularly serious when there is a salary differential between the locally and federally financed programs. For example, Toledo, Ohio, reports that its substitute teachers get $20 a day for six hours of instruction while Head Start pays $18 for four hours in much smaller classes.

Reporting an estimated shortage of 1,000 teachers for New Jersey, a spokesman for the New Jersey Education Association said:

"Many supervisory positions with attractive salaries are opening up under the Elementary and Secondary Education Act. This has taken some of our best and most experienced teachers out of the classroom."

In Connecticut, the number of unfilled vacancies—a total of 422 one week before school opening—is about twice that of the same time last year. The state has 24,000 teaching positions.

Emergency License in Use

Dr. William H. Flaherty, Deputy Commissioner of Education, said the trouble, seemingly alleviated in the last five years, was worse this year. There are fewer candidates for most positions, except in social studies and men's physical education, he added.

Maine, which employs 10,000 public school teachers, reported 501 vacancies at the last pre-opening inventory, with English, science, mathematics, industrial arts, music, guidance and—for the first time this year—social studies among the critical fields.

At the request of local school superintendents, the State Commissioner this year authorized a "temporary emergency license" for persons with only two years

of post-high school education.

In Illinois, with 110,000 teachers, including 25,000 in Chicago, Verne Crackel, deputy superintendent of instruction, reported that local school superintendents call this "the most critical year in the last 8 to 10 years."

"Heretofore, we've come up with the needed teachers but I don't think we'll get them this year," he added.

Illinois is urging housewives and others with bachelor's degrees to enter teaching to alleviate the emergency.

When Martin Essex, Ohio's State Superintendent of Instruction, called together local school leaders last month, he was told that between 1,500 and 2,000 teachers would have to be recruited before schools open.

A spokesman for Ohio said that about 2,000 teachers were being used for instruction under the Federal programs provided by the Elementary and Secondary Education Act of 1965, including 1,500 elementary school teachers who have been hired for remedial programs.

Ohio's education authorities are trying to overcome the shortage through several steps. They have appealed to retired teachers, they are trying to find 17,000 former teachers who have left to raise families, they are trying to persuade college seniors to go into teaching and they are issuing emergency calls through the news media.

Ohio experts estimated that almost one-third of all those who leave college with full preparation for teaching never actually enter the teaching field.

Missouri reported "the situation is pretty bad"—with a shortage of about 1,600 at last count. Indiana, which faced a serious shortage a month ago, has averted the crisis by calling back retired teachers, enlisting housewives and raiding neighboring states by instituting high salary schedules.

Shortage in All Fields

"The [manpower] shortage is general, not only in teaching, but in our region there is a shortage in every line, even in the department stores," William E. Wilson, Indiana State Superintendent, said.

Kentucky, with a shortage of about 1,000 teachers, is issuing emergency certificates to persons without a completed college education.

"Many young men would be available to us if it were not for the Vietnam War, and many more are staying on in college for graduate work because they feel that if they started to teach, they'd be called up in the draft," said Dr. Harry M. Sparks, Superintendent of Public Instruction.

But he conceded that salary remained the major roadblock.

"Business and industry are getting the college grads before we can, at $1,000 more a year, even though we have

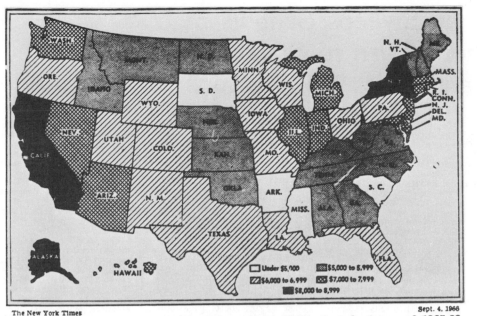

The New York Times

Sept. 4, 1966

The average salaries for teachers, state by state, during the school year of 1965-66

Legend:
- Under $5,000
- $5,000 to 5,999
- $6,000 to 6,999
- $7,000 to 7,999
- $8,000 to 8,999

raised our salaries by $500," he added.

Underlining the nationwide shortage of industrial arts teachers, Wisconsin's State Superintendent, William C. Kahl, said that city school systems

would have to run larger classes in that field, while small school systems might have to drop industrial arts programs entirely. The Job Corps has drained off A spokesman in Texas estimated that Federal funds for

the aid of schools with large numbers of disadvantaged pupils had created positions for about 10,000 teachers, often "draining off" the surplus that existed in the metropolitan areas.

Dr. Max Rafferty, Califor-

nia's State Superintendent, said:

"Call us any year and we have a shortage." But he expected things to be worse this year. He said between 800 and 1,200 provisional credentials would have to be issued this year, compared with 400 a year ago.

Other states reporting shortages were North Carolina, Pennsylvania, Montana, Rhode Island, Vermont, Maryland, Minnesota, Nebraska and Oklahoma. Georgia, which loses teachers to higher-paying Alabama and Florida, reports the worst shortage in its educational history.

Salary differences, often between neighboring states, also add to many local or regional problems. For example, the average teacher's salary in Ohio is $6,550, but in neighboring Michigan it is $7,200 and in Indiana $7,300.

Nationally, average salaries range from $8,600 in California and $8,400 in New York to $4,300 in Mississippi. New York City's scale now ranges from $5,400 for beginning teachers to $11,950 at the top.

Mrs. Elizabeth McGonigle, president of the New Jersey Education Association, said that "although teacher income has gone up, in economic status teachers are still behind the other professions requiring equivalent preparation."

September 4, 1966

PAY OF TEACHERS REPORTED RISING

Militancy Called Key Factor by Department of Labor

WASHINGTON, Dec. 9 (AP) —Teacher salary increases, lagging for years by some standards, are accelerating, especially in big cities, according to a Labor Department report.

New teacher militancy and a stronger bargaining position in some states are given as possible reasons in the report, prepared for the next monthly edition of The Labor Review.

But pay scales still vary widely from city to city.

"In 1966," the report said, "it was possible for a teacher in a city of 100,000 or more to earn as little as $2,950 or as much as $12,698 annually."

The average is $6,862, the report said.

Reasons for Lag

The report, by Arthur Sackley of the Bureau of Labor Statistics, depicted the lag in teacher salary increases with these figures:

¶Annual increases averaged 4.6 per cent from 1939 to 1951, but dropped to 4.2 per cent from 1951 to 1965.

¶The percentage of pay gains for big-city teachers have fallen behind factory workers and most other occupational groups in the last five years. Fringe

benefits have also trailed these groups.

¶Salaries are not growing in proportion to teacher demand in the classic supply-demand sense, but tend to be dependent on the average income of the population served. Thus, teachers who follow the flight to the suburbs earn more than those who stay in the city, where an influx of low-income families can dilute the tax base.

Since 1961, the over-all salary increase for teachers has been 17.4 per cent, but the increase for teachers in cities of 100,000 or more has been only 12.1 per cent.

The report declared, however, that "there is some evidence from improvements in salary scales in 1966 that the rate of increase is accelerating again, particularly in the largest cities."

As possible reasons the report cited the following:

¶"A rising tide of official action" among states and cities in favor of giving teachers more bargaining rights.

¶"A new militancy" among teachers, reflected in part by a doubling in size of the American Federation of Teachers of the American Federation of Labor and Congress of Industrial Organization to 125,000 members since 1959.

¶"Increasingly forceful policies, including more resort to sanctions against school systems," by the million-member National Education Association, chief rival of the Federation of Teachers.

The report also cited "increased frequency of strikes, threats of strikes and sanctions, mostly in the big cities."

December 10, 1966

Militancy Sweeps Schools in U.S. as Teachers Turn to Strikes, Sanctions and Mass Resignations

By DAVID R. JONES
Special to The New York Times

WASHINGTON, June 10—Charles Cherubin, a Baltimore teacher, stood on the back of a black paddy wagon recently and led his students in singing the alma mater.

The Baltimore police waited respectfully until the song had ended. Then, with Mr. Cherubin firmly under arrest for picketing the school despite a court injunction, the police slammed the door shut and hauled the teacher off to the city courthouse.

Mr. Cherubin's picketing was one man's protest against the way the Baltimore schools were being run, and he was not alone. Before the two-day protest strike was over, nearly 200 teachers were arrested.

The furor shocked many of Baltimore's citizens, who never thought they would see the day when teachers went on strike. But it was merely dramatic evidence of the militancy that is sweeping these days through classrooms around the nation.

More Group Action

School and college teachers across the country, fed up with lagging salaries and a lack of voice in policy-making, are looking more and more to strikes, sanctions, mass resignations and similar tactics to change matters.

Teacher organizations and school boards are increasingly facing each other across the bargaining table in an effort to resolve their differences.

Most experts agree that the teacher militancy is being heated up right now by the rivalry between the fast-growing American Federation of Teachers and the powerful National Education Association. Each organization is striving to outdo the other in the race for teacher allegiance.

The trend toward militancy has broad implications because it may affect the nature and cost of American education. Most authorities agree that increased pressure for higher pay will drive up taxes. And there is already evidence that teachers are moving deeply into the traditional policy-making prerogatives that have been jealously guarded by school administrators.

"The adjustment to collective negotiations is a formidable undertaking for legislators, boards of education, school administrators and teacher organizations," says Dr. George W. Taylor, the University of Pennsylvania's labor relations ex-

pert. "Together they have to invent the future."

"There's a tremendous ferment in the school systems throughout the country," says Charles Cogen, president of the American Federation of Teachers, in Chicago. "Conditions in the schools have been allowed to deteriorate to such an extent that any person who's really interested in proper education must be in a state of revolt against what we now have."

"There is no doubt in my mind that the issue of collective negotiations in public education must rank high on any priority list of imperatives for education in the United States in the late nineteen-sixties," says Dr. Harold V. Webb, executive director of the National School Boards Association, Evanston, Ill.

Aggressiveness by N.E.A.

"Strikes are illegal, yet teachers are calling them, and making gains with them," observes Sam Lambert, the executive secretary-elect of the National Education Association in Washington. "The N.E.A. in the future, I'm certain, will be much more aggressive and much more action-oriented toward local problems than ever before."

There have been sporadic teacher strikes for years, but the trend is sharply upward. The Bureau of Labor Statistics recorded only 35 teacher work stoppages in the decade through 1965, but there were 36 in 1966 alone. Eleven other stoppages occurred in the first quarter of this year, and there is no slowdown in sight.

Teachers in Maywood, Ill., have voted to strike the schools there, and some walkouts are expected in Michigan, where more than a score of districts are engaged in contract talks. Eleven teachers were recently arrested and fined for striking in Woodbridge, N. J.

Albert Shanker, president of New York City's United Federation of Teachers, has warned that a school shutdown is "practically inevitable" there on Sept. 11 because the board of education has so far not made an offer on major union demands.

The teachers have voted to call for mass resignations, rather than formally striking, to avoid penalties under the state's new antistrike law.

All across the nation — from New York City and Detroit to South Bend, Ind., and Portland, Ore., — teacher-representatives are sitting down with school

boards to bargain new contracts covering wages and working conditions for the coming academic year.

The American Federation of Teachers won its first written contract in 1957, and Dr. Robert E. Doherty, a Cornell University labor relations authority, estimates that about 100,000 teachers are now covered by "comprehensive contracts that differ little from labor-management agreements in private employment." Other experts figure more than 200,000 teachers are now covered by "substantive" contracts.

The upsurge of teacher militancy is part of a broader restiveness among the nation's 10.5 million public employes. Many authorities believe unionizing teachers could have deeper impact than unionizing other workers because it involves the nation's educational system. Labor leaders think unionizing teachers is important in erasing the stigma of union membership among white collar workers.

Strikes by teachers are considered illegal, either by stature or common law, in all 50 states. But teachers are generally free to negotiate if they do not strike. And eight states lately have enacted laws providing machinery for such bargaining.

Most authorities agree that the teacher revolt is rooted in deep-seated dissatisfaction over salaries, which the N.E.A. says average about $6,821 a year. This is less than the average pay of construction workers ($7,525) and draftsmen ($6,945). Salaries of urban teachers have tripled since 1939, but weekly earnings of factory workers have quadrupled.

The pay problem is complicated by the impersonality that seeps into school systems as they grow in size, these authorities say, leaving the teacher frustrated over what he thinks is a lack of ability to shape the educational process.

This has become a particular irritant, the experts add, as more career-oriented men come into teaching.

The membership rivalry between the federation and the association is an important contributor to the turmoil. The Baltimore strike, for instance, was an outgrowth of a struggle between the two organizations, which will compete in a June 16 election for the right to bargain for teachers.

Dr. Lewis E. Harris, executive director of the Ohio School Boards Association, says that in this battle "for dominance,

each must make new strides to heighten the organization's standing in the eyes of the men and women they are 'courting'."

"Neither group can afford to stand still, each must offer more than the other," Dr. Harris adds. "As a consequence, each group will try to strengthen its memberships' hands in determining how the school will be run."

The A.F.T., an affiliate of the American Federation of Labor and Congress of Industrial Organizations, was energized in 1961 when its 5,000-member New York City local won the rights to represent 40,000 teachers. With that boost, and a subsidy from Walter P. Reuther's Industrial Union Department, the teachers union membership has soared from 61,000 to 136,000 in six years.

The union, headquartered in an old house not far from the gaudy night spots on Chicago's Rush Street, pursues traditional trade union practices of collective bargaining, supports strikes to back up its demands, and places heavy emphasis on bread and butter issues. It is composed almost entirely of classroom teachers and is strongest in the big cities.

The N.E.A., headquartered in a luxurious big building in downtown Washington, has for years been the nation's most influential educational organization. It conducts widespread legislative and research programs on behalf of nearly one million members, many of whom join as a matter of professional rote.

The association has traditionally been under the conservative influence of state affiliates, which reflect a strong rural and small town bias, and has been dominated by supervisors rather than teachers. It historically accented "professionalism" and has shunned strikes.

But a series of stunning election wins by the federation—starting in New York and spreading to Philadelphia, Detroit, Chicago, Boston and Cleveland—has shocked the association into action lately. The organization is now shucking its conservative mantle, giving militant teachers more voice, and jumping into the fray with sanctions and even strikes.

"The organization of New York was the bellwether," says Wesley A. Wildman, a University of Chicago labor relations expert. "The N.E.A. got frightened to death and had to respond. They tossed and turned, had to act like a union."

The association traditionally

pressures recalcitrant school systems with "sanctions," which brand a state as undesirable and make it unethical for teachers to work there.

Early this week the association imposed sanctions on Florida. This backed up the Florida Education Association, which had accused the state of reneging on a promised salary increase.

The association still does not officially promote strikes, but in 1965 it wiped out a policy forbidding them. Affiliates conducted four strikes in Michigan alone last June. The Massachusetts affiliate recently went on record favoring the right to strike for teachers.

The federation "does have some advantage over us," concedes Allan M. West, head of the association's field operations and urban services. "They can start with a big program geared to the present, and we have to change. They're gambling that they can recruit the teachers faster than we can change. I don't think they can."

The two organizations, in their monthly publications, trumpet the "victories" they are achieving over the opposition. Many of these amount only to a codification of existing practices. But most authorities agree that both organizations are winning significant gains.

The vast majority of contract demands center on higher salaries and related benefits, and settlements almost always provide for such gains.

Fringe Benefits

The association says that a review of 200 agreements negotiated in Michigan last year, for instance, showed record-setting salary increases averaging $400 to $700 a year against common increases of $100 to $250 in previous years.

The range of contract benefits seems almost limitless. Many contracts specify the length of the school day, provide arbitration of grievances, or put limits on the work a teacher must do each day.

The benefits include ceilings on class size (New York); "freedom from interference in the conduct of the class, including the grading of students" (Inkster, Mich.); a promise to hire 100 special teachers (New Haven, Conn.); insurance to pay for cars damaged in school parking lots (Milwaukee) and making all extracurricular activities voluntary (East St. Louis, Ill.).

Philadelphia teachers recently won the right to veto any transfer. Those in Newark, N. J., now have a voice in the use of Federal aid. The Jersey City, N. J., contract calls for a master plan to achieve full segregation.

Many contracts provide that teachers be freed from non-teaching duties because, as one federation official notes, a "teacher doesn't go to college to learn how to teach children to eat a peanut butter and jelly sandwich."

The Stratford, Conn., contract frees teachers from collecting money for noneducational purposes, hauling books, duplicating instructional materials, or keeping daily attendance records.

A number of contracts—such as the one in Livonia, Mich.—give teachers added voice in selecting textbooks and instructional materials and shaping curriculum. That contract also allows teachers to join the school board in recommending those to be named principals and department heads.

The federation local in East St. Louis, Ill., last summer won what one official calls "20 pages of dynamite" when the school board settled on contract terms 30 minutes before a strike that had threatened to disrupt the opening of school.

The agreement makes extracurricular activities voluntary,

cuts back the classes to be taught, calls for room assignments based on seniority, and prohibits any "change in teaching conditions" unless the majority of teachers in the building "desire the change."

Mr. Cogen, of New York, has asserted, that the federation "would place no limit" on the items subject to bargaining. He looks "for a great expansion in the effective scope of negotiations" in such fields as class size, curriculum, hiring standards, book selection, and "anything having to do with the operation of the school."

"Boards are going to have to work more actively with the troops," says Mr. Lambert of N.E.A. "Teachers are bound to be involved now in personnel policies. This is no longer going to be a unilateral action of the board, but something the board works out with the teachers organization."

Dr. Harris of the Ohio School Boards Association says, "Almost every facet of decision-making has become fair game in the teacher organizations' drive for greater recognition. The term 'working conditions' is being sketched to include the entire school operation, from how much tax millage will be sought to how many pupils will be taught in a class."

"The drive is for the making of administrative decisions within limits set by negotiated agreements," notes Dr. Taylor of the University of Pennsylvania. "This means a drastic change in the way supervisors and principals have run things, and this is what most employe organizations want."

This trend is deeply disturbing to most school board members and principals, who feel it is dangerously eroding their authority. "If the boards are going to have the legal responsibility for running the schools,"

says Dr. Webb of the school boards association, "the boards must have the decision-making authority that will stick."

"The board of education is not comparable with the management of a business or industry," adds Dr. Webb. "There is no profit factor in the operation of public schools. The schools belong to the citizenry—not to any individual or group—and the school board acts and serves as the representative of the people."

Everyone agrees that rising teacher militancy will drive up the cost of education and increase taxes. One reason for these predictions is a prevailing feeling that school boards and local politicians, inexperienced in bargaining and unwilling to face the prospect of strikes are likely to bend to teacher threats and try to scrounge up the money somewhere.

While no one doubts that the teacher unrest will channel more money into schools, there is disagreement over whether that alone will improve education. The teacher organizations say that it will, but some experts are not so sure.

"The greatest concern of the public about collective negotiations in education is not simply whether teachers are entitled to 'a better break' but whether the process will improve or decrease the chances of developing an educational program adapted to the needs of a changing world," says Dr. Taylor of the University of Pennsylvania.

"Whether or not the effective performance of that useful — indeed necessary — function of employe organizations can be reconciled with the public demand for extensive improvements in the quality of education and in the productivity of the educators is a momentous cuestion," he adds.

June 11, 1967

Above Controversy:
The Versatile Teachers' Assistant

By NANCY HICKS

A small group of women sat in the second-floor office of a Brooklyn intermediate school one Friday afternoon recently, enjoying potato chips and lavish praise.

They were a group of paraprofessionals attending a party given in their honor by the school's reading teachers.

For a month, they had helped the teachers set up an individualized reading program, administering placement tests to 1,100 pupils, grading them and helping to set up groups.

The following Monday, when the program began, they were in the classrooms offering assistance to teachers and children.

Although the term paraprofessional has many meanings and many facets, it is becoming synonymous in New York with educational assistant, an intensively trained high school graduate who helps a teacher much the way a nurse helps a doctor.

The School Aide Program, begun in 1957, was essentially designed to relieve teachers

of such nonteaching chores as lunchroom duty and hallway patrol.

The 1964 Head Start Program brought a new type of aide, the family worker, who served as a liaison between the child's home and the school.

The paraprofessionals, said Rose Pernice, assistant director of the Board of Educa-

337

tion's Bureau of Auxiliary Personnel, "are aides, not maids."

"They won't just wipe the windowsill, they'll also read a story," she said.

New York City has 17,000 paraprofessionals — 7,000 school aides and 10,000 in all other categories. Among the latter group are the educational assistants, who usually work directly in a classroom with a teacher.

Because the paraprofessional program is essentially financed with money from Title I of the Elementary and Secondary Education Act of 1965, most paraprofessionals other than school aides live in poverty areas. About 85 per cent are Negro and Puerto Rican.

Paraprofessionals are becoming one of the most valued components of urban education today (one Brooklyn district invested all its decentralization funds in paraprofessionals). They also seem to be about the least controversial group in the urban schools today.

"I think we have tapped one of the greatest resources I have ever been in contact with," said Gladstone Atwell, director of the Bureau of Auxiliary Personnel. "They are fantastic."

"They are mature women, well-dressed on their little salary [an average of $2.25 an hour]," he went on. "They have a professional air, and they genuinely want to improve education.

"They are talented."

To become a paraprofessional in a school, a person has to live in the school district and meet the income criteria. She is hired by the principal.

She undergoes an intensive two-week orientation and then, for several weeks, spends half the day observing in the classroom and half in training. Once she is in the classroom full time, she and the teacher train together several times a month.

For other positions, such as family worker, which do not require a high school diploma, workers are encouraged to take equivalency test to become eligible to advance.

The long-range goal in using paraprofessionals is to improve education, Mr. Atwell said. By working in the classroom, the auxiliary personnel sharpen the teachers' skills, and they are able to provide great individual attention to the children.

January 9, 1969

BIRTH DROP BRINGS TEACHER SURPLUS

Worst Job Market Since the Depression Is Reported

WASHINGTON, July 27 (AP) —The World War II baby boom has passed through the nation's public schools, leaving in its wake the worst job market for teachers since the Depression.

No relief is in sight for the next decade, according to the National Education Association, which predicts that the teacher surplus will double by 1976.

Unless new jobs are created, the association said in a private memorandum to its staff, overproduction of teachers will reach 100,000 to 150,000 annually. And each year 15,000 to 35,000 experienced teachers who quit teaching want to return to school jobs, officials of the education association said.

Scope Is Described

The job picture is further complicated by the fact that financially pressed school districts are cutting back on programs and the size of their teaching staffs. In addition professionals laid off by business and industry are turning to the field of education in search of work.

"The situation is completely unlike anything we have faced since the Great Depression of the nineteen-thirties," the National Education Association's Research Department said in the memorandum.

"Not only beginning teachers but persons with above-average experience and qualifications are unable even to find vacancies for which to apply."

High school employment has also been hit, but the full impact of unemployment will probably not reach that educational level until the mid-nineteen-seventies, the association said.

The job pinch is just beginning to be felt at the college level. The Cooperative College Registry, originally formed to find qualified instructors, now finds its role changing—it is looking for jobs.

Mrs. Elizabeth S. Fisher, executive director of the registry, said that, of 6,139 persons with doctorates who registered for jobs, 34 per cent were still without work last week. Fourteen of those who found jobs are not going into teaching.

"Many of these people are having to settle for less," said Mrs. Fisher. "They don't get university-level jobs and have to take jobs in junior colleges and high schools and business. In one case, a man began driving a taxi rather than teach at a level below his degree."

Letter from Syracuse

She said that the number of persons with master's degrees still seeking jobs for the start of the school year was even greater, but she had no figures available of applicants and jobs.

Underscoring the bleak outlook, Syracuse University's School of Education sent the following information in a letter July 1 to its elementary education students:

"Among our current graduating class, less than half have positions for next year. It appears that at least a third of our graduates will not be employed come September. The situation among State University of New York graduates is even worse; in June, less than 30 per cent of the Oswego, Cortland and Potsdam graduates had teaching positions."

As examples of the tight job market in elementary schools, the Syracuse letter noted that, among area school districts, one had 400 applicants for six openings; another had more than 300 applicants for each.

The situation is not confined to New York or any other geographical area. Throughout the United States, teachers are finding job openings few and far between.

Roy Archibald, an official of the National Education Association in California, said that he had advised friends to look for jobs in the mountains but that "they came back and said they're not hiring out there, either."

In the past, Los Angeles has sent recruiters across the country looking for teachers. Now it has a waiting list with hundreds of names.

The letter from Syracuse's School of Educatin concluded: "Blame it on the pill or whatever, but the cause of all this appears to be a reduction in the birth rate."

"Give it some serious thought before you get so far into a program that it's impractical to change," the letter warned its elementary education students. "We are fairly certain [that] the situation that confronts us will not go away overnight."

July 28, 1971

*'s education
too important to be left to educators?*

Teachers
And Power

*The Story of the
American Federation of Teachers.
By Robert J. Braun.
287 pp. New York:
Simon & Schuster. $7.95.*

By MARIO D. FANTINI

"The American Federation of Teachers — led by its strongest affiliate, Local 2, United Federation of Teachers (who have made "U.F.T." a household term to most New Yorkers) — is determined to control the public schools of America by waging an all-out war against any of its enemies, whether they be parents, students, school boards, politicians or minority communities, all in the name of education. Modeling itself after the American Medical Association and the American Bar Association, the teachers' union is after a strong, disciplined national organization that will negotiate contracts escalating teachers' demands without genuine responsibility to any one, certainly not the public." This is the warning of Robert J. Braun, education editor of the Newark Star-Ledger, in his fascinating account of "Teachers and Power." Since he first covered a teacher strike in Perth Amboy, N. J., in 1965, Braun has become an intimately involved observer of teacher strikes, including the two prolonged affairs in New York City (1968, the Ocean Hill-Brownsville crisis) and Newark (1970), which he skillfully recounts and analyzes.

Braun points out that after the U.F.T.'s awesome display of power in the 36-day New York strike in 1968, few could doubt that a real political war was being waged in our schools. Alarmed, outraged, the author hopes that this book will jolt those "who believe that education is too important to be left to educators, who believe that the battles should be not

Mario D. Fantini is Dean of Education, S.U.N.Y., New Paltz, N. Y., author and co-author of several books, including "The Disadvantaged," "Community Control and the Urban School," and the forthcoming "Public Schools of Choice: Alternatives in Education."

for control over the schools, but to rid them finally of any form of control by special interests, who believe that popular control, while often illusory, is yet desirable." To the author, the innocent victims of this political war are the educational consumers themselves: students and parents.

Since he is dealing with a national institution second only to defense in expense, and involving 50 million people, Braun pulls no punches in his indictments:

"Because it is a union first and foremost, its organization is geared to war, to servicing strikes, to collecting new members, to protecting teachers — whether or not they deserve protection — never considering the possibility that teachers, as surrogate parents, should really derive their true protection from the pure love they provide for their children and the respect they earn in a community, a neighborhood or a town. A.F.T. leadership behaves like the leadership of any other established union — that is, with an eye to staying in power as long as possible. Although it pays considerable lip service to local autonomy and union democracy, the national trains its reps to mold opinion, to exploit fears, if necessary, to promote paranoia and hysteria and even racism among its teachers, for the war must be won."

Braun maintains that "educationally the A.F.T. has produced little beyond the M.E.S. (More Effective

Schools) — a collection of the most generally agreed-upon and, until late, unchallengable educational improvements — small classes, extensive psychological care, team teaching, and so on." It is not surprising that he also argues that "the union hardly has displayed a depth of understanding of either the political or the educational process which would motivate a community willingly to turn over its schools to its kindly command. And there is little in the history, its present operations or its leadership, to indicate that the A.F.T. would know what to do with the public schools of the nation should it manage to assume control through contract — beyond, of course, increasing salaries, decreasing workloads, picking up more members and strengthening leadership control at the top."

While these may be startling revelations to many citizens, they represent concerns some of us have had for a number of years, especially those who have been close to the urban action. Braun is essentially correct in his assessments: teacher organizations do appear to be on a collision course with the public.

The struggle for teachers' rights started in Chicago in the 1890's. It was led by Margaret Haley, whose incessant criticism of the failure of big corporations to pay school taxes won her a reputation as "the lady assistant mayor," that "opinionated, nasty, unladylike woman" and more. It took time to overcome the chronic timidity of female teachers, but in 1897 the "hard-driving Miss Haley finally convinced them to form the Chicago Federation of Teachers." Haley and her raiders wanted and ultimately achieved a salary of $900.

Among the heroes of the early days of the movement for teachers' rights was John Dewey, one of the first members of the teachers' union in New York City. Dewey gave the New York Chapter a strong philosophical base; he envisioned a strong teacher organization committed to responsive community service and dedicated to the principles of democracy. The American Teacher, which became the official voice of the teachers' union, carries the slogan "Democracy in Education: Education for Democracy."

By the time the Depression rolled around, Chicago was again the scene of teacher unrest and, in 1933, John M. Fewkes led a group of teachers in raids on the city's largest banks. Teachers' salaries were being held back, and in their place scrip was doled out to be redeemed once large corporations paid municipal taxes. There was an eruptive episode, and it served to highlight the differences between the National Education Association — which was company-aligned, ruled by school administrators, and encouraged teachers to return their salaries to keep school systems from bankruptcy — and the teachers' union, whose members would sooner break bank windows than continue to starve.

Divisive elements posed severe strains on the union during the thirties: a Midwest-New York split, an A.F. of L.-C.I.O. split, the Communists vs. the non-Communists. It remained for George Counts, prominent educational philosopher and author of "Dare the Schools Change the Social Order," to try to pull the union together. He received assistance from the theologian, Reinhold Niebuhr. (Other notables in the story of the A.F.T. include Samuel Gompers, Walter Reuther, John L. Lewis, Mike Mansfield, Paul Douglas, Hubert Humphrey, Albert Einstein.)

The modern era of teacher unionism belongs to Dave Seldon, president of the A.F.T., Charles Cogen, first U.F.T. president, and Albert Shanker, president of U.F.T. Under these men, the A.F.T. has grown — begun to build strong locals in some of our major cities (the A.F.T. is considered city-oriented) and pressed national teacher unification. For the past few years the A.F.T. (with about 950 locals) and its larger

national rival, the National Education Association (N.E.A.), with nearly 9,000 affiliated locals, have been talking merger. In the last decade the dominant power in the N.E.A. has shifted from school administrators to classroom teachers. This change fits neatly into the projected aspirations of the A.F.T., which is almost completely teacher-oriented. (A recent event not included in the book gives further credence to Braun's thesis that the A.F.T. is after a professional-teacher monopoly. In April, 1972, a potentially prototypic merger was announced in New York State between the 85,000 member U.F.T. and the 105,000 member New York State Teachers Association.)

Yet, since Braun's verdict that the A.F.T. is guilty of growing misuse of power is final, in all fairness to the A.F.T. the reader should keep certain factors in mind. He should note that this is a se-
tive story and not a *definitive* history of the American Federation of Teachers. Braun's purposes are more to expose than to instruct. For instance, we may be left with the mistaken impression that increased teacher militancy, including strikes, is an exclusive A.F.T. strategy. But the number of strikes, work stoppages and interruptions in service reported by the rival N.E.A. in 1961-62 was merely one, while in 1969-70, it reported 181.

There are various inconsistencies in Braun's argument. For him the A.F.T. today is somehow both "bankrupt" and "potent." And while Braun does note that teachers were an oppressed group, he moves almost too quickly into making them oppressors. He seems to want to make sure that we all realize that power, even in the hands of schooled professionals, inevitably corrupts, and is used for selfish not public interests.

As Braun is making his telling and alarming points, it is difficult to understand why he did not strengthen his case by spending some time on the institutional causes of increased teacher power. No book that deals with public-school teachers can escape the cold fact that they work in an institution forged in the 19th century, with a hierarchal, monolithic structure. Teachers, no less than students and parents, are imprisoned by this outmoded institution. It was never meant

to deal with an urbanized, technologically advanced, pluralistic society groping toward universal education for survival. The author, as a journalist, an outside observer looking in, cannot completely sense what the teacher's life is like inside the school. Teachers are forced to behave in certain ways by the institution. If we accuse teachers of outdated behavior, it is also, in part, the result of their outdated institution.

Furthermore, when teachers are isolated every day in eggcrate school rooms — trying to cope with human and cultural diversity that they were never adequately prepared to deal with and sensing the increased public demand for accountability — they are pressed to respond largely in ways that make sense within the institution itself. Their suggestions for improvement usually include smaller classes, remedial services, special classes for the non-adjusters — in brief, more of the same old measures. (These measures not only cost more money, but are being increasingly criticized as to their value.) This does not make the teachers' actions right; it only partially explains them. But the basic problem lies not so much with the teacher, the student or parent, but with the institution, which is in urgent need of reform. This fundamental point is difficult to glean from the book. To be sure, we have expected and not received from professional educators the statesmanlike leadership necessary for this reform, but we must also realize that few of us can rise above the environment that shapes us. Ironically, for the teachers to achieve control of a dying institution is a futile feat indeed, if their control is not directed at its renewal.

It's also important to note that teachers unify not only to increase their political and economic power but also to protect themselves against unfair pressures and demands. Repressive school administrators and get-tough-on-education legislatures unite teachers. Desperation attempts at educational reform — such as community control, a voucher plan that obviates public schools, performance-contracting with private firms, no schools at all — are also threatening to people who are trying to play by the ground rules of an established, albeit debilitating institution that finds it necessary to contract for police-guard protection.

It would be a serious mistake to blame individual teachers, either for the general crisis in American education or for the behavior of professional organizations. That would be a simple answer to a complex problem. There are thousands of individual teachers dedicated to child growth and leading a national struggle for reform

through educational alternatives within the framework of public schools — with or without the support of A.F.T. or N.E.A. affiliates. Teachers' unions are not the same as teachers. Braun expresses the deep disappointment many of us have felt in what the A.F.T. could have done for school reform:

"Sadly for an organization which has the muscle and skill to join with students, parents and others concerned with significant reform of education, the A.F.T. has all but betrayed its founding principles, including those articulated by

its most prized member, John Dewey....

"As a protest organization, and not the educational establishment it aspires to be, the teachers' union might have become the central organizing force for all the diverse elements which, within the public schools, are demanding change. Oriented to local concerns, allied with what should be their natural allies — parents and students — organized teachers might have been able to provoke reform, even through mass action like strikes, while still maintaining a sound enough base among the local gentry to

ensure competitive salaries and tolerable working conditions, something that every worker deserves."

Braun's story of the American Federation of Teachers is a courageous and hard-hitting report. He has given us much that was hidden from the public. He has dared to say the emperor wears no clothes. While there will undoubtedly be disagreement with Braun's assessments, it is difficult to criticize his attempt to deal openly with the intricate and controversial politics of the teacher - power movement in America. ■

May 28, 1972

Teachers

Merger Is in The Air

The nation's 2.1 million teachers constitute one of the largest special-interest groups. But it has been only in the last decade that the teachers have become fully aware of their potential power through organized action. The turning point came with the first big-city collective bargaining agreements with the teachers unions in the 1960's.

But many spokesmen for the profession consider the continuing rivalry between the two major organizations — the National Education Association (N.E.A.) and the American Federation of Teachers (A.F.T.), the C.I.O.-A.F.L.-affiliated union—a roadblock to the full exercise of teacher power. Last week, a merger of the giants moved closer to what is widely regarded as an inevitable agreement. A large block of classroom teachers from the urban areas, members of both the N.E.A. and the A.F.T., formed

a National Coalition for Teacher Unity with the stated purpose of bringing about a merger within the next two or three years.

Conditions for a merger have been improving steadily. The N.E.A., with its 1.1 million members, has long since given up its earlier posture as a professional organization opposed to such labor practices as collective bargaining and strikes. In many disputes, it has recently been as militant as the unions. Moreover, from its original rural and conservative orientation that often had a strong Southern flavor, the N.E.A. has transformed itself into a strongly integrationist and educationally progressive force.

The A.F.T., under the leadership of David Selden, the national president, has stopped deriding the N.E.A. (which also includes school administrators—the teachers' bosses) as a "company union." Mr. Selden, an ardent supporter of the merger, seems convinced that although the A.F.T. has only 280,000 members, the union's tightly organized strength in such big cities as New York, Washington and Detroit, is more than a match for the N.E.A.'s huge but more diffuse armies.

In the past few years, merger advocates dipped their toes in the water with some local unity agreements, including those in Los Angeles and New Orleans. But the most emphatic boost, prior to last week's coalition, came earlier this

year when Albert Shanker, president of New York City's United Federation of Teachers, the A.F.T.'s flagship local, engineered a merger with the N.E.A.'s New York State Teachers Association. The merged group, the new United Teachers of New York, was seen by many as the prototype and forerunner of the national move.

Substantial obstacles to a full merger nevertheless remain. The N.E.A. is split on the issue. Its more numerous and militant classroom teachers favor it. But many of the administrators, particularly at the state level, as well as the association's own bureaucracy, are less enthusiastic. To them, a merger means the submerging of their own powers. Moreover, they draw much of their strength from non-urban politics, and they fear domination by the union leadership.

N.E.A. insiders also say privately that the timing for a merger is unfavorable to them. They make no secret that their association is in a leadership crisis. Although most of its old guard has been retired, the men and women currently in charge represent an interregnum, while internal reorganization and the search for new leaders continues. Ballots on constitutional changes which would make a merger easier will be counted in January, but the forecast is that a stalemate between the progressive membership

and the state organizations will throw the final decision onto the convention floor in June.

Under such conditions of internal turmoil, it is not surprising that even some pro-merger N.E.A.'ers express concern that Mr. Shanker at present is so dominant a personality that a merger might have all the aspects of a union takeover. These observers consider Mr. Selden more conciliatory and less intimately involved than Mr. Shanker with George Meany's trade union hierarchy.

Despite these immediate obstacles, most observers on both sides agree the question is not *whether* but *when*. They cite the fact that even increasing numbers of school administrators, particularly in the cities, have moved closer to the union view of collective bargaining. They see themselves increasingly not as the bosses but as the teachers' allies in the fight with the politicians over funds and in the skirmishes with local community groups over teachers' rights and powers.

At any rate, last week, the new coalition for a merger claimed affiliates in 150 cities in 34 states and the support of 400,000, or over one-third, of the N.E.A. membership, as well as of the entire, more tightly disciplined A.F.T.

—**FRED M. HECHINGER**

December 24, 1972

Class 4-4: Educational Theories Meet Reality

By JOSEPH LELYVELD

On a bulletin board in the office of Public School 198, next to the time clock on which the teachers punch in and out, was a newspaper clipping making nearly official a constant theme of the most fervent school reformers.

The clipping quoted the new school Chancellor, Dr. Harvey B. Scribner, as calling the schools "oppressive and authoritarian" and citing in ironic terms their "capability" for "sifting their students into social classes."

Joseph G. Schumacher—a mild, avuncular figure who has presided as principal over P. S. 198 since it opened 11 years ago at 96th Street and Third Avenue, where the silk-stocking district slopes into East Harlem—did not find an accusation in the Chancellor's remarks. Instead, he said he hoped Dr. Scribner would come to a session of the principals' association and amplify them.

But in classrooms along the quiet corridors of the school, as in classrooms throughout the city, the process of "sifting" that the Chancellor condemned was taking place as a matter of routine, on the widely debated assumption that a student's ability to learn has some vital connection with the particular place he occupies in a school. Specifically, the process was taking place in room 217, in Class 4-4.

Dorothy Boroughs, a brisk, energetic and strongly committed young teacher who is usually among the first at the school to punch in, was telling 9-year-old Michael Smuckler that he was being transferred to Class 4-5.

The order of numbers assigned to the classes had been deliberately jumbled to disguise their significance, but Michael did not have to be told that 4-5 was the top class of the fourth grade, the so-called "I.G.C." — intellectually gifted children.

"My mother will be very proud," he said. "She'll probably take me out to dinner or something like that."

In the jargon of educators, Michael is an "advantaged" youngster (meaning, in effect, middle-class).

Recently expatriated from Brooklyn, he has just been enrolled by his mother in a judo class so he can protect himself on the streets. "I didn't want to learn karate," he confided gravely. "You can kill someone with that.")

The class he leaves, 4-4, is the second class of the grade, sometimes known as the "G" class. The initial has become so detached from its meaning that administrators have to pause to recall that it stood for "gifted."

The presumption is that all the pupils in the class—there are 30—are able to read at what is calculated by "objective" standards to be the grade level. The fact is that 12 students are still laboring through reading materials designed for second-graders.

In other words, they have moved at half the expected pace in their first three years of school though they are bright, without obvious impediments to learning and well-behaved by the traditional standards—so much so that Miss Boroughs is likely to call on her most docile students to "jump around a little." Students in 4-3, 4-2 and 4-1 are generally less actively engaged in school.

Only two pupils in Miss Boroughs's class were above grade level when the semester started—Michael Smuckler and Regina Fusco, who made it to 4-5 a day ahead of him.

The sifting has not stopped there, for two children from 4-3 are moving up a rung to 4-4. And they were preceded by Cecil Robinson, the class wit, who became such a favorite of Miss Boroughs in summer school that she plucked him from a lower class of the grade and made him 4-4's unofficial toastmaster.

In all, five children have been added to the class since school started and 11 subtracted. The flux is not expected to end with the reorganization of classes according to reading scores. This is because there is a normal turnover in the school population every year of about 30 per cent, reflecting the mobility or breaking up of families (the Park Avenue families as well as the East 99th Street ones).

Thus, calm as it is—Mr. Schumacher calls it a school with a "soul"—P.S. 198 is in a constant state of upheaval beneath the surface.

Guidance counselors say that new class assignments are part of an effort to impose order on a disorder that is beyond the control of schools and that assignments represent careful professional judgment of where individual children will learn best.

The principal oversees the sifting process but frowns on it. "There is a lot of snobbery connected to the I.G.C. classes," he maintains.

To no one's surprise or consternation, the assignments to classes that are as "homogeneous" as possible according to reading skills also prove to be aligned with the stretched-out social-economic scale.

This scale can be easily traced in the district from which the school draws its students, a 14-sided jigsaw piece that reaches as far north as East 100th Street, south to East 88th Street, and from Fifth Avenue to First Avenue.

The top class, 4-5, is almost wholly middle-class and only one-third black and Puerto Rican, in a school that last year found more than 70 per cent of its students in those communities.

In 4-4, a pupil who walks down the hill from Fifth Avenue and Park Avenue is automatically in a minority. Some parents see this as unfair. Mrs. Sally Stearn, whose son Michael is known to the rest of the class as "the hippie" because of his long blond hair, has been demanding that Mr. Schumacher reassign her son to the I.G.C. Most of his friends are there, she says, and they call him a "dummy" for not being with them.

Miss Boroughs's register is a rich catalogue of exotic

Dorothy Boroughs, teacher of Class 4-4, with two of her pupils

Class 4-4, with a student teacher and Miss Boroughs at the ends of the top row

names. There are Javier and Desirée, Hajnalka and Sharaie. Too often prosaic translations are allowed — Andres becomes Andy, Sandalio gives way to Sandy, and Anibal Rosado shyly asks if he can be known as Charley because some of the children have been calling him "Animal." Called Charley, he regularly forgets that the name refers to him and he fails to respond.

The only homogeneity in 4-4 that leaps to the eye is that of childhood itself. Chromatically the class shades from ivory to ebony and if the children have observed that, they do not show any signs that they find it significant.

So far skin color has come up for discussion only once —when Miss Boroughs asked the children to name some Indian tribes. One mentioned the Iroquois, another "the redskins."

Miss Boroughs held up a library book that pictured an Indian chief with tangerine-colored skin.

"Is a white person's skin really white?" she asked. Bronzed by weekends on the beach at Westhampton and tennis played while school was closed for Rosh ha-Shanah, the teacher was her own best answer.

"For some reason," she went on, "people thought they needed skin colors to talk about each other. I don't know why they decided that. It hasn't really helped."

The children seemed willing to leave it at that.

Class 4-4 is equally accepting of patriotic rituals. Unless the teacher forgets, which is rare, the mornings begin with the Pledge of Allegiance and a singing of the verse of "America" that starts "Our fathers' God, to three. . . ."

Capping a discussion of symbols the other day, Miss Boroughs noted that "the flag is a symbol of our country—does anybody know what the red stands for?"

"Blood," a child said.

"Whose blood?"

"Kennedy's," suggested Fred Fiandaca, who was not

yet 3 years old when the President was shot.

Miss Boroughs, who drives to school every morning from her East Side apartment in a four-year-old convertible that is missing three hubcaps and a radio antenna, welcomes the grouping of classes by skills. She thinks this is necessary to give an experience of success to students who might otherwise lag in a setting where they cannot compete effectively.

Success leads to confidence, she believes, and confidence creates the possibility of a commitment to learning.

If, as is often maintained, the teacher's expectations are crucial in the performance of the pupil, then Class 4-4 should be in for a good year. Asked for a realistic estimate of the limits on her pupils' reading improvement, she unhesitantly replied, "There are no limits."

Her own involvement with the children is not limited by the time clock in the school office. In past years she has invited pupils to her apart-

ment, gone to theirs, taken them to the beach, or ice skating.

In the course of a day she seeks both spontaneity and order from her class, for to her mind both are essential for learning.

Of course, sometimes she gets spontaneity when she wants order.

The other day, on a class trip to Staten Island, Miss Boroughs grouped her students on Richmond Terrace, above the ferry slip, and attempted to focus their attention on the Verrazano-Narrows Bridge. Suddenly, Matthew Phillips, started dancing, completely oblivious of the bridge.

Later in the afternoon, the teacher laughed and did a couple of dance steps herself on the sidewalk outside P.S. 198 as she recalled that moment. But at the time she had been angry.

"I started shouting like an ogre or a witch," she said. "At times like that I ask myself, 'What am I doing here? What is it all about?'"

October 9, 1970

Class 4-4:

The Gifted Often Hide Talents

By JOSEPH LELYVELD

Early this semester, a teacher at Public School 198 stopped by Class 4-4 to alert her colleague there, Dorothy Boroughs, to the promise and abilities of one of her new students, a bright-eyed youngster named Raymond Mercado, who had managed through most of his first four years of school to conceal his natural eagerness.

Occasionally he was troublesome and was expelled from his classroom. More often he was so withdrawn as to appear sluggish, even slow. In fact, in the third-grade last year he was placed in what is called an "under-achieving" class. The placement semed to become a self-fulfilling prophecy, for he was still reading on the second-grade level when the year ended.

This had dismayed and surprised Raymond's mother, Mrs. Melva Mercado. Without being pushed, she says, this same boy taught himself the alphabet before he was 3 and learned to recognize simple words.

A Matter of Faith

Miss Boroughs was grateful for the signal from her colleague. As an experienced teacher, she knows how alert and even lucky a teacher has to be to recognize whatever it is that makes an individual child blossom out in a class the size of 4-4, which now has 28 pupils.

She believes as a matter of faith, she said, that there is something special about each child. But faith is not enough, for some children seem to shrink into themselves in school, possibly because they think that is what the adults there expect, or possibly because their interior world proves more interesting than the one the school offers.

"You have to keep looking for opportunities to get to know each child," Miss Boroughs said, "but the school process doesn't give you many chances to be alone with individual children. When one of them shines, it may be for a minute and you may be looking the other way."

Raymond really shone for the first time this year outside the classroom. On a class trip to Staten Island, he suddenly threw off the time-serving listlessness with which he attends to his classroom chores and revealed himself as a vivacious 9-year-old, leaping to the end of the subway car to watch the receding tunnel, gaily taunting his friends, then grandly treating them to pretzels on the ferry.

The next day Miss Boroughs posted an abstract and difficult puzzle on the blackboard, a chart on which the letters of the alphabet were represented by similarly colored symbols, each a box enclosing a set of concentric circles.

'Decoding' a Sentence

The trick was to withstand the dizziness all those circles tended to induce and "decode" a sentence transcribed in the symbols. Raymond was the first to perform the feat, decoding the message with greater accuracy than the student teacher, Blanche Goldberg, a 20-year-old Hunter College senior.

Elated by his success, Miss Boroughs jokingly offered him the reward of a kiss, which he declined with a blush. So she gave him a book of stories and puzzles as a prize and a "commendation card" for "good thinking."

The next day Raymond had a reward of a kind for his teacher. He brought to class a book he had purchased with the allowance he receives from his father, a prospering cabinetmaker and contractor; then he made a great show of avid reading. The book was "The War of the Worlds," H. G. Wells's fantasy of the future.

That afternoon, after the other children left, Raymond asked his teacher to bend down so he could whisper something in her ear. When she did, he kissed her.

Another Commendation

The next commendation card for "good thinking" (an ordinary index card inscribed by the teacher with an orange "magic marker") went to Matthew Phillips, another youngster whose brightness and eagerness could easily be missed in the classroom setting.

For Matthew is sometimes sloppy—losing homework or forgetting to do it—and invariably kinetic—acrobatically rocking on his chair, standing on it, or sliding below the desk till he is horizontal to the floor, then sitting up again, his face an impassive mask but his feet still dancing out of sight.

The smallest boy in the class, he is reported to be the best fighter.

One morning last week after the Pledge of Allegiance, Miss Boroughs challenged the class to tell her what "indivisible" meant. "It means something that can't be seen," Fred Fiandaca replied.

"Visible" and "invisible" and "divisible" and "indivisible" were then distinguished on the blackboard. Miss Boroughs asked the class for other examples of words in which the prefix "in" negates

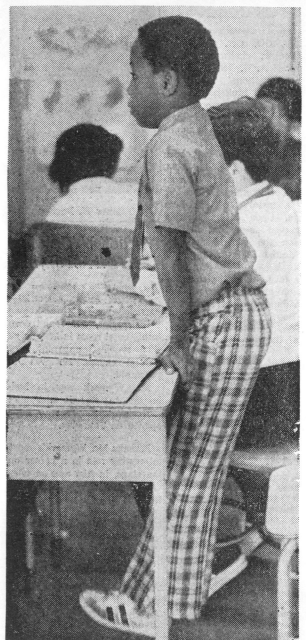

Matthew Phillips is one of many children whose gifts are more easily recognized outside the classroom than in it. Of himself, he said, "I think faster than I speak."

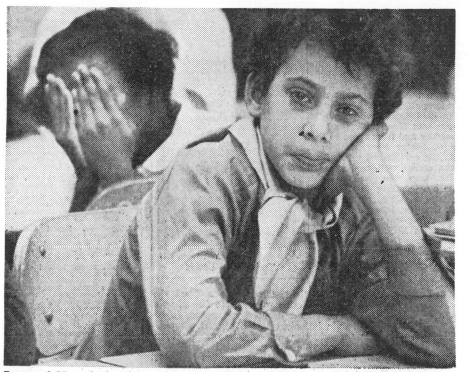

Raymond Mercado in Class 4-4 at P.S. 198. Put into a slow class because of "sluggishness," he later decoded a sentence transcribed in symbols faster than student teacher.

what follows. Having asked the question, she suddenly realized how hard it was for a class of 9-year-olds, for she herself could only think of such words as "inopportune," "indecisive" and "indiscreet."

It was Matthew who finally came up with what she later called "the answer to a maiden's prayer."

"Ooh, ooh, I know," he cried. "Independence and dependence."

"Matthew is the little genius this morning," the teacher beamed, out of astonishment and relief.

Matthew lives with his mother and 17-year-old sister in a two-room apartment on East 97th Street that is neat and brightly painted but so tiny that he sometimes has to do his homework on the fire escape. Some school psychologists see "a poor self-image" as a natural product of such a "disadvantaged background."

But Matthew takes his self-image from his mother, a proud and lively woman who was active 14 years ago in the Montgomery, Ala., bus boycott that launched the civil rights movement and Martin Luther King. Of himself he says, "I think faster than I speak."

Put another way, he may lack some of the vocabulary and facility in language by which the schools distinguish their "intellectually gifted" children, but not the gifts.

In Class 4-4 Matthew and Raymond are not the only gifted children whose gifts are sometimes easier to recognize outside the classroom than in it. Some children who are the picture of alert curiosity in the schoolyard seem to turn inert when they take their seats.

Miss Boroughs isn't sure why this is so, or what can be done about it in the schools as they are. But she tries to meet the pressing needs of individual children.

Stella Pistorio, an inward, dark-eyed girl, caught her attention one morning last week.

Growing up with four brothers and sisters in a small apartment, Stella sometimes finds it necessary to protect herself by drawing into a shell. When the class went to Central Park to see the leaves turning one afternoon last week, Stella withdrew from the group to gather chestnuts.

Balm of Companionship

The next day the class gratefully received those same chestnuts and, at Miss Goldberg's instigation, turned them into necklaces. Stella, who had made the project possible, withdrew again and sat by herself in the back of the room.

At noon, Miss Boroughs asked if she wanted to spend the lunch hour with her and accompany her to her bank. Stella came, put the top on her teacher's convertible up and down, and followed her to a supermarket where Miss Boroughs purchased her usual lunch, a container of cherry yogurt.

Little was said about Stella's earlier unhappiness. But the hour of undemanding companionship with her teacher was healing, and that afternoon Stella worked contentedly with her classmates.

Giving her class a homework assignment the other day to write down a list of the things or experiences they find "beautiful," Miss Boroughs offered an example from her own experience.

"I think it's very beautiful when you are working and you are learning," she said. "That's my special feeling. But I think it's most beautiful when you go out to do something by yourselves, your own thing, because that's what learning is all about."

At that instant, the class seemed enticed, if not enthralled. But a few moments later a number of students had tuned out again.

"Anibal," Miss Boroughs said in an exasperated voice, spying one of those whose attention had drifted off, "are you on this planet? In this class? 4-4, Room 217, P. S. 198, 1700 Third Avenue, New York City, New York State, U.S.A., planet Earth? Where are you?"

Anibal Rosado smiled an inscrutable little smile; then he looked away.

October 21, 1970

Class 4-4:
Parents Go to School, Too

By JOSEPH LELYVELD

When it was time for the noon recess on the second day of Open School Week, the total number of parents who had come to visit Class 4-4 seemed to be holding steady at the level of zero.

"We must be the saddest class in the world," the teacher, Dorothy Boroughs, remarked to the children as they formed a ragged line by the blackboard. "Nobody's come. If you told all your friends you were giving a party and nobody came, how would you feel?"

The mixed plaintiveness and irony of the teacher's appeal may have had an effect, for when the only week in the year in which the schools are officially proclaimed "open" ended yesterday, the parents of 11 of the 27 children in Class 4-4 had put in an appearance.

Some of those who came indicated they did so mainly on account of pressure from their children. "If I hadn't gone, Desirée would never have let me hear the end of it," said Mrs. Bernice Fleming, whose daughter is among the five pupils in the class able to read on a fourth-grade level.

Searching for an explanation for the tepid response earlier in the week, Miss Boroughs wondered aloud whether "apathy" might have something to do with it. She recalled a chance meeting at a hot-dog stand on Columbus Day (when school was closed) with Nelson Cerda—a voluble, alert youngster who had not been doing his homework—and his mother.

Reason for Absence

The teacher stopped the young mother and voiced her complaint. Reading no response on Mrs. Cerda's face, she retreated in embarrassment, almost regretting having made the effort.

Neither Mrs. Cerda nor her husband were among the parents who came to school this week. But apathy was not the reason. Both parents leave for work before their son leaves for school—the mother to a garment-district job sewing buttons, the father to a delivery job at a jewelery shop.

Nelson himself is the best witness to their concern for his progress in school. His mother understands English

but is shy about speaking it, he explains. But the moment Miss Boroughs left them that day at the hot-dog stand, Mrs. Cerda sternly warned her son in Spanish of the punishments he would face if he missed another homework assignment. He hasn't.

Few parents would be as quick to absolve the schools from any taint of failure as Miguel Santana, who sat next to his son José yesterday morning as the class read a story about a squirrel who mistook a red balloon for a big piece of candy.

"There is no such thing as a bad school or a bad teacher," Mr. Santana declared. "I tell my son a school is like a church. You go to church to get close to God. You go to school to get close to knowledge."

Example of Earnestness

Mr. Santana proved his earnestness about this proposition a few weeks ago when José accidentally stuck a pencil into the palm of his hand and was sent home from school with a note suggesting he be taken to a hospital for a tetanus shot. The father sent him straight back to class with a note demanding that nothing be allowed to interrupt the boy's lessons in the future.

But if this approach is unusual, there are also few among the parents of the children in 4-4 who attempt to judge the school on the basis of such abstruse and

abstract standards as reading scores or curriculum. Their standards appear to be more direct—what they can see in their own children and what this says about how highly the school values them.

Mrs. Ramona Carril's only son, Andy, had a turbulent time in his first few years at P.S. 198 and she found herself visiting the school nearly every week. When she came this week it was only the second time in the semester, for Andy seems content with school at last.

"It's the best thing that has happened to me. I'm so happy," Mrs. Carril said.

Another Reason

When Arthur Fleming, Desirée's father, went to the school yesterday morning, it was his first Open School Week visit in the nine years that he has had children in the school. Again, it was not apathy that kept him away but a bitter conviction that children and parents who live north of 96th Street were not on an equal footing in the school with youngsters from affluent families to the south.

"I had the feeling I would blow up any time I went near there," said Mr. Fleming, a correctional officer at the state facility in Ossining who proudly wears the red-black-and-green Black Liberation button.

But Desirée was doing well in school and that gradually persuaded her father that

"they must be doing something right."

One recent evening he went to a parents' meeting and met Miss Boroughs. He liked her for being young, involved with the children and wearing miniskirts, and for the impression she gave that her life outside the school was at least as eventful and vivid as her life inside.

"She seemed very much together," he said, "not like those terrible, old teachers in their horrible-looking clothes who only liked to shout at kids."

The fact that Miss Boroughs sometimes also shouts did not faze him. "Children need discipline," he said.

So pleased was Mr. Fleming by what he saw yesterday morning that he returned to school in the afternoon to cut the pumpkin at the class's Halloween party.

For the last two weekends Room 217, where Class 4-4 meets, has been the scene of a different kind of open-school function. This was arranged by some person or persons gifted with feline agility who apparently walked the narrow top of a wall that abuts the school, ignoring shards of glass placed there as a deterrent, and a possible 30-foot fall. From the wall the visitors clambered up to a window-sill and broke in.

Their rewards were meager. The first time the visitors made off with a box of 10-cent plastic puzzles and

Miguel Santana, who sets a high value on school, came to class with son José, left

magic tricks that Miss Boroughs had hoarded as rewards for pupils who had distinguished themselves. On their second foray, the intruders discovered a stapler.

It was Desirée Fleming who suggested that the police be asked to lay a trap for the burglars this weekend. Miss Boroughs responded by proposing that the students write letters to the officers and men of the 23d Precinct station on East 104th Street.

Andy Carril thought he had a better idea. He wanted the class itself to rig up "something electric so they get a shock." But the epistolary approach won out and Miss Boroughs called on Carlos Andwjar, a youngster with a seraphic countenance who had not been paying attention, to suggest an appropriate salutation for the letter.

Carlos hesitated, then replied gravely, "Dear Children."

Laughing with the rest of the class, the teacher asked, "Carlos, to whom are we writing?" Carlos shrugged.

"Dear Local Policemen," suggested Javier Romero.

"Dear Brave Men," called out Andy Carril.

"Is that a logical beginning?" the teacher asked.

"No," Shaun Sheppard said. "Some cops are chicken."

Faced with a delicate issue, Miss Boroughs called for a vote. "Dear Brave Men" won by a wide margin.

Most of Class 4-4 takes an improvisational approach to spelling. Here are some excerpts from the letters, before they were corrected and sent:

"Today we found a footprint and how big it was. We're asking you to protect

Photographs for The New York Times by NEAL BOENZI

Mrs. Bernice Fleming, present at the urging of her daughter, Desirée, left, shares a laugh with Miss Dorothy Boroughs, teacher, right, amid decorations for the Halloween party.

our class from crimanels . . .

"We want a siren so wcn they cross the door the siren go's on and you get them ..."

"Class 4-4 has a problom. We have been stolen two times. And we hope we don't get stolen a third time . . ."

Class 4-4:

A Contest
For and With Individuality

By JOSEPH LELYVELD

"Miss Boroughs," exclaimed Andy Carril in a soft voice that sounded more surprised than concerned, "you're turning red."

His observation caught Dorothy Boroughs, the teacher of Class 4-4, midway in a declamation about how frustrated and bothered she felt when she had to struggle for the class's attention. Thrown off guard, the teacher stepped back and enjoyed her first good laugh of the afternoon. "I'm glad you were watching me," she said.

That day, during the lunch hour, the teacher had closeted herself in a storeroom adjacent to the school's office to type up an overdue paper for a graduate course in education at Hunter College. The paper was on a book she had read with avid interest, George Dennison's "The Lives of Children," which describes the public school system as "a horrendous, life-destroying mess."

One-Sided Discussion

The unusually difficult afternoon that followed in her fourth-grade class had almost seemed an illustration of the book's assertion that in the public schools "the schoolchild's chief expense of energy is self-defense against the environment."

First, there had been a discussion in which Miss Boroughs attempted to put across the notion that the children might try to remember the names of writers whose books they had really enjoyed and look for other titles by the same writers when they went again to the library; that discussion was mostly one-sided. Then a spelling review dragged on too long, forcing the teacher to postpone a planned lesson on subtraction. And now the afternoon was almost done.

"Individual" had been the spelling word on which the class had snagged. When Miss Boroughs asked for its meaning, definitions of other words floated to the surface, the jetsam of previous lessons.

'That's It'

"Something that can't be divided?" proposed Desiree Fleming, harking back three weeks to a discussion of the word "indivisible."

"Something that separates," said Nelson Cerda, offering a phrase that had won the teacher's approbation when the word in question had been "departure."

"It's a person," said Shaun Sheppard finally.

"That's it," said Miss Boroughs, glancing at Raymond Mercado whose dreamy, aquamarine eyes seemed focused on a point beyond the windows, perhaps the backs of Park Avenue apartment houses two blocks distant.

"Raymond is a particular kind of individual," she said. "He's always doing his own thing. If we're all looking to the left, he's looking straight to the right. Raymond, did you know the meaning of 'individual'?"

"Yes."

"What? What is it?" challenged Matthew Phillips.

"I forget," said Raymond.

"Let's just cut the individuality for a few minutes," Miss Boroughs pleaded with a sigh, "until we can get through these words."

Attaching a negative value to "individuality," however ironically, was a demoralizing way for a teacher to end a school day. Of course Miss Boroughs wants individuality in her students, none of whom she regards as being hopelessly beyond her reach. But there never seem to be enough hours in the day, or days in the year for her to reach them all on an individual basis.

One reason the Dennison book (one of the most widely praised in the recent spate of books on educational reform) had appealed to her

was that it focuses on the relation between individuality and learning. Children learn best from adults, the book argues, when they are engaged in real relationships, not when they are regarded mainly as vessels to be filled.

Class Numbers 27

But for such relationships to flourish, the book maintains, small primary schools are essential. In fact, "The Lives of Children" was based on the experiences of a school (the First Street School, now defunct) that had four teachers for only 23 students, with no administrative overhead.

Public School 198 has 58 teachers and guidance counselors, plus 12 teaching aides, for 924 students; Miss Boroughs herself has a class of 27.

Maybe new types of public schools are needed, she sometimes thinks, or maybe the big schools would be more successful if the chronological grades were abolished and students were encouraged to move freely from one "skills center" to another.

She feels increasingly that the sorting of students into grades tends to undermine the whole purpose of education, for it assumes that students learn and grow at uniform rates. Before long many students are unable to function at their so-called "grade level," a term that describes the administrative needs of their school rather than their own growth. If they are not advanced, they are exposed to a stigma that will be difficult to overcome.

Personal Conflict

But in an ungraded school would students really acquire the skills and standards of work that the world presumably is going to demand from them one day?

Miss Boroughs herself, she recalls, learned reading and spelling and arithmetic not as a result of her own free

choice, but from relentless drilling in parochial schools in Queens.

Miss Boroughs is a poised and experienced teacher, but she feels torn: She believes in self-discipline strongly enough to have hanging over her desk in her otherwise modish studio apartment on the East Side William Ernest Henley's poem "Invictus" (" . . . I am the master of my fate/ I am the captain of my soul"). But does self-discipline in schools come from drilling or freedom? And wherever it comes from, shouldn't there be fun in learning and discovery?

Her course at Hunter hasn't guided her to the answers—as yet. In fact, nearly every week—despite resolutions to avoid getting caught in debates—she finds herself asking the instructor why he assumes that the schools can or should survive as they are.

And nearly as regularly something in his responses makes her feel that she has been misunderstood and she finds herself protesting: "But I'm not a radical!"

The instructor is William Goldstein, a Trumbull, Conn., high-school principal who sprinkles his comments in class with allusions to a wide variety of authors and regularly proclaims his openness to ideas on education advanced by those he classifies — "with affection," he says—as "the dreamers."

Sees Pain in Learning

But the subject he is teaching is "Administration and Supervision," so his first concern in the course is the survival, not the restructuring, of the schools as they are. "I don't think," he said the other evening, "that an educational ambiance, an educational milieu, can survive in an atmosphere of raw unrestrained innovation."

There must be pain in learning, Mr. Goldstein maintains, and the schools should withstand "educational he-

without structure," protested a woman. "They need to know what time to go to gym and what time to go to assembly. What you're attempting to do is not possible."

"But we've done it," the first teacher said.

Miss Boroughs laughed approvingly, but a high-school teacher at the other end of the first row said he could see dangers in the approach. "What if you have a student in your fifth-grade class," he asked, "who decides he wants to stand at an easel for six or seven hours and spend the whole day painting?"

"We hope," replied the first teacher," we can give him that freedom."

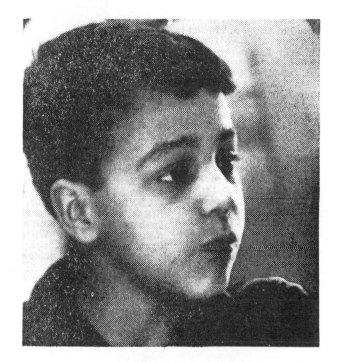

donists" who propound "the bizarre formula that interest equals entertainment." An even more pressing need, as he presents it, is to withstand the onslaught of "disruptive" students and radical students whose radicalism is "media-induced."

School administrators can "listen" to such students but not "respond" to them, he says.

'Not Possible'

At the class's last session one of the students described in ardent terms his efforts to "unstructure" his fifth-grade class so that students could develop interests and pursue them. Both the students and their teacher were finding it hard to get used to freedom in the classroom, he said.

"But children can't exist

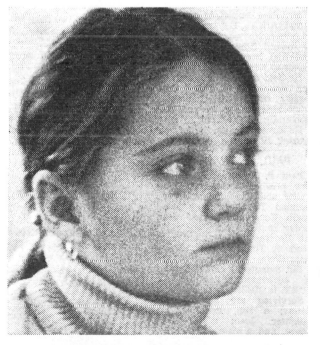

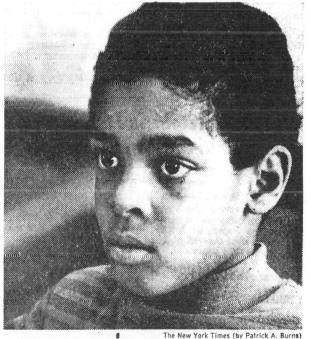

The New York Times (by Patrick A. Burns)

Some of students in Class 4-4, from top: Israel Valle, David Badillo, Raymond Citron and Hajraika Fülop. Their teacher, Miss Dorothy Boroughs, is attempting an individual approach to education within a large organizational framework.

November 16, 1970

Class 4-4:

Up the Reading Ladder

By JOSEPH LELYVELD

Javier Romero moved with the solemnity of one engaged in a ritual. In his own mind it was a tiny commencement, for he had just climbed up a rung in Class 4-4's reading program, becoming the fifth member of a small élite able to read slightly above what is calculated to be their "grade level."

He didn't put it quite that way himself, for the concepts of an élite and a grade level had not crossed his mind. Instead, he reported, in grave, hushed tones, "Miss Boroughs said I can move from Red to Tan."

The colors—there are 12 of them—mark off different stages of the reading program, each of which comes with a set of brief texts appropriate to it. Thus when the whole class is reading, each student can be working at his own speed and level, no matter how sharply these diverge from the rate and level of the youngster next to him.

'Laboratory' in a Box

Once his teacher, Dorothy Boroughs, had given him a nod of approval after checking his answer to questions on the reading in "Red," Javier stepped to the table at the back of the room where the "reading laboratory" is kept in the box in which it was originally packaged by its publisher, Science Research Associates of Chicago. Next to that is another box, one that holds brown envelopes in which students preserve their finished work.

Javier brought his envelope back to Miss Boroughs. On its cover she wrote "Red" in red with a Magic Marker above the words "Blue," "Brown and "Green," each inscribed by her in the appropriate color when he finished earlier stages of the program. This done, Javier was authorized to carry out the final part of the ritual by untacking his name from the square of red paper on the bulletin board and moving it to the tan.

So far this semester that ritual has been acted out 59 times in Class 4-4 (at least once by each of the 27 fourth

Photographs for The New York Times by PATRICK A. BURNS

Javier Romero placing his name in Tan group, Class 4-4's top reading group. He joined four other members of small élite able to read slightly above their "grade level."

graders) as the children moved up in reading. According to the measures built into the Science Research Associates program, the average improvement has been four-fifths of one whole grade. Of the 12 students reading on a second-grade level in September, only five are still stranded there.

In 4-4 the first of the three R's overshadows everything else. The reason is not that Miss Boroughs is caught up with some new method in this most fad-ridden area of teaching.

Committed to neither the so-called "phonics" nor "look-say" approach to reading instruction, she is ready to try almost anything in order to end the school year with a class of confident, eager readers. Otherwise, she knows, many of her students will be doomed to careers as misfits in the schools.

The improvement in reading scores presumably also reflects improvement in reading, but what does it say about confidence, eagerness and involvement? Miss Boroughs answers that she likes the "individualized" program because it has given some of her students their first real experience of success in school, and that involvement cannot follow from failure.

Individual Attention

She also likes it because it frees her to deal with the children one at a time. At the start of every hour devoted to the program Miss Boroughs goes to the blackboard and asks, "Who wants help?" Hands shoot up and she writes down the names of children who will read aloud to her, Mrs. Celenia Ingenita, her teaching aide, or Joanne Guidotti the new student teacher from Marymount College.

Usually that is the last time Miss Boroughs has to address the class as a whole until the period is over. By then most of the children will have sat for five to 10 minutes with one of the adults in the room.

The reading texts are never more than 15 paragraphs. They range in difficulty from "Orange 1"— which discusses dinosaurs without using the word, apparently because it is regarded as too difficult—to "Silver 12," an excerpt from something Jawaharlal Nehru once wrote about the nature of civilization. Expressed in grades, this range is said to be second through seventh.

In the first weeks of the semester this reading program dominated the school day, but Miss Boroughs realized that it was far from adequate to meet the reading needs of the class because it did little to promote the notion that reading was not the only end of reading.

Soon she started handing out library books to the pupils, keeping track of what they read and how often they came back for new titles.

And simply for the fun of it—since that is one of the things reading is supposed to be — she regularly read a story to them herself, starting with Roald Dahl's "Charlie and the Chocolate Factory."

Many Like Math

Arithmetic came on slowly but steadily as the second main area of concentration. Among the pupils who re-

Sharaie Blue, another member of the Tan group, receiving individualized reading instruction from teacher, Miss Dorothy Boroughs. The reading program has given some of her students their first real experience of success in school.

spond brightly to any presentation of a mathematical concept are some who start to quiver with anxiety when called on to read. The other day when Miss Boroughs prescribed an especially stiff dose of math exercises, half the class broke out in applause and cheers.

More recently spelling has been added as a third concentration, with the words emerging not from any standardized list but from the reading and random experiences of Class 4-4. Penmanship and social studies have hardly been touched as yet, and four of the six textbooks distributed to the class have rarely been used.

In part this is because of Miss Boroughs's own pre-occupation with the reading problem; in part, it reflects her fear that the standard history text the class has would petrify its quickening interest in reading.

"I just can't throw the book at them," she explains. "And we don't have the time yet to cover the same ground in more imaginative ways."

In other words, she has made up her mind to be more loyal to her own sense of what it is the specific children she teaches really need and can handle than to a standarized syllabus designed for children of their age in general.

Disagreement Tolerated

This mild rebellion on her part is tolerated by her superiors at P.S. 198 because they are also preoccupied with the reading problem and because they have seen that Miss Boroughs usually gets results.

This fall the school has two new reading programs —one for beginning readers in the lower grades in which letters are presented as cartoon characters and the combining of them is presented as a game, the other for older pupils who have never made much headway.

These pupils are sent to a reading clinic three times a week where they are given individual exercises to develop their "word-attack," "decoding" and "comprehension" skills — the sum of which, say the experts in the teachers colleges, is the mysterious activity known as reading.

In their polemical writings, educational reformers have contended that the only thing mysterious about reading is how the schools have managed to make it arduous. Thus Paul Goodman once identified the main obstacle to reading as "going to school."

Miss Boroughs still thinks that reading is a problem for many pupils, and not merely because of the schools. "It's like ice skating," she told her class the other day. "If you want to do it really well, you have to do it often."

Class 4-4:
A Rule Is Bent to Give Shaun a Chance

By JOSEPH LELYVELD

At the start of the third week of school this fall the children of Class 4-4 were told by Miss Dorothy Boroughs, their teacher, that a new student was about to join them. His name was Shaun Sheppard and, as the teacher explained it, he was really in the fifth grade but was going to remain in their class.

"They call it 'traveling,'" she said. "He'll be traveling in our class."

The aim of this unusual arrangement was to enable Miss Boroughs to continue working with Shaun, who had made good progress with her help the previous two years but still had a long way to go if he was not to be hopelessly stranded in school.

Shaun could not be formally enrolled in Miss Boroughs's fourth-grade class because he had already been left back once and that was the limit, according to school regulations. Besides, though he was thought to be more than two years behind in reading, there were other fifth graders who were much worse off.

What made him different was Miss Boroughs's belief that she could make a difference in his life and the willingness of her superiors to ease the rigidities of the system so she could try. But if schools had analysts to calculate risks and probabilities the way insurance companies have actuaries, then Shaun Sheppard would probably be recorded on a computer printout as the student in Class 4-4 with the lowest educational expectancy.

Bright and Sturdy

This would fly in the face of everything that is most obvious about Shaun himself —his lively intelligence, his feeling for stories and language, his gift for sketching and painting, and his self-sufficient emotional sturdiness, none of which could be easily missed or overlooked in a classroom.

But a computer would not have to assume equality of opportunity as the schools do when they demand that learning take place at a uniform rate. It would know, without asking why, that not many students catch up in school after falling two years behind, and that students coming from families that have been on welfare for two generations, as Shaun's has, tend to fall behind first.

One Life 'Messed Up'

Shaun's mother, Josephine Sheppard, knows this better than any computer. Her own life, she says, was "messed up because I never learned what I was supposed to know."

As she bitterly recalls it, she was assigned to a class for retarded children in school, though it was and is obvious that she didn't belong there. Then she dropped out altogether from Mabel Dean Bacon Vocational High School here after giving birth to Shaun at the age of 17, which was 11½ years ago.

With her own experience in mind, she says learning is what will save Shaun, "the only son I have." Three years ago she approved Shaun's being left back to repeat the third grade. She says she approves his studying with a fourth-grade class now, for it means he still has a fighting chance to move ahead with the skills he needs and not be pushed on to oblivion, which is what high school became for her.

Miss Boroughs first met Shaun when he was going through the third grade the second time. In those days he was regarded as a discipline problem and could hardly read.

But when she came into his class as a "cluster teacher" to read stories and poems, with the aim of showing that reading has a purpose, Shaun quickly won her over with the radiance and gentleness of his smiles, his eagerness to sit next to her as she read, his complete absorption in the stories, and his quickness in committing to memory verses by poets such as Robert Louis Stevenson on subjects such as rain and snow.

That year and last, Shaun's reading improved to the point that he was nearly able to handle material designed for the third grade; with the progress he has made this fall he is now almost up to the fourth grade.

But he still has a strained and erratic relation with words and numbers on paper. Having to read aloud to his teacher or his class still seems to embarrass him slightly, causing him to sit tensely, curl his hair nervously with a finger and vibrate his knees like a jackhammer under the table.

Performance Varies

Sometimes he will go to the blackboard and write "tor" as the first three letters of "taught" or subtract 678 from 1,000 and come up with the answer 789. But when he concentrates, he often works well and, on occasion, manages to express himself not just well but elegantly.

For instance, the other day Miss Boroughs was trying to get the class to tell her that she should use multiplication to solve a problem she had put on the blackboard. "Well, what should I do with these numbers? Should I cook them?" she asked, baiting the class. "What would I get if I cooked them?"

It was Shaun who called out, "A numbers soufflé."

Similarly, when Class 4-4 wrote letters to Blanche Goldberg, a student teacher who was moving to another class, it was Shaun who wrote, "Your times table work in Class 4-4 was very good and I may add superb, Miss Goldberg." Urging her to keep up the good work, he also advised, "Sock it to the facts, Miss Goldberg."

Miss Boroughs cautiously broached the idea of switching from Class 5-2 to 4-4 to Shaun when he visited her classroom early in the semester to give her a tiny bottle of dime-store perfume for her birthday. At first he said, "Maybe." A week later he said "Yes."

She then promised him that he could return to 5-2 whenever he liked and, whatever happens, that he would be promoted to the sixth grade in June.

Sunless Apartment

Shaun lives with his mother and infant sister in a small, well-scrubbed but roach-infested tenement apartment that is below street level and gets so little natural light it might almost be under water. Heroin addicts sometimes pass the apartment on their way to the basement to shoot up. Because of them, the Sheppards keep gates on all the windows and a large dog.

He has a room and television set to himself. Television, he says, is "where I learn." It also may be where he picks up words like "soufflé" and "superb."

Plaster is crumbling from the wall above his bed and his landlord only invites his mother to move out when she complains. But Shaun has handsomely decorated the wall with his own painting of Mickey Mouse.

Usually he is late when he comes swinging out of the building every morning, passing through the front door, which is missing its glass pane. From there it is a block and a half to school.

Miss Burroughs is encouraged by Shaun's work this year because she thinks he is experiencing some success and gaining a stronger sense of his own powers. In part, this may have something to do with a crush he has on Desirée Fleming, one of the best readers in the class.

Recently in the midst of a reading lesson, Desirée taunted him, "Shaun, you'll never catch up."

"I be I will," he shot back, adding softly and wistfully as she glided away, "Maybe I will and maybe I won't."

Whatever the reason, he shows signs of bearing down. The other evening he mentioned a spelling test with 40 words on it that Miss Boroughs has promised for this week. Asked if he would study hard, he smiled and replied, "I'll have to get ready to face the dangers of school."

December 7, 197

Class 4-4: Day of Judgment Is Mostly a Delight

By JOSEPH LELYVELD

"Now sit still, BECAUSE . . ."

Dorothy Boroughs's voice suggested the teasing solemnity of a magician about to pronounce his "presto." With a flourish, she reached into a brown envelope and extracted a sheath of printed white papers.

"What's going to happen?" she asked.

"Report cards!" a dozen excited voices replied.

Frightened and fascinated, as if bracing for the worst, the children of Class 4-4 edged forward on their seats as their teacher called out their names. Almost in every case, the name came with a reassuring capsule summary of the report.

"Sharaie," Miss Boroughs called, "an excellent report card." Or, "Cecil, pretty good but not great."

One of the few students in the fourth-grade class who approached Judgment Day confident that he was in a state of grace was Israel Valle. When he got his card, he ran his eye down a column of 15 "excellents" (out of a possible 20) and beamed. It was the best report card in the class.

His mother, Mrs. Maria Valle, was not surprised, either. "He's very intelligent," she said when Israel, a champion returning with a trophy, met her in the playground and handed over the card.

By contrast, Javier Romero had the harrowed look of one who had just escaped disaster. "I didn't get no U's," he told his mother. U stands for unsatisfactory; the fact that he had excelled — done very well — 11 E's for excellent — seemed hardly to have made an impression.

The report cards used in elementary schools here these days are a little less terse and a little less rigid in their classifications than report cards used to be.

A Generous Grader

There are only four grades —G and F for good and fair, in addition to the extremes of E and U—but the subjects to which these are applied are broken down into the vital skills they demand.

Instead of being told that his child is good in reading, a parent may find a fair next to "recognizes new words,"

Photographs for The New York Times by MICHAEL EVANS

Israel Valle shows his mother the best report in his class

an excellent next to "reads with understanding" and a fair next to "shows an interest in reading."

In addition, there is room for comments by both teachers and parents on the back of the cards. And if the parent is of Hispanic origin and shaky in English, the whole report comes in Spanish.

Miss Boroughs thinks of herself as a strict and demanding teacher, but confesses to being a generous grader when it comes to report cards.

It is one thing to scold a child for failing to do a particular assignment properly, she says, for his failure is specific and immediate. It is quite another thing, she believes, to tell him he is a failure generally, for he may take it to be the last word on his prospects in school.

Thus Miss Boroughs several times disregarded a Board of Education guideline that says no child should be graded above fair if he is not reading on what is held to be "grade level." Several of her children had done very well in reading, even if they were not quite yet where they should be, she said, and she wanted them to know she was pleased.

The 27 report cards she filled out last weekend at home gave her 999 opportunities to hand out U's (540 in the 20 categories under the headings of reading, oral language, written language and science, plus 459 in the 17 categories of what once was called "deportment" where the only other grade is S for satisfactory). In all, she gave only 13 U's, and only five children received them.

The teacher labored the hardest on the comments. Although she was concerned not to make too much of report cards, she also wanted, she said later, to put down something really personal about each child. In the process, she often more than filled the small inch-deep box provided for the comments, overflowing into the margins of the box provided for the next marking period.

If 4-4 was filled with child actors, some blurb writer could have had a field day snatching phrases from Miss Boroughs's reviews.

"A delightful, clever boy," she called Andy Carril. "An enthusiastic learner," she said of Fred Fiandaca. "Really fun to teach," ran her comment on Matthew Phillips. "Preciosa," meaning precious or beautiful, was the Spanish word she found for Maria Rivera.

A Year of Progress

Andy's mother, Mrs. Romana Carril, was nearly moved to tears by the report card her red-haired son presented to her on the eve of his ninth birthday.

It contained five excellents, 13 goods, two fairs and not a single U. Last June, sorrowfully and resentfully, Andy brought home a report card from his third-grade class containing only one good, 12 fairs and eight U's. Before Tuesday, he had never received an excellent in school.

The teacher's comment last year was brief and blunt: "Andy has not been doing well due to his behavior in school."

This year he has so overcome the idea of failure that when Miss Boroughs asked him recently whether he

could ice skate, his unhesitating response was: "How do I know? I've never tried."

Matthew Phillips came bustling home with his report card in an attaché case that is nearly half his own length, which is only 49 inches. He dropped the case by the door in the kitchen and called out to his mother, "I got my report card today, Ma."

Then he headed to the rear of the small railroad flat to turn on the television set and watch a program called "Lost in Space." About 20 minutes later, when he returned to the kitchen to pick up a tuna-fish sandwich for dinner, he discovered that what he had said about the report card had not registered with his mother.

"It's bad, Ma," he said. "Eight U's."

But by then, his mother, Mrs. Jean Phillips, had the card in her hand and was reading Miss Boroughs's comment, which said her son was "always alert and contributed a great deal through his clever comments." Then she turned it over and found the grades—mostly goods and excellents, no U's

To discourage competitiveness, each report card carried the printed caution that "No two children are alike." Matthew's mother and most of the other parents in the class did not seem to require that warning, for they did not read the reports to discover the relative standing of their children.

In a number of her comments, Miss Boroughs tried to make propaganda for more reading at home or special application to the spelling list by the worst spellers over Christmas vacation. Only a handful of parents sent comments back in the space provided for that purpose.

In a few homes the report cards did not bring glad tidings. Parents and children in these homes told of earnest colloquies and, possibly, a few tears. There may even have been some dire warnings of what would happen if improvement were not shown. But, in the literal sense, Class 4-4 seemed to have come through report-card week unscathed.

December 17, 1970

Class 4-4:
An Occasion for Sadness

By JOSEPH LELYVELD

For three months after she received a curt notice that the tenement building in which her family had its small railroad flat was about to be demolished, Mrs. Felicita Romero searched for an apartment nearby that would make it possible for her to keep her two sons at Public School 198.

It was a hopeless search, for there is more demolition than construction taking place in the East 90's these days.

Housing officials told her there was no point in adding her name to one of the long lists of those waiting for places in city projects. And the private relocating agency whose signboard was nailed to the front of her building on Second Avenue offered only one apartment—in a building eight miles away in Queens, which was, for Mrs. Romero, another world.

By last week there were only three families left in her building, and addicts, winos or other displaced persons had twice broken into vacant apartments and started fires.

Boys in Another School

Mrs. Romero still had not found a place to live but decided she had no choice but to squeeze her sons, husband and herself into her mother's apartment on East 27th Street. While she continued her search, the boys—Javier, who is 9 years old, and Aurelio, 6—could enroll at Public School 116 on East 33d Street.

In Class 4-4 at P.S. 198, word that the Romeros were moving aroused feelings of loss and injury, especially in the teacher, Dorothy Boroughs, who had once called grave, solicitous Javier "the best monitor I ever had."

Nearly every afternoon Miss Boroughs leaves school burdened with more papers and books than two hands can carry: Javier always stayed by her side until she reached her car, providing the extra hands.

"As a teacher, you have to try to harden yourself to

this," she remarked. "Children come and go all the time."

In P.S. 198's office, such comings and goings are called "transactions." Last Monday there were 11 of them; 9 out and 2 in. Since school began in September, moving and demolition have caused the enrollment to drop from about 1,000 to 930. Class 4-4 is now down to 26 children—a net loss of eight.

The average turnover in the school runs to about 30 per cent a year, according to its acting principal, Mrs. Charlotte Schiff, who said there were other schools in which it was even higher. The constant flux, Mrs. Schiff said, raises questions about the significance of the average reading scores published each year by the Board of Education on a school-by-school basis.

On a child-by-child basis, the flux simply adds to the discontinuity in education that a student usually experiences inside a single school as he is passed from teacher to teacher and grade to grade.

Miss Boroughs could speak of the need for a teacher to harden herself to the loss of a favorite child, but on Javier's next-to-last afternoon in her class she impulsively kissed him and said, "I'm going to miss you very much."

On the last afternoon she gathered the class around his desk and presented him with a book she had bought and a note, on her stationery with her name in lavender art-nouveau lettering addressed to "Master Javier Romero."

The note said: "Thanks for being such a cooperative and interesting member of our class. Please do not forget us."

Javier seemed astonished by all the attention, almost dazed.

The look had not quite worn off by the time he put in his appearance at his new school. Both Javier and his brother were wearing neckties and black shoes Mrs. Romero had carefully shined for

the occasion. As they waited in the office to be placed in classes, Aurelio worked away at his notebook, doing examples in addition he made up for himself in order to demonstrate his prowess; Javier nervously drummed his fingers on the arm of his chair.

7 Times 5 Is . . .

"The boys are raring to go, they're ambitious," a secretary in the office noted approvingly.

Miss Veola Harper, an assistant principal, called Javier into a side office and tested his reading ability by asking him to read a story about a raccoon. Then she asked him to count by fours. When he got to 28, Javier stumbled and had to count on his fingers.

His reading was good enough to convince Miss Harper that he belonged in the top class on the grade—known by the teachers at P.S. 116 as 4-1 but called 4-320 whenever students are around, in a hopeless effort to hide from them the fact that the classes are grouped according to skills.

Class 4-320 was just leaving for gym when Javier and Miss Harper reached the room. Once again Javier had drawn a poised and attractive teacher. Her name was Susan Jaffe and as introductions were made, she extended her hand to shake that of her new student. In response, Javier stuck out his left hand.

"How about the other one?" the teacher asked, laughing.

Holding him close to her as she spoke, Miss Jaffe announced to the class: "This is Javier. He'll be in our class. Go up to him in gym and say 'hello.' When we get back to the room, we'll welcome him formally."

Javier had a wary, alert look when he took the last seat in the last row after Miss Jaffe assigned it to him.

"I don't want you to get scared when you see all of these," the teacher said as she piled 10 textbooks and

workbooks on his desk, not one of which had been in use in his old school.

Then she informed him that loose-leaf notebooks, like the one he was carrying, were banned from the school. The principal, Miss Hazel R. Mittelman, considers them messy.

Next, Javier was told that 20 spelling words were handed out every Monday, leading to regular tests; also, that he would be expected to learn the multiplication tables. Finally, the new student heard that the class had nearly finished its study of the explorers in social studies and was about to move on to the founding of the American colonies.

Almost immediately it became clear also that two students speaking at once invited trouble in 4-320. The girl sitting next to Javier spoke out of turn and was quickly rebuked. "Will you wait, young lady?" Miss Jaffe said. "That's being extremely rude to your classmate."

In 4-4, talking when another student had the floor was much less likely to irritate the teacher than failure to pay attention; the explorers had been almost totally ignored; math concepts were stressed rather than memorizing times tables; formal tests came irregularly, usually without much fanfare; textbooks were rarely used, and desks were arrayed in clusters, not in orderly rows all facing front.

Knowing there are bound to be differences between any two classrooms, Miss Boroughs had assumed that Javier would have considerable adjusting to do in his new school. Specifically, she had a premonition that his new teacher would already have started long division, a subject she had yet to touch. So last week she hastily gave him a cram course.

Luckily, 4-320, like 4-4, still had that frontier to cross. As for the differences that were apparent, Javier hardly seemed to notice them. He was too busy trying to fit in.

Class 4-4:
Teacher Veers Between Elation and Despair

By JOSEPH LELYVELD

Ever since Javier Romero transferred out of Class 4-4 to another school, depriving its teacher of her favorite monitor, his old friends in the class have been sending him regular bulletins on its progress.

"Oh!" Lori Spellman began a recent letter. "Felix took over your job. Felix is doing fine on his new job. But Miss Boroughs is still having trouble with homework. Ray M. now don't do so much homework, if you ask me. He just do a little bit."

The part about Felix Herrera was news, for he had probably been the student in 4-4 most frequently in trouble with the teacher, Dorothy Boroughs. His difficulties had to do with an offhand attitude to homework assignments and his large size, which combined with a certain imprudence and lack of stealth, made him stand out in the midst of an uproar.

Felix hadn't grown any smaller and his performance on homework was still erratic. Yet, without knowing exactly how it happened, everyone recognized a subtle transformation. Felix was on good terms with the teacher and good terms with himself, more likely now in a tight situation to be the accusor than the accused.

Lori's report on Raymond Mercado's casual ways wasn't news at all. In a discussion of the imagination the other day, Miss Boroughs asked the children whether there were any daydreamers among them. Raymond was jolted out of a state of self-immersion by the discovery that everyone was looking his way.

With the wending of the school year into its second semester, transformations — and the lack of them—have been much on the teacher's mind, causing her to veer between elation and despair

'Brightest' Moment

Her brightest moment came on a day when she felt overwhelmed with administrative chores. Seemingly there was no time for teaching, so she asked the children to take out their library books and read. And that's what they did, in happy and complete absorption. Miss Boroughs, who had coaxed,

Felix Herrera

begged and harrangued them to read for pleasure, felt like crying "Eureka!"

"We've made a breakthrough," she proclaimed proudly a few days later. "Everybody is reading books!"

Israel Valle, with his chin on his hand and his hand on his desk, seemed almost to be drinking the words off the page. "Look at Israel," exclaimed the teacher. "He really likes what he's doing."

Raymond Cintron, one of the few students who wasn't doing much of anything at that point, took the hint and promptly put his chin on his hand. But that didn't make the book before him more interesting.

Desirée Fleming called out that she was on chapter 13. Stella Pistorio said she was on chapter 5. Ralph Ingenita wanted it known that he had reached chapter 4. All had started different books at different times. "They like to tell me what chapter they're on," the teacher said.

At the end of the afternoon, children converged on the blackboard and took turns writing in upper and lower case letters of all sizes with numerous exclamation points: "reaD!!" "rEAD!!" "READ" and "ReAD!" Over and over again.

The explosion of imperatives had started quietly when Miss Boroughs wrote "Read!" next to a homework assignment a few weeks ago. She didn't remember which child was the first to copy her. Like the reading itself, it had just seemed to happen.

Rise in Reading Skill

Of course, it didn't just happen. Twelve of the 25 students in the class were reading on a second-grade level in September. None was ready for the fourth-grade books they were supposed to use. Now—after five months of stress on reading skills— 15 are reading on or above grade level.

Class 4-4's reading "breakthrough" lifted its teacher's spirits, but they soon sank again. The pressures she felt seemed to emanate from outside her classroom.

There was a series of changes in the schedule of the paraprofessional assigned to the room, followed by a switch of paraprofessionals. There was difficulty with a parent who hadn't responded to her requests to come to school; then Miss Boroughs felt she got less support than she deserved from a supervisor when the parent did show up. Finally, she discovered that some students she taught last year were having to work their way again through reading materials they had completed with her.

"I've had a very bad two weeks in the system," Miss Boroughs said. She felt so depressed, she said, that she had even thought for a moment of splurging on a charter flight to Switzerland on the coming holiday weekend —"to restore my mental health."

Irritation Contained

Soon she realized that some of the irritation she couldn't vent elsewhere was falling, unfairly, on the heads of children in 4-4 when they committed such relatively minor infractions of the routine as failing to bring sneakers on gym days, leaving library books home, or bring incomplete homework.

To contain that irritation, Miss Boroughs worked out an elaborate scheme involving a

chart in the back of the room on which a child's name would be posted if he committed such a misdeed. That way, she explained to the class when she unveiled the chart, "I won't have to be miserable from yelling all the time and you won't have to be miserable hearing me yell."

On top of the chart was a dictionary definition of the word responsibility: "That for which one is answerable or accountable." Below were the days of the month to which the names would be tacked. The idea was that the teacher would calmly order the posting of the names, that she would refrain from yelling, and that the children involved would learn the meaning of "responsibility." The result, she said, would be "a happy room."

From the beginning, Miss Boroughs had her own doubts about the project. "I'm doing something educators say you should never do," she said. "They always tell you, 'Never make a negative chart.'"

Second Thought Taken

Raymond Mercado's name went up first for some math homework he didn't do. Raymond Mercado's name went up second for failing to complete another assignment.

Four more names went up the first day. Five more names went up the second day. Among them was Raymond Mercado's. Then Miss Boroughs noticed that he was blushing.

On the third day, there were no names. Owning up to the children, Miss Boroughs told them she had made a mistake. "I didn't do it to be mean," she said, "but it was."

"The educators were right," she said later, "It was an appalling idea."

Class and teacher were both in a relaxed mood yesterday when they went to the Whitney Museum to see Alexander Calder's "Circus," an array of acrobats, clowns, trick riders, wild animals and circus paraphernalia, fashioned from wire, cork, rags and bottle tops.

A museum official pointed out that every figure had moving parts. Yvonne Prileau wanted to know where the slot was for the penny that made them move. Hajnaika Fulop thought there was probably a button.

355

Another Calder work was on display in the sculpture court, a large sheet-metal piece the artist had called "The Snuck." The man from museum said that Calder was more than 70 years old.

"I wouldn't want to see him if he looked that old," Stella Pistorio remarked. "But maybe he doesn't look old. Maybe he keeps in shape, always running around making things."

Miss Boroughs said "snuck" was a made-up word, which left Stella wondering why an old man would enjoy so childish a sound. "Snuck, snuck, snuck," said Stella, trying to make sense out of it.

"Snock, snock, snock," she muttered. Then she gave up.

Class 4-4: Teachers Ponder Union Attitude on Problems

By JOSEPH LELYVELD

Dorothy Boroughs led Class 4-4 to the cafeteria and left the children there for lunch, then carried her container of apricot yogurt to the library. Other teachers brought cottage cheese, raw carrots, pastrami sandwiches, Danish pastry and mugs of coffee.

It wasn't a rained-out picnic, but a chapter meeting of the United Federation of Teachers, which at Public School 198, as in the city at large, is solidly, even intrinsically, a part of the school establishment.

Kenneth Munson, the chapter chairman, and Flora Karbelnik, its delegate, opened the meeting by telling the teachers they would all be told soon whom to write to in Albany and what to say to defeat legislation that would authorize financial aid to parochial schools. "That's the first target of our legislative action," Miss Karbelnik declared.

Then Mr. Munson turned the floor over to the school's acting principal, Mrs. Charlotte Schiff, who had been invited to talk about the difficulties of getting Federal funds for special programs in the school.

Mrs. Schiff confers formally with the chapter chairman once a month and informally nearly every day, but her appearance at the union meeting was unusual. She was there, Mr. Munson explained, not as the principal but as an expert on the subject she was discussing and as a "good unionist," having joined the U.F.T. the year it started organizing and playing now an active role in the Council of Supervisors and Administrators, which recently got a charter from the A.F.L.-C.I.O.

While the principal was speaking, Miss Boroughs finished her yogurt. Keeping busy, she then filled out the necessary forms to obtain a bus so she could take her class ice skating in Central Park next month.

With the children due to return to their classrooms, Mr. Munson closed the meeting by saying there would be an urgent topic for discussion at the next one.

Later he said that this was the subject of "the disruptive child," a hardy perennial at union meetings, which had become a matter of special concern now, he said, because of the abolition of special classes in which such students could be segregated and the placing of restrictions on suspensions.

Teachers in the school say that chapter meetings have been concerned almost exclusively with working conditions and political matters that touch the schools, such as the parochial schools issue. There has been no discussion at chapter meetings of classroom reforms, a subject that has lately been emphasized by the union's president, Albert Shanker, in his public statements.

Mr. Shanker gave a talk to the union's Elementary School Committee on Charles E. Silberman's book, "Crisis in the Classroom," but P.S. 198's representative to that committee, Mrs. Bertha Gladstone, was unable to attend. Later she went to a lecture on the so-called British infant school and concluded there was "nothing new" in the informal approach to teaching that Mr. Shanker and Mr. Silberman have been advocating.

The real problem in schools these days, says Mrs. Gladstone who teaches fourth-graders, is that teachers are expected to turn all their students into "intellectuals." Not enough is done, she says, to stress the dignity of manual labor.

For eight years before Mr. Munson was elected U.F.T. chapter chairman in September, the job was held by Michael Rosenberg, a young teacher of music who was elected by the eight other members then in the chapter one day while he was out to lunch and, as he says, then "grew up with the union." Now among the 56 teachers in the school there are only three nonmembers, including two of the three blacks.

The eight years engraved a somewhat saturnine expression on Mr. Rosenberg's face. He has always thought of himself as strongly in favor of the labor movement and the cause of racial integration. Eight years ago, he says, that was a "far-out" position; now he finds it's considered "neo-conservative."

During the 1968 teachers' strikes that grew out of the dispute in the Ocean Hill-Brownsville demonstration district he even heard himself called a "racist." Naturally, he says, he is bitter. "New York is gone," Mr. Rosenberg has concluded. "The whole city is on a downhill slide."

Last June, after his wife had been mugged in the lobby of their Bronx apartment house with their small child looking on, Mr. Rosenberg moved his family to Fairlawn, N. J., and gave up the chairmanship so he could concentrate on his new responsibilities as a homeowner.

According to Mr. Munson, most complaints at P.S. 198 have to do with working conditions—the cancellation of a "prep" period in which a teacher is supposed to be freed from classroom duties, an abbreviated lunch hour, or assignment for two consecutive years to so-called "difficult" classes. So far, however, he has had to present no formal grievances.

Like his predecessor, Mr. Munson is deeply troubled by changes he has seen. Coming from a conservative background, he resisted joining the union for five years. Then he had what he calls "my road to Damascus." Now, he finds, the liberal values that led to that conversion are under attack "before they could take root."

Criticism Is Rejected

Other teachers, probably a minority, feel a different kind of malaise. Theirs concerns the union itself and what they see as the tendency of many teachers to react bitterly and personally to the slightest criticism of its stands.

"They take the position that you can only be a union man if you agree with the union on everything, that members who disagree are, somehow, not unionists," said a teacher in the chapter who complained that it never addressed itself to the question of what teachers can do to accomplish more in classrooms.

Whatever else they did, the strikes apparently simplified the issues involved in union membership for the young teachers who started their careers in the last two years. Miss Olive McNeil, one of the black teachers, said the Ocean Hill-Brownsville strikes

356

made her decision to stay out of the union "automatic."

Jeanette Campbell, who started teaching this year, used the word "automatic" to describe her decision to join. "The union has the power," she said. "If you want to bring about change, that's where you have to do it."

The same reasoning recently led Miss Boroughs to give up her resistance to U.F.T. membership.

She had been a hold-out all the years Mr. Rosenberg was organizing the chapter.

During the 1968 strikes she was one of only two teachers who went into the school to teach, not because she was convinced the union was wrong about Ocean Hill-Brownsville, but because she thought the strike tactic fundamentally wrong and damaging to children.

This fall Mr. Munson never even thought to ask Miss Boroughs whether she had changed her mind. But when she heard there were only four nonunion members left among the school's teachers, her assumption that nonunion teachers represented some kind of force collapsed.

"Why am I perpetuating this myth?" she asked herself. "The union doesn't need my $7 a month in dues. They're the power. Who am I kidding?"

Still Opposed to Strikes

Miss Boroughs still is opposed to strikes or the threat of strikes by teachers. And, though she recognizes that the wages the union has won have helped make it possible for her to ski in Chile, tour Japan and buy a Pucci dress, she still feels the contract establishing those wages makes the school too "teacher-centered" as opposed to "child-centered."

The week she filled in her union card she was angered when her children lost their one hour a week with the science teacher because the school had directed him to take the hour for a "prep" period owed him under the contract, thereby averting an overtime payment.

Last week, Miss Boroughs was told to take an hour off from teaching for the same reason. She said she would rather spend the hour with her class and write off the overtime.

February 23, 1971

Class 4-4: A Visitor From the Front Office

By JOSEPH LELYVELD

"Best behavior!" commanded Harvey Dagen, the young teaching assistant in Class 4-4.

The cue for his warning was the appearance in the classroom doorway of the assistant principal, Edmund Fried, who had come, armed with a clipboard, for a formal "observation" of a social-studies lesson.

The commotion his entrance caused seemed to amuse Mr. Fried but also to make him slightly self-conscious. "Where do you want me to hide?" he asked Dorothy Boroughs, the teacher.

She indicated a table in the rear of the room, which she had hastily covered with a cloth of yellow baize only a few moments earlier. Then she handed him a "lesson plan" detailing the "aim," "motivation," "procedures" and "conclusion" of her lesson, which was to deal with Spanish explorers of the 16th century.

Miss Boroughs had been worrying about the lesson plan for a week but had not actually committed any thoughts to paper until the lunch hour that day. Normally she prepares lesson plans only to satisfy the demands of her supervisor but never works from them preferring to work with students on an individual basis wherever possible and keep her lessons as informal and spontaneous as she can.

"I've never been a lesson-plan teacher," she remarked. But this was a command performance: Mr. Fried had specified that he expected a plan and wanted it to deal with social studies, a subject Miss Boroughs had deliberately neglected in the first half of the year in order to stress reading.

That emphasis had paid off. Twelve of the 24 children who had been in her class since the fall had gone ahead as much as two grades in reading, according to measurements built into the reading program she used; none had gained less than one grade.

Her first venture into social studies made use of a book on Negro heroes of the American past and present that Mr. Fried made available. She thought the children would find this more lively than the prescribed textbook, which starts with the explorers.

Faced with what she regards as the pressing needs of her students to gain confidence in their own abilities, Miss Boroughs would endorse Charles E. Silberman's wry comment in his book, "Crisis In the Classroom," that "the obsession with the explorers is one of the mysteries of American schooling."

The day before Mr. Fried's visit there was a hint of what a mystery the explorers were to some members of Class 4-4 as well. The textbook said that Jacques Cartier, the French explorer, had sailed for the New World in 1534. "How long ago was 1534?" Miss Boroughs asked.

"Two years," said Benny Winslow. Nelson Cerda realized that it must have been longer. "Six years," he suggested.

The immediate result was a lesson, improvised on the spot, not planned in advance, on how long a time 437 years really is and what it would have been like to live 437 years ago. Following it up, Miss Boroughs asked the children to imagine they were living in 1534 and to write essays on that theme.

Stella Pistorio thought life without television or electricity was bound to be primitive. So she wrote: "I woke up from sleeping on the tree. I got water from the river to take a bath. I ate leaves for breakfast."

That lesson gave rise to the one Mr. Fried was to witness. Unlike any other taught by Miss Boroughs this year, the demonstration she staged for her supervisor turned on an elaborate fiction — that 4-4 was being transported back in time to the 16th century.

Nelson Cerda was asked to say the magic words to accomplish the transporting. Then Miss Boroughs said, "Call on somebody and ask if he's in Europe," adding with a touch of irony she couldn't suppress, "Some nice cooperative child — he'd better say 'yes.' "

"Israel," said Nelson, calling on Israel Valle, who last week, once again, had received the best report card in the class. "Super-Israel," Miss Boroughs had called him then.

Now, obliging as ever, Israel agreed that he was in Europe. Next, Miss Boroughs asked the children to enact the roles of various explorers, then call on their classmates to guess whom they were trying to portray. "There's no women explorers," Stella objected, sounding a note for liberated women.

Discovery of Pacific

Cecil Robinson, an ardent fan and imitator of the comedian Flip Wilson, offered his best idea of the way his television hero might portray the discovery of the Pacific Ocean by Balboa if, by some mishap, he found himself booked into a fourth-grade class.

"The Pacific!" Cecil exclaimed, his hands spread wide and his eyes fixed on the concrete horizon across Lexington Avenue. "Sacre bleu! The Pacific!"

Mr. Fried laughed and said, "You have some great actors in this class. With all the Spanish-speaking kids here, Cecil, you had to say 'sacre bleu?' "

Trying to bring the lesson to a formal conclusion as prescribed in some teaching manuals, Miss Boroughs asked, "Why are we studying the explorers?"

"Because he's here to watch," said Shaun Sheppard knowingly, nodding in the direction of Mr. Fried.

"Fooled you, Shaun," the assistant principal declared. "I know about them already."

On his way out, Mr. Fried noted that Pizarro was the only Spanish explorer mentioned in the text who had not been mentioned in the lesson. He told Miss Boroughs that later on he would go over with her the comments that filled two sheets on his clipboard.

It had been the first time, in 24 weeks of the school year, that a supervisor spent some time in Class 4-4 to assess the quality of the teaching going on there. The discussion, Miss Boroughs ruefully commented after Mr. Fried's departure, had not been up to par.

What may actually have been for many children the most engrossing discussion of the year had occurred the week before when she taped a poster to the blackboard that had caught her eye one weekend while she was shopping.

'White Man's World'

It was a large color photograph of a black boy dressed all in white and seated in a room in which every inch of wall and floor and every object had been whitewashed. Its title was "White Man's World."

In bringing it to the class's attention, the teacher was not trying to make any point of her own. She was merely curious to see what they would make of it, thinking it might present a good opportunity for self-expression.

First the teacher asked the pupils to write down their thoughts about what the poster was supposed to represent. For one reason and another, about one-third of the children in Class 4-4 don't live with both their parents. Perhaps as a result, many imagined that the boy in the poster had been stranded.

"He looks like if his mother and father went away or died and some person adopted him and he doesn't like him or her," wrote Nelson Cerda, who has always lived with both his mother and father.

Racial Point Ignored

Only one child, Raymond Mercado, noted that the boy was black. In the discussion, it became clear that the propagandistic point of the poster was lost on these nine-year-olds — or rejected by them — because none was prepared to accept the proposition that the world did not belong to him and his classmates.

"Do you think it's possible for a black boy to think the world really belongs to white men?" the teacher asked.

"No!" the class thundered.

Shaun Sheppard — a fifth-grader assigned to the class so that Miss Boroughs could continue working with him — is about two years older than the other children and aware of many things that have not touched them. Expressions like "Power to the People!" and "Right on!" come easily to him. Either in spite or because of this, Shaun was most emphatic in denying that it's a "white man's world."

"It's everybody's world," he declared. "Japanese, Jewish, Pastrami . . ."

Class 4-4 has yet to be affected by the current budget crisis in the schools. But three times in two days last week Miss Boroughs had to go to meetings called to focus the concern of teachers and parents over the threatened cuts.

Tactics Discussed

At the first meeting, the acting principal, Mrs. Charlotte Schiff, urged support for a bus trip to Albany to protest outside the state Legislature. One parent proposed that school be closed for a day to underscore the protest. When the proposal was put to a vote, it resulted in a tie.

"Get another parent from the hallway," Mr. Fried quipped. Then, in graver tones, he declared: "We have to be heard once and for all."

The next day the proposed bus trip was a thing of the past as plans were laid for taking part in the demonstration outside City Hall called for tomorrow. Mrs. Schiff told the teachers that consent slips for parents to sign would be distributed so that fifth and sixth graders could go to the demonstration as an "educational experience trip."

Class 4-4: Weekly Study at Local Parochial School

By JOSEPH LELYVELD

Once a week six members of Class 4-4 leave school an hour early and cross Lexington Avenue to St. Francis de Sales Roman Catholic School where they are led, gently but firmly, into discussions of feelings that wax and wane inside them.

The more troublesome of the feelings that are talked about at the parochial school —anger or loneliness or boredom—are not hidden at Public School 198. But there, as in most schools, the emphasis is generally on containing them in the interests of orderly instruction. Once contained, they usually go unmentioned.

Some teachers encourage students to think about their feelings in the hope of encouraging free expression in writing. More rarely—as happened last week in one third-grade class at Public School 198—this may be done to relieve a tense situation in the classroom.

The Subject Is Anger

The young teacher in that class, Miss Roberta Korn, got her children talking and writing about anger—how they feel it and why—after acknowledging to them that she had allowed herself to become too angry over an incident of misbehavior.

One of her children, Antonio Beltran, tried to explain how such situations go out of control. "When I scream," he wrote, "I throw a book because when I want to get mad I feel like I am going to hit somebody. And when I hit somebody the teacher screams at me."

For the nuns and lay teachers at St. Francis de Sales, the inner lives of children are a stock in trade. There, and at many of the other Catholic schools to which 80,000 public-school children in the city are dispatched each week in the "released time" program, the memorization of catechism has largely given way to discussions of emotions children feel and situations that give rise to them.

The attempt is to weave religious doctrine into the discussions so that it really touches the life of the child. "Catechistics have undergone a revolution," a nun asserted.

Preparing for Communion

Ralph Ingenita and Stella Pistorio, two pupils from Class 4-4, are being prepared for their first communion in a class taught by Sister Mary Hildegarde Kogler.

Last Wednesday the nun read rapidly through an account of the conversion of Saul of Tarsus on the road to Damascus, then — without making explicit the connection she had in mind — showed a filmstrip about a young caveman who became enraged when a squirrel bit him and killed the animal, only to be overcome by a feeling he could not name. Sister Mary Hildegarde did not name it, either.

"When I was growing up," she said, "they told us it was a little voice. It's not really a little voice. It's a feeling you have."

One of the children suggested that the feeling was Jesus. The nun seemed to think the answer had come too easily so she let it stand without comment and returned to talking about a feeling that "keeps bothering you."

Finally—almost reluctantly, as if giving the feeling a name might kill off the children's understanding of what she meant—the teacher put the word "conscience" on the blackboard.

Ralph, who had been following her with rapt attention, raised his hand and made what was, for him, a long speech.

"I know another thing what conscience means," he declared. "If you break your mother's best dishes and tell your mother your friend did it, conscience says you are lying."

Asked afterward whether he had been talking about any particular incident of broken dishes, Ralph firmly insisted that he had made up the example.

In another classroom, the most accomplished pupil in Class 4-4, Israel Valle, was happily drawing a picture of something "nasty and horrible" he had done recently, to fulfill an assignment of a lay teacher, Miss Constance Archambault. She had promised that the drawings would not have to be shown to anyone.

While the children worked, a phonograph played a record of soft, rhythmic folk music with religious lyrics ("Into your hand we commend our spirit/Oh, God, we commend our hearts. . . .")

The words "selfishness," "pain," "sadness" and "hell" were grouped on one side of the blackboard, juxtaposed against "sacrifice," "love" "happiness" and "heaven" on the other.

A bulletin board was decorated with photographs of wounded civilians and soldiers in Indochina under a legend that said: "If anyone says he loves God but hates his brother, he is a liar."

Israel was drawing a picture of himself hitting his younger brother. At the bell, Miss Archambault told the children to tear up their drawings so no one would learn the secrets they contained.

Later she offered this explanation of her approach to teaching:

"It's all in the context of loving each other. I try to do this with my children. I don't always succeed. Sometimes I grind them into hamburger. But sometimes it's so wonderful I have to refrain from dancing on the ceiling."

The nuns at St. Francis de Sales are the first to wonder about the effectiveness of the teaching they do in the 45 minutes they spend each week with the children from P.S. 198.

"Our thinking is ahead of our practice," declared Sister Marita Murphy who runs the released-time program, which is officially known as the Confraternity of Christian Doctrine.

Beyond the Classroom

"It's a drag," said Sister Mary Hildegarde. "Forty-five minutes. What can you do?"

The nuns belong to an order called Holy Union of the Sacred Hearts, which allowed them to quit wearing their religious habits two years ago.

They see themselves as giving the children an inner strength that will help them withstand the violence on the streets where they live. But the nuns are just as interested in doing something about the conditions on those streets themselves.

"The action is in the streets," one declared.

"Politics is where the action is," said Sister Marita, who hopes to spend her summer working with prisoners from the Men's House of Detention.

Parochial schools have powers of expulsion no public school has. Occasionally that power is brandished over the heads of the troublesome pupils at St. Francis de Sales. But Sister Patricia Deasy, the principal, says the emphasis in recent years has been on helping such students, not getting rid of them.

Mrs. Natalie Zucker, a guidance counselor at P.S. 198, confirmed this. She said the Catholic school had even been ready to take in children who were having trouble in the public school when it appeared that a change of scene might help.

Matter of Security

Fred Fiandaca, a pupil in Class 4-4, will be going to St. Francis de Sales next fall, but not because of any trouble he is having. On the contrary, Fred is happy with P.S. 198 and his teacher, Dorothy Boroughs, is happy with him.

But his mother has heard and read a lot about problems in public schools—specifically drug problems — and hopes that, by this change, she will be able to shield her son from them as he enters into adolescence.

Stella Pistorio, who sits next to Fred in Class 4-4, said that her mother had warned her that she and her little brother would be sent to the Catholic school if either of them were ever left back.

Asked how she would feel about that, Stella replied: "Terrible. Yuck! They're so fussy. They make you wear a uniform, and if you don't wear a uniform, they kick you out."

A new pupil in the class, Kathy Brugueras, transferred out of a Catholic school, St. Ann's on East 110th Street, because her family thought standards would be higher at P.S. 198.

"All they used to teach me was religion, religion, religion, religion," Kathy said, voicing the dissatisfaction that was felt.

A Familiar Face

Another recent admission to Class 4-4 is Donna Smith, but she cannot be called a new pupil because she spent several weeks in the class last autumn before transferring to a school in East Harlem. Donna has changed classes three times this year and schools four times in the last two years.

Understandably, she was a bit disoriented when she returned to 4-4, calling her teacher Miss Owens for the first week and walking east to go home after school when she should actually have been walking west. Now she seems to have her bearings and to be at ease. The other day when 4-4 visited the Metropolitan Museum of Art, the two newcomers, Kathy and Donna, held hands all the way.

For Miss Boroughs—herself a product of a parochial school, St. Bartholomew's in Elmhurst, Queens—the comings and goings from her class, including the weekly excursions to St. Francis de Sales, sometimes all seem part of a hidden conspiracy to disrupt her teaching.

Twenty students are usually left in the room after the released-time children depart, but nothing new can be undertaken. The nuns, who have to dismiss their regular classes at lunchtime on Wednesdays to make room for those children, can commiserate.

"It must be very difficult," Sister Patricia said.

The New York Times/Neal Boenzi

Israel Valle, the most accomplished student in Class 4-4, with Constance Archambault, a teacher at St. Francis de Sales School. There, "released time" children are encouraged to explore their feelings in a religious context.

March 31, 1971

Class 4-4: Books Battle The Tube in Uphill Fight

By JOSEPH LELYVELD

On the final day of school before the start of the spring vacation last week, Dorothy Boroughs, the teacher of Class 4-4, waged a brief campaign on behalf of books, libraries, museums and the great outdoors, in the hope of weakening slightly the immobilizing magnetism of television.

Even when school is in session, most of the children in the class spend more time manning their positions in front of the tube than they do on any other activity in their lives except sleeping.

If Marshall McLuhan, the media prophet, is correct, "The TV child encounters the world in a spirit antithetic to literacy." In a spirit antithetic to TV, Miss Boroughs made sure that each child went home with enough books from the class library to keep him absorbed during the vacation.

Book Inspection

Checking to see that no one would be caught short, she asked the children to hold up their books. Suddenly a canopy of 80 or so volumes stretched across the classroom.

Then she urged them to make dates to meet at the public library on 96th Street. Hajnalka Fulop, who passes the library twice each day on her way to and from school, was the one child in the class who said she had never been inside.

"They won't let me go," she said.

"Who won't?" asked the teacher.

"My uncle, my mother and my aunt," said Hajnalka, who came to this country 20 months ago from Cluj in Rumania, speaking Hungarian, some Rumanian and no English. Now, because of special instruction at school and a few thousand hours in front of the television set in her uncle's apartment, she expresses herself in her new language as well as any child in the class.

Like many of the children in 4-4, Hajnalka usually isn't permitted to go outside after school because her family worries about her safety. Miss Boroughs suggested they might worry less if she told them she was meeting her classmate Stella Pistorio at the library.

The teacher's campaign for livelier vacations proceeded with a brisk walk to Central Park, where everyone had lunch in the sun, and a brief visit to the Museum of the City of New York, which has a special exhibit on addiction called "The Drug Scene." The park and the museum will be available during the holiday, she noted.

A television set with the word "BUY!" taped to its screen was part of the exhibit. Harvey Dagen, the teaching assistant in Class 4-4, tried to spell out for Jose Santana the intended message—that television fosters the notion that happiness and euphoria can be easily purchased.

"Whatever you see on TV you want to buy," Mr. Dagen said, "not because you really want it but just because you saw it on TV."

"I really want it," Jose protested.

"Sometimes," said Mr. Dagen with a knowing nod that seemed to say, "not often."

"Yeah," Jose agreed doubtfully.

Addicts Commonplace

Shaun Sheppard, who often passes addicts waiting to buy drugs in the hallway of his tenement, pointed to a needle, spoon and eyedropper — the tools of the drug scene—and repeated an explanation of their use he had heard on television.

"They showed them on 'Room 222,'" remarked Cecil Robinson. A few children nodded to indicate they had seen that program.

On the way back to school, while the class was waiting on a traffic island in the middle of Park Avenue for a red light to change, Yvonne Prileau playfully smacked Benny Winslow on the cheek. "You remind me of someone I hate," she said tauntingly. The line happened to come from an ancient Abbott and Costello rerun she had watched on television the previous afternoon without smiling even once.

Yvonne's mother, who works for the Post Office as a deliverer on a shift that starts at 1 A.M., wakes up at about the time her daughter gets home from school and insists that Yvonne finish her homework before starting to watch television.

TV Set of Her Own

There are two sets in the house and Yvonne is an only child, so, like a surprising number of children in the class, she has one reserved for her exclusive use. Usually her set is still on when she falls asleep at night, and her father, a barber whose shop has fallen on hard times as a result of the long-hair fad, has to tiptoe in and turn it off.

Yvonne usually keeps her set tuned to Channel 11, which has a stronger pull on the juvenile market, according to ratings, than any other station available here. If she finishes her homework in a hurry, she can see "Magilla Gorilla," a cartoon show that goes on at 4 P.M.

'Lucy's' Second Generation

After that she watches an uninterrupted series of TV reruns beginning with chapters of the "Superman" serial that are often as much as 20 years old. Most of the reruns are sugary situation comedies, which rank second only to cartoon shows, according to surveys, in the affections of the 6-to-11 age group.

The prevalence of hoary reruns in their television diet would seem to undercut one of Professor McLuhan's hypotheses—that "today's television child is attuned to up-to-the-minute 'adult' news—inflation, rioting, war, taxes, crime, bathing beauties."

Channels 5, 9 and 11—which vie with one another for the afternoon and evening children's market that the network channels have abandoned as insufficiently lucrative—make a point of showing reruns during the hour and a half in which Channels 2, 4 and 7 show news each evening.

Television may offer the children what the professor calls "all-inclusive nowness," but that "nowness" can take the form of an "I Love Lucy" show their mothers may have seen when they were in the fourth grade.

Often the children will watch a program they have seen before, but the factor of predictability only enhances its appeal. A few moments after "Lost In Space" started the other evening, David Badillo knew that the spaceman family's pet robot was about to become a victim of a kind of mechanical elephantiasis and that the youngster in the family would then crawl inside the robot's enlarged body to spin a few dials and reduce it to normal size.

The youngster would almost be crushed inside the shrinking robot, David warned, but there was no reason to fear because the father would pull him to safety. And so it came to pass, to David's immense satisfaction.

The Badillos have four sons and only one television set in their tiny rear apartment. Two sets have been stolen in recent years. Sometimes there is spirited debate over what program to watch. David, who is the second son, says he usually gets his way.

When he is fighting with Dennis, his older brother, he explained, "I always pretend to cry, then my mother yells at Dennis and makes him let me watch my program." Tony, the next brother, has not become shrewd enough to turn this strategy against David.

"He watches 'Popeye' and 'Magilla Gorilla,'" Tony hastened to point out, obviously expecting that his brother would lose status because of his craving for cartoon shows.

"So? So?" David retorted. "Lots of people dooze."

"Baby!" taunted Tony, who is two years younger.

"So? So?" said David. "I didn't say I was a man."

In the last couple of weeks before the vacation, David and a number of other pupils in Class 4-4 started showing up in school without completed homework. Eventually Miss Boroughs cut back on the assignments so no one would have an excuse for not finishing them. "They broke me," she admitted.

The exercises that gave them the most difficulty required the rearranging of sets of scrambled sentences in a logical sequence so they told a coherent story. Possibly because of the fast cuts and sudden reversals of fortune in the television programs they watch, the children found it hard to grasp the idea that there was one sequence that was more logical than any other.

Cecil Robinson, the best comedian and entertainer his classmates ever see "in person," always finishes his homework but sometimes not before 11 P.M.

Cecil's slowness—not of wit, obviously, but of pace—is legendary in the class. "Cecil Robinson," Miss Boroughs exploded one afternoon, "you waste an incredible amount of time." As always happens at such moments, he looked so astounded that his teacher found it impossible to sustain her anger.

"You're a good student now," she said, softening, "but you'd be a super-student if you didn't waste so much time, a human computer. You'd frighten us with your brain power."

In part, Cecil's lack of urgency may be related to the timelessness — another way, perhaps, of describing "all-inclusive nowness"—of the television world in which he spends much of his life. Except on weekends when his older sister takes him bicycle riding in Central Park, he is rarely permitted to go out of the city housing project in which he lives.

Last summer a stranger tried to lure him across the street by promising him candy. When his parents heard the story they immediately thought of drugs.

So on the afternoon his vacation started, Cecil went home and turned on the TV. Five hours later he was still watching it. "I've got it all worked out," he said, spreading his hands wide in a characteristic show-biz gesture. "I'll start my homework on the fifth day. That will give me five days to finish it."

Asked what else he would do, Cecil heaved his shoulders in a shrug. "I'll sit and I'll think and I'll bite my nails," he said. "I don't know what I think about but I sure do a lot of thinking."

Class 4-4: Childish Fantasy Is More Than Make-Believe

By JOSEPH LELYVELD

Unknown to the rest of the school, unicorns, dragons, monsters too monstrous to be named, Martians, beautiful princesses with hair like golden flax, their paladins and frenzied, battling frogs have been inhabiting a drab lunchroom for teachers in the depths of Public School 198.

These creatures are metamorphosed each week out of a small group of ordinary, relatively docile children from the school's third, fourth and fifth grades under the direction of Richard Lewis, a visiting teacher who functions as a kind of impresario of children's fantasies.

Mr. Lewis, who has edited several anthologies of imaginative writing by children, operates on the theory that their creative powers do not have to be developed so much as excavated from the rubble under which they are buried by society in general and the schools in particular.

Obtains Grant

Armed with a grant from the New York State Council on the Arts to demonstrate how such powers might be released in traditional school settings, he came to P.S. 198 at the start of the year and volunteered to help a group of children express their inner reveries in a variety of art forms.

Six teachers, including Dorothy Boroughs of Class 4-4, were asked to name two children each for what was described merely as a "poetry class."

She had taken a couple of stabs herself, by then, at provoking strong, vivid writing from the children in her class but had been discouraged by the results.

On her last try, the class discussed the nature of imagination and concluded it was concerned with things that were "make-believe" and "not real." Miss Boroughs had browsed through a book called "Wishes, Lies and Dreams," in which the poet Kenneth Koch described his methods of teaching writing to children, so she then asked the children to use their imaginations and write about wishes they felt strongly.

Not Easy

Their imaginations did not take flight on command. Desirée Fleming seemed to be remembering an earlier discussion about new year's resolutions. "I imagine that Class 4-4 would do all their homework and not give Miss Boroughs a headache," she wrote.

Israel Valle, 4-4's star student, headed his composition "My Imagination" and wrote: "I'll be the most richest boy in the world and earn as much money as I could, like a zillion dollars. That is my imagination."

José Santana wrote: "I wish to be like Matthew in math." And Matthew Phillips, the mathematics whiz of the class, plaintively asked, the next time the teacher assigned a composition, "Do we have to use our imaginations again?"

Miss Boroughs concluded that conveying a real notion of creativity would take more time than she could spare from her tasks of sharpening the reading and math skills of the class, so she did not renew her effort.

Reaction Mixed

When the invitation to Mr. Lewis's sessions came, she reacted with both skepticism and gratitude. On the one hand, she doubted that much could be achieved in an hour a week, the time allotted by the school for the program. On the other hand, she thought it just barely possible that some of her children would seize the chance.

Shaun Sheppard, whom she has been teaching for the last three years, was an obvious choice, for she had been drawn to him in the first place by his feeling for language and stories. Shaun's absorption in his own inner world is so strong, it almost seems possible to hear the hum of his reveries.

For her other choice, she played a hunch. Nelson Cerda, a voluble child with a piping voice and dark shadows under wide, watchful eyes, sometimes looks distracted to the point of being dazed in class. But when he tunes in, no child is more alert, more wholly present.

Lets Children Lead

It is a bedrock conviction for Mr. Lewis that the reveries of children are powerfully concerned with reality, not make-believe. So he tries to let the children chart the direction and pace of their meeting with him, making as few demands as possible.

A rumpled man in his mid-30's, he started off the first class by talking about dreams. Some children denied ever having any, but Nelson Cerda was quick to pick up the thread. "I can switch the channels of my mind whenever I want," he declared.

The TV metaphor required no explanation. Instantly, children were comparing the mind to a projector and talking about "mind pictures." Mr. Lewis then intervened and asked them to draw some of their "mind pictures."

Shaun was more "uptight" in these early sessions than Nelson, according to Mr. Lewis who finds an obvious explanation in the fact that Shaun, at 12, is two years older than his classmate. That puts him two years further away, in Mr. Lewis's ardently Wordsworthian view, from a young child's freshness of vision.

The mind picture Shaun drew turned out to be a copy —well-executed in the sense of being accurate—of a comic-strip Porky Pig. Nelson's picture was hard to identify, only tentatively sketched but strange and arresting. It was a scene of violence involving four figures, but whether they were animals or human or some combination of the two was not clear. Nelson didn't say and Mr. Lewis purposefully never asked.

In the weeks that followed, Nelson's interest in these classes never flagged, while Shaun's intensified. Soon the older boy drew a picture of a monster that was obscure in its meaning but seemingly deeply felt, not traceable to any obvious source outside himself.

Mr. Lewis constantly mixed the forms of expression. One week he brought in a tape recorder so the children could record stories as they improvised them, another week he let them work with a Polaroid camera. Often he encouraged them to enact something physically before they tried to portray it in words and pictures.

361

The results were not the sort of finished works that get tacked to bulletin boards for parents to see. Some of them were far more expressive, however, and maybe even dangerous — or so Nelson may have thought, for he had the daring to turn his preoccupation with violence into drawings that were unmistakably sexual. If he expected condemnation from Mr. Lewis, he did not get it.

One week the teacher invited a friend, Arthur Tress, a professional photographer, who arrived with a duffle full of costumes—capes, crowns, horns, swords and monster masks. The children dressed themselves and took parts.

Shaun became a unicorn. Nelson became a bearded king. He also quickly asserted himself as the main author of an improvised story — about a king who wanted to capture a unicorn to present to the princess he was marrying.

'Congratulations'

Then, functioning as a director, Nelson arranged the other children in a series of tableaux that Mr. Tress photographed. In the school's playground, in less than an hour, the children created an elaborate narrative in pictures.

Last week, sauntering into the room, Nelson called out to Mr. Lewis, "Congratulations!" The teacher was sitting on a desk beside a dark-haired young woman with a vulnerable expression and Nelson, mischievously, had decided to regard her as Mr. Lewis's daughter: Hence, his greeting. Nelson has found that Mr. Lewis is rarely nonplussed by comments most adults in schools would find intolerable.

The young woman was introduced as Laura Simms. A storyteller by occupation (and by virtue of unusual gifts), she had been invited by Mr. Lewis to tell stories that might evoke some kind of expressive response from the children.

But before any story could begin, Nelson had to run her through a series of tests. Bright-eyed with the thrill of his audacity and impudence —which never show up in his regular classroom—Nelson declared, "I just have to look at you and I know I don't like you."

Miss Simms looked puzzled and a little stunned. Then, responding to the bright eyes rather than the words, she smiled.

Nelson smiled back but was not quite ready to lift' his siege. First he pointed to a hole in one of the guest's socks, then he noted that her socks were mismatched and demanded to know why.

"That's another story," she replied sweetly, explaining she had wanted to wear sandals without any socks that morning as a way of welcoming the spring. Then, finding it was really too chilly, she decided she would keep the sandals on, even if she had to wear mismatched socks.

Other Interruptions

At that point, it seemed, Nelson decided to put her on probation and allowed her, finally, to begin the story she had come to tell. But in a moment he was interrupting again.

"Can I get comfortable?" he asked. Without waiting for an answer, he sprawled across two desks.

There were other interruptions, mostly from Nelson, but the intervals between them lengthened and Miss Simms was able to relate the narrative of a strange and bloody war between two armies of frogs that erupted recently, she said, near a village in Malaya.

At first, recumbent like a Roman emperor, Nelson tried to appear jaded and bored. At one point, he even slipped off the desks and wandered to the doorway in an ostentatious display of restlessness, only to be drawn back again by the story and the fascination with the visitor that had kept his eyes fixed on her from the moment he entered the room.

In a soft voice, Miss Simms described the eerie peace that came over the village just before the frogs went to war. "You were there?" Nelson asked.

"I heard the story," she replied.

"It sounded so good and so relaxing," he said, "I thought you were really there."

This was the ultimate tribute and Miss Simms let her pleasure show. Later, when Mr. Lewis asked the children to crouch down to imitate frogs—old frogs, dying frogs, jumping frogs—Nelson was one of the most eager amphibians in the room. But he was surpassed by Shaun who absolutely unself-conscious for a moment—rendered an aging frog with great pathos.

A moment later and Shaun was at the window, inviting a classmate who was passing by on the sidewalk, David Badillo, to come in and hear Miss Simms tell another story.

"You better not throw none of us out just because you brought David in," Nelson warned Mr. Lewis in his high voice. "You better not throw me out!"

Class 4-4: Shaun, a Profile of Progress

By JOSEPH LELYVELD

Shaun Sheppard, the grand old man of Class 4-4, marked his 12th birthday last week.

"It's getting scary," said his teacher, Dorothy Boroughs, who has taught Shaun for the last three years, rescuing him from the pattern of failure and deepening estrangement in school that afflicts masses of children.

Shaun, who is two years older than any other child in the fourth-grade class, has been having the best of his seven years at Public School 198.

Far from feeling resentful over finding himself out of step with the friends with whom he entered school, he believes he still has a chance —unlike many of them—to unlock the mysteries of the classroom.

His facility in school may not have caught up yet with his remarkable felicity in life, but Shaun can joke about his situation. On a trip to Central Park with 4-4 a few weeks ago, he was challenged by a youth on roller skates to identify the class. "We're the midget ninth grade," he boasted.

Miss Boroughs worries because she knows that Shaun is already on borrowed time. Somehow, she hopes, she will be able to keep him in her class for another year in his unique status in the school as an ungraded student.

But adolescence and junior high school are almost upon him. This coming September Shaun will be a sixth-grader on the records, regardless of his classroom assignment. Thus the slow rebuilding of his damaged confidence in his ability to learn cannot continue much longer: Ready or not he will have to go.

The sense of a deadline weighs heavily on Miss Boroughs, who taught for two years in a junior high school, then switched to elementary school teaching because she wanted to work with children before they had been hopelessly alienated and doomed.

The deadline weighs less heavily on Shaun, in part because his first four years of unrelieved failure in school left him with a habit of resignation. Shaun accepts the theory that he has the ability to be branded a "success" in the school's terms, but he is full of skepticism about this ever happening.

The other day he did a better job than any other student in the class on a project on which the teacher had laid great stress. The assignment was to prepare a comic strip, model, drawing or perform a skit on any book the children had enjoyed so that their classmates would be moved to read it. "A sharing project," it was called.

Shaun, who lives in an illlit tenement apartment below street level and near an air shaft that is usually ankle-deep in refuse, chose to illustrate a chapter from a book called "Henry and Ribsy." In it, Henry assumes the task of carrying out the garbage from his suburban home for the sake of a 15-cent weekly increase in his allowance.

Apt to Carp

After Shaun presented a miniature stage set in a shoe box showing the boy stomping the garbage into a can, Miss Boroughs commented: "It just shows, Shaun . . ."

"That you have the brains if you'd only use them," Shaun interrupted, smiling brilliantly as he finished her sentence. The teacher relished his mimicry.

But some times Shaun seems to Miss Boroughs to be deliberately removing his attention from a lesson he is having trouble grasping in order, it seems, to spare himself the pain of having tried and failed.

Then the teacher is apt to carp. "You drop out if it's any kind of strain on your brain," she complained once. "Lots of things are difficult. That's what you're here for. That's what a teacher is here for."

The issue of ultimate success or failure overshadows all his efforts at learning. "What do you see as the end of all this? Where are you going?" Miss Boroughs asked him the other morning when he came in with part of his homework undone.

Asked the same questions herself, she says she could imagine Shaun as "an oceanographer, an artist or a racketeer." All she wants is to insure him a choice, she said.

Shaun's grandmother, who lives in the neighborhood, sometimes talks about when Shaun will strike it rich as a doctor or football star. His mother, who has been on welfare since he was born, says she would prefer him to be a doctor. Shaun himself leans to the gridiron. To both him and his mother, the two futures seem equally fanciful and remote.

Alarm Clock Broken

By necessity, the Sheppard household is fixed and stranded in a timeless pres-

ent. Daylight hardly enters the small apartment. The alarm clock broke weeks ago, so it is the television set that usually tells the time. Shaun himself is the only one with a set schedule and routine and often this gives way to needs that seem more pressing.

In kindergarten he was absent from school more days than he was present. In first grade, days absent and present balanced exactly. Since then there has been a gradual improvement in attendance, but he has been out 28 days so far this year, twice as many as any other child in 4-4.

On the morning of his birthday, Shaun did not show up in school. "He can't get by doing only 75 per cent of the work," said Miss Boroughs, who had brought a small present for him. "He needs to do 175 per cent."

At 9:30, giving in to her impatience, the teacher stepped out of the classroom and called his home. The phone rang 15 times before Shaun answered in a sleepy voice.

Mother Out

"Happy birthday," she said. "Are you coming to school?"

"I don't know," he replied. "My mother had to go out."

Normally when Shaun's mother needs to go out—to the stores, welfare office or clinic—he has to stay home unless arrangements have been made for his grandmother or a friend to sit with his infant sister, Robin.

He prefers going to school, he says, but takes his disappointments in stride, navigating between home and school as best he can, in the recognition that sometimes their demands are in competition and it is impossible to satisfy them all.

Misses Vermont Trip

His balance in these matters survives disappointments greater than missed classes.

The Saturday before his birthday Miss Boroughs was going to Vermont with friends and made arrangements with his mother to take him along for a weekend of hiking and kite-flying. But when she banged on his apartment door to pick him up, Shaun said his mother was not home and he was not supposed to open the door for anyone.

Miss Boroughs waited for nearly an hour, then shouted through the door that she would have to leave without him. Shaun had been hoping for a trip to Vermont with his teacher since she took a classmate of his there last year, but he called back soothingly, "That's all right."

He was absent the following Monday, but Tuesday he showed up with a painstakingly lettered note from his mother explaining the absence ("I had to take care of something") and regretting the missed excursion ("I hope there will be a next time.")

The note from the mother, Josephine Sheppard, was a tangible sign of a slight narrowing of the gulf between Shaun's home and the school. Two years ago Mrs. Sheppard, a blunt and quick-witted young woman, got into an argument in the school office and was told—as she now recalls it—never to return.

Her first favorable contact with the school in all the years Shaun has gone to school there, came less than two months ago when she followed a phone call from Miss Boroughs with a visit to the classroom—to Shaun's complete amazement and delight.

She told the teacher then that she had never learned to read properly in school. Miss Boroughs reported that Shaun's reading was steadily improving, but that he did not yet have a "reading habit."

Soon after the visit, Shaun proudly reported that he and his mother had stayed up one night reading together. The book was Roald Dahl's "Charlie and the Chocolate Factory," an outlandish and funny tale for children.

Home Gets Credit

Miss Boroughs hopes for more backing of this kind. She recognizes that the qualities that have made Shaun the student to whom she has devoted the most attention in her teaching career—his sturdiness, quickness and sublime sense of fun—all can be traced to his home.

Four weeks ago, when Miss Boroughs received a form from the principal's office asking her to state her preferences for her own class assignment next semester, she thought first of Shaun and what would become of him. Two proposals took shape in her mind: Maybe she would try to get him into a private school on scholarship or maybe she would ask to accompany the whole of 4-4, Shaun included, to the fifth grade.

But neither of these ideas nor any other seemed practical to her in terms of the system, so she never returned the form.

Shaun does not think of himself in some future incarnation when he thinks of a truly accomplished student. Instead, he thinks of someone like the 14-year-old boy on his block who is known there as "Genius."

The other afternoon he ran into Genius on Lexington Avenue and called on him to demonstrate his prowess.

"Tell us what sex is," Shaun demanded.

"Sex," the youth responded in an expressionless voice, "is the form of reproduction practiced by humans and other higher animals."

"Attaboy Genius!" said Shaun, with a laugh. "Keep that brain turning!"

Class 4-4:

A Dip Into the Joys of Poetry

By JOSEPH LELYVELD

The time came this week for Class 4-4 at Public School 198 to write letters of hail and farewell to its departing student teacher, Mrs. Gabriella Corrigan. "You are my fourth best student teacher," Fred Fiandaca wrote.

That sounded scathing, for the class has had precisely four student teachers since the school year began. But Fred offered a more generous interpretation: The first student teacher was the best, he explained, and so were the second, third and fourth. Put another way, Mrs. Corrigan was peerless except for her peers.

Fred packed another surprise into what he wrote for the last lesson taught by Mrs. Corrigan in the class. The lesson rounded off a series in which she had labored to quicken the interest of the children in poetry. This time the poets were supposed to be the children themselves.

One of Fred's two poems got off to a start that sounded odd, spring in Central Park notwithstanding:

How lovely in the English
    wood
And on the English mead...

Before he could be charged with plagiarizing, Fred amiably let it be known that he had found the lines in an anthology and decided it would be useful to quote them at the start of his poem. He did not have to cite the example of T. S. Eliot, for Mrs. Corrigan readily accepted quotation as a valid technique.

Madelyn Cotto and David Badillo, who sit near each other, were moved to write of caterpillars in almost the same words. But Lori Spellman's muse spoke in the words of Lori Spellman on the theme of peace:

Everyone likes peace.
Peace is a good thing to
    have around.
I like peace and you do too,
    I think?

Mrs. Corrigan, a Hunter College senior who traveled to the school every morning from Bensonhurst, backed into the teaching of poetry. Her professor had advised her to set up an "interest corner" in the classroom, a place reserved for the pursuit of a particular subject or activity. It was Dorothy Boroughs, 4-4's teacher, who suggested it might be reserved for poetry.

Keeping Things Going

The corner turned out to be a table near the center of the room with a box on it; in the box were pieces of heavy paper with poems stapled to them. For a few days some of the children delved into the box, then the delving ground to a halt.

How to sustain the momentum of lessons started in her classroom by other teachers —and make them add up to something coherent — has been a worrisome problem for Miss Boroughs all year long. There have been the four student teachers and two full-time teaching assistants (one of each at any given time), plus three regular "cluster" teachers specializing in music, science and geography.

Kindly visitors have also offered to teach lessons. For instance, there was the mathematics expert who said she was available to teach a lesson on positive and negative numbers. Miss Boroughs said the class was working on measurements. "Positive and negative numbers were what I had in mind," the visitor persisted.

"There are too many people for the kids, too many new things," Miss Boroughs commented later. "The teacher has to be too busy creating opportunities for each person to perform when it's the kids who should be performing."

Since January, Mrs. Corrigan's professor from Hunter, Dr. Richard Smolens, has actually been conducting a graduate course at Public School 198 that focused on this problem.

Breaking Out

"Utilization of Multiple Personnel" was its formal catalogue title, but Dr. Smolens had the broader purpose of breaking the shell of loneliness that encloses many teachers so they could talk with easy candor about the whole enterprise of teaching, and eventually consider the possibility of new approaches.

Miss Boroughs went to Dr. Smolens's first session, but dropped out of the course, feeling fed up with special projects and courses with fancy names and bis promises. "They never get down to the child," she complained at the time. "It's hypocrisy. You just sit around and talk jargon. Think what you could do if you gave that time to the kids."

At the same point she also reached a quiet pact with her teaching assistant for the semester, Harvey Dagen, that they would not squander 4-4's time on a project in bilingual education in which they both were supposed to be taking part.

As far as she had been able to tell, the project involved teaching beginning Spanish to children who were unlikely to benefit, in part because little atention was paid to the fact that many of them already know Spanish.

Growing Into the Job

Mr. Dagen, a young musician who had drifted into teaching at the start of the school year because he needed a job, agreed eagerly. What he wanted most was the experience of teaching.

He had asked to work with Miss Boroughs, he recalls, because she struck him as "a very together lady" and "a relentless teacher who was really out for the kids."

His own attitude to the children was undergoing a revolution then. "When I started I was very up-tight about getting the respect of kids," he said. "My big thing was getting kids to listen to me. But I really didn't like them at all."

Then he started working with children on an individual basis and, as he expresses it, "it was like fantastic." Once he stopped seeing them as a mob, he said, he found depths of patience and feeling inside himself he never really knew to be there.

Increasingly, Miss Boroughs relied on him to give special help to children who hit snags in her class. His presence in the room, and Mrs. Corrigan's also gave her a connection to Dr. Smolens whom, she decided, she had judged too hastily.

She had vowed to have "nothing to do with anyone in the school except the children." But the professor —a bearded man who wore turtleneck sweaters and drove to school in a battered Volkswagen covered with graffiti — proved more interested in offering practical suggestions than in convoluted discussions of theory. So she started to let down her defenses.

Visit to Another School

Last week Mrs. Corrigan reported to Miss Boroughs on a visit she had made, at Dr. Smolens's instigation, to a school where a few venturesome teachers had banded together to organize "open classrooms," freeing their children—not to mention themselves —from conventional group instruction by giving them a measure of responsibility for their own learning.

The school was P.S. 42, an aged brick pile at the corner of Hester and Orchard Streets on the Lower East Side, which was designed to be as open as a penitentiary.

In the first class Mrs. Corrigan and three other student teachers from P.S. 198 stepped into there that morning, they found the teacher, Norma Brooks, off in a corner leading a chorus line of four boys through a dance to the theme from the movie "The Third Man." Hardly breaking step, she explained the class was getting ready for a dance festival.

No one had to be reprimanded or told what to do, but all the children who were not dancing were working intensely on a wide variety of activities. The single exception was a girl who seemed to be holding herself out on the periphery, dancing a few steps in one corner of the classroom, fondling a guinea pig in another. Finally she gravitated to a table where children were painting.

The walls of the room had been brightly painted by the class—in violation, the teacher was later told, of regulations forbidding "mutilation of public property." The effect was as personal as a living room.

Later Miss Brooks asked the student teachers if they had any questions. "Yes," said Mrs. Corrigan, taking a deep breath. "How'd you do it?"

When she returned to P.S. 198, she repeated her first impression to Miss Boroughs. Miss Boroughs said she would try to visit P.S. 42 and see for herself.

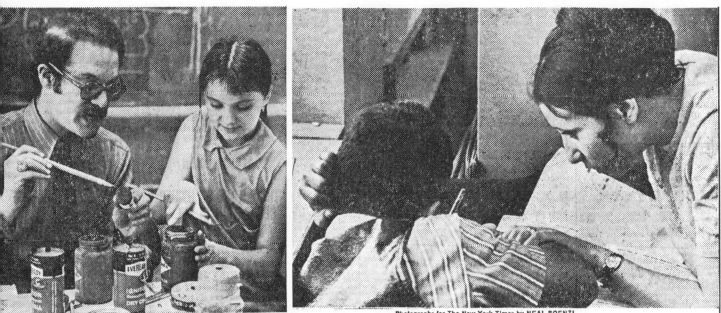

Photographs for The New York Times by NEAL BOENZI

Above, Mrs. Gabriella Corrigan, a student teacher, tries to quicken interest of a member of Class 4-4 in poetry. Left, Harvey Dagen, a teaching assistant, directs an experiment in the class. He described Dorothy Boroughs, 4-4's teacher, as "a very together lady."

Carlos Andujar was chosen to lead Mrs. Corrigan by the hand to a table in the back of the room when the time came for her to receive her letters from Class 4-4. The girls came first, one by one,

and the student teacher kissed them all.

Then came the boys. Jose Santana and Matthew Phillips bent down to be kissed but Cecil Robinson leaned

backwards and shook hands stiffly, as the class laughed.

"He's a regular Anibal," said Jose, referring to the absent Anibal Rosado, the shyest child in the class.

Before she left, Mrs. Corrigan handed Miss Boroughs a gift and a note. "I only hope," it said, "that I am able to establish in my class the type of attitude and goodwill I see in yours."

May 21, 1971

Animation of an 'Open Classroom' Generates Curiosity

By JOSEPH LELYVELD

First came the chimes, then the voice, calmly but cryptically promising great truths. Mystical experiences don't happen often in public schools, otherwise Class 4-4 might fairly have expected something in that line.

The chimes, which interrupted a lesson on fractions, merely heralded an invitation on the intercom system for all 55 teachers of Public School 198 to stay in the building after punching out on the time clock. There would be a meeting with two teachers from another school who had "opened up their classrooms."

"What do you think that meant, 'opened up their classrooms?'" Dorothy Boroughs, 4-4's teacher, asked the children.

Hajnalka Fulop thought an open classroom was one that was "still open at 3:30." Matthew Phillips suggested it

was one in which "the teachers can come in and go out."

"What about the kids?" the teacher asked. The very idea made Matthew giggle.

"Who thinks we have a closed classroom?" Miss Boroughs continued. Hands of half the children floated uncertainly into the air.

Visit to Another School

"When people talk about open classrooms," the teacher said, attempting to spell out the mystery, "they're really not talking about whether the door is open or shut. They're talking about ways of learning. In open classrooms the children make more choices about what they want to do each day. They make almost all the choices. The teacher is there to help them."

Miss Boroughs took a breath. "How does that grab you?" she asked.

"I wish we could do that," said perky Yvonne Prileau.

"You'd talk your head off all day if we could," Shaun Sheppard wisecracked.

"Come to the meeting," the teacher said, with a look that seemed to show she was less than fully serious but amused, even tantalized, by the thought.

"If you really like the idea," she said, "maybe we can have it here, too."

A few days earlier Miss Boroughs had asked her principal, Mrs. Charlotte Schiff, for a morning off so she could visit Public School 42 on the Lower East Side where three teachers had created open classrooms on their own initiative, without waiting for special funds or supervision.

Miss Boroughs had decided she should see them after her own student teacher, Mrs. Gabriella Corrigan, returned from a visit to P.S. 42 saying they were "unbelievable" and "fabulous."

In the first classroom she visited there—a busy second-grade class crowded with pets and children's work, including vats for pickle-making—one girl sent shivers through Miss Boroughs by placing a gerbil on the back of her neck, another went to work plaiting her long hair.

Incessantly, she was barraged by eager children asking her to "give" them words —that is, spell them so they could be used in stories.

Kenny Reed, a solemn 7-year-old who attached himself to the visitor, haltingly but proudly read to her a story he had dictated to his teacher, Zina Steinberg, about the best day any child could have at the circus.

"I was telling the lion trainer to let me stay at the circus and help him . . . I was on the flying trapeze . . ." his story rhapsodized. "My brother Anthony and

Central Park became a schoolroom for Class 4-4 this week as the youngsters spent a day flying kites and reading on the park's lawns

me got in the cannon. They lit the fuse and they pulled the string and we went flying over the flying trapeze and landed in the net. We were human cannonballs."

Miss Steinberg had mimeographed the story so that Kenny and the other children in the class could read it. In fact, she had five volumes of stories and poems by the children in her class, each of whom kept his own writing notebook.

The bravura of the narratives impressed Miss Boroughs. She was also struck by the relatively low level of noise in a room in which small children were allowed to work independently. But when she commented on this, Miss Steinberg mistook her meaning and tried to explain why it wasn't even lower.

"There are some kids with very yelling voices," she said. "If you go into their homes, you know why. It's the only way they ever get heard."

Benefits of Home Visits

Miss Steinberg and the teachers with whom she is working feel strongly that regular home visits can be crucial for successful teaching—a radical contention in a system in which the teaching day, as a matter of contractual obligation, now ends at 3 o'clock sharp. Often they stay on in the neighborhood of the school into the evening.

"If you just leave at 3, nothing is possible," one teacher declared. In fact, the teachers have committed themselves to a program of home visits in a formal proposal they drew up asking official support for 15 open classrooms at P.S. 42 next year. (The proposal is now foundering, as far as they know, on a low level of the school system's extended chain of command.)

The question of how much time a teacher should commit to work hung in the

air unexpressed when two of Miss Steinberg's colleagues, Norma Brooks and Linda Sessoms, appeared at P.S. 198 for the teachers' meeting on the open classroom.

As it happened, none of the children in Class 4-4 took Miss Boroughs up on her invitation to the meeting. And only 12 members of the faculty attended. Most of these were enrolled in a course given by Prof. Richard Smolens of Hunter College, who had invited the two teachers to the school.

Urges Discretion

On the way up the Franklin D. Roosevelt Drive to the school, Dr. Smolens had asked the two teachers not to stress the extra time and money they lavish on their classrooms.

He didn't want them to leave an impression, he explained later, that new approaches in teaching could only be effective through devotion beyond the call of duty.

So when Miss Brooks said that she checked up on the progress of her students by giving regular tests, there was confusion and even skepticism in her audience. How could tests be given, one teacher wanted to know, if the children were working individually at their own level and rates?

"You may have to prepare four or five separate tests," Miss Sessoms said.

"If you do that," asked Jeanette Campbell, a first-year teacher at P.S. 198, "when do you have time to teach?" The answer was that the teachers spend hours outside school preparing curriculum materials, games and tests. But diplomacy won out and it was never clearly stated.

The visitors answered all the questions put to them, but their answers did not seem to pierce a general

sense of reservation in the room that was largely unexpressed except in further questions, whispered aside and dubious looks.

So the discussion never advanced. Long after the visitors explained how they tested their students, conferred with them regularly on an individual basis, kept detailed records on their strengths and weaknesses and checked all their written work on a weekly basis, a teacher asked, "How do you know if they're getting the skills they need?"

"Can I ask you something?" Miss Brooks shot back. "That teacher standing up in front of a class of 30 students, what more can she know about what they are all really learning?"

Dr. Smolens sat glumly in a corner. A discussion on which he had counted to spark a sense of excitement and possibilities in the school had left him, instead, with stale, unwanted reflections on the isolation and habitual defensiveness of teachers.

As the meeting broke up, the visitors asked to see Miss Boroughs's room. Largely as a result of Dr. Smolens's influence, there have been more changes in the last couple of weeks in the layout of Room 217, where Class 4-4 spends its days, than in the previous eight months.

Small Areas Set Up

Tables and bookcases that had been pushed against the walls now jut into the room, forming small areas for the pursuit of particular activities. As yet, these corners haven't been put to heavy use, but Miss Boroughs looks on them as a start.

"I'm finally getting with it in this classroom," she remarked one morning as she hung a sign the children had painted proclaiming the existence of a "Math Corner."

But when it came to showing the room to Miss Brooks and Miss Sessoms, she said she felt "mortified." Room 217 looked drab to her, she said, in comparison to their classrooms. The visitors, who teach in a school that has had no major renovation in 73 years, said it looked luxurious.

Miss Boroughs said it had become obvious to her that the open classroom could be an effective answer to the alienation masses of children feel in schools. But she seemed uncertain as to how far or fast she herself would move in that direction.

Off to Central Park

By the end of the week debates over educational theory and practice had faded. The supreme reality was spring, so Miss Borough led 4-4 into Central Park for a day of kite-flying and reading on the park's piebald lawns.

Carlos Andujar's kite was emblazoned with a dragon. Fred Fiandaca had a 39-cent Skyway Special, showing an astronaut sailing through space. But the most magnificent kite of all was a $4 gold and brown eagle on clear plastic that Cecil Robinson had purchased with four allowances at F.A.O. Schwarz.

The eagle caught a small breeze. "He's up," Cecil cried, standing still in his tracks. Then it plopped into the dust. "He's down," said Cecil.

"What's the matter, bird, are you afraid?" he asked. Then, all of a sudden Cecil grasped the idea that he was supposed to run. "There he goes," he cried, clomping off across the field.

"Look at Cecil's eagle!" Yvonne Prileau called to her friend Sharaie Blue. Cecil's kite soared higher than all the others.

"I see the eagle," said Sharaie, "but I can't see Cecil."

May 29, 197

Class 4-4:

It Was the First Good Year for Stella

By JOSEPH LELYVELD

It's the time of the school year when the air turns heavy and stale in the afternoons, and teachers douse the lights to give their classrooms an illusion of coolness; when school librarians call a halt to the circulation of books; when teachers' mailboxes are stuffed with forms, insistent demands for data to pin down their most elusive sense of a child's possibilities: the homestretch, the last lap, the time for summing up.

In Class 4-4, 9-year-old Stella Pistorio offered a startling summing up of her own. It sounded like pure whimsy, but Stella presented it as pure fact. "This was my first year in school," she declared.

She meant, or seemed to mean, that previously she had resided on school days at Public School 198 only physically and under protest. This year, for the first time, the whole Stella Pistorio has been present.

Carlos Andujar found Stella's existential leap bewildering.

"No one here was in my class last year," Stella said with a smile that seemed to dare him to contradict her. "What about me?" Carlos asked. "And Fred and Madelyn? And Maria and Benny?"

Stella cocked her head to one side and widened her grin until it was almost touching the frame of her straight dark hair. "I don't like you giving me that fish eye," she said.

History of Trouble

Translated, that seemed to mean she didn't like Carlos' remembering that last year she had been constantly angry and withdrawn, constantly in trouble. Mrs. Charlotte Schiff, now the acting principal but last year the supervisor responsible for Stella's grade, recalls that no child in the entire third grade was in her office more often.

Stella rarely produced any homework, often refused to

respond when called on in class and sometimes hit out at other children who tried to impinge on the tight little circle she drew around herself.

One day Mrs. Schiff asked Stella what she wanted to be when she grew up, and Stella gave one of the two or three answers most schoolgirls have for that question. She said she wanted to be a teacher.

Grasping the chance to offer positive encouragement, Mrs. Schiff promised to help if only Stella would settle down, do her homework and help her brothers and sisters with theirs.

"I don't think that really got to her," said Stella's mother, Mrs. Mary Ann Pistorio. "To tell the truth, it didn't get to me. I mean, doing your homework and becoming a teacher, it's as if everything in life was school."

An alert, self-aware young woman, Mrs. Pistorio has a persistent sense of humor that, somehow, she has been able to preserve despite crushing burdens. Her first child was born a few days after her 16th birthday and she had four more before she was 22. Stella, her second, she delivered herself in a tenement apartment on East 95th Street.

Later her marriage broke up, so she went to work to support her children a few days after the fifth was born. She has worked ever since, sometimes at three jobs at once, because, she says, she doesn't believe in going on welfare.

All this Mrs. Pistorio recounts without the faintest trace of self-pity. It may be that the kitchen has to double as a living room in her narrow walk-up apartment on the fifth floor of a five-story tenement—every other room is used as a bedroom—but the children are well-dressed and the family has a good feeling about itself.

That feeling has been especially strong this year, for Mrs. Pistorio has managed to get by working at only one job and has started to think seriously of remarriage.

"We're going to have a father and he's Slovak," Stella announced one morning in school. "Did you ever hear of that language?"

But Mrs. Pistorio feels sure that is not why it was hard to keep Stella home from school this winter when she was ill, or why she always insists on doing her homework before playing when she gets home in the afternoon.

"It's the teacher more than anything," the mother said. "She's the kind that's the same inside school as she is outside. She's real."

The touchstone of the reality of the teacher, Dorothy Boroughs, in the mind of Stella's mother is that Mrs. Pistorio finds it possible to think of her without thinking of school. One evening she was walking near the apartment house Stella had pointed out to her as the one in which Miss Boroughs lives when her eye was caught by an ad for Tuborg beer in a grocery store window.

Association With Beer

The ad showed a model with long blond hair proclaiming to the avenue, "Tuborg is my thing." Mrs. Pistorio thought the model looked strikingly like her daughter's teacher. The thought pleased her, and now she often thinks of the beer ad when she thinks of Miss Boroughs.

The first encounter between Stella and her teacher, back in September, was not promising.

"Leave me alone," Stella demanded, firing off her words like artillery shells, when Miss Boroughs tried to mediate between her and another student with whom she was arguing.

Stella's old pattern of withdrawal set in. Sometimes she even insisted on sitting by herself in the back of the room. But Miss Boroughs made a point of showing in quiet ways that she liked her and enjoyed her company —for instance, keeping Stella with her on her lunch hour.

Before long the tension seemed to seep out of Stella. The minuscule left-handed

lettering in her notebook, reminiscent of an ant's footprints, grew to fill the space between the lines. She even sent a valentine to Fred Fiandaca, who sat next to her.

Recently, Miss Boroughs received a computer print-out of her children's scores on the citywide reading test they took April 1. Of the 24 children who had been in the class for the better part of the school year, eight had registered a gain in reading comprehension of better than a grade and a half. Stella, reading on grade level for the first time in her school career, was one of the eight.

Over-all, these 24 were said to have gained an average of 1.1 grades in comprehension since they were tested last year: par for the course. Their average of 4.6 was just a shade below what it should have been.

But Miss Boroughs was disappointed. The fact that one student, Fred Fiandaca, had shot up to the sixth grade and five others were reading on a fifth-grade level did not outweigh in her mind the fact that half the children, after her constant stress on reading, were said to be a decimal point or more under the calculated grade level.

Shaun Sheppard, a 12-year-old whom she had been helping in reading for three years, had the lowest score. Miss Boroughs had been warmed by the thought, when she watched Shaun taking the test, that she had never seen him concentrating so hard. But she had also noticed that he was too intent on avoiding error and never finished many of the questions.

Special Programs

By contrast to 4-4, Class 4-5 averaged out on the seventh grade. 4-5 is the so-called I.G.C. for "intellectually gifted children," a high proportion of whom come from privileged homes. None of the three other fourth-grade classes managed to touch the fourth grade on the statistical index.

Thus, as happens in most city schools, a heavy majority of fourth-graders proved to be significantly behind in reading. But thanks to special reading programs, Mrs. Schiff reported proudly, P.S. 198 this year had more children scoring above grade level than below in grade two.

Late as it is in the school year, 4-4 continues to undergo change like an unstable chemical compound. At one time or another, 41 names have been on its register, but only 26 now remain.

The 41st belongs to Miguel Ramos, an intense, often solemn child who transferred to P.S. 198 with only six weeks left to go from PU LIC SCHOOL 161, the FIORELL H LA UARDIA SCHO L, which has had some letters stolen from the facade of its building at Amsterdam Avenue and 133d Street.

Schools Are Identical

Superficially, the change should have been easy for Miguel, for P.S. 161 and P.S. 198 are identical twins, having been built from the same set of plans 12 years ago. In his old school he was in Room 219; now he's in 217.

"We was next door all the time and you didn't come to

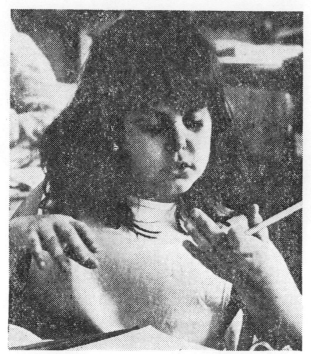

The New York Times/Patrick A. Burns

Stella Pistorio, 9, summarized her past school year in Class 4-4 saying that "This was my first year in school."

visit us," Desiree Fleming said when the coincidence was pointed out in class the other day.

But the shift had been especially rough on Miguel. In his old class he had sought praise for diligence and attentiveness, even when this meant being picked on by less orderly children. In 4-4, his penchant for sitting apart with folded hands seemed eccentric.

The fabric of relationship that holds 4-4 together started to weave itself around the newcomer. Until Miguel arrived, Anibal Rosado had been unanimously recognized as the shyest child in the room. Now Anibal was speaking for Miguel the way Nelson Cerda had made a point all year of answering questions directed at Anibal.

"Miguel doesn't have a book to read," Anibal piped up one morning in what was, for him, an attack of logorrhea.

"Is he too shy to speak for himself?" asked Miss Boroughs.

The thought that he didn't have to seemed to give a moment's pleasure to Miguel, who allowed himself a tight-lipped smile. The smile seemed to be flickering toward an open grin, but Miguel brought it under control.

Class 4-4: A Sense Of a Job Well Done

By JOSEPH LELYVELD

With less than 60 minutes left to the school year, Anibal Rosado kept a promise yesterday to Class 4-4 by softly crooning a solo.

It was the first time anyone in the room had heard him sing. The shyest child in the class, his face always had reflected excruciating embarrassment whenever the possibility was so much as mentioned. If he had to sing at all he would say, it would be on the last day of school.

The expression of pain returned fleetingly when he reached the last stanza of "Raindrops Keep Fallin' on My Head." But the final line had an unexpected appropriateness to the time and place that helped erase it.

"Because I'm free-ee," Anibal sang, "nothin's worrying me-ee."

No curtain fell at that instant as it should have, for Dorothy Boroughs, 4-4's teacher, still had report cards to distribute and textbooks to collect. But there was a feeling in the room that probably comes only once a year to most classrooms, a feeling of completion.

Quality the Criterion

The report cards themselves were mostly an anticlimax, for when it came to setting down her final thoughts about each member of the class, Miss Boroughs found herself dwelling more on their qualities as children, rather than their shortcomings, or even their strengths, as students. Incomplete assignments, missed academic opportunities and other irritations then faded into the background.

It was not that the teacher was being overcome by sentiment. She was simply ready now to step back and look at the whole picture, like a traveler attempting to fix a particularly pleasing vista in his memory.

Of Andy Carril, who had been in almost constant trouble with her in recent weeks, Miss Boroughs wrote:

"Andy is quite a charming fellow. I hope he'll be charmed into reading a book a week over the summer."

The teacher was reminded of the difficulties. "I can't remember what was bothering me," she said.

Maria Rivera, more captivating than ever in a new starched dress and white shoes bought for the last day of school, received a report card in which the sugar coating was more noticeable and heartfelt than the rebuke it covered.

"Maria is still lovely and delightful," it said. "She is also still a disappointment in her attitudes to her work."

"He Won't Forget"

The sharpest written comment was reserved for the parents of a child who, Miss Boroughs wrote, "seemed to come to school each day burdened with problems from home."

Of another student whose scholastic progress had been less than she had anticipated, the teacher could remark with hope: "All my harassment—that's not the right word, I mean my prodding—will do him good next year. He won't forget."

But she did not have to count on wistful forecasts for a sense of accomplishment. There were numerous tangible gains. Yvonne Prileau, who used to have trouble with the simplest subtraction problems, now understood fractions and division. Sheer diligence had made a student of Cecil Robinson, and it was possible now to worry that Sharaie Blue read too much.

Sharaie and her friends Desirée Fleming and Lori Spellman would go to the class that is supposed to be reserved for "intellectually gifted" children along with Israel Valle and Nelson Cerda.

11th-Hour Reprieve

At one point, stolid Benny Winslow had been threatened with being left back. Until 30 minutes before the report cards were distributed he was due to be dropped into a slower class. But he had worked hard in recent weeks and was promising to go to summer school, so Miss Boroughs changed his assignment for September and told him he would be going to Class 5-1 along with most of his classmates.

But the intangible gains were really the ones that moved her. There was the feeling Class 4-4 had for itself.

Tuesday morning Fred Fiandaca and Jose Santana managed to sneak past the monitors charged with preventing children from coming up to their classrooms early in the morning. As soon as they entered the room, they pulled chairs over to their teacher's desk and opened a serious discussion of the shooting of Joseph A. Colombo Sr. last Monday.

"They knew I would be glad to see them and be interested in what they had to say," the teacher said. "That made me feel good."

Or there was the way Nelson Cerda had insisted on going along when Miss Boroughs took 11 children from the class to Jones Beach for a cookout Monday afternoon, one of several special excursions that marked the final week. Nelson is a closely protected only son whose father decided he had better stay at home.

A Note Undelivered

It took five phone calls for Miss Boroughs to reach the father at the midtown jewelry shop where he works as a messenger in order to reassure him on his son's safety. The news that he could go made Nelson incandescent.

Only later did the teacher discover how much it had meant to him. A melodramatic note he had written to his father but never had the bravado to deliver slipped out of his pocket in the station wagon in which she returned with the children from the beach.

In it, Nelson had threatened to run away from home. "If you can't trust me, you can't trust nobody," he wrote. "Say good-by to my sister and my mother. I am sorry to have wasted your time."

Poignantly, the note was signed with his first name, his middle initial and a question mark.

Miss Boroughs knew Nelson came from a warm and happy home and the note was no cause for concern. Its ardor also told her that he came from a happy class.

About half the children were in new clothes yesterday morning. Many of them brought gifts and notes for their teacher.

"Dear Miss Boroughs," Sharaie Blue had written, heedless of the danger of overstatement, "Thank you for teaching me all the things I did not know."

A Pen for the Teacher

Stella Pistorio had said more than once that she planned to bring her teacher a gift on the last day of school and Miss Boroughs had given her a sermon on why she shouldn't.

Tuesday evening, weighing her feelings on the matter against her teacher's, Stella had taken all the money she had managed to save since her ninth birthday 10 months ago—it came to $12—and walked down Lexington Avenue to 86th Street where she selected a pen.

She had given Miss Boroughs a pen at Christmas time, too. But this time to fool her, Stella packed it in a box big enough for a handbag.

The teacher brought her own gifts, paperback books for each child that were intended, so all the inscriptions explained, "To start you on your summer reading!" There was also a mimeographed reading list with 16 titles, preceded and followed by Miss Boroughs's entreaties to "Read! Read! Read!"

The inscription in the book Shaun Sheppard got had three extra exclamation points. Shaun also got a special appeal to join Miss Boroughs and as many as 10 other children from Class 4-4 in the same classroom next Tuesday when summer school begins.

"I'll be waiting for you here Tuesday morning," the teacher said. "If you sleep late, you can still come."

Shaun was as noncommittal as he could be, but Miss Boroughs pressed her plea. Monday morning Anibal Rosado had reported that he had seen Shaun hanging from the back of a Madison Avenue bus last weekend. All Miss Boroughs's fears about what the streets could do to Shaun, who is now 12, seemed to her to have been confirmed.

José Santana, Israel Valle, Raymond Mercado and Madelyn Cotto said they might go to Puerto Rico during the summer. Cecil Robinson, Benny Winslow and Matthew Phillips expected to visit relatives in the South. Shaun has a three-week scholarship to a camp sponsored by the Boys Club of New York. Stella would be going to day camp for six weeks.

No one's plans were more uncertain than the teacher's. Summer school would last six weeks. Then she thought she might go to India as a tourist or attend a teaching

Maria Rivera

Yvonne Prileau

Miguel Ramos

Matthew Phillips

Fred Fiandaca

David Badillo

Anibal Rosado

Hajnalka Fulop

CLASS
4-4
P. S. 198
JUNE, 1971

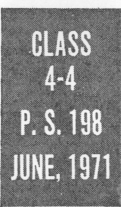

Israel Valle

Shaun Sheppard

Sharaie Blue

Ralph Ingenita

Nelson Cerda

Stella Pistorio

Cecil Robinson

Raymond Mercado

Miss Dorothy Boroughs

Kathy Brugueras

Madelyn Cotto   **Carlos Andujar**

Desiree Fleming   **Oliver Niles**

Benny Winslow   **José Santana**

Andy Carril   **Lori Spellman**

Photographs for The New York Times by JACK MANNING

institute at Cuernavaca, Mexico, that describes itself as "a meeting place for humanists whose common concern is the effect of social and ideological change on the minds and hearts of men."

School for Teacher

Somewhere along the way, if she did not want to forfeit a $1,200 raise that would bring her salary to over $15,000, she would also have to take a two-credit course —virtually any two-credit course—at a graduate school here.

To get pay raises under the Board of Education's rules, teachers must constantly keep going back to school, whether they expect to learn anything or not.

When she left school yesterday afternoon, she still had not been officially notified as to her class assignment in September. All she had learned was that she would be receiving neither her first nor second choices.

Last week Mrs. Charlotte Schiff, the acting principal, had said that only one teacher in the school would be in that position. Because she is about half-way up on the seniority list, Miss Boroughs had assumed she could not be that one.

On the next-to-last day of the semester, however, the principal had been informed that 17 of the 55 teachers at Public School 198 were being "excessed" out—that is, assigned to other schools in the district as a result of the budget crisis.

The school, Mrs. Schiff said, would have eight fewer classes in September unless, once again, the extent of the crisis was being exaggerated for political effect.

Miss Boroughs went home asking herself why she worked in such a system and how much longer she could maintain her feelings of independence inside it. The question depressed her, but then she remembered a visit she had received in her classroom yesterday from Ralph Ingenita two hours after the final dismissal of the school year.

Tuesday afternoon in Central Park, Ralph played on a softball team for which Miss Boroughs batted cleanup. The team lost, but Ralph now wanted her expert advice on whether he should become a catcher or an outfielder. Miss Boroughs didn't know why he assumed she knew the answer, but she was delighted to be asked.

"I ask myself why I go on," she said when she described the visit. "Well, that's why."

THE END OF THE SCHOOL YEAR

The New York Times/Jack Manning

July 1, 1971

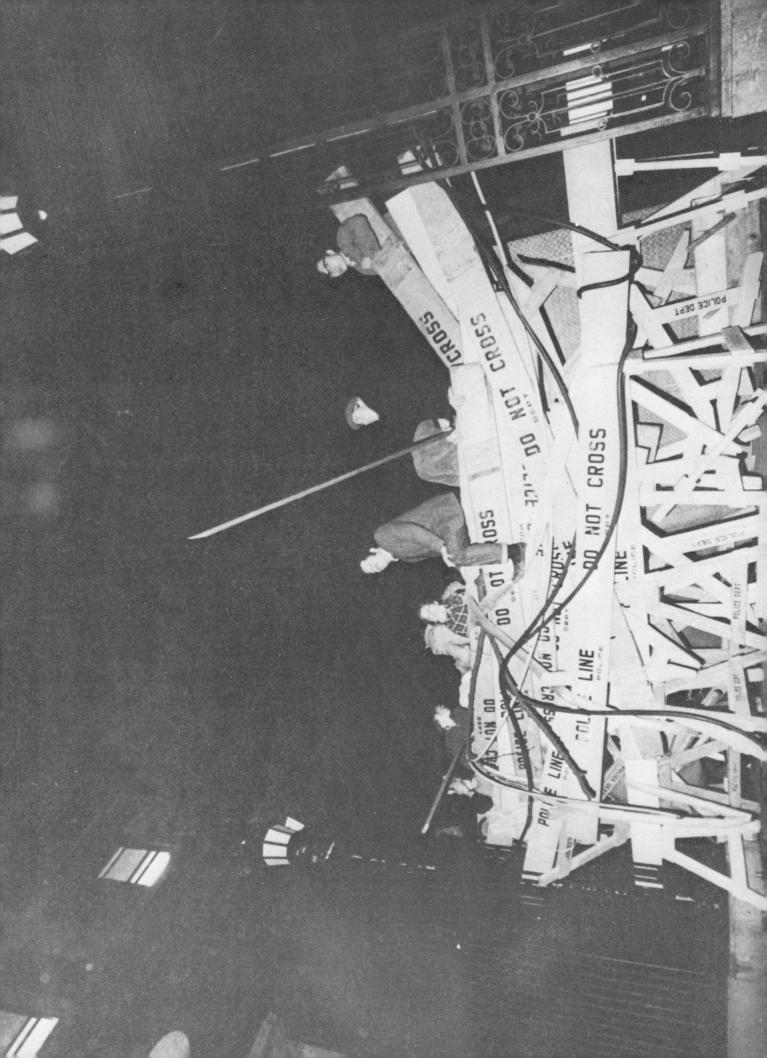

Higher Education

To Teach
Men to Know How to Be Free

In colleges today courses in basic human knowledge replace traditional electives.

By IRWIN EDMAN

Professor of Philosophy, Columbia University

A FEW weeks ago there was a front-page headline in THE NEW YORK TIMES informing the public that Harvard had abandoned the elective system. This was in a special sense news because it was at Harvard under President Eliot that the elective system had been developed in its most extreme form. But it had long been well known to those following educational changes in this country that many colleges had been substituting a more or less prescribed curriculum for a miscellany of courses freely elected according to the judgment—or whim—of the individual student.

What are the reasons for this shift in opinion in the colleges with respect to the values of a required curriculum of free election? What brought on the elective system? What has produced the reaction against it?

A set, required program is no novelty in American colleges. The elective system is, in any long view, the novelty. On the traditional American campus there was a fairly settled curriculum which, with negligible variation, all students followed.

Mathematics, the classical languages, rhetoric, moral philosophy and Christian ethics and apologetics; these were to influence the mind and character of the teachers or preachers for whose training the traditional New England colleges were primarily founded. Colleges had pretty much identical programs, and students spent four years not only in the same dormitories but in the same courses. They graduated having studied identical subjects in identical ways.

There are several reasons why the old-fashioned, prescribed curriculum went by the boards. In the first place, there were new subjects coming into the educational picture. Colleges, especially those which formed part of great universities, were developing new fields of knowledge: physical sciences, economics, psychology, anthropology, fine arts and music, modern languages. In the second place, the older curriculum was dying because of both internal decay and the changing preparation of the students coming to college.

The dead languages had come to be taught in a manner deadly enough to all living interest on the part of students. They were taught as mere conjugations, as exercises in grammar. Psychologists began to question how much "mental discipline" there was in fighting in every collegiate generation the subjunctives of Caesar's campaigns. Even lovers of the classics began to wonder how much a taste for the best that has been known

and thought in the world was promoted by hours spent with the ablative absolute. Mathematics did not to the non-mathematical-minded seem to promote clear thought, nor rhetoric to produce good writing.

A CURRICULUM designed to train teachers and preachers came less and less to meet the needs of young men—and young women—destined to all sorts of careers, many of them unknown when American colleges were founded.

The elective system, moreover, began to develop at a time when there was a growing emphasis in both education and society on the "individual." The curriculum, educators began to think, should be designed to fit the needs and satisfy the interests of the student rather than to fit the student into the molds of an already fixed program. Students were encouraged to study what they pleased; all that was required in some universities was that students choose sixteen out of the four hundred or more courses not infrequently to be found in a college catalogue.

Stephen Leacock, the Canadian professor and humorist, once wrote an anecdote of the elective system at its extreme. He had, he reported, met an American student during the summer vacation. He asked him what he was going to take in the way of courses that autumn. "Turkish, music and architecture," the student promptly replied. "Do you expect to be choirmaster in a Turkish cathedral?" Mr. Leacock asked. "No," said the student, "those courses come at 9, 10 and 11 o'clock."

There was another tale, equally apocryphal, that one student at Yale chose only courses that were given on the ground floor. Up to the present time at Harvard, practically the only required course for all students is English A (which can be evaded by a proficiency test).

For almost twenty years before the war there had been increasing suspicion that such a complete miscellany of courses as was possible and even probable under the elective system scarcely constituted an education at all, if education is interpreted as some development of understanding of man's place in nature and society and the character of man himself.

BUT the elective system continued despite protests against it, and behind its continuance lay certain feelings, deep if not always expressed. One was the conviction current among more teachers and

students than would always admit it that it did not matter so much what a student studied as whom he studied with. There was also the sentiment, endorsed by affectionate alumni, that it really did not matter what a student studied at all, or even if he studied, so long as he caught by osmosis the common temper of a given college and shared an urbane life with well-bred young men in the shadow of ivy-clad walls.

The heyday of the elective system could never have been quite so bad as it is now pictured to have been, nor was freedom of election generally as free in its extreme form as it was for a time at Harvard. Some distinguished critics of the free-choice program seem to have survived it themselves and to some degree even to have profited by it. And even at its most miscellaneous, under the elective program students used some common sense in selecting courses that had some relation to one another.

BUT there is no question that complete freedom of election in college courses is generally regarded as a failure. Colleges began to correct their error by requiring a certain concentration and distribution of courses. Students were obliged to take a fixed number of courses in science, in social science and in the fields of literature and philosophy. Nearly all colleges required a basic year's work in English composition, in one natural science, in one modern language, in philosophy.

But still something was missing. Graduates of the same college often had only the thinnest of common backgrounds. Graduates of different colleges had often no common intellectual background at all. Alumni of reputable institutions would ruefully recognize, ten years later, that college had given them no coherent view of the world. They would discover that in the major areas of nature, society and human experience they could not put two and two together. Students found by the time that they arrived at their degree that freedom led only to emptiness and chaos. The elective system did not seem to insure a unified awareness of the past, nor a sense of one's responsibility in

College vista—Dormitory Triangle at the University of Pennsylvania.

the world: in other words, an intelligent comprehension of the present. One could get a degree without having had anything entitled to be called an education.

THE recognition of these facts lies behind the emphasis, in a very new form, of the latter-day prescribed curriculum. About twenty-five years ago Columbia College initiated a course, now widely adopted or adapted in many other places, called contemporary civilization, a required freshman course for all students, in the history and structure of present-day society. A few years later there was a course called general honors, for a limited number of students, a course in the great books of the Western tradition.

St. John's College has made famous the idea that the essence of a liberal education is in a reading of a selected list of the great masterpieces of the Western World. Columbia has since made a course in the readings of twenty-five or more masterpieces, from Homer to the present time, a required course for all freshmen. A similar course in the basic sciences, required of all students, will soon be obligatory. A similar general scheme is now proposed at Harvard.

No one thinks that these courses are educational magic. But it is believed that they will provide for students two diverse goods of what has come to be called, in terms of the Harvard report, a "general" as contrasted with a "special" education. The first good is that of a generalized awareness of the nature of the natural world, the character of modern society, and, as displayed in great literature, human nature itself. The second good is that of a common background, urgently necessary in a democracy composed of so many diverse strains, interests and types of persons as is our own. Education is an education in a basic fact: we are all in the same boat. This new conception of general education insists that everyone, to whatever special career he is destined, should know what the nature of that boat is, what sort of seas it has traversed and is likely to run into, and what in general is the basic nature of one's self and of one's fellow-passengers.

THE elective system is not completely dead. In most institutions it continues to be recognised that talents and interests differ. But the colleges are very widely now committing themselves to the proposition that there is a common world which we must all understand, a common human nature we all share, a common history which we all inherit. That is what college educators now have no hesitation in prescribing. And it looks as if students enjoy the prescription very much and, what is even more important, are benefiting by it. The colleges are simply requiring a program that will provide the basic common understanding needed by citizens who are to be intelligent enough to know how to be free.

September 30, 1945

EDUCATION IN REVIEW

Survey Indicates the Difficulty Encountered By Women Attempting to Enter College

By BENJAMIN FINE

Difficult as it may be for the returning veteran to enter the overcrowded colleges and universities of this country, the situation is far more serious for the potential women students. Co-educational and women's colleges in all parts of the country report record enrollments; thousands of qualified women applicants are being turned away because of insufficient facilities.

A study of thirty typical institutions, conducted by this department, reveals an unprecedented condition—never before in their history have women's and co-educational colleges been swamped with so many women candidates. Not only the big name institutions but even the lesser known colleges are finding it virtually impossible to admit all competent students. In many instances the September rolls have been closed at this early date.

As in the case with the men's colleges, housing is one of the chief bottlenecks in the women's institutions. Filled to capacity, the colleges cannot expand their dormitory quarters nor provide additional living facilities. Many of the housing projects supported by the Government are restricted to veterans and thus do not help the women's colleges.

Probably one of the most important reasons why women are finding it difficult to get into college is that veterans receive priority in most institutions of higher learning. Many colleges report that they are putting aside most of the vacancies for the veterans, even though it may mean that civilians, men and women alike, are to be kept out.

Sons and Daughters

Despite the fewer opportunities for women to get into a college or university, more women are applying for higher education than ever before, THE TIMES survey disclosed. Several college presidents suggested that the GI bill, which provides free educational opportunities for the veterans, is partly responsible for the greater number of women who are seeking admittance. Because the veterans do not have to pay for their college education, many families can now afford to send their daughters to a college or university, using the funds that would have gone in normal times for their sons.

Women's colleges in particular report record enrollments and unprecedented applications from women. In some instances the number of applicants has increased as much as 100 per cent over previous years. Such well-known institutions for women as Bryn Mawr, Mills, Randolph Macon, Mount Holyoke, Vassar, Sweet Briar,

Bennington, Smith, Wilson and Wellesly report that they are receiving more applications this spring for September than ever before in their history. Thousands will have to be turned away.

Typical of the overcrowding of women's colleges is the situation at Mount Holyoke. Applications are running more than 20 per cent ahead of those on file at the same time last year. Requests for admission to advanced standing have been so heavy that the list for the coming year closed Feb. 1. Enrollment for the present year is 1,149; the normal peacetime figure is 1,000.

Applications Doubled

Similarly, the New Jersey College for Women reports that it has on hand twice as many applications for fall admission as it had a year ago. Because of the large number who are applying, several hundred will have to be turned away for lack of space. Further South, Newcomb College, women's division of Tulane University, reports that it has received 100 per cent more applications this year than in previous years.

At co-educational as well as women's institutions the crowded conditions prevail. At the University of North Carolina 600 women students have been rejected thus far for the Fall quarter—the largest number the university has ever had to turn away. Women students at Bucknell University face an unusually difficult problem. Because of the lack of civilian men, Bucknell admitted an average of 200 women students during each of the war years as compared with a pre-war admission of 130 women each year. The university took over the men's fraternity houses as residences for women.

With men students returning to the campus in large numbers, the fraternity houses are being turned back to the men. As a result the university expects to admit a maximum of forty women next September—only a small percentage of those applying. What will happen to the women who are rejected at Bucknell? Unfortunately, many will find, when applying elsewhere, that a similar situation exists on almost every campus and that former men's quarters which were turned over to women are now being reconverted to men's dormitories.

At a Small College

Whether it is a small New England college, a large Midwestern university, a Southern institution or a college in the Far West, the story is the same. For example, Colby College in Maine

reports that three times as many women are applying for admission now as in the past. For the spring term 137 men were accepted, but not one woman. The number of available dormitory rooms limits the women students who can be admitted.

Most women's colleges have a fixed enrollment and find that they cannot expand as much as the co-educational or men's institutions. Smith College is a typical example. Enrollment is limited to 2,000 undergraduates. Although the number of applicants for the incoming freshman class in September is higher than ever before, the size of the college will not be increased.

Similarly, applications for admission to Wilson College are topping all previous figures—thus far there has been a 100 per cent increase over the record-breaking total of last year. However, enrollment will be the same next fall as it has been in the past; the student body is limited to 400

At Oakland, Calif., Mills College is experiencing the same type of record-breaking demand for admittance as are the Eastern institutions. For this semester 35 per cent more applications have been received than for last year; on the basis of present trends, the college reports, competition for admission will be even greater than in the past few years. Hundreds of applicants will be turned away.

Because of the housing situation Marietta College is discouraging applications from women. Sixteen women were admitted this semester as compared with 263 men. Although up to now Marietta has not given priority to men students, this policy is being changed because of lack of housing for women. Campus housing facilities have been given over entirely to women, but they are now filled to capacity.

Priority to Veterans

For the first time in the 100-year history of Marshall College in West Virginia, the enrollment of full-time first-year male students outnumbers women six to one. Boston University reports that three times as many men students were admitted this semester as women students. Co-educational institutions, giving top priority to veterans, are taking the men students at the expense of the women. That is one reason why the students are flocking to the women's colleges.

During the past few years there has been a consistent increase in the number of women students seeking admission to Indiana University. This term 350 women could not be accommodated because of the overcrowded housing situation. The University of Illinois is discouraging women from enrolling because of the lack of room.

Judging from the reports of the college and universities reached in the survey, the situation for women students will remain critical for the next year or two. Many educators are confident that constructive action will be taken once the problem becomes generally known.

April 14, 194

Record College Enrollment Brings Big Expansion Plans

400 Institutions in U. S. Propose to Build at Cost of $1,250,000,000—Tuition Rates Are 50% Above the Pre-War Level

By BENJAMIN FINE

Faced with a record enrollment this fall, American colleges and universities are planning a huge expansion program, a nation-wide survey conducted by THE NEW YORK TIMES has shown.

Institutions of higher learning everywhere report that they still are overcrowded and in need of more buildings, equipment and supplies. They are seeking competent instructors and other faculty members. Many centers indicate that because of inflationary prices they must turn to alumni or friends for funds to help balance budgets.

The cost of obtaining a higher education has jumped again. More than half of the nation's colleges raised their tuition rates in the last year. It now costs 50 per cent more, in tuition fees alone, to go to college than it did before the war. Similar increases have taken place in rooming costs and other fees paid by students.

An over-all picture of "what's happening to higher education" shows that this fall, for the first time since the post-war expansion began, fewer veterans are on the campus. The peak in veteran enrollment under the G.I. Bill of Rights was reached in December, 1947, when 1,157,966 ex-service men were in college. This fall the veteran enrollment has dropped to a little more than 1,000,000.

THE TIMES' study indicates that 2,400,000 men and women are attending the 1,800 liberal arts colleges, professional and technical schools, junior colleges and teacher-training institutions in the nation. This is just about 50,000 more than were enrolled in the fall of 1947. Sixty-eight per cent of the colleges said that they believed their peak in student enrollment had been reached this fall, while the other 32 per cent predicted that their registration would go still higher in the immediate years to come.

Despite the over-all enrollment increase, the current study showed that the liberal arts colleges had a drop of 5 to 10 per cent in the last year. Sixty per cent of the liberal arts colleges reached in the survey reported that their 1948 enrollment was greater than it was in 1947, while 40 per cent said it

was the same or less. Some of the large state universities as well as privately controlled institutions reported enrollment drops as high as 10 per cent. On the other hand, a number of large colleges continued to expand.

It costs considerably more to go to college this fall than it did a year ago, the study indicated. Tuition rates and other college expenses have gone up steadily in recent years. Fifty-five per cent of the colleges and universities reported that their tuition fees had been raised in the last year, while virtually all said that the tuition rates had gone up since Pearl Harbor.

Tuition Up 50 Per Cent

Back in 1941-42 the average tuition fee of 410 representative liberal arts colleges and universities, both public and private, was $250 annually. In 1947-48 the fee had jumped to $338. This fall it averages $366, an increase of nearly 50 per cent since 1942. Room fees and other expenses connected with the classroom and campus have gone up proportionately.

Even though student fees have increased, the colleges and universities are concerned at the rising prices that they must face. A number point to the increased faculty expenses, as well as the higher costs for equipment, buildings and other supplies needed in the operation of an institution, as partial explanation for the tuition increases.

A major item of cost, the colleges report, is the building program that is in blueprint stage everywhere and already has begun on many campuses. Four hundred liberal arts colleges and universities report that they plan to spend $1,250,000,000 for new buildings, or an average of approximately $3,000,000 a college. At this rate higher education faces a huge building program that may reach in the neighborhood of $5,000,000,000 in the next decade. Eighty-eight per cent of the colleges have made plans for a building program.

Lack of Facilities Reported

More than half of the colleges report that they do not have sufficient facilities for all the students on their campuses. Throughout the land veterans and non-veterans still are living in quonset huts, makeshift temporary buildings and other improvised quarters. The campuses are dotted with "veterans' villages" that house single and married students.

Conditions are somewhat better as far as laboratories and instructional space are concerned. According to the survey, 75 per cent

of the colleges have sufficient laboratory facilities for their student bodies. However, many point out that their laboratories gradually are becoming obsolete and soon will have to be replaced if they are to keep pace with the rapid changes of science.

To meet the increased enrollment a majority of the colleges and universities plan to add to their faculties. Sixty-five per cent of the liberal arts institutions report that they are seeking additional men and women as teachers. Three hundred representative colleges and universities indicate that they will need well over 3,000 instructors, or an average of ten for each college in the land. If that same ratio held for the 1,800 institutions of higher learning, it would mean that more than 18,000 college teachers were needed immediately.

But it is difficult to obtain adequately trained persons to teach on the college level, the educators declare. Forty-two per cent of the colleges and universities report that they are unable to get all the qualified faculty members needed. Cited is the growing shortage in critical fields, particularly in the physical sciences. Many institutions have had to dig down deep in the barrel and come up with teachers who under ordinary circumstances and in normal times would not be employed for college teaching.

In mapping expansion programs, many colleges are concerned with future trends. They are not certain whether the present record enrollment will continue or whether a drop can be expected. In certain divisions of higher education a decline already has been noted, although the overall figures show that general enrollment is greater than it ever has been in this country.

Nearly one-third of all the colleges — 32 per cent — believe that enrollment will continue to increase, but 68 per cent feel that it already has reached its peak. Most colleges are of the opinion that if a decline is to take place it will be gradual and only temporary.

Few responsible educational officials think that the pre-war level of enrollment will return. They hold that the present high plateau —just about double the 1941 figures—will continue for several years and then will rise again. A number of colleges, particularly those in the small, private category, intend to reduce their total enrollment and return to their previous status. One-fifth of all the institutions responding in the survey said they would cut their enrollments as soon as was possible.

Admission Difficulties

Perhaps within another year or two it may be easier for students to gain admittance to college, but THE TIMES' survey indicates that it still is difficult at present. Many institutions report that they are unable to accept all the qualified students who apply for admission. Actually 250 colleges said that they had to turn away 130,000 students who had applied either as entering or as advanced students, or an av-

erage of more than 500 students a college.

These figures may be misleading, however, as frequently a student applies to more than one college. In fact, several colleges complained that the multiple choice among students seeking admittance had reached the point where it was becoming costly and troublesome. Some of the colleges said that they were uncertain until the last moment as to just how many accepted students actually would report for instruction.

A significant trend is found in the number of entering students, where a decline has taken place for the first time since the upward swing began. For all students the entering class is approximately 570,000, compared with 600,000 in the fall of 1947. The drop of 20,000, or 5 per cent, may be indicative of the future enrollment trend for the next few years, the college officials say. However, THE TIMES' survey shows that 42 per cent of all colleges and universities had a greater entering undergraduate class in 1948 than they had in 1947.

Fewer Veterans Noted

The decline in the proportion of veterans on the nation's campuses, while not great, indicates that the downward trend has begun. Ninety per cent of all colleges and universities report that their 1948 veteran enrollment is less than it was a year ago. They expect that the drop will continue in the next several years as the number of veterans who have not taken advantage of the G.I. bill for free tuition gradually decreases. At present approximately 40 per cent of all students are veterans, compared with 50 per cent in 1947.

It is in the freshmen classes that the veteran drop is noticeable. For example, it is plain that New England's colleges and universities, representing a trend shown elsewhere, are beginning to "demobilize" from the war. The freshman class at Middlebury College in Vermont will have only a 12 per cent veteran representation. Entrance in the peak year of 1946 was composed of 85 per cent of veterans. Last year the figure was 44 per cent. Harvard University will have 16 per cent veterans among the 1,200 freshmen entering the college.

The Massachusetts Institute of Technology reports 12 per cent of veterans among the entering class, compared with 50 per cent two years ago. Tufts College lists these percentages to show how the veteran enrollment is dropping: seniors, 87 per cent; juniors, 67 per cent; sophomores, 39 per cent, and freshman, 28 per cent. Dartmouth College, which in 1946 had 523 veterans enrolled, compared with 243 civilians, will have less than 10 per cent veterans this year.

New Registration Records

Despite the gradual falling off in enrollment, many institutions are setting new records this fall. Bowling Green State University, with 4,500 students, is triple its pre-war enrollment of 1,600. The University of Delaware's undergraduate enrollment has topped 2,200 for the first time in its history. Similarly, enrollment

Iowa State College has reached a new peak of 10,000 students.

Colleges and universities in Illinois have 134,337 students enrolled for the fall semester, a 2 per cent decrease from a year ago. Teachers' colleges showed an increase in enrollment of 4 per cent over the 1947 totals, junior colleges dropped 6 per cent, women's colleges decreased 5 per cent and universities were down 3 per cent in total enrollments. Four-year colleges showed a slight increase of 1 per cent.

Enrollment in the graduate or professional schools continues at its record peak. Graduate schools report that more students are applying for admittance to their departments than ever before. Thousands of qualified students are being turned away because of insufficient facilities. The colleges express concern at the large numbers of students who cannot continue with their graduate studies.

Ninety-two per cent of the nation's universities have higher enrollments in their graduate or professional schools this fall than they had in the fall of 1947. Only lack of facilities, they point out, stands in the way of still greater numbers going into these advanced institutions or into professional schools for further training. Conditions are particularly difficult in medicine, dentistry and engineering.

U. S. Giving $100,000,000 For Research in Colleges

Most Extensive Work in History Under Way, Survey Shows—Industry Adds $25,000,000 —'Applied Sciences' Get Lion's Share

By BENJAMIN FINE

Aided by funds from the Federal Government and private industry, American colleges and universities are engaged in the most extensive research program in the history of higher education.

In the current academic year, the Federal Government will give 200 institutions more than $100,000,000 for research purposes, and industry will contribute close to $25,000,000. This is an estimated increase, for both the Federal Government and private industry, of 500 per cent over the funds of pre-war years.

A survey of sixty colleges and universities, together with interviews in the leading Government agencies, conducted by THE NEW YORK TIMES, shows the tremendous position that research has attained on the campuses. Many institutions report that the bulk of their research is directly subsidized by Federal funds. For the most part, the Federal money is concentrated in the larger universities and big-name technological institutions.

Although various United States agencies provide funds, the largest proportion comes from the Department of Defense, the Atomic Energy Commission, the Department of Agriculture and the Federal Security Agency.

Literally hundreds of projects are under way in almost every field of learning. However, the "applied sciences" are receiving the lion's share of the research funds. More than one-third of all Federal funds goes for the engineering sciences, while the physical and medical sciences account for nearly half. Eighty-two institutions report that they are sponsoring 4,000 engineering research projects at a cost of $35,000,000.

Many educators interviewed by this writer are worried lest the colleges and universities "slant" their research too heavily in the direction of applied projects at the expense of fundamental research. They warn that a large proportion of the projects are geared toward practical problems despite the need for theoretical research. Other officials fear that the highly concentrated research program, placed in a few specialized areas, will "freeze out" the smaller colleges and harm the whole field of research.

A few college educators also warn that the long-range results of a huge Government-sponsored program may prove harmful. They fear that once the colleges and universities become dependent upon Washington, there may follow an attempt to control the institution's policies. They add that this has not happened as yet, but is possible in the future.

No Attempt to Control Seen

Most of the educators reached in the study said that the Government had not attempted to influence their curricula. They pointed out that the money that came to the campus, whether it was $50,000 or $5,000,000, came with no strings attached. Primarily, they said, the Government is interested in results, and does not interfere with the college administration.

With the exception of the veterans' programs, Federally financed research at colleges and universities represents the largest single expenditure of Federal funds in education. Every state has one or more of these projects, although the bulk is concentrated in the Northeast.

Some criticism has been voiced by the college officials over the lack of systematic approach to the granting of funds. They charge that on occasion the "connections" of the university heads may have considerable influence in the amount of money that can be obtained from the Government. On this issue the Hoover Commission said bluntly:

"At present grants for research purposes are being made on a hit-and-miss basis, making the award of research grants, in effect, a new form of patronage."

The Hoover Commission suggested that research awards be made "with due recognition given to their impact on the educational program of our higher institutions of learning." It advocated the creation of a National Science Foundation.

Industry Increases Aid

Although Federal grants are zooming, industry also has increased its contributions to the colleges and universities for research purposes. Reports received by THE TIMES indicate that support from industry has increased five-fold.

The reports reflect the vast increase in Federal research funds this year as compared with those in 1941-42—the last pre-war year. The University of Cincinnati, for example, is getting $600,000 this year, as compared with $50,000 in 1941. The University of Kansas is receiving $309,000, whereas it received nothing before the war. This year the University of Michigan will receive $5,000,000, as compared with $13,386 eight years ago.

This money is allocated for numerous projects. Some institutions list scores of them. Harvard University, for example, shows research work in such fields as astronomy, biology, biochemistry, dental medicine, acoustics, electronics, dermatology, nuclear physics, public health, physical chemistry, solar research and biophysics.

The Navy conducts one of the most intensive college research programs. It consists of 1,200 projects in 200 institutions, with a total expenditure of $20,000,000 a year. Nearly 3,000 scientists and 2,500 college and university graduate students are actively engaged in basic research projects of interest to the Navy.

"The basic research program has made available to the Navy the advice and counsel of many of the outstanding scientists in the country," Navy officials say. "They have provided their knowledge either through individual consultation, or through membership on advisory panels and participation in symposia. At the same time, through its subsidization of many projects making use of graduate students, it has indirectly aided in the training of essential future scientists."

AEC Allots Millions

Next in importance on the campus is the research program sponsored by the Atomic Energy Commission. During the 1948-49 year the Commission allocated $10,000,000 for the support of research in colleges and universities, exclusive of the research carried on in Commission-owned laboratories operated by the academic institutions under contract. Fully 1,000 research persons are employed on the projects, located in approximately 150 institutions.

Another $17,000,000 was spent for research in government-owned laboratories or facilities operated for the AEC by colleges or universities.

Typical of the university research programs is that at Boston University. During 1949-50 it will receive $500,000 from the Government and from industry to support fundamental research in a variety of fields—ten times as much as it received in 1941-42. The major portion of the grants and contracts by the Government are sponsored by the Air Force, the Air Matériel Command, the Office of Naval Research and the Public Health Service.

The largest single project at Boston University is in the general field of physical optics, with emphasis on aerial photography. The university's optical research laboratory was established after the war to serve the educational needs of the university, both as a training center for graduate students and as a research facility in this important branch of physics.

Another large project concerns the physics of the upper atmosphere and involves the use of the V-2 and other types of rockets to send physical instruments into the upper atmosphere for recording and transmitting measurements of physical conditions.

Other Fields Represented

Although the two largest Government-supported research projects are administered under the supervision of the physics department, smaller projects also are carried out in such fields as psychology, chemistry, biology, biochemistry, pharmacology, geochemistry and physiology. Grants also have been made in most of these fields by industrial concerns and by nonprofit foundations.

"Federal contracts for research projects in the university have been extremely free of any control, leaving to our own faculty and research scientists a maximum amount of freedom to follow their own judgment as to what should be done within the general limits of the projects," the officials point out. "There appears to be little if any direct or indirect effect of such projects on either the curriculum in Boston University or on the type of research projects under investigation."

For the most part the college and university officials declare that the money given them by the Federal Government has proved beneficial. They point to enriched offerings in graduate work, to an expanded curriculum and to greatly stimulated interest in research as immediate results.

Advantages Are Cited

Typical of the comments is this, by Dr. Leonard Carmichael, president of Tufts College:

"We have been better able to recruit and maintain staff members with research interests, to increase the number of active investigators connected with the college by supporting them partially from research funds and to give research training to both undergraduate and graduate students under the active supervision of trained investigators. Our courses of study have also become broader and more numerous due to the presence of a larger number of professional individuals who can be placed on a schedule of part-time teaching and research."

On the other hand, a number of highly placed educators warn that the vast Federal subsidy can become dangerous if it ever gets out of hand. They point to the possibility of "interference" and "control" as part of the price that may have to be paid.

These dangers have been stressed by Dr. Henry M. Wriston, president of Brown University, who is also head of the Association of American Universities. Dr. Wriston observes:

"Government support of research is dangerous if it deflects the basic intent of the university, or takes too much time and energy from this program, if the terms are so onerous as to restrict activities."

"Gadget Research" Criticized

Spokesmen at the University of Washington express their fears this way:

"There has been a tendency in the case of contract research for the military departments to emphasize what might be called 'gadget research' rather than basic investigations. There is a strong feeling here that this type of project distracts attention of good research men from their basic work and that 'gadget' developments such as special weapons should be left to the military services to be conducted in their own premises.

"A policy now being implemented at this university will provide that no contract research be accepted without provision for graduate fellowship training, with the graduate student and the instructor completely free to determine what work is to be done by students. This, it is hoped, will obviate the employment of students merely as technicians or helpers on projects which do not further their graduate programs."

Similarly, officials at the University of Minnesota declare that "institutions which receive Federal funds for research should guard against any wholesale shift from basic fundamental research to applied research." Dean Thorndike Saville of the New York University College of Engineering observes that "we accept only projects of a truly fundamental nature, of a character of interest to our staff, or one which contributes appreciably to the training of the graduate students."

Resentment is expressed by the smaller colleges and universities at the emphasis placed by the United States agencies on the "big-time" institutions. This attitude is best stated by Dr. Sidney J. French, faculty dean at Colgate University.

Wider Distribution Urged

"It seems to us highly important," Dr. French maintained, "that Federal funds for research purposes be widely enough distributed to include the smaller, typically undergraduate colleges, so that research will not be confined, alone, to the large universities. Otherwise, there is danger that scientific work in the smaller colleges will tend to atrophy. There are already definite signs that this is happening. The evidence clearly indicates that the smaller colleges have in the past trained considerably more than their share of the nation's leading scientists."

On the whole, the college and university presidents and administrative officials are satisfied with the $100,000,000 or more that they are receiving from the Federal Government. They are realistic in their views. In large measure they subscribe to this position, voiced by the University of Michigan:

"The research projects supported by the Federal Government have benefited the university by giving our faculty an opportunity to pursue research that we could not otherwise afford."

December 5, 1949

Rise in Colleges Sets Record; 150 Registered in Two Years

By BENJAMIN FINE
Special to THE NEW YORK TIMES.

WASHINGTON, March 19—Since the end of World War II this country has experienced a record growth in higher education. During the last two years, for example, more than 150 colleges and universities have been added to the list of recognized institutions of higher learning in the United States Office of Education directory—more than in any comparable period in American history.

The current higher education directory, which has just been made public, lists 1,808 colleges and universities, compared with 1,728 a year ago—an increase of eighty in twelve months. To date in 1950, eighteen additional colleges have been reported to the Office of Education and, before the year ends, it is estimated that another fifty institutions will be added to the directory, to raise the total for this country to 1,875—a record for this or any other nation.

The greatest increase was registered at the junior and community college level, Dr. Earl J. McGrath, United States Commissioner of Education, declared in an interview yesterday. About 50 per cent of the new institutions founded since the end of the war have been the two-year colleges.

Junior Colleges in the Lead

Pointing out that the United States is on the threshold of an unprecedented growth of its higher educational facilities, Dr. McGrath predicted that the junior-college movement would take the lead in this development. There are 500 recognized junior and commuting colleges in this country today. Within ten years, Dr. McGrath predicted, the number would double, going to 1,000.

At the same time, he estimated that the over-all college enrollment in the United States would continue to increase. Before the war, colleges and universities had a total student enrollment of less than 1,500,000. This figure has risen to 2,500,000 for the current academic year, and, according to Dr. McGrath's prediction, it will reach 3,000,000 in less than a decade.

"The institutions being established to meet the increasing demand for higher education are chiefly of two types," Dr. McGrath said. "About one-fourth are specialized professional and technical schools and more than half are junior or community colleges.

"The development of community colleges gives promise of making two years of education beyond the high school readily available to most young people, in an institution near their homes and where they can find programs suited to their needs at relatively low cost."

Dr. McGrath added that the tremendous growth in higher education represented an expression of the American philosophy that educational opportunities should be extended to all our youth. Through the community college movement, he pointed out, higher education will become available to all boys and girls, whether they want an academic program or want to take technical or vocational courses.

Role of the Two-Year College

Many of the new institutions now being founded, Dr. McGrath disclosed, were either free, or have low tuition charges. Although some of the established four-year colleges and universities may be concerned lest the community colleges take away some of their enrollment, that is not likely to happen, according to Dr. McGrath. Rather, he said, the two-year colleges would tap new groups of students who do not go to any institution at present.

Pointing to California as an example, the commissioner observed that the enrollments in that state had increased in the four-year colleges, despite the tremendous increase in community and junior college enrollments. He added that the "fears of the four-year college officials are not well-founded."

Based on present trends, enrollment in higher education will be divided among the two-year, four-year and technical institutions. Dr. McGrath added that "I do not think that we have reached the end of our growth in higher education on any level." However, the greatest increase, he predicted, would be on the community college level.

A survey conducted by the Office of Education revealed that, in twenty-four states, one or more communities were planning to establish junior and community colleges during the next year or two. Dr. McGrath predicted that there would be "at least" fifty new junior and community colleges founded annually for the next ten years—a far greater number than ever before in the history of higher education.

An analysis of the Federal statistics indicates that, last year, eighty-nine additional recognized colleges and universities were added to the official directory. At the same time, nine colleges were dropped, making a total record gain of eighty in twelve months. In 1948-49, fifty-one colleges were added, while ten were dropped, resulting in a net increase of forty. With another seventy-five additional colleges and universities expected to be added in 1950, the total gain in recognized institutions of higher learning for the last three years reached the unprecedented figure of 195.

Of the eighty-nine additional colleges and universities added to the United States Education Directory last year, forty-five were junior and community colleges, twenty-six were professional institutions, and eighteen were four-year liberal arts colleges. A comparable proportion is expected to take place in the institutions to be added to the directory this year.

According to the Office of Education, the value of college buildings, ground and equipment has increased by almost $1,000,000,000 since 1940, having risen from $2,-754,000,000 to $3,692,000,000. Since the war, the Federal Government, exclusive of the Department of Defense, donated about $300,000,000 to the colleges and universities in the form of surplus property and equipment.

The increase in enrollments in the regularly established colleges and universities has put a severe strain on the physical plant, Dr. McGrath observed. The needs for additional plant facilities have been met temporarily in most institutions by the use of surplus Federal property. However, the institutions are moving rapidly to develop additional permanent buildings.

Dr. McGrath indicated that a sample of fifty-three institutions in thirty-two states and accounting for 14 per cent of the total college enrollment, showed that permanent buildings costing $300,-000,000 had been completed or begun between September, 1945, and July, 1948. A tremendous buiding program is under way on college campuses in every part of the United States.

Mark of Democratic Society

The unparalleled growth in higher education enrollment and facilities is a concrete manifestation, Dr. McGrath said, of the fact that in a democratic society "we believe in giving our young people an opportunity to develop their individual talents for their own personal benefits and for the improvement of our society at large."

"It stands as a symbol before the world that we are not fearful of developing the intelligence of our people," Dr. McGrath added. "We believe that the more they know the better citizens they will be and the more productive members of society they will become. This extension of educational opportunities is one of the surest safeguards for the perpetuation of our liberties."

A strong system of higher education, the Commissioner suggested, would prove valuable in strengthening the elementary and secondary school programs of the country. He pointed out that higher education serves as a great source of power in the preparation of teachers for the public school system and helps "extend the frontiers of knowledge."

Copies of the higher education directory will be made available through the Superintendent of Documents.

March 20, 195

Colleges Shift From the Arts As Students Call for Science

By BENJAMIN FINE

A gradual swing away from the liberal arts and humanities is occurring on the American college and university campuses. Greater stress is being placed on the natural and applied sciences, and on professional subjects in general.

This trend began right after World War II, when large numbers of veterans flocked to the "practical" or technical courses that might help them to make a living more quickly. It gained momentum from the Korean conflict that re-emphasized the need for technically trained men.

A survey of 100 representative institutions conducted by THE NEW YORK TIMES shows that, in comparison with enrollments ten years ago, proportionately fewer students are in the liberal arts than in the technical and professional fields.

Sharp Cut In Faculty Rolls

The decline in enrollment in the last two years, with the drop anticipated for the next academic year, has cut sharply into the faculty rolls. Some institutions report they will be forced to dismiss 20 to 30 per cent of their instructors. A study of these figures indicates the most drastic cuts will be in the humanities and liberal arts. The liberal arts field has 6 per cent fewer professors this year than last. In the natural and applied sciences only 1 per cent of the faculty members were dropped, while the faculties in medical and related sciences gained 7 per cent.

College authorities report that while they can retain all their chemistry, physics and applied science professors, they must reduce the rolls of full-time professors of English, foreign languages and the humanities. Indeed, the fields of foreign languages, English and history seem to be the hardest hit. The number of students in these courses has declined, resulting in the dismissal of faculty members, or, as frequently happens, the non-replacement of those who resign, retire or leave.

Moreover, the survey indicates the colleges and universities expect in 1952-53 to have 19 per cent fewer students in the humanities, social studies and liberal arts. At the same time the natural and applied sciences expect a decrease of only 5 per cent. This will mean, of course, that the faculty members in the liberal arts once again will be cut more severely than those in the other departments.

However, the decline in the liberal arts enrollments is not universal. Some institutions report an increased interest in the humanities, with larger enrollments. This is true particularly of those institutions that have earned national reputations as centers of the liberal arts.

Even so, the over-all picture is one of young men and women more practical-minded and more interested in professional and technical fields than were those of a decade or more ago.

What has caused the recession of interest in the liberal arts? Many educators believe that the turn to technical and professional subjects is part of a gradual evolution of the role that higher education can play in present-day society. They point to the emphasis placed on technical subjects by the military services, by war-related industries and by research divisions of the Government itself, putting a premium on technical skills.

The importance of the liberal arts and the humanities does not register as effectively in the minds of many students as does the significance of "getting a job that pays a lot of money."

Typical of the responses received by THE TIMES is this statement by Dr. Colgate W. Darden Jr., president of the University of Virginia:

"I believe there has been a decrease in interest in the liberal arts during the past ten years. Technical and professional subjects appear to attract more students now than in previous years."

Dr. Darden suggests it is not certain just how much influence the growth of atomic power has had in swinging students away from the humanities, but, he says, "the growth in the opportunities for earning a living in such work has been, in my opinion, largely responsible for the increase in the number of students enrolled in the physical sciences."

Similarly, Deane W. Malott, president of Cornell University, formerly president of the University of Kansas, said enrollment figures in recent years seemed to indicate a definite trend to the technical and professional fields.

"The physical sciences have attracted greater number of students as a consequence of the recent atomic advances," he reported. "At Cornell, at least, there is a corollary in an upsurge of interest in the social sciences—partially a result of the problems posed by the leap-frog strides made in physical science."

A number of college heads pointed to the veterans' enrollment after World War II as having influenced the growth of scientific curriculums.

Reversal of Trend Seen

For example, Dr. Victor A. Coulter, Dean of the College of Liberal Arts at the University of Mississippi, said the ex-service men from 1946 to 1950 showed a decided trend toward professional curriculums. When, compared with 1941, the student body doubled in 1946, the University of Mississippi premedical enrollment quadrupled.

A spokesman for the Louisiana State University and Agricultural and Mechanical College suggested that the times apparently demanded some kind of specialization by students, or at least the students seemed to think so. For that reason, technical and professional subjects attract more students than before World War II.

That the situation may change is indicated by some of the educators. This view is held by West Virginia University: During the period immediately after the war, when the university had a large influx of veterans, there was a strong trend to technical and professional subjects, particularly in engineering and medicine. Veterans also were attracted to programs set up as preparation for careers in such fields as agriculture, business and journalism.

"At the present time," the university spokesman says, "the liberal arts subjects are holding their own with good prospects of an increase in demand."

Educators everywhere urge that students take courses in the liberal arts courses and the humanities, asserting that a thorough grounding in the liberal arts is especially important in the troubled era that confronts the world. Our democratic way of life would be strengthened, many contend, if our youth had a solid program based on the humanities and the social sciences.

W. Emerson Reck, vice president of Wittenburg College, holds that a strong liberal arts program is valuable to society because it develops in the individual the ability and the desire to achieve his highest potentialities.

In the opinion of Sister M. Honora, president of Marygrove College, Detroit, society needs a strengthening of the moral fibre of its citizens, a dissipation of a widespread ignorance of the essence of the Western culture and of the place of this culture in a united world.

'V. B. Alexander, vice president of Antioch College, remarks that "scientists and technicians without a liberal education, turned out in too great numbers, may be positively dangerous in the long run, because wise use of our technological and scientific apparatus depends on a broad and informed view of history and culture."

At no time has there been greater need for human understanding, observes Dr. T. E. Strevey, dean of the University of Southern California. Holding it is important that we understand our own heritage and that of others, Dr. Strevey adds that a liberal arts program with its stress on human understanding and with a positive approach to essential values, is of the greatest importance to society.

One of the most pressing problems in the world of learning, according to Dr. Laurence J. McGinley, president of Fordham University, is to provide in better fashion for the dissemination of knowledge at an accelerated rate. He notes that we are piling discovery on discovery and releasing forces that defy the imagination and challenge man's ability to control them. He adds:

"Those who are charged with the heavy responsibility of using these new forces for right ends must have well-rounded personalities, characterized by wide intellectual interests and a deep and broad human sympathy. They must have a sense of the eternal verities, the capacity to distinguish, to see things as they are, and in their relations."

Vice President Nils Y. Wessell of Tufts College believes the liberal arts are important in the education of all students as "a way of life and the fortress we are preparing to defend."

The president of Tulane University, contending that universities, and in particular liberal arts colleges, are a principal source of democratic ideals, says students with a good liberal arts education are the least likely to become associated with communism.

The 'Terribly Normal' Class of '52

By PENN KIMBALL

THE class of 1952, taking leave of the sheltering elms during these bright June days, looks on the world with an air of sad resignation and incurable hope. Neither mood deserves to be mistaken for the capital sins so often ascribed to alternating generations of American youth. This year's senior is no starry-eyed idealist. He's not a curled-lip cynic either. He is, in most respects, just terribly normal—a condition, all the same, his terribly normal elders may find upsetting to contemplate.

Military service is uppermost in the mind of the average boy graduating from college this month, although the tension and jitters that went with former draft uncertainties have subsided. The draft is accepted, with no show of zeal, as part of "the system," but the senior is at least relieved to know where he stands. He appears, to the interested observer, to be adjusted, fatalistic perhaps, about the immediate prospect of spending the next two or three years of his life in uniform.

He seems, furthermore, to be looking right through those years as pioneers might let their gaze skip past a desolate foreground to fix on purple mountains beyond. The important departure from this analogy is that the graduating student appears to be staring stark, straight ahead, rather than upward. He talks about exploring plateaus, not peaks. His life goals —even as expressed by those who do not identify themselves as "draft bait" —are modest and practical, though not the shallow and single-minded pursuit of economic security that many of us off campus have been led to believe.

In terms of long-range but somewhat unadventuresome objectives, then, the class of '52 might be described as self-confident and optimistic. It is self-confident as regards individual ability to surmount the knotty problems of starting late on both a career and a family, both of which are denied the majority right away by the pressure of circumstances. It is optimistic that the world situation in general will somehow work itself out, at least in no worse fashion than the era of strain and simmering conflict which is all that the class of '52 has ever known anyway throughout the thinking span of its whole adolescence.

For the class of 1952, be it recalled, was born two decades ago in the darkest years of economic depression. Pearl Harbor, in this instance, fell upon the consciousness of fifth-grade children. As high school students, this generation watched the sun break out briefly,

only to be eclipsed almost at once by post-war ideological strife. Then, with the close of sophomore year in college, came Korea.

IN the memory of these youngsters, only Franklin D. Roosevelt and Harry S. Truman have ever been President; the New Deal or Fair Deal is all they have ever seen in Washington. Social security, big government, foreign aid, the cold war against communism—all of these are as commonplace, and as taken for granted, as T-shirts or crew cuts. A lot of seniors will be voting for the first time this fall, but the issues of their formative age have largely been decided, it seems, without the help of passionate debate in the quads.

This strikes one as odd when viewed against the American tradition of rebellion and revolt on the campus—one recalls the "lost" generations and hotbloods of the Twenties and Thirties who talked in contemptuous tones of the way previous generations had fumbled the ball. Panty raids and spring riots notwithstanding, this crop of seniors rates itself on the phlegmatic side, blaming the hovering "dead spot" of future military duties for casting a pall on their boyish enthusiasms.

Whatever the reason, the college visitor finds the class of '52 sober without being earnest, quizzical rather than questioning, pretty strong-minded and pretty sophisticated. It is, on the whole, a very likable lot, disarmingly frank and surprisingly urbane. If this generation nurses a complex at all its vice is an almost excessive balance, an overpowering care not to commit its emotions too deeply to anything.

These generalities, rashly advanced on a topic always hot to the touch, are based on a few talks with some representative members of the graduating class at Columbia College. The New York City school last week awarded degrees to some 527 young survivors of a class which arrived on Morningside Heights four years ago at the same time as a brand-new university president named Dwight David Eisenhower.

"I DON'T care how much they talk to you about geology and geography," Eisenhower declared to the class of '52 that first September, "but I hope the day never goes by that you don't have some fun, that you don't enjoy life. * * * I know what it means to a human being to believe that he has done something that day that is worth while."

The advice,

making allowances for changing times and circumstances, seems to have stuck in the minds of the class. And the recipients, making allowances for the local peculiarities which exist in all institutions of learning, are possibly not too far off the broad pattern of college seniors elsewhere. "On the whole, I suppose our bunch is quite ordinary," says Columbia's 1952 class president, Ira Hoffman. "but we think of ourselves as a little more open-minded, though a lot more narrow in ambition, than when we came in. We have a good sense of humor; most of us don't take anything too seriously and all of us are wondering when we'll ever get set."

COLLEGE administrators point out that these seniors are not just a little younger than the ex-G. I.'s who passed through the educational system just ahead of them (only eighteen Columbia seniors this year were still studying under the G. I. Bill). Gone with the old khakis and new babies, says a Columbia dean, is "an emotional lift and buoyancy on the campus. In comparison to the returned veteran, these 21-year-olds seem singularly lacking in high spirits and enthusiasm."

Faculty members also report a big change in their classes: "Getting back to normal has meant finding once more that our students lack experience by which to link their classroom courses with the outside world. The class of '52 has been more insulated, more passive in the aggregate than its immediate predecessors."

What do Columbia seniors say of themselves? A composite impression of their main spheres of interest might produce this:

THE DRAFT

"Most of us expect to lose our educational deferments

ALMA MATER

and revert to 1-A in the draft at the end of June. But nobody is sure. A lot of us really don't believe in educational deferments on principle, but as long as they're offered you can't blame us for trying all the angles that are within the rules. Our dope is that the local boards are waiting for us to graduate to stick us at the top of their list, so, if there are any commission deals kicking around, we want to get in on them. Military service is just so much time out of our lives. We want to get it over with—as painlessly as possible. We're all thinking and planning about what we'll do when we get out.

"Nobody thinks our group is having it any rougher than other generations before. The hardest thing on us is that the draft has been hanging over our heads for so long; it hit the others before they thought too much about it. After we found out we could finish college, we more or less took it in stride. Now we are operating back on a week-to-week basis again, especially those who are aiming for a professional school in the fall."

THE WAR

"No, we don't think in terms of combat during our military hitch. Maybe we just don't want to think about it that way. The truth is that the war in Korea seems very remote; very few in our circle of friends have been touched by it. A lot of us, those without older brothers maybe, can't remember much about the last war, when it comes to that, except as Boy Scouts in salvage drives. Our own impression is that things will continue to muddle along much as they have—for another ten or fifteen years. It's all so much bigger than we are."

MARRIAGE

"Our generation of girls is ready for marriage, but the boys don't feel very marriage-minded with no income and a few years in the Army staring them in the face. A few seniors who have been going steady for a long time are getting married after graduation. One reason is that the girls are saying: 'It's June—or never.' It's quite a problem. Some of us didn't invite our best girls to Senior Week; it just didn't seem fair to keep them on the string.

"We want to get married all right, but we want to do it

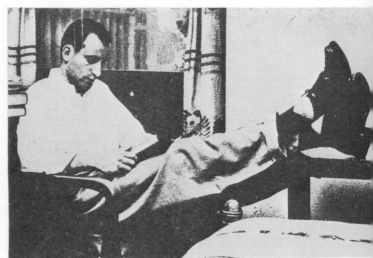

CLASS PRESIDENT Ira Hoffman, Brooklyn, N. Y., has been accepted for medical school next fall and expects his draft service to be deferred. He hopes to be a psychiatrist

NAVAL RESERVE commission was earned along with bachelor's degree by Philip Sh— Lawrence, Mass., who also worked his way through school. Active duty lasts three years

when we can afford to be definitely thinking of a family. We couldn't take the step now without depending on help from the girl's family or our own parents. A lot of us don't want to do it that way. So we refuse to get serious and try to play things so we don't get tied up. When the time comes, there's a lot to think about besides an emotional kick. A guy has to think of his wife and family as a business asset, too, and analyze his girl's good points and bad points from that point of view as well as considering looks and intelligence."

JOBS

"The minority who got their military service out of the way between high school and college are sitting pretty, of

course. But the big companies seem willing to hire the draft eligibles, even if only for a month or two. The offers range from $250 to $350 a month, including the training period, but we try to look behind that starting salary. Sure, we'd like to latch on to something before the draft catches up with us, but we're looking for opportunity, too.

"WE don't want the company where we think we might get lost in the shuffle. We don't want to get bogged down with too much emphasis on seniority. We want to be able to advance as fast and as far as our ability will let us. We want something with a little satisfaction, a sense of performing a service in it, if we

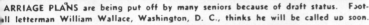
ARRIAGE PLANS are being put off by many seniors because of draft status. Football letterman William Wallace, Washington, D. C., thinks he will be called up soon.

OB MARKET is strong for this year's crop of college graduates. Aldo Ippolito, North arrytown, N. Y., served overseas as a G.I. and was business manager of The Jester.

can, something that gets some respect in our home community.

"We're not indifferent to the dough—far from it. But just money or fancy security plans aren't what we're after. Maybe there isn't much we can do about changing the world. Nobody can stop you from working at something you like, though, and making a contribution to your own small group or profession and winning some recognition that way."

If politics, religion, international affairs, Government corruption and similar subjects are not reported here in eloquent, youthful phrases, the reason offered is that the college seniors of 1952 do not volunteer to declaim in that way on those issues. That is

not the same thing as saying the class of '52 is indifferent to intellect, for conversation in dorms at Columbia is liberally sprinkled with Plato, T. S. Eliot and other learned references to the compulsory course in Humanities A. And the evidence is strong that the pendulum is swinging away from purely sensate values among our college kids, tabloid accounts to the contrary notwithstanding.

THE night before classes ended this year, it is true, a noisy crowd of Columbia undergraduates besieged the girls' dormitories of near-by Barnard College by the light of torches and fireworks. After carrying off assorted bits of underwear (most of them

thrown out the windows by co-operative females) the rioters started fires in public waste-baskets, set off stench bombs and cannon crackers, demonstrating for two hours before fifteen radio cars, fifty patrolmen and a police emergency truck carried the battle. An eminent columnist, surveying the wreckage, concluded that this form of spring madness was probably a throwback to the days when knights wore delicate tokens from their ladies on the outside of their armor.

Columbia seniors, more realistically, mark the occasion as a testimonial to the suggestive power of mass-circulation magazines, and contend that the crowd was swelled by a lot of neighborhood kids. The fact of the matter, they report, is that very few young collegians showed much taste for direct encounter with Barnard girls, and contented themselves with shouting and singing. "In other years we let off steam by throwing water containers and lighted paper out the window," says Class President Hoffman. "We're a little ashamed of the panty raid; it was so unoriginal."

The moral tone of the class of '52, according to Columbia's dean of students, Nicholas McKnight, has been "pretty high and pretty sober, with no indication of an eat-drink-and-be-merry attitude." Senior Winston Fliess, a pitcher on the varsity baseball team and an active fraternity man, observes: "We watched the G. I.'s in the classes ahead, and I think the reaction of a lot of us was in the direction of being a little less crude on dates and around the fraternity house. I don't know if our morals are any better than theirs, but at least the fellows are more discreet now. We don't want to be Boy Scouts, but we don't want to be hoodlums either."

ALTHOUGH Columbia has seen its share of political ferment through the years, the class of '52 by its own testimony is pretty apathetic, especially for a Presidential year. "These fellows have a lot more confidence, maybe, in their elders than our generation ever showed," a professor remarks. "Politics seems to touch very few." Max Frankel, former undergraduate editor of The Spectator, the campus paper, says "I think perhaps we are not quite as

conscious as college graduates may once have been of becoming leaders in society. Politically, I don't believe this class will swing the national balance very much, either way."

A strike against the college administration by C. I. O.-organized cafeteria and maintenance workers this spring, an event which in former times might have aroused Columbia undergraduates to a boil, was regarded with bland indifference by all except tiny minorities aligned on each side of the dispute. Not a lecture was missed; not a class postponed. Bill Wallace, a strapping football tackle with a B average, thinks young folks "are as interested in liberal causes as they ever were, but they worry more now whether their own economic position as a college man is going to keep its value."

WALLACE, who expects to be drafted soon, talked to representatives of twenty companies this spring about his own economic future. Five small concerns backed away when they heard about his draft status, and he wasn't interested in four others. Of the other eleven, nine made concrete job offers, and several took him on expense-paid tours of their home plants.

He didn't take the highest bid, or the surest future. "I think if a man has ability and wants to work he doesn't have to worry too much about security. He can make his own security." He chose a training program in insurance salesmanship, because "I think I'll get the feeling that I'm producing something that might do somebody some good, and I like the idea of being my own boss."

If this sounds unusual, there's James Hurley, who has had lots of job offers because he performed his military service after finishing high school and also acquired some

business experience running the student laundry agency at Columbia. Hurley nearly signed up with a carpet company at $300 a month, then backed down at the last minute. "I decided I would rather do what I want to than just make money, and the thing that I'm interested in is prison reform."

LAWRENCE GROSSMAN, former managing editor of The Spectator, hopes to make law school this fall if he isn't drafted. "I want to be a good lawyer and a credit to the profession, but I don't feel a driving ambition to get to the top. This class may possibly feel frustrated by our inability to do anything about the big picture. It's a big job for us just to get ourselves and our own family and our own career going; it's too frightening a proposition to try to think in terms of tackling problems of a lot of other people, too. We're all looking for a peaceful life and a quiet life, within the bounds of our personal philosophy, among people we like. We figure we'll make our contribution to soci .y in the way we lead our inc. .idual lives."

There it is, the class of '52, already sounding a little like its own twenty-fifth reunion, perhaps. So hard-headed, so analytical, so down-to-earth and, very possibly, feeling a trifle alone and abandoned. Safe now in the wide, wide world.

$350,000,000 Research Aid Irks Colleges by 'Imbalance'

By BENJAMIN FINE

American colleges and universities will spend a record total of more than $350,000,000 for research projects during this academic year. Most of this money—about $300,000,000—has been granted by the Federal Government. Business foundations and individual donors are providing the rest.

Ninety per cent of the money is earmarked for research in the physical or biological sciences. Only a fraction is set aside for research in the humanities. Virtually none of the Government's funds will be devoted to the social sciences or liberal arts.

This "imbalance" is causing concern among educational leaders. They see in the continued trend toward the physical sciences a gradual weakening of the humanities and note an emphasis on applied rather than basic research.

These views were elicited in a study conducted by THE NEW YORK TIMES dealing with the research programs conducted by the American institutions of higher learning. Detailed information was obtained through a sampling of fifty representative colleges and universities. This was supplemented with data provided by the American Council on Education and the National Science Foundation.

Campus research in this country has grown at a phenomenal rate during the last decade. In 1940 higher education reported that it spent about $20,000,000 a year for all research. Only a small amount came from the Federal Government. Research grants have risen 1,500 per cent since then.

For 1952-53 the Federal Government has allocated $340,000,000 for scientific research and development at nonprofit institutions. This represents an increase of $40,000,000 over the previous year.

Funds administered by the Department of Defense now make up more than 50 per cent of the total, with the Atomic Energy Commission following with 35 per cent.

The Federal Security Agency provides 6 per cent and the Department of Agriculture 5 per cent of the total funds.

Spokesmen for the National Science Foundation estimated that of the $340,000,000 granted by the Federal Government to nonprofit institutions for research about $300,000,000 would be allocated to colleges and universities.

Of this amount, about half is under the direct supervision of the educational institutions, while the other $150,000,000 is earmarked for large-scale projects away from the campus but under educational direction. In the latter category are several atomic research centers.

Although the amount provided by business, industry and foundations cannot be determined with accuracy, THE TIMES study indicates that $50,000,000 to $75,000,000 is spent annually on research by the colleges. Industry is offering more research funds today than ever before, but it cannot keep pace with the huge sums provided by the Government.

Half of Income Provided

The American Council on Education has appointed a special committee on institutional research policy, headed by Dr. Virgil M. Hancher, president of the State University of Iowa, to study the question of Federally sponsored research and determine what can be done to counteract the emphasis on the physical sciences.

A preliminary investigation showed that grants for research from the Federal Government now constitute, in some institutions, more than half of their total operating income from all sources.

"It is becoming clear that these vast funds for research are having significant effects, often unrecognized, upon the procedures and objectives of the institutions that receive them," the committee warned.

"The concentration of support on the physical sciences, to the virtual exclusion of the humanities and social sciences, may distort existing relationships among the various disciplines with regard to undergraduate and graduate instruction as well as to research."

Dr. Arthur S. Adams, president

of the American Council, observing that concern was not over the amount of money spent for research itself, which was regarded as worth while and necessary, said:

"The real issue is that in our judgment the humanities and the social sciences are not receiving an adequate proportion of this support."

If more money is being spent on the physical sciences than on the social sciences, he continued, the former at once receives top priority in institutional attention, draining support from the latter.

Effect on Future Teachers

Another danger, said Dr. Adams, is a shift in the proportion of personnel trained in research activities among the various disciplines. Young people who will be the future teachers are largely prepared in the graduate schools.

If the preponderance of financial support in the graduate schools, including fellowships, is in the physical sciences, Dr. Adams reasoned, the number trained for the social sciences and the humanities will be limited.

"This is the reason why even now it is difficult to find enough highly competent teachers to round out the departments," he went on. "All teachers may be in short supply when we need them ten years hence. If the present imbalance continues we shall have a particularly serious shortage of competent teachers in the important areas of the humanities and social sciences.

"These are matters of national significance which merit the careful attention of educators and of those who direct the research policies of the Federal Government."

Educational leaders believe too much emphasis is put on applied research. Of the $340,000,000 spent by the Government on educational research $173,000,000 is listed for applied research and $71,000,000 for basic research. And while the money for applied research increased nearly $30,000,000 from 1951 to 1952 the amount for basic research decreased more than $4,000,000.

Role of Basic Research

The universities have traditionally been the source of basic research in the United States, Dr. Alan T. Waterman, director of the National Science Foundation, declared.

Warning universities against committing a large share of their research and their staff resources to applied work, especially in the standard scientific subjects, he said:

"The growing imbalance between applied and basic research and its effect upon our educational institutions are of concern to the National Science Foundation and other Federal and private agencies, as well as the universities.

"No nation can afford to neglect basic research, since it is the source of knowledge from which come the great forward steps not only in weapons but also in medicine, agriculture and technology in general. It is the responsibility in accepting Federal support to work out an appropriate balance between applied and basic programs, so that basic research and the training of young scientists will not suffer."

College and university presidents are disturbed over the emphasis on applied research, as well as the dearth of research funds for the liberal arts.

For example, Princeton University spent $2,647,651 for organized research during the fiscal year ended June 30, 1952. Of this $136,526 came from endowment, $235,288 from the Eugene Higgins Trust, $709,063 from corporations, foundations and other sources, and $1,566,774 from Government-aided projects.

Low Social Sciences Ratio

Research in the natural and applied sciences took $2,224,029, while $423,622 went for the social sciences and humanities. One-fifth of Princeton's income was Government reimbursement for research in the natural sciences.

Similarly, at the University of Illinois, with $8,000,000 spent for research, a ratio of $7 to natural sciences for $1 to the social studies existed. Provost C. R. Griffith warned that funds for the natural sciences were out of balance with those for the broad area of human relations.

At the University of Minnesota research in the natural sciences took $5,251,913, while the social sciences received $159,974. Dean Theodore C. Blegen of the graduate school said:

"The neglect of the humanities is one of our most serious educational and research problems—serious because of the importance of history, philosophy, literature and the arts in interpreting for our generation the values and heritages of democratic civilization."

At Boston University, where $2,000,000 was spent for research in the last year, the emphasis is upon natural sciences. Dean Chester M. Alter of the Graduate School urged more funds for basic research in economics, sociology, anthropology, political science and human realtions.

For Wider Sponsorship

"To right the imbalance," he said, "we need a recognition on the part of business and industry that basic research in humanities and social sciences may contribute to the future solution of some of the most important problems facing their organizations, just as their technical problems have been solved in the past by scientific research."

Dr. Leonard Carmichael, president of Tufts College, noted an upward trend in support from foundations and industry for research activities. However, most of the money spent by the college for research, chiefly in the natural sciences, came from Government agencies. Of $998,855 devoted to research during the last academic year $618,884 went to natural sciences.

The University of Vermont allocated $320,693 for research in the natural sciences and $3,379 in liberal arts and humanities. Dr. Charles E. Braun, coordinator of research, believed the humanities, history, languages and philosophy needed more research funds.

At the University of Washington, $1,775,000 has been spent on research in the natural sciences this year and $225,000 in the social sciences.

Marquette University has a budget of $143,247 for research, all of which is allocated for the natural sciences.

The University of Florida reported that it would spend $5,000,000 for research, two-thirds of which would come from thirteen Government agencies. Only $75,000 will be available for social science research—$50,000 for the Bureau of Economic Research and $25,000 in education.

At Cornell University, where the 1952-53 funds amount to $16,350,000, about 1,250 projects are under way, Dr. Theodore P. Wright, vice president for research, observed that while social science research was coming into better balance with research in the other sciences, the humanities continued to lack support.

From New York University the suggestion was made by James W. Armsey, assistant to the chancellor, that an active campaign be undertaken to educate future donors, governmental and private, to the necessity of increasing knowledge of human beings and the ways in which their loyalties to high values may be developed.

A vast majority of educators believe that more attention should be paid to research in the liberal arts, the humanities and the social studies because democracy needs moral as well as physical strength.

Classified Allocations for College Research

The following table shows the amount of money allocated in 1952-53 for research in representative colleges and universities in the United States. The funds are divided according to whether they come from the Federal Government, states, industry, foundations or other sources. The amounts for natural science and the social sciences and humanities are listed, as reported by the institutions:

COLLEGES	Federal Government	State	Industry	Foundations Others	TOTAL	Natural Sciences	Social Sciences Humanities
Alabama Polytechnic Inst....	$108,267	$11,522	$52,028	$1,558,351	$1,730,170	$1,715,170	$15,000
Amherst	75,561	......	......	80,806	156,367	146,367	10,000
University of Arkansas......	850,000	700,000	......	50,000	1,600,000	1,434,000	166,000
University of Boston	......	......	......	......	1,998,316	......	......
Bucknell University	16,000	......	......	2,500	18,500	18,500	......
California Inst. of Technology.	2,000,000	......	......	......	5,000,000	......	......
University of Cincinnati......	572,000	......	......	985,000	1,557,000	1,497,000	60,000
Clark University	99,819	......	7,500	22,775	130,094	43,574	86,619
Colgate University	6,000	......	4,000	35,000	45,000	16,000	29,000
Cornell University	10,425,000	3,475,000	1,013,000	1,437,000	16,350,000	14,850,000	1,150,000
Duke University	690,934	......	46,951	324,566	1,062,181	849,745	212,486
University of Florida........	3,300,000	......	......	1,700,000	5,000,000	4,925,000	75,000
Fordham University	168,654	......	15,341	19,086	203,081	152,846	50,235
University of Illinois	3,704,219	3,301,121	......	1,410,909	8,416,249	7,213,928	1,202,321
University of Kansas.........	......	300,000	......	942,833	1,242,833	1,135,188	107,645
University of Kentucky.......	......	......	......	......	1,750,000	1,450,000	300,000
Lafayette University	......	11,000	12,000	42,000	75,000	......	......
Marquette University	18,256	......	......	18,336	143,247	143,247	......
Michigan State	175,077	......	374,388	46,393	595,858	536,258	59,600
University of Michigan.......	6,889,616	......	517,703	2,059,003	9,466,322	7,024,567	2,441,755
University of Minnesota......	3,531,811	727,744	391,666	760,665	5,411,886	5,251,912	159,974
New York University........	2,415,000	......	......	2,850,000	5,265,000	......	......
University of North Carolina.	192,684	160,795	......	94,918	448,399	285,559	162,839
Northwestern University	1,095,232	......	313,815	1,754,814	3,163,862	2,430,038	733,823
University of Pennsylvania...	1,817,902	......	......	1,668,092	3,485,994	3,082,677	403,317
Princeton University	1,566,774	......	......	1,080,577	2,647,651	2,224,029	423,622
Rensselaer Polytechnic Inst...	450,000	......	225,000	75,000	750,000	750,000	......
University of Rhode Island...	371,763	......	40,659	2,325	414,747	414,747	......
University of St. Louis.......	251,000	......	9,000	140,000	400,000	400,000	......
University of Texas..........	1,272,204	......	......	911,465	2,183,669	1,830,147	353,522
Tufts College	793,000	......	205,000	......	998,855	618,884	376,371
Union College	......	......	......	......	189,638	189,638	......
University of Vermont.......	233,579	42,218	12,962	35,312	324,071	320,693	3,378
University of Virginia........	583,013	14,000	......	31,685	633,710	611,260	......
Stanford University	3,182,964	......	368,516	326,542	3,878,022	1,031,048	389,448
University of Washington....	1,321,000	115,000	......	543,000	2,000,000	1,775,000	225,000
University of Wisconsin......	991,989	2,027,931	......	1,198,604	4,218,524	85%	15%

College Endowment Income

The investment income of the endowment funds used to run fifteen of the nation's major colleges is, on the average, now coming more from common stocks than from any one other form of investment, according to a survey by Vance, Sanders & Co. Of the $800,000,000 of investment money held by these big colleges, an average of 44.7 per cent is invested in common stock and 41.2 per cent in bonds, 6.45 per cent in preferred stocks and 5.73 per cent in real estate mortgages. Harvard's fund of more than $300,000,000 is about 49 per cent in common stocks and about 44.6 per cent in bonds. Trinity College has about 68 per cent of its $7,000,000 fund in common stocks and about 26.2 per cent cent in bonds. Oberlin, with an investment fund of about $27,000,000, has the biggest holdings of preferred stock, notably about 17.5 per cent. Harvard is getting a return of about 5 per cent on common stock holdings, compared with about 2.7 per cent from the fixed-income section of the account. As a consequence, less than half of the Harvard portfolio is producing about 64 per cent of the income.'

COSTS AT COLLEGE REACH NEW PEAK

Loss of the Gifted Feared as Tuition Tips $1,000 and the Total $2,000 a Year

GRANTS HELP STUDENTS

But Scholarships and Loans Have Not Caught Up With Need, Educators Observe

By BENJAMIN FINE

It costs more to go to college today than ever before.

Tuition rates, fairly stable until World War II, have just about doubled in the last ten years. Room, board and general expenses are at record highs.

As colleges and universities reopen this month, students will face another round of tuition increases. The officials do not like this upward spiral any more than do the parents—but they are helpless in the face of their own rising costs.

A sampling of typical colleges and universities, made by The New York Times, shows that the better known institutions now charge $600 to $1,000 for a year's tuition. It is not uncommon for the engineering, medical or other technical and professional schools to charge $1,000 or more.

Even the municipal and state-supported colleges are increasing their rates. Frequently the colleges, both public and private, impose "a general tax" on the students to serve as a catch-all for higher fees:

Fear of Excluding Talent

Many college and university officials are afraid that the high fees will keep talented students away. And they are convinced that if the costs go any higher, economics rather than talent will determine who attends college.

Some colleges are beginning to expand their scholarship programs to help needy students. Business and industry also are offering more scholarships and awards. The National Merit Scholarship Corporation, set up last week with a $20,500,000 grant from the Ford Foundation and Carnegie Corporation, is an important step in this direction.

But educators recognize that thus far only the surface has been scratched. It is estimated that each year 250,000 gifted high school graduates do not enter college because of the high costs.

The United States Office of Education recently reported that from 1940 to 1955 tuition rates in 120 publicly controlled institutions rose from an average of $70 to $132, or 89 per cent. The comparable tuition rise for students in seventy-six privately controlled institutions was from $328 to $599, or 83 per cent.

Whereas fifteen years ago the average student could plan to attend college at a total cost of about $1,000 a year, today he must figure on close to $2,000. Attendance at women's colleges is even more costly.

Mitigated by Aid to Students

This fall some Ivy League colleges will charge $1,000 for tuition. For example, the rate at Princeton University is $1,000. Last year it was $850, and in 1949-50 it was $700.

The total cost to a student at Princeton in 1946 was about $1,400. This year it will be $2,150. The university has a program of scholarship help, student loans and employment. More than 35 per cent of the undergraduates received help from such sources last year.

Yale increased its fee this year from $800 to $1,000. In 1949 it was $600. In the last five years the room and board charges increased from $700 to $800. The minimum budget for a student, excluding travel, will be $2,200 this year. Ten years ago it totaled $1,343.

A typical New England institution—Amherst College—reports that its tuition has increased from $450 to $700 in ten years. This is the way the student's money will be spent this fall, compared with the way it was spent five and ten years ago:

	1954-55	1949-50	1944-45
Tuition	$700	$550	$450
Room	225	200	200
Board	400	340	320
Fees	95	60	50
Personal	350	350	300
Total Cost	$1,770	$1,500	$1,320

While the fees have gone up, the Amherst scholarship program is four times as large this fall as it was ten years ago. Before World War II, $50,000 was awarded in scholarship aid each year. This year the aid will exceed $200,000.

From all indications the colleges will have larger student bodies in the next decade than in the last. But a greater number of the gifted may be "deprived" of a higher education.

"Good students are being frozen out and their numbers will increase unless remedies are found," said Dr. John F. Morse, director of admissions at Rensselaer Polytechnic Institute. Tuition there in 1949-50 was $700; a year ago it was $800, and this fall it is $1,000.

Dr. Morse suggested two possible remedies: Scholarship funds must be increased sharply and immediately; students and parents must recognize that a college education is not a four-year expense but a lifetime investment to be financed over a long period.

Cornell University has raised its tuition this fall from $750 to $850, compared with $400 in 1944-45. The total cost for a four-year education there is estimated at $8,800, compared with $5,200 ten years ago.

G. I. Bill, Expiring After Twelve Years, Has Been, It Is Agreed, an Outstanding Success

By BENJAMIN FINE

On Wednesday the G. I. Bill of Rights set-up for veterans of World War II on June 22, 1944, expires. In twelve years, nearly 8,000,000 ex-servicemen attended school and college, took on-the-job training or worked on farms. The whole program cost the Government $14,500,-000,000.

Educators began last week to take stock of this great educational venture. At one time college campuses were swamped with veterans. A total of 2,200,000 veterans took advantage of the G. I. Bill to go to college or graduate school, with up to $500 in tuition fees, and subsistence grants ranging from $75 to $110 a month from the Government.

There were misgivings at first. But the educators soon found that the veterans were characterized by maturity and strong motivation. The veterans were substantially older than their civilian classmates. And they wanted to make up for lost time.

Perhaps the situation at Yale University is typical of the institutions that found their campuses overcrowded with ex-servicemen. Some 15,000 veterans attended Yale in the twelve years. A maximum of 5,900 were enrolled during the spring term of 1947. Yale found that scholastically the vets did better work than the other students. But, as Richard R. Shank, head of the veterans' affairs program at Yale puts it, the University benefited also from the rise in standards achieved by the veterans.

Benefits Conferred

The G. I. Bill, educators generally agree, opened avenues of educational opportunities to wide numbers of veterans qualified in every way except financially. It did so without directly subsidizing schools. Nor were the administrative controls too objectionable. Many veterans continued their education at the graduate level. This, of course, increased the country's supply of research scientists and Ph.D. scholars to teach as well as to man posts in private industry.

The G. I. Bill discounted the theory, held in some quarters, that only those able to afford it should take graduate studies. It has given impetus to a fellowship program sponsored by industry and the Federal Government.

The Columbia University campus probably had the largest number of G. I.'s of any institution. Some 85,000 veterans have attended Columbia since the program began. The peak year was reached in 1947 when 17,733 ex-servicemen were enrolled, comprising 74 per cent of the male student body.

Contrary to expectations, few veterans gave up before completing their educational objectives. The ease and completeness with which the ex-G. I.'s fitted into the academic environment proved heartening.

"Veterans seem to be more interested in public affairs and world problems, and in equipping themselves for sound citizenship," one official summed up. "They have brought to our campuses an atmosphere of serious purpose and a sense of responsibility."

The G. I. program is bound to have lasting results. It has trained 238,000 teachers, 450,000 engineers, 180,000 doctors and nurses, 113,000 scientists and 36,000 clergymen.

There is little doubt that the veterans brought a sense of maturity previously unknown to college campuses. This view was best expressed by Dr. Herold C. Hunt, Under Secretary of the Department of Health, Education and Welfare and former Chicago school superintendent and Harvard University professor.

High Level of Achievement

"Having shared the experience and responsibility of winning World War II," he said, "many veterans came to college with a deeper sense of values than those who came directly from high schools. Their seriousness brought good scholarship and a high level of achievement. The progress they are now making in their peacetime pursuits confirms this observation.

"As a former superintendent of schools, I have observed the benefits of the G. I. Bill of Rights at first hand. I feel that inestimable good has come from educational and training opportunities the bill made possible."

According to Dr. Henry T. Heald, president of New York University who recently has been named as president of the Ford Foundation, the G. I. Bill was one of the most enlightened pieces of legislation enacted by Congress in the wake of any military effort in which the nation has been engaged.

Educators in all parts of the country, in almost every type of institution, speak highly of the G. I. program. Dean Fred W. Ajax, coordinator of veterans' affairs at Georgia Institute of Technology, says, "The veterans' program was worth every cent spent by the Government, both to the individual veteran and to the country. Federal aid to higher education in peacetime is more than justified by the results of the federally sponsored G. I. Bill."

Under Handicaps

Not only were the G. I.'s ambitious and eager to complete their courses, but many worked under tremendous handicaps. Some 600,000 disabled veterans received vocational rehabilitation, some of them in colleges. A striking example is the Tulane University veteran who had lost both hands and one eye but completed an architecture course with an outstanding record.

Many institutions created veterans' divisions. Brown University set up a separate college for ex-servicemen in the fall of 1946 for men whose academic background was not up to those of the regular students. All, however, who had the equivalent of a high school education had been told by Uncle Sam that they could go to college. College gave them this chance to show that acquired maturity and greater incentive to learn could offset any deficiencies of previous training.

They took the same course under the same faculty and with the same grading system as the students of the regular college. The only differences were that their classes and laboratories were held in the late afternoon and evening (thus utilizing the Brown plan during off-hour periods) and they did not participate in any extra-curricular activities. They made good. Most of them were able to transfer successfully to the college proper.

Although in the main the G. I. program did an excellent job, in its early years some unscrupulous promotors made financial killings. They organized phony trade schools or other institutes to get a share of the free tuition funds. Some G. I.'s, in these schools, spent Government money on ballroom dancing, toying with photography or taking up horseback riding. The Government cracked down in 1948, when the Veterans Administration tightened up its requirements.

Now the Korean veterans, 350,000 strong, are on the nation's campuses and in the classrooms—not a large number, in comparison with their predecessors. But they are being made welcome by educators impressed with the success of the World War II veterans.

July 22, 1956

COLLEGE CHEATING CALLED CUSTOMARY

Special to The New York Times.

CHICAGO, March 5—A college professor said today that systematic cheating appeared to be the "custom rather than the exception' at many major universities in the nation.

Philip E. Jacob, director of college collateral courses and summer school at the University of Pennsylvania, reported the results of surveys in a paper before the twelfth national conference on Higher Education.

His report was extracted from his newly published book, "Changing Values in College."

He said that the college graduate held high respect for sincerity, honesty and loyalty but was not inclined to censure those "who choose to depart from these canons."

"For instance," he said, "standards are generally low in regard to academic honesty, systematic cheating being the custom rather than the exception at many major institutions."

He said frequent cheating "is admitted by 40 per cent or more at a large number of colleges, often with no apology or sense of wrongdoing."

He pictured college students as "gloriously contended, unabashedly self-centered, with no resolve to win others to their views, and quite often, politically irresponsible and, quite often, politically illiterate as well."

The conference is sponsored by the Association for Higher Education, a department of the National Education Association.

Study Discloses Faculty Salaries

The average salary for the nation's college faculty members is $5,243. This is disclosed in the most comprehensive survey yet undertaken of salary schedules in the nation's colleges and universities made by the research division of the National Education Association.

The report, published in the current N. E. A.'s quarterly research bulletin, shows that, on the average, municipal universities pay the highest salaries, with state universities running second. Larger colleges pay more than the smaller ones. Public institutions pay more than non-public institutions.

A geographical breakdown shows faculty salaries vary considerably from one part of the country to another. The highest average, $5,758, is paid in the Far West. The lowest, $4,799, is paid in the Southeast. This difference of nearly $1,000 shows up in all ranks of teachers and in all types of institutions.

Limited Opportunities

Though administrative positions in the $25,000 to $30,000 bracket are not unknown, and salaries of $10,000 or more for straight teaching during the academic year can be cited, over-all financial opportunities for teaching and administrative personnel are limited. The

average college president receives $11,314; the average full professor, $7,076; the average associate professor, $5,731, the average assistant professor, $4,921 and the average instructor, $4,087.

The shortage of competent teachers can be charged to a number of contributing causes, but, the N. E. A. bulletin notes, insufficient salaries stand as the most significant and important cause. Employing officials lack the necessary funds to enter the free competitive market to obtain the services of superior teachers in the numbers needed by today's educational system.

Devoted Teachers

The investigation further discloses that many of the higher educational institutions are forced to take unfair advantage of the devotion of their staff members. Many superior teachers remain in the classroom year after year because of their sincere belief in the worth of their efforts and dedication to their work, the report points out. In many other instances, however, mediocre and even inferior work in the classroom is condoned simply because funds are not available to attract and hold superior teachers.

The study is based upon replies from 730 degree-granting institutions as well as from 258 junior colleges. B. F.

COLLEGE IS CALLED NO MARRIAGE BAR

Special to The New York Times.

BOSTON, June 24—The high attrition rate at women's colleges was attributed tonight to women's fear of missing marriage.

Dr. David Riesman of Philadelphia, a social scientist, presented the view in a speech to more than 800 delegates to the seventy-fifth annual convention of the American Association of University Women.

In spite of "good statistical evidence" that women can earn their degrees and still find a husband, a third or more drop out after the freshman year, Dr. Riesman said. He recently was appointed Henry Ford 2d professor of social sciences at Harvard University.

Dr. Riesman said that if "the romance of far-flung possibly unmarried careers attracts few college women, it should also be noted that the images held as to the ideal spouse have departed quite widely from the dreams of romantic love that were popular a generation ago."

The social scientist expressed confidence that an education could be given women that would prepare them for the highest and best eventualities of marriage and career, "while also helping to sustain them if it turns out that family life alone does not prove wholly absorbing."

'COLLEGE BOARDS' FOR 85,000 TODAY

Examinations Test Capacity of Students to Do Well as Undergraduates

USED ACROSS COUNTRY

Requirement Reflects Rise in Enrollments and Better Selection Procedure

By LEONARD BUDER

Throughout the United States and in many foreign countries, 85,000 young Americans will take tests today that could have an important bearing on their next four years and perhaps their entire lives. The tests are the "college boards," so-called because they are offered by the College Entrance Examination Board.

How the students do on these examinations will play a role in determining whether they will be admitted to a college of their choice. One hundred and seventy colleges and universities in the United States are members of the board and require prospective students to take "college boards." Four hundred other institutions last year used the examinations for some students.

A record total of 250,000 students will take the "college boards" this year. Besides March, tests are given in December, January, May and August. The 1955-56 total represents an increase of 80,000 applicants in one year. The increase in the last five years is 175,000. Before World War II, the figure was 23,214 candidates.

The greatly increased use of "college boards" in recent years reflects the rise in college enrollment. But it is also a measure of the colleges' desire to improve their selection procedures. College enrollment this year is 3,000,000 students, a record high. But it is little in comparison with what is expected to come. A 75 to 100 per cent increase within the next fifteen years is predicted.

Within 75 Miles of All

No student will have to travel more than seventy-five miles to take the examination. If there is no testing center near by, the Educational Testing Service — which administers and helps prepare the examination for the board — will set up a special facility, even for just one candidate.

The test will get underway today at 9 A. M. when candidates break the red seal on the Scholastic Aptitude Test. It has two sections. One is verbal, designed to measure ability to read with understanding and discrimination and skill in dealing with word and thought relationships. The other is mathematical, to measure aptitude for handling quantitative concepts.

Some institutions require just the aptitude test. Others require candidates also to take various one-hour achievement tests. These are given in the afternoon. They cover English composition, chemistry, biology, physics, intermediate and advanced mathematics, social studies, French, German, Italian, Greek, Spanish and Latin.

With the exception of the General Composition Test—given in May—which has essay questions, and the English Composition Test, which may have essay questions, all of the achievement tests, as well as the morning aptitude test, are "objective." This means they consist of "short answer" or "multiple choice" questions.

The thousands of papers—last year there were 413,030—will be sent to the Educational Testing Service in Princeton, N. J., for grading by machine.

Five Weeks for Grading

Within five weeks after the candidate has taken the test, the board will report his scores to the colleges concerned. The tests do not have a passing or failing grade. They are scored according to a scale that runs from 200 to 800.

The scores are used by the colleges as only one measure of the student's ability and academic preparation. Other factors considered include school grades, rank in class, recommendations and interviews. Each college decides for itself whom it will admit.

The board was founded around the turn of the century. Each college then had its own admission requirements, and the preparatory schools were buffeted by these cross-currents of diverse standards. The board—composed of representatives of member secondary schools and colleges—brought about some uniformity in admission requirements.

At the beginning and for many years to come, the "college boards" consisted solely of essay-type tests. Whereas in the objective test a student has to select the right answer, in an essay test he must supply the answer on his own and present it in an acceptable manner.

An essay-type test, to be effective, required a homogeneous body of knowledge so that it could be sampled within the limitations of the test and the time available. This homogeneity was achieved by the sale of syllabi and old tests to the schools.

The system worked well while the group tested remained relatively small—most of the candidates for college admission came from a select group of private eastern preparatory schools—and the college requirements remained fairly stable.

Then students from public schools began to clamor for admission to college.

Objective Test Since 1925

In 1925, the board gave its first objective test. Seventeen years later it dropped essay tests from its major testing program. According to William C. Fels, associate director of the board, a reaction had set in against the essay tests because they tended to restrict teaching. In addition, he noted, far greater accuracy was possible with objective tests. On the essay test, the scorer had to rely on his subjective judgment.

The emergence of the objective test, however, has caused some division among educators.

By using objective tests, which cover a lot of ground and seek to be fair to all students, some critics have charged the board has relieved high schools of the necessity of meeting certain standards in order to qualify their students for admission to college. With the old essay tests, and the definition of requirements, they contend, a school knew what was expected of it and had to comply if it wanted its students to do well on the tests.

Because they do not have to adhere to certain standards, the criticism runs, some schools shove cultural subjects into the back seat of the curriculum, if they do not put them out of the academic vehicle altogether. Students can now get a good score even if they have never read a complete book, it is charged.

The old "college boards," another contention holds, gave the schools a check on their teachers. If a student with ability did not get a good score it could mean that the teacher had been remiss. Since the new aptitude tests are intended to give students who received "poor" teaching almost the same chance as their more fortunate counterparts, it is said, a school now does not know whether a student received a high mark because of its teaching or in spite of it.

"The essay test provided a way of spotting superior students," commented the head of one institution with recognizably high academic standards. "It showed quality mind, not grades. It gave insight into a student's background, which may or may not have correlation with a student's success in college, but which is nevertheless important to the college. Many students get high marks on the test, but how do you spot the fewer superior students?"

The board's side was recently explained by Mr. Fels at board headquarters, 525 West 117th Street, adjacent to the Columbia University campus.

Despite the charge that schools are reducing their programs to the least common denominator, he said, there has been no decline in the ability of students to do college work. In fact, he asserted, there are more students who are now able to do the work colleges require than ever before.

The "college boards" do not ignore reading or writing, he continued, even though they do not test them the same way they once did. "The more reading and writing a candidate does," Mr. Fels said, "the better scores he will get."

He added that it was "conceivable that a very able candidate could get into college without ever having read a complete book." If the candidate were that able, he commented, he would deserve to go.

To the charge that the "college boards" no longer provided a "check" on the candidate's teaching, Mr. Fels replied:

"The Scholastic Aptitude Test is designed to give a student a chance to show if he is capable of doing college work, regardless of whether his school prepared him well. We are testing the student's aptitude, not the teacher's ability. A student's success in college depends on many factors besides the teaching he received in secondary school."

However, the effects of good teaching or poor teaching, Mr. Fels asserted, would show on the various achievement tests.

As for the quest for superior students, he said that the candidates who received top scores in the aptitude test would tend to be the superior students.

Miss Mary E. Chase, vice president and director of admission for Wellesley College, said a recent study by the college confirmed this.

The College Entrance Examination Board and the Educational Testing Service are mindful of the need to improve the examinations in the light of new findings, new requirements and changing circumstances. Research is always underway and one new test that is now being studied for possible addition to the entrance battery involves essay questions.

March 17, 1956

High School Seniors' Agony

Competition for admission to college today has created an unprecedented time of intense study, worry and waiting.

By CHARLOTTE DEVREE

THIS is a dreadful year for the young who are now seniors in high school and want to go to college next fall. Competition for places at college is so sharp and apprehension over the outcome of the mass race for them so severe that the months ahead are unjokingly referred to as the winter agony—the time of senior panic.

Students jockey cannily for position in deciding which colleges to apply to; they take exquisite care in filling out application forms; they measure themselves closely against those who sit beside them. There is anxious mark-watching and a high-strung approach to many arduous examinations. Tension will reach its crescendo in May, when the colleges begin mailing letters of acceptance or rejection. Then there will be shrieks of triumph or quiet tears in corridors and locker rooms.

Getting into college has never been so competitive. It is as if our competitive society had expressly devised this gruelling initiation rite for its promising adolescents. Senior year in high school has moved farther and farther from the ideal of a calmly fruitful pursuit of knowledge. Many educators, parents and students wish this were not so, and recognize the wish as vain.

For the trouble is, there simply is not enough college education of desired quality to go around. Population and wherewithal have gone up since the war—many who did not go to college themselves can now afford college for their children. And colleges have not expanded to meet the demand.

It is at the heart of the difficulty that so many parents want their children to go to Ivy League colleges or other long-established schools of nearly equal prestige. (In the South, the Midwest and the West, there are still colleges whose enrollments are below capacity.)

Teachers, principals and headmasters whose job it is to advise students in college selection agree that the concentration on schools with magic names greatly heightens the competitive nature of the college-entrance race. Many parents equate the best-known with the best. There is great hankering for the finest possible education, for social prestige and economic advantage. "I want you to make Cornell," a father said to a boy. "When you look for a job, the man behind the desk may be Ivy League. He will be impressed." Inordinate pressure is often put upon youngsters, and can be tragic for those who have no chance because of their marks. "Please pull my father off my back," a senior near tears begged his teacher. "He won't speak to me if I don't get into Harvard." Though many parents are not so blindly ambitious, Ivy-League-itis has infected a multitude.

STANDARDS of admission have shot upward. Parents who got into top-notch colleges on medium marks and good all-around qualifications cannot understand why their sons and daughters can't. When they belatedly become aware of today's competition, parents demand of principals, "Why wasn't I warned?" Mothers and fathers are angry and frustrated.

College-aspiring high school seniors themselves have come to believe that their future will be affected by the standing of the college that accepts them. Their pride is involved, their stature is at stake. But not everyone who dreams of an Ivy League college applies. Those whose marks average less than the 90's know it is all but useless, and are advised against trying. Even so, last year 2,200 tried for 285 places at Williams, 3,000 for 650 at Tufts.

Such colleges, with their high scholastic standings, are known to have top-quality entering classes with high numbers of valedictorians and editors of secondary school magazines. A good college selection adviser, noting that a boy's marks hover in the middle 80's, can say immediately to which rank of college he might realistically apply. Another list of colleges will be appropriate to B-minus, or C-plus. Though there are very bright youngsters studying in all of them, colleges tend increasingly to be stacked according to academic reputation. This makes the competition for admittance all the keener.

AND so unpleasant realities invade the senior year, realities that can seem quite unfair, that appear to work to the disadvantage of solid youngsters who happen not to be brilliant. Much heartache is avoided by a wise selection of colleges to apply to—and it is sensible to choose a number in different categories, to reduce the risk of being left out altogether. But the best advice cannot guarantee an admission; and, for this reason, some young competitors are afflicted with indecision even at the last minute—after masses of catalogues have been studied and many campuses visited.

A boy with an 87 average, whose first choice is an excellent Midwestern university that might in all reason accept him, worries because four brighter boys in his class have made it their second choice, and are likely to displace him. A girl ninth from the top of her class, her heart long set on a magic-name institution and a career in archaeology, is jittery because four other girls, two above her and two with impressive extracurricular records, are applying. Surely the college won't take all five from one secondary school.

Sometimes students become secretive and won't tell friends which college is their first choice. And sometimes they show generosity, changing a second choice to give another a better chance at his first. Frantic discussion about the choice of college is endless among seniors, at home and at school. In suburbs and cities telephones ring, in preparatory schools there are dormitory bull sessions. Everyone tries to plot the best possible track to the post.

THERE is no limit to the number of colleges one can apply to, though four to seven is usual. Having taken all factors into account by the beginning of the senior year—size, co-ed or not, location, cost and, above all, the possibility of acceptance—the applicant now frets over the accuracy and tone of application-form answers. It is not good to be too egotistical in one's autobiography; seniors write and rewrite their 500-word compositions about themselves and why they want to go to college. Letters of recommendation from important people who don't know you are pointless, whatever your parents say to the contrary. You ought not to load an application with material not asked for, with special pleas from alumni (or -ae), since this only puts the admissions dean's back up. If you want to go to Yale, and your marks up to mid-November qualify you but you are told that Yale can take only half its qualified applicants, you cannot afford a slip on the application form.

AND you must make a good impression on the college representative when he comes to your school, or when you call on him—not too eager, not too shy. Seniors in public high schools go to grooming classes, boys borrow Ivy League jackets if they don't own them and practice saying "sir," girls find hats and gloves for the important interview. Slurs in speech are corrected, postures improved before mirrors. The less fortunate in looks groan at their reflections. In private schools, too, students agonize over the impression they will make.

But everyone involved in this great obstacle race knows that the most important criterion in college acceptance everywhere is marks. Other factors are much less vital—the search for the "well-balanced, all-round student" is a thing of the less competitive past. So the very bright slave for still better marks, lest a fraction of a point make some dreadful difference. Those who rank in the top 80's and low 90's bone to raise their marks to the top echelon. And so on down the line. The intense pressure of mark-watching, begun for some in freshman year, mounts in the senior. But the entire secondary school record counts and there is fine calculating.

IF a boy whose major is history lacks a science credit, he may choose biology rather than physics or advanced math, on the ground that biology is easier, and he will get a higher mark. Another may confess that, in a homework paper, he is more likely to solve a problem by a known method than to experiment with a new one lest he lower a mark.

Mark anxiety is most apparent in the big public high schools. In one senior class of over a thousand—of whom 80 per cent want to go to college — students know their numerical standing in the class as they know their own names; and they know the fraction of a point that divides them from the next above them. Even in those private schools where there is an effort to minimize competition, mark anxiety is unavoidable. In a progressive private school that places the greatest possi-

ble insistence on the quality of the high-school years for their own sake, a senior who graduated last June (he was a top student and later went to Harvard on scholarship) wrote:

"The year has been a bad one for me, for it has marked a distortion of values in school. This year my interest in schoolwork has generally gone only as far as the mark, and the mark's importance in my college record. The integrity of individual assignments or reports is lost in a whirlwind of college applications."

FOR college candidates, senior year is as full of exams as Switzerland of mountain peaks. College boards, required by 200 colleges and suggested by 400 more, are given several times during the year all over the country. These test achievement in fourteen subjects—chemistry, social studies, languages, and so on. They pit students from different kinds of schools against each other on an equal basis.

"After a College Board," one girl said, "I shake like crazy." Her friends said they do, too.

Some colleges specify the date on which they wish applicants to take College Boards, so that sets of them may have to be taken more than once to qualify for more than one college.

Then there are the New York State Regents' exams, for admission to New York State colleges. There are the Merit Scholarship exams, and others for scholarships in special fields, awarded by business firms. Ambitious students may take several scholarship exams on the theory that, even if they do not win a scholarship, a good mark will help toward college admission.

Many educators feel that in most of these exams a student's months of laboriously boning up may show to too great advantage. Colleges do wish to discover promising youngsters who are not grinds. The College Board Scholastic Aptitude Test, the famous S. A. T., is designed to show native promise chiefly because (it is thought) it cannot be boned for. For this reason the

S. A. T. mark is of greatest importance. But competitive pressure for a good S. A. T. mark is so great that the technique of boning even for S. A. T. has been developed.

THIS three-hour test is top-secret. Question books are numbered so that they may all be accounted for and turned in as soon as the exam is over. But questions from examinations of previous years are the subject-matter of S. A. T. cram classes given Saturday mornings off campus, for a fee, by high-school teachers. Children become so familiar with old S. A. T. questions that they could no doubt draw up an S. A. T. themselves. Frequently they raise their scores (marked from 200 to 800 by machine) by perhaps a hundred points between a dry run at the end of junior year and the real thing in the senior.

S. A. T. cram classes may add not one whit to true knowledge, but they appear to be excellent training in competitive winning. And they do lessen anxiety a little, in that they often assure a higher score. "You have to know some tricks you don't learn in school," seniors say.

THE moral atmosphere around the young who take S. A. T. cram classes is not disapproving. It is the attitude of elders on campus and off that the kids might as well do whatever they can to try to get into the college of their choice.

Thus, determined youngsters will undergo any amount of pressure to make their goal. It is no wonder that, as months go by, some will suffer a lapse of confidence, feel pushed into a corner. "I think we're fighting for something we won't get," one boy said. "I think the colleges are trying to keep us out." Some will have sleepless nights, and arrive haggard at classes; they will cut down on parties in favor of study. And all of them will wish that senior year might be less strenuous, more full of the enjoyments they feel are due to seniors.

Yet these pressures are nothing to what they might be if every youngster of college

capacity in the country were competing. It has been estimated that about 200,000 qualified youngsters a year do not think to apply, for lack of money. Uncounted others, because the very idea of going to college does not exist in their backgrounds, are among those who choose commercial courses in high school and go to work afterward. Altogether, it is said, almost half the country's young with good minds do not go to college.

And severe as the pressures are now, they are nothing to what they will be in the near future. Those now trying to enter colleges are lucky, having been born at the tag end of the low birth-rate period of the depression; soon the unluckier ones of the greatly increased wartime and post-war birth-rate periods will be coming along.

Almost three and a half million go to college now; in eight years, the number of eligibles is expected to exceed five million, even on the present basis of economic and social selectivity. And still we will be no nearer the goal of affording college educations to all worthy youngsters.

WHAT can be done about the pressures that constitute senior panic? Educators say that realism in parents and a warmly secure atmosphere at home that is encouraging without being overambitious make up the greatest gift parents can give children caught in the competitive squeeze. There is not much else parents can do, except pay the bills.

But the best of attitudes and the best of plans for easing the agonies of senior year are thought to be merely palliative. In the near future, authorities believe, something bigger will have to give. Vast sums of money, public and private, are obviously needed to expand college facilities and to expand them fast. It is agreed that money ought to go immediately to the tightest point in the tightening bottleneck—college faculty salaries. "You can put up buildings in six months," one educator sums up, "but it takes a little longer to develop a biochemist."

New College Boards for Juniors

In the last five years, the number of high school students taking College Entrance Examination Board tests in their junior year has been growing rapidly.

Because 250 colleges use the Board's Scholastic Aptitude Test as one of their admissions criteria, 126,000 juniors took it last year either for practice or for guidance. The Scholarship Qualifying Test, required by many scholarship donors, was taken by 172,000 juniors. They must retake the tests in their senior year.

Dual Purpose

Last week the College Board announced a new dual-purpose test that will replace the aptitude and scholarship tests for juniors. Seniors may also take it in place of the present scholarship test.

The new test, intended primarily for juniors, is expected to be taken by about 500,000 students in 15,000 schools in October.

Called the Preliminary Scholastic Aptitude Test, it will give the junior a forecast of his senior-year performance on the Scholastic Aptitude Test when it is taken for college admission.

More important, from the viewpoint of the schools and colleges, it will give the high schools, early in the junior year, an indication of their students' college capabilities. The board hopes this will lead to earlier advice on a "good and realistic" choice of college. Moving the choice of a college into the junior year should simplify the admission problem for both applicant and college.

Two-Hour Test

The new preliminary aptitude test will be a two-hour version of the three-hour Scholastic Aptitude Test. It will use the same kinds of multiple-choice questions and measure the same verbal and mathematical abilities. Separate verbal and mathematical scores will be on a scale ranging from 20 to 80, a gradation parallel to the S. A. T. scale of 200 to 800. This will make it easy for guidance officers to relate the preliminary test scores with the admissions test results.

The board also named a special committee of school and college officials to study the growing problems of college admissions.

March 8, 1959

A MACHINE MARKS 1,000 TESTS WRONG

But Error in College Board Grades Is Also Traced to Human Frailties

By LEONARD BUDER

An error by a new electronic scoring machine and some man-made mistakes that went undetected by the machine have caused confusion and concern over the results of the College Entrance Examination Board tests given last December.

As a result of the errors, wrong scores were reported for perhaps 1,000 of the 300,000 test papers written across the nation. In some instances students were given scores for tests they did not take.

The Educational Testing Service, which administers the college boards, expects to mail out the last of the corrected scores within a few days.

The scores are among the factors used by many colleges and universities to guide them in selecting candidates for admission.

The testing service, whose headquarters are at Princeton, N. J., is also sending an explanation of what went wrong with the December scores, in an effort to allay the unfounded concern that the December tests may not be valid.

According to a spokesman for the testing service, the mix-up resulted from these factors:

¶The failure of the new data processing machine to read some of the student identification numbers placed on the answer sheets.

¶The failure of some candidates to copy their identification numbers correctly on the answer papers.

Many Concerned

For the most part the errors were in the scores reported in achievement tests—not the more widely taken aptitude tests.

But the mix-up was sufficient to cause considerable concern and confusion among those affected.

"You can imagine how much concern there was before we found out that a mistake had been made," one parent commented yesterday. "Just picture the despair that resulted when, because of an error, a youngster was informed that he did very poorly in a subject and when he thought this might keep him out of the college of his choice."

The machine that erred was placed in operation some months ago. It is capable of scoring 100 examination sheets a minute. It can "sense" a candidate's pencil-marked responses on the answer sheet, accumulate a count of right and wrong answers, and automatically punch raw score totals into cards that are fed into a general purpose computer.

The machine also "reads" and punches—when it is functioning properly—various information about the candidate.

Each candidate taking an examination is given a seven-digit identification number. He writes this number on his answer sheet —along with his name for checking purposes—and also must put the number in code or "machine readable language" by marking appropriate boxes on a grid.

February 3, 1961

EDUCATOR URGES TESTING INQUIRY

Challenges Standards and Validity of Choice Series

By ROBERT H. TERTE

A critic of the educational testing industry called yesterday for an investigation of the entire matter of mechanized testing.

In proposing such a study, Prof. Banesh Hoffman of the Queens College Mathematics Department said the minimum concern of such an inquiry should be the problem of policing tests to ensure that they met high standards.

Professor Hoffman charged that the testing services, instead of providing just difficult questions, offered multiple-choice questions with a choice of ambiguous answers.

This practice produces a question that "in the case of good students does not measure understanding of science so much as understanding of the workings of the mind of the test makers," he said.

Professor Hoffmann also challenged the scientific validity of some of the explanations offered by a major testing service

College for Children Ruled Duty of Parents

JACKSON, Miss., March 21 (UPI) — The State Supreme Court said today that parents had an obligation to provide their children with a college education if they could afford it and the children were capable.

Specifically, it ruled that courts had a legal right to compel a father to provide funds for a college education for his minor child the custody of whom had been awarded to the mother.

Justice James G. Holmes expanded on the ruling to assert that in this day a college education might be necessary to enable a person to discharge the duties of good citizenship.

The Yalobusha County Chancery Court was upheld in ruling that E. C. Pass, who owns farm land near Water Valley, must increase the support payments for his daughter Nancy from $50 to $90 a month so that she might attend the University of Mississippi.

March 22, 1960

in defense of its own multiple-choice questions. He said that the explanations had produced evidence about the quality of test makers that scholars "may well find disturbing."

Professor Hoffmann, who was trained as a mathematical physicist, made his charges in an article entitled "Testing," appearing in the October issue of Physics Today.

The explanations to which he objected were prepared and distributed by the Educational Testing Service of Princeton, N. J., after the publication of an article by Professor Hoffmann in the March issue of Harper's. In this article he pointed out as "defective" a number of sample questions in a booklet describing the Science Achievement Tests of the College Board.

Professor Hoffman emphasized that he had selected the service as his principal target because "one makes the strongest case by criticizing the best test makers, not the worst."

Among the explanations by the testing service that he challenged was one that stated that the superior student, in answering a particular science question, "should realize that the classical concepts of matter and chemical change provide the framework in which the question is asked"—rather than the concepts of modern physics.

"Why should the superior student realize that he is to use only the 'classical' concepts that E. T. S. has in mind?" Professor Hoffman said.

October 12, 1961

393

Cheating Rising in City Schools

By MARTIN TOLCHIN

Increase Attributed to Competition for College Places

Cheating is increasing among the city's high school students, especially those near the top of their classes who are competing for the limited number of openings in Ivy League colleges.

This pattern emerged from interviews with hundreds of students at a dozen schools, where midterm examinations are now in progress. Most of the principals and teachers at other schools agreed that there was an increase in cheating.

The prevailing view was that the youths were responding to the spiraling demand for high grades made by college admissions officers. The pressures are likely to intensify as society's demands increase for highly educated experts able to digest and extend scientific material.

Pointing up this contention were reports that the worst offenders are students who could get good grades without cheating and that honors classes were the most affected. Interestingly, the least cheating was found in vocational high schools and the most in academic high schools, where a higher proportion of students plan to go to college.

A minority of principals and teachers dissent strongly from the idea that cheating is increasing. They consider cheating something that flourishes in all ages regardless of pressures, society's demands, the intellect of students, their class standing or competition for college.

But student polls conducted by two of the city's best math and science high schools found widespread cheating and there is evidence that teachers, through ignorance, indifference or desire to see students get good marks, sometimes help them to cheat.

Also there is such strong suspicion that students cheat on College Entrance Examination tests that students have been hired to take the courses of coaches believed to have obtained advance copies of the tests. Thus far this counter-espionage has failed to turn up solid evidence against the coaches.

Last June, however, two good students, one the son of an assistant principal, were caught stealing a college board test.

When the school withheld their diplomas for a time, "the boys were contrite, but the parents were outraged at the punishment,' their principal said.

In candid discussions held in classrooms, gymnasiums and study halls, often in the presence of principals and teachers, the students labeled as a myth the once-popular concept that the worst students were most prone to cheat, for sheer survival. The faculty generally agreed.

"The dropout who can only raise his mark from a 40 to a 45 doesn't have the motive of the kid aspiring for college, where the difference between an 88 and a 93 is crucial," said Abraham H. Lass, principal of Abraham Lincoln High School in Brooklyn. "The pressure to cheat is greater because the pressure for grades is greater."

Louis K. Wechsler, principal at the High School of Music and Art in Manhattan, said that those caught cheating "were always students who didn't have to do it—there was no need for it at all."

Many Are B Students

"They were B kids who wanted to make an A," he said. "They shared the motivations of the A kids, and maybe the abilities, but they didn't work as hard."

Students taking midterms at one of the better high schools last week chalked crib notes across the blackboard. The proctor, who came in late, failed to notice them. The principal, informed of the incident, said that "you're dealing in every school with an unusually high percentage of teachers who don't know what they should do automatically."

The editor of the student newspaper at an academic high school, an honor student whose average was in the 90's, described at length how he had cheated with others on the oral comprehension portion of a foreign language regents.

Collaborating with a group of honor students, who corroborated the incident, the youths communicated with each other by moving their pen points up, down, left and right, to indicate A, B, C, or D.

Honor students in other academic high schools described in detail how they communicated "true" or "false" on examinations — by slumping left or right, by scratching left or right, by earlugging, by resting their chins on one, two, three or four fingers.

An honor student said that she wrote ponies on the inside of thick rubber bands, stretched to the fullest, which she then wore into class on her pony tail. Others wrote on their nails, palms, cuffs, and the underneath side of their ties.

When an incredulous teacher asked if they felt embarassed or guilty, the girl with the pony tail said that guilt and embarassment over low marks were worse than what she experienced by cheating.

At a high school where the student average is 89, a student said that he had cheated because "there are so many kids with a 90 that you need to do better."

The students also practiced what they called:

¶Unconscious cheating — "Your eyes happen to fall on a sheet of paper. You see an answer. You can't get it out of your mind."

¶Altruistic cheating — "If you're fairly smart, and your friend needs to cheat off you, how can you turn him down?"

¶Weak ego cheating — "If you don't have the self-confidence and you think the kid next to you is smart—it's just curiosity."

¶Scholastic cheating—"It's like studying. I write what I don't know on a small sheet of paper over and over, maybe 10 times, and when I get through I know most of it. I take in what I don't know."

Teachers Turn Backs

Teachers sometimes help students cheat. They have been seen acting out the oral comprehension portion of foreign language Regents, texts and of stressing the right answer by voice inflection. Some proctors busy themselves in their newspapers, turn their backs on the students, or even leave the room. A guidance counselor at Stuyvesant High School explained:

"The penalty for cheating on Regents examination is so severe that the teacher is likely to ignore it. If somebody's caught, the person who catches him is put on the spot. Can you prove it? Do you want to ruin the boy? Do you want to be marked lousy by the other teachers?"

At one such school, a senior with a 97 average was caught cheating on a Regents test. All of his Regents marks were invalidated and he repeated his senior year. He was ultimately accepted by one of the four prestige colleges that had accepted him in the first place.

Brooklyn Technical High School employs roving teams of teachers to proctor the proctors by going in and out of the examination rooms.

"We don't put temptation in their way," said Frank Stewart, acting principal. He believes the system is effective.

Some educators question, however, whether this approach hits home, where they think the trouble lies. Dr. Alexander Taffel, principal of the Bronx High School of Science, explained:

"There is a group of parents who exaggerate the importance of being at the very top, and therefore create in their children the idea that high achievement isn't good enough—it's got to be the highest achievement."

Many principals reported that after each semester they were besieged by parents who implored them to raise their children's marks, citing college admission requirements.

Dr. David Abrahamsen, a psychiatrist who specializes in the problems of children and youths, asserts:

"If parents were more aware of their child's limitations, there wouldn't be so much cheating."

The psychiatrist, a consultant to the State Department of Mental Hygiene, said that he had treated hundreds of cheaters, and found that cheating was seldom an isolated phenomena. It is usually associated with lying, stealing, and general deception, he said.

Some educators blame the schools and colleges for stressing marks and depersonalizing the students.

"You're not known by your name but by your average," a guidance counselor said, echoing the complaint of many students.

November 22, 196

The Fourth R— The Rat Race

By JOHN HOLT

MOST of what is said and written about the tremendous pressures for high grades that burden so many young people today implies that schools and colleges are not really responsible for these pressures, that they are the innocent victims of anxious and ambitious parents on the one hand, and the inexorable demands of an increasingly complicated society on the other. There is some truth in this, but not much. Here and there are schools that have been turned, against their will, into high-pressure learning factories by the demands of parents. But in large part, educators themselves are the source and cause of these pressures. Increasingly, instead of developing the intellect, character and potential of the students in their care, they are using them for their own purposes in a contest inspired by vanity and aimed at winning money and prestige. It is only in theory, today, that educational institutions serve the student; in fact, the real job of a student at any ambitious institution is, by his performance, to enhance the reputation of that institution.

This is true not only of colleges and universities. I have heard teachers at secondary and even elementary schools, in reply to the just claim that students were overworried and overworked, say that if students were less burdened, their test and examination scores would go down and the reputation of the school would suffer. I can still hear, in my mind's ear, the voice of a veteran teacher at a prestigious elementary school saying at a faculty meeting that if the achievement-test scores of the students did not keep pace with those of competing schools, the school would have to "close its doors"—and this in spite of the fact that it had a long waiting list of applicants. I know of a school in which, at least for a while, the teachers' salaries were adjusted up or down according to the achievement-test scores of their classes.

Not long ago, I went to an alumni dinner of a leading New England preparatory school and there heard one of the faculty, in a speech, boast about the percentage of students who had been admitted to the college of their first choice, the number who had gone directly into the sophomore class at college and so on. The tone was that of a manufacturer bragging that his product was better than those of his competitors. Conversely, when the faculty of a school meets to discuss the students who are not doing well in their studies, the tone is likely to be that of management considering an inferior product, one not worthy of bearing the company's name and which they are about to drop from the line. There is sometimes concern and regret that the school is not doing well enough by the child; much more often there is concern, and resentment, that the child is not doing well enough by the school.

I DO not think it is in any way an exaggeration to say that many students, particularly the ablest ones, are being as mercilessly exploited by ambitious schools as they are by business and commerce, which use them as consumers and subject them to heavy and destructive psychological pressures.

In such schools, children from the age of 12 or 13 on are very likely to have, after a long day at school, two, three or more hours of homework a night—with more over the weekend. The load grows heavier as children get older. Long before they reach college, many children are putting in a 70-hour week— or more. As Paul Goodman once put it, children have not worked such long hours since the early and brutal days of the Industrial Revolution.

One of my own students, a girl just turned 14, said not long ago, more in a spirit of wry amusement than of complaint, that she went home every night on a commuter train with businessmen, most of whom could look forward to an evening of relaxation with their families, while she had at least two or three hours more work to do. And probably a good many of those men find their work during the day less difficult and demanding than her schoolwork is for her.

Schools and colleges claim in defense that they are compelled to put heavy pressure on students because of society's need for ever more highly trained men and women, etc., etc. The excuse is, for the most part, untrue and dishonest.

The blunt fact is that educators' chief concern is to be able to say, to college-hunting parents on the one hand, and to employe-hunting executives on the other, that their college is harder to get into, and therefore better, than other colleges, and therefore the one to which the best students should be sent and from which the best employes and graduate students can be drawn.

In a recent private talk with some of the teachers at a men's Ivy League college, I said that the job of our universities was not to provide vocational training for the future holders of top positions in business, government, science and the learned professions; it was to help boys and girls become in the broadest sense of the word, educated adults and citizens. In return, I was asked a most interesting and revealing question: If a college does not turn out future "leaders," where in future years, will it get the money for its alumni fund, the money it needs to stay in the prestige race? Where indeed? A difficult problem. But not one that should be the primary concern of educators, and certainly not one that justifies the kind of pressure for grades that is now bearing heavily on more and more children.

WHAT are the effects of these pressures? They are many—and all harmful. They create in young children an exaggerated concern with getting right answers and avoiding mistakes; they drive them into defensive strategies of learning and behavior that choke off their intellectual powers and make real learning all but impossible.

On older children, like the teen-agers I now teach, the effects are even wider and more harmful. This is perhaps the time in a growing person's life when he most needs to be free of pressure, when he needs the most time, leisure, solitude and independence. It is at this period in his life that he becomes most sharply aware of himself as a person, of the need to know who and what that person is, and of the fact that he can and will to a large extent determine who and what that person becomes. In short, it is at this time that he begins not only to know himself but also consciously to create himself, to feel intuitively what Thoreau meant when he said that every man is his own masterpiece.

A person's identity is made up of those things—qualities, tastes, beliefs — that are uniquely his, that he found and chose and took for himself, that cannot be lost or taken from him, that do not depend on his position or his success or other people's opinion of him. More specifically, it is the people that he admires; the books, the music, the games, the interests that he chooses for himself and likes, whether or not anyone else likes them, or whether or not they are supposed to be "good" or "worthwhile"; the experiences that he seeks out for himself and that add to his life.

An adolescent needs time to do this kind of seeking, tasting, selecting and rejecting. He needs time to talk and think about who he is and how he got to be that way and what he would like to be and how he can get there. He needs time to taste experience and to digest it. We don't give him enough.

IN addition, by putting him in a position where he is always being judged and where his whole future may depend

on those judgments, we require the adolescent to direct his attention, not to who he is or ought to be or wants to be, but who *we* think he is and want him to be. He has to keep thinking about the impression he is making on us —his elders, the world. Thus we help to exaggerate what is already, in most young people, a serious and crippling fault— an excessive concern with what others think of them.

Since our judgments are more often than not critical, unfavorable, even harsh, we exaggerate another fault, equally serious and crippling —a tendency to imagine that other people think less well of them than in fact they do, or what is worse, that they do not *deserve* to be well thought of. Youth ought to be a time when people acquire a sense not just of their own identity but also of their own worth. We make it almost certain to be the very opposite.

In this competition into which we have driven children, almost everyone loses. It is not enough any more for most

parents or most schools that a child should go to college and do well there. It is not even enough for most children themselves. More and more, the only acceptable goal is to get into a prestige college; to do anything else is to fail. Thus I hear boys and girls say, "I wanted to go to so-and-so, but I'm not good enough." It is outrageous that they should think this way, that they should judge themselves stupid and worthless because of the opinion of some remote college admissions officer.

THE pressures we put on our young people also tend to destroy their sense of power and purpose. A friend of mine, who recently graduated with honors from a prestige college, said that he and other students there were given so much to read that, even if you were an exceptionally good reader and spent all your time studying, you could not do as much as half of it.

Looking at work that can never be done, young people tend to feel, like many a tired businessman, that life is a rat race. They do not feel in control of their own lives. Outside forces hurry them along with no pause for breath or thought, for purposes not their own, to an unknown end. Society does not seem to them a community that they are preparing to join and shape, like the city of an ancient Greek; it is more like a remote and impersonal machine that will one day bend them to its will.

My students ask, "How can I defend myself, the real person within me, against society?" Having asked the question, they gloomily decide that it cannot be done. This is, I think, what Paul Goodman meant when he said that we have imposed on the élite of our younger generation a morale fit for slaves. We

have not given them a sense of mission and vocation, but of subjection and slavery. They do not seek more knowledge and power so that they may one day do great work of their own choosing; instead, they do their tasks, doggedly and often well, only because they dare not refuse.

Along with their sense of mission, we destroy to a very considerable extent their sense of joy, both in work and in leisure. Thoreau once wrote: "The truly efficient laborer will not crowd his day with work, but saunter to the task surrounded by a wide halo of ease and leisure." The man is badly cheated who has never felt that he could not wait to get back to his work and, so feeling, hurled himself into it with fierce joy. Not only is he cheated; he probably has never done much work worth doing.

Nor do our young people, on the whole, get much more joy out of their pleasures. They are not much re-created by their recreation. We, their elders, say that this is because their amusements are trivial; but even when this is true, it is so to a great extent because we have left them so little time or energy for anything more serious. A member of the Boston Symphony told me not long ago that the music programs of even our best suburban schools do not compare with those he knows in the Midwest, simply because college pressure leaves so few students time for serious practice.

EVEN the songs the young sing for fun have little fun in them, but are mostly tragic, bitter, angry, defiant. They seem to sing them, as they do most things that they do of their own choice, as a way of shaking their fists under the noses of their elders. No fad is more sure to succeed among

the young than one they think the adults won't like.

I think of a student of mine, years ago, kept on campus weekend after weekend for not having his work done—presumably so that he could use the time to get it done. On one such weekend, I found him working on one of his hobbies, a small printing press. In exasperation I said to him, "If you'd just do the things you have to do and get them out of the way, then you could be free to do the things you *want* to do."

With tired wisdom, much greater than mine, he said, mildly: "No, you can't. They just give you more things you have to do."

It is truer now than it was then. Schools cannot bring themselves to say, "That's enough." No matter how high they raise the hoop, if a child manages to jump through it, they take it as a signal that they must raise it still higher.

THE gross effects of these pressures are painfully evident. Along with an increase in psychological disturbances we have increases in suicide, in the use or overuse of alcohol and in drug-taking. We also read of a great increase in all kinds of cheating, not among unsuccessful students, but among superior students whose grades would be very good even if they did not cheat. It

is no small thing that large numbers of our young people, supposedly our ablest and best, are becoming convinced that they must cheat in order to succeed; that success is so important that it justifies the cheating.

But the broader and more general consequence of the pressure for grades is that it has debased and corrupted the act of learning itself. Not by what we say but by what we do, by the way we hand out rewards and prizes, we convince many young people that it is not for the joy and satisfaction of understanding that we learn, but in order to get something for ourselves; that what counts in school and college is not knowing and understanding, but making someone *think* you know and understand; that knowledge is valuable, not because it helps us deal better with the problems of private and public life, but because it has become a commodity that can be sold for fancy prices on the market. School has become a kind of racket, and success in school, and hence in life, depends on learning how to beat it.

CAN schools and colleges be persuaded to do away with, or greatly reduce, their demands for high grades? There are many reasons for thinking they cannot.

First, they do not seem aware of the harm that their competition for prestige is doing to American youth and American education. In fact, they take quite an opposite view, talking about higher standards and upgrading education.

Second, they would say that they have found from experience that it is the students with high test scores who have the best chance of staying in college. But this is because so much of their teaching is *based* on getting high test scores; if they reduced the importance of exams and marks, they would reduce the need for getting only those students who were good at taking exams.

Third, the colleges would say that unless they make entrance difficult by demanding high test scores, they will have too many applicants to choose from. But they have too many as it is, and must ultimately make many choices on the basis of criteria other than test scores. Why not make these criteria more important, and if they still have too many applicants, choose from them by lot? Under such a system, a student applying to a popular college would know that his chances of being admitted were slight, but would feel, if he was not admitted, that it was chance that had kept him out—not that he was no good.

PERHAPS a number of prestige colleges could be persuaded to agree to say jointly that they would admit some fixed percentage of applicants each year, despite low test scores, if the applicants had other important qualifications. If they found, as I believe they would, that such students were on the whole as useful and valuable as students getting very high scores, they could raise the percentage. Such a policy would encourage primary and secondary schools and teachers to work for goals other than high test scores, and it would give hope to at least a number of very talented young people who are not good at taking exams.

But if the colleges cannot be persuaded to give up, or moderate, their competition for

prestige and for high-scoring students who will enhance that prestige, then the schools should resist them. A good place to begin would be by attacking the notion that only at a prestige institution can one get a good education.

I have known, and know, students at prestige colleges who are not interested in their courses and for whom college has not been an exciting or stimulating experience. I know other bright and able boys and girls who have been, and are being, very much excited and stimulated at institutions that have much less prestige, or none at all.

It may well be true that a non-prestige institution has fewer first-rate scholars or teachers, but it is probably true that such as there are have more time for and interest in their really able and curious students. And the students, themselves under less pressure, have more time for them.

Most important of all, the schools and their teachers must do all they can, by word and deed, to destroy the notion that education is a race against other students to win the favor of someone in authority. They must put in its place the idea that what is important—and here I use the words of the late President Griswold of Yale—is "the desire and the capacity of the individual for self-education; that is, for finding meaning, truth and enjoyment in everything he does."

A. B.='Academic Bureaucracy'

A university professor complains that a lush undergrowth of nonteaching administrators is choking the groves of Academe.

By JOHN Q. ACADEMESIS

ACADEMIC HIERARCHY—Compared with administrators, teachers are the low men on the university totem pole.

Drawings by James Flora

THE most striking change in American higher education during the past generation has been not the increase in the proportion of young people going to college (although this seems little short of miraculous), nor the increased number of imposing buildings and other physical facilities (even though some of them are breathtaking), nor the proliferation of courses (difficult as this may be to justify in view of our goal of a well-rounded education to develop the individual potential). Towering over all has been the phenomenal growth of administrative personnel. This largely nonteaching bureaucracy, which has shot up like a child with abnormal glands, today equals, at some institutions, the number and cost of the teaching staff.

Statistics have little meaning in examining the facts of this growth, for so much depends on how one defines the unit of count. Some illustrations are more to the point. Consider University X. Twenty-five years ago, one definite part of its administrative work was done by one person, aided by a secretary. Ten years later, with no change in the size of the job, there were a director, an assistant, a receptionist and two secretaries. Today, still with no basic change, there are a director, an associate director, an assistant to the director, a receptionist and three secretaries. Or, take Division K in another university, which has had a fixed enrollment for many years. Twenty years ago, the administrative force of the division consisted of a dean and a secretary-assistant. Today, besides a dean, there are two associate deans, two vice deans, and a battery of secretaries and assistants.

Then there is the business side of the university. Consider so simple a matter as the purchase of a typewriter ribbon for departmental use. Two telephone calls and a written requisition (four carbon copies, please), properly coded, speed the request on its way. After being returned twice for detailed changes and amplifications, the request is approved. A week later, a messenger appears—but with four ribbons and of the wrong color. Two weeks of negotiation follow and after several more forms are executed (four carbon copies, please) one ribbon as originally ordered is delivered.

THIS, of course, should close the matter, but comes the sixth of the next month and the department is charged with five ribbons. This includes the four ribbons returned. Two months and eight letters later, that matter is cleared up. Meantime, a labor-saving machine has rendered a mid-monthly sheet to inform one that five typewriter ribbons have been purchased, and at the end of the month another sheet arrives indicating the total expenditures for ribbons and how much is left for ribbons for the balance of the year. This continues for several months until the machine begins sending corrected statements on all of these matters. Estimated total cost for one typewriter ribbon: $85.

Examples could be multiplied ad infinitum and ad nauseam. The particular facts vary from one institution to another, but the trend is obvious. Just as an article in Fortune magazine once revealed how seven employes can be made to do the work of one, so various American universities are now

EXTRACURRICULAR ACTIVITY — The time spent by the faculty on administrative details adds up to a serious loss of teaching.

showing how two administrators, three secretaries, one receptionist and one teacher can do the work the last-named used to do all by himself. Apparently the "law" set forth by that sly professor, C. Northcote Parkinson, in his book "Parkinson's Law"—which shows how continuous growth in administrative personnel occurs, regardless of its contribution to the main task or need for such personnel—operates in higher education in the United States even as it does in government and industry.

What do these administrators do? They are in conference. With whom? The students? Not if they can be avoided. The faculty members? If necessary, these can be sandwiched in between conferences. Chiefly, administrators are in conference with each other. Since each school, college or division of a university has its own plethora of administrators, each group confers not only among themselves but also with every other administrative group within the university. This explains why the lowly faculty member has such difficulty in seeing an appropriate administrator, even when it is necessary. And faculty members being as lowly as they are nowadays, necessity is not always easy to prove.

This need for conferences among themselves is so emphasized at some universities that the administrators are housed conveniently near each other and far away from the students and faculty they theoretically are to serve. For example, the deans and associate deans and assistant deans of men and women at one university have been moved to adjacent offices, several blocks from the undergraduate classrooms and dormitories where, in a more naive era, they were wont to serve. Incidentally, this continuing series of conferences is attended by certain health hazards for administrators, chiefly shown by the increased number of ulcer victims. Ulcers, as every one knows, are an occupational disease resulting from chronic conferencitis.

WHAT do they do at these conferences? Some of their work is top-secret or classified information, related to the safety of the institution or conceivably of the confrères. But the nature of other items of their agenda can be gathered from its impact upon the faculty. Just as an élite of public guardians needs all kinds of data to plan for the masses in authoritarian states, so university administrators spend much time devising forms, questionnaires and report outlines to be returned by the lowly faculty for their own future welfare.

The information thus requested ranges from measurements of the number of square feet in an office or classroom to teaching records, examination grades, absence reports, classroom temperatures, research under way, number of pages published (book reviews not included) and transportation facilities used during the past month.

And since each administrator must have these and other sundry reports for his very own, the faculty is kept quite busy. Thus, one professor filled out eleven reports on his research activities during an eighteen-month period, which must interfere, of course, with the research work he has time to do.

IT is well known that these reports from the faculty are never read by the administrators, for that is not the purpose of the collection. Basically, they are intended, first, to keep the secretaries of the administrators busy, and if possible increase their number, thus inflating the ego of their employers; and, secondly, to impress the faculty and fellow administrators. Good administration tends to be measured by the show of activity, with relatively little attention to the nature of the activity.

The phrase "lowly faculty" has been used several times, and advisedly so. Today, the faculties at our large universities work for the administration rather than the reverse, as was the case in earlier days. The relative status of administration and faculty is revealed in a myriad of ways, many of them minor and thus highly significant.

CONSIDER the matter of secretarial service. A teacher may be the most distinguished and aged professor on the campus, but he answers the telephone himself and greets his students in his simple office. Compare this with a graduate of three years ago, now a member of the administrative staff. Quite quickly he acquires a secretary, then a receptionist, and soon even an appointments secretary. Some offices noted here and there have blossomed forth with a staff messenger to carry precious documents from one administrative sanctum to another.

Whereas lowly professors function for years in carpetless offices with unadorned walls and a single telephone for a dozen men, once a young graduate of theirs becomes a member of the administrative staff, he rates a wall-to-wall carpet, art creations on the walls, an executive-type desk and chair and an inter-com system to link him with the administrative world.

From one well-known university comes this choice illustration of relative status. Prior to the outbreak of Asian flu in the academic year 1957-1958, the institution obtained a limited amount of vaccine. Because of its scarcity the following order of priority was established for its distribution: medical students and nurses at the top, followed by administrative officials, service staffs and students. The faculty was not included. Actually, this order was not maintained after the vaccine arrived; it was given to anyone who applied. What is significant is the announcement of the administrator in charge.

THE truth of the matter is that the teachers in our large universities are the low men on the totem pole. The administrators look down their noses at the faculty; research faculty members look down their noses at teachers; the latter take it out on the students and find therapeutic outlets in extravagant exercises in semantics, concerned chiefly with the importance of a liberal education.

These distinctions, of course, have nothing to do with the abilities of the relative strata; in fact, a waggish friend has improved upon the epigram attributed to George Bernard Shaw. The friend puts it this way:

Those who can, do.
Those who can't, teach.
Those who can teach, do.
Those who cannot, become administrators.
Those who can administer, do.
Those who cannot, work for the government.

What is the effect of this creeping bureaucracy upon the educational process? This, after all, is the acid test. The author believes it to be a grave threat to the field of his lifetime devotion, both because of certain immediate consequences and because of others more remote. He is at one with Milovan Djilas, who contends in his study of "The New Class" that the devastating effects of communism lie in the rise and menace of a bureaucratic class; and with those members of the United States Congress who admit that the Federal bureaucracy is powerful to the point of overshadowing their own legislative initiative and action.

SOME of the more apparent weaknesses and dangers of this creeping bureaucracy in the field of higher education are these:

First, in regard to the administrative conduct of affairs, there develops a Christmas-tree chain of command. It works like this: The lowly professor has a need. He communicates this to his department chairman, who in turn presents the matter to one of the deans, who, if the matter is deemed of sufficient importance, will present it to the main dean. This dean then hies himself to the next stage in the hierarchy of command, and so it goes until the level of decision is reached.

Good administrative etiquette calls for an undeviating respect for this chain of communication, so that the No. 4 man on the totem pole dare not receive any communication from anyone except the No. 5 man. Logical as this seems on organization charts, it presents certain grave difficulties and dangers.

ONE is that the strength of the chain depends on the strength of its weakest link - the least able man in the series. Then, aside from deliberate misrepresentation en route—and many faculty members know cases of this kind—there is always the possibility of rays of information being refracted by the media through which they pass. I have often wondered, in recent years, what my requests sounded like by the time they reached the level of decision.

Somewhere along this line decisions are made, but where and by whom is not always clear. The system offers admirable opportunities for hedging and passing the buck. Nor can faculty members be consulted, no matter how great their competence on a given subject. They cannot be consulted because they are not in the chain of command.

Thus, one university with a nationally known expert in the field of publication has never once consulted him on matters regarding the university's own publication program. Another university plagued with labor troubles has never availed itself of a labor conciliator on its faculty. Decisions by a bureaucracy are merely announced, as *faits accomplis.*

A second difficulty is that the growth of the bureaucracy has expanded enormously the number of persons with whom the lowly faculty member must curry favor. Time was when only the dean and the department chairman mattered. Now the entire chain of command may have to be taken into consideration, for it is one of the devious aspects of the bureaucrat in action that, as Djilas has pointed out, he finds himself at war with anything which he does not administer. A large and powerful bureaucracy, then, places a premium upon service to its ends, and these tend not always to coincide with the primary function of the teacher.

THIS manifests itself particularly in regard to promotions. Two groups of faculty members tend to be promoted: those whose work is so outstanding that they must be promoted, and those who serve the administration. True, most universities now have standardized procedures and rules governing promotions, but in interpreting them the administration at many universities reminds one of children at play. Both groups play by the rules, but they change the rules when and as it is expedient for them to do so.

It is clear that the abnormal growth of a non-teaching bureaucracy makes for a general reduction in university efficiency. This is not only because mere size makes it unwieldly but also because administrators become involved in wrangling with one another as well as in justifying themselves to one another.

More important is the undoubted fact that the efficiency of the faculty is reduced. The proportion of time faculty members must give to the meeting of administrative details is far from humorous. The writer has carefully noted and tabulated his own experience. These administrative requirements account for from two to three weeks' time out of every fifteen which are considered a term of academic teaching. Multiplied for an entire faculty this represents a serious loss. A friend, always inclined to take a light view of serious matters, suggests that faculty members today need to retire at 70 because they cease to have the energy to meet all the detailed demands of the non-teaching bureaucracy.

Finally, there is the financial cost of maintaining this administrative plethora. The

exact facts are difficult to determine, since financial reports of universities are not always open to the scrutiny of inquiring faculty members, nor are they sufficiently clear in their distinction between

teaching and administrative costs.

BUT the price is high and few American universities, especially in this day of inflated costs, are in a position to indulge in the luxury. Increased salaries for teachers, coupled with increased status, would go far to improve the effectiveness of higher education in the United States. The non-teaching bureaucracy stands in the way of both.

Many university teachers today are convinced that much, perhaps most, of this administrative plethora makes no contribution to the main business of a univerrity, which is the teaching of young men and women. It is highly significant that the European universities which trained so many of the top scientists now in the service of the national defense of this country have

managed to get along without such a non-teaching bureaucracy. An educational Clemenceau who would rise and say, "WE TEACH," might prove as effective as the first World War Premier, who replied to all diversionary suggestions by saying, "I WAGE WAR."

IT would be unfair, of course, to close without paying tribute to many able administrators who eat out their hearts and bend their bodies to the breaking point in the work that is necessary to make a university a good place to teach and learn. But this article is not concerned with them or the necessary tasks which they perform. Its subject is the luxuriant underbrush which hampers the growth of the needed forest, and obstructs those who seek their proper pursuits in it.

October 12, 1958

College President— Idea Man or Money Man?

Instead of the intellectual leader he once was, one of them declares, pressures have forced him to become largely a fund-raiser, to education's loss.

By HAROLD TAYLOR

"**M**Y plea then is this," said Woodrow Wilson of Princeton University, "that we now deliberately set ourselves to make a home for the spirit of learning . . . ."

It is the task of the college president to make a home for the spirit of learning, although in contemporary America he is seldom free to think of his mission in ideas of this size. He is too absorbed in operating the business of learning to occupy himself with its spirit. His position as an educator has in fact become impossible. For the spirit of learning is a delicate plant that grows only in the most favorable of environments. It is nurtured by love and trust, it grows in the warmth of friendly association of minds, it responds to the encouragement, support and leadership of those who understand it because they have experienced it deeply.

The college president of previous generations was an educator, a scholar, often a clergyman, a *teacher*—a man who symbolized as well as administered

a community of scholars. He read a great deal, he spoke often to his students and faculty, at chapel, at daily or weekly college assemblies, on questions of moral and intellectual substance. He expressed in his person and in his daily work the results of learning and the experience of serious thought. At his best he was both a man of thought and a man of action, one who devoted himself to making real the life of the mind.

The college president of the second half of this century is not this. He is called upon to administer an organization that directs, among other things, a real estate development, a public relations program, a fund-raising and financial apparatus, and a community ranging from 500 to 40,000 in size lodged in a chain of small hotels. He is more like the mayor of a small town than an intellectual leader, more like the executive of a business corporation than an educator. Money is what he talks about, while bankers, politicians

and industrialists have the privilege of talking about education.

THE underlying causes of this shift in the character of the college presidency are dangerous to American society. They are dangerous because they force education and its leaders to concern themselves with organizing and administering academic manpower rather than with improving the quality of education. "The dilemma is," says one commentator, "unless an institution is run by a learned man, you may be left with an institution and no learning."

There are two main causes for the change in the role of the college president—the radical expansion of the educational system to accommodate an expanding population, and the lack of funds to support the expansion. The practical problems of organization and finance have overwhelmed the colleges and have made it impossible for college presidents to keep up with the demands placed upon them. At the same time the urgency of the problems has often persuaded boards of trustees to seek out administrators and men of business experience to serve as college presidents.

There are new buildings to be planned and built, administrators to be hired, faculty members to be appointed, and funds to be found for all of these. Next year, and in each succeeding year, we will need from $300 million to $500 million more than we are now spending to deal with the needs of the colleges and universities. In ten years the national budget for higher education must move from the present $4.5 billion to at least $8.5 billion. Each college has to find for itself its own portion of this ...mount.

What does this mean for the college president? In the case of one president of a distinguished institution of the liberal arts in the Midwest it has meant sitting in the waiting room of a lumber company along with the other salesmen, awaiting an audience with a company executive to whom he may present the needs of the private colleges of his state. His plea for support may mean a gift of $500 to $10,000 to be spread among approximately twenty colleges. The college president spends his time in other waiting rooms, at luncheons, cocktail parties, dinners, wherever potential donors are gathered together.

IN the case of state and municipal university presidents it means active involvement with political leaders, boards of regents and legislative lobbyists for securing adequate appropriations in the state budget, along with a public relations program built to advertise the university to the state, to the city, to the country.

It also means continual consultation with architects, contractors, alumni leaders, business men, real estate executives, public relations experts, lawyers and bankers, in order to coordinate all the components of the university program. In addition, it means an endless round of speeches to alumni, civic and national groups and radio and television broadcasts on the subject of the virtues of education and its financial needs. Almost every public statement from the college president now has to do with the need for money, almost every conference and public event planned by educational institutions has as its primary or secondary purpose to attract attention to the need for funds.

AS a result, most public discussion of education is concerned with practical and immediate requirements—the demand for scientists and engineers, the needs of industry for educated manpower, the pressures for teachers, for buildings, for higher pay. Even when education itself is discussed the topics are technical—how many years should be spent on what subjects, how large should the schools be, how can television be used to economize in teaching

time, how large can college classes be, what should be the faculty-student ratio?

We have become so used to discussing education in these terms that the mind, the spirit, the quality, of the American experience is seldom mentioned and seldom missed. It is as if education had no spiritual content, offered no joy, no intellectual delight, but were only a matter of subjects to be taken for material reasons and external purposes. Education has become all structure and academic content, when it should in fact provide a rich experi- ence in the enjoyment of ideas and human values.

The forces that have shaped the role of the president have also affected the attitudes of the faculty. Their efforts as teachers have been distracted by the continued need for money. That faculty salaries have fallen so far behind the salaries of other professions and vocations is not merely a cause of personal discomfort and deprivation to college faculty members. It is a severe handicap to the teacher in the fulfillment of his mission. He is compelled to be more conscious of his place in the competitive market for academic talent, more concerned about promotion in the hierarchy of the faculty.

In addition, he is caught by the same administrative forces

Colgate University.

which have trapped the president. He is called upon for service in many new ways— committees for buildings, for administrative surveys, for faculty salaries, for appointments, for curriculum, for scholarships—and so becomes involved with time-consuming tasks in administration. At the same time, he is asked to plan new courses, new educational programs for the expan-

Vassar College.

sion of his college, and to teach more students without decreasing the number of courses he offers.

This not only lowers the intellectual vitality of the college community, but has a direct effect on the position of the president in relation to his faculty. As the faculty becomes more involved in administration, the members inevitably become less inclined to grant freedom of decision either to their own elected representatives or to their administrative officers. It is thus difficult for the president to exercise appropriate educational leadership without seeming to threaten the prerogatives of the faculty. The increased bureaucracy of the modern college isolates the president from his students and faculty, and makes it impossible for him to share in the intellectual life of his community.

SO urgent are the financial needs that the scholar-president may find that all of his time has disappeared into fund-raising and business management, while by default the role of educational leadership is assumed by the faculty as a whole. In this situation, the system of faculty committees often serves to resist educational change rather than to initiate it, with faculty groups holding each other in check by the sheer variety of their conflicting interests and opinions.

New plans, no matter how exciting or from whatever source, may be picked away, bit by bit, until the luster of the original idea is gone and in its place is a neutered thing that has been able to survive the voting machinery of several committees and the faculty body.

What, then, is the solution?

The solution lies exactly where the two main problems occur—in the financing and administration of higher education. Both are incredibly inefficient. It is as if the editors of, and contributors to, magazines were responsible not only for maintaining the quality of the ideas and the writing, but also for collecting sufficient advertising and circulation to finance themselves.

IT must become the full responsibility of boards of trustees to finance the institutions they serve. The role of the president in financial matters should be to present educational ideas and needs in such a way that they can be understood and recognized as imperatives, not only by trustees, but by alumni, faculty members, students and the general public.

The college president must have time to read, to talk with his students and faculty, to listen, to learn. The moment to decide, as eventually he must, about the direction his college should take, or about issues of academic freedom, or Federal aid to education, or the relation of science to the arts, or the controversy over progressive vs. traditional theory, is not just before he makes a public statement to the press, but after years of continual study and critical thinking, through daily association in his university with those who are themselves concerned with such issues.

Otherwise, the educator can give no leadership to public policy in exactly the area where such leadership is crucial. Instead, he must take his opinions secondhand from others. Rather than leading opinion, he follows it in search of funds.

AS matters now stand, in a public-relations culture, the president learns the ways of the organization man, and because he must present his institution to the public as if it were the gem of all institutions, he is unable to think creatively on bigger issues. He is forced into chauvinism, and talks less of education in the dimension of its humanity and total scope than about the virtues of the particular institution he represents.

What is called for is a radical reorganization of the American college to reinstate the educator in the role which is his. Each board of trustees should contain a nucleus of full-time, if necessary salaried, members whose prime responsibility is to organize the fundraising and financial affairs of the institution. At present, board members, no matter how public spirited, are able to give to the problems of their institutions only such limited time as their business, professional and personal lives allow. But the chairmanship of a trustee committee on development or finance requires the whole of each week every week and the skill and decisiveness of a first-rate surgeon.

Similarly, the chairmanship of the board of trustees demands the full time of a well-educated, interested, experienced man of affairs no less than does the chairmanship of the board of directors of any large organization. It also requires an understanding of education, a belief in the freedom of the faculty and president to form educational policy, and a deep conviction that cultural and intellectual

Ohio State University.

values are of key importance to the life of a democratic society.

In the college itself, the financial and fund-raising duties should be delegated by the president to a vice president or provost who works directly with trustees in maintaining the financial position of the college.

OFTEN today we find that the president of a university has been appointed specifically because of his management and fund-raising abilities, with the educational duties assigned to vice presidents and deans. In some instance this works well, at least as far as finance

Drawing by Vernon Howe Bailey.
Wellesley College.

is concerned. But in the long run, under this arrangement, the influence of the university in the national life will decline.

The president, to whom we must look for final decision in matters of educational and cultural policy, remains the titular head of his institution, yet is not equipped to speak and to act as an educational authority or as an intellectual. Administrative efficiency may be dangerous if, in such circumstances, it is not based on the resources of an informed and broad-reaching mind.

It is also true that the situation of the college faculty can be remedied only by the application of large sums of money to support its enterprises. It is unfair to place upon the faculty both the psychological and the administrative burdens of financial problems. Members can be released to return to their real purpose of teaching and scholarship only by the provision of sufficient funds to relieve them of administrative responsibilities and financial concerns.

There are those who will say that money is not the answer, and of course they are right. Money is simply the necessary condition under which the an-

swer can be found. The point is that teachers and educators are unable to achieve ease of mind and freedom to be themselves under the wearing pressures of a competitive society. They are not armed for such combat. Or, if they are, their combats distract them from the true tasks of learning.

WE come once again to the question of what America wants. Do we want composers, scientists, writers, philosophers, poets, teachers, clergymen, public officials and citizens who can bring their creative gifts to enrich the spiritual life of the American people? Do we want a society whose military and material power is tempered with a love of humanity and a sense of justice? Do we want a civilization that honors the arts and the sciences as instruments for the enrichment of human life?

If we do we must support our schools and colleges with a generous and bold program of public and private funds— for buildings, for teachers' salaries, for scholarships. We should not make beggars of our educators, salesmen of our college presidents. If we continue to do so we will develop under the present system a breed of educational executive who in his personal and public character represents the material values of American society and who has learned very well how to reproduce his kind among the student bodies of this country.

To achieve the ends our democracy seeks will require massive support from the Federal and state governments for our colleges—grants for buildings, a national scholarship and loan program for students, fellowships for graduates. It will require equally strong support from corporations, alumni, parents and individual donors, for faculty salaries and other needs. But if we are to have colleges that are homes for the spirit of learning, we must first make it possible for men of learning to live there.

April 12, 1959

PUBLISH OR PERISH—

The familiar threat to "publish or perish" still makes life miserable for university professors, according to a report published in the current issue of Ohio State University's Journal of Higher Education.

Replying to a survey of 126 leading American colleges and universities by Prof. Bill G. Rainey of Murray State Agricultural College in Oklahoma, more than three-fourths of the university presidents indicated that publication has a strong influence on employment and promotion; the rest said that it has some effect. About 75 per cent of university teachers write professionally, the report said, and all the universities surveyed give some type of aid to teachers who are writing.

Of the senior college presidents replying to the survey, nearly half considered outside writing an important criterion in hiring and promoting faculty, and all acknowledge its influence. Only about 40 per cent of the college teachers write professionally, however, although nearly all the presidents said they encouraged it.

Junior college presidents consider publication less influential, with less than one-fourth reporting that it had a positive effect on salary increases. But about 40 per cent considered it an important consideration for employment and promotion.

February 19, 1961

Colleges Step Up Faculty Raids In Rivalry for 'Name' Professors

By FRED M. HECHINGER

A shortage of top-level academic talent has transformed faculty recruiting into a frantic competition, little short of institutional piracy.

Every lure, from outbidding a rival university on salary to offers of appointments with almost non-existing teaching duties, is being used to capture "name" academicians.

The traditional gentlemen's agreement to halt raiding not later than May, in the interest of campus stability, has been abandoned. High-pressure recruiting now continues throughout the year.

These key facts have emerged from a New York Times study of professional recruiting across the country.

One spokesman characterized the situation as "strictly a seller's market" in which the most sought-after professors virtually write their own tickets. This does not usually apply to the lower echelons, below associate professors. There are approximately 283,000 college and university faculty members, from instructor to full professor. No separate statistics for full professors, the top echelon, are available.

Faculty salaries for 1961-62 ranged from an average of $6,033 for instructors to an average of $11,595 for full professors. According to the most recent statistics published by the American Association of University Professors, Harvard leads with an average salary of $18,750 for its full professors.

One president of a large urban university in the East said that the "going offer" in raids on the most desirable scholars was $20,000, with a promise of no more than one course of teaching a year. Often that teaching assignment is even cut in half—one course every other semester. The president said that in the past month he had to intercede in more than half a dozen cases to try to block the raid.

Observers call most serious the fact that many of the outstanding faculty members devote less and less time to the teaching of undergraduates.

They also point out that weaker institutions, intent on improving their image rapidly, are trying to buy prestige by using a few prominent scholars

as window dressing while the rest of the faculty continues to be underpaid. This threatens to widen the gap between the academic stars and the supporting cast.

Another widespread complaint is that institutions with sizable foundation or Government grants are able to lure outstanding talent away from rivals that have slowly and laboriously built up departments of quality but lack glamorous crash projects.

Raiding Morality Defended

On the credit side, it is widely conceded that the long-term effects will be to give outstanding scholars the kind of prestige and reward they have long been denied. This can be expected to upgrade the more routine conditions, too.

Dr. William J. Baumol, Professor of Economics at Princeton and chairman of the committee on salaries of the American Association of University Professors, said that he saw nothing immoral in hiring exceptional faculty members at higher salaries so long as the institution's general quality and strength was built up at the same time.

What is wrong, he said, is the establishment of one spectacular chair as bait, surrounded by low salaries.

Although there has been criticism of excessive research and consultant work, Dr. Baumol said that the fact was that these services were desperately needed, with not enough people capable of providing them.

"I often say 'no' and then feel guilty; but I also feel guilty when I sit on the train to Washington going away from the campus," he said.

He said that raiding had been intensified as a result of higher specialization.

"Sometimes it's easier for me to talk to colleagues in other departments than to some of the specialists in my own," he said.

Money Is Chief Lure

What are some of the factors that make faculty members eager to move? A spokesman at the University of Chicago said that "money is it." But he conceded that there were other important lures.

"We can't compete with the scenic beauty of Palo Alto in California," he said. "And let's face it, too, that the determining factor in the decision is the wife and the family."

Urban universities, unless they can become deeply involved in neighborhood development and urban renewal, face increasing handicaps.

"The urban university, if it wants to keep open at night, has to have good faculty housing and schools for the children nearby," the Chicago spokesman said.

Dr. Putnam F. Jones, dean of the Graduate Faculty at the University of Pittsburgh, said that a "university in upper New York State" had tried to get one of his economists by offering, in addition to a $6,000 raise, a university-paid insurance, retirement and annuity, plus full four-year tuition payment for all of the scholar's children at the colleges of their choice.

Pittsburgh had earlier abducted the same professor from Chicago.

Another talking point is to let an outstanding scholar point out other scholars, anywhere in the country, with whom he would like to build a particularly strong department—and promise to try to get them as a tie-in. Pittsburgh said that it had lost some anthropologists when the Indiana University started bidding hard for them to make up such a constellation.

A check with Indiana showed that they were able to get three anthropologists last week, among them a leading African and Latin-American specialist from Pittsburgh and another from Northwestern University. Both had associate professors, but were immediately moved into full professorships.

Indiana's move toward an outstanding department was supported in part by a $2,300,000 Ford Foundation grant for graduate international studies.

Getting a man who wants to specialize in a newer field of strong interest to him is a powerful lure. Indiana took an economist from the graduate business school at the University of Nebraska, without a special financial carrot.

"He is interested in transportation and public utilities, and we are building an Institute of Urban Development, with economists and business school experts cooperating," a spokesman said.

"But we're also losing them," he admitted. Rutgers University in New Jersey had just taken a professor of the classics by offering him a department chairmanship.

Few institutions like to talk about their losses, whereas they advertise their acquisitions. The fear is that faculty departures signify lower prestige. However, although university administrators like to boast about new appointments, they are understandably reluctant to talk about the terms lest they make the next foray more costly or lower the morale of the home forces.

One administration member at Yale, who called the present recruiting "strictly a dog-eat-dog business," pointed with pride to the acquisition last year of Prof. C. Vann Woodward, the historian. Professor Woodward had been at The

403

Johns Hopkins University and was offered a Sterling Professorship at Yale where his son is an undergraduate. He was given a one-year leave of absence by Yale as his first year there. Thereafter, his teaching schedule was to consist of one seminar so that he would be free to devote himself to writing.

Teacher Wins Promotion

By contrast, Yale last year lost Dr. E. G. Begle, nationally noted director of the School Mathematics Study Group concerned with high school mathematics reform. Only an assistant professor at Yale, where the mathematicians appeared more concerned with university mathematics than lower school curriculum revision, Dr. Begle accepted a full professorship at Stanford's Graduate School of Education.

Dr. Kingman Brewster, provost at Yale, said:

"You've got to enjoy fishing without catching all the fishes."

He said that the high-quality institutions in the East were doing relatively little effective raiding of each others faculties because their salary scales and general conditions were not sufficiently different. As a consequence, he said, "natural inertia keeps people from moving."

These institutions, he noted, merely try to replace faculty members they lose, often through retirement, or to "fill in weak spots."

He said that, except for the metropolitan areas, the Eastern universities gain from the fact that there was "no bumper-to-bumper commuting problem" and that these institutions, although comprehensive in academic scope, were still communities of scholars and not sprawling giants.

Other Factors in Decision

He listed these attractions that, in the process of raiding, are often more important than increased salaries:

¶Liberal university-financed housing loans.

¶Generous research support in terms of money and time.

¶A fellowship policy to attract first-rate graduate students.

¶The assurance that the lower echelons of the faculty are also well-paid and generously treated.

However, he said that the decision between accepting or turning down offers from comparable institutions was most likely to be influenced by climate, smog, the conditions of the local public schools and the distance to the suburbs.

"New York City, for example, is either a major attraction or a deterrent," he said. "You either like it a lot or it's repulsive."

Whereas Eastern spokesmen

talk of the attraction of their institutions, a Stanford representative pointed to "the westward tilt of the continent." He cited the example of the chairman of Anthropology Department at Columbia University going West to take a professorship at Stanford. Similarly, the chairman-elect at New York University, will be a professor on the California campus next year. Three senior faculty members from the Columbia Law School and one from Cornell were also listed as following the westward tilt.

Threat From the West

Stanford and the University of California are probably among the most effective—and respected—large-scale threats to the Eastern "repositories of talent," as one academic expert in New York put it. Stanford's special attraction, in addition to its considerable wealth and ideal climate, is its almost unlimited expanse of land. Much of this is available at token rentals for professors who want to build their own homes.

Perhaps even more important, part of this land has been converted into a giant "research park" for private industrial laboratories. This makes the consultants' territory just about as convenient and compact as the adjoining campus itself.

A Stanford spokesman said that the box score for 1961-62 was not yet available, but that in 1960-61 the university had gained thirty professors and lost only one.

Dr. Robert J. Wert, vice provost, said that he considered as important as all the tangible lures the fact that Stanford was developing its programs and departments "across the board." The really good person, he said, cannot be attracted by a flashy offer unless the whole department "looks good."

Spend Less Time at Job

Jacques Barzun, dean of the Graduate Faculties at Columbia University, said that faculty-pirating practices failed to add to teaching manpower but merely transplanted it. In the process, the transplanted teachers tend to teach less each time.

He told of an approach by "a wealthy Western university" to one exceptionally good professor. The offer was $2,000 more than whatever his salary might be—plus $1,000 for every semester hour of teaching he chose to do. An average undergraduate one-term course consists of three semester hours.

Dr. Barzun called this "official recognition of absurdity"—payment on a piece-work basis to reward the teacher for doing what ought to be his basic job.

He listed these among other current practices:

¶"The-band-of-brothers idea," or the growing practice among faculty members to say: "If Joe goes, I go, too." This, he stressed, is not a matter of personal friendships but a result of team work on foundation projects or other research grants.

¶Snaring a noted academician with the promise that once he has established a new department and got it going, he would not have to do anything by way of administration or teaching. "This is a form of sterilization," Dr. Barzun said.

¶Stockpiling, or the practice of building up larger staffs of prominent faculty members than necessary, either for purposes of prestige or to bag grants or contracts later on. He said that this practice was confined largely to the Western institutions.

Competition Is Evaluated

Charles H. Peake, Vice President for the Academic Disciplines at the University of Pittsburgh, charged that some of the "excessive competition" was coming from "upstart institutions" that wanted to build prestige by establishing "professional landmarks outside their general range." He said that the safety brake to slow this trend was that "good scholars fortunately do not want to go to places where they can't find good graduate students."

The more serious competition, Dr. Peake said, comes from institutions with a real potential for rapid but solid expansion. In face of competition from grant-supported programs, universities can only hold their own by developing their own research institutes so that they "can offer package deals." He pointed to the loss of an African specialist who will only have to teach one course in his new station.

"In many places, the trend is to get three people instead of one to take care of both research and teaching," he said. He said that "the code of ethics of when you can recruit is gone."

Small Colleges Hard Hit

The raiding parties also hit the smaller colleges of high quality. Wesleyan University in Middletown, Conn., reports that after one of their professors of classics had written a successful book, he was bombarded with offers.

The president of one large state university told him to come and write his own ticket. He offered the professor his own department, if he did not like the existing one, a Wesleyan spokesman said. The scholar turned down the offer as "preposterous."

However, this was only a respite for Wesleyan. The University of Rochester managed to be sufficiently persuasive.

Dr. Joseph C. Palamountain Jr., Wesleyan's provost, said that the competition had moved from mathematics and the sciences to the social sciences. It is rapidly growing in the creative arts, but has not yet seriously affected the humanities, he asserted.

Dr. Palamountain pointed to a successful recruiting venture in getting an economist who had been with the Bureau of the Budget and a visiting professor at Stanford.

"We don't go very far in the direction of lighter teaching loads because we are a teaching institution," he said. "We try to match salaries with other offers. Fortunately there are some people who like New England."

"We lose if somebody needs a big hunk of physical equipment or wants a large team of specialists," he said. "But we are attractive to teachers who want to work alone or across the many disciplines."

Dr. Palamountain said that once a man whom the department wanted was spotted "the attempt at seduction has to take place at a rapid rate." If it takes more than two months, it usually ends in failure.

As the competition in the academic field gets stiffer, some institutions are successfully raiding the two institutions that originally took some of their most valuable members away from the campus—Government and industry. Yale, for example, last month announced that William R. Bennett Jr. would leave Bell Telephone Laboratories to become an associate professor of physics and applied science to help develop the new undergraduate engineering department.

Chicago has raided the National Science Foundation and come away with John T. Wilson, who will become assistant to the president and Professor of Psychology. It also carried off Donald McClure from the Radio Corporation of America and has appointed him Professor of Chemistry.

For other recent appointments, Chicago has gone to the Union of South Africa, British Columbia, Canada and Venezuela. The University of Pittsburgh confirmed the greater recruiting effort abroad.

Historians at Chicago point out that what may seem momentarily alarming is not a new phenomenon in American academic history. They recall that the only reason the university was able to start operations in 1892 was because its president, William Rainey Harper, was a pastmaster at raiding faculties across the country.

June 10, 196

The Emerging U. S. University Is Called a Model

Kerr of California Delivers 3d Godkin Talk at Harvard

By JOHN H. FENTON
Special to The New York Times

CAMBRIDGE, Mass., April 25 — The American university that is emerging from the present ferment in the "education industry" will serve as a model for the rest of the world, a California educator said tonight.

At a time when knowledge is "central to the conduct of an entire society," Dr. Clark Kerr, president of the University of California, told a Harvard audience that "mountain ranges" of higher education were forming.

Already three groups of universities, following the industrial strength and population centers were forming "great plateaus" of interconnected educational centers, Dr. Kerr said. He spoke in the last of three annual Godkin lectures in Sanders Theater, adjacent to Harvard Yard.

For a National Foundation

In the two earlier lectures, Dr. Kerr described the broadening scope of the university as creating a "multiversity," and he called for a national foundation for higher education parallel to the National Science Foundation.

The lecture series was established in 1903 in memory of

Associated Press
Dr. Clark Kerr

Edwin L. Godkin, British-American journalist who founded The Nation and edited the New York Evening Post. The 1963 series was concerned with "The Uses of the University." The lectures eventually will be published in book form by the Harvard University Press.

Dr. Kerr, who directs the education of 58,600 students on seven campuses in California, said the Pacific coastal complex of universities in his state had 36 per cent of the American Nobel laureates in science and 20 per cent of the members of the National Academy of Science.

The largest plateau, said Dr. Kerr, ran from Boston to Washington. It embraces 46 per cent of the nation's Nobel winners in the sciences and 40 per cent of the members of the National Academy of Sciences.

The third of the plateaus, he said, was made up of the Big Ten and Chicago with 10 per cent of the Nobel laureates and 14 per cent of the membership of the National Academy of Sciences.

A fourth plateau appears in the process of development in the Texas - Louisiana area, Dr. Kerr said.

In discussing the idea of the "multiversity" in the first lecture, Dr. Kerr said it was a concept of combining undergraduate instruction, graduate and professional education and research and the American idea of service to the state and nation.

The leadership of such an establishment, said Dr. Kerr, calls for mediators rather than giants as among past university presidents.

"The mediator, whether, in government or industry or labor relations or domestic quarrels, is always subject to abuse," said Dr. Kerr. "He wins few clear-cut victories; he must aim more at avoiding the worst than seizing the best."

He went on:

"Out of fragments, experiments and conflicts, a kind of unlikely consensus has been reached: undergraduate life

He Sees 'Mountain Ranges' of Higher Education Forming

seeks to follow the British, who have done the best with it, and the historical line that goes back to Plato—the humanists find their sympathies there. Graduate life and research follow the Germans, who once did the best with them, and an historical line that goes back to Pythagoras—the scientists lend their support to all this.

"The 'lesser' professions (lesser than law and medicine) and service activities follow the American pattern, since the Americans have been best at them, and an historical line that goes back to the Sophists —the social scientists are most likely to be sympathetic. The resulting combination does not seem plausible but it has given America a remarkably effective educational institution.

"A university anywhere can aim no higher than to be as British as possible for the sake of the undergraduates, as German as possible for the stake of the graduates and the research personnel, as American as possible for the sake of the public at large—and as confused as possible for the sake of the preservation of the whole uneasy balance."

Where a community has a soul, acting as a single animating principle, said Dr. Kerr, "the multiversity has several of them, several of them quite good, although there is much debate on which souls really deserve salvation."

April 26, 1903

'The Knowledge Industry'

The delivery of the Godkin Lectures at Harvard by Clark Kerr, president of the University of California, gave personal meaning to his prediction of a bridge linking the East Coast "ideopolis," which runs from Boston to Washington, with the nation's other great concentration of university centers on the West Coast. These intellectual focal points together are already home base for 82 per cent of all American Nobel Prize winners.

Dr. Kerr's lecture is important beyond statistics which might be misread as regional boasting. He has put aside clichés and tried to assess the vast changes under way in higher learning. When he forecasts that the university of the past is to be replaced by the "multiversity" of the future, he talks about more than size. When he considers the importance of Federal grants, he refuses to act out the old political tribal dance of Federal control versus institutional autonomy.

When he lists the vast contributions made by scholarship and research to the physical sciences and hints at similar revolutions in knowledge about to explode in the biological sciences, he eschews the chant of the "need for balance" by offering equal academic time and grants to all other fields. "The only certainly wrong decision is that the balance of today must be preserved for tomorrow," he warns. Support must be on the basis of merit, need and future productivity.

Especially challenging is Dr. Kerr's prediction that what the railroads did for the second half of the last century and the automobile for the first half of our century may be done for the rest of this century by "the knowledge industry," with the university at its center. M.I.T., for instance, has already become at least as closely related to industry and government as Iowa State ever was to agriculture.

The rapid shift from past priorities does not imply that universities ought to face their future as rudderless ships driven by currents of governmental and societal pressures. Mr. Kerr cautions that "the university may now again need to find out whether it has a brain as well as a body." We agree that in this attempt a National Foundation for Higher Education, created on the model of the National Science Foundation, would be of value—not to maintain artificial balances but to determine new areas of merit and promise —in the arts, international studies and other fields.

But more active leadership must also come from within the universities themselves. Too often faculties tend to be liberal toward everybody else while being excessively conservative about changes in their own departments.

Perhaps the problem most urgently in need of tackling is the dangerous decline of interest among research-oriented faculty members in the quality of undergraduate education. That is where reforms must begin to assure that "the knowledge industry" will not run out of steam by forgetting its most essential resource—individual human talent.

May 5, 196

WHERE THE TIME GOES

A typical week's schedule for a professor with an eight-hour teaching load.

HOURS	MONDAY	TUESDAY	WEDNESDAY	THURSDAY	FRIDAY	SATURDAY
9-10	Prepare senior class	Teach freshman class	Teach freshman class	Prepare senior class	Give exam to freshman class	Teach freshman class
10-11		Coffee	Write letters of recommendation	See book salesman	Argue with department chairman	See students who can't wait till office hours
11-12	Teach senior class	Office hours	Teach senior class	Teach senior class	Office hours	Teach senior class
12-1	Lunch	Luncheon meeting of faculty committee	Lunch	Lunch	Lunch	Drive to meeting of high-school teachers
1-2	Read latest journals		Lunch	Fill out questionnaires from dean, Government and two high schools	Correct examination papers	
2-3			Office hours			
3-4	Short departmental meeting	Find error in research paper	Referee paper submitted to a research journal	Answer mail		Give lecture
4-5		Try to correct error		Write report for national committee	Receive visiting lecturer	Discussion
5-6			Referee a research proposal			Dinner
6-7	Dinner	Dinner	Dinner	Dinner	Dinner with visitor	
7-8	Work on research paper	Prepare two classes	Proofread previous research paper	Go to movies		Drive home
8-9						
9-10			Read detective story	Find way of correcting error in research paper	Prepare two classes	Go to sleep early
10-11	Prepare class					
11-12						

June 2, 196

Colleges Study Their Portfolios As Financial Burden Increases

Boom in Enrollment Prompts a Change in Emphasis to Common Stocks— Buying-Power Drop Noted

By ROBERT FROST

With the financial burden on higher education climbing steadily as a result of increasing enrollment, privately endowed colleges and universities are taking a closer look at their investment portfolios.

Administrators must use their endowment funds not only to provide income for current demands, but also to "protect their dollars" against the inflationary trend of the economy.

These funds, primarily supported by gifts from alumni, have in the past been managed very conservatively. High-grade corporate bonds were usually given preference over more risky common stocks.

In recent years, however, the emphasis has shifted. As one bank officer, charged with the counseling of several endowment funds, explained: "Investments in good quality growth stocks will enable schools to benefit from increased earnings and dividends, and in the long run provide better yields than similar fixed-income situations."

Part of the shift has been caused by the continued decline in the buying power of the dollar. At Cornell University this problem "seems to be uppermost in our minds at present and may require a reshaping of our portfolio with greater emphasis on equity," it was said.

Aggressive Stand Seen

Most endowments are structured on the "balanced fund" concept, which seeks to get maximum income and also allow for appreciation. Some of the larger universities, which do not rely as heavily on endowment income, have tended to take a more aggressive position, stressing appreciation.

While endowment earnings help to meet the compelling needs of the present, investment counselors warn that too much stress on income could be detrimental to a fund's overall purpose.

Frank Grady, a vice president at the United States Trust Company, which services 13 schools, has found that "most schools deal more with the need for current income, causing a constant battle to get long-term growth." He cautioned that "portfolios too heavy on income are being shortsighted and unfair to future generations."

Paul A. McMannus, vice president of the Investment Advisory and Custody Division of Chase Manhattan Bank, one of whose accounts is Columbia University, stated in an interview that schools that set a "target return are handicapping appreciation by pressuring income."

Book Value Cited

Although many schools try to keep yields at about 4 per cent of the endowment's market value, "the real test," the financial vice president of a large university observed, "is the return on book value."

Based on book value, nearly all schools earn in excess of the 4 per cent target. The University of Rochester estimates its earnings on market value at 3.21 per cent, but at book value, the price actually paid on investments, it is a healthy 7.03 per cent.

Earnings of even small endowments may yield more than a half million dollars, while the funds of large universities return several million dollars annually. This revenue is normally used for faculty salaries, scholarships, building programs and other similar current expenditures.

Harvard University is the most heavily endowed school in the nation, with the market value of its fund at over $843 million. For the fiscal year ended June 30, it earned more than $28.5 million.

Following Harvard is Yale, with $392 million; Massachusetts Institute of Technology, $267 million; University of Chicago, $252 million; Princeton and Rochester with $230 million each.

College and university endowment funds are most heavily invested in oil and petroleum producers and public utilities, which may represent as much as 25 to 30 per cent of a school's fund.

Favored Stocks Listed

The list of endowment fund favorites includes Standard Oil Company (New Jersey), Texaco, Inc., International Business Machines Corporation, American Telephone and Telegraph Company, Gulf Oil Corporation, General Motors Corporation, Eastman Kodak Company, E. I. du Pont de Nemours & Co. and General Electric Company.

Although endowment funds are not normally used for speculation, one investment counselor at a large New York bank suggested that a small part of the fund should be invested in cyclical investments, such as textiles, steels or trucking, for short-term profits.

The University of Rochester, which maintains such an account, capitalized handsomely on investments in Xerox and Control Data, while these companies were in the growing stage. Princeton owns 16,439 shares of Xerox with a book value of $77,385 or an average cost per share of about $4.75.

Princeton applies the following criteria in selecting investments: (1) the right industry (noncyclical in general); (2) leadership in that industry; (3) quality of management; (4) research or technical competence; (5) relatively low labor costs; (6) growth of company in industry and growth of industry, and (7) for some companies, the ability to compete in world markets.

Although common stocks and bonds consume the major portion of endowment investment, some schools have purchased considerable amounts of real estate, both for profit and with an eye toward future campus expansion.

Stanford University, with over 15 per cent of its endowment in real estate, has developed a shopping center and industrial park. Besides being "very profitable," Stanford reported, its industrial park "has attracted new science-orientated industries to the campus."

At Syracuse University, the feeling has been that "well located real estate holdings offer real promise of capital appreciation." It holds approximately 10 per cent of its endowment in real estate, including a hotel in New York City.

The Boston Fund, which annually conducts a study of college and university endowment funds, found in a recent survey of 48 schools with endowment funds totaling over $4 billion that 55.9 per cent of these funds were in common stocks, 32.9 per cent in bonds, 7.8 per cent in real estate, 2 per cent in preferred stocks and 1.4 per cent in other investments.

Interviews with several bank trust officers disclosed that the trend in college and university endowment funds today was to keep 55 to 60 per cent invested in quality common stocks, about 35 per cent in high grade bonds and the remainder in "selected situations" such as real estate.

Many colleges and universities, realizing the difficulty of trying to make investment decisions with "too many people to satisfy," have set up committees of two or three trustees with authority to make these decisions for the entire board

Tenure Issue

By FRED M. HECHINGER

Although a number of flashy cases and accompanying student protests recently have moved academic tenure into the center of public attention, the debate over it actually is a perennial one. The spring issue of the AAUP Bulletin, the quarterly of the American Association of University Professors, published last week, is full of specific cases. So is every preceding issue.

The procedures involved differ from institution to institution. But the common denominator is a specific probationary period, especially in the lower ranks of academia, which leads either to permanent employment and tenure or to a notice, generally at least one year ahead of time, to look for a berth elsewhere.

Once tenure is given, the teacher's position remains assured until he reaches retirement age or decides to go elsewhere on his own accord.

At Harvard, for example, instructors' appointments end automatically after a three-year period unless a promotion to assistant professorship can be offered at that point. The assistant professorship consists of one non-renewable five-year term. During the fourth year, the assistant professor is told whether he is to be promoted to permanent rank. If not, he has one year to look elsewhere.

Trustees' Decision

As part of the legacy of reform left by Dr. James B. Conant, who preceded Nathan M. Pusey as Harvard's president, the ad hoc committee which passes on promotion to permanent appointment must include distinguished scholars in the candidate's field from outside Harvard. The final decision, based on the committee's recommendation (which, in turn, has had the benefit of expert review by the appointee's department), is left with the president and ultimately the trustees.

All associate professors and full professors at Harvard (and most other institutions) are on permanent tenure.

At public institutions, the probationary period is frequently shorter and tenure may be given to the lower ranks, even after three years or less, without promotion to associate professorships.

However, a member of the budget committee which deals with tenure matters at the University of California said recently: "We have our own way of preventing this from leading to the accumulation of deadwood. If a young man with tenure doesn't work out, we just don't promote him, and he goes elsewhere in a hurry."

Why has tenure become the most basic condition of employment in the academic world? The most persuasive reason for the tenure system is the protection of academic freedom. If a professor's right to take an unpopular stand, politically or academically, is essential to free inquiry and honest scholarship, then ironclad safeguards must be built into the system. Freedom of this kind cannot exist without a protection of the scholar's livelihood. The experience of economic blacklisting in the entertainment industry during the so-called McCarthy period underlined the close link between freedom of thought and economic security.

Even in academic terms, the absence of tenure protection might lead to the suppression of certain scholarly and scientific views, as has happened in the Soviet Union over such issues as genetics and as happened in the United States over Darwin's evolution theory.

Why the Controversy?

On a less exalted level, tenure may simply give stability to academic quality by preventing trustees and other "outsiders" from tampering with the academic appointment and employment system.

In addition, academic salaries were until recently so far below the scale of rewards in other fields requiring similar talent and preparation that security was an essential substitute for affluence.

Why, then, has the issue of tenure become a cause for public controversy?

One major reason is not tenure but the qualities which lead to tenure. Undergraduates across the country—from Berkeley to Yale—feel neglected. They charge that too little promotion and tenure opportunities are being granted to those faculty members whom they respect as teachers. These students therefore are putting pressure on the senior professors as well as on the university presidents and their advisory committees to give greater weight to a faculty member's action in the classroom than to his research or publication output.

But while the controversy, with its catch phrase of "publish or perish," gets most of the attention, new problems are hidden beneath the surface. With the academic market weighted in the professors' favor, institutions are understandably eager to offer promotion and tenure to those faculty members who can be expected to be more than short-term transients. Tenure offers the teacher a lifetime berth, but there is nothing to prevent him from pulling up stakes a year later and moving to another university—often one that offers less teaching for more money.

An intangible cause of imbalance is the fact that extreme youth has taken over in mathematics and science. Productivity in those fields can be measured rapidly. Experience seems to be less important than the absence, in the words of one young scientist, of a hardening of attitudes.

The result is comparable to the morale problem created in the Army and Navy when the Air Force turned out youthful generals on the assembly line. The humanities and social sciences, which rely on experience and maturity, thus lag behind the sciences in terms of tenure appointments and promotions.

Those responsible for the tenure decision face a dilemma. Like the college admissions dean, they are expected to gamble on future performance; but whereas the admissions expert need worry only about a student's next four years, the tenure committee has to project a lifetime of promise.

Tomorrow's students may be demonstrating because of today's leniency.

None of this absolves departmental politics of blame for some abuses of the tenure system—especially when it is used to keep out faculty members who disagree with the dominant "school" within departments. The use of tenure to suppress academic freedom internally is as harmful as the external loss of such freedom through lack of tenure.

Fritz Machlup, professor of economics and international finance at Princeton and past president of the AAUP, makes a convincing case for tenure—even on the issue of preventing the accumulation of deadwood. Without tenure, he points out, the temptation is to say, "Let's try him for another year." If tenure decisions are taken seriously, the tough standards of "up or out" make quality control more effective.

Like Congressional immunity, tenure can be abused. It may protect mediocrity and occasionally even irresponsibility. But the arguments in its favor remain more persuasive than the objections. Virtually every recent controversy illustrates not the flaw in the tenure system but the need to adjust the yardsticks by which candidates for tenure are to be judged in the light of changing conditions in academia.

'Publish or Perish'

Why Prof. Edelweiss Has Little Time for Junior

By ROBERT LANGBAUM

THERE is indignation these days over the so-called "publish-or-perish" policy by which professors are rated in our universities. The catch phrase is used as if it described a senseless and brutal mechanism for depriving good teachers of their jobs and students of adequate instruction.

This shows how little the public understands about our universities and the changes that have taken place in them since World War II. Protests without an adequate knowledge of the facts could end by swelling the pressures, already so formidable in our democracy, for a kind of genial mediocrity. They could end by defeating their own purpose—to achieve good university teaching.

Editorialists and others who assert that "teaching comes first" wonder why the universities should encourage professors to divert their efforts from their primary job of teaching and why universities should let anyone go who satisfies the students even if he fails to satisfy the publishing requirement. This argument turns on a false set of alternatives. It suggests that some faculty members publish while others are good teachers. The plain fact, however, is that in any university the best and most successful teachers are also the men who are known, or on their way to becoming known, for their publications. There are, of course, exceptions—the famous scholar who is a bore in class, the great teacher who has published little if anything—but they *are* exceptions.

The notion that there is something incompatible between teacher and scholar probably derives from a mistaken idea of justice that would have the blessings of this world equally distributed. If one man is handsome, another ought to be intelligent; if one is rich, another ought to be virtuous; if one is a good scholar, another ought to be a good teacher. Fortunately for the universities, however, this last division of blessings does not apply. Both qualities are usually found in the same man, because publication and teaching require the same talents—intelligence and articulateness. That is why universities consider successful publication an index of successful teaching. Indeed, the work that goes into publication is often a positive *condition* of good teaching.

THE thing that distinguishes university from high-school teaching is not only the subject matter but the professor's attitude toward it. In a good university course, students ought to get from the professor a sense that the subject is a living thing, being continually made and unmade by living men. They learn from this to respect the subject and to be critical of contributions to it—to see it not as academic fiddling but as a bold and hazardous adventure. Some may even be inspired to embark for themselves on the adventure of enlarging knowledge.

In most cases, it is publication, and the work which precedes it, that gives a professor intimate engagement with his subject which students sense and from which they catch fire. But the professor's scholarship is not only good for students; it is, in most cases, necessary for the professor if he is to stay alive intellectually. For most men of energy and talent, teaching is not and cannot be a full-time career. The university system is, in fact, predicated on the idea that the kind of man who would be willing to make teaching a full-time career is probably not of university caliber.

Most professors teach only nine hours a week. Senior men may teach six hours or less. Although the hours in class represent only a fraction of the time spent in preparing for

classes; in reading examinations, term papers, masters' theses and doctoral dissertations; in sitting on committees and doing routine administrative chores, it remains true that university teaching is still not quite a full-time job. Those professors who make it so have always the uneasy sense that they are stretching the work. Because the universities do not consider teaching a full-time job, they demand evidence of some other activity relevant to their interests — an administrative job often being accepted in lieu of publication.

WHY not get rid of the publishing requirement, then, and by increasing the hours in class *make* teaching a full-time job — and thus help solve the teacher shortage? The problem here is that if university teaching were to become, like high-school teaching, a full-time job, the universities would no longer attract men capable of giving first-class *university* courses. And without time or energy to grow intellectually, professors already in the universities would lose ground until in time they would know only as much as they needed to teach their courses—which for undergraduate courses is not very much. They would cease to be effective university teachers because students would no longer sense an extra depth of knowledge or a position in the adult world based on something other than attending to them.

While a small amount of teaching is stimulating and refreshing for a man of intellect, too much teaching can dull the mind and drain energy without giving much in return. Since it keeps a man from his own work, it can lead to a depressing sense of unfulfillment, of doing something less than a man's work.

Original scholarship, on the other hand, seems like a man's work because it is the activity in which a professor competes with, and is judged by, his peers. In teaching, he always has the advantage of age and experience over his students. Their plaudits, though gratifying, cannot be a real measure of his intellectual achievement.

WHILE the successful teacher-scholar is the ideal, there are not,

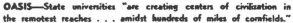

OASIS—State universities "are creating centers of civilization in the remotest reaches . . . amidst hundreds of miles of cornfields."

and never will be, enough of them to go around. They constitute a majority of the faculty only in the five or six very best universities. Universities farther down the scale are lucky if they can boast one or two such men in each department. Although some critics rail at these academic "big shots" because they are unavailable to most students, especially to undergraduates, the fact is that distinguished professors are unavailable in relation to the demand for them—because so many students want to crowd into their classes. The truth is these men actually teach *more* than their share of students.

The usual complaint is that Junior cannot get a course with the famous Professor Edelweiss; or if he does, that Edelweiss has little time to give him outside class. Now the university ought, as far as possible, to see that Edelweiss gives at least one course open to qualified undergraduates, but Junior must also realize that he gets the benefit of Edelweiss in all his courses because Edelweiss's presence has attracted faculty and students of a higher caliber than would otherwise have been at the university. If conferences with Edelweiss are short, Junior might

INSPIRED—Writing a book engages a professor with his subject and students in turn "catch fire."

well reflect that 10 minutes with him may be worth hours with a lesser man.

If Junior does not agree, if he would rather have from his teachers less distinction and more time, then he is the kind of student who ought to have gone to a college rather than a university. The university offers the advantages of size — celebrities, good libraries and laboratories, a cosmopolitan and intellectually vibrant atmosphere—but the prospective undergraduate must be prepared to find it impersonal

and hard on the nerves. If he needs a cozier atmosphere, then college is the place for him.

COLLEGES and universities are often indiscriminately mixed up in criticisms of higher education, by which critics usually mean undergraduate teaching. But while teaching undergraduates is the sole purpose of colleges, it is only one of the three main purposes of universities. As centers for the advancement of learning, universities are also concerned with teaching graduate students and with research.

This does not mean that colleges are inferior places, of course. Many colleges have higher intellectual standards than many universities, and the size of some of our mammoth state universities can cancel out the advantages. There is a laudable trend nowadays, started at Harvard and Yale, to have the undergraduate spend his college years in one residence house with a resident faculty, where he can feel himself a member of a small community while still taking advantage of a university's cosmopolitan stir and bustle.

IT is important that prospective undergraduates and their parents clearly understand the differences between colleges and universities. It is important that teaching problems stemming from the brutal overcrowding of our universities not be blamed upon the publication requirement, for even colleges try to get as many professors as they can who publish. The real problems have to do with the university's change of position from the periphery to the center of American life.

In the old days, when university education was considered a luxury for all except the relatively few people entering the professions, the universities served a privileged minority. Now that our highly technological society has made undergraduate and sometimes even graduate education a necessity for most middle-class jobs, more people are trying for a higher education than we have space or qualified teachers for.

Another problem is that university research, which used to be considered academic and remote from public affairs, has in the nuclear and space age become one of the foundations of national power

NEGLECTED—The usual complaint about academic "big shots" is that students rarely see them after class.

and survival. The result is that teaching and research are becoming harder to reconcile than ever, because the demand on each has increased so enormously. The danger is that these pressures will force some faculty men to become all teacher and others all researcher, when the university system depends for its quality upon the combination within the same man of both functions.

But the underlying reason for all the attention being paid to universities just now is that they are flourishing as never before. Never before has the American public taken university education so seriously. Never before has the university professor, once patronized as an unworldly, ineffectual figure, been taken so seriously. This applies not only to the scientists who make world-shaking discoveries, but also to the scientists and social scientists who are consulted by government and big business and to professors of humanities who run the apparatus of our cultural life, awarding fellowships and prizes and providing much of the copy printed in the book reviews and better magazines. Indeed, the universities today are subsidizing American culture by supporting a large proportion of the people who make it.

THEN, too, the universities, especially the state universities, are doing yet another job—one that never gets discussed. They are creating centers of civilization in the remotest reaches of our conti-

nent. The university town is a remarkable place where, often amidst hundreds of miles of cornfields or empty ranch lands, one can find a first-rate library and a book store where the best books, periodicals and phonograph records are sold. The university brings in famous concert artists and lecturers, gives plays and even operas, and may provide the town with an art museum.

All these benefits are available to the local population and their generally elevating effect can be seen in a quality of life far superior to that in other towns, and sometimes even cities, of the state. Electronics and other sophisticated industries have begun moving into university towns because they provide a suitable cultural setting for the high-class personnel they need. It is also too little realized in the current racial crisis how much light has radiated from the Southern university towns.

The university student comes not merely to a school, then, but to a center of civilization, where he can participate in a special way of life that derives much of its quality from the personal distinction of the faculty. The increased wealth and prestige of the universities have attracted men into the academic profession who in the old days would not have entered it, because it would have meant renouncing the world—or at least the chance of influencing it. Now that they find the university precisely the platform from which to influence the world, more and more of the intellectual life of

DEFENSE—If a professor is fired for not publishing, his colleagues often liken him to Socrates.

A chemistry professor at N.Y.U. in class and in his lab (below right). His dilemma: striking the best balance between teaching and research.

The idea that students suffer because university professors spend too much time on research is a canard, says a university professor. Academic distinction is not to be measured by hours spent in class; it's the quality of teaching that counts.

the country is centered in the universities. Our students are being taught by some of the biggest names in American intellectual life.

This raises problems, because these high - powered professors are often away, sometimes more than they should be, on research grants and lecture tours. They are also, in the competitive bidding for their services, being offered fewer and fewer hours of teaching and sometimes no teaching at all. These problems could and should be solved, however, by simple agreement among the universities that, barring exceptional cases, anyone who is to be considered a member of the faculty must teach and be in residence for a specified minimum period of time.

WHAT about the great teacher, the rare and exceptional man who publishes little if anything yet pours out his talent in ways that are fruitful for his colleagues as well as his students? There has always been a place for such a man; he can be found in universities with the most exacting standards. The difficulty, however, is to be sure he is an exceptional case. Sympathetic colleagues have a way of discovering, when a man is to be let go for not publishing, that he is the greatest teacher since Socrates — who did not publish either. One of the best features of the university system is the principle that, when bidding for promotion, the professor competes not only with his local colleagues but with his peers in universities all over the country. This prevents professors from turning their departments into societies for promoting each other. It prevents the teaching staff from encouraging each other in mediocrity.

As for the majority of professors, those who are needed to man the classrooms but do not come up to the ideal of the teacher - scholar, their role is to work toward the ideal, for to do so is to support it and to support the proper standards. What the university really wants, or should want, is some sign that the professor is intellectually engaged. With the expansion of the universities, we are going to have to employ many teachers who will publish little, but this is no reason for attacking the principle of publication itself.

We should recognize that if we do not come up to the ideal of the teacher-scholar, then the deficiency is in us, not in the ideal. If we scrap it, we will inevitably substitute one that is derived from the requirements for the man who only teaches. This substitute ideal would, I am afraid, put such a premium on mediocrity as to make the universities suffocating—indeed, uninhabitable — places for first-rate teachers and students.

CAMPUS RULE

Students Turn to World Politics As College Regimes Decline

By FRED M. HECHINGER

In a world of government crises, the fall of a student government is not sensational. But as a sign of campus trends, the demise of the Student Board, the undergraduate government at Columbia College, after a fifty-three-year history, is interesting. Victim of alleged political scandals and an overwhelming vote of no-confidence, the student governing body has not only been deposed, but is not being replaced.

Columbia's government crisis, which will be reviewed in the February issue of "Columbia College Today," the alumni magazine to be published this week, took the following course:

In 1959, the Columbia Daily Spectator, the student newspaper, exposed what it called the worst case of election fraud in the college's history. Charges included stuffing the ballot boxes.

After lingering conflicts, a petition for an "Abolish Board" referendum received more than 700 signatures last May and the ensuing vote was 935 to 167 for letting the government expire on Jan. 1. Since then, a proposal that a new student assembly replace the old board has been voted down 690 to 378. Columbia College is now without a student government.

Action at Brown

Early last month, at Brown University, in another revolt against undergraduate governmental institutions, the president of the government's stu-dent court recommended that the court be abolished. The student government group approved, although this is still subject to ratification.

George H. Wales, the student court president, said no useful purpose was served by the court because of its limited and hazy jurisdiction and lack of business. Students in trouble had a choice of asking for trial by the court or reporting to the dean of students.

At the University of Connecticut last term, a battle was fought between student representatives and the administration over the latter's attempt to take over student activity fees and determine the budget for all campus activities. The battle ended in a compromise, with the administration agreeing to accept an advisory role.

At other colleges, peaceful change rather than revolution resulted in a conversion from a single-body student government into legislative and executive bodies, partly in search of more efficient administration.

The Reasons

What are the reasons for a combination of unrest, change and an apparent increase of student skepticism toward their governments?

At Columbia, according to the alumni magazine, lack of confidence on the part of the dean's office gave the student board only a semblance of power. Academic spokesmen explained that, with the heavy burden of studies, undergraduates best qualified to represent the students lack the time to assume the burden. Those who "choose to run" are often the campus counterpart of the ward politicians and therefore antagonize both the college administration and the electorate.

Furthermore, with increasing academic domination by the graduate divisions of a large university with an enrollment of 23,000, the 2,600 undergraduates tend to feel like a small cog in a large machine.

Outward Turn

Commenting on the bigger picture, Scott Keech, a spokesman for the National Student Association, said that revived undergraduate concern with national and international problems has turned students outward—away from campus government to the country and the world. Student "political parties" are beginning to overshadow student government.

After years of apathy at least the leadership group is emerging with interest in issues of war and peace, nuclear policy and the fate of the United Nations. Domestically, Mr. Keech said, civil rights is the rallying cause. He added that the reappearance of conservative student opinion, though a minority movement, has helped to infuse controversy and new life.

Such organizations as "Voice" (liberal and pro-Democratic) at the University of Michigan, "Toxin" (civil rights and peace), "Advance" (liberal Republican) at Harvard, "Challenge" (for discussion rather than action), at Yale and "Polit" at Oberlin are increasingly holding the attention of the articulate minority. Mr. Keech estimates that active groups number no more than 3 to 5 per cent of the nation's students—"about the same percentage as in adult society."

Other student political groups, not confined to any particular campuses, are the Congress of Racial Equality and the student contingent of the National Committee for a Sane Nuclear Policy. The right-wing Young Americans for Freedom occasionally join the conservative Intercollegiate Society of Individualists, as in their combined White House picketing to urge nuclear testing.

Junior John Birch societies spring up tentatively here and there, but they appear to attract little more permanent support than the pro-Soviet Progressive Youth Organizing Committee, a front at the other extreme of the spectrum.

The influence of student political parties on national and international affairs may not be great, but students feel that their voice is hardly less effective than that of the general population—and perhaps better informed.

On campus, by contrast, students feel that college administrations often pay little more than lip service to student governments' importance and not infrequently treat it as a nuisance. If this has led to disenchantment, need it be permanent? A footnote offers hope that it need not.

From Amherst comes word that, after years of decline in concern for the student government, the past two years have seen a strong resurgence. The reason given is that, after a growing feeling of uselessness, a Student Committee to the Faculty, part of the regular Student Council, has been welcomed as a partner in planning the college's future. The answer appears unmistakably that students are responsive if they are considered responsible.

AID FOR STUDENTS IN SIT-INS URGED

A.C.L.U. Asks Colleges to Defend Those Arrested

By FRED M. HECHINGER

The American Civil Liberties Union told the nation's colleges and universities yesterday that it was their duty to protect the constitutional rights of students arrested for taking part in public demonstrations against racial segregation, civil defense programs or nuclear tests.

The civil liberties organization added that the colleges and universities should go beyond the defense of the rights of college students to engage in public protests.

When students run into police difficulties off the campus, it said, the colleges and universities should see that they are assured of fair trial, defense by counsel and protection against police abuse. The colleges were even urged to seek or furnish bail for such students.

The A.C.L.U. also told educational administrators that "no disciplinary action should be taken by the college against a student for engaging in such off-campus activities as political campaigning, picketing or participating in public demonstrations, provided the student does not claim without authorization to speak or act in the name of the college or one of its student organizations."

The sweeping policy pronouncement was included in a 16-page revised pamphlet on "Academic Freedom and Civil Liberties of Students in Colleges and Universities."

Urged on Admission Policies

The institutions were also warned against denying admission to a student "who has been expelled from another college because of his arrest in connection with a conscience-motivated activity," including sit-ins, picketing, riding of freedom buses and other civic protests.

The most controversial aspects of the policy statement are likely to be found in a section on "Students as Private Citizens."

On the one hand, the statement demanded that "in their nonacademic life, private or public, students should be free from college control," unless they had harmed the institution's educational function or injured or endangered the welfare of others in the academic community.

But even though the civil liberties group denied the colleges' right to interfere with the students' private activities, it appeared to extend the colleges' responsibility beyond the educational boundaries by urging the institutions to protect students legally, if their private, off-campus actions got them into trouble.

"Unless college authorities act in behalf of students," the statement said, "there is the very real danger of alienation" and the possibility that students may turn to undesirable, self-serving outside agencies for aid. This was an apparent attempt to reconcile what might appear as something of a double standard, giving the student complete off-campus freedom while assigning to the college full responsibility for protecting the student.

The following were listed among student freedoms that the committee was seeking to protect:

¶Freedom to discuss and pass resolutions, distribute pamphlets and circulate petitions.

¶Freedom to participate in student government and leadership, subject to reasonable standards of scholastic eligibility, set up by the administration for major student offices.

¶Freedom to join clubs, invite speakers and publish newspapers and magazines.

Dr. Louis Hacker of Columbia University is chairman of the union's academic freedom committee.

'Forgotten' Student

Higher education's mass enrollments have created a seller's market in which the student is likely to become a surplus commodity or the forgotten man. This warning was sounded last week by Logan Wilson, president of the American Council on Education in a 178th Founder's Day convocation at Franklin and Marshall College.

"Because others are standing in line to take the places of the dropouts, there is a danger of becoming indifferent, if not callous, to the sources of discontent and the causes of failure," Dr. Wilson warned.

He did not suggest that the increasing neglect of students was a deliberate university or college policy. But, he said, the pendulum has swung from expecting too little of our colleges and universities to perhaps expecting too much, with the individual student increasingly "crowded out of the picture."

"The faceless anonymity that I. B. M. cards, drop cards, seat numbers and I. D. numbers represent," and "the depersonalization of the student," he added, could endanger the purposes of higher education.

He announced that next year's annual meeting of the powerful council would be devoted to "the student in higher education." He urged an end to the trend that had made relief from teaching the highest status symbol for faculty members, then said that colleges must halt the trend by rewarding good teaching.

Concession Ends Three-Day Protest At U. of California

By WALLACE TURNER
Special to The New York Times

BERKELEY, Calif., Oct. 2—A three-day student demonstration on the University of California campus ended tonight with a minor concession from the university administration.

Clark Kerr, president of the university system, said the school would review the duration of suspensions imposed on eight students. The suspensions had been "indefinite."

It also will not press trespass charges against a man arrested by the Berkeley police yesterday and held all night in a police car.

"But the District Attorney may want to prosecute him," said Mr. Kerr.

The charge was lodged against Jack Weinberg, 24 years old, a Congress of Racial Equality member but not a student. Students were responsible for his being held in a police car on the campus from 11:45 A.M. yesterday until about 8 tonight.

When the announcement of the agreement was made tonight, a crowd of about 4,000 students quietly left the campus.

Observers said that many of the hard core of about 300 demonstrators were — like Mr. Weinberg — not students.

The dispute arose after the university announced Monday that it was applying its rules on political conduct to all the campus.

Area Is in Dispute

The specific area involved is a strip 25 feet wide and 60 feet long outside the Sather Gate entrance. Although a part of the campus, the area is outside a pair of pillars and was thought by many to be public property.

The university had permitted use of this strip for political fund solicitation, recruitment for political purposes, and recruitment of persons for social protests. All these activities have been prohibited on the university campus.

After representatives of student organizations were unable to change the university's position, the protest developed. Students first sought to take over Sproul Hall, the administration building, and then the so-called Hyde Park area in front of Sproul Hall, which has been traditionally set aside as a place for student oratory.

February 10, 1964

October 25, 1964

October 3, 19

CAMPUS PROTESTS A BAN ON POLITICS

BERKELEY, Calif., Nov. 10 (UPI)—The University of California student free-speech movement received impetus today when graduate students and teaching assistants joined in defiance of university rules forbidding on-campus political activity.

Some 100 teaching assistants and graduate students signed petitions protesting the university ban during a rally at the school's main plaza. They also manned tables in the plaza in defiance of rules prohibiting solicitation of membership and funds for outside political activities.

Mike Abramowitz, who led the protest, said the graduate students and teaching assistants felt "very strongly about this and wish to be considered a part of the protest."

He and two other members of his group took the list of protestors to the administration office in Sproul Hall and presented it to the associate dean, Peter van Houten.

Several hours after the demonstration, the university president, Clark Kerr, and the Berkeley campus chancellor, Edward W. Strong, issued a statement that warned that students who violate the rules "will be subject to penalties through established procedures." This would mean suspension or expulsion.

Berkeley Students Stage Sit-In To Protest Curb on Free Speech

1,000 Occupy Administration Building After University Ignores Ultimatum —Political Activities Are an Issue

By WALLACE TURNER
Special to The New York Times

BERKELEY, Calif., Dec. 2—Demonstrating students took possession of the University of California administration building today.

About 1,000 supporters of the Free Speech Movement moved into the corridors of Sproul Hall about noon.

Some were still there late tonight. Many slept and others read while still others sang. There was no attempt by the campus police to remove them.

The doors to Sproul Hall were locked at 7 P.M., Pacific standard time (10 P.M., Eastern standard time), as is customary, with many of the demonstrators still inside. Guards at the doors permitted those who wanted to to leave, and a steady stream of departures joined a crowd of about 1,000 outside.

"The time has come for us to put our bodies on the machine and stop it," said Mario Savio, a student leader, in a speech on the steps of the building as the demonstration began. "We will stay until the police remove us."

Mr. Savio, a philosophy major and a frequent speaker in the several months of demonstrations, rejected the plea of the student body's president, Charles Powell, not to demonstrate further.

Mr. Powell had pleaded with a crowd of several thousand gathered in the plaza by the modernistic Students Union Building "do not do this thing."

Joan Baez, the folk singer, helped draw the crowd, as she has at other demonstrations on the campus.

Civil Rights Songs

She sang various civil rights movement songs, including "We Shall Overcome," and urged the students who went into Sproul Hall to "have love as you do this thing and it will succeed."

The sit-in was one of several that have come about here on this 27,500-student campus since classes began in late September.

There was a near-riot on Oct. 1 when police were prevented for 32 hours from taking away a non-student they had arrested.

The issue originally was a plea for the right to recruit and solicit money for off-campus activities. After early demonstrations eight students were suspended, but they were ordered reinstated by the university regents two weeks ago.

The regents also ordered the university administration to enforce discipline on the campus here.

The regents said that students should be able to organize political activities on the campus. They also should be held accountable for their off-campus political activities that had campus beginnings, the regents said. This was a change in the direction sought by the student group.

In the two weeks since then, an uneasy truce has existed.

Reports were published in The San Francisco Examiner, a Hearst paper, that called the Free Speech Movement "Marxist-dominated."

Last week, letters were mailed by the university administration to Mr. Savio, Arthur Goldberg, his sister Jackie Goldberg and Brian Turner.

They were advised that charges had been made against them in connection with their campaign against the university administration.

The charges included one that they had incited students to resist the police on Oct. 1 when a police car was immobilized. Mr. Savio was also accused of biting a policeman.

Yesterday the Free Speech Movement demanded that the charges against the four be withdrawn, that the university promise that no more charges of similar nature would be made, and that no new rules inhibiting freedom of political activity be made.

The ultimatum was ignored. The noon speeches in the plaza and the sit-in in Sproul Hall followed.

Air of Festivity

There was an air of festivity accompanying the beginning of the sit-in. The student body at this campus is unusually picturesque in its dress and grooming. The beards and long hair and guitars were much in evidence along the corridors of Sproul Hall. At least one young man came in barefoot.

Beneath a table a young mother sat with her baby taking milk from a bottle. Nearby, oblivious to the songs and high noise level, a young girl sat reading a language lesson. Free Speech Movement functionaries in armbands directed traffic.

A class in Spanish was organized on the first floor, but it became a songfest.

796 Students Arrested as Police Break Up Sit-In at U. of California

University of California students face line of policemen outside the university administration building in Berkeley

By WALLACE TURNER

Special to The New York Times

BERKELEY, Calif., Dec. 3 —The police arrested 796 University of California students in 12 hours today, dragging many on their backs down flights of stairs to end a sit-in demonstration. The mass arrests were made in removing demonstrators who took possession of the administration building on the campus last night. The Free Speech Movement, the protesting student group, retaliated by calling a student strike. Faculty members, at a special meeting, gave evidence of some support for the students. The dispute over students' political and protest activities has shaken the university for almost three months. The strike was called after Gov. Edmund G. Brown ordered early this morning that sit-in demonstrators be removed by force from the corridors of Sproul Hall, the administration building. Mr. Brown said that the students' action constituted "anarchy." Charges of police brutality were made as a result of the removals and arrests today. In this 27,500-student university, the effectiveness of the strike was difficult to measure. In the morning pickets wheeled in front of the doors of all the classroom buildings and, although students continued to pass through the lines, there were reports that many classrooms were empty.

Clark Kerr, president of the university, issued a statement tonight declaring that the Free Speech Movement represented an "understandable concern" last September but that it "has now become an instrument of anarchy and of personal aggrandizement."

Representatives of about 75 of the 82 academic departments at the university, in a meeting this afternoon, found that about 20 departments were functioning normally in the face of the strike. Prof. Charles Hulten, chairman of the Journalism Department, said that individual faculty members would decide tomorrow whether to hold classes.

A meeting of 500 of the 1,200 members of the faculty voted a resolution this afternoon stating that the university faced a "desperate situation."

The faculty members favor new and liberalized campus rules for political activity and setting up a committee to which students could appeal administration decisions on penalties for violating university rules on political action.

Plan Telegram to Brown

The resolution also asked "that all pending campus action against students for acts occurring before the present date be dropped."

At the meeting, faculty members drafted a telegram to be sent to Governor Brown. It condemned the use of the California Highway Patrol on the campus and the exclusion of faculty members from Sproul Hall.

Last night about 1,000 sit-in demonstrators filled the corridors of Sproul Hall before the doors were locked at 7:00 P. M. They sat there, sleeping, singing, studying and talking until about 3:10 A. M., when Edward W. Strong, the chancellor for this campus of the multi-campus university, went to Sproul Hall.

Mr. Strong read a statement asking the students to leave. A few did, but most stayed. They had put up barricades at the stairways and were concentrated on the second, third and fourth floors.

The police took an elevator to the fourth floor and began removing students there.

Capt. Larry Waldt of the Alameda County sheriff's office made the estimate of the number of students arrested.

By midday, the routine was standard, as illustrated by the arrest of Jean Golson.

When she found herself at the head of the line of demonstrators, Sgt. Don Smithson of the Berkeley police force told her, "You are under arrest for trespass and unlawful assembly."

Another Berkeley policeman held a microphone to record her answers and the sergeant's statements. A third made notes on a booking form.

"If you talk out, you will not be charged with resisting arrest, but if we are forced to carry you out, you will be charged with resisting arrest," the sergeant said.

'Female on the Way'

Miss Golson said she would not walk out. A number was held to her chest and her photograph was taken. The Berkeley police pulled her by the arms for a few feet and then turned her over to two sheriff's deputies from Alameda County. They dragged her quickly down the corridor on her back, shouting, "Female on the way."

At a booking desk, she was pulled erect and was fingerprinted. Then she was pulled into an office for searching by two matrons from the sheriff's office.

Then she was dragged back into the elevator, where other girls were being held. When the elevator was full, the girls were taken to the basement and were loaded into a van for transportation to the county jail.

The bail schedule was $75 each on the trespass and unlawful assembly charges and $100 for resisting arrest.

Total Bail Is $150,000

Booking officers at the Alameda County sheriff's office said that about 25 of the demonstrators posted bail soon after being booked. Meantime, lawyers, parents and others were meeting with a municipal judge attempting to obtain an order freeing the demonstrators on their own recognizance. The total bail involved will be more than $150,000.

For men, the handling was significantly different once they were turned over to the sheriff's deputies after arrest. Those men who would walk were jogged down four flights of steps to the basement. Those who remained limp were dragged by the arms down the steps, departing to the cries of "Good luck" from their friends.

There were about a score of sheriff's deputies whose job was to drag the men down the steps. As the day passed, their humor became more acid. Some bumped the buttocks of their male prisoners as they dragged them down the stairs.

"There'll be some sore rumps in jail tonight," one deputy said.

After the corridors of Sproul Hall were closed, a floor at a time, the litter of the sit-ins remained. There were empty fruit cartons, crushed soft-drink cans, a guitar, stacks of textbooks, sleeping bags and blankets and scores of notebooks with lecture notes in them.

Shouts 'This Is Wonderful'

When Mario Savio, a protest leader, was taken away by the police, he shouted, "This is wonderful—wonderful. We'll bring the university to our terms."

Another leader, Arthur Goldberg, said as he was led away, "Good! The kids have learned more about democracy here than they could in 40 years of classes. This is a perfect example of how the State of California plays the game."

Mr. Savio is a New Yorker who is the president of the Berkeley Chapter of Friends of S.N.C.C., the Student Nonviolent Coordinating Committee. He was involved last spring in recruiting demonstrators who slept in at the Sheraton Palace Hotel. He was arrested on a charge of disturbing the peace. He also worked in the S.N.C.C. program in Mississippi last summer.

Another leader of the Free Speech Movement is Bettina Aptheker. She is a member of the W. E. B. DuBois Club, which has been described by Department of Justice sources as a front among college students for the Communist party.

The dispute that led to the arrests began last September when the university administration announced that it would no longer permit the use of a strip of campus property for soliciting political funds and recruiting protests demonstrators.

The students objected, and a series of demonstrations resulted. Eight students were suspended and the demonstrations were stepped up.

Last month, the university regents ordered that the students be permitted to recruit demonstrators and collect political contributions on campus. But the regents said the students must be held accountable for off-campus violations of the law in projects begun on campus.

They also said that discipline must be tightened.

Earlier this week, four students received letters from the administration indicating that they were to be disciplined, and perhaps expelled. Yesterday the newest demonstration began in protest.

Conservatives Quit Group

The Free Speech Movement was organized with an executive committee of about 60 members, each representing some campus organization. Initially, conservative groups belonged, including the Young Republicans, but these recently disassociated themselves.

The leadership is concentrated in an 11-member steering committee that appears to be dominated by representatives of campus chapters of the Congress of Racial Equality, the Young Socialist League, the Young Socialist Alliance, Slate (a student political organization) and the W. E. B. DuBois Club.

Policemen drag student from administration building where the strike was called by "free speech" advocates.

At a noon rally of about 5,000 students, Steve Wiesman, leader of the Free Speech Movement, called for an investigation of what he termed police brutality. He also demanded the removal of the police "from this campus now and forever" and the removal of Mr. Kerr as president of the university.

In his statement tonight, Mr. Kerr denied that freedom of speech had ever been an issue and said, "The protest has been over organizing political action on campus."

Mr. Kerr accused the Free Speech Movement of violating the law, of intolerance, distortion of the truth, irrationality, indecency and ill will.

In Sacramento, Governor Brown said, "We're not going to have anarchy in the state of California while I'm Governor, and that's anarchy. I did plan to go to Berkeley, but I have other things to do."

Opposition to the Free Speech Movement was in evidence here today. Some students standing at the noon rally held signs reading "Throw the Bums Out" and "Law Not Anarchy—The Majority of Students Do Not Support This Demonstration."

A Rebel on Campus
Mario Savio

Special to The New York Times

BERKELEY, Calif., Dec. 8 —The leader of the Free Speech Movement on the Berkeley campus of the University of California is a 6-foot-1 student who has taken to wearing neckties lately—and is flat broke. Mario Savio celebrated his 22d birthday today, looking forward to three more semesters before graduation. Then he will have to look for a full-time job "when the Free Speech Movement is over." Mr. Savio, who weighs 195 pounds, is slender and his sandy hair makes him look taller—it stands on his head as if it had not been combed in two weeks.

Man in the News

Yesterday Mr. Savio, a philosophy major, was dragged from a microphone in view of 13,000 students and faculty at a meeting called to settle a campus dispute on rules governing political activities.

Clark Kerr, president of the university, who had just left the microphone, said that he was astounded. Mr. Savio was also astounded.

"I thought they might turn off the microphone," he said today.

Had Mr. Kerr allowed him to talk, he acknowledged "we would have been dead."

He eventually was able to speak, but the man who introduced him was a member of the faculty.

Mr. Savio's father works as a machine punch operator in Los Angeles. His parents live in Glendora, having moved there from New York, where Mario was born on Dec. 8, 1942. He was graduated at the head of his class of 1,200 from Martin Van Buren High School, and attended Manhattan College on a scholarship received as a result of a high-school physics project.

Mr. Savio later transferred to Queens College, changing his major from physics to philosophy. When he enrolled the University of California last year his grade average was 3.9, just a shade off perfect.

"My grades have suffered

United Press International

Grades fell when politics claimed his interest

from my political interests," he remarked today, smiling.

Mr. Savio was suspended from the university in early October, and although he was reinstated by order of the regents in November, he has not attended classes.

"I intend to withdraw before the end of the semester and re-enter next semester," he said, "if they'll allow me to do that."

At his victory tonight in winning recommendations from the Academic Senate for the relaxation in rules his organization has been working toward, Mr. Savio was jubilant. He also was wearing a blue suit that was pressed and a white shirt and tie. Gone was the fleece-lined coat he wore during the weeks of the controversy.

As he walked to a press conference to comment on the action of the faculty senate, students were singing "Happy birthday, Mario" and shouting congratulatory words to him.

When he was asked to say what all the turmoil meant to him, Mr. Savio said he would have to borrow from the ninth chapter of "Moby Dick" by Herman Melville. He quoted:

"Woe to him who would try to pour oil on the waters when God has brewed them into a gale."

Pressed to explain why he threw away a semester of school work to risk expulsion for campus agitation, he said: "I spent the summer in Mississippi. I witnessed tyranny. I saw groups of men in the minority working their wills over the majority. Then I came back here and found the university preventing us from collecting money for use there and even stopping us from getting people to go to Mississippi to help."

"I suppose I'll end up as a professor," he declared.

The youth said he first became interested in political activity in 1963 when he came to the Berkeley campus and was introduced to the civil rights movement.

He was arrested in the Sheraton Palace Hotel in San Francisco last spring during a sleep-in staged to back Negro demands for equal job opportunities. He was tried and acquitted by a jury.

Last summer in Mississippi, Mr. Savio spent the early weeks in Holmes County in the north, then moved to Mc-Comb, a tinderbox of racial tension. Once, in Jackson, he said, he and a local Negro and another white from New York were assaulted by two men armed with clubs.

"I outran them, and the Negro outran me," he said. "The other white man ran the wrong way and was caught and beaten."

At the end of the summer, he returned here to his studies, determined to better his grades. Then he encountered the change in rules by which the university sought to limit use of the campus for political activities and the recruitment of students for off-campus demonstrations.

THE STUDENT LEFT: SPURRING REFORM

New Activist Intelligentsia Is Rising on Campuses

By FRED POWLEDGE

On a recent Saturday night, a group of University of Chicago students gathered at an apartment for a party. There was no liquor and no dancing and no talk about basketball, student politics or sex.

Instead, the young men, in sport coats and without ties, and the young women, in skirts and black stockings, sat on the floor and talked about such things as "community organization," "powerlessness" and "participatory democracy."

The host, Bob Ross, a 22-year-old graduate student in sociology who is the son of a factory worker, opened a window and found a cold bottle of beer on the fire escape. He offered it to a visitor and explained:

"I guess it seems pretty strange. I suppose some of us feel that we don't have time to drink or dance. We're too busy trying to change the world."

The young people in Chicago, and their counterparts in a dozen other college communities, are part of a new, small, loosely bound intelligentsia that calls itself the new student left and that wants to cause fundamental changes in society. Last week these young people, or people who feel the same as they, picketed in favor of academic tenure for professors at St. John's College. Some of them participated in the recent New York school boycott.

They organized the Northern demonstrations and sit-ins that followed the civil rights uprising in Selma, Ala., and some of them went to Selma to help there.

They believe that the civil rights movement, the emergence of poverty as a national cause, and the possibility of nuclear extinction make fundamental change mandatory.

Small Letters Preferred

They do not deny that they are a lot like the young radicals of the thirties in their aspirations. Some of them, who liken their movement to a "revolution," want to be called radicals.

December 9, 1964

Most of them, however, prefer to be called "organizers." Others reply that they are "democrats with a small 'd'" or "socialists with a small "s". A few like to be called Marxists.

Most express contempt for any specific labels, and they don't mind being called cynics. Few have allowed themselves to develop a sense of humor about their work; they function on a crisis footing.

They are mindful that their numbers are tiny in comparison with the total in the nation's colleges. Now, as before, the great majority of their fellow students are primarily interested in marriage, a home, and a job.

Forming Own Religion

Jeffrey Shero, a 23-year-old Texan, sat recently in the student union building at the University of Texas, drinking bitter institutional coffee and explaining his own particular cynicism in this way:

"This generation has witnessed hypocrisy as has no other generation. The churches aren't doing what they should be doing. There is lie after lie on television. The whole society is run and compounded on lies.

"People are manipulated. The kind of ethics that our parents preached are not practiced, because we now see how our parents really live.

"We are the first generation that grew up with the idea of annihilation. In a situation like this, you have to go out and form your own religion."

About 70 others were interviewed recently in New York, Chicago, San Francisco, Atlanta, Newark, Louisiana, and Austin, Tex.

Skeptical of Communism

Although a few displayed a tendency to defend the Soviet Union as an example of the sort of society they want to create, the great majority of those questioned said they were as skeptical of Communism as they were of any other form of political control.

Their conversations indicated that they were neither directed nor inspired by Communism, as some of their critics have alleged. "You might say we're a-Communist," said one, "just as you might say we're amoral and a-almost everything else."

Although one of their goals is the elimination of the evils of a middle-class society, many of them come from middle-class, middle-income families.

They believe that the only way out of the nation's problems is through the creation of a new left. They reject many of the old leftist heroes, whom they describe as "sellouts"; they want to write their own philosophy, and they want to

create an alliance between the millions of American whites and Negroes who have no economic or political power.

Most of them express skepticism about their own chances of success, but they want to invest the rest of their lives in the cause.

One of them, Richard Rothstein, a 21-year-old worker in a district of Chicago that contains poor whites, Negroes, Mexicans and Puerto Ricans, was graduated from Harvard and was a Fulbright scholar at the London School of Economics. His father is a Federal civil servant.

Working From Within

"We reject the idea that you can bring change through getting elected to the legislature and then handing down change from the top," he said. "Somehow, under that system, the poor still get treated poorly."

Mr. Rothstein is attempting to work from within to organize the residents of his adopted neighborhood into political groups.

It is this theory of "community organization" that is being practiced by almost all of these youth organizations now. The idea is to use the labor movement's techniques to organize deprived people around a central complaint.

Jobs and Traffic Lights

The complaint may be poor housing, inferior schools, unequal job opportunities, capital punishment, the need for a traffic light at a busy corner, or the impersonality of a college administration.

There is little talk among the activists about racial integration. Some of them consider the subject passé. They declare that integration will be almost as evil as segregation if it results in a complacent, middle-class interracial society.

"The civil rights movement has a built-in dead end," said one young man, "because when most of the basic civil rights issues are settled there still won't be enough jobs for everyone."

Said William Strickland, the executive director of the Northern Student Movement: "We have come to see that the attainment of full freedom transcends the secularity of 'civil rights.'

"Something more is needed: A movement which confronts the structural barriers to equality and enables people to assume the responsibility for their own lives."

Bias at the Bottom

As a result most of the efforts at community action are based on grievances that arise from racial discrimination, but they are not aimed at eventual desegregation.

Some exponents of the community-action approach point out that young activists in the Southern movement, who orig-

inally worked almost exclusively in the fields of public accommodations or voter registration, are now talking more about other forms of organization.

Albany, Ga., was the scene of Selma-type demonstrations in the summer of 1962. Now a day-care center is being organized there.

In Newark, workers of the Students for a Democratic Society are trying to organize a Negro neighborhood that is faced with the probability of destruction through urban renewal.

Inside the college communities, some of the young people have found student freedom to be the issue around which a movement may be built.

On the campuses of a number of universities, the student leftists are planning demonstrations, marches, and political action around the issues of conscription, academic freedom, the war in South Vietnam, disarmament and poverty in general. They hope that an important side effect will be increased enrollments in the organizations they represent.

At present there is no reliable index of the strength of the student left. The hard core amounts to about 500 persons. However, thousands may rally around them from time to time in support of a given cause.

In the North, the movement is being run by a handful of organizations, along with a number of smaller or less important groups. The major groups are Students for a Democratic Society, the W.E.B. Du Bois Clubs of America, the Northern Student Movement and the Student Nonviolent Coordinating Committee.

Port Huron Statement

Students for a Democratic Society was organized in June, 1962, at Port Huron, Mich., by "a band of young intellectuals who got most of their immediate inspiration from the sit-in movement," according to one of the founders, Tom Hayden, a 25-year-old Detroit native.

The Michigan meeting produced a 63-page paperback document called "The Port Huron Statement" that concluded as follows:

"We seek the establishment of a democracy of individual participation governed by two central aims: That the individual share in those social decisions determining the quality and direction of his life; that society be organized to encourage independence in men and provide the media for their common participation."

Students for a Democratic Society is affiliated with the League for Industrial Democracy Inc., a nonprofit educational institution founded in 1905 by Jack London, Upton Sinclair and Clarence Darrow.

It claims a national membership of 1,700 in 44 chapters, along with 50 staff members. It

operates or cooperates with community action projects in Newark; Baltimore; Chester, Pa.; Cleveland; Chicago; Cairo, Ill.; San Francisco; Austin, Tex.; Hazard, Ky.; Boston, and New Brunswick, N. J.

New York Headquarters

The group publishes an extensive list of essays, most of them written by its own members. The office is at 119 Fifth Avenue in New York. The president is Todd Gitlin.

The W. E. B. DuBois Clubs of America started in San Francisco about three years ago. The organization is named for the Negro leader who helped found the National Association for the Advancement of Colored People and who later turned to Communism.

Last June the clubs became a national organization. The preamble to its constitution states:

"It is our belief that this nation can best solve its problems in an atmosphere of peaceful coexistence, complete disarmament and true freedom for all peoples of the world, and that these solutions will be reached mainly through the united efforts of all democratic elements in our country, composed essentially of the working people allied in the unity of Negroes and other minorities with whites."

Last October, J. Edgar Hoover, the director of the Federal Bureau of Investigation, wrote that the DuBois Clubs had been spawned by the Communist Party, U.S.A., and that the clubs' ideology was one of "discord, hate and violence."

Hoover Viewed as Threat

Many members reply that Mr. Hoover is part of the reactionary force that the DuBois group believes is the greatest threat to American society.

One DuBois member on the West Coast, Bettina Aptheker, a 20-year-old University of California student, explained her philosophy this way:

"The basic thing is destroying or eliminating the corporate monopolies and nationalizing the control of the industries in the hands of the people.

"If this were done, a lot of other things would follow. There would be an elimination of the race thing, elimination of the preparations for war.

"That's the long-range thing. On a short-term basis, we should do whatever can be done within the present confines of the System—things like voter registration and political education.

"Being a member of the DuBois Club, I am also a Socialist, and I see the fight for further political freedom at Cal and the fight for civil rights in the rest of the country as part of the over-all fight to change the System. Any democratic movement to further the rights of the people is part of the democratic move toward Socialism."

Daughter of Writer

Miss Aptheker, an American history major, is the daughter of Herbert Aptheker, a writer on Negro history and director of the Institute for Marxist Studies here. She calls herself a "Marxist Socialist."

She believes that "at present the Socialist world, even with all its problems, is moving closer than any other countries toward the sort of society I think should exist. In the Soviet Union, it has almost been achieved."

Robert Heisler, a 19-year-old sophomore at City College in New York, and the local co-ordinator for the club, shares the view of Miss Aptheker.

"The Soviet Union and the whole Socialist bloc are on the right track," he said. "They have broken loose from some of the basic problems that are at the heart of this country's social system.

"I don't mean that we're calling for a blueprint, a carbon copy of what they do. But I do believe that the Soviet Union and the Socialist bloc—including the new nations in Africa and Asia—are more on the way to getting this than is the United States at this point."

The DuBois Club claims a national membership of more than 1,000. Chapters are currently active in Madison, Wis.; New York City; Minneapolis; Chicago; Detroit; Los Angeles; Albuquerque; Berkeley; Oakland, Calif.; San Francisco; New Paltz, N. Y.; Philadelphia; New Jersey; Portland; Pittsburgh and Boston.

Phil Davis, the 25-year-old national president, is a hefty, bushy-haired young man who wears open-necked dress shirts and rough yellow boots, and who takes home $46.15 a week from his office in San Francisco. He calls himself a Socialist.

The Northern Student Movement was founded in 1961 as the Northern wing of the Southern-based Student Nonviolent Coordinating Committee.

The Northern group concentrates on tutorial programs and community organization in the Northern Negro ghettoes. It has field projects in Boston, Hartford, Detroit, Harlem and Philadelphia.

The Northern movement says it has 73 campus affiliates, 28 field secretaries, about 40 full-time volunteer workers and a constituency of about 2,000 students. The national office is at 514 West 126th Street, New York.

The Student Nonviolent Coordinating Committee, the inspiration for all the organizations of the new student left, was founded April 17, 1960. About 300 persons, almost all Negro youths heartened by the sit-ins that had started two and one-half months before in Greensboro, formed the Temporary Student Nonviolent Coordinating Committee. Their statement of purpose spoke almost exclusively of the virtues of nonviolence.

"By appealing to conscience and standing on the moral nature of human existence," it concluded, "nonviolence nurtures the atmosphere in which reconciliation and justice become actual possibilities."

The committee started out in a tiny office in Atlanta, upstairs from Dr. Martin Luther King Jr.'s headquarters. It had two employes. Now, more than a dozen campaigns later, it has 237 paid staffers. Twenty of them work in Northern Friends of S.N.C.C. offices and 25 in the Atlanta office. The others work in cities like McComb, Miss., and Selma, Ala.

The organization still retains its youthful, interracial composition, but its members have grown more cynical as the battle progresses. It now has 65 to 70 automobiles, more than 50 short-wave radio units, long-distance trunk lines and a ledger in which it can write its own airplane tickets.

Asked if the organization has adopted any defensive weapons, a member replied: "Yes. Our bodies."

On issues that involve the Southern campaign, S.N.C.C., or "Snick" as it is often called, and the Friends of S.N.C.C. can rally immediate Northern support. Most of the protests that issued from the North last week over the Selma crisis were organized by their people.

The organization is too involved in the highly realistic issues of Southern voting and the like to spend much time on academic freedom, conscription or ending in the war in Vietnam. Many Northern college students are active in its projects in the South in the summer time, community-organizing in the North during the academic year.

The Student Nonviolent Coordinating Committee has tended more and more toward political organization in recent months. Next summer's project, for example, will be centered on bringing pressure to bear in Washington to provide equal representation in Congress for Southern Negroes.

Other organizations have formed as a result of its experiences in the South, and in some cases standard civil rights groups have altered their programs to accommodate those who believe in a new radicalism.

The Southern Student Organizing Committee was formed a year ago in Nashville to seek the involvement of Southern whites in the rights movement and is closely aligned with S.N.C.C. One of this group's first projects will be to seek the abolition of capital punishment in Tennessee.

Many members of the Congress of Racial Equality, a Northern group established in 1943 and devoted primarily to nonviolence, are working now on community organization. The group experienced a fundamental change last summer when some of its leaders declared that "demonstrations for demonstration's sake" were no longer a useful weapon.

Sharing 'Powerlessness'

The members of the student left are hesitant about predicting the success or failure of their efforts. Most of them see the movement as one without end. The expression "not in my lifetime" occurs frequently in their conversations.

One man who has watched them feels confident that they will succeed in most of their aims. He is Dr. Neil J. Smelser, the 34-year-old editor of the American Sociological Review and the assistant to the Berkeley chancellor for student political activity. His job was created as a result of last fall's rebellions at the Berkeley campus.

"The students of the thirties considered themselves intellectuals," he said in an interview. "They were Marxists. They were concerned with wealth, and their friends were the workers.

"The student intellectuals of this generation now find their friends among the Negroes and Puerto Ricans and Mexicans. They share powerlessness with the minority groups. They're students and they have relatively little power and they're frustrated."

Dr. Smelser believes that "this movement will be as successful as the thirties' movement because it's as closely linked to the inevitable process of social change as the thirties' movement was."

Another faculty member at the University of California detects a note of sadness in the situation. Lewis S. Feuer, social scientist at Berkeley and a writer on the subject of student movements, said:

"The sad thing is that so many of these people have a sympathy for anything that's anti-American."

"The new student movements, by and large, differ from the older ones in that they believe in direct action," he said. "They don't lobby; they don't bother with legal procedures. They say 'By golly, we'll turn up with 500 people and compel the agreement to take place.'"

He believes that liberal student groups of a more moderate nature will come into existence to represent "the people who want to solve these problems through the traditional American democratic-liberal approach." But he adds:

"On the other hand, as long as there is an illness in America that makes some people look to others—Castro, Mao, or anyone else who comes along—this sort of thing will persist.

"Whatever makes in our society for any sort of emotional rejection of American character will cause this feeling, and this movement, to persist."

May 15, 1965

COLLEGIANS ADOPT A 'BILL OF RIGHTS'

Say Administrators Should Be Campus Housekeepers

By FRED POWLEDGE
Special to The New York Times

PHILADELPHIA, March 28 — A group of Eastern college students declared here this weekend that college administrators should be no more than housekeepers in the educational community.

The modern college or university, they said, should be run by the students and the professors; administrators would be "maintenance, clerical and safety personnel whose purpose is to enforce the will of faculty and students."

A manifesto, which is not likely to be adopted by any college administrator, was adopted in draft form at an all-day meeting yesterday at the University of Pennsylvania. About 200 students attended the meeting, 45 remaining until the end when the "Student Bill of Rights" was adopted.

The 200 youths were from 39 colleges in the Philadelphia and New York areas, Harvard, Yale, the University of California at Berkeley, and from schools in the Midwest.

Their political beliefs represented a spectrum of campus activism. Some are members of campus chapters of the W.E.B. DuBois Clubs of America; one represented the National Student Association.

Many said they were independent of any student-left group. All appeared to believe that the wave of campus rebellion that started in Berkeley last fall should be brought to all American campuses.

National Panel Discussed

There was not complete agreement on the methods that should be employed to bring it there. A key portion of the manifesto, proposed after hours of discussion, had been the pledge that, in order to achieve their demands, the students would not hesitate to start a general academic strike. The provision was voted down, 27 to 11.

The students then went on to discuss the possibility of forming a national coordinating committee to channel campus protest movements. They failed to reach agreement on this by 9 P.M. Saturday, which was the time the Christian Association Auditorium, where they met, closed. The question was to be settled at some later point.

A recurring theme in the meeting was that colleges and universities had become servants of the "financial, industrial, and military establishment," and that students and faculty were being "sold down the river" by administrators.

Among the provisions of the manifesto were declarations of freedom to join, organize or hold meetings of any organization and to extend the freedoms of speech and assembly to the campus; abolition of tuition fees; control of law enforcement by the students and faculty; an end to the Reserve Officer Training Corps; abolition of loyalty oaths; student-faculty control over curriculum, and a number of safeguards against what the students considered wrongful search and seizure.

The conference, titled "Democracy on the Campus," was held under the auspices of the Emergency Civil Liberties Committee, which was formed in 1951 "to help meet the growing menace to the Bill of Rights."

One of the participants at the conference was the folksinger and pacifist Joan Baez, who announced that she was about to start an "Institute for the Study of Nonviolence" in the Carmel, Calif., area.

Miss Baez said the institute would admit 10 or 15 students for six-week sessions, and that they would study nonviolence while remaining "politically active."

STUDENTS PROTEST BERKELEY OUSTER

But 'Dirty Word' Advocates Fail to Rouse Crowd

By WALLACE TURNER
Special to The New York Times

BERKELEY, April 22 — Leaders of the Free Speech Movement at the University of California tried unsuccessfully today to provoke the school's administrators into actions that would arouse lagging student support.

The resurgence of bitterness stemmed from the dismissal of one and suspension of three students last night.

The disciplinary steps were an outgrowth of the so-called "dirty word incidents" of last month. At that time four-letter vulgarisms were shouted over a loudspeaker and printed on signs in an effort to maintain the impetus of last fall's free speech demonstrations.

Last night the acting chancellor, Martin Meyerson, announced the dismissal of Arthur L. Goldberg, 23 years old, of Los Angeles, a graduate student in education who has been in the forefront of the campaign this year.

Michael Klein, 25, of Berkeley, a graduate student in English, and Nicholas Zegintzov, 25, from Britain, a graduate student in business administration, were suspended until next fall. David A. Bills, 19, of Belvedere, Calif., a freshman in letters and science, was suspended for the reminder of this semester.

An angry response built up overnight among the student movement's leadership, which in the past has been able to use similar administrative actions as the means of touching off mass demonstrations.

A noon rally in the plaza before Sproul Hall, the scene of countless demonstrations, attracted a crowd of about 1,500. As the speeches wore on the students remained apathetic. Throughout the rally speakers made references to the lack of militancy among the students. There was sympathy shown for Mr. Goldberg, however.

Most of the veterans of past Free Speech Movement meetings were back today. They came up to the university from the Berkeley Veterans Memorial Building, where they are on trial on charges growing out of a mass sit-in demonstration in Sproul Hall.

Mario Savio, a former student who was prominent in last year's campaign, spoke at length today.

The mood of the speakers at the rally was demonstrated by Robert Starobin, a teaching assistant in history, who declared: "Very soon they [the administrators] are going to make a false move and we're going to crush them."

At one point in the rally it appeared that the university administration might be about to give the students a new cause.

The rules provide that public address systems for the meetings will be supplied by the university and will not be used after 1 P.M.

After 1:15 P.M., the dean of men, Arleigh Williams, notified the speakers that the microphone was about to be turned off, but that another would be set up across the plaza, where the sound would not disrupt other activities.

The speakers refused to move and brought out their own microphone, provided by Mr. Savio.

Then two campus policemen appeared and the student leaders watched them approach with every indication of happiness. But the policemen only repeated the request to move the meeting to another location.

The meeting broke up in time for Mr. Savio and his co-defendants to get back to Municipal Court for the afternoon session of their trial.

Later a statement on the rally was issued by Neil J. Smelser, the special assistant to the chancellor. He said that the group had violated the university rules on free speech and warned that disciplinary action might be taken.

Vietnam Comes to Oregon U.

By MITCHEL LEVITAS

EUGENE, Ore.

NEVER had the pleasant, placid campus of the University of Oregon been through anything like this. The Erb Memorial Student Union, usually deserted on a Friday night, was jammed with 3,000 standing, sitting, milling people. Raw freshmen argued fearlessly with senior professors. Platoons of "Greeks" —fraternity men—debated with intellectuals they ordinarily ignore as "smokies." "Between choosing one extreme or another," patiently explained a smokie, "there is another alternative—think."

As he spoke, one happily unthinking student waved aloft a sign on which was written nothing at all. A pert coed decorated her sweater with a card that carried the sensible entreaty: "Let's make love, not war." Carefully watching it all from the sidelines—and later in the thick of things—were two Eugene policemen, dressed in plainclothes for the evening.

The occasion was a marathon protest against United States policies in Vietnam, and fo. 12 straight hours nothing else seemed to matter. Finally, after 400 sandwiches, £0 gallons of coffee, 30 speakers, nine "seminars," three folksingers, two poetry recitations and an edgy interlude of drunken jeering and brief violence punctuated by an exploding firecracker and a flying golf ball that narrowly missed its human target, the evening-till-morning demonstration stumbled to a weary finish. "This has been a great success as a campus event," anthropology professor David F. Aberle, 47, organizer of the meeting, told 250 survivors who stood beneath the cool gray morning sky. "As to its success as an event of national importance, that's a wide open question."

And one that is being raised with a growing insistence at colleges and universities across the country. Called a "Teach-In" on many campuses—a slogan that blends the politics of protest with the decorum of academia— the demonstrations began at the University of Michigan on March 24, spread to Columbia the next day, and by now have been staged at about 30 schools, ranging from the predictable (Berkeley) to the unexpected (Texas).

NOT for 25 years, since the nation and its halls of learning bitterly argued whether or not to intervene against the menace of Nazi Germany, have the campuses echoed to similar organized outcries on a foreign policy issue.

Somewhat belatedly, the State Department is hastily dispatching "truth squads" to schools where the opposition is loudest. Another indicator of official concern over the "Teach-Ins" was the irritable reaction of that normally soft-spoken Georgia gentleman, Dean Rusk. "I sometimes wonder at the gullibility of educated men," the Secretary of State snapped, "and the stubborn disregard of plain facts by men who are supposed to be helping our young to learn—especially to learn how to think."

Rusk was uncharitable. There is no guarantee that a Ph.D. in physics, say, is insurance against political gullibility, or a key to Revealed Truth about a situation as perilously complex as Vietnam. Men with sheepskins can behave like sheep, too. Yet there is no denying that a respectable segment of the American academic community is opposed to United States policy in Vietnam, and even many of those teachers who back the Government and refuse to sign up as "Teach-In" participants are not all that certain of their stand.

THE demonstration at the University of Oregon on April 23-24 originated with a phone call to Professor Aberle from Marshall Sahlins, an anthropologist at Michigan who had thought up the "Teach-In" idea, and who knew Aberle as a former colleague at Ann Arbor.

A slender man with thinning black hair fringed by strands of silver, Aberle feels "uncomfortable" picketing or marching for a cause. He is less concerned with ideology than with facing what he considers his moral and social responsibilities. Back in 1952, for example, he had accepted an appointment at the Walter Hines Page School of International Relations at Johns Hopkins, at the time headed by Owen Lattimore. Then Lattimore came under fierce Senatorial attack based on his alleged Communist sympathies, and for Aberle the issue boiled down to whether he should still accept the job, or decline it because of the uproar. He took the offer, remaining until 1960.

A year later he became chairman of the anthropology department at Brandeis, but resigned with his British-born wife, Kathleen, also an anthropologist, after she was called on the carpet by Brandeis president Abram L. Sachar for a speech during the Cuban missile crisis. Addressing a student group, Mrs. Aberle had expressed the hope that nuclear war would be avoided, but added that if the showdown developed into a limited war, "I hope Cuba will win and the United States will be shamed before all the world, and its imperialistic hegemony ended forever in Latin America."

Rather than call their protest a "Teach-In," the Oregon organizers decided at the outset to fly the banner of a "Faculty-Student Committee to Stop the War in Vietnam." "A 'Teach-In'," said Prof. Lucian Marquis, director of the university's Honor College, "suggests an immediate grievance, like a civil rights sit-in. To use that concept here we thought would be falsifying the situation." "Besides," added Prof. George Streisinger of the Institute of Molecular Biology, "the term suggests a protest against the university administration, which it certainly wasn't."

Oregon's president, Arthur S. Flemming, who was Secretary of Health, Education and Welfare under President Eisenhower, firmly supported the committee's right to protest. Enhancing the university's long-established reputation for protecting academic freedom, Flemming in 1962 won the American Association of University Professors Meiklejohn Award for allowing students to hear speakers of their own choice, specifically Gus Hall of the Communist party, at a time when Hall was being barred on other campuses. This time, Flemming cooperatively made the Student Union available for the Vietnam demonstration, and by officially "recognizing" the rally as a university event, he enabled coeds to stay up all night —if they attended (o said they did).

Meanwhile, Aberle's group plunged into the hectic job of signing up supporters, planning the meetings, and finding off-campus speakers. Everyone agreed that Oregon's senior U.S. Senator, Wayne

New York Times photographs by SAM FALK

"A respectable segment of the academic community is opposed to U.S. policy in Vietnam." The result: a new form of campus protest called the "Teach-In."

five departmental chairmen signed up, along with 104 other faculty members and 190 students—opinions ranged all the way from those who thought the U.S. position in Vietnam was blatantly immoral to those who thought it was merely untenable. Within the inner circle, it was more important that the United States had helped obstruct free elections in Vietnam (specified under the Geneva agreements of 1954) than that there had never been free elections in Hanoi; anger over growing U.S. military involvement overshadowed parallel aid from China, the Soviet Union and North Vietnam; doubts about a future U.S. role in Southeast Asia were louder than fears concerning Red China's aims for the area.

"Believe me," said Aberle, puffing on an ever-present cigarette and leaning back in a chair in his small corner office in the Science Annex,

Morse, a vehement critic of United States policy, would be the ideal big gun. The pacifists wanted one of their own, so they got David McReynolds of the War Resisters League. Professor Marquis had heard about Stanley Sheinbaum, an economist at the Center for the Study of Democratic Institutions who had been on a University of Michigan technical-aid project in Vietnam under the Diem regime, and Sheinbaum agreed to speak. Someone, Aberle doesn't remember who, thought of Robert Scheer, a writer for Ramparts magazine who had recently returned from Vietnam, and Scheer accepted, too.

TEACH-IN—The University of Oregon at Eugene is one of 30 schools where faculty and students have gone through the partly educational, partly evangelistic, thoroughly tiring experience of the night-long "Teach-In" to protest the U.S. role in Vietnam. Clockwise from bottom left: a question from the audience; entertainment; guest speaker Senator Wayne Morse of Oregon, a critic of U.S. policy; heckling from the rear of the hall; time out.

THE line-up was strictly anti-Government, as befits an all-out protest, though among the organizers and sponsors—

"I'd much rather teach and do research than fight this thing. The kind of publicity I need are articles in professional journals. But what we have in Vietnam is a schizophrenic situation, a war that is not a war by a government that is not a government. And we refuse to recognize a stable regime in Peking, a stable regime in Hanoi, a stable National Liberation Front. This could lead us into World War III but we're acting like the man who jumped off the Empire State Building and shouted as he passed the 24th floor. 'So far I'm all right.' "

Passionate politics like this was a recent phenomenon on the Oregon campus, which only last November chartered its first right-wing Young Americans for Freedom club and its first left-wing group, Students for Socialist Action, an amalgam of Marxists and non-Marxists. "We're not sufficiently structured to worry about ideology," cheerfully explained Mike Harpster, a graduate history student and one of the many native Californians who have carried the seeds of political awareness from the rich soil of Berkeley to virgin lands up north.

"I was surprised," said Cathy Neville, editor of the Daily Emerald, "but since this protest was organized a few weeks ago Vietnam has replaced civil rights as the most serious topic of discussion." "Even the Greeks have been talking about it," said John Luvaas, president of the student government, "and among students in general Vietnam has been running the subject of girls a pretty close race."

Two groups of students in particular decided—at the last minute—to protest the protest demonstration. Paul Medlar, a sophomore pre-med student, initiated a petition urging those who favor the United States staying in Vietnam to show up at the all-night meeting wearing white shirts and blouses; more than 800 signed the petition. At the same time, two earnest freshmen, Bill McCarter and Jim Mead, organized a picketing cadre, thriftily using some signs imported from other campuses where similar opposing forces had already met.

"We disagree strongly with those who want to pull out of Vietnam," said McCarter, a lanky, trim figure in a suit and tie. "But we really respect the atmosphere of their demonstration. If it accomplishes nothing else, it at least

will make a lot of people who didn't know or care about Vietnam really think about it. And that's what the democratic spirit is all about."

The democratic spirit overflowed the Erb Memorial Union the night of the rally, despite a light drizzle and threats of heavy rain.

At about 7:15 McCarter's pickets unloaded a pile of signs from the back seat of a yellow Cadillac convertible. There were rumors that some Law School students might show up with a supply of eggs to throw, and that the Greeks would come bearing tomatoes. The messages on the placards seemed to match the mood of uneasy expectation: "Welcome Comrades — Viet Cong Headquarters Upstairs," "Reddish Professors Turn Out Yellow Pinks," "Oh Hell, Let's Pull Out—Who Cares About 15,-000,000 Vietnamese."

The incoming crowd ignored the marchers, and after circling about for a few minutes, the pickets climbed a wide staircase to the second-floor ballroom. There they quietly took up positions on the fringes of the packed hall, dotted with white shirts and blouses. A thousand people occupied folding chairs on which were pamphlets protesting the war in Vietnam, along with the State Department White Paper and an analysis of the document by journalist I. F. Stone, whose credentials include a book accusing the U.S. of having plotted the Korean War. Outside the hall, hundreds of students stood shoulder-to-shoulder in the adjacent upper lobby, crowding a table for donations to offset the estimated cost of $1,500 to transport speakers, pay for janitorial services, and mimeographing.

The meeting began promptly at 7:30. In a few words of welcome, Aberle greeted "those who came to protest, those who came to be informed, and those who disagree with us." It was a mild prelude to a series of fiery speeches.

Senator Morse, former dean of the Oregon Law School, was first up, and stayed up for 90 minutes. If words were bullets, he would have defeated the Administration single-handed.

Morse gave credit to the "Teach-Ins" as the most important single factor behind President Johnson's Baltimore pledge to hold "unconditional discussions" on Vietnam. At the same time he said that "a return to the Geneva accords

is the last slim hope for peace." Otherwise, Morse predicted, "if we keep up our unilateral policy, 12 months from tonight there will be hundreds of thousands of American boys fighting in Southeast Asia—and tens of thousands of them will be coming home in coffins." The crowd leaped to its feet in a standing ovation, while the pickets jiggled their signs in silent disapproval. His speech over, Morse fielded a few hostile questions with ease ("Can we wait until China becomes a nuclear power?" "Why do you say we can't win the war in the air?") then sat down to another ovation.

Thus primed for more protest, the audience attentively listened while Ramparts magazine's Scheer argued that Vietnam is "America's Hungary" because, like the Russians, "we are trying to push our way of life onto a people that want none of it." Economist Sheinbaum, who ought to know, reported that the staff of the University of Michigan aid program in Vietnam was heavily infiltrated with C.I.A. agents. Pacifist McReynolds took the line that President Johnson deceived the voters by switching to a "Goldwater policy" in Vietnam after the election, an opinion widely shared among "Teach-In" organizers.

THE speeches continued until 12:20 A.M., with the ballroom crowd as large as ever. Meanwhile, on the main floor of the Student Union, a more personal form of education took place as a dozen informal debates were waged in the midst of a jostling mob. One student carrying a sign that said "Stop Communism in Southeast Asia" was challenged by a social scientist. "Your sign says nothing about methodology," he argued, and the discussion was on.

In the glass-walled "Fishbowl," a curved, spacious room with tables and a jukebox, Jim Peterson, a sophomore political-science major, sat with pretty blonde Carol Chislett, a freshman liberal arts student. "A lot of the students here don't know what they're talking about when they argue Vietnam," she said. "I didn't know anything and that's why I came." Added Peterson: "Now this is an education. I have no sympathy with the aims of this protest, but it would be a crime to miss it."

Wandering through the crowd were two bewildered members of the Stanford track team, in town for a race with Oregon the next day. They were uninterested in the meeting, "but what else is going on in Eugene tonight?" one murmured in disappointment.

Following a 30-minute break after the main speeches, part of the demonstration was scheduled to move outside for more speeches (brief ones) and folk-singing. Instead, it stayed indoors because of the threat of rain, the fear that students might drift away in the open air, and the belief that possible trouble from rowdy students would be easier to control in the ballroom. Trouble did erupt, but it was not easy to control.

STANDING in the rear of the hall were about 100 students, many of whom had used the recess as a cocktail hour. No sooner did the speeches begin than heckling, jeering and catcalls drowned them out. One speaker who had a German accent was interrupted by cries of "Heil!" Another, who was perfectly audible, was stopped by shouts of "We can't hear you."

The uglies were confronted by sweating Dean of Students Donald M. DuShane, who tried to mollify them. The hecklers laughed, and went on booing. When a policeman tried to eject a blond youngster, his companions grabbed the arm and yelled: "You got free speech, man. Stand up for your rights." Instead, the kid defiantly went limp, telling the policeman: "I'm a juvenile. You better not hit me." Finally, in a desperate maneuver, the folk singers came on to quell the outburst. As they began to sing "Over Jordan," the cry went up "The Vietcong want to cross the Mekong."

After 40 tense minutes, the atmosphere simmered down. The hecklers departed and the speakers went on as before, denouncing the U.S. for "the most immoral actions it has ever taken," pleading for the recognition of Red China, and arguing that, like the French in Algeria, the U.S. would win the world's respect by pulling out of Vietnam "with no loss of face." "All this nauseates me," said Steve Munson, former president of the campus Young Republican Club.

If the early part of the formal program was only loosely "educational," the hours from 3 A.M. until dawn more fully redeemed its pedagogic aims. After another break, for coffee and sandwiches, the participants joined nine seminars. There, looking remarkably alert, they quietly argued various aspects of the Vietnam conflict: Was the "domino theory" a plausible forecast of eventual U.S. defeat in all Southeast Asia? Could the United Nations help to end the war? How relevant was the breakup of monolithic Communism?

Most seminars were led by sponsors of the protest, but they made no effort to control the discussion. "You can't duplicate this in a classroom," said Chuck Webster, a freshman. "I've learned an awful lot." Sophomore Jane Isaacs was amazed by the "frat types" who stayed to disagree. "There are 500 people in those seminars—and this is Oregon!" she exclaimed.

AS the sun rose over Eugene, 250 sleepy souls trudged back to the ballroom to conduct the penultimate part of the program: hearing reports from the seminar leaders and voting on a "policy proposal" that summed up the night's work. The resolution preserved the polemic tone of the opening speeches. The U.S. was condemned for military actions "not directed towards the welfare of the people of Vietnam," for its "unilateral intervention" and for "wilfully misrepresenting the facts concerning the war."

As for proposals, the document demanded an immediate cease-fire, that the U.S. "abandon its policy of containment and confrontation of Communism for an active policy of coexistence based on extensive economic aid . . . ," and the convening of an international conference, including the National Liberation Front, to supervise "free elections in North and South Vietnam." The resolution passed, 233 or 234 (the bleary tellers couldn't tell) to 9. With that, the group adjourned for another outdoor rally "to show our strength," as Aberle said, wearily. A few more remarks by students, faculty and two members of the clergy and the protest at Oregon was over.

But not forgotten. At the tables in the "Fishbowl," in the wooden booths at Maxie's, a local beer joint, and through

the hi-fi at the New World coffee house, the debate over Vietnam continued the next day. They were even talking about it at the Paddock, a dimly lit, upholstered watering place favored by the Greeks. "I know my parents are for the U.S. staying," said pretty Barbara Kimball as she eyed a pizza "but the demonstration pretty well convinced me that we ought to go."

THOUGH the speeches at some "Teach-Ins" may often be more shallow than profound, and the atmosphere perhaps more propagandistic than scholarly, the roots of protest are nurtured by legitimate longings.

One is the desire for clarity among academics, and Vietnam is an issue riddled by moral and intellectual contradictions. Another desire stems from the larger battlefield of the cold war—the fear that after the nuclear-test-ban agreement, Goldwater's defeat and President Johnson's promises, the chance for a "reconciliation" with Moscow seems to be slipping away; according to this reading of events, bitter disappointment has bred angry discontent.

Then there is the question of the democratic process itself. Oregon's Aberle may be swayed by enthusiasm when he proclaims "a new form of citizen communication." But university president Flemming is undoubtedly correct when he says that, regardless of whether the communicants are right or wrong, "if we don't have this kind of discussion and debate, if we don't encourage the trend of getting people involved, then our form of government is in trouble."

The "Teach-In" movement was born at the University of Michigan after heavy criticism of an original plan for a one-day faculty "work moratorium" to protest U.S. policies in Vietnam.

The notion of a "strike," while sufficiently dramatic, was so controversial that it diverted attention from the basic aim of the protest group. During a meeting on the night of March 17 they were batting around alternative ideas such as night classes or a vigil, when anthropologist Sahlins suddenly interrupted the discussion. "Hold everything!

I've got it!" he shouted. "They say we're neglecting our responsibilities as teachers. Let's show them how responsible we feel. Instead of teaching out, we'll teach in—all night."

Though "Teach-In" organizers may make an effort to round up a Government partisan, most demonstrations are one-sided affairs, for which the sponsors make no apologies. "There's something bizarre about that suggestion," says philosophy professor Arnold S. Kaufman, a leader of the 200 University of Michigan faculty members who joined the U. of M. protest movement. "The mass media are filled with the Government position."

Nevertheless, Kaufman and his colleagues were enough concerned about the objection that, in addition to the open seminars, they set aside four hours of the 8 P.M.-to-midnight speechmaking portion of the program for questions from the floor (a schedule that was abridged because two bomb scares emptied the hall).

Vietnam critics range from a small cadre of sympathizers with the new, far-out left who want the U.S. to pull out of Vietnam tomorrow, to nonpolitical types aroused mainly by the fear—by no means shared unanimously—that the war may well lead to a nuclear holocaust. Somewhere in the middle are "peace" strategists such as Seymour Melman of Columbia and Anatol Rapoport of Michigan; politically minded scholars who worked actively for the Johnson-Humphrey ticket; and civil-rights militants for whom Vietnam is the overseas version of Selma.

There are exceptions, of course.

At Oregon, "Stop the War" organizers tried hard to win over Prof. James Klonoski, a political scientist, chairman of the Eugene CORE chapter, and an aide to Hubert Humphrey during the Presidential primaries of 1960. Klonoski declined to join up, "even though I support the Government by something like 50.1 per cent to 49.9 per cent. At the risk of sounding simplistic, like Richard Nixon, it's a matter of having to confront the evil."

Historian Paul Dull backs the Government somewhat more strongly, but would not,

if asked, join a counterdemonstration. "It would be too closely identified with the campus Young Republicans," says Dull.

THE result, at Oregon and elsewhere, is a partial vacuum, filled by dissent. Escalating the argument, the newly formed Inter-University Committee for a Public Hearing on Vietnam has scheduled a national "Teach-In" this Saturday in Washington, D. C.; the group aims to round up at least 500 professors from all over the U.S. for a daylong meeting. After delicate negotiations which transformed the event from a protest to a debate, Presidential adviser McGeorge Bundy has agreed to appear, emerging from the sanctuary of his office in the White House basement to confront George Kahin, a Cornell University expert on Southeast Asia, as the main speakers of the occasion. The moderator will be the distinguished Columbia professor of philosophy, Ernest Nagel.

While it is too early to predict the ultimate result of the "Teach-In" movement, its campus impact has been considerable. Audiences are sizable and mostly sympathetic.

Then, too, the activist academic—strengthened by his role as a professional scholar—is in a formidable position to shape opinion.

To a degree that pains Dean Rusk, at least, he is succeeding.

No one among the protest leaders at Oregon claimed to represent a majority of faculty or student opinion. Many who attended the rally simply were curious or, like their elders, concerned and perhaps confused. Among those in the crowd who were undecided about the wisdom of U.S. policy in Vietnam, undoubtedly more people became critics than supporters, scarcely surprising after hearing 12 hours of mostly one-sided discussion. Yet the real significance of the "Teach-Ins" lies deeper. They are catalysts not only for the conversion of ideas, but for the dispersion of ideas. And when interest replaces apathy, the growth of a meaningful consensus will take care of itself.

Coast Regents Set Up Students' Code

By GLADWIN HILL
Special to The New York Times

LOS ANGELES, May 29—Eight months after the outbreak of disorders at Berkeley—eight months of recurrent trouble, endless debate and a bewildering succession of surveys and reports—the first remedial measures to stabilize the huge University of California are finally crystalizing.

On July 1, Dr. Clark Kerr, its president, will put into effect a new code of regulations for student conduct in an effort to avoid the confusion that underlay the initial occurrence of trouble last fall.

The difficulties started when Berkeley campus officials banned the use of a patch of campus ground for recruiting and fund-raising by students and outside organizations in support of off-campus civil rights demonstrations.

The new code gives individual students virtually unlimited rights of advocacy but sharply limits action collectively to one's calculated not to disrupt university operations. It excludes outside, nonstudent agitators, and maintains university jurisdiction over students' off-campus conduct.

Changes Under Way

In the second major aspect of the current university ferment—structural changes to bridge the gap between administrative and academic realms—resolutions are less concrete but progress is definitely under way.

At last Friday's monthly meeting of the institution's 24-member Board of Regents, Dr. Kerr presented a two-page outline of reorganization principals and was authorized to draft specific steps for implementing them.

His presentation was made even as the regents' meeting, under the chairmanship of Gov. Edmund G. Brown, was formally receiving from its special Forbes Committee a much-publicized report called the Byrne Report. This $75,000 study by a staff of outside experts headed by Jerome Byrne, a Los Angeles lawyer, called the university's official structure archaic in many respects. It said this obsolescence was much to blame for student discontent not having been dealt with effectively.

Subject of Controversy

The report, released a fortnight ago, has become a subject of intense controversy. Dr. Kerr's blueprint, obviously prepared with the regents' sanction and incorporating some themes of the Byrne Report, evidently represented an effort to neutralize the report as the sole basis or battleground of discussion and planning of structural overhaul.

The regents are an unpaid board of prominent business and professional men and women—supplemented by eight state officials—who meet for two days monthly. The Kerr proposals would relieve them of trivia dating from days when the university was small; would assign all operational matters, such as professors' leaves, to the chancellors of the respective campuses, with coordination by the university president, and would focus the regents' effort on the broad dimensions dealt with by the board of directors of a business corporation.

The nine campuses of the university are scattered over 500 miles. Each, of necessity, has operated with a large degree of autonomy, even about what courses it would give.

The areas in which the campuses were responsible on the one hand to the university president and on the other to the regents have, however, been blurred.

A major aim of the reorganization—which, Dr. Kerr emphasized, has been under way during the entire seven years of his tenure — is to sort out and clarify these lines of responsibility and communication.

The last eight months have brought a gradual settling-down of the turbulence—distinctive to the Berkeley campus—that reached its peak in the sit-ins last December that involved more than 800 persons, mostly students.

Dr. Kerr, who at one point submitted his resignation, now says he has no intention of leaving the university. Dr. Martin Meyerson, who succeeded Dr. Edward W. Strong as Berkeley chancellor after the trouble started, got an informal vote of confidence in an appearance before the regents last week.

The original Free Speech Movement had failed to take cognizance of "a significant and growing minority of students who want to lead lives less tied to financial return than to social awareness and responsibility." It also assessed the curriculum as "an intricate system of compulsions, rewards and punishments" directed too much toward graduate work in a narrow field.

The leaders of the State Assembly and Senate, meanwhile, announced they intended to ask for an investigation of the institution. Others directed their fire on faculty members' supplementary income from outside consultant work, calling it "moonlighting." They threatened to take it into consideration in future salary appropriations.

The new regulations for student conduct are the product of five months of work by a nine-member regents' committee headed by Theodore R. Meyer, a San Francisco Lawyer.

The committee canvassed the views of university officials, the faculty and student groups. The Free Student Union was solicited for opinion, Mr. Meyer said, but did not respond. The final version of the code, completed only last week, was approved by all the university chancellors and by the Academic Council, the universitywide faculty body.

"Students have the right of free expression and advocacy," the code says. "The time, place and manner of exercising speech and political activity shall be subject to regulations adopted by the chancellors of the respective campuses. Such regulations shall require orderly conduct, noninterference with university functions or activities, and identification of sponsoring groups or individuals, and shall provide for one or more open discussion areas."

Group Activities Listed

Nonuniversity speakers may be invited to address meetings on campuses only by registered student organizations and upon prior notification to the chancellor, who may specify the chairman of the meeting and require that the speaker "be subject to questions from the audience."

Student government organizations (which vary as to voluntary or compulsory membership) may take formal positions on "university-related issues." Voluntary-membership groups may take positions on "nonuniversity-related issues" if they specify they are not speaking for the whole student body.

Individual students and registered student organizations "may take positions on any issue." The primary requisites of a registered organization are that it consist of university personnel and be otherwise acceptable to the chancellor.

Fund-raising will be confined to registered student organizations, "generally recognized charitable organizations, public service agencies, and university or university-related groups."

The display and distribution of printed propaganda is limited to university personnel under "time, place and manner regulations" discretionary with chancellors.

"A student," the code concludes, "may not be disciplined for off-campus conduct unless such conduct affects his suitability as a student. Political action, as such, shall not be deemed to affect suitability."

Protest Against Vietnam War To Begin on Berkeley Campus

By WALLACE TURNER
Special to The New York Times

BERKELEY, Calif., Oct. 10 —A major protest against American involvement in Vietnam will begin on the campus of the University of California Friday.

But within a few hours after it starts, this protest will move off the campus in a "peace march" to the Oakland Army Terminal, where all the action is expected to take place.

That is as good a symbol as any of the different tone that exists on this campus this year, in contrast to the bitter conflicts of the autumn months of 1964.

The upcoming protest will be in the hands of the Vietnam Day Committee. A few people connected with the university have a place in the executive committee but mostly they are persons like Jack Weinberg and Jerry Rubin, former students.

The Berkeley students appear interested but uncommitted.

The organizers of the demonstration said today that there would be companion demonstrations next weekend around the world and in 70 American cities. A spokesman said "demonstrations have been promised in three Iron Curtain countries." He said these were Poland, Czechoslovakia and Hungary.

Among the American cities where demonstrations are planned, the spokesman listed Los Angeles, Portland, New York, Boston, Philadelphia, Baltimore, Washington, Chicago, Detroit, Madison, Wis., and Macon, Ga.

A new committee protesting about Vietnam appeared here last week. This is the Faculty Peace Committee. Some observers thought it was organized to provide a respectable organization for faculty members to join.

The activist talk of the Vietnam Day Committee this past summer, and the committee's futile attempt to stop movement of troop trains with pickets, have given it a bad name that appears to have inhibited some from joining.

This year a broad range of political and economic thought is represented at tables set up in the plaza before Sproul Hall. There are anarchists, socialists, conservatives, radicals, and the Free Student Union, the successor to last year's wildly successful Free Speech Movement.

But no one has been able to find an issue with which to flay the university administration.

A new chancellor is in control on this campus, Roger W. Heynus, formerly of the University of Michigan. New rules, giving complete political freedom so long as no disturbance is committed, have been in force. Speakers say about anything they please, mostly at noon.

Almost every noon hour some group with a student member has a permit to use the Sproul Hall steps for a public meeting. The attendance at Vietnam Day Committee meetings has appeared to disappoint its directorate. The university will not try to prevent the use of its campus for the rally next weekend, but it has refused to dismiss classes as the committee demanded.

The Faculty Peace Committee drew the biggest crowd of the year last week, perhaps 600 at the peak. The total enrollment of the Berkeley campus is about 27,000, so that these 600 represented less than 3 per cent of the student body, if all had been students, which many were not.

October 11, 1965

Voice of the New Campus 'Underclass'

By THOMAS R. BROOKS

THE entrance to the national office of the Students for a Democratic Society is between two vacant store fronts on East 63d Street between Glenwood and University, not far from the University of Chicago but well within the slums of Woodlawn. Like everything else on the street, the leaflet-sized placards in the S.D.S. doorway are tattered and torn. One is the inevitable reproduction of a SNCC (Student Nonviolent Coordinating Committee) poster showing Negroes and whites clasping hands beneath the appeal: "Come Let Us Build a New World."

The others are photographic reproductions, too, including the cover of an S.D.S. Bulletin with a striking picture of a begrimed white boy standing in the backyard of a poverty-stricken neighborhood in Cleveland, and one of two demonstrators moving toward the camera ahead of a crowd of policemen, television cameramen and a train. Over this is a typed caption: "Cops chase S.D.S. pickets who are attempting to stop California train which is carrying troops to suppress the Revolutionary movement of the Vietnamese people."

At the head of the stairway, with its peeling green and white paint and chipped plaster walls, one finds what some students have come to view as the command center of student opposition to the war in Vietnam. Within this warren of badly scarred offices crowded with battered desks and wobbly chairs, telephones ringing and typewriters clacking, a group of some 15 young people, in their early twenties and late 'teens and mostly male, worked around the clock one day recently to get out a referendum to the S.D.S. membership on the so-called "Draft Program," a proposal that S.D.S. agitate, educate and organize around a "legal" antidraft campaign. Posters of all sorts and conditions abound—"Stop Escalating Now," "Vote for Mad," and "Make Love, Not War" are just a few of the catchier slogans.

"They told me this job would take 15 minutes," a girl running an Addressograph machine said. "But I've been here three hours already."

In another office, several young men collated the 18-page mimeographed S.D.S. Bulletin carrying general news of S.D.S. as well as the referendum. Periodically, an elevated train rumbled past, rattling windows and drowning out the incessant conversation.

"This is alienating work," said Jeff Shero, Bulletin editor and S.D.S. vice president, as he stapled Bulletins, "so we can talk." Shero, a soft-spoken 23-year-old Texan who looks out at the world through troubled eyes, went on to say that he was taking a year off from his studies at the University of Texas "to help the organization out." Asked about his draft status, he answered that he was "C.O.'ing it," having applied for conscientious-objector status some time back. The referendum, he explained, was essential because the draft program had been "selected" for attack by the Government. "The June S.D.S. convention decided that any program that might involve legal or political recriminations against the organization should be submitted to the membership," he said.

ONE suspects that S.D.S. members —at least some—are flattered by the attacks on them from President Johnson as well as a number of other eminent public figures, including Senators Dodd, Dirksen and Jackson and Attorney General Katzenbach. In truth, the Attorney General did not attack so much as explain. Asked by newsmen about Communist influence in S.D.S., he said that in such groups "you are likely to find some Communists involved" (something not denied by SDS people). Asked if Communists were leaders, he said, "By and large, no."

Katzenbach announced that the F.B.I. had started a national investigation of groups backing the anti-

427

CLOSE QUARTERS—In the corridor outside S.D.S. national headquarters, the Chicago Committee to End the War in Vietnam, whose offices are down the hall, holds a meeting. The two groups, whose memberships overlap, work together.

draft movement. He also said that while he disagreed "strongly and violently" with the young antidraft demonstrators, they had the right to express their views and opinions. The S.D.S., however, viewed all this—and the stronger statements—as open attacks on S.D.S. and as Red-baiting.

Shero, however, also seemed disposed to view these attacks as a public-relations boon, a gift from the enemy opening up the opportunity to reach thousands of students.

"We figured," Shero told me, "if we'd mimeographed on our machines for 10 years we wouldn't have got as much attention as we got overnight because of the attacks on us." Then he added: "Whenever they attack us, you see, in our reply, we ignore the attack and talk about the war." As for the question of Communism: "That's irrelevant when bombing children in Vietnam." Besides, Shero insisted, "we have no line—the rationale is not all drawn out. We're a very beautiful group because so many different people are able to work together."

THE S.D.S. people, these children of liberal, middle-class parents, are concerned about poverty, civil rights and the war in Vietnam. They spurn, however, parental solutions; they are scornful of the War on Poverty, skeptical about the voting-rights legislation, suspicious of President Johnson's willingness to negotiate in Vietnam. But their own war against poverty has not gone too well; Negroes are running the civil rights struggle. So, the escalation of the war in Vietnam not only horrifies these youngsters, it also offers them a target that fulfills their need for commitment and demonstrations aplenty to absorb their energies.

S.D.S., of course, is not the only antiwar group on campus. The old pacifist organizations, such as the American Friends Service Committee, the Fellowship of Reconciliation and the War Resistors' League, and the peace-movement groups, such as the Committee for a Sane Nuclear Policy, Turn Toward Peace and many others, all have college contacts, members and chapters. The new Marxist-oriented groups, such as the May 2d Movement (named after an antiwar demonstration of a few years ago) and the Du Bois Society clubs, are also active in antiwar agitation.

In addition, a number of so-called *ad hoc* committees, such as the New York and Chicago Committees to End the War in Vietnam, have sprouted up. But these are united-front, or umbrella, committees—rather than membership organizations—embracing a wide range of campus and non-campus antiwar and peace groups.

There are about 100 of these around the country, loosely tied in with the National Coordinating Committee to End the War in Vietnam, whose headquarters are in Madison, Wis. Frank Emspak, a 22-year-old zoology graduate who is chairman, has announced plans for a national convention in Washington, D.C., over the Nov. 26-28 weekend, bracketing a SANE-initiated March on Washington for Peace in Vietnam scheduled for Nov. 27. Emspak says emphatically: "We're not in the business of writing programs. The local groups decide what to do. We're a communication and coordination organization with agreement on a minimal slogan."

S.D.S. is represented on the National Coordinating Committee along with representatives from various local groups and national organizations, including M2M, the Du Bois Society and others. Local S.D.S. chapters have been influential in the formation of a number of local End the War groups. In New York City, for example, S.D.S. and the New York Committee to End the War in Vietnam share the same office at 1165 Broadway. S.D.S. according to its president, Carl Oglesby, "plans to concentrate on the education program on the campus and in the community, not on mass demonstrations. We hope that the National Committee in Wisconsin will take over the organization of demonstrations." But Oglesby does want S.D.S. to explore the possibilities of a student strike along the lines of those in France over Algeria and in Japan over the Japanese-American treaty several years ago.

Relations between S.D.S. and the National Coordinating Committee are not always smooth. "Everyone and his brother is a member of the steering committee," S.D.S. National Secretary Paul Booth told me, "and I wouldn't want them making decisions for my membership." Who will do what where, I suspect, will be determined by the relative strength of the various members of this uneasy coalition. Roughly speaking, and with considerable overlap, the M2M is a big thing in the East, S.D.S. in the Middle West and the Du Bois Society on the West Coast.

MEANWHILE, S.D.S. is the largest single radical student group on or around the nation's campuses. It claims a membership of 3,000 (spokesmen say that at least twice as many participate in its activities) with 90 chapters around the country a national staff of 12 people and an annual budget of $80,000. Single staff members are paid $12.50 a week—when they get paid—plus rent. S.D.S. has rented two floors in a nearby house for use as a staff apartment. "We eat together a lot," one staff member said. Married staffers are paid $70 a week and are expected to pay their own rent.

PROTESTING THE PROTESTERS—Iowa collegians assail S.D.S. (Students for a Democratic Society) and its antidraft stand.

S.D.S. is not entirely a traditional campus-based organization. It has some 50 volunteers, living on subsistence pay raised out of local chapter funds, working in some 10 poor neighborhoods in Northern cities. Many of these are in the slum neighborhoods that surround our major universities—such as those around Columbia University in New York. S.D.S. members seek to organize the residents into community unions, battle urban renewal, agitate for control of poverty programs by the poor, and work to form new political groupings of the poor.

The S.D.S. missions to the poor have been undergoing a change since a group of youngsters under the leadership of Tom Hayden, an S.D.S. "founder," moved into the Clinton Hill area of Newark and formed the Newark Community Union Project. N.C.U.P. is the prototype and most successful of such S.D.S. projects.

The youngsters who join N.C.U.P. as "community organizers" exist on a Spartan diet — mostly peanut-butter and jelly sandwiches and powdered milk. At first, these lay brothers of the poor roam the neighborhood getting acquainted, taking surveys — "Does your landlord provide heat?"—as a way of meeting residents and getting to know their grievances. Then come informal meetings and more formal protest organizations on a block basis. Rent strikes are encouraged, along with sit-ins in city offices aimed at securing housing inspection and enforcement of building codes. In Newark, such tactics have paid off in needed repairs, regularized garbage collection and the shelving of an urban-renewal project that would have displaced residents.

DESPITE this modest success, S.D.S. has had difficulty in keeping projects of this type going. Last summer, there was a shift in emphasis from the problems of the poor toward the building of opposition to the war in Vietnam. The S.D.S. Oakland Community Union Project for example, apparently spent most of its time "combating Selective Service," according to a report in The S.D.S. Bulletin. On Manhattan's West Side, a similar group spent its time handing out antiwar leaflets to the crowds at New York's Shakespeare Festival. Literature tables were set up in the street as a means of distributing antiwar literature and engaging passers-by in "educational debate." Street-corner meetings were also held.

Susan Schwartz, an attractive Radcliffe graduate now a French instructor at New York State University in Stony Brook, L. I., who lives on the Upper West Side, told me: "We're trying to create a permanent radical constituency by linking up peace issues with domestic issues." It is an effort that has its hazards. Miss Schwartz, the daughter of a Hartford, Conn., eye specialist, recalled street-corner speakers being pelted with eggs, tomatoes and bottles. "The police," she said, "did nothing. All the neutrals were driven away and the situation got kind of ugly and frightening. We had to have the police escort us to the subway."

This West Side group plans door-to-door canvassing this fall "on questions of peace, housing, schools and other community issues." It has opened a store-front community meeting place, largely staffed by Columbia students, and "hopes to lay the basis for a Congressional campaign in 1966." Despite the groping for community support, the group seems to draw its strength from what might be termed the Columbia University "surround," where the S.D.S. constituency is to be found.

THE S.D.S. constituency is that new intellectual underclass growing up around our universities—students, college dropouts, graduate students, graduates who have started on their careers but who have not left the university neighborhood (especially in the larger cities), teaching assistants and professors in the lower ranks. It is a mobile class, shifting with ease from Berkeley to Cambridge and all points between.

The traditional constituency of the left, the working class, is pretty much given up as lost, having fallen prey to the unions and the Democratic party, pillars of the Establishment in S.D.S. eyes. Informed estimates place at least a third, if not more, of S.D.S. membership among graduate students, dropouts, graduates and others who make up the new underclass.

The S.D.S. president, Carl Oglesby, may well be the representative man of this new underclass. "There is something very Emersonian about belonging to S.D.S." he told me. Though a member of only several months' standing, he was elected—perhaps the better word would be "chosen"—at the last S.D.S. convention in June after a long debate over whether or not S.D.S. should elect officers at all.

Holding office or having officers seems to some in the movement "a form of oppression." Vice President Shero, for example, who is something of an anarchist, has proposed a referendum that would abolish the offices of president and vice president. He believes the organization is "over-structured." When he was asked about the office of national secretary, he said: "Don't worry, we'll get around to abolishing that, too." However, debate over this issue was temporarily resolved last June when Oglesby was elected to office.

The story of Oglesby's involvement in S.D.S. and his election tells a good deal about the style of the movement as well as about its uncertainties. Note, for example, that Oglesby at 30 is the same age as many of the teaching assistants, section men and younger professors who actually teach S.D.S. students in college. Also, though a new boy, he is of an age with the S.D.S. elder statesmen and founders.

WHEN I interviewed Oglesby in the Greenwich Village apartment of a friend, he was dressed casually in a yellow pullover, white shirt, dark brown slacks, white socks and nondescript black shoes. As he talks, he uses his hands expressively and his eyes are sharp and quizzical behind black, thin-rimmed glasses. He is tall and thin and, with his beard and brown hair, he looks rather like the middle-period D. H. Lawrence.

One is not surprised at all to discover that Oglesby is a playwright and a would-be novelist. He has had two plays, "The Peacemaker" and "The Hero," produced at the University of Michigan; another, "The Season of the Beast," was produced by the Margo Jones Theatre in Dallas, Tex., and closed, says Oglesby, "by fiat" of the Board of Directors for being "anti-fundamentalist." "The Peacemaker" also was given a reading by the Actors Studio here in New York. Oglesby told me that he would not now finish his first novel, finding it no longer "relevant," though he has hopes of writing another.

Oglesby is one of the few S.D.S.'ers who can claim a working-class background. He was born in 1935 in Akron, Ohio, the son of a rubber worker. His parents, now divorced, came from the South: his father from South Carolina—"He came North to get rich in a factory"—his mother from Alabama. Asked about family politics, Oglesby said, "My family is completely non-political, kind of pale Democrats. My father believes in the union and that's about it."

After graduating from the Akron public schools, Oglesby entered Kent State University. By his own account, he was not very happy there. "In 1953," he told me, "there wasn't any movement discernible from Kent." But, he adds, "I really wasn't entitled to complain. I had the option of leaving." Which he did, moving to New York, where he almost succeeded in getting a play produced on Broadway. After a year, he went back to Kent, where he met his wife-to-be and married her.

Then came a time of odd jobs, including a stint in the mill room of a rubber factory. "It was a tough place," he says. A job as a technical writer at Goodyear came as a welcome break. Later, "somewhat over-ecstatic" at the acceptance of his first play by the Dallas theater group, Oglesby packed up wife and daughter and took off for Maine where he spent "three really beautiful months."

But the money ran out and he became a technical writer again, this time with Bendix Systems Division at Ann Arbor, Mich., where he was soon promoted to supervisor of his department. Meanwhile, he re-

entered school, hoping to get his B.A. degree from the University of Michigan as well as perhaps win the university's Hopwood Literary Prize. "Bendix," he told me, "was very tolerant about employes going to school during working hours. It's part of corporate liberalism. They thought I was kind of eccentric, but despite myself I became the fair-haired boy of upper management."

Still, though Oglesby believed that "American society was so bad that there can't be anything between me and it" he felt ashamed about "drawing a moral blanket over the fact that for eight

hours a day I was a hireling in the cold war." At about this time, he became involved in an S.D.S. project "to get a grass-roots theater going." The project didn't but Oglesby did within S.D.S.

He did some research on the war in Vietnam and published some lengthy communiqués on the subject in The S.D.S. Bulletin. Then came a series of soul-searching conversations with S.D.S. leaders Rennie Davis and Todd Gitlin over: "What to do with my life?" At the time of the teach-ins last year, S.D.S. offered Oglesby two jobs, one with a community project in Boston and the other as research director

in Ann Arbor. He accepted the latter, despite possible financial hardship for his wife and three young children.

The election as S.D.S. president, Oglesby told me, "was an emotional experience for me and the organization, too." I asked him if he ascribed his election to the swing within S.D.S. toward organizational concentration on the anti-Vietnam war issue. He thought not. "I was the oldest of the lot [of five] running," he told me, "and consider that the people are perplexed over what happens when you leave school. Is it possible to stay with the movement when you take on a job and family re-

PRESIDENT—Carl Oglesby, 30, dropout, playwright, technical writer: "There is something Emersonian about belonging to S.D.S."

NATIONAL SECRETARY—Paul Booth, 22, Swarthmore, says, "We fill the void left by the nonexistence of an adult left."

ALLY—Frank Emspak, 22, chairman of the National Coordinating Committee to End the War in Vietnam, with which S.D.S. works.

FIELD SECRETARY—Jane Adams, 22, Southern Illinois University graduate, visits local chapters as S.D.S. campus organizer.

sponsibilities? My willingness to come to them from a $12,000-a-year job and to throw myself on their willingness to sustain us was moving to them." Oglesby added that he "wanted to push away" the nomination—"I felt that it was obtrusive of me"—but he also felt himself "becoming a moral center for people though I tried not to be."

THIS kind of mystique is as important to the S.D.S youngsters as is morality and the need for consensus. "The movement" of which S.D.S. is a part depends on consensus just as much as—if not more than—President Johnson. "The Trotskyites," Paul Booth, S.D.S. national secretary, in the course of a discussion about the umbrella-type End the War in Vietnam Committees, "are so new to the coalition that they don't know how to act. So, the first thing they do when they come in is to form a faction immediately. And, no one knows how to handle them."

It seems that as a result of this "Trotskyist" factionalism at least one new left united-front group actually has had to take votes on important decisions. "Within the new left," Booth said, "you know, we work for consensus, but how can you get consensus if there is an already committed bloc?" He shook his head regretfully, saying, "The self-destructive forces within the coalition really shouldn't be underestimated. Outside of meetings, though, things work O.K."

Booth, a 22-year-old Swarthmore graduate, class of 1964, who majored in political science, told me, "I was brought back partly to repoliticalize the movement." Booth's parents were both active in Americans for Democratic Action and before his disillusionment with liberalism Paul worked—in 1960—for the Democratic National Committee. His father, a New Dealer, was chief of the Unemployment Security Bureau's Division of Program and Legislation before becoming a professor of social work and economics at the University of Michigan. Paul's mother worked as a psychiatric social worker in Washington, D. C., where Paul grew up.

He is an intense, lanky young man with curly, light brown hair, with hazel eyes bright in a triangular face. Walking to lunch, wearing a dark madras jacket, white shirt and stringy tie, dark slacks, he was oblivious of the pencil perched above his right ear. His words tumbled out in haste trying to catch up with his rapid strides along the sidewalk. "We contend that young people don't want to fight, so why don't they test it by allowing choice, offer something that builds. Work in Watts, with SNCC, in the Peace Corps—this should be seen as high a duty as burning a village." We stepped into the best restaurant on the block—not very good but one step above cafeterias and drug-store counters — and Booth said, "This is where the local poverty warriors eat."

Booth worries over what he calls "our mumbling articulateness in the face of questions about our politics. We do have a sound critique of coalition politics [the alliance of liberal, labor and civil-rights forces advocated by people like Michael Harrington and Bayard Rustin] and we should articulate. We've got a lot to say to the world." S.D.S., Booth believes, "is filling the void left by the non-existence of an adult left."

DESPITE disclaimers, however, S.D.S. does owe something to an adult left. Seeking a "sustained community of educational and political concern . . . bringing together liberals and radicals, activists and scholars, students and faculty," S.D.S. originated in 1960 as the revived student department of the League for Industrial Democracy, a tax-exempt Socialist-oriented educational organization founded in 1905 by Upton Sinclair, Jack London, Clarence Darrow and others and dedicated "to increasing democracy in our economic, political and cultural life." The L.I.D., too, is experiencing a revival under its new executive secretary, 27-year-old Tom Kahn, and chairman, 38-year-old Michael Harrington.

Recently, however, the two organizations have parted company. The separation followed S.D.S.'s increasing participation in action programs that clearly transcended the limits imposed by law on tax-exempt organizations. S.D.S., in short, did not want to be

inhibited by the L.I.D.'s tax exemption, nor did S.D.S. want to jeopardize the exemption. However, a joint statement, issued by Kahn and Booth, did say: "We do not conceal the fact that political differences between the two organizations have emerged in recent times."

The S.D.S. Port Huron Statement, drafted in 1962 and considered its founding document, contained denunciations of colonialism, Communism and anti-Communism. This summer, however, the S.D.S. convention struck from its constitution clauses barring "advocates and apologists" of totalitarianism and opposing "authoritarian movements both of Communism and the domestic right" because these sections were "negative and exclusionary" and "smacked of Red-baiting." "The New Left," The S.D.S. Bulletin said in reporting the deletions, "should not concern itself with this Old Left tactic."

The L.I.D was no more pleased about this development than it was about a Viet Cong romanticism among some of the S.D.S. The Viet Cong are fighting "at bottom a legitimate war of liberation," says Oglesby. There is also a strong feeling that the S.D.S. antidraft program pushes demonstrations to the point of defeating their purpose—peace in Vietnam—by hardening the opposition, freezing out the middle ground, and bringing an end to debate. There have been some counter-demonstrations, angry verbal exchanges and occasional fisticuffs on campuses recently.

Recent weeks have been rather trying ones for the S.D.S. "We're in trouble all right," Paul Booth told me, "but such trouble I can live with. The organization is booming." S.D.S. leaders expect to double their membership shortly and hope to hit 10,000 before the year is out. But one suspects that they are now recruiting only the converted; for example, a "super late news" item in The S.D.S. Bulletin: "University of Chicago students have been piling into the office all morning to sign membership cards. One fellow said, 'If you are going to be Red-baited, I want to be on the list.'" Or, there is the girl who joined at a University of Chicago meeting I witnessed. She said: "I've always *felt* this way; member or not, it made no difference. But now I have to tangibly show I'm committed."

EDITOR—Jeff Shero, 23, taking a year off from the University of Texas to run The S.D.S Bulletin, says he is "C.O.'ing it."

STAFF PHOTOGRAPHER—Dee Gorton, 23, University of Mississippi, provides pictures for The Bulletin and campaigns.

That day, the Chicago S.D.S chapter picked up 20 new members, bringing total membership to about 50—and this, I am told, is a big chapter.

Until now, S.D.S. has been very lax about dues: "When we split—you know, left the bourgeoisie," Oglesby told me, "we left all those habits behind, like paying dues." But, worried lest its antidraft stand cause a drop-off in contributions from the "richies" and "friendly institutions," the S.D.S. leadership has intensified both recruitment and the collection of dues.

THE S.D.S. draft referendum is couched in terms that emphasize its value as "a tool for expanding the antiwar movement." First, The S.D.S. Bulletin discusses its "relevance" as a "central factor in the lives of millions of people." Among the "possible approaches to the draftable kids" are tables outside physical-examination centers for distributing leaflets along the lines of "Why are they trying to draft you?" and urging that "kids file Form 150," a request for C.O. classification. Help should be offered in filling out such forms, "strictly legal, unlike 'draft refusal.'"

Speaking engagements at high schools should be sought along with debates with military recruiters. Organizing around an antidraft program, The Bulletin goes on, provides the opportunity to educate listeners about the "basic facts about the war in Vietnam, the undemocratic nature of the draft itself, and serves to illustrate the connections between the University and the military establishment."

The program opens up opportunities for protest, too. According to The S.D.S. Bulletin, "the act of filing for C.O. is, in itself, a gesture of personal protest."

On campus, the authorities should be stopped from turning over class-rank information to the military. (S.D.S. believes that the extension of the draft may hit students in the bottom quartile of their class this winter.) Recruiters "should be the focus of attention, challenged to debate, accused by picket signs of participation in war crimes." Ditto, the R.O.T.C. Demonstrations may also be aimed at local draft boards.

THE antidraft referendum, as is often the case with S.D.S. policy-making, embraces activities already under way in some individual chapters.

There is, incidentally, no hard cut-off date for the vote, return of ballots and the count. "S.D.S. chapters," Oglesby told me, "have the right to act autonomously and a lot have been moving independently on this [the antidraft program] already."

S.D.S. members, for example, were active in the International Days of Protest, Oct. 15 and 16, which brought out some 80,000 in protest marches and demonstrations across the country. In Ann Arbor, 38 people were arrested in an S.D.S.-sponsored draft-board sit-in. The North Carolina S.D.S. chapter marched against the biological weapons center at Fort Bragg—without discernible results, however.

In Oakland, S.D.S. members have handed out leaflets at recruiting centers urging young men of draft age to file C.O. forms. They also tried unsuccessfully to stop a troop train. "How did we know when the trains were coming — answer—spotters up the line," reported Paul Booth in the summer S.D.S. Bulletin. (Booth spent the summer working in the S.D.S. Oakland Community Project.) But, he added: "All the dramatic troop train demonstrations and other demonstrations have still not added up to more than a handful of arrests."

"Like Berkeley last year," Booth told me, "the draft thing contributes to student class consciousness."

Todd Gitlin, a member of the S.D.S. National Administrative Committee, also believes that the antidraft program will rally broad student support. "Originally," he said, "I was more excited about rallying ordinary kids. Then they read me an interview with the head of the Michigan Selective Service. This worthy gentleman pointed out that there were 76,000 students in Michigan (presumably this includes part-timers, kids in junior and community colleges, etc.), and that 20,000 of the lousy brats would be drafted. If such is the case, the campus should be fertile soil for an antidraft movement."

SOME S.D.S. members, however, do not agree. Lee Webb, another member of the S.D.S. National Administrative Committee, put his opposition in these terms: "The antidraft issue is not the best one around which to organize a mass opposition to the war. . . . [It] raises just those emotional cold-war issues that make it a terrible choice. . . . S.D.S. should be concerned most with broadening the base of opposition to the war, not with escalating the antiwar movement to more militant tactics." To paraphrase Webb, if S.D.S. members are arrested, it should be because the Government can no longer tolerate "mass dissatisfaction" with its foreign policy, not because of an antidraft program. "We see the linkage between the war and that program," Webb said, but "most people will not—they will see us only as draft dodgers."

The S.D.S. youngsters, incidentally, while they admire those who protest by burning their draft cards are not likely to emulate them. As one S.D.S. member put it: "Is going to jail for three years,

ANTI — At the University of Iowa, undergraduates demonstrate against organizations like the Students for a Democratic Society

say, going to help the peace movement?" Those who burn their draft cards in protest, like young David J. Miller, who burned his in New York City several weeks ago and was subsequently arrested, are members of avowedly pacifist organizations and not of S.D.S. in most cases. S.D.S. is not a pacifist group.

"We're not against violence, per se," Oglesby told me. "We don't like it. Who does? But we're not pretending to be pacifists. The aim of the antidraft program is to make it possible for people who feel as we do about the war to do something about it." S.D.S., I was told, is interested in expanding the definition of conscientious objector to include those who in their conscience object to particular wars as well as those who are against all wars.

Another group opposed to the present antidraft program is the New York-At-Large chapter of S.D.S., most of whose members believe in the workability of a liberal-labor-civil-rights coalition in politics, a belief in Establishmentarianism frowned upon by most of the rest of S.D.S. Steve Max, an articulate former S.D.S. staff member, fears that S.D.S. faces "a progressive narrowing of options." The combined effect, he argues, "of the incautious attitude taken toward the Viet Cong, the removal of statements in our constitution differentiating our politics from Communist ideologies, and the antidraft proposal is to cut off S.D.S. from many individuals and groups who are not to its left. The total, uncalculated effect is to alienate present friends and prospective allies."

EVEN the supporters of the antidraft program, it seemed to me as I talked to them, approached it warily. They are a little nervous about what they consider the pro-

gram's "legal ambiguities." The day the referendum was sent out, a page was added explaining possible legal consequences. A number of letters have come into the S.D.S. national office raising essentially the same question, "Are we engaged in a *draft-dodging* program?" (Italics mine.)

David Gilbert, a 21-year-year-old Columbia University senior, philosophy major and former Eagle Scout, spoke to a floor meeting of about 20 at Carman Hall recently on the S.D.S. antidraft program. "My mother called me up," he said, "all upset about me now doing something illegal." Gilbert paused, then added: "Well, no one laughed, so I guess we've all got mothers." To set all such troubled minds at ease, Booth and other S.D.S. leaders repeatedly insisted to me: "We are legal."

"We've become a bit too Vietnam-oriented," Steve Kindred, a husky Chicago University history major told me. Kindred's father is an Iowa Methodist minister and Steve himself has just returned to Chicago after a year of working with peace groups in England. Speaking of plans for the Chicago S.D.S. chapter, he said: "We don't want to get stuck on crisis issue stuff." The Chicago group is forming working committees on foreign policy, domestic social change and university reform. It also plans an "inquest" that will "get the facts out" on Vietnam. The French and Italian press are to be "researched" for material to present to the inquest. "We're trying to fit in a general framework and reach as wide a base as possible," Kindred told me. But, he added, draft program publicity "helped get people here."

Carl Davidson, president of the University of Nebraska S.D.S. chapter, insists on describing S.D.S. as being "extremely antitotalitarian,

against both Fascism and Communism." (The quotation is from The Daily Nebraskan.) Although S.D.S. is only a few weeks old at Nebraska, Davidson reports a dozen members, the sponsorship of a teach-in on Vietnam, a proposed study of rules and regulations on campus, and a look into the possible unionization of university service employes. All this is traditional S.D.S. campus activity.

THE antidraft program is a departure on a new course. It is rooted in aversion to the horrors of the Vietnam war. At the moment, S.D.S., I would say, is content to look no further. Some S.D.S. members may believe that the Viet Cong are fighting "a revolutionary war"; others agree with Oglesby that the war is fought by the United States "under the banner of cold-war colonialism." Most, I suspect, would agree with young David Gilbert, who told a group of Columbia students: "I wouldn't say North Vietnam is a democratic ideal but it is the only viable regime in the country"—meaning all of Vietnam.

Neither do the S.D.S. youngsters see Communist China as an aggressor; the U.S. seems to them to be playing that part. They simply are not concerned about the possibility of Chinese Communist domination over Asia; China is remote and perhaps revolutionary still. India, once a rallying point for idealists, is no longer, especially since her refusal to grant a plebiscite in Kashmir. Socialism and neutralism in the underdeveloped countries, say S.D.S. spokesmen, "in many places should be encouraged."

Beyond this, they do not go. In sharp contrast to radical movements of the past, even a short decade ago, there is no discussion or debate over the nature of the Soviet Union or

of Communist China. At their age, Stalin, the Stalin-Hitler Pact, Hungary, even Khrushchev's revelations are already dim history. During most of their nonage, the Communist monolith has, in fact, been falling apart, or so they believe. Besides, the S.D.S. generation is a most ahistorical generation. Unlike earlier radicals, they do not relate themselves to any radical tradition. There is little or no citing of texts in the Marxist manner.

S.D.S. is planning a December membership conference "to look at ourselves intellectually and organizationally." Among the topics of discussion—the list is almost endless — is the question of "coalition." With whom? The Du Bois Clubs, M2M, etc., on the one hand, or the L.I.D., the A.F.L.-C.I.O., Socialist party and Reform Democrats on the other? Communism and the national liberation movements as well as "the structure of power" in the United States are due for scrutiny. The parental League for Industrial Democracy has been asked to participate.

Still, one suspects that it is the antidraft program that will shape the S.D.S.'s immediate future. As Oglesby told me: "It appears our resources are being allocated for us by the Administration." And, he might have added, television, the press and other mass media. In this context, what will happen may depend upon Government reaction. But it will also turn on the response of the new university-created underclass to a tighter draft and to the S.D.S.'s antidraft program. Campus polls, so far, show that students favor President Johnson's approach to the Vietnam war over that of the S.D.S. But no one has polled the new underclass. What they will do and how that will affect S.D.S. no one at present can say.

November 7, 1965

STUDENTS OF LEFT SET UP COLLEGES

'Counter-Universities' Called Mirror of Campus Revolt

By PETER BART
Special to The New York Times

LOS ANGELES, Dec. 11 — Joseph Byrd is a soft-spoken, scholarly young graduate student and teaching assistant at the University of California at Los Angeles who discusses most subjects with wry detachment. When he talks about the plight of the university student, however, his face registers passionate indignation.

"The university student today is the single most exploited individual in our society," the 27-year-old Mr. Byrd declares. "Fortunately, students at long last are awakening to this fact."

Mr. Byrd and some fellow students have recently decided to ameliorate the problem. They have taken over a shabby loft building in downtown Los Angeles and established a new educational institution to fit their own design. Called the New Left School of Los Angeles, it is one of a series of roughly similar "counter-universities" that are springing up around the nation.

In the last few months at least seven institutions have been established—in San Francisco, Chicago, New York, Los Angeles, Gainesville, Fla., Austin, Tex., and Palo Alto, Calif.—and still others appear each month.

The founders of the new schools, which are often called "counter-universities" or "anti-universities" to signify their rejection of all that ordinary universities stand for, are not especially interested in achieving formal accreditation or in building themselves into giant organizations.

"Our interest is to provide the sort of intellectual vigor that has disappeared from the established universities," says Dr. Paul Krebs, 31, director of the six-month-old Free University of New York, 20 East 14th Street.

This, he notes, ultimately involved the Free University in subjects considered taboo by established institutions. Its course offerings include such subjects as "Life in Mainland China Today," "Hallucinogenic Drugs: Uses and Social Implications" and "Search for the Authentic Sexual Experience."

"We're seeing the beginning of what I think will be a real proliferation of the student-formed counter-university," says Paul Jacobs, a writer and lecturer who has taught at the New School in San Francisco. "The new schools mirror the massive student revolt against society."

Variety of Approaches

The institutions vary in many ways. Some, like the New School in San Francisco, are operated under the auspices of a specific organization belonging to the so-called "new left" —in this case the Students for a Democratic Society—and orient their courses toward political activism.

Others, like the Free University of New York or the New Left School of Los Angeles, say they are independent of any organization and try to offer courses of a broader cultural orientation.

In general, the schools have no plan to adopt the formal accoutrements of a university — accreditation, the right to grant degrees, establishment of four-year undergraduate programs. The only institutional formality is tuition, which at the Free University amounts to $24 for a first course running 10 weeks, and lesser amounts for other courses.

All the newcomers acknowledge, however, that they owe their origins to the increasingly aggressive student-led new left movement. As such, the institutions try to hold up an ideological umbrella that encompasses all shades of left-wing opinion —anti-Vietnam groups, civil rights groups, the students for a Democratic Society, Socialists and even Communists.

The institutions are of modest size. The School of Chicago has an estimated total of 300 students and 39 instructors who meet at church in the Negro section of the West Side. The Free University of New York also has 300 students and 39 teachers.

Many of the students continue to be undergraduates or graduate students at formal universities, attending the counter-universities at night and without credits.

Faculty Is Cited

The faculty of New York's Free University includes Milt Rosen, chairman of the Peking-oriented Progressive Labor party; David McReynolds, field secretary of the War Resisters League, and James Mellen, a political science instructor at Drew University.

Dr. Krebs says he was an assistant professor of sociology at Adelphi University until he was dismissed after traveling to Cuba in 1964. Although he acknowledges he is a Marxist he insists that the Free University is not tied to any single ideology.

Similarly, Joseph Byrd in Los Angeles says he considers himself a radical but intends to keep his New Left School "non-sectarian." The school's "associates" or founding sponsors include Harvey Wheeler, co-author of "Fail Safe," who is a fellow at the Center for the Study of Democratic Institutions in Santa Barbara; Dorothy Healey, chairman of the Communist party for Southern California, and Theodore Edwards, Los Angeles chairman of the Socialist Workers party.

Mr. Byrd says that acknowledged Communists put up a substantial portion of the $1,100 needed to start the school but that the party has at no time attempted to dictate school policies.

Mr. Wheeler, however, finds that too many of the school's students reflect a "suffocating Marxist commitment." Mr. Wheeler said he had agreed to become a sponsor because he supported the right of students to "reject society."

The New Left School, started only two months ago, is in dismal shape financially. Its enrollment is only about 100, but Mr. Byrd believes his institution will expand as a result of the growing student resentment over exploitation."

By exploitation Mr. Byrd means the sort of "depersonalization" and "regimentation" that he and friends believe helped trigger the Free Speech Movement at Berkeley. The University states in its prospectus that university students today are "treated like raw material to be processed for the university's clients—the business, government and military bureaucracies," it continues, "have been systematically dehumanized, deemed incompetent to regulate their own lives, sexually, politically or academically."

However, Joseph Tussman, a philosophy professor at the University of California's Berkeley campus says that "it's easy to indict many aspects of our universities but it's wrong to write them off as lost causes."

Mr. Tussman, who was approached to be a sponsor of two counter-universities but declined, has, instead, focused his attention on an experimental college within Berkeley. The college, which has 150 students, focuses on reading and writing and breaks away from the "deadly lock-step pattern" of the course system.

"The paradoxical thing about the so-called counter-universities is that despite their radical aims they fall right back on the old pattern of courses and lecturers," Professor Tussman says.

Although the students of the new left encountered rejection from many professors, they nonetheless solicited help from enough young faculty members to put together a teaching staff. At a recent evening session at the New Left School one professor was lecturing on "Planning and the Constitution," another on "Introductory Marxism."

"I Do Not Fear or Reject the Impending Vietcong Victory in Vietnam. I Welcome It."
— Prof. Eugene D. Genovese

Study in Academic Freedom

By ARNOLD BEICHMAN

THIRTEEN years ago Rutgers University forced the dismissal of two professors who had claimed protection of the Fifth Amendment in appearances before the Senate Internal Security Subcommittee. Questioned under oath about past or continuing membership in the Communist party, the two men—a professor in the College of Pharmacy for 27 years and a teacher of classics for four years—declined to answer and cited their constitutional guarantees against self-incrimination.

A Faculty Committee of Review recommended "no further action be taken" against the professors following their refusal to testify. Nevertheless, on Dec. 12, 1952, the Rutgers Board of Trustees, supported by the then university president, concluded a two-and-a-half-month debate by voting, 39-12, that unless the two men testified by the end of the year before the Senate subcommittee, their teaching appointments would be terminated. The professors ignored the ultimatum and on Dec. 31 they lost their jobs.

On Election Day last month another battle over academic freedom at Rutgers came to a different ending. The Republican nominee for Governor of New Jersey, State Senator Wayne Dumont, had conducted a bitter campaign ostensibly against an expelled Communist party member, now a professed "Marxist and Socialist," teaching and enjoying tenure at Rutgers. Actually, Dumont's real target was incumbent Gov. Richard Hughes, for having refused to pressure the university into firing historian Eugene D. Genovese, a 35-year-old associate professor who had declared at a campus teach-in on April 23:

"I do not fear or reject the impending Vietcong victory in Vietnam. I welcome it."

If public concern can be measured by election results, New Jersey voters were unmoved by Dumont's campaign outcries. Hughes won by 354,000 votes, a record margin in the state. Even Republican leaders who made pilgrimages to New Jersey to extol Dumont's other virtues—the pilgrims included Dwight D. Eisenhower and Govs. George Romney of Michigan,

William Scranton of Pennsylvania and John Chafee of Rhode Island—carefully steered clear of the Genovese issue. Only Richard M. Nixon echoed Dumont's protests over l'affaire Genovese. Such leading New Jersey Republicans as United States Senator Clifford Case and C. Douglas Dillon were openly critical of Dumont's tactics.

THE general dismay over the character of Dumont's campaign revealed the remarkable change in attitudes toward academic freedom since the expulsions at Rutgers 13 years ago. This time, demands for capitulation by the university were solidly opposed by the university's administration and its lay governing boards. More predictably, in a letter to Rutgers president Mason Gross, Genovese's colleagues in the history department expressed their support in this fashion:

"Some may assert that because he has described his intellectual position as Marxist, Professor Genovese cannot therefore perform acceptably as a scholar. The test here, we believe, would be the professional evaluation of the articles that he has published and the books that will appear within the next few months. Members of our department hold widely varying beliefs in religion, in ethics and in social and political philosophy, but we do feel strongly that none of these beliefs in itself disqualifies a man as a teacher or a scholar."

The most important outside backing, of course, came from Governor Hughes. He refused to interfere, he said, on the assurance by Rutgers that Genovese "had observed the [university's] prohibition against using the classroom to mention his personal political viewpoint [and] that his position at the university is based not upon his political opinions but upon his reputation as a scholar."

IN its most significant aspects, the Genovese case raised the problem of locating the outer limits of academic freedom more sharply than it had for years. The limits change with the times, and the times are changing.

It has been quite obvious, for example, that with the gradual weakening of the Communist party on the

American campus, Communist membership alone is no longer regarded as it once was by many people—as evidence of scholarly incapacity and, therefore, grounds for refusing academic tenure.

One debate nowadays is whether "Marxists, Socialists" and others who do not belong to any "subversive" apparatus should enjoy the protections of academic freedom. Or, to consider the issue from the opposite political perspective, does a university have the right to fire a professor with tenure for praying that the Ku Klux Klan will win in the South? Though some liberals would squirm at the notion of defending a racist, the principles of academic freedom demand protection for professorial free speech. And what about the professor who raises a storm about sex, not politics?

For example, a University of Illinois botany professor without tenure wrote a letter to the college newspaper saying he saw "no valid reason why sexual intercourse should not be condoned among those sufficiently mature to engage in it without social consequences and without violating their own codes of morality and ethics." The university fired him in 1961 over the protests of the faculty. Two years later the American Association of University Professors officially censured the administration for the dismissal.

Hughes's statement on Genovese defined the conventional bounds of academic freedom: a professor can speak on an off-campus soapbox as long as his classroom does not become a propaganda forum for his "personal political viewpoint." But the soapbox and the classroom are often indistinguishable as far as the public is concerned; in fact, it is being argued that in his role as teacher the professor is entitled to use his classroom as a soapbox and can hardly avoid doing so.

Such questions demonstrate the difficulty of specifically defining academic freedom. (Can any freedom ever be inclusively defined?) To complicate the issue, the professor not only enjoys rights as a teacher; he is a scholar and citizen, too, and each of his three roles involves problems of academic freedom that provoke overlapping controversies.

The 'Genovese Case' —started by the controversial statement of the Rutgers professor (left) to a campus teach-in last April (below)—once again raises the question: What does a teacher have the right to say, both in and out of his classroom?

THE academician who stirred the latest debate is a specialist in Southern history and the institution of slavery and the author of a recently published book, "The Political Economy of Slavery." A lean man with black curly hair, Genovese lives with his second wife on the top floor of a decrepit three-story Greenwich Village walk-up near the Hudson River. Brooklyn-born, he went to New Utrecht High School and was attracted, he recalls, to children of "left-wing families." While at Brooklyn College, at 17, he became an open Communist party member and organizer for the Communist-front youth organization, American Youth for Democracy. But because of disagreements on Communist party tactics, he was expelled three years later, he says, charged with being "anti-Semitic, anti-Negro and a Browderite right-wing deviationist."

"The real reason for my expulsion," Genovese explains, "was I zigged when I was supposed to zag. Actually, I should have been expelled because I was violating party discipline."

Eventually he got his degree from Brooklyn College and was inducted into the Army. After 10 months at Fort Dix, he was discharged for having been a Communist party member, a fact he had not concealed from the authorities. Attending Columbia University graduate school, he received his Ph.D. in 1959 with a dissertation entitled "The Agricultural Reform Movement in the Slave South." His first teaching job was at Brooklyn Polytechnic Institute in 1960 and in 1963, having complied with the New Jersey loyalty oath prohibition against membership in "subversive" organizations, he was appointed an assistant professor at Rutgers. Last spring he was promoted to associate professor with full tenure. Genovese has recently applied for a year's leave of absence to complete another book on slavery.

GENOVESE'S political credo is fairly simple. He is contemptuous of the American Communist party, less contemptuous of the Soviet Union, strongly sympathetic—with some minor reservations—to Communist China. He feels congenial toward the Italian Communist party, "the closest to any radical movement in the West in finding the road to Socialism in the West."

Genovese's April 23 teach-in speech and a long essay-review he wrote in 1963 in Science and Society of a book by Dr. Herbert Aptheker, a pro-Moscow Communist intellectual, reveal the usual left-wing preference for the political

"double standard." American foreign policy is rarely, if ever, morally acceptable; the policies, domestic and foreign, of the "Socialist" (meaning Communist) countries are always defensible, "despite wars and revolutions, despite the deformation of Stalinist bureaucratism, despite the most painful curtailment of civil liberties." If some countries are dominated by Moscow it is because, "unfortunately, no small country can be truly and completely independent, especially in foreign policy, so long as the cold war continues."

So dedicated is he to "Socialism" that Genovese ridiculed Aptheker's "illusory pronouncements" about the effects of nuclear war. "Does Aptheker mean that if several hundred million people were to be killed, one of the two social systems could not emerge victorious? If so, he is talking nonsense, for even the destruction of the United States, the Soviet Union, Western Europe, and much of China would not preclude the victory of the Socialist forces across Latin America, southern Asia and Africa. . . .

"Mao Tse-tung's comment on this matter is unanswerable: 'If I thought,' he is reported to have said, 'that being afraid of nuclear war would prevent it, I should be terrified of it!' Certainly no Marxist can believe that the bourgeoisie would not fight, if cornered, unless there were no hope—none whatever—of its own survival . . . [Aptheker's] subsequent remarks about several hundred million casualties in a nuclear war are, like all pacifist handwringing, irrelevant."

IT is these passages which candidate Dumont exploited and which, Genovese claims, distorted his political position, making it appear that he favored nuclear war, believed world war inevitable and coexistence impossible. In a postelection interview, Genovese said he was no longer "a Leninist" although he believed that "Leninism is a great force and has validity in the world today." He doubted that "American capitalism would give up peacefully, but Socialism should build on the idea of a peaceful transition.

"If, however, the state breaks down," he added, "and refuses to use the democratic process, then the workers should defend themselves with arms."

Concerning China, he said that he was becoming "alarmed at the increasingly theoretical rigidity of the Chinese." He scoffed at China's assertion that Russia is going capitalist as "just demagoguery." On the other hand, he thought "it is monstrous to say that China is guilty of aggression. It's because she has been so much under the threat of aggression that she has behaved this way."

"How about the attack on Tibet?" I asked.

"Nasty," he replied.

Genovese believes that Marxist Socialism in the West has no future, "unless it takes an unambiguous position on civil liberties and democratic values. Socialism must take a new look at American institutions and see what is positive in America." He paused and added with a smile, "I'm getting conservative as I grow older."

THE basic academic freedom issue raised by the Genovese case concerned the rights of an academician, as a citizen, to discuss anything he wants, whether he is an expert in the subject or not. This thesis was recently summarized by Prof. Robert A. Nisbet of the University of California at Riverside, who wrote in the current issue of The Public Interest:

". . . it is, today at least, the very essence of academic freedom that a faculty member's views on matters outside his stated professional competence—however shocking these views may be, however suggestive prima facie of want of ordinary intelligence or moral responsibility—shall not be held against him when he is being considered for retention or promotion. Academic freedom, so conceived, justifies itself not by what it grants the individual but what it does for the university. We have learned that it is absolutely necessary to the search for, and the communication of, knowledge. It is an essential attribute of the university; not a special privilege of the individual."

A somewhat different viewpoint was expressed by Dr. Grayson Kirk, president of Columbia University. In an essay adapted from his last commencement day address and published in the Columbia University Forum, he declared:

"Academic freedom for a professor means that his career may not be jeopardized by the expression of his views to his students or to the public. But however much a professor may assert his rights as a citizen to speak out on

CAMPAIGN ISSUE—A picket demands Genovese's ouster as a teacher during New Jersey's recent governorship battle.

any topic, he ought to think twice before he makes a ringing public declaration on a controversial subject, particularly if it is far removed from his own field of scholarly competence. He should hesitate before doing so simply because no matter how loud or sincere his disclaimers, he can never entirely shed his scholar's gown.

"It may well be that when he seeks to take off his academic gown he will have beneath it only the emperor's clothes, but he cannot escape a certain popular presumption of intellectual authority—and he has the responsibility not to abuse it. A scholar has an implied professional commitment to approach all issues in the spirit of a judge rather than as an advocate. . . . When a scholar fails to keep this admonition in mind in the long run he puts in danger the public acceptance of the essential integrity of the university."

Prof. Richard Hofstadter, Columbia's Pulitzer Prize-winning historian and co-author of "The Development of Academic Freedom in the United States," believes that professional competence is no longer the test. "Now the question is, basically, the rights of a professor as a citizen," he said in an interview. "Today, the model for academic freedom should be civil liberties.

"Perhaps it should be one's moral imperative to think

twice before speaking. Yet most voters make decisions without much information and, of course, the experts can be wrong. It's up to the public to know that the professor of mathematics is wrong about the Dominican Republic but the professor of mathematics isn't thereby obliged to shut up.

"Usually, I should add, these warnings against half-baked opinions are made when the opinions are heterodox. One rarely hears such warnings if the professor agrees with public policy, however stupid that policy may be."

Prof. Walter Metzger of Columbia is co-author with Hofstadter of "The Development of Academic Freedom in the United States." For 10 years he has been a member of the potent Committee A of the American Association of University Professors, which investigates issues of academic freedom and tenure. Metzger feels strongly that a professor should not use his lectern as a pulpit and should avoid irrelevant discussion. He cites the A.A.U.P. principle on academic freedom: "The teacher is entitled to freedom in the classroom in discussing his subject, but he should be careful not to introduce into his teaching controversial matter which has no relation to his subject." Yet, concedes Professor Metzger, this caveat is "unenforceable because the classroom is as private as the confessional."

THE academic profession seems agreed that a professor is entitled, as a scholar, to argue any position within his area of expertise even though that position may represent a minority of one. The test is the quality of his scholarship and research.

Much more controversy surrounds the professor's role as teacher in the classroom and citizen in the public forum. Rutgers University regulations on academic freedom provide that "outside the fields of instruction, research and publication . . . the faculty member shall be free from institutional discipline unless his actions or utterances are both reprehensible and detrimental to the university."

Is the teacher free to press his political opinions in the classroom? Theoreticians of academic freedom offer no clear answer, but in practice it seems that more militant professors have seized the

right and university administrations have been more or less compelled to back them up. The alliance is based on two factors: the greater bargaining power of the individual professor in a society that has elevated education to new eminence, and the increased politicalization of the American campus.

"The academic market place has changed greatly," explains Prof. Richard P. McCormick, acting chairman of the Rutgers history department and the official university historian. "In the old days a man expected to remain an assistant professor for six years before he got tenure. Today this is out the window. If you've published one book, you're an associate professor—with tenure. The old slogan—'publish or perish'—doesn't apply any more. Today it's 'publish and prosper.'

"At the same time, something is happening in the academic profession. It is becoming more politically committed and concerned. Therefore, the academic community must clarify its responsibility and its understanding of that responsibility in dealing with a political problem on the campus and in the classroom."

Some professors believe a man's political views should be pushed in the classroom; not only should he have a commitment, they say, but he should also preach it."

Professor Genovese believes that as a teacher, not only does he have a right to discuss his political beliefs in the classroom, but the subject he teaches makes such discussion inevitable. "I teach Southern history and Negro history up to the present day," he said, "and I must discuss civil rights. Whatever I say in my analysis of the civil rights battle is affected by my politics. You can't avoid these issues.

"On the other hand, I don't believe in digressions because they're an insult to the students. A man has a professional responsibility to teach his material. Yet the material often overlaps between past and present. The history of abolitionism, for example, shows how the dynamics of a small, unpopular group in America affected politics through the radicalism of its stance. It can be related to present problems and the students can draw their own conclusions.

"It happens that I don't

teach abolitionism this way because I'm distrustful of historical analogies and I don't push them too far. But if I wanted to direct this comparison between the abolitionists and contemporary extremist groups I would regard that as O.K. as long as there was no proselytizing.

"As for propagandizing in the classroom, everybody does it and I do it minimally. I regard propagandizing in the classroom as distasteful because it's a captive audience. A professor who isn't teaching his subject will acquire a reputation accordingly and suffer professionally. But if he's skillful in relating his political views to his material, that's a strong prima-facie case that he's a good teacher.

"Of course, the classroom lends itself to all kinds of abuses. If you're going to have maximum freedom of inquiry, you have to suffer windbags, fools and people with axes to grind. The question is whether the university is strong enough and self-confident enough to absorb these abuses in order to do the job it has to do. If it isn't, then you can't have universities."

"The Common   Good"

The most widely accepted definition of academic freedom is the "Statement of Principles" adopted in 1940 by the American Association of University Professors jointly with the Association of American Colleges. The assumptions which underlie the statement can be syllogized as follows: (1) universities exist for "the common good"; (2) "the common good" depends on "free search for truth and its free exposition," which embraces the concept of academic freedom; (3) academic freedom is therefore a guarantee of "the common good."

By this reasoning, academic freedom is not merely a desirable goal of society but an essential

attribute of our culture. Its foundations were built by men like Spinoza, Galileo, Darwin and Freud, who were reviled in their time by powerful adversaries in church and state. Today, the academic profession demands virtually complete permissiveness without ever having really debated whether academic freedom is an "absolute." But rather than allow that freedom to be restricted and the teacher intimidated, the profession would tolerate extreme rightists or leftists on faculties, or even non-political academic charlatans. Thus, a biologist who taught the discredited Lysenko theory of genetics would be scorned, but probably not fired.

The scholar is accordingly granted even greater rights and privileges than the lawyer or doctor. The lawyer or doctor may be punished by an organization of his colleagues or by the state for professional misconduct, but the academic community argues that the worst a teacher should suffer is a rebuke for almost any act short of murder or using four-letter words in his classroom (and even on the latter issue there is disagreement among today's academic avant garde). Any policing is to be done by the academic community but there is little agreement on how the policing is to be done, and none at all regarding punishment.   —A.B.

PROF. DANIEL BELL, chairman of Columbia's sociology department, believes a professor invariably brings his intellectual prejudices into the classroom. Yet as long as they are openly labeled as prejudices, not "true knowledge," then the professor has a right to do so.

"A man is hired to teach a subject," said Bell. "As long as he does not conceal contrary evidence, he has a right to his beliefs. For example, he may be a great admirer of the Soviet Union. But if he denies the existence of famines under Stalin, if he denies the facts about the Soviet Union, then that's another matter. In any case, other faculty members are free to combat him."

Professor Bell's chief objection to the Dumont campaign in New Jersey was the Republican candidate's statement that academic freedom "does not give to a teacher in a state university, supported by taxpayers' money, the right to advocate victory of an enemy in war, in which some of his own students may very well lay down their lives in the cause of freedom."

"This is really a most threatening statement," said Bell. "The taxpayers' money supports the one person out of seven who today earns a living by working for some branch of government or a government agency. But according to Dumont, somehow if you're working for the Federal, state or city government your free speech rights are restricted, unlike the rights of citizens in private employment. This is setting up a double standard."

The greater liberality of faculty members, college administrations and the general public toward academic freedom is unquestionably due to the tremendous importance of higher education in the country today. This change in atmosphere is recent. Professor Hofstadter, in his book "Anti-Intellectualism in American Life," has noted that while "anti-intellectualism in various forms continues to pervade American life . . . at the same time intellect has taken on a new and more positive meaning and intellectuals have come to enjoy more acceptance and, in some ways, a more satisfactory position."

Thus, Rutgers president Mason Gross warned that "the consequences for Rutgers would be disastrous" if the university deviated from the principles of academic freedom in the Genovese case. Gross said he feared "censure and probable loss of accreditation. This, in turn, would result in loss of faculty and great difficulty in recruiting new faculty." Loss of accreditation could also mean difficulty for Rutgers students who apply to graduate schools.

In short, the college teacher today lives in a seller's market. If he is halfway good and productive he can pick his employer and expect rapid promotion. And in a seller's market the academician has the kind of power over his terms of employment that he lacked in previous generations.

FLEXING its muscles, the academic profession has now begun to discuss the need to examine hiring policies by university administrations. Since dismissals on ideological grounds can be masked, especially if the faculty member lacks tenure, full disclosure of hiring policies would make it tougher for officials subsequently to fire a professor on some pretext that would not arouse the suspicions of the A.A.U.P.'s vigilant Committee A.

Committee A veteran Walter Metzger says: "In America, academic dismissals on any ground are infrequent; academic dismissals based on utterances are still more infrequent. In the major institutions intramural relationships have a benign, if not a halcyon, appearance. What is significant about the extreme example, the case that seldom occurs, is the illumination it throws on morbid tendencies that lie beneath the smiling surface and often escape our view."

In this double meaning, the Genovese case revealed its share of morbidity and hope. It may also have provided a glimpse into the future.

In an era of the antihero, the antitheater, the antinovel and anti-art, will the professor seeking self-realization subvert himself into becoming the anti-academician?

December 19, 1965

A Polite Encounter Between the Generations

By EDGAR Z. FRIEDENBERG

THE recent U.S. National Student Association conference on "Student Stress in the College Experience" was notable in several respects. U.S.N.S.A. is an organization of student governments which was formed just after World War II and now includes most of the major colleges and universities in the country—about 300 in all. Some 30 of these, selected to represent the widest possible variety of institutions — from Princeton to Randolph-Macon, Tuskegee and the University of California—were invited to send two students and one faculty member each as delegates, and in addition about 30 other adults were present, either as representatives of the various sponsors of the conference or as special consultants, like myself.

Despite its small size, a little over 100 altogether, this conference is of general interest, I believe, because it is indicative of a major, and long overdue, change in the status of at least a segment of American youth. The student leaders who participated in it were not, to be sure, typical of their contemporaries, most of whom are not college students at all. But they are representative at least in the sense that these are the youngsters who are "making it," and making the most of the educational opportunities our society affords. Since our society assumes that youth should be in school or college, they may justly be taken as examples of the best it—if not they—can do.

The issues the students led us to concentrate on, and the way we dealt with those issues, tell us a great deal about American youth and its place in society today. Our discussions showed at work the basic processes in the confrontation between the generations, and how the relationship between them is changing—has already changed enough to require that students and their national organization be treated with the respect due them. Students have been under stress, as we all have, for a long time; but this was the first time a group of middle-aged professionals, who had reason to suppose themselves influential, had gone so far out of their way to hear what the students thought these stresses were.

THE most fundamental and pervasive "stress" to which they referred over and over in their discussions they called "alienation"—though they never succeeded in saying precisely what they meant by it. Indeed, the discussions at the conference were annoyingly clumsy, intellectually; the students seemed to feel no responsibility for precision or style. Their manner, in fact, deprecated such qualities as indications that the speaker must be inauthentic and insincere or too detached from his experience. Many of the students seemed also to value their own ignorance and imprecision as proof that they were "democratic," requiring no special qualifications of themselves or their leaders—though this, as Ortega y Gasset stated clearly 40 years ago in "The Revolt of the Masses," is the distinctive attitude of a mass society rather than a democratic one.

Well, a mass society is what we have now, and one of the delights it affords is that of listening to an obviously sensitive, intelligent and earnest Swarthmore student punctuate his deeply felt comments on obstacles to communication by saying "you know?" every time he had a specific point to make, when the burden of his complaint was that we *didn't* know.

Nevertheless, he succeeded in making his point. Alienation was manifest and communication was impeded by factors more fundamental than poor use of language. The responses of the adults were, by and large, indeed inauthentic. We were too polite, which can also be a form of patronage and contempt. One reason why these youngsters feel alienated from us is that we do not show our real feelings and our real skills in our dealings with them; we try, instead, to put them at their ease, gain their cooperation and establish a basis for working together without making excessive demands on them.

Many students complained that professors were too busy to see them or take any interest in them as people. This is a serious charge, but what I find more distressing is that the students sounded as if they had never seen a professor absorbed in his profession. They find our preoccupation with research and writing often phony and self-seeking. They had no idea at all of what they might have learned by watching us or helping us at an authentic scholarly job—even if we *were* too occupied with it to be nice to them. *This* is where we have failed them — and their comments proved it, though they did not make this charge specifically.

The discussion also showed in more subtle ways that the students were probably justified in calling one of their major sources of stress "alienation." By and large, we adults had great difficulty even in understanding that what made their experience in college stressful was that they felt it to be meaningless and isolated. This kind of statement conveyed nothing to most of the adult participants; we wanted to hear something quite different. Partly, this was because we suspected that a lot of the youngsters were only pretending to be alienated because it was fashionable—and the Princeton, Randolph-Macon and Smith delegates, among others, admitted that they couldn't meet the high standards of alienation that were being set at the meeting, probably because the schools they attended were too small to alienate them properly. But a more important reason why we could not dig the youngsters who complained of being alienated was that as adults we had largely lost the capacity to understand anyone who was trying to speak of his total state of being.

We wanted symptoms, specific points of conflict, problems that we could deal with professionally. The youngsters speaking of alienation, wanted us to understand that this need of ours to analyze, rationalize and set up procedures for dealing with categories of experience *was itself* what they meant by alienation—the very heart of the process of bureaucratization they were talking about. Most of us couldn't see it; we went on solemnly citing the deplorable rise in suicide and mental illness among college students and asking delegates to explain it. They could only reply that they could not, though they could conceive that one might be driven mad by being treated as a statistic.

PERHAPS inevitably, the predictable misunderstandings about sex arose to divide adult and student members of the conference. Some of us were concerned about rising rates of pregnancy among high school and college girls, and being thereby convinced that sexuality must put a lot of stress on students, insisted that they must put a lot of stress on it. We were prepared to sympathize with the ardor and misery of youth constrained by a puritanical social order to feel either guilt or frustration, and to consider practical measures, like providing better contraceptive information, for reducing tension. But while students undoubtedly experience strong sexual desires that cannot be gratified very satisfactorily within a college environment, they do not usually consider sex a source of stress because they do not break up their life into pieces like that. What concerns them is the quality of life itself, in which sex plays an important part, but not a very distinctive one.

The stress, as they see it, comes not from sex but from living in a society which prevents people from having human contact with their sexual partners, especially if they are young. Even sexual relationships become shallow and sporadic in a society that affords the young no privacy and not enough jobs, in which they must accept an interim, sub-adult status that delays marriage for 10 or 15 years after puberty; in which competition and status-seeking induce young men and women to make use of each other while denying them the opportunity to get to know one another.

These youngsters experience their situation as a state of isolation, a loss of intimacy or relatedness. To offer them tolerance of greater sexual freedom instead of a better chance to know and love one another does not help. Many of them feel they cannot use the contraceptive information they already have, for example, because the whole experience of love-making would lose its essential meaning if they approached it as entrepreneurs approach a business venture, calculating the risks and girding their loins to meet emergencies.

MANY young people today find the older generation's emphasis on sex as artificial, and repugnant, as the Marxists' rigid economic determinism. This conflict in viewpoint resulted in a head-on clash on the second evening of the conference, after which it became much more taut and productive. A highly dramatic Ivy League professor who came on in the role of a defender of the freedom of youth attacked several of the delegates for having used the phrase "24-hour intervisitation rules" to refer to the admirable practice of allowing young men and women to visit each other in their dormitories at their discretion. What had infuriated this teacher was what he took to be the hypocrisy implied by so pedantic a phrase. "My God, '24-hour intervisitation rules'!" he cried. "You know damned well that means. . . ."

At this point, he lapsed into language inappropriate to the conference and perhaps unintelligible to readers east of Berkeley. He intended, as he later said, to shock the people, student and faculty, whom he had identified as conservatives or administration finks. It was not they, however, who resented , is statement so much as the liberal youngsters who had been laboring since puberty to make it clear that this was not the central issue in their demand for freedom of access to one another; what they want is an opportunity for private, unself-conscious *social* intercourse, without having to keep an eye on either the door or the clock. It seemed altogether fitting, therefore, that the delegate who rose after a moment of

stunned silence to put this professor down was one of the abler and more rhetorically gifted leaders of the 1964 Free Speech Movement.

AFTER this open encounter, the tone of the conference improved immensely. Both students and adults became more direct and "authentic" in their discussion, and while we never produced an inventory or an anatomy of student stress in the college experience, we did begin to understand our own differences better.

The chief reason for this, I judge, is that we adults renewed our memories of what it was like to be more open and honest, and could therefore begin to grasp how distressing our particular kind of maturity might be to the young. The students, as they finally became convinced that we really did want to understand them, began to realize that they were wasting a real opportunity through posing and the linguistic and philosophical ineptitude that a decade of pretentious but bad education had left them with. They became ashamed of their own inauthenticity.

The moment of truth came, appropriately enough, in the last session of the conference, when the Swarthmore delegate was attempting a critical summary of the proceedings. Each time he became blocked by his own inarticulate emotion, the audience applauded him warmly and indulgently—until finally he lost his temper. "I don't know why it is," he almost snarled. "Whenever anybody here becomes especially incoherent, the conference seems to like it better. The hell with it!" And he sat down, having finally succeeded in ripping through the veil he had been picking at and reweaving for four days. This time, there really was applause.

THE quest for authenticity —what a Reed College student delegate called "the real nitty-gritty"—in the midst of alienation was the source of stress to which the conference kept returning, no matter where it started or how it tried to shift its ground. It would seem to be the central conflict, at least for middle-class adolescents—and I should think for lower-status youngsters, too, though for them the conflict is more externalized; they are more aware, that is, of the

fraud and duplicity that surround them and less aware of their own implication in them.

I do not mean by this to ignore or minimize hard factors like unemployment or poverty or the probability of being drafted into a war as cruel and dangerous as any and more dishonorable than most. These dominate the destiny of American youth today, and it is tragic that they should. What I am trying to emphasize is that, threatening as these conditions are objectively, youth does not complain about them much — or not nearly so much as it has a right to. What the young do complain about is living in a society that makes their lives senseless and incoherent.

Unemployment, poverty and even war, though evil, do not in themselves constitute a betrayal — we never promised them a rose garden. But a life in which these and even the apparently more amiable aspects of a mass society invade every moment and distort every relationship is not tolerable. Among male college students generally, for example, there seems to be a much bitterer resentment that the draft now requires students to complete their academic careers without interruption (thus destroying the opportunity to take off and reflect about what, if anything, the work means) than there is resentment of the draft itself. And policies like that of the Utah Selective Service System, whose regional director has asserted that the deferments of students who demonstrate against the war will be subject to special scrutiny, further suggest that the entire system is contemptible and will be used to suppress dissent.

THERE are several reasons why youth complains more about the quality of life than about the specific factors that impair life. Much of the integrity of the young depends on the fact that they are self-centered. This makes them less compromising and political but also less curious about the unpleasant realities that have to be dealt with and how they work. Generalized complaints are also safer for a relatively powerless segment of the population to make than specific indictments of the adult authorities who control them. Our tolerance and wish to be understanding and helpful would, I suspect, diminish

rather rapidly if the students got down to specific cases.

Nevertheless, what is wrong with any system is always specific, however valid the general malaise it produces. To complain of alienation, moreover, is to be not only too general but also too subjective. It suggests that the alienated might be satisfied by improvements in their relationships with others and with social institutions instead of by improvements in others and in institutions that would make them worth relating to. To define misery and discontent primarily as problems of adjustment is one of the oldest ploys used by our society to disarm the troublemakers among its young. In fact, we have so powerfully institutionalized this defense against recognizing that students might have something valid and realistic to complain about that we can no longer escape it even when we want to.

The conference on "Student Stress in the College Experience" was sincerely searching for real difficulties, but the money and sponsorship came primarily, as it happens, from organizations concerned with guidance and mental health because listening to students has come to be defined as their responsibility. Conversely, educational reform can best be justified in our society if it can be demonstrated that existing practice is not merely vicious or vacuous but emotionally disturbing.

There can be no better evidence of the alienation of students than our assumption that their difficulties ought ordinarily to be dealt with by alienists rather than by lawyers, who might defend their rights, or by architects, who might design them dormitories to live in, or by people acting in their personal rather than their specialized capacities. Yet we adults went to the conference and we listened, concentrating as hard as we could on understanding what students' lives are like. Why? What brought out such an expensive array of academic and administrative talent?

Concern for youth and goodwill toward them were certainly among the reasons. Common status-seeking — the desire to be in on something that might turn out to be important—was surely another. But these are not new and were certainly not enough to account for the meeting's hav-

A conference of students and adults
throws light on a most striking feature of today's
campuses—the phenomenon called 'alienation.'

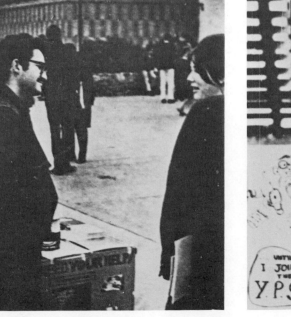

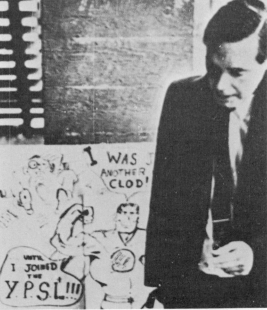

"THE ALIENATION SCENE" — Since the 1964 student riots at the U. of California at Berkeley, a special area on campus has been set aside for protest groups. These pictures show the range of interests, from the religious move-ment, Bahaism, which emphasizes man's spiritual unity, to sex freedom, to the Y.P.S.L. (Young People's Socialist League). "Adults are accustomed to quiescent, apolitical youth, docile in pursuit of self-interest."

ing been held. Was it an indication that youth is beginning to command more respect in society or is the explanation more complex?

I suspect it is more complex. The past year of increased student political activity at Berkeley and elsewhere would in an" case have alarmed adults accustomed to a quiescent, apolitical youth, docile in the pursuit of self-interest. But the fact that the sharp increase in student involvement coincides with, and is partly a response to, the more serious moral ambiguities in our society, makes it seem more threatening.

So long as students concentrated on the civil-rights movement, they did not generate more anxiety than could be borne. Our official position on civil rights is not ambiguous, and the social conflicts that make up the civil-rights struggle, though murderous, may be viewed as attempts by benighted local authorities to resist a morally defensible, if ponderous, national social system. But Vietnam and Santo Domingo have been something different and worse. Even if one could accept American policy as having been basically moral in its intent—as I suppose most young Americans do, though I do not—one would still be appalled by the duplicity with which it is being conducted.

THERE really is something rotten in America today, and it is making Hamlets of some of our youth. It has also turned a good many adults into Claudiuses or Gertrudes—they, too, tried for as long as they could to deal with Hamlet's behavior as if it were a problem of stress and mental health. This, I fear, is the cause of much of our present concern about youth. Unless youth accepts the society we have built, there can be no

succession, and what we know as America will be lost.

Our concern about the young is therefore valid, but there is a note of panic in it stemming from our own guilt. When we ask, "What is disturbing them?" we mean also, "How much do they know about what is really going on, and will they buy it?" When we ask, "Are their protest movements Communist-dominated?", we are also asking, "Can they really be convinced, without having been tricked or misled, that our way of life has become viciously irresponsible and destructive? Is it, after all, so obvious that even the young can notice it for themselves?"

These seem to me good questions to ask; we ought to have raised them sooner. If there are grounds for hope in the answers, they lie in the fact that the values affirmed by the protesters, including their right to dissent, are far more deeply rooted in our culture than the policies against which they are directed (though I should not like to argue this point with an Iroquois). And so far, the more basic values have survived, though they have not prevailed.

Appalled though I am by our present course and our persistence in it, it seems only fair to acknowledge that we have shown more moral outrage at our own conduct than I would have thought our culture could muster. By and large, it has been possible to defend the right to protest with the legal instruments our society provides. People do experience freedom — among other things—in this country, and though the young enjoy relatively little of it, they are probably getting enough to taste. It isn't Instant Freedom, and nobody dispenses it, like LSD, on cubes of sugar. The odd thing, in fact, is that so many *do* get hooked on something so slow-acting and bitter.

Strains in Teacher—Student Relationship

To the Editor:

Gen. Lewis B. Hershey's announcement that a draft deferment will be based upon college students' standing in class, as well as tests that will be administered, adds one more strain to the student-teacher relationship—a relationship upon which there are already too many strains.

There was a time in America when a student merely had to pass his courses and a student and teacher could work together with this objective and degrees of excellence in mind. Now the classroom work is put in doubt by a whole host of examinations which re-evalue the education that the student receives—the graduate record examination, the legal aptitude tests, the medical aptitude test, the Selective Service test, etc. The standards of graduate schools have risen sharply. A student without a "B" average in his major can expect that his college education is terminal.

For those who succeed, there is a whole raft of incentives by the Federal Government, private foundations and universities—incentives in terms of cash money, as well as scholarships. In many respects, perhaps, graduate students are making more money going to school than they will make during the first years upon entering their profession. Carrots and sticks have multiplied in the collegiate educational process.

Anxiety Over Failure

It is not surprising in the midst of this outside management of the collegiate educational process that friction should develop between teachers and students, reflecting students' anxieties as to whether they are going to make the grade or be consigned to the dump heap.

The additional introduction of the draft system makes the

misery of the student greater and the punitive powers of the professor more terrifying. The professor who marks a student down not only prevents him from continuing his education, but consigns him to the swamps of Vietnam.

We have come a far distance in American education from the days when James Garfield could say that his concept of a college education was Mark Hopkins at one end of the log and a student at the other. Yet this remains the essence of the learning situation, and no matter how many comprehensive examinations a student passes, nothing will happen to him until he comes into close contact with a truly creative mind.

This kind of relationship can provide the motivation for achievement, the insights for learning and creating in a field as well as the guidance to achieve.

Guidance for Achievement

Jonas Salk, when he was receiving his honorary doctorate at The City College, made exactly this kind of reference to his graduate professor at the University of Michigan as an explanation for his ability to push back frontiers in his field.

The teacher-student relationship is in some respects a parent-child relationship. If it becomes mechanized, determined by outside agencies, and dominated by the punishment which the teachers' marking may bring about, it cannot succeed.

It should be remembered that it is basic to behavior that the animal, including the human animal, when frustrated, either engages in aggressive behavior or does nothing. The carrot and the stick will serve no purpose once this state has been achieved. Frustrated students can be expected to rage against their teachers or to become "beat."

JOHN A. DAVIS
Chairman
Dept. of Political Science
The City College
New York, Feb. 10, 1966

BERKELEY REPORT URGES REFORMS

Faculty Group's Plan Seeks Broad Experimentation

By FRED M. HECHINGER

A blue-ribbon faculty committee of the University of California's troubled Berkeley campus yesterday recommended sweeping changes intended to open the door wide to experimentation. But while the professors went all out for academic reform, they appeared determined to hold the line against direct student participation in top-level policy-making.

The committee's 42 recommendations include the establishment of a powerful new board to bring about and supervise innovation and the appointment of a top-ranking administrator to preside over such reforms in curriculum and operations.

The powers of the board would include even the granting of degrees for programs not represented in the traditional departments. This recommendation was so dramatic that one faculty member, in a dissenting report, attacked it as the creation of "a university within a university."

The 200-page report, which was released here and in Berkeley, Calif., borrowed from innovations and reform steps in colleges and universities across the country. It touches on aspects of academic life ranging from selection and grading of students to the activities of the faculty.

It includes a proposal to create a new degree — the Doctor of Arts, as a substitute for the Ph.D., for persons interested in college teaching rather than research.

The report recommends that students be asked to help in rating the teaching quality of faculty members, but it rejects the growing demands that undergraduates be permitted to sit on faculty and administration committees.

Student Demands Backed

"The typical faculty member does not get called for committee service until he has reached tenure rank," the report explains. Students who lack experience "with the intellectual and pragmatic aspects of campus life" therefore should not be given "professional responsibility for educational policy," the committee maintains.

Apart from this determined stand against direct student participation in policy-making, which is gaining ground on some campuses, the report liberally supports most student demands for greater attention to their education. It urges the faculty and administration to consult the views of students on educational policies affecting both the entire campus and individual departments.

The nine-member committee was appointed by Berkeley's Academic Senate 10 months ago in the wake of the student demonstrations that shook the 27,000-student campus late in 1964.

Charles Muscatine, professor of English, is the committee chairman. The Academic Senate, which is the campus faculty body, will begin consideration of the proposals next Tuesday. If approved by the Senate, the proposals would then have to be accepted by the Berkeley chancellor before they could be implemented.

A Channel for Heresy

The committee report rejects most existing attempts to reform general education. It warns that the introduction of one or a few required general education courses on western civilization or the great books "would be a monolith of massive proportions and bureaucratic impersonality." But it concedes that it is not enough to rely on "that good will of individual faculty entrepreneurs" to bring about change.

Thus the most dramatic proposal is the establishment of a seven-member Board of Educational Development and the creation of a special Vice Chancellor—in charge of "experiments which do not readily find protection within a regular department"—to receive, foster and support new ideas, courses and programs.

The vice chancellor, who would virtually be patron saint of academic heresy, would also be in charge of securing special funds from public and private sources. He and the new board would be authorized to sponsor new bachelor's degree programs for experimental courses.

Ad Hoc Courses Urged

This dramatic proposal led George C. Pimentel, professor of chemistry, to warn in his minority report:

"We may well find it difficult to live with our own creation." He said that so powerful a board, with virtual autonomy, might "establish curricula that are incompatible with existing colleges."

In what appears to be a direct reaction to that aspect of the students unrest that has had to political teach-ins and even to the establishment of so-called Free Universities in many parts of the country, the committee urges the offering of "ad hoc courses" on topics that might be determined each term by the new board "to supply the relevant scholarly and intellectual background to subjects of active student concern."

In addition, the report requests the creation of a small number of new posts called Professorships of the University. These professors would be appointed for three years, would carry "the highest status, privileges and emoluments," would be confined to no department and would leave the scholars "free to investigate and teach as they please."

Pass or Fail Courses

In a mass of other recommendations, the committee would introduce the freshman seminar, pioneered by Harvard, which permits some students in their first year to work independently under a senior professor.

It would, in the tradition of such institutions as Antioch and Bennington, give liberal credit for field study, such as work in hospitals, industry and outside research.

It would permit students to take a limited number of courses on the basis of a mere passing or failing mark, thus encouraging them to take difficult courses outside their major field without fear of depressing their over-all record. This approach has been successfully introduced at Princeton University and Knox College, Ill.

The report says that Berkeley fully intends to "maintain its eminence in research." But it warns that "we find no place on the faculty for researchers who are not teachers." It asks those who want to be "isolated scholars" to find their proper places in research institutes and industry.

Stress on Teaching

To improve teaching it recommends "faculty-wide experiment with the use of student comments, greater scrutiny and recognition of the teaching ability of younger faculty members, and general improvements in the training and apprenticing of graduate students as teachers. But it also warns that no particular "devices or gimmicks" will bring about improvements "if a fidelity to teaching is not part of the atmosphere of the campus.

Among other key recommendation are the following:

¶Every recommendation for tenure must be accompanied by a formal dossier on the candidate's teaching performance, including evidence based on class visitations."

¶On an experimental basis, during the 1967 winter quarter, students send evaluations of all their undergraduate courses directly to individual faculty members, as a basis for later consideration of a permanent system of student evaluation of courses.

¶Students, at any stage of their careers, be eligible for supervised independent study "involving any proportion of their time justifiable by sound educational reasons."

The proportion of lecture courses be decreased in favor of discussion sections, small classes, seminars, tutorial and even "cooperative student self-instruction."

¶Departments in which faculty members teach too few freshmen and sophomore courses be reorganized.

After disclosing that the typical Berkeley undergraduate is taught by teaching assistants or graduate students in almost one-third of his classes, the report asks drastic reforms.

"The ratio of regular faculty to students at Berkeley is extremely unfavorable as compared with liberal arts colleges or with the leading private universities with which we compete for faculty," the report says.

In its reform proposals of the graduate program, the report urges that language requirements be dropped whenever they are merely "formal and external baggage."

"We should decrease the number of hurdles in the graduate curriculum by elevating admissions standards, then simplifying examination requirements correspondingly," the report says.

In proposing the creation of the Doctor of Arts degree, especially for careers in teaching rather than research, the committee suggests that by requiring virtually the same preparation but relinquishing the demand for a dissertation, many able persons could be salvaged for effective college teaching.

March 18, 1966

SURVEY DISCOUNTS STUDENT PROTESTS

Leftists Numbered at 1% —Civil Rights Tops Issues

The notion that American college students are, in general, "angry" and "up in arms" was disputed yesterday in a study issued by the Educational Testing Service in Princeton, N. J.

The report, based on responses from college deans, found that the number of students who took part in protest activities last year seldom exceeded 8 per cent of the college's enrollment.

The "organized student left," the report said, probably accounts for "less than 1 per cent of the total student population." It added that there was a correlation between student leftists and certain protests, such as those directed against United States policy in Vietnam.

But last year more American colleges had student protests over campus food service and dormitory rules than over the nation's policy in Vietnam, the study showed.

"For any specific issue," the report noted, "the number of institutions where protests have occurred constitutes a clear minority when viewed against the totality of colleges and universities."

The study was conducted by Dr. Richard E. Peterson, an associate research psychologist in the testing service. It was based on a questionnaire survey of deans of students at 850 four-year colleges and universities over the nation.

When all the responses were combined to form a national picture, the report said, the following emerged:

"Issues pertaining to instruction, faculty and freedom of expression rarely evoked organized student activism.

Civil Rights First

"Issues bearing on personal freedoms and student participation in the administration of the college somewhat more often generated protest.

"Civil rights matters locally were the single issue most frequently cited by the deans (38 per cent of them) as leading to student activism."

Campus food service, the study found, ranked second as a protest issue, prompting organized protests at 29 per cent of the colleges and universities.

This was followed by protests over dormitory rules (28 per cent of the institutions), American policy regarding Vietnam (21 per cent), dress regulations (20 per cent) and insufficient student participation in campus policies (19 per cent).

The study found that the total enrollment of an institution was a significant factor in influencing protest activity "only when size is very big." Of 50 public universities in the study with enrollments of more than 10,000 students, 56 per cent had protests over civil rights and 68 per cent had demonstrations over the nation's Vietnam policy.

Although student unrest may not be as widespread as some persons believe, Dr. Peterson said, there "are substantial numbers of students willing to make known publicly their antagonism to existing situations —especially those situations where there is a perceived moral contradiction or hypocrisy."

"Students actively concerned with broad social and moral issues," he continued, "are undoubtedly concentrated at the high end of the intellectual ability distribution; they are bright enough to detect and comprehend some of what ails American society.

"In this vein, judging from the relative peace at teachers' colleges and technical institutes, it would seem that the intellectual interests of the student activists tend toward the liberal arts and sciences; their commitments are more toward ideas than jobs."

University Project Cloaked C.I.A. Role In Saigon, 1955-59

By MAX FRANKEL
Special to The New York Times

WASHINGTON, April 13— Michigan State University was disclosed today to have provided the support and cover for operations of the Central Intelligence Agency in South Vietnam from 1955 to 1959.

It did so while operating a seven-year, multimillion-dollar technical assistance program that trained police and other public officials for the regime of President Ngo Dinh Diem at the behest of the United States Government.

The intelligence agency's involvement was disclosed by Ramparts magazine and Stanley K. Sheinbaum, former coordinator of the university's Vietnam project, an economist who is now with the Center for Democratic Studies in Santa Barbara, Calif.

They cited the C.I.A.'s involvement in support of charges that Michigan State and other universities "on the make" were lending scholars to Government agencies in exchange for lucrative contracts and exciting overseas assignments.

Prof. Ralph Smuckler, acting dean in the Office of International Programs at Michigan State, confirmed the role of the C.I.A. in the Vietnam project, which he headed. He described the Ramparts article as false and distorted in many respects, but he acknowledged there had been a reluctant relationship with C.I.A. agents.

Ramparts, an iconoclastic West Coast magazine founded by Roman Catholic laymen, has been especially outspoken against United States policy in Vietnam. Its article makes the following major points:

¶The university neglected scholarship and suspended its critical function in society by obediently serving American policy in Vietnam and advising "on the very writing of South Vietnam's Constitution." One professor, Wesley Fishel, was described as instrumental in helping to install Ngo Dinh Diem as President of South Vietnam and selling him on the technical assistance program that brought Michigan State $25-million worth of projects.

¶At least five men hired by the university as "police administration specialists" and given "faculty rank" operated in Saigon as a separate unit in "counterespionage and counterintelligence" assignments.

¶In helping to train South Vietnamese internal security forces, the university project at first "actually supplied them with guns and ammunition" and directed an operation that at one point had only four university persons among 33 police specialists recruited throughout the United States.

¶Some university reports were written to please President Diem and to protect the project, under which some professors were earning nearly twice their normal salaries, tax free, and were gaining rapid promotion. The project was canceled by President Diem in 1962 because he was displeased with the critical articles by some professors.

Prof. Robert Scigliano, a former assistant chief of the project, said he had not read the Ramparts article closely but described as "absolutely correct" the report that the university had operated as "cover for a C.I.A. team" until July, 1959.

He said he had written a book generally critical of the project and the Diem regime that alluded to this. But he was upset, he added, by Ramparts' "inaccurate" quotation of him.

Professor Smuckler implied some difficulties in severing the C.I.A. connection.

"It may not have been right to get into it," he said in a telephone interview from the campus in East Lansing, Mich. "We were caught and felt we had to follow through."

The university tried to rid itself of the connection as early as 1956, he indicated, but it took until 1959 to terminate the arrangement.

Other university officials, from President John A. Hannah down, said they would not dignify the charges with a formal reply and could not deal with the massive job of rebutting its points one by one. However, James Dennison, the university spokesman, who played a small role in the Vietnam project, said, "Whatever Professor Smuckler says is our reply."

Prof. Alfred Meyer of the Michigan State political science department said it was now conceded at the university that there had been some fronting for the C.I.A. But he said that the full story was in dispute and was not likely ever to be known.

Professor Meyer said that Dr. Hannah had alerted the Academic Council to expect a hostile article in Ramparts and had conceded that there was "a certain amount of substance" in its allegations.

Professor Smuckler had hired Rampart's informant, Mr. Sheinbaum, for the Vietnam project. He said he may, as the article states, have been the first to tell Mr. Sheinbaum that the men "borrowed" from the Government for the project were C.I.A. agents interested in police and other "countersubversion" activities. These men were nominally from the Department of the Army.

But almost everything else in the Ramparts article struck Professor Smuckler as distorted or wrong.

He disputed its calculation of the cost of the Vietnam project, its portrayal of the relationship with the agency, its account of the circumstances under which the university project was ended and its basic argument that universities had no right to engage in foreign operations.

The C.I.A., which declined immediate comment on the article, is known to have had various operational relationships with universities. In recent years, the agency is said to have limited itself to more or less open dealings with academic consultants and with research institutions.

In 1950, the agency contributed $300,000 to the creation of the Center for International Studies at the Massachusetts Institute of Technology and sustained it with subsequent grants in return for many studies of the Soviet Union and Communist activities. The relationship did not become public until it had virtually ended several years ago, but M.I.T. found that the disclosure hurt its other activities abroad an aroused resentment and controversy among faculty member.

Since then, other educators have expressed concern about the C.I.A.'s involvement in academic and foundation activities. Officials of the Kennedy and Johnson Administrations have contended that no infiltration of educational activities has been authorized in recent years and the few formal dealings were well known to the heads of cooperating institutions.

Harvard and some other universities have long refused institutional ties and have let individual scholars decide whether they wish to have any dealings with the intelligence agency.

Professor Smuckler made the following contentions:

¶The university never obtained more than $1-million a year for the work, but advised on Government projects and spending that involved many additional outlays. Up to 50 university people at a time served the project in Vietnam

¶The employes "borrowed" from the Government were intended for police training and not for operations, and were "held accountable" to the project. Soon, however, the university became dissatisfied with the evident link to C.I.A. men and "we did, as soon as we could with responsibility, withdraw" from that part of the arrangement.

¶Many of the project members were far from passive or uncritical about the Diem Government and aroused its displeasure with their writings, though others disagreed.

Moreover, a number of publications show that "a certain amount of academic production" resulted from the university's involvement, Professor Smuckler said.

STUDENTS PROTEST C.I.A. RECRUITING

Agency Curtails Interviews at Columbia as Result

A student protest yesterday forced Columbia University to curtail a series of student interviews with a personnel recruiter for the Central Intelligence Agency.

The recruiter was scheduled to interview about 25 students this week to discuss employment opportunities in the C.I.A. But a demonstration sponsored by Students for a Democratic Society disrupted the interviewing.

More than 100 protesting students congregated on a staircase in Dodge Hall, outside the room where the interviewing was scheduled to resume after a lunch break, and demanded that the C.I.A. recruiter join them in a question-and-answer session. A few students tried to enter the interview room, but were barred by university security guards.

Alexander Clark, director of Columbia's office of university placement and career planning, conferred with Dr. Lawrence H. Chamberlain, vice president of the university, and then called off the remaining interviews.

Mr. Clark said that the C.I.A. recruiter "couldn't hold interviews under the circumstances." He criticized the demonstrators for "blocking other students from the opportunity to seek employment" in the interviews with the recruiter, Harry Russell. He had arrived on the campus yesterday. Some interviews were held in the morning.

Mr. Clark said students interested in seeking C.I.A. employment would be referred to the agency's local field office. The C.I.A. has a phone number in the Manhattan telephone book. But the listing does not include an address.

The leaders of the student demonstration asserted in a statement that the university "should do nothing to cooperate" with C.I.A.

Mr. Clark said later that it was the university's policy to permit any legitimate business firm or Government agency to discuss possible career plans with students.

William Kahn, proctor of the university, said no disciplinary action was contemplated against the student demonstrators.

Stanford War Critics

To the Editor:

A news article in The Times on Nov. 14 reported that the American Civil Liberties Union has urged 900 university presidents to resist subpoenas and other efforts by the House Committee on Un-American Activities "to obtain membership lists of campus organizations critical of American policy in Vietnam"; and that it has specifically criticized the administrations of the University of Michigan and the University of California at Berkeley for complying with such subpoenas last August without first attempting legal resistance. [Editorial Nov. 15 "Freedom on Campus."]

The A.C.L.U.'s position is of course not a stand on the merits of the Vietnam war. It is quite simply a demand that university administrations firmly resist all attempts to intimidate students who maintain dissenting opinions. The A.C.L.U.'s plea is so obviously proper that it should not have had to be made at all. We share the A.C.L.U.'s regret at Berkeley's and Michigan's easy compliance with the subpoenas.

Unhappily, we have to point out that these two universities are not the only institutions the A.C.L.U. could have criticized. Last July Stanford University received a similar subpoena from the committee, and quietly turned over the lists of students' names. In failing even to "pursue the quite orthodox and risk-free procedure of seeking to have the subpoenas quashed," as the A.C.L.U.'s statement has put it, our university has missed an opportunity to set a valuable precedent.

DAVID S. NIVISON
Professor of
Chinese and Philosophy
DONALD H. DAVIDSON
Professor of Philosophy
Stanford University
Stanford, Calif., Nov. 17, 1966

April 14, 1966 | November 16, 1966 | November 28, 1966

The Student Scene: Angry Militants

By NAN ROBERTSON
Special to The New York Times

MADISON, Wis., Nov. 19—The prevailing mood among student political and social activists in the fall of 1967 is powerlessness. It is also bewilderment, dissension and anger.

The University of Wisconsin here is one of the angriest campuses in the nation. Tomorrow, Navy and Marine recruiters are expected. So, reportedly, are 200 sheriff's deputies and policemen. There may be a clash with students protesting the war.

In the spring of 1962, an observer journeyed across the United States, visiting 10 campuses and interviewing hundreds of students and professors.

That year, three movements embroiled activists. They were civil rights; the new student right, led by the militant Young Americans for Freedom, and the peace movement, which focused on the banning of the atomic bomb and the fear of genetic distortion.

Five of the 10 campuses were revisited this month. They were Harvard University at Cambridge, Mass.; the University of California at Berkeley, the University of Texas at Austin, Grinnell College in Grinnell, Iowa, and the University of Wisconsin.

Everywhere, both the spirit and the movements of 1962 had changed dramatically. What has happened? This:

¶The civil rights groups have vanished. The white liberals have entered the New Left or the peace movement, or both, and almost all their activity revolves around Vietnam. The Negro students are flocking to separatist groups that encourage race pride and self-pride.

¶The peace movement is entirely engaged in anti-Vietnam war, anti-draft issues. It is impossible to tell exactly how many students oppose the war, but opposition ranges across the spectrum of student ideology —be it active or passive, white or black, Republican or Democratic.

¶The super-patriotic Young Americans for Freedom of 1962 have nearly shriveled away.

¶The left of 1967 is far more radical than the left of 1962. The New Left of 1967 also exhibits some striking similarities to the New Right of 1962. Politically, the most extreme students in the New Left advocate revolution and tend towards anarchism. The moderate members are really liberal Democrats with a radical vocabulary.

¶A growing social concern has drawn thousands of previously uninvolved students into welfare movements, particularly on campuses in big cities. These students make no noise and no headlines, but in terms of numbers they represent the most important single social commitment in 1967. Five years ago they might have chosen to enter the civil rights movement—or to do nothing.

Meantime, the vast middle gets on with the business of going to school: growing, learning, reaching some kind of truce with the status quo. These students look milk fed, scrubbed and not much involved with anything besides books and dating.

The number of militant activists of every stripe has not increased significantly over 1962. At most, they still range from 1 to 10 per cent of the student population. But their tactics, ideology and rhetoric are far more extreme.

What are today's issues? Overwhelmingly, they are Vietnam and what the students regard as the sickness of society.

"The war, the war," said one college administrator. "It's getting so that I can't talk or think about it anymore. A meeting on student loans comes as a relief."

The Promise Fades

The bright promise of 1962, that peaceful, simple protest—a sit-in, a boycott, a picket line —could change, indeed, had already changed deeply rooted institutions and prejudices, has turned into the ugly disruptions of 1967.

The nonviolence and Christian love of the Rev. Dr. Martin Luther King Jr. has given way to tear gas, clubs and hatred at some colleges and draft-induction centers. Many who found the student scene exhilarating in 1962 find it depressing today.

The 1967 students have no American heroes. The last time around, President Kennedy and Barry Goldwater could arouse enormous fervor.

This fall, Governor Rockefeller, Robert F. Kennedy, Ronald Reagan, Mayor Lindsay, Senator Charles Percy and Mark Hatfield are popular, but the passion is missing. Some voice a we-see-through-him-he-wants-to-be-President distrust of Robert Kennedy.

Furthermore, the Young Democrats and Young Republican clubs largely have become speakers' bureaus or paper organizations.

By at least 4 to 1, the Young Democrats at Harvard, with 800 dues-paying, but largely inactive, members, believe that President Johnson has betrayed his 1964 campaign promises about Vietnam and oppose his 1968 candidacy. The President of the Young Democrats at the University of Texas is equally disaffected.

Vocal students express a sometimes irrational hatred of President Johnson and Secretary of State Dean Rusk. Most students find the judgment extreme and unfair, but the vocal ones call the President a "murderer" for escalating the war.

The most charitable thing they say about Mr. Rusk is that he is "intractable," or perhaps "a blithering idiot."

Many who are close to them say the campuses, in both their activity and apathy, reflect a sickness in American society.

The New Left, for example, led by the Students for a Democratic Society, seems to be experiencing what Prof. William Appleman Williams of Wisconsin calls "a moral revulsion against the bland righteousness of a society shot through with failures."

Products of Society

The New Leftists are both a product of, and a reaction against, a society they despise and call grossly materialistic, hypothetical and inhumane. They see divisions — white against black, rich against poor, world humanity against the United States in an unpopular war. They see no hope in America.

Prof. Stanley Hoffman of Harvard says that in 1962, "Some students here were disaffected with their Government, but it was still their Government. They had the basic trust of people brought up to believe it was really theirs.

"They now believe even their Government may be a bunch of liars and cheats."

Like the extreme right-wing students of 1962, the extreme left of 1967 is by and large suspicious of the mass media, liberal teachers and liberal textbooks, the Communist Party, U.S.A. and the Soviet Union.

Michael Lerner, for instance, a Berkeley student, calls the Soviet Union "the second most important imperialistic power in the world—next to the United States."

New Leftists can also be dogmatic, noisy, skilled at disruptive tactics, philosophically confused, unwilling to compromise, and fascinated with rhetoric, other characteristics of the young Americans for Freedom in 1962.

The on-campus New Left gurus include Michael Ansara of Harvard, a 20-year-old major in history and literature, and Robert Cohen of Wisconsin, a 24-year-old philosophy student and teaching assistant, who is in danger of dismissal because of his anti-war activities.

Students hold both of them in awe for their brilliance and dedication to radical causes. Each has a carefully articulated radical philosophy, although neither offers a blueprint for revolution or major change.

Mr. Cohen, however, will say that Cuba has best met its "historical possibilities" toward being a "free, rational and happy society" and that she has done this with far fewer resources than the United States.

Still Rational Discourse

On the left, there is still rational discourse about issues, even the war; it is the order of the day in meetings at Harvard and Grinnell.

Similarly, Texas has been calm, although resentment of another sort still lingers from a student rebellion last spring against strict controls over rallies. ("This campus could blow up any minute over some silly little university rule," said Mary Morphis, the student editor.)

At both Texas and Grinnell, however, the nucleus of the New Left sometimes seems to be made up of intellectual hobbits—warm, lovable and a little furry minded.

At Wisconsin and Berkeley it is different. The radicals of the left there shout down opposition, stifle debate over the war, or student power, or faculty power, and call for the destruction of the "corporate-military system," which, they say, includes the universities.

"It's oppressive—this place is really getting sick," said Joel Brenner, editor of The Wisconsin Daily Cardinal.

"The extremists have broken down, intellectually and psychologically," he said. "Instead of asking themselves: 'What is the problem? What can be done about it?' They're asking: 'What is the most radical thing to do?'"

Across the country, the radical intellectual students are reading "Repressive Tolerance" by Prof. Herbert Marcuse, a German-born philosopher, who now teaches at the San Diego campus of the University of California. Its thesis is that a liberal society, by encouraging debate and tolerance, emasculates and submerges any radical arguments or alternatives.

On all five campuses visited, the New Leftists were beginning to argue that the "higher morality" of their protest against an unjust war superceded individual rights such as free speech. The most radical among them displayed total scorn for individual liberties.

Prof. John Silber of the University of Texas, a liberal philosopher who is widely respected on the campus, produced a harsh indictment of extremists of the left.

Furiously, he said:

"They are the new Fascisti."

He went on:

"They are indistiguishable from the far right. One group wants bloody revolution. The other wants to blast the world. They share a contempt for rational political discussion and constitutional, legal solutions.

"Both want to be pure. They know nothing about the virtue of compromise. They know nothing about the horror of sainthood or the wickedness of saints."

The extreme leftists, Professor Silber said, are "Kamikaze liberals," who would "dive down the funnel of a battleship to assert their principles."

Even their radical faculty heroes have begun to turn against the leftists. At Wisconsin, Professor Williams, a socialist, whose stinging critiques of American foreign policy, are read eagerly by New Leftists, said of them:

"They are the most selfish people I know. They just terrify me. They are acting out a society I'd like to live in as an orangutan.

"They have no experience of the way the world really works, or of coalition politics. They say: 'I'm right and you're wrong and you can't talk because you're wrong.' They think the university president should be leading the revolution — it's ludicrous."

A Liberal Mourns

Meantime, the liberal new chancellor of the Madison campus of the university, until recently a popular sociologist, sat forlornly in his big office atop Bascom Hill. He talked of the resentments and mutiny within the students and faculty that followed a bloody put-down of a sit-in Oct. 18 against a recruiter for Dow Chemical Company, which makes napalm.

The chancellor, William Sewell, had just been hooted down the night before at a student forum.

"I'm worried sick," he said. "They talk of tearing the society down, remaking it over. Nobody says how. What has happened here has happened in the cities. They are turning from protest to disruption, and the protesters will use force."

Mr. Sewell also spoke of the anger the legislators in the state capitol, near the bottom of Bascom Hill, felt toward the protestors. There have been rumblings about cutting the university budget and of restricting the out-of-state enrollment.

About 28 per cent of the undergraduates are from out of state, most of them from the cities of the Eastern Seaboard or Chicago. It is from this group, as in 1962, that the liberal-left activists come.

At Berkeley, Texas and Wisconsin, the gulf is widening between once sympathetic faculty members and the student left.

Prof. Robert H. Cole of Berkeley, who helped draft a resolution after the Free Speech movement in 1964 that led to drastically liberalized university rules, said:

"I was a revolutionary in 1964 — a faculty Young Turk. Now I'm an administrator, and I'm tired, very very tired. We all are."

George Mosse, a history professor at Wisconsin, who is easily one of the most popular and stimulating men on campus, had this to say:

"The essence of a university is the personal relationship and dialogue between some interesting professors and some interested students. The tactics of confrontation will end this dialogue. It's already becoming more difficult."

The Draft Issue

These tactics center now on the draft.

Unquestionably, the vast majority of male students would serve in the armed forces if drafted. The left, however, wants to disrupt the draft by blocking campus recruiters, sitting in at induction centers, burning or mailing in draft cards, or urging potential draftees to flee to Canada.

David Pratt of Texas, a member of Students for a Democratic Society, who served in the Army three years, explained another approach:

"Use any means. Get stoned before you get down to the induction center. Say you're schizoid, a queer. Refuse to sign a disclaimer saying you are not a member of any subversive organization.

"File for conscientious objector. It takes more time. You can't be classified or drafted if your case is under appeal."

Perhaps a more typical anti-Vietnam, anti-draft view comes from Richard Beahrs, the head of the student body at Berkeley. He described himself as a "Percy - Lindsay - Rockefeller - type Republican" in his voting pattern, but "very, very liberal" in terms of the national outlook.

He said:

"They say you can't pick your wars. Well, why not? You're the person who's putting his life on the line and has to take the life of others."

Oct. 21, 1967, has become a sacred date on the campuses. Students revere those who joined the peace march then to the Pentagon.

Everywhere, they point out students who were tear-gassed, or smashed over the head by Federal marshals, or jabbed by soldiers with bayonets.

"It's like German dueling scars," said Prof. Joseph F. Wall of Grinnell, who has been active in the peace movement since 1962.

The opposition to the war and the pull of the New Left have drawn the uncommitted mass of students at Harvard toward the left.

"In 1962 they were armchair liberals. Now they're armchair radicals," complained Harlon Dalton, president of the campus Young Democrats.

In other universities the middle has been alienated. At Texas, where the orientation is traditionally right of center, anyway, Professor Silber worries about his students taking what he calls nineteen-twenties "Herbert Hoover" stances about the poor, believing they are poor because they are lazy or stupid.

"Year after year I have sent students into slum projects," he said. "I have had to take them deeper and more intimately every semester before they became touched and ashamed by the injustices and inequities of our social life."

Negroes Move Away

Still another, more dramatic, alienation can be found on campus—that of the black separatists. There are enough Negro students now for them to coalesce, which is exactly what they have done.

Go to Wisconsin and you will see them off together in a corner of the Student Union Rathskeller. Go to Berkeley and you will see them in a little knot near the steps of Sproul Hall. Go to Grinnell and you will find them at certain hours in the North Lounge of the Forum.

At Grinnell, the only one of the five campuses visited where a strong all-Negro group had not formed into an official society, the white students call the North Loungers "the subculture."

It is difficult to tell precisely how many Negro students are on a campus because anti-discrimination laws forbid identification by race on registration forms.

However, Negro students interviewed seemed to have a clear idea of their numbers, and two surveys—at Texas and Berkeley—confirmed their estimates.

At Berkeley, with 28,000 students, there are 400 to 500 Negroes. Those who belong to the Afro-American Students Union, formed 18 months ago, will not reveal the size of the membership. Some Negroes are in both the union and a Negro fraternity—there are four—or a sorority, of which there are two.

At Harvard, with 15,000 students in the university, there are about 200 Negroes. About 75 belong to the African and Afro-American Society. This was formed in 1963.

At Texas, with 29,000 students, there are some 250 Negroes. Many belong to the Negro Alliance for Progress, formed in 1967.

"They form less than 1 per cent of the student population, which gives you a good idea of the state of higher education in Texas, said Lloyd Doggett, the student government president. He did not know that the percentage was little better at the other campuses.

At Wisconsin, with 33,000 students, there are probably 300 Negroes. Twenty-five belong to Concerned Black People, a political group formed under a slightly different name a year ago. About 80 more belong to three all-Negro fraternities and one Negro sorority.

The almost universal reaction of white liberal and radical students to the separatist movement is hurt and dismay. They remember the happy days, when it was "black and white together."

Yet, anyone who cares to question the Negro students, who are eager to talk, discovers that a sense of self-pride, race pride and group identity is being fostered in these new organizations.

Moreover, according to Charles Hamilton of Harvard, "They inculcate responsibility and concern for black people."

Willie Howard of Wisconsin said that Concerned Black People was developing leaders in the professions who "will uplift the black people."

'Never Let You Forget'

Lenneal Henderson of Berkeley, speaking of the white students, whose numbers engulfed him, said:

449

"They never let you forget you were black. We decided to remember we were black.

"We decided to remember our African heroes, our American heroes and our culture. We decided to stop hating ourselves, trying to look like you, bleaching our hair, straightening our hair. In high school, I used to hold my big lip in."

Then Lenneal, a handsome, light tan youth, said:

"Now I wish I were 39,000 shades darker."

Dwain Harris of Texas, president of the Negro Alliance for Progress, said: "All of us are proud that we have something to identify with. Every black man in this country is in some way feeling awareness of himself—who he is and what he is, and trying to find himself."

Dwain, who is from Houston, burned a Confederate flag on the Texas campus recently. "It gave me a feeling of real satisfaction," he said.

White students angrily reproached him for burning the flag, he said, telling him that "their Southern daddies fought and died for that flag."

But, he said: "You go in their rooms and you see the Confederate flag plastered all over the walls, and you see it flying from their car aerials and on the bumper stickers with the words 'Forget, hell.'

"All that means to you as a black man is slavery," he said. "It's objectionable. If they're going to hang on to that flag I don't want their friendship."

Only at Grinnell, where the Negroes are split between the middle-class students and the lower-income scholarship students, do most want to lead an integrated life.

Still, there is frustration and ambivalence. Roy Walker expressed it this way:

"If I go with the soul-music group in the North Lounge, I'll be categorized as a traditional Negro by the whites. If I don't, the soul group will call me an Uncle Tom. I want to develop as an independent individual."

He said his "deepest hurt" had come at college when his white room-mate of two years, to whom he is very close, mistook him for another Negro student. Roy seemed to be saying:

"Maybe they really do think we all look alike."

The Berkeley Negroes spoke warmly of the educational opportunity program that has brought most of them to campus on scholarships and tutored them "to make sure we succeed and don't just wither away" in the intense academic competition.

There are strains and pressures, but by and large the Negro students appear healthy and tough-minded, even though all the expressions of the black separatist movement do not.

At Berkeley the other day, James Nabors, a Negro, yelled racist insults at an all-white group of 1,200 gathered below Sproul steps.

"You're the cream of the crop! Well, you look like cream," he said, sneering. "I'm gonna skim you off!"

His listeners remained silent or giggled nervously.

A Student Explains

Paul Glusman, an adherent of Students for a Democratic Society, explained the listeners' feelings.

He said:

"I don't like it when they say, 'We're going to take over this country and paint it black.' They spend half their time attacking the white liberals as sellouts.

"But I think it is incumbent on us to be accommodating because of their subjugation. It's just a stage they're passing through."

Two days earlier, Afro-American members led by Nabors seized a noon rally from Volition, an Ayn Rand-Laissez faire capitalism group that has swallowed up the Young Republicans. The date for the rally had been promised long before by the university, which gets at least one request a day for one.

"I've been denied so long that anything I take is right," Nabors shouted. In defending a Negro accused of killing an Oakland policeman and wounding another, for whom the Afro-Americans are raising money, he said:

"Huey P. Newton committed the crime of protecting black women first, black children second and white policeman last."

Nabors is the outer limits of black racism heard on the campuses today.

In most cases the Negro societies ban whites from their meetings. The Berkeley students are also touchy about the word "Negro."

"Negroes is equivalent to nigger. It's a name the white man gave us," Lenneal Henderson said. "America has Chinese-Americans and Italian-Americans. We come from Africa and they call us Negroes."

Stokely Carmichael is their man of the hour. Martin Luther King has receded. In discussing black power, the term Carmichael brought into currency, Frank Jenkins, the president of of Afro-American Student Union, said:

"It's the same thing as Jew power. You got the Liebermans and the Goldbergs working away for each other in New York. The Italians help themselves, too. We're giving a birth to an economy and a culture you've stolen from us.

"We're 15 per cent of the population. We should have 15 per cent of the economic power. We ought to be in control of the ghetto."

Some militant Negro students oppose the draft and almost all oppose the war in Vietnam. However, they do not participate generally in white anti-war protests.

Lenneal Henderson, who will resist the draft, said:

"White people intellectualize. We have a different reason for not going. We haven't enjoyed the benefits of this society. The whites are resisting as citizens. We resist on the ground that we aren't citizens. He who has no country shouldn't fight for it."

Concern for Poor

Yet, alongside the campus bitterness and shouting about race and war, there is something else—the growing student participation in working with the poor.

This is especially true at Harvard and Berkeley, and what is happening there is reflected on most campuses in great urban areas.

The biggest organization of any kind at Harvard is 60-year-old Phillips Brooks House, a volunteer agency. It has 1,200 members and its budget has gone from $52,000 in 1962 to $127,000 in 1967.

At Berkeley, some 3,000 students—10 per cent of the stu-

dent population, and ten times the number of those in Students for a Democratic Society—are active in such work.

The student government at Berkeley, which now controls $250,000 each year, has shifted big chunks of money from the university band and glee club to the Clearinghouse, a campus information center where volunteers can discover what work they do do among the poor.

The thrust of Phillips Brooks House was changed. Five years ago, volunteers were simply placed in agencies that worked with the poor.

"We didn't have any self-contained programs," Benjamin Barnes, the student president of Phillips Brooks House, said. "The emphasis was on offering social services. Now we are devoted to social change."

The volunteers from Phillips Brooks House have developed tutorial programs in public schools and in housing projects in Boston slums. They have hired professional consultants to guide them.

The volunteers also speak of a growing number of medical and law students who want educations for other reasons than students did in 1962. Now, they say, many seek training so they may defend and succor the poor.

Many observers believe this strain of social thought will persist after the angry demonstrators of today are gone.

Certainly, many teachers and administrators are now saying to the demonstrators: "Enough."

One professor said:

"It's nasty, it's nasty. Kids have got to learn the limits that must be enforced."

Another said:

"They're pushing the liberals too far. The students don't have a prayer against the university."

The other night, two visiting fathers at the Wisconsin campus were worrying aloud. They spoke of the dissension and the shouting and of their children's threats to grind the university to a halt.

Then they turned to a friend. He was a permissive liberal, who had raised his son on Dr. Benjamin Spock. The son is now a leader in Students for a Democratic Society.

"Ultimately and inevitably," said the third father, "They all become 30."

2 KILLED, 40 HURT IN CAROLINA RIOT

Negro Students Trade Fire With Police and Troops

By The Associated Press

ORANGEBURG, S. C., Feb. 8 —Two Negro college students were killed and more than 40 were wounded tonight in the fourth straight night of violence on the campus of South Carolina State College, a predominantly Negro school.

Killed were Sam Hammon, 18 years old, and Delano Middleton, 17. Young Hammon was killed outright in a blast of gunfire between students and law enforcement officers, and the other youth died a short time later.

At least one law enforcement officer was wounded. He was identified as State Highway Patrolman D. J. Shealy, who was struck in the head by a bullet. He was not believed to be seriously injured.

The police said Cleveland Sellers, a field coordinator for the Student Nonviolent Coordinating Committee, was among those wounded. He was hit under the left arm.

The Orangeburg police said the shooting erupted after students set fire to grass on the campus. The fire occurred on a grassy slope that borders the campus alongside U. S. Route 601.

An Associated Press Staff Photographer, Dozier Mobley, who witnessed the gunfire, said a group of 50 to 75 Negroes standing on the campus at the crest of the slope opened fire as city firemen and policemen moved in to put out the blaze.

Mr. Mobley said policemen and National Guardsmen stationed across the highway charged up the embankment after the firing began. One of their number was hit as he climbed the slope.

Several students fell as the officers opened fire, Mr. Mobley said. During the next hour, ambulances entered and left the campus as the wounded were taken to hospitals.

About 100 National Guardsmen were on duty in the city of 15,000 persons 40 miles south of the state capital at Columbia. About half of them were deployed with city and state officers near the campus when the shooting broke out. The remainder were stationed in other parts of the city.

Additional Guard units were held in alert at nearby Edgefield.

Mr. Sellers, 24 years old, who had said earlier he was on the scene to observe and not to lead students in their demands for fuller integration of the community, was not believed seriously hurt.

It was the fourth straight night of violence in Orangeburg, triggered Monday night when the operator of a bowling establishment, All-Star Bowling Lanes, refused to admit Negroes. Before tonight's violence 13 persons had been injured, and rioting had damaged several stores in the downtown area.

Student leaders, who had submitted a list of seven grievances to the Orangeburg City Council, staged a "prayer-in" during the early evening, and later held a meeting in a ball park near the campus.

Officers said that these meetings went off without trouble.

February 4, 1968

Faculty Warns Columbia on Its Expansion Policy

By J. ANTHONY LUCAS

Seventy faculty members at Columbia University warned yesterday that the university's current expansion policy would aggravate racial tensions in the Morningside Heights area.

The Faculty Civil Rights Group, in a report adopted last December but released today, said the university's "oil slick" expansion plans would create a "garrison enclave" both physically and psychologically separated from the surrounding community.

It called on the university to commit itself to "the revival of an ethnically and economically integrated and balanced community on Morningside Heights" and to revise its expansion plans to serve those ends.

The 28-page report and accompanying resolution marked a new stage in the developing debate over Columbia's role in the community.

However, the university declined to be drawn into the debate yesterday. John J. Hastings, director of Columbia's Office of Public Information, said the university would have "no comment" at this time.

Immanuel Wallerstein, associate professor of sociology and chairman of the civil rights group, said that the report, which had been submitted to the university administration last January, led to a series of discussions between the group and university officials.

"We didn't come to blows, but neither can I say we got very far," Professor Wallerstein said. "The university said it was in sympathy with our objectives, but disagreed with certain details of our approach.

"We plan to keep continuing pressure on the university to see if we can get it to live up to what it says its ideals are."

The report was drawn up by a small committee headed by Peter Haidu, assistant professor of French, and was adopted by the full group last Dec. 13. Professor Wallerstein said the delay in releasing it was due chiefly to printing problems.

At the same time the group adopted a four-point resolution calling on the university to implement the report's aims.

Among other things, the resolution urged the university to undertake "an energetic campaign to provide low-and middle-income housing" for a mixture of community, faculty and students; development of a comprehensive policy for "community service" on Morningside Heights in cooperation with other institutions in the area; and "cooperation with community representatives in the planning and operation of all programs."

March 27, 1968

Wider Role for Students Urged In Columbia Advisory Report

Columbia University has released two controversial reports concerning student rights and discipline that were prepared by members of a special 15-member advisory committee of students, faculty and administration representatives.

Both reports, released in response to student pressures, call for a shaping of university policy and decision-making.

The Advisory Committee of Student Life, which put out the reports, was formed by Dr. Grayson Kirk, the president of the university, following a demonstration that disrupted the annual awards ceremony of the Columbia Naval Reserve Officers Training Corps in 1965.

The majority report, endorsed by the five members of the administration, the five faculty members and one of the five students on the committee, called for a significantly greater advisory role for students in decision-making at Columbia.

The other four student members entered a minority report that said the majority opinion offered "too little and too late" and charged that "a few of the majority proposals would even reduce rights traditionally and properly enjoyed by students."

They called for "real student power" in helping to form university policy.

The committee submitted its reports to Dr. Kirk last August after almost two years of hearings, research and deliberation. The report was released by the university late Tuesday.

In a letter to the president of the Student Council, Dr. Kirk said, "Final decisions on such issues cannot and should not be taken quickly or lightly."

The majority report recommended the appointment of a "cabinet level" director of student affairs who would report directly to the president on all nonacademic matters involving students.

Also suggested were a student-faculty-administration committee on student affairs and a judicial body to rule on student disciplinary issues. In both cases, the university president would have the veto power.

Among the proposals of the minority was one for a tripartite committee that would determine all nonacademic university policy subject only to the approval of the Columbia trustees.

Aaron W. Warner, a professor of economics, was chairman of the advisory committee.

April 21, 1968

300 Protesting Columbia Students Barricade Office of College Dean

By DAVID BIRD

Three hundred chanting students barricaded the Dean of Columbia College in his office yesterday to protest the construction of a gymnasium in Morningside Park and a defense-oriented program participated in by Columbia University. The protest against the gymnasium extended at one time to the building site, where students tore down a section of fence before being driven off by 30 policemen. The students say that construction of the gymnasium would be "racist" because it would deprive Negroes in the area of recreational facilities. The charge against the defense program, the Institute for Defense Analysis, was that it supported the war effort in Vietnam. The protest, organized by the leftist Students for a Democratic Society, had the support of other Columbia campus groups. Representatives of several Negro organizations unrelated to Columbia joined the protest. Among the groups were the Harlem chapter of the Congress of Racial Equality, the Harlem Committee for Self-Defense, the United Black Front, and the New York chapter of the Student Nonviolent Coordinating Committee, which is headed nationally by H. Rap Brown. The protest began shortly after noon when about 500 students gathered around the sundial in front of Low Memorial Library, Columbia University's main administrative building. From the sundial, the demonstrators surged up the steps toward the Low building to take their protest directly to the administration.

The Low building was closed, however, and the demonstrators were turned back by university security guards. Behind the guards stood about 150 members of a counter-demonstration group, the conservative-oriented Students for a Free Campus.

The S.D.S.-led students gathered around Mark Rudd, Columbia's S.D.S. president, who read a letter from David B. Truman, vice president of the university, offering to meet with the group immediately in the McMillan Theater, on the Columbia campus.

The boisterous group shouted down the offer. The students then marched to the site of the new gymnasium, at 113th Street and Morningside Drive, where they tore down a section of chain link fence around the area being cleared for the $11.6-million gymnasium. The police moved in, wielding billy clubs, and arrested one student, Fred Wilson.

The protesters marched four blocks back to the university campus, where Mr. Rudd again addressed the group at the sundial. "We're going to have to take a hostage to make them let go of I.D.A. and let go of the gym," he shouted.

With that, Mr. Rudd led the group to Hamilton Hall, the administrative building for Columbia College, the undergraduate arm of the university.

A Protest 'Forever'

At Hamilton Hall, Mr. Rudd took a stand in front of acting Dean Henry S. Coleman's office. He said Mr. Coleman had been selected as the group's hostage.

Mr. Coleman, formerly director of admissions at Columbia, became acting dean in June, 1967, when Mr. Truman, then dean of Columbia College, was named vice president and provost of the university.

Mr. Rudd urged the group to remain in Hamilton Hall and outside Mr. Coleman's office, until its demands were met, and vowed that the group would stay there "forever" if necessary.

Dean Coleman was not in his office at the time. He appeared a few minutes later, elbowing his way through the crowd, and stood next to Mr. Rudd at the door of his office. Mr. Rudd asked the crowd: "Is this a demonstration?" and the crowd boomed back, "Yes!"

The university recently instituted a rule banning any demonstrations in buildings on the campus, and so the question and answer were obviously meant to point up the group's defiance of the rule.

"Are we going to stay here until our demands are met?" Mr. Rudd asked, and again, there was a booming "yes" from his followers. The demonstrators then chanted, for several minutes, "Hell no, we won't go."

Dean Coleman, who stood and listened to the chanting, finally said, "I have no control over the demands you are making, but I have no intention of meeting any demands under a situation such as this."

A voice from the crowd shouted "get on the phone." Dean Coleman replied, "I have no intention of calling the president or vice president of the university under condition such as this."

The group started singing "We shall not be moved." Leaders of the protest urged the demonstrators to remain in the hall outside Dean Coleman's office, and they promised that food and drink were on the way. Dean Coleman turned and entered his office.

Soon boxes containing soft drinks, carrots, bananas, cake and oranges were brought in.

After the demonstrators had been outside his office for more than an hour, Dean Coleman came out and said, "I repeat, I have no controls over your demands."

He warned, "It's getting too crowded here and we're going to have trouble." The Dean then went back into his office. The student leaders drew up a written list of demands.

The demonstration was spearheaded by an informal steering committee established at 2 P.M. by representatives of the Society of Afro-American Students, the Students for a Democratic Society and the Columbia Citizenship Council, a group that does tutorial work in the neighborhoods surrounding Columbia.

In addition to demanding that Columbia end construction of the Morningside Park gymnasium and sever its links with the Institute of Defense Analysis, the steering committee also called upon the university to:

¶Terminate all disciplinary actions pending against students as a result of previous demonstrations against the gym and grant a general amnesty to all participants in the current protest.

¶Lift the ban on campus demonstrations.

¶Resolve all future disciplinary action against students at open hearings before students and faculty members.

¶Use its good offices to obtain dismissals of charges against those who participated in demonstrations at the gymnasium site in the past.

Six students are on probation at Columbia as a result of their participation in protests at the gymnasium site and several persons, including the Rev. A. Kendall Smith, have been arrested.

Dean Coleman, after reviewing the demands, told the students that Mr. Truman had seen the demands and was willing to meet in Wollman Auditorium "now." A steering committee of the protesters met briefly and turned down the offer of the meeting, unless they received a written guarantee of amnesty for the protesters.

Mr. Truman later, in an interview in his office in Low Library, said the answer to the amnesty demand was "no." He said he was prepared to have the demonstrators remain in Hamilton Hall "until they get tired."

Once the students had taken over Hamilton Hall, no campus security guards were in evidence and there were no city police anywhere on the campus. By the early morning, the number of demonstrators had grown to about 400.

Shortly after the blockade of the dean's office began, red crepe and posters bearing the likenesses of Lenin, Ernesto Che Guevara and Malcolm X, the black nationalist who was assassinated in Harlem, were pasted on the walls.

A group of eight Negro youths stood guard outside Dean Coleman's office. At about 10 P.M., a group of Columbia students scuffled briefly with the guards,

One student showed a copy of a leaflet that he said was being distributed in Harlem. It said: "Stop Columbia from taking over Harlem. Black students at Columbia are holding a dean captive and have taken control of the administration building . . . Go to Columbia and help the black students NOW . . ."

At 11:15 P.M. Dean Coleman said he intended to stay in his office "throughout the night if necessary." He refused any other comment.

There were at least two other Columbia faculty members who remained in the dean's office.

Outside the office, Omar Ahmed, an organizer for the United Black Front said: "We have been running a long campaign against Columbia. This is part of the continuing attack. This is going to be a very hot summer for Columbia University."

Mr. Ahmed said his group intended to "keep up the pressure on the gym, on Harlem Hospital and on Delano Village, which Columbia University bought."

Delano Village is a Harlem housing development bought by Columbia to house staff members of Harlem Hospital, which is affiliated with Columbia. Black organizations charge Columbia has evicted Negroes to make room for hospital personnel. The organizations also blame Columbia for allegedly poor conditions at Harlem Hospital.

The Student Nonviolent Coordinating Committee, one of the most militant black organizations in the country, urged "all people who understand the urgency of this struggle to support the students, community people and their allies."

"It should be crystal clear that the issue at stake is the control by local people of their community and the institutions within their community, and the right of black people to protest injustices perpetrated

Columbia students sitting in Hamilton Hall yesterday listened to speakers protest against university's policies

The New York Times (by Neal Boenzi)

upon them by institutions such as Columbia University," S.N.C.C. said.

The group's spokesman said that I.D.A. "works on military projects aimed at the oppression of the people of Vietnam" and "develops riot equipment to commit mass genocide against black people here in the U.S."

Groups Invited

William Sales, a 25-year-old Columbia graduate student who is working on a doctorate in international affairs and who is a member of the five-man steering committee leading the protest, said all off-campus groups participating in the demonstration had been invited by the steering committee, which is composed entirely of students.

While demonstrators filled the corridors of Hamilton Hall, some playing guitars and others sharing blankets and engaging in discussions, Mr. Sales summarized his feelings about Columbia's relations with its neighboring black community.

"They're trying," he said, "to Bogart Harlem," explaining that he meant act toward Harlem like Humphrey Bogart, the late movie star.

Shortly after 1 A.M., about 50 counterdemonstrators gathered around a statue of Alexander Hamilton about 20 feet from the besieged building and sang choruses of "The Ballad of the Green Berets," a song extolling the heroism of Special Forces troops fighting in Vietnam.

Fred Wilson, the 19-year-old student arrested at the gymnasium site, was charged with assault, criminal mischief and resisting arrest. He was said to have knocked down three policemen when they tried to stop him from pulling down the fence.

Plans for the construction of the gymnasium have been troubling members of the Negro community as well as some city officials and Columbia alumni. The building is to be erected on a steep rocky slope in Morningside Park, which separates Columbia, on Morningside Heights, from Harlem.

The university signed a 100-year lease with the city for the site in 1961, with rent set at $3,000 a year. The arrangement provided that Columbia build a separate gymnasium and swimming pool for the Harlem community.

Columbia's relations with its neighbors in Harlem have been strained for several years.

One of the problems has been Columbia's expansion, which has resulted in the university's acquisition of more than 100 buildings in the last few years and the eviction of many longtime residents of low-cost rent-controlled housing.

Concerned about crime in its area, Columbia bought many hotels that were well-known havens for prostitutes and narcotics addicts and attempted to evict these tenants, but some community groups objected, saying Columbia should have undertaken the rehabilitation rather than the eviction of the residents.

Recently, when Columbia began attempts to rehabilitate some of its tenants, the efforts were denounced in leaflets.

April 24, 1968

Columbia Closes Campus After Disorders

Office of President Is Seized—Dean Freed but Protest Widens

Columbia University students expanded their protest early today, invading two more buildings after the Morningside Heights campus was closed following a second day of tumultuous demonstrations.

By early this morning, the demonstration involved Hamilton, Fayerweather and Avery halls as well as the Low Memorial Library office of Dr. Grayson Kirk, the university president. Dr. Kirk's office was seized yesterday, a day also marked by the release of Acting Dean Henry Coleman, who had been held captive in his Hamilton Hall office for more than 24 hours.

With the demonstration growing in magnitude, the police established a command post on the Columbia campus at the request of university authorities for the first time in three years.

Classes Canceled

The closing of the campus was ordered last night and resulted in the cancellation of classes for 1,500 students. Later Dean David B. Truman, vice president of the university, said classes today would be held as scheduled.

Campus activities in general were carried out normally yesterday, as only about 150 students of the 27,500 enrolled at the university were involved in the seizure.

But a university spokesman said sessions scheduled for Hamilton Hall, where one-third of the college's classes are held, had been canceled yesterday.

Many students were openly resentful of the demonstration, and last night, as a light rain fell, about 200 gathered outside Low Library, which houses President Kirk's office, chanting: "Get 'em out. Get 'em out."

Gym Is Opposed

Principally, the demonstrators are seeking to halt construction of a controversial new gymnasium in Morningside Park, a project depicted by some members of the university and surrounding community as a wrongful use of public property; and an end to the university's ties with the Institute for Defense Analysis, an organization the demonstrators contend not only aids the war in Vietnam, but also devises methods to control protests here.

In addition, the demonstrators were seeking a guarantee of amnesty for all who took part in the protest.

Last night, after an emergency meeting dealing with the demonstrators' demands, a faculty committee made the following recommendations:

¶A halt in the gymnasium construction.

¶Continuation of the association with the Institute for Defense Analysis.

¶No declaration of amnesty.

¶Establishment of a tripartite committee to try the student demonstrators. President Kirk had no comment on the recommendations. He may accept or reject them, or forward then to the university's trustees for action.

Just before 2 A.M. today the university issued a statement saying that President Kirk had indicated that he would put before the trustees a college faculty recommendation that the trustees consider suspending construction of the gymnasium and inviting Mayor Lindsay to designate a group to meet with the university on the question.

Barry Gottehrer, the head of the Urban Task Force, who was on the scene, said the Mayor would be willing to consider the matter.

In the evening, Manhattan Borough President Percy E. Sutton said that he, City Human Rights Commissioner William H. Booth, State Senator Basil A. Paterson and Assemblyman Charles B. Rangel had met with Dr. Kirk to make the university aware of potential danger in the anger of the Harlem community toward the gymnasium.

Mr. Sutton, speaking at a news conference at the Harlem branch of the Congress of Racial Equality, 307 West 105th Street, said Dr. Kirk had agreed to call a meeting of the Board of Trustees as soon as possible.

Asked when that might be, Mr. Sutton replied, "I assume tomorrow."

Also present at the news conference, in addition to those described by Mr. Sutton as participants in the meeting with Dr. Kirk, were Victor Solomon, chairman of Harlem CORE, and Omar Ahmed, vice chairman of the National Conference of Black Power.

During the news conference, it was noted that each of the elected officials—all of them Democrats—had introduced legislation in Albany during the last few years to rescind Columbia's use of the park land.

Arthur Williams, another activist who was present, said there would be "massive retaliation if one head is touched."

However, no police action was taken yesterday, officials said, in an effort to avoid increasing tensions.

But policemen—in uniform and in plainclothes—were grouped on and around the campus.

Policemen on Alert

Some of the policemen were in the ground floor security office of Low Library, the university's main administration building and the site of Dr. Kirk's invaded office. Others were across Broadway in the basement of a Barnard College dormitory, and about 40 patrolmen waited in a temporary field headquarters in the basement.

Last night, members of the Tactical Patrol Force were on alert just outside the campus.

Until yesterday, no city policemen had been summoned to the Columbia campus since May 8, 1965, when about 200 demonstrators forced the postponement of a ceremony at which commissions were being distributed to members of the university's Naval Reserve Officers Training Corps.

Twenty policemen were invited to the campus by the university to restore order during the 1965 demonstration.

Previously, the police have gone to the Columbia vicinity during panty raids, but a Columbia spokesman said such outbreaks were largely focused on streets bordering the university so that the police did not have to enter the Columbia campus.

By 9:30 P.M., between 25 and 50 city policemen were on the campus to protect campus property, according to the office of J. W. Whiteside, director of buildings and grounds for the university.

According to the police, city policemen normally do not enter private property, such as a university campus, unless invited. Should the police have evidence of a crime on a campus, the police said, they would respond without invitation from university officials.

The protest began shortly after noon Tuesday with an attempt to take the issues directly to the administration by storming the offices in Low Library. Turned back by guards, the demonstrators proceeded to the site of the new gymnasium, off the campus at 113th Street and Morningside Drive, where they tore down a section of chain-like fence around the area being cleared for the $11.6-million structure.

A short time later, the protestors, led by Mark Rudd, campus president of Columbia's Students for a Democratic Society, marched to Hamilton Hall, the ivied main building that is the headquarters for Columbia College, the men's undergraduate school, where Dean Coleman was later blockaded in his office.

Hamilton Hall, which is near Amsterdam Avenue at 116th Street, was occupied by the largely white membership of S.D.S., joined by Negro students and some Harlem residents. When at about 5 A.M. the Negroes asked the whites to leave, declaring that the whites were not committed enough to radical action, including violence, Mr. Rudd led a group of about 60 white students to Low Library, north of 116th Street, midway between Broadway and Amsterdam Avenue.

Late in the afternoon the Students for a Democratic Society held a strategy session to plan further action. Mr. Rudd advocated the seizure of more campus buildings, but was voted down by those who wanted to concentrate on lobbying with other students in support of the society's demands.

Mr. Rudd left the crowded meeting in a rush. He announced he had resigned, but later reconsidered, attributing his announcement to the strain of the last two days.

Meanwhile, members of the society had proposed a student strike today.

Many members of the S.D.S. are deeply troubled over their relationship to the Negro students and Harlem residents who ejected them from Hamilton Hall. Some felt it was necessary for the Negroes to take control.

"It's very important for blacks to have their own thing, to develop solidarity," said a graduate student in sociology.

"Blacks have to assume their own positions of leadership," added John Hendrickson, a law

The New York Times (by Carl T. Gossett Jr.)

Demonstrators gather on steps leading to Hamilton Hall on Columbia University campus

student, "and this is one way of doing it."

"We just didn't have the same commitment," added Henry Reichman, a junior, who had been sleeping in the lounge of a dormitory. "Some of the blacks were actually willing to die. It made me wonder what my commitment really was, and it frightened me."

When the whites moved on Dr. Kirk's office, some gained access by brushing past security guards and entering the front door. Others clambered up an outside grating and entered a window.

Among the students inside was Linda LeClair, the 20-year-old New Hampshire girl who was the focus of attention on the university's campus last week when she was reprimanded by Barnard College authorities for living off campus with her boyfriend.

President Kirk was not in his office when it was seized, but he was on campus and appeared at the closed faculty meeting late in the day.

Inside Dr. Kirk's office, some students hurled papers and books to the floor, damaged fixtures in the private bath-

room, helped themselves to a supply of cigars and pasted to the window signs reading: "Liberated Area. Be Free to Join Us."

The students also pasted up photographs of President Kirk that they found in the office. One was decorated with a red mustache.

The opposition of other students to the demonstration evidenced itself in direct action at one point when Mr. Rudd appeared at a window in Dr. Kirk's office to say that the demonstrators were ready to stay indefinitely. Eggs were

thrown from the crowd on the sidewalk below. The eggs missed their target and splattered on the building's granite face.

A member of the steering committee, Edward Hyman, a Columbia junior, said he had had a two-hour meeting with Dean Truman during which the dean had said that "construction of the gymnasium in Morningside Park was a matter of principle" with both him and Dr. Kirk.

Dean Truman, according to Mr. Hyman, said that the university could "not capitulate to community pressure" and that Columbia had legal rights to build the gymnasium, and that "legality alone determines both morality and justice."

For a while around noon yesterday the students moved out of the president's office and into the hallway. Security officers rushed in and rescued a Rembrandt painting entitled "Portrait of a Dutch Admiral," valued at $450,000.

At one point, the protesters broke wires in the office, cutting off telephone communication with the outside. This kept them from knowing what was going on at the other building.

"What's happening at Hamilton?" the students shouted to newsmen outside.

At Hamilton, the protesters were preparing to release Dean Coleman. Desks and chairs piled against the building's front door were pushed aside and a pathway was cleared between the militants who had seized the building.

The tall, lean administrator strode out calmly and briskly, showing no sign that he had been unsettled by the experience.

Mr. Coleman was accompanied by two other college officials who had spent the night inside the office with him. They were the university proctor, William Kahn, and Daniel Karlinsky, a college public relations man.

Dean Well Treated

Dean Coleman said they had been treated "very nicely—we had more food than we possibly could have eaten."

He said: "We ate, drank and played cards. We attempted to do some reading and we talked a lot."

After he left Hamilton Hall, he walked quickly across the rainswept campus to the faculty meeting in Havemeyer Hall, just off Broadway and north of 118th Street.

The students offered no explanation of the brief opening of the Hamilton Hall barricade to free Dean Coleman after more than 24 hours, but he said they had told him they were disturbed by reports of a spread in the disorder.

Within an hour after he had

been freed, Dean Coleman was back in the midst of the crowd in front of Hamilton Hall, calming a conflict developing between the Negro demonstrators inside the building, their white allies on the steps and a group of burly athletes who were shouting racial epithets at the demonstrators.

"We're having a faculty meeting to try and solve this," he said. "But we can't meet if we have to continually come out here and police this situation."

Just before the dean's return, the barricade was parted again to let newsmen in to hear a statement from the demonstrators.

Standing in front of posters of Che Guevara and Malcom X that had been pasted on the walls of the building's lobby, a Negro student, Raymond Wells, read from a typewritten sheet.

"Black university students have barricaded themselves here," he shouted, "to protest the white racist university that encroaches on the Harlem community."

Then he said that the university "had raped the minds of black people through the I.D.A."

Outside Groups Expected

He announced that outside Negro groups would arrive on the campus during the evening to augment the militant force. But as daylight began to fade, university security forces began locking the gates to the campus and affixing printed signs saying: "No Classes Tonight April 24." Only one gate remained open.

Then as night fell, architecture students took over the architecture school in Avery Hall, between 117th and 118th Streets on the east side of the campus and not far from Low Memorial Library.

The students were given permission to remain in the building until 1 A.M. in support of the Low and Hamilton demonstration, but they said they would stay all night if necessary. The architecture students were joined by other young people, almost all of them white.

The students were still in Avery after the 1 A.M. deadline passed.

At 1:45 A.M., protesters — mostly graduate students—began slipping into Fayerweather Hall, just to the east of Avery. Fayerweather is the seat of the graduate faculties in history, economics and sociology.

The Avery group drew up a resolution in support of the demonstration, calling upon the university to adopt an "expansion policy that does not overrun adjacent areas" and demanding a university effort to recruit more black and Puerto Rican students and greater university recognition of students and community groups in formulating university policy.

While the demonstrators remained inside Hamilton, Low Library and Avery, about 300 students were meeting in Ferris Booth Hall to discuss the situation. A clear majority were in favor of the protest and against the gymnasium.

Among the demonstrators in the library was a student reporter for the campus radio station, WKCR-FM, who said in a telephone conversation recorded for broadcast that students had rifled Dr. Kirk's files and photocopied many documents, some allegedly showing the connections between the university and the Institute for Defense Analysis. Dr. Kirk was in the same building conferring with members of his administration about the demonstration.

At 11 P.M., a Columbia security guard, Ernest Wood, took into custody a young man allegedly leaving the campus with six philosophy and law books he was said to have taken from the low library.

The young man was taken to the West 126th Street station house for questioning and later booked on a burglary charge. He was identified as Peter Henig, 24 years old, of 600 West 115th Street. The police said he was not a Columbia student.

Columbia's history of troubles with its community actually has involved two communities — the people on Morningside Heights and those in adjoining West Harlem.

Columbia has long maintained that opposition to its policies has for the most part, reflected the views of a minority of residents in the two communities. But the opposition has attracted widespread publicity, the university contends, because it has been led by a vocal group of people seeking either political or personal gain.

The troubles largely began about 12 years ago, when Columbia began acquiring buildings on Morningside Heights to meet the expanding housing and educational needs of its students and faculty. The university also sought to rid the area of the many narcotics addicts, prostitutes and so-called undesirables who lived in cheap, run-down hotels.

The acquisition of buildings angered many people who were not undesirables and who were forced to leave low-rent apartments and buildings in which they had lived for many years. Both whites and Negroes were dislocated and they, and their supporters, have at times helped to form the basis of opposition to Columbia on other issues.

Columbia is still acquiring buildings in the area, but is making a more sensitive effort than in the past to relocate the tenants. In recent years, those who say they represent the community have critized Columbia for interfering in the community life and not doing enough for the community.

The university is attempting to develop programs of assistance for Harlem with the aid of a $10-million grant from the Ford Foundation. But that effort has been troubled, too, because of opposition within Harlem at Columbia's approach.

The New York Times (by Larry Morris)

Police watch without taking action last night as a student lifts box of food up to demonstrators in Low Library. Students have occupied offices in library since early yesterday.

April 25, 196

456

COLUMBIA HALTING WORK ON ITS GYM; SUSPENDS CLASSES

But Students Remain in Five Seized Buildings—School Closed Until Monday

DEMONSTRATIONS GO ON

Kirk Refuses Amnesty for Protesters — Policemen Scuffle With Faculty

Columbia University announced early this morning that it was halting work on the gymnasium that had set off a student protest. It also said it was closing the university until Monday, and was postponing any police action on campus.

The announcement, made just before 3:30 A.M., followed a brief scuffle between plain-clothes policemen and faculty members who had lined up in front of Low Library.

Despite the announcement, the students remained in the five buildings they had occupied.

Dean David B. Truman, the vice president of the university, who made the announcement, said the administration's decision to postpone police action had been taken at faculty urging.

Acted at Mayor's Urging

He said that the suspension of work on the gymnasium had been made at the request of Mayor Lindsay and would remain in effect "until further notice."

The scuffle between policemen and faculty members took place after a delegation of deans attempted earlier to dissuade Dr. Grayson Kirk, the university president, from calling in the police.

The brief scuffle outside the entrance to the police command post on the tension-filled Morningside Heights campus brought hundreds of students on the run to the scene.

As the conflict subsided, one of the faculty members, Prof. Richard L. Greeman of the French department, raised a hand that had been bloodied by a head wound, while one of his colleagues shouted:

"This is our university. It does not belong to the police."

Faculty Group Forms

The flurry broke out not long after the protest, which began on Tuesday, took a new turn when faculty members banded together to guard five buildings seized by students against the possibility of police incursions.

By 3 A.M. today, it was reported that 100 policemen were on the campus.

Professor Greeman said he had been hit on the back of the head by a stick held by a policeman after two other policemen had seized him.

The confrontation took place at 2:30 A.M. when two dozen plainclothes men, who apparently did not identify themselves, sought to enter Low Library.

As the students raced toward the library, the faculty members, who were wearing white armbands, called to them to

stay out of the fighting. However, some joined in.

After the battle, as some of the faculty members groped for spectacles that had been knocked to the ground, others were joined by students in the chant: "Kirk must go, Kirk must go."

Sid Davidoff, a mayoral assistant who had been inside the building, emerged to tell the crowd that had swelled to more than 500 that no students had been arrested, and that the building had not been taken over by the police from protesting students who were also inside, on another floor.

Key Demand Rejected

Yesterday afternoon, Dr. Kirk had refused to grant demonstrating students their key demand—an amnesty covering all participants in the protest, which is primarily directed against construction of a new gymnasium in Morningside Park.

Late in the afternoon, Dr. Kirk said that an amnesty concession would "destroy the whole fabric of the university community" by making a sham of disciplinary procedures at Columbia.

At that time, student demonstrators held control of four buildings and were picketing at several others in a tense protest that had disrupted academic life on the normally contemplative campus since Tuesday afternoon.

At 1 A.M. today, the students had extended their hold to a fifth building, the Mathematics Building, near Broadway at 118th Street.

Shortly after its seizure, according to Isaiah Sheffer of the theater arts department, the faculty was told by Acting Dean Henry Coleman that the police would soon be called "to maintain order."

Furor at Meeting

His announcement created a furor at the meeting, and later a delegation of deans met with Dr. Kirk to attempt to persuade him not to use the police.

As the tension increased, another faculty member, Seymour Melman, professor of industrial engineering, called the Mayor's office and was told that a mayoral aide, Barry Gottehrer, was on his way to the campus. Dr. Kirk was also understood to have consulted with the Mayor.

A few minutes later, Dean Coleman went before a crowd of 800 opponents of the demonstration who were gathered in Ferris Booth Hall. When they applauded his appearance, he told them there was "little reason for applause."

He said, "It is a very unfortunate day for Columbia

OUTSIDE THE GATES: Charles Kenyatta, Harlem Mau Mau leader, addressing a crowd gathered outside entrance to Columbia campus at Broadway and 116th Street last night.

University. The president of the university just spoke to the Mayor of New York and asked him to supply us with a sufficient force to maintain law and order."

He added, "We in no way feel this is the end of all our troubles."

It was not immediately known what action the police would take.

Faculty members lined up three deep at the entrance to Hamilton Hall and took up positions outside the other student-occupied buildings.

One of the faculty members outside Hamilton, Quentin Anderson, an English professor, said he and his colleagues had taken their position there because "to clear up Hamilton Hall with police would only precipitate action that could damage the university."

He said that although faculty members had differing views on the issues of the protest, they were united in their attitude toward the use of the police. He said they intended to maintain their posts as long as there remained any threat that the police might try to take the building.

Out on the dark campus, couriers hurried from building to building, spreading the word of the latest developments among the demonstrators.

Attendance Down

University officials said that 2,500 of the 10,000 students who usually attend cl... es on a Thursday were prevented from doing so by the demonstration.

For the second straight night, evening classes were canceled by the university because of the demonstration. Gates of the campus were locked, a they were on Wednesday nigh

The student demonstrators have demanded an amnesty as a precondition to formal negotiations to end the demonstration, which is aimed principally at halting the construction by Columbia of a new gymnasium in Morningside Park, and at ending Columbia's association with the Institute for Defense Analysis, a 12-university consortium that does research for the Federal Government.

Proposal From Faculty

In an attempt to end the dispute, a special faculty committee representing some 100 faculty members proposed last night that the students should evacuate campus buildings, in return for which the teachers would refuse to meet with their classes "until the crisis is resolved."

The committee, headed by Prof. Alan Westin of the government department, also asked the trustees to authorize the

immediate cessation of excavation at the Morningside Park construction site.

In addition, it proposed the delegation of all disciplinary matters in the current dispute to a tripartite committee consisting of students, faculty members and representatives of the administration of the university.

The faculty commitee said that "until this crisis is settled we will stand before the occupied buildings to prevent forcible entry by the police or others."

Despite the absence of formal negotiations, informal efforts to end the protest continued with intermediaries shuttling between Low Memorial Library, the university's administrative center, and the occupied buildings to talk to leaders of the Students for a Democratic Society and Negro leaders who are spearheading the protest.

Opposition to Tactics

Throughout the day, it was evident that mounting opposition to the tactics, if not the objectives, of the S.D.S. and the black student groups was emerging among faculty members and students.

The Mathematics Building was seized at 1 A.M. today by about 30 white students who went in through a window. They escorted two cleaning women from the building, then barricaded the door with desks and chairs.

Shortly after the seizure, four policemen were posted at the door.

The situation at Columbia yesterday was this:

¶No classes were held at Hamilton Hall, the main undergraduate classroom building, or at Fayerweather Hall, a social sciences building. Hamilton was occupied by some 50 Negro students and their off-campus supporters from black activist groups. Fayerweather was held by about 100 white social science students.

¶According to the university, some classes were held in Avery Hall, the architecture building occupied by about 100 white students, and normal activities were conducted in Low Memorial Library except in the area around Dr. Kirk's office, where about 60 students were in control.

¶Mass picketing of up to 200 students was conducted in Low Plaza, just below the celebrated statue of Alma Mater, and smaller groups of pickets marched under partly cloudy skies outside Kent, Schermerhorn, Dodge, Havemeyer and Lewisohn Halls, the Mathematics and Philosophy Buildings and the Law School.

The pickets did not attempt

to interfere with the movement of students, and classes were conducted normally in those buildings. There were no pickets at Uris Hall, the business administration building, or at many other university buildings.

¶Opponents of the demonstration grew more vocal. About 350 met in the Columbia gymnasium and some urged violent action to break the student demonstrators' hold on the four buildings they controlled. The opponents were dissuaded from precipitous action by acting Dean Henry S. Coleman and Jack Rohan, the basketball coach.

¶The police remained on the campus, but were out of sight except at Low Memorial Library, where about a dozen were posted around the building and another 20 to 30 were kept inside. No effort was made by the police to remove any students from the occupied buildings.

Last night, as tensions rose on the campus, 50 young people bearing signs and chanting "Columbia out of the park, support the student strike" began a march from 72d Street up Broadway toward the university.

But at 100th Stree. they were stopped by four students from the Students for a Democratic Society, who warned them that a huge crowd was gathered at 116th Street and advised them to abandon their signs and try to reach the campus in small groups.

At 116th Street, Charles Kenyatta leader of a small band of militants known as the Mau Mau and other black activists addressed a crowd, while about 100 burly white youths, some of whom made racial slurs, blocked the campus gate. Faculty members attempted to disperse the crowd.

Just before 10 P.M., about 20 Negroes said they wanted to come on the campus while the burly youths and other whites called, "Hold that line," and tried to keep them out.

City policemen dispersed the crowd blocking the gate.

Dean Coleman, using a megaphone, urged the crowd, which included Columbia students, to "cool it" and to let the marchers through.

The crowd parted and the Negroes, led by Dean Coleman and Assistant Chief Inspector Eldridge Waith led the march through the campus and onto Amsterdam Avenue.

Some of the marchers, who were 600 strong when they reached Amsterdam, went to the gymnasium site where they heard a brief speech by Mr. Kenyatta. Members of the Tactical Patrol Force of the Police Department were stationed at

the site. The crowd then dispersed.

Complicating efforts to end the campus dispute was a split between Negro students holding Hamilton Hall and white students led by the Students for a Democratic Society holding the other three buildings and conducting the picketing.

Student leaders and university sources said that although the objectives of the two groups were largely similar, they had broken over tactics, with the Negroes advocating more militance than the whites were prepared to accept.

At 1 A.M. on Wednesday, a university official said, the Negro students and their off-campus supporters in Hamilton Hall made it clear to the white students there that if they did not leave the building, they would be forcibly evicted. The white students left.

At 12:15 this morning, the Negro students inside Hamilton Hall issued a statement accusing the university of following "racist policies" and setting forth four demands and outlining terms for negotiation.

The demands were: halting construction of the gymnasium, dropping charges against all persons involved in the protest, breaking all faculty and administrative ties with the Institute for Defense Analysis, and granting a general amnesty for the students involved in the protest.

The statement continued: "When the university has stopped construction of the gym and granted an amnesty we will consider the question of negotiation with the university.

"We are prepared to remain here indefinitely until these conditions are met. We have established a cafeteria with adequate stores for all contingencies. A physician is in charge of the infirmary, morale is high. Our sanitation teams are maintaining the excellent condition of the building."

The statement was read by Ray Brown, a member of the steering committee of the Student Afro-American Society who spoke from the top of a short flight of steps to newsmen, who entered the hall by climbing over a barricade of desks, chairs and filing cabinets in the main doorway.

The briefing was the first formal conference of its type since the hall was occupied. Bundles of bedding, clothing chairs and benches were set up in a not untidy arrangement on the ground floor.

Several students wearing maroon armbands and identified as "marshals" flanked Mr. Brown as he spoke.

Yesterday afternoon, a group opposed to the demonstration collected 1,500 signatures on a petition to the administration deploring "the tasteless, inconsiderate and illegal manner" of the protest and urging severe punishment for the participants.

The campus came to life yesterday when a group of about 50 students appeared at Fayerweather Hall and demanded permission to enter. The building had been occupied by student demonstrators since shortly after midnight.

Several of those attempting to enter the building pushed their way to the door and some pounded on it, but the door was kept closed by students peering out from inside.

As the antidemonstration chants grew louder, they were matched by shouts of "Strike, strike," from supporters of the S.D.S. who were drawn to the area of grassy lawn and irises by the noise. But no police came to the scene.

Finally, Prof. Amitai Etzioni, an internationally renowned sociologist, took a bullhorn and addressed the students, who now numbered about 300.

Declaring that he was largely in sympathy with the objective of the demonstration, Professor Etzioni warned: "The disruption of the educational process goes against what you are after."

He was promptly challenged by Professor Greeman, who said, "There can be no education and no thought that is divorced from action."

Dean Coleman, who was held hostage for 23 hours in Hamilton Hall early in the demonstration, urged students to remain calm.

Dean Gets an Ovation

Mr. Coleman also declared: "I personally have no intention of seeing 2,500 of the students at Columbia College let down because of the actions of 200." The comment drew loud applause and a standing ovation from the students.

In Low Memorial Library, meanwhile, a news conference at which President Kirk and Vice President David. B. Truman were to speak, was delayed more than half an hour

until about 2:30 P.M. because talks with the student demonstrators were still being conducted.

Finally, Dr. Kirk, a portly man in a gray suit, white shirt and striped gray tie, and Dean Truman, a short dark man in a lighter gray suit, appeared before a battery of microphones to answer reporters' questions.

They seemed grim and quickly made it clear that the talks had produced no progress toward a settlement.

Dr. Kirk emphasized that "we have exercised great restraint in the use of police and security forces because at almost all costs, we wish to avoid physical confrontation."

The demonstration began shortly after noon on Tuesday.

At that time S.D.S. members and sympathizers moved into Low Library in an attempt to dramatize their demands for cessation of excavation for the gym, and termination of the university's affiliation with the

Institute for Defense Analysis, among other demands.

Turned back by guards, the students went to the site of the gym excavation at 113th Street and Morningside Drive and tore down a section of fence around the area being cleared for the $11.6-million building.

Then the students marched to Hamilton Hall and blocked Dean Coleman in his office. He remained there until midday Wednesday.

It was there that differences between the Negro and white students developed. Negro leaders of several activist groups including the Student Nonviolent Coordinating Committee, the Harlem Self-Defense Committee, and the Congress of Racial Equality, threw their support behind the black groups, and the white students were ordered to leave.

They moved to Low Memorial Library, leaving Hamilton Hall in Negro hands.

The demonstration spread early yesterday to Avery Hall, then to Fayerweather Hall.

April 26, 1968

1,000 POLICE ACT TO OUST STUDENTS FROM FIVE BUILDINGS AT COLUMBIA; MOVE IN AT UNIVERSITY'S REQUEST

Proposal by Kirk to End Dispute Spurned by Faculty Group

By SYLVAN FOX

A handpicked force of 1,000 policemen moved onto the Columbia University campus early today and began ordering student demonstrators out of five buildings the students have occupied in a tense, week-long protest.

The police moved with stunning suddenness at 2:30 A.M. while most of the city and much of the campus and its surrounding neighborhood slept.

As the hour for the police assault approached, tension

mounted sharply on the campus as groups of students held informal meetings. At 1:45 A.M., when word reached the Mathematics Building that "a bust," or police raid, was imminent, student demonstrators began strengthening their barricades and girding themselves for the assault.

WKCR, the campus radio station, at 1:30 A.M. reported that a police move appeared close, and it urged students to remain in their dormitories.

Move Delayed

The raid originally had been scheduled for 1:30 A.M. It was postponed several times because of what police officials described as "tactical delays."

A high police official said

later that the raid had been delayed to wait until Harlem was asleep.

Wearing helmets and carrying flashlights, they fanned through the darkened campus, which they had divided for purposes of the assault into seven sectors that were designated "target areas."

These were Hamilton, Avery and Fayerweather Halls, the Low Memorial Library and the Mathematics Building—all occupied structures — and the areas of 115th Street and Morningside Drive and 116th Street and Amsterdam Avenue.

Target Gets Priority

Hamilton Hall, which Negro students and a scattering of off-campus black activists had

occupied since the student uprising began last Tuesday afternoon, was the first police target.

As the police moved on Hamilton Hall, other policemen issued an ultimatum to the students occupying Low Library, demanding they leave peacefully or be ejected.

Speaking over a bullhorn, a white-helmeted policeman called to "the occupants" of Hamilton Hall, saying: "We want you to come out and come out now. We are authorized by the trustees of the university. This is it. Come out now. You made your point. Come out now."

It was understood to be the hope of the police commanders

459

that they could remove the Negro students with a minimum of force, thus making it easier for them to evict the white students from the four other occupied campus buildings.

The police commanders, who led a force that included 200 men from each of five precincts, were said to be carrying written instructions from Police Commissioner Howard R. Leary to use necessary force but to show restraint in their handling of the students.

As the first move in their coordinated attack, the police at 2 A.M. severed all telephone service and water supplies to the five occupied buildings. The student protesters had depended heavily during the demonstration on telephone communication to keep in touch with the situation in each of the buildings they held.

Meanwhile, pockets of students, many huddled under blankets against the chill night air, moved from building to building trying to see what was going on. And outside the Low Library, where about 200 students gathered in a milling crowd, a "town crier" with a bullhorn issued minute-by-minute bulletins about events leading up to the raid.

Mr. Leary, accompanied by two representatives of the university administration, was directing the opation on the campus. Chief Inspector Sanford D. Garelik supervised the force, which included members of the Emergency Service Division, policewomen and detectives, as well as uniformed patrolmen.

University Made Request

The police acted in response to a request from the administration of the university it was understood. Under normal procedure, the police would take no action on the campus, which is private property, unless formally authorized to do so by university officials.

The police intervention came after a day of futile efforts to resolve the Columbia dispute by peaceful negotiations and mediation. The Columbia administration proposed a peace plan, but it was rejected by a key faculty group as inadequate.

The decision to request the police to move into control of the troubled campus was made about 5 P.M., according to high police officers.

During the next few hours, the operation, which had been planned long before on a contingency basis, was carefully reviewed by police commanders.

At midnight, the selected task force members assembled at each of five nearby station houses. An hour and 40 minutes later, the 1,000-man force grouped at the West 100th Street police station and prepared to move onto the campus.

Throughout the operation, the campus was tightly sealed. The police blocked all entrances in an attempt to prevent any off-campus groups sympathetic to the demonstrators from going to their support.

Faculty Intervenes

Police intervention had loomed as an almost constant prospect since the student uprising began. Last Friday morning, some 25 plainclothes policemen armed with clubs moved on Low Library at the request of university officials. There was a fracas as members of an Ad Hoc Faculty Group stood at the southeast entrance to the building and refused to permit the police to pass.

During the clash, one member of the faculty was struck on the head by a club and injured, although not seriously.

A faculty delegation immediately went to Dr. Grayson Kirk, the president of Columbia, and urged him to defer any police action until attempts to mediate the dispute had been exhausted. Dr. Kirk agreed to give the Ad Hoc Faculty Group, which has led mediation efforts, more time to seek a peaceful solution.

But ever since the confrontation, tension ran high on the Morningside Heights campus, which has about 17,500 students.

Over the weekend, rumors flew around the campus that some police action would be taken against the demonstrators on Sunday night to permit the university to reopen yesterday morning.

No action came, however, as mediators continued to seek a way out of the deadlocked dispute.

Police Remain

In the meantime, the police remained on the campus as a visible but inactive presence. About 20 policemen stood guard around Low Library. Several policemen were posted at 116th Street and Broadway and at 116th Street and Amsterdam Avenue—the only two campus gates that remained open when the university was officially

closed Friday—to permit students and employes to enter.

The police had been requested to enter the campus by the university authorities on Thursday. It was the first time since May, 1965, when a campus demonstration disrupted graduation ceremonies of the Naval Reserve Officers Training Corps, that a police force had been asked to enter the university grounds.

The move by the police early this morning reflected the university administration's evident decision that negotiations and mediation had failed.

Earlier in the day, Dr. Kirk had offered a four-point peace plan that he said carried out "the essential spirit" of a faculty group's proposals to end the demonstration.

Leaders of the Ad Hoc Faculty Group, however, promptly declared that Dr. Kirk's plan fell far short of their proposals for drastic revision of Columbia's disciplinary machinery and abandonment of plans for the construction of a controversial gymnasium in Morningside Park. These were additional developments during the day:

¶A brief but angry clash erupted when supporters of students occupying President Kirk's office in Low Memorial Library and four other buildings attempted to smash their way through a human wall erected around Low by students opposed to the campus protest.

¶Theodore W. Kheel, the labor mediator, stepped into the Columbia dispute in an attempt to find a third-party solution.

Governor's Help Sought

At a meeting of the Ad Hoc Faculty Group last night, a proposal to ask Gov. Rockefeller to establish arbitration procedures to end the dispute was rejected.

But the faculty members who had been meeting in the Philosophy Building most of the day, approved a resolution asking Mayor Lindsay to intervene personally, according to one member of the group.

The group member said that two of the Mayor's aides had informed him that if the Ad Hoc Faculty Group requested the Mayor's help, the aides would recommend that Mr. Lindsay offer his services.

For the second day, there were no classes at Columbia yesterday. The university — except for Barnard, Teachers College and units removed from the Morningside Heights campus — was officially closed, as it had been on Friday.

Early this morning, about 450 students collected around the sundial in the center of the Columbia campus to listen to speakers urging support for the demonstrators.

One student speaker said he had been informed at 11:45 P.M. that "in the event of a bust" — a police raid on the demonstrators — members of the Ad Hoc Faculty Group planned to circle the occupied buildings and interpose themselves between the police and the demonstrators.

The student urged those sitting around the sundial to remain there until they saw the faculty members taking up positions, then to join them.

Shortly after midnight, the campus was a strange and eerie place. Japanese music drifted from a window of Fayerweather Hall, one of the occupied buildings, and a show of red, blue and white lights payed on a window of the building. Everywhere else on the campus, there was almost deathly silence.

Dr. Kirk said last night that "in the present circumstances there will be an announcement on the radio each morning at 6 A.M. as to when classes will be resumed."

Dr. Kirk's announcement of his four-point plan, issued by the Columbia information office in midafternoon, brought a glimmer of hope to a campus that has been gripped for days by fear that it was heading for a potentially bloody confrontation between the police and demonstrating students.

In his plan, Dr. Kirk said he was prepared to accept a faculty committee recommendation for establishment of a tripartite disciplinary commission composed of students, faculty members and members of the administration and to appoint members recommended to him by the three-member faculty committee.

Dr. Kirk also said he would "recommend to the trustees that the statutes of the university dealing with disciplinary matters be re-examined in the light of the recommendations to be submitted by the tripartite commission."

Further, the Columbia president said "matters such as the question of uniform penalties" for students involved in the protest would be referred to the tripartite commission, which he proposed should consist of seven students, eight faculty members and three representatives of the administration.

The idea of uniform penalties for the demonstrators had

been proposed by faculty leaders as an alternative to the total amnesty that the student demonstrators have been demanding as a precondition to any formal negotiations to end the protest. Uniform penalties would mean that student demonstrators would receive token punishment, probably nothing more than letters of warning from the administration.

Amnesty Is Rejected

The Columbia trustees and large numbers of faculty members have supported Dr. Kirk's rejection of amnesty. Aside from the letter of warning, the punishment for the demonstrators could range through probation, suspension or outright expulsion.

However, six leaders of the protesting group, including Mark Rudd, the Columbia chairman of the Students for a Democratic Society, are on probation because of earlier protests and even a letter of warning on top of probation would bring mandatory expulsion.

In his statement, Dr. Kirk said that he would "recommend to the trustees that they authorize me to proceed with discussions" on the problem of the gym in Morningside Park. Excavation work at the gymnasium site was halted at the request of Mayor Lindsay on Friday, and it is widely felt on the campus that work will never be resumed.

"I commend and fully share the objectives of the resolution adopted by the Ad Hoc Faculty Group on April 28," Dr. Kirk said in his statement. He went on to say that he was confident that his proposals "carry out the essential spirit of those proposals."

But a leader of the Ad Hoc Faculty Group, who asked not to be identified, said of Dr. Kirk's statement: "There's no give here."

Views of the Faculty

The faculty member said that Dr. Kirk had said only that he would recommend that disciplinary affairs be "re-examined," while the Ad Hoc Group had called in its resolution for establishment of a tripartite commission that would have "ultimate judicial review on all matters affecting university discipline."

The faculty member said also that Dr. Kirk's statement indicated only that he would undertake further discussion of the Morningside Park gymnasium plan. The Ad Hoc Group, it was noted, had called for the creation by Mayor Lindsay of a panel to review the gymnasium plan, adopt an alternative to the present plan and, if the alternative involved keep-

ing the gym on its present site, submitting the matter to representatives of Harlem, where there has been strenuous opposition to construction of the gymnasium.

"He's taking the posture of a neutral party," the ad hoc leader said of Dr. Kirk.

As Dr. Kirk's statement was circulating around the campus, where thousands of students milled around and held informal meetings, Mr. Kheel arrived outside Hamilton Hall, which is occupied by Negro students and a scattering of off-campus black activists.

Mr. Kheel was with Dr. Kenneth Clark, a City College psychology professor and the president of the Metropolitan Applied Research Center.

The two men waited outside heavily barricaded Hamilton Hall, normally the focus of Columbia College undergraduate classroom activity, for about 45 minutes. Then, at 1:45, Dr. Clark was invited inside.

Kheel on Crutches

Fifteen minutes later, Mr. Kheel, carrying two metal crutches to ease the strain resulting from a recent leg operation, was summoned inside.

The mediator, who has participated in settlements of transit strikes, newspaper strikes and a host of other labor disputes, climbed the tables and filing cabinets blocking Hamilton Hall's door. When some students reached out to aid him, he said: "No help, please I can make it."

Mr. Kheel remained in Hamilton Hall, meeting for about three hours with leaders of the Society of Afro-American Students, which, with the Students for a Democratic Society, has been leading the protest.

Afterward Mr. Kheel said that he and Dr. Clark had "made several suggestions for a possible resolution and the leaders have agreed to study the suggestions." He declined to divulge the nature of the proposals.

Mr. Kheel, who was joined in the Hamilton Hall talks by Dr. Clark and William H. Booth, the city's Human Rights Commissioner, then left for conferences with representatives of the Columbia administration.

He met for two hours with Dr. Kirk and David B. Truman, the vice president of the university.

"We had informal discussions with President Kirk and Dean Truman," Mr. Kheel said of his talks with the administrators. "We made some suggestions."

Before he entered Hamilton Hall, Mr. Kheel, who is chairman of the board of the Metro-

politan Applied Research Center, said he had gone to Columbia at the invitation of Dr. Clark, who met with students in Hamilton Hall on Saturday.

While Mr. Kheel met with Negro students in Hamilton Hall, opponents of the protest, who have organized a group called the Coalition of the Majority, maintained a solid blockade around Low Library, where student demonstrators have occupied President Kirk's office since the uprising began on Tuesday afternoon.

About 250 antiprotest students stood shoulder to shoulder along the west side of the domed and pillared building vowing to prevent any food or medical supplies from reaching the demonstrators inside. The blockade, which was totally effective, was erected at 5:15 P.M. Sunday and maintained day and night.

At 3:35 P.M., as reports circulated on the campus that several of the students in Low Library were suffering from diarrhea and were running low on food, an attempt was made to breach the blockade.

About 60 supporters of the demonstration, which is aimed principally at halting construction of the Morningside Park gym and ending Columbia's association with the 12-university consortium known as the Institute of Defense Analyses, began marching around Low Library chanting "Food, food, food."

The foes of the demonstration locked arms and formed a solid wall along a hedgerow that skirts the building. Behind the wall of students, several faculty members wearing white arm bands braced themselves for trouble.

On their third circuit of the library building, the chanting supporters of the demonstration turned from the red brick walkway and threw themselves against the line of opposition forces.

Fists swung wildly as about 40 supporters and an equal number of opponents of the demonstration broke into open conflict for the first time.

"Hold that line, hold that line," the opposition forces shouted. "We're trying to get food up there," a student screamed.

"They're welcome to come out any time they want to," a majority coalition student replied.

While the battle raged, supporters of the demonstration hurled sandwiches, oranges, grapefruits and cigarettes to the demonstrators poised on the second floor ledge outside Dr. Kirk's office. Much of the food fell short of its target, but some was caught by the demonstrators amid cheers from their supporters below.

Another Fight Flares

The violence subsided after few minutes as faculty members moved between the fighting students and separated them. But moments lafter, another fistfight erupted a short distance away. This, too, was halted by the faculty members who walked up and down the line urging the students on both sides to "cool it."

Although about 30 policemen were within 100 feet of the scene of the violence, they did not move to interfere. One police official, explaining that "we don't go in unless there is a cross-complaint," said: "This is an administrative thing. It's a scholastic thing."

The failure of the police to take any action was a disappointment to at least one demonstrator on the ledge outside Dr. Kirk's office.

"We want the real cops," he cried as fist-fighting broke out. His remark was understood to reflect the feeling of some of the most militant demonstrators that a violent confrontation with the police would prove to the world the "brutality" of American society and the need for revolutionary change.

No attempt was made by opponents of the demonstration to blockade any building except Low Library. In the other buildings, food moved freely to the demonstrators and they entered and left the buildings at will.

A leader of the Coalition of the Majority said no effort was being made to cut off supplies to the other buildings because "Low Library is a symbol of the administrative center of our university" and because "we don't have enough people."

At 6 P.M., as the potential danger of another confrontation between the opponents and supporters of the demonstration increased, about 40 policemen were moved into position along the west side of Low Library between the two student groups.

During the evening, several outside groups brought food for the beleaguered students occupying Hamilton Hall and the Low Library.

At about 9 P.M. 200 persons, mostly Negroes, gathered at the entrance to Columbia at 116th Street and Amsterdam Avenue —one of the two gates along with the one at 116th Street and Broadway that remained open—and sent a delegation of six persons into the campus carrying food for the students in Hamilton Hall.

The police checked each box of food before permitting the bearers to enter the tightly sealed campus.

An hour later, about 35 persons, white and Negro, were allowed to pass through the

Amsterdam Avenue gate with food. They went to Hamilton Hall first, but when they were informed there that food was plentiful, they moved to the blockaded Low Library.

The police there, however, would not permit the food to be passed in to the students occupying President Kirk's office.

500 Reported Involved

Estimates of the number of demonstrators who occupied the five buildings at Columbia varied. Student leaders claim about 1,000. Most faculty sources put the figure closer to about 500.

In addition to holding Dr. Kirk's offices in Low Library, the students are occupying Fayerweather Hall, Avery Hall, the Mathematics Building, where they have flown a red flag and declared the building a commune, and Hamilton Hall, which is held entirely by Negro students.

Two other buildings are occupied by students seeking to avoid their take-over by the demonstrators. One is held by a group of general studies students, and the other, Uris Hall, is held by a group of business students.

The New York Times (by Barton Silverman)

MARCH ON CAMPUS: Units of the police force moving toward center of the Columbia University campus at midnight last night. Scene was Amsterdam Avenue at 116th Street.

April 30, 196

Combat and Compassion at Columbia

By A. M. ROSENTHAL

It was 4:30 in the morning and the president of the university leaned against the wall of the room that had been his office. He passed a hand over his face.

"My God," he said, "how could human beings do a thing like this."

For hours Grayson Kirk had heard the sounds of Columbia in chaos—the police sirens, the smashing of glass, the chants of "Kirk must go," the shrieked obscenities.

Now the campus was quiet except for the taunts and shouts of the arrested students waiting to be taken away in the paddy wagons. They did not reach the room in which Dr. Kirk stood.

He wandered about the room. It was almost empty

of furniture. The desks and chairs had been smashed, broken and shoved into adjoining rooms by the occupying students, who had just been led down the stairs, manacled and whistling "We Shall Overcome."

Dr. Kirk picked his way slowly among the dirty blankets, half-eaten sandwiches, comic books and tin cans on his spattered green rug. He looked around for some of his mementoes.

"I think I found one," he said. "An ashtray."

He was still neat and dapper but his face was gray and he seemed to move and walk in a trance. So did almost everybody in the room. A policeman picked up a book on the floor and said: "The whole world is in these

books; how could they do this to these books?" and put it down.

Dr. David B. Truman, vice president of the university, was there, too, exhaustion on his face. He wandered through the suite, back and forth from wrecked room to wrecked room and at one point he said, almost to himself, "Do you think they will know why we had to do this, to call in the police? Will they know what we went through before we decided?"

A police inspector strolled over to Dr. Kirk and silently showed him something he had just picked up from the floor that a student had left behind—a piece of iron pipe tied to a bit of rope. "What is it?" Dr. Kirk asked. The inspector looked surprised.

"A knuckle duster," he said.

"Unbelievable," Dr. Kirk said.

Somehow the whole night seemed unbelievable, a mixture of moods that seemed to have no relationship to each other; violence and compassion, talk of hatred and death and talk of gentle philosophies, ugliness of action and of speech, and moments of tenderness, a place of learning become a place of destruction.

"Columbia is finished," a student said as he heard the smashing of glass in the Mathematics Building.

"It isn't, it isn't," the girl next to him said. "Please, please," she was weeping. The boy walked away and the girl stayed and for a long time she cried, standing in the dark.

Smothered in Obscenity

Most of the university was dark. Lights showed from a lamppost here and there but they seemed somehow just to accentuate the grayness of the campus rather than brighten it. Everybody moved in shadows,

462

alone or in groups running from building to building to try to put their bodies between the police and the doors, or just to watch and see what was happening to Columbia.

There was no one tone or feel to the night—except perhaps a general sense of desolation. There was instead a sensation, as one walked about the campus, of isolation and remoteness, of incident, emotion and tempo.

There was, at times, a sense of almost being smothered in a stream of obscenity. It was not casual obscenity that came from angry students, but hard, cold and directed at target—a policeman, a newspaperman, a stranger, and most particularly at anybody older.

Three middle-aged men were standing near Hamilton Hall, just beyond the fringe of the crowd. A young man walked by, stopped, peered in the gloom and screamed in a voice strangled with fury:

"I hope you old . . . die! I hope all you old . . . die. Go ahead and watch us and die!"

A Sense of Fear, Too

And then, a few paces away and a few moments later, a young woman, hardly older than the young man but with a white armband worn by faculty members, spoke softly and kindly to the same men and told them how she certainly did not approve of occupation of the buildings by the students but said that the administration had handled it all wrong and that at least the boys and girls in the buildings had made Columbia awake to what they felt in their souls.

One of the men asked her then if she would go out with a "colored man." The young instructor said that she certainly might but somehow she indicated that that did not seem to be exactly to the point.

Some of the students outside the buildings seemed seized with a kind of nervous exhilaration. They leaped up and down, laughed and one boy shouted "go it bear, go it man."

There were others who almost trembled with fear, not so much for themselves but at what they were seeing on their campus.

On the steps of one of the buildings, as the police moved and swayed in unison to shoulder through the blockade of students before the door, a boy and a girl stood with their arms around each other.

"Come, Petey," the girl kept saying. "Come away. I don't want to see any more. Come away, Petey, please Petey." They stayed, moving back a few steps from time to time, then forward again and just did not seem to be able to go away, though they looked so forlorn.

EXPLAINS ACTION: Dr. Grayson Kirk, left, president of Columbia University, with Dean David B. Truman at a news conference yesterday discussing the use of police.

There were students who flung themselves passionately into danger, rushing past policemen to guard the doors with their bodies. And there were a few students who concentrated, quite coolly, at urging others into danger.

A line of silent policemen was drawn up at the far edge of the lawn in front of the Mathematics Building, keeping the crowd well away from the doors. A few hundred students stood behind a hedge, a dozen feet away from the police. One young man stepped over the hedge and kept shouting: "Come on, step over, join us, move up."

Some of the youngsters did and moved up to the police line. The young barker stood back, well away from any policeman's reach and kept up his pitch.

There were moments of plain, almost tangible hatred between some of the students opposing the demonstrations and some of them supporting the youngsters barricaded in the buildings.

"Go home and wash, you little tramp," one boy shouted at a demonstrator.

"Wash your dirty mind," she shrieked back.

But in a shadow here and there some students who could not understand each other did try to.

"I came here for an education," said a boy wearing a jacket and tie. A jacket and tie had suddenly become a protest uniform of its own—protest against the protesters.

A girl wrapped in a blanket against the chill moved toward him a few steps.

"Yes, so did I," she said.

"But don't you think that this is part of education — to be part of the world?"

"Is it education to break into buildings and just go ahead and smash and smash? Is that education?"

The boy was not angry and neither was the girl when she said:

"No, I am not for violence but the administration wouldn't do anything, don't you see?"

They sat down in the damp grass and for a while, softly but quite urgently, talked to each other.

There was, on the campus, really only two groups of participants throughout the long night who seemed to be in any relationship to each other and to have any significance—the students and the police. There were faculty members with their armbands who rushed from group to group, there were observers from Mayor Lindsay's office, there were reporters and cameramen but only the police and students seemed to have any real role at all.

Before the police arrived in force, moving according to an intricately detailed precinct by precinct plan of operation, the campus was alive with rumors that this was to be the night of the bust. Across from Low Memorial Library a knot of students was kept informed of the latest rumors through a loudspeaker — "We hear they are moving up a couple of trucks with barricades." "They've got patrol wagons out on the streets."

Almost nobody left the campus and there were mo-

ments when there was a sense of the curtain going up — and of anticipation.

When the police arrived, marching in formation from various parts of the campus, a couple of hundred students formed a kind of barricade in front of the police command post, a series of rooms on the first floor of a wing in Low. The police let them stay for a long time just keeping enough room for policemen to come and go.

There were scores of plainclothesmen in casual clothes and when one of them clouted a young man who had shoved or taunted them there were indignant cries from the crowd: "Show your badges!"

A uniformed policeman on the outskirts said: "I guess the idea is, O.K. to sock somebody who hasn't got a badge. College education."

Around the campus there were a few policemen and plainclothesmen who delivered themselves, to each other, of four-letter opinions of some of the students but for the most part the police were silent throughout the evening. Some of them seemed almost fond, in a professional way, of the students.

"Pretty good crowd," said one officer strolling about the campus. "A little singing, a little moving, that's all right. Not much running, that would be bad, running. Not too hard to handle."

But sometimes there were blackjacks used during the night, and fists, and the edge of hatred on the campus of Columbia was as sharp as a knife. There were students who were hurt and there were students who pretended they were hurt. One boy was pulled out of the Mathematics Building, dumped fairly gently on the ground to await the patrol wagon and, a moment later, began shouting "police brutality." Everybody laughed.

But in other parts of the campus there were students with bloody heads. And for every student with a bloody head there were 50 who saw him and were filled with a sense of horror.

Whatever the degree of harsh force that grew out of the police's orders to clear the buildings of students, there was no sense of satisfaction in the command post.

Police Commissioner Howard R. Leary moved among his senior officers, received reports of the progress of the clearing process, but nobody talked of triumph or victory, but just of a quite nasty job.

The Commissioner left Low about 5 A.M. The patrol wagons were drawn up in front of the building and from behind the steel mesh students inside taunted the few adults on the steps.

"I'm going to rape your daughter," a young man shouted.

"First they arrest the workers and now they arrest the intellectuals," came a girl's shriek from the wagon.

Somebody laughed and said: "Intellectuals," and there was a stream of curses from the wagon.

The Commissioner did not laugh. Near him, a few steps above, a thin boy in jeans shouted something about students having been beaten.

"Is this what your parents slaved and worked for to send you to college, so you could break up the university," one of the adults, who had walked onto the campus, screamed at the boy, moving toward him.

"Leave him alone," said the Commissioner, "leave him alone."

That was about 5 o'clock in the morning. The students had been pushed out of the campus onto Broadway. They stayed for hours and so did Grayson Kirk, in his office one flight up in Low.

Kirk Says All Steps Necessary Will Be Taken for Peace

By SYLVAN FOX

Dr. Grayson Kirk, the president of Columbia University, warned yesterday that he would use "all measures necessary to restore peace" in the face of continuing violence on the Morningside Heights campus.

"I think it is important for me to state," he said at a news conference in the austere, columned rotunda of Low Memorial Library, "that if disciplinary probation, suspension or even permanent expulsion must be dealt to any number of students, this action will be taken."

Dr. Kirk issued his stern warning after a chaotic morning in which the Columbia campus, scene of a crippling student uprising that began on April 23, had been plunged into a frenzy of violence. Sixty-eight persons were injured.

Fires burned in campus buildings, leading to an immediate Fire Department investigation of the possibility of arson. Hundreds of students roamed the campus in the pre-dawn hours and many hurled bricks at the police and they smashed windows and doors of university buildings.

Waves of policemen, who earlier had peacefully removed student demonstrators from a campus building the students had seized, swept through the university grounds clubbing, kicking and punching student protesters, who flung back rocks, taunts and obscenities.

Responding to rumors of further planned outbreaks on the campus, Columbia last night canceled its evening class schedule and closed the campus to all but resident students.

City policemen stood guard at the entrance to virtually every campus building. It was the first time policemen had been stationed on the campus since May 9.

Although the campus was sealed, a rally in support of the student uprising was held shortly after 6 P.M. outside the university gate at 116th Street and Amsterdam Avenue.

About 500 persons gathered in front of the gate and almost 1,000 more stood on a bridge that crosses Amsterdam Avenue from Kent Hall to the Law School. One hundred policemen were in the area, but there were no disturbances.

Rudd Addresses Rally

At the rally, Mr. Rudd said there were "hundreds of plainclothes men" in the crowd, "and they are here to provoke us."

He asserted that the strike leaders would like to "sit down at the bargaining table" with the administration, "but they're not going to let us because these men are bourgeoisie."

"This university is building on the sweat of the black people and other people of this university and they can't keep it up," Mr. Rudd said. "They can't turn us around. We'll strike."

His last word brought an insistent response of "strike, strike" from the crowd.

The actions of the student protesters early yesterday and Tuesday night drew strong condemnation from the 12-member executive committee of the Columbia faculty.

But the moderate Students for a Reconstructed University, which had broken with the more radical Strike Coordinating Committee in a disagreement over tactics, charged that "the administration provoked" the disturbance by starting disciplinary action against student demonstrators.

A spokesman for the Strike Coordinating Committee charged that Columbia "can only attempt to solve problems by the use of repressive force, of police force." He accused the police of having beaten students with billy clubs and of having charged into a campus building with pistols drawn.

A spokesman for the Police Department denied the police had drawn their pistols. But three New York Times reporters saw policemen carrying their guns in their hands. No shots were fired, however.

Negroes Threaten to Quit

In another development, 100 Negro students at Columbia threatened to leave the university if any Negro students were suspended or expelled as a result of their roles in the protest.

In a letter to Dr. Kirk signed by "The Black Students of Hamilton Hall," the students said some had received letters summoning them to their deans for disciplinary discussions.

When it was first seized on April 23, Hamilton Hall was occupied by white and Negro students. A few hours later, the latter ordered the whites to leave. The Negroes then occupied the building until they were removed, without violence, by the police on April 30.

So far as could be ascertained, no black students occupied Hamilton Hall when it was seized for the second time on Tuesday.

Columbia University has a total of 17,500 students. Of that number, 2,700 are in Columbia College, which has classrooms and offices in Hamilton Hall.

About 125 of the college's students are Negroes. A university source said that there were about 350 Negroes enrolled in the university.

A total of 177 persons were arrested during the early morning police sweep through the campus, according to court sources, bringing to almost 1,-000 the number of arrests resulting from the four-week uprising. The university said at least 48 of those seized yesterday were not connected with Columbia.

At least 68 persons were injured in the violence. Like the 48 injured when the police raided the campus on April 30, most of them were students. But the total included 17 policemen, many of whom were struck by bricks thrown by student protesters.

The police staged several charges across the campus and into its buildings in the early morning.

In one that took place at about 4:30 A.M., a tall, red-haired member of the Tactical Patrol Force was seen cracking a student across the skull with his nightstick. Bleeding, the student fell to the ground. As he lay there, in sight of several newsmen and students, a second uniformed policeman bent over him and struck him again with his nightstick.

The youth was taken by stretcher from the campus by volunteer medical personnel.

Asked at 5:15 A.M. if he was satisfied with the way his men had behaved during the campus police action, Police Commissioner Howard R. Leary said: "No comment. No word at all."

Deputy Commissioner Jacques Nevard, who is in charge of press relations for the Police Department, responded to the same question by saying: "We have no reason not to be pleased."

"Force must be used by the police to overcome deliberate resistance," Mr. Nevard said later, "and the use of it does not constitute brutality. Only an excessive amount of force constitutes police brutality."

Hamilton Hall Seizure

The violence erupted on the campus after 250 student protesters, led by the leftist Students for a Democratic Society, had seized Hamilton Hall, the center of the men's undergraduate college, for the second time in a month.

The seizure was ostensibly intended to protest the suspension a short time earlier of Mark Rudd, the 20-year-old junior who is the campus S.D.S. leader, and three of his supporters. They were suspended for refusing to appear at their dean's office, as requested, to discuss their role in the protest as a prelude to disciplinary action.

Hamilton Hall itself was cleared with virtually no violence at about 2:30 A.M. yesterday, some 10 hours after it had been seized. But a short time after the student protesters were removed through tunnels below the building, fires broke out in Hamilton and elsewhere around the campus, students began hurling bricks, and the clashes with the police ensued.

Mr. Rudd, who was arrested by a plainclothes policeman who had infiltrated the S.D.S., was charged with riot, inciting to riot, criminal trespass and criminal solicitation. If convicted, he could be sentenced to more than six years in prison. He was released in $2,500 bail posted by his father, Jacob Rudd of Maplewood, N. J.

Two others, Martin Kenner, 27 years old, of 174 West 189th Street, and Anthony Sager, 23, of 855 West End Avenue, were charged with conspiracy, riot and inciting to riot, and were held in $5,000 bail each. Their connection with Columbia was not immediately ascertainable.

Radical Castigated

The highest bail, $7,500, was imposed on Edward J. Hyman, a mustached Columbia radical charged with riot and inciting to riot. Criminal Court Judge Hyman Solniker set the high bail after Mr. Hyman had said he was a nephew of Supreme Court Justice Mitchell D. Schweitzer and the Supreme Court justice had called the claim "an unmitigated lie."

In his statement on the crisis, Dr. Kirk noted that the "necessary evacuation" of Hamilton Hall and the arrest of the first group of demonstrators, of whom there were about 130, was "gratifyingly peaceful."

He said that after Hamilton Hall was cleared, however, "action developed, with a reported 1,000 people ranging through the campus in uncontrolled violence."

Dr. Kirk said seven buildings had suffered extensive damage; more than 100 bricks had been gouged from campus walks and hurled at windows, and fires had been set by burning manuscripts and other valuable, and even irreplace-

able, papers taken from professors' offices.

In addition, the university president said "A potted tree was dragged 20 yards across a terrace and dropped on a police vehicle parked in an in-

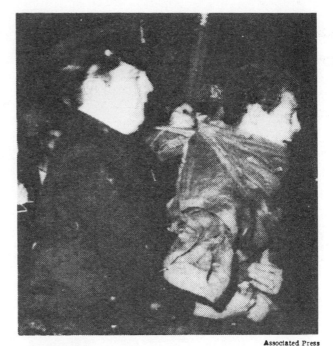

Associated Press

A protester being hustled from campus by a patrolman

terior court almost 100 feet below."

Dr. Kirk said that the student strike committee had made it plain that "theirs is a political action—one that goes far beyond their grievances with the university."

May 23, 1968

Columbia Rebels Find Disruption Pays

By NAN ROBERTSON

A significant number of students at Columbia University have acquired a new and shocking belief. They believe that disruption pays.

They have discovered that the use of force and the tactics of intransigent confrontation can engulf the classic democratic processes of compromise and negotiation.

The radicals have learned different lessons from the assassination of Senator Robert F. Kennedy than some. The most extreme seem to see no connection between the violence and unreason that struck him down, and the tactics that provoked violence on their own campus.

In interviews, they expressed the belief that the assassination

was yet another manifestation of sickness in the American society they despised and an illustration of why more violence was inevitable.

Yet, it is true they have achieved something, and it is more than some people may think. Their rebellion brought results and, possibly, long-needed reform.

They have shown the university and the outside world that they cannot be ignored — and that they are angry. They have forced the suspension of construction of the gymnasium in Morningside Park that became a symbol of racism and exploitation to them and to some residents of Harlem. They have focused attention on the university's affiliation with the Institute for Defense Analyses, a link that a university committee

last week recommended be broken. And they have generated widespread support for substantial reform of the university's administrative structure, which has not been altered since 1810.

The response to these calls for structural reform has brought the beginnings of tangible action. A faculty executive committee, a committee of trustees and student groups will work through the summer on proposals for the restructuring of Columbia University.

But in making these gains, the student rebels paid a heavy price. More than 70 have been suspended from the university, a move that in many instances is tantamount to their expulsion since they cannot be readmitted without submitting formal applications that are unlikely to be received favorably. Still more suspensions are expected during the months ahead.

Felony Charges Faced

In addition, several of the student rebel leaders face serious felony charges growing out of the two police raids on the campus and could be sent to prison for as much as seven years.

Moreover, for the most extreme campus radicals, who had hoped through the uprising to mobilize broad community support that would extend far beyond the university itself, the response of Harlem was disappointing and demoralizing. While some community support was manifest on Morningside Heights, efforts by the student protesters to win the backing of large numbers of Negroes never succeeded.

But in the process, a small radical core succeeded in traumatizing and embittering an entire campus, pulling large numbers of neutral or hostile students and faculty toward the left. The catalyst, as always, was the bloody intervention of the police—every cause needs its martyrs as well as its

465

demons. Committed radicals know this better than most.

Aim Was a Radical Campus

Student protest leaders have said publicly that their aim had been to "radicalize the campus." Columbia's administration now concedes that this phenomenon has occurred.

The protesters who struck the campus may force the resignation of President Grayson Kirk and others. Theodore W. Kheel, one of the nation's most imaginative and successful mediators, called the situation now "beyond repair—the only thing that will put Columbia together again will be Kirk's resignation and a clean slate. You can't patch it up with Humpty-Dumpty methods."

It is crucial to distinguish among the three key groups in this student uprising.

There are the white radicals, most intransigent of them all, led by and clustered around the New Left Students for a Democratic Society. Behind these, very quietly, are a handful of members of the Progressive Labor party, a Maoist group.

There are the black militants, with whom Mr. Kheel and others talked during the crisis days, following April 23—and found to be extraordinarily disciplined, pragmatic and principally concerned about the Harlem community protesting the gym. They were removed peaceably from Hamilton Hall, the campus building they joined S.D.S. in seizing to dramatize their opposition to the gym, one week after occupying it.

An Offshoot of S.D.S.

The third group of strikers calls itself Students for a Restructured University. Liberal and left-liberal in leaning, these students still think of the S. D.S. as their mentor.

They broke away from the white radicals after charging verbal intimidation, manipulation of their aims and support, and total contempt on the part of some radical leaders for the rights and opinions of those who disagreed with them.

This last group, like the black students, does not speak of revolution in the society. They hope to reform the university. Yet, "if we succeed, it will be because of the radicals," said John Thoms, leader of the moderates in S.R.U.

A survey conducted by Columbia's Bureau of Applied Social Research found that 58 per cent of the students and 51 per cent of the faculty who responded to a bureau questionnaire supported the objectives of the student uprising, but the survey showed that 77 per cent of the responding faculty mem-

bers and 68 per cent of the responding students opposed the tactics of the protest.

The findings were based on a questionnaire mailed to about 2,000 faculty members and 3,400 students. A 50 per cent response from each group was obtained.

All the protest groups operated against a background that included several sources of malaise on the Columbia campus: Many students and faculty members considered the university administration remote and inaccessible; the structure of the institution did nothing to discourage the faculty's predisposition to pay far more attention to its teaching and research than to its role in governing the university; there were few if any effective channels for student-faculty-administration dialogue; the student body was deeply troubled by the war in Vietnam, the draft, racial tensions in the United States.

Against this background, the university in September, 1967, ordered a ban on demonstrations within campus buildings. The ban provoked immediate protests by leftist students and set the stage for the uprising

Spearheading the uprising was the S.D.S. group, headed by 20-year-old Mark Rudd. It is the group that has baffled and fascinated outsiders and kept the Columbia strike boiling for six weeks — the longest sustained student boycott in the history of American universities. What are they like, why are they angry, what do they want?

A Pattern Emerges

After extensive interviews with Columbia's radical student leaders, a pattern in their backgrounds emerges. It is strikingly similar to the pattern evident across the nation, which surfaced following long interviews by The New York Times of student political and social activists at a dozen other campuses last November and again in April.

The activists are typically very bright and predominantly Jewish, usually reared in affluent or financially comfortable families in the big cities and suburbs of the Eastern Seaboard. They are students of the humanities rather than the sciences. Their fathers came of ago during the Great Depression of the nineteen-thirties and were often insecure about money and jobs, if not downright needy.

Many of them are now successful in the professions or creative fields. They are permissive parents, politically oriented toward liberalism and the left.

The New York Times

WORRIED OFFICIALS: Dr. Grayson Kirk, right, president, and Dr. David B. Truman, vice president of Columbia University, crossing campus after a meeting of school's professors April 28. The meeting condemned seizures.

The overwhelming majority of radical leaders at Columbia said their parents had been sympathetic to their protests: more loving than judging. The proud "my son, the revolutionary" response of Mrs. Jacob Rudd, mother of Mark, was absolutely typical.

In private conversations, Columbia's white radical leaders often seem extremely appealing, by contrast with a public posture that has appeared at times to be truculent, rigid and obscene. Many of them are sensitive, thoughtful and express idealistic goals.

A Paranoidal View

The most extreme possess a simplistic and almost paranoidal view of history and events, seeing every part and cog of the establishment as being in interlocking conspiracy or combined interest with

every other against the oppressed — including students. These also seem self-righteous and absolutely bent on having their own way.

"Their moral arrogance is incredible," said Allan Silver, an assistant professor of sociology and a leftist who was an important member of the faculty committee trying to negotiate with the strikers in the early stages of the rebellion.

A professor who said he could not be quoted by name because he is a member of a faculty committee to restructure Columbia shared Mr. Silver's view of the hardliners. "These students," he said, "would exact a conformity from others that makes Joe McCarthy look like a civil libertarian."

Moreover, the tactics they have used in seizing buildings, holding hostages, rifling admin-

The New York Times

Student perched in window of building near campus signaling to rebel demonstrators on June 4, commencement day.

istration files and keeping other students from attending classes does not disturb them.

"The coercion we have used is insignificant compared to the coercion used by this university," said Ron Carver, a student who was badly beaten by the police in one of the clashes. "The use of the police is an example—it brings it home."

Another radical leader, Lewis Cole, argues like most other protesters that Columbia students had exhausted every legal channel of protest such as picketing, petitions and rallies.

"It is regrettable that people can't attend classes and continue their normal function," he said. "But I would say our ends did justify the means—they are the only means allowable to us. Our rights and needs have been consistently unsatisfied."

Parallel With Labor

Mr. Cole and others compared the student strike to labor strikes and sit-downs where "people are hurt because they can't go to work."

The assassination of Senator Kennedy produced such conclusions among the radical students as this, from Robert Dillon, a member of S.D.S. and the Strike Coordinating Committee:

"What creates the violence in this country is the political decay. The decay is what brought on the assassination. I am absolutely against the use of terrorism and I don't think the taking of Kennedy's life had anything to do with leftists.

"This country must be rebuilt. In the process the old order will repress such a movement. They repressed it with police at Columbia and they repress it with political assas-

sinations. The weaker they get, the more violent and depraved they become."

J. Michael Nichols, a leader of the Students for a Restructured University, expressed a similar view of the assassination. He said:

"This just demonstrated how peaceful tactics in America are being choked at the core. The people who advocate peaceful change seem to be the ones who get struck down. And the result among their followers is frustration. It looks like more people are going to start listening to those who say that you have to fight back. This is the logical outcome of a system that beats you down all the time instead of listening and trying to help."

He likened the police who put down the demonstrations at Columbia to Senator Kennedy's assailant.

Even some of the striking students who are not radicals are saying now that while they do not agree with the tactics of Mark Rudd and his followers, the more extreme group has élan, tenacity and courage.

Log-Jams Are Broken

And a senior told Warner R. Schilling, a professor of government who allied himself with the student antistrikers: "I feel like I just wasted three and a half years trying to change this university. I played the game of rational discourse and persuasion. Now there's a mood of reconstruction. All the log-jams are broken—violence pays. The tactics of obstruction weren't right, weren't justifiable, but look what happened."

George Keller, editor of the alumni magazine Columbia College Today, said the response of the "civil liberatarian leftist" segments of the faculty to this was reflexive:

"A chill goes up their backs when they hear it. They recall the Joe McCarthy times when all those people stood by and said: 'I don't agree with McCarthy's tactics, but he's cleaning up America—clearing out all those Reds and fellow-travelers.'"

The faculty remembers, but the students do not. They were toddlers when the late Senator Joseph R. McCarthy of Wisconsin investigated communism in a way that bought widespread charges that he trampled on civil liberties and constitutional rights, intimidating a nation. He is ancient history to them.

Further, radicals everywhere have read and absorbed the political philosophers of Herbert Marcuse, a professor at the University of California in San Diego. In his essay on "Repressive Tolerance," a key passage reads:

"I believe that there is a

'natural right' of resistance for oppressed and overpowered minorities to use extralegal means if the legal ones have proved to be inadequate. Law and order are always and everywhere the law and order which protect the established hierarchy. . . . "

The students have also been exposed for almost a decade to the example of conscience set by the Rev. Dr. Martin Luther King Jr. and the tactics of non-violent civil disobedience in the civil rights cause.

But a professor who is sympathetic to almost all the aims and grievances of the students, if not their tactics, said they did not make a further connection. It is that Dr. King was willing to violate a law he believed to be unjust and then suffer the consequence of his actions by going to jail.

"The students don't want to be punished and yet they want moral support for their actions," he said. "They argue that Dr. King had to go to jail because he violated properly enacted laws whereas they are being ruled by fiat—Columbia's trustees are not democratically chosen; they elect themselves to the board.

"What the worst of them don't see in their priggish moral fervor is that this kind of Anthony Comstock-thinking leads to banning books and smashing saloons."

Ideologically, the white radical students at Columbia and elsewhere in America are hard to pin down, particularly with the labels of the Old Left of the nineteen-thirties.

Soviet Union Detested

They read Marx, Marcuse and the tracts of Ernesto (Che) Guevara; they admire Cuba, but do not necessarily believe that the Cuban type of revolution could succeed here; they detest the Soviet Union as bureaucratic and imperialistic and they abhor the rigidities of the Communist party U.S.A. Some believe themselves to be Maoists, others call themselves Marxists or Socialists or anarchists.

The S.D.S. supporters say again and again that they do not have a "blueprint" for changing society, although they often talk about "participatory democracy" as a doctrine of their movement. This is a concept that purports to take representative democracy one step further to give each person a voice in the decisions and processes that affect his life. Despite endless discussion and votes by students within the seized campus buildings, however, opponents accuse S.D.S. of verbal intimidation and "manipulatory democracy."

Ron Carver, who has worked

long and with the sincerest dedication to try to change the lot of the black poor in the South, said the first goal of S.D.S. was to clarify the role of the university in the community, "burst the lie" that Columbia was a benevolent force and "educate" people to the fact that it was really an exploitive landlord with tremendous real estate holdings.

He said the second S.D.S. objective was to change that role.

"It's wrong to say that just because we don't have a blueprint we're not correct in wanting to change that political role—or not correct in understanding in which direction the change has to go."

The response of the fiery Mr. Rudd was different. When one Columbia official asked him what his program was, he shouted back: "I don't have a program. I have a vision of a better world than yours, you mother——!"

Society Seen As Fat

A response to ideological questions from many Columbia radicals, including Ted Gold, a former vice chairman of S.D.S., was: "I suppose I'm a Marxist, but not by reading books—by looking at society"—a society they see as fat, smug, hypocritical and inhumane.

This is an important clue for people who tend to dismiss rebellious students at Columbia and elsewhere simply as spoiled, rich, bored children who want what they want right now, but are not sure what it is.

Professor Silver elaborated:

"The radical leaders and their sympathizers are often among the most morally committed students in America. The 9-to-5 life, the mortgage, the ranch house in the suburb —they're running away from that.

"My generation ran away from a suffocating lower-class environment. Where in America do you run? Who employs an intellectual? Where do you own your own mind? Where but the universities? They know it before they get here."

Professor Silver cited a survey taken several years ago among freshmen entering Columbia College, the nucleus of the present revolt. Forty-four per cent said they wished to become teachers.

In Search of a Home

"A lot of them come here seeking a permanent home. They find a filthy house. They perceive the arbitrary authority of the professors, the pressures of grades, of graduate schools, the draft, early specialization. these are real problems.

"They really want to get at

society, but they're not in American society here. They're young. They have no access to power. The only thing they can force to respond to them is the university—tolerant of their ways, vulnerable, a soft touch.

"But they are sons of the academy more than they would like to admit," Mr. Silver said. He mentioned one of the S.D.S. proposals this spring that a course on student rebellions should be offered for credit in every division of the university.

"Isn't that a tribute to the academy—for credit, yet?" he exclaimed. "The university is the base and object of their political style."

Ripe for Revolt

Columbia was particularly ripe for revolt. All the ingredients were there.

There was President Kirk, described in many interviews with students and faculty as "totally remote" from them, speaking only to the board of trustees, what one student called "the very image of the corporate bay window." During the worst of the Columbia crisis, he was called "timid and indecisive" one moment, "rigid, arbitrary and ungenerous" the next.

With President Kirk was the board of trustees, a self-perpetuating body heavy with corporate personalities, particularly real estate men, elected not by alumni—a widespread practice at other universities— but by themselves.

There was the faculty before the revolt, many of them described by students as distant, absorbed in their own research and consulting at the expense of their teaching, an excessive amount of their time drawn to the graduate side.

There was tiny Columbia College, seat of the revolt, engulfed in an enormously top-heavy graduate structure. Its student population is 2,700 in the university's total of 17,500.

'Comradeship of Battle'

And there was student frustration. Despite the ugliness and trauma among students and faculty, the strikers over and over express feelings of community, drama, meaning; what Columbia's vice president and provost, David B. Truman, called "the comradeship of battle."

At last they mattered. They were noticed. They had some say-so.

Jonathan Shils, a bright and engaging S.D.S. supporter with a long personal history of service among the poor, called the four weeks of crisis, "Probably the happiest month of my life, in terms of what I've thought and what I've done. The affirmation of faith in self has been just tremendous."

Mike Nichols, executive vice president of the Student Council this year, who began with the radicals and then became one of the leaders of S.R.U., expressed a similar view:

"I never really felt a part of Columbia before. I now feel I belong. I recognize the faculty and other students." He and many others called it a learning experience that became more relevant to them than much of their book learning.

Faculty Is Criticized

Still others had harsh things to say about how the faculty was "exposed" during the long crisis. They spoke of the squabbling among professors of different views; the confused rushing about in vain attempts to mediate between the Columbia administration and the students; the faculty's "naivete" and inconsistencies of thought.

"I could see more clearly than the great professors I'd admired all the years. It was the end of my political innocence," said Mr. Shils. "The faculty was so impressed when the trustees met with them. They were disgusting. All the great faculty heroes are walking around naked."

In students' minds, their strike has also served to lump Vice President Truman, regarded by many as a liberal and able political scientist, with the villains—President Kirk and the board of trustees.

Columbia's polarization of camps and the sprouting of bitter distrusts that may go on for years are classic phenomena, according to Seymour Martin Lipset, a sociologist at Harvard University and a perceptive observer of the new student politics. Professor Lipset made these points:

¶The more violent the confrontations, the better, in the radicals' view. Violence by the police shows that if you scratch a liberal or the "tolerant" system, the basic repressive tendencies will be unmasked.

¶The universities are peculiarly susceptible to this kind of direct action because most American campuses are liberal in bent, if not in fact.

¶Students and faculty operating in the tolerant atmosphere at most universities are not dogmatic enough to reject forcefully even outrageous positions if they seem to contain some seed of merit. Dialogues are conducted among civilized gentlemen. Administrations and faculties have a horror of invoking the police.

Finally, what distinguished Columbia from other rebellions sparked by similar discontent was the presence of a radical student leader who had the talent to seize the moment and

manipulate it to his goals— Mark Rudd.

An All-Out Drive

"It was all-win, no-lose with Mark," one professor remarked. "He and the kids around him want to contribute to the convulsive state of affairs which involves polarization. You've got to choose between the board of trustees and Mark Rudd. Some choice! Who needs it? 'We can't give up,' they said —by which they meant 'We can't negotiate.' That's Rudd's triumph."

The crucial counterpoint to this was the administration's failure to move for the entire week following the start of the uprising on April 23. Meanwhile, in the five student-occupied buildings and on campus, the rebellion became institutionalized. Time was on the students' side.

"We allowed the activity of the demonstrators to become customary and accepted," said Vice President Truman.

Finally, on April 30, the Columbia administration summoned the police. The police used extreme care while removing the black students occupying Hamilton Hall. But the kid gloves were off for the white revolutionaries. The sight of blood, of skulls cracked open, the screams, the sudden frightful face of violence in the protected and genteel enclave absolutely traumatized faculty and students alike.

The role of shouted hatreds and obscenities during Columbia's agony is fascinating but cloudy. What one administrator called the "Get Dad" and "naughtiness" syndrome—the wicked children shocking their parents and the outside world —is perhaps part of the explanation.

One further clue might be a pamphlet by Che Guevara on "Vietnam and World Revolution," circulated widely among radicals on the Columbia campus.

"A people without hate cannot triumph over a brutal enemy," said one passage. "How close and bright would the future appear if two, three, many Vietnams flowered on the face of the globe with their quota of death and immense tragedies, with their daily heroism, with their repeated blows against imperialism, obliging it to disperse its forces under the lash of the growing hate of the peoples of the world!"

This passage was reflected in the graffiti at Columbia that paraphrased Guevara: "Two, three, many Columbias."

Other theories were advanced by George Keller and Professor Silver.

"The language reveals an attitude of disrespect," said

Mr. Keller. "Mark Rudd was putting down Nobel Prize winners and distinguished teachers in words that were profane and spiteful. It makes everybody equal. It reduces everybody to the lowest.

"Those kids said: 'We have the answers. We know the truth. We can eliminate poverty—it's no big deal, you guys are all hung up.' Guys who have given 20 years to the race question, left-wing and reformist action, were being told they didn't know how to go about it by a 20-year-old kid."

Professor Silver, however, said the use of obscene language might be a manifestation of a deep-seated wish of white radicals to identify with the rhetoric and argot of the poor.

"Obscenity is very much a feature of proletarian life, of black city life. They chose this style instead of the genteel university style they are revolting against," he said.

The repeatedly shouted slogan of "Up against the wall, mother," taken from the line of a poem by LeRoi Jones, concludes: "This is a stick-up." Some believe that the reverse side of the coin is what the police say in Harlem when they frisk suspects, front to the wall. Others believe what the students meant was the revolutionary final solution of a back to the wall, facing the firing squad.

Now Columbia is quiet, perhaps for a long, cool summer. The S.D.S. is setting up its "liberation schools" in the city. The S.R.U. and the executive committee of the faculty will attempt to use the breathing spell to suggest reform.

At the Columbia commencement last week, Prof. Richard Hofstadter said such reform could not be carried out, "though it can be begun, in a moment of crisis." He said that friends had asked him: "How can Columbia go on after this terrible wound?"

He replied: "How can it not go on? The question is not whether it will continue, but in what form."

COX REPORT FINDS COLUMBIA POLICY 'INVITED MISTRUST'

Study in Disorders Holds Administration Conveyed 'Authoritarian' Attitude

REBEL TACTICS SCORED

By SYLVAN FOX

The Cox Commission, which investigated the campus uprising that crippled Columbia University last spring, issued a strong indictment of the institution's administration yesterday.

The commission said the administration of Columbia—including its trustees—"too often conveyed an attitude of authoritarianism and invited mistrust."

The five-member commission also condemned the "disruptive tactics" of student rebels. It warned that "the survival—literally the survival—of the free university depends upon the entire community's active rejection of disruptive demonstrations."

At the same time, the commission said in its 222-page report that the police employed "excessive force" when they cleared campus buildings that students had occupied, that the quality of student life at Columbia was "inferior in living conditions and personal associations" and that Columbia's faculty and administration functioned as "rival bodies."

Set Up by Faculty Group

The Cox Commission was set up on May 4 by the Executive Committee of the Faculty as a fact-finding body to look into the disturbances that swept the 215-year-old university last April and May.

The commission was charged by the faculty committee, which had been established four days earlier by an extraordinary meeting of the entire university faculty, to develop a chronology of events on the campus during the crisis and to determine its underlying causes.

The report was issued after the commission held 21 days of hearings at which 79 witnesses were heard, including students, faculty members, administrators, trustees and community figures. The transcript of the hearings was 3,790 pages long.

The writing of the report was done largely by the commission chairman, Archibald Cox, a Harvard Law School professor and former Solicitor General of the United States.

Mr. Cox said at a news conference yesterday in the World Room of the Graduate School of Journalism at Columbia that although representatives of Students for a Democratic Society and the Student Afro-American Society boycotted the hearings, his panel was able to talk informally with radical and black students at Columbia.

Covers Last Spring's Crisis

The commission's work covers only the crisis of last spring. Since then, significant changes have occurred at Columbia, which has remained generally quiet during the fall term that began late last month.

Construction of a controversial gymnasium in Morningside Park has been halted by the university pending consultations with the Harlem community. The university has severed its institutional ties with the Institute for Defense Analyses, a consortium that does military research for the Government, although William A. M. Burden, a university trustee, remains on the board of I.D.A.

Both were key demands of the student protesters last spring.

In addition, Dr. Grayson L. Kirk retired as president of Columbia in August and was replaced by Dr. Andrew W. Cordier, as acting president. Dr. Cordier promptly took apparently successful steps to restore an atmosphere of calm and reconciliation on the campus.

Commenting on the situation before these changes occurred, the Cox Commission said that Columbia's administration relied too often on "evasive improvisation" in dealing with campus problems and it declared that "the scale of priorities at Columbia all too regularly put the students' problems at the bottom."

"The hurricane of social unrest struck Columbia at a time," the report said, "when the university was deficient in the cement that binds an institution into a cohesive unit."

Among the report's other major findings were these:

¶One of the causes of the spring disturbances was Columbia's "unhealthy relations with her neighbors" in Harlem and on Morningside Heights. "Columbia cannot flourish in Upper Manhattan until it establishes a new and sounder relation with its present neighbors," the report said.

¶In the months preceding the student seizure of five campus buildings during the last week in April, students were left uncertain by the administration's inconsistent actions about precisely what kind of demonstrations were acceptable on the campus.

¶Although the protest that began on April 23 was spearheaded by a small group of New Left and militant black students, it quickly drew widespread support among moderate students and faculty members.

Grievances Widespread

"We reject the view that ascribes the April and May disturbances primarily to a conspiracy of student revolutionaries," the report said, adding that the grievances of 1,000 students in the occupied buildings and another 1,000 supporters outside the buildings were felt by "probably a majority" of the university's 17,500 students.

¶The commission rejected the view that most of the moderate support for the protest materialized only after the police cleared the occupied buildings on April 30.

"The trauma of the violence that followed police intervention intensified emotions," the report said, "but support for the demonstrators rested upon broad discontent and widespread sympathy for their position."

¶The violence that occurred at Columbia on April 30 and May 22 when the police cleared seized buildings resulted largely from "miscalculations" by the administration and the police about the number of students in the buildings and the mistaken belief that there would be no opposition to the police among students gathered outside the seized buildings.

¶Methods must be found quickly by which students can "meaningfully influence the education afforded them and other aspects of the university activities."

Dr. Cordier was not immediately available for comment on the report. A spokesman for the university said the acting president had not seen it.

Most members of the board of trustees could not be reached.

469

Those who were reached had no immediate comment because they either had not received or had not yet had an opportunity to study the report.

Spokesmen for S.D.S. were not immediately available for comment.

The report is divided into three major sections: "Conditions Giving Rise to the Disturbances," "History of the Disturbances" and "General Observations."

Tied to External Events

Among the conditions that the commission said set the stage for the disturbances were the war in Vietnam, racial strife in the United States, the university's strained relations with its neighbors, the lack of any clear sense at Columbia of whether disruptive demonstrations were acceptable, and the conditions under which students and faculty live at Columbia.

"At Columbia," the report said, "as at other universities, students' opinions cover the entire spectrum of political life. But two issues command unusually broad agreement among the young and engage their deepest emotions: the peace movement and racial justice. Both were causes of the April disturbances."

These two issues became exemplified for many by Columbia's plan to build a gymnasium in Morningside Park, which borders the university, and by the university's links to the Institute for Defense Analyses.

It was the demand that construction of the gymnasium be halted and that Columbia end its connections with I.D.A. that sparked the protest that flared on April 23.

The Cox Commission said it was convinced that the Harlem community was now opposed to construction of the gymnasium in the form that Columbia planned it and said the university should have been "more open-minded toward abandonment of the gym site or radical alterations of the planned construction and use."

As planned, the gymnasium was to be used partly by the university and partly by the community, with separate entrances for each.

Related to the problem of the gymnasium was the problem of Negro students.

"Columbia, like other universities," the report said, "has scarcely faced the extraordinary difficulties that face black students in the transition from a society permeated by racial injustice to one of true equality of opportunity."

And related to the black students and the gymnasium was the problem of Columbia's relations to Harlem and Morningside Heights.

"The record before us is filled with the strongest criticism of Columbia's conduct in relation to its noninstitutional neighbors both in Harlem and on Morningside Heights," the report said. "The criticism comes from faculty, students, political figures and neighborhood organizations. Their testimony is confirmed by our inquiries in knowledgeable circles."

The criticisms cited include Columbia's "indifference" to the poor, the "manner in which Columbia has pushed her physical expansion" and the university's "harassing tenants in order to evict them."

Still another problem at Columbia, the commission found, was the neutral role of the faculty, which "did not participate in institutional decisions and, therefore, could contribute little to provide the university with internal coherence."

In the absence of any coherent role, the report said, the faculty became "more and more remote from the problems of student life and general university policy not directly related to formal instruction."

"The authoritarian manner [of the administration] on one side, and aloofness [of the faculty] on the other were mutually reinforcing", it added.

"We are persuaded," the report said, "that the faculty's remoteness from the worries and grievances of students and its lack of vigilance vis-a-vis the administration were significant factors in the development of an atmosphere in which student unrest could reach the point of combustion."

S. D. S. Activities

In a discussion of the Students for a Democratic Society, the commission declared that "one of the causes of the April disturbances was the organized effort of a tiny group of students, within S.D.S., whose object was to subvert and destroy the university as a corrupt pillar of an evil society."

"We cannot estimate the number of hard-core revolutionists." the report goes on, "but we are convinced that it was tiny.

"Unfortunately, the failure of both the administration and much of the faculty (although the erred in different directions) to distinguish the former group from the great body of students genuinely concerned with improving the university not only left the university philosophically and tactically unprepared for the crisis but also prolonged its duration."

The report had high praise for the leaders of the Ad Hoc Faculty Group, a loosely knit group of teachers who sought to mediate the dispute, commenting that they had "a much truer understanding of the issues and nature of the conflict than any revealed by the administration or trustees."

But the commission found that the group's attempts to delay police intervention on the campus actually "increased the risk of violence and the shock of the administration's decision to call the police."

The report concluded on an optimistic note, expressing confidence that if students were given a significant voice in the affairs of the university, they would gain "a more sophisticated" understanding of the university's problems and complexities. At the same time, teachers, trustees and alumni would gain a greater understanding of "the true needs and aspirations of students" thus converting the spring crisis "into a creative source of renewal."

October 6, 196

Troops Sent to U. of Wisconsin to Help Police Quell Disorders

900 in Guard Called

Special to The New York Times

MADISON, Wis., Feb. 12—Gov. Warren P. Knowles ordered 900 Wisconsin National Guard troops to the University of Wisconsin campus today after 3,000 students disrupted classes for the fourth day.

Shouting pickets in support of Negro student demands moved from one major campus building to another throughout the day to block many students from entering classrooms.

Mr. Knowles said he had called the Guard in response to a request from Mayor Otto Festge of Madison.

It was believed to be the first time the Guard had been called up in the current wave of student disorders.

The first Guardsmen arrived in Madison about 9:30 P.M. and set up camp at the Dane County Fairgrounds and at an armory in Madison.

The troops will probably move onto the 32,000-student campus before classes begin tomorrow morning.

Mr. Knowles said that the Guard would "assist local officers to restore order to the University of Wisconsin campus."

"The university will not be closed down," he said.

By midafternoon, 400 riot-equipped policemen from Madison and surrounding areas had moved onto the campus to break up the picket lines.

At least four persons were arrested, though the police and demonstrators avoided violent confrontations.

Demonstrations broke out last Friday in response to demands from Negro students that the university increase Negro enrollment and faculty members, and set up Afro-American studies, with the faculties to be selected by Negro students.

Chancellor H. Edwin Young said that the university would seek to enroll more Negro students and hire more Negro teachers, but that students would not be permitted a voice in the hiring or dismissal of faculty members.

A spokesman for Governor Knowles said the decision to call up the Guard had been reached by the local authorities after police contingents complained of fatigue following two days of round-the-clock duty.

A National Guard spokesman, Capt. David Zweifel of Madison, said the Guard had been instructed to "use the minimum

Youths trying to disrupt bus service at the University of Wisconsin campus in Madison are held back by policemen

Associated Press

force required to maintain law and order."

Drivers of campus buses refused to enter the university area after students had locked arms to halt traffic.

Chicago Protest Continues

Special to The New York Times

CHICAGO, Feb. 12—The University of Chicago today offered a controversial teacher, whose retention had been demanded by student demonstrators, one more year on the university faculty. She declined.

Leaders of the demonstrators who were occupying the university's administration building for the 14th day expressed anger at the conditions of the offer, described as a "terminal appointment."

The university's earlier refusal to renew the contract of Mrs. Marlene Dixon, an assistant professor of sociology, had led not only to the take-over of the administration building but also to picketing and disorders elsewhere on the campus.

The new offer to Mrs. Dixon was at the recommendation of a seven-member faculty committee, headed by Mrs. Hanna Gray, assistant professor of history. The committee was set up after protests over Mrs. Dixon's ouster, scheduled to become effective in September.

The committee concluded that Mrs. Dixon had been an "energetic, warm, dedicated, open and compelling teacher," but had not demonstrated "incisive competence for inducing advanced students in the highest levels of scholarship." The committee insisted her sex and political beliefs had not entered into consideration. Mrs. Dixon describes herself as a radical politically.

February 13, 1969

Nixon Letter Hails Notre Dame For Tough Stand on Disruption

By NAN ROBERTSON

Special to The New York Times

WASHINGTON, Feb. 24 — President Nixon has strongly praised the president of the University of Notre Dame for his stern disciplinary response to student disrupters.

In a letter released by the White House today but not yet received by the Rev. Theodore M. Hesburgh, Mr. Nixon condemned campus protesters for violence and vandalism and said they had "grossly abused" the rights of the majority of students.

Last week, Father Hesburgh spelled out what is believed to be the toughest policy on student disruptions yet enunciated by any major American university in the course of recent disorders.

The priest is a noted liberal who has been a leader in the civil rights movement. He actively opposed the late Senator Joseph R. McCarthy and has resisted right-wing attempts to interfere with the operation of universities.

In a "Dear Ted" letter, Mr. Nixon praised Father Hesburgh for his "forthright stand."

"A fundamental governing principle of any great university is that the rule of reason and not the rule of force prevails," the President wrote. "Whoever rejects that principle forfeits his right to be a member of the academic community."

The President thus endorsed Father Hesburgh's rule of prompt expulsion if students do not stop obstruction or disruption tactics.

Mr. Nixon further disclosed that he had instructed Vice President Agnew to discuss with the nation's Governors, meeting here Wednesday and Thursday, "what action, consistent with the traditional independence of American universities, might be taken at the state and Federal levels to cope with the growing lawlessness and violence on our campuses."

The President said the means used by "a small, irresponsible minority" of students reflected

471

an impatience with the democratic process, an intolerance of legitimate authority and "a compelte disregard for the rights of others."

Father Hesburgh, in an eight-page open letter last Tuesday, warned of on-the-spot expulsion of any student or teacher who disrupted normal campus operations.

He said that anyone who substituted "force for rational persuasion, be it violent or nonviolent, will be given 15 minutes of meditation to cease and desist."

Then, he said, demonstrators would be asked for campus identity cards. Those producing cards would immediately be suspended and given five minutes more to stop demonstrating before being expelled from the university. Those without cards would not be considered members of Notre Dame and would be subject to arrest as trespassers.

"Without the law," Father Hesburgh's statement said, "the university is a sitting duck for any small group from outside that wishes to destroy it, to incapacitate it, to terrorize it at whim. Somewhere a stand must be made."

His policy statement, released Feb. 17, came three days after Father Hesburgh had met with President Nixon at the White House.

A White House spokesman said the priest, in Washington for a meeting of the Civil Rights Commission, had stopped by briefly to see Mr. Nixon. What the two talked about was not disclosed.

The President's letter was signed and sent out Saturday. Father Hesburgh's secretary in his South Bend, Ind., office said today by telephone that the letter had not yet been received and that the priest was in Bogota, Columbia, for a meeting of the Council on Higher Education for the American Republics. She said she did not know his exact whereabouts.

THE PRESIDENT'S LETTER

Following is Mr. Nixon's letter to Father Hesburgh:

DEAR TED:

I share your concern over the recent disorders that have paralyzed campus after campus across the country in recent weeks, and I want to applaud the forthright stand you have taken.

As you know, the issues raised by the protesting students range from minor reforms within the academic community to major concerns of national policy.

But the means some students—a small, irresponsible minority—have employed reflect an impatience with democratic processes, an intolerance of legitimately constituted authority, and a complete disregard for the rights of others.

Violence and vandalism have marked many of these protests, and the rights of the majority of the students have been grossly abused.

If the integrity of our universities is to be preserved, then certain principles must be re-established and certain basic rules enforced. Intimidation and threats remain outlaw weapons in a free society.

A fundamental governing principle of any great university is that the rule of reason and not the rule of force prevails. Whoever rejects that principle forfeits his right to be a member of the academic community. The university administrator who fails to uphold that principle jeopardizes one of the central pillars of his institution and weakens the very foundation of American education.

I have directed the Vice President in meetings in Washington this coming week with the Governors of the 50 states to discuss what action, consistent with the traditional independence of American universities, might be taken at the state and Federal levels to cope with the growing lawlessness and violence on our campuses. I would appreciate it greatly if you would take the time to give him your views on this matter.

With warm regards,
Sincerely,
RICHARD M. NIXON

February 25, 196

Armed Negroes End Seizure; Cornell Yields

By JOHN KIFNER
Special to The New York Times

ITHACA, N. Y., April 20—Carrying 17 rifles and shotguns, Negro students at Cornell University marched out of the Student Union Building today, ending a 36-hour occupation.

A few minutes later, rifle-carrying students stood by in front of the cottage that the Negro students used as their headquarters, while university officials signed an agreement.

This called for the dean of the faculty, Robert D. Miller, to recommend to a full faculty meeting tomorrow that a judicial proceeding against five black students "be nullified."

The administration also capitulated to a series of other demands by the Afro-American Society, including:

¶University legal assistance against any civil charges arising out of the occupation of the buildings.

¶A promise that the university would press no civil or criminal charges or other forms of punishment against the occupiers and would assume all responsibility for damages to the building.

¶Twenty-four-hour campus police protection for the Afro-American center and the cooperative residence used by black students two nights ago.

¶An investigation into the cross-burning and into an attempt by fraternity men yesterday to break back into Willard Straight Hall, which resulted in a fist fight in which four students received minor injuries.

¶The possibility of a new campus judicial system, which black students would cooperate in devising.

The Negro students seized Willard Straight Hall at 6 A.M. yesterday, routing 20 sleeping parents visiting the campus for Parents Weekend, and a number of university employes.

At 4:12 this afternoon, more than 100 Negro men and women walked out under a red-and-white banner proclaiming "Welcome Parents" through the unchained steel gates and heavy wooden doors of the rambling, mock Gothic building that is the center of campus activity.

The seventeen rifles and shotguns were carried by the group, two in cases, the others held openly. Several students wore bandoliers of rifle or shotgun ammunition, and others carried spears made by fastening knives, to poles or homemade clubs.

Fists Are Clenched

White members of Students for a Democratic Society, who had cleared a path through the crowd of several hundred people gathered in front of "The Straight" raised clenched fists and cheered. There were a few scattered jeers.

The withdrawal from the building followed more than 11 hours of meetings of an augmented Faculty Council yesterday and today, and negotiations this afternoon between the administration and the black students.

Before the agreement was reached, visiting parents were hustled out of their guest rooms in Straight Hall and into the chilly morning by shouting Negro students; four students received minor injuries in a fist fight when fraternity members tried to break back into the building; many Parents Weekend activities, including a convocation speech by President James A. Perkins were canceled and tension mounted on the campus.

But observers here noted that there has been growing resentment among the faculty—particularly among senior members of the history and political science departments and in the agriculture school—toward the black students' activities and demands.

Three weeks ago, about 600 faculty members—the largest faculty meeting in recent Cornell history—voted that a joint student-faculty disciplinary board had jurisdiction over the five black student cases and some observers felt there was a strong possibility they might repeat the action tomorrow.

"I do not want to teach at

472

Associated Press

Armed students leaving Cornell's student center. Edward L. Whitfield, head of Afro-American Society, is at right.

an institution where arms are carried openly, or for that matter, crosses are burned," Clinton Rossiter, a Senior University Professor of American Institutions and one of the university's best known names, said tonight.

Method at Issue

The judicial proceedings over the cases growing out of demonstrations last December have been the main point at issue. The Negro students contend that the demonstrations were political acts against the university, and thus the university was a party to the dispute and should not sit in judgment.

Other issues grew out of the alienation felt by many of the 250 Negro students on this 14,-000-student campus. Many of the members of "Afro" are especially recruited slum students, who feel the education they are getting here is relevant only to the white world.

The Negro students complain that their leaders were kept under threat of suspension for months following the December demonstrations, which sought a separate "black college," and that hostility had mounted against them among the white students.

The Negro students presented a bizarre sight as they marched from the buildings on the gently rolling Arts Quadrangle, escorted by about 10 campus policemen. Negroes flanked the procession, their rifles carried at the ready, some with cartridges in the open breeches.

Behind them, the Negro students left the litter of their occupation in Straight Hall. Mattresses and cushions had been pulled into the cafeteria where most of the students slept.

In the Memorial Room, some high light fixtures had been ripped out, several candy machines had been rifled and walls bore slogans like "Kill the fraternity honkies."

White students stared goggle-eyed and silent as members of the group wound their way to the Afro-American headquarters.

When they reached the building, most of them moved onto the cottage porch of the cottage, while the riflemen took up positions on the steep lawn and steps.

Steven Muller, the university's vice president for public affairs, and W. Keith Kennedy, the vice provost, conferred briefly on the steps with Edward L. Whitfield, a husky sophomore from Little Rock, Ark., who is the chairman of the Afro-American Society.

Then the two university officials walked into the three-story building with Mr. Whitfield. They emerged 20 minutes later.

The Afro-American leader read the agreement from the bottom of the steps and the university officials signed the typewritten document.

Statement Read

Then another "Afro" member, wearing two bandoliers of shotgun shells, read a statement saying that the group had occupied Straight Hall "to demonstrate to the university our continued commitment to the fact of the illegitimacy of the faculty-student boards and its insistence upon judging black people without 1) jury of our peers, 2) being the legitimate body to deal with a case of such political magnitude.

"We further decided that the time had come to stand up and let this community know that threats on the lives of black women will not be tolerated."

The statement said that the group had left with the understanding that the university would carry out the agreement, but warned that "failure on the part of the university to do so may force us to again confront the university in some manner."

The existence of arms in Straight Hall became known this morning when the university's division of safety and security confirmed that a rifle with a telescopic sight, two gun cases and several hatchets had been taken into the building at 10:35 last night.

The university announcement quoted Mr. Whitfield as having said that the weapons were obtained for self-defense.

Asked whether today's display of guns violated any laws, an officer on duty at the Ithaca Police Headquarters said:

'It's Still a Free Country'

"It's still a free country. You can carry a gun if you want to."

The officer said that anyone over 18 years old could legally carry a shotgun or a rifle in public, and that no permit was required. He added:

"Of course, he may not threaten anybody."

Speaking at a university news conference after the agreement was signed, Mr. Muller said the black students had obtained the guns because they felt "life was increasingly at stake," and "these events led them to fear for their safety."

Mr. Muller said he had signed the amnesty agreement "to prevent a growing and imminent threat to life."

"We were working in a limited area of options," he explained. "It is very clear that we do not as a university have the resources to assure that life and property were not endangered."

He said that to eject the armed students from the building the university would have had to call in civil authorities and wanted to avoid it.

The Negro students were permitted to retain their guns, he said, because of "a very real fear that they were subject to reprisal."

April 21, 1969

473

Shotguns and Tear Gas Disperse Rioters Near the Berkeley Campus

A tear gas canister fired by the police explodes amid demonstrators and passers-by near the university campus

United Press International

By **LAWRENCE E. DAVIES**
Special to The New York Times

BERKELEY, Calif., May 15 — Policemen with shotguns and National Guardsmen with tear gas opened fire on rioters along Telegraph Avenue near the University of California here this afternoon, incapacitating scores of persons. Two hours after the first clash 21 persons had been arrested, several of them on felony charges. Gov. Ronald Reagan, about three hours after the trouble began, ordered the National Guard to active duty to supplement two of the Guards gas dispersal teams already on hand. His press spokesmen refused to disclose the number of troops involved. The Governor, with the concurrence of local officials, also imposed a curfew on the city, forbidding loitering between 10 P.M. and 6 A.M. and out-

lawing parades, assemblies, and sound permits, with any violations to be treated as misdemeanors. The rioting began in protest against the university's taking over "People's Park," a tract of land owned by the institution but improved in recent weeks by hippies, yippies, nonstudents and others as a playground and gathering place.

Most of the injuries, hospital spokesmen said, appeared to have resulted from the use of birdshot by the police.

By evening, Telegraps Avenue and nearby streets were littered with bricks, rocks and broken glass but most of the direct confrontation between the police and protesters was limited to the first hour of violence.

The balminess of the evening, however, caused law enforcement leaders to maintain their vigil.

A spokesman for City Manager William C. Hanley said no order had been given to the

Berkeley police to use birdshot. The operational field commander is Sheriff Frank Madigan, but his whereabouts were not disclosed.

The spokesman estimated at least 300 law enforcement personnel were engaged in the operation but observers put the number at double or triple that figure. Policemen were on hand from Oakland, San Francisco and a half dozen or more other cities.

At Herrick Hospital, the nurses lost count of the numbers and an aide said most of the victims were taken immediately into surgery.

Late in the evening the number of injured stood at about 75, including at least 15 policemen who suffered minor hurts and were treated by a county doctor. Arrests totaled almost 40, with charges ranging from obscene gestures toward a policeman. The bail ranged from $100 to $18,000.

The shooting started near the Sather Gate entrance of the Berkeley campus after a dem-

onstration attended by 1,500 or so at Sproul Hall Plaza. At the rally's conclusion, Dan Siegel, the student president-elect, shouted:

"Let's go down and take over the park."

Shortly afterward a platoon of Alameda County sheriff's deputies opened fire into a crowd standing on a roof at Dwight Way and Telegraph Avenue, near the campus. National Guardsmen arrived soon afterward and they tried to control the rioters by firing tear gas.

Among those wounded early in the fracas were Don Wegers, a reporter for The San Francisco Chronicle, and Daryl Lembke, San Francisco bureau chief for The Los Angeles Times.

A state highway patrolman, whose name was not disclosed, was stabbed.

Governor Reagan had never lifted a state of extreme emergency that he declared for the campus and its immediate environs on February 5 while confrontations between the police and striking students led by members of the Third World Liberation Front were almost a daily occurrence.

The Third World Front is a group, found on a number of San Francisco Bay area campuses, made up of students of minority ethnic and national backgrounds. It includes usually the Black Students Union and representatives of Asians, Mexican-Americans and American Indians.

The Governor's proclamation enabled the sheriff to call upon the National Guard and the state highway patrol to keep order on the campus.

A critical situation had been building for the last day or two since Dr. Roger W. Heyns, chancellor of the Berkeley campus, served formal notice that the university would evict the "people's park" patrons and place a steel mesh fence around the 445 by 275 foot area owned by the institution. It covers most of a square block at the corner of Haste and Bowditch, near the campus.

Worked for Weekends

Several hundred policemen had appeared at the park before 5 A.M. and "dispossessed" a small group of "trespassers" in preparation for the start of the fence erection an hour later.

Squads of laughing, singing hippie types had been busy at the site for several weekends, transforming the $1-million property — destined eventually for student housing and, more immediately, for playing fields —into a park.

They had spent a reported $700 for turf, with which they

RETURNED: A demonstrator throwing a tear gas canister back at the police during yesterday's violent rioting in Berkeley, Calif., near the University of California campus.

covered part of the bare ground and have spread sawdust over some of the rest. They also brought in striped swings to delight children and installed benches and tables for picnics.

Someone dubbed the result "power to the people park," which was shortened on a sign to People's Park. A corner bulletin board carried a schedule of activities so that residents and nonresidents, students and nonstudents, who arrived with picnic baskets or sandwiches in brown bags could stop to read on their way to a picnic table.

There were three apple trees and colored balloons and a steel triangle like a chuck wagon dinner bell, which they called a "bulldozer alarm," to alert them when the police might be about to descend on the area.

Art Goldberg, one of the leaders of the Free Speech Movement on the Berkeley campus more than four years ago, said recently that the university had purchased the land because the Berkeley police department had asked it to.

"They're trying to drive the students and the street people out," he asserted, a statement that has been denied by the administration.

4 Kent State Students Killed by Troops

6 Hurt as Shooting Follows Reported Sniping at Rally

By JOHN KIFNER
Special to The New York Times

KENT, Ohio, May 4—Four students at Kent State University, two of them women, were shot to death this afternoon by a volley of National Guard gunfire. Six other students were wounded.

The burst of gunfire came about 20 minutes after the guardmen broke up a noon rally on the Commons, a grassy campus gathering spot, by lobbing tear gas at a crowd of about 1,000 young people.

In Washington, President Nixon deplored the deaths of the four students in the following statement:

"This should remind us all once again that when dissent turns to violence it invites tragedy. It is my hope that this tragic and unfortunate incident will strengthen the determination of all the nation's campuses, administrators, faculty and students alike to stand firmly for the right which exists in this country of peaceful dissent and just as strongly against the resort to violence as a means of such expression."

In Columbus, Sylvester Del Corso, Adjutant General of the Ohio National Guard, said in a statement that the guardsmen had been forced to fire after a sniper opened fire against the troops from a nearby rooftop and the crowd began to move to encircle the guardsmen.

Frederick P. Wenger, the Assistant Adjutant General, said the troops had opened fire after they were shot at by a sniper.

"They were under standing orders to take cover and return any fire," he said.

This reporter, who was with a group of students, did not see any indication of sniper fire, nor was the sound of any gunfire audible before the Guard volley. Students, conceding that rocks had been thrown, heatedly denied that there was any sniper.

Gov. James A. Rhodes called on J. Edgar Hoover, director of the Federal Bureau of Investigation, to aid in investigating the campus violence.

At 2:10 this afternoon, after the shootings, the university president, Robert I. White, ordered the university closed for an indefinite time, and officials were making plans to evacuate the dormitories and bus out-of-state students to nearby cities.

Robinson Memorial Hospital identified the dead students as Allison Krause, of Pittsburgh; Sandy Scheuer, of Youngstown, Ohio, both coeds; Jeffrey Glenn Miller, of 22 Diamond Drive, Plainview, L. I., and William Schneider. The hospital said it had no address for Mr. Schneider.

Students here, angered by the expansion of the war into Cambodia, have held demonstrations for the past three nights. On Saturday night, the Army Reserve Officer Training Corps building was burned to the ground and the Guard was called in and martial law was declared.

Today's rally, called after a night in which the police and guardsmen drove students into their dormitories and made 69 arrests, began as students rang the iron Victory Bell on the Commons, normally used to herald football victories.

A National Guard jeep drove on to the Commons and an officer ordered the crowd to disperse. Then several canisters of tear gas were fired, and the students straggled up a hill that borders the area and retreated into buildings.

A platoon of guardsmen, armed—as they have been since they arrived here with loaded M-1 rifles and gas equipment—moved across the green and over the crest of the hill, chasing the main body of protesters.

The youths split into two groups, one heading farther downhill toward a dormitory complex, the other eddying around a parking lot and girls' dormitory just below Taylor Hall, the architecture building.

The guardsmen moved into a grassy area just below the parking lot and fired several canisters of tear gas from their short, stubby launchers.

Three or four youths ran to the smoking canisters and hurled them back. Most fell far short, but one landed near the troops and a cheer went up from the crowd, which was chanting "Pigs of campus" and cursing the war.

A few youths in the front of the crowd ran into the parking lot and hurled stones or small chunks of pavement in the direction of the guardsmen. Then the troops begain moving back up the hill in the direction of the college.

The studen s in the parking lot area, numbering about 500, began to move toward the rear of the troops, cheering. Again, a few in front picked up stones from the edge of the parking

Ohio National Guardsmen advancing over the campus of Kent State University yesterday behind a screen of tear gas

lot and threw them at the guardsmen. Another group of several hundred students had gathered around the sides of Taylor Hall watching.

As the guardsmen, moving up the hill in single file, reached the crest, they suddenly turned, forming a skirmish line and opening fire.

The crackle of the rifle volley cut the suddenly still air. It appeared to go, as a solid volley, for perhaps a full minute or a little longer.

Some of the students dived to the ground, crawling on the grass in terror. Others stood shocked or half crouched, apparently believing the troops were firing into the air. Some of the rifle barrels were pointed upward.

Near the top of the hill at the corner of Taylor Hall, a student crumpled over, spun sideways and fell to the ground, shot in the head.

When the firing stopped, a slim girl, wearing a cowboy shirt and faded jeans, was lying face down on the road at the edge of the parking lot, blood pouring out onto the macadam, about 10 feet from this reporter.

The youths stood stunned, many of them clustered in small groups staring at the bodies. A young man cradled one of the bleeding forms in his arms. Several girls began to cry. But many of the students who rushed to the scene seemed almost too shocked to react. Several gathered around an abstract steel sculpture in front of the building and looked at a .30-caliber bullet hole drilled through one of the plates.

The hospital said that six young people were being treated for gunshot wounds, some in the intensive care unit. Three of the students who were killed were dead on arrival at the hospital.

One guardsman was treated and released at the hospital and another was admitted with heat prostration.

In early afternoon, students attempted to gather at various area of the Commons but were ordered away by guardsman

Tar entum Valley Daily News via Associated Press

A girl screams as fellow student lies dead after National Guardsmen opened fire at Kent State

and the Ohio Highway Patrol, which moved in as reinforcements.

There were no further clashes, as faculty members, graduate assistants and students leaders urged the crowd to go back to the dormitories. Brig. Gen. Robert Canterbury, the commander of Guard troops on the Kent State campus, said today that no warning had been given to the students that the troops would shoot.

General Canterbury, at a campus news conference said in reply to questioning that no official order had been given to open fire.

"The situation did not allow it," he said. "The emotional atmosphere was such that anything could have happened. It

was over in two to three seconds."

He said a guardsman "always has the option to fire if his life is in danger."

"A crowd of about 600 students had surrounded a unit of about 100 guardsmen on three sides and were throwing rocks at the troops," he said. "Some of the rocks were the size of baseballs. The troops had run out of tear gas."

Governor Rhodes, who had ordered the National Guardsmen onto the campus Saturday after students began looting stores and breaking windows in the downtown area, said "a complete investigation" would be made into the shootings.

"We have called on both the Ohio Highway Patrol and the National Guard to conduct a

complete investigation and supply us with full reports," the Governor said. "When we have full and detailed information, we will make a report and announce any further actions that may be necesasry.

"In the meantime, we are urging additional investigations of this incident by the Portage County prosecutor, the Federal Bureau of Investigation and the Untied States District Attorney for this area."

But a bizarre atmosphere hung over the campus as a guard helicopter hovered overhead, grim-faced officers maneuvered their men to safeguard the normally pastoral campus and students, dazed, fearful and angry, struggled to comprehend what had happened and to find somehting to do about it.

Big Man on the Campus: Police Undercover Agent

By ANTHONY RIPLEY
Special to The New York Times

ALBUQUERQUE, N. M., March 28—There is a new man on campus among the freaks and fraternity men, the athletes and the esthetes, the bookish types and the bomb throwers. He is the spy.

He has not come to study Russian or Chinese or to prepare himself to infiltrate some foreign nation. Instead, his mission is to watch the students, the faculty and the off-campus crowds.

Though such undercover activity was almost unheard of five years ago, it has now become almost a permanent institution on the American college scene.

It is the product of student turmoil—rioting, bombing, arson, strikes, demonstrations—and the widespread drug problem.

The police defend their undercover tactics as the only practical way to enforce drug laws and to keep watch on radical campus activities, which, they fear, might trigger disturbances in the surrounding community.

What is happening around the country shows up in sharp relief at the University of New Mexico. In fact, reports from college campuses coast to coast indicate there is nothing at all extraordinary about such incidents as these:

¶A semi-undercover state policeman, Jack E. Johnson, was seen on the campus from the fall of 1969 to the summer of 1970. He generally tried to blend in with the students and carried a Brownie Instamatic camera. His presence was publicly announced on several occasions. Once he was spotted and identified at a closed faculty meeting and was asked to leave. Mr. Johnson is now back on uniformed patrol duty near Albuquerque.

¶Two city narcotics agents were discovered by students living in Coronado Hall, a dormitory for men. The agents left quietly soon after they were identified and both city and university officials confirmed their presence.

¶A city policeman using false press credentials posed as an Associated Press photographer during demonstrations last spring protesting the invasion of Cambodia. Howard Graves, the AP bureau chief in Albuquerque, complained to the police, who promised it would not happen again.

¶Unspecified law enforcement agencies requested permission to place undercover agents on the campus but were refused by university officials.

Displeased but Helpless

Like most of the officials at the other colleges that reported similar incidents, school officials here were not pleased with the snooping but felt helpless in keeping undercover men from either enrolling as regular students or mixing with off-campus crowds.

"We do not condone or encourage such activity," said Harold W. Lavender, vice president for student affairs. "Neither can we prevent it. We've had opportunities to deliberately enroll undercover agents and we have, in high dudgeon, turned them down."

John S. Todd, an assistant to the Albuquerque city manager who is responsible for police matters, said undercover men were assigned to the university area whenever there were "specific instances of illegal activity" such as narcotics use. Agents are also assigned, he said, when "feeling is developing" over a campus political issue or national political issue.

Mr. Todd said it was only "prudent" to watch radical activities that might spill over from the campus to the surrounding city.

The bulk of the nation's undercover work is done by local police officers or outsiders hired by the state, county or city police, according to the campus reports. Probably the best known undercover man in the United States, M. L. Singkata Thomas Tongyai, known at Hobart College in Canandaigua, N.Y., as "Tommy the Traveler," was one of these.

He was hired by the local sheriff's office and, according to an Ontario County grand jury, "advocated violent forms of protest" among student radicals. He took part in a police drug raid on the Hobart campus last June 5.

Other Campus Watchers

But Federal agencies, particularly the Federal Bureau of Investigation and United States Army intelligence, have also been watching campuses.

A series of United States Senate committee hearings have detailed the extensive surveillance activities of the Army at such widely separated places as New York University, Northwestern University and Colorado College. However, the Army, under public pressure, has announced it has cut back its civilian watching programs in the United States.

Recent public disclosure of the contents of F.B.I. files stolen March 8 from the bureau's office in Media, Pa., show that it has regularly used informants to watch radical activities at Haverford College.

The F.B.I. has been active elsewhere, too, according to the campus reports. "There's someone here I think you should meet," a University of Illinois student shouted last fall to a group of protesters in front of the Champaign, Ill., county courthouse. "That man there, in the blue jacket, with the camera, works for the F.B.I."

A young, clean-cut man in a blue windbreaker, whom the student identified by name, said nothing and continued to take pictures of the demonstrators, who were protesting acquittal of a former Champaign police officer charged with murder in the death of a black store clerk.

Drug Control Efforts

Charles Travelstead, special agent at the Urbana, Ill., office of the F.B.I., declined to comment on the incident but said the agency did use "confidential informants who share our concern in the vital areas of terrorism and bombings."

"If an individual cooperated with us and incurred expenses," he continued, "he would be reimbursed for out-of-the-pocket expenses."

Much of the undercover activity surrounds anti-drug efforts by the police, who insist that a man in uniform only scares away pushers and buyers.

A survey released in February by the National Institute of Mental Health reported one-third of the 10,000 students on 50 campuses who were interviewed admitted that they had smoked marijuana and one-seventh of the total reported that they were regular users.

At Yale University, an undercover agent named George Miller last November was involved in the arrest of 90 young people on assorted drug charges. Most were not students, but were drifters and dropouts among the so-called "street people" who gather near university campuses across the nation.

A leaflet called "View from Behind Bars" was circulated after the arrests and described the activities of Mr. Miller, who was hired by the New Haven police:

"Lots of people are still muttering how Good Ol' George couldn't possibly do that. The stark reality is that George Miller was an incredibly slick agent. He tripped with us, went to rallies with us, turned on with us. He dressed in purple and yellow and wore hip glasses. . . . He waved to us and smiled at us. He was accepted and trusted.

"Some people muttered a few things about not trusting him. But we're all paranoid, right?

"And in the end, George busted our friends. . . . So what does it all mean about our lives? About who we trust and how we really relate to one another? And how do we prevent another George Miller from coming around again?"

Other surveillance methods are also used.

In Miami, Seymor Gelber, chief assistant State's Attorney for Dade County, made a study of campus police at 210 colleges and universities for a doctoral degree from Florida State University. He said 14.1 per cent of those studied admitted using telephone recording devices. Among 28 colleges of over 20,000 students each, the use of wiretaps was 25 per cent.

Though some of the undercover men say infiltration is a difficult task, others find it easy in the open, accepting atmosphere of college life.

At the University of Kansas, a 19-year-old undercover narcotics agent told The Associated Press:

"I just went into the dorm and acted stupid. I got into conversations and got to know them. Then I asked where I could get the stuff and they told me."

His work led to a series of early morning raids by 150 agents on the campus at Lawrence, Kan.

At the University of Michigan, Ann Arbor Police Lieut. Eugene Staudenmaier makes no pretense of being undercover as he attends almost all political rallies.

Recently he attended a workshop during a campus peace conference. Someone recognized him and complained. He stood up, identified himself and the workshop members voted to allow him to stay. He left a short time later.

"I don't like this polarized situation where police and students are stereotyped as natural enemies," he said.

At Ohio State University last April, two young men up front in a crowd of rioting students were later identified as undercover state policemen. Their pictures were published in the student newspaper, The Lantern.

The university's 58-man campus police force, armed with .38 caliber revolvers, night sticks and chemical disabling agents, keeps an undercover squad of six men. They are supplemented by undercover Ohio State policemen and Columbus city policemen.

At the University of Texas at Austin there was "Duke," who arrived in a new car with mod clothes and who made fiery speeches during student union demonstrations a year ago. He was indicted, but never arrested, and the charges against him were later dropped.

At Northwestern University it was a girl, "Connie," who moved into the apartment of two off-campus radicals and, according to one Northwestern activist, "hung around the campus and was mildly friendly."

Last May, when the police were called during an argument between her and one of her roommates, she identified herself as a member of the "Red Squad" of the Chicago police department. She disappeared the next day.

At the University of California at Berkeley it was a city police officer, Roland Soliz, who had been on campus under the name of "Roland Guzman." He joined Students for a Democratic Society, the Young Socialist Alliance, the Radical Student Union and various Mexican-American groups before he was uncovered by the student newspaper, The Daily Californian.

Associated Press

M. L. Singkata Thomas Tongyai, who was known as "Tommy the Traveler."

Former undercover agents, though useless once identified, do have a future. Gerald Kirk, a University of Chicago student who said he worked for the F.B.I. from 1966 to 1969, has been touring the country in the last few months, speaking six nights a week. The topic of his speech is "Inside the Spider's Web."

Students Revive
Good Old 1950's

By ANDREW H. MALCOLM

A year after student anti-war protests closed dozens of colleges and universities across the country, thousands of the same youths are caught up in a new pursuit —nostalgia for the good old days. For these people, the good old days mean the nineteen-fifties.

From New England to California, college students are jamming old-style rock 'n' roll concerts, paying $5 to see old Howdy Doody kinescopes and sitting bleary-eyed through all-night "movie orgies" of Hopalong Cassidy episodes.

At "come as you were" parties and mock high school proms and sock hops—complete with crepe paper decorations—girls wearing pleated skirts and ponytails and boys in tight, pegged pants, T-shirts and carefully combed but greased hair dance once again to such "oldies" as "At the Hop," "Silhouettes" and "Teenager in Love."

Buffalo Bob, the jolly television host who daily led 15 million youngsters through the Howdy Doody do's and don'ts during the fifties, is packing his former Peanut Galleries into college auditoriums these days where, with tears in their eyes, they sing the old songs and commercials and play the familiar games.

Now 53 years old, Buffalo Bob Smith is booked well into next year. By then, there will be Howdy Doody records, watches, sweatshirts, bags, jewelry, hot pants and a singing group called Howdy Doody and the Peanut Gallery.

"There's no doubt about it," said Ray B. Browne, director of Bowling Green University's Center for the Study of Popular Culture, "this nostalgia among college students is a real groundswell. And it's much more than just a fad."

Mr. Browne, other faculty, students and campus observers around the country attribute this phenomenon to many causes. But one stands out: a desire among the youths to turn away from the social, technological and political turmoil of recent years and to seek a reassuring security among familiar memories.

"The fifties were a good, safe period," said one teacher. "Besides, they almost have to go back there. That's where they came from and that's what they know."

The students' nostalgia is selective. "They don't remember the pimples," said one professor.

Whatever the reasons, they are having fun. At the University of South Carolina one recent evening, 1,000 students raised such a clamor singing "It's Howdy Doody Time" with Buffalo Bob that school officials were drawn from other buildings to see what was happening.

"It's the kind of feeling you didn't think you'd get until you were 50 and watching James Bond movies on TV," said Harry Hope, a sophomore.

At Harvard University last month, Buffalo Bob drew 2,300 students. As he appeared on stage, one girl screamed, "Oh! Oh! It's all coming back."

"I went because it was the event of the year as far as I was concerned," said Peter Lemieux, a senior. "Buffalo Bob brought back a great carefree time for me," added Rick Tilden, also a senior. "It was a fitting way to cap off my college career."

At Yale University's Ezra Stiles College, the dining hall was recently decorated like a high school gymnasium, complete with borrowed basketball baskets hanging from the ceiling, colored crepe-paper streamers and a disk jockey babbling out record dedications.

At Ohio State University, the Beach Boys and Chuck Berry were well received and one local radio station broadcasts only "oldies but goodies" from the fifties. Many parties feature that era's dress and some coeds are wearing a boyfriend's ring on a chain around their neck.

Several students at the University of Illinois spent an entire night last weekend watching old Mighty Mouse and Hopalong Cassidy episodes.

An annual dance at the University of Chicago was replaced last week by a sock hop, complete with a free shoe check and door prizes. Admission was free to students wearing any two of the following: greased-back hair, black leather jacket,

March 29, 1971

ponytail, letterman's sweater, bobby socks, saddle shoes or bright red lipstick.

Also included were showings of such regular 1950 television fare as "The Lone Ranger" and "Sergeant Preston of the Yukon." "The Lone Ranger just evokes a flow of security," commented one student. "You knew who were the good guys, who were the bad guys and everything turned out all right."

"We noticed at our regular parties that whenever an older song was played people seemed to have a special kind of enjoyment," said Dave Martin, a senior at Princeton.

As a result, students there have held several "oldies nights" this year, including a revival of the "Yale Prom," an old institution dropped by Yale last year because of financial problems. A number of Princeton students have written home to have their old clothes sent out.

At Stanford, one dorm holds weekly rock 'n' roll or twist parties. Some 1,700 students recently jammed a concert by ShaNaNa, a 12-man group that sings such songs of the fifties as "Blue Moon," "Teen Angel," "Little Darlin'" and "Jailhouse Rock." The same group had Yale students dancing in the aisles at a concert in New Haven last week.

"Our music bears directly on the lives of our listeners," said Edwin Goodgold, the group's manager. "Obviously the past is more simple and less painful than the present. It's been lived through. In a world with very few standards left, the past offers those standards whether you live by them or not.

'Hypocrisy and Violence'

"The music evokes memories of those days when rebelling was much simpler—sneaking a cigarette, guzzling a beer, going to a drive-in or a jaunty strut in front of the candy store. They weren't debating about wars or drugs then."

Philip Zimbardo, a social psychologist at Stanford, said: "Today's youth is threatened by an uncertain future, alienated from traditional values and turned-off by the hypocrisy and violence they see about them. So they trip out on the past they can relate to and which they can control."

Others see the popularity of nostalgia as an alternative to the feverish political activity of students in recent years. "How can you possibly link Howdy Doody to the Vietnam war?" asks David McClelland, a Harvard professor.

"Today's college student," said Doris Kearns, an assistant professor at Harvard, "missed out on the college life of panty raids, clubs and big weekends. They had politics instead. And think some students may feel they really missed something."

Mr. Browne, whose Bowling Green center investigates such

The New York Times/William E. Sauro

Buffalo Bob Smith at an autograph session in Korvettes

phenomena, fears the implications of nostalgia's strong popularity.

"When you get afraid of contemporary life and start looking back to the good old days too much," he said, "you become unrealistic. You don't participate in current life and you tend to try to solve today's problems with yesterday's attitudes."

Charles Wendell, a student at New York University who paid $5.50 to see a Buffalo Bob revival, said:

"I grew up with Howdy Doody and that show shaped my life in many ways. I cried when it went off the air in 1960. It was great to see Buffalo Bob again. But I got mugged on the way home. That shows how much the world has changed for the worse."

May 17, 1971

Youth Rebellion of Sixties Waning

By DOUGLAS E. KNEELAND
Special to The New York Times

PALO ALTO, Calif., Oct. 23 — The great youth trip, that heady, sometimes breathtaking, sometimes frightening, rollercoaster ride that careened through the late years of the nineteen-sixties and plunged headlong into this decade, is slowing down and may be almost over.

Two or three years ago, a member of the administration of Stanford University here recalled the other day, he was entertaining a group of students at his home when he asked: "Who are your heroes? Whom do you really admire?"

After a few awkward moments in which nobody spoke, a young man replied.

"Us," he said. No one disputed him. And he may have spoken for a generation of high school and college students, of young people in general.

This fall it is still almost impossible to find individuals who are heroes to the young. But the self-worship of the youth cult, the easy assumption that youth has all the answers, is dying, too.

At Dartmouth College in Hanover, N. H., Peter Willies, a senior from Weston, Conn., declared recently that he "distrusts our generation as much as any other."

And at the University of Wisconsin in Madison, Gerald Peary, a bearded, 26-year-old graduate student who had been a political activist, took an even harsher view.

"The youth revolution has turned sour," he complained. "There's no indication that this generation will be any less piggy than the rest. I'm a skeptic."

Quality of Life

That is a hard judgment, one not many people, particularly of the younger generation, would be willing to make. More would be likely to agree with Robert W. Fuller, president of Oberlin College, who gave a more positive interpretation to what seems to be essentially the same phenomenon. Noting that youth today seem to feel "ineffectual" about bringing about "institutional change" in the country, he added:

"The students I've seen have been talking about more personal issues. There is a desire for greater quality of life in the private sphere as opposed to the reformist zeal and the personal price you have to pay for change."

Whatever the interpretation, the young, whether in college or high school or working, are undergoing some major changes in their attitudes and approaches to life. This was the conclusion drawn from visits to and reports by correspondents of The New York Times from a score

The New York Times

At the University of Southern California, touch football tempers political activism

of campuses and 10 large cities from Maine to California.

With the war in Vietnam becoming less visible, with the draft lottery accepted as more equitable, with the 18-year-old vote a reality, with a lagging economy threatening the affluent society and, perhaps, with just plain passage of time, some distinctly new patterns are emerging among young people.

They are more serious, but having more fun. They are studying more but relaxing more. Their concern for the problems of the world contin-

ues, but their search for solutions has generally narrowed to what they can do as individuals, usually on a local level.

Their radicalism, where it exists—and it exists in many places—has become a more personal matter and not something to be constantly paraded in the streets.

"Though the rhetoric superficially resembles the typical radical charges of past years," said a Boston University student describing activists at the crowded Commonwealth Avenue campus, "the action they seek differs considerably.

"Where student leaders would have called for a march for peace. Now it's for teach-ins

and lobbying; where they would have moved to take over a building and harass its occupants, now the problems are hashed out over a cup of coffee; where unnegotiable demands flew across the streets through megaphones, now requests for forums between students and more responsive administrators come in the form of telephone calls and letters."

Dread Is Reduced

Among other things, the young's dread of working in or with the Establishment seems to have lessened, but most want to do something self-satisfying and constructive.

All in all, their sense of apocalypse has diminished. They have become—to cite some descriptions that are frequently encountered — more patient, more tolerant, more cynical, more skeptical, more apathetic, more subdued, more prone to take the longer view, more mature.

"No one is burning inside for immediate upheaval, or even drastic change," a Harvard senior said, "figuring perhaps that there isn't much to be done anyway—that the apocalypse is not just around the corner after all, that anarchy may not be the answer, that the wheels of government and society aren't going to change much regardless of what students do or say."

Among noncollege youths, most of whom tend to be some-

what more conservative, but still upset by the war in Vietnam and occasionally by other problems, the words may be different, but the feelings can be similar to those expressed by the Harvard man.

Mellowing Process

"I don't give a damn," said a 19-year-old Ohio State dropout who works in an office in Coral Gables, Fla. "The war, the bombing, the waste and all that —its so insane that it isn't worth getting mad about."

The uneasy calm that descended on the nation's campuses last year after the major upheavals that followed the Cambodia incursion and the shootings at Kent State and Jackson State seem to have mellowed into something much less than euphoria but much more than alienation. In fact, alienation, a key word in any campus discussion last year, seldom arose this fall.

Last year, as the colleges went silent, the word was out to "watch the high schools, that's where the real action is." This fall, if Boston, Pittsburgh, Washington, Charlotte, Miami, Chicago, St. Louis, San Francisco, Los Angeles and San Diego are any indication, high school students are following the quiet paths of their older brothers and sisters.

"Their definitely is a lot less militancy among students," said Ted Tishman, editor of the student paper at Taylor Allderdice High School in Pittsburgh, echoing words heard across the nation. At a school that had had racial fights and antiwar demonstrations in the past, he added:

'Little Tension'

"Nobody's bugging anybody else. There has been little tension and no discussion of antiwar activity. It seems passé. The kids are not politically active. They seem to be turning inward. There has been a big attendance at football games."

Harder to put a finger on in the over-all picture is the attitude of black youths. Over the last few years, most of them have tended to shun the militant radical movements and the hippie-style counter-culture as the conceits of a well-to-do white middle-class that could afford to play at politics and poverty.

On campuses, for instance, most blacks have concentrated their efforts on matters that they considered of paramount interest to themselves. With the battle for black studies won at many institutions they seem to be concerning themselves primarily with working with college administrations for the admission of more minority students.

The New York Times/D. Gorton

University of Southern California students in a relaxed mood. The tense atmosphere on campuses has eased.

Cracks in the Wall

Like their white counterparts, black student leaders appear to be more interested in working quietly and forcefully through the system rather than taking their grievances into the streets.

Although the trend is not widespread, there also seem to be some signs of cracks in the wall of separatism between blacks and whites. Blacks and whites are fraternizing more on some campuses. At Harvard for instance, a white student noted that where three years ago all the blacks sat together in a dining hall in a sort of self-enforced segregation, they now mingle freely with their white friends without risking the contempt of other blacks.

Many things, most observers agree, are responsible for the changes that are appearing among youth across the nation.

There is an acceptance among the young that the war in Vietnam is being ended. It is happening more slowly and less conclusively than they would like, but most are convinced that they have exhausted, without avail, their efforts to persuade the Nixon Administration to speed up the process.

The draft lottery has eased the anxiety of many young men and at least given others a certain choice to make when their number comes up.

Berkeley Disillusionment

The lagging economy has made scarce jobs more attractive to some and has put pressure on others to work harder in high school and college to meet stiff competition for jobs or for advanced education. Many more youths also seem to be working part-time or seeking such work while they are going to school to meet higher costs, achieve more independence or ease the demands on families that are feeling the economic squeeze.

The 18-year-old vote has had an effect that is difficult to measure. In many college communities, for instance, hundreds and in some cases, thousands of youngsters have registered. Most insist that they intend to vote and there are some indications that many are using that as a rationalization for not taking a more activist role on current issues. However, most also seem pessimistic that their votes will bring about much change.

Even at the University of California in Berkeley, where youthful workers helped last April to produce a radical-moderate deadlock on the City Council, there is disillusionment.

"So we elected three radical councilmen." said Barbara Kane, a senior in sociology. "What difference did it make? It's the same City Council."

Another factor that has contributed to the changing attitudes of the young has been the yielding over the last few years by many colleges and high schools to most demands for revisions in rules and curriculum.

Many Changes Cited

Dress codes have been dropped and course requirements changed in high schools across the country. Countless other demands, as varied as the imagination of local student leaders, have been met. At Palo Alto High School, for instance, the administration has even agreed to stop ringing bells between classes, since some students found them annoying.

At many, if not most, colleges, dormitory rules have all but evaporated. At quite a few, birth control information and contraceptives are distributed at the college dispensary. Required courses have been curtailed. Great numbers of new courses requested by students have been offered.

At the University of Michigan, for example, courses may be taken for credit in the history of the blues, comics and their place in American literature, science fiction, and the history of the student movement in the United States; which may be symptomatic of something.

All the battles may not have been won in all places, but it is hard to find many schools now where reforms seem to be of overwhelming importance to the students.

"At our rap sessions, students are encouraged to express their views and criticism of the educational system and society," said Dr. Jean Hausler, a high-school teacher and counselor in Miami. "We don't try to appear all-knowing. Perhaps for the first time we are listening to their complaints and adjusting our thinking accordingly. I am beginning to be optimistic about our relations now. I wasn't last year."

As important as all the other reasons, perhaps, is an apparently growing conviction among many young people that they have survived years of crises, conflicts and turmoil, of war, assassinations, riots and demonstrations and that now is a time for settling down, for pursuing individual interests, even pleasures.

Return to the Fifties

There is a temptation to view the new attitudes as a return to the fifties, when another generation felt the need for respite from years of war and personal displacement. Some people do.

"It seems like a return to the nineteen-fifties," said Josh Peckler of Massapequa, L.I., a sophomore at Brandeis. "There's more booze, more nice clothes, the music's becoming less radical and softer—Carole King and James Taylor—and people seem to be getting into their middle-class shells and worrying about their future."

He said that more people seemed to be talking about grades, medical school, law school "and less about what's really happening, less about politics, less about universities and less about themselves."

While many people would disagree that there has been a return to the mood of the fifties, he touched on a number of the external aspects of change that are apparent in most sections of the country.

As the use of marijuana has spread through more segments of the population, it no longer serves to divide the "hip" from the "straight." Perhaps for that reason, beer and liquor are no longer put down among the young as the "drugs" of an alien culture. And wine has soared in popularity, sometimes in partnership with marijuana, but more and more for itself.

At Stanford, as at many other places, the social pressure to use marijuana seems to be lessening.

Wine Is Popular

"Not using pot doesn't exclude you from the 'in' group any more," Jim Millea, a senior, explained. He said wine had become extremely popular with upper classmen because "you can keep drinking it and still converse sensibly and you can show off your intellectual wares by becoming a connoisseur of wines."

Despite the increased acceptance of alcohol among the young, the use of marijuana does not seem to have dropped noticeably. However, in most places the use of hard drugs and hallucinogens is reported to have peaked and probably to have declined.

Another visual mark of change has been in clothing styles. As radical groups have all but disappeared from most colleges and high schools and the street people have virtually vanished from many of their old haunts, the street-fighting uniforms, the Army surplus look, the blue jeans and work shirts, and the costumes of the "freaks," the tie-dyed, thrift shop and frontier scout styles, have become rarer and rarer.

With some exceptions, notably at colleges and high schools in the South and in other rural areas that frequently lag behind the national pacesetters, students are dressing up more—not high-style, but neater, cleaner and brighter.

Here-and-Now Stressed

"Duke is probably a few years behind some of the Northern universities in clothing," a student at the institution in Durham, N. C., said, "and the work shirt and jeans are becoming more and more the style here."

But the new trend is taking hold in many areas.

"As concern with the future seems to fade in importance and urgency," a University of Michigan student said, "the here-and-now has gained in significance. Clothing styles have changed from the studied drabness of two years ago, to a variety of stylish, and colorful, but distinctly 'student' fashions.

"Bold color combinations, floral shirts, Indian and embroidered fashions, cowboy boots and wild hats. Anything goes any time."

And at Brandeis, Susan Giavaris, a sophomore, said:

"Socially speaking, Brandeis is coming together, which is incredible. It's getting straight, baby. There's a whole new influx of skirts and sweaters. It's an incredible freak-out. All of a sudden this summer I went out and bought dresses. Why? I felt like feeling good."

October 24, 1971

The Jesus Movement Spreading on Campus

By DOUGLAS E. KNEELAND
Special to The New York Times

PALO ALTO, Calif., Dec. 25 —A new interest in religion, which in some ways resembles the rise of radicalism in the late nineteen-sixties, is taking root on many of the nation's recently becalmed college campuses.

Some of the fascination is intellectual and is reflected in increased enrollment in religion classes. Some of it represents a personal search for human and spiritual values and may draw the seeker to Eastern as well as Western theologies.

But campus observers in many parts of the country agree that the most visible manifestation of this is in the rapid spread of nondenominational, Fundamentalist, evangelical Christianity.

Just as the radicals gained adherents because of the wide disenchantment among the young with existing political and economic institutions, the Christian movement is attracting many who are disillusioned with the established churches and the quality of American life, including some facets of the so-called counterculture.

Both movements have been nourished by a pervasive sense of malaise, by a conviction that old ways have failed and by a search for truth. But, while the growing Christian movement comes at a time when the radicals are in decline on campuses, there is little evidence that the constituencies overlap, that many frustrated political activists are seeking solutions in the spiritual.

The Christians, as they prefer to be called, who make up what is known on campuses as the Jesus Movement, tend to resent being identified as "Jesus freaks," a term usually applied to street people who have frequently dropped out of the drug scene and occasionally out of radical politics to commit their lives to Christ.

"Most of the Jesus people I know seem to come out of the mainstream of life," said Jerry

so clearly a kind of Linus blanket."

The Rev. David Roper, a minister at the Peninsula Bible Church, a nondenominational, evangelical institution that has 15 young internes working with Stanford students, took a somewhat different view.

"One thing is the disenchantment of kids of late with science," he said. "They're hungry for something that's real. There's still a lot of skepticism there, but I see a lot of kids responding to Jesus."

Sipping coffee at a local restaurant, the baldish, serious minister marveled at the growth of the Jesus Movement at Stanford in the last year or so.

"Sometimes it reminds me of a story they tell about the French Revolution," he said with a trace of wonderment in his voice. "You know about the woman who saw a man running after a mob and called out to him, 'Don't follow them. They'll lead to destruction. And the man answered, 'I have to. I'm their leader.'"

Forthright About Beliefs

"These kids are aggressive, they're forthright about their religion, they're unashamed."

Still pondering the sudden upsurge in the movement, he

added, almost as an afterthought:

"I suppose it has something to do with the climate of despair."

The young Christians themselves, from one end of the country to the other, tend to explain their commitment in open, simple terms.

"Freshmen year I saw that what I thought was Christianity was really only 'churchianity,'" said Mark Hoffmann, an earnest, short-haired senior at Stanford who majors in biology. "After I had an intellectual understanding of where I was at and what the alternatives were, I realized in my own mind that I needed Jesus. Two guys who knew Him personally told me what knowing Him meant and then I took the step to go to Him and say, 'Lord, I need you.'"

"I have a real hang-up about the term 'Jesus freak,' because it denotes someone easy to explain away," said Kathleen Polasowski, a junior majoring in social studies at Wayne State University in Detroit. "I've been committed to Christ for two years. The movement will grow. It's really beautiful. We praise God for His goodness."

And at Boston University, which has a small but enthu-

The New York Times/Andrew Sacks
Scene at "Word of God" group meeting in Ann Arbor, home of University of Michigan

A. Irish, a professor of religion at Stanford University here, which has a large contingent of new Christians. "I think an awful lot of them are right out of middle-class and upper-middle-class homes."

"I think there's more going on in theology," he went on. "I think it's an authority structure in a society that's at a loss for authority structures. There's a real authoritative simplicity about the evangelical Christian position that's very appealing.

Sense of Community

"Another factor is that it's a kind of discipline in a society that doesn't take discipline very seriously.

"A third thing is community —there's a real sense of community among people who are part of this movement."

Shaking his head thoughtfully, he added, "The only time that it scares me is when it's

siastic chapter of the Campus Crusade for Christ, one of several evangelical bodies that are actively engaged in spreading the movement across the nation, Joseph Battaglia, a fully committed member, explained:

"When one comes into a commitment with Jesus Christ, it's total. And when one's life is transformed through this total commitment, you've got to believe He's true. The present Jesus Movement bears this out, because people are committing their lives to Him."

There is no question that the movement is growing rapidly, but total numbers across the nation are almot impossible to obtain. Like the radicals before them, the new Christians usually start out with small, extremely dedicated groups such as the one at Boston University, which has about 15 members. By fervent proselytizing and by the example of their own lives, these groups frequently expand dramatically in a few months.

As with the radicals in their formative years, the movement's development seems to be spotty and somewhat unpredictable. Reports by campus correspondents of The New York Times from a score of colleges indicate that at some schools the movement has become perhaps the single most visible force on campus, while at others it has not arrived or is in an early stage where its impact has been negligible.

Large Massachusetts Group

At Amherst, Mass., for example, Campus Crusade for Christ has six full-time staff workers and more than 300 active members out of 24,000 undergraduates at the University of Massachusetts. At Amherst College, the Crusade claims only about a dozen members out of 1,200 students, while at Smith in nearby Northampton it reports 40 members out of an enrollment of 2,400.

The new Christian group at Wayne State in Detroit is estimated at only 50 out of 35,000 students, while at the University of Michigan in Ann Arbor, which has a student body of similar size, several hundred are reported to be in the Jesus Movement. On the Ann Arbor campus, the largest group is said to be the Word of God Community, which started with a prayer meeting of 10 people in 1967 and now has a membership of about 400, more than half of them Roman Catholics.

And so it goes around the country. Dartmouth and Brown in the Ivy League have small but deeply committed groups. The University of Chicago reports no apparent Jesus Movement, but the University of Illinois has well over 100 of the new Christians. At the University of Minnesota, the number is estimated at 200 and at the University of Colorado in Boulder a member said that there were "maybe 75 committed Christians when I got here three years ago; now there are several hundred."

Influence Seems Large

Again, as with the radicals, the new Christians' influence may often appear to be out of proportion to their numbers. Two hundred or 300 active new Christians may represent a small percentage of students on a campus, but, in a year when most students are shunning movements of any kind, they loom large by comparison.

At Stanford, for instance, most persons close to the movement place the number of committed new Christians at about 300 out of more than 11,000 graduate and undergraduate students, but this probably makes them the largest cohesive group on campus. They publish a mimeographed newspaper, The Fish, and meet in 20 separate Bible study groups, an increase of 16 in the last two years. Most of them also attend Seminar 70, a cluster of Bible seminars held each Sunday morning in campus classrooms.

On a recent rainy Sunday at final examinations, more than 160 straggled into a large lecture hall, wet and bedraggled, but greeting one another with cheerful smiles and friendly hugs.

In a few minutes, a guitarist started picking and singing, "Sing that sweet, sweet song of salvation and let the people know that Jesus lives."

Soon the room reverberated with:

And when you know a wonderful secret
You go out and tell it to your friends,
That a life that's filled with Jesus
Is like a street that never ends.

After another song and some announcements, the meeting broke up into seminar groups in smaller classrooms to take up such subjects as "Mere Christianity," "The Gospel of Matthew," "A Song for You," "Christology," and "The Joy of Discovery."

Forty-eight youths crowded into the "Joy of Discovery" class, described as "a workshop in Bible study designed to help you develop a lifetime habit of exploring the Book." It was taught by David Wilbright. Before beginning the class, he asked, as is the custom at all the seminars, if anyone had any problems to share with the group.

Hey, Pray for Her

A slender, dark-haired girl volunteered that she was soon getting married and that she had found herself becoming so self-centered that she had resented when her parents asked her to paint the bathroom.

"I just want to stand in the forgiveness of the Lord," she said.

"Hey, Mary, pray for her," Mr. Roper said softly.

"Let peace and calm come into her life," Mary prayed.

In the "Christology" seminar, Jack Crabtree, a 1971 Stanford philosophy graduate who is a Peninsula Bible Church interne, was discussing the Atonement. Declaring that Jesus died on the cross to expiate the sins of man before and since, he went on to say that God had been impressed.

"He said, man, that's a quality sacrifice," the slim, young lecturer said, his eyes shining behind his glasses. "I like what you did. That's my Son, man. That's a quality sacrifice."

Waiting a moment for it to sink in, he added, "That's pretty exciting."

Most of the new Christians seem to agree, but there are others in the campus religious community across the nation who are not so excited about the whole Jesus Movement and its scorn for traditional churches, its total acceptance of the Bible as the given word of God, its every real belief in the presence of the Holy Spirit and its joyful expectation of the Second Coming.

Some Couples Break Up

"I had a student in this office who had come down from a Jesus high," said B. Davies Napier, dean of the chapel and a professor of religion at Stanford. "He said it was like having been on a drug high for a number of months. He thought it was fraudulent."

"Another tragedy from my point of view," he went on, "is the number of couples who are breaking up, where one member gets picked up by the 'Jesus freaks' and the other can't accept it."

Dean Napier's criticism, though harsher than most, was typical of the attitude of many campus ministers.

For the last decade or more, large numbers of them had been preaching social activism, the importance of the church's reaching out beyond its doors to play a role in the community. Now, with traditional churches barely holding their own at most schools and admittedly being in some difficulty, they are worried by the great growth of the apolitical, Bible-oriented Jesus Movement, which shuns social involvement.

"The Jesus Movement is not going to lift a finger to change the status quo," Dean Napier said disapprovingly. "They're waiting for the Second Coming and Christ is going to take care of all that."

CONFEREES BACK 900 MILLION FUND TO AID EDUCATION

4-Year Plan to Spur Science Gives 295 Million in Loans —Scholarships Omitted

By BESS FURMAN
Special to The New York Times.

WASHINGTON, Aug. 21—A four-year Federal education bill devoid of scholarships was approved today by Senate-House conferees. It would cost about $900,000,000 and be chiefly designed to spur science education.

The compromise bill goes first to the Senate, with passage assured. In the House, acceptance is also generally predicted.

The main provisions of the bill specify $295,000,000 for student loans and $300,000,000 to help schools buy scientific equipment.

Both Senator Lister Hill and Representative Carl Elliott, the Alabama Democrats who sponsored the legislation, were gratified at the results of the prolonged conference sessions on Tuesday, Wednesday and today.

Said Representative Elliott: "I think we have an excellent bill."

Said Senator Hill: "It has many good provisions."

However, Senator Hill deplored the lack of scholarships.

"The House struck scholarships out," he said. "The Cooper amendment on the floor of the Senate seriously damaged the scholarship concept and stripped the Senate conferees of their bargaining power with the House conferees."

Regrets Scholarship Ban

Senator H. Alexander Smith, Republican of New Jersey, joined Senator Hill in expressing regret at "not getting a scholarship program which would have given national recognition to intellectual achievement." Senator Smith said that, except for the scholarships, the compromise provisions closely paralleled the program requested by President Eisenhower and constituted "a positive step forward."

The amendment sponsored by Senator John Sherman Cooper, Republican of Kentucky, which was eliminated today by the conferees, would have reduced scholarships to $250 annually each.

The extensive loan program adopted by the conferees would be administered by institutions of higher learning, as in the House bill, instead of by state boards, as the Senate bill asked. This was a victory for the Administration.

The conferees also accepted a vocational education program not sought by the Administration. It was softened, however, by a Senate amendment tying the funds closely to training in skills necesary for defense industries.

The chief features of the compromise bill follow:

¶Loans—$295,000,000 for four years. The amounts would be $47,500,000 the first year; $75,-000,000 the second year; $82,-500,000 the third year; $90,000,-000 the fourth year. Up to $1,000 could be borrowed by a student each year, with interest at 3 per cent to start one year after graduation.

Half the amount of the loan would be forgiven to students going into teaching after graduation and continuing to teach for five years. The House bill had no forgiveness provision.

¶Science equipment—$300,-000,000 in matching grants to the states at the rate of $75,-000,000 each year. Private schools would be eligible for equipment. The House had asked $60,000,000 a year, but the Senate prevailed.

¶Institutes for teachers to learn counseling—$28,000,000. at $6,250,000 the first year and $7,250,000 each of the three other years.

¶Institutes for training foreign language teachers—$29,-000,000 at the rate of $7,250,-000 each year.

¶Fellowships — estimated at $59,400,000. Amounts would be about $4,800,000 the first year; $12,200,000 the second year; $19,900,000 the third year; and $22,500,000 the fourth year. Included would be allowances for dependents as well as stipends for teachers improving their skills. Stipends would start at $2,000 the first year and increase to $2,400 the fourth.

¶Guidance, counseling and testing —$60,000,000, at the rate of $15,000,000 a year for grants to be matched by the states.

¶Centers for teaching little-known modern languages—$32,-000,000 at the rate of $8,000,-000 a year.

¶Research and experimentation on better educational use of television, radio, and audiovisual aids — $18,000,000 of which $3,000,000 would be authorized for the first year and $5,000,000 for each of the three succeeding years.

¶Vocational education in skilled trades necessary for defense—$60,000,000 at the rate of $15,000,000 a year.

¶Improvement of state educational statistics — $6,500,000, with $1,000,000 authorized the first year; $1,500,000 the second, and $2,000,000 for each of the third and fourth years.

Authorized also was a scientific information center to which no specific sum was assigned. It would be partly financed by the National Science Foundation.

The first estimates of the staff of the Senate Labor and Public Welfare Committee on the cost of the compromise legislation was $887,400,000.

August 22, 1958

Sharing the Costs

17 Colleges Pool Facilities To Cut Their Expenses

As costs and enrollments rise, the nation's thousand or so smaller private colleges find it harder and harder to meet the demands on their modest endowments and budgets.

United States Office of Education officials believe that one of the answers is cooperative effort by groups of neighboring institutions to enlarge their programs, or by coordination to do their present jobs more economically.

Last week the Fund for the Advancement of Education made a small grant to a group of seventeen Virginia colleges to further their cooperative efforts. The $12,600 grant will enable the group to buy a filmed course of lectures by historian Arnold J. Toynbee, which the member colleges will use as the basis for a credit course.

This is one of a dozen or more cooperative efforts which are suggested and administered by a central agency, University Center of Virginia, Inc., set up by the colleges.

By working as a group through the center, each institution is able to afford lectures by twenty-five or thirty leading scholars each year. Exchanges of professors enable colleges to offer courses they lack by paying only a share of the exchange professors' salaries. Cooperative summer schools can together offer a full curriculum, with each institution having to provide only a part. Cooperative adult education and library services also are offered.

One of the notable benefits, according to Center Director Herbert W. K. Fitzroy, has been the stimulus which cooperative action has given to research.

Clearing House

The center, acting as a clearing house, asked each institution to submit standard application forms for the kind of research it could best do. The center then sought foundation aid, which the applying institutions had to match. From virtually nothing, research activity has grown to 153 grants in six years and resulted in the publication of forty-three books and seventy-nine monographs.

Some other groups of colleges, notably one composed of Amherst, Mount Holyoke, Smith and the University of Massachusetts, are also going deeply into cooperative enterprises. The Virginia group, Office of Education officials said, has been receiving a lot of attention from other colleges recently because of the effectiveness of its central organization.

April 26, 1959

485

The nation's women are the principal victims of rising education costs. A major reason: parents are more inclined to scrape up money to finance the education of sons than daughters. This is a conclusion of a survey by the American Association of State Universities and Land Grant Colleges, which covered its ninety-four members. The survey was published last week.

Even in the relatively low-cost state institutions, tuition and fees for state residents rose more than 71 per cent in the past eight years; room and board increased 27 per cent in the same period.

Recent reports indicate that only 55 per cent of girls in the top 10 per cent of high school graduates enter college. In the fall of 1959, 39 per cent of all girl graduates, compared with 54 per cent of the boys, went on to college after completing high school.

Girls Priced Out of College Education; Universities Fight State Rules

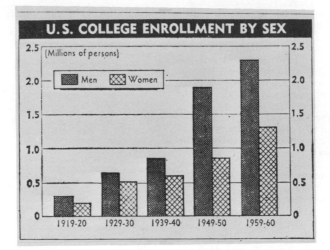

The chart shows the college enrollment ratio, men to women, since 1919. Men get more family financing than women.

The association's survey attributes the lag in large part to the low priority that families give to the education of women when funds are limited. As costs rise, parents offer less objection to borrowing against the future to educate their sons, the survey found. It recorded that "parents felt the sons should get whatever money was available because the daughters would soon marry." The report noted, however, that the United States Department of Labor predicts that young women will work outside the home for about twenty-five years, mainly after their children are grown.

Other factors which the survey said made it less difficult to finance education for men, as compared to women, are better opportunities for men to gain higher vacation and school-year earnings, and larger scholarship grants to men which often come from sources not available to women, such as athletics and engineering.

June 11, 1961

Not Such B.M.O.C.'s

The stands may still roar for the heroes on the gridiron, but on the campus a different view of them prevails.

By **WILLIAM BARRY FURLONG**

ONCE it was an article of high faith that you had to be a football hero to get along with the beautiful girls. That is still largely true *off* the college campus. *On* campus the status of the college football player is in decline. "It used to be a fashion to worship football players," says a senior at a Midwestern college. "Today it's the fashion on campus to knock them."

In the old, idolatrous days, the college football hero had a spectral, not to say supernatural, quality. Red Grange was a galloping ghost. The Four Horsemen were not just any set of jockeys; they were of the Apocalypse. The very names of the heroes reflected the robust dimensions of their legend: Bronko and Pug, Bulldog and Marchie, Ruffie and Eggs ("You get in his way, you'll get scrambled").

In those days the antic mummery of a college week-end—the games, the pageantry, the touch of the bacchanal—was not so much a homecoming as a coronation. Legend fed imagination and imagination fed legend.

WHAT has happened to make today's football hero a non-hero on campus? The change is due largely to the population expansion and other forces which required colleges to raise mental standards. Naturally, its heroes are going to reflect that change in taste and outlook. College students have simply put them outside their cultural orbit. "We go to the games and cheer," said one co-ed, "but really, they're not a part of us."

To a certain extent, the "football system" fought for exactly this: a place apart—and a little above—the general student body. But the "system" didn't work out as expected. Instead of the players being admired and envied for the special privileges they enjoy on campus, they are now regarded indifferently (except among those whose whole orientation is physical). In fact,

By permission Broadway Music Corp.; and Leo Feist, Inc.
SONGS TO CHEER BY—The image of the football hero of other days was enhanced by tunes like these.

the general student body now appears to dislike a system in which a "Mickey Mouse with muscles" can enjoy special privileges not available to the rest of the student body and most spectacularly not available to the student who is merely intelligent.

WHAT about these special privileges?

Financially, they frequently include the historic "ride" offered athletes — tuition, room, board, and books. At many colleges, the football player is offered a "job" on campus to justify a small salary paid him. In some cases, the alumni offer tidy "gifts" — autos, money, high-paying jobs for little work in the summer or the assurance of a good job after graduation. (Many of these "gifts" violate the rules of the National Collegiate Athletic Association — the governing body of college sports — but the rules have long been honored more in the violation than in the observance.)

Otherwise, the special privileges range from details- i. e., one college forbids scholarship students from owning cars on campus, but makes an exception for football players on athletic scholarships- to broad, if subsurface, concessions on the academic level. The extent and nature of these privileges is not uniform; some colleges simply demand more of — and give less to — football players than do other colleges. But there is a conspicuous uniformity in the way the colleges — coaches, deans, and students — talk about the academic problems of athletes on campus.

The coaches — almost all coaches — maintain an enchanting ambivalence about their players. Publicly, they insist that the players are measuring up to the tougher academic pace of today's college culture. Privately, they concede that they must still recruit about three players for every one who will survive long enough to play varsity ball as a senior. Most of the rest fall prey to academic problems, although a few get homesick, get married, get injured, or get hired away by other colleges.

The deans tend to support the public attitude of the coaches — that the players are superbly qualified for college. It is part of the rationale for big-time football, a sort of national chorale of deans chanting, "Whatever *other* colleges may do, *we* maintain the strictest academic standards for students playing football."

THE cry has become more acute under the rising academic pressures of recent years. The dean of students at the university mentioned above says: "Six years ago, the football players here avoided wearing the jackets and letters they had earned. Today, they're proud to wear them. They know they're just as good academically as the next guy. They can't stay here unless they get the grades."

The students, less ingenuous, more intimate with the situation and its harsh realities, insist that many of the players who *do* survive academically do so only with extraordinary help and stretching of academic standards.

THEIR attitude toward the situation varies with many factors. Among them: whether the school has a winning team (they'll overlook many "privileges" to bask in an unbeaten season); how important football is to the school (as, say, a fund-raising device or simply as a game) and how many privileges are actually extended specially to the football player. Quite clearly, many, many students resent not the players but the system which gives the players so many special privileges. Here is a sampling of opinion collected recently.

Sorority girl — "The dumb boy who is a football player has a better chance of getting through college than the dumb boy who isn't."

Another co-ed: "We kind of hate football players. We break our necks to get a B and they show up twice a year and get the same grades we do. And everybody knows they get all the tips on exams ahead of time."

Male senior who roomed with a football player last year — "I resented it terribly when I found out how he was getting through school. It's bad enough he got all the extra help we didn't get, but when the tutors arranged for by the athletic department gave him the answers to the tests he didn't know enough to write them down. He was

a wonderful guy, the warmest person in the world. But I resented it when I found out his diploma will look as good as mine."

Male senior who is enthusiastic about football — "I'd be stupid not to know the bad doesn't go on. Sometimes the football players have the blue [exam] books all filled out before anybody else takes the exam. But I think the good outweighs the bad. The football player has a job to do. I say let him do it."

That seems to reflect the status of the football player on campus today. He is there to do a job, just as the janitors, the electricians, the groundskeepers are there to do theirs. His attitude toward his job determines, in large part, how he'll be accepted in the college community. If he ventures into the general culture of the college community, he'll be accepted enthusiastically by the other students. But if his job — football — is his whole life, then there is a precipitous decline in popularity.

Most assuredly, the beautiful girls will date him, particularly if he's "cool" or a "good 'face' man" — that is, handsome. But they'll be careful not to brag too loudly about it. There's no status these days in dating a football hero who's known around campus as a "dumb jock." One co-ed says, "The only person it really matters to is your father. He thinks it's a big deal."

ON this campus, the football player finds that the top fraternities no longer will make concessions to him. "Of the top five houses, not one would pay a football man to get him to join," says one fraternity man. The "payments" were usually in the form of forgiven dues and forgotten initiation fees — perhaps $200 to $500 a year, depending on the fraternity.

If the status of the football hero on campus is in noticeable decline, then it is only a matter of time before that decline becomes conspicuous off the campus. For, as their fathers did before them, so today's college students will see as heroes in life the types of persons that struck them as heroes on campus.

Who are they? What sort of person has supplanted the football hero on campus?

In some colleges it is the editor of the student paper, in others it is the director of the drama group or music group. There is reason to believe that, as the trend from the physical to the cerebral continues, the exceptionally

The gridiron star's falling star — "There's no status these days in dating a football hero."

Drawing by Abner Dean.

HERO?—Harold Lloyd in a gridiron spoof, "The Freshman."

THE FOUR HORSEMEN—Miller, Stuhldreher, Crowley, Layden.

intelligent student will enjoy greater popularity (though it is apparent that he will have to indulge in more than studies —just as the football player must indulge in more than muscle-building—to win that popularity.)

At this particular college in the Midwest, the rising cam-

pus figure is clearly the student politician. "If you really want to 'climb' on this campus," says one co-ed, "the people you have to know are the ones who run the campus organizations."

A number of girls were asked to name those they wanted most to date and those they thought their best girl

friends wanted most to date. The overwhelming response was for the president of the Student Council.

The dean of students reflected this view, not only as it applied to his campus but as it applied to a number of other colleges. "The campus politician makes good copy

for the campus newspaper every day," he said. He riffled through a pile of college newspapers on his desk.

"Look through these—the campus politicians are all over page one in every paper. You don't see too much about individual football players, even on the sports page."

November 26, 196?

NEW WANDERLUST

College Students Seek Maturity Through 'Leave' From Campus

By FRED M. HECHINGER

More than five qualified applicants are currently competing madly for every available place in next year's freshman class at Harvard, Yale and Princeton. It may therefore come as something of a surprise that before the current academic year ends at least 120 undergraduates at Harvard alone will have departed voluntarily because they felt that, at least for a while, they would rather be somewhere else. The great majority of these students, and their fellow escapists at other colleges, will be coming back to their original campuses a year or two hence to finish their undergraduate work.

The relatively new phenomenon of the "leave of absence" was described in detail by C.

Boyden Gray in the Oct. 27 issue of The Harvard Crimson's Weekly Review. A spot check by The Times at other colleges shows that while the number of students who interrupt their studies, for reasons other than academic financial or health deficiencies, varies greatly from campus to campus, the trend is unmistakable.

Radcliffe's Dean of Students estimated that about 25 to 30 girls take the equivalent of leaves every year.

General Restlessness

At Colby College, in Maine, 14 students left "on their own" in the past three years, seven having since returned.

Lawrence College, in Wiscon-

sin, reports that there is a noticeable increase in temporary leaves — last year 12 students went off on various travel expeditions abroad and in the United States. Most of them have come back.

What appear to be some of the reasons? A general restlessness among students is undeniable. It has already led to a substantial increase in student transfers from one college to another. The trend toward earlier marriage and the tendency among students to take dating and romance before marriage more seriously have meant that girls not only transfer to a college closer to their husband's station but also follow the trail of potential husbands.

But the increase in leaves of absence points to a different restlessness. Dr. Elliot Perkins, Master of Harvard's Lowell House, in comparing pre-war students to today's generation, said that before admission became highly competitive, college was mainly "an experience to be lived." Now it has become

something to be "exploited," and many students therefore feel that they would be better able to make the best of the colleges' resources if they first sought greater maturity.

Dr. John J. Conway, Master of Leverett House, added that greater selectivity in admitting students leads to greater sensitivity. Able students are often plagued by serious self-doubts — a drive to prove themselves in a non-academic setting.

The reasons why students take time off are startlingly similar in different places. George T. Nickerson, dean of men at Colby, told of a student who "just plain couldn't settle down because courses had no meaning." Another student "thought he wanted an entirely different experience" went to New Zealand to work and study.

The frustration of standing on the sidelines — absorbed with theory while others act — has had some impact. Barnard released a girl who, committed to integration, "had to" work in the South. The Peace Corps has had similar effects.

Healthy Basis

But a Radcliffe spokesman also felt that the greatest number are propelled by a vague sense that they are not quite ready to take advantage of what higher education might offer them. The trend has a healthy basis and students are usually welcomed back, without excessive obstacles.

John U. Monro, dean of Harvard College, said: "The important thing is breaking stride. After 14 straight years of education, a lot of students get restless." They want to run their own lives, get out of the academic competition, break away from institutions. But he added, it is important not to generalize—what may be good for one student may be wrong for his roommate.

Richard C. Carroll, associate dean of Yale told the Crimson editors that statistically the students who stayed out longer tended to do better after they returned. Mrs. Mary I. Bunting, president of Radcliffe, agreed, pointing out that "the lock step isn't good for everybody." This was strikingly illustrated when Hamilton College, at Clinton, N. Y., this year gave one boy the year off "just to read."

It is tempting to read lofty aims into every trend. Some young people have been hurried along the educational road too fast and too rigidly by overly college-conscious and prestige-seeking parents. Others simply lack sufficient self-discipline to resist the impulse to do right away things that might sensibly be postponed. Making college the normal routine for so many in some instances has devalued its meaning: instead of a privilege, it looks like a chore, and the grass suddenly looks greener off-campus.

Affluence can lead to aimlessness. A spokesman at Hamilton College pointed out that the well-to-do are more likely than scholarship students to go off in search of adventure.

But because some restlessness is the result of justified dissatisfaction, colleges are trying to build escape hatches into their plans. Six of the Big Seven women's colleges (Bryn Mawr, Barnard, Wellesley, Mount Holyoke, Smith and Vassar, but not Radcliffe) have long permitted students, if they can show good reason, to take their senior year at one of the other five colleges and then come "home" for commencement.

More Opportunities

Lawrence College, like many other institutions, offers many more opportunities for students to work at off-campus "field stations," such as the Argonne National Laboratory.

Such outlets reduce youthful wanderlust. But many colleges build traveling itself right into their curriculum. A representative of Stanford University in California said there had been no increase in the number of temporary withdrawals, since the university operates permanent campuses in Germany, France, Italy and Japan. About one-third of all students spend at least half a year abroad.

Compared to the real academic casualties — about half of each year's total freshman class across the nation falls by the wayside — the temporary leaves of able students may seem a minor problem. But as a trend, it shows the kind of ferment that must be taken into account at a time of change, if the changes are to meet the future.

November 4, 1962

SEARCH FOR NEGRO STUDENTS

Leading Northern colleges and universities are making a collective effort to reach into the South to bring talented Negro students to their campuses.

The Ivy League (Brown, Columbia, Cornell, Dartmouth, Harvard, University of Pennsylvania, Princeton and Yale) and the Seven Sisters schools (Barnard, Bryn Mawr, Mount Holyoke, Smith, Vassar, Wellesley and Radcliffe) have undertaken an unprecedented joint "talent search."

The effort is remarkable because it is based on cooperation among the very institutions which normally compete with each other and tend to play the admission and recruiting game pretty close to the chest.

"Negro students are discouraged before the fact from applying to our schools," Charles E. McCarthy, Jr., assistant admissions director at Yale, said last week while on a recruiting trip for all 15 institutions in Kansas City, Mo.

"Our job is to tell them that not only admission but also scholarships are available," he said.

Henry S. Coleman, director of admissions at Columbia College, praised the collective effort because "we do not have a member of the staff to devote full time to this."

On his field trips, Mr. McCarthy seeks to establish lines of communications with high schools which have previously not even considered the Ivy League for their students.

He meets with high school guidance counselors, teachers, and students, referring potential candidates to two or three of the colleges which he thinks will be most suitable for them.

Mr. McCarthy will take a four-week trip through the Deep South in December, when he plans to visit South Carolina, Georgia, Alabama, Mississippi and Louisiana.

In addition, undergraduates from the Northern colleges are

October 20, 1963

PRESIDENT SIGNS COLLEGE AID BILL

Hails It as Most Significant Education Act in History, a Monument to Kennedy

By United Press International

WASHINGTON, Dec. 16 — President Johnson signed legislation today setting up a $1.2 billion program to help colleges build classrooms, laboratories and libraries. He called it the most significant education bill in history.

The measure authorized $835 million in grants and $360 million in low-interest loans over three years. It is designed to meet needs for a wave of students who will be entering colleges through the decade.

In hailing the bill at a White House ceremony, the President indirectly noted that it authorized the first broad assistance program for colleges since the Land Grant Act a century ago.

Praises Supporters

The bill is an authorization measure and must be followed by legislation providing the funds. If fully used, the program would generate up to $3 billion in new construction at 2,100 educational institutions.

Mr. Johnson paid tribute to President Kennedy for having fought for the program, and to members of Congress of both parties who had supported it.

He called it a monument to Mr. Kennedy, saying no subject had been closer to his heart.

He referred to those who had channeled the bill through the House and Senate: Senator Wayne Morse of Oregon and Representatives Adam Clayton Powell Jr. of Manhattan and

Edith Green of Oregon, all Democrats.

"This is the most significant education bill passed by the Congress in the history of the Republic," the President declared.

He predicted that "this will go down in history as the Education Congress of 1963."

But he said it was no time to stop in meeting educational needs. He urged the approval of other Administration proposals, particularly aid to primary and secondary schools, and Government support for adult education programs.

Under the program signed today, colleges will match Federal grants on a 2-to-1 basis. They will supply at least a quarter of the total project cost when seeking the authorized 50-year loans.

The program is open to privately endowed and church-connected schools as well as those publicly owned and financed. But no funds may be spent on chapels or divinity schools, nor on sports arenas or other auditoriums charging admission.

Classrooms built under the grant program must be designed for instruction in the sciences, mathematics, engineering and modern foreign languages. The bill set aside 22 per cent of the undergraduate grants for junior colleges and semi-professional technical institutes.

The President used about 50 pens to sign the bill, passing them out afterward to those in the audience. One each went to Mr. Morse, chairman of the Senate Labor and Public Welfare subcommittee that had worked on the bill; Mrs. Green, the Senator's counterpart in the House, and Mr. Powell, chairman of the House Education and Labor Committee.

GIFTED DISPLACING RICH AT IVY 'BIG 3'

Harvard, Yale and Princeton Are Taking Fewer Sons of Prominent Families

NEW UPPER CLASS SEEN

Accomplishment Is Reported to Be Replacing Wealth as the Key to Status

By ROBERT TRUMBULL

Fewer scions of socially prominent families are taking the traditional academic road to Harvard, Yale and Princeton. The heirs of wealth are being edged out in the "Big Three" universities by better-qualified students.

One result of this trend is the growth of a new kind of upper class in the United States, in which membership is obtained by accomplishment rather than inheritance.

These conclusions grew out of a study of the New York Social Register by Gene R. Hawes, a free-lance writer and editor who has been closely associated with various university publications. When he published his findings in an article in the latest issue of Columbia College Today, a quarterly magazine at Columbia University, wide interest was aroused in educational circles.

"The frantic competition for the prestige colleges after the war has forced many sons of the rich into the frathouse and drum-majorette kind of schools," the Princeton Alumni Weekly commented in an editorial on the Hawes article.

'Radical Change' Seen

The Williams Alumni Review remarked, in a review of the Hawes article, that the new academic trend has accompanied the emergence of an "aristocracy of the able," replacing the aristocracy of the wealthy. The movement represents a "radical change" in the direction of "meritocracy," the magazine said.

The analysis of the New York Social Register, 1963 edition, by Mr. Hawes showed that while nearly two-thirds of the men listed went to Harvard, Yale or Princeton, fewer than half of their sons have followed in their fathers' footsteps to the Big Three.

The flood of academically qualified veterans applying for university admission after World War II forced the Big Three to choose between social atmosphere and intellectual quality in the student body, Mr. Hawes says.

"Intellect won, though not easily or decisively," he notes. "Gradually, painfully, the upper-class colleges severed as amicably as possible their links with the least-qualified members of the prominent families."

'Social Colleges' Rank High

As a result, Mr. Hawes says, students at "the leading social colleges" now rank among the top 10 per cent nationally for intellectual attainment.

"Upper-class students who could not meet the academic demands have had to go elsewhere to college," Mr. Hawes says. He adds, however, that some socially prominent applicants who could qualify to enter the Big Three preferred other schools for their "different kind of atmosphere."

Although almost two-thirds of the men listed in the Social Register went to one of the three colleges, the rest have dispersed themselves widely among more than 100 other institutions, Mr. Hawes found.

This would amaze the British, "whose upper class almost to a man has attended only Oxford and Cambridge," Mr. Hawes remarks.

In his investigations, Mr. Hawes found that an earlier change of significance in college attendance patterns occurred after the Civil War. Before the war there were "venerable" colleges in almost every eastern state, where most of the powerful families lived, so that traveling to a far-away school was "not only difficult but pointless."

New Fortunes Created

Then American business organizations expanded on a national scale, increasing old fortunes and creating new ones.

"The new national upper class warily recognized new members, centered its work and its homes more and more on New York, grew well accustomed to travel by rail, and started sending its sons away to college," Mr. Hawes says.

Why, in this period, didn't more of the upper-class families living in New York send their sons to Columbia? Because, Mr. Hawes answers, Columbia opened its doors to immigrants' sons—"predominantly Jewish, Irish and Italian"—who "seemed not only deficient in money, manners and cultural interests but excessively prone to taking academic work seriously."

Gradually, up until just before World War II, Mr. Hawes says, "scions of the upper class were joined in college by more than equal numbers of young men from the middle class, and even some numbers of the lower class sons who possessed great skill in athletics."

More Changes After War

The end of World War II further changed the social complexion of the famous schools, according to the Hawes findings.

Yet social class remains a matter of concern to college administrators, Mr. Hawes says, because it is from families of great wealth that the schools have to get their money.

Nevertheless, says Mr. Hawes, "a new kind of American upper class is slowly being forged," in which ability is more important than wealth. It combines "the best of the old upper class and the most talented of the lower and middle classes."

"The new alignment of 'haves' and 'have-nots' according to highly developed talents rather than accumulated wealth and social position may have fundamental consequences for American democracy," Mr. Hawes concludes.

STUDENT LOANS AID 600,000 IN 6 YEARS

WASHINGTON, Sept. 12 (AP)—About 600,000 students have been helped to obtain or continue a college education by loans available under the National Defense Education Act, the Office of Education reported today.

This was one of the highlights in a review of actions taken under the legislation, which was enacted six years ago this month.

Students from kindergarten through graduate school have been helped, the office reported.

Among other achievements, it said that the act had resulted in the training of 42,000 skilled technicians to meet critical manpower needs, and the granting of 8,500 graduate fellowships, a first step toward meeting the need for many more college teachers.

More than $1 billion in Federal funds have been expended at all levels of education, public and private, under provisions of the act. The law is scheduled to expire on June 30, 1965, but bills before the House and Senate would extend and expand the programs.

The some 600,000 students in 1,574 colleges and universities who have received loans under the program have borrowed about $453 million. The Federal Government puts up about $9 to every $1 provided by the educational institution.

ENROLLMENTS SET COLLEGE RECORD

Total Soars Past 5 Million —Increase Exceeds 10%

WASHINGTON, Dec. 2 (AP) — Enrollment in the nation's colleges and universities soared to a record total of 5,320,294 students this fall, an increase of 10.8 per cent over the 4,800,332 listed in the fall of 1963.

The Office of Education reported this today. It said the increase reflected the fact that postwar babies were now reaching college age in increasing numbers.

"This impact is expected to be just as great next year," the office said.

Students entering college for the first time and taking degree-credit courses increased by 17 per cent this fall in contrast to an average rise of approximately 7 per cent annually for the last 12 years.

These first-time students totaled 1,234,806 compared with 1,055,146 a year ago, 1,038,620 in the fall of 1962 and 1,026,087 in the fall of 1961.

Thus, the increase between the fall of 1961 and the fall of 1964 was 20.3 per cent, with practically all of it coming this year. First-time students are freshmen with no prior college education.

Students working toward bachelor or higher degrees number 4,987,867 this fall at 2,135 institutions.

In addition, 332,400 students 60,000, or 22.3 per cent, more than last year — are enrolled in special one-, two- and three-year programs to equip themselves for employment. Most of the work in such programs is not creditable toward a bachelor's degree.

The total enrollment by those working for degrees broke all records for the 13th consecutive year. The 4,987,867 students more than doubled the 2,469,000 enrolled 10 years ago and ran 10 per cent above the total of 4,528,516 in the fall of 1963.

Of this fall's total enrollment, 3,441,814 students, or about two-thirds, are studying full time.

The proportion of women among the degree-credit students edged up slightly for the eighth consecutive year, from 38.4 per cent to 38.8 per cent. There were 1,936,106 women enrolled last fall, compared with 1,738,989 a year earlier and 1,467,243 in the fall of 1961.

4 Colleges Found Another, Using a Gift of $6 Million

New England Schools to Try to Lower Cost of Quality Education

By FRED M. HECHINGER

Three leading private New England colleges and a state university announced yesterday that they would join in the creation of a new coeducational liberal arts college in western Massachusetts made possible by a $6 million gift from a single donor.

Hampshire College, as the new institution will be called, is named after Hampshire County, its home county. The college is expected to serve as a testing ground to determine how high-quality education can be offered at substantially reduced cost. It is expected to admit its first class of 250 freshmen not later than September, 1969, with plans for an eventual total enrollment of 1,000.

Smith and Mount Holyoke Colleges, both women's schools of the high-prestige Big Seven; Amherst College for men, and the University of Massachusetts will give the new institution their full "academic support." This will include a sharing of faculty and joint planning of courses and departments. The presidents of the existing colleges will be members of Hampshire's first board of trustees. Harold F. Johnson, a retired 69-year-old lawyer of Southampton, L. I., who was a member of Amherst's class of 1918, pledged the initial $6 million.

A site of 350 acres is already owned by, or under option to, the new college in the area of South Amherst and Hadley. The future campus in the Connecticut River Valley is roughly equidistant from the four supporting institutions—about five miles from each.

The site consists of rolling land, much of it farmland, with open fields, small forests of spruce and some apple orchards. To the north, it looks up the Connecticut Valley and to the south lies the Holyoke range of hills.

Mr. Johnson's interest in the creation of a fifth college in the area is reported to have been aroused by a proposal written in 1958 by a joint faculty committee of the four institutions. Entitled the "New College Plan," the prospectus attracted nationwide attention as a possible pilot project that would permit the expansion of prestige higher education through the sponsorship of new colleges by leading old ones.

In addition, the plan called for dramatic departures from the traditional use of faculty time and talent, with stress on independent study, and with an economical cooperation between a number of institutions.

Although the plan failed to get the hoped-for dollar support from foundations, elements of the cooperative approach were subsequently adopted by the four colleges. For example, a joint department of astronomy was established. Students and faculty members often study and teach on campuses other than that of their home college.

New Women's School

Library exchanges by station wagon have reduced the expense in stocking each campus with some of the more specialized volumes. An educational FM radio station is also jointly operated.

The new institution will be created to extend these exchanges of courses and teachers and the cooperative use of facilities.

Hampshire College, since it will be free from the traditional commitments governing curriculum, alumni, departmental divisions and faculty vested interests, is expected to engage in experimentation to determine whether the costs of education can be substantially reduced without the damage to quality and prestige that is thought to attend the expansion of relatively small institutions.

In a somewhat different move, St. John's College in Annapolis, Md., created a new branch in Santa Fe, N. M., a year ago. However, the two institutions are operating under one board and president, whereas Hampshire College will have its own governing body and chief executive.

Earlier this year, Hamilton College, a men's college in Clinton, N. Y., announced that it would create a coordinate women's college near its campus. Similar plans have been discussed but not finally approved by Wesleyan College in Middletown, Conn.

Hampshire's curriculum will be developed with an eye to the prevention of unnecessary proliferation of courses. If a high-quality, specialized course is offered by one of the neighboring institutions, it will be considered more sensible to let the students travel to the course rather than import the course itself.

Extraneous and often costly features, such as intercollegiate athletics and fraternity houses, will be eliminated.

It is estimated that the initial plant will require a total expenditure of about $15 million. Tuition and board, by rough guess, will be in the neighborhood of $3,000 a year, which is expected to cut the per capita cost of education to the school. A faculty of about 50 professors is expected, but many appointments will be made jointly with the other institutions.

In addition to Mr. Johnson and the presidents of the four institutions, the first board will include Charles W. Cole, president emeritus of Amherst and former ambassador to Chile, and Winthrop S. Dakin of Amherst, a lawyer.

An interim organization, the Hampshire College Educational Trust, has been formed to conduct the planning of the college. Charles R. Longsworth, formerly assistant to the president at Amherst, is chairman of the trust.

PRESIDENT HAILS NEW COLLEGE AID

Signing Bill, He Says Loans and Grants Will Enable Thousands to Enroll

By JOHN D. POMFRET
Special to The New York Times

SAN MARCOS, Tex., Nov. 8 —President Johnson returned today to the college from which he graduated 35 years ago and signed the pioneering higher education bill.

The students at Southwest Texas State College gave the institution's most famous alumnus an enthusiastic reception despite a drenching rain that forced the ceremony indoors.

Speaking in the college gymnasium, the President heaped praise on the last session of Congress for having done "more to uplift education, more to attack disease . . . , more to conquer poverty than any other session in all America's history."

"Too many people, for too many years, argued that education and health and human welfare were not the Government's concern." Mr. Johnson said. "And while they spoke, our schools fell behind, our sick people went unattended and our poor fell deeper into despair.

"But now, at last, in this year of Our Lord 1965, we have quit talking and started acting."

140,000 to Be Helped

President Johnson told his audience of 3,500 students and teachers that the Higher Education Act of 1965, which provides new scholarship, loan and work opportunities, would enable 140,000 young people to go to college "in the next school year alone."

He said of the legislation:

"It means that a high school senior in this great land of ours can apply to any college or any university in any of the 50 states and not be turned away because his family is poor."

The $2.3 billion program, over three years, also expands Federal grant-in aid programs for construction of college facilities and purchase of equipment.

The law sets up a National Teacher Corps to provide teachers for elementary and high schools in poor areas. But while the first-year authorization for the entire program is $852 million, Congress has appropriated only $160 million so far—with no funds for operating the Teacher Corps. The Administration expects to get the rest of the money for the year ending next June 30 in a supplemental appropriation next year.

Mr. Johnson told his audience the people expected the Federal and state governments to work together to achieve "an education system that fits the needs of the 20th century." He added:

"I want to make it clear . . . that the Federal Government . . . intends to be a partner and not a boss, in meeting our responsibilities to all the people." Mr. Johnson declared. "The Federal Government has neither the wish nor the power to dictate education."

While the greeting that the President received at his alma mater was warm, the welcome given him by 2,000 Job Corps trainees at Camp Gary, outside San Marcos, was warmer.

Mr. Johnson, who dedicated the Job Corps training center last April, touched down at the center in his helicopter for a visit before going on to the college.

The Job Corps trainees are for the most part poor, untrained, uneducated youths, 16 to 21 years old, who have dropped out of school. They are learning occupations at the center.

They were standing behind a rope at the airstrip. When the President approached, those in the rear surged forward, trying to see him, say hello to him and shake his hand, Mr. Johnson had to step back to avoid being pushed back.

As he walked along the rope, trainees who already had seen him ran behind the crowd and farther down the line, to try to shake hands with him again.

The President quickly fell in with their mood. He flipped his hat to an aide, who fielded it neatly, and later shed his raincoat despite the drizzle.

In the welding shop the President talked earnestly with several boys. He asked Isaac Dillon, 17 years old, of Bogalusa, La., why so many youths dropped out of the Job Corps.

"Some come here thinking it's a joy place," the welding trainee replied.

The President asked David Pearce, 17, of Mangum, Okla., if he liked the Job Corps and if he would be willing to pay taxes to support it after he got out and got a job. The youth answered yes to both questions.

"I'm betting on you fellows, and I believe you're going to make it," Mr. Johnson told the Oklahoma youth. "But don't let me down."

In his talk in the gymnasium, Mr. Johnson told how he had left the campus to teach in an elementary school in the Mexican-American neighborhood of Cotulla, Tex. He was a teaching principal during the 1928-29 school year. He took the job to earn money so he could complete college.

The superintendent of the Cotulla school system at the time, William T. Donaho, was in Mr. Johnson's audience today, and the President asked him to stand. Mr. Donaho, now 79 years old, lives on a ranch at Floresville, Tex., and came here at the President's invitation.

Today was by far Mr. Johnson's most strenuous since his surgery on Oct. 8 to remove his gall bladder and a kidney stone. He seemed to be enjoying himself, but he was tired after his speech and went directly to his helicopter for the 55-mile flight to his ranch.

There he signed several other bills, including the Sugar Act of 1965. This measure allocates the $10 million annual sugar market in the United States between domestic and foreign producers for the next six years. Domestic producers will get 65 per cent of the market, and 31 foreign nations will get the rest.

The Higher Education Act provides scholarships of from $200 to $1,000 a year for qualified, needy students. It authorizes Federal guarantees of low-interest loans to students and expands grants to institutions to enable them to pay students up to $500 a year for work.

The measure authorizes grants to states to strengthen community-service programs of colleges and universities, such as extension services and research programs designed to assist in the solution of housing, poverty, transportation, recreation and youth problems.

It authorizes programs to improve libraries. It also provides for assistance in upgrading the academic standards of weak colleges. It would do this through Federal aid for cooperative arrangements between institutions for faculty exchanges, joint use of libraries and faculty improvement programs.

The President, acting before a midnight deadline, tonight disposed of his legislative chores for this year by signing the last 15 bills remaining before him. Among the bills was a measure providing Federal assistance for victims of hurricane Betsy.

SHOPLIFTERS RAID YALE'S BOOKSTORE

27 Caught in 3 Weeks— Problem Called National

Shoplifting was described yesterday as the No. 1 problem facing college bookstores throughout the country.

The problem was cited yesterday by Charles L. Willoughby, general manager of the cooperative store at Yale University. He said that "we have apprehended at least one student a day for the last three weeks."

A total of 27 Yale students were apprehended for shoplifting in his store during the three-week period. Mr. Willoughby said. He added that the cooperative, a two-story rubblestone structure on Yale's central campus, lost $90,000 to shoplifters during the last fiscal year.

"Our shortage has been doubling in the last two years," Mr. Willoughby said in a telephone interview.

"The problem here is no greater than at any other college store," he said. "This is just a nationwide pattern."

The shoplifters at Yale include a wide range of undergraduates, graduate students, foreign students and even a divinity student accused of taking a textbook on the Bible, according to Mr. Willoughby.

"This is a pathetic thing." he added, referring to the divinity student.

Mr. Willoughby said he could offer no explanation for the sharp increase in shoplifting by college students at Yale and elsewhere.

He added that shoplifting by students was not confined to the campus store, but extended to retail stores throughout the university area.

The student shoplifters are turned over to the New Haven police, Mr. Willoughby said. He noted that the university usually withheld action until court action had been taken but that student shoplifters faced eventual suspension from school.

"What concerns us most," he went on, "is what effect this sort of thing could have on a student's career. He could be suspended, could be prevented from entering graduate school, could get a police record."

Carl E. Forsberg, director of the Columbia University bookstore, said last night that shoplifters were "caught daily" in his store, but that he did not discern any recent increase.

"I do not think it's on the increase." he said. It's always there. Maybe they [other college stores] have just become aware of it. We have been aware of it for some time."

November 13, 1965

N.Y.U. Forming School of Arts To Go Beyond Technical Skills

By SAM ZOLOTOW

New York University has organized a School of the Arts, which will seek to carry training a step further than a conservatory does. The school, said to be the first of its type in the United States, will be divided into three institutes: performing arts, film and television, and visual arts programs in painting and sculpture.

The announcement was made yesterday by Dr. James M. Hester, president of the university. Dr. Robert W. Corrigan, professor of dramatic literature at the university, was appointed dean of the collective institutes.

The first to start, in the fall of 1966, will be the performing arts section. The opening of the Film and Television Institute is planned for 1967 and the visual arts division in 1968.

"The creation of the new school," Dr. Hester said, "is in keeping with New York University's urban orientation and its tradition of adopting new approaches to learning in the city."

The university is furnishing $500,000 toward the first year's operation of the performing arts program. An additional $1 million will be sought from foundations. The combined procedure will apply to the other two institutes "to make this thing more than a piece of paper." a spokesman said.

Listing the advantages of the School of the Arts over a conservatory, Dr. Corrigan said:

"In a conservatory, the young artist is primarily trained in the techniques of his art. Because we believe the artist must also have a well-developed mind and imagination as well as a mastery of technique, the university is a more suitable place for training.

"Most schools stop right at the point where the young person of talent needs training the most. If we believe that training must be continuing, then we must be constantly making opportunities available to the artist as he matures and grows."

Professional artists will be employed in the three institutes as master teachers. They will work with students to meet the special needs of each one.

The theater program calls for a junior repertory company to appear for invited audiences, and one with advanced performers to give public performances. A Theater Center is to be formed for rehearsal, experimentation and discussion by actors, directors and playwrights.

The emphasis of the Film and Television Institute will be placed on training for the field, management training and experimentation. In the visual arts area, there will be training programs for artists and apprentices, with students participating in major projects undertaken by the master teachers.

THE LIBERAL ARTS FIND A DEFENDER

Columbia Report Challenges Early Specialization at Cost of General Studies

RELATION TO LIFE URGED

Bell, of College's Faculty, Asks Course in Problems of the World Today

By FRED M. HECHINGER

Columbia College began yesterday a defense of general education on its own campus and throughout the country.

Daniel Bell, a professor of sociology, appointed by the dean of the college as "a committee of one," opened a sharp counterattack against the viewpoint that general education must be sacrificed to the demands of earlier specialization.

The report, which is expected to be debated by faculty members at Columbia and throughout the country, specifically challenged the opinion expressed earlier by Jacques Barzun, dean of faculties and provost at Columbia University, that the liberal-arts tradition in the colleges was dead or dying.

Instead of abandoning the college years to specialization, Professor Bell said, colleges should expose undergraduates to Greek and Roman history at the start of their college studies, and they should be required to relate their general education, when they reach their senior year, to such questions as urban renewal and world economy.

Expansion Proposed

In his appeal for the re-establishment of the once central position of the liberal arts, Dr. Bell urged the following:

¶That Columbia College be expanded by 50 per cent — from its present enrollment of 2,700 to about 4,000.

¶That all students be offered a new set of general education courses in their senior year in which they would relate the liberal arts to such specific areas as urban renewal, the development of new states, the problems of the public bureaucracy and the philosophy of science.

¶That the required freshman course in contemporary civilization be extended from one year to one and a half years, with special stress on Greek and Roman history in the first term.

November 18, 1965

493

¶That every student, in addition, should be required to take a one-term course in economics, sociology, government, anthropology or geography.

¶That all students should take a two-year mathematics-physics or mathematics-biology sequence.

In a 312-page analysis called "The Reforming of General Education," Dr. Bell challenged the growing belief that improvement of the high schools has made much of the colleges' general education program obsolete or redundant.

He charged that the high-school reforms had not been nearly as effective as was often contended. He warned specifically that many students entered college with woefully inadequate knowledge of English.

"The hue and cry to foreshorten the college years to speed the boy into sophomore standing and spin him into graduate school in his senior year—these are not only destructive of the college; they are, more sadly, destructive of the student himself," Dr. Bell said.

Dean Barzun said on the telephone yesterday that he had not read the report. He added: "I am sure Dan Bell has done a superb job. If there is some disagreement with what I have said, so much the better for the fun of the debate."

Despite his defense of general education, Professor Bell asserted that much of the present program was in need of change. He described the present science requirement as "a mishmash."

Minimum Standards

Dr. Bell called for the abolition of freshman English. But to make this step possible, he said, all Ivy League colleges should require certain minimum writing standards for admission.

The current "modishness" of offering college-level work in the humanities in high school, "will quickly wear out," he declared, because students at that age lack the maturity to draw meaning from such studies.

Dr. Bell described as his most radical departure from past general-education programs the proposal of a "third tier"—after acquisition of general cultural background and the study of a discipline—in which the liberal-arts experience is made relevant to modern life and contemporary problems.

For example, students majoring in the social sciences would, in their senior year, take a course in "the development of new states," relating economic, political and social theories to the development of a society from rural to industrial life.

Similarly, students majoring in science might be required to take a senior course that examined the philosophical and social inmpact of science on contemporary problems.

March 1, 1966

Relaxed Campus Rules Reflect Liberalized Attitudes on Sex

By JONATHAN RANDAL

A favorite off-campus student haunt at Cornell University is a basement coffee shop called The Unmuzzled Ox. Founded by a Lutheran pastor, it takes its name from the Bible verse: "Thou shalt not muzzle the ox when he treadeth out the corn."

The verse, from Deuteronomy xxv, 4, reflects as accurately as possible a trend among some university authorities to let students run their own lives—especially sex lives.

Student involvement in civil rights causes, where civil disobedience has brought about major changes in the law, has led some undergraduates to question all rules. This questioning is perhaps the most evident in students' attitudes toward parietal rules, the regulations governing life and order within university grounds.

With some notable exceptions, a survey of Columbia, Cornell, Fordham, New York University, Princeton and Yale finds growing reluctance by university officials to legislate "in loco parentis."

If anything, university authorities, by their own admission, have been purposely slow in adjusting regulations governing student behavior to what has been called "the permissive society" and "the sexual revolution."

"Older universities tend to drag a bit over change in social customs," a dean at one Yale residential college said, expressing what was by no means an isolated view. James B. Laughlin, assistant dean of students at Princeton, said: "I don't think we gain any respectability by being in the forefront."

But there has been change, especially in the relaxation of rules on visiting hours for women in men's dormitories. Most of the universities surveyed now allow women to visit men's dormitories at least until midnight on Saturdays.

For example, Columbia, which banned women visitors in men's dormitories for the first 209 of its 212 years, extended the visiting hours last winter. Now women may visit until midnight on Fridays, instead of the former 9 P.M., and until 1 A.M. Sunday, an hour longer than before. The university also dropped the requirement that room doors be kept slightly open during visits.

Even at Fordham, a Roman Catholic university and the strictest of those surveyed, rules were liberalized last spring, although liquor and women are still banned from the dormitory rooms of its 487 boarders.

Fordham sophomores and juniors are now allowed to sign out—rather than obtain a pass from the dean of men's office— to be away from their dormitories until 1 A.M. on school days. On weekends, boarders can sign out until 3 A.M. Also, the hours for arising and going to bed have been abolished.

Not one university official interviewed expressed dissatisfaction with the results of the liberalized rules—although several said they had expected serious trouble. But the number of rule infractions has remained constant—and low.

Universities do not make public information about rule infractions. But it is generally believed that none of the schools has to deal with more than half a dozen violations of visiting hours every year. Many involve forgetfulness of only a few minutes in getting girls out of dormitories by the deadline.

Cornell Revising Code

And while university officials do not like to make predictions, it is considered likely that the rules will be further relaxed. Cornell, for example, is in the process of rivising its social code.

The university officials appeared less worried about students' sexual behavior than they are by the use of narcotics and drugs. While no university official would say that drugs posed a serious problem among undergraduates now, their serious concern for the future was summed up by one dean who crossed his fingers.

Increasingly the attitude of university authorities is that discretion, rather than rigid morality, should be the gauge of student sexual behavior.

George S. May, dean of Yale College, said: "We are not interested in the private lives of students as long as they remain private." Another Yale official, Richard C. Carroll, dean of undergraduate affairs, said: "Don't think we are trying to protect the honor of young men and women. It's ridiculous to think you can."

Ruth Darling, assistant dean for residence halls at Cornell, where junior and senior girls have virtually no curfew, said: "We don't ask what they do and don't want to know. We don't ask because the girls are presumed to be responsible." But she added that "we know that all are not responsible."

The greater tolerance by university officials reflects changing parental attitudes and growing student touchiness.

Parents Also Changing

One university official recalled the case of a student who was discovered in bed with a girl in his dormitory room well after visiting hours. The boy's parents found nothing out of order in his behavior and were astonished that the university took a dim view.

Not so many years ago such serious infractions of campus rules would have led to automatic expulsion. Today, especially with men students risking the draft if expelled, the trend is to study the motivation. For example, if the couple had been going together, were in love, had been to bed before, then such factors would amount to extenuating circumstances.

Many infractions now are handled by disciplinary probation or less severe action.

Even the majority of students who honor the letter and spirit of the rules are increasingly sensitive about the university's right to run their lives for them.

"If the university moves to tighten parietal rules," one Cornell student said, "even the prudish Quakers among us will take a libertarian line."

Much of this attitude stems from student involvement in the civil rights movement, where civil disobedience has brought both rapid change and general antagonism to respecting certain laws for their own sake. More tolerant legal decisions on pornography and movie moral codes are also credited with creating a permissive, questioning attitude to all regulations.

Dean Harris A. Schwartz, assistant dean for residence halls at Columbia, said: "Students today are too bright to be treated as children. They should be allowed greater permissiveness but without letting them destroy themselves or hurt themselves for the future."

But in many a student's mind undergraduate demands for liberalized rules have a certain logic since most universities have given them greater academic freedom than ever before.

The current college generation is almost uniformly credited with being the brightest best prepared and hardest working ever to matriculate. In most of the surveyed universities, the traditional cut system — limiting the number of lectures that could be missed— has either been abolished for all but freshmen courses or is in the process of being abolished.

Still, there is a lack of clarity and logic in some student demands, which at times gives the impression of anarchy.

"When it comes to who sleeps with whom, the university must stay out of my life," Mr. Schwartz said, imitating an imaginary student. "But the university has the right, indeed the responsibility to provide contraceptives and birth control information. When it comes to the draft, I want the university to write a letter to my draft board."

Talking to students, university officials and teachers leave the impression that sexual revolution or not, most undergraduates are only slightly less conservative in their behavior than their counterparts of 15 years ago.

As one university professor said: "Some undergraduates' behavior may not seem moral to me. But in many cases, it is much more honest in terms of their own morality."

What has changed most noticeably is that sex is now openly, often clinically discussed.

"I don't think sex was the big issue" behind student demands for liberalized parietal rules, one Columbia senior from California said. "I think it was pretty much a question of does the university treat us as adults or as kids. They keep telling us we're supposed to be mature and responsible. It was sort of incongruous for them not to treat us that way."

The availability of off-campus housing is considered more important than rules in determining the undergraduates' attitudes towards sex. At N.Y.U., Columbia, Fordham, and Cornell many students live off-campus where university officials do not enforce any visiting hours.

But at Yale and Princeton, visiting privileges are considered extremely important because virtually all undergraduates live in dormitories and college girls are in relatively short local supply. Student newspapers at both Yale and

Princeton have come out in favor of coeducation.

Princeton Complaints

Princeton students tend to feel their situation is the unhappiest. Cars are banned on campus, the local hotels are considered too strait-laced and, in the words of one disgruntled undergraduate, "the little ladies who rent rooms to dates on weekends are ferocious."

Apparently typical of many Princeton students, one junior acknowledged that "you have to be terribly unlucky to be caught," but said he abided by the visiting hours he hated.

At Princeton students may have female visitors Sunday through Thursday until 7 P.M., Friday until 9 P.M. and Saturday until midnight.

In New York City, almost a quarter of Columbia College's 2,700 students live off-campus. Last year more than four out of five students answering a dean's office questionnaire said the main reason they lived off-campus was dissatisfaction with women's visiting hours in the dormitories.

At Cornell, about 45 per cent of the 7,142 male undergraduates live off-campus in a nearby residential section known as college town. A 20-year-old junior girl estimated that as many as 150 of Cornell's 2,398 coeds were living with Cornell boys in college town.

"If you're a junior or a senior, you only have to check in at the dorm once a day," she said. "Most parents don't know and don't want to know."

Did any of the girls living with boys tell their parents? she was asked. "That," she replied, "depends on how you brought up your mother."

April 25, 1966

Now a Degree Is Path to Power

By FRED M. HECHINGER

In the past, when education was described as the nation's first line of defense or as the individual's road to opportunity, the lines had the ring of do-gooders' bromides. Last week, a socio-economic commentator, David T. Bazelon, pointed to a new trend—the emergence of education as the tangible asset that buys economic, technological and ultimately political power in modern America.

The issue here is not the one posed by the rather offensive "public service" advertisement in the New York subways which says: "Education is for the Birds (the birds who want to get ahead)." The ad is mainly concerned with the drop-outs and their difficulty in finding jobs. The Bazelon theory is concerned, not with low-level employment, but with high-level power.

Mr. Bazelon, author of "The New Class in America," to be published early next year, writes in the current issue of Commentary that power in the corporate and technological society is passing to "the propertyless New Class." This influential group gained status, not through the amassing of personal riches, but through prestigious positions in private or public organizations and the physical comforts and prerogatives attached to these positions. The passport to these outposts of power and prestige is the academic degree and educational qualification.

The influence of higher education is growing rapidly. In 1960, some 2,000 institutions of higher learning enrolled about 3.2-million students. By now, the annual enrollment is already past the five-million mark. By 1980—in a conservative estimate—the number of persons above the age of 25 who have completed four or more years of college will be 14.4-million.

The trend is unmistakable. While higher education in the past was of economic interest only to the relatively few professional people—the teachers, ministers, lawyers and doctors—it is now the crucial stepping stone to power and status in business, government and the general management of society. It is no longer just the adornment of gentlemen and ladies.

On the contrary, higher education is a prime investment. A decade ago this was recognized only in discussion of the problems of underdeveloped countries, or of the crash program of industrialization in the Soviet Union.

Growing Relationship

It is this growing relationship between education and top-level politico-economic power that has been behind the so-called college admissions rat race, especially the frantic drive to get into the high-prestige colleges. It is in these institutions that academic ability competes most furiously with the old clientele of wealth and family background. Gene R. Hawes, a college admissions expert, reported that while nearly two-thirds of the men listed in the 1963 edition of the New York Social Register went to Harvard, Yale and Princeton, fewer than half of their sons followed in their footsteps. Their place has been taken by the educationally nouveaux-riches (or those who want to enter that bracket) from the public schools.

Those who always hoped for the greater power of education in the management of society may be tempted to hail the trend as the coming of the millenium. Indeed, reliance on education rather than on inherited power or accumulated wealth does move the United States closer to the American dream of the open society—as does the effective rivalry of the new, so-called Red Brick Universities with the Oxford-Cambridge establishment in Great Britain.

But with the advent of higher education as negotiable currency for the attainment of power and prestige in the corporate and technological society, new problems arise.

Whatever may have been the limitations of higher education as the mere adornment of the well-born (and some occasional newcomers admitted to the club) it had the advantage of being unrelated to the marketplace. While this option contained the germ of irrelevance, it also gave scholarship the opportunity for true independence.

Occasionally, of course, pragmatic inroads were made on this ivory tower, with its luxuriously generalist devotion to things cultural. Germany's frenetic dash for hegemony at the beginning of the century turned its universities into high-quality professional trade schools. American universities, in search of better medicine and law, were excessively influenced by this trend for a while. Even before this, the advent of the land-grant colleges had put these new institutions in the service of the agricultural and industrial revolution.

As higher education becomes the passport to power, the in-

495

dependence of educational goals and content is threatened by off-campus considerations and pressures. This, more than anything else, explains the crowding out of the generalists' (or liberal arts) education and the crowding in of career- and power-oriented specialization.

If higher education is the passport to technological and managerial as well as governmental power, then the liberal arts content of education may quickly come to be regarded as the non-functional and therefore superfluous remnant of the ornamental past.

Understandably, the young men and women (and their parents) in search of power and success through the investment in higher education have their eyes on the returns on the investment. The danger is that higher education will turn out to be so functional that the emerging new leadership will at best be a-cultural and at worst anti - cultural. Modern thought and esthetics then would turn into the equivalent of those functional, styleless shopping centers or culturally neutral, factory-modern public schools.

Even more serious, since planning in government, industry and social legislation is properly a priority of the new leadership's concern, this could lead to a mapping out of the future by people who have no intellectual roots in the past.

Alarmed voices are being raised, such as that of Columbia's sociologist Daniel Bell ("The Reforming of General Education," Columbia University Press), to warn against the fragmentation of a society in which highly educated specialists are unchecked by generalists with a broader and longer vision.

Since it is unlikely that personnel directors will go out of their way, except in commencement speeches, to support an education that is more than functional training for efficiency, the colleges and universities may have to fight the curriculum battle without much outside help.

But they will have to be careful not to pose as protectors of the doomed status quo of general education as a prerequisite to the green pastures of specialization. Perhaps the victorious banner will be that of a new fusion of cultural and pragmatic education so that the New Class will not increasingly be one of efficient, boorish automatons.

COLLEGE SUICIDES REPORTED ON RISE

Total for Year Is Estimated at 1,000 Campus Deaths, With 9,000 Attempts

By HAROLD M. SCHMECK Jr.
Special to The New York Times

WASHINGTON, Oct. 3 — During 1966 there will be 1,000 suicides among American college students, according to estimates in a study made public today.

The same study estimates that 90,000 students will threaten suicide and one in 10 of these will actually make the attempt. The estimates are projections based on a recent survey of colleges, together with evidence from earlier published studies of suicides.

A "pressure-cooker" emotional atmosphere on today's college campus was cited as a contributing factor in student suicides.

Speakers at a news conference today on the suicide study said the number of such student deaths seemed to be rising. But they added that it was impossible to tell how many of these deaths resulted simply from an increase in the number of college students and the increasingly broad variety of persons now going to college.

Sees Shortage of Help

The study is published in the October issue of Moderator, a magazine aimed at top-ranking students. Philip R. Werdell, editor of the magazine and author of the study, said the impetus for the study had come from a conference on student stress held last year.

Mr. Werdell estimated that as many as 10 per cent of the nation's 6½-million college students had emotional problems serious enough to warrant professional help, but he said that college mental health programs were not extensive enough to reach more than half of that total.

Dr. Edwin Schneidman, co-director of the Los Angeles Suicide Center, said he believed the figure of 1,000 suicides among college students in a year's time to be conservative.

Dr. Schneidman, who is also a consultant on suicide problems for the National Institute of Mental Health, took part in the news conference with Mr. Werdell and others.

In keeping with the "pressure-cooker" aspects of the modern competitive college life, speakers at the news conference said it was their impression that suicides were most likely to come at or near examination time. Dr. Schneidman said graduate students had a higher suicide rate than undergraduates.

Student Group Involved

The National Institute of Mental Health is sponsoring a series of current studies on student stress and how to deal with it. The study program, an outgrowth of the conference on stress last year, is being conducted through the National Student Association in whose offices here the news conference was held today.

The survey made public today estimated that suicide was the second most important cause of death among college students.

"Students die of little else than accidents (37 per cent) and suicide (34 per cent);" the study said, quoting a report from University of California at Berkeley. Altogether, the national suicide rate among students appears to be 50 per cent higher than that for Americans in general, the article in Moderator added.

The over-all national suicide rate is estimated at 11.6 per 100,000 population for the year 1965, in which there were 22,560 suicides, according to figures available from the Public Health Service.

On the

By FRED M. HECHINGER

When John U. Monro resigned a week ago as dean of Harvard College to become Director of Freshman Studies at Miles College, a struggling Negro college in Birmingham, Ala., he focused on the nation's Negro colleges the dramatic attention they seldom get.

Miles College's basic condition and Dean Monro's mission serve as a simple primer on the problems and goals of the great majority of the nation's 123 Negro colleges which still enroll the majority of all Negro undergraduates.

Founded 62 years ago under the auspices of the Christian Methodist Episcopal Church, Miles is the only college in the fiercely segregationist Birmingham metropolitan area to which the city's annual class of 4,000 Negro high school graduates may aspire.

By 1960, however, Miles was bankrupt. Lack of books and Ph.D.'s had led to its disaccreditation. As it was about to shut down, Lucius H. Pitts, an optimistic and courageous Negro educator who, 52 years ago, was born as the seventh son of a Georgia tenant farmer, agreed to take on the presidency (at $7,500-a-year) and try to save the institution.

Dr. Pitts sent students out with tin cans to collect money for the library. Racist police authorities halted the door-to-door campaign but the national publicity started contributions rolling in.

Today, with the library stocked and 15 Ph.D.'s on the faculty, Miles is within grasp of re-accreditation. But its day-to-day problem was less to satisfy the accrediting agency than to find ways of making educable the hundreds of Negro youngsters who sought admission — the freshman class takes in about 400 a year. Their past schooling could not be relied on to equip them for higher education.

When Dean Monro was asked: "Why Miles?" he replied, "Because the man asked me down." The man was, of course, Dr. Pitts, and he had asked Dean Monro three years ago to come during the summer and help groom poorly educated youngsters for the freshman year and to transform a traditionally

Ailing   Negro   College

rrelevant freshman program into a curriculum that could excite the students.

Under the new program, for example, freshman social studies start with questions of local elections and voter registration and with the organization of the area's anti-poverty program.

"When we tested these youngsters, the intelligence scores showed nothing, but when we got them into the classroom, things happened," Dean Monro said. The answer, he said was to forget about the tests and work directly with the students.

This, then, is the story of Miles, as brought to public attention by Dean Monro. What is the larger story of the nation's Negro colleges?

Although a few Negro colleges opened in the North before the Civil War, none granted a bachelor's degree until after 1865, and the great rush to found Negro colleges began during Reconstruction, largely under missionary auspices.

About 200 such institutions were established, much like the Protestant and Catholic institutions of some 50 years earlier, with more faith and determination than funds and intellect. More than half of them had disappeared by the turn of the century, a mortality rate about equal to that of the white colleges of the era.

Today, 49 private Negro colleges (37 of them still church-related) survive. The remaining 72 are either junior colleges or state colleges.

Originally, the private Negro colleges were almost entirely supported, governed and staffed by whites, and only gradually was control shifted to Negro administrators and faculty (often as a result of the increasingly rigid segregationist laws) and even some predominantly Negro boards of trustees.

Although some of the Negro colleges had a tradition of high courage and silent defiance of the South's racism, the atmosphere was more often one of educational and social conservatism. While many Negro college campuses became the only meeting places of Negro and white intellectuals in the South, penalties for any challenge to the restrictions of the region were too brutal to be risked

by many Negro faculty members. Loss of a job meant the end of a career.

The remarkable fact was not that so many Negro colleges minded their own business but that some, such as Fisk and the cluster of Negro institutions around Atlanta, became the frontline of the battle for social justice and intellectual freedom.

David Riesman and Christopher Jencks, two noted social critics, reviewed the history of the American Negro college in the Winter 1967 issue of "The Harvard Educational Review." They described the understandable effort to copy the white institutions, partly as an attempt to overcome the "outrageous injustice" of the hostile surroundings.

"The cumulative result of all this was that the Negro college of the 1950's was usually an ill-financed, ill-staffed caricature of white higher education—which was, after all, easy enough to caricature," they wrote.

Many of the Negro colleges had adopted the worst attributes of the worst of the white colleges—"the intervening trustees, the domineering but frightened president, the faculty tyrannized by the president and in turn tyrannizing the students . . . the emphasis on athletics, fraternities and sororities."

Like Nigerians "wedded to a University of London syllabus," too many of the faculty members used to "cling to a pallid version of the academic tradition, itself in need of revision," the Riesman-Jencks critique said. "Insecure and marginal, they became insistently pedantic."

This, they stressed, was far from the total picture. At the head of the Negro academic procession, as they put it, stand a handful of well-known private institutions such as Fisk, Morehouse, Spelman, Hampton, Howard, Tuskegee and Dillard, and an even smaller number of public ones. Other analysts would include Bennett, Talladega, Knoxville and Lincoln University.

But, these observers add, while the great majority of the Negro colleges, quite understandably, "stand near the tail end of the academic procession," even the leading ones are at present only "near the middle . . . comparable to

. . . small and not very distinguished sectarian colleges or fairly typical state colleges." The average Negro college, they found, pays the faculty only 75 to 80 per cent of what the typical white college pays.

Ironically, the significant improvement of the Negro student's position in the nation's predominantly white—and especially the high-prestige— institutions may make the upgrading of the Negro colleges even more difficult. The cream of Negro youth is now skimmed off and enrolled, with scholarship support, in these colleges. While this trend is essential and, if anything must be speeded, it does not help the struggling Negro college.

This is why the Miles-Monro episode is important. Neither Dr. Pitts nor Dean Monro has visions of turning Miles into an instant Alabama Harvard. On the contrary, Dean Monro, recognizing that half of each year's freshman class will for the foreseeable future fail to go beyond a year or two in higher education, speaks of offering a freshman science course that will make the best of what for many will be their last chance at formal science instruction.

The immediate mission, in other words, is not one more blurred carbon copy of mediocre white education, but a boost of the education, the aspirations and the opportunities of great masses of Negro youngsters whose prior education has been stunted by the tradition of exclusion and neglect.

The Riesman-Jencks analysis puts it somewhat differently. It suggests that colleges such as Miles are beginning to play the role of private commuter colleges, serving their urban constituency in much the same way as the small Jesuit colleges used to serve theirs.

Different Negro colleges will seek different ways, most of them with the ultimate goal of integration. But the chapter begun at Miles and dramatized by Dean Monro's personal commitment stresses the urgency of the search for new, unconventional and pragmatically relevant ways to let these colleges serve a new generation of Negro youth, without regard for the dictates of standard college catalogs.

IVY LEAGUE SHIFTS ADMISSION GOALS

Variety Now More Important Than Geography—12,354 Accepted as Freshmen

By WILLIAM BORDERS
Special to The New York Times

NEW HAVEN, April 16 — The Ivy League colleges are moving swiftly away from geographical distribution as a major standard in admitting students.

With something that they call "student diversity" as the new criterion, the eight Ivy League colleges are enrolling more Jews, rejecting more preparatory school students, and tending to ignore the postmark on the application.

Yesterday, when the schools sent out their 12,354 highly prized letters of acceptance, one, undoubtedly, went to the archetypal Episcopalian from Greenwich and another to the farmer's son from Montana, for balance.

But, increasingly, letters also are going to the promising Negro from Newark and to the public high school student from the Bronx and other areas relatively close to the Ivy League schools.

"Of course, we still send our recruiting people to out-of-the-way places like Nevada, but there's really as much diversity in taking Harlem, Park Avenue and Queens," said R. Inslee Clark Jr., the dean of admissions at Yale.

According to Dean Clark, Yale has almost completely abandoned the goal of geographical distribution, which most Ivy League colleges were pursuing a decade ago to insure their status as national universities.

To broaden the character of the student body, special consideration was given to an applicant from a remote state like North Dakota or Mississippi, and the system tended to discriminate against the big Eastern cities, particularly, New York.

Jewish Enrollment Rises

Since metropolitan New York is the home of 40 per cent of the nation's 5.6 million Jews,

497

the move away from the system is cited as a possible reason why Jewish enrollment in some Ivy League schools has increased sharply.

At Yale, more than 20 per cent of the freshmen this year are Jewish. Ten years ago the figure was 10 per cent.

There, and at the other schools, deans said the residence of applicants had declined in importance as personal factors, such as economic background, had gained.

"I got into the Class of 1950 at Harvard because I was from Idaho," said Fred L. Glimp, Harvard's dean of admissions, "and now I run a policy that's really the reverse of the one I benefited from."

It was in the nineteen-thirties that Harvard decided to start giving an edge to applicants from outside the East, Mr. Glimp explained. At the time, 75 per cent of its undergraduates were from New York and New England.

Twenty years later, with the percentage from New York and New England nearly cut in half, "we suddenly said: 'wait a minute, maybe we're neglecting our own back yard,' so we're pulling back on this geographical distribution thing," he said.

Deans at the Ivy League colleges also cite the mobility of modern Americans as a reason for paying less attention to where they live.

"If a boy moves from Rye to Shaker Heights, has anything about him really changed?" one dean asked.

Background Counts

Although most of the Ivy League colleges still give some slight preference to applications from states or regions that seem under-represented, background is often more important. As John T. Osander, Princeton admissions director, said:

"It's not the place they're from, really, but rather some sense of a different background that we're looking for."

As an example, he mentioned a member of a 4-H club in Missouri who would be important to Princeton's diversity because he was interested in farming, not because his home

was 1,000 miles from the campus.

The desire for diversity has also brought a sharp decline in the number of Ivy League students from the Eastern preparatory schools. For example, 60 per cent of the present Yale freshmen are from public high schools, compared with 40 per cent 10 years ago.

St. Paul's School, one of the most select preparatory schools in the country, sent 35 per cent of its graduates to Yale, Harvard and Princeton last year, about half the number it was sending 15 years ago.

The decline has distressed St. Paul's sufficiently so that last spring, immediately after the Ivy League admission letters had been sent out, the school's rector, the Rev. Matthew M. Warren, visited Yale and Princeton to lodge strong protests with the university presidents.

The change in what the Ivy League is looking for is also reflected in the recruiting effort, which the colleges are vastly intensifying, despite their contention that they could fill their dormitories with bright men even if they did not solicit a single application.

The admissions deans have established elaborate alumni reporting systems in which graduates scout for their alma mater in their home towns. Harvard has seven such alumni committees searching New York City alone.

This year there were 45,591 applications for the 7,688 places in the freshman class at the eight colleges. Five colleges reported more applications than a year ago—the biggest increases were 12.8 per cent at Cornell and 12.6 per cent at Columbia.

The biggest downward change was a 3.3 per cent decrease in applicants at Brown, where there were 4,800 applications for 710 places.

Harvard appeared the most confident of being the first choice of its applicants—it sent out only 1,340 acceptances for 1,200 places in the freshman class, a narrower margin than any of the other seven.

Although total enrollments have grown only slightly, the Ivy League schools have expanded their admissions offices.

Ten years ago, Yale had two full-time men, who made recruiting visits to a few hundred secondary schools a year. Now the staff has grown to 15, and the number of schools visited is 1,200.

"Many of the places where we're looking for students now were places where they just didn't used to think in terms of Yale," Dean Clark said. "Erasmus Hall in Brooklyn, for example, was very surprised to see our man when he started going there last year."

Presumably because of Yale's expression of interest, six boys from Erasmus Hall applied for the present freshman class, and four of them were accepted.

The new recruiting efforts, particularly in New York City, is a possible reason for the increase in the number of Jewish students at Yale.

"Take the Bronx High School of Science," Dean Clark continued. "Until three years ago, we didn't do any recruiting there at all, even though it's one of the best public schools in the country. Now we do, and we get more people from there, and I suppose many of them are Jewish."

Like other Ivy League schools, Yale has said over the years that it never had any religious quotas, although the number of Jews in each class in the late nineteen-fifties "tended to be between 103 and 109," according to Rabbi Richard J. Israel, the Jewish chaplain.

Figures Inexact

Rabbi Israel based his estimates on questionnaires each incoming freshman fills out—after he has been accepted—for religious guidance. The original application blanks do not have questions about religion.

Although the figures are inexact, partly because, as one chaplain put it, "Jews cannot be precisely identified," they indicate substantial increases in Jewish enrollment in most of the Ivy League schools since World War II.

Now about 40 per cent of the

undergraduates at Columbia and the University of Pennsylvania are Jewish. The figure is thought to be between 20 and 25 per cent at Yale, Harvard and Cornell, and between 13 and 20 per cent at Dartmouth, Princeton and Brown.

But admissions officers scrupulously avoid conceding any knowledge of the religious make-up of a class. When asked about the sharp and recent rise in the number of Jews at Yale, Dean Clark said:

"Is that right? I honestly hadn't noticed. In this office, our only concern is quality."

In some cases, such as at Pennsylvania, the figure is little changed from the nineteen-forties. In others, such as at Princeton, the change, for whatever reason, was dramatic.

"When I came here in 1948, there were perhaps 75 or 100 Jews in the whole school," Rabbi I. M. Levy, a chaplain at Princeton, said. "Now there are more than 100 per class.

"The general atmosphere in this country brought about the change. Americans simply became disgusted with discrimination."

"But that new liberalness goes only a certain distance," Rabbi Levy added, expressing a vague suspicion, shared with some other rabbis, that there is still some subconscious anti-Semitism effected by such devices as the preferential treatment of alumni sons or vestiges of geographical distribution.

The Ivy League colleges, which will be taking only 1 per cent of the 843,000 American youths expected to enroll as freshmen next year, still have enough applicants to turn down three for every one they accept.

The deans, therefore, acknowledge the possibility of a class that is dominated by Jews, by New Englanders, or even by football players.

"If some year we got to the point where something like that had happened," Dean Clark said at Yale, "well, maybe we'd have to re-evaluate our system. But at the moment, we get a pretty diverse group just by seeking the very best we can get."

April 17, 196

More Colleges Go a Courting

By M. A. FARBER

A couple of years ago, The Daily Princetorian gave the nearly all-male university $500 for the "cause of coeducation at Princeton."

The student newspaper, a persistent crusader for the enrollment of women on a large scale, said that "we thought it fitting to make the first contribution toward that far-away Nirvana."

It now seems likely, however, that the investment will yield a quicker return than the editors of 1965 contemplated.

Like many other single-sex institutions, Princeton is moving toward some kind of coeducation. No uniform method of achieving the goal nationally has emerged, but the aim itself is being increasingly approved.

In late 1966, Yale University invited Vassar College to consider a union of the two institutions. The student paper at Harvard University, which is virtually coed as a result of its close ties to Radcliffe College, said: "We know what they're after. And we like it."

The Other Side

Advocates of coeducation contend that separate institutions isolate the students from "life as it is."

They distort normal relationships, it is charged, make an exaggerated thing of weekend socializing and lessen the opportunity for genuine, prolonged exchange of ideas between the sexes.

It is also said that coeducational colleges can attract and hold students more easily, can operate more economically and can provide a greater variety of programs.

Combined schooling was not always preferred, particularly among the older private institutions in the East.

But the barriers, eased if not removed in much of the West and parts of the South years ago, are falling in all regions today and largely because the men's institutions, as much as the women's, want them down.

There are, essentially, three approaches to mixing the sexes in undergraduate education, and all are being tried by the colleges and universities making changes.

The first might be called pure coeducation. Here men and women are part of the same institution, with one faculty and one administration.

A second approach is the coordinate college. Under this arrangement, two or more colleges share classes and student activities to varying degrees but have independent leadership and admission policies. Examples are Columbia College (men) and Barnard College (women), and Brown University (men) and Pembroke College (women).

A third form involves little or no formal link between institutions but simply an agreement permitting students to take some courses or use some facilities on either campus. Generally, in this case, the institutions are farther apart geographically than in the coordinate college scheme.

For instance, Wellesley College, in Wellesley, Mass., a Boston suburb, and Massachusetts Institute of Technology, in Cambridge, signed a pact of this sort last May. But the institutions stressed that each should retain "its own character, tradition and autonomy."

Bryn Mawr (women), Haverford (men) and Swarthmore (coed)—all near Philadelphia—have similar agreements among them.

Of the three approaches to coeducation, the coordinate college appears to be favored the most by single-sex institutions that are switching.

This is the route chosen by Kenyon College in Gambier, Ohio, which plans to open a women's institution in 1969, and by Hamilton College, which started Kirkland College for women on its Clinton, N. Y., campus last September.

Other male institutions reportedly considering this method include Williams, in Williamstown, Mass.; Colgate, Hamilton, N. Y., and Wesleyan, Middletown, Conn.

Nor are existing women's colleges excluding a reverse attempt. MacMurray College in Illinois opened a coordinate college for men in 1955; Mills College in Oakland, Calif. is reviewing the possibility of following suit.

Vassar, after it decided in November not to affiliate with Yale, announced that it would draw male students to its Poughkeepsie, N. Y., campus by either starting a coordinate college or by persuading a men's college to open a branch at Vassar.

Yale, with the break-off, also disclosed that it would establish a college for women of its own in New Haven.

Kingman Brewster Jr., Yale's president, said the new college would have its own faculty and an independent curriculum coordinated with that of its parent institution. He predicted "a very large amount of overlap and cross-registration" between the male and female units.

A "personal" preference for the coordinate college has also been expressed by the president of Princeton University, Robert F. Goheen. Dr. Goheen said last May that some type of coeducation at Princeton was inevitable and could come within the next 10 years. A university committee studying the matter is expected to make its recommendations by June.

The Princeton president noted last year that the prime reason for adopting coeducation "won't and shouldn't be that Princeton's social life is warped."

He said that "this is certainly one consideration" but that more important questions were what Princeton could offer to women and what women could bring to "the intellectual and entire life" of the university.

"I am persuaded," he concluded, "that in mixed classes you get a fuller range of sensitivities and points of view than when girls and boys study alone."

January 12, 1968

Black Studies Off To a Shaky Start, Beset by Rivalries

By STEVEN V. ROBERTS
Special to The New York Times

BERKELEY, Calif., Nov. 22 —Black studies programs are making a slow start on many college campuses this year as they face sharp competition for staff, money and space from established departments and from one another.

Most college administrators believe that the programs will gradually expand and achieve full academic status. A few, however, feel they are just a fad that will eventually wither away when student activists turn to other issues.

These conclusions emerge from interviews with students, faculty and administrators of black studies programs in 20 colleges and universities across the country.

No precise figures are available, but officials of the American Council on Education estimate that hundreds of campuses have instituted some form of black studies program.

These range from a few scattered courses at the University of Oklahoma to a study and research center at Cornell that may eventually become a separate college.

Several Western colleges have also started "chicano" (Mexican-American) studies programs, and the University of California here has Asian and Native American programs as well. Some Eastern schools, such as the City College of New York, have started Puerto Rican programs.

Many of these programs were instituted only after militant students demanded them with violent rhetoric and occasionally violent action. They were thrown together hastily during the spring and summer, and now they usually show it. One example is here at Berkeley.

Last winter, the Third World Liberation Front, composed of minority group students, called a four-month student strike in support of its demand for an independent Third World College. In March, the faculty approved a more modest proposal for an "experimental department," which might someday become a college.

By the time administrators were designated they had only about 10 weeks left to recruit staff and design a curriculum

for the current semester. None of the courses offered by the ethnic studies department is listed in the college catalogue, and no one is even sure how many there are, with estimates ranging from 35 to 41.

Just a few weeks ago the department finally got adequate office space. And, because ethnic studies was instituted after the current budget was adopted, money for it has been squeezed out of existing programs and the department complains that it is getting far less than was promised.

Beyond immediate organizational problems, however, the debate over black studies centers on two interrelated, but distinct, issues: academic standards and political control.

Black Staff a Problem

In academics, the biggest problem is finding qualified staff, particularly black staff.

"There are simply not enough to meet the demand for them," said Dr. Lawrence Silverman, vice chancellor for academic affairs at the University of Tennessee. "Inevitably, we are being forced to turn to the faculty of black colleges. And yet when we meet with the administrators of black colleges they plead with us not to raid their staff. Unfortunately, if we do this we shall contribute to the destruction of black colleges."

The problem is compounded by the reluctance of some Negro scholars to teach in black studies programs. "They're still worried that the future of black studies is not guaranteed," said one black administrator. Another said: "They don't want to be harassed or dictated to by black students and they don't want to compromise their academic or professional integrity."

Moreover, such colleges as Dartmouth, in Hanover, N. H., and the University of California at Santa Barbara, find it difficult to attract Negroes to their isolated campuses. Santa Barbara has only one full-time teacher in its black studies department this year; six others commute one day a week from San Francisco or Los Angeles.

In addition to using part-time teachers, some departments are using more whites than they would like. Others are employing instructors without the usual academic qualifications. At Berkeley, courses are given by graduate students who have not completed work on higher degrees or by outside experts, such as the director of a local antipoverty program.

Some Administrators Pleased

Some administrators see a virtue in this necessity. "We're trying to get away from the kind of course the establishment type would offer anyway," said Douglas Davidson, assistant to the coordinator of

ethnic studies at Berkeley. One Dartmouth faculty member suggested that black studies could provide "a spark to a dragging institution" and force a re-evaluation of many academic shibboleths.

The presence of black scholars, however, does not guarantee campus harmony. Men who have long believed in the ultimate goal of integration often find it difficult to communicate with separatist-minded students. Dr. Sethard Fisher, 29-year-old chairman of the black studies department at Santa Barbara, was forced to resign recently when students charged he was not "relevant to the black experience.

Probably the second biggest problem is money. New programs and faculty members often put tremendous pressure on budgets that are already strained to the limit. At Antioch, the administration had to strip $500,000 from existing programs to finance a new institute on racial problems. Many schools are looking for foundation grants to subsidize their programs.

State institutions have it even worse. Chancellor Glenn S. Dumke of the California State College System recently vetoed the appointment of Marvin E. Jackman, a well-known black militant, as an instructor at Fresno State. The chancellor reportedly feared reprisals from the State Legislature, which last year passed several laws curbing student demonstrators.

Legitimacy Was Doubted

A year ago many faculty members doubted the legitimacy of black studies as an academic field. Some still have qualms, but most now seem to accept the idea as long as a student is "trained in the basic disciplines," as Dr. Henry A. Bullock, director of ethnic studies at the University of Texas put it. "This is an anxiety every black intellectual has had," he said. "I refuse to send students into an occupational blind alley."

However, "black studies" remains an undefined term on many campuses. "We're not sure at this point what black studies are," said Prof. Troy Duster, a Berkeley sociologist. "The amount of confusion in the department is not a problem, it is to be expected at this stage. We have to institute new procedures, and new criteria for courses and faculty. There's really no other way."

Courses offered here this fall are typical. They include black world history, Afro-American economics, Swahili, and Afro American art and culture. The other programs include such titles as the Native American in Contemporary Society, Introduction to La Raza (Mexican-American), and Comparative Asian Student Movement.

The primary aim of black studies is to teach the black student about his own culture, to improve his self-image, and to analyze current problems from a new perspective. Blacks would often like whites to understand these things as well, and in many schools whites form a large percentage of the black studies enrollment. At Texas, for instance, which has few blacks, the enrollment is 85 per cent white.

In a few places, such as Cornell, black hostility is so obvious that few whites want to participate in the program. "We have neither the time nor the resources to operate a race relations project wherein well-meaning but inexperienced and dysfunctional white students would occupy positions that might be better filled by blacks," declared James Turner, director of the African Study and Research Center.

Another major aim of black studies is to make education "relevant" to the problems of minority communities and prepare students for dealing with them. Cornell is planning a sort of "junior year in the ghetto." Dartmouth provides the chance to spend a full quarter working either in Fourth Bay College in Sierra Leone, the Roxbury ghetto of Boston, or the Institute of the Black World in Atlanta.

Along with academic problems, many colleges are facing the political question of who will have ultimate control over black studies programs. In some cases, black students are demanding control in order to promote a particular ideology for political programs.

Militants at San Francisco State, scene of a long and violent strike last year, contended recently that they had "taken control" of the black studies program and were using it to extol the virtues of the Black Panthers. The school's president, S. I. Hayakawa, said that the militants had launched a "reign of terror" and were threatening faculty and students who disagreed with them.

At Duke, about 25 blacks left school when the university would not let them control the black studies department or frame courses with "a consistent ideology . . . toward the ultimate goal of black federation."

In most cases, however, students want control simply because they "can't trust the faculty" to implement the kind of program they want, according to one Radcliffe girl. This can lead to considerable tension.

At Berkeley, there is a growing disagreement between students and the administration over the proper criteria for awarding a degree. At Santa Barbara, students demanded that white faculty be kept at a minimum and that only blacks be hired as teaching assistants.

Control of the program also carries great symbolic importance to young blacks. "They want something that is their own," said one black scholar. Dr. Fisher, who was forced out by rebellious students, said: "They have legitimate idealistic motives. They're sensitive to the subordination of blacks and other minorities in this country and want to find a way out of it."

Or as Robert Mason, chairman of the Black Students Union at Santa Barabara, put it: "Only blacks are capable of making decisions concerning blacks."

Most university officials do not agree. They are trying to give black students large advisory roles while reserving for themselves the right to make final decisions.

"When students demand autonomy without presenting a program, there is often trouble," said W. Todd Furniss of the American Council on Education. "But when they lay out what they want, both sides can often agree. The faculty usually says, 'Yes, that's what we'd do.'"

Campus disruptions have been minimal so far this year. Many white students are concerned mainly with Vietnam, and are no longer very interested in black studies.

Moreover, many blacks are now occupied with the difficult bureaucratic task of implementing the decisions made last year and realize that massive demonstrations could set back the progress of black studies.

When the Berkeley administration, for instance, refused the students' suggestion to hire Dr. Nathan Hare, the leader of the strike at San Francisco State last year, the students decided the issue was not important enough to risk a fight.

But if progress does not come fast enough, and on terms acceptable to the students, there is plenty of fuel around for future conflagrations, especially since most colleges have more black freshmen this year than ever before.

"It's very difficult for whites to fight racism," said Dr. Roscoe C. Brown Jr., director of black studies at New York University. "But it's also very difficult for blacks to have patience."

Increasing Campus Crime Spurs Security Measures

By ANDREW H. MALCOLM

Until this fall, Libby Honeycutt, a 21-year-old senior at the University of South Carolina in Columbia, walked to the library in the evenings without a worry. Not any more.

There have been three rapes and several other assaults on campus since September. Now when Miss Honeycutt goes out at night, she telephones for an escort. An Alpha Phi Omega fraternity member, working in a new security program, drives her to her campus destination in a university car.

The University of South Carolina is not alone in its concern with crime. At many colleges and universities across the country there appears to be an increase in campus crime. Administrators are responding—often at student urging—with new security measures.

As a result of this concern, which is especially strong in holiday periods when campus crime is at a peak, many school security forces have rapidly grown into sizable, well equipped police departments.

There has always been some crime on the nation's 3,000 university and college campuses, ranging from indecent exposure and petty theft to armed robbery and isolated cases of murder.

Although no nationwide statistics are compiled, administrators and informed security officials believe campus crime is on the rise. They generally attribute the apparent increase to the growth of crime in adjacent communities, to larger student populations, to society's general permissiveness and to better statistical records.

These authorities can draw no clear picture of who is committing the crimes, but they believe nonstudents are involved in most cases on urban campuses.

In New York City, for example, arrest records show that the majority of serious crimes in city universities are committed by outsiders who find university buildings rich preserves on which to prey. Officials at the New York schools say theft has shown the sharpest rise amid a general increase in campus crime in recent years.

At the University of Arizona, Robert L. Houston, a vice president, said: "Twenty years ago our biggest problem on campus was a panty raid." But this year, he noted, there have been 18 assaults on students.

After several such assaults at Rutgers University, a group of students last month disrupted a Board of Governors meeting and staged a sit-in at a dean's office to demand additional security.

There were five rapes at the University of California at Santa Barbara in 1970 compared to none the year before. The crime rate of Colorado State University doubled in 1970, with $10,000 in property stolen in November alone.

Rutgers reported one armed robbery in 1969 and 13 in 1970. At Harvard, where officials began keeping figures this fall, more than $18,000 in property was stolen from the freshman dormitories between the opening of the school year in September and Nov. 9.

During the Stanford-Purdue football game Oct. 2, thieves took almost $3,000 in clothes, radios and stereo tape players from several rooms and cars on the Palo Alto campus. Reported theft losses there in 1969 totaled $117,757 — more than 10 times the 1965 figure.

Faced with political disruptions and the increased crime, many school, already hardpressed financially, have had to create police departments complete with fleets of vehicles, radio networks, arsenals, student night patrols and even plainclothes detectives.

At South Carolina, security now costs almost $30 a year for each of the 15,000 students. Thirty-seven policemen (three times the 1968 force) patrol the 206-acre urban campus, each packing a .38-caliber Colt.

Even so, Miss Honeycutt said, "I just never go out alone at night anymore. The girls are just too scared."

Instead, as posters throughout the women's dormitories urge, she and perhaps 60 or 75 other women nightly use Alpha Phi Omega's free car service. In addition, members of Pi Kappa Alpha are on call to walk with women on campus after dark.

More Funds Sought

"In effect," said George A. Key, security director, "we're covering a small city of 20,000 people with all the attendant problems."

Mr. Key said it was difficult to solve such problems in the open atmosphere of an urban university campus. During the 12 months ending last June 30, he reported, $60,289 in property was stolen on campus. Only $8,641 worth was recovered.

The university recently spent $200,000 to illuminate some dark areas, to fence in others and to clear trees and shrubs that formed excellent hiding places for would-be attackers.

The trustees will seek $17,000 more from the Federal Government and $1-million from the state for further security measures.

Two university buses provide nightly transportation, and coeds may park after dark in no-parking zones that are closer to their rooms than the lots. Many women take self-defense courses, while others carry sharpened nail files or small cans of irritant spray for protection.

On the night of Nov. 18, largely at the initiative of Howard Comen, an energetic junior, four casually dressed students began patrolling the campus from 8 P.M. to 2 A.M. Equipped with flashlights and radios, they report anything suspicious to the campus police. In recent days they sighted a break-in at a gym, some unauthorized peddlers, a stolen auto and a leaking gasoline tank on a parked car.

"We're just another pair of security-conscious eyes on campus," said Rick Pozniko, a junior who joined the force after a friend was raped.

Although sexual assaults arouse the most fear and emotion, the major campus crime problem is theft. Students tell of thefts from their rooms even during brief walks to the drinking fountain down the hall.

"The smaller the item the faster it moves," said one policeman. Most popular these days are stereo tape players, radios, television sets, purses, wallets, clothing and office machinery.

The reasons for the rise in campus crime are varied.

There are more students and buildings to guard.

Full-time enrollment this fall was 5.8 million, or 2 million more than in 1960.

Students are generally more affluent than their parents' generation was, and they have more valuable property, such as record players and cars.

More students and outsiders need money to buy drugs, officials say. Many transients are attracted by campus life styles.

There are fewer restrictions on students—at many schools women's hours have been eliminated—and this has resulted in more time when dormitories, once locked throughout the night, are open to intruders.

John Marchant, president of the International Association of College and University Security Directors, said part of the increase was due to better reporting by an increasingly professional corps of campus policemen.

The long-term effects of the crime and new security steps are difficult to assess. They are diverting thousands of dollars from educational needs.

For instance, officials at Holy Cross, in the light of recent crimes, revised upward their estimates of the cost of admitting women. More guards and lights will be necessary, they decided.

Fear for Freedom

Others in the academic world are beginning seriously to fear that crime and the campus reaction to it will mean less openness and freedom in the universities.

The New York Times/Dave Underwood

Gwen Edge leaves car provided by Alpha Phi Omega fraternity at University of South Carolina in a new security program. Gary Naylor drives and George Psomas is at right.

A number of schools, including South Carolina and Rutgers, already check the identities of all persons entering and leaving certain buildings.

"I think campuses are on the verge of tightening up, said Audie Shuler, security chief at the University of Florida in Gaines-ville, who is regretfully considering several "very severe security measures" to help his 55 men guard the school's 3,600 acres.

One step would involve sealing off little-used portions of the campus at night. A group of buildings would be enclosed by a steel fence, and the perimeter would be regularly checked by armed patrols.

"Nobody would buy such a plan now," the chief said, "but in another year or so I think they would. It's the least expensive way."

January 2, 197

New College Trend: Women Studies

A new academic discipline is rising on the nation's campuses: women studies.

More than 60 colleges and universities around the country, apparently taking a hint from the black studies movement, are offering women studies courses this year. A year ago, only a handful of schools offered such courses.

The trend toward women studies, which has affected such schools as Yale, Cornell, Princeton, Wellesley and Northwestern, appears to have been generated not only by the women's liberation movement but also by pressures from students, teachers and alumnae who believe women are not getting fair academic treatment.

The trend has encountered some opposition, however, from faculty members who believe such fields as black studies and women studies are divisive and academically unsound.

Women as a Group

In general, women studies courses treat women as a group that has its own history, a unique role in society and special problems. The courses involve such matters as the contributions of women to science, history, literature and political science; discrimination against women, and the treatment of women in different societies.

At San Diego State College in California, 10 elective courses are offered. Fifty women and 20 men are enrolled in a course called "Contemporary Issues in the Liberation of Women," under the direction of Dr. Roberta Salper, 31 years old, a dedicated women's liberationist, The class examines such issues as abortion, divorce laws, contraception, sexual attitudes, child care and the role of minority group women.

At Princeton, where women were admitted last year, a similar course explores the impact of women on such social problems as drugs, racism, unemployment and pollution. Seventy-five per cent of the students in the course are men.

An idea of the purpose of such courses is provided by the San Diego State program's statement of purpose, which declares that the movement is "an attempt to repair the damage done to women by the omissions and distortions of traditional education and to illustrate at least one way of releasing the power and potential of more than half the population of this country."

"If it hadn't been for women's lib protests," said Dr.

Salper from her West Coast office, "we wouldn't have this program at San Diego."

Stephanie Serementis, a neurobiology major at Cornell, believes there is discrimination against women students.

"I fight to be recognized in class," she said, "and if I'm a success, the teacher thinks I must be an exception to the female race."

At San Diego State, about 50 male professors recently attacked that school's program as "a radical innovation."

At Cornell, a questionnaire on the issue was distributed to the faculty last spring. Half of the 185 who responded supported the program and half opposed it.

An engineering professor, whose name was not disclosed by the university, commented on the questionnaire:

502

At Douglass College of Rutgers University, New Brunswick, N. J., Mary McCarthy's novel "The Group," is discussed in a course called "Educated Women in Literature." Dr. Elaine Showalter, 29, leads study of portrayal of women.

"The idea is slightly absurd. Why don't you stop these attempts at fragmentalizing higher education and devote yourself to real scholarship?"

A humanities teacher called the program a "disaster."

"Black studies is divisive enough," he said. "Female studies would inevitably be aimed toward political goals, which I am far from sharing."

Other authorities disagree.

"There are compelling reasons right now for an intellectual focus on women," said Dr. Jennie Farley, academic coordinator for female studies at Cornell.

"Take a problem like the population explosion," she said. "If we are to encourage women to have fewer children, we must give them some satisfactory alternatives to being only housewives and mothers."

Ella Kusnetz, a Cornell senior, said women studies were valuable to her as a student.

"I wish they had been offered when I was a freshman," she said. "I've never been as interested in academics. Female studies is a new reference, I have some identity now as a woman."

At Douglas College of Rutgers University, a women's school, a substitute for freshman English is "Educated Women in Literature," a course that concerns the portrayal of women in modern American literature. The class, led by Dr. Elaine Showalter, 29, recently discussed Mary McCarthy's description of women in "The Group," her novel about eight Vassar graduates.

"The direction the new courses will take is unclear," said Florence Howe, assistant professor of English at Goucher College, who is considered an authority on women studies by faculty members throughout the country.

"Nonetheless," she added, "the courses are multiplying rapidly."

Title Is Vague

Miss Howe is the director of the Modern Language Association's Commission on the Status of Women in the Profession, which is investigating the equality of women teachers. She has established a clearing house at Goucher for information on women studies.

The enrollment of men in the course at Princeton is at least partly a result of its vague title, "Political Modernization."

"Originally I thought the course was about underdeveloped nations," said Robert P. Thomas, a bearded sophomore from Washington. "It was a complete shock to find out what this was all about. Although I was a bit skeptical, I decided it would be a good time to find out what women's lib is all about."

"The majority of guys are all for women's lib as a result of taking the course," he said.

In a recent seminar involving nine students, eight of whom were men, the instructor, Dr. Kay Boals, 26, posed a question about Betty Friedan's "The Feminine Mystique."

Friedan Book Discussed

"Did you find Friedan's argument that there's no such thing as a happy housewife true?" she asked.

The New York Times/William E.Sauro

Dr. Kay Boals, 26, at Princeton, where she conducts a course that looks into the impact of women on drugs, racism and other issues. Men form 75 per cent of class.

"Of course not," replied Mr. Thomas.

"But Friedan mentioned there were large numbers of suicides among the housewives she studied," argued a classmate.

"In the U.S. women either have to do their thing with grandchildren, or go out and get work," observed Mr. Thomas.

"But so many women over 40 can't get interesting jobs," said another student.

"Look, it's not just women who can't find interesting work," asserted Jonathan Winder. "I worked in a warehouse this summer where all these guys did was rip out slips from other forms. It

may be chauvinistic to say, but I don't think women ever had it so good."

"The question isn't to decide who's oppressed but to end oppression of both men and women," said Dr. Boals. "However, that man ripping papers has it better than a woman caught in 'the mystique,' because her job is never finished."

The one woman student, Sherri Peltz, a junior, remained silent throughout the class.

In an interview later she explained: "I generally feel intimidated being the only girl and therefore find it difficult to say what I'm thinking."

January 7, 1971

Pass-Fail College Grades Gaining Favor

By ANDREW H. MALCOLM

As the school year draws to a close on college and university campuses, there is mounting evidence that perhaps as many as three-quarters of the nation's 3,000 institutions of higher learning have turned to the simple pass or fail method of grading as a flexible, though limited, alternative to the traditional A through F marks.

While exact nationwide figures are not available, interviews with school officials and some representative studies show that many of the schools adopted some form of pass-fail in at least a few courses during recent years largely as a result of student pressures for grading changes.

A handful of other schools, such as Simmons College in Boston and the University of California at Santa Cruz, use the pass-fail system almost exclusively.

Major Goals of Pass-Fail

Advocates of pass-fail, mostly in the humanities and generally students, based their demands on two major goals: That it encourages students to experiment with broadening courses outside their major field without fear of hurting their academic average; and that it removes the competition for grades that sometimes distorts the learning process and makes the letter grade the goal rather than the learning itself.

"Pass-fail helps open horizons," says Prof. Seymour Slive of Harvard, "and that's what we're all about."

The critics, often in mathematics and the sciences, contend, on the other hand, that pass-fail destroys academic standards and that students without the reward of an A to strive for, simply do the minimum work necessary to pass.

Graduate School Resistance

In addition, the system is encountering stiff resistance from graduate schools, especially in medicine and law, where admissions committees have historically relied on undergraduates' letter grades as an indication of an applicant's potential.

For instance, in 1969 William W. Hassler of Indiana (Pa.) University took a survey of 230 graduate school deans. He found that 214 preferred letter grades and 69 would not accept a student with all pass-fail grades, even if he had good faculty recommendations.

Such resistance, however, has not stopped the steady

growth in adoption of pass-fail, although it may have limited the number of times a student takes such courses.

Although similar grading systems have been used in Europe and elsewhere for many decades, pass-fail's impact in the United States was minimal until the nineteen-sixties when student demands for academic reforms gained strength.

Discernible Changes

A recent study of 434 schools by Roy S. Burwen, director of institutional research at San Francisco State College, found that half the institutions had altered their grading system within the last five years. And three-quarters of those changes were to allow some pass-fail grading. Many other schools were cautiously considering similar reforms.

According to some educators, the desire among students for pass-fail is rooted in their high school experience where many felt they were "scored, graded, tested and measured to death," as Michael Brennan, dean of Brown's Graduate School, put it.

There is no standard pass-fail system. Each school adopts and adapts those characteristics that fit its needs. Typically, each term a student may take one course outside his major field under pass-fail, receiving the usual letter grade in the others.

Written Evaluations

Ideally, the P or F grade is combined with a detailed, written evaluation of the student's work by the instructor, although in many cases the teacher is not told who are his letter grade students and who is on pass-fail. The conversion from letter grade is made by the registrar.

Some schools have gone so far as not to record any F grades. This, according to many educators, is part of a general desire to eliminate from grading the threat of academic failure, with its social, economic and emotional consequences.

"Pass-fail will definitely continue to grow," said Mr. Burwen, "because it is regarded as a nonpunitive grading system, and many would like education to work by the carrot rather than the stick."

"There is the possibility of allowing more ungraded work," adds Ernest May, dean of Harvard College, "but no one talks of abandoning graded work."

Mixed Results Recorded

Studies of the effects of pass-fail so far have produced mixed results.

Many instructors, such as Hans H. Penner of Dartmouth, believe that students who take their school's version of pass-fail "tend to do minimum amounts of work," often to gain more time to spend on other courses.

"I never take pass-fail if I really want to do the work," concedes Wayne Tanaka, a Harvard junior.

Like many graduate deans, Russell Simpson of Harvard's Law School, believes "pass-fail is really pass-pass. No one flunks."

Figures for last fall at Harvard appear to support him. That term, 1,320 undergraduates took pass-fail courses. Only 12 failed.

Matter of Interpretation

At Princeton, however, Dr. Edward Sullivan, dean of the college, reported that pass-fail had produced substantially more failures. And, he noted, "people interpret what scanty data we have on pass-fail pretty much according to their own prejudices."

Nonetheless, student utilization of pass-fail continues to grow at many schools. At Duke, for instance, where a recent student referendum found 95 per cent in favor of continuing pass-fail, 10 per cent of the undergraduates took a course under pass-fail last fall. This spring the figure grew to 13 per cent.

At Harvard about 25 per cent take pass-fail courses at any one time, and most take at least one during their undergraduate years.

"I'm not worried about the student who is an English major and decides to take computer science or astronomy on a pass-fail basis," said Mrs. Helen Hay, assistant to the dean of the Graduate College at the University of Illinois.

"I am worried," she added, "about the English major who takes English courses pass-fail."

For despite some acceptance of pass-fail by graduate school officials, English, history or any other majors with sizable numbers of P's on their transcripts are liable to encounter problems when applying to graduate school.

"I had intended to take all my courses pass-fail," said Mark Ethridge, a senior at Princeton, "but then I decided on grad school, and it's almost impossible to get accepted if your transcript is full of just plain passes."

"Pass-fail courses complicate the graduate admissions process enormously," said Dr. Marvin Bressler, who heads a commission reviewing undergraduate education at Princeton.

"To the extent you eliminate grades," he added, "you prejudice the system against people from nonprestigious schools. We'll take a person with all A's from Podunk over one with all C's from Harvard, but if both have a bunch of passes, you pick the one from Harvard."

Elimination of specific letter grades in many applications has forced graduate admissions officials to give greater weight instead to written faculty evaluations and scores on the national Graduate Record Examination.

Examination Limitation

However, many bemoan this development because the test, perhaps unfairly, measures a student on only one day's performance, while a grade point average spans four years.

And they are wary of attaching too much importance to faculty recommendations, which are generally favorable, especially from those dubbed "puffers."

"After you read the 10th letter from the same teacher claiming that each student is the best he's ever had," said one official, "you begin to get suspicious."

To eliminate some of this suspicion, at least one institution, Yale's Law School, is considering establishing a file of recommendation letters indexed by professor to check what he wrote about previous students.

In addition, evaluations of students in classes of several hundred are viewed as meaningless.

Despite the problems, however, Dean Brennan of Brown, who is also an officer of the Association of Graduate Schools, believes that use of pass-fail will increase, though not totally replace, letter grades. And the graduate schools, he said, will eventually adjust to the situation.

Already, he added, there is serious discussion among deans over revising their graduate application forms to provide additional material for judging an applicant's potential.

Such changes might include greater stress on a more elaborate personal statement by the student on such topics as why he wants to pursue graduate work or what books he has read recently and his views of them.

Beyond that, the evolution of a new academic measuring system raises important questions for colleges. By opting for pass-fail, Mr. Burwen said, many colleges have chosen to evaluate a student's individual progress without providing the grades used by employers, parents and others as a form of "social certification."

Eventually, he said, there may have to be a whole series of independent agencies certifying competence through licensing examinations, much like those existing for doctors and lawyers.

June 7, 1971

Study Finds College Is Means to More Satisfying Life

Factors Other Than Pay Affected, Says Carnegie Report

By GENE I. MAEROFF

College attendance causes many measurable differences in a person's life style in addition to the widely recognized increase in lifetime earnings, according to a new report sponsored by the Carnegie Commission on Higher Education.

The report, "A Degree and What Else? The Correlates and Consequences of a College Education," is one of a series produced under the auspices of the commission. It is to be published later this fall.

A preview of the report was given yesterday at a news conference in Washington by Dr. Clark Kerr, chairman of the Carnegie Commission.

In the foreword to the report, a copy of which was obtained by The New York Times, Dr. Kerr wrote:

"Going to college—any college—does give to the individual a chance for a more satisfying life and to society the likelihood of a more effective community."

Dr. Kerr said in a news release that persons who had gone to college tended to be as follows:

¶More liberal and tolerant in their attitudes toward and in their relations with other individuals and groups.

¶More satisfied with their jobs.

¶More highly paid and less subject to unemployment.

¶More thoughtful and deliberate in their consumer expenditures.

¶More likely to vote and to participate generally in community activities.

¶More informed about community, national and world affairs.

The conclusions in the report are based on an analysis of data gathered by social scientists over several decades.

"The years of higher education are a period of delayed commitment and a moratorium during which most students are encouraged to examine issues, to reconsider their own standards, values and identities and to lay plans for their own role in society," Dr. Stephen B. Withey wrote in the report's concluding chapter.

He is program director of the Institute for Social Research at the University of Michigan and was the author of three of the eight chapters in the report.

In a chapter devoted to a discussion of the way in which college graduates use the media, the report says that "the greater one's education, the greater the dependence on the printed media."

Total family income—within various groups (percentage distribution of families)

Education of family head	Mean income in 1968	Number of cases	Less than $3,000	$3,000 –4,999	$5,000 –7,499	$7,500 –9,999	$10,000 –14,999	$15,000 or more	Total	Median
0–5 grades	$4,000	143	52	22	13	7	4	2	100	$2,920
6–8 grades	6,300	410	33	16	19	14	13	5	100	5,170
9–11 grades, some high school plus noncollege	8,820	402	17	15	20	17	22	9	100	7,260
12 grades, completed high school	9,480	415	6	12	18	24	29	11	100	8,940
Completed high school plus other noncollege	9,890	264	5	14	18	20	31	12	100	9,060
College, no degree	10,830	329	14	9	12	17	31	17	100	9,610
College, bachelor's degree	13,030	239	6	10	14	13	29	28	100	11,240
College, advanced or professional degree	16,460	109	3	6	6	15	31	39	100	13,120

Report prepared for Carnegie Commission on Higher Education shows direct relationship between years of education and earnings. Data in tables on this page are from studies made in various years in 1960-1970 period.

Relationship between education and marital adjustment indices (in percent)

Marital adjustment indices	Educational attainment		
	Grade school	High school	College
Number involved	(553)	(950)	(362)
Evaluation of marital happiness:			
Very happy	38	46	60
Above average	16	25	22
Average	41	27	17
Not too happy	5	2	1
Not ascertained			
TOTAL	100	100	100
Frequency of feeling inadequate:			
A lot of times; often	10	13	10
Once in a while; once or twice	34	42	53
Never	53	42	33
Not ascertained	3	3	4
TOTAL	100	100	100
Report of marriage problem:			
Had problems	33	44	45
No problem	56	50	51
Inapplicable*	5	2	1
Not ascertained	6	4	3
TOTAL	100	100	100

*Refers to 50 people who evaluated their marriage as "not too happy" and therefore were not asked whether or not they ever had problems.

The New York Times   Oct. 6, 1971

The better educated, it was noted, seemed to be happier in marriage and more introspective about behavior.

Education of respondent and indices of parental adjustment (in percent)

Indices of parental adjustment	Educational attainment		
	Grade school	High school	College
Number involved	(646)	(955)	(337)
Report of problems in raising children:			
Mentioned problems	71	76	75
No problems	27	23	24
Not ascertained	2	1	1
TOTAL	100	100	100
Number involved	(424)	(632)	(224)
Frequency of feelings of inadequacy:			
A lot of times; often	15	16	19
Once in a while; once or twice	22	33	40
Never	60	47	37
Not ascertained	3	4	4
TOTAL	100	100	100

Figures on parental problems are similar, but the better educated were found more sensitive to parental role.

It says, however, that although college graduates spend "far less time" viewing television than nongraduates, the amount of time is still greater than that the college graduates give to all other mass media combined.

Also, according to the report, college graduates are "much more likely" that nongraduates to consider themselves Republicans.

In an examination of several studies of the relationship of education to income, the report

Education and workers' attitudes toward their jobs* (in percent)

	Education			
	0-11 grades	12 grades	College, no degree	College degree
Number involved	(975)	(854)	(407)	(383)
Job is:				
Enjoyable	70	78	82	89
Pro-con	22	16	14	8
Drudgery	7	4	3	2
Not ascertained	1	2	1	1

* The question was: "On the whole, do you feel that the work on your present job is drudgery, or is it all right, or do you enjoy your work?"

College graduates are happier in their work, the report says, because they have easier access to desirable jobs.

reinforces the belief that the more education one has, the more money he is likely to earn.

But it says there are "exaggerated notions" about the dollar value of higher education. The "main thrust," according to the report, is more subtle.

College-educated people hold jobs that expose them to fewer risks of accidents and income losses and depend less on physical capacity and, thus, are more sympathetic to the aging process and offer more advancement, the report says.

In closing, the report cites the need for more studies to determine the effect of higher education in the light of changing social conditions.

$100-Million Ford Grant To Aid Minority Education

6-Year Program to Help Black Colleges, Individual Students, Ethnic Programs

By M. A. FARBER

The Ford Foundation announced yesterday a six-year, $100-million program to improve the quality of a limited number of predominantly Negro private colleges and to provide various minority students with individual study awards at most types of institutions.

McGeorge Bundy, president of the foundation, said the program marked the largest single commitment of funds by the foundation since he assumed office in March, 1966.

Mr. Bundy said that the program was addressed to "the central problem of American society—the failure to achieve equal opportunity for members of America's racial and cultural minorities."

Reversal of Priorities

The grants to Negro colleges, he said, will bolster the "stability, independence and quality" of institutions that are important not only to blacks but also "to the country as a whole."

As a result of the program, nearly 80 per cent of the foundation's aid for the general improvement of American higher education from 1973 to 1978 will be devoted to minorities—almost an exact reversal of priorities from 1968, when the proportion was 21.7 per cent. The share designated for minorities in 1972, the first year of the new program, is 45.7 per cent.

Mr. Bundy, at a news conference, said that "any program of the magnitude" of the one for minorities was bound to restrict what the foundation could do in other areas of higher education. But, he added, "we will continue to be in business" with colleges and universities on a variety of issues, "except we will not be giving other large-scale institutional grants."

Decision for Colleges

As many as 10 of the more than 60 four-year private Negro colleges will receive a total of about $50-million in the next six years for student financial aid, curriculum and instructional changes, faculty salaries and professorial chairs, endowment and special projects, including scholastic help for "disadvantaged" students.

Officials of the foundation said the main focus of this aspect of the program would be on the undergraduate level, with the colleges determining how funds will be spent and with some of the Ford funds available only when matched by new funds raised elsewhere by the colleges.

"The colleges are going to have to tell us what they want to do with the grants," said Harold Howe 2d, the foundation's vice president for education. "We don't have a blueprint for each of these institutions and the institutions are not all similar."

The first colleges chosen for the program are Tuskegee Institute in Tuskegee, Ala.; Hampton Institute in Hampton, Va.; Fisk University in Nashville; and Bendict College in Columbia, S. C. While all but Benedict have some master's degree programs, all are primarily undergraduate liberal arts colleges.

Puerto Ricans, Mexican-Americans and American Indians, as well as blacks and other minorities, will be eligible for the individual study awards for the junior and senior years of college and graduate work.

About $40-million has been earmarked for this part of the program, which will emphasize graduate and perhaps profes-

October 6, 1971

507

McGeorge Bundy, third from left, the president of the Ford Foundation, making the announcement yesterday. From left: Luther Foster, president of Tuskegee Institute; James Lawson, the president of Fisk University; Mr. Bundy; Roy Hudson, the president of Hampton Institute; Harold Howe 2d, head of the educational division of the foundation, and Benjamin Payton, the president of Benedict College. The meeting was at the Ford Foundation.

sional studies. Award winners, named by the community colleges they attend or, on the graduate level, by panels of minority scholars, can use the awards at any institution they elect.

In addition, $10-million has been set aside by the foundation for the development of ethnic studies and curriculum materials, probably at graduate schools, and for project-oriented assistance as other "ethnic colleges" and Negro institutions not included in the main Ford effort.

The foundation is also considering aid for the establishment of a national commission to help black colleges in long-range planning.

The over-all program represents more of a substantial expansion in dollar terms of an earlier Ford interest, and a recasting of that interest, than it does a new departure for the foundation.

Public Colleges Skipped

From 1960 to last month, the foundation gave $37.4-million to 67 of the 100 or so Negro colleges and universities, public and private. In its new program, direct aid to the Negro institutions is confined to the private colleges, and is highly selective with regard to them.

The foundation concluded that it could have greater impact with fewer institutions and that the public colleges were essentially the responsibility of government.

There were about 160,000 students in all the Negro colleges in 1970 and 104,000 of them were in public institutions, according to a recent report by the Ford Foundation.

In addition, 310,000 black students attended predominantly white institutions, it said. As recently as the mid-1960's, a majority of black students were enrolled in the Negro colleges.

The foundation has also funded individual study awards for minorities in the last five years, at a cost of about $6-million a year by 1970. More than 2,000 students—mostly at the graduate level—have benefited from these awards, Ford officials said. They estimated that 1,200 to 1,500 new students each year might profit from the broadening of the awards announced yesterday.

Vernon E. Jordan Jr., executive director of the United Negro College Fund, described the new Ford action as "a landmark decision" in response to the "anguished cry" for aid by private black colleges.

"I believe that the path Ford has charted may be a turning point in enabling these minority-oriented schools not only to survive, but to realize the potential which they possess for enriching all of American life," Mr. Jordan said in a prepared statement.

The United Negro College Fund has helped raise and distribute about $130-million for private Negro colleges since 1944.

Negro colleges, like many institutions of higher learning in the country, are going through a financial crisis. But experts generally agree that the Negro colleges, because of a historically weaker base of financial support, are in particular fiscal trouble.

Expenditures of Ford Foundation's Office of Higher Education and Research
Fiscal years (Oct.-Sept.), in millions of dollars

	1968 Actual	1969 Actual	1970 Actual	1971 Actual	1972 Budget	1973 Projected Budget
Minorities	$ 7.9	$ 8.6	$10.5	$11.6	$12.8	$18.0
Other Higher Education	28.6	28.9	23.0	17.6	15.2	5.0
	$36.5	$37.5	$33.5	$29.2	$28.0	$23.0
Minorities Proportion of Higher Education	21.7%	22.9%	31.2%	39.9%	45.7%	78.3%*
Proportion of Other Higher Education	78.3%	77.1%	68.8%	60.1%	54.3%	21.7%
	100.0%	100.0%	100.0%	100.0%	100.0%	100.0%

Source: Ford Foundation   *This percentage is expected to remain steady until 1978-79

In 1968, Ford Foundation allocated one-fifth of its higher education funds to minorities and four-fifths to general uses. By 1973, the proportions are scheduled to be reversed.

"The black colleges have entered this period thin and starved, not sleek and fat," Mr. Howe said. He said that, when compared to the size of their budgets, the Ford grants to the Negro colleges were "equivalent to giving Harvard or Yale a quarter million dollars."

Last February, the Carnegie Commission on Higher Education recommended a tripling of Federal support for Negro colleges. Yesterday, in a move unrelated to the Ford announcement apparently unrelated to the Ford announcement, the Department of Health, Education and Welfare disclosed that Negro colleges received $125-million in Federal aid in 1970, a "16 per cent increase over the previous year."

Last year, when the department released figures for 1969, it said the Negro colleges received $122.1-million in 1969. However, a spokesman for the department said yesterday that the 1969 figure was actually $107-million.

Many Negro college leaders have charged that Federal aid to their institutions has been inadequate or too conditional on terms they cannot meet. The colleges receive about 3 per cent of all Federal aid to higher education.

Mr. Bundy said yesterday that Ford grants to Negro colleges would be planned "so they can be adjusted to the needs of the institutions" as Federal and state programs emerge.

Urging increases in both public and private assistance to "particularly promising" Negro colleges, Mr. Bundy said it would be "gravely misleading" to suggest that the new Ford program satisfied the colleges' needs. "Those needs are very much larger than this program," he said.

Ford's "heightened commitment" to black colleges "should in no way be interpreted as support of segregated education," Mr. Bundy said. He noted that the colleges did not bar students of any race and that "full integration is likely to come to many of these colleges only if their quality continues to improve.

"The central point is that it is important for American society that institutions under black leadership and with a tradition of service to black students have an opportunity to thrive and share fully in our national efforts in higher education," he said.

The new grants are not the largest ever given by the foundation. In the early 1960's, for example, the foundation gave $349-million to 16 universities and 68 colleges, in a "challenge grant" program. Negro institutions were not selected for the program.

Mr. Bundy said that half the expenditures of the foundation's domestic divisions were now "going out in various forms in the struggle for equal opportunity." The foundation spent $196-million last year, in the United States and abroad. It has assets of $3-billion.

October 10, 1971

Professors' Unions Are Growing

By M. A. FARBER

The unionization of professors, a movement that is beginning to realign economic, political and academic power on many campuses, has emerged as a leading and contentious issue in higher education.

Collective bargaining agents for professors have been recognized at 133 of the country's 2,500 colleges and universities in the last several years. Hundreds of other campuses have adopted looser arrangements for negotiation.

Ten to 15 per cent of the half-million teaching faculty in the nation are subject to collective agreements beyond their individual contracts, or will soon be, and expansion is in prospect.

Campuses with bargaining range from Yakima Valley College in Washington to Rutgers University in New Jersey, from the Polytechnic Institute of Brooklyn to Central Michigan University, from Massasoit Community College in Massachusetts to Green Bay Technical Institute in Wisconsin.

About half the total faculty covered by bargaining are employes of the two New York systems: the State University and the City University.

"A specter that has been haunting higher education—the specter of collective bargaining —is now a living presence," observed Dr. William B. Boyd, president of Central Michigan University.

"The unthinkable became thinkable, then bearable, and soon may be taken for granted," he said. "While I have no crystal ball, my hunch is that we are more apt to see the emergence of unions for presidents and deans than to

National Education Association.

see a reversal in the movement of faculties toward unions."

Major drives to win the allegiance of professors and obtain exclusive bargaining rights are being waged by three rival organizations—the National Education Association; the American Federation of Teachers, A.F.L.-C.I.O., and the American Association of University Professors.

Officials of the N.E.A., which previously shunned unionization as "unprofessional," trek from campus to campus, their suitcases laden with pamphlets that say unionization spells "dignity" as well as "security" for professors.

In a campaign at Fordham University, the A.A.U.P. invoked the encyclicals of three Popes on the right of labor to organize; and on another campus, it challenged the very existence of a competing local organization.

Yet the A.A.U.P., despite a commitment by its national council last month to step up bargaining efforts, remains deeply divided over unionization and the association's involvement in it.

Pros and Cons Weighed

The quandary of the A.A.U.P.

American Federation of Teachers.

—will the advantages of bargaining outweigh the drawbacks—is not unlike the predicament of many professors who never expected to see campus unionization.

Some faculty members, especially in the senior ranks, argue that bargaining is incompatible with the cooperative traditions of a profession that they believe is largely self-regulated. They caution that it will erode the "diverse" character of colleges and universities and result in a "leveling" of quality and a turn away from rewarding merit.

Other professors, equally adamant in their regard for educational quality, assert that the real power on campus has been usurped by administrators and public budget officials. They hold that the right and needs of professors can only be met through collective action supported by more muscle than that vested in the typical faculty senate.

"Like many faculties, we thought about this endlessly," said Dr. I. Leonard Leeb, a social scientist at Polytechnic Institute of Brooklyn.

"One would have thought that collegiality was enough but, in fact," he added, "the university is a group of autarchic entities out to promote their own self-interests. And, in times of financial retrenchment, it becomes necessary to get together and fight for whatever the administration has to hand out."

"Power," remarked Richard Hixon, an A.F.T. official, "used to be a dirty word among faculty—professors would throw up their arms and say 'Oh, we don't want power'. Well, no more. The other day I was at a meeting on unionization at the University of Illinois—I expected about 65 professors to attend, out of 3,100. About 1,000 showed up.

Mr. Hixon described bargaining as "the last conservative alternative on campus."

"It may have its revolutionary aspects," he said, "but it works within the system."

The appeal of unions has been heightened by what Dr. Joseph W. Garbarino of the University of California calls "the end of affluence" in higher education.

Salaries are not rising as fast as in the mid-1960's; research and teaching posts are being cut back and promotions curtailed; and relatively few posts are opening to a crush of new applicants.

A mood of acrimony prevails in many faculty clubs and lounges as legislatures demand that professors spend more time in the classroom with larger numbers of students. Students themselves seek influence over faculty appointments, and critics charge that tenure does more harm than good by protecting "dead wood."

Profound Effect Expected

Dr. Boyd, in an article in Liberal Education last month, noted that more professors and their families "take unionism for granted," particularly since public school teachers organized. And many junior faculty, like students, he said, are "present-minded . . . they are not believers in deferred pleasure. They want benefits now."

Since only a handful of contracts are more than a year old, unionization had had less of an impact on campus conditions than on attitudes. Yet many educators are convinced that bargaining will ultimately

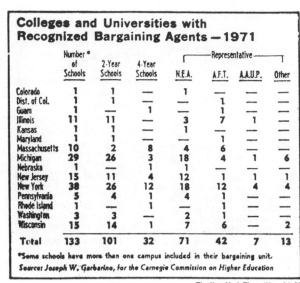

Colleges and Universities with Recognized Bargaining Agents — 1971

	Number* of Schools	2-Year Schools	4-Year Schools	Representative			
				N.E.A.	A.F.T.	A.A.U.P.	Other
Colorado	1	1	—	1	—	—	—
Dist. of Col.	1	1	—	—	1	—	—
Guam	1	—	1	—	1	—	—
Illinois	11	11	—	3	7	1	—
Kansas	1	1	—	1	—	—	—
Maryland	1	1	—	—	1	—	—
Massachusetts	10	2	8	4	6	—	—
Michigan	29	26	3	18	4	1	6
Nebraska	1	—	1	1	—	—	—
New Jersey	15	11	4	12	1	1	1
New York	38	26	12	18	12	4	4
Pennsylvania	5	4	1	4	1	—	—
Rhode Island	1	—	1	—	1	—	—
Washington	3	3	—	2	1	—	—
Wisconsin	15	14	1	7	6	—	2
Total	**133**	**101**	**32**	**71**	**42**	**7**	**13**

*Some schools have more than one campus included in their bargaining unit.

Source: Joseph W. Garbarino, for the Carnegie Commission on Higher Education

The New York Times/Nov. 14, 1971

have a profound effect on expenditures and programs.

"Make no mistake about it, the advent of bargaining will result in radical changes in the nature of colleges and universities in the next decade," said Dr. David Newton, vice chancellor for faculty and staff relations at the City University.

Current negotiations cover virtually every faculty concern: book space and secretarial help in offices, sabbaticals and funeral leaves, the privacy of personnel files, salaries, work loads and schedules, class sizes, curricular policies, standards of academic freedom and rules governing tenure.

"We'd gladly bargain on everything that takes place in the university, including the improvement of instruction," said Jim Williams, a top organizer for the N.E.A.

The most significant gains for faculties, so far, according to negotiators on both sides of the table, are broad grievance clauses that provide for review and, sometimes, arbitration of a variety of administrative decisions, especially regarding employment.

Force for Greater 'Parity'

On the whole, unionization has not produced dramatic salary increases; it has been a force for greater "parity" in pay among professors.

A number of contracts contain provisions that have not been fully implemented. For example, the contracts signed by the City University in 1969 —City was the first major university to engage in bargaining —stipulate that every faculty member would have a minimum of 120 square feet of private office space. Many professors still have closer to three square feet.

The "paradox of faculty unionism" to date is that the greatest gains have accrued to faculty on the margin of institutions — lecturers and part-time instructors; nonteaching professionals such as librarians and counselors; and professors at the "lower-level" campuses of university systems, Dr. Garbarino said.

Dr. Garbarino, who is preparing a study on "creeping unionism and the faculty labor market" for the Carnegie Commission on Higher Education, said that regular, full-time faculty "have shored up some of their benefits from possible attack but otherwise have gained the least from bargaining." For them, he said, unionization has been "essentially defensive in character."

Before 1969 bargaining was all but confined to community colleges. Even now the two-year institutions with recognized agents represent three-fourths of all institutions with agents. But the movement is spreading to four-year colleges and universities, both public and private.

Trend in the States

Six states account for 118 of the 133 institutions with bargaining agents—New York, Michigan, New Jersey, Wisconsin, Illinois and Massachusetts, in that order.

States where faculty interest in bargaining is just beginning to be expressed include Hawaii, Maine, Connecticut, Iowa, Delaware, Kansas, Indiana, Vermont, Georgia and Louisiana.

The growth of bargaining in the public sector has been facilitated by the passage of public employe relations laws or similar measures in 19 states. Many other states are expected to follow suit in the near future.

The prospects for unionization at private institutions, which employ 30 per cent of all faculty, were much enhanced in 1970 when the National Labor Relations Board assumed jurisdiction at private colleges and universities with gross incomes of more than $1-million.

Two months ago the labor board denied a challenge by Fordham University to its jurisdiction saying that faculty members at private institutions are "entitled to all the benefits of collective bargaining if they so desire."

The A.A.U.P. has moved to obtain bargaining rights at Fordham and New York University, and is considering an attempt at Columbia University as well.

A representation election is generally held when an organization secures petitions from 30 per cent of the unit for which it wants to bargain. In a few elections, such as at Pace College two weeks ago, faculty have rejected bargaining.

Range of Problems

The A.A.U.P. has more than philosophical problems in undertaking bargaining. Like the A.F.T., it needs considerably more funds. The N.E.A., which many professors see as less tradition-bound than the A.A.U.P. and less militant or aggressive than the A.F.T., has, by far, the largest budget and staffs of the three organizations.

A number of observers believe that, unless the A.A.U.P. make a concerted effort at unionizing, the N.E.A. will become entrenched in the four-year institutions.

Many administrators, caught off guard by unionization, are only now starting to assess it. Some maintain that the costs of financing contracts will be prohibitive; others — like some members of the A.A.U.P.— stress that the faculty are managers as well as employes of an academic institution and could lose more in tradeoffs at the bargaining table than they stand to gain.

"I don't have the same bugaboos about bargaining that some of my colleagues have," said Robben W. Fleming, president of the University of Michigan. "But the next five or 10 years will be very much of an experimental period in this area. It will be a real shakeout."

Campus Homosexuals Organize To Win Community Acceptance

By ROBERT REINHOLD

In defiance of taboos that have prevailed for generations, thousands of college students are proclaiming their homosexuality and openly organizing "gay" groups on large and small campuses across the country.

No one knows exactly how many are involved, but in growing numbers they are forming cohesive campus organizations for educational, social and political purposes, often with official sanction and with remarkable acceptance from fellow students. However, a number of psychiatrists and psychologists are somewhat uneasy about the ready availability of homosexual social activities in the presence of impressionable adolescents whose sexual identities are not fully crystallized.

By organizing, the gay students hope to build a sense of community among gay young men and women and to disabuse their heterosexual classmates and the outside community of what they feel are damaging myths about homosexuality.

From conversations with officials and homosexual students on half a dozen college campuses from Boston to Los Angeles, as well as reports from campus correspondents at 15 other schools, it would appear that the gay students have made substantial strides in changing attitudes.

To do so, they hold dances and parties, run gay lounges and offices on campus, operate telephone "hot-lines" for emergency problems and counseling services, publish newsletters, and provide speakers to address fraternity, dormitory and faculty groups.

They will, for example, provide advice and comfort over the phone to a student troubled by his attraction to his roommate. In regular meetings the students engage in discussions on such topics as the church and the homosexual and plan tactics for the repeal of sodomy laws. And in their parties they seek to provide, quite candidly, the kind of relaxed setting for "dating" and sexual contact that heterosexual students enjoy.

For the most part they are indistinguishable in appearance from their "straight" classmates. But such is their new presence that the National Student Center Association recently opened a division called the National Gay Student Center. And yesterday at Queens College in New York, more than 100 college psychologists and counselors from 30 colleges gathered to meet with gay students and discuss the delicate problems of dealing with young people who are troubled by their homosexuality.

Negligence Discerned

The counselors were told by Dr. Ralph Blair, director of the Homosexual Community Counseling Center in New York, that a national survey of deans, college counseling directors and homosexual students indicated that the schools' attitude toward their homosexual students constituted "the greatest single example of negligence" in their profession.

It was an assertion that was largely confirmed in the interviews with homosexual students.

Typical, perhaps, of the new breed is Larry, an easy-going youth with medium-length brown hair and clean-cut good looks. He was once an officer of the Interfraternity Council at the University of Southern California, where he was selected as one of the "outstanding seniors" last June for his leadership and academic abilities.

But shortly before graduation he announced to his friends, professors and family that he was a homosexual. And he began to organize the Gay Liberation Forum, a group of 30 or so homosexuals on the Los Angeles campus who will soon bring suit against the university's trustee in an attempt to gain recognition.

'Terrifying' Isolation

In organizing, Larry, now a 23-year-old graduate student, would like to save others from the eight months of "terrifying" isolation he went through as a junior when he first realized his homosexuality.

"I was isolated and I was upset—because I was looking at my own gayness through heterosexual eyes," he recalled the other day in an interview in the living room of the large, well-furnished Los Angeles apartment he shares with his lover, a U.C.L.A. student.

"I wanted to change it, but I didn't feel I could tell anybody —and the school really offered no counseling. But when I began reading on the subject I realized that there were millions of men and women who were gay and were indistinguishable—and that it was not a sickness."

"We have to reach the general student and explode the myths," he went on, "and we have to reach the gays in a supportive way. We are cut off from our church, family, jobs, our friends, not because we are gay but because of society's attitude toward gays."

As college organizations, the gay groups feel they have a special function in cushioning the young homosexual from the often agonizing experience of "coming out," the emotionally wrenching period during which he recognizes his sexuality and makes tentative contact with other homosexuals. By providing a "positive" atmosphere for social contacts, they seek to provide an alternative to the harsh noisy "gay bars" where contacts are usually superficial and sex-oriented.

While the colleges have generally maintained a hands-off attitude toward the groups, some officials harbor worries.

While sympathetic with the plight of homosexuals, Dr. Benson R. Snyder, a psychiatrist who is a dean at the Massachusetts Institute of Technology said he was worried about 18-year-olds "who are uncertain about their identities getting caught in an exploitative situation."

But others disagree. Dr. Robert Liebert, a psychiatrist at Columbia University, argues that "there is simply no basis for believing that an individual who is on the path of developing a reasonably fulfilling heterosexual life prior to the emergence of the Gay Liberation Movement will be moved from the course because of a gay lounge and militant gay movement on campus."

Official Recognition

Whatever the case, gay groups have found little difficulty in achieving recognition as official campus organizations at such diverse schools as Boston University, Columbia, Cornell, Illinois, Colorado, Stanford, City College and the various University of California campuses. At the University of Minnesota, the leader of the local gay liberation group, Jack Baker, was recently elected president of the student association.

The Student Homophile League at the University of Massachusettt in Amherst, which works out of an office on the balcony of the student union, is getting $835 this year from the student activities fund. It recently attracted about 150 students from central Massachusetts colleges for a Halloween dance on the campus and several men came in drag.

At Columbia University, a group called Gay People at Columbia set up what is believed to be the first gay lounge in a dormitory—over the strenuous objections of the college's dean but with faculty and student support. Last week, two of the students occupied the office of Dean Carl F. Hovde and won an agreement for school furniture for the lounge, located in the basement of Furnald Hall.

Arm Around a Friend

And across the country at U.C.L.A., Don Kilhefner, a former Peace Corpsman who founded a Gay Liberation branch at the university, strolled across the sunny campus one recent Saturday afternoon with his arm around a male friend. They got scarcely a glance from other students.

But at a handful of schools, the homosexuals have encountered official obstacles, mostly from older administrators and trustees. Their organizations have been barred from the University of Texas at Austin, San Jose and Sacramento State Colleges in California, the University of Kansas, Pennsylvania State, the University of Florida at Tallahassee and U.S.C. At San Jose, a California judge ordered the college to accept the group, and lawyers are preparing suits in most of the other cases.

For the most part, the gay groups are not very political, although a few small factions have tried to identify the gay homosexual cause with movements for radical social change. The memberships are predominantly male; at a few institutions, such as Stanford and Colorado, women have formed separate lesbian groups.

150 Groups Reckoned

Steve Werner of the National Gay Student Center in Washington estimates that there are 150 homosexual groups on campuses and says that many more are forming. Still, the organizers agree they are reaching only a small fraction of the homosexuals in college. The Kinsey report of 1948 said that 10 per cent of American men experienced long periods of predominantly homosexual behavior.

At the root of the new movement is an assertion by the gays that, contrary to prevailing medical opinion, homosexuality is not necessarily a mental disorder. For this reason, much of their effort goes into "consciousness raising" among homosexuals to instill a sense of worth. Many of the groups have speakers who visit and "rap" with psychology and sociology classes and with counselors.

"It's difficult going through psychology classes and constantly being told you are sick and less than good," said Benjamin Hemric, a sociology major at C.C.N.Y.

The groups appear to be most successful at schools isolated from large urban areas and where there are few social outlets. Thus, strong gay organizations exist at Cornell, Massachusetts, Rutgers, Maryland and Colorado.

Other Students' Hostility

The students say that their lives on these and other campuses are made difficult not necessarily by official harassment, but the personal hostility and indifference a student may encounter when his roommates or fraternity brothers learn of his homosexuality. The rate of suicide among homosexual students is said to be unusually high.

Even the existence of formal groups has not dispelled the fear. The Stanford Gay Students Union finds almost nobody comes when meetings are held on campus, and a medical student there reports that he was warned by a doctor to be "more discreet" about discussing his homosexuality with others.

In Boston, the Student Homophile League attracts young people from many colleges in the area. Every Friday night, after choir practice clears out, they filter into the basement of an Episcopal church on Beacon Hill to hear lectures, talk, dance, listen to music and drink punch.

"So many kids are sitting in dormitories tonight. They don't know who they are or what they are supposed to do," said one of the leaders the other night. "They know they are gay and they are going through the worst crisis of their lives. Here they can come to a church and affirm their gayness openly."

Among the participants was an affable freshman from Tufts, 18 years old, who said he "just wanted a place to go—I'm really very alienated from most of the gay scene—the campiness, the tackiness."

There was also a boyish-looking M.I.T. junior, a fraternity member, who said he was "not really decided yet" about his sexuality.

To at least some college administrators, the fact that young people must flounder so during such trying periods in their lives is very much a fault of the schools. Dr. William M. Birenbaum, president of the Staten Island Community College, told the Queens College meeting that the colleges owed their homosexual students a full opportunity to learn and grow.

"If the university is embarrassed by this commitment to do what decency says it should do, then it is a sign of our weakness," he said.

Nation's Collegians Turning to Courses Keyed to Job Goals

By ROBERT REINHOLD
Special to The New York Times

BOSTON, Dec. 19—Students at American colleges and universities are showing unusual interest this fall in courses of study that are closely keyed to vocational goals.

Undergraduate enrollment in such fields as premedicine and prelaw, social work, psychology, journalism and nursing has generally risen this fall.

In part, the pattern seems to reflect the current economic situation. There have been continuing declines, for example, in enrollment in such areas as engineering, education and physics, paralleling a sharp drop in employment opportunities in those fields.

This is one of the conclusions that emerge from analysis of two recent nationwide statistical studies on college enrollment—one by the Carnegie Commission on Higher Education and the other by Dr. Garland G. Parker, vice provost of the University of Cincinnati. It has been generally confirmed by The New York Times in interviews with directors and students on a dozen campuses across the country.

The patterns are not fully consistent throughout the country, and definitive statistics are elusive. The picture is further clouded by the creation on many campuses of experimental courses that cut across traditional departmental boundaries and therefore defy direct comparison with courses in previous years.

Still, the new trend is well illustrated by the situation in biology, which is probably the most popular course of study for aspiring physicians. The Carnegie study reports that the number of new students entering biology this fall was up by 16 per cent over last year's number in a survey of 357 institutions.

Medicine is one of the few fields in which there is still a shortage of trained personnel; medical schools have previously reported a dramatic rise in applications.

At Harvard, the number of biology majors rose from 194 to 248 last semester. And enrollment in organic chemistry, a prerequisite for medical school, has nearly doubled in two years. Latecomers are compelled to watch the lectures on television.

Rise at Cornell

Similarly, the percentage of entering freshmen at Cornell who indicated that they planned to major in biology jumped from 20 per cent in 1969 to 22 per cent in 1970 and 26 per cent this fall.

And at Berkeley, more than half of the freshman class of 3,000 is taking introductory chemistry this fall, requiring televised lectures and night classes.

"There seems to be both negative and positive reasons for this," said Mrs. Barbara Boga, a premedical adviser on the California campus. "The glut of Ph.D.'s and the bad teaching market are one reason. And of course everybody has been talking about the shortage of doctors."

Conversely, enrollment in subjects linked to fields severely affected by the economic slowdown has suffered heavily.

For example, registration in aeronautical engineering at the Massachusetts Institute of Technology has plunged from 687 students in 1969 to 385 this year.

Economic forces are not the only factors at work. The flux of current events and the heightened social awareness of young people appear to have had an effect.

For instance, Prof. John K. Fairbank's course on modern China experienced a doubling of enrollment this fall in the wake of the American rapproachement with Communist China. At the same time, an offering on modern Vietnamese history at the same school has suffered an enrollment drop of about half.

Simultaneously, there has been a surge in enrollment in Chinese language courses despite generally falling registration in foreign language studies. Stanford University reports that over the last two years, the ranks of students of Chinese and Japanese language have swelled by 25 per cent.

One of the most rapidly growing areas of study is journalism and communication arts, where they are offered, despite the fact that the job picture in the news industry is not very bright at this time. Journalism registration at the University of Wisconsin jumped from 181 last semester to 246 this fall.

"Students see journalism as a way to get involved in the world in an active way," said Edwin R. Bayley, dean of journalism at Berkeley. "It is a manifestation of their discontent with the establishment."

"Journalism has more scope than anything," said Don Irwin, a 21-year-old journalism major at Wisconsin. "It's an ever-changing field."

Another very popular field is psychology, which leap-frogged ahead of government and English as the largest undergraduate major at Dartmouth this year, according to the college. The same thing is happening at the University of Michigan and at the University of Pennsylvania, where psychology enrollment has doubled from 1,300 students in 1968 to 2,600 in 1971.

Dr. Burton S. Rosner, the department chairman at Pennsylvania, offered an explanation.

"A lot of people are interested in psychology because they think it can help solve their own psychological problems," he said. "At the same time, psychology has become more intellectually rigorous, so that easy solutions are not plentiful. Those seriously interested in the nature of man now find that there is more to psychology than before. Fi-

Shifts in College Course Enrollments Between Fall 1970 and Fall 1971

UNDERGRADUATE	% Increase	GRADUATE	% Increase
Social Work	+35.9	Forestry	+65.8
Nursing	+27.1	Nursing	+58.9
Urban Studies	+25.8	Architecture	+46.9
Forestry	+21.9	Psychology	+18.2
Biological Sciences	+16.0	Business	+10.9
Psychology	+12.5	Theology/Religion	+9.9
Architecture	+8.6	Education	+9.8
Fine and Performing Arts	+8.6	Ethnic Studies	+6.7
Agriculture	+6.7	Medicine	+4.9
Theology/Religion	+4.7	Agriculture	+4.6
Sociology	+4.5	Social Sciences	+3.4
Social Sciences	+4.4	Law	+3.0
Business	+4.3	Fine and Performing Arts	+2.7
	% decrease	Social Work	+2.3
Engineering	—17.1	Urban Studies	+1.1
Ethnic Studies	—12.1		% decrease
Education	—8.7	Engineering	—7.8
Humanities/History	—2.3	Sociology	—4.4
Physical Sciences	—1.7	Physical Sciences	—2.7
		Humanities/History	—2.1
Source: Carnegie Commission on Higher Education		Social Sciences	—0.9

The New York Times/Dec. 20, 1971

nally, many want to go on to clinical work. They see this as a concrete way of dealing with social problems."

There appear to be shifts of student interest even within fields.

At Harvard, professors in social relations report a marked growth in "self-understanding" courses and a drop in "social action" ones. Thus, offerings in personality psychology are up, apparently at the expense of sociology.

To some, this is a reflection of a new introspective mood on campus.

Other popular areas include ecology, urban studies and city planning, theology and agriculture. However, ethnic studies, which came into vogue two years ago, experienced a 12.1 per cent decline in new students this year, according to the Carnegie study.

The mainstays of liberal education — English, the fine arts, history, philosophy—have not fallen by the wayside. The Carnegie report found only a small decline (2.3 per cent) in new humanities students.

December 20, 1971

Colleges Expand Modern Psychiatric Aid

By JANE E. BRODY

The college health service, long viewed by students as good only for doling out aspirin, patching up athletes and diagnosing the common cold, is now emerging as a leading counseling and treatment center for student sex and psychiatric problems.

While the majority of campus health centers still maintain a conservative, in loco parentis approach to student health, dozens of them at large and small schools around the country have begun to provide such modern services as sex counseling, contraception, abortion referral, venereal disease treatment and help with drug and psychiatric problems.

The trend has generated surprisingly little controversy,

partly because administrators believe that such services are important to the students' effective functioning and partly because parents seem glad to be relieved of the burden.

A number of universities—from the University of California at Berkeley to the University of Nebraska and Princeton—are involved in the trend. A new health plan at Yale University represents what many consider to be the epitome of the revolution in the scope and quality of services offered to college students.

Since July 1, Yale students, faculty members, employes and their families have been served by a prepaid group practice housed in a new $5.5-million health center that offers a veritable cafeteria of medical serv-

ices, including obstetrics, pediatrics and sex therapy of the Masters and Johnson type.

In partial explanation of this approach, Dr. Daniel S. Rowe, the jack-of-all-trades pediatrician who oversees the operation, said in an interview the other day, "We feel the university should be a pioneer in delivering new methods of medical care." He said that dozens of groups had visited the new center and he received letters daily from other universities inquiring about Yale's program.

At Yale, as at dozens of other colleges around the country, much of the innovation in student health care has come in sex-related areas to meet needs created by changes in student life styles and mores.

Yale's sex-related services date to 1969—the first year of co-education. Dr. and Mrs. Philip Sarrel, a gynecologist and a social worker, respectively, who were the innovators in this area, estimate that they have since been visited by 75 per cent of Yale's undergraduate women.

Vasectomies Available

Yale, like many other large universities, has for several years been supplying students with the "morning-after" pill for emergency contraception, as well as with a wide variety of more conventional birth control aids. This fall Yale added vasectomies to its list of available options.

In addition to Dr. Sarrel, who works out of the mental hygiene department, Yale employs one full-time and four part-time gynecologists and a nurse-midwife.

Yale is just one of dozens of colleges across the country that have recently hired gynecologists, at least on a part-time basis. Several schools have also opened birth control clinics.

At the University of California, Berkeley, the contraceptive clinic that opened two years ago is visited by 4,000 to 6,000 students a year. The University of Nebraska handles 50 to 60 contraceptive cases each week, even with a charge of $15 each. New York University is scheduled to open a contraceptive clinic soon.

Changing Times Cited

The University of Michigan set up a separate gynecology clinic last fall, which was visted by 900 students in September. And at Boston University, a gynecologist who was hired in October to work six hours a week is already booked up months in advance.

In explaining his hiring of a gynecologist, Dr. Samuel E. Leard, Boston's director of student health services, said, "It was done in recognition of changing times—if you start having dorms wide open, it adds to problems along gynecological lines."

Barnard's director, Dr. Harriette Mogul, said her service offered birth control and abortion referrals because "we would rather have the information dispensed here, where we are sure of its accuracy, than have our students search on their own."

There has been surprisingly little parental opposition to decisions like Barnard's. When a similar program at the University of California, Los Angeles, was described to parents of entering freshman last summer, the reaction was highly favorable. One father remarked, "Thank God the pill is there for my daughter's protection."

The smooth introduction of contraception at the University of Michigan was aided in an unusual way by the student newspaper, The Michigan Daily. Fearing that publicizing of the fact that contraceptives were being given to minors would stir up opposition among the conservative Board of Regents, the newspaper chose not to run a story on the contraceptive clinic.

Student reaction to these changes in service have been mixed. While most are grateful to have something available, many complain about the long waits for appointments to see the gynecologist and, in some cases, about the high cost. Duke University charges $25 for a pelvic examination and birth control prescription; at UCLA the cost, which includes

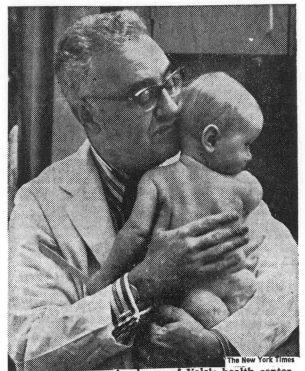

The New York Times
Dr. Daniel S. Rowe, in charge of Yale's health center.

an educational session, is $22.

Several institutions, strapped by a tight budget for student health, found that charging for contraceptive services (even though other health services are free) was the only way they could be made available.

At Princeton, where the university pays the cost of student visits to three local gynecologists, one coed remarked, "There's a general feeling that the examination is cursory and that the doctors don't really care. They're just there to dispense contraceptives."

Most institutions offer pregnancy testing without charge, and a number of colleges offer some sort of abortion counseling, usually in the form of referral to agencies with the necessary contacts.

At the University of Georgia, one coed who turned to the health service when she found herself with an unwanted pregnancy said, "They really helped me through a terrible time. They really seemed like they cared, and you know, I think they really did."

At the same time that college health services have upgraded services related to students' physical well-being, they have also done much to expand and improve the care given to emotional health. Nearly all of the three dozen colleges questioned reported they had recently expanded their psychiatric staff.

Pressures Are Eased

The University of Colorado is one of several that now has

a campus psychiatrist on call nights and weekends. Dr. James E. Marquardt, who administers the Colorado health center, said, "Such around-the-clock service is necessary because suicide is the second most frequent cause of death in the college age group."

Michigan State University maintains seven branches of its counseling service around campus so that students with emotional problems can find help more easily. Many institutions also train dormitory counselors to handle uncomplicated problems.

Barnard's psychological unit recently went to battle for some students who were "anxious" about a freshman English composition assignment that involved writing a personal essay that was then attacked by the instructor. "When we recognize an unfair university pressure, we try to get it corrected," Dr. Mogul explained.

For the most part, drug-related problems are handled within the general psychiatry program. Although many colleges have drug education programs, few have organized drug treatment facilities. City College of New York was recently awarded a $50,000 grant from the City University to hire two drug counselors and establish a drug abuse program.

Most of these improvements in college health services have come about despite a shortage of funds and even though de-

livery of health care is not the raison d'être of an educational institution.

At some colleges the changes were prompted by student pressure; at others, they were initiated by new, enlightened administrators who attracted young, dedicated staffs.

For generations, college health services have tended to be staffed by older men—general practitioners who want partly to retire from pressures of private practice. When 37-year-old Dr. John R. Curtis took over at the University of Georgia three years ago, the average age of the four doctors on the staff was 65. Most of the two dozen staff members added since are 20 or more years younger.

Dr. Marquardt at Colorado remarked, "More doctors are finding the college campus stimulating and more younger doctors are now coming to work at college centers."

Dr. Mogul at Barnard noted that doctors were beginning to see the campus health center as " a chance to help young people develop a good doctor-patient relationship in what is for many of them their frist experience with a doctor on their own."

"It's an exciting field with potential for doing very good things," she added.

At Yale, where 9,000 students and 9,000 other members of the college community already belong to the new health plan, Dr. Rowe said: "Medically speaking, students are just not very interesting. They're just too healthy. Doctors tend to view the job more as a babysitting operation than a stimulating medical service."

However, by including patients from infancy to old age, Dr. Rowe believes Yale has found a good way to attract a top notch medical staff.

Despite the obvious progress made at many institutions, students still find plenty of cause for complaining about the quality of care. Just as all dormitory food is automatically labeled "garbage," students have a hard time finding a good word to say about college health care.

Although some of their complaints have the ring of truth, many reflect a basic lack of understanding of what medicine can and should do. Students find it hard to accept the fact that there is still nothing more than symptomatic relief for the flu and common cold.

As Dr. Rowe pointed out, "At college, the student needs a mother substitute to tell him when to gargle and stay in bed."

January 1, 1972

Women on the Campus Find a 'Weapon'

By BETSY WADE

A shadow no bigger than a woman's hand appeared on the American campus as the seventies opened and now, two years later, that shadow has lengthened. Some believe that it may touch every American college by the end of the decade, bringing with it, like the student uprisings and the black revolution, profound change in American academic life.

For years, women teachers and other professionals had seen a decline in their ranks, a constriction in promotions and an increasing number of closed doors, despite a rise in the number of women college graduates.

The first counterattack was a single letter of complaint written by one woman. There have since been hundreds, but the impact has been remarkable beyond the numbers.

The weapon the women are using is an Executive order forbidding holders of Federal contracts to pursue discriminatory employment practices. The Federal contracts with colleges and universities involve money in the millions, and they sometimes constitute a college's margin of survival.

Federal statistics on academic employment of women disclose, with unequivocal clarity, a weeding-out process that leaves few women holding responsible positions.

At the end of the sixties, women were earning 42 per cent of the bachelor's degrees awarded in the country, 37 per cent of the master's degrees and 13 per cent of the doctorates.

In 1969, women constituted barely 19 per cent of the total American faculty, and one calculation—not made by the Government—put the figure at 10 per cent in the more prestigious schools. By rank, 34.8 per cent of the instructors' posts were held by women, 28.7 per cent of the assistant professorships, 15 per cent of the associate professorships, and 9.4 per cent of the full professorships. The higher the fewer—across the board.

This was the setting in which Dr. Beatrice Sandler, then the compliance officer of the Women's Equity Ac-

tion League, a three-year-old national organization, wrote the letter that started the stir.

She had noted that Executive Order 11375, signed in 1965, had been amended in 1967 to specify that it "expressly" bars discrimination against women by all Federal contractors and that such employers must take "affirmative action" to insure that "applicants are employed and that employes are treated during employment, without regard to their race, color, religion, sex or national origin."

Dr. Sandler's complaint, made on Jan. 31, 1970, was an open letter to the Department of Labor and was directed against all universities holding Federal contracts, and the University of Maryland in particular.

Since that day, 350 similar complaints have been filed against other American universities and colleges. The Women's Equity Action League, known as WEAL, has initiated 260 of the actions. The complaints are now directed to the Department of Health, Education and Wel-

fare, which has been designated by the Department of Labor as the enforcing agency for contracts with colleges.

The complaints already touch more than 10 per cent of the 2,556 colleges and universities in the country and, in the words of one woman activist, the potential is 100 per cent.

The actions are "class actions" in the main—that is, they are attacks by groups that maintain they are victims of discrimination, rather than actions by individuals. Class actions are favored, ac-

WOMEN AND HIGHER EDUCATION
(1969 statistics)

Student Enrollment

YEAR	ALL INSTITUTIONS		JUNIOR COLLEGES		GRADUATE	
	Total Female	% Female*	Total Female	% Female*	Total Female	% Female*
1950	727,270	32	77,599	36	65,262	27 ('49-'50)
1955	931,194	35	112,021	36	73,608	29 (Nov. '55)
1960	1,339,367	37	170,325	38	97,373	28 ('59-'60)
1965	2,173,697	39	321,712	38	196,000	32 (Est.)
1970	3,135,000	41 (Est.)	593,000	40	347,000	37 (Est.)

Source: American Council on Education

*are % of total enrollment

Earned Degrees (In per cent)

YEAR	ALL DEGREES		BACHELOR'S		MASTER'S		DOCTOR'S	
	Male	Female	Male	Female	Male	Female	Male	Female
1949-50	76	24	76	24	71	29	90	10
1955-56	65	35	64	36	66	34	90	10
1959-60	66	34	65	35	68	32	90	10
1965-66	62	38	60	40	66	34	88	12
1968-69	60	40	58	42	63	37	87	13

Source: American Council on Education

Faculty Rank (In per cent)

RANK	ALL INSTITUTIONS		2-YEAR COLLEGE		4-YEAR COLLEGE		UNIVERSITIES	
	Male	Female	Male	Female	Male	Female	Male	Female
Professor	24.5	9.4	7.1	3.6	22.0	11.2	30.1	9.9
Associate	21.9	15.7	10.1	13.4	23.3	17.1	23.8	15.1
Assistant	28.2	28.7	15.2	17.0	30.8	31.6	29.4	30.7
Instructor	16.3	34.8	38.7	45.6	15.8	29.6	11.5	35.7
Lecturer	3.3	4.6	0.8	1.3	5.2	6.5	2.7	4.0
No ranks	3.4	3.3	23.1	14.6	1.4	1.4	0.3	0.3
Other	2.3	3.5	5.0	4.6	1.4	2.5	2.2	4.2

Source: American Council on Education

Basic Salary (In per cent)

SALARY	ALL INSTITUTIONS		2-YEAR COLLEGE		4-YEAR COLLEGE		UNIVERSITIES	
	Male	Female	Male	Female	Male	Female	Male	Female
Below $7,000	6.2	17.0	10.9	16.6	6.0	17.8	5.3	16.2
7-9,999	21.7	45.6	35.7	52.7	30.0	48.8	13.1	38.8
10-11,999	20.6	17.6	22.2	15.4	24.1	15.7	17.9	20.7
12-13,999	17.4	9.9	15.8	9.8	15.9	8.8	18.1	11.3
14-16,999	15.5	6.1	10.5	4.6	12.5	5.5	18.6	7.4
17-19,999	9.1	2.0	1.2	0.1	6.3	1.8	12.7	3.2
20-24,999	6.3	1.2	0.4	0.1	3.7	1.0	9.3	2.0
25,000 +	3.1	0.5	0.2	0.7	1.5	0.6	4.9	0.3

Source: American Council on Education

cording to Margaret Gates, now the compliance officer of WEAL, because the burden of an action would be intolerable on a single secretary or instructor who challenged her employer.

The Federal official in charge of enforcing the Executive order on campus; J. Stanley Pottinger, head of the office of civil rights of the Department of Health, Education and Welfare, has urged WEAL to use class actions because of the relatively easier task of showing a "pattern of discrimination" on a faculty through numbers, salaries or time between promotions.

In theory, the machinery of the Executive order works this way. The university assesses its situation and gives the Government and affirmative action program with goals and timetables for repairing imbalances, taking into account the pool of available people in the area. If the Government accepts the program, the contract is let and then, in theory, the contractor is checked at intervals to see if it is making a good-faith effort to fulfill the goals and timetables. Failure to meet the timetable is not automatically disqualifying, but some results and actions must show.

Columbia stumbled early on. The university went through a certain amount of discussion with H.E.W. in regard to the minority-group hiring aspect of the 1965 Executive order. After a show-cause order by H.E.W.,

The New York Times/Mike Lien
Dr. Beatrice Sandler, whose complaint spurred women's push for jobs on campuses

Columbia submitted an affirmative action plan on Dec. 3, 1969, which was tentatively accepted on Jan. 27, 1970. Soon thereafter, Columbia fell under the eye of WEAL, which filed a complaint on May 11, 1970.

The situation seesawed. Columbia produced a second affirmative action program, which was rejected last Nov. 4. The immediate issue was not discrimination or lack of it, but a void on the statistical record: Columbia was unable to present data on hiring, salaries or job categories as they related to minority groups or to women.

On Dec. 5, it was disclosed that $688,000 in Federal contracts had been held up pending the outcome of Columbia's effort to gather data.

As the year ended, a university spokesman said that the data would be collected within a few weeks. A new affirmative action program would then have to be drawn up and submitted.

The actions against universities under the Executive order have not been without their critics. Sidney Hook, professor of philosophy at New York University, asserts that the "effect of ultimata

to the universities to hire blacks and women under threat of losing crucial financial support is to compel them to hire unqualified Negroes and women and to discriminate against qualified non-blacks and men."

Dr. Sandler, who is now in charge of the Project on the Status and Education of Women at the Association of American Colleges in Washington, takes issue with this. A report she made says that it would be illegal to force an employer to hire an unqualified person and that further, no reverse discrimination is allowed.

January 10, 197

Campus Racial Tensions Rise As Black Enrollment Increases

By THOMAS A. JOHNSON

Racial tensions, distrust, some fist fights and a near total segregation in all but classroom activities characterize the relationships between black and white students on many major American college and university campuses.

Many campuses have separate living arrangements, some authorized, and others ignored by housing officials. Separate tables in the dining halls are so commonplace that students go without second thought to either a "black" or a "white" table.

College "dailies" have, in many cases, been forsaken by black students who have preferred to print news about themselves and the black community in weekly or monthly publications bearing Yoruba or Swahili names.

"Music War," in which whites turn up the volume on "hard rock" or "country and Western" tunes to the discomfort of black students and in which the blacks retaliate with "soul" sounds, have become one of the most common of the dormitory confrontations. And they

lead, frequently to scuffles. Officials are hard put to find visiting musicians for concerts that would appeal to both racial groups.

At Kent State University in Ohio, complaints by black students that they were excluded from the basketball cheering squad resulted in the creation of two cheering squads, one black, one white, that alternated during recent games.

"I had no idea there were such racial tensions here," said Mrs. Gertrude Huebner, a member of the Michigan State Regents when the education officials heard testimony both for and against the setting up of two "Afro-American" housing units at the University of Michigan at Ann Arbor.

"I thought we were doing so well," she said. "I'm just very depressed."

Government agencies and the police have been brought into some campus racial difficulties. A white student at Northwestern University has complained to the Federal Housing and Urban Development agency that a predominantly black dormitory there represents discrimination against him in housing.

In San Francisco State College, a white student has complained to the United States Attorney's office that he was kept out of a black studies course and asked that office to help in protecting his civil rights.

Enrollment Rise Cited

Interviews with administrations, faculty and students at several major colleges showed that the current uneasiness was a direct outgrowth of the dramatic increase in nonwhite enrollments on what had been almost all-white, middle-class campuses.

Generally, no effective measures have been employed to avoid cultural clashes between the new "proud-to-be-black" students and whites who had little or no previous contacts with racial minorities.

Among the interviewed were 20 student journalists at major institutions. All but two of them used such terms as "tense," "expectant," "hostile," "frustrating," "threatening" and "polarized" to described black-white relations.

Student journalists at the University of Florida at Gainsville (548 blacks out of 23,000 students) and the University of Arkansas at Fayette (175 blacks out of 12,000 students) reported little or no racial frictions.

In some informal sessions, white students on several other campuses, however, confided that they had "expected blacks would want to be integrated into [white] campus life" or at least be "grateful for getting into a good school."

There were some admissions of racial prejudice and deliberate attempts by whites to harass the black students. They said also, that there was greater likelihood that campus and town policemen would harass more black students than whites.

Whites Are Rejected

In addition, the interviews with black students showed a widespread and aggressive rejection of whites, except on the very necessary level of instructor, administrator or, perhaps, roommate.

Dianne Howell, a graduate student of psychology at the University of California at Berkeley, likened her white classmates to "the wallpaper." "They're there. They are just there," she said.

Miss Howell is a recent graduate of Barnard College, Columbia University, where she said that blacks and whites were also polarized. She expressed a fear that is widespread among black students. She said:

"I am not here to be some white person's 'black experience.' I am here to obtain a skill the black community needs."

Some white instructors, after expressing shock and dismay, will confide that they consider much of the black aloofness from white campus life to be a fear of competing with whites.

Black instructors, acknowledging the "insecurity" and "adjustment problems" of black students, add, however, that they are probably the "largest

group of non-middle-class street blacks" ever to go to the major universities and to "freely express" black cultural patterns that are different from whites'.

"The top priority of most black students is simply getting out of school," said Harold Cruse, author of the "Crisis of the Negro Intellectual" and director of the Center for Afro-American and African Studies at the University of Michigan.

Separatist Feelings

He said that the black aloofness from general campus activities "is a continuation of the separatist feelings going on among a number of blacks, especially younger people and especially freshmen and sophomores here."

Black enrollment in colleges and universities was 680,000 in 1971, according to census figures, compared to a white enrollment of 8,087,000. In 1960, the black enrollment was some 287,000. About 56 per cent of the black college students attend predominantly white institutions where very few blacks attended a decade before.

The increases were spurred by the black urban rebellion in the middle and late nineteen-sixties, by war-on-poverty and foundation-sponsored programs supporting black college recruitment and by a growing black consciousness that preached a need "for nation-building skills."

A survey by the National Scholarship Service and Fund for Negro Students conducted among some 54,000 high school students preparing for college in 1970 and 1971 showed that some 67 per cent of the black students, from all sections of the country, thought racial integration was both good and necessary, compared to 6 per cent who said it was bad.

A number of educators and close observers contended that the college experience tended to radicalize all students, and that blacks were especially affected since they were now living in a strange, predominantly white atmosphere where they banded together for reinforcement.

The survey said also that 90 per cent of the group gave their life's objective as a desire to "help my people."

There appears to be less friction on the major "commuting campuses," like New York's City University or the University of California at Los Angeles, where students return nightly to neighborhoods that are mostly segregated.

Most of the friction occurs in dormitories. A major dormitory controversy is now continuing on the Ann Arbor campus of

the University of Michigan where some black students are attempting to create "an Afro-American and African Cultural residence hall."

The Michigan Regents recently rejected the proposal for the hall, saying that it would lead to segregation in university-owned housing.

The proposal calls for the creation of special facilities for 400 students in two dormitories that would "provide an Afro-American and African living experience." It would not be restricted to black students.

Lee Gill, a black student leader who supports the plan, said that he had names of more than 30 white students who would want to move into such a living arrangement. A bearded and articulate "graduate" of Chicago's teeming South Side, Mr. Gill described the move as "blacks seeking a power base on campus." He said that other student groups already had such bases.

Gayle Nelson, a Detroiter who is president of Black Women of Stockwell (dormitory), has insisted that the plan would help "to end the polarization of the races."

The housing director, John Feldcamp, who is white, supports the plan as "a positive attempt to get at student racial problems." He said that it would be no different from living arrangements on campus centering on special interests like German, French, chemistry and biology.

Barbara A. Meyer, a white sophomore who is a resident adviser at the South Quadrangle, opposes the housing plan and said that she had conducted a survey that showed 87.5 per cent of the students in her quadrangle opposed it also. She said that students were beginning to settle their disputes in their present integrated setting.

The local National Association for the Advancement of Colored People and the Jewish Cultural League have also gone on record as opposing the special housing units, contending that they were tantamount to segregation.

'A Black Agenda'

In some cases, black students have gone deeply into the general campus life—into student government and fraternities— but "with a black agenda."

At Stanford University, the student president, Douglas McHenry, who is black, called the campus actions by black students "attempts to solidify our gains in recent year and to map new strategies."

The gains, he said, are getting blacks onto the campuses, getting black studies programs

and getting universities involved in the social needs of nearby black communities and in the prisons.

He said that this was not easy, because white interests did not often coincide with the interests of today's black student, and he gave his own experience as an example.

He and other black students at Stanford who had been active in the Black Student Union decided to take over the Student Body and to use the organization's annual $300,000 budget —normally used for student activities — for the social needs of Palo Alto's minority communities.

He said that while black students made up less than 6 per cent of the total, "black students are more politically and socially conscious, so we were able to take over the Student Body organization by building the first, effective political machine here."

"We immediately started dealing with setting up car pools to take families to visit relatives in prison, day-care centers for poor children, ambulance programs," he said. "The white students saw what we were doing, and they organized, voted to take all the funds except enough to run the Student Body office. They made me a general with no bullets."

Seek Out One Another

A tall, slender youth from a middle-class Southern California family, Mr. McHenry stroked the first, uncertain growths of a beard and told a black visitor:

"Sure, we seek out one another. Worst part of my campus life was when I was a freshman and had to walk clear across the campus to find another nigger.

"I can't afford to waste time with whites—that skiing, smoking dope—they can afford to fool around for four years trying to find out who they are. I know who I am. I'm a man who owes success to my folks and to my community."

The pages of Nommo, a black student monthly at the University of California, Los Angeles, reflects the same sense of identity with the black community, rather than with school activities. Nommo is Swahili for "the power of the word."

"We founded Nommo because The Daily Bruin refused to print black news," said the editor of Nommo, Miss Sonji Walker, although Daily Bruin staff members have denied the accusation.

"When they did print it," Miss Walker said, "we could never rely on them to print it accurately. They just didn't care and we needed a publication that did care."

Asked to evaluate the black-white relationship on campus, Miss Walker said, "It's not cordial, not friendly — really a business relationship, a necessary relationship, since we must deal with them."

Potentially Explosive

She said: "People ask us if the white student is more liberal than his parents. I say no, they're just more sophisticated. They're upset with us on campus because they want us to 'be grateful,' to show 'them' some gratitude. Why should we?"

A number of university officials have termed the black-white cultural gap on college campuses potentially explosive. Most, however, express bewilderment.

John Hicks, the assistant to the president at Purdue University, where racial battles have occurred, told a gathering recently at the school's Black Cultural Center that Purdue was "basically a white, middle-class, Midwestern university" and, referring to black students, said: "We don't know many things we should know or do many things we should do."

And while school officials seek ways to avoid or lessen the clashes in attitudes and interests this terms, some express a growing fear that next fall will bring an even greater number of black student enrollments to those "basically white and middle-class" campuses.

Many colleges have pledged to raise their black enrollments to a percentage equaling the national black population of about 12 per cent.

PRESIDENT SIGNS SCHOOL AID BILL; SCORES CONGRESS

Terms Rejection of Stricter Limit on Busing a 'Retreat From Responsibility'

By ROBERT B. SEMPLE Jr.
Special to The New York Times

WASHINGTON, June 23— President Nixon signed today a bill making major innovations in Federal aid to higher education but sharply criticized Congress for not having provided strict and uniform limits on school busing.

In a statement issued shortly after he signed the measure, Mr. Nixon described the bill's antibusing provisions as far less effective than his proposals. His aides left little doubt he intended to carry the issue into the fall campaign.

"Confronted with one of the burning social issues of the past decade and an unequivocal call for action from the vast majority of the American people, the 92d Congress has apparently determined that the better part of valor is to dump the matter into the lap of the 93d," Mr. Nixon said.

'Congressional Retreat'

"Not in the course of this Administration has there been a more manifest Congressional retreat from an urgent call for responsibility."

John D. Ehrlichman, the President's senior adviser on domestic affairs, said later at a news conference that Mr. Nixon still hoped Congress would act on the Administration's antibusing proposals. He said that if Congress did not do so, the President would "go to the people" during the campaign to attempt to rally support for a constitutional amendment.

The President devoted more than half of his message to the busing issue, though the anti-busing provisions constitute a fraction of the complex education bill.

Principles of U.S. Aid

Regarded in some quarters as a landmark piece of legislation, the bill would establish three principles of Federal aid that could have a major impact on colleges and universities:

¶For the first time, the bill would provide nearly every institution of higher learning with Federal money that the schools could use as they wished.

¶The legislation would establish, as a matter of national policy, that every college student who could not afford the cost of his education would get some financial help from the Federal Government.

¶The bill would take Federal assistance away from any graduate school or public undergraduate college that discriminated against women in its admissions policies.

In addition, the measure contains Mr. Nixon's proposal to provide $2-billion over the next two years to help communities that are in the process of desegregating their grade schools and high schools, his plan to create a National Institute of Education to conduct and coordinate basic and applied educational research, and his proposal to establish a new National Student Loan Association. The association would purchase existing student loans from banks, thus providing the banks with fresh capital to make new loans.

The cost of the bill is estimated at more than $20-billion, although the funds must still be provided for in separate appropriations. A major cost item is the new Federal scholarship programs, which would provide Basic Educational Opportunity Grants to needy students.

The maximum grant would be $1,400 a student, although each student would be geared to a sliding scale based on the size of the student's family and income. The total grant could not exceed one-half of the cost of attending college, but the measure also authorizes other grant and loan programs to help the student make up all or part of the difference.

However, the busing issue dominated the President's statement, much as it had the debate in the House and Senate.

Mr. Nixon said Congress had provided neither clarification, guidance, nor relief on the busing issue.

"Congress has not given us the answer we requested," he said. "It has given us rhetoric. It has not provided a solution to the problem of court-ordered busing; it has provided a clever political evasion. The moratorium it offers is temporary; the relief it provides is illusory."

In its final form, the bill delays the implementation of court orders requiring busing "for the purpose of achieving a balance among students with respect to race" until all appeals have been exhausted, or until Jan. 1, 1974.

Mr. Nixon's original proposal plans until the middle of 1973. Mr. Nixon's moratorium would also have applied to all busing decisions, rather than busing orders—in the language of the bill—aimed at "achieving would have imposed a 'moratorium,' or flat prohibition, on any further court-ordered busing a balance among students with a respect to race."

Mr. Nixon's aides believe this is an important distinction; they feel a judge could order busing but deny any intent to achieve precise racial balance.

The measure "applies only to certain kinds of orders," Mr. Nixon said in his statement.

"An adroit order-drafter may be able to prevent any effective application of this law," he added.

Representative Carl D. Perkins, chairman of the House-Senate conference committee that shaped the final bill, disagreed strongly on this point.

"The busing provisions will bring uniformity of legal procedures on this issue for the first time," the Kentucky Democrat said.

"He [Mr. Nixon] just wants to keep the busing issue alive. He played politics with it as far as he could and he's still trying to keep it up."

Mr. Nixon also took exception to Congress's failure to draw uniform national guidelines for school busing to guide the courts in their decisions after the moratorium on new busing expired in 1973.

Mr. Nixon had proposed a series of guidelines as part of his original plan. They would have limited the degree of court-ordered busing for grade school children and allowed districts that are now required to bus children "far in excess of reasonable standards" to seek relief.

April 4, 1972

Suddenly, There's Room To Spare

Only a few years ago there was a general panic about getting into college — there were too many applicants for the seats available. Today, the situation has been reversed: Two months before the new academic year, it is estimated that there may be as many as half a million vacancies in a total of 8 million seats.

For many colleges, the vacancies will aggravate an already serious financial situation. With overhead costs for the coming semester largely fixed — faculty positions filled and facilities to be maintained — any vacancies will widen the budget gap.

What are the reasons for this sudden change? A telephone survey last week of some key institutions in 13 Western states provided these answers:

● *High costs.* College and university officials believe that tight money and ever-rising tuition are keeping many students away.

● *Changes in the draft law.* It is no longer necessary to attend college to avoid military service.

● *A weak job market.* Several administrators pointed out that a college education is no longer an ironclad guarantee of a good job. Far from it, in fact. Unemployment among recent graduates is high.

But there are other less tangible reasons. A growing revolt has been building against the educational lockstep which used to keep young people in the classrooms for 16 continuous years or more from kindergarten through commencement. Colleges no longer frown on interrupted studies, particularly after high school graduation and during the college years. But it makes planning for facilities more difficult.

The temporary attraction of the counter-culture also adds to the enrollment problem. One college admissions expert said: "Just look around the edge of the campuses today, from Harvard to Berkeley, and count the number of kids sitting on rugs peddling homemade belts, jewelry, sandals and candles. These are all part of the student crowd that hasn't enrolled."

Finally, the colleges, failing to anticipate these dramatic changes in supply and demand, have overbuilt. In many instances, particularly with regard to the public institutions, it is less a case of too few students than of too many new places.

The most serious potential consequence of the vacancies is the snowballing effect it has. Institutions affected this year will undoubtedly try to reduce their overhead for the following year. Since salaries account for about 75 per cent of the budget this means reductions in faculty.

Coming at a time when Ph.D.s are already in oversupply, this leads to more Ph.D. unemployment. It is estimated that close to 40 per cent of all Ph.D.'s have traditionally been employed as a teachers.

This trend, in turn, will cause more young people to question whether college-going offers the best career opportunities. And so the problem is likely to accelerate at least until there is a marked change in the employment picture.

Some of the snowballing effects became evident last week when the American Council on Education pointed to a National Science Foundation survey which showed that first-year, full-time graduate science enrollment decreased by 5 per cent between 1970 and 1971. During the same period, virtually all areas of science experienced reductions in first-year employment.

Apart from cutting their overhead, what are the colleges likely to do about their critical situation?

Predominantly residential institutions which are unable to attract enough out-of-town students will increasingly make an appeal for commuting students to take up the slack. This may make some campuses less cosmopolitan in the years ahead.

The University of California Board of Regents earlier this month, faced with a drop in students transferring from other institutions, voted to lower entrance requirements for such students. The Regents also reduced their estimates for long-term growth. They said they now expect the university centers to enroll between 128,000 and 137,000 students 10 years from now — 30,000 to 50,000 less than originally estimated. Present enrollment is about 101,000.

Colleges and universities across the country can be expected to make a special pitch for part-time students, particularly among the middle-aged and women who must still tend their children. This is ironic because the universities, during their recent decade of plenty, had been negative and sometimes downright rude to part-timers and women, looking down their noses at what one dean called "the subway circuit." Now many experts expect that clientele to be courted as never before.

—**FRED M. HECHINGER**

July 23, 1972

519

The Flowering Of a Campus Hybrid

The two-year community college seeks to meet the rising need for training after high school.

By FRED M. HECHINGER

THE new American search for a wide-open door to higher education has led to a new American solution: the two-year community, or junior, college. Like many American educational solutions, it has the pragmatic charm of being flexible and serving different students in different ways.

For some students, who have no scholarly ambitions but would like the basic benefits of the general education provided by traditional colleges in the freshman and sophomore years, the junior colleges offer a "terminal" program in the conventional liberal arts. Since no American course of study is considered complete without a sheepskin, these students leave with an Associate of Arts (A.A.) degree.

For a second group—and a rapidly increasing one—the community college, being located within commuter radius, offers the opportunity to live at home for two more years, while getting the full academic benefit of the first two years of college. These "transfer students" gain easy admission to high-quality colleges and universities, provided, of course, that their record is good and their promise satisfactory. To the parents, the benefits may be these: to be able to keep younger and not-so-mature youths under home supervision a little longer and to reduce significantly the fast-rising cost of "going away to college." For the colleges, this development means spending less money for real estate and dormitories. (This aspect does not apply to the older group of private, residential junior colleges which, however, in many other respects resemble the public community college variety.)

FOR a third group of students, the community colleges hold out up-to-date vocational or technological training, adorned with an overlay of basic general education and made respectable by the college label. This "trade and tech" category, though still fighting for rec-

FRED M. HECHINGER, *education editor of The Times, wrote "The Big Red Schoolhouse" and was co-author of "Teen-Age Tyranny."*

ognition in more snobbish scholarly circles, is little else than the 20th-century adaptation of the old agricultural and mechanical colleges.

The unique attraction of this new American hybrid is that all these diverse purposes are served on the same campus, thus giving students a maximum number of opportunities to change academic careers without loss of time or face. Many a student who had mistakenly thought himself a scholar, now doesn't flunk out altogether; instead he finds a satisfying niche as an electronics technician or a nurse. Thus, these multipurpose institutions become instruments of sorting as well as of education.

Why the new trend? Secretary of Labor W. Willard Wirtz recently appealed for universal schooling through the 14th grade. The Educational Policies Commission warned that, unless junior colleges become part of free and universal public education, millions of youngsters will be ill-equipped to deal with life in America's future. The powerful American Council on Education, giving support to these demands, charged that the traditional colleges neglect the need for post-high-school vocational, technological and subprofessional scientific skills. It predicted that unless American education trained more people both for the service industries and as "clusters" of technicians to support the scientists, engineers, professors, master teachers, computer experts and scores of others, the paradox of simultaneous manpower shortage and unemployment would be heightened.

DR. NORMAN C. HARRIS, an expert in technical education at the University of Michigan, documented the need with such "Help Wanted" advertisements as these:

"Accountant—must be trained in business data processing."

"Electronics technician — transistor circuit knowledge essential."

"Secretary—shorthand required, experience on all common office machines."

It is argued that the instrument of any dramatic extension of education, if it is to become a nationwide reality, will be the two-year community, or

junior, college. Will it work? Should it be offered free, supported by the taxpayer, to all American youth?

Today, the answers to these question range from an enthusiastic "yes" to a belligerent "no." The universal public junior college is regarded by some as the greatest American academic innovation since the establishment of the land-grant colleges 100 years ago. To others the movement appears a gigantic boondoggle, intended to extend the professional educators' power and influence without any real effort to concentrate on educational excellence.

WHAT is the present status of the community junior college? (The word "community" is important in a description of the new trend because private junior colleges have an established tradition, some of them as the outgrowth of the earlier finishing school concept for girls without high academic ambitions, others as feeders into some of the best four-year colleges.) Today, nearly 400 public community colleges are in operation, and new junior colleges are being started at the breathtaking rate of 20 to 30 a year. In Florida, for example, the trend has been marked by an increase from three to 28 junior colleges in the past six years. New York has 34; Michigan 16, with five more in planning. Dr. Harris estimates that a conservative forecast would show 600 such colleges by 1970, with an enrollment of 1.5 million.

The community-college idea has caught hold, especially in California, and in order to take a look at the proposed future as it is already being lived there, this reporter inspected campuses from Los Angeles to San Francisco. In addition, present operations and future plans of the community college movement were discussed with the presidents of over 30 of these institutions.

Seventy-three community colleges are in operation, and 95 per cent of all California youths have a two-year college within commuting distance of their homes. Moreover, any California high-school graduate who does not live within the commuting radius of such an institution may pick a college outside his area, with the understanding that his home community will pick up the cost of this education and reimburse the college of his choice.

PROVING GROUND—California, with 73 community colleges already in operation, leads the nation in the trend to the two-year junior college. Shown here, a campus view of San Mateo College, which this fall expects an enrollment of more than 18,000 students.

THE first impression, during a visit to any of the campuses, is one of enormous enthusiasm. Administration, faculty and students appear caught up in an infectious spirit of adventure. Even where the scholastic quality is spotty—and it sometimes is— the excitement of being on the educational frontier has an intangible but omnipresent effect.

The campuses have a clean, prosperous look. Students are cheerful, relaxed and confident. Although there is the inevitable sprinkling of bearded freshmen, the Eastern affectation of unkempt attire is generally absent. Campus rules prohibit shorts for men and both shorts and slacks for girls, but the outdoor informality of California survives the more formal dress.

FACULTY members compete with each other for the privilege of showing off their departments. "What do you think of this place?" is the typical question. The visitor arriving on the El Camino campus in suburban Los Angeles was greeted from all sides with an almost juvenile sense of triumph over the fact that one of the local science teachers had just been featured in a national picture magazine. An expressed desire to sit in on classes is not met —as it is in more traditional colleges and universities—with a worried scanning of the catalogue in search of an outstanding professor. Instead, there is a sweeping invitation to go into any classroom. The open door is partly a way of life, partly a reflection of supreme pride and assurance. The teacher in charge of a fully equipped beauty parlor is as anxious to welcome the visitor as the instructor of English history.

Who attends junior college? Theoretically, any resident of California who has graduated from high school. Graduates who are in the upper 12 per cent of their high-school classes may enter any one of the University of California campuses without further examinations. Those in the top third of their class may go to one of the network of state colleges. The rest are eligible for junior or community college attendance.

But although this rule implies that the lowest academic group is shunted off to the community colleges, this is not true in practice. Many students who could automatically have entered the selective university campuses choose instead to take their first two years at the local community colleges. This reduces the cost of their academic career, since the community colleges are free and the student continues to live at home.

ESSENTIALLY, the community college program on each campus is divided into two streams — the so-called transfer program and the trade and technical division. The transfer students are simply the equivalent of the freshmen and sophomores in colleges across the country. Their courses are essentially the required and elective studies which prepare them for their majors. (Of course, not all academic students actually do transfer; many conclude their studies at the end of the second year and receive an Associate of Arts degree.)

The vocational and technological departments, on the other hand, are geared to the manpower needs of modern technology, business and the service industries. They are to modern America what the A & M colleges of the last century were to a nation that tried to break away from the exclusive, scholastic tradition of the European universities. But they are also a significant break with the vested vocational education interests of the high schools where both teachers and equipment often belong to a past era.

THE occupational programs of the California junior colleges can by no means be described as a uniform curriculum offered by each of the institutions. Since the colleges belong—as the term "community" college implies—to the local scene, they respond to local pressures, needs and preferences. Practically all junior-college administrators believe that they must offer the . semi-professional programs, such as nursing, electronics, X-ray technology, drafting, surveying, medical and dental technicians' training, secretarial and accounting work. But a growing

number give equal time and space to (and fight for equal prestige for) bricklaying, carpentry, toolmaking, automobile repair, printing, food trades and others.

"Look at the changes of our vocational curriculum, and you can spot the changes in the economy, almost from year to year," said an administrator at El Camino College with its 22 classroom buildings and a day-and-evening enrollment of 13,000. He pointed out that radio and even television technicians' courses had shrunk in enrollment in direct proportion to the phenomenal growth of advanced electronics. One small classroom contained about $125,000 worth of microwave equipment so modern that the college had not yet found a qualified instructor to operate it.

Throughout the "trade and tech" stream of the junior colleges, academic prestige takes a back seat to what Dr. James B. Conant has called "marketable skills." Thus fender repair gets as much attention as high-level industrial design. On dozens of campuses, students are building ultramodern model houses which are sold in open bidding and trucked away to become somebody's suburban home. The college beauty parlors by special nonprofit arrangement with local shops, permit commercial appointments so that students, after basic practice on dummies, can get real experience.

A typical campus legend at El Camino concerns a past football star. The story about him, however, features not his touchdowns but the fact that, within a few years of graduation, he had made a small fortune as the operator of a series of vacation-resort beauty salons.

TO keep this vital aspect of the junior college curriculum technologically up-to-date and geared to the labor market, each department has its local advisory group, composed of industry experts, which meets with the college faculty and administration, counsels on future courses, and reviews and criticizes the existing work. Periodically, retraining leaves for teachers are arranged.

The link between the consumer scene and the "trade and tech" curriculum was demonstrated by a story told

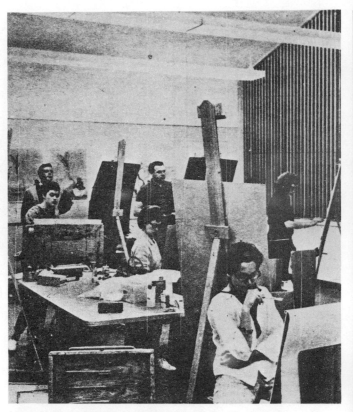

CULTURAL COURSE—A painting class at San Mateo. A community college may fulfill many diverse educational needs on a single campus.

in one of the refrigeration departments. Four years ago, the refrigeration advisory committee had asked the college to eliminate the training of repair personnel. "The business experts told us that it is cheaper to buy new units than to repair old refrigerators and air conditioners," a director of technical training said, "but within three years, the consumer made himself heard. People balked at the idea of educated-in obsolescence. Now we're training repair men again."

"We are not academic," said the director of one vocational program with nonacademic pride. The sense of a direct relationship with the contemporary world was underlined by a visit to the modern printing technology workshop at Los Angeles Trade and Tech. This institution is in the heart of a nonaffluent section of the sprawling city. Much of the printing-trade enrollment appeared to be Negro. The institution's president, when asked how it was possible to ignore the anti-Negro employment barriers in the printing industry, replied: "We don't ask

questions about color. We train able students. When the unions and the employers ask for men we certify that they are qualified—and they are accepted."

WHEN a Russian delegation from the Soviet Technikums—the counterpart of the technical program of the junior colleges—stopped in at a precision-toolmaking class, the leader of the group appeared to ridicule the time apparently wasted on minute refinements applicable to mass-production industry. The teacher, a Rumanian refugee, replied with a cold smile: "Some of the boys and girls we train will be working on intercontinental missiles, and I want them to be on target."

If the "on target" philosophy characterizes the vocational-technological side of the California junior-college movement, what about the academic transfer curriculum?

Inevitably, it is more conventional. Like freshman and sophomore programs everywhere in regular four-year colleges, the instruction ranges from poor to good, with an occasional peak of excellence.

TECHNICAL COURSE—Video technique is taught at San Mateo's KCSM, one of two junior-college TV stations in California.

The junior-college propaganda line has always been that, whereas first and second-year students in four-year colleges never meet the senior faculty, the two-year college brings even the lowly freshman into immediate contact with the entire range of teachers. This is a public-relations myth: The truth is that, with few exceptions, the junior colleges do not have a senior faculty in the sense of a traditional university with an undergraduate college.

AFTER admitting this, it might be well to add that the difference is relatively slight in practice. While many of the junior-college instructors are upgraded high-school teachers, many freshman-class instructors at universities are graduate assistants.

The primary advantage of the open-door policy—admitting any holder of a high-school diploma—is that the process of sorting and selection can be carried out without the rat-race that results from college admissions barriers. True, about 50 per cent of those who are admitted drop out; but they will not go through life with the self-pitying complaint of never having been given a chance.

"We don't have much tradition, but maybe we are better off without it," said one college president. This leaves the door open to an amazing variety of approaches. Suburban El Camino has all the posh atmosphere of a middle- and upper-middle-class campus, except possibly during the busy evening session. Urban

Los Angeles Trade Technical has the flavor of a city college, with a predominance of minority-group students who want to use education as the traditional American escape hatch from lower-class life. Rural, scenic and architecturally grandiose Bakersfield is sufficiently remote from populated urban centers to ignore the "commuters-only" label of the community college movement. It offers comfortably collegiate dormitories which have attracted a share of out-of-state and even foreign students.

FRESNO CITY COLLEGE—one of the older campuses, inherited from a state college—has the well-settled smugness of the established institution, with a well-stocked library and a lived-in look. By contrast, the brand-new campus of San Mateo College, which has outgrown its urban confinement and moved atop a cliff in a windblown expanse of wide-open spaces, has the look of the future. Its giant glass-and-steel library is still awaiting shipments from one of those new commercial firms which, like fish hatcheries, specialize in stocking magnificent new libraries with books. Despite the enthusiasm and success of the California junior-college movement, its leaders are strangely defensive. They appear conscious of a feeling among traditional college faculties that they are too closely linked to the high schools. Indeed, most of the colleges had their start—and many still remain—under the auspices of the local superintendent of schools.

Although a fierce intramural argument over the issue is still unresolved, the trend appears in the direction of independence from the schools, with separate local college boards. But salary scales, which rarely pierce the $11,000 ceiling, are not much higher than those of high-school teachers.

LACK of tradition is everywhere in the air, and depending on the onlooker's point of view it can be alarming or refreshing. There is little question that growing pains abound. In some instances, the administrators' enthusiasm borders on immaturity. When a college president hands out tourist-type mementos (manufactured, of course, in the occupational workshops), he suggests the promoter rather than the educator.

The well-intentioned theory that the daily proximity of liberal-arts transfer students would inoculate the vocational and technical students with the virus of general education is not yet proved in observable practice. Although vocational students must assume a certain minimum of academic work, the injection does not appear to take too readily. The proximity of the two worlds is useful because it permits transfers from one to the other, but the fusion of the two remains a dream. Budding beauticians and electronics technicians tend to regard required world history as a chore.

YET, the over-all impression is one of an educational success story. There is little doubt that California's phenomenal ability to absorb growth and influx of population has been immeasurably aided by the community colleges. Last July Secretary Wirtz announced that job prospects for junior-college graduates in the technical and vocational fields are excellent—and this means that the state with the most complete two-year college system is bound to be ahead. In addition, the junior colleges — as both a buffer and a feeder system—have played a vital role in protecting the academic quality of the state universities, without closing the doors on universally available higher education.

Women Ph.D.'s Are Increasing in Number But More Are Needed to Fill the Gaps

By BENJAMIN FINE

A growing number of women are now entering graduate schools, according to a report by a faculty-trustee committee at Radcliffe College. But despite the great need for trained personnel, prejudice against women Ph. D.'s dies hard. The 135-page Radcliffe study indicates that the number of higher degrees taken by women has tremendously increased in recent years. Nonetheless, a wide gap still exists between the proportion of superior men and women who continue with their graduate work.

The report says there is need for more women with advanced training. They play an important part in education, especially in the women's colleges, where they ordinarily compose a majority of the faculty. Women, the study notes further, help to make a reservoir of highly trained specialists in a variety of fields; the present acute shortage of skilled personnel might be eased if more women were encouraged to continue with their education. In a 1955 study, "America's Resources of Specialized Talent," Dael Wolfle and a commission found that a small percentage of women capable of earning a doctor's degree elect to work for it.

The Wolfle commission learned that although the number of girls who finish high school is approximately the same as the number of boys, and the distribution of intelligence equally balanced, the similarity ends there. Nearly two-thirds of the qualified boys enter college and 55 per cent remain to graduate. Only 42 per cent of the girls go on to college, and 37 per cent graduate. On the graduate level the disparity is even greater: 5.6 per cent of all men college graduates receive their Ph. D.'s, in contrast to less than 1 per cent of women college graduates.

Need for Skilled Workers

Women, the Radcliffe study points out, can help to ease the shortages in many fields. Skilled hands are needed in a host of professions and occupations. Not only is there a shortage of engineers and scientists, but also of linguists, anthropologists, economists and statisticians.

Radcliffe studied 400 of its graduates who had received Ph. D.'s. The reluctant conclusion is reached that as a group, these graduate students, now mostly college teachers, have not distinguished themselves unduly. For example, the women professors cannot keep pace with their male colleagues in the matter of research or in published papers.

"The relatively low productivity of Radcliffe Ph. D.'s can hardly be ascribed to their training as such," the study notes. "It is more likely to result from the environment in which they find themselves, the tradition of scholarship, the amount of time and facilities available for research and writing, and the attitude of their colleagues and the college administration."

Are the women good as teachers, if not as scholars? From all accounts, the women do just as good a teaching job as men. Actually, the question of sex is not a factor, college presidents who employ both men and women faculty members say. It all depends upon the individual.

Evaluation of Teachers

The best evaluation of the man versus woman teacher was made by Dr. Harold Taylor, president of Sarah Lawrence College, which employs both men and women on its staff. He says:

"I do not believe that quality in scholarship or in teaching depends on the sex of the scholar-teacher, or the quantity of publications. Many of the country's best teachers publish little; some of our best scholars are not good teachers.

"The ideal must always be the scholar-teacher—one who knows a very great deal about his chosen field of knowledge and who teaches out of the richness of his intellectual experience. Whether or not the member of a college faculty publishes research or produces creative work is a personal matter, just as is the question of whether or not individual faculty members make public addresses, are active on committees or in professional organizations.

"The teacher must always find a large part of his creative expression in his work with students and he must be judged by the way in which his students learn, not by the external criteria of the quantity of his publications."

It is true, though, as the Radcliffe study shows, that at present the woman teacher has to be better than her male colleague in order to get ahead on the campus. This is particularly true for those who seek administrative posts.

Attitude of Husbands

Married women professors are at a disadvantage, the report indicates. One factor is the attitude of their husbands. Unless the husband approves his wife's efforts to combine a career with her marriage, neither the marriage nor the career is likely to be a success. Then, too, a wife may be offered an opportunity in a different locality from her husband's job and thus feel unable to accept it.

Sometimes women with families take part-time teaching jobs. There were twenty-nine Radcliffe Ph. D.'s working part-time, according to the study. Most of these women have taken several years away from their careers or have restricted themselves to part-time work only. In consequence, their record of professional progress is somewhat uneven. The records reveal a conflict between family and professional responsibilities which has almost invariably been resolved in favor of family, and especially of children.

But, as one of the women professors expressed it: "It is harder for qualified women to be promoted than for men, and the reasons, I suspect, are intangible. Some, certainly not all, men who are in a position to recommend promotion in a women's college are second or third rate and feel insecure with good women. It is harder for a single woman professor than for a married man to carry on the social life and entertaining which is a factor in promotions."

The survey says that this "grousing" is too frequent to be dismissed. Perhaps through these expressions the women teachers show their defensiveness, insecurity and rationalization. They may even show a sense of inadequacy or frustration. But in any case, the report concludes, they do show a severe psychological handicap for the single academic women. It is not easy to do first-rate work if one is seriously bothered with problems of status and discrimination.

EDUCATORS SCORE STUDIES FOR PH.D.

Report Asks Wide Changes —Speed-Up and Tightening on Admissions Urged

By BENJAMIN FINE

The nation's graduate schools came under sharp attack yesterday.

A committee of four prominent educators called for drastic revision of the studies leading to the Master of Arts and Doctor of Philosophy degrees. The educators said they were "shocked" at some of the existing practices. Their views were given in a report to the Association of Graduate Schools.

It is particularly essential to strengthen the advanced degrees, the report said, because of the growing demands for men and women with Ph.D's in all fields.

The Committee on Policies in Graduate Education consisted of Dr. Marcus E. Hobbs, dean of the Graduate School of Arts and Sciences, Duke University, chairman; Dr. Jacques Barzun, dean of the Graduate Faculties at Columbia University; Dr. A. R. Gordon, dean of the University of Toronto's Graduate School and Dr. J. P. Elder, dean of the Graduate School of Arts and Sciences, Harvard University.

'Uncertainties Are Noted'

The committee said the Ph.D. program was "tortuously slow and riddled with needless uncertainties." Frequently it is "inefficient and traumatically disagreeable to the bewildered and frustrated candidate," the report stated.

April 29, 1956

The committee criticized the length of time required to get a doctorate degree in the graduate schools. Unlike students in other professional schools, such as medicine and law, where a definite timetable is set for the degrees, the Ph. D. candidate does not know how long he will take to complete his work.

Candidates for a Ph.D. must expect to work at least four years for the degree, the committee said. It pointed out that not infrequently a candidate would take ten to fifteen years.

Why this length of time? The educators report:

"Financial need, to be sure, often comes into the picture. But all the same we know that too many programs have taken too many years simply because faculty members and the graduate office have failed to give hard-headed advice at the right time, have shied away from making their students work hard enough, and have generally thought a well-bred air of amateurishness more gentlemanly and becoming than down-to-earth efficiency."

Many worthy candidates, the report suggested, are stymied because of financial reasons. As a result, "all too often the files of the dean's office become a last repository for uncompleted thesis projects," the committee said.

The type of work a candidate takes to get a Ph. D. is not always of top quality, the report asserted. The committee said that "we see many a man less mature, less self-poised and less confident after two years in a graduate school than he was as an inspirited college senior!"

What of the end result?

The committee was harsh in its evaluation of the "emerging Ph. D." It said he was not an educated man who combined "wide-ranging learning with an attitude of simplicity and vividness, and who commingles good taste with an excited curiosity."

"Rather," it said, "he likely has become a sort of expert plumber in the card catalogues or other areas and neither as teacher nor scholar will he throw off this inhibiting heritage."

The committee made these recommendations to improve the Ph. D. program:

¶The whole program should not take more than three years of residence.

¶Admission requirements should be tightened. Candidates for the Ph. D. should show that they can write respectable English and have a proficiency in two foreign languages.

¶A member of the faculty, acting as an adviser, should deal with the individual candidate.

¶Two courses should be required: A "pro-seminar" during the first year and seminar the second year.

¶The thesis should show/ evidence of ability, research and competence in developing original work.

A 'Consolation Degree'

The committee also criticized graduate schools for their Master of Arts programs. Frequently the M. A. is viewed a "consolation degree" for those who cannot get the Ph. D., it said. Or it may be a "quick degree," representing superficial performance, the report added.

It is important to "rehabilitate" the master's degree, the committee declared.

The educators recommended that work for the master's degree take one and one-half years to complete. The candidate would be required to write an essay of seventy-five to 125 pages.

"If we do not take some steps toward defining and tightening the Ph. D. program," the committee concluded, "and toward rehabilitating the A. M., we shall gradually lose the power to get our own houses in order. For doctors and masters will be called for the next decade with a resistless intensity."

EDUCATION PH.D.'S ARE GRADED LOW

Report Finds Mathematics and Physics Attract Better Students

ACADEMIC NEEDS NOTED

Conant Finding That Small High Schools Are Short of Courses Is Backed

By FRED M. HECHINGER

A nation-wide study of academic background and personal abilities of all of the Ph.D's produced in one year shows that physics and mathematics have captured most of the talent.

By the same criteria, education has attracted the lowest share of top-level intelligence.

The study also vindicates an earlier warning by Dr. James B. Conant that small high schools are unable to provide an adequate academic challenge.

Every high school with fewer than 100 graduates in 1958 was found below the national norm of doctorate production. All the high schools in the largest class-size category of 800 or more students in their graduating classes were found to produce three times as many doctorates as would be expected of them, according to the national norm.

The study was carried out by Lindsey R. Harmon, director of research, Office of Scientific Personnel, in the National Academy of Sciences. It was supported by the National Science Foundation and the United States Office of Education. The report will be published today in the weekly magazine Science.

Two Fields Lagging

It is apparent, the report said, that the physical sciences and social sciences are "the outstanding fields at the higher ability levels, followed closely by arts and humanities, with the biological sciences and education lagging far behind."

The study found "that the fields of biology and education have not been able to attract their proportionate share of individuals of highest intelligence."

Since these fields "are certainly inherently as challenging as those in the physical sciences," the report concluded that "there is a failure somewhere, probably at the high school level or even earlier, to present adequately these challenges to the bright young people who eventually attain doctorate degrees."

The study started with a list of all of the 8,930 doctorates awarded in 1958. After eliminating about 13 per cent who had been graduated from foreign high schools and those for whom no high school information was available, the survey followed up the remaining 6,259 recipients.

Other Findings

Among other important findings of the survey were these:

¶The Northeastern States as a whole outproduce the rest of the country in Ph.D.'s by almost 50 per cent.

¶The Mountain States are 50 per cent above the national norm in the production of biological science Ph.D.'s.

The yardsticks used for the study included intelligence tests; an adjusted ranking in the high school class; grade-point averages in mathematics and science and the Army General Classification Test.

It was found that one person in 3,100 of any one year's approximate Ph.D. age group in the nation actually attained a doctorate.

Even at the highest ability level tabulated, above the "genius" classification, only one person in five actually attained the doctorate. The report concluded that there remained "a substantial reservoir of under-developed ability."

Survey Finds Science Students Have Best Chance for Stipends

Those With Less Ability Are Said to Hold Edge Over Top Graduates in Social Studies and the Humanities

By FRED M. HECHINGER

Students of natural science who have relatively poor ability have a better chance of getting financial support for graduate study than do superior students in the social sciences and humanities. A recent nation-wide report on the academic and financial standings of graduate students showed that studying "the right thing at the right school" was a surer road to a stipend than was intellectual excellence.

The study was carried out by the National Opinion Research Center of the University of Chicago under joint sponsorship of the National Academy of Sciences, the Social Science Research Council and the American Council of Learned Societies.

Dr. M. H. Trytten, director of academy's Office of Scientific Personnel, said the findings showed that the financing of graduate students was "precarious and opportunistic."

Dr. James A. Davis, director of the study, said they showed a system "wasteful in terms of the working lives of the country's brightest young people" and suggested that the country was a long way from "providing real encouragement for excellence."

One-Fourth in 7 Schools

The report found that one-quarter of all students seeking either master's degrees or doctorates were enrolled in the nation's seven largest graduate schools. These are Columbia University, New York University and the Universities of Chicago, California in Berkeley, Michigan, Wisconsin and Minnesota. Furthermore, graduate study was found to still be a man's world. About 82 per cent of the graduate enrollment is male.

The 190-page report is entitled "Stipends and Spouses—the Consumer Finances of Graduate Study in America."

It said that "the impoverished graduate student putting himself through school by washing dishes in a beanery" had practically disappeared. But it said that today's financially comfortable graduate students had got that way be devoting too much time to fairly high-paying professional employment that seriously cut into their academic work.

"Within each stage and control group, natural science students who are seen as poor Ph.D. material have almost the same chance for a stipend as social science and humanities students who are rated as superior or exceptional, and a better chance than social science and humanities students who are rated as competent for Ph.D. work," the report said. It went on:

"Public university students who are rated poor Ph.D. material have almost the same chance for a stipend as private university students rated superior or excellent."

Three-fourths of all graduate students in public universities get some form of stipend, the report said. It found that in private institutions about 70 per cent of the graduate students in the top colleges got them and about half in the smaller universities received them.

The median income of graduate students was found to be about $400 a month. An average of 15 per cent of this is spent on education. Stipends are the single most important source of income. This category includes scholarships and research or teaching assistantships. Almost half the students receive $150 a month or more from these sources. Most of the aid money is provided by the students' own universities.

Other sources of income, in the order of their importance, are income from a wife's or husband's employment, from part-time jobs, savings, veterans' benefits, full-time work, investments and borrowing.

Young scholars are highly conservative in borrowing for personal financing. The report said:

"It appears that the students decide how much money they need to prevent them from going into debt, then raise it, even if this means cutting down seriously on their academic progress."

Don't Take Full Load

Students frequently were found to be taking "as many courses as they can literally afford, and no more."

As a result, the study found that two-thirds of all graduate students who relied on outside employment completed less than two-thirds of a full-time academic load in a typical year.

Fewer than one-fourth of all students expect any financial aid from their parents, usually because the students do not consider such support necessary, the report said.

Of all groups of graduate students, only the fathers of children appear to have serious financial troubles.

In terms of religious background, about half the sample were brought up as Protestants, one-quarter as Roman Catholics and 13 per cent as Jews. Twenty-five per cent of the sample shifted from an original denomination to "none." This change was found most frequently among Jewish students and least frequently among Catholics.

The survey, begun in 1958, was based on a national sample of 3,000 arts and science graduate students from twenty-five institutions, representative of 63,000 graduate students then enrolled in American universities. The study excluded students in professional fields such as law and medicine.

September 3, 1961

Washington

Enter the Academic Bum or Perpetual Student

By JAMES RESTON

WASHINGTON, June 9 — Bob Hope's advice to this year's college graduates on going into the world was "Don't!" After the stock market slump, he told the Georgetown University graduates, things were so bad, even for holders of A. T. & T. stock, that when he put a dime in a coin telephone the other day, a voice said: "God bless you, sir."

It was the merriest moment of the annual cap and gown parade, and darned if a lot of the most intelligent graduates are not taking his advice. They are not going into the world. They are staying on in their privileged ivy-covered sanctuaries. For a remarkable number of them—a majority in many of the best colleges—college graduation is what high school graduation was a generation ago—a sunny interlude between one educational institution and another.

The Devalued Diploma

This was probably inevitable and in many cases, maybe most, it is desirable. Mass education has devalued the college diploma. To stand out from the mob, many men and women feel that graduate work is essential; to meet the increasingly high demands of the scientific and professional worlds, college graduates now think they have to keep going into post-graduate studies.

And yet it is hard to avoid the conclusion that American education is out of balance: about a third of our best high school graduates don't go to college, and about a third of our best college graduates won't leave college until it is almost too late to consider anything but the academic life.

Much has been said, and is being done, about the waste of the bright ones who won't go to college; less about the others who won't get out. Yet there is a new class of perpetual students in America, spawned by prosperity, who think of education not as a preparation for life but as an escape from the more strenuous life of competitive business and squabbling nations. In another generation we used to deplore about this time of year the athletic bum, who put sports ahead of everything else; now we have the academic bum, who puts books ahead of everything else.

Money produced them both. A good tackle and particularly a good passing quarterback could get an athletic scholarship anywhere in America; now a good student can pile up fellowships all over the world. The tax structure has produced the foundation; the foundation has produced vast sums for graduate studies and research fellowships; foreign aid has piled up millions of dollars in counterpart funds in other countries which provide all in education grants overseas.

Like every good thing, however, this creates its own problems. Now the bright boy can be financed through graduate school, get a Fulbright or a Ford grant after that, have it renewed for another year or two, and find himself at 30 living a pleasant life, and meanwhile escaping the draft on a series of student deferments.

526

A Matter of Choice

At the end, your perpetual student usually lives a useful life. He teaches, and teachers are in short supply. Or, increasingly, funds and competition for good minds being so prevalent, he can negotiate a research or writing position.

This does not mean that he is not making a contribution to the nation, but the fact remains that the United States is getting a smaller percentage of its best minds into the public service today than any other major country in the Western world, and this at a time when it needs good brains in the municipalities, legislatures and executive departments of the various governments.

This is often not the fault of the student. His parents and teachers often encourage the cult of graduate degrees. The atmosphere of the time encourages them to choose the higher pay of business or the quieter life of the campus. The agonies of the political struggle are well known and usually held in some contempt. So on graduation day, when most students are in doubt, it is easy just to go on to graduate school and then it becomes increasingly difficult to leave.

The athletic bum was a limited problem: he was a drag on the classroom but he put on a good show and, when his talents declined, he soon went away. The academic bum is more serious. His talents increase with the years. He has the gifts the nation needs more now than ever before, and the question is not whether he is using them to advantage—he usually does in the end—but whether he is using them where they would do the most good.

Matters Of Degree

By CLIFTON BROCK

THE first Master of Arts degree awarded in the New World was won in 1655 by a Harvard student who produced a thesis titled, "Every Perfect Being Can be Perfectly Defined." Who today would dare dispute him, or even attempt to say what he was talking about? As recently as 1765 a Cantabridgian named Belknap was successful in obtaining his M. A. with an opus labeled, "Did Adam Have an Umbilical Cord?" (Belknap maintained that he did not.)

Today we may smile condescendingly at such treatises. We are the learned sons of an electronic age. But one may wonder if, two or three hundred years hence, our descendants may not smile at such mid-twentieth-century titles as "Metamorphosis of the Nervous System in the Lumbrosacral and Caudal Regions of the Frog" (Harvard), "The survival of Adrenalectomized Cats in Experimentally Induced Pseudo-Pregnancy" (Princeton) or "Asexual Inheritance in the Violet" (Cornell).

WHEREVER we look, we find what appears to be ridiculous treatises, including many submitted for Ph.D's. Texas University, which some might expect to be provincial, has awarded the Ph.D. for a work on "Uses of the Subjunctive in King Alfred's Old English Version of Boethius's 'De Consolatione Philosophiae.'" Another Texas student, perhaps doing his research on dark nights, investigated the "Histological Changes in the Fallopian Tubes of the Oppossum During the Phases of the Oestrous Cycle." And at Columbia a candidate for a graduate degree produced a work titled "A Comparative Study of the Breathing and Speech Coordinations of Laryngectomized and Normal Subjects, Including an Evaluation of the Relationships Between the Breathing and Speech Coordination of the Laryngectomized and their Judged Intelligibility."

Readers may well wonder at the verbal and intellectual gymnastics which go into the writing of academic dissertations. Why are such apparently abstruse subjects chosen? Ignorance may explain the early Harvard writings, but what can explain those of our own day?

There are those—including many who hold the Ph. D.—who say that ignorance is still an adequate explanation. A more valid explanation would appear to be, not ignorance, but the opposite—too much knowledge. There is in Ecclesiastes an oft-quoted line to the effect that there is nothing new under the sun. One reason for such dissertation subjects as those mentioned above is that, under our system of graduate education, the candidate for an advanced degree is required to find what the Bible says he cannot find—something new about which to write a dissertation.

AN academic dissertation has been defined as a "formal treatise based on original research in partial fulfillment of the requirements for a doctor's degree." The key words are "original research." In 1960, the latest year for which accurate figures are available, 9,829 Ph.D. degrees were awarded by American universities, the bulk of them in Education (1,590) and the fewest in Journalism (8). With that many fishers at the scholastic pond, it would take an academic Izaak Walton to pull out anything original. Under the circumstances, a student can hardly be blamed for selecting, as one recently did, the topic: "Blood Changes During Emotional Stimulation in the Goat."

All this is not meant to imply that most Ph.D. dissertations are frivolous. Many esoteric studies — including some mentioned here — have practical applications—indeed, may represent important research. Several years ago a student analyzed "The Effects of Arsenic, as Used in Poisoning Grasshoppers, Upon Birds." As Rachel Carson demonstrates in her new book, "The Silent Spring," the indiscriminate use of such pesticides has had a serious effect on the bird population in many areas. And, of course, there are always dissertations which deal with timeless subjects like "The Relation Between Religion and Science" or "The Policy of the United States Toward Industrial Monopoly."

STILL and all, the requirement of originality combined with the proliferation of knowledge drives many students to extremes wondrous to the layman. And the layman can hardly be blamed. Today, even specialists in the same field often cannot understand each other. Many a chemist would have to run to his reference books before reading a colleague's work on "The 3a-methylhexahydroindans."

Most students consider the process of obtaining a Ph. D. in a modern American university a cross between an extended desert march and a medieval inquisition. It was not always such an ordeal. The requirements for an M. A. at Harvard in its early days, for example, were a good deal simpler than they are today. Historian Samuel Eliot Morison notes in "Three Centuries of Harvard, 1636-1936" that there was a saying at the time: "All a Harvard man had to do for his master's degree was to pay five dollars and stay out of jail."

The discerning reader may have noticed a curious difference between these early Harvard theses and the dissertations of today. In the old days, even though other requirements were lax, the title of the thesis itself had to be cast in the form of a question or a positive statement. The candidate for a degree was required to adopt a position and could be called upon to defend this position. Today there is no such stricture. The modern candidate may choose a topic which would, on the face of it, seem to defy argument—e. g., "Some of the Factors Which Influence the Composition of Cabbage and Their Relation to the Quality of Sauerkraut."

SOME years ago one Carroll Atkinson, who evidently found the road to a graduate degree rather rocky, summarized the experience in a book titled "True Confessions of a Ph.D."

"The Ph. D. stands alone," he wrote, "a living monument testifying to the mighty effort of the man or woman who attains one—but unfortunately a monument that too often resembles a tombstone because the holder of the degree

527

in the process has become withered both mentally and physically as a result of the sacrifices that are required to secure this recognition. . . ."

Why do they do it? Some say it is a matter of vanity. Karl Marx, Ph. D., never missed a chance to remind his less-educated comrades that they were far from being his intellectual equals. This explanation may fit in many cases, but it does not apply to the Einsteins, the Schweitzers and the Oppenheimers, among many others. From the titles of their dissertations, we may not be able to understand what these men were writing about, but we know that somewhere to someone, the work means something.

On the other hand, there are other scholastics who will continue to discourse learnedly on such a subject as "A Study of Two Methods of Teaching Bowling to College Women of High and Low Motor Ability," or, "An Analysis of the Aerodynamics of Pitched Baseballs."

IN RUSSIA, TOO

AMERICAN scholars have no monopoly on seemingly bizarre dissertations submitted for advanced degrees. Premier Khrushchev had a few words to say about theses in the Soviet Union recently in an address he delivered before the Central Committee on the state of agriculture in the U.S.S.R. Herewith an excerpt, as reported in The Current Digest of the Soviet Press (Vol. XIV, No. 12):

"I would like to mention some of the subjects that have been prepared for the degree of candidate or doctor of sciences. I will say beforehand that I do not know what guided the people who chose these subjects, or what guided the people who reviewed them.

"The Kharkov Veterinary Institute accepted a work by

NYET—"The Biomechanics of the Gait and Carriage of the Horse" did not impress Premier Khrushchev.

V. N. Zemlyansky, presented for the degree of doctor of biology. Its title was: 'Concerning Certain Patterns in he Biomechanics of the Gait nd Carriage of the Horse as Factors Influencing Its Basic Productivity.' [Stir in the hall. Laughter.] These are the conclusions the author of this doctoral dissertation arrived at:

" '(1) The rapidity of a horse's movement, one of the indices of its work usefulness, depends chiefly on the length and frequency of the stride. [Stir in the hall. Laughter.]

" '(2) Trotters at various stages of training have strides with the following phases: at low speeds a hold phase and a shift phase; at high speeds a hold phase, a shift phase and two phases of free suspension.' [Stir in the hall. Laughter.]

"Apparently the author of the dissertation was awarded a doctor's degree, and our statistics on the number of scientists in the Soviet Union were increased by one. I don't know—let the scientists not condemn me for this—perhaps this 'suspension' is needed, but I am convinced that a 'scien-

tific' work like this one will do no good. [Applause.]

"Or take another example. R. E. Aluoya defended a dissertation at the Estonian Agricultural Academy on the subject: 'Study of the Microclimate in the Cow Barns of the Estonian Republic.' The dissertation consists of the following sections: the state of cow barns and their construction in the Estonian Republic; design characteristics of the cow barns studied; the number of microbes in the air in cow barns; the chemical composition of the air in cow barns.

"Any person with a sense of smell who goes into a cow barn can tell you the composition of the air. [Laughter. Stir.] We do not need any special instruments for this. We can get along without research on the composition of the air in cow barns. What we need is higher beef production. Apparently, they think differ-

ently in the Estonian Agricultural Academy, the source of this dissertation.

"In the Biology Institute of the Belorussian Republic Academy of Sciences, A. P. Krapivny defended a thesis for the degree of candidate of biology on the following subject: 'The Ecology and Economic Importance of the European White Stork, the Black Stork and the Common Gray Heron in Belorussia. I admit my ignorance. I have never seen a black stork, and I don't know whether or not they are to be found in Belorussia. I'll take this scientist's word for it if he says that the black stork does exist there. I can't be sure perhaps this dissertation will do our great-grandchildren some good, but I don't really think so. In any case, Soviet money should not be wasted on research on the white and black storks and gray herons of Belorussia."

ON THE BALL—The national pastime has come in for learned study; e.g., "An Analysis of the Aerodynamics of Pitched Baseballs."

November 4, 1962

YALE SETTING UP M. PHIL. DEGREE

2-Year Graduate Program Will Be Like a Doctorate Without a Dissertation

NEW STANDARDS ON WAY

Traditional Master's Study to End in 1968—Spur to Teacher Training Seen

By WILLIAM E. FARRELL
Special to The New York Times

NEW HAVEN, May 12—Yale University announced today the establishment of a new graduate degree, the Master of Philosophy, designed to help satisfy the demand for more college teachers as well as to raise the requirements for the master's degree.

Dean John Perry Miller of the Yale Graduate School said the Master of Philosophy degree would be awarded to students who had completed all of the requirements for the degree of Doctor of Philosophy except for the writing of the dissertation.

The M. Phil. degree is the first of its kind in the country and will become effective for graduate students entering Yale in the fall of 1968. It will generally take two years of study to earn. Acquiring a Ph.D. requires a minimum of three years of study and usually runs to four and often five years.

A Shift in 1968

When the new program is implemented in 1968, the university will discontinue the traditional Master of Arts (M.A.) and Master of Science (M.S.) degrees, which usually require only a year of graduate study. Exceptions to this policy,

the university said, will be in special programs designed to train persons in industrial administration, public service and as secondary-school teachers.

In addition the M.A. and M.S. degrees will continue to be offered to Yale College seniors who have managed, during their undergraduate careers, to complete a full year of graduate study. These students will receive both the bachelor's degree and the master's degree after four years' work.

In a statement outlining the new program, Dean Miller said:

"For over a decade there have been demands that our leading graduate school establish a new degree which represents substantially greater achievement than the typical Master of Arts or Master of Science degree, but which places less emphasis upon research than the Ph.D.

"I believe that Yale's new degree is an appropriate answer to this demand."

Need for Research

He added that intensive research, such as that required by a Ph.D. program, was "a prerequisite for imaginative and effective teaching in much of the curriculum of our colleges and universities."

"But there are many teaching positions, especially concerned with general education in the first two years of college, which can be filled by talented teachers who have achieved the level of training represented by the new Master of Philosophy degree," the dean continued.

Dean Miller said he was "hopeful that other universities will join us in awarding the Master of Philosophy degree and that many institutions will offer holders of this degree teaching appointments that may lead eventually to tenure professorships."

Several weeks ago the Select Committee on Education of the University of California, Berkeley, suggested the establishment of a Doctor of Arts degree, which would be a doctorate that did not require a written dissertation. However, the proposal has not been implemented, largely because of objections from faculty members who argue that such a degree would seriously depress the value of the Ph.D.

GRADUATE STUDY FACED BY CRISIS

Schools Fail to Keep Up With Sharp Rise in Applicants

By FRED M. HECHINGER

The country's graduate schools are facing a floodtide of applications and a crisis of shortages in staff and facilities. Within three years it may be more difficult to get into a graduate shool than it has been to get into an undergraduate one.

These warnings are being issued by experts in higher education, who cite the new pressures for advanced degrees. They believe that quotas on graduate school admissions are inevitable.

"Tomorrow's headlines, ulcers and broken hearts will be products of the graduate school situation," Arnold L. Goren, dean of admissions at New York University, warned yesterday in a special report in the university's Alumni News.

As recently as 1960, there were only 300,000 graduate students in the United States, but by 1970 there are expected to be 800,000, Mr. Goren said. About 500,000 are now enrolled. He predicted that the pressures would rapidly build "to a point where many, many qualified applicants will have to be rejected."

Already Critical

A spot check by The New York Times indicated that other experts in the field not only agree with these forecasts, but assert that the situation is already critical, at least in the high-prestige institutions.

John Perry Miller, dean of Yale University's Graduate School, said the number of applications in some departments this spring has been "just tremendous."

Actually the build-up has been dramatic ever since the early nineteen-sixties—an indication that the trend is not a freakish one, inspired perhaps by the desire of students to stay out of the draft.

Mr. Goren, citing the trend at N.Y.U., said applications rose from 3,222 in 1963 to 4,287 in 1964 and to 4,809 last year—a 50 per cent increase in a two-year span. Incomplete figures indicate a further increase of 21 per cent for classes starting next September.

The trend toward increasing graduate study is in line with the over-all development of American education. At the turn of the century only about 6 per cent of the country's youths completed high school, compared with over 70 per cent today. Until World War II only a minority of young people attended college. Today close to

half of each high school graduating class moves on to a campus.

The technological, scientific and highly specialized society has few jobs for those with little education, but offers promising careers to those with advanced degrees. All this has steadily increased the pressure for more college students to go on to graduate study.

More Fellowships Available

Moreover, since the American tradition is for families to want their children to do better than the parents, an additional rung on the educational ladder symbolizes such achievement.

In addition, greater numbers of young people are now able to postpone the day when they must be self-supporting. And an increasing number of Federal and private fellowships are taking the financial hardship out of graduate study.

Dean Miller of Yale said that the graduate department of English there had 522 applications last year for 40 places, and that applicants this year for the same number of vacancies has risen to 575.

In history and economics, too, there were more than 10 applicants for every place, he said. "We often turn down 30 people with Woodrow Wilson fellowships in one year," the dean remarked. This might be considered the equivalent to turning down high school valedictorians with merit scholarships for admission to college.

"In good graduate departments the pressure is already worse than in the undergraduate colleges," Dean Miller said.

Dean Goren said, "We are very ill-prepared." He blamed the fact that graduate schools had "no bureaucracy, no hierarchy, no guidance counsellors comparable to the staffs of the high schools and the colleges."

Guidance Called Lacking

The high schools and the college deans of admissions are in close contact with each other, he pointed out, whereas in the graduate schools "everything is done by academic departments." Thus, he suggested, there is less opportunity for planned expansion and proper guidance for admission.

"A particularly distressing aspect of the impending graduate school crisis is that many people have no concept of what a graduate school is," Mr. Goren said.

"Some think it is simply an extension of the undergraduate college. They think it is possible to graft on to every college a few additional faculty members, extra seats in the library and maybe a batch of bunsen burners and — presto, you have created a graduate school."

What makes solutions difficult all the experts say, is the need for leading researchers and scholars as well as close per-

May 13, 1966

529

sonal supervision of the graduate students by experienced professors, all the experts warn. For example, the City University of New York, which was formed in 1961, was able to graduate only two doctoral students—its first—last year.

Dr. Allen M. Cartter, who conducted graduate education studies as vice president of the American Council on Education and will assume his new post as chancellor of New York University in August, confirmed the build-up of pressures across the country.

He said the graduate schools would be hardest hit by applicants in 1969, when the colleges' record freshman classes will start moving to advanced study. In that year about one million applications can be expected— 10 times the number in 1950.

Between 1950 and 1965, the proportion of college students who move on to graduate work has doubled, from 10 per cent to 20 per cent of all bachelors' degree holders, Dr. Cartter said.

"In 1965 about 100,000 actually entered graduate schools, but by 1975 more than twice that number of entering graduate students can be expected," he said.

One result is the fact that students apply to five or more graduate schools to improve their chances.

This will greatly aggravate the universities' admissions problems on a level where administrative facilities are already inadequate.

Most experts appear to agree that the high-quality institutions, both public and private, will establish quotas on the number to be admitted. They see as the only alternative a deterioration of quality, with serious consequences to all levels of education.

Dean Goren of N.Y.U. urged undergraduates who want to go on to advanced studies to be sure to know what will be expected of them, in examinations and achievements.

Report by Graduate Students Asks End to Formal Tests and New Stress on 'Learning'

By HENRY RAYMONT

A study sponsored by the American Political Science Association has concluded that graduate students are working under a climate of "threat and fear" of failure and suggests alternatives to restore "learning and enlightenment."

In a preliminary report on almost a year of research, the authors — five graduate students — called for the elimination of formal examinations. They contended that the present system of testing "perverts instead of serves" scholarly goals.

The study received immediate attention — and high praise — at the opening session yesterday of the association's annual conference, which will last through Saturday and which has already drawn more than 5,000 political scientists to the city.

Instead of relying on standard examinations for evaluating a student's capacity, the association was asked to urge universities to devise alternatives. Among them were the submission of two or more "publishable" papers and more flexible tests, possibly combining oral and written examinations to suit the abilities of the individual candidates.

Some Professors Criticized

The report rejected arguments by those who would like to give students control over the curriculum. It also emphasized the shortcomings of professors who leave the choice of subject matter to their students.

Kenneth Sharp, a Yale government student and one of the authors of the report, elaborated on this point:

"We find that the professor who asks his students to determine what subjects they want to discuss is in reality paralyzing discussion. Rather than offering alternatives among which students might choose, he is simply abdicating his role."

The report called for a balanced discussion on study programs "embracing both students and faculty," asserting that what was needed "is not the abolition of all structure, but the proper structure."

The nature of the issue and the fact that it was considered by the association's governing council yesterday morning in advance of the conference's formal program reflected a new concern in the 66-year-old academic society.

"We are witnessing a historic shift from the image of the student as a disciple to the student as a colleague," Prof. Karl W. Deutsch of Harvard, the association's incoming president, said at the end of a two-hour discussion of the report. More than a fourth of the association's membership of about 15,000 is made up of students.

Many of these young scholars and some young professors who advocate greater social and political change are challenging their elders at the association's meetings in the Commodore Hotel.

The discussion of the graduate studies report was marked by typical classroom give-and-take, with the political science professors saying they were impressed by the depth and scholarly substance of the study, even though it was sharply critical of the academic system.

"Our great concern," said Morris J. Blachman, a government student at New York University and another of the authors of the document, "is that more flexible methods be developed to evaluate the individual abilities of students."

Alternatives Favored

Professor Deutsch observed: "I agree with you that the grading system should not be so restrictive as to be stifling. Students should be evaluated in more than one dimension. Some work better at a leisurely pace and might say, 'I'm a fuddy-duddy like Einstein,' and others seem to work better under pressure, like McGeorge Bundy. The system ought to recognize the value of both."

The report, based on research among the government departments of 61 universities, suggested that the findings could be broadened to encompass American graduate studies in general. It represented the median student in his fourth year of graduate work as being 27 years old, married, beset by fears of failure and treated by the faculty as if he were still an undergraduate.

"Today, fear is the dominant motif in the life of the graduate student—if his future depends on his successful completion of the present graduate obstacle course," the report said.

To overcome the threat of failure, it went on, students tend to concentrate on short-run strategies based on "psyching out" the faculty "on what might be asked," so that "the real goals—education, learning and enlightenment—get subsumed by the more obvious performance criteria, like grades, exams and the degree itself."

"The sense of threat and fear," the study went on, "is heightened by the way the graduate student feels he is often treated by the faculty: 'In most departments, he is regarded as the object, rather than the subject of decisions.'"

The association voted $12,000 to undertake the research after finding itself besieged with complaints from young scholars at last year's annual meeting. The other authors of the paper were Douglas Bennett of Yale and Frederick Eisele and James Paul of New York University.

June 23, 1966

September 3, 1969

Deans Say Lag in U.S. Aid Hinders Graduate Schools

By M. A. FARBER
Special to The New York Times

WASHINGTON, Dec. 4—The quality of many of the country's leading graduate schools is being seriously threatened by the loss of millions of dollars in Federal fellowships and other support, according to deans of those schools.

Many top graduate schools, including Harvard, Yale, Wisconsin and Stanford, have reduced enrollments by as much as a third in response to the erosion of outside financial aid for students whom the universities cannot fully subsidize. At the same time, over-all graduate enrollments have increased slightly, with the greatest gains at newly expanding state universities.

Among the graduate schools that have been hardest hit by the drying up of Federal, and sometimes state, assistance are many that were rated most effective in program and highest in faculty caliber in a recent national poll of professors by the American Council of Education.

Find 'Mediocrity' Fostered

Over the last decade, many of these schools have come to rely heavily on such outside support.

Their deans argue that fund cuts aimed to stem a supposed oversupply of doctors of philosophy are sapping the strength of the finest doctoral programs and fostering "mediocrity" while not significantly denting the total production of new doctorates.

Such views were repeatedly expressed in interviews with the graduate deans of Harvard, Cornell, Yale, Stanford, Chicago, Princeton, Brown and Columbia Universities. The deans were attending a three-day annual meeting here on the Council of Graduate Schools in the United States.

"Ironically, the bellwether graduate schools that have set a standard of excellence will, in the next few years, be fighting for the very existence of departments and programs and of the graduate school as we know it," said Dr. Aaron Lemonick, dean of the graduate school at Princeton. "What is at stake is a loss of national excellence in doctoral education that the country can ill-afford."

Cites Need for Discussion

"The educational process at the Ph.D. level requires the bringing together of certain numbers of students with other students and with faculty," observed Dr. Michael Brennan, the graduate dean at Brown. "They have to be there and be able to talk to each other. What good is a seminar with only two students?"

Dr. Brennan said that the "weakest" graduate schools were insulated from Federal and foundation retrenchment because they did not attract students who merited nationally competitive awards, because they received a minimum number of Federal fellowships allocated to institutions, and because they often depended for student support on teaching assistantships financed by state governments. "Instead," he said, "the institutions of highest quality are forced to contract, denying space to students of promise who are then compelled to accept a lesser education."

"One thing is apparent—the graduate schools are facing hard times" Dr. Donald W. Taylor, graduate dean at Yale, told the 500 educators at the meeting here.

Presents Happier View

A number of the educators, however, were more sanguine.

Dr. J. Boyd Page, the graduate council's president, said that the drop in funds in the last several years was forcing a reassessment of graduate studies and had led to a "reassertion of pride in the best system of post-baccalaureate education in the world."

He said that it would take "more optimism than I have" to believe that Congress will authorize substantial new funds for graduate education in time to benefit the "current generation of graduate students." But the prospects for passage of pending legislation that would ultimately aid the graduate schools "seem very good," he said.

Perhaps the most sensitive issue at the meeting, which ended today, was the so-called "Ph.D. glut." The deans generally seemed to agree that too much had been made of an alleged oversupply of doctorates.

They conceded that an adequate, perhaps excessive, number were being produced in certain disciplines and that this should be curbed. Yet they stressed that other fields needed even more graduates with doctorates, that the future requirements of society were still unsettled and that focusing attention on "the numbers game" detracted from the more crucial question of the quality and character of graduate studies.

A resolution overwhelmingly adopted by the educators said that the council "views as a disservice to the long-range public interest the uniformed and often exaggerated emphasis on the increasing number of Ph.D. degree holders in the U.S."

Dr. Page, on the basis of a broad survey of schools in October, reported that, "contrary to widely held expectations," total graduate enrollment in the fall of 1971 including masters and doctoral candidates but excluding such professional areas as law and medicine, rose by 1.4 per cent. In 1969, however, the increase was 7 per cent; in 1970, 8 per cent.

"The leveling off of the enrollment curve reflects diminished support and the current employment situation," Dr. Page said, "but it is significant that students continue to seek advanced education in growing numbers."

The deans of the leading graduate schools traced a good part of their woes to the elimination or reduction since 1968-69 of fellowships and traineeships from the National Science Foundation, National Defense Education Act, National Aeronautics and Space Administration, National Institutes of Health, National Institute of Mental Health and Public Health Service, as well as from such private sources as foundations.

Estimate of Loan

Several of the deans estimated that the combined loss for all graduate schools in the country, including cuts in aid for institutional development buildings and libraries, amounted to hundreds of millions of dollars.

Leading schools have cut enrollments largely because they cannot afford to pick up much of the slack. Many deans at top schools contended that the majority of their applicants needed substantial aid and that many would turn to other schools if they could not get it.

At Harvard, the entering class of 550 students this fall is down 40 per cent from three years ago; at Yale, the decline is 30 per cent from 1969; at Brown, 24 per cent from two years ago; at Cornell, 15 per cent from two years ago. At Columbia, the entering class is down from 850 to 650 students since 1967; at Princeton, down from 569 three years ago to 400; at the University of California, Berkeley, and the University of Wisconsin, both down 20 per cent over two years.

A number of these schools, in addition to limiting enrollment, are already consolidating or suspending certain programs — sometimes, the deans acknowledged, to the advantage of the institution.

December 5, 1971

Census Shows Big Rise in Schooling

By JACK ROSENTHAL
Special to the New York Times

WASHINGTON, Dec. 7—The Census Bureau issued new evidence today of the educational transformation that has occurred in the United States in the space of a single generation.

According to a new population survey report, the typical American now has almost four more years of education than he did as recently as 1940. A greater proportion of adults have now been to high school than had been to elementary school at that time.

There has been even more dramatic change, the report showed, among young adults, particularly young blacks.

The report also documented a strong relationship between the amount of schooling and later earnings, a finding that bears on the current controversy over a new study by Christopher S. Jencks of the Harvard School of Education.

The educational gains reported by the Census Bureau apply to all regions, men and women, blacks and whites, cities and suburbs.

The proportion of Americans aged 25 and over who have had four years of college or more has almost tripled since 1940, going from 4.6 to 12 per cent.

The proportion who have completed at least four years of high school has more than doubled, going from 24.5 per cent to 58.7.

And the proportion who have not gone to high school at all had dropped sharply, from 60.4 per cent to 24.8.

As a result of these changes, the median education level nationally is now 12.2 years. That is, half of all adult Americans now have finished high school and spent some time in college.

In 1940, by contrast, the median was 8.4 years, meaning the mid-point of educational attainment was only a little more than elementary school. The upgrading in schooling has been so pronounced, in fact, that elementary school completion has disappeared as a routine category of measuring educational attainment.

These signs of change, covering the whole adult population, mask still-sharper gains in schooling among young adults. For example, the median education level among those aged 20 and 21 is 12.8 years —almost a year of college. Among persons aged 65 to 74, the median is 9.1 years—just over a year of high school.

The new census report demonstrated striking gains for blacks in an absolute sense. Among all blacks, educational attainment has nearly doubled since 1940. Then, it was 5.7 years of schooling. Now it is 10.3 years.

Even on a relative basis, the historic gap between black and white levels has thus closed somewhat. But blacks as a whole still lag almost two years behind the white median of 12.2 years.

At the same time, the report showed that the gap is closing much faster at younger age levels. Among whites aged 20 and 21, for example, the median education level is now 12.8 years. For blacks of those ages, it is 12.4 years—less than a half-year behind.

Even in the South, where both black and white schooling levels remain slightly behind other regions, the gap is the same — 12.7 years for whites and 12.3 years for blacks aged 20 and 21.

The report, like earlier studies, found a strong relationship between schooling and income. The more years of school completed, the higher one's annual earnings.

For instance, among employed men who earned $15,000 or more last year, the median education level was 15.2 years—more than three years of college. Among those who earned less than $3,000, the education median was 10.7 years, less than three years of high school.

The highest education level was for white collar workers earning $15,000 or more—16.3 years, or part of a year of graduate study. The lowest was for farm workers earning less than $3,000—8.7 years, or part of a year of high school.

Such findings appear to confirm criticism of the conclusions of a three-year study by Mr. Jencks and six colleagues at Harvard, recently published under the title, "Inequality: A Reassessment of the Effect of Family and Schooling in America."

Mr. Jencks's study found very little relationship betweeen how much peope learn in school and how much they earn in later life.

Mr. Jencks responded to his critics in a telephone interview, saying: "The tables are right. The association between schooling and income is there. What remains a mystery is why."

"No one has been able to show a strong relationship between higher income and higher grades, or any other measure of educational performance, like standardized tests."

His study showed that college graduates who did somewhat poorly on standardized tests earn only a little less than those who made average scores. Conversely, the Jencks team found, high school graduates with high test scores earn considerably less than average college graduates.

"My own hunch," he said, "is that there are two important explanations. One is that many employers pay for people's credentials—and you just can't get into many occupations without credentials.

"The other half of it is that someone who has gotten through college presumably was pretty good at figuring out what the teachers wanted. Then he goes on to a job and is even better at figuring out what the boss expects."

The new census report, "Educational Attainment, March, 1972" (P-20, No. 243) is based on a Current Population Survey of some 39,000 households in 1,863 counties across the country. Copies are available for 65 cents from the Government Printing Office, Washington, D.C. 20402.

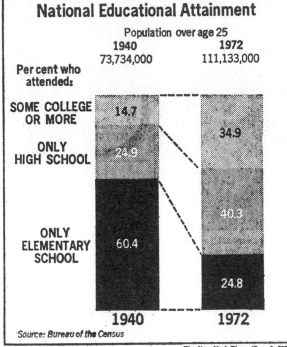

National Educational Attainment

Population over age 25

	1940	1972
	73,734,000	111,133,000

Per cent who attended:

	1940	1972
SOME COLLEGE OR MORE	14.7	34.9
ONLY HIGH SCHOOL	24.9	40.3
ONLY ELEMENTARY SCHOOL	60.4	24.8

Source: Bureau of the Census

The New York Times/Dec. 8, 1972

ONE VIEW OF HIGHER EDUCATION

Index

Environment: influence on IQ, 7; and academic achievement, 8, 42-43, 306-08, 350; influence on women Ph.D.'s, 524
Ethical Culture, 52
Evening schools 4, 6

"Fads and frills" program: defense of, 2; and tax strike, 45
Failure, 114: in public schools, 6, 160-69, 208
Family, weakened by schools, 8
Faubus, Gov. Orval E., 221-23
FBI, 427-28, 478-79
Federal aid, *see* Funding of public schools
Federal Security Agency, 376
Feinberg Law, 65, 71
Ferguson, Herman, 286
Fifth Amendment, 214; and tenure, 435-39
Finances, *see* Funding
Fine Arts: and Cornell University, 28; at NYU, 493
First Amendment, 79, 87
Folsom, Marion B., 39
Ford Foundation, 115, 140, 152, 258, 388: sponsors use of video tape, 140; on the "School Without Walls", 175-76; and decentralization, 272-73, 282; and the U.F.T., 278; announced plan for "community control", 279; financing of "community control", 282; and funding of black colleges, 507-09
Foundations: influence on schools, 246; and research grants, 382
Fourteenth Amendment, 214, 253
Freedom: of students, 5, 9, 191-200; within public schools, 16; of public schools from federal control, 40; in elementary classroom, 347; teaching of, 372-73; of speech and assembly on college campuses, 421; of expression, 446; *see also* Free Speech Movement; Compulsory education; Discipline
Free schools, 179
Free Speech Movement, 441, 475: at Berkeley, 415-18, 421
Free Universities, 445
Friedenberg, Edgar Z., 197-98
Fuentes, Luis, 283, 286-87, 303-04, 313-14
Fund for the Advancement of Education, 258
Funding colleges and universities, 21, 24, 82, 144, 421: by endowment, 27; and research, 376-77, 382; and function of college president, 400-03; and investment portfolios, 407; and Federal education bill, 485; and federal aid, 489-90; and black studies, 500-01; and the black colleges, 507-09; federal aid, 531
Funding non-public schools, 75, 176-77: federal aid, 39-41; state aid, 85-87
Funding public schools, 6, 19, 140: federal aid, 14, 32-34, 37-40, 42-44, 77, 144; interest on school debt, 37; federal report of problems, 38; school bonds, 40; crisis in, 45-46; statistics by state, 47; state aid, 48; for educational research, 112; school bonds, 112; and Ford Foundation, 115, 153, 272-73; research, 122; Carnegie Corporation, 123; federal aid for busing, 239; for Puerto Rican students, 258; from foundations, 246-47; and decentralization, 272-73; in successful programs, 311-12

Galamison, Milton A., 260-63, 274. appointed to Board of Education, 288-89; on NYC decentralization plan, 289-90
Gardner, John W., 123
Generation Gap, 440-44
Genovese, Eugene D., 435-39
Geochemistry, 377
G.I. Bill, 388
Gifted students, 110-12, 117-21: mothering of, 160-69; description of in classroom, 342-43; and college costs, 387
Goodman, Paul, 179, 196: influence in Philadelphia, 178
Goslin, Willard E., 49-50
Grades, 482, 504-05: reform system, 49; under criticism, 52; in "School Without Walls", 175-76; abandonment of, 199; pressures for, 395-97; effects on student-teacher relationship, 444; in graduate school, 530
Graduate degrees, 524-25, 527-29, 531
Graduate programs, 27, 518: increased enrollment, 36, 375-76; and research grants, 377; admission to, 444; and vocational goals, 512-13; and women, 524; and "academic bums", 526-27; increased applications to, 529-30; overcrowding of, 531; years required in, 533
Greek, 20
Green, Edith, 490

Growth sciences, 160-69
Guidance: program established in Pasadena, 49; effect on students, 197-98

Half-day session, 36
Handicapped, schools for, 2, 4, 121, 132, 155
Harlem Preparatory School, 247
Harvard University: and compulsory chapel, 23; gates (illustration), 26, 56; spurns U.S. loans, 70; study of pre-school child, 160-69; 209, 479-80: and the CIA, 447; black students at, 482
Hayden, Tom, 429
Head Start, 150-72
Henry Street Settlement, 4
High schools: and student strikes, 5; compared, 15; institution of junior highs, 19; national survey (1952), 32-34; overcrowding in, 34-36; money spent in, 38; in poor districts, 42-43; federal aid to, 45-46, 72-74: curriculum reform of, 110-14, 121-27; and the new math, 129; and paperback books, 136-38; language laboratories in, 139; Nova High School, 151; as damaging to students, 180; and students' hair, 192; and competition, 394; and Ph.D. candidates, 525; *see also* Academic and Vocational high schools; Integration; Student protests
High schools, junior: instituted, 19; to be abolished, 267
Higher Horizons, 269
History, ancient, advocated at Columbia, 493-94
Holt, John, 179, 196-97: on "The Rat Race", 395-97
Home economics: as a fad and frill, 2; and progressive education, 12
Homework, 54, 114, 130
Homosexuality, 511-12
Hoover, J. Edgar, 419
How Children Fail (Holt), reviewed, 196-99
Hutchins, Robert Maynard, 27, 62

IBM, 147
Illiteracy, 11, 36
Independent study, 445
Industrial arts, 19
Industry, private: influence on segregated schools, 4; influence on universities, 376-77
Inflation, 45
"In loco parentis", 494-95
Institute for Defense Analyses, 465, 469
Integration, 212-42, 247-72: response of Southern Governors to, 219; Congressional drive to upset, 220-21; U.S. Army used to enforce, 221-23; and "evasive schemes", 224; at the University of Georgia, 225-26; at the University of Mississippi, 226-28; statistics re extent of, 231; displacement of teachers, 233-34; tensions among students, 250-51, 309-11, 516-18; protest on behalf of, 262-63; pairing of schools, 264, 268; statistics regarding, 268; curtailment of open enrollment, 271-72, and the New Left, 419; and black colleges, 451
Intellect, 110-11
Iowa State University, 132
IQ: correlated with schooling, 102; influence of emotions on, 103; linked to heredity, 104-05; and the environment, 106, 120, 157, 160-69; effect of schools on, 209; influence of teacher on, 244
IQ Tests, 4, 6-7
IS 201 (NYC), 269-70, 278, 281-82, 284, 287
Ivy League colleges, 394: and Latin, 20; admission to, 22; and college chapel, 23; students' reactions to communist scare, 63-65; and search for black students, 489; gifted students at, 490; and admission practices, 497-98

James, William, 51
Jencks, Christopher, 209, 497
Jensen, Arthur, 169
Jesus Movement, 483-84
Jewish students, 22, 497-98
John Adams High School, 180
John Birch Society, 55
Johnson, President Lyndon B., 41-42, 159, 424, 489-90, 492
Journalism, 512

Kagan, Jerome, 168, 173
Kennedy, President John F., 228-30, 489-90: advocates aid to schools, 40-

school, 111-12; and the President of Radcliffe, 123; damage done to, 168; and guilt, 172-73; protested school pairing, 264; on the status of, 323; and college admission, 374, 499; marriage and college, 389; entitled to college education, 393; decreased enrollment of, 486; and rape on college campuses, 501-02
Women studies, 502-03
Women's colleges: foundation, 21; and record enrollments, 374; and high attrition rate, 389; new college for, 491; and Lesbianism, 511-12; and college gynecologists, 512-14; and "affirmative action", 515-16; and federal assistance to graduate schools, 518; and the Ph.D. degree, 524
Women's Equity Action League, 515-16
World of Our Own, A (Prescott), 100-01
World War I, 6
World War II, 32, 377

Xerox Corporation, 146

Yale University, 26-27, 388, 479-80: compulsory chapel challenged, 23; spurns U.S. loans, 70; and faculty recruitment, 403; announces Master of Philosophy degree, 529
Young, Whitney M., 123

Zoning, 271-72: Department of Health, Education and Welfare on, 233-34; protest against, 264; upheld by Court of Appeals, 265; *see also* School districts